TO THE STUDENT: A Study Guide for this textbook is available through your college bookstore under the title STUDY GUIDE FOR BUSINESS LAW and COMPREHENSIVE BUSINESS LAW by Elizabeth M. Crocker and Ann R. Henry. The Study Guide can help you with course material by acting as a tutorial, review, and study aid. If the Study Guide is not in stock, ask the bookstore manager to order a copy for you.

Business Law

Note to the Student

Dear Student,

If you winced when you learned the price of this textbook, you are experiencing what is known as "sticker shock" in today's economy. Yes, textbooks are expensive, and we don't like it any more than you do. Many of us here at PWS-KENT have sons and daughters of our own attending college, or we are attending school part-time ourselves. However, the prices of our books are dictated by cost factors involved in producing them. The costs of typesetting, paper, printing, and binding have risen significantly each year along with everything else in our economy.

The prices of college textbooks have increased less than most other items over the past fifteen years. Compare your texts sometime to a general trade book, i.e., a novel or nonfiction book, and you will easily see substantial differences in the quality of design, paper, and binding. These quality features of college textbooks cost money.

Textbooks should not be considered only as an expense. Other than your professors, your textbooks are your most important source for what you learn in college. What's more, the textbooks you keep can be valuable resources in your future career and life. They are the foundation of your professional library. Like your education, your textbooks are one of your most important investments.

We are concerned, and we care. We pledge to do everything in our power to keep our textbook prices under control, while maintaining the same high standards of quality you and your professors require.

Wayne A. Barcomb
President
PWS-KENT Publishing Company

The Kent Series in Business Law

Labor and Employment Law
Cihon and Castagnera

The American Legal System
Davidson and Jespersen

Business Law: Principles and Cases, *Third Edition*
Davidson, Knowles, Forsythe, and Jespersen

Comprehensive Business Law: Principles and Cases
Davidson, Knowles, Forsythe, and Jespersen

Business and the Legal Environment
Jennings

Real Estate Law, *Second Edition*
Jennings

International Dimensions of the Legal Environment of Business
Litka

The Structure of the Legal Environment: Law, Ethics, and Business
Shaw and Wolfe

Essential CPA Law Review, *Seventh Edition*
Thompson and Brady

Business Law
Principles and Cases
Third Edition

Daniel V. Davidson
Radford University

Brenda E. Knowles
Indiana University at South Bend

Lynn M. Forsythe
California State University, Fresno

Robert R. Jespersen
University of Arkansas at Little Rock

PWS-KENT Publishing Company, Boston

PWS–KENT
Publishing Company

Acquisitions Editor: Rolf A. Janke
Production Editor: Susan L. Krikorian
Compositor: Progressive Typographers
Text Designer: Nancy Lindgren, Susan L. Krikorian
Cover Designer: Nancy Lindgren
Manufacturing Manager: Ellen J. Glisker
Cover Printer: New England Book Components, Inc.
Text Printer/Binder: Arcata Graphics/Halliday Lithograph

PWS-KENT Publishing Company is a division of Wadsworth, Inc.

Printed in the United States of America

3 4 5 6 7 8 9—93 92 91

Library of Congress Cataloging-in-Publication Data

Business law: principles and cases/Daniel V. Davidson . . . [et al.].
    p.   cm.
    Includes indexes.
    ISBN 0-534-91882-4
    1. Commercial law—United States—Cases.   I. Davidson, Daniel V.
KF888.B817   1989
346.73′07—dc19   89-3076
[347.3067]   CIP

To the memory of my mother, Jane Davidson, and to my wife, Dee

To Paul, for his unconditional love and support

To James M. Poptanich and Vicky L., Aileen B., and Robert J. Zollweg

To Shirley

About the Authors

DANIEL V. DAVIDSON received both his B.S. and his J.D. degrees from Indiana University. He has taught at Central Connecticut State College, St. Cloud State University in Minnesota, the University of Arkansas, and California State University at Fresno. He is currently serving as the Chairman of Accounting, Finance, and Business Law at Radford University in Virginia.

Professor Davidson has been the recipient of four different awards for teaching. In 1975, he was named Outstanding Teacher of the Year at Central Connecticut State College. In 1979, he received the Outstanding Faculty Award from Beta Alpha Psi, and, in 1980, he was named the Razorback Award winner as the Outstanding Business Professor, both at the University of Arkansas. In 1984, Professor Davidson was awarded the Meritorious Performance Award at California State University, Fresno.

Professor Davidson is an active member of the American Business Law Association and its Southern regional. He has held each of the offices of the Southern Region, most recently serving as president for the 1982–1983 term.

BRENDA E. KNOWLES received a B.A. *magna cum laude* from the University of Evansville, an M.A. from Miami University, and a J.D. from the Indiana University School of Law. She is Associate Professor of Business Law at Indiana University at South Bend, where she has been the recipient of a system-wide, all-university teaching award, the Amoco Foundation Excellence in Teaching Award. She has also been an associate with the Danforth Foundation, which encourages effective teaching and seeks to humanize teaching and learning in the academic community, and is a member of Beta Gamma Sigma.

Professor Knowles specializes in research on employment discrimination, antitrust, and intellectual property law. She publishes her work in professional journals and recently won an award for her research. In addition, she has been recognized both nationally and locally for her professional and civic accomplishments.

Professor Knowles is an active member of the American Business Law Association, which she currently serves as Second Vice President, and various regional associations. More specifically, she is a past President of the Tri-State Regional. Licensed to practice law in Indiana, she is a member of the American, Indiana State, and St. Joseph County Bar Associations.

LYNN M. FORSYTHE is Professor of Business Law and Director of Graduate Business Programs at California State University, Fresno. She received her B.A. from the Pennsylvania State University and her J.D. from the University of Pittsburgh School of Law and is licensed to practice law in both California and Pennsylvania.

Professor Forsythe has been an estate and gift tax attorney for the Internal Revenue Service and has taught business law, administrative law, government regulation of business, real estate law, business ethics, and estate planning. She is the author of numerous articles on business law and the teaching of business law. She has held the positions of staff editor and reviewer and of coeditor for the *Journal of Legal Studies Education* and is currently the Editor-in-Chief for the 1987–1989 term.

Professor Forsythe is a member of Beta Gamma Sigma; the American Bar Association, for which she chairs subcommittees and panels, including an American Law Institute–American Bar Association program; and the American Business Law Association, for which she served as program coordinator for the 1983 annual meeting and as liaison to the National Conference of Commissioners on Uniform State Laws. She is currently a member of the Executive Committee of the American Business Law Association. Having previously held each of the other offices of the Western Business Law Association, she served as president in 1986–1987.

ROBERT R. JESPERSEN is Professor of Business Law at the University of Arkansas at Little Rock, where he has served as associate dean of the College of Business Administration and as director of the M.B.A. Program and of the Executive Development Program. He holds A.B. and A.M. degrees from Columbia University and a J.D. from the University of Houston.

Professor Jespersen has practiced law in both Texas and Arkansas. He has served as Assistant Attorney General of Texas and has been a member of the faculty of the University of Houston and an administrative officer at Columbia University and Princeton University.

Professor Jespersen served three years in Africa, first as headmaster of the Kurisini International Education Center in Dar es Salaam, Tanzania, and then as senior advisor to the Association of African Universities in Accra, Ghana. He is a former president of the Southern Regional Business Law Association and is a member of Beta Gamma Sigma. He is currently President of the American Business Law Association.

Preface

Law cannot be made simple, nor can it be made easy. However, it is our strong conviction that law does not have to be made any more difficult than it already is, and it is on that premise that we have written this basic text for undergraduate students. The purpose of *Business Law: Principles and Cases, Third Edition,* is to make the myriad topics of business law comprehensible to the beginning student by using plain language, relevant and realistic examples, pertinent cases, and an easy writing style. While we do not intend to familiarize students with all the technical intricacies of the law, we do hope to stimulate their interest in those intricacies and to make them aware of how the law affects their lives.

No matter what discipline a business student selects as a major field of study, that student will encounter many legal issues during his or her professional life. A substantial number of those issues will undoubtedly fall within the areas covered in this text—among them, contracts, sales, commercial paper, debtor–creditor relations, agency, partnerships, corporations, government regulations, property protection, and international business. This text cannot supply the solutions to all the potential legal problems involved in these areas, but it can help one in recognizing the legal issues that such problems present and in deciding when to seek the appropriate help. The study of this book will not make anyone into a lawyer, but it should make one aware of when a lawyer is needed.

The book is divided into ten parts, with the divisions based on the traditional topical areas of business law. Such an approach allows the instructor to select those topics germane to any course in which the text is used. It is suitable for use in a single-semester, comprehensive-coverage course or as the text for a multiple-semester, sequential series of courses. While the text is not specifically geared to the CPA examination, it does cover each of the business law topics included in the examination, and thus should be of considerable value to the accounting major.

Part I, "Foundations of American Law," introduces the student to the American legal system by examining the logic behind the law and the reasons for studying business law. Chapter 2 explains the structure of the court system and the place of the United States Constitution in our legal system. Chapter 3 introduces tort law and the concept of private duty. Chapter 4 focuses on the area of criminal law and the concept of public duty. The next chapter is an unusual and distinctive feature of the book. It leads the student, step-by-step, through the stages of a civil lawsuit, with explanations of *what* is being done at each stage of the proceedings and *why* it is being done. Chapter 6 is also distinctive, exposing the student to two professional relationships: the attorney–client relationship and the legal liability of the accountant. Chapter 7 introduces the student to business ethics.

Part II deals with the topic that forms the foundation of business law: the law of contracts. Although the modern complexities of business have led to a number of specialized areas of law, contract law forms the base upon which these specialized areas are built. A sound understanding of contract law is therefore essential to an understanding of the various other areas of business law. Chapter 8 explores the development of contract law and the different classifications of contracts. Chapter 9 looks at the formation of the agreement between the parties—the area of offer and acceptance. Chapter 10 discusses the concept of consideration—the exchange of value between the parties that makes the contract enforceable. Chapter 11 points out the limitations on who can enter a contract—the concept of capacity. Chapter 12 focuses on illegal agreements, underscoring the requirement that, to be valid, a contract must have a legal purpose. Chapter 13 examines the voluntary nature of the contract—the concept of reality of consent. Chapter 14 looks into the occasional need for formality in contract law and the need for a written agreement. Contracts between two parties often affect the rights of a third person not a party to the contract; Chapter 15 explores some of the rights—and duties—of the third persons so affected. Chapters 16 and 17 deal with the release of some contract obligations, or discharges, and the remedies available for nonperformance of other contract obligations.

Part III, "The Law of Sales," introduces the Uniform Commercial Code (UCC), the modern, comprehensive law that governs many commercial transactions. Although any contract for the sale of goods falls within Article 2 of the UCC, very few people are aware of their rights and duties in this area. Merchants need to be especially cognizant of the different legal aspects of sales law. Of special interest and growing importance are warranties and product liability, which are the subject of Chapter 21. The recent consumer movement has made both these areas particularly important to any business that deals in goods.

Commercial paper, which is the focus of Part IV, is another area governed by the UCC. Millions of checks are issued every week to pay bills, to purchase goods and services, or to receive cash. Every loan made involves the use of some type of promissory note. Both checks and promissory notes are types of commercial paper and both are governed by Article 3 of the UCC. Knowing how and when to use a negotiable instrument can be extremely important to a business, especially in terms of profit generation and liability.

Part V, "Debtor–Creditor Relations," offers a more comprehensive coverage of this subject than that offered in any other business law text we have seen. Three detailed chapters are devoted to secured transactions; two chapters focus on bankruptcy and alternatives to bankruptcy. We have given these topics such extensive coverage for several reasons. These are two of the most difficult areas in business law to master, and the extra coverage allows us to go into greater detail in our explanation, resulting in a better treatment of the fundamental concepts. The breakdown of secured transactions into three chapters emphasizes the major stages of a security interest from creation through enforcement. The breakdown of bankruptcy into two chapters emphasizes the alternative nature of the options available to the debtor. Chapter 31 deals with the Bankruptcy Reform Act, the Bankruptcy Amendments and Federal Judgeship Act of 1984, and the general concepts of a "straight" bankruptcy under Chapter 7. This chapter also explains why the Bankruptcy Reform Act was declared unconstitutional and how the 1984 Amendments have clarified this area of law. Chapter 32 examines the alternatives to a "straight" bankruptcy, both within bankruptcy law and under traditional state laws.

Part VI devotes three chapters to a very important area of business law: the law of agency. Agency is a specialized type of employment in which one person is authorized to represent another in business transactions. Without the law of agency, modern business as we know it would be impossible. Thus, a thorough knowledge and understanding of this area is of special importance to a business student. We decided not to combine agency with the general topic of employment for two reasons. First, agency is an important enough topic to stand alone. Second, nonagency employment is primarily an aspect of contract law, a subject covered earlier in the text, and as such is controlled by government regulation, which is the focus of Part VIII.

Part VII, "Business Organizations," consists of nine chapters. The first three examine the partnership as a business form: its formation, operation, and termination. Chapter 38 provides a detailed discussion of the problems involved in winding up this particular type of business. The next six chapters deal with many aspects of the corporation as a business form. Included are chapters on the formation of a corporation, the operation of the business, and the management of the firm. Also included is a timely chapter that explains the effects of mergers, consolidations, and other acquisitions of the corporation. The last two chapters in Part VII treat the topics of franchising—another timely subject—and securities regulation. Because so many corporations use securities as a source of funds, familiarity with securities regulations is an important consideration in avoiding liability for securities fraud. The Foreign Corrupt Practices Act, partially enforced by the Securities and Exchange Commission, is included in the coverage of this topic.

Part VIII, "Government Regulations," is another unique feature of the text. It not only covers the major antitrust statutes but also explains the theories that justify government regulation of business. Also included are chapters on consumer and environmental protection, one of the most controversial areas of modern business law, and labor and fair employment practices. The chapters in Part VIII deal comprehensively with the environment within which all American businesses must operate, and an awareness of these issues is essential to a successful business career.

Part IX, "Property Protection," examines a number of diverse yet related topics: real and personal property, bailments, insurance, wills, estates, and trusts. These chapters provide the student with some of the basic information needed to protect personal assets. Chapters 49 and 50 deal with the acquisition, transfer, and protection of personal and real property. Chapter 51 covers the topic of insurance, the protection of that property from hazards. Wills, estates, and trusts—the planning of an estate to provide for one's heirs and family—are the subjects of Chapters 52 and 53.

Part X is another unique feature of our text. This section, "The Emerging Business Environment," discusses the topics of international business and computers and the law. Our intent here is merely to provide an overview of these increasingly important areas, which promise to have a substantial impact on the future path of business and of business law. Thus, although the coverage of any single issue is limited, the overall treatment effectively introduces each of the topics.

Multinational corporations present special problems—and special opportunities—for the future, and some awareness of the legal issues to be faced in this area will be extremely important for the successful business person of the future. As society increases the demands it makes upon corporations, the business leaders of the future will need to respond to these demands or face ever-increasing government regulation. The pervasive nature of computers in our world justifies a separate chapter dealing with the topic of how computers and the law must interrelate.

CHANGES IN THE THIRD EDITION

We have made some changes in the text to improve our coverage and to make the book an even better teaching/learning tool. Throughout the book we have replaced cases, selecting cases that are more recent and also selecting cases that illustrate a particular topic better than the cases being replaced.

The law of bankruptcy changed in 1984, and our coverage of bankruptcy has been totally modified to reflect these changes. Of special interest here is the new pro-creditor approach of the new bankruptcy coverage. We have also revised chapters dealing with business ethics and with computers. These two areas promise to offer much legal controversy in the years ahead.

The Test Bank has been improved and upgraded, providing instructors with numerous options and a larger number of potential questions. There are also more transparencies, together with some new, more illustrative replacement transparencies.

We feel that these changes make an already strong text even stronger.

Chapter Outlines

PEDAGOGICAL DEVICES

The topical outlines that begin each chapter alert the student to what the chapter will cover and help to provide a structured study approach.

Marginal Notes and Glossary

Brief, semitechnical definitions for key terms appear in the margins throughout the text. These marginal notes are not intended to be complete definitions but, rather, to provide a working understanding of the phrases without disrupting the student's efforts to read the material. More complete definitions are provided in the Glossary, and the student may also want to consult a law dictionary for even more detail.

Cases and Case Index

The text uses numerous condensed cases to illustrate a variety of legal points. These include both classic, landmark cases and many of the most recent decisions pertaining to business law. The actual court opinions have been "briefed" into a four-part format for instructional purposes: a statement of facts, the issue upon which the decision hinges, the holding of the court, and the reasoning behind the holding. The Case Index at the end of the book allows the reader easy access to this material. A number of hypothetical cases intended to illustrate particular points of law also appear in several places throughout the text.

Illustrations

The text includes many helpful illustrations—flowcharts, diagrams, legal forms and documents, summary and comparative tables. A list of these follows the table of contents.

Summaries

The text of each chapter closes with a narrative summary of the material presented in the chapter. The summaries are not meant to completely cover the material but, rather, to aid the student in a general review.

Questions and Case Problems

Each chapter ends with a number of questions and problems, some dealing with the principles and terms covered in the chapter and some designed to test general comprehension of the material. Most chapters include case problems that are based on actual court opinions. Since these problems give the case names and citations, students can look up the actual cases to compare their answers and reasoning with those of the court. These chapter-ending questions and problems can be used as a study tool in reviewing the material, as classroom discussion material, or for out-of-class writing assignments.

Appendixes

Four appendixes provide easy access to actual source material referred to in text discussions and in footnotes throughout the book. Appendix A includes Articles 1–9 of the Uniform Commercial Code; Appendix B presents the United States Constitution; Appendix C contains the Uniform Partnership Act; Appendix D contains the Revised Uniform Limited Partnership Act with the 1985 amendments.

SUPPLEMENTAL ITEMS

Study Guide

Elizabeth Crocker and Ann Henry, both of the University of Arkansas, have prepared a comprehensive Study Guide to accompany the text. This Study Guide contains materials designed to help the student master the subject and its vocabulary.

Instructor's Manual

The Instructor's Manual outlines each chapter's material in the form of teaching hints. A segment called "Trouble Spots" highlights those areas that traditionally confuse students because of the complexity of the material or the language of the law. This section suggests methods of avoiding these traditional problems by calling the student's attention to them in advance. The Instructor's Manual also includes answers to the text's chapter-ending questions and problems.

Transparencies

A set of more than fifty acetate transparencies is available to help instructors graphically illustrate some of the more difficult concepts presented in the text. These consist for the most part of illustrations not contained in the text; they include summary charts, legal documents, and various other facsimile items.

Test Bank Booklet and Computerized Test Banks

For each chapter of the text, the Test Bank provides the following types of questions: ten true-false, aimed at both application and vocabulary; five multiple choice, aimed primarily at application; five matching, with seven possible matches, so that the process of elimination is largely excluded; and one short essay or discussion question. This mix provides sufficient flexibility and enough possible questions to satisfy the needs of most instructors. A computerized test bank of the same items is also available.

A STATEMENT OF GRATITUDE

Trying to put a textbook together "from whole cloth" is difficult under the most ideal of conditions. To do so when geographically separated is even more difficult, and we could not have done it without the help, support, encouragement, and belief of the following people:

Rolf Janke, our editor and emotional guru. His help and encouragement from day one were invaluable, and his enthusiasm provided the necessary adrenaline whenever we began to tire.

Kathleen Tibbetts and Laura Mosberg, Rolf's assistants. Laura and Kathleen were always there with the details, correspondence, and communications necessary to coordinate our multiregional writing efforts.

Susan Krikorian, our production editor, who managed to take our individual quirks and grammatical eccentricities and turn them into a well-written textbook, and did so with never (well, hardly ever) a complaint voiced to us.

And a special thanks to Dick Crews, who guided us through two editions before he got promoted. His support was invaluable, and his promotion well-earned.

We also wish to express our gratitude to The American Law Institute, which granted us permission to reprint excerpts from the *Restatement (Second) of Contracts* (copyright 1982 by The American Law Institute; reprinted with the permission of The American Law Institute), *Restatement (Second) of Torts* (copyright 1977 by The American Law Institute; reprinted with the permission of The American Law Institute), and *Restatement (Second) of Agency* (copyright 1958 by The American Law Institute; reprinted with the permission of The American Law Institute).

Finally, our thanks to the many reviewers who read over our manuscripts and offered constructive criticism to strengthen the finished product. Throughout, they were critical, supportive, and encouraging. Their efforts and inputs were essential to the final product.

A NOTE TO THE STUDENT

As you read this text, you may find yourself occasionally frustrated by the use of such terms as *generally, usually, ordinarily, in most cases, as a rule,* and the like. When that happens, remember this: most business law is based on state law, and there are many variations among the several states. These variations make it impossible — and unwise — to make definite statements about some legal subjects. In addition, although there *are* general rules of law, there are also exceptions to the general rules. Since space and time limitations would make it impossible to list all these exceptions in any one introductory text, we have gone with the majority rule unless otherwise noted.

Also remember that if these generalities are frustrating for you, they are equally frustrating for your instructor, for attorneys who are arguing these principles in the various courts of the land, and for the judges who have to decide the cases being argued!

It is our sincere hope that we have put together a text that is not only a valid educational tool but also a book that is enjoyable to read. Business law is a serious and important topic, but it is also a potentially entertaining and interesting one. This book is designed to emphasize the importance and seriousness of the topic while underscoring the interest it contains. We feel that we have been successful in our efforts, and we hope that you agree.

Daniel V. Davidson
Brenda E. Knowles
Lynn M. Forsythe
Robert R. Jespersen

Contents

List of Figures

Business Law

PART 1

Foundations of American Law

Ignorance of the law is no excuse. The basic truth of this old adage seems simple and obvious. However, the simplicity of the truth hides the complexity of the law. Each citizen — and resident — of this country has "constructive notice" of the law. Each person is expected to be aware of, and to abide by, all the laws of the land. Yet the enormity of "the law" makes such an expectation an exercise in futility. No one person can really *know* "the law," but every person is expected to obey it. Thus, a built-in contradiction exists in the system.

This opening part of the book will introduce the reader to the law as it exists in the United States. Broad legal philosophies will be briefly presented. The American legal system will be outlined. The concept of private duty and torts will be introduced, as will the concept of public duty and crimes. A civil lawsuit will be explained. Finally, a special legal-professional area will be examined, and business ethics will be discussed.

The opening part — and each of the other parts to follow — will shed some light on and offer some insights into areas that the reader may not have previously explored. A thorough knowledge of law takes years of specialized study, and this text alone will not provide it. But it will begin to open the doors of understanding for the student and to remove that "ignorance of the law [which] is no excuse."

CHAPTER 1

Introduction

WHAT IS THE RELATIONSHIP BETWEEN LAW, ORDER, AND JUSTICE?

Law

Sanctions Coercive means

Criminal law That body of law dealing with public wrongs called crimes

Negligence Failure to do something that a reasonable person would do, or doing something that a reasonable and prudent person would not do

Procedural law Methods of enforcing rights or obtaining redress for their invasion; machinery for carrying on a lawsuit

This book is about understanding the law of business. Before we begin our study, however, we must answer a basic question: what is *law?* There are many definitions, ranging from the philosophical to the practical. Plato said law was social control. Blackstone said it was rules specifying what was right and what was wrong. For our purposes, however, we shall define law as *rules that must be obeyed.* People who disobey these rules are subject to **sanctions** that could result in their having to do something they would not voluntarily do, such as paying money to someone or going to jail. Our society has many kinds of rules, but not all rules can be considered "law." For example, a rule in baseball says that after three strikes you are out. That is not law. All laws are rules, but not all rules are laws. What differentiates a law from a rule is its *enforceability*. People who do not follow the rules in baseball are not hauled into court. They are simply ejected from the game. In contrast, people who break laws can be hauled into court and made accountable for their actions.

There are many different kinds of legal rules. One kind defines a definite way of making a contract or a will. A second forbids certain kinds of conduct; **criminal law** is an excellent example of this kind of legal rule. A third category has been established to compensate persons who have been injured because someone else breached a duty. For example, when an automobile manufacturer builds a car negligently, and its **negligence** is the direct cause of an injury, the manufacturer may have to pay the injured person money damages. Finally, there are rules that our legislative bodies and courts establish to take care of their everyday business. For example, all states have a rule concerning the maximum number of days defendants have before they must answer a lawsuit. This is called **procedural law.**

We shall view the law as consisting of a body of rules that establish a certain level of social conduct, breaches of which are grounds for enforcement in courts of law. The enforcement could consist of one of three legal remedies: (1) paying money damages, (2) being subject to a court order that directs a person to do or not do something (an injunction), or (3) going to jail or prison. The law is not unlike the controlling function in management, in which a standard is established (a law), performance is measured against that standard (the facts), and actual performance is corrected so the standard can be achieved (through the use of a legal remedy).

Order

The manner in which the law usually looks at *order* is in the form of a legal command issued by a judge. But we are not concerned with order in that sense. Another way of looking at order is as *the absence of chaos.* Chaos, as you know, is confusion and total disorganization. If the laws of a society were always followed and never broken, perfect order would result. There would be no crime, and everyone would be safe. For example, no one would run red lights and cause injuries to others; all orders would be legal and no one would break them; and neighbors would get along with neighbors without arguing. History tells us that no society in which there was perfect order has ever existed. Our society would come very close to perfect order if we allowed ourselves to be treated as though we were in the military. All police states have a great deal of order but very little justice. Nazi Germany was an example of this condition.

The words *law* and *order* are often linked together. It is natural to link them because if the law is followed, there will be order. It is precisely because the law is not followed all the time by all the people that there is not perfect order. Society is always somewhat chaotic and disorganized. One of the reasons people do not always obey the law is because often they are not aware of what the law is. For example, every contract, whether oral or written, could be organized in such a way that it would always be legally enforceable. But since not everyone knows the law of contracts, it is quite impossible for all contracts to be legally enforceable. For this reason, the law presumes that all citizens know the law, whether, in fact, they do or do not. This position, theoretically at least, creates an incentive for all citizens to study the law. If the law did not presume that everyone knows the law, more chaos would be created than exists already. In that case, individuals accused of breaking the law would have an excellent defense in that they did not know they were breaking it. Our educational system plays an important role in allowing us to learn the law. A perfect society, of course, would not need any laws. Until that day arrives, every society will have to establish certain laws designed to create order.

Justice

Just as all life is a search for reality, all law should be a search for justice. Although justice *is* fairness, the concept of fairness is less abstract than that of justice and thus is easier for us to deal with on a practical level. For example, when a millionaire accused of murder obtains the best criminal trial lawyer in the country to defend him and is either acquitted or receives a small sentence, many people ask: is that fair? When you were a child and saw bullies pick on someone smaller than themselves and extract whatever they wanted, you probably asked yourself the same question. Is that fair? In these situations, the results are clearly unfair and are therefore unjust. Seemingly, as Lenny Bruce once said, ''They call it the Halls of Justice because the only place you get justice is in the halls.''

There are two kinds of justice: commutative and distributive. **Commutative justice** attempts to give all persons what is due them. It places everyone on an equal footing. An example of commutative justice is a contract that requires a person who sold some property for $60,000 to carry out his part of the bargain even though he subsequently discovers he could have sold the property for $80,000; the law will usually not take into account that he was a high school dropout and that the person he dealt with was a college graduate. **Distributive justice,** on the other hand, does not place everyone on an equal level. It holds that some people should get more and others less because people are unequal, and it is up to ''justice'' to establish equality through a disproportionate allocation of benefits. Distributive justice could be used as a philosophical basis for the federal government's affirmative action programs, which attempt to make up for past unconstitutional discrimination. In a free society such as ours, the best we can do is *seek* to achieve justice. We can only attempt

Commutative justice
The attempt to give all persons their due on the assumption that all persons are equal

Distributive justice
The attempt to ''distribute'' justice in a way that considers inequalities among individuals

to approximate it. It is improbable that we could ever achieve perfect justice in every case.

The Nexus: Practicability

"The law," then, is really a system consisting of law, order, and justice. Combined, they make up the American legal system. All the elements should be balanced in perfect equilibrium so that one element does not adversely affect any other. If we had total order, we would have very little justice; if we had total justice, we would have very little order. The *nexus* (link between elements) of the two concepts is the point of *practicability.* For example, to achieve perfect justice with respect to traffic violations, we would have to have jury trials with counsel to ascertain precisely whether a citizen did in fact violate the speed limit. However, the costs of such a venture would be so prohibitive that no municipality or other local jurisdiction could afford to pay for it. Accordingly, most traffic courts tend to achieve "assembly line" justice rather than perfect justice. Such is the practicability inherent in the relationship between law, order, and justice.

THE LAW AS AN ARTIFICIAL LANGUAGE SYSTEM

Even though the law uses English words to describe its various elements, do not be lulled into complacency. Many terms used in the law are also used in everyday speech, but they have totally different meanings in the law. This text will define the terms for you, either in the chapter or in the Glossary at the back of the book. The list of terms is seemingly endless: *offer, acceptance, consideration, guaranty,* and so on. Since the terms may have different connotations within the law, be on guard for subtle shifts in meaning. If you are in doubt, reread the passage again or check for other definitions in the Glossary. In addition, it is impossible to discuss the law intelligently without reference to some words that are limited to the law for their definition. For want of a better term, these words are called **jargon.** Examples include *estoppel, appellee, assignee, bailee, causa mortis, caveat vendor, quid pro quo,* and *codocil.*

Jargon The technical terminology of a particular profession

You make no assumptions when you study a foreign language; therefore, make none about the law. Remember these three rules about our artificial language system, and you will encounter minimal difficulty in mastering this material:

1. Legal terms may appear to be synonyms for everyday words, but they are not.

2. Legal terms may have more than one legal meaning.

3. Some legal terms have no relation to everyday language.

THE LAW OF BUSINESS

The law of business began as a private system administered outside the regular law courts in England. It was called the **law merchant** because it was administered in courts established in the various merchant guilds. It was eventually integrated into the English **common law** court system. Today the law of business includes contracts, sales, commercial paper, secured transactions, agency, partnerships, corporations, and insurance.

Law merchant Those rules of trade and commerce used by merchants in England after 1066

This textbook could be called a primer in **preventive law**. As a businessperson, you should understand the legal implications of what you are doing; as a consumer, too, you will find such understanding valuable. If you understand the issues raised here and can apply your knowledge to particular business situations, you may save yourself great expense later. For example, when you study the Statute of Frauds, you will learn that if two persons enter into a contract that is reduced to writing and only one of the two parties signs the contract, only the party who signed the contract can be sued on it. That means the party who did not sign the contract has two options: (1) to comply with the contract if acceptable or (2) to breach the contract knowing that the other, in general, cannot sue successfully. The party who signed it has no options. That person must comply or stand ready to be sued. This is because the Statute of Frauds states that certain contracts must be in writing in order to be enforceable. Therefore, a party cannot be sued on such a contract unless that person signed it. If a tenant signed a lease but the landlord did not, the tenant could be sued on the lease, but the landlord, in general, could not. Business is a very practical subject; accordingly, the law of business is also very practical.

Another reason for studying the law of business is that it will help you develop valuable decision-making skills. It will also sensitize you to particular situations in which you will need the assistance of a lawyer. In real estate transactions, for example, you will discover that the buyer or seller will need the assistance of a lawyer *before* an earnest money contract is signed rather than after. Skillful legal draftsmanship in drawing up the contract is where a lawyer can be most useful.

WHY STUDY THE LAW OF BUSINESS?

Common law The unwritten law that is based on custom, usage, and court decisions; different from statute law, which consists of laws passed by legislatures

Preventive law Law designed to prevent harm or wrongdoing before it occurs

A legal system must be reasonable. The laws under which people live must be based on assumptions that are provable. These various assumptions can be proved through reliance upon facts. The law stating that persons driving motor vehicles must stop at red lights and may proceed on green lights is based on the fact that chaos would result if busy intersections did not have lights or stop signs. Speeding laws are reasonable since it can be demonstrated that the faster that automobiles are allowed to travel on busy streets, the greater the number of accidents. Laws must also be applied reasonably. A law stating that persons will have property taken away from them if they do not pay for the property is certainly reasonable; but it would not be reasonably applied if a person stopped paying for the property and, with nothing more, the property were summarily removed by the person to whom the money was owed. The person owing the money would first have to be told that the money was due and payable and then be given a chance to say why the money could not be paid. Then, if the

WHAT ARE THE NEEDS OF A LEGAL SYSTEM?

The Need to Be Reasonable

money were still not paid, the person to whom the amount was due could repossess the property through legal process.

The Need to Be Definite

The law must be definite, not vague. For example, a law stating that all contracts "in excess of approximately $500" must be in writing would not clearly specify when a contract must be in writing. The Statute of Frauds, however, states that all contracts in excess of $500 must be in writing, which makes it very clear: if one has a contract for $499.99, it need not be in writing; a contract for $500.01 must be in writing. Sometimes the law is unable to state so precisely what one must do in all circumstances. In such cases, the law uses the word *reasonable* instead of setting precise parameters. If an automobile hits a pedestrian and causes injury, the pedestrian may sue the driver of the vehicle. In this situation, the law does not state that speed in excess of a particular amount is sufficient to find the driver at fault. If all you had to go on was that the speed limit was fifty-five miles per hour and the car was going fifty miles per hour, would you find the driver at fault? You simply do not have enough facts. You would need to know more about the driver. Did the driver have a current operator's license? If the driver had to wear glasses when driving, were they worn? Was the driver intoxicated or otherwise under the influence of drugs? Did the driver get enough sleep the night before? One could continue seeking facts about the driver, the automobile, the road conditions, the time of day, and so on. Under these conditions, the law would ask the question: was the driver's conduct reasonable under the circumstances? If so, it will be written off as an accident; if not, the driver will be liable for any injury caused the pedestrian. In the final analysis, the law provides an answer. Thus, the law is definite.

The Need to Be Flexible

Community property
Property owned in common by a husband and wife as a kind of marital property in a form of marital partnership

It is not a contradiction in terms to say that the law must be both definite and flexible. The law needs to be definite in order to establish a standard. The law also must be flexible so that it can be applied in many different *individual* situations. For example, in many **community property** states, the divorce court judge has flexibility in dividing the community property of the two parties. If a couple, both aged twenty-five, have a community estate of $500,000 and there are no children to consider, how much should each get? You simply do not have enough facts to answer the question. What if the man is a brain surgeon with a yearly income of $300,000 and his wife is a high school dropout with no employment skills? Their joint community property amounts to $500,000. A division of $400,000 to the wife and $100,000 to the husband might be appropriate under those circumstances. In the future, the husband can always go out and earn much more than his wife because he has a skill that people will pay for. In such a situation, a judge would be persuaded by the skill of the advocates as well. If lawyers are not persuasive, their clients will get less. Yielding to persuasion makes our system flexible. If all trees did not bend in the wind, they would break. Our legal system is like those trees: it must bend without breaking.

Because people depend on it to guide their actions, the law needs to be practical and oriented to action rather than thought. This is not to say that there are not some very thoughtful ideas behind the law, but it is *not* a philosophical system; it is a *real* system. One can prove or not prove just about anything in a philosophical system, because it is not real. The law, however, must deal with real issues. Real issues are created by real people. These issues take the form of a legal conflict. For example, say a world-famous concert pianist earns over $200,000 per year. While driving home one night her car stalls at a railroad intersection. The pianist attempts to start the car but to no avail. A train is rapidly approaching. She decides to abandon the car and flee, but the doors and windows are all electrically controlled and are jammed. The train hits the car, and the driver's hands are crushed by the collapsing metal. Suit is brought, and it is decided that the automobile manufacturer was negligent in constructing the vehicle. It is currently medically impossible to rehabilitate the hands so that they can again play a Chopin etude. The law cannot wave a magic wand and replace the hands. In general, all the law can do is to assess money damages and give the pianist the present value of what she would have earned from playing the piano for the rest of her life. That is not an ideal solution, but it is a practical one. If the law were not practical, it would be useless.

The Need to Be Practical

If we had the best set of laws imaginable but no one knew of them, they would be useless. Therefore, all laws must be published. It is for this reason that the law properly presumes that all persons know the law.

The Need to Be Published

If a controversy exists and it is possible to use the legal system to resolve it, one thing is certain: at some point in the future, the matter will be finally resolved. It may not be resolved to the satisfaction of the person who "won" the case, but it will be resolved. In this sense, the law is like a political election. On election day, someone wins and someone loses. The outcome is final. In criminal law, if the defendant wins the case in trial court, that is the end of the matter. The prosecutor cannot appeal in most situations. A defendant who is convicted in trial court can appeal to the highest court in the state system. If the defendant does not gain a reversal, that is the end of the matter, unless the United States Supreme Court chooses to review the case. The process is much like a ping-pong ball that keeps bouncing back and forth until someone finally wins and the ball comes to rest. Many cases end in a **settlement.** That means the matter is not carried to trial, but rather the parties agree to end the matter on their own. The settlement agreed on is incorporated into the court's final judgment. In criminal cases, the same sort of process is called **plea bargaining.** More than 75 percent of all cases, criminal and civil, are disposed of in this manner. However the process is accomplished, it results in a final judgment. Figure 1.1 outlines the needs of a legal system.

The Need to Be Final

Settlement A form of legally binding agreement that "settles" a lawsuit

Plea bargaining Process of settlement used in criminal cases

Figure 1.1   The Needs of a Legal System

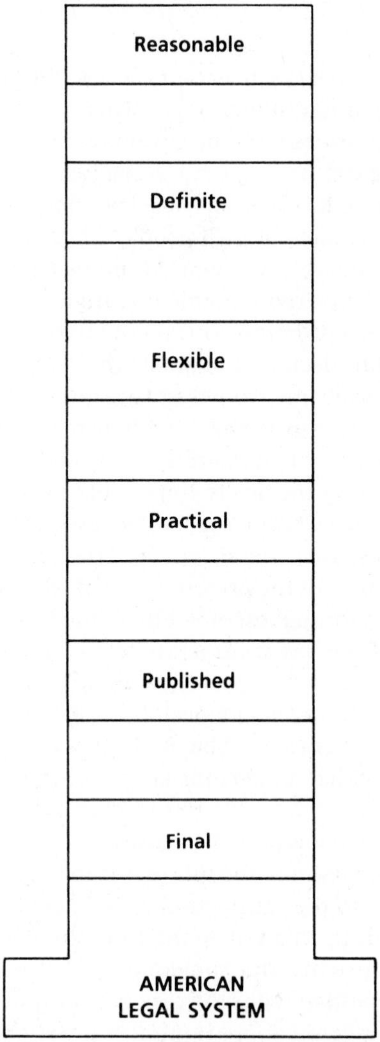

Reasonable
Definite
Flexible
Practical
Published
Final
AMERICAN LEGAL SYSTEM

WHAT ARE THE PURPOSES OF A LEGAL SYSTEM?

Achieving Justice

As previously discussed, justice is basically fairness. Sometimes we achieve it and sometimes we don't. In the law of business, we deal more with commutative justice — giving each person his due — than with distributive justice. In a contract, for example, commutative justice gives each person that to which the person is entitled under the contract — no more, no less. The rule of *caveat emptor* (let the buyer beware) is an example of how the law allocates risk in a business transaction. If the buyer does not thoroughly examine the goods before they are bought, the buyer will be prevented from seeking redress in the courts if what is bought does not conform to the buyer's expectations. If the buyer had examined the goods before the purchase, flaws could have been discovered and the sale might not have been made.

There is a trend, however, to introduce elements of distributive justice into the law of business. The courts, legislatures, and administrative agencies are attempting to reallocate the risks of business transactions by taking into account the status of the parties. For example, in 1976 the Federal Trade Commission established a new rule concerning consumer transactions that resulted in more protection for the consumer. You will learn more about this matter in Chapter 22, on the holder in due course doctrine.

Another limit placed upon the doctrine of commutative justice is that of **unconscionability.** An eighteenth-century English case provides an excellent working definition of unconscionable contracts as contracts that are so unfair "no man in his senses and not under delusion would make [them] on the one hand, and no honest and fair man would accept [them] on the other."[1] Our legal system must always consider that some contracts ought not to be enforced even if they fully comply with all the rules concerning contract formation. You will learn more about this subject in Chapter 12, on reality of consent.

Unconscionability
Condition of being so unreasonably favorable to one party, or so one-sided, as to shock the conscience

Providing Police Power

Since justice is the ultimate purpose of a legal system, providing police power may be viewed as an intermediate purpose of a legal system. When most students see the term *police power,* they usually envision a person in a blue uniform with a badge and gun. That is just one part of the power we call police power. Police power is inherent in all governments. This power allows for the creation and enforcement of laws designed to protect the public's health, safety, and general welfare.[2] Laws and ordinances concerning police, fire, sanitation, and social welfare departments in state and local governments stem from this power.

Maintaining Peace and the Status Quo

Ever since the days of ancient England, one of the clearest purposes of the law has been to "keep the King's peace." All modern torts and crimes can trace their origin to a simple breaching of the King's peace. Today, laws that govern the relationships between private individuals, such as the laws governing assault, battery, trespass, and false imprisonment, are private forms of keeping the peace. Allied with keeping the peace is the concept of maintaining the status quo — that is, keeping things the way they are. It is natural for the law to maintain the status quo unless changing things will benefit society. In cases where irreparable injury is alleged, it is possible, upon a proper showing, to obtain an **injunction** from a court that will maintain the status quo until the matter is finally resolved.

Injunction A court order prohibiting a person or persons from doing a certain thing or, on the other hand, ordering that something be done

---

[1] Earl of Chesterfield v. Janssen, 28 Eng. Rep. 82, 100 (Ch. 1750).
[2] Drysdale v. Prudden, 195 N.C. 722, 143 S.E. 530, 536 (1928).

Providing Answers

On a philosophical plane, the law should be just; but on a practical plane, it should provide answers. Sometimes the answers the law provides are not satisfactory answers. If a person sues a neighbor concerning a nuisance the neighbor is allegedly creating, and the neighbor wins the case in trial court, the person who sued can appeal the decision to the next higher court. In most states this higher court is called an **appellate court.** If an appellate court rules in favor of the person who allegedly created the nuisance, a further appeal may be taken to the state's highest court. In that court, however, the person who originally sued may win and thereby receive a satisfactory answer. Your business law professor may be more interested in raising questions for you to consider than in providing answers, which is as it should be in a college classroom. That same person, however, as a practicing lawyer, would be more interested in obtaining answers for clients than in raising legal questions. A legal system in which there were no answers would be ridiculous.

Appellate court A court that has the power to review the decisions of lower courts

Providing Protection

The law protects all kinds of interests. You have already seen that the law concerns itself with protecting individuals. The tort law of assault and battery is a classic example of protection of the individual. The law also protects persons less obviously when it protects their **civil rights.** Civil rights laws are extremely important in modern litigation and have their historical antecedent in the first ten amendments to our federal Constitution. The Constitution appears as an appendix to this book; it would be worthwhile for you to refresh your memory about its features at this time. Persons are protected in the free exercise of their speech, are free to choose or not to choose a religion, can peacefully assemble, and may petition their government for a redress of grievances (a rarely used freedom). The right to keep and bear arms, the right to be free of unreasonable searches and seizures, the right against compulsory self-incrimination, the right to a grand jury, the right against double jeopardy, the right to a jury trial, and the right to bail are just some of the more important civil rights.

Civil rights The rights in the first ten amendments to the Constitution (the Bill of Rights) and due process and equal protection under the Fourteenth Amendment

The government is also in the business of protecting *itself.* A government's self-protection is an ancient right that goes back to Roman law. It is based on the concept that if the sovereign is **sovereign,** it is a contradiction in terms to allow the sovereign to be attacked legally. This rule still stands, although somewhat altered in that the federal government and many states have passed special statutes allowing suit for torts to be brought against them.

Sovereign Above or superior to all others; that from which all authority flows

Lastly, the law is concerned with the protection of property. All property is either personal or real. *Personal property* is all property with the exception of real property. In general, if property is movable, it is personal property. *Real property,* on the other hand, is land and whatever is affixed to land, like a house. Our legal system has a variety of laws that protect property.

Enforcing Intent

The law of contracts is based on *freedom of contract.* It is this rule that allows each of us to be our own legislator. We make our own laws as long as the contracts into which we enter do not violate the general principles of contract law. For example, you may wish to enter into a contract with a supplier of goods. You may want to make the contract today so that it will immediately bind the other party. Perhaps you have found a good price and do not think you will find a better one. Your problem is that you do not presently have the money to pay for the goods. You know that you could easily resell the goods for an immediate cash profit within ten days after delivery of the goods. You should then seek a provision in the contract stating that the buyer will pay the seller for the goods eleven days after receipt of the goods. Of course, if you cannot resell the goods within ten days, you will have a problem, but that is a question of business judgment and not one of law.

Both criminal law and civil law are directed toward rehabilitation. Criminal law should, among other things, rehabilitate the criminal. If people who enter jails or prisons are not rehabilitated by the time they leave, all we are doing is maintaining free hotels for criminals. Civil law is directed toward the rehabilitation of debtors. The Constitution gives Congress the power to make laws concerning bankruptcy. Bankruptcy laws have developed to the point that anyone can use the protection of the law to escape financial difficulty and to create a new financial life. For example, take a twenty-five-year-old university honors graduate. The graduate decides to enter the computer software business because of her knowledge of computer programming. At first, business booms. The decision to expand is made, and banks help in financing a major expansion. Suddenly the market shifts and the business finds it has much more in debts than in assets. Is it not fair to allow this person to seek protection under the bankruptcy law and begin again? What is the alternative? To allow this person to spend the rest of her working life trying to pay off the debt would be counterproductive. Let her start afresh and profit from her mistakes.

Providing Rehabilitation

One of the major characteristics of the American legal system is that it facilitates the making of commercial transactions. For example, if everyone had to have cash to purchase an automobile, the number of automobiles sold in the United States would be reduced by millions. To a great degree, our society is built upon the automobile. The steel, energy, and transportation industries are directly related to the automobile. Accordingly, the extension of credit for the purchase of automobiles greatly facilitates trade. The use of checks and credit cards also accelerates commercial transactions. The taking of a security interest in goods expedites trade to persons who might otherwise not be in a financial position to make the purchase. The United States legal system, which reflects its public policy, fosters free and open competition and facilitates trade. This characteristic of the legal system has done much to make the United States the business and financial giant it is today. Figure 1.2 outlines the purposes of a legal system.

Facilitating Commercial Transactions

Figure 1.2   The Purposes of a Legal System

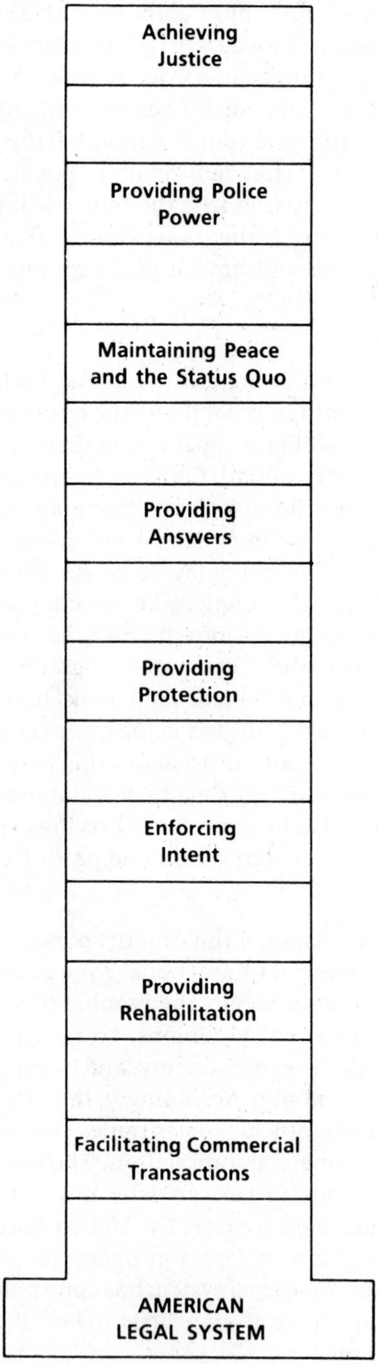

Achieving Justice
Providing Police Power
Maintaining Peace and the Status Quo
Providing Answers
Providing Protection
Enforcing Intent
Providing Rehabilitation
Facilitating Commercial Transactions

AMERICAN LEGAL SYSTEM

Our legal system is based upon the Constitution, treaties, statutes, ordinances, administrative regulations, common law, case law, and equity. These elements of the American legal system are interconnected. Each of the elements is separate, but when the elements are interconnected, they make up the system. It is important to think of these elements as a system, since a change in one element cannot be considered in isolation. Such a change will affect one or more parts of the system. In a civil rights suit, a person may allege a violation of constitutional rights (Fourteenth Amendment), a statutory right (Civil Rights Act of 1964), an administrative regulation (Equal Employment Opportunity Commission), past decisions of the court **(stare decisis)**, and equity (if all else fails, the person should win because it is fair). There are provisions in our legal system for taking a case filed in state court and removing it to a federal court. The important thing to remember is that all the parts are interrelated and that the whole is more than the sum of the parts.

A *constitution* is the *fundamental law of a nation.* It may be written or unwritten. The British constitution is said to be unwritten. Clearly, the United States Constitution *is* written. It allocates the powers of government and also sets limits on those powers. Our founding fathers knew that all tyrants had two powers: the power of the purse and the power of the sword. The Constitution places the power of the purse exclusively with the Congress and the power of the sword with the executive branch. Our third branch of government — the judiciary — has neither the power of the purse nor the power of the sword, and yet it has the power to decide the constitutionality of the laws passed by Congress. In the case of *Marbury* v. *Madison,*[3] the United States Supreme Court for the first time applied the doctrine of **judicial review.** That case held that the Supreme Court has the power to decide whether laws passed by Congress comply with the Constitution. If they do not, they are unconstitutional and thus of no force or effect. We shall discuss the unique nature of the Constitution, and the *Marbury* v. *Madison* case, further in the next chapter.

Our states also have constitutions, and they are the fundamental laws of those jurisdictions. The Constitution, however, is the supreme legal document in the United States; any conflict between it and state constitutions will result in the latter yielding to the federal document.

Treaties, which are *formal agreements between two or more nations,* are the only element of our legal system that does not stem from the Constitution. Treaties are made, not with the authority of the Constitution, but under the authority of the United States. This difference is important, since the power to make a treaty is a function of sovereignty and not one of a constitution. In most cases, treaties require enabling legislation passed by Congress. In the case of *Missouri* v. *Holland,*[4] it was established that statutes passed in accordance with a valid

[3] 1 Cranch 137, 2 L.Ed. 60 (1803).
[4] 252 U.S. 416, 40 S.Ct. 382, 64 L.Ed. 641 (1920)

WHAT ARE THE SOURCES OF THE AMERICAN LEGAL SYSTEM?

Stare decisis To abide by, or adhere to, decided cases; policy of courts to stand by decided cases and not to disturb a settled point

Constitutions

Judicial review The power of the courts to say what the law is

Treaties

treaty cannot be declared unconstitutional. Once made, treaties also become the supreme law of the land.

Statutes

Statutes are the *acts of legislative bodies.* They command or prohibit the doing of something. The word *statute* is preferred when one is referring to legislative acts, in order to distinguish it from such other "laws" as ordinances, regulations, common law, and case law. The best example of state statutory law is found in the Uniform Commercial Code (UCC) (see Appendix A). All fifty states, the District of Columbia, and the United States Virgin Islands have adopted this law. It is the subject of many of the chapters contained in this book. The UCC covers the following subjects: sales, commercial paper, bank deposits and collections, letters of credit, bulk transfers, documents of title, investment securities, and secured transactions.

Ordinances

Ordinances are *laws passed by municipal bodies.* Cities, towns, and villages, if incorporated, have the power to establish laws for the protection of the public's health, safety, and welfare. These entities are to be distinguished from counties, which generally do not have legislative power. Counties usually have the power to enforce state laws within their boundaries.

Administrative Regulations

Administrative regulations are *rules promulgated by governmental bodies created by the legislative branch of government,* such as the Federal Trade Commission on the federal level and an insurance commission on the state level. These bodies have unusual powers, which will be discussed in Chapter 45. The rules and regulations of these entities have the full force and effect of law.

Common Law and Law Merchant

Common law consists of "those principles and rules of action, relating to the government and security of persons and property, which derive their authority solely from usages and customs of immemorial antiquity, or from the judgments and decrees of the courts recognizing, affirming, and enforcing such usages and customs."[5] *Law merchant,* on the other hand, is the body of rules used by merchants that was based on usage and custom. This is the predecessor of the modern law of business.

Case Law

Case law exists in the many reported cases emanating from federal and state courts. It is quite often up to judges to interpret statutes in order to apply them to actual cases and controversies. These interpretations place what lawyers call a "judicial gloss" on the statute. You will not know what a particular statute really stands for until you have read not only the statute but also the cases that have interpreted that statute. *Case law,* then, is *the law as pronounced by judges.*

Stare decisis is an ancient doctrine that means *the question has been decided.* For example, if a particular legal point is well settled in a certain jurisdiction, then a future case with substantially the same facts will be decided in accor-

[5] Western Union Tel. Co. v. Call Pub. Co., 181 U.S. 92, 21 S.Ct. 561, 45 L.Ed. 765 (1901).

dance with the principle that has already been decided. It is for this reason, as well as others, that lawyers do a great deal of legal research. An opportunity to "make law," as it is called, occurs when a legal point is in conflict. For example, many states are divided into various judicial districts, and each of these districts may issue written legal opinions. If two or more districts have published conflicting opinions on a particular point, and the state's supreme court has *not* issued an opinion on the point, the time is ripe for the creation of a new rule, statewide, that will resolve the matter once and for all.

Equity has been defined as *a body of rules applied to legal controversies when there is no adequate remedy at law.* These rules are based not on technicalities but rather on the principles outlined by Justinian during his reign as the Byzantine emperor of Rome (A.D. 527 – 565): "to live honestly, to harm nobody, [and] to render to every man his due." These rules were developed outside the common law courts in England by an officer of the king called the chancellor. Today the rules of law and equity are joined into one system. The injunction is an equitable remedy, but before our courts will issue an injunction, the person requesting it must show proof of an inadequate remedy at law. For example, if your neighbors are burning rubber tires on their property and the prevailing wind carries the obnoxious odor directly across your property, it will destroy the peaceful use and enjoyment of your land. In general, no amount of money damages would be sufficient to allow them to continue to burn rubber tires. In that case, you would have an inadequate remedy at law, and you could request that the court issue an injunction to stop your neighbors from burning those tires. In a larger sense, however, equity may be viewed as a doctrine that results in the legal system's adhering to the principle of fairness. Figure 1.3 outlines the sources of the American legal system.

Equity

Our legal system is divided into two branches: federal and state. American lawyers must learn not only the law of their states but the law of the federal courts as well. In addition, lawyers must know the *majority rule.* The majority rule is simply the rule that a majority of states has adopted. Quite often, there is also a minority rule that a smaller number of states follow. Rarely, if at all, do the states agree on everything.

HOW IS THE LAW CLASSIFIED?

Federal Versus State Law

As discussed earlier, our system consists of both common and statutory law. The European legal system, however, does not have a common law. It is totally statutory. The statutes are grouped into codes, and the codes are administered by judges. Judges do not make law in the European system. On the other hand, judges in England and the United States have the power to "make law."

Common Versus Statutory Law

Another dichotomy in our legal system is its division into civil and criminal law. *Civil law* is *private law wherein one person sues another person. Criminal law,* however, is *public law in which a government entity sues a person;* for example, if a

Civil Versus Criminal Law

Figure 1.3   The Sources of the American Legal System

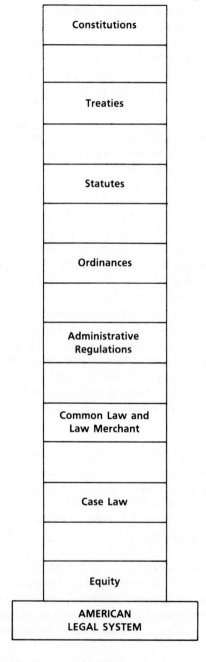

person becomes violently abusive and attacks another individual, and thus inflicts bodily harm upon the innocent individual, the district attorney as the representative of a government entity may prosecute the attacker for assault. If convicted, the attacker may go to jail or prison. In addition, the person who was injured may sue the attacker in court for money damages. The additional suit would not constitute **double jeopardy** or its civil law equivalent, **res judicata,** since there are two different theories of action: civil and criminal.

Double jeopardy A rule of criminal law that states that a person will not be twice exposed to conviction for the same offense

Res judicata A rule of civil law that states that a person will not be twice exposed to liability for the same wrong

Substantive Versus Procedural Law

Substantive law deals with *rights and duties given or imposed by the legal system. Procedural law* is devoted to *how those rights and duties are enforced.* For example, the law of contracts is substantive law. The law of pleadings describes how one goes about enforcing those rights or duties. A controversy over the matter of contractual consideration or the lack of it is a substantive matter, but how one goes about getting that matter into a court is a matter of procedure. Where one files the lawsuit, what must be alleged, how one serves the lawsuit on the defendant, and how long the defendant has to answer the allegations are all examples of procedural law. This book is devoted primarily to *substantive* law.

SUMMARY

Law consists of rules that must be obeyed. These rules must be obeyed because they can be enforced in courts of law. Order is the absence of chaos. Our legal system strives to create and to maintain order. Justice is fairness. Commutative justice seeks to give each person what is due him or her. Distributive justice seeks to give each person more, or less, than what is due. The goal of distributive justice is to balance the unequal distributions that exist in society. Our legal system seeks constantly to balance law, order, and justice. Its ultimate goal is to achieve equilibrium.

The law is an artificial language system. It uses words from everyday conversation, but it adds different meanings. It also uses words that are unique to the law. The law of business includes contracts, sales, commercial paper, secured transactions, agency, partnerships, corporations, and insurance. By studying the law of business, you will learn how to avoid legal problems. If legal problems should develop, however, this knowledge will sensitize you to their ramifications. As a result, you will know when an attorney should be consulted.

A legal system needs to be reasonable, definite, practical, published, and final. A legal system should be directed toward achieving justice. It does so by properly utilizing police power; by keeping the peace or maintaining the status quo when irreparable injury is threatened; by providing answers; by protecting people, property, and government; by enforcing intent; by rehabilitating people; and by facilitating commercial transactions.

As you can see, our legal system is like a three-dimensional chess game in which a move in one subsystem can affect other subsystems. The sources of the American legal system are constitutions, treaties, statutes, ordinances, administrative regulations, common law, the law merchant, case law, and equity. The law is a multifaceted, bifurcated system of federal and state law, common and statutory law, civil and criminal law, and substantive and procedural law.

DISCUSSION
QUESTIONS

1. Why do you think St. Augustine said that states without justice are robber bands enlarged?

2. Are law, order, and justice equally weighted parts of our legal system, or do one or two outweigh the other? Explain.

3. Why is the law an artificial language system? Turn to the Glossary and look up five legal terms whose meanings in the law differ from their meanings in everyday usage. Look up five legal terms that have meanings unique to the law. What are the definitions?

4. What rational arguments can you make for *not* having a knowledge of the law? What arguments can you make for having a knowledge of the law?

5. What is the primary purpose of issuing an injunction?

6. The Federal Tort Claims Act allows the United States government to be sued under certain circumstances. Why do you think this statute was enacted? Why are intentional torts exceptions to the law?

7. What is stare decisis? Once a question has been decided, is there no way for the rule to be changed?

8. The UCC was developed by the National Conference of Commissioners on Uniform State Laws and the American Law Institute. What advantage is there to such an organization?

9. Jeremy Bentham (1748–1832), an English lawyer, is best known for his utilitarian philosophy that the object of law should be to achieve the "greatest happiness of the greatest number." Discuss the implications of the following statement based upon your knowledge of common versus statutory law.

> Do you know how they make [common law]? Just as a man makes laws for his dog. When your dog does anything you want to break him of, you wait until he does it and then beat him. This is the way you make law for your dog, and this is the way judges make laws for you and me. They won't tell a man before-hand. . . . The French have had enough of this dog-law; they are turning it as fast as they can into statute law, that everybody may have a rule to go by. . . . (Bentham, 5 *Works* 231.)

10. On numerous occasions, Mochan telephoned a person and used language that was obscene, lewd, and filthy. After the person complained to the police, Mochan was indicted and convicted of a common law misdemeanor since there was no criminal statute covering obscene telephone calls. Discuss the outcome of this case with respect to the rule that our laws need to be published. (*Commonwealth* v. *Mochan*, 177 Pa. Super. 454, 110 A.2d 788 [1955].)

CHAPTER 2

The American Legal System

THE FEDERAL CONSTITUTION

The Constitution of the United States is unique for two reasons: it is the oldest written national constitution, and it was the first to design a government based on the concept of a separation of powers. It was created in reaction to the tyranny of English rule. England has an unwritten constitution and a system of government that tends to merge the legislative, executive, and judicial functions. In contrast, our written constitution created a governmental structure with three separate "compartments" and a series of checks and balances whereby the power of one "compartment" is offset by that of the others.

Because their study of history taught them that all tyrants had at least two powers — the power of the purse and the power of the sword — our founding fathers placed the power of the purse (fiscal and monetary) in the legislative branch of government and the power of the sword (armed forces) in the executive branch. They gave the third branch of government the power that ultimately was to be called the power of *judicial review*. This power allows the third branch of government to make the ultimate decision as to where and how the other two powers may be properly exercised. We shall discuss this power in greater detail later.

Allocation of Power

Legislative Power

Article 1 of the Constitution creates a Congress consisting of two houses: the Senate and the House of Representatives. Congress has the power to levy and collect taxes, pay debts, and pass all laws with respect to certain enumerated powers, such as providing for the common defense and general welfare, regulating commerce, borrowing and coining money, establishing post offices and highways, promoting science and the arts, and creating courts inferior to that of the Supreme Court.

Executive Power

Article 2 creates the executive branch of government by creating the offices of president and vice-president. The president is the commander-in-chief of the armed forces of the United States. In addition, the president has the power to make treaties and to nominate ambassadors, judges, and other officers of the United States. The Senate must confirm all presidential appointments. Without Senate confirmation, the appointee can not take office. The vice-president serves for the president when the president is unable to serve, and is also the president of the Senate.

Judicial Power

Article 3 vests the judicial power of the United States in one Supreme Court and in such other inferior courts as Congress may create. All federal judges in the United States are nominated by the president; if they are confirmed by the Senate, they serve in office for the rest of their lives, during good behavior.

The actual wording of Article 3 limits rather than expands the judicial power. Limitations placed on the power flow from the words "**cases . . . [and] controversies**" that appear in Section 2. In general, the federal courts are limited to hearing and deciding cases and controversies only. Constitutional law has evolved to the point where, today, the following areas are not within the realm of cases and controversies:

Cases and controversies Claims brought before the court by regular proceedings to protect or enforce rights or to prevent or punish wrongs

1. advisory opinion
2. moot point
3. lack of standing
4. political question

Advisory opinion A formal opinion by a judge, court, or law officer on a question of law submitted by a legislative body or a government official but not presented in an actual case

The doctrine of the separation of powers requires that our courts deal only with judicial matters. An **advisory opinion** is one wherein the executive branch refers a question to the judicial branch for a nonbinding opinion. That is not the purpose of our judicial system. Accordingly, whenever a member of the executive branch requires an advisory opinion, the question will be referred to the justice department within the executive branch for an opinion of the attorney general. In our system of government, the attorney general is the appropriate person to issue an advisory opinion. The following case illustrates that the judicial power is limited to real controversies and does not encompass advisory opinions.

Muskrat v. *United States*
219 U.S. 346 (1911)

In 1902 Congress made an allotment of certain lands to the Cherokee Indians. Congressional legislation authorized suits to be brought against the United States to determine the validity of any acts of Congress passed since that act.

FACTS

Did Congress have the power to confer this jurisdiction?

ISSUE

No. Such conduct is not authorized.

HOLDING

The exercise of judicial power is limited to cases and controversies. Not every violation of the Constitution can be redressed in our courts, only actual cases and controversies. Therefore, the congressional legislation purporting to grant authority to determine the validity of an act of Congress is not within the powers granted to Congress in the Constitution because it is not a "real, earnest, and vital controversy between individuals."

REASONING

The federal courts will hear only cases that are appropriate for a judicial solution. In the case of *Defunis* v. *Odergard*,[1] the Supreme Court stated that the question of whether a student should be admitted to a law school was a **moot point** because by the time the Court could have issued its opinion, the student would have been on the brink of graduation. Accordingly, as an example of judicial efficiency, it chose not to write an opinion on the merits of the suit.

Moot point A subject for argument that is unsettled or undecided; a point not settled by judicial decision

Only persons who can assert that they have actually been harmed or injured have **standing** to sue. For example, if you saw a person punch someone in the nose, you would not have standing to sue the aggressor for assault and battery. The person who was hit would have standing to sue since he was injured, not you. The following case discusses one aspect of standing.

Standing Legal involvement; the right to **sue**

[1] 416 U.S. 312 (1974).

Flast v. *Cohen*
392 U.S. 83 (1968)

FACTS   A federal taxpayer brought suit to prohibit the spending of federal monies to finance instructional materials in parochial schools. The spending was authorized under the Elementary and Secondary Education Act of 1965. The suit was based on the grounds that such expenditures were in violation of the First Amendment guaranteeing freedom of religion.

ISSUE   Does a taxpayer have standing to sue?

HOLDING   Yes. In such a case a taxpayer does have standing.

REASONING   "The fundamental aspect of standing is that it focuses on the party seeking to get his complaint before a federal court and not on the issues he wishes to have adjudicated." The party seeking relief must have a personal stake in the outcome of the controversy so as to assure a *concrete* awareness. Under certain circumstances, a taxpayer may have a personal stake in the outcome. Therefore, there is no absolute bar to a federal taxpayer suit. This case raised the sole question of the standing of individuals who assert only their status as taxpayers. Since the taxpayer in this case successfully asserted that this legislation exceeds specific constitutional limits, he had standing to sue.

Political questions
Questions concerning government, the state, or politics, which are thus more properly settled at the ballot box than in the courtroom

Judicial restraint A holding or pressing back from action by a court

Even though many **political questions** in our society involve real controversies, the doctrine of our courts is that they will not hear them. This rule is based on the concept of **judicial restraint.** For example, if a citizen should assert that a state is not based on a republican form of government, that claim would not be heard in our federal courts since it is a political question. Also, if a citizen should think that our nation's foreign policy is incorrect, our courts could not be used to debate the point since it is a political question. But is *legislative apportionment* — the ratio of legislative representation to constituents — a political question? The following case resolved that question.

Baker v. *Carr*
369 U.S. 186 (1962)

FACTS   The plaintiffs alleged that the apportionment of the state legislature under Tennessee state law was unequal since rural voters had greater representation than urban voters.

Is state legislative apportionment a political question and therefore **nonjusticiable**?

ISSUE

No. It is a constitutional question and is therefore justiciable.

HOLDING

REASONING

The claim of the **appellants** that "they are being denied equal protection is justifiable, provided discrimination is sufficiently shown . . . the right to relief under the equal protection clause is not diminished by the fact that the discrimination relates to political rights . . . the nonjusticiability of a political question is primarily a function of the separation of powers . . . the question here is the consistency of state action with the federal Constitution. We have no question decided, or to be decided, by a political branch of government coequal with this court . . . when challenges to state action respecting matters of the administration of the affairs of the state and the officers through whom they are conducted have rested on claims of Constitutional deprivation which are amenable to judicial correction, this court has acted upon its view of the merit of the claim."

Nonjusticiable Not subject to the jurisdiction of a court

Appellants Persons who appeal the decision of a lower court to a higher court

━━━━━━━━━━━━━━━━━━━━

Now that you know the four limits that constrain judicial power, we shall consider the one concept that has expanded judicial power. When you read the Constitution, you will not find the specific power of judicial review mentioned. That is because it is a court-created power. The chief justice of the United States in 1803, John Marshall, created this doctrine of the law in the landmark case of *Marbury* v. *Madison.*[2] This power is based on an interpretation of the Constitution that our courts may examine the actions of the legislative and executive branches of government to ascertain whether those actions conform to the Constitution. If they do not, the courts have the power to declare those actions unconstitutional and therefore unenforceable. Thus, the Supreme Court can declare an act of Congress invalid. This concept of judicial power does not exist in England, where the Parliament is supreme. Therefore, the branch of government that has neither the power of the purse nor the power of the sword has all the power, in a sense, because it has the power to say what is right. Since 1803, the power of our courts to judicially review all actions of the legislative and executive branches of government has gone unchallenged. It is the keystone of our doctrine of the separation of powers. Furthermore, this power of the Supreme Court to invalidate legislation also extends to all state legislation because of the supremacy clause of the federal Constitution.

The Watergate crisis may be remembered by some as a low point in American history. However, it may actually be viewed as a high point with respect to the doctrine of judicial review. In 1974 President Nixon was ordered to produce the now famous Watergate tapes for use in a federal prosecution.

[2] 1 Cranch 137, 2 L.Ed. 60 (1803).

President Nixon claimed executive privilege and rejected the order to turn over the tapes to the federal prosecutor. The Supreme Court, in a unanimous opinion, denied his claim and ordered him to release the tapes. The rest is history. President Nixon complied with the order of the Supreme Court, a constitutional crisis ended, and Nixon became the first president to resign from office.

The following case contains the most famous Supreme Court opinion. It created the doctrine of judicial review.

Marbury v. Madison
1 Cranch 137, 2 L.Ed. 60 (1803)

FACTS

Mandamus A type of writ that issues from a court of superior jurisdiction commanding the performance of a particular act specified therein

Congress enacted a statute that revised the federal judicial system. In accordance with that law, President John Adams signed the commission for a Washington, D.C., justice of the peace, William Marbury, but the commission never reached him. The new president's secretary of state, James Madison, withheld Marbury's commission. Marbury sought relief by filing an action in the Supreme Court asking that Madison show cause why a **mandamus** should not be issued directing Madison to deliver his commission.

ISSUES

1. Does Marbury have a right to the commission?

2. If he has a right, and that right has been violated, does the law afford him a remedy?

3. If he is entitled to a remedy, is mandamus the appropriate remedy?

HOLDINGS

Yes to the first two issues, and no to the third.

REASONING

Writ A mandatory precept issuing from a court of justice and couched in the form of a letter ordering some designated activity

"The peculiar delicacy of this case, the novelty of some of its circumstances, and the real difficulty attending the points which occur in it require a complete exposition of the principles on which the opinion to be given by the court is founded. . . . It only remains to be inquired whether [the remedy] can issue from this court. . . . If this court is not authorized to issue a **writ** of Mandamus . . . it must be because the law is unconstitutional, and therefore absolutely incapable of conferring the authority, and assigning the duties which its words purport to confer and assign. . . . The act to establish the judicial courts of the United States authorizes the Supreme Court to issue Writs of Mandamus in cases warranted by the principles and usages of law, to any courts appointed or persons holding office, under the authority of the United States. . . . However, the Constitution says that the Supreme Court shall have original jurisdiction in all cases affecting ambassadors, other public ministers and consuls, and those in which a state shall be a party. In all other cases, the Supreme Court shall have appellate jurisdiction. . . . The authority given to the Supreme Court, by the act establishing the judicial courts of the United States, to issue Writs of Mandamus to public officers, appears not to be warranted by the Constitution, and it becomes necessary to inquire whether a jurisdiction so conferred can be exercised. . . ."

The powers of the legislature are defined and limited. . . . It is a proposition too plain to be contested, that the Constitution controls only legislative acts repugnant to it; or, that the legislature may alter the Constitution by an ordinary act. . . . Certainly all those who have formed written constitutions contemplate them as forming the fundamental and paramount law of the nation, and consequently, the theory of every such government must be, that an act of the legislature, repugnant to the Constitution, is void. . . . It is emphatically the province and duty of the judicial department to say what the law is. . . . If two laws conflict with each other, the courts must decide on the operation of each. . . . If, then, the courts are to regard the Constitution, and the Constitution is superior to any ordinary act of the legislature, the Constitution, and no such ordinary act, must govern the case to which they both apply. . . . Thus, the particular phraseology of the Constitution of the United States conforms and strengthens the principle, supposed to be essential to all written constitutions, that a law repugnant to the Constitution is void, and that courts, as well as other departments, are bound by that instrument."

Figure 2.1 outlines the allocation of Constitutional power.

Figure 2.1 Allocation of Constitutional Power

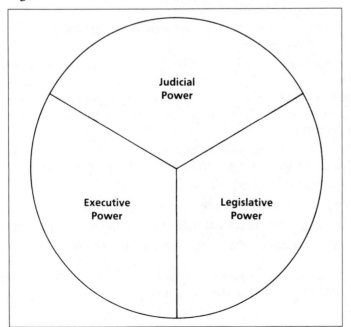

Limitation of Power

Habeus corpus The name given to a variety of writs issued to bring a party before a court or judge

The original Constitution that was signed on 17 September 1787 contained a number of rights pertaining to individuals. The ancient and most celebrated prerogative writ in English law was the right to **habeus corpus.** This right may be used by all persons who have been deprived of their liberty. The writ is addressed to the person who detains an individual; it commands that person to produce the individual in a court and requires that court to determine whether the person has been rightfully detained.

Another right established in the Constitution was that no bills of attainder were to be passed by Congress. A *bill of attainder* is a "legislative trial" whereby a person is judged a felon or worse by act of the legislature and not by a court of law.

Ex post facto After the fact; pertaining to an act or fact occurring after some previous act or fact

Congress was also denied the right to enact **ex post facto** laws. For example, if a citizen entered into a transaction that was perfectly legal in January, Congress would be prevented from declaring that transaction illegal in a statute passed after January.

Other individual rights, such as trial by jury in most criminal cases, were contained in the original Constitution, but those just mentioned are particularly notable.

The Bill of Rights

Four years after the Constitution was signed, the first ten amendments to the Constitution were passed. They further protected individual rights. They may be summarized as follows:

1. freedoms of religion, speech, press, assembly, and petition of government
2. the right to bear arms
3. no quartering of soldiers in private homes during times of peace without consent of the owner
4. no unreasonable searches or seizures; warrants issued only on probable cause
5. right to a grand jury, no double jeopardy, no compulsory self-incrimination, due process of law, and no taking of private property without just compensation
6. right to a speedy and public trial and an impartial jury; right to confront accusers and witnesses and to have the assistance of counsel
7. right of trial by jury in civil cases
8. no excessive bail or cruel and unusual punishment
9. retention of other individual rights beyond the ones enumerated
10. granting of further rights to the state and the people

The Fourteenth Amendment

In 1868, Congress amended the Constitution to enable the rights contained in the Bill of Rights to apply to state law as well:

Figure 2.2 The Current Constitutional Situation

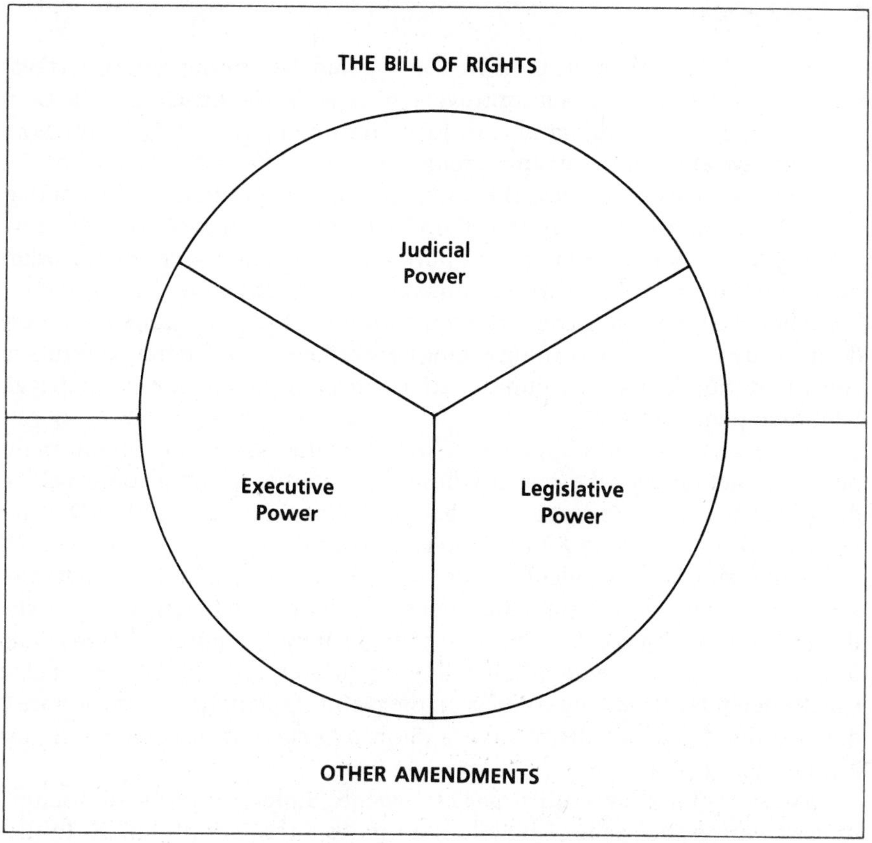
THE BILL OF RIGHTS
Judicial
Power
Executive
Power
Legislative
Power
OTHER AMENDMENTS

> No state shall make or enforce any law which shall abridge the privileges or immunities of citizens of the United States; nor shall any state deprive any person of life, liberty, or property, without due process of law; nor deny to any person within its jurisdiction the equal protection of the laws.

Figure 2.2 depicts the current Constitutional situation.

THE COURTS

The basic concept with respect to our courts is one of *jurisdiction.* Quite simply, jurisdiction is *the legal power of a court to decide a particular matter.*

Jurisdiction

For our purposes, we shall examine four aspects of jurisdiction:

1. subject matter jurisdiction
2. jurisdiction over the person

3. concurrent versus exclusive jurisdiction

4. venue

In our discussion of the Constitution, we said that the Supreme Court was limited to deciding cases and controversies. In addition, Article 3 of the Constitution defines the **subject matter jurisdiction** of the Supreme Court as all cases in law and equity arising under the Constitution, the statutes of the United States, and all treaties. The article goes on to explain the extent of that jurisdiction. Suffice it to say that the Constitution grants extensive subject matter jurisdiction to the Supreme Court. A state juvenile court, on the other hand, is limited solely to hearing matters concerning children. If an adult were brought before a juvenile court, the court would lack jurisdiction, since it may decide only matters concerning youngsters. Likewise, a federal bankruptcy court may not decide a criminal matter, since its jurisdiction is limited to bankruptcy matters.

Once a court has the appropriate subject matter jurisdiction, it must also have jurisdiction over the *persons* whose rights, duties, or obligations will be decided by the court. For example, if both the **plaintiff** and the **defendant** are residents of state X, state X has jurisdiction over them. On the other hand, if only the plaintiff is a resident of state X while the defendant is a resident of state Y, then it is possible that state X does not have proper jurisdiction over the defendant. In such a case, it is probable that the more appropriate forum would be a federal court, for reasons that will be stated later. If the plaintiff wanted to sue the defendant in a state court, then the plaintiff might have to go to state Y and sue the defendant there, since a *defendant's* state of residence is almost always appropriate.

All states have laws called *long-arm statutes.* Suppose a resident of state Y drives a car on the roads of state X and injures a resident of state X. In that situation, the courts of state X would have jurisdiction over the person of the resident of state Y, since it would be unfair for the resident of state X to have to go to state Y to sue. Under these laws, a state can also exercise jurisdiction over corporations that are incorporated in one state, have offices in a second state, and do business in a third state. In that situation, the courts of all three states would have **in personam** jurisdiction over the corporation.

Lastly, if a state cannot obtain in personam jurisdiction on either of these grounds (residency or long-arm statutes), another approach can be used. If an individual or a corporation has property in one state but resides in another, the state in which the property is located can exercise jurisdiction over the property on the basis of what the law calls **in rem** jurisdiction.

In cases of either in personam or in rem jurisdiction, notice to the defendant must be properly served by process. Proper **service of process** includes *actual notice,* where one is personally served by an officer of the court, or notice served publically in a newspaper. Notice in a newspaper would be used in those cases where actual notice could not be obtained after a reasonable attempt to do so. In that case, it is called *constructive service.* With regard to long-arm

Subject matter jurisdiction The power of a court to hear only certain kinds of questions

Plaintiff A person who files a lawsuit; the person who complains

Defendant A person who answers a lawsuit; the person complained about

In personam Directed against or with reference to a specific person

In rem Directed against a thing with reference to no specific person and consequently against or with reference to all whom it might concern

Service of process Delivery, in person or otherwise, of a writ or notice to the person named so as to inform that person of the nature and terms of the writ or notice

statutes, proper notice is usually service at the office of the state's secretary of state.

In certain cases, both state and federal courts may exercise jurisdiction. If so, it is called *concurrent jurisdiction.* On the other hand, certain matters can be heard only by federal courts; this is called *exclusive jurisdiction.* Examples of exclusive jurisdiction are suits in which the United States is a party, some areas of admiralty law, bankruptcy, copyright, federal crimes, and patent cases.

Venue

Once a court establishes that it has proper jurisdiction over the subject matter and the person, it must then ascertain whether proper venue exists. *Venue* literally means "neighborhood." In a legal sense, however, it means *the proper geographical area or district where a suit may be brought.* For example, if both the plaintiff and the defendant are residents of the same state, then in personam jurisdiction exists in that state's court. But which state court? The question is usually answered with respect to the area in which a particular court is located and in which the defendant's residence is also located. Also, venue could be proper in the area in which an incident, such as an automobile accident, occurred. The venue laws of each state spell out in great detail the appropriate court in which the filing of the suit would be proper.

Conflict of Laws

Conflict of laws is *the legal doctrine that resolves any variance between the laws of two or more conflicting jurisdictions.* It deals primarily with the subject matter jurisdiction of any particular court. For example, assume that a citizen of state A entered into a contract with a citizen of state B while both of them were residing in state C. The contract concerned goods that were located in state D, and the goods were to be shipped to state E. While the goods were in transit, they were stopped and taken by a citizen of state F who was a creditor of the citizen of state A. What should the citizen of state B do to get the goods? In which state should suit be filed? What law should that state apply? The law of state A, B, C, D, E, or F? It could be that the citizen of state B would win were the laws of states A, C, or E applied, but would lose were the laws of states B, D, or F applied. We will not attempt to resolve this question in this text, since it is clearly too complex for a first course in the law of business. You need only be aware of the complexity of this matter and the often quite simple solution to the problem — that is, the contracting parties agree ahead of time that if there should be any dispute concerning the contract, the laws of a particular state would apply. That is called preventive law.

Federal Courts

In addition to the general grounds discussed previously with respect to jurisdiction, there are two specific grounds for federal jurisdiction:

1. federal question
2. diversity of citizenship

Plus amount in controversy.

Federal question jurisdiction derives directly from Article 3 of the Constitution. *Federal questions* are *questions that pertain to the federal Constitution, statutes of the United States, and treaties of the United States.* Also included today are all regulations of federal administrative agencies. For example, if a person were denied a job because of race, that would raise a federal question, since such discrimination would raise questions of violations of the Constitution, federal statutes, and federal regulations as well. If a publishing company brought an action asserting that its copyright had been infringed upon by another publishing company, it would raise a federal question, since copyright is both a Constitutional and a statutory question. States do not have the right to issue copyrights.

A basis of federal jurisdiction that is distinct from federal question jurisdiction is diversity of citizenship. For example, if there is a federal question, there is no need for diversity of citizenship. If there is diversity of citizenship, there is no need for federal question jurisdiction. *Diversity of citizenship* exists *when the plaintiff is a citizen of one state and the defendant is a citizen of another.* It also exists *when one party is a foreign country and the other is a citizen of a state.* The primary reason for this basis for jurisdiction is that if a citizen of state X had to file suit in state Y in order to obtain jurisdiction over that person, it is possible that the court of state Y might favor its citizen over the citizen of state X. In that case, the plaintiff could file suit in federal court.

When federal jurisdiction is based on diversity of citizenship, there is a further requirement for the majority of the approximately seventy-five thousand cases that are filed in federal courts annually: a *minimum amount* in question. Title 28, Section 1332(a), of the United States Code now requires that the amount in question exceed $50,000 in diversity cases. This new amount, which took effect 18 May 1989, was established in the Judicial Improvements and Access to Justice Act, signed into law 19 November 1988. Cases in which the federal courts have exclusive jurisdiction do not have a minimum amount requirement. The purpose behind the amount is to prevent federal courts from dealing with trifles. This rule complies with an ancient Latin legal maxim: *de minimus non curat lex* ("the law takes no account of trifles").

Most federal cases are highly complex, and the precise amount is a matter that sometimes is not known until after the lawsuit is filed. Accordingly, the courts look to the amount that the plaintiff, in good faith, has determined to be the amount in dispute. This is called the *plaintiff viewpoint rule.*

Figure 2.3 depicts the two grounds for federal jurisdiction.

Specialized Courts

Congress has, from time to time, created courts of limited jurisdiction. At present, these courts include the claims court, court of military appeals, court of international trade, and the tax court.

Congress has created *federal district courts* in every state. Each state has at least one; some states have many. Rhode Island, for example, has one district, whereas Texas has four. The courts contained in each district constitute the general trial courts of the federal system.

Figure 2.3 The Two Grounds for Federal Jurisdiction

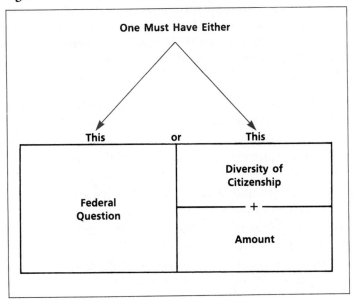

All the district courts are grouped into circuits. Currently there are thirteen circuits. Each circuit has a court of appeals in which appeals from the trial courts are heard. For the most part, the decisions of these *circuit courts of appeals* are final. In a very few cases, further appeal may be made to the Supreme Court.

The *Supreme Court* sits at the apex of the American judicial system. *It is the only court created by the Constitution.* It has nine judges, called justices. They are nominated by the president, confirmed by the Senate, and serve for life, as do all federal judges except those appointed to serve in the specialized courts.

As mentioned previously, the Supreme Court must hear certain cases. These cases arise under the following conditions:

1. whenever the highest state court declares a federal law invalid
2. whenever the highest state court declares a state law valid in situations where it was challenged by application of a federal law
3. whenever a federal court declares a federal statute unconstitutional and the government was a party to the suit
4. whenever a federal appellate court declares a state statute invalid on the grounds that it violates federal law
5. whenever a federal three-judge court has ruled in a civil case involving an equitable remedy

Certiorari A writ used by the court in order to review a case

Certiorari, which means *"to be more fully informed,"* is used whenever the Supreme Court desires to hear a particular case even though there is no right of appeal. It is through this device that most cases are heard in the Court. No hard and fast rules exist in connection with this route other than that a minimum of four justices must agree to hear the case. Nevertheless, there are certain situations where this route is followed:

1. whenever two or more circuit courts of appeals have conflicting rules with respect to the same question
2. whenever the highest state court has decided a question in such a manner that it is in conflict with prior decisions of the United States Supreme Court
3. whenever the highest state court has decided a question that has not yet been determined by the Supreme Court
4. whenever a circuit court of appeals has decided a state law question that is in conflict with established state law
5. whenever a circuit court of appeals has decided a federal question that has not yet been decided by the Supreme Court

State Courts

All states have *inferior trial courts.* These include justice courts (courts presided over by justices of the peace, most of whom are not lawyers), municipal courts, juvenile courts, domestic relations courts, traffic courts, small claims courts, and probate courts. For the most part, they are not *courts of record*—that is, there is no record of the trial. In cases of appeals from their decisions, there is a *trial de novo,* "a new trial," in a court of general jurisdiction.

The more significant cases involving matters of state law originate in *courts of general jurisdiction* (courts having the judicial power to hear all matters with respect to state law). In some jurisdictions, there are two courts on the same level. One court is charged with resolving all **questions of law;** the other, with resolving all matters of **equity.** An example of a question of law is a suit seeking money damages. Most business law cases fall into that category. Equity questions involve the issuing of an injunction. Rarely, if ever, do business law cases involve the issuing of an injunction.

Questions of law A term used in contrast to *fact;* questions to be decided by the court

Equity The spirit and habit of fairness, justness, and right dealing that should regulate human intercourse

Each state has at least one *court of appeals.* It is usually called the supreme court, but not always. In New York State, for example, the "supreme court" is a court of general jurisdiction, whereas the Court of Appeals is the highest court in the state. Sometimes there are also intermediate courts of appeals, as in the federal system.

Figure 2.4 describes how a typical state system and the federal system make up the American judicial system.

ARBITRATION

Arbitration is *the submitting of a dispute to the judgment of a person or group of persons called arbitrators.* The final decision of the arbitrator or arbitrators is called an *award,* and generally it is binding on the parties to the arbitration. Many states

Figure 2.4   The American Judicial System

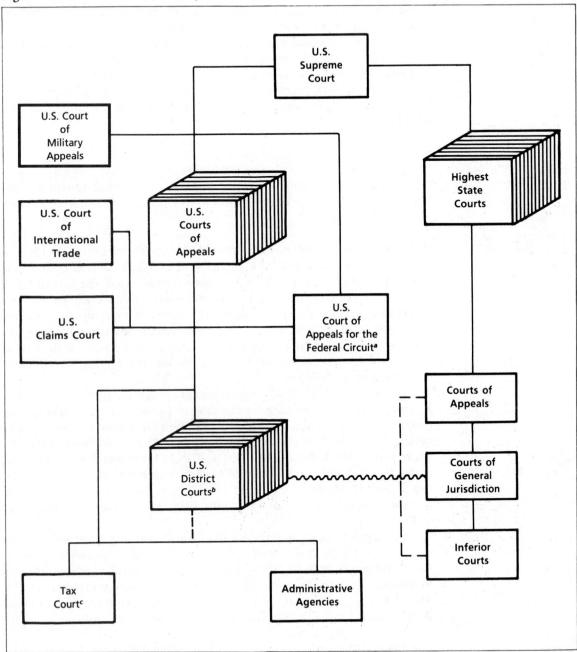

Note: Solid line(——) denotes direct appeal; dotted line (– – –) denotes appeal in some cases; wavy line (〰〰)
denotes removal jurisdiction.
[a] Takes appeals from some specialized courts.
[b] Bankruptcy courts exist as units of the district courts.
[c] In some cases, there is direct Supreme Court review.

have statutes that provide for arbitration and the enforcement of their awards in the courts of the state. At one time, the law did not favor arbitration because it was considered a means of avoiding the judicial system. Today that is no longer the case. Retired Chief Justice Warren Burger of the United States Supreme Court has gone on record as favoring the greater use of arbitration and other legitimate means of resolving disputes without having to go to the time and expense connected with getting a case through the court system. There is no reason to suspect that Chief Justice William Rhenquist disagrees with Burger.

HOW TO FIND THE LAW

We have already referred to some legal cases in this and the previous chapter. Other cases will be cited in succeeding chapters. If you should want to go to the library and read any one of these cases in its entirety, you will have to know how to find the law.

Federal Court Cases

If you were looking for the case *Mitsubishi Motors Corporation* v. *Soler Chrysler-Plymouth, Inc.,* 473 U.S. 614, 87 L.Ed.2d 444, 105 S.Ct. 3346 (1985), for example, you would find it in any one of three sources. First, the United States Government Printing Office publishes the official *United States Reports.* The case would be found on page 614 of volume 473. Alternatively, you could also find it on page 44 of the 87th volume of *Lawyers Edition, Second* published by the Lawyers Cooperative Publishing Company. Lastly, you could find the case in the 105th volume of the *Supreme Court Reporter,* published by the West Publishing Company, at page 3346.

All cases decided by the circuit courts of appeals are found in the *Federal Reporter.* If you were looking for the case of *United States* v. *Douglas Aircraft Company,* you would find it at 169 F.2d 755 (9th Cir. 1948). You would go to volume 169 of the *Federal Reporter,* Second Series, and would turn to page 755. There you would find the case. The (9th Cir. 1948) means that the case was decided by the Ninth Circuit Court of Appeals, which sits in San Francisco and hears cases from district courts in Washington, Montana, Oregon, Idaho, Nevada, Arizona, Alaska, Hawaii, and California. The case was decided in 1948.

U.S. district court cases are found in the *Federal Supplement Series.* If you were looking for the case of *Hoeflich* v. *William S. Merrell Co.,* you would find it at 288 F. Supp. 659 (E.D. Pa. 1968). Following our established procedure, look for volume 288 of the *Federal Supplement.* The case would be found on page 659. The (E.D. Pa. 1968) means that the case was decided in the United States District Court for the Eastern District of Pennsylvania in 1968.

State Court Cases

The *National Reporter System* contains seven regional reporters for state cases, plus two separate state reporters. They are as follows:

1. *Atlantic Reporter* — Connecticut, Delaware, Maine, Maryland, New Hamp-

shire, New Jersey, Pennsylvania, Rhode Island, Vermont, and the District of Columbia Municipal Court of Appeals

2. *Northeastern Reporter* — Illinois, Indiana, Massachusetts, New York, and Ohio

3. *Northwestern Reporter* — Iowa, Michigan, Minnesota, Nebraska, North Dakota, South Dakota, and Wisconsin

4. *Pacific Reporter* — Alaska, Arizona, California, Colorado, Hawaii, Idaho, Kansas, Montana, Nevada, New Mexico, Oklahoma, Oregon, Utah, Washington, and Wyoming

5. *Southeastern Reporter* — Georgia, North Carolina, South Carolina, Virginia, and West Virginia

6. *Southwestern Reporter* — Arkansas, Kentucky, Missouri, Tennessee, and Texas

7. *Southern Reporter* — Alabama, Florida, Louisiana, and Mississippi

8. *New York Supplement*

9. *California Reporter*

SUMMARY

The federal Constitution is unique because it created the doctrine of separation of powers. As a result, our government is divided into three distinct branches: legislative, executive, and judicial.

The judicial power is not unlimited. For example, courts may not issue advisory opinions or decide moot cases or political questions. In all cases, the plaintiff must have standing to sue.

The doctrine of judicial review was created by Chief Justice John Marshall in the landmark case of *Marbury* v. *Madison.* The doctrine represents an expansion of judicial power, since it allows the Supreme Court to determine whether a statute passed by Congress is in compliance with the Constitution or whether the executive branch has acted in accordance with the Constitution.

Our court system is based on the concept of jurisdiction. Jurisdiction means the power to speak the law. It is divided into subject matter jurisdiction or in personam jurisdiction and can be either concurrent or exclusive. A federal court's jurisdiction is based on either federal question or diversity of citizenship jurisdiction. In all diversity cases, the jurisdictional amount of $10,000 must be met. Federal courts are specialized, district, appellate, or supreme. Venue, on the other hand, is a question of whether the case is filed in the proper court.

All cases reported in the federal or state systems may be found by referring to the *National Reporter System.*

DISCUSSION QUESTIONS

1. Why is our federal Constitution considered unique?
2. What is the significance of the case of *Marbury* v. *Madison?*

3. Where is the constitutional protection of habeus corpus found? What does the term mean?

4. What is meant by the term *jurisdiction?*

5. What is a federal question?

6. Why do some state courts have only one court of general jurisdiction, whereas others have two?

7. What is meant by this citation: 234 S.W. 358 (1946)?

8. In *Baker* v. *Carr* the issue of state legislative apportionment was determined to be a judicial question and not a political question. What arguments can you make that it really was a political question and therefore nonjusticiable? Why do you think the Supreme Court acted as it did?

9. The highest court in a state determines that a state law violates the federal Constitution. Can that decision be reviewed by the United States Supreme Court, or is the decision of the state court final?

10. Go to the nearest law library and determine who was counsel for the plaintiff in *Flast* v. *Cohen.*

CASE
PROBLEMS

1. The text indicates that a moot point is one that is undecided. If that is so, would a case be barred in which the parties carefully stipulated all the facts: a so-called test case? (*Chicago & Grand Trunk Ry.* v. *Wellman,* 143 U.S. 339 [1892].)

2. Does a taxpayer have standing to sue the federal government challenging the creation of a Christmas postage stamp for the reason that it violates the establishment of religion clause of the First Amendment? (*P.O.A.U.* v. *Watson,* 407 F.2d 1264 [D.C. Cir. 1968].)

3. Was the conducting of the Vietnam war by presidential authority, without a congressional declaration of war in accordance with Art. I, Sec. 8, Cl. 11 of the Constitution, a "political question"? (*Mora* v. *McNamara,* 389 U.S. 934 [1967].)

4. Does segregation of children in public schools on the basis of race, even though the physical facilities and other "tangible" factors may be equal, deprive the children of the minority group of equal educational opportunities? Discuss with respect to the Fourteenth Amendment. (*Brown* v. *Board of Education,* 347 U.S. 483 [1954].)

5. The plaintiff sued the defendant in a New York court. The defendant was served in person at his residence in the state of Connecticut. Does the New York court have jurisdiction to grant the plaintiff appropriate relief? (*Garfein* v. *McInnis,* 248 N.Y. 261, 162 N.E. 73 [1928].)

6. Producers of chemicals used for pesticides sued the U.S. Administrator of the Environmental Protection Agency challenging Section 3(c)(1)(D) of the Federal Insecticide, Fungicide, and Rodenticide Act (FIFRA). That

section allowed parties to submit disputes to binding arbitration. The producers alleged that the law violated Article III of the U.S. Constitution by allocating to arbitrators the function of the courts. The District Court held that the Congress acted unconstitutionally by assigning judicial powers to arbitrators. On appeal, did the Supreme Court affirm or reverse? Why? (*Thomas* v. *Union Carbide,* 473 U.S. 568, 87 L.Ed.2d 409, 105 S.Ct. 3325 [1985].)

CHAPTER 3

Torts

OBJECTIVES OF TORT LAW

Tort law is concerned with a body of "private" wrongs, whereas *criminal law*, which we shall study in the next chapter, is concerned with "public" wrongs. The laws have evolved over hundreds of years to support the protection of an individual's rights with respect to property and person. Tort law, therefore, reflects civilized society. Torts provide a mechanism for persons who have been wronged to seek remedies in our court system. In general, the remedy sought is money damages. The way that people avoid committing these wrongs is to adhere to various "duties." For example, society recognizes a duty to refrain from physically injuring other persons or their property. Society also recognizes a duty to refrain from humiliating others.

Because tort law recognizes certain duties, it raises the question of exactly which rights society should protect through the imposition of duties. For example, should society recognize as a wrong only behavior that was intended to be a wrong? Or should society recognize as a wrong not only intended wrong but also an unintended wrong that was due to someone's negligence? Should society also recognize as a wrong unintended behavior in which the person was not negligent? These are the questions that we shall discuss in this chapter.

Society has developed the body of tort law to resolve social and economic policy questions. The law has to take into consideration the social usefulness of the conduct of persons, the interests asserted by the plaintiff, the justification (if any) for the defendant's conduct, the economic burden that would be placed upon the defendant if liability were imposed, the question of spreading the cost of liability from one to many persons, and the unique problem of respecting past decisions and yet maintaining flexibility within the legal system by providing solutions to modern problems.

This chapter discusses intentional torts, negligence, and strict liability. Figure 3.1 depicts the three theories of tort liability. *Intentional torts* are those wrongs in which the persons charged must have acted in such a manner that they either wanted to harm someone or knew that what they did would result in harm. Suppose that someone said something offensive about you, and you said, "If you don't stop that, I'll punch you in the nose." If that person did not stop it, and you punched him in the nose, the law states that you were wrong. You committed the tort of *battery* on the other person. (Provocation is not an

THEORIES OF TORT LIABILITY

Figure 3.1   The Three Theories of Tort Liability

TORT LIABILITY THEORIES		
Intentional Torts	Negligence	Strict Liability

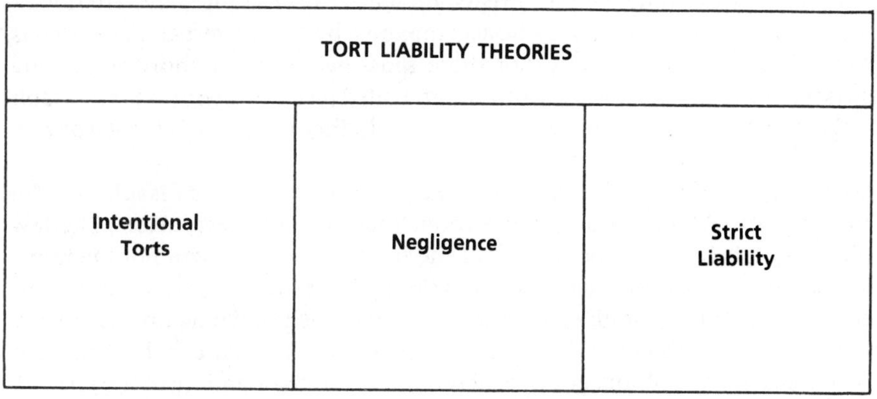

issue here, since the law does not recognize the privilege of striking someone unless you are struck first.)

The law of *negligence* is based on a concept of fault in which the areas of morals and law have been intermingled. The question raised here is how society apportions the costs of accidents. Society must often make a moral statement when an injury occurs. Suppose a child darts out from behind a parked car an instant before the driver's car reaches that point; the driver immediately brakes in an effort to avoid hitting the child but is unable to stop in time to avoid the accident. In all likelihood, this accident would be considered unavoidable — it occurred without any negligence on the part of the driver. The child, even though injured, would be denied any compensation from the driver for the accident.

On the other hand, if a child walking across the street in a designated crosswalk was hit by an automobile because the driver was drunk or the car's brakes were faulty, society says that the driver breached a duty to drive the car in a reasonable manner. Accordingly, the driver will have to pay for damages suffered by the child. Although the child is just as injured in the first example as in the second example, society denies compensation in the first case but not in the second.

Strict liability finds persons liable even if their conduct was unintentional or nonnegligent; that is, even if it wasn't their fault, they're liable. Some activities are classified as either ultrahazardous or abnormally dangerous, and if injury results from either of those situations, the actor will be held liable. For example, suppose you have a pet rattlesnake in a sealed glass cage and you place the cage in your back yard with signs on the fence that say: Danger — Poisonous Snake, Beware. If the snake somehow gets out and bites someone, you will be held liable. The law would prevent you from trying to prove how careful you were. It would say that your rattlesnake caused injury, and you will simply have to pay.

INTENTIONAL TORTS

Assault

Assault is the threat or reasonable apprehension that one person will strike another. For example, verbal threats, no matter how belligerent, are not an assault. The verbal threat must be accompanied by some overt act. The threats can be used to show intent, but there must be some act short of actually striking the other person. Pointing an unloaded pistol at a person is an assault if the other person has no way of knowing whether the pistol is loaded or not.

Battery

Privilege A particular or peculiar benefit or advantage beyond the common advantages of other citizens; a right, power, franchise, or immunity held by a person beyond the course of the law

Some legal authorities have defined *battery* as a consummated assault. It is the touching or striking of another without that person's permission. The law places a high value on the dignity of the human body and will not tolerate a contact that is without *consent* or **privilege.** For example, removing a chair from a person who briefly stood up and began to sit down again is a battery when the person hits the floor. The key element in that case is that the actor intended the natural consequence of removing the chair: falling to the ground.

As far as the law is concerned, it is the same as pushing the person to the ground. On the other hand, if the removal of the chair had been unintended, then there could not have been a battery. The following case is an example of the extent to which the law will go in order to protect a person's interest.

Childs v. Berry
597 S.W.2d 134 (Ark. App. 1980)

Childs apprehended Berry while he was in the process of burglarizing Childs's building. Childs kicked Berry and then carried him to a building and handcuffed him. Sometime later Childs called the police.

FACTS

Is this sufficient evidence of false imprisonment, assault, and battery?

ISSUE

Yes.

HOLDING

"... Appellee was apprehended, kicked several times, while on the ground, and was compelled to accompany [Childs] to the home of Harry Childs who admitted that he attempted to strike appellee; appellee was required to accompany [Childs] ... to a building where appellee was handcuffed to a column. One and one-half hours later, appellee was taken into custody by police and remained in jail for three weeks. . . ."

REASONING

There are two forms of defamation: *slander* and *libel*. The reason for the two forms, each of which has different elements, is that each was developed in a different English court. Slander, which is spoken defamation, was developed in the English church courts (the ecclesiastical courts that had jurisdiction over spiritual matters). Libel (written defamation) was developed in the Star Chamber (an English common law court that had jurisdiction over cases in which the ordinary course of justice was so obstructed by one party that no inferior court could have its process obeyed). The tort of defamation is an exception to the First Amendment's guarantee of free speech. Accordingly, United States courts have changed some of the common law rules.

Defamation

Slander is spoken communication that causes a person to suffer a loss of reputation. The common law rule distinguished between *slander per se* and *slander per quod.* Slander per se occurs when a person says that another person is seriously immoral, seriously criminal, has a social disease, or is unfit as a business or professional person. In those cases, there is no need to prove actual damages. Slander per quod is any other type of oral defamatory statement.

Slander Any oral statement that tends to expose a person to public ridicule or to injure a person's reputation

Libel is written communication that causes a person to suffer a loss of reputation. There are also two kinds of libel. *Libel per se* is libelous without

Libel Any *written* or printed statement that tends to expose a person to public ridicule or to injure a person's reputation

having to resort to the context in which the remark appeared. For example, if a newspaper printed a story that referred to a person as a ''known assassin for hire,'' there is no need to show the context of the statement. On the other hand, *libel per quod* requires proof of the context. For example, suppose a television talk show host says that a particular woman just gave birth to a child. In order to prove that it was libel, the woman would have to prove that she was not married and that she had not made public knowledge of her cohabiting, but unmarried, private life. The following case describes how American courts have tailored the English doctrine to our own situation with respect to public officials.

New York Times Company v. Sullivan
376 U.S. 255 (1964)

FACTS   Sullivan was a city commissioner in Montgomery, Alabama. He alleged that he had been libeled by the *New York Times* when it carried a full-page advertisement in which certain charges were made against the city with respect to the treatment of Dr. Martin Luther King, Jr.

ISSUE   ''To determine the extent to which the constitutional protections for speech and press limit a state's power to award damages in a libel action brought by a public official against critics of his official conduct.''

HOLDING   This was not libel because there was no showing of *malice*.

REASONING   ''. . . Debate on public issues should be uninhibited, robust, and wide-open, and . . . it may well include vehement, caustic, and sometimes unpleasantly sharp attacks on government and public officials. . . . The constitutional guarantees require, we think, a federal rule that prohibits a public official from recovering damages for a defamatory falsehood relating to his official conduct unless he proves that the statement was made with 'actual malice' — that is, with knowledge that it was false or with reckless disregard of whether it was false or not. . . . We hold that the Constitution delimits a state's power to award damages for libel in actions brought by public officials against critics of their official conduct.''

The *New York Times* case is a landmark in American jurisprudence. Since 1964, the Supreme Court, in a number of cases, has extended the holding to ''public figures'' as well as public officials. A public figure is a person who has a degree of prominence in society. Thus, a person who chooses to become active in society and who not only receives but actually solicits attention in the media would be classified a public figure. Furthermore, the court has extended the definition of a public official to include mere candidates for public office, as well as incumbents.

False imprisonment is the detention of one person by another against the former's will and without just cause. This tort protects a person from the loss of liberty and freedom of movement. For example, if after the end of a college class your professor locked the door and said that no one could leave the room, that action would be false imprisonment. Sometimes standing in a doorway and refusing to let a person pass is also false imprisonment. On the other hand, being stopped by a store detective when there is just cause to consider the person a shoplifter is not false imprisonment.

False Imprisonment

A growing body of law concerns situations that fall far short of assault but, for public policy reasons, have been recognized as a tort by the courts. The law will protect an individual from suffering *serious indignity* that *causes emotional distress.* This right, however, is balanced against the interest of the state in not opening the courts to frivolous and trivial claims. In this context, liability has been found where an airline unreasonably insulted a passenger on an aircraft. Also, liability was found where a bill collector unreasonably humiliated a debtor. In that regard, you should know that federal law now specifically controls the activities of bill collectors, and the court-made rules concerning liability have been modified by the federal statute. Liability has also been found where a mortician displayed a dead body without its having been embalmed. In that case, damages were recovered by near relatives.

Mental Distress

Under common law, there was no tort of invasion of privacy. Recently, however, our courts have begun to recognize that unwarranted invasions of privacy are **actionable.** Liability has been found for the public disclosure of private matters, such as wiretapping a private citizen's telephone without permission. The use of a famous person's name or photograph without permission is an invasion of privacy when the name or the photograph is used to promote a commercial product.

Invasion of Privacy

Actionable Furnishing legal grounds for an action

In common law, trespass was the most common tort. Today, the general tort of "trespass" has evolved into some of the specific torts we have already discussed, but trespass remains as the tort used to define *actions that protect both real and personal property interests.* A person who ventures onto the land of another without permission is a trespasser. The only question is one of damages. Even if the person trespassed through mistake and did no harm, there will be "nominal" damages, say one dollar. If, on the other hand, the person had trespassed before and had been warned, then more than nominal damages would be assessed in order to compensate the owner for the unwarranted invasion of land. Of course, the trespasser will be liable for any damages done.

Trespass

Conversion

Conversion occurs when a person intentionally exercises exclusive control over the personal property of another without permission. In such a case, the converter is liable for damages. If a person actually obtains possession of the property lawfully but is then told by the owner to return it and does not do so, that person is still a converter. Once damages are paid, there is no need for the converter to return the property. If return is sought, the proper action is one for **replevin.**

Replevin A personal action brought to recover possession of goods unlawfully taken

Fraud

Fraud is an extremely complex tort. It concerns the misrepresentation of a material fact made with the intention to deceive. If an innocent person reasonably relies on the misrepresentation and is damaged as a result, the injured person may successfully sue for fraud. Accordingly, there are five elements of fraud:

1. A material fact (not an opinion) was involved.
2. The fact was misrepresented (a falsehood).
3. The falsehood was made with the intent to deceive *(scienter).*
4. The falsehood was one on which another person justifiably relied (reliance).
5. That person was injured as a result (damage).

For example, whenever a jeweler sells a rhinestone as a diamond with the knowledge that it is a rhinestone, the action is fraud. Whenever a bank customer obtains a loan on the basis of a false financial statement, it is fraud. Whenever a landowner sells "one hundred" acres of land with the knowledge that it is only fifty acres, it is fraud. Whenever a corporation solicits persons to buy stock for the purpose of building a new plant when in reality the corporation wanted the money to pay off existing liabilities, it is fraud. The list is endless. Figure 3.2 outlines the intentional torts discussed in this chapter.

Defenses to Intentional Torts

Consent

Even though a tort has been committed, the law may not compensate the injured party if, in fact, that person consented to the tort. Most cases involve issues of **implied consent.** The law will not infer consent unless it is reasonable under the circumstances. For example, football players obviously batter each other throughout the course of a game. Therefore, even though the tort of battery may have been committed, it is not actionable, because the law views each player as having consented to the touching. However, if a player intentionally exceeds the implied consent, he may be liable for the tort.

Implied consent A concurrence of wills manifested by signs, actions, or facts, or by inaction or silence, which raises a presumption that agreement has been given

Privilege

Beyond the permission that can be received either expressly or implicitly, there is a nonvoluntary defense that the law recognizes. Because the law seeks

Figure 3.2 Intentional Torts

SPECIFIC TORT	DEFINITION
Assault	The *threat* or reasonable apprehension that one person will strike another
Battery	A consummated assault
Defamation	Slander (spoken) Libel (written)
False Imprisonment	The detention of one person by another against his or her will and without just cause
Mental Distress	The suffering of a serious indignity
Invasion of Privacy	Unwarranted invasions of privacy are actionable
Trespass	Actions to protect real and personal property from invasions
Conversion	Occurs when a person intentionally exercises exclusive control over the personal property of another without permission
Fraud	The misrepresentation of a material fact made with the intention to deceive

to protect certain social interests more than others, it developed the concept of privilege. Privilege is recognized in the following situations:

1. If someone moves to strike you, you have the ancient privilege of self-defense.

2. Retail businesspersons have a privilege to detain persons who they reasonably believe have committed theft.

3. Persons whose property is stolen have the privilege of going onto another person's property in order to retrieve it.

4. Judges and legislators have the privilege of saying things that might be slander under other circumstances in order to stimulate debate and encourage independence of thought and action.

Necessity

Whenever a person commits what would otherwise be a land trespass for self-protection, the law recognizes that necessity would disallow the landowner nominal damages. For example, if you were in a boat on a lake and a storm suddenly developed, you could enter a private cove, tie up to a private dock, and find shelter on the land in order to protect yourself. There would be no trespass.

Truth

Truth is the best defense with respect to the tort of defamation. If an individual accuses a businessperson of being a crook and is sued for defamation, the individual will win if it can be proved that the businessperson is a "fence" for stolen property. Figure 3.3 depicts the defenses to intentional torts.

NEGLIGENCE

Negligence exists when four conditions are met. First, the defendant must have owed the plaintiff a duty. Second, the defendant must have breached the duty. Third, the breach of that duty must be the actual as well as the "legal" cause of the plaintiff's injury. Fourth, that injury must be one that the law recognizes and for which money damages may be recovered.

Duty

We live in a legal system in which we all have a duty to protect other persons from harm. The question the courts must examine is what degree of duty exists under what specific circumstances.

The *reasonable-and-prudent-person* rule has been established in negligence law in order to determine the "degree" of duty. Figure 3.4 may be helpful in explaining this point.

In the discussion on intentional torts, we emphasized that the key element in finding liability is determining that the defendant intended harm. For example, if a defendant points a gun at the plaintiff and pulls the trigger, we can determine that the defendant intended some sort of harm to the plaintiff. We infer intent from overt behavior. Negligence stands in sharp contrast to intentional torts. Referring to Figure 3.4, you can see that with respect to intentional torts, we all have a simple duty to avoid liability-causing behavior. However, with respect to negligence, we all have a "reasonable" duty to avoid

Figure 3.3   Defenses to Intentional Torts

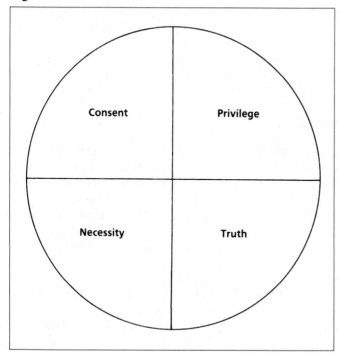

Consent	Privilege
Necessity	Truth

Figure 3.4   Theories of Liability

INTENTIONAL TORT	NEGLIGENCE	STRICT LIABILITY
Simple Duty to Avoid	Reasonable Duty to Avoid	Strict Duty to Avoid
Fault		No Fault
Foreseeability		

this type of behavior. This standard is more difficult to define, explain, and apply than is the standard of simple duty. Generally, however, the law states that *reasonable duty is a standard of ordinary skill and care, based on the facts of each individual case.*

If, while you were quietly fishing on the shore of a lake, you saw another fisherman one hundred feet away fall out of his boat and begin to drown, does the common law place on you a duty to help him? The answer is no, because you did not create the hazard in the first place. On the other hand, suppose you owned a boatyard on the lake and the fisherman rented his boat from you. If the boat sprung a leak because it was defective when rented, thereby causing the fisherman to drown, then you would have breached your duty to rent safe boats. You created the harm in the second situation but not in the first.

Ignore for now the part of Figure 3.4 that deals with strict liability. When we discuss strict liability later in the chapter, be sure to go back to the illustration. It will help cement the various duties in your mind. For now, you should know that both intentional torts and negligence are based upon the concept of *fault*. Strict liability has nothing to do with fault. All theories of liability, however, have to do with **foreseeability.**

Foreseeability The knowledge or notice that a result is likely to occur if a certain act occurs

Foreseeability deals with the likelihood that something will happen in the future. It is not very difficult to see that if you point a loaded gun at someone and pull the trigger, you will cause that person harm. But suppose you get in your car and drive down a dark street, within the speed limit and with your lights on. A child darts out from behind a parked car, and you hit the child. Were you negligent, or was it merely an unavoidable accident? This is a more difficult question, because it concerns foreseeability.

In order to test for a duty in any particular situation, the law has constructed a person against whom the conduct of the defendant will be compared. This purely hypothetical person is known as the *reasonable and prudent person* — not perfect, merely reasonable. Three areas help to define the reasonable and prudent person: knowledge, investigation, and judgment.

Knowledge

As the amount of knowledge existing in the world increases, so does the amount of knowledge that the reasonable and prudent person is expected to possess. In this sense, therefore, the law presumes that we have complete knowledge of the law. If we did not have this rule, it would be silly for us to have any legal rules at all, for if we had no knowledge of the law how could we be expected to obey it?

Investigation

Before you drive a car, for example, the law presumes that you will have ascertained that the brakes are working properly. If you are a drug manufacturer, the law presumes that you will have discovered that your drug does not cause any harmful side effects; if it does, you will have violated the standard of care of a reasonable and prudent person.

Judgment

You have heard some people say that one person has "good" judgment, or that another has "bad" judgment. The law measures both persons against the same standard. In a tort case, the defendant had better have acted reasonably or else he will be found to have breached the duty of reasonable care. We have no hard and fast rules here. The outcome always depends on the facts of each case. A missing fact, once supplied, can change the outcome. Therefore, before we begin any activity, the law expects us to ask ourselves such questions as: what is the likelihood that this particular activity will harm someone else? If harm might come, what is the likelihood of the extent of the harm? What must I give up in order to avoid the risk to others?

Let's say that you just got a new rifle and want to zero it in for the deer season. You find an isolated field in the country and set up a target at the base of a bald hill three hundred yards away. No one else is present. After firing the first shot, however, you begin to attract a crowd. Assume that with each shot the crowd gets larger. At what point do you decide to stop shooting in order to avoid injury to an innocent person? The decision to stop involves the exercise of reason. The exercise of reason is judgment.

Statutory Standard

In some cases, the law solves the problem of limits, such as we have just raised, by providing a standard contained in a statute. For example, most laws state that when it begins to get dark, all drivers are required to turn on their car lights. If, while traveling down a road at night without your lights on, you hit and injure a pedestrian, the law will conclude that you breached a standard of reasonableness, no matter what your excuse. Most of these statutes provide a criminal penalty, but that penalty is truly irrelevant in a civil proceeding, such as a tort case. The majority rule is that breaching the statutory standard is **negligence per se.** In a minority of states, breaching the statutory standard is only "some evidence of negligence" and is not conclusive.

Negligence per se
Inherent negligence; negligence without a need for further proof

Breach of Duty

In general, the plaintiff has to prove that the defendant caused injury by not adhering to the standard of the *reasonable and prudent person.* In some cases, however, that strict requirement of proof is relaxed. In these cases the law has developed the doctrine of *res ipsa loquitur,* which means "the thing speaks for itself." It applies in situations where circumstantial proof is sufficient. In order to apply solely circumstantial evidence, the injury must be such that it meets the following three tests: (1) it ordinarily does not occur in the absence of someone's negligence; (2) it must be caused by a device within the control of the defendant; and (3) the plaintiff in no way has contributed to his or her own injury. For example, if a patient submits to an operation to remove infected tonsils and leaves the operating room with a surgical instrument imbedded in her throat, there is no need to require direct testimony on the point. It speaks for itself. The physician was negligent.

Causation

The heart of the law of negligence is causation. Causation has two components: actual cause and proximate cause.

Actual Cause

The law determines whether *x* is the actual cause of *y* by raising the question of whether but for *x, y* would not have happened. This is called the *but-for test*. For example, a defendant in an automobile accident case may have failed to signal a turn properly. But if the accident would have happened even if he had signaled properly, the failure to signal is not the actual cause of the accident. It fails the but-for test.

Proximate Cause

After actual cause has been established, the scene shifts to what the law calls *policy questions*. Such questions have nothing to do with whether the defendant actually did the act. What is decided here is whether the law should hold the defendant liable or not. At some point the law will say, "Enough." Beyond this point the defendant will not be held liable. In order to solve these policy questions, the law has developed a three-pronged test:

1. What is the likelihood that this particular conduct will injure other persons?

2. If injury should occur, what is the degree of seriousness of the injury?

3. What is the interest that the defendant must sacrifice to avoid the risk of causing the injury?

For example, if it is determined that the defendant was negligent with respect to Tommy, but Bob tried to rescue Tommy and suffered some injury as a result, the defendant will be held liable for Bob's injuries as well as Tommy's because it is foreseeable that people will try to rescue someone in peril. The following case is considered by experts to be the landmark case with respect to proximate cause.

Palsgraf v. *Long Island Railroad*
284 N.Y. 339, 162 N.E. 99 (1928)

FACTS   Palsgraf was standing on the defendant's platform when another passenger attempted to board a train that was already moving. A railroad employee attempted to assist the passenger, but in the process a package the passenger was carrying fell on the rails and exploded. The shock of the explosion caused some scales at the other end of the platform to fall, thus causing Palsgraf's injury.

Was the employee's act of knocking an apparently harmless package onto the platform the proximate cause of Palsgraf's injury?

ISSUE

No. Such a result was not foreseeable.

HOLDING

"Here, by concession, there was nothing in the situation to suggest to the most cautious mind that the parcel wrapped in newspaper would spread wreckage through the station. If the guard had thrown it down knowingly and willfully, he would not have threatened the plaintiff's safety, so far as appearances could warn him. His conduct would not have involved, even then, an unreasonable probability of invasion of her bodily security. Liability can be no greater where the act is inadvertent."

REASONING

The concept of harm is so self-evident that it seems unnecessary to mention it. However, if the plaintiff is not injured, the defendant will not be held liable in damages. For example, a driver speeding down a road at 180 miles per hour is clearly breaching the duty to drive in a safe and reasonable manner; but if a person is not injured thereby, no one can successfully sue for negligence.

Harm

Assumption of the Risk

The common law developed a doctrine in which the defendant will win if it can be proved that the plaintiff assumed the risk. The law calls this *volenti non fit injuria.* For example, have you ever examined the outside of a cigarette package? It bears this note: "Surgeon General's Warning: Smoking by pregnant women may result in fetal injury, premature birth, and low birth weight," or "Quitting smoking now greatly reduces serious risks to your health," or "Cigarette smoke contains carbon monoxide." A longtime cigarette smoker who contracts lung cancer and sues the cigarette manufacturer will most likely lose, because the manufacturer will defend on the basis of the plaintiff's voluntarily assuming the risk.

Defenses to Negligence

Contributory Negligence

If a plaintiff had been wearing a black raincoat at night and, while jaywalking across a street, had been hit by a car that was exceeding the speed limit, the defendant could assert that the plaintiff actually contributed to the injury. If the state in which the case was being heard followed the rule of *contributory negligence,* and if contributory negligence were successfully asserted, the plaintiff would lose because contributory negligence would **bar** recovery.

Bar In the legal sense, to prevent or to stop

Comparative Negligence

In a growing number of jurisdictions, the doctrine of contributory negligence has been replaced by the doctrine of *comparative negligence.* Here, the fact finder (usually the jury) determines to what degree the plaintiff contributed to his injury. Provided that the plaintiff did not contribute more than 50 percent to his injury, the percentage will be used in making the ultimate award of damages. For example, if he is injured to the extent of $100,000 in damages but contributed 35 percent to his injury, he will be awarded $65,000 instead of losing completely, as he would under the doctrine of contributory negligence. The following case is an application of the rule in federal court.

Lewis v. *Timco, Inc.*
716 F.2d 1425 (5th Cir. 1983) 74 ALR Fed. 293

FACTS   Lewis was injured while working as a crew member on a drilling barge. He was employed by Timco. His injury occurred when a design defect in a piece of equipment he was using caused it to malfunction resulting in a cable wrapping itself around him.

ISSUE   "Whether the doctrine of comparative fault applies in a product liability suit . . . under the maritime jurisdiction of the federal courts."

HOLDING   The doctrine of comparative fault applies in a product liability suit under the maritime jurisdiction of the federal courts.

REASONING   If the injury did not occur solely through the malfunction of the equipment but occurred as a result of *both* the equipment and the operator (Lewis) then the recovery of money damages must be reduced by the degree to which the plaintiff contributed to his injury. "Admiralty courts have long engaged in the exercise of comparing plaintiff's negligence to both fault and nonfault based upon the liability of plaintiffs . . . comparative fault has long been an accepted risk-allocating principle under the maritime law. . . . We are persuaded that general considerations of fairness and efficiency support a comparative fault defense in (this) action."

STRICT LIABILITY AND PRODUCT LIABILITY

Referring back to Figure 3.4 we recall that with respect to intentional torts, we all have a duty to avoid such behavior. With respect to negligence, we all have a duty to use reasonable care. We now examine two situations in which the law states that our duty is absolute to avoid such behavior, regardless of whether we are at fault or not.

Whenever a person undertakes an extremely hazardous activity and it is foreseeable that injury could result from it, that person will be held "strictly liable" if injury does result, whether or not the person was at fault. *Strict liability* means *without regard to fault.* For example, if you use explosives on your property and by so doing cause windows to be blown out of an adjoining neighbor's house, you will be held liable no matter how careful you were in handling those explosives. The following case created this doctrine of the law.

Rylands v. *Fletcher*
L.R. 3 H.L. 330 (1868)

The defendants were mill owners in Lancashire, England. They constructed a reservoir on their land. The water in the reservoir broke through and flowed into an abandoned coal mine shaft. The flooding of the well overflowed into the adjoining property owner's coal mine and caused injury.

FACTS

What should a landowner's liability be for the nonnatural use of the land if it causes damage to another?

ISSUE

The landowner should be liable for the abnormal use of land.

HOLDING

The lower court said, "We think that the true rule of law is that the person who for his own purposes brings on his land and collects and keeps there anything likely to do mischief if it escapes, must keep it at his peril, and if he does not do so is **prima facie** answerable for all the damage which is the natural consequence of its escape." The House of Lords (the highest "court" in England), however, said that the rule applies only to nonnatural use of land versus ". . . any purpose for which it might in the ordinary course of the enjoyment of land be used." Therefore, the rule applies only to abnormal activity.

REASONING

Prima facie At first sight; on the first appearance; on the face of it

---

Through the development of the doctrine of strict liability, our courts have shifted emphasis from ultrahazardous activity to dangerous activity. The *Restatement (Second) of Torts,*[1] Section 402A, has established the rule with respect to products: a vendor will be held liable for a product containing a defect sufficient to make the product unreasonably dangerous to a person who uses the product, provided that the product has not been substantially changed. The following case illustrates this point.

---

[1] *Restatement (Second) of Torts* is a publication of the American Law Institute that states the current version of the common law of torts. An authoritative source, it is used by courts but is not binding on them.

Greenman v. *Yuba Products, Inc.*
59 Cal.2d 67, 377 P.2d 897 (1963)

FACTS   Greenman's wife bought him a Shopsmith power tool for Christmas. While he was using the tool, it struck him and inflicted serious injuries. He sued the manufacturer for negligence.

ISSUE   Is proof of negligence required if the facts reflect that a product was defectively manufactured?

HOLDING   No. Liability will attach without any showing of negligence.

REASONING   "A manufacturer is strictly liable in tort when an article he places on the market, knowing that it is to be used without inspection for defects, proves to have a defect that causes injury to a human being. The purpose of such liability is to insure that the costs of injuries resulting from defective products are borne by the manufacturers that put such products on the market rather than by the injured persons who are powerless to protect themselves. . . . To establish the manufacturer's liability it was sufficient that plaintiff proved that he was injured while using the Shopsmith in a way it was intended to be used as a result of a defect in the design and manufacture of which plaintiff was not aware that made the Shopsmith unsafe for its intended use."

SUMMARY

Tort law is designed to protect an individual's rights with respect to person and property. To do this, the law uses the device of "duty." Tort law deals with "private" wrongs, whereas criminal law deals with "public" wrongs.

There are three theories of tort liability: intentional torts, negligence, and strict liability. Intentional torts are those in which a person either intended to harm someone or knew that harm would result from the action. Intentional torts to persons are assault, battery, defamation, false imprisonment, mental distress, and invasion of privacy. Intentional torts to property are trespass and conversion. The defenses of consent, privilege, necessity, and truth apply to both categories.

Negligence is the unintentional causing of harm that could have been prevented if the defendant had acted as a reasonable and prudent person. Strict liability is a separate basis of tort liability because it has nothing to do with either intent or negligence. Our legal system has declared that certain activities are so dangerous that if harm results, the actor will be found liable.

Central to a discussion of all three theories of liability are the concepts of duty and foreseeability. Duty means a certain kind of conduct and therefore is action oriented. Intentional torts establish that one has a duty to avoid them.

Negligence establishes that one has a "reasonable" duty to avoid it. Strict liability, on the other hand, establishes a strict duty so that no matter how reasonable the conduct, there is automatic liability if harm occurs. Foreseeability concerns thought rather than action. If the hypothetical reasonable and prudent person would have foreseen harm, then there is liability.

1. What are the objectives of tort law?
2. A person decides to go shopping at the XYZ Department Store. While in the Sportswear Department, the store detective suspects the person of stealing a swimsuit. The detective approaches the person and says, "Excuse me, but would you mind if I asked you a few questions?" The person responds with, "Well, I'm really in quite a rush. I'm on my lunch hour and I have to get back to work." Nevertheless, the person submits to the questioning. The questioning lasts for twenty minutes. Has there been a false imprisonment? Would your answer be any different if the detective had said, "Excuse me, I suspect you of stealing swimsuits. Would you mind if I asked you a few questions?"
3. A hotel waiter asks a male guest, "Is this woman your wife or your mistress?" Is the hotel liable for the waiter's insult? Would your answer be any different if the waiter had asked, "Is this woman your wife or your daughter?"
4. Someone knocks on your front door; after you have admitted him, he accuses you of having a "loathsome" disease and of being a rapist. Has he committed a tort against you? Would your answer be any different if he said the same things in the presence of another person?
5. Why is it that intentional torts, negligence, and strict liability all involve the issue of foreseeability?
6. We all have a duty to protect other persons from harm. How does tort law resolve the question of the extent of that duty?
7. A manufacturer of chemical products markets suntan oil without sufficiently investigating the fact that under certain circumstances the vapors of the product become inflammable. Suppose a person uses the product, and as he rubs the oil on his chest, it ignites and burns him. Can he successfully sue the manufacturer for its negligence? Why?
8. It can be scientifically proved that pollution in the smoke stacks of a steel plant in Beaumont, Texas, is carried in the clouds over the Gulf of Mexico and deposited on the city of Orlando, Florida. It is also known that the pollutants carry cancer-causing chemicals. On what theory can a person who contracted cancer while living in Orlando successfully sue the steel plant? Discuss your answer with respect to proximate cause.
9. Because you love skydiving, you decide to open a parachute-jumping school. Before students can take the training and make a jump, you

require that they sign a voluntary statement that frees you of all liability if they should be harmed. A student makes a jump, but the parachute fails to open. On the basis of those facts, could you be successfully sued for wrongful death? Would it make any difference if it develops that the student simply did not pull the ripcord?

10. A gorilla escapes from a traveling circus, enters a shopping center, and destroys $347,500 worth of property. Will all suits be successful against the circus, or can the circus win if it proves it was not at fault?

CASE
PROBLEMS

1. The defendant entered a hotel dining room carrying a walking stick under his arm. He approached the plaintiff and threatened to ''whip the hell out of'' him if he didn't sign an apology prepared by the defendant. Has an assault occurred? (*Trogden* v. *Terry*, 172 N.C. 540, 90 S.E. 583 [1916].)

2. The defendant threw a punch at Larry, intending to hit Larry when he did so. Unfortunately, he missed Larry with the punch. Instead he struck Daryl. The defendant had no intention of striking Daryl at any time. Has the defendant committed a battery on Daryl? (*Carnes* v. *Thompson*, 48 S.W.2d 903 [Mo. 1932].)

3. The defendant published the following: ''These progressive dealers listed here sell Armour's Star Bacon in the new window-top carton.'' If one of the dealers listed specialized in kosher meat exclusively, has a defamation taken place (kosher meat dealers do not deal in bacon)? (*Braun* v. *Armour & Co.*, 254 N.Y. 514, 173 N.E. 845 [1930].)

4. An insurance company investigator went onto the plaintiff's property and peeked into the plaintiff's window. Has a tort or torts occurred? (*Souder* v. *Pendleton Detectives*, 88 So.2d 716 [La. App. 1956].)

5. The plaintiff was employed as a mechanic on a cruise ship. He was injured when a weight fell on him when he was repairing the machine containing the weight. Will a federal court apply the doctrine of comparative negligence in such a case? (*Schaeffer* v. *Michigan–Ohio Navigation Co.*, 416 F.2d 217 [6th Cir. 1969] 7 ALR Fed. 493.)

6. The defendant falsely asserted that his warehouse was fireproof. Based on the assertion, the plaintiff deposited his goods in the warehouse and was issued a warehouse receipt which stated that the defendant would not be liable for loss owing to fire. A fire occurred and the goods were destroyed. What would be the result and why? (*Rosenblatt* v. *John F. Ivory Storage Co.*, 262 Mich. 513, 247 N.W. 733 [1933].)

7. The defendant shot the plaintiff's dog while it was in the process of attacking the defendant's sheep. Will the defendant win the lawsuit on the basis of privilege? Why, or why not? (*Granier* v. *Chagnon*, 122 Mont. 327, 203 P.2d 982 [1949].)

8. The plaintiff fell down an unlighted stairway in the defendant's public

building. The plaintiff's injury occurred at night. A city ordinance required that stairways in buildings open to the public be constantly lighted. Discuss with respect to the tort of negligence. (*Monsour* v. *Excelsior Tobacco Co.,* 115 S.W.2d 219 [Mo. App. 1938].)

9. The defendant operated an amusement park ride in which it could be observed that some patrons fell down because they could not maintain their balance on a moving belt. The plaintiff observed the ride, paid for a turn, and fell down, fracturing his kneecap. Discuss with respect to assumption of the risk. (*Murphy* v. *Steeplechase Amusement Co.,* 250 N.Y. 479, 166 N.E. 173 [1929].)

10. The plaintiff's estate sued the defendant for the plaintiff's death owing to carbon monoxide poisoning. The defendant manufactured a wall furnace that heated the motel room in which the plaintiff's body was found. The wall furnace was installed in 1957 and had not been substantially changed by 1972, the year of the plaintiff's death. Discuss. (*Jahnig* v. *Coisman,* 283 N.W.2d 557 [S.D. 1979].)

CHAPTER 4

Crimes and Business

WHY STUDY CRIMINAL LAW?

You may wonder why a business law textbook contains a chapter on criminal law. Our reason for including this brief overview of crimes is that businesses are constantly confronted with the *effects* of such crimes as embezzlement, forgery, and fraud, to cite only a few of the kinds of crimes that will be discussed later in the chapter. To prevent a crime from happening, or to deal effectively with a crime once it has occurred, you have to know what the crime is and what the legal ramifications are.

OBJECTIVES OF CRIMINAL LAW

The objectives of criminal law are the protection of persons and property, the deterrence of criminal behavior, the punishment of criminal activity, and the rehabilitation of the criminal.

Protection of Persons and Property

Someone once said that a lock was designed to keep an honest person honest. It is for the same reason that the state declares certain conduct to be illegal. The state believes that all persons and their property should be protected from harm. In Chapter 3, you learned that tort law also protects persons and property. The difference between tort law and criminal law is that tort law results in money damages, whereas criminal law results in loss of freedom by sending a person to jail or prison. Private interests are served through the awarding of damages. The public interest is served by punishing criminal activity. If all persons respected everyone else's person or property, there would be very little reason for criminal law.

Deterrence of Criminal Behavior

A key to the hoped-for reduction in criminal behavior is that our criminal laws present a sufficient **deterrent** to antisocial behavior. The presumption inherent in criminal law is that if we make the punishment sufficiently harsh, persons who might do something criminal are prevented from doing so because they fear punishment. If enough people fear the punishment, they will not commit a criminal act.

Deterrent A danger, difficulty, or other consideration that stops or prevents a person from acting

In our society, however, the Constitution states that there shall be no cruel and unusual punishment. Certainly, if our laws allowed the death penalty for even minor offenses, there would probably be fewer minor offenses. But is that just? To lose one's life for stealing a loaf of bread seems too high a price to pay for fewer loaves of bread being stolen. The problem is to decide how much punishment will deter criminal behavior without going too far.

Punishment of Criminal Activity

Since we most likely will be unable to deter all criminal activity, our laws accept that a certain level of criminal activity will exist in society. Accordingly, we punish criminal activity for punishment's sake. There is no such thing as a free lunch: if a criminal takes something without paying for it, the criminal law makes that individual pay for it through deprivation of freedom for a period of time.

Rehabilitation of the Criminal

Once convicted, a criminal will begin to serve a sentence in a jail or prison. But that is not where our criminal justice system ends. Our government has designed various programs to educate and train criminals in legitimate occupations during the period of incarceration. Upon release, therefore, there should be no reason to return to a life of crime. Sometimes a sentence is suspended; that is, it is not put into effect. In such cases, the court supervises the individual's activities to ensure that they have learned from their mistakes. Figure 4.1 depicts the four objectives of criminal law.

Figure 4.1   Objectives of Criminal Law

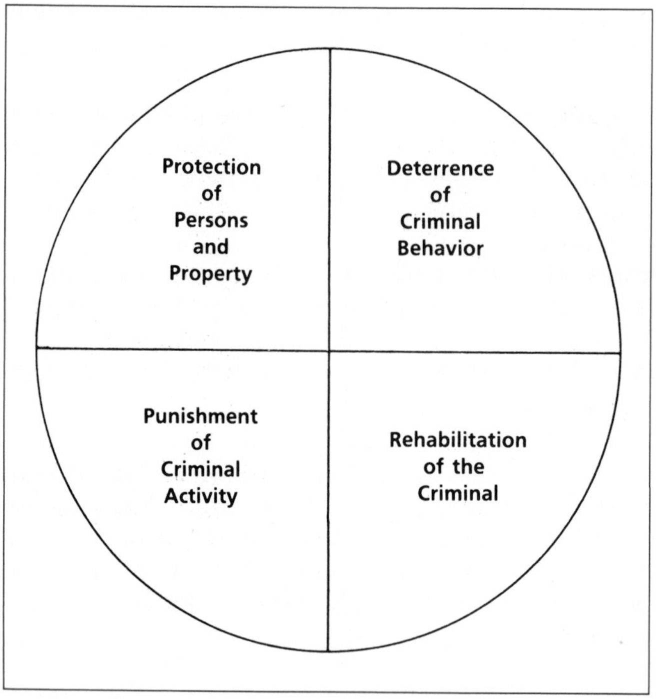

BASES OF CRIMINAL RESPONSIBILITY

All crimes are defined as consisting of two elements: a criminal *act* and an appropriate *mental state.* If only one element is present, there can be no crime. For example, if you decide that you are going to rob a bank and then do nothing about it, you have not committed a crime. Similarly, if a cigarette you are smoking in a motel ignites the draperies in your room and causes the motel to burn down, you have not committed a crime. In the latter case, you may be liable in tort for negligence, but you have not committed the crime of arson.

The Act

The law will impose criminal liability for an illegal act that is voluntarily committed. For example, if you were kidnapped and your abductor forced you to rob a bank under threat of death, obviously the act of robbing the bank was not voluntary. On the other hand, what about a failure to act? In that respect, the following case is informative.

Jones v. *United States*
308 F.2d 307 (D.C. Cir. 1962)

FACTS   The defendant failed to provide for an infant, thus causing the infant's death by malnutrition. The defendant was not the child's mother.

Was the defendant's failure to act a violation of a legal or a moral duty?

It was a violation of a moral duty; thus it is not actionable.

A failure to act that amounts to a failure of a moral duty will never result in criminal liability. Only a failure to act that violated a statute or breached a contractual duty, a failure to perform as volunteered, or status as the parent or guardian of the infant would have resulted in the failure of a legal duty on the part of this defendant.

To be held criminally responsible for an illegal act, the actor must intend to do that which is done. Various terms have been used to describe this mental state: *consciously, intentionally, maliciously, unlawfully,* and *willfully,* to name just a few. These terms once had a place in our **jurisprudence** as the concept of mental state was being developed, but today our approach to the problem is more systematic. This current approach involves the use of one of five terms. Since the term used depends on the specific requirements of the statute and shows more specifically the *degree* of intent than the older terms, the approach is thus more systematic. The terms used are as follows:

Mental State

Jurisprudence The philosophy and science of law

1. *Purpose*—An actor acts with purpose if it is his conscious objective to do that which is done.
2. *Knowledge*—An actor acts with knowledge if he is aware of what he is doing.
3. *Recklessness*—An actor acts with recklessness if he disregards a substantial and unjustifiable risk that criminal harm or injury may result from his action.
4. *Negligence*—An actor acts in a criminally negligent way if he should have known that a substantial and unreasonable risk of harm would result from his action.
5. *Strict liability*—An actor will be held strictly liable if he acts in a manner that our criminal law declares criminal even if none of the above four elements is present. The justification for this theory is that it is used primarily for crimes that have a light punishment—for example, violating public health laws with respect to the sale of food. This theory is also used in statutory rape cases simply because our society has a vested interest in protecting our youth.

The following case shows that the application of the principle of knowledge is a required mental state.

Lambert v. California
355 U.S. 225 (1957)

FACTS   Lambert was arrested in Los Angeles for violating a municipal ordinance that required anyone who had been convicted of a felony in any state to register with the police if he or she remained in the city for more than five days.

ISSUE   Does the ordinance violate the due process clause of the Constitution when it is applied to a person without personal knowledge of it?

HOLDING   Yes. Some showing of knowledge is required by due process.

REASONING   "The rule that ignorance of the law will not excuse . . . is deep in our law, as is the principle that of all the powers of local government, the police power is 'one of the least limitable.' . . . On the other hand, Due Process places some limits on its existence. Engrained in our concept of Due Process is the requirement of notice. . . . We believe that actual knowledge of the duty to register or proof of the probability of such knowledge and subsequent failure to comply are necessary before a conviction under the ordinance can stand."

Figure 4.2 depicts the two bases of criminal responsibility.

SERIOUSNESS OF THE OFFENSE

Criminal law classifies all offenses according to their level of seriousness. On this basis, it distinguishes three categories of offenses. These categories are, from least to most serious, respectively, misdemeanors, felonies, and treason.

Misdemeanors

Misdemeanors are minor offenses that are punishable by confinement of up to one year in a city or county jail, a small fine, or both.

Figure 4.2   The Bases of Criminal Responsibility

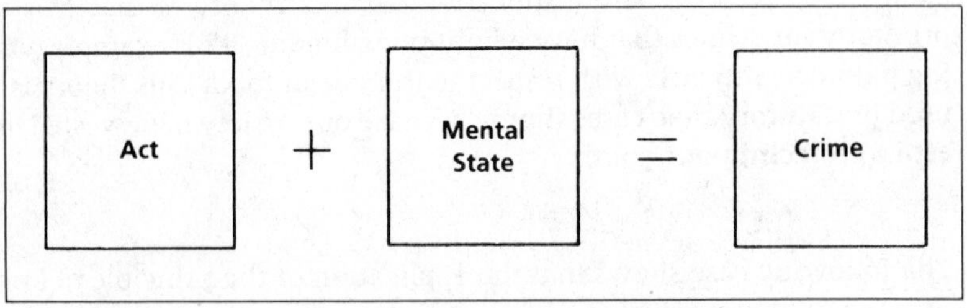

Figure 4.3 The Seriousness of the Offense

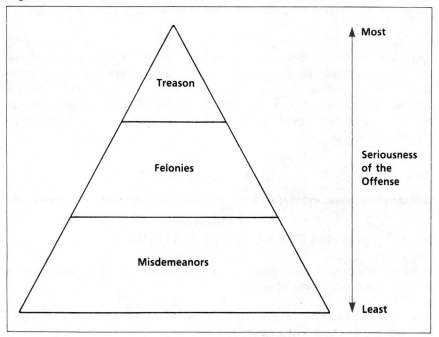

Felonies are *major offenses punishable by confinement from one year to life in a state or federal prison, a large fine, or both.* In some states special capital felony statutes provide for the sentence of death.

Treason is *the most serious offense against the state.* It consists of *waging war against the state* or of *giving aid and comfort to our enemies in time of war.*
    Figure 4.3 depicts the seriousness of the offense.

There is insufficient space in this introductory business law text to list all of the common crimes. We will, however, mention selected crimes that have applications for either detection or prevention in the marketplace.

Arson is *the intentional burning of any property by fire or explosion.* Originally this crime was restricted to the burning of a house. Today the crime has been expanded to include the burning of all real property and just about all personal property.

Burglary is *the breaking and entering of a structure with the intent to commit a felony.* Originally this crime was restricted to the breaking and entering of a house at night, but it too has been expanded to include more activity.

Felonies

Treason

SELECTED CRIMES

Arson

Burglary

Embezzlement	*Embezzlement* is *the taking of money or other property by an employee who has been entrusted with the money or property by his or her employer.*

Forgery	*Forgery* is *the making or altering of a negotiable instrument or credit card invoice in order to create or to shift legal liability for the instrument.* It generally consists of signing another person's name to a check, promissory note, or credit card invoice or altering an amount on any of those documents. To win any such case, the state must prove that the accused acted with the intent to **defraud,** as illustrated in the following case.
Defraud To deprive a person of property or of any interest, estate, or right by fraud, deceit, or artifice	

In re Clemons
168 Ohio 83, 151 N.E.2d 553 (1958)

FACTS   The defendant drew a check on a nonexisting account in an existing bank in order to obtain something of value.

ISSUE   Is the drawing of a check on a nonexisting account in an existing bank forgery if it is done with the intent to defraud?

HOLDING   Yes. This is a forgery.

REASONING   "In order for a check to be considered a genuine instrument the [drawer] must have a right to make such order, i.e., he must have money in the drawee bank. . . . [But] . . . we . . . hold that . . . a person is guilty of a false making of a check where the check is drawn upon a bank in which the [drawer] has no funds or deposit account and is calculated to induce another to give credit to it as genuine and authentic, even though such person signs his own name thereto and likewise that one who utters such a check [with knowledge of its falsity] is guilty of forgery."

Fraud	*Fraud* is a broad term that covers many specific situations. The English courts were very slow to criminalize fraudulent behavior, preferring to let tort law handle most situations. Over the years, however, legislation was passed in both England and the United States to overcome the rather insensitive view of "[we] are not to indict one for making a fool of another."[1] Today most states have statutes that cover variations of what is generally called *theft by deception.*

1 Regina v. Jones, 91 Eng. Rep. 330 (1703).

For example, if a seller of goods created the impression that certain goods were worth $1,000 when, in fact, they were worth only $10, the action would be theft by deception if the purchase were made.

Larceny is *the wrongful taking and carrying away of the personal property of another without the owner's consent and with the intent to deprive the owner of the property permanently*. The most common forms of larceny are shoplifting and pickpocketing. The use of force is not needed.

Larceny

Robbery is a form of aggravated theft. It is basically *larceny plus the threat to use violence or force*. The following case distinguishes a good-faith belief from the bad faith required for criminal intent.

Robbery

People v. *Butler*
55 Cal. Rptr. 511, 421 P.2d 703 (1967)

Butler got into an argument with his employer over the question of wages due him. Guns were drawn, shots were fired ... and Butler took his employer's wallet.

FACTS

Will the mistaken belief that one had a right to property negate the felonious intent necessary for a robbery conviction?

ISSUE

Yes. A good-faith belief will negate intent to commit robbery.

HOLDING

"It has long been the rule in this state and generally throughout the country that a bona fide belief, even though mistakenly held, that one has a right or claim to the property negates felonious intent."

REASONING

There is a growing tendency in many states to hold corporations criminally responsible when their officers and agents commit criminal actions in the execution of their office. Punishment is usually in the form of a fine. If a fine is assessed against the corporation for the criminal activity of its officers and agents, who really suffers? The officers and agents? No, because they will have been separately tried and convicted for their behavior. The stockholders do. The question then is: should innocent stockholders suffer the loss in the form of lower earnings?

A Comment on Corporations

A Comment on the Racketeer Influenced and Corrupt Organizations (RICO) Statute 18 U.S.C. § 1961 et seq.

The RICO statute was made law in 1970. Since that time, Congress has amended the law, and many courts have interpreted many of its sections. The definitions of terms used in the statute are found in section 1961. Section 1962 lists the activities that are prohibited. Criminal and civil penalties are found in section 1963, and sections 1965 to 1968 cover procedural rules.

According to the law's legislative history, it was the intent of Congress to remedy a serious problem: the infiltration of criminals into legitimate businesses as both a "cover" for their criminal activity and as a means of "laundering" profits derived from their crimes.

Since the law focuses on legitimate business activities, it continues to present a concern for all business organizations. The following case extends the definition of a business "enterprise" to include public as well as private entities.

United States v. *Grzywacz*
603 F.2d 682 (7th Cir. 1979)

FACTS The District Court convicted three former police officers of violating the RICO statute by using their former status to solicit and accept bribes from various businesses.

ISSUE Does the term "enterprise" as defined by 18 U.S.C. 1961 (4) include public entities as well as private entities?

HOLDING Yes.

REASONING "Consideration of past precedent, legislative history, and the plain words of the statute convince us that the RICO statute admits of a broader, less constricted interpretation. We believe that public entities and individuals may constitute section 1961 (4) enterprises through which racketeering is conducted."

SELECTED DEFENSES

The four classic defenses to criminal liability are duress, insanity, intoxication, and justification.

Duress

Duress exists when *the accused was coerced into criminal conduct by threat or use of force that any person of reasonable firmness could not resist.* Not all states have this defense, and those that do have differences with respect to the crimes to which it is applicable. The following case cites the three essential elements of the defense.

United States v. *Contento-Pachon*
723 F.2d 691 (9th Cir. 1984)

The defendant was convicted of unlawful possession with intent to distribute a narcotic substance. During the trial, the defendant attempted to introduce evidence of duress. The trial court excluded it.

FACTS

Should the court have allowed the evidence to be introduced?

ISSUE

Yes.

HOLDING

There are three elements to the defense of duress:

REASONING

1.   an immediate threat of death or serious bodily harm
2.   a well-grounded fear that the threat will be carried out
3.   no reasonable opportunity to escape the threatened harm

The defendant offered evidence on each of the three elements. Therefore, his evidence should have been allowed.

Insanity exists when, *as a result of a mental disease or defect, the accused either did not know what he was doing was wrong or could not prevent himself from doing what he knew to be wrong.* This defense has been under increasing attack for a variety of reasons, but chiefly because after almost two hundred years the definition is still ambiguous. It has been applied to less than 1 percent of all criminal cases and has been successful in only a very small number of those cases.

Insanity

Lipscomb v. *State*
609 S.W.2d 15 (Ark. 1980)

Lipscomb was convicted of robbery and sentenced to fifteen years' imprisonment. He argued that the trial court erred in not making a pretrial determination of his insanity plea.

FACTS

What is the proper test to determine if the defendant is not guilty by reason of insanity?

ISSUE

The proper test is whether the defendant could conform his conduct to the law or appreciate the criminality of his conduct.

HOLDING

REASONING   Prior law used the test that "the existence of an insane delusion is a defense to a crime only when the imaginary state of facts, if real, would justify or excuse the crime." Today, the proper test is that "a person is not criminally responsible for his conduct if at the time of that conduct, as a result of mental disease or mental defect, he lacked the capacity either to appreciate the criminality of his conduct or to conform his conduct to the requirements of the law."

Intoxication

Intoxication may be either *voluntary* or *involuntary*. Voluntary intoxication is not a defense unless it negates the specific intent required by a statute. For example, the crime of rape is said to require a general intent. Intoxication, therefore, would not be a valid defense. On the other hand, assault with the intent to commit rape is said to require specific intent. In that case, intoxication could be a valid defense. Generally, involuntary intoxication is a good defense. Involuntary intoxication could occur if one were forced to drink an alcoholic beverage against one's will or without one's knowledge.

Justification

Justification exists when *a person believes an act is necessary in order to avoid harm to himself or to another person.* The key to this defense is that whatever the person does in order to avoid harm must be lesser than the harm to be avoided. For example, sometimes property has to be destroyed in order to prevent the spread of fire. Also, a druggist may dispense a drug without a prescription if to do so would save a person's life.

THE LAW OF CRIMINAL PROCEDURE

Criminal procedure is the *area of law that deals with the judicial process in a criminal case.* It is concerned with assuring criminal justice without infringing upon individual rights. The drafters of the United States Constitution were determined to avoid the excesses and abuses that had been faced under English rule. As a result, the area of criminal procedure was very important. There was a desire to protect the rights of the individual to the greatest extent possible without making law enforcement impossible.

Due process The proper exercise of judicial authority as established by general concepts of law and morality

Equal protection Treatment of all persons before the courts as any other person would be treated before the courts

Bail The procurement of release of a person charged with a crime by assuring his future attendance in the court

The Constitution contains numerous criminal procedure provisions and protections, among them the guarantees of **due process** and **equal protection.** The defendant must be informed of the charges against him, must be tried before an impartial tribunal, must be permitted to confront witnesses against him, and cannot be compelled to testify against himself. The defendant is entitled to a speedy trial, may not be held subject to excessive **bail,** and may not be subjected to cruel and unusual punishment if convicted. No citizen may be subjected to unreasonable searches and seizures, and the only evidence that may be admitted at trial is evidence properly and lawfully obtained. Figure 4.4 depicts the stages of criminal procedure.

Figure 4.4 The Stages of Criminal Procedure

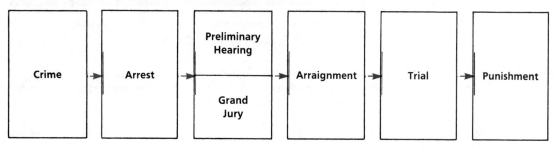

The law carries a *presumption* of innocence until the defendant is proved guilty, and the burden of proof that must be satisfied in a criminal trial is the heaviest such burden in American jurisprudence. The state must convince the jury of the defendant's guilt **beyond a reasonable doubt,** or the defendant must be acquitted.

A police officer acting with probable cause may arrest and accuse an individual of committing a crime, or the arrest may occur under a warrant issued by a judge. A police officer who has probable cause to believe that a crime has been committed, or is being committed, may take the suspect into custody without obtaining a warrant. If an arrest warrant is used, it must be issued by a judge based on probable cause. The judge may find probable cause to believe that a crime has been committed only on the basis of a sworn, written complaint that names the person to be arrested or adequately describes him.

Once arrested and charged with criminal conduct, the accused must be given a preliminary hearing. At the preliminary hearing, a magistrate determines whether there is probable cause to proceed to a trial. Should the magistrate decide that there is no probable cause, or that there is not enough evidence to proceed to trial, or that there is virtually no chance to obtain a conviction, the charges against the accused will be dropped, and the accused will be released from custody.

A **grand jury** may also be involved in the pretrial stages of criminal proceedings. A grand jury is a panel charged with determining whether there is reason to believe that a person has committed a crime. After hearing the evidence presented by the prosecutor, the grand jury will issue an **indictment** if it believes that the accused has committed a crime. The state will then proceed to trial on the basis of this indictment.

The following case raises the question of whether an indictment must be dismissed if, at times, unauthorized persons are present during a session of a grand jury.

Beyond a reasonable doubt The degree of proof required in a criminal trial, which is proof to a moral certainty not subject to any other *reasonable* interpretation

Grand jury A jury whose duty it is to receive complaints of criminal conduct and to return a bill of indictment if convinced a trial should be held

Indictment A written accusation of criminal conduct issued to a court by a grand jury

United States v. Computer Sciences Corporation
689 F.2d 1181 (4th Cir. 1982)

FACTS   The District Court dismissed all fifty-seven counts in an indictment because on five occasions during an eighteen-month period some unauthorized persons were present during a session of the grand jury.

ISSUE   Does Rule 6 (d) of the Federal Rules of Criminal Procedure require dismissal of the indictment?

HOLDING   No.

REASONING   Under the general rule, the counts must be dismissed if unauthorized persons are present during the deliberations of a grand jury. However, ''[a] review of the record satisfies us that the invasions of the grand jury proceedings were rare, inadvertent and nonprejudicial to any defendant. . . . [E]ach situation should be addressed on a *sui generis* basis. . . . In the course of a grand jury investigation lasting eighteen months, intrusions by unauthorized persons occurred on [only] five occasions. . . . Each intrusion was brief, lasting no more than a minute or two. . . . Each intrusion brought the proceedings to an abrupt halt, and no testimony was taken in the presence of the unauthorized persons. . . . Attainable reality, not perfection, here suffices. . . . [But] [p]rosecutors should not consider what we have written as in any way amounting to an encouragement to depart from scrupulous compliance with Fed.R.Crim.P. 6 (d). . . . ''

Arraigned Called before a court to enter a plea on an indictment

Nolo contendere A plea in a criminal proceeding that has the same effect as a plea of guilty but that may not be used as evidence of guilt

Once the grand jury has issued an indictment or the magistrate at a preliminary hearing has determined that probable cause exists, the accused is **arraigned.** At the arraignment, the accused is informed of the charges against him, and, if necessary, the court appoints an attorney to represent the defendant. The defendant than enters a plea to the charges pending against him. If the plea so entered is guilty or **nolo contendere,** the court moves to the sentencing stage. If the plea is not guilty, a trial date is set and bail is determined, if appropriate.

At the trial, the state has the burden of proving its case beyond a reasonable doubt, and it must satisfy this burden within the established rules of evidence. Any violation of the rules of evidence will result in the exclusion of the improper evidence, and often the exclusion of the evidence will destroy the state's case. When this happens, the defendant will be acquitted.

If the defendant is found guilty, the court moves to the sentencing stage. Sentencing is governed by legislative guidelines to some extent, but the guidelines are normally very broad and somewhat vague, and a great deal of judicial discretion is usually involved in sentencing.

Criminal law is designed to protect persons and property from harm. In addition, it should deter criminal behavior. The best protection, of course, is the absence of criminal activity. However, since there is always bound to be some criminal activity, the law should punish criminals for their wrongful acts and try to rehabilitate them while they are incarcerated.

Criminal responsibility is based on two essential elements, one physical and the other mental. The physical element is an overt act. The mental element is actually one of the following: intent, negligence, or strict liability. There is a similarity to tort law, but the interests that are protected are different. Tort law protects private interests, whereas criminal law protects public interests. Accordingly, one can be held liable twice for the same act, once in tort law, and once in criminal law. This is not double jeopardy (a second prosecution after the first trial for the same offense) because there are two distinct bases of liability.

All crimes are either misdemeanors or felonies. Misdemeanors are the less serious crimes; felonies, the more serious. Treason, on the other hand, involves acts to overthrow the government on the part of a person who owes allegiance to that government.

The selected crimes discussed in the chapter are arson, burglary, embezzlement, forgery, fraud, larceny, and robbery. The defenses mentioned are duress, insanity, intoxication, and justification.

The law of criminal procedure is very technical. An individual suspected of committing a crime may be arrested only upon probable cause, either by the arresting officer or by a judge issuing an arrest warrant. Once arrested, the accused is entitled to a preliminary hearing that requires another finding of probable cause in order to proceed to a trial. A grand jury may also be used, issuing an indictment if it believes that the accused has committed a crime.

If there should be a trial, the state must prove its case beyond a reasonable doubt, and it must do so under numerous constitutional guarantees, such as due process, equal protection, and the rules of evidence. Only upon conviction may an accused person be sentenced to a fine or imprisonment.

1. With respect to the individual citizen, what is the meaning of the following quote from *Lanzetta* v. *New Jersey*: "No one may be required at peril of life, liberty, or property to speculate as to the meaning of penal statutes"?

2. Of the four objectives of criminal law, which should have precedence over the others? Why? Which should have the least precedence? Why?

3. If merely thinking about a crime is not punishable under criminal law, why are both the act and the mental state required in order to decide criminal responsibility?

4. If a restaurant cashier takes money that rightfully should have been placed in the restaurant's checking account, what crime, if any, has been committed? Why?

5. If a house were on fire during a drought, would a volunteer firefighter who dynamited the surrounding houses in order to save the rest of the community have any criminal responsibility? Explain.

6. In 1951, twenty-one corporations were convicted on criminal price-fixing charges in violation of federal antitrust laws and were fined a total of $822,500. The judge who sentenced them said, "The real blame is to be laid at the doorstep of corporate defendants and those who guide and direct their policy." What is to be gained by society when fines are inflicted on corporations rather than imposing prison sentences on those officers and agents who actually committed the criminal activity?

7. An individual's business is losing money. She decides to burn down her place of business, collect the proceeds of her insurance, and start over again. The building burns down, but a drifter sleeping in the building at the time was burned to death. What is the liability for the actor: arson, homicide, both, or neither? Why?

8. If an individual was observed entering a store yard at night and carrying a ladder and a bag of tools, could that person be convicted of attempted burglary?

9. The Model Penal Code is a proposed criminal code that many states have used to revise and modernize their criminal laws. It consolidates larceny, embezzlement, false pretense, extortion, blackmail, fraudulent conversion, receiving stolen property, and all other similar offenses into the one general offense of theft. What advantages can you find to this approach?

10. Crimes are either *mala in se* (morally wrong) or *mala prohibita* (wrong because the law says they are wrong). To which category does the crime of arson belong? To which does income tax evasion belong? Why?

CASE
PROBLEMS

1. A New York statute made it a crime for a person to have no visible means of support and to live without employment. Such a law is commonly called a vagrancy statute. Discuss the legality of the statute with respect to the two bases of criminal responsibility. (*Fenster* v. *Leary*, 20 N.Y.2d 309, 229 N.E.2d 426 [1967].)

2. A defendant was accused of having been involved in a heroin distribution scheme. He attempted to introduce evidence of duress. The evidence was that he was in a "depressed" state, that he was tense and nervous, and that if he hadn't involved himself in the scheme, there would have been "consequences." Should the trial court have allowed the evidence? Why? (*United States* v. *Hernandez*, 608 F.2d 741 [9th Cir. 1979].)

3. RICO was designed to apply to legitimate businesses that had been infiltrated by criminals. Can RICO be used against criminals who operate illegitimate businesses such as a gambling business? Why? (*United States* v. *Cappetto*, 502 F.2d 1351 [7th Cir. 1974].)

4. Federal law requires that government attorneys appearing before grand juries be "specifically directed" by the Attorney General. (See 28 U.S.C. 515 [a].) A government attorney appeared before a grand jury pursuant to a letter from an assistant attorney general. Is that proper grounds for a dismissal of the indictment? Give reasons for your answer. (*United States* v. *Agrusa,* 520 F.2d 370 [8th Cir. 1975].)

5. A fifteen-year-old was tried as a juvenile for being in the company of another boy who stole a woman's wallet. He was confined for up to six years (until he was twenty-one). If he had been convicted of the same crime as an adult he would have been fined $5 to $50 or jailed for not more than two months. Discuss with respect to the reason, or lack thereof, for the length of his confinement. (*In re Gault,* 387 U.S. 1 [1967].)

6. If, as a judge, you had to choose between protecting society or rehabilitating the offender, which would you choose and why? (*People* v. *Levy,* 151 Cal. App.2d 460, 311 P.2d 897 [1957].)

7. The defendant was convicted of embezzlement. In his appeal, he argued that he was not guilty of the crime since the money came into his possession as the operator of a collection agency, and, as an independent businessman, he could not have been the employee or agent for the business that lost the money. Discuss. (*State* v. *Riggins,* 8 Ill.2d 78, 132 N.E.2d 519 [1956].)

8. A lawyer was retained to represent an individual accused of disorderly conduct. In a meeting with his client, the lawyer said that his fee would be $200 and that he would need an additional $2000 to buy the silence of the arresting officer. In fact, the arresting officer subsequently told the lawyer that the client was not in any trouble and that the matter would be dropped. Nevertheless, the attorney kept the $2200. Discuss. (*Graham* v. *United States,* 187 F.2d 87 [1950].)

9. The defendant was convicted of assault with intent to murder. He argued that he could not have had the mental intent to murder since, prior to the assault, he became voluntarily intoxicated. Discuss. (*Roberts* v. *People,* 19 Mich. 401 [1870].)

10. May a wife who is regularly beaten by her husband use deadly force to defend herself? (*People* v. *Jones,* 191 Cal. App.2d 478, 12 Ca. Rptr. 777 [D.C. App. 1961].)

CHAPTER 5

Anatomy of a Civil Lawsuit

THE PROBLEM

Nic Grant, a college sophomore, had saved some of his earnings from a part-time job to take his girlfriend, Nancy Griffin, to dinner at the most expensive restaurant in town, Chez Joey. This was an important date for him, and he wanted to impress Nancy with his interest in her. What better way, he thought, but to spend a lot of money? After all, deeds speak louder than words.

That night he called for Nancy at seven o'clock and took her to the restaurant, which was on the top floor of the town's tallest building. As soon as the elevator door opened, he knew he had made the right decision. It was beautiful. The interior was exotic. Soft music could be heard in the background. The head waiter ushered them to their table, and the waiter quickly appeared to take their order. They ordered a delicately dry white wine to go with their fresh swordfish, the specialty of the house. The wine was served. It had a marvelous bouquet and superb aftertaste. Nic could see that Nancy was having a wonderful time. When the swordfish was served, it was partially covered with a sauce that had an unusual taste. Since neither of them had had swordfish before, they took no further note of it and ate the fish.

Using his newly obtained credit card, Nic paid the bill. He said goodnight to Nancy at eleven o'clock and was home by eleven-thirty. Before he went to bed, he felt some rumbling in his stomach, but he discounted it as merely experiencing new food. He couldn't sleep, however, and things got worse. He called out to his roommate, Tom. Tom knew that he had to get Nic to a hospital. It was one-thirty in the morning. Tom carried Nic to his car and drove him to the closest hospital with an emergency room.

Nic spent the next five days in the hospital; lost his job because he didn't show up for work Monday night; and failed to take his mid-term examinations, which caused him to drop out of college for the semester. Nancy, who didn't have a job, suffered the same physical problem Saturday night and also dropped out of school. Tom, who finished the semester, which included a course in business law, advised Nic to consult a lawyer to see if there was anything that could be done for him.

Nic called the local bar association, and they referred him to an attorney. Nic called the attorney and was given an appointment. At the interview Nic recounted for the attorney, Lyn Carroll, all the facts of that fateful evening. The attorney asked whether Nic had gotten in touch with the restaurant, and he said no. Attorney Carroll said that something could be done about the matter. Nic was relieved. Ms. Carroll said that she might be able to help Nancy as well. A call was made to her, and the three agreed to meet on Monday to discuss, read, and sign the client–attorney contract. At the meeting, Ms. Carroll produced this document for all to sign. A copy of it is shown in Figure 5.1. As indicated in the contract, payment was to be based on a **contingency fee.**

CLIENT'S INTERVIEW WITH A LAWYER

Contingency fee A fee that is possible but not assured; a fee stipulated to be paid to an attorney for services rendered in conducting a suit or other proceeding only if the case is won

In the interviews with her clients and in subsequent telephone conversations, the information displayed in Figure 5.2 was obtained by Ms. Carroll. On the basis of this preliminary information, Attorney Carroll obtained medical releases from both clients in order to obtain the hospital and medical records. Nic merely turned over his copy of the credit card invoice reflecting payment for the meals. The medical release appears in Figure 5.3 on page 80.

After reviewing the file, Ms. Carroll wrote to the university that Grant and Griffin had been attending for proof that they had been withdrawn from classes after 17 June 1988, as well as to Grant's former employer for proof that he had been fired on 20 June 1988. Once all the material requested was in the file, the preliminary investigation came to a close. It evidenced that they had

INVESTI-GATION OF THE FACTS

Figure 5.1 Client–Attorney Contract

AGREEMENT

THIS CONTRACT entered into, by, and between NIC GRANT and NANCY GRIFFIN, herein referred to as CLIENTS, and LYN CARROLL, hereinafter referred to as ATTORNEY, WITNESSETH:

1. Clients hereby retain and employ attorney to represent them in the prosecution of their claim and cause of action for damages sustained by them as a result of eating food at Chez Joey on 17 June 1988 at 9876 Appian Way, Smithville, Texas, resulting in injuries and damages to clients.

2. Clients agree to pay attorney for her services rendered pursuant to this employment contract at the rate of one-third (33⅓ percent) of the net amount recovered, if any.

3. All necessary and reasonable costs, expenses, investigation, preparation for trial, and litigation expenses shall be initially paid for by attorney and then deducted from the amount of any settlement or recovery, and the division between the parties shall be made after deduction of said expenses. Furthermore, clients shall reimburse attorney for all such costs and expenses even if no recovery is made or, in the alternative, if the costs and expenses should exceed the amount of the recovery.

4. Attorney agrees to undertake the representation of clients in the prosecution of the above claims and causes of action, using her highest professional skill to further the interest of said clients in all matters in connection with their claims and causes of action, and to diligently pursue said claims and causes of action.

5. No settlement or other disposition of the matter shall be made by attorney without the written approval of clients.

IN WITNESS WHEREOF, the parties hereto have executed this instrument in triplicate originals this 26th day of June 1988.

CLIENT _____
                                NIC GRANT

CLIENT _____
                              NANCY GRIFFIN

ATTORNEY _____
                               LYN CARROLL

---

both eaten contaminated swordfish, based on a chemical analysis of the contents of their stomachs, and had contracted food poisoning. (The term *ptomaine poisoning* was used beginning in 1870 to include various nitrogen compounds formed during the decomposition of proteins. Today, however, it has been determined that most food poisoning is due to other factors, including bacteria, especially salmonella organisms, as well as chemicals.) At this point, Ms. Carroll sat down and wrote the letter displayed in Figure 5.4 on page 81.

Figure 5.2 Preliminary Information

ACTIONS	INFORMATION	
	Nic Grant	
	4321 South Medford, Apt. 32	
	Smithville, Texas 88903	
	(123) 521-2394 (Home)	
	NONE (Work)	
	DOB 21 May 1968	
	Nancy Griffin	
	1234 North Mitford, Apt. 9B	
	Smithville, Texas 88909	
	(123) 522-4932 (Home)	
	NONE (Work)	
	DOB 24 Dec 1969	
Get Credit Card Copy	Date of Injury	17 June 1988
	Place of Injury	Chez Joey
		9876 Appian Way
		Smithville, Texas 88906
	Nature of Injury	WARRANTY: Breach of Implied Warranty of Merchantability — Contract — Sale of Goods (UCC)
Get Hospital and Doctor's Records	Treatment	Grant — Doctor's Hospital 18–22 June 1988
	Physician	Billy Lee, M.D. Professional Building Smithville, Texas 88901
	Treatment	Griffin — none
	Physician	Alfred Lowens, M.D. 8323 Farkleberry Lane Smithville, Texas 88901

Upon receipt of the letter of notice, Mr. Durand called his insurance company and informed them of its contents. The insurance carrier immediately assigned an adjuster, Angus McPike, to the case. Mr. McPike got in touch with Ms. Carroll to ascertain the nature of the injuries and discovered the information shown in Figure 5.5 on page 82. On the basis of this information, the adjuster attempted to negotiate a settlement by offering $1454.15 to Mr. Grant and $175.00 to Ms. Griffin. Since the offer covered only out-of-pocket medical expenses, it was rejected, and Ms. Carroll filed **suit** on 24 July 1988.

NEGOTIATION OF SETTLEMENT

Suit Abbreviation of "lawsuit," the formal legal proceeding used to solve a legal problem

Figure 5.3   Medical Release

MEDICAL AUTHORIZATION

TO: _____

I hereby authorize and request you to allow my attorney, LYN CARROLL, free access to any and all hospital and/or medical records or reports in your possession or custody and, upon request of LYN CARROLL, to furnish to her, at my expense, a full and complete report concerning your medical examination and treatment of

_____

_____
Date

_____
        Name

_____
        Address

FILING OF THE SUIT

Complaint In civil practice, the plaintiff's first pleading

Summons A writ requiring the sheriff to notify the person named that the person must appear in court to answer a complaint

Figure 5.6 (pages 82 to 83) shows the Plaintiff's Original Petition. After this **complaint** was filed, the clerk of the court issued a summons and delivered it to the sheriff so that he could serve the summons along with the complaint on the defendant. A **summons** is *a court writ that tells the defendant to answer the complaint within a certain period of time*. Both the summons and the complaint were in this case personally delivered to the defendant. Since the defendant is a corporation, they were delivered to Mr. Durand, the registered agent for the corporation. Figure 5.7 (page 84) displays a copy of the defendant's answer.

At this point in the proceedings, the issue is *joined,* meaning the plaintiffs have sued the defendant in a court of law and the defendant has filed an answer. Before trial, it is the duty of both counsel to simplify the legal issues, amend their complaint and answer, and limit the number of expert witnesses, if any.

PRETRIAL PROCEEDINGS

Now begins what is called the discovery process. *Discovery* is a general term that applies to *a group of specific methods of narrowing the issue*. The reason lawyers use the process is that it results in either shortening the actual trial, if there is one, or eliminating the need for a trial if the case is settled before trial. If one side can see that there is no way they could win the suit, it is in their best interests to settle the case. The "scope" of discovery is very broad. Accordingly, one can discover all that is relevant even if the evidence could not be introduced at trial. The test is that it must be reasonably calculated to lead to admissible evidence.

A *deposition* is *the reducing to writing of a witness's* sworn *testimony outside of court.* This is done routinely today either to preserve testimony for someone who, for good cause, may not be able to be present at the trial or it is done to subsequently impeach the witness when the party does appear at trial and gives evidence that conflicts with what he or she gave at the time the deposition was taken. To **impeach** a witness is *to demonstrate to the jury that the person is untruthful.* For example, if a witness in this case said that she saw both Nic and Nancy at Chez Joey's on June 17 but later at the trial contradicted her own

Depositions

Impeach To call into question the veracity of a witness by means of evidence brought forth for that purpose

Figure 5.4   Letter of Notice

LYN CARROLL, J.D.
Attorney at Law
Suite 654
Smithville Savings Building
Smithville, Texas 88905

6 July 1988

Mr. Joseph E. Durand
President
Chez Joey, Inc.
9876 Appian Way   RE: *Nic Grant and Nancy Griffin* v. *Chez Joey, Inc.*
Smithville, Texas 88906   **d/b/a** Chez Joey

Dear Mr. Durand:

I have been retained by Mr. Nic Grant and Ms. Nancy Griffin to represent them in a cause of action arising from their having dinner at your restaurant on 17 June 1988 and, as a direct result, having contracted food poisoning. My investigation indicates that their injuries were caused by having eaten contaminated swordfish, which is a breach of the implied warranty of merchantability and is thus actionable under the Texas Uniform Commercial Code, Section 2-314.

Should you or your liability carrier wish to discuss this matter with me in order to achieve a just and equitable settlement, please get in touch with me within twelve days from the date of this letter. If I do not hear from you or your representative within that period, I shall file suit against you without further notice.

Sincerely,

Lyn Carroll

LC:rj
cc: Mr. Grant
cc: Ms. Griffin

D/b/a Abbreviation for "doing business as" that is used whenever one person operates a business under another name

Figure 5.5   Summary of the Insurance Adjustor's Findings

DAMAGES

Mr. Grant
1. Cost of meal $67.00
2. Trans. to hosp.   5.00
3. Hospital bill   1250.15
4. Doctor bill   137.00
5. Lost wages   unknown
6. Tuition for 1 sem.   550.00
7. Books   75.00
                            TOTAL $2084.15

Ms. Griffin
1. Doctor bill $175.00
2. Tuition for 1 sem.   550.00
3. Books   60.00
                            TOTAL $785.00

                      GRAND TOTAL $2869.15

Figure 5.6   Plaintiff's Original Petition

Plaintiff's Original Petition
No. 23465

NIC GRANT	) **IN THE DISTRICT COURT**
and	)
NANCY GRIFFIN	) **MALFUSIA COUNTY**
V.	) **STATE OF TEXAS**
Chez Joey, Inc.	) **156th JUDICIAL DISTRICT**
d/b/a/ Chez Joey	)

TO THE HONORABLE JUDGE OF SAID COURT:

NOW COME NIC GRANT and NANCY GRIFFIN, hereinafter called PLAINTIFFS, complaining of CHEZ JOEY, Inc., a domestic corporation doing business in the State of Texas as Chez Joey, hereinafter called DEFENDANT, who may be served with citation by service upon their statutory agent, JOSEPH E. DURAND, 9876 Appian Way, Smithville, Malfusia County, Texas, and for cause of action would respectfully show unto the court that:

I

On or about 17 June 1988, plaintiffs had dinner at Chez Joey restaurant. They ordered, were served, and consumed the specialty of the house, broiled swordfish with house sauce. Mr. Grant paid $67.00 for the two meals. Later that evening plaintiffs became violently ill, had high temperatures, vomited, lost control of their bowels, and

Figure 5.6   (continued)

required medical and hospital attention. A subsequent examination of the contents of their respective stomachs revealed that the swordfish was contaminated, thus causing the plaintiffs to contract food poisoning.

II

Defendant's breach of the implied warranty of merchantability is a violation of the Texas Uniform Commercial Code, Section 2-314, the pertinent portion of which is quoted verbatim:

> (1) Unless excluded or modified . . . a warranty that the goods shall be merchantable is implied in a contract for their sale if the seller is a merchant with respect to goods of that kind. Under this section the serving for value of food or drink to be consumed either on the premises or elsewhere is a sale.

III

As a result of defendant's breach of the implied warranty of merchantability, plaintiffs have incurred, and will continue to incur, various medical expenses; they have suffered, and will continue to suffer, pain; Mr. Grant has been unable to work and has lost wages in the sum of $600.00, and his ability to earn in the immediate future has been temporarily impaired; plaintiff's have suffered a loss of tuition incurred in the course of furthering their education by having to drop out of school.

WHEREFORE, plaintiffs pray judgment against defendant in the sum of $10,000.00, their costs, and all other proper relief.

LYN CARROLL
Attorney at Law
Suite 654
Smithville Savings Building
Smithville, Texas 88905
(123) 525-1234

testimony, the deposition would be used to show the jury that the witness is unreliable. A deposition may be obtained from any party or witness.

Interrogatories

Interrogatories are *written questions from one side to the other.* The result is the same as in depositions in the sense that there is a written record of answers to questions. But it is also different because both the questions and the answers are written, and thus the answers are not so spontaneous as in a deposition. While the answer is made under oath, the respondent has the time to think out and carefully phrase the written answers to the questions posed. Interrogatories may be obtained from all parties to the lawsuit but not from all witnesses — that is, if a witness is neither a plaintiff nor a defendant (the two groups that comprise the parties), an interrogatory may not be obtained.

Figure 5.7   Defendant's Answer

Defendant's Original Answer
No. 23465

NIC GRANT and	) **IN THE DISTRICT COURT**
NANCY GRIFFIN	) **MALFUSIA COUNTY**
V.	) **STATE OF TEXAS**
CHEZ JOEY, INC. d/b/a/CHEZ JOEY	) **156th JUDICIAL DISTRICT**)

TO THE HONORABLE JUDGE OF SAID COURT:

COMES NOW CHEZ JOEY, INC., d/b/a/ CHEZ JOEY, defendant in the above styled and numbered cause, and for answer to Plaintiff's Original Petition would respectfully show unto the court:

I

Defendant denies each and every material allegation contained in Plaintiff's Original Petition.

WHEREFORE, having fully answered, defendant prays that the complaint be dismissed, for his costs, and for all other proper relief.

JONES, MURPHY, SABBATINO, and SCHWARTZ
Suite 1010
First National Bank Building
Smithville, Texas 88905
(123) 525-9876

By _____
    ATTORNEYS FOR DEFENDANT

On 14 August 1988 a copy of this answer was mailed to Ms. Lyn Carroll, attorney for plaintiffs, Suite 654, Smithville Savings Building, Smithville, Texas 88905.

By _____
    JEFFERSON JONES

Production of Documents and Things

In many lawsuits, testimony alone is insufficient to win the case. In our case, since the testimony of Nic and Nancy would be insufficient, Ms. Carroll will introduce the records of the two doctors, the hospital, and the credit card invoice. Because of the circumstances of this case, Ms. Carroll may also request the production of records in the possession of Chez Joey reflecting when and where the fish was bought, as well as any internal communications used in its kitchen explaining the procedure used in preparing swordfish. The legal form used to obtain those documents is called a **subpeona duces tecum.**

Subpeona duces tecum A court order to produce evidence at the trial

Whenever the physical or mental condition of a party to the suit is in question, the court may order that party to submit to an examination by a physician. In this case, it is not so much the present condition of the plaintiffs as their physical condition on June 17–18 that is in question. Therefore, an examination at this point will probably not be pursued.

Physical or Mental Examination

One party can serve upon the other party a written request for an *admission,* which takes the form of *a question asked by one party to which the answer is either yes or no.* If the party who is to respond fails to answer in a stated period of time (usually thirty days), the matter is deemed admitted. Figure 5.8 depicts the five discovery devices.

Request for Admission

As a result of the discovery process, the attorneys for Chez Joey inform their client that the law of implied warranties with respect to merchantability imposes an absolute liability upon the merchant (Chez Joey) for the fitness of the food. It makes no difference that the restaurant did everything it could reasonably do to prevent such injury from occurring. Mr. Jones recommends settlement for $5,000. Mr. Durand accepts the advice of counsel. Ms. Carroll informs her clients of the offer and recommends rejection. Nic and Nancy agree, and the case goes to trial.

The Result of Discovery

At this point, it is most likely that Lyn Carroll would introduce a motion for a summary judgment because no substantial fact questions appear to be in dispute; it is merely a matter of applying the law. In such a case, a motion for summary judgment is appropriate. The motion will be granted if, after a review of the pleadings, depositions, affidavits, and other filings it appears that there is no genuine issue of any material fact. Nevertheless, let us assume that there is an issue of fact and continue with the process.

Motion for a Summary Judgment

Most states require prospective jurors to complete a juror information form, which elicits information on which the respective attorneys base their questions to the jury in what is called the **voir dire** examination. This is an important part of the trial. The information offered by the jurors in response to the questions from counsel are used by counsel as the basis of their challenging jurors as biased and thus ineligible for service. In this case, for example, if a potential juror worked for Chez Joey, Ms. Carroll would challenge that person and request that the judge excuse the person. On the other hand, if one of the prospective jurors was a student at Nic and Nancy's university, Mr. Jones would examine the student very carefully to see whether he or she would favor a fellow student.

THE TRIAL

Jury Selection

Voir dire An oath given to jurors stating that they swear to answer truthfully all questions asked them in order to determine their competence to serve on the jury

Figure 5.8 Pretrial Proceedings

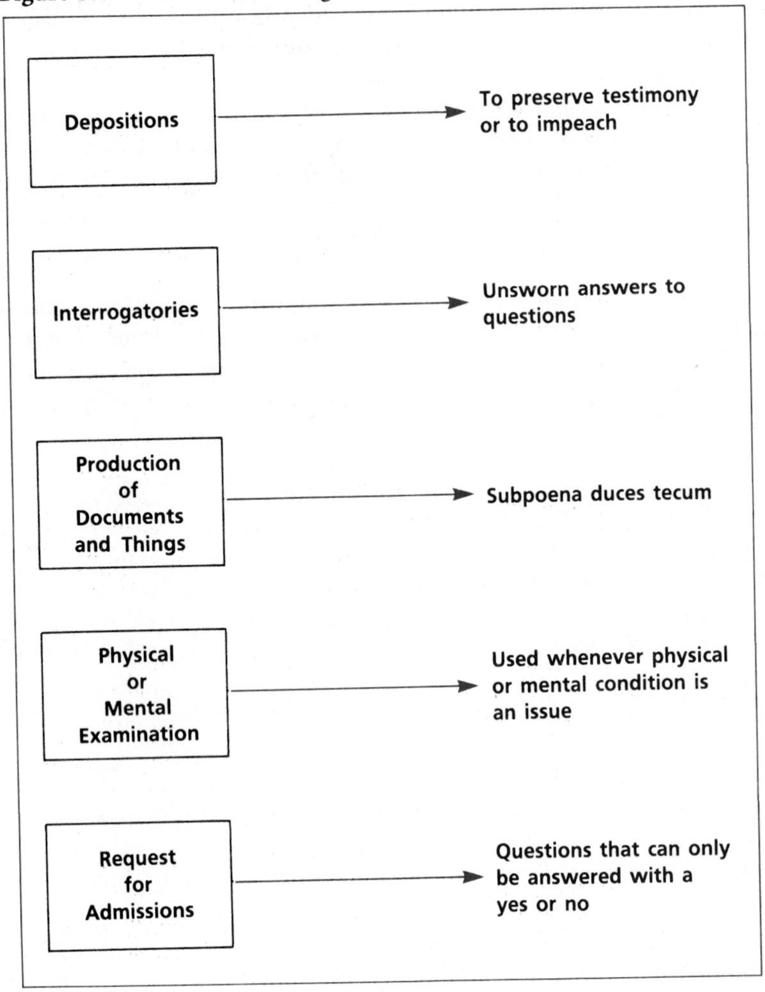

Depositions	To preserve testimony or to impeach
Interrogatories	Unsworn answers to questions
Production of Documents and Things	Subpoena duces tecum
Physical or Mental Examination	Used whenever physical or mental condition is an issue
Request for Admissions	Questions that can only be answered with a yes or no

Opening
Statements
After the jury is chosen, each side has an opportunity to tell the jury what it intends to prove.

Direct
Examination
Ms. Carroll questions her witnesses.

Cross-
Examination
After Ms. Carroll questions each of her witnesses, Mr. Jones has an opportunity to question them. Skillful use of cross-examination by competent counsel is the best means we have at present to ascertain the truth of the matters brought up in direct examination. (This process continues until Ms. Carroll has no other witnesses to call. At that time Mr. Jones directly examines his wit-

nesses, and Ms. Carroll cross-examines them until the defense has no further witnesses to call. At that time, both sides "rest" their cases.)

After both sides have rested, each has an opportunity to persuade the jury by going back over the testimony and laying out all the facts that were proved in court and then drawing conclusions from those facts that best support its position. Thus, the attorneys take the same set of facts and draw opposite conclusions.

Closing Arguments

At the conclusion of closing arguments, the judge discusses the law with the jury and charges them to answer certain questions with respect to the evidence **adduced** at trial. After the jury withdraws from the courtroom, they deliberate and reach their decision, called the *verdict*. At that time the verdict is announced in open court. In this case, the jury, whose members are referred to as **petit jurors**, held for the plaintiffs for $7500. The judgment is the court's official decision and appears in Figure 5.9.

Judgment

Adduced Given as proof

Petit Jurors Ordinary jurors comprising the panel of twelve for the trial of a civil or criminal action

Figure 5.9 Court's Judgment

IN THE 156th DISTRICT COURT OF MALFUSIA COUNTY, STATE OF TEXAS

NIC GRANT and NANCY GRIFFIN	))	**PLAINTIFFS**
V.		
CHEZ JOEY, INC. d/b/a/ CHEZ JOEY	)	**DEFENDANT**

No. 23465

JUDGMENT

On the 10th day of November 1988 this cause came to be heard, plaintiffs appearing in person and by their attorney, LYN CARROLL, and defendant appearing in person and by his attorneys, JONES, MURPHY, SABBATINO, and SCHWARTZ. All parties announcing ready for trial, a jury composed of Mae Brown and eleven others of the regular panel of the petit jurors of this court was selected and impaneled and sworn according to law to try the issues of fact arising in this cause. After the introduction of all the evidence, the instructions of the court, and the arguments of counsel, said jury retired to consider its verdict, and after deliberating thereon returned unto court the following verdict:

We, the jury, find in favor of the plaintiffs, Nic Grant and Nancy Griffin, and assess their damages as $5000.00 and $2500.00, respectively.

MAE BROWN, FOREMAN

Figure 5.9 (continued)

IT IS, THEREFORE, BY THE COURT, CONSIDERED, ORDERED, AND ADJUDGED that the plaintiffs, NIC GRANT and NANCY GRIFFIN, have and recover of and from the defendant, Chez Joey, Inc. d/b/a/ Chez Joey the sums of $5000.00 and $2500.00, respectively, plus their court costs herein expended. Said judgment shall bear interest from this date until paid at the rate of TEN PERCENT PER ANNUM.

ENTERED this 10th day of November 1988.

_____
DISTRICT JUDGE

APPROVED AS TO FORM:

_____
Attorney for Plaintiffs

_____
Attorneys for Defendant

Appeal

At this point, attorneys for Chez Joey could file a notice of appeal and thus have an opportunity to be heard in a higher court; but since the decision is in accordance with the law, no appeal is filed and the case finally comes to an end. Chez Joey now owes the plaintiffs $7500. Figure 5.10 depicts the stages of a trial.

NOTE: FINALITY

In this chapter, you have witnessed one of the great virtues of the law: finality. Whenever a cause of action has been litigated and reduced to a judgment and all appeals have been exhausted, the matter finally comes to an end. In that case the doctrine of res judicata applies. *Res judicata* means that whenever a court issues a final judgment, the subject matter of that lawsuit is finally decided between the parties to the suit. This doctrine prevents further suits from being brought. The matter finally comes to rest.

The following case discusses the question of the appropriateness of applying the doctrine of res judicata.

Cotton States Mutual Ins. Co. v. Anderson
749 F.2d 663 (11th Cir. 1984)

FACTS

An insurance company challenged the constitutionality of Georgia's no-fault insurance statute. On appeal from the trial court's decision, the State of Georgia (Anderson) raised the question for the first time that the insurance company was estopped from raising the question of the unconstitutionality of the statute because it had raised an almost identical argument in prior litigation.

Will the doctrine of res judicata prevent a litigant from relitigating the same issue if it is raised for the first time on appeal and not in the trial court?

ISSUE

Yes and no.

HOLDING

The reason the issue was not raised in the trial court was because the other case had not been finally decided prior to the time when this trial court announced its decision. Therefore, it is understandable that it would be raised for the first time on appeal. Res judicata is proper "if the issue in the subsequent proceeding is identical to the one involved in the prior action, the issue was actually litigated, and the determination of the issue was necessary in the prior action." However, the court chose to exercise its discretion and not apply the doctrine because "[f]ederal courts must be slow to declare state statutes unconstitutional" on the basis of the important principle of federalism. The court then went on to analyze the statute and found that it was not unconstitutional.

REASONING

SUMMARY

Lawsuits are based on factual circumstances. The facts create the legal issues. Therefore, it is up to the client to reveal all the facts to his or her attorney. If all the facts are not known, the attorney might draw the wrong legal conclusion. Physicians work the same way. They need to have all the relevant facts before they can draw a medical conclusion. If the facts warrant a lawsuit, the first thing the attorney should do is to apprise the potential defendant of liability and seek to settle the case without filing suit.

Attorneys' fees are an important consideration in deciding whether the client should sue. The case that we discussed involved a contingency fee arrangement, whereby if the plaintiffs had lost the case, their attorney would have received no fees. There are two other bases for attorneys' fees, which are not mentioned in the chapter: flat rate and hourly rate. In those cases, the attorney would have received compensation whether or not she had won the case. Whatever fee arrangement exists, it is mentioned in the contract, either oral or written, that creates the attorney–client relationship.

Before a lawsuit is filed, the attorney has a duty to investigate the facts to determine whether sufficient evidence exists to justify litigation. Before filing suit, however, an opportunity is usually provided the defendant to settle the matter.

Figure 5.10 The Stages of a Trial

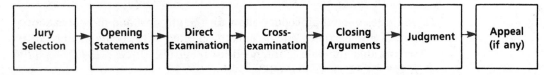

After suit is filed, the discovery process takes place. Discovery is designed to "narrow" the legal issues, thus enhancing pretrial settlement or reducing the duration of the actual trial. Trial is the last stage of the preappellate process.

The doctrine of res judicata means that when a court issues a final judgment, the subject matter of the case cannot be relitigated between the same parties.

DISCUSSION QUESTIONS

1. Refer to the attorney–client contract and answer this question: if Lyn Carroll spent forty-five hours on this case but lost the lawsuit, would she be due the reasonable value of her services instead of the 33⅓ percent she would have received if she had won? Explain your answer.

2. Would Attorney Carroll have had a more difficult time proving her case if Nic had paid for the meals in cash? Why?

3. Give one reason for the rejection of the first offer to settle the case for $1454.15 and $175.00. Explain your answer.

4. What is a deposition?

5. What is an interrogatory? How does it differ from a deposition?

6. What is a subpeona duces tecum?

7. What is the reason for using a request for admission?

8. What are the stages of a trial? Explain each one.

9. Why didn't the defendant appeal the decision of the trial court?

10. What is res judicata?

CASE PROBLEMS

1. A deposition was used in a trial instead of the person appearing as a witness. If the rules of civil procedure allow this only if the party offering the deposition has been, after due diligence, unable to procure the attendance of the witness, what do you think would constitute "due diligence"? (*Hertz* v. *Graham*, 292 F.2d 443 [2d Cir. 1961].)

2. The defendant objected to interrogatories that asked him to define a dishonest act in general and to state if certain acts were dishonest. If interrogatories are to be "liberally construed," should the questions be allowed? (*Leumi Financial Corp.* v. *Hartford Accident & Indemnity Co.*, 295 F. Supp. 539 [S.D.N.Y. 1969].)

3. The rules of discovery are quite broad but are they broad enough to include the opposing party's expert witness report? (*Franks* v. *National Dairy Products Corp.*, 41 F.R.D. 234 [W.D.TX. 1966].)

4. The rules of civil procedure allow for the physical and mental examination of all "parties." The defendant objected to his being examined, asserting that the rule is intended for plaintiffs. Discuss. (*Schlagenhauf* v. *Holder*, 379 U.S. 194 [1964].)

5. Is the purpose of the rule that allows for a request for admission the discovery of information or the elimination at trial of having to prove points that cannot be fairly contested? (*McSparran* v. *Hanigan,* 225 F. Supp. 628 [1963].)

6. Should an appellate court consider an argument that was raised for the first time on appeal if the argument was based on a case that was decided after the trial in this case? (*Davis* v. *United States,* 413 F.2d 1226 [5th Cir. 1969].)

7. The Federal Rules of Civil Procedure provide, *inter alia,* that a motion for a summary judgment "shall be served at least ten days before the time fixed for the hearing" on the motion. Can a trial court grant a movant's *oral* motion for a summary judgment? Why? (*Hanson* v. *Polk County Land, Inc.,* 608 F.2d 129 [5th Cir. 1979].)

8. When Ms. Carroll questions her witnesses in direct examination, one of the grounds Mr. Jones can use in objecting to her questions is that of relevancy. Relevancy is defined as " . . . having any tendency to make the existence of any fact that is of consequence to the determination of the action more probable or less probable than it would be without the evidence" (Fed. R. Evi. 401). Ms. Carroll asks Nic these two questions:

   a. "Why did you decide to go to Chez Joey?", and
   b. "What did you eat prior to dining at Chez Joey?"

   Mr. Jones objects to both questions on the grounds of relevancy. You are the judge. Rule on the objection. Give reasons for your answers.

9. The judge participated in examining the witnesses by asking various questions. By so doing, the judge helped or hurt one side or the other. If a trial judge has a duty to make clear to the jury the facts and circumstances pertinent to the case, do you think that either attorney has a valid ground to object? Discuss. (*United States* v. *Ostendorff,* 371 F.2d 729 [4th Cir. 1966].)

10. *Hearsay* is defined as a statement, other than one made in court, that is offered to prove the truth of the matter asserted. An exception to the hearsay rule exists for records of regularly conducted business activities. Discuss with respect to the case of *Grant* v. *Chez Joey, Inc.*

CHAPTER 6

The Attorney – Client Relationship and the Accountant's Legal Liability

THE ROLE OF THE ATTORNEY

Agent A person authorized by another individual to act for that individual, normally in the conduct of business

Principal The employer of an agent; the person who gives authority to the agent to represent his or her interests.

Independent contractor One who contracts to do a job or perform a task, but according to his or her own methods and not subject to the control of the employer

As we discussed in Chapter 5, the attorney–client relationship is largely governed by contract law. The client will normally hire an attorney to represent the client in a particular matter. The attorney will then perform the agreed services for a fee. The amount of the fee should be agreed on in advance, along with any other factors the parties need to negotiate or settle. The more aspects the parties agree to in the contract, the fewer areas subject to disagreement later.

The client should be aware that the attorney may occupy different types of legal roles while representing the client. The attorney may, in some instances, be acting as an **agent** for the client. In such a role, the attorney is subject to the absolute control of the **principal,** the client. In other instances, the attorney will be acting as an **independent contractor** who is representing the client. While acting in this capacity, the attorney is not subject to the control of the client. The client will have determined the *ends* to be accomplished, but the attorney/independent contractor is responsible for the *means* chosen to accomplish those ends. The attorney must choose means that comply with the Code of Professional Responsibility and state statutes, regardless of the client's

92

desires. An understanding of the role played by the attorney will often prevent misunderstanding by the client.

The Anglo-American legal system is based on a unique premise. Early in the development of English common law, it was determined that the *adversarial process* should be followed in trials. Under the adversarial process, *each side to a lawsuit is to present its case in its most favorable light.* Neither side to the lawsuit is required to present "the truth." Rather, the finder of fact (the jury, or the judge if there is no jury) is expected to find the truth by examining the conflicting evidence presented by each adversary.

The plaintiff in a civil case, or the state in a criminal case, will present evidence and testimony in a manner that best supports the plaintiff's own viewpoint. All the evidence is expected to show why the plaintiff—or the state—should win the case. Once the plaintiff has completed the presentation, the defendant takes a turn. The defendant will then present evidence and testimony to best support the defendant's viewpoint. This evidence may be intended to refute the evidence of the plaintiff—or of the state—or to support the position of the defendant. Once the defendant has completed the presentation, the finder of fact will deliberate over the evidence and testimony presented by both sides. It is generally felt that by hearing what each side feels are its strongest arguments, the truth will be found by an impartial third party, the finder of fact.

To help the finder of fact resolve the legal conflict, certain "burdens of proof" are imposed by the law. As noted in Chapter 4, in order to obtain a criminal conviction, the state must provide proof *beyond a reasonable doubt* for its case. In other words, a *reasonable* person could not doubt the truth of the state's evidence. In civil cases the plaintiff has the burden of proof, but not to the same degree as in a criminal proceeding. The plaintiff will have to prove the case by **clear and convincing proof** or by a **preponderance of proof.** Both these tests require the plaintiff to establish sufficient evidence that the plaintiff's position is most likely the truth. A failure to satisfy the necessary burden of proof will result in a verdict for the other party.

Clear and convincing proof A degree of proof that tends to establish the truth in a case beyond a well-founded doubt

Preponderance of proof The greater weight of evidence; a degree of proof that makes the conclusion sought more likely than not

To practice law in the United States, a person must be admitted to the bar. Admission to the bar is governed by state bar associations, state statutes, and state courts. Each state has its own bar association; admission to the bar in one state does not mean admission to any other state's bar. The normal requirements for admission to a bar include graduation from a law school, passing a state bar examination, and presenting satisfactory proof of high moral standards.

Bar membership is a jealously guarded privilege. Once attained, it carries with it certain duties and responsibilities. Attorneys who are admitted to the bar are expected to conduct their professional—and even personal—lives in an appropriate manner, to act in a way that reflects favorably on the profession, and to adhere to the Code of Professional Responsibility. In addition, each attorney is deemed an officer of the court, and as such must act appropriately.

As an *officer of the court,* an attorney "is responsible for the purity and fairness of all his dealings in court."[1] The attorney must avoid obvious misconduct, such as fraud, deceit, or dishonesty; refrain from serving as counsel in any cases in which the attorney expects to appear as a witness; refrain from asserting unwarranted or improper legal claims; report to the court any frauds perpetrated against the court; and avoid any appearance of impropriety.

Privilege

In order for the adversarial process to work, each attorney must adequately represent his or her client. To do so, the attorney must have access to any relevant information the client possesses. The concept of attorney–client *privilege* was developed to facilitate attorney–client communication by *protecting the attorney from being forced to divulge to third parties any communications with the client.*

The purpose of privilege is to preserve the secrets and confidences of the client. It is generally felt that only by ensuring confidentiality can the client feel free to discuss any matter with the attorney. In addition, the protection afforded by privilege allows the attorney to obtain information beyond that which the client might otherwise volunteer.

Before privilege will be recognized, the communication must be secret and confidential. The type of communication that is protected by privilege is either legal advice of any kind sought by the client from a legal advisor or any communications made in confidence by a legal advisor to the client. Such communications are permanently privileged and protected against disclosure by either the attorney or the client unless the client waives the protection.

The existence of privilege is denied when the attorney is aware of any intent by the client to commit a criminal act. Under such circumstances, the attorney may reveal the plan and any other information needed to prevent the commission of the criminal act.

The following case illustrates how far the courts are willing to go to protect attorney–client privilege.

Kevlik v. Goldstein
724 F.2d 844 (1st Cir. 1984)

FACTS   Kevlik was driving an automobile in Derry, New Hampshire. In the automobile with him were his brother and another person, Southmayd. The three were allegedly stopped by the Derry police, unlawfully arrested, beaten, and denied medical attention. All three were charged with disorderly conduct and resisting arrest and with simple assault. At trial, all three were acquitted of all charges.

---

[1] *In re Application of Griffiths,* 162 Conn. 249, 254 (1972).

As a result, all three men filed suit against the city of Derry. Southmayd, on the advice of his father, retained an attorney named McNamara, of the law firm of Wiggin and Nourie, to represent him in the case, paying a $200 retainer at the time. Southmayd met with McNamara after McNamara filed an appearance, and the full story was told to him. When McNamara learned the extent of the case, he withdrew as Southmayd's attorney, citing a conflict of interests since his firm represented the Derry police department's insurer. When the Kevliks got to trial, they sought to have the firm of Wiggin and Nourie disqualified owing to a conflict of interest and to the access the firm might have to privileged information between McNamara and Southmayd, which might harm their case.

Does an attorney–client privilege exist in this setting? Is there a conflict with the Code of Professional Responsibility and the firm of Wiggin and Nourie?   **ISSUE**

Yes, to both issues. Southmayd had made confidential communications with McNamara, and the information that had been communicated to him could be harmful to the case being presented by the Kevliks.   **HOLDING**

The withdrawal of McNamara from the case prior to any trial was irrelevant. At the time of the communication between McNamara and Southmayd the attorney–client privilege became applicable. A subsequent withdrawal did not change the nature of the communications made earlier.   **REASONING**

    The Kevliks intended to call Southmayd (who had previously settled out of court with the city of Derry) as a witness. The possession of the information communicated to McNamara by Southmayd gives the appearance of impropriety. Such an appearance of impropriety is a violation of the Code of Professional Responsibility. An attorney who possesses information relevant to the controversy at hand of such a delicate nature must disqualify himself. Accordingly, the firm of Wiggin and Nourie must be disqualified in this case.

In many respects, accountants occupy a position similar to that occupied by attorneys. Attorneys are governed in their professional conduct by the Code of Professional Conduct and by state statutes. Accountants are governed by generally accepted accounting principles (GAAP) and generally accepted auditing standards (AICPA). Accountants must also comply with codes of professional ethics and with state statutes. Both attorneys and accountants are highly trained and strictly regulated professionals.

    Accountants are governed to a great extent by the *contracts* they make with their clients. The terms of the contract go a long way toward defining the duties of the accountant to the client. However, an accountant who is independent is hired to provide services as an *independent contractor*. The client establishes the ends to be attained in the contract, but the accountant selects the means for attaining those ends on the basis of professional judgment, GAAP, and GAAS.

THE ROLE OF THE ACCOUNTANT

Accountants perform much of their work for the use and benefit of *third persons*— persons who are not a party to the contract. These third persons may have rights against the accountant as third-party beneficiaries under the contract, even though they are not a party to the contract. In addition, accountants may face liability to third persons under various statutes. These statutory provisions are designed to protect the investing public from securities manipulations or the general public from tax evasions and frauds.

Common Law

Under the common law, accountants face three types of potential liability. They could be found liable to their clients for any breaches of contract. They could also be found liable to their clients under tort law for negligence or for fraud. And in certain circumstances, they could be found liable to third parties under tort law for negligence or fraud.

When an accountant enters a contract with a client, the accountant owes the client a duty to honor the terms of the contract. Any failure to honor the terms of the contract or to perform the contract within the stated time period will constitute a breach of contract. Once a breach is established, the client can sue for— and collect— any reasonable and foreseeable damages that arise as a result of the breach. (For a detailed discussion of remedies for breach of contract, see Chapter 17.) The potential liability is normally substantially higher than the fees the accountant is to collect. For example, a simple tax return preparation may carry a fee of $40. But if the accountant makes an error, he or she faces fines of at least $100, plus any interest and penalties imposed on the client.

The accountants are governed in their dealings with clients not only by the terms of their contracts but also by standards imposed by law. Accountants are expected to exercise reasonable care in their dealings with clients. But the degree of care deemed reasonable is measured against a hypothetical person, a prudent accountant. In other words, accountants must exercise the degree of care and skill normally possessed by members of the accounting profession. A failure to satisfy this degree of care and skill will make an accountant liable *in tort* to the client.

An accountant will be deemed guilty of *negligence* if he or she fails to exercise the care and skill that a reasonable, prudent accountant would exercise under similar circumstances. Although this test requires accountants to meet the demanding standards of the accounting profession, it does *not* make them absolutely responsible for the accuracy of their work. So long as accountants satisfy generally accepted accounting principles and auditing standards and act in good faith with integrity, they will not be liable for simple errors in judgment. By the same token, accountants are not *required* to discover every impropriety or **defalcation** in their clients' books and records. However, if these defalcations or improprieties have gone undiscovered because of negligence, the accountants will be liable for any losses suffered by their clients due to the negligent failure to discover the problem.

An accountant may be liable for *fraud* under two different circumstances:

Defalcation The acts of a defrauder in the commission of the fraud

findings of actual fraud or of constructive fraud. An accountant's intentional misstatement of a **material fact** to mislead the client will result in a finding of **actual fraud,** provided the client relies on the misstated fact to his or her detriment. Actual fraud against the client is very unusual for an independent accountant. **Constructive fraud** will be found if the accountant is grossly negligent in the performance of duty. The accountant who is so negligent as to "disregard the truth" will be deemed guilty of fraud.

The duty an accountant owes to third persons is frequently misunderstood. Again, the major tort theories are negligence and fraud. But the third person is not in **privity of contract** with the accountant, so the right to sue for damages is less obvious. The third person must prove not only that the tort occurred but also that the accountant owed a duty to the third person to perform the work properly.

In order for a third person who is injured by the negligence of an accountant to seek remedies for the negligence, the third person must show that the accountant knew the work was being done for the benefit of the third person. In some jurisdictions, the accountant must know the work was intended for a particular third person. In other jurisdictions, it is sufficient to show that the third person was part of a group that would normally rely on the work of the accountant. For example, a negligently prepared financial statement used by the client in a loan application could subject the accountant to liability to the bank if the accountant knew the statement was to be used as part of the loan application. But the same statement would not subject the accountant to liability to the bank if the accountant could not have known the statement would be used in the loan application.

Third persons may also seek recovery for fraud committed by the accountant, whether actual or constructive fraud. Any third person who can show that he or she relied on the accountant's work and that the work was fraudulently prepared can collect damages for the fraud from the accountant. Notice that there is no need to show any expectation of reliance or usage by the third person to recover for fraud.

The following case originally set the standard for third-party proceedings against accountants based on constructive fraud.

Material fact A fact a reasonable person would rely on in deciding whether to act

Actual fraud Intentional misstatement of a material fact for the purpose of inducing action by the other party

Constructive fraud Fraud in effect, although not in intent

Privity of contract The connection or relationship that exists between two or more contracting parties

---

Ultramares Corporation v. Touche
255 N.Y. 170, 174 N.E. 441 (1931)

Fred Stern & Co. hired Touche to prepare certified financial statements, which were to be used in seeking credit for its operations. Stern had falsified its financial records, adding $700,000 to its accounts receivable, among other things. Touche did not discover these falsifications, although it should have done so. Touche prepared and certified the statements, and Ultramares extended credit based on the statements so certified. In fact, Stern was insolvent and could not

FACTS

repay the loans received. Touche was sued for negligence and fraud in its preparation of the statements.

ISSUE   Was the failure of Touche to discover the falsifications sufficient to prove constructive fraud?

HOLDING   Yes. The certification form used by Touche could not honestly be believed by the auditors. A lack of honest belief amounts to constructive fraud in this case.

REASONING   Touche was negligent in failing to discover the alterations in the records. The negligence prevented the possibility that it could honestly believe the certification. Certification of statements that cannot be believed amounts to gross negligence, and gross negligence operates as constructive fraud against unforeseen third parties. Touche certified that the statements were true to their personal knowledge. In fact they had no knowledge of the matter. Such a certification is grossly negligent. Ultramares relied on these statements. Touche is liable to Ultramares.

Federal Securities Statutes

The Securities Act of 1933 and the Securities Exchange Act of 1934 each impose potential civil and criminal liabilities against accountants. These two acts are covered in detail in Chapter 43. In this section, we examine only the liabilities and responsibilities of the accountant under the acts.

Under the Securities Act of 1933, the accountant is quite vulnerable to civil liability. The accountant may be found liable to anyone who purchases a security covered by a **registration statement**. If the accountant prepared any financial statements included in the registration statement and if the statement *contains* a false statement or *omits* a material fact, the accountant is potentially liable. Any purchaser of the **security** need only show that he suffered a loss on the security. That establishes his case. The accountant must then disprove liability. The only defense that will disprove liability is a showing that the accountant made a reasonable investigation of the information; that the accountant reasonably believed his work was correct, complete, and truthful; *and* that he did *in fact* believe that the work was correct, complete, and truthful. Unless the accountant can prove a lack of liability, he is held liable for any loss suffered by the purchaser.

The Securities Exchange Act of 1934 is less biased against the accountant. The accountant still faces potential civil liability, but the purchaser has a substantially heavier burden of proof. In order to hold the accountant liable for any false or misleading statements made in the financial statements, the purchaser must prove three things:

1.   The price of the security was affected by the false or misleading statement.

2.   The purchaser relied upon the false or misleading statement in making the purchase.

3.   The purchaser was not aware of the inaccuracy of the statement.

Registration statement   A statement that must be filed with the Securities Exchange Commission before a security can be offered for sale

Security   Any note, stock, bond, certificate of interest, or investment contract, or any interest or instrument commonly known as a security

Even if the purchaser can prove all three necessary elements, the accountant may not be liable. The defense to civil liability under the 1934 Act is a showing of **due diligence** and good faith in preparing the statement.

An accountant may also face criminal liability under both the 1933 and the 1934 Acts. If it is shown that the accountant *willfully* made false statements or *willfully* omitted material facts, the accountant faces a potential fine of up to $10,000, up to five years of imprisonment, or both. The following case dealt with the issue of the criminal liability of accountants.

Due diligence A fair, proper, and common degree of care that persons of ordinary prudence would exercise in the same circumstances

United States v. Simon
425 F.2d 796 (2nd Cir. 1969)

Harold Roth was the president of Continental Vending Machine Corp. and owned approximately 25 percent of Continental. He also managed Valley Commercial Corp., an affiliate of Continental. Roth regularly borrowed money from Valley for his personal stock market transactions, after having Valley borrow the money from Continental. In 1962 Roth was unable to repay $3.5 million to Valley; thus Valley could not repay its $3.5 million debt to Continental. As a result, Roth put up $2.9 million in collateral to secure the loan. The auditors certified that collateral in excess of the loan amount was being held by Continental, although they knew this was not true.

FACTS

Were the auditors guilty of criminal conduct due to their knowing certification of false financial statements?

ISSUE

Yes. No showing of intent to profit is necessary to establish criminal liability; merely proving intent to certify a false statement is adequate.

HOLDING

The auditors were aware of all relevant facts in the case. Despite their knowledge of the true facts, they certified a false statement and filed that false statement with the SEC in violation of the Securities Exchange Act of 1934, Section 32.

REASONING

Many accountants derive a substantial portion of their incomes from preparing tax returns for clients. Professional preparation of tax returns can carry substantial potential liability for the preparer.

If the preparer *negligently* understates the tax liability of the taxpayer, the preparer can be fined $100.[2] If the preparer *willfully* understates the tax liability of the taxpayer, the penalty increases to $500.[3] In addition, making a false

Internal Revenue Provisions

---

[2] Internal Revenue Code, Section 6694(a).
[3] Ibid., Section 6694(b).

return or aiding in the preparation of a false return is a crime punishable by a fine of up to $5000, imprisonment of up to three years, or both.[4]

In addition, the Tax Reform Act of 1986 has added or amended the penalties imposed on the taxpayer for various violations of the Internal Revenue Code. For example, a failure to pay taxes carries a penalty of 1 percent per month, as compared to the penalty prior to the Reform Act of ½ percent per month.[5] The penalty for negligence under the new law is 5 percent of the taxes due, and the scope of negligence is expanded to include any failure to make a reasonable effort to comply with the Code and any careless disregard of the rules of Internal Revenue.[6] This is in addition to any conduct that would have been negligent under the prior laws. The fraud penalties have also been increased, from 50 percent to 75 percent. However, the higher penalty rate is only applicable to the portion of the tax underpayment that is fraudulent, and the taxpayer is allowed to prove that the underpayment is not fraudulent.[7] In any of these cases, the tax preparer may be liable to the taxpayer for these penalties if the preparer is the party who is responsible for the penalty assessment.

Privilege

Unlike the attorney–client relationship, the accountant–client relationship does not carry automatic privilege for confidential communications. Any accountant–client privilege that exists does so only by express state statute. The vast majority of states do not recognize any privileged communications between accountant and client. Even if state law recognizes the privilege, no federal court will recognize it or honor it in a federal court proceeding.

At the present time, there are seventeen different states that recognize the existence of an accountant–client privilege.[8] The statutes are not identical, so even in these seventeen states broad, general statements about the nature of accountant–client privilege cannot be made. Some of the states grant the privilege only to CPAs, while others extend the privilege to all public accountants. Some of the states deny the existence of the privilege in any criminal or bankruptcy proceedings, but allow it otherwise. And some of the states are unclear as to whether the privilege belongs to the accountant or to the client. In at least two of the states (Illinois and New Mexico) court opinions have interpreted the privilege as belonging to the accountant and *not* to the client.

In the following case, the issue of the extent of the privilege was involved. Notice how narrowly the court defined the privilege, and to whom it belongs.

---

[4] Internal Revenue Code, Section 7206.

[5] Ibid., Section 6651 as amended by Section 1502 of the Tax Reform Act of 1986.

[6] Ibid., Section 6653 as amended by Section 1503 of the Tax Reform Act of 1986.

[7] Ibid.

[8] The states that have adopted some form of accountant–client privilege are: Arizona, Colorado, Florida, Georgia, Illinois, Indiana, Iowa, Kentucky, Louisiana, Maryland, Michigan, Missouri, Montana, Nevada, New Mexico, Pennsylvania, and Tennessee. In addition, Puerto Rico recognizes the privilege.

People v. *Zimbelman*
572 P.2d 830 (Colo. 1977)

Knox and Zimbelman each owned one-half of the stock in Balto Industries, Inc. Knox was in poor health and desired to sell his share of the business so he could retire. Zimbelman prepared financial statements and a general report on the company, which he presented to Knox in conjunction with an offer to buy Knox's shares. Zimbelman misstated the position of the company and otherwise committed fraud in these reports.   **FACTS**

After the sale was completed, Knox died. His family discovered the fraudulent representations that Zimbelman had made and filed civil and criminal charges against Zimbelman for the fraud. In the criminal proceedings, the state of Colorado called Hook as a witness. Hook had prepared financial statements and had audited the books of Balto shortly before the reports prepared by Zimbelman. Colorado statutes provide for accountant-client privilege, and Zimbelman asserted this privilege in an effort to prevent Hook from testifying.

Can Zimbelman assert the accountant-client privilege in this case in order to prevent Hook from testifying?   **ISSUE**

No. Balto Industries, Inc., and not Zimbelman, was the client, so only Balto can assert the privilege provided by the statute.   **HOLDING**

The Colorado statute is very specific. Only the client possesses privilege, and since the corporation is a legal person, only Balto in this case had the privilege. Zimbelman was not the client, despite his 50 percent ownership of the stock of the corporation. If the corporation had asserted the privilege, the testimony of Hook would have been disallowed. But since Balto did not assert the privilege, the testimony was allowable. (Based on the testimony of Hook and others, Zimbelman was convicted of the criminal charges brought against him.)   **REASONING**

An accountant's *working papers* are those papers and documents prepared by the accountant during the course of the employment; they are used in preparing the final financial statements. These working papers are the *accountant's* property, and not the property of the client. The client is entitled only to the finished work product. The accountant needs the working papers as proof of the care and quality of the work performed. They are to be treated confidentially and protected zealously. But they are never to be turned over to the client. To do so is to stand defenseless in the face of lawsuits for negligence, fraud, or statutory liability.   **Working Papers**

SUMMARY

The Anglo-American legal system follows the adversarial process. Each side to a case or controversy presents its evidence in its most favorable light. The finder of fact decides the facts of the case on the basis of these conflicting presentations. In order for the process to work, skilled advocates are needed. Attorneys fulfill the roles of skilled advocates in the United States. An attorney is admitted to the bar and acts as an officer of the court in representing the client. One aspect of the role of legal counselor for the client is the concept of privilege. Communications made between an attorney and a client are legally protected from disclosure for so long as the client desires confidentiality.

Accountants face multiple types of potential liability for the work they perform. Under common law principles, the accountant may be liable to a client for breach of contract or to a client or third persons for negligence or fraud. In addition, there are potential civil and criminal liabilities under federal securities laws for errors of commission or omission in preparing financial statements for use in registration statements. The Internal Revenue Code also provides for both civil and criminal liabilities for errors made by tax preparers.

The concept of privilege, so important to the attorney–client relationship, does not apply to accountants. There is no common law privilege for accountants, nor any federal court privilege. The working papers prepared by an accountant belong to the accountant, not to the client. An accountant's working papers are extremely important as proof of the quality of the work performed.

DISCUSSION QUESTIONS

1. What is the theory behind the adversarial process as a method of finding facts in a trial?

2. What is the purpose of attorney–client privilege, and when does this privilege exist?

3. What standards are used to determine whether an accountant is guilty of negligence? Are these standards appropriate, or should some other standards be used?

4. What must a third person prove in order to hold an accountant liable for constructive fraud? For actual fraud? Why are these two types of fraud treated differently?

5. What are the standards for holding an accountant civilly liable under the Securities Act of 1933? Under the Securities Exchange Act of 1934? Why do these acts have different standards?

6. Roberts is subpoenaed to appear in a federal court to testify against his former client, Smith. One of the questions asked of Roberts concerns a confidential communication between Smith and Roberts. Before Roberts can answer the question, Smith objects, asserting that the communication is privileged. What result should occur if Roberts is a former accountant of Smith? If Roberts is a former attorney of Smith? If there is a different answer, why?

7. Betty, a CPA, negligently prepared financial statements for use in a registration statement covered by the Securities Act of 1933. Phillip purchased some of these securities and has lost a large amount of money on his purchase. Phillip has decided to sue Betty to collect damages. What must Phillip do in order to be able to collect damages from Betty in this case?

8. Attorney Jones learns that her client is planning to commit a robbery in order to pay the fees for the defense Jones is preparing for the client. Jones has learned the time, place, and manner of the planned robbery. What should Jones do in this case?

9. Mike, an accountant, prepared the tax returns for Diane in 1987. In his preparation of these returns, Mike disregarded several of the new provisions of the Tax Reform Act of 1986. As a result, Diane's tax liability has been understated by $1000. The Internal Revenue Service audited Diane's return and discovered the understatement of her liability. Diane has settled her tax audit with the IRS and is now seeking remedies against Mike. What results should occur, and why?

10. Gary, a CPA, has prepared financial statements for Apex, Inc., for the past several years. Gary was recently fired by Apex, and the president of Apex has demanded that Gary surrender all his documents and data concerning Apex to the president, including any working papers in Gary's possession. What should Gary do in this situation? Why?

1. Lang was general counsel for First National Bank. Several shareholders of the bank sued the bank's board of directors for alleged mismanagement of bank funds. The plaintiffs attempted to get Lang to aid them in this suit. The board of directors sought a court order to prevent Lang from associating with the plaintiffs or to disclose any secret information he obtained from the board. What was the result? (*Housler* v. *First National Bank of East Islip*, 484 F. Supp. 1321 [E.D. N.Y. 1980].)

2. Sam, an attorney, sued Rose, his former client, for legal fees allegedly earned but not paid. Rose and her attorney sought the right to inspect Sam's work records from the earlier case. Sam refused to produce the records, citing privilege rules. What was the result? (*Brandt* v. *Smith*, 634 F.2d 796 [5th Cir. 1981].)

3. An accounting firm certified the overstatement of several factors of its client's financial statements. These statements were then used in a registration statement covering securities the client was issuing. The auditors were found not to have used "due diligence" in their work. What would need to be shown in a suit by investors under the 1933 Securities Act? (*Escott* v. *BarChris Construction Corp.*, 283 F. Supp. 643 [S.D. N.Y. 1968].)

4. Drake purchased stock in Thor Power Company based on fictitious financial statements. The statements were certified by Peat, Marwick. Drake sued Peat, Marwick for applying inappropriate accounting procedures.

CASE PROBLEMS

Peat, Marwick defended by arguing that it did not profit from the allegedly inflated security prices. If the suit is filed under the Securities Exchange Act of 1934, what will be the result? (*Drake* v. *Thor Power Tool Co.,* 282 F. Supp. 94 [N.D. Ill. 1967].)

5. A CPA firm was hired by a real estate management company to prepare various financial statements. All of the statements prepared were listed as "unaudited," being based solely upon the books and records of the management company and not verified by the CPA firm. The CPA firm discovered some "missing invoices," but did not follow up on the discovery. In fact the "missing invoices" were a cover-up for a major embezzlement of company funds. The tenants sued the CPA firm for constructive fraud for failing to follow up on the "missing invoices." What was the result? (*1136 Tenants* v. *MacRothenberg and Company, New York Law Journal* [No. 3305], 1971.)

6. Nay was the president and principal stockholder of First Securities, a brokerage firm. Ernst and Ernst, a CPA firm, performed the audits for First Securities for twenty years. During that twenty-year period, Nay induced Hochfelder and others to invest funds in allegedly high-yielding escrow accounts. In fact, the accounts were fictitious, and Nay was converting the funds to his own personal use. Upon the suicide of Nay, the fictitious nature of the accounts was discovered. Hochfelder sued Ernst and Ernst for his losses, alleging a violation of the Securities Exchange Act of 1934 in the auditing of the records of First Securities. There were no allegations of fraud or intentional misconduct by the CPA firm, but rather a charge of negligent nonfeasance for failing to discover the fraud. If the CPA firm had done nothing improper in its auditing practices, should it be held liable for not having discovered this fraudulent program implemented by Nay? (*Ernst & Ernst* v. *Hochfelder,* 425 U.S. 185 [1976].)

7. A businessman hired a CPA firm to prepare financial statements for his businesses. The firm was aware that the statements so prepared were to be used for the procurement of additional financing and also for the purpose of obtaining investors so that the businesses could be incorporated. The CPA firm accepted the job and guaranteed that its report of the business would be accurate for any category within $5,000. The final statements submitted by the firm misstated the Accounts Payable total of the business by $33,689. The businessman used the statements prepared by the firm to obtain additional financing and also incorporated a portion of the business, again using the statements prepared by the firm. The corporation has filed suit against the CPA firm, alleging negligent preparation of the financial statements. The firm is defending on a lack of privity of contract and on allegations of contributory negligence. What should the court rule? (*Ryan* v. *Kanne,* 170 N.W.2d 395 [Iowa 1969].)

8. Emle sued Patentex for alleged patent infringements. One of the attorneys representing Patentex in the case had formerly served as an attorney for

Emle. Emle objected to the presence of this attorney as a representative of Patentex and sought his removal from the trial. The grounds asserted by Emle for the removal of the attorney was a possible violation of the attorney-client privilege. What should the judge rule? (*Emle Industries, Inc.* v. *Patentex, Inc.* 487 F.2d 562 [2nd Cir. 1973].)

9. A Rhode Island corporation was seeking financing from Rusch. In order to ascertain the financial condition of the corporation, Rusch asked for certified financial statements. Levin, a CPA, prepared the statements so requested. These statements represented the corporation to be solidly solvent. In fact, the corporation was insolvent and near bankruptcy. On the basis of the statements prepared by Levin, Rusch loaned the corporation $350,000. The corporation subsequently went bankrupt, and Rusch lost over $120,000 from its loan. Rusch has sued Levin for fraudulent or negligent misrepresentation in the preparation of the statements, and Levin has based his defense on a lack of privity of contract between himself and Rusch. What result should occur? (*Rusch Factors, Inc.* v. *Levin,* 284 F. Supp. 85 [R.I. 1968].)

10. The shareholders of Clute, Inc., proposed a merger between Clute and Synkloid to the shareholders of Synkloid. To further the merger, these shareholders presented financial statements of Clute to the shareholders of Synkloid. These financial reports were false and misleading. The merger took place soon thereafter, and the shareholders of Synkloid lost over $1.5 million owing to the false statements included in the reports. Weck, on behalf of the shareholders of Synkloid, sued the majority owners of Clute for the fraud they perpetrated. Weck called Peat, Marwick, Mitchell Co. accountants to testify as to the financial reports in question, which they had prepared. These accountants from Peat, Marwick asserted accountant–client privilege and refused to testify. Assuming that the case occurred in a state that recognizes accountant–client privilege, must Peat, Marwick comply or may they assert the privilege as a bar to testifying? (*Weck* v. *District Court,* 408 P.2d 987 [Colo. 1965].)

Business Ethics

ETHICAL THEORIES

The study of ethics and ethical principles is well known in philosophy, but it is relatively new to business. Business students have long been used to "hard and fast" answers and theories in their courses. "Debits equal credits" is a given in accounting classes, and accounting students can tell at a glance if the debits and credits are equal. If they are not equal, the student knows that a problem exists and can then attempt to find the problem and resolve it. However, the fact that the debits and credits are equal does not guarantee that there is no problem. An error could still exist, but it is not as obvious. Business ethics is somewhat similar to this latter situation. Studying ethical theories and principles is not nearly as "hard and fast" as most business courses, and problems are not nearly as obvious in an ethical setting as they are in the example above. Yet, questions of ethics — particularly questions of *business* ethics — are among the most important questions that the business person of this era will face.

Ethics can be defined as the system or code of morals of a particular person, religion, group, or profession.[1] Such a definition does not provide much help

---

[1] *Moral Issues in Business,* 3rd ed., Barry (Belmont, Cal.: Wadsworth, 1986), p. 5.

in the area of business ethics, however, because the "group" is too diverse to have a single system or code of morals. Similarly, "business" is not a single profession like law or medicine. And while it is probably true that some people "worship the almighty dollar," business cannot properly be viewed as a religion. Thus, for most people, the study of business ethics comes down to an analysis of the system or code of morals of a particular person — the particular business person whose conduct is being evaluated. Unfortunately, the ethical standard too often applied is the ethical standard of the observer, and not that of the observed person. In order to properly treat the ethical issues of a business person, some framework must be established for analysis, and some basic understanding of the ethical parameters of business needs to be developed.

Before a framework for the analysis of business ethics can be developed, some decisions must be made as to what values and standards are being measured, and on what basis the measurement is being made. There are two broad categories of ethical theories. Ethical theories may be based on *consequential* (teleological) principles or on *nonconsequential* (deontological) principles. Consequential principles judge the ethics of a particular action by the consequences of that action. Consequential ethics determine the "rightness" or "wrongness" of any action by determining the ratio of good to evil that the action will produce. The "right" action is that action that produces the greatest ratio of good to evil of any of the available alternatives. The two major theories of ethical behavior under the consequential principles are egoism and utilitarianism.

Consequential and Nonconsequential Principles

Nonconsequential principles tend to focus on the concept of duty. Under the nonconsequential approach, a person acts ethically if that person is faithful to his duty regardless of the consequences that follow from being faithful to that duty. If a person carries out his or her duties, the greatest good occurs *because* the duty of the individual is carried out. If each individual carries out his or her duty, society knows what to expect from each individual in any given situation. This provides for greater long-term continuity than would arise if every individual based every choice on the consequences of each particular action, and society imposes duties to maximize the values that society wants. The categorical imperative advanced by Immanuel Kant in the late eighteenth century is the best known theory in support of the nonconsequential principles of ethics.

The doctrine that self-interest is the proper goal of all human action is known as *egoism*.[2] In this doctrine, each person is expected to act in a manner that maximizes his or her long-term interests. In so doing, society benefits because each individual acts in a manner that produces the greatest ratio of good to evil, and the sum of these "good-producing" actions is the greatest good for the society.

Egoism

[2] Ibid., p. 36.

One common misconception of egoism is that all egoists are hedonistic seekers of pleasure. This concept focuses on pleasure as being equal to one's best interests. In fact, an egoist may well choose to act in a "selfless" manner because doing so will further the long-term self-interests of that person to a greater degree than will any short-term pleasures he or she may enjoy. An egoist may be willing to make a personal sacrifice today in order to receive some benefit in the future, and doing so is consistent with the doctrine of egoism. Similarly, an egoist may simply obtain self-gratification from performing acts that benefit others, so that such actions further one's long-term interests by increasing one's satisfaction.

In the same manner that an individual may follow egoism, so may an organization. From an organizational perspective, egoism involves those actions that best promote the long-term interests of the organization. Thus a corporation may establish a minority hiring program or a college scholarship program and in so doing may well be acting in a totally egoistic manner. Such programs may advance the long-term interests of the corporation by improving its public image, by reducing social tensions, or by avoiding legal problems that might otherwise have arisen. The short-term expenses incurred in such programs are more than offset by the benefits to be derived in the future, so that the programs may appear to be generous and public-spirited when in reality they are undertaken for "selfish" reasons.

Utilitarianism

The other major consequential approach is utilitarianism. To a utilitarian, the proper course of conduct is that which produces the greatest good for the greatest number. Rather than focusing on the interests of the individual, utilitarianism focuses on the interests of the society. The appropriate act is that act that best serves the interests of the social group as a whole, regardless of the impact on any given individual or subgroup of the social group. In theory, a utilitarian does not care if the "good" is immediate or long-term. The only concern is whether the "good" to be derived—whenever it is derived—is the greatest possible "good" available among the alternatives.

There are two primary types of utilitarianism, act utilitarianism and rule utilitarianism. Act utilitarianism is concerned with individual acts and the effect on the social group that such acts will cause. To an act utilitarian, each individual must act in the manner that will produce the greatest net benefit to the group, even if such acts involve the breaking of a rule. To an act utilitarian, telling a "little white lie" may be the ethical thing to do if telling the truth would cause more harm than telling the lie, or if telling the lie would produce more good than would result from telling the truth.

A rule utilitarian believes that a strict adherence to the rules of the social group will, by definition, produce the greatest good for the greatest number. A rule utilitarian follows all the rules of the society without exception unless the society decides that some specific exceptions are needed to make the rule more ethical. Since the ends justify the means, and since the rules strictly define the means, the proper course of conduct is simple. Follow the rules, and the proper ends will be attained automatically. This principle applies across the board, whether the acts are those of an individual or of an organization within the society. The rules reflect social values, and obedience to those rules maximizes social values and social good.

The nonconsequential principles of ethical theory are best exemplified by the categorical imperative developed by Immanuel Kant, a German philosopher of the eighteenth century. Kant felt that there were universal moral principles that existed without regard to the circumstances of the moment. When people follow these universal moral principles they are acting ethically. When they do not follow these universal principles, they are acting unethically. Individual variations and consequences are irrelevant. The universal moral principles impose a duty on each person, and the performance of that duty is what determines the "rightness" or "wrongness" of any action.

The Categorical Imperative

To Kant, there were perfect duties and imperfect duties. Perfect duties were things that a person must always refrain from doing; imperfect duties were things that a person must do, but only on certain occasions. For example, a perfect duty might be that a merchant must never cheat a customer. An imperfect duty might be that a merchant may need to contribute to charity, but only occasionally, and based in part on the merchant's ability to make a contribution at a particular time.

Based on his theories, Kant developed his "categorical imperative." The categorical imperative, simply stated, says that each person should act in such a way that his or her action could become the universal law. Each person is expected to act as every person ought to act in a perfectly ethical and moral world. The rules to be followed are unconditional, and adherence to those rules is imperative. If each person carries out his or her *duty* by following the "universal law" then society will be properly served by each individual.

This approach to ethics is also applicable to organizations. An organization is judged in the same manner as an individual; the organization is expected to obey the categorical imperative, just as an individual is expected to obey it. The organization is to act according to its duty, with its actions being judged against the universal law standard—would such conduct be proper if all organizations were to act in the same manner? The organization would be expected to act in a manner that discharged its duty to every aspect of society, which would include a recognition of the rights of others and the duty owed to others.

Whether consequential or nonconsequential, these theories provide a possible framework for evaluating the ethics of business and the people who operate business. Unfortunately, there is no universally accepted theory or approach to ethics in general, let alone to business ethics. However, each firm in the business environment can select a theory of ethics to follow in developing its own ethical approach to conducting its business. But to do so, the business person must also take into account some other factors, which we will now discuss.

THE CHANGING SOCIAL ENVIRONMENT

Over the years, business has changed, and as business has changed the attitudes of society toward business have changed. The early days of commerce featured primarily local trade, with mainly hand-crafted goods produced and sold by local merchants and craftsmen. Under these circumstances, the rule of *caveat emptor* was followed, and the success of any business was, to a great extent, dependent upon the reputation of its operator.

Eventually, business began to industrialize and gained an increased capacity for productivity. As business began to produce more, it was able to expand its geographic market from local to regional. This expansion caused a minor change, although the buyer still had to beware. No longer could the buyer expect to be personally acquainted with the seller. Although the reputation of the seller remained important, much of the spread of that reputation was now by hearsay. The buyer and seller were becoming separated by distance.

As industrialization continued to expand, transportation and communication began to grow and develop. The advent of the railroads allowed truly national business operations for the first time. With the opportunity to deal on a national scale, manufacturers became aware of "economies of scale." The age of "bigger is better" had arrived. Now caveat emptor took on more meaning. The buyer could no longer rely on a seller's reputation, since sellers began to combine into trusts, and the available substitutes for any seller's products began to decline.

For the first time, the public expectation of business made a drastic change. The public began to request government intervention to protect the consumer and the workers—the "little guys"—from Big Business. And the government responded with what business must have felt was a vengeance. The Interstate Commerce Commission, the various antitrust statutes, the Securities and Exchange Commission, and a myriad of other agencies and acts were passed in relatively rapid succession. The list of alphabet agencies and acts seemed endless to business.

Why did this happen? Business did not meet the expectations and the demands of the public. Was business acting illegally? In most cases, no! Was business acting unethically? From our contemporary perspective, it probably was; from a historical point of view, probably not. The key element to remember is that in most cases business was being conducted in a manner that had been socially and legally acceptable up to that point in time. However, the societal perspective was changing and the demands of the society were moving in a new direction, and business refused to recognize these changes. When businesses did not respond to what society demanded, the legislatures intervened to force businesses to respond.

In the following case, the stockholders of a corporation challenged a decision by the board of directors that would have resulted in a reduced profit picture for the firm. Notice how the court defined the *duty* of the corporation. After reading the case, think of how a similar case might be resolved today.

Dodge v. Ford Motor Co.
170 N.W. 668 (1919)

The Dodge brothers as shareholders of Ford Motor Company brought suit to compel the payment of dividends by the company and for other relief under the laws of the state of Michigan. At the time of the suit, Ford Motors had assets in excess of $132 million, total liabilities of just over $18 million, and a capital surplus of nearly $112 million. Ford was at that time paying a dividend of 5 percent *per month* and had also paid "special dividends" of $41 million in the five prior years, or $20 per dollar of stock. Henry Ford declared that henceforth there would be no special dividends and that certain socially beneficial programs would be started with the financial support of the Ford Motor Company.

FACTS

May the board of directors of a corporation place the interests of the public ahead of the interests of the stockholders of the corporation by discontinuing these special dividends and by rerouting funds for nonbusiness purposes?

ISSUE

No. The directors have a duty to the business and to the stockholders and must honor that duty. Directors may not change the goals of the business in order to devote themselves to other purposes.

HOLDING

The directors of a corporation have a duty to be exercised in good faith, the duty to operate a business. The first duty is to the shareholders and to the business. Any acts that are detrimental to the business are not to be taken, even for humanitarian purposes. Humanitarian acts should be conducted by individuals with their personal funds and not with corporate funds. (Note: Ford Motor Company was ordered to pay a special dividend of $19 million in addition to the regular 5 percent per month dividend it had been paying.)

REASONING

Many business executives today argue that American business is too regulated. These people see domestic business drowning in a sea of bureaucratic red tape while less regulated foreign firms are assuming control of the economy. They want to be unfettered, set free from the "excessive" regulations and allowed to freely compete with foreign producers.

Although this attitude can be justified from a purely economic position, it fails to take into account the "social contract" between business and society. This social contract defines the permissible scope of business conduct, and it goes beyond the purely economic issues. Society wants more from business than profits, and business *must* accept this mandate if business is to survive. To do otherwise is to breach the social contract.

The social contract theory basically posits that business can only exist

THE SOCIAL CONTRACT THEORY

because society *allows* it to exist and that business must satisfy the demands of the society if it is to be allowed to continue. If business does not satisfy the demands of society, society will change the rules of the game, and in so changing the rules, the permission that business now has may well be revoked. Society today expects—and demands—more from business than mere profits. Environmental concerns, consumer safety and protection, and quality of life must also be provided for in the production process. If these added demands cause costs to rise, so be it. If business as we know it will not meet these demands voluntarily, the demands will be met by regulation—or by society's changing the form of business.

THE PROBLEM OF BUSINESS ETHICS

There is a basic problem facing any business in its efforts to be "ethical": there are no fixed guidelines to follow, no formal codes of ethics to set the standards. The legal profession has a Code of Professional Responsibility; the medical profession has its Hippocratic oath; the accounting profession has a code of ethics; the real estate industry has a code of conduct; other professions have codes to guide them. But business has no code, no "road map" of ethical conduct. The closest thing business has is the law. If a business obeys the law, it is acting legally, and it is seemingly meeting its minimum social requirements. However, this forces business into the sea of red tape, and it makes business *reactive*—responding to legislative demands rather than establishing its own path.

Given this problem, what can be done to provide a solution? At the present time, probably nothing in the large sense. But each industry can attempt to develop a code of ethics for that particular industry, in much the same manner that the real estate industry has developed a code for its members. And if an industry-wide approach will not work, each firm can develop a code of ethics for its employees.

The Human Element

Too often in the past business has acted as an amoral institution. Workers were expected to leave their personal values at the front gate when they reported to work. The workers were expected to be loyal agents of the employer. If a course of conduct was good for the employer, it was to be followed by the employee. If a course of conduct was not good for the employer, the employee was not to follow it. The attitudes and opinions of the employees were ignored.

This attitude was described—and then rebutted—by Alex C. Micholos in his article "The Loyal Agent's Argument."[3] This argument runs as follows:

1. As a loyal agent of some principal, I ought to serve his interests as he would serve them himself if he had my expertise.

2. He would serve his own interests in a thoroughly egoistic way.

[3] *Ethical Theory and Business,* 2d ed., Beauchamp and Bowie (Englewood Cliffs, N.J.: Prentice-Hall, 1983), p. 247.

3.   Therefore, as a loyal agent of this principal, I ought to operate in a thoroughly egoistic way in his behalf.

In order to operate in a thoroughly egoistic manner, a person acts in the way that best advances his or her interests, presuming that everyone else is doing the same thing. If each person maximizes personal interests, the society as a whole will be better off.

The gist of the loyal agent's argument is that the loyal agent will put the principal first in any conflicts of interests. The agent is more concerned with being *first* than with being *nice*. However, there is a weakness to the argument, and Micholos spends the balance of his article rebutting the basic premise of the loyal agent's argument. Too many people feel that a loyal agent, if acting in a truly egoistic manner, has a license — if not a duty — to act immorally and unethically if doing so will advance the interests of the principal. Micholos feels that the truly loyal agent must exercise due care and skill in performing his or her duties and must act in a socially acceptable manner while furthering the interests of the principal.

In the following case, the court had to deal with the issue of an employer allegedly terminating an "employment at will" situation, when the employee alleged that the termination was due to her refusal to continue an experimental formula that was potentially harmful to the persons who might use it. Notice how the court treats each of these conflicting issues in its opinion.

Pierce v. *Ortho Pharmaceutical Corporation*
399 A.2d 1023 (N.J. Super. 1979)

Pierce, a doctor, was employed by the defendant as the director of a medical research team. One of the projects the team was involved with was a liquid treatment for chronic diarrhea designed to be used by infants, children, and the elderly. The original formula contained a very high concentration of saccharin, the use of which was objected to by the plaintiff. The defendant's management pressured the team to begin clinical and human testing of the product, but the plaintiff refused to begin the testing, preferring to wait for approximately three months until a substitute formula without the saccharine could be developed and be ready for use. As a result, Pierce was relieved of her duties as director of the research team and pressured into resigning her position with the firm.   **FACTS**

May an employment at will be freely terminated by the employer at any time and for any reason, even if that reason involves a violation of public policy?   **ISSUE**

No. There is an exception to the right of the employer in an employment at will to discharge an employee at any time and for any reason. If the discharge   **HOLDING** is in violation of public policy, the discharge is wrongful and the employee is entitled to damages.

REASONING   There is a growing trend among the states to restrict the absolute authority of the employer in an employment at will, particularly when the employee is a professional whose activities might involve violation of a professional code of ethics. In addition, in this case the employer's desired actions might have also involved a threat to the public health and welfare.

On retrial, the court may want to consider the ethical issues of the medical profession, the issue of public health and safety, and the Hippocratic oath in determining whether the plaintiff was wrongfully discharged in violation of public policy despite the "at will" nature of the employment.

If you refer to the chapters on agency (Chapters 33, 34, and 35), you will discover that the agent has a duty to obey the *lawful* orders of the principal. The agent is not empowered, or allowed, to follow unlawful orders. The loyal agent's argument is an excellent model for agents to obey, provided that the agent remembers that there are limits to loyalty. A corporation — or any other principal — will do well, likewise, to remember that the agent is a person, and that as a person the agent has certain attitudes, values, and principles to which he or she must be true if he or she is to be happy in life or in work.

The Legal Aspect   The American legal system contains numerous "ethical" components. For example, a person is presumed innocent until proven guilty. Each person is entitled to due process of the law and to equal protection under the law. There is a right against self-incrimination and a right to legal counsel in criminal proceedings. Freedoms of speech and religion, among others, are guaranteed by the Constitution.

Business law also attempts to reflect the morality of the society and to promote ethical conduct in the realm of business. The law of sales imposes a duty on the parties to a sales contract to act in good faith. Bankruptcy is designed to give an *honest* debtor a fresh start. As already discussed, agency law imposes the duties of good faith and loyalty on the agent. And there are other examples of the ethical and/or moral aspects of business law.

The laws regulating business have developed to a great extent under the social contract theory. Governmental regulations of business were enacted initially — in many cases — in response to a public demand for protection from the abuses and excesses of "big business." The antitrust laws discussed in Chapter 46 were intended to control business and to protect the ideal of a free and competitive economic society. The abusive practices of the railroads, the oil companies, the meat packers, and others led to a public outcry for reform and to governmental intervention in response to these outcries. Eventually these same laws were used to combat other perceived wrongs committed by the business community. For example, the Federal Trade Commission has begun to require corrective advertising from firms deemed guilty of misleading or deceptive advertisements in an effort to increase the sale of their products. The following case deals with an allegedly deceptive advertising campaign. Note how the FTC attempts to force the advertiser to use honesty in its commercials.

Federal Trade Commission v. *Colgate-Palmolive Co.*
380 U.S. 374 (1964)

FACTS

Colgate-Palmolive and its advertising agency developed a "mock-up" of sandpaper to demonstrate the moistening abilities of the Rapid Shave product developed by Colgate. The FTC challenged the advertisement as false and deceptive and issued a cease-and-desist order against both Colgate-Palmolive and the advertising agency.

Colgate-Palmolive objected to this cease-and-desist order for several reasons. First, it was alleged that Rapid Shave really could shave sandpaper but that it took approximately eighty minutes for the sandpaper to be sufficiently soaked to allow the shaving. Secondly, the use of sandpaper on television was inappropriate since, when televised, real sandpaper looks like colored paper, whereas the Plexiglas-and-sand "mock-up" *looks* like sandpaper when televised. Both the defendant and the hearing examiner at the administrative hearing felt that the actual moistening time or the use of the mock-up was material or misleading to the public.

ISSUE

Is the use of an undisclosed mock-up and the creation of the conception in the mind of the viewing public that it is seeing an actual experiment as opposed to a simulation an unfair or deceptive trade practice in violation of the FTC Act?

HOLDING

Yes. Any fact that may induce a prospective purchaser to select one product instead of another is material. Misrepresenting such a fact is a prohibited deception in violation of the Act.

REASONING

It has been held to be a deceptive and unfair practice to have an advertiser tell the public that it can rely on something other than the word of the advertiser without more to substantiate that word. In this case the public is being told that it can rely on the demonstration of the moisturizing abilities of the product and on the product's ability to shave sandpaper quickly and smoothly. In fact, it is being shown something entirely different. The undisclosed use of sand-coated Plexiglas in the commercials is a material deception, and such a practice must be halted. The ruling of the FTC is reinstated by the court.

The apparent success of the antitrust laws encouraged both the public and the government in the use of statutes to coerce business into meeting the demands of the public. The consumer movement of the 1960s led to a number of protective statutes by both the federal and the state governments. The federal government was most concerned about protecting consumer credit, based on the importance of credit in our modern society. However, there were also federal statutes that dealt with consumer product safety. Similarly, the state governments enacted safety statutes and also dealt with home solicitation. In each of these areas, the government became involved only after a perceived problem was identified, public demands for protection were raised, and the business community failed or refused to meet the demands of the public.

The decades of the 60s and the 70s also saw an increased public awareness of — and concern over — pollution of the environment. Again, a number of protests and a great deal of public action were ignored by the business community in general, and once again governmental intervention was the tool used to correct the problem. These governmental environmental protection statutes were intended to clean up the environment so as to protect the quality of life for our population, our wildlife, and for future generations. Again, the government only became involved after the business community failed to present any viable solutions to the problems concerning the public.

The areas of consumer protection and environmental regulation are each covered in Chapter 47. The statutory treatment of these problems provides relatively rigid and potentially expensive protections to the public. Similar protections could have been developed by the business community with a great deal less rigidity and a great deal less expense had business merely been willing to meet the challenge directly on its own. Instead, by waiting until the government told it what to do, business faces a much stricter regulatory environment in which to operate.

The labor movement is another example of the stubbornness of business to face a developing situation, which led to a multitude of regulations. Business refused to recognize the union movement, and it refused to bargain collectively in good faith with the workers. As a result, the workers obtained statutory rights to unionize and to bargain collectively. These rights are, again, rigid and technical and more stringent than they would have been had business given the same principles voluntary recognition. In a similar vein, we find such matters as occupational safety, civil rights of the employees, and a number of other areas rigidly regulated owing to the unwillingness of business to self-regulate. These topics are dealt with in some detail in Chapter 48.

In each of these areas and in a number of others the social contract theory is obvious. Society recognized a problem and demanded certain corrective steps be taken to alleviate these problems. Business had an opportunity to take the corrective steps in a fashion devised by business, but failed — or refused — to do so. The government then stepped in to resolve the problems in a rigid, statutory manner when no informal solutions were advanced by business.

Despite a continuing attempt by many businesses to avoid the problem of business ethics in the hope that it will "go away," there are contemporary ethical problems that illustrate the seriousness of the issue. In addition, recent court opinions show an increased judicial awareness of the social responsibility of corporations. Several years ago, Ford Motor Company engineers discovered a potentially hazardous defect in the construction design of the newly developed (at the time) Ford Pinto. The defect presented the possibility of a gas tank rupture, with a resulting fire hazard, if the Pinto was subjected to a rear-end collision. However, Ford's management applied a cost-benefit analysis and determined that it was cheaper for the corporation to pay damages in the lawsuits that were likely to arise due to the design defect than it was to recall the cars and correct the defect. With hindsight, it is obvious that the management made an improper decision from a cost perspective. But what about the ethical issues raised by this decision? How many consumers lost confidence in Ford over this act? How does the public feel about the case and its implications?

More recently, the courts awarded Pennzoil a multibillion dollar settlement in a lawsuit against Texaco for Texaco's conduct in attempting to prevent a merger between Pennzoil and Getty Oil. The court based its decision on the *unethical* interference and conduct of Texaco.

Other cases will undoubtedly arise in the future, and the likelihood of liability for unethical conduct may be the spur needed to force business to recognize and to honor its ethical obligations.

American businesses need to develop a model, a framework, of ethical behavior. While it is highly improbable that a single model can be developed that will apply equally well to every industry within the American economy, it is possible to suggest a general outline for business that can then be tailored by each industry to the particular needs and demands of that industry. For example, business should probably lean toward the consequential ethical theories rather than toward the nonconsequential theories. Consequential ethical theories are more easily understood, and more readily accepted by the general public than the more esoteric concepts that go with a nonconsequential approach.

Business should also consider its public relations image in deciding how to proceed within the consequential area. A utilitarian approach, one concerned with the greater good of the society, would be more acceptable to society than an egoistic approach. Society already tends to view business as *egotistic* and many people seem to have trouble distinguishing between egoistic and egotistic. To avoid this problem of comprehension and understanding, business should probably select the utilitarian approach. Such an approach also fits into the Social Contract theory, which business must already satisfy if it is to be "allowed" to continue.

Business should avoid "hard and fast" rules because of the changing

THE PROBLEM CONTINUES

A SUGGESTION FOR BUSINESS

social environment, especially with the rapid changes of the modern technological age. This does not mean that business should not have rules and standards but, rather, that the rules and standards should be flexible enough to
change as society and the business environment change. Business should also
advocate the Loyal Agent argument, with the loyal agent of the business acting
as an agent should — with the best long-term interests of the principal in mind.
This means that an agent should act in a proper and legal manner to further the
best interests of the principal, and should not be encouraged to take short cuts
in the short run for immediate profit without regard to the rules or the interests
of society.

Businesses should also learn to work with the government in establishing
statutory regulations of the business environment whenever possible. By taking a proactive rather than a reactive role, business can not only protect its
own best interests but also use its active stance to show that business cares
about society and the interests of the public. This would not only improve the
public relations posture of business but would also show a serious effort to
conform to the social contract.

The development of a comprehensive business ethic will not be easy, nor
will it be greeted with open arms by many business leaders. However, the
alternative is excessive regulation, public distrust, and a general malaise in the
business community. Steps can be taken that will benefit both business and
society. To do so can only be good for business.

SUMMARY

Over the history of this country, the social environment in which business
operates has changed drastically. As the social environment has changed, the
demands of society on business have also changed. Business has been slow to
recognize or to accept these changes, however.

The social contract theory basically says that business must respond to the
demands of the society, or the society is permitted to change the rules of the
game to ensure business will comply. If business does not act as society demands, society will have the legislature enact rules to force compliance.

Even if business wants to act ethically, it is difficult for business to do so.
There are no clear-cut guidelines for business to follow in adopting a code of
ethics, and interfirm agreements as to what should be done could be challenged as a conspiracy in violation of the antitrust laws. Still, some effort must
be made. Business can make this effort by recognizing the human element, the
fact that its employees are humans with human wants, desires, and values.
Business needs to also recognize the legal aspect, in that unless business
responds voluntarily, the legislature will often intervene. Finally, business
needs to recognize that the courts are beginning to recognize an ethical aspect
of conduct. Cases like the Pinto case and the Pennzoil-Texaco case will help to
establish a new line of precedent concerning business ethics and the liability of
the firms that fail to toe the ethical line.

1. What is the "social contract" theory, and how does it affect the role of a corporation within the society in which it operates?

2. Do you feel that a state supreme court today would resolve the fact situation presented in *Dodge* v. *Ford Motor Co.* in the same manner as the Michigan Supreme Court did in 1919? Why?

3. Should the federal government develop a model code of ethics for all businesses in the United States to follow? If so, why? If not, who should develop such a code?

4. What should be considered in the establishment of a code of ethics for any particular business?

5. Explain the "loyal agent's argument" as described by Micholos. What, if anything, is wrong with the argument?

6. Should a legal system be concerned with ethical issues and moral values, or should it only be concerned with the allocation of justice?

7. What could/should business do to prevent further federal regulations requiring "ethical" conduct in the business environment?

8. Do you agree with the recent "ethical" opinions of the courts in such cases as the Pinto case and the Pennzoil-Texaco case?

9. The FTC has recently become active in the area of advertising, requiring corrective advertising in a number of cases. Do you feel that corrective advertising is an appropriate remedy when a firm is found guilty of false or misleading advertising?

10. Is business ruled by a "game theory" in which bluffing is a proper part of the game, or is business obligated to act in an honest and forthright manner without regard to any "game theory"?

1. Bayard was a truck driver for McLean Trucking. He had been employed by McLean for over twenty-two years and was also the union shop steward at the company's plant. Bayard was sent by McLean to pick up a load of goods. The load exceeded the state maximum weight limit, and Bayard refused to drive the truck with the excessive load on board. As a result of this refusal, McLean discharged Bayard. Can McLean legally fire Bayard under these circumstances? (*Bayard* v. *National Labor Relations Board,* 505 F.2d 342 [1974].)

2. The directors of A. P. Smith Manufacturing adopted a resolution stating that the corporation was making a $1500 donation to Princeton University and that the donation was in the best interests of the firm. A number of shareholders have objected to this contribution as an improper use of corporate funds. Is such a contribution appropriate for the firm? (*A. P. Smith Manufacturing Co.* v. *Barlow,* 98 A.2d 581 [N.J. 1953].)

3. Duke Power Company employed ninety-five employees, fourteen of

whom were black. The company revised its hiring and promotion policies so that a high school diploma and a minimum score on an intelligence test were both required in order to be hired or promoted. Thirteen of the black employees challenged this new standard as discriminatory and violative of their rights. Should a company be able to impose such employment and promotion standards? (*Griggs et al.* v. *Duke Power Company,* 401 U.S. 424 [1970].)

4. The secretary of labor, acting under the provisions of OSHA, passed a standard limiting occupational exposure to cotton dust. Representatives of the cotton industry challenged the standard as unreasonable since there was no cost-benefit analysis to support the standard. Should such a standard be upheld only on the basis of a cost-benefit analysis, or are there more important ethical considerations involved? (*American Textile Manufacturers Institute, Inc.* v. *Donovan,* 452 U.S. 490 [1981].)

5. The Securities and Exchange Commission charged Steadman with numerous violations of federal securities laws and regulations. At an administrative hearing, the SEC presented evidence that Steadman was guilty of securities frauds, conflicts of interests, and other wrongful acts. The administrative law judge upheld the SEC on the basis of preponderance of the evidence and imposed severe sanctions against Steadman. Steadman has objected to the sanctions, arguing that such severe treatment cannot be justified on the basis of a mere preponderance of the evidence but rather should require at least clear and convincing proof. Do you agree with this argument? Is it ethical to deny a person the right to engage in his or her normal occupation for any extended time on such evidence? (*Steadman* v. *Securities and Exchange Commission,* 450 U.S. 91 [1981].)

6. Utah Pie Company entered the frozen pie market in Utah in 1957. At the time, Continental Baking Company, among others, was already in the frozen pie market. Utah Pie immediately gained a large percentage of the market, due in part to the fact that it was the only supplier that had a plant in the state of Utah. In an effort to regain its market share, Continental Baking began to offer its frozen pies to its Utah customers at a lower price than it offered them elsewhere, and even at a price below its direct costs. Utah Pie objected to such practices, alleging that in setting such low prices, Continental was in violation of federal antitrust laws. Can Continental's actions be justified from an ethical perspective (without regard to antitrust laws) under either an egoistic or a utilitarian analysis? Did Continental act in compliance with the Social Contract theory? (*Utah Pie Co.* v. *Continental Baking Co.,* 386 U.S. 685 [1967].)

7. The Federation of Homemakers, a consumer protection group, challenged the labeling of frankfurters as misleading, and asked the Secretary of Agriculture to enforce the Wholesome Meats Act more strictly. The central issue in the challenge was the use of the term "all meat" on frankfurter labels when, in fact, the frankfurters could contain up to 15

percent nonmeat ingredients. The Secretary of Agriculture resisted the group's challenge, asserting that in the meat industry the term "all meat" was generally understood to mean that some nonmeat additives could be used. Should the manufacturers of frankfurters be allowed to label their product as "all meat" when it is really only 85 percent meat and the remaining 15 percent filler? Why? (*Federation of Homemakers* v. *Hardin,* 328 F. Supp. 181 [D.C. D.C. 1971].)

8. Park is the chief executive officer of Acme Markets, a retail food chain. Acme Markets was charged with storing its food in a building contaminated by rodents, a violation of the Federal Food, Drug, and Cosmetic Act. The government charged both Acme Markets and Park for violations of the act. Park asserts that he is not guilty of the charge since he told another officer of the firm to correct the problem and that he should not be held responsible for the other officer's failure to act properly. Evaluate Park's argument from a loyal agent perspective and from a general ethical perspective. (*U.S.* v. *Park,* 721 U.S. 658 [1975].)

9. A registered investment adviser was in the habit of secretly purchasing securities for himself, advising his clients that the securities he had purchased were good long-term investments, and then selling his own holdings in the securities when the market price rose, in part due to the investments of his clients. Evaluate this conduct from an ethical perspective. (*SEC* v. *Capital Gains Research Bureau,* 375 U.S. 180 [1963].)

10. The employees of Gissel Packing Company were considering the formation of a union under NLRB guidelines. The president of the company learned of the union drive and decided to persuade the employees that joining a union was not in their best interests or the best interests of the company. In a talk to the employees, the president pointed out that the company was not that solid financially, and that a strike would probably result in the closing of the plant and the loss of a great many jobs. In a subsequent letter to the employees, the president asserted that the organizing union was a "strike-happy outfit" that would destroy the profitability of the firm and force a plant shutdown. The union lost the NLRB election, and filed an unfair labor practice charge against the company and the president for the preelection communications. Evaluate the conduct of the president in this situation. (*NLRB* v. *Gissel Packing Co., Inc.,* 395 U.S. 575 [1969].)

PART 2

The Law of Contracts

The law of contracts forms the foundation of business law. Virtually every aspect of business involves contracts, as does much of a person's normal life. When you rent an apartment, you sign—or orally agree to—a contract known as a lease; when you take a job, you enter a contract of employment; any purchase of goods, services, or real estate involves some form of contract. Loans are evidenced by a type of contract known as a promissory note. Even the marital relationship is a type of contract.

This part of the book will examine the traditional elements of contract law—the so-called common law of contracts. Later parts will consider various special types of contracts, among them sales, commercial paper, secured transactions, and insurance. These specialized forms are probably more familiar to you than the basic form and may seem more timely and relevant. However, you must keep in mind the fact that all of these specialized forms are merely variations of the basic form. The common law elements are present in each special contract; thus, you must understand those common law elements before you can properly utilize these specialized forms.

CHAPTER 8

An Introduction to the Law of Contracts

THE IMPORTANCE OF CONTRACT LAW

Of all the aspects of law examined in this text, none is probably as significant overall or as pervasive in your life as the law of contracts. Virtually every personal or business activity involves contract law — activities like charging a birthday gift on a credit card, buying and insuring a car, leasing an apartment, writing a check, paying for college, and working at an establishment covered by an employment agreement. These are but a few of the ways in which the law of contracts impinges on our daily lives. On a grander scale, the effects of international contract law even seep down to our gasoline tanks, since we receive OPEC oil as a result of international contracts. Thus, the law of contracts affects our most mundane activities, as well as some rather sensational ones, such as *surrogacy* contracts (whereby women agree contractually to have babies for infertile couples) or lawsuits between famous "live-in" couples involving *palimony* (requests by one member of an unmarried couple that the other pay alimony or a similar form of financial support after the couple's breakup). Accordingly, in this chapter, we deal with broad categories of contracts and contractual situations. In later chapters we shall consider many of these topics in more detail as we attempt to understand an area of the law that is as old as Moses, yet as new as today's developments.

Commercial Law Contracts

Mercantile Having to do with business, commerce, or trade

Free enterprise Freedom to conduct a legitimate business for profit

When most of us think of the word *contracts,* we envision the **mercantile** world. Indeed, our system of **free enterprise** has historically stressed the importance of freedom of contract and a corresponding protection of contractual rights. It was not always so. Blackstone's *Commentaries on the Laws of England,* first published in 1756, devoted 380 pages to real property law, while only 28 pages concerned contracts. Thus, to Blackstone the law of contracts apparently was a subdivision of the law of property rather than the independent branch of law we know it as today.[1]

Part of the reason for this lies in the historical development of contract law. Although always broadly a part of the common law, mercantile traditions grew out of the law merchant, which represented the accumulation of commercial customs from as early as Phoenician times. The mercantile courts were separate from courts of law, and the merchants (or guilds) administered their own rules and customs. Hence, the evolution of commercial law remained outside the mainstream of legal development until fairly late in English history, the end of the seventeenth century.[2] In the late 1800s, after the assimilation of the law merchant into the common law, several acts of Parliament dealt with commercial law subjects.

Not surprisingly, then, various legal bodies in the United States, influenced by these English precedents, penned a wide variety of statutes covering American commercial law (for example, the Uniform Negotiable Instruments Law and the Uniform Sales Act). By the 1930s several such acts existed. Because each state had not completely adopted these acts, however, commercial remedies differed from state to state. Moreover, these acts were already somewhat outmoded and thus not reflective of modern commercial practices. For these reasons, and especially to effect an integration of these contradictory statutes, in the 1940s the American Law Institute and the National Conference of Commissioners on Uniform State Laws began to prepare what we today call the Uniform Commercial Code.[3]

The UCC, as the Uniform Commercial Code is commonly known, revolutionized prior approaches to commercial transactions by viewing commercial transactions as a single subject of the law.[4] The drafters saw, for example, that a sale of goods may constitute one facet of such a transaction. They also realized that a check may be used for payment of the purchase price of the

---

[1] A. G. Guest, ed., *Anson's Law of Contracts,* 25th ed. (Oxford: Clarendon Press, 1979), p. 1.
[2] Paul Conway, *Outline of the Law of Contracts,* 3rd ed. (Irvington-on-Hudson, N.Y.: American Legal Publications, 1968), p. 10.
[3] Bradford Stone, *Uniform Commercial Code in a Nutshell* (St. Paul, Minn.: West, 1975), pp. 1–2.
[4] Ibid., p.3.

goods or that, alternatively, the seller may retain a **security interest** in the goods to ensure payment of the balance of the debt. An examination of the Uniform Commercial Code reveals articles on sales, **commercial paper,** bank deposits and collections, and **secured transactions,** which correspond roughly to the scenarios described above. The UCC has fulfilled its original goals of simplifying, clarifying, and modernizing the law governing commercial transactions; permitting the continued expansion of commercial practices through custom, usage, and agreement of the parties; and making uniform the law among the various jurisdictions (Section 1–102[2] and Comment 1). Louisiana, while it has incorporated some of the articles of the UCC into its commercial laws, is unique in that it has not wholly adopted the UCC. Most states' commercial statutes, with minor variations, have reproduced the UCC articles in their entirety. Excerpts from the Code are included in Appendix A.

In addition to the Uniform Commercial Code, the National Conference of Commissioners on Uniform State Laws has drafted other statutes for possible adoption by the states. Examples include the Uniform Partnership Act and the Uniform Consumer Credit Code, among others. As discussed, these laws have regularized commercial transactions so that transactions from state to state will be more consistent with each other. Such uniformity fosters predictability of result without necessarily sacrificing the law's capacity to change when commercial practices dictate change. You will need to check your particular jurisdiction to see whether your state has adopted these uniform acts and codes or whether it instead relies on its own statutes to cover these legal areas.

Common Law Contracts

The existence of statutes concerned with commercial contract law should not overshadow the importance of common law contracts. Many doctrines regarding modern-day contracts stem from "judge-made" law, those decisions growing out of contractual disputes from earlier times. Contract disputes being decided on a daily basis in jurisdictions around the country significantly add to this body of precedents. In addition, even the UCC states that common law contract law supplements the UCC in those areas where the statute is silent. It is appropriate, then, that most of our discussion in the succeeding chapters will center around *common law* contract principles—that is, principles derived from the judgments and decrees of courts.

Definition of a Contract

As you would expect, there are many definitions for the word *contract*. In general, a *contract* is *a legally binding and legally enforceable promise, or set of promises, between two or more competent parties.* Put another way, a contract is a "promise or set of promises for the breach of which the law gives a remedy, or the performance of which the law in some way recognizes as a duty."[5] Most of us intuitively understand what a contract is. Still, situations exist that may at first glance appear to be contracts but are not. An illustration should suffice.

Let's assume that you are a Rolling Stones fan. The Stones are in the

Security interest An interest in personal property or fixtures that secures payment or performance of an obligation

Commercial paper Negotiable instruments; checks, drafts, notes, and certificates of deposit; instruments that are used as credit instruments and/or as substitutes for money and that are governed by Article 3 of the UCC

Secured transactions Credit arrangements, covered by Article 9 of the UCC, in which the creditor has a security interest in certain assets of the debtor

[5] *Restatement (Second) of Contracts,* Section 1 (1981).

United States for a concert tour. You are extremely anxious to attend a concert because, given Mick Jagger's age, you fear that this may well be your last chance to see them. A friend promises you tickets to the show, and you are of course elated. Two days later, your friend calls to tell you he is taking an "old flame" instead of you. As you hang up, one of your thoughts — besides killing your "friend" — may be to sue him. After all, you had an agreement, and he has broken a promise to you.

Did your agreement give rise to a legally enforceable contract? Will a court protect your expectations and award you damages? The short answer is probably no. Most courts would see this situation as a breached social obligation, not a breached contractual obligation. Nevertheless, one occasionally reads of people suing in small claims courts for the expenses incurred in driving to pick up a date and finding that they have been stood up. If the plaintiffs win these "contract" actions (and sometimes they do), the results are generally overturned if appealed, because the more settled rule would call such situations broken social obligations, not breached contracts. Put another way, you should be aware that a court will not call all agreements "contracts."

Contrast this situation with one in which you call a Stones' ticket outlet, give the staff member your credit card number, and order two concert tickets. When you arrive at the box office days before the concert, you are informed that the tickets have been sold to someone else. Can you successfully sue this time? Perhaps you can, because this situation is less social and seems instead to have created binding *economic* obligations on both sides. Thus, to protect your economic expectations, a court could call this a contract and award you damages. Hence, the part of our definition that alludes to a "legally enforceable" or "legally binding" agreement is quite significant and reminds us that not every promise, agreement, or expectation gives rise to a contract. In essence, a contract is any agreement between two or more parties that a court will recognize as creating legally binding duties and obligations between the parties.

Elements of a Contract

Given the law's emphasis on promises or mutual assent, it is not surprising that the first requirement for a valid contract is an *agreement*. Basically, an agreement consists of an offer and an acceptance of that offer. The law necessarily looks at the agreement from the viewpoint of a reasonably prudent person and asks whether such a person would believe that an offer and an acceptance had actually occurred.

Second, the agreement must be supported by *consideration,* something bargained for and given in exchange for a promise.

Third, the parties must have *capacity,* or the legal ability to contract.

Fourth, the contract must be based on the *genuine assent* of each party. If such assent has instead been procured by fraud or duress, for example, courts may set the contract aside.

Fifth, the subject matter of the contract must be *legal.* The legality of the bargain would be questionable, for instance, if the parties agreed to do something that would violate a statute or **public policy.**

Sixth, in some cases a contract must be in *proper form*. Despite the fact that courts ordinarily will enforce oral contracts (even though it is risky to contract orally because of the difficulties of trying to prove exactly what was said), some categories of contracts must be in writing to be legally effective.

In summary, to be valid, a contract must embody: (1) an agreement, (2) supported by consideration, (3) made by parties having the capacity to contract, (4) based on these parties' genuine assent, (5) grounded in a legal undertaking, and (6) expressed in proper form, if applicable. We shall discuss each of these requirements in detail in succeeding chapters. For the time being, however, try to use this information to analyze why the court reached the result it did in the following case.

> **Public policy** The general attitude of the public toward certain conduct; the public sense of morality, good conduct, and acceptable behavior to which citizens must conform

Griffin v. Griffin
699 P.2d 407 (Colo. 1985)

FACTS

When the Griffins were divorced in 1979, the divorce decree gave custody to the mother but incorporated a separation agreement stating that both parents would participate equally in the education of their child. Among other things, the parents agreed to select their child's school jointly and to participate jointly in school-related activities such as parent-teacher conferences. In 1980, Mr. Griffin went to court to prevent Mrs. Griffin from enrolling their son in a Tibetan Buddhist school. He argued that his wife's unilateral decision had denied him his right to participate in the selection of his son's school.

ISSUE

Was the provision in the separation agreement relating to the parents' joint selection of a school for their son an enforceable contract that gave Mr. Griffin the right to select his son's school?

HOLDING

No. The provision was merely an agreement to agree and not an enforceable contract. In the absence of an enforceable contract, the selection of schools and the power to control the child's education rested with the custodial parent under Colorado law.

REASONING

The provision in the separation agreement relating to the selection of a school was unenforceable because the agreement neither selected a school nor by its terms provided a means of resolving disagreements concerning the selection of schools. In essence the parties had merely agreed to agree, or to reach agreement at some future time regarding their child's education. Under the general rule, such agreements were unenforceable because a court has no power to force the parties to reach an agreement and cannot grant a remedy. This rule was particularly appropriate for a situation such as this one, because any attempts to force the parties to agree might lead to further discord, which would not be in the best interests of the child. The court was therefore reluctant to substitute its own judgment as to the choice of a school, since it was a stranger to both the child and the parents and thus ill-equipped to make such important choices. In the absence of an enforceable agreement relating to the child's education, the power to control the child's education remained with the custodial parent, the mother, under Colorado law.

FROM STATUS TO CONTRACT AND BACK AGAIN

As mentioned earlier, the development of contract law occurred relatively late in English legal history. One reason for this stems from the social hierarchies set by the feudal society that prevailed throughout Europe between the eleventh and thirteenth centuries. In such a rigid, stratified society, each person occupied a special status, or social position. Consequently, one's social circumstances determined the rights owed to one and the conduct expected of one. For example, feudal lords owed few duties to lowly serfs; but serfs owed their lives to their lords.

Imagine the disruptive effect contract law, which calls for the performance of mutual duties and obligations, would have had on such a social order. It is not surprising that property law assumed foremost importance during these times. If a serf were the property of the lord, courts did not have to bother with protecting what the state would consider the serf's rather trivial expectations. Accordingly, the development of contract law was unnecessary.

Yet, as England became a commercial center, the law merchant and contracts became more important. Moreover, during the social and political reforms of the late eighteenth and nineteenth centuries, the rise of capitalistic ethics brought with it demands for freedom of contract. This political emphasis on the importance of the individual and of private property accelerated the growth of what we now call contract law. To a largely agrarian society dedicated to self-reliance and individualism, protection of expectations and enforcement of obligations took on added importance. The demise of a status-oriented society ushered in a contractually oriented social order.

Ironically, as an aftermath of the industrial revolution, the twentieth century has witnessed numerous restrictions on the nineteenth century's adoption of virtually unrestricted freedom of contract. Legislatures and courts in the last century have curtailed freedom of contract. Labor laws, environmental protection statutes, consumer enactments — these are a few examples of how lawmakers have lately restricted freedom of contract. Similarly, through common law decisions, courts have hampered the continued development of freedom of contract by protecting individuals who have little bargaining power even *after* these persons have consummated a contract. The doctrine of *unconscionability,* which we mentioned in Chapter 1, and about which you will learn more in Chapters 10 and 13, is a perfect example of this. Suppose two parties have bargained. If, in the court's opinion, one of them (usually a corporation or business entity) had grossly superior bargaining power, or leverage, over the other, the court will sometimes set such contracts aside on the grounds of unconscionability—that is, because *the contract is shockingly oppressive or grossly unfair to one of the parties.* (Do not, however, make the mistake of believing *you* can rely on this remedy to get out of each and every contract for which you belatedly wish to avoid responsibility!) Such developments have convinced some commentators that we have actually moved from "status" to "contract" and back to "status" again.

It is possible to categorize or distinguish contracts in various ways. These categories are not always mutually exclusive, and several different terms may apply to the same contract.

CLASSIFICATIONS OF CONTRACTS

The distinction between formal and informal contracts comes from the method used in creating the contract. As you may recall, in early common law times, the contracting parties generally engaged in certain formalities (hence the term *formal*). To be valid, for example, a contract had to be under seal; that is, the document had to be closed with wax and imprinted with one's insignia, or distinctive mark. Nowadays, very few contracts have to be under seal because most jurisdictions have abolished the need for certain classes of private contracts or instruments to be under seal. A seal, if used, does not affect the legal validity of most contracts. This trend toward eliminating the necessity for sealed, or formal, contracts demonstrates that the need for ceremonies and formalities to ensure validity has largely passed. The more common category of contracts today consists of *informal* (or simple) contracts. In these, the emphasis is not on the form or mode of expression but instead on giving effect to the promises of the parties. Informal contracts do not require a seal. Such contracts may be either oral or written and in fact may even be implied from the conduct of the parties.

Formal Versus Informal Contracts

As you have learned, every contract has at least two contracting parties. The person who makes an offer (called the *offeror*) generally promises to do something or to pay a certain amount if the person to whom the offer has been made (called the *offeree*) will comply with the offeror's request. Usually, then, in return for this promise, the offeror demands a certain act or a certain promise of the offeree as acceptance. The form of the acceptance demanded determines whether the contract is a *unilateral contract (promise on one side only)* or a *bilateral contract (promises on both sides)*.

Unilateral Versus Bilateral Contracts

If the offeror promises to pay the offeree $50 for plowing the offeror's garden, this contract is unilateral. Only one person (the offeror) has promised to do anything. The offeree accepts the offer by doing the requested act (that is, plowing). By *performing* the act, the offeree *accepts* the offer.

In contrast, if one party (the promisor) makes a promise and the other party (the promisee) accepts the offer by promising to do the requested act, a bilateral contract exists because there are promises on both sides of the agreement. To use the same example, assume the offeror promises to pay the offeree

$50 if the offeree will promise to plow the offeror's garden. When the offeree accepts by so promising, an exchange of promises has occurred, and a bilateral contract has resulted.

Valid, Voidable, Void, and Unenforceable Contracts

A *valid contract* is one that *is legally binding and enforceable.*

In contrast, a *voidable contract* is one that *may be either affirmed or rejected at the option of one or more of the contracting parties.* The agreement is nonetheless valid until it is rejected or disaffirmed. For example, if a person buys a car in the belief that it has been driven only 50,000 miles when in actuality it has 250,000 miles on it, that contract may be voidable on the basis of fraud or misrepresentation. However, the contract is valid and fully enforceable *until* the buyer disaffirms it.

Void agreements, though they may outwardly appear to be contracts, can never have any legal effect. They *are unenforceable and never become contracts because they lack one of the essential elements of a contract.* An agreement to murder someone is void and cannot be enforced because it lacks the element of legality.

On the other hand, it is possible to have a seemingly binding contract that *will not be given effect in a court of law.* Suppose, for example, that the contract involved is one that must be in writing (such as a contract for a sale of goods priced at $500 or more); if the contract is oral, it will be *unenforceable.* Note that otherwise the contract appears to meet all the criteria of a valid contract.

Express Versus Implied Contracts

An *express contract* is one in which *the parties set forth their intentions specifically and definitely,* either in writing or orally. Most contracts are of this type.

Conversely, an *implied contract* is one that *must be discerned or inferred from the actions or conduct of the parties.* Even though the parties should have expressed their intentions more clearly, it is still possible to conclude that a true contract exists. We often call these agreements *contracts implied in fact* because, based on the facts, it is possible to say that despite the absence of explicit language to this effect, the parties intended to create a contract.

Assume, for example, that two parties have had a well-known, years' long understanding that grain will be accepted when delivered. If one party takes grain to the elevator and the elevator refuses to accept it, the facts of the parties' prior, long-standing relationship and their previous conduct may allow a court to enforce this agreement as a contract implied in fact. But in the case that follows, the judge refused to find a contract implied in fact.

Rouse v. Peoples Natural Gas Company
605 F. Supp. 230 (D. Kan. 1985)

FACTS   Lorena G. Rouse sued Peoples Natural Gas Company (Peoples) for breach of an implied employment contract. Although there was no written employment contract between Rouse and Peoples, she argued that a contract implied in fact arose from certain provisions in Peoples's employment manual and from Peoples's prior conduct, including Peoples's promoting her, giving her positive performance evaluations, and increasing her salary. Rouse contended that Peoples's termination of her employment with the company was not in accordance with the procedures set out in the employment manual and thus represented a breach of Peoples's employment contract with her.

Could the terms of an employment manual form the basis for an implied contract?

ISSUE

No. An employment manual that only represents a unilateral expression of company policy could not alone be the basis for an implied contract.

HOLDING

The evidence was undisputed that Peoples's employment manual was a unilateral expression of company policy. Rouse in no way had bargained for her position on the basis of the policies defined in the manual, and there was no mutual asset or meeting of the minds with respect to these employment policies. Given these facts, under the law of Kansas, neither Peoples's employment manual nor Peoples's prior conduct could form the basis for an implied contract.

REASONING

An *executory contract* is one in which *some condition or promise has not yet been completed by one or more of the parties.* For instance, if one person agrees to buy a television set from Honest John's, the contract is executory; the television still has to be delivered and paid for. If the buyer pays for the television, the contract is likewise executory, although technically the buyer has executed his or her part of the contract.

Executory Versus Executed Contracts

As you may have surmised, an *executed contract* is one in which *all conditions or promises have been fully completed or performed.* In the last example, when Honest John's delivers the television set, the contract will be executed. Neither party has anything further to do.

One type of implied contract deserves special attention. This is a contract implied in law, or a *quasi contract.* Lawsuits alleging quasi contract as the basis for recovery may also be called suits for **unjust enrichment.** Under certain circumstances, the law will "create" a contract for the parties, despite their wishes and intentions, in order to prevent the unjust enrichment of one party. In these circumstances, even though it may be clear that the parties did not actually contract with each other, the parties will be treated as if they had contracted. A *contract implied in fact,* which was discussed earlier, is also an implied contract. It differs from a contract implied in law in that sufficient facts or evidence of conduct exists for a court to find that the parties actually meant to contract with each other. Their transaction was perhaps a bit sloppy; that is, we might wish for more explicit language. But we can with some certainty conclude that the parties intended a binding agreement between themselves. A contract implied in fact is thus a "true" contract. In contrast, a *contract implied*

Quasi Contracts Versus Contracts Implied in Fact

Unjust enrichment
Benefits unfairly received or retained by a person and to which the person is not entitled unless the person pays the reasonable value of them

in law is a fiction engineered by a court so as to effect justice between two parties. Unlike a contract implied in fact, this is not a "true" contract, hence the name quasi contract.

The result in the following case turns on this very distinction.

Hirschmann v. U.S.
11 Cl. Ct. 338 (1986)

FACTS   Jan Victor Hirschmann, the assistant Chief of Medicine at the Veterans Administration (VA) Medical Center in Seattle, Washington, submitted a request for a twelve-month extended leave for educational purposes on December 8, 1983. The request included six months' leave at full pay for training in London, England; but questions arose within the VA as to whether it should pay for leaves involving training outside the United States. Dr. Hirschmann eventually took the leave without pay from September 1984 through September 1985 and then sued the VA for the six months' pay he claimed the VA had arbitrarily and capriciously withheld from him.

ISSUE   Did the United States Claims Court have jurisdiction to hear Hirschmann's complaint under the Tucker Act, which states that the Claims Court has jurisdiction to "render judgment upon any claim against the United States founded either upon the Constitution, or any act of Congress or any regulation of an executive department, or upon any express or implied contract with the United States?"

HOLDING   No. The Tucker Act reaches only claims based on contracts implied in fact, not contracts implied in law. Thus, the Claims Court had no jurisdiction to hear Hirschmann's claim.

REASONING   A contract implied in fact necessitates circumstances indicating that the parties have in fact come to a "meeting of the minds" and have agreed to take upon themselves corresponding obligations and liabilities. A contract implied in fact, then, requires the same contractual elements as an express contract—mutuality of intent, consideration, and lack of ambiguity as to the offer and acceptance. In contrast, a contract implied in law exhibits no agreement between the parties but arises instead from the law's imposing a duty in order to prevent injustice. Because Dr. Hirschmann at best could prove only a contract implied in law rather than a contract implied in fact, the Claims Court did not have jurisdiction over his claim for breach of an implied contract.

An illustration should help to clarify further the difference between a contract implied in fact and a contract implied in law. Assume that Mattie is sitting on her front porch when a painting crew drives up. Actually, the painting crew has the wrong address (111 Riverside instead of 1111 Riverside). Mattie allows the crew to paint her house and later tries to argue that since she had not asked for the services, she should not have to pay for them. To prevent the unjust enrichment of Mattie at the painters' expense, most courts will force Mattie to pay the painters for the benefit she has received (a newly painted house) or, put another way, for the **detriment** suffered by the painters (the cost of their supplies, services, and so on). Mattie would be liable in quasi contract or a contract implied in law only for the reasonable value of the services rendered; the painters cannot "gouge" her by charging, after the fact, an exorbitant price. A contract implied in fact does not exist here because nothing in the facts suggests that Mattie and the painting company had dealt with each other before the crew arrived at Mattie's house. Evidence of an intention to contract, however sloppy the execution of the contract, would have made this a true contract, or a contract implied in fact. Instead, the court *creates* a contract — a quasi contract or contract implied in law — to prevent the unjust enrichment of Mattie.

> **Detriment** Any loss or harm suffered by a person or property

Do not be misled into believing that every time one person receives a benefit, a quasi-contractual recovery will be possible. Remember that the policy underlying such recoveries is the avoidance of injustice. Mattie has to pay because she knowingly allowed the painters to proceed. Had she not been present, however, the painters would probably be unable to hold Mattie liable because the services were conferred on her as a result of the painters' negligence or mistake. (They had come to the wrong house.) In these circumstances, it would not be inequitable to allow Mattie to retain the benefits bestowed on her. By the same token, a person who confers a gift (for example, let us assume Mattie's brother contracts with a painting company to redo Mattie's dilapidated house as a surprise for her) or one who volunteers a service, say a neighbor, who decides to paint Mattie's house while Mattie is away for the weekend, will not be able to recover later from Mattie in quasi contract either. The same will be true of a person who buys supplies in a mistaken belief there is a contract, or who incurs foreseeable difficulties and later tries to make the recipients of the services pay for these extra costs or services on a quasi-contractual theory. Still, it is wise to remember that courts can, in a given circumstance, create a contract in order to avoid injustice.

Analyze the following case in light of these principles.

Perkins v. *Daugherty*
722 S.W.2d 907 (Ky. App. 1987)

FACTS

Perkins, in partnership with Kindred Homes, Inc. (Kindred), began developing Crosswoods Subdivision. Daugherty, a licensed engineer, was retained to do the engineering and contracting work for the subdivision. There was no written contract between Daugherty and the developers; rather, he worked by verbal agreement. Perkins and Kindred later dissolved their partnership, each taking a portion of the property. Daugherty, however, continued to work on Kindred's portion of the property and planned to complete his work on Perkins's property, as well, after finishing Kindred's. Daugherty still had no written contract with either Perkins or Kindred. Daugherty subsequently worked on Perkins's property until it became apparent that Perkins had obtained the help of another engineer for the project. At that time, Daugherty sent Perkins a bill for $18,256.52. When Perkins did not pay the amount due, Daugherty filed an engineer's **lien** against Perkins's property. This action, in turn, led Perkins to sue Daugherty for damages allegedly incurred by the wrongful filing of the lien. Daugherty **counterclaimed** for the amount of the bill, plus interest on the lien.

Lien A legal charge or encumbrance against property

Counterclaimed Presented a cause of action in opposition to the plaintiff's

ISSUE Should Daugherty receive compensation for the work done for Perkins on the basis of either a contract implied in fact or a contract implied in law?

HOLDING Yes. Daugherty should receive compensation based on a contract implied in law.

REASONING The evidence was insufficient to show a contract implied in fact. However, Daugherty could recover on a contract implied in law owing to Perkins's unjust enrichment. A contract implied in law is not based on a contract but is a legal fiction invented to permit a recovery where the law of natural justice says there should be a recovery as if promises were made. Courts may allow such a recovery regardless of the intentions of the parties and may even, in some cases, violate such intentions. Perkins's requests that Daugherty begin working for him as soon as possible, Perkins's knowledge that Daugherty had begun the work, and the substantially lower fee charged Perkins by the second engineer as a result of Daugherty's previous efforts entitled Daugherty to an award based on a contract implied in law.

SUMMARY Probably no area of the law affects us as often as the law of contracts. Commercial law, especially the Uniform Commercial Code's integration of older statutes and common law rules, has become increasingly important in the United States. For the first time many statutes exist that attempt to harmonize areas of the law that previously varied from state to state. Besides statutes, the common law has also spawned numerous contract principles that affect the legal environment of business. Although the word *contract* has many definitions, a common one states that a contract is a legally binding and legally enforceable promise or set of promises between two or more competent parties.

To have a valid contract, six requirements are necessary: (1) an agreement, (2) supported by consideration, (3) made by parties having the capacity to contract, (4) based on these parties' genuine assent, (5) grounded in a legal undertaking, and (6) expressed in proper form, if applicable. Historically, contracts were of minor importance because a feudal social order was uninterested in protecting parties' expectations. With the advent of freedom of contract and rising industrialism, contract law had outstripped property law in significance by the nineteenth century. Ironically, today the law appears to be swinging back to a concern with status, as evidenced by protective statutes and common law decisions. Contracts may be classified as formal or informal; unilateral or bilateral; valid, voidable, void, or unenforceable; express or implied; and executed or executory. These categories are not necessarily mutually exclusive. A contract implied in fact consists of evidence of sufficient facts or conduct from which a court can conclude that the parties intended a binding agreement between themselves. A contract implied in fact is thus a true contract. A quasi contract, or contract implied in law, is not a true contract. It is a different type of implied contract in which a court will create a contract for the parties, despite their wishes and intentions, in order that justice may be served. However, not every situation in which a benefit has been conferred gives rise to a quasi contract.

DISCUSSION QUESTIONS

1. Define the term *contract*.
2. Distinguish between a contractual obligation and a social obligation.
3. Name and define the six requirements for a valid contract.
4. Why do some commentators state that the history of contract law has swung from status to contract and back again?
5. Explain the following categories of contracts: (1) formal, (2) informal, (3) unilateral, (4) bilateral, (5) valid, (6) voidable, (7) void, (8) unenforceable, (9) express, (10) implied, (11) executory, and (12) executed.
6. What are the legal requirements for showing a quasi contract?
7. What is the Uniform Commercial Code, and why is it important?
8. Suppose Joan asks the bank for a loan. What kind of a contract would result from the bank's granting her this loan?
9. A contract involving an interest in land (such as a contract for the sale of a house) must be in writing. What is the legal effect of an oral contract in this situation?
10. What is the difference between a contract implied in fact and a contract implied in law?

CASE PROBLEMS

1. Michael and Mary Dursteler entered into a written contract to sell their mink ranch to Michael's brother, Dennis, and his wife Gloria. The contract provided for a down payment of $10,000 and periodic payments thereafter. The parties also agreed to establish an interim partnership to operate the business while the buyers became acquainted with mink ranching. Within a few months, the parties found themselves at odds over various issues that had not been addressed in the contract, including how the partnership would initially raise the money to run the ranch, how the buyers would secure food for the mink, and how the partnership would report its income and expenses. Was there an enforceable contract between the parties? If there was none, could the buyers nonetheless sue the

sellers for the value of the benefits the buyers had conferred on the sellers (e.g., the $10,000 down payment, $850 in feed, etc.)? *(Dursteler v. Dursteler, 697 P.2d 1244 [Idaho App. 1985].)*

2. Lucille and Carl Mjolsness were divorced in 1970 after twenty-four years of marriage. Immediately after the divorce, the Mjolsnesses began seeing each other again. Four months later, Carl moved into a house Lucille had purchased with her own funds and began living with Lucille and their children. Carl made no monetary contribution toward the purchase of this house; since he was disabled, his income consisted entirely of governmental benefits. Although Lucille alleged that Carl had agreed to pay $70 per month for room and board, Carl made no such payments but did perform household maintenance and repairs. When Lucille filed suit to make Carl leave the premises in 1980, Carl contended that he was entitled to a one-half interest in the house on an implied contract theory. Was Carl correct? *(Mjolsness v. Mjolsness, 363 N.W.2d 839 [Minn. App. 1985].)*

3. Carlotta and Stephen D'Onofrio lived together for several years prior to their marriage in 1971. The birth of their only child, Stephanie, preceded their marriage by four years. Before they were married, they had signed a "Prenuptial Agreement" in which Carlotta, for $1000, gave up the right to any of Stephen's real estate should their marriage end in divorce. When the D'Onofrios divorced in 1984, this agreement became a part of their divorce decree. Carlotta at the time argued that this antenuptial agreement was void because it was inequitable, grossly unfair, and unconscionable. Was such an antenuptial agreement enforceable in a divorce action under New Jersey law? *(D'Onofrio v. D'Onofrio, 491 A.2d 752 [N.J. Super. 1985].)*

4. Dr. Chanda took twenty-eight rolls of already developed Super-8 movie film to a Fotomat outlet in Melbourne, Florida, in April, 1980, in order to have the film images transferred to videotape as a way of saving the images, which were deteriorating. This film contained depictions of his honeymoon, his graduation from medical school, his son's birth, and other events of great sentimental value to Chanda. The Fotomat clerk prepared an order form that contained a conspicuous, bold-type statement that limited Fotomat's liability for loss, damage, or delay during film processing to the replacement cost of a nonexposed roll of film and/or a blank cassette of similar size. Fotomat expressly disclaimed liability for all other loss or damage. Dr. Chanda read this clause, asked the clerk about it, and signed it. The film was later lost and never found. Dr. Chanda sued for damages, arguing that the limitation of liability provision was unconscionable. Should the court set this contract aside on the grounds of unconscionability? *(Fotomat Corporation of Florida v. Chanda, 464 So.2d 626 [Fla. App. 1985].)*

5. Arduini was a tenured teacher who had begun his duties for the 1979–80 school year on 27 August 1979. On 13 September 1979, Arduini received

a "contractual continued service notification" that stated his salary for the 1979–80 school year and included a copy of a liquidated damages policy adopted by the school board on 6 August 1979. This policy allowed the school district to deduct 4 percent of the contract salary as liquidated damages from the pay of any teacher who resigned on his or her own initiative during the school year. When Arduini resigned from his position on 19 October 1979, the school board, in accordance with this policy, withheld 4 percent of Arduini's salary. Arduini sued, arguing that he was not bound by this liquidated damages policy because it was not part of the contract between him and the school board. The school board contended that the liquidated damages clause was part of a unilateral contract formed between Arduini and the board when he had begun performance of the act contemplated by the contract (commencing his teaching duties). According to the board, Arduini thus had accepted the contract and the liquidated damages clause some time after 13 September 1979, when he had received official notice of the policy. Who was correct? *(Arduini v. Board of Education of Pontiac Township High School,* 441 N.E.2d 73 [Ill. 1985].)

6. Mary Dobos was admitted to Boca Raton Community Hospital with a condition serious enough to cause her doctor to order around-the-clock nursing care. The hospital, on Dobos's doctor's orders, asked Nursing Care Services, Inc., to perform nursing services for two weeks while Dobos was in the hospital and for a second two-weeks' period while Dobos was at home. Mrs. Dobos, who was mentally alert during the at-home period, later argued that she should not be liable for Nursing Care Services, Inc.'s fees because she had neither signed a written contract nor orally agreed to be liable for these services. Should Dobos be liable for the $3,723.90 in fees, and, if so, under what theory? *(Nursing Care Services, Inc. v. Dobos,* 380 So.2d 516 [Fla. App. 1980].)

7. Michelle Marvin alleged that in 1964 she and Lee Marvin had entered into an oral agreement that while they lived together, they would share their earnings and property and hold themselves out to the public as husband and wife. She took Marvin's name and allegedly agreed to give up her career as an entertainer and singer in order to devote her time to Lee as a companion and homemaker. She asserted that in return Lee had agreed to provide her with financial support for the rest of her life. Michelle and Lee lived together until 1970, when he asked her to leave his household. Upon Lee's subsequent refusal to provide further support for her, Michelle sued him for one-half of the property acquired during their relationship. Could one party to a nonmarital relationship sue the other for a distribution of property in the absence of an express contract if the parties' conduct demonstrated an implied contract or some other tacit understanding between them? *(Marvin v. Marvin,* 557 P.2d 106 [Cal. 1976].)

8. McGrath and Hilding agreed to be married in November. They built an

addition to Hilding's home at a cost of $7900. McGrath contributed one-half of this sum. The marriage was on the rocks by February. McGrath reconciled with her first husband and started to buy another house with him while she was still married to Hilding. McGrath claimed Hilding should be forced to convey to her a one-half interest in his house as he allegedly had promised he would or, alternatively, he should pay her the $3950 she had advanced for the extension, in order to avoid Hilding's unjust enrichment at her expense. Hilding argued that McGrath's misconduct and the extra expenses resulting from the addition had eliminated any unjust enrichment on his part. Who should win and why? (*McGrath* v. *Hilding*, 394 N.Y.S.2d 603 [N.Y. 1977].)

9. The Strupps had borrowed $68,500 from People's Bank & Trust Company (People's) for use in their farming operations. The Strupps had promised to repay the loan out of their 1980 crop harvest. But owing to a drought in 1980, the Strupps had defaulted on part of this loan. However, as a result of this drought, they became eligible for a Farmers Home Administration (FmHA) disaster emergency loan. The Strupps hoped such a loan would give them sufficient funds to operate their farm for the 1981 growing season and also allow them to pay off the loan on which they had defaulted. An FmHA official assured the Strupps that they were eligible for such an emergency loan and furthermore that they would be able to get an "interim loan" from a commercial lender that would permit them to begin their 1981 plantings while the FmHA processed their loan. People's agreed to become this "interim lender" based on several phone conversations with FmHA officials in April and June. In reliance on these agreements, People's advanced $72,851.88 to the Strupps. During the summer, the Strupps began divorce proceedings. As a result of these marital problems, Mr. Strupp deeded back to the original owner a farm he had been buying on a land contract because he decided to give up farming. The FmHA then refused to close the emergency loan because the FmHA had intended to use this farm to secure the Strupps' repayment of the loan. The FmHA soon afterward called People's to advise it that the FmHA loan would not be closed owing to the unavailability of the land as security. After the FmHA's cancellation of the Strupps' loan, People's sued the Government for the amount extended to the Strupps in the interim loan. Had People's' dealings with the FmHA provided the basis for the Claims Court's jurisdiction over claims brought against the Government for either an express or implied in fact contract? (*People's Bank & Trust Co.* v. *U.S.*, 11 Cl. Ct. 554 [1987].)

10. On 12 May 1978, Siders purchased a home from the Odaks. She also executed an option agreement permitting her to purchase an additional 1.3 acres of adjoining land at any time within 3 years from the date of purchase on giving 30 days' written notice. Hence, the option was valid until 12 May 1981. In February, 1981, Siders orally notified the Odaks of

her intent to exercise this option. The parties later disagreed about whether the Odaks had waived the requirement of a written notice. Nonetheless, the Odaks ultimately refused to sell Siders the additional acreage. When Siders sued to have the optioned land conveyed to her, the Odaks contended that the option agreement was a unilateral contract that could be accepted only by full performances (i.e., the actual purchase of the land) prior to the expiration date of 12 May 1981. Were the Odaks correct? (*Siders* v. *Odaks*, 513 N.Y.S.2d 549 [N.Y. App. Div. 1987].)

CHAPTER 9

Contractual Agreement: Mutual Assent

THE FIRST STEP IN CONTRACT FORMATION

Bona fide In good faith; honest; without deceit; innocent

Agreement is the essence of a contract. Once there has been a *valid offer* by the offeror (the person making the offer) and a *valid acceptance* by the offeree (the person to whom the offer is made), we are well on our way to having a legally binding contract, because there are generally few problems with consideration, capacity, genuine assent, legality, and proper form, the remaining requirements for a contract. On the other hand, precisely because these two aspects of contract formation are so important, courts will closely examine the words and conduct of the parties to determine whether a **bona fide** offer and acceptance are indeed present. From common law times, numerous rules have developed for checking the authenticity of the offer and the acceptance. Broadly speaking, under these rules it is fairly difficult to contract, because courts require rather clear-cut statements that the parties are freely and voluntarily entering into a particular agreement. Conversely, under the Uniform Commercial Code, a court can more easily imply a bona fide offer and acceptance from the conduct of the parties, even if the parties have omitted terms like price, mode of payment, or mode of delivery. We shall discuss the reasons for these developments in this chapter.

The assent of both parties to the agreement is a requirement of this important phase of contract formation. This assent must be mutual, and the parties must agree to exactly the same terms. In short, both parties must actually intend to be bound to the terms embodied in the offer and acceptance. Without mutual assent, there can be no agreement.

MUTUAL ASSENT

Given the necessity for mutual assent, the question of how to judge whether the parties have mutually assented naturally arises. If you are in a particularly mischievous mood, you may say to a friend, "Tom, I'll let you buy my stereo outfit for $100; that's the offer." Since Tom knows the components are worth at least $1,000, Tom quickly says, "I'll take it." Has there been a valid offer and acceptance here? Do you have to sell the stereo, or will you be allowed to say that you were kidding and did not intend to make an offer?

THE OBJECTIVE THEORY OF CONTRACTS

Common law rules tell us that the offeror must exhibit a clear and present intent to offer. You fairly straightforwardly enumerated the terms of the offer, it seems. Would it nevertheless be apparent from your statement that you were only kidding?

Whether or not a valid offer exists is judged by an **objective** standard. To decide whether an offer has been made, common law requires us to put ourselves in the offeree's place (that is, in Tom's shoes) to ascertain if a reasonable offeree would believe that you were serious in offering the stereo at this price. Since your words and conduct will be judged by an objective (instead of **subjective**) test, your secret intent (for instance, that you were joking and did not really want to sell the stereo) cannot be shown. Hence, in this example a court may well find that you have made a valid offer to Tom.

Objective Capable of being observed and verified without being distorted by personal feelings and prejudices

Subjective Capable of being observed and verified through individual feelings and emotions

Obviously, this result depends heavily on the facts. If you are clearly jesting, are excited, or are even visibly angry, details supporting the existence of these facts might lead to a different result. A word to the wise should be sufficient: beware of making "offers" you do not mean, since under both the common law and the Uniform Commercial Code you may be stuck with them.

The following case illustrates these important concepts.

City of Everett v. Estate of Sumstad
631 P.2d 366 (Wash. 1981)

Petitioners Mr. and Mrs. Mitchell are the proprietors of a small secondhand store. On 12 August 1978 the Mitchells attended Alexander's Auction, where they frequently had shopped to obtain merchandise for their own use and for use as inventory in

FACTS

their business. At the auction the Mitchells purchased a used safe with an inside compartment for $50. As they were told by the auctioneer when they purchased the safe, the Mitchells found that the inside compartment of the safe was locked. The safe was one of two safes that were part of the Sumstad estate. Several days after the auction, the Mitchells took the safe to a locksmith to have the locked compartment opened. The locksmith found $32,207 inside. The Everett Police Department, notified by the locksmith, impounded the money.

ISSUE   Was there in fact a sale of the safe and its unknown contents to the Mitchells at the auction?

HOLDING   Yes. There was a sale of the safe and its contents, as revealed by the terms of the agreement in light of the surrounding circumstances.

REASONING   The objective manifestation theory of contracts stresses the outward manifestation of assent made by each party to the other. The subjective intention of the parties is irrelevant. A contract has, strictly speaking, nothing to do with the personal, or individual, intent of the parties. A contract is an obligation attached by the mere force of law to certain acts of the parties, usually words, that ordinarily accompany and represent a known intent. The inquiry, then, focuses upon the outward manifestations of intent by a party to enter into a contract as judged by the reasonable meaning of a person's words and acts. If the offeror, judged by a reasonable standard, manifests an intention to agree in regard to the matter in question, agreement is established. Here the facts showed that the auctioneer had told the bidders that both this safe and the other one had come from an estate, that both were still locked, that neither had been opened, that the required combinations and keys were unavailable for either, and that all sales were final. Furthermore, there was no statement in which the auctioneer reserved the rights to any contents of the safe to the estate. Under these circumstances, reasonable persons would conclude that the auctioneer had manifested an objective intent to sell the safe and its contents and that the parties had mutually assented to enter into that sale of the safe and the contents of the locked compartment.

OFFER

Let us look more closely at this first phase of reaching agreement, the offer. An *offer* generally involves *an indication (by a promise or another commitment) of one's willingness to do or refrain from doing something in the future.* An offer implicitly invites another person to assent to the promise or commitment so as to seal the bargain.

Clear Intention to Contract and Definiteness of the Offer

Given this definition, an offer must show a *clear intention to contract* and be *definite* in all respects if it is to be a genuine common law offer. An agreement to agree at some future time, for example, lacks these prerequisites of a common law offer. Similarly, statements of opinion, statements of intention, and preliminary negotiations do not result in bona fide offers because they lack definiteness. But reasonable people will differ as to what is a clear, definite offer and what is instead only preliminary negotiations or dickering. Since these are questions of fact that a judge or jury may later decide, caution is of course desirable. If you want to make an offer, be specific in all particulars. On the other hand, haggling or dickering lacks this definiteness regarding the details of the transaction and your intentions. Such preliminary negotiations are ordinarily too vague to constitute a valid offer. Winning or losing a lawsuit may turn on such minute distinctions as how a court will interpret the words expressed by the parties. For example, are the words, " I can send you two carloads at $5000 per carload" identical in intent to "I offer to send you two carloads at $5000 per carload"?

The case that follows demonstrates that courts will not enforce agreements that are vague and indefinite in their material, or essential, terms.

Smith v. Smith
375 So.2d 1138 (Fla. App. 1979)

FACTS

In 1972 the husband and wife acquired a home at the purchase price of $65,000, title to which was held by them as **tenants by the entireties.** It was listed for sale by the parties when they were on the verge of seeking dissolution of their marriage at a price of $125,000. In the event of a sale, each was to share equally in the net proceeds. During a court hearing about the dissolution of their marriage, the husband told the court that because of his love for his wife and children and his desire to show her that he was making an honest effort to correct the past conduct that had led to his wife's seeking a divorce, he had deeded his interest in the real property to her by **quitclaim deed.** This was done with the understanding that the wife would reconvey to the husband his one-half interest in the home upon his rehabilitating himself. However, the time frame was not clearly specified by the parties. The husband continued to make the mortgage payments. Although the record reflects that the husband engaged in a course of conduct that indicated a good-faith effort to save the marriage, the wife decided to file for dissolution. Prior to filing in May 1977, however, the wife, without the knowledge of the husband, executed a quitclaim deed to the property to her brother, Gary Hale, in April 1977.

Tenants by the entireties An estate that is held by a husband and wife jointly by conveyance and that carries a right of survivorship

Quitclaim deed A deed conveying from the grantor to the grantee such rights as the grantor possesses, if any; a deed of conveyance that carries no warranties or assurances of its validity or genuineness

ISSUE

Was the agreement in which the husband had conveyed his interest in the marital home to his wife legally enforceable?

HOLDING

No. The agreement was too indefinite to constitute a binding contract.

REASONING

A fundamental principle of the law of contracts is that in order for a contract to be binding and enforceable, it must be definite and certain as to its terms and obligations. Indefiniteness as to the duration of an agreement can be fatal to its being found enforceable as a binding contract. The record in this case reflected no agreement as to duration; the parties merely spoke of the agreement's being conditioned on the husband's making an effort to rehabilitate himself. Neither of the parties was able to testify as to any precise (or even approximate) time limit set or understood by either of them. Similarly, there was no evidence that the husband had actually intended to convey his interest in the property on a permanent basis. Indeed, it was manifestly clear that he had had no such intention: he was merely making a good-faith gesture in support of his promise to help "make the marriage work." Since the deed from husband to wife was ineffective to convey his interest in the homestead, the wife's subsequent quitclaim deed to Hale was also ineffective because she was attempting to transfer her husband's one-half interest to her brother, an interest that she did not legally possess at the time.

Despite what the *Smith* case illustrates about the common law's requirement that an offer be definite in all its material terms, you should be aware that the Uniform Commercial Code relaxes this common law prerequisite in several significant ways. For instance, the UCC in Section 2–204 states that a contract for sale under the Code will not fail for indefiniteness as long as the parties have intended to form a contract and a reasonably certain basis for giving an appropriate remedy exists, even though one or more of the terms of the agreement have been left open. In addition, the UCC contains several so-called gap-filling provisions whereby the court can supply the terms omitted by the parties, including price, place of delivery, mode of payment, and the like.[1] Moreover, the Code validates **output** and **requirements** contracts, both of which would be too indefinite for common law courts to enforce.[2] Because the Code is predicated on the idea that commercial people — merchants — want to deal with each other, it has eliminated some of the ticklish technicalities that impeded contract formation under the common law. You will learn more about this and other revolutionary changes in the common law brought about by the Uniform Commercial Code in Chapters 18–22.

Output contract A contract that calls for the buyer to purchase all of the production of the seller during the term of the contract

Requirements contract A contract in which the seller agrees to provide as much of a product or service as the buyer needs during the contract term

Advertisements and Auctions

The law in general does not treat *advertisements* as valid offers, but rather as *invitations to deal, or statements of intention to sell certain merchandise*. Advertisements are characterized in this fashion because they usually lack sufficient specificity to become offers. Instead, the law views advertisements as invitations for persons to come in and make offers for the types of goods and at the prices indicated in the advertisements. A contrary rule that advertisements are offers would presuppose that a merchant has an unlimited supply of merchandise. Thus, the principle that advertisements are not offers protects merchants from the hardships that a contrary rule might produce. On occasion, though, an advertisement, catalogue, circular, price list, or price quotation will be detailed enough for a court to say that a valid offer exists. Such a result, however exceptional, sometimes occurs, as the following case demonstrates.

---

[1] See Uniform Commercial Code, Sections 2–305, 2–309, and 2–310.
[2] Ibid., Section 2–306.

Harris v. *Time, Inc.*
237 Cal. Rptr. 584 (Cal. App. 1987)

Joshua Gnaizda, the three-year-old son of a prominent Bay Area attorney, received an offer from Time, Inc. (Time) in an envelope that contained two see-through windows that only partially revealed the envelope's contents. One window showed Joshua's name and address. The other revealed the following statement: "JOSHUA A. GNAIZDA, I'LL GIVE YOU THIS VERSATILE NEW CALCULATOR WATCH FREE Just for Opening this Envelope Before Feb. 15, 1985." Beneath the offer was a picture of the calculator watch itself. However, upon opening the envelope, Joshua's mother realized that the see-through window had not revealed the full text of Time's offer. Specifically, printed below the picture of the calculator watch were the following additional words: "AND MAILING THIS CERTIFICATE TODAY!" Thus, the see-through window did not allow these words to be visible before opening the envelope. The certificate itself clearly required that Joshua purchase a subscription to *Fortune* magazine in order to receive the free calculator watch. Joshua's father, suing on his son and Mark Harris's behalf for $15,000 in punitive damages, contended that Time's failure to supply Joshua with a calculator watch represented a breach of contract.

FACTS

Was the text of the unopened mailer an offer rather than an advertisement?

ISSUE

Yes. The text technically constituted a bona fide offer. However, the frivolous nature of the lawsuit mandated its dismissal.

HOLDING

The law usually treats advertisements as merely invitations to bargain, not offers. However, an advertisement can constitute an offer and can form the basis of a unilateral contract if it calls for performance of a specific act without further communication and leaves nothing for future negotiation. The text of Time's unopened mailer technically represented an offer to enter into a unilateral contract: the promisor had made a promise (i.e., to give the recipient a calculator watch) in exchange for the performance of an act by the promisee (i.e., the opening of the envelope). Hence, this communication represented an exception to the general rule. Once Time had made an offer proposing the formation of a unilateral contract and the Gnaizdas had supplied the required consideration by opening the envelope and exposing themselves to the sales pitch within, there was an enforceable contract, assuming the Gnaizdas had given Time notice of their performance. But because of the legal maxim *de minimus non curat*—"the law disregards trifles"—the case had to be dismissed owing to the inappropriateness of a court's being used as a vehicle by those whose only real damage is feeling foolish for having opened junk mail.

REASONING

Normally, courts will require a showing that the merchant has placed some limitation on the advertised goods before courts will find an offer was made by the advertisement. For example, the merchant may have placed a time limit, such as "for one day only," on the advertisement. Or the merchant may have placed a quantity limit, such as "while they last" or "to the first ten customers," on the advertisement. In such a situation, the courts are somewhat more likely to find that the advertisement is an offer and not an invitation to deal, or negotiate. Again, the objective standard of what a reasonable person would have thought will be the deciding factor.

Auctions are similar to advertisements in that the seller is not actually the offeror, although he or she may appear to be offering the goods for sale through the auctioneer. In reality, the bidder is the offeror. For there to be a sale, the seller must accept the bid. The seller can even refuse to sell to the highest bidder unless the auction is publicized as "without reserve." In this type of auction, the seller must let the goods go to the highest bidder; he or she cannot withdraw the goods if the price bid is too low. Once the auctioneer lets the hammer fall, the seller has accepted the bid. But until this point, the bidder can withdraw the offer and thus avoid the formation of a contract of sale. Section 2–328 of the Uniform Commercial Code covers these points, which will be discussed again in Chapter 20.

Communication of the Offer to the Offeree

Another requirement for a bona fide offer embraces the fact that an offer must be *communicated* by the offeror (or his or her agent) to the offeree. At first glance, this rule may seem nonsensical. How, you may ask, can a person accept an offer if he or she is ignorant of it? Believe it or not, that sometimes happens. For example, assume two parties have been haggling over the terms of a real estate transaction. After much correspondence, the would-be buyer (offeree) writes, "Okay, you win. I'll pay $80,000 for the land." A day later, the offeror (seller) coincidentally arrives at the same figure and writes, "This is my final offer. I'll sell the land for $80,000. Take it or leave it." If the seller later wants to sell to someone else, he or she probably can, because most courts would hold that there has been no valid acceptance by the first party. This is true because, *at the time* of the would-be buyer's purported acceptance, there had been no offer to sell the land for $80,000 communicated to the person. And, as we have mentioned, an offer has no legal effect until it is communicated to the offeree. The above correspondences would be likened to identical offers crossing in the mail, each asking for and necessitating an acceptance before there could be a valid agreement.

This requirement of communicating the offer to the offeree sometimes arises in the context of *general offers*. Although most offers are made by one person to another, offers made to the general public or a similar class of large numbers of persons are perfectly legal. A reward (such as for the arrest and conviction of the persons who have been vandalizing an office complex) represents the best example of a general offer. Even though some case results to the contrary exist, most courts will require that the party who performs the act contemplated by the reward (here, the identification of the vandals so as to lead to their prosecution and conviction) must have known of the reward and have intended the act as acceptance of that offer. In essence, then, under this view even a general offer must be communicated to the offeree in order for a valid acceptance to occur. A person who coincidentally had identified the vandals without knowledge of the reward would be ineligible to receive the reward under the rule followed in a majority of jurisdictions.

Usually, offers will comply with the above rules and will be legally effective. The next question that often arises concerns the *duration* of the offer; that is, how long will it remain open? Basically, there are four methods for terminating an offer: (1) lapse, (2) revocation, (3) rejection, and (4) acceptance.

Duration of the Offer

It is quite possible that the offeror will set the life span for the offer by stating in the offer when it will terminate. This sets up the potential **lapse** of the offer. For instance, an offer may state, among other things, "This offer will remain open for thirty days." If after thirty days the offeree has not responded to the offer, it automatically lapses. The offeror is under no legal duty to communicate the fact that the offer has lapsed to the offeree. After thirty days, the offeror can make the same offer to anyone else without worrying about facing a lawsuit from the first offeree.

Lapse The expiration or the loss of an opportunity because of the passage of a time limit within which the opportunity had to be exercised

In many cases, no time is stated in the offer. How long does the offeree have before he or she must respond in these situations? To avoid lapse, the offeree must accept within a reasonable time. Determination of what constitutes a reasonable time becomes a question of fact to be decided by a judge or jury. The trier of fact will consider such things as industry conditions, customs, and usages of trade. In volatile commodities markets, an offer may lapse in a matter of moments. On the other hand, given a downturn in the real estate market, a period of days or weeks may be a reasonable time if the offer involves a sale of real property. To avoid such uncertainties, it makes sense for the offeror to state specifically when the offer lapses.

Lapse may also occur by operation of law. This means that, irrespective of the wishes of the parties, an offer automatically lapses upon the following events: (1) the death or insanity of the offeror or offeree; (2) the **supervening** illegality of the subject matter of the offer; and (3) the destruction of the subject matter involved in the offer. In other words, if Joe Olivetti offers to sell his car to Joan Hays but dies before she accepts, the offer automatically lapses. Joe's estate does not have to inform Joan of his death. Similarly, if two days after Joe makes the offer, his city passes an ordinance stating that sales of private cars without safety stickers are illegal, Joe's offer will lapse if the car does not have a sticker. By the same token, if lightning strikes the car and destroys it, the offer has lapsed as well. Again, no communication to Joan is necessary in these last instances either.

Supervening Coming or happening as something additional or unexpected

Another method of terminating an offer, besides lapse, is **revocation.** Under common law, the offeror possesses virtually unlimited rights to revoke at any time before acceptance. This is true whether or not the offeror uses the word *revoke,* as long as an intention to terminate the offer is clear.

Revocation The cancellation, rescission, or annulment of something previously done or offered

In general, revocation is not effective until it is communicated to the offeree. Interestingly, such communication may be effective whether communicated directly or indirectly. Using our earlier example, Joe may state bluntly, "Joan, I revoke my offer to you." Alternatively, Joan may hear that Joe has sold the car to Len Hill. There has been an effective revocation in either case.

Usually, Joe will be dealing only with Joan or, at most, with a few parties. This is not the case with a general offer to the public. If Joe has lost his prize Dalmatian, Jake, and has offered a reward for the return of or information about the dog, he need only revoke his offer in the same manner (or medium) in which he has made the original offer. Because it would be too burdensome to require Joe to communicate with every possible "taker" of his offer, public revocation suffices. It is even effective against a person who has not seen the advertisement and who later comes forward with information about Jake.

Methods do exist for taming this seemingly unlimited power of revocation by the Joes of the world. Joan may prohibit Joe's power of revocation by forcing Joe to promise to keep the offer open for a stated time. The promise itself will not protect Joan from revocation. But if she takes an **option** on the car, Joe is legally bound to hold the offer open for the period of time agreed upon. Joan will have to pay Joe for the option; but once she does so, he cannot sell the car to anyone else during the option period without breaching this option contract. Usually, Joan is under no obligation to exercise the option. If she does not, Joe can keep the money or other consideration paid to him for the option. If Joan does exercise the option, normally the money paid for the option will be subtracted from the purchase price. Depending on the bargaining position of the parties, however, this is not always the case.

Another exception to the rule that an offeror can revoke an offer at any time before acceptance comes from the Uniform Commercial Code, Section 2–205:

> An offer *by a merchant* [emphasis added] to buy or sell goods which by its terms gives assurance that it will be held open is not revocable, for lack of consideration, during the time stated, or if no time is stated, for a reasonable time, but in no event may such period of irrevocability exceed three months.

The Code demands that merchants, as professionals, keep their word even if they have been given no consideration for their assurances. Simply put, the Code dramatically changes the common law doctrine regarding the offeror's right to revoke when the offeror is a **merchant** and the other provisions of Section 2–205 have been met.

Lastly, the doctrine of **promissory estoppel** may prohibit offerors from revoking their offers. Under this theory, offerors will be prevented (estopped) from asserting a defense otherwise available to them (generally that they as common law offerors have the right to revoke the offer). In order for Joan, the offeree in our earlier example, to assert this doctrine successfully, she must show (1) that Joe, the offeror, promised or represented to her that he would hold the offer open; (2) that she relied on these promises or representations; (3) that she suffered a detriment thereby (maybe she passed up another car because she thought she would get Joe's); and (4) that injustice can be avoided

Option A privilege given to the offeree, for consideration, to accept an offe at any time during a prese period, with the understanding that the offer cannot be revoked during the stated period; a contract to keep an offer open for some agreed-upon time period

Merchant A person who regularly deals in goods of the kind or has the knowledge or skill peculiar to the practices or goods involved in the transaction

Promissory estoppel A doctrine that prohibits a promisor from denying the making of a promise or from escaping the liability for that promise because of the justifiable reliance of the promisee that the . promise would be kept

only by forcing the offeror to leave the offer open. In several cases, plaintiffs have used this doctrine to cut off the offeror's power of revocation.

Thus far, we have dwelt on the offeror's power to terminate the offer. The offeree, of course, may refuse the offer and thereby terminate it. This power of termination is called **rejection.** Like revocations, rejections are not effective until communicated by the offeree to the offeror. Thus, Joan may reject Joe's offer by telling Joe she is no longer interested in the car.

The usual rule holds that an offer cannot later be accepted after lapse, revocation, or rejection, because after these events the offer has expired. However, if the parties are nonetheless still willing to deal, there may be a valid agreement subsequent to one of these events. The parties generally are not obligated to continue the transaction, though, unless they find it advantageous to do so.

For a good example of some of the concepts about which we have been learning, including the application of promissory estoppel in a real life context, read the next case.

Rejection A refusal to accept what is offered

Zeman v. Lufthansa German Airlines
699 P.2d 1274 (Alaska 1985)

Zeman was a contractor who in October, 1978, had offered to build a thirty-six-unit building for Lufthansa German Airlines' (Lufthansa's) accommodations for its personnel in Anchorage. Lufthansa in January, 1979, had sent Zeman a letter saying "as soon as we are able to convince ourselves that the completion of the building will be within a fortnight, the agreement we have in mind can be signed." Zeman responded that he was confident he could meet the occupancy date required and that he looked forward to entering into an agreement with Lufthansa. Zeman proceeded with the construction of the building intended for Lufthansa. He also consented to a judgment against himself for delinquent payments on the property acquired for the building owing to his belief that Lufthansa's signing of the lease would provide funds for paying off these delinquencies. However, Lufthansa informed him in late July, 1979, that the airline would not be staying in Zeman's building. Zeman could not find other renters and therefore, in late 1979, lost the building to the bank that had financed the construction. Zeman thereafter sued Lufthansa for breach of contract and promissory estoppel. The lower court granted Lufthansa's motion for summary judgment.

FACTS

Did Zeman have a binding contract with Lufthansa? If not, could promissory estoppel be applied against Lufthansa to force the airline to live up to the alleged agreement with Zeman?

ISSUE

Summary judgment was inappropriate because substantial issues of fact existed as to the interpretation of certain ambiguous letters between the parties. Thus, the case was **remanded** to the trial court for a determination of whether there was mutual assent between the parties and of certain facts to ascertain whether Zeman alternatively would be able to pursue his promissory estoppel theory.

HOLDING

Remanded Sent back to an inferior court for further action

REASONING   The trial court had found that there was no mutual assent between the parties, that there was instead only a nonbinding agreement to agree. Yet because the record in this case had contained evidence that could reasonably be interpreted to indicate definiteness as to mutual assent and material terms, a reversal of the summary judgment as to these issues and a remand of the case for trial was necessary. Moreover, it was not clear whether Zeman had substantially changed his position in reliance on any of Lufthansa's statements. Zeman, in order to make out a case of promissory estoppel, must be able to show that: (1) the action induced amounted to a substantial change of position; (2) it was either actually foreseen or reasonably foreseeable by the promisor; (3) an actual promise was made and itself induced the action or **forbearance** in reliance thereon; and (4) enforcement would be necessary in the interest of justice. Zeman had argued that he had undergone substantial changes of position in reliance on Lufthansa's statements even though he had always intended to build the apartment complex. Thus, a remand of the case to the lower court was necessary to determine the substantiality of the costs associated with accelerated financing for the project and with furnishing the apartments for Lufthansa's special requests. If either of these costs proved substantial, Zeman could pursue the promissory estoppel theory. Otherwise, he could not.

Forbearance   A refraining from action

ACCEPTANCE

Acceptance is the usual mode of terminating an offer. As noted earlier, this represents a significant moment for the offeror and offeree because they now have an agreement. Barring problems with consideration, capacity, genuineness of assent, legality, or proper form, a binding contract now exists.

Acceptance involves the *offeree's assent to all the terms of the offer.* Because this is so, the offeree's intention to be bound to the total offer must be clear. Hence, the offeree's uncommunicated mental reservations will not be binding on the offeror. As with offers, courts apply the objective test to see whether the acceptance is valid. That the acceptance is oral, written, or implied (such as through an act like cashing a check) generally does not affect its validity, so long as the offer has been communicated to the offeree (or the offeree's agent), and it is the offeree (or the offeree's agent) who accepts. The case that follows illustrates these points.

Moore v. Kuehn
602 S.W.2d 713 (Mo. App. 1980)

FACTS   After fire had damaged Kuehn's building, Moore was contacted by an insurance adjuster employed by the company with which Kuehn had coverage about a written estimate for the necessary repair work. The adjuster approved Moore's estimate of $7600 and instructed Moore to submit a written proposal to Kuehn in that amount. When Moore did so, Kuehn told him that he, Kuehn, wanted to look over the proposal more closely before signing it. However, he told Moore, "The roof ought to be fixed, so get on it." Moore proceeded to do all the repairs suggested in the proposal.

Kuehn retained his copy of the proposal but never signed it. After the completion of the work, the insurer settled with the Kuehns for $12,069.48, based on Moore's $7600.00 estimate and the separate estimates of two other companies that had aided in the restoration of the building. Kuehn received a check in the amount of $12,069.48 and wrote out checks to the three companies involved in the rebuilding. Moore's check from Kuehn, however, was in the amount of only $5500. Kuehn assured him that the balance of $2100 would be paid when Moore finished a small number of specified items that needed completion or correction. Moore did so, apparently to Kuehn's satisfaction, but was thereafter told by Kuehn that he could not pay him owing to insufficient funds. Moore's subsequent extrajudicial attempts to recover the claimed balance due and the payment for extras were unsuccessful. Kuehn claimed there was no contract between him and Moore for the completed repairs and the extras.

Was there a valid contract between Kuehn and Moore due to Kuehn's acceptance of Moore's proposal regarding repairs?

ISSUE

Yes. There was such a contract, so Moore was awarded $2531 in damages.

HOLDING

It is a well-settled rule of law that a written offer may be orally accepted. The result is an oral contract embodying the terms of the writing. In light of this rule, there could be little doubt that Moore and Kuehn had entered into an express oral contract for the repair of the roof. Upon receiving the written proposal, Kuehn had told Moore, "The roof ought to be fixed, so get on it." The only offer made to Kuehn at that point, and the only offer to which his acceptance could conceivably have had reference, involved Kuehn's property. The terms of that writing necessarily controlled the oral contract established at that point. Moreover, Kuehn's silent acquiescence in and acceptance of Moore's performance of the other repair work listed in the proposal constituted an implied acceptance of the contract as it related to those items. The manifestation of acceptance of an offer need not be made only by the spoken or written word; it may also come through the offeree's conduct or failure to act. The evidence indicated that the writing was the sole offer made by Moore to Kuehn; that Kuehn was aware of the terms of that offer; that he instructed Moore to complete one of the items proposed; that he subsequently permitted Moore, without objection, to complete all the work proposed in the writing and in fact cooperated with him in one facet of the job; and that he accepted the benefits of Moore's performance. There was no evidence that Kuehn had either questioned the necessity of any of the proposed repairs or contested the proposed contract price. In view of this evidence, Kuehn's contemporaneous refusals to sign the proposal were such that they indicated that he had in fact impliedly assented to Moore's full performance in accordance with the proposal. Consequently, the trial court was justified in finding a contract to have existed between the litigants for the repairs listed in the proposal.

REASONING

Under common law rules, an acceptance has to be not only clear but also unconditional. This is called the *mirror image* or *matching-ribbons rule* of common law. In other words, the acceptance must match, term by term, the

Mirror Image Rule

provisions in the offer. Any deviation from these terms, whether by alteration, addition, or omission, makes the acceptance invalid and tantamount to a rejection of the offer originally made.

Any deviation from the terms of the offer brings about a qualified acceptance, known as a *counteroffer*. Counteroffers terminate offers unless the original offeror is willing to accept the terms of the counteroffer. As we have seen in other contexts, such offerors are not obligated to do so unless they still want to deal. Therefore, if you desire to enter into a contract with the offeror, you should pay close attention to the language of the acceptance. Mere inquiries, requests, and terms implied by law, if part of the acceptance, do not invalidate it. Thus, if Joan says, "I'll take the car at $2000 as you offered, but I'd like you to throw in the snow tires," we probably have a valid acceptance (Joan's added statement is a request). Contrast this with Joan's saying, "I accept *if* you throw in the snow tires." The latter statement sounds more like a provision or a condition and may make the purported acceptance legally ineffective unless Joe is prepared to let Joan have the snow tires as part of the deal.

Note the following case in which the court applied the mirror image rule in concluding that the writings reflected a counteroffer and thus the lack of any mutual assent to the terms of the purported agreement.

Loeb v. *Gray*
475 N.E.2d 1342 (III. App. 1985)

FACTS

Reformation An equitable remedy whereby the court changes the wording of a contract to remove a mistake and to make the agreement conform to the terms to which the parties have originally agreed

The Loebs sought **reformation** of a contract for the sale of real estate and for **specific performance** of the contract as reformed. The real estate purchase agreement the Loebs had signed as purchasers gave them the right to lease the land for oil, gas, and other minerals without the consent of the sellers, the Grays. The real estate listing agreement, however, reserved to each of the sellers one-fourth of the mineral rights during the lifetime of each, including the exclusive power to execute oil and gas leases.

ISSUE

Should the court grant reformation of the agreement involving the Loebs and the Grays?

HOLDING

No. It could not grant reformation as a remedy because no contract existed between the parties.

REASONING

To constitute a contract between two parties, the alleged agreement must manifest the parties' mutual assent to the essential terms and conditions of the subject about which they are contracting. For a contract to exist, there must be an offer and an acceptance; and to create a binding contract the acceptance must comply strictly with the terms of the offer. An acceptance containing terms that vary from those offered constitutes a rejection of the original offer and becomes a counterproposal that must be accepted by the original offeror before a valid contract is formed. Here, the terms of the real estate listing agreement gave the sellers the exclusive right to execute oil and gas leases with respect to the property in question, whereas under the terms of the real estate purchase agreement the buyers would have full power and authority to do so. The inconsistency reflected in these two documents on this essential term of the alleged contract revealed that no meeting of the minds of the parties had occurred as to the power to execute oil and gas leases. Without mutual assent, there could be no contract formation. And, without a meeting of the minds, there was nothing to reform.

Specific performance
An equitable remedy provided by the courts when monetary damages would be insufficient and the object of the contract is unique and in which the court orders performance of the contract exactly as agreed

The Uniform Commercial Code continues its relaxation of common law rules in Section 2–207 by permitting a contract to arise between the parties even if the offeree adds terms or includes different terms in the purported acceptance. This provision of the UCC reflects the drafters' knowledge of commercial realities, specifically the fact that buyers and sellers in commercial settings generally exchange their respective forms (for example, purchase order forms or order acknowledgment forms), which may contain contradictory terms. Rather than hamper commercial dealings by judging the inconsistent terms under the common law rule that any variances in the material terms of the offer and acceptance constitute a counteroffer and hence a rejection of the original offer, the UCC drafters permit a contract to arise between the parties if the offeree has definitely indicated his or her acceptance of the offer. Section 2–207 furthermore sets out a scheme for determining what the operative terms of the contract will be in these circumstances. For instance, between merchants the additional terms automatically become part of the contract without the offeror's consent unless the original offer expressly requires the offeree to accept the terms of the offer; the additional terms materially alter the contract (that is, they would unfairly surprise or be unduly oppressive of the offeror); or the offeror has notified the offeree that he or she will not accept the new terms. This same section of the Code additionally states that conduct by both parties that recognizes the existence of a contract is sufficient to establish a contract for sale even though the writings of the parties do not otherwise establish a contract. You will learn more about these concepts in succeeding chapters. But you should at this point at least have some appreciation of the alterations of common law rules embodied in the Code and the underlying rationales for these changes.

Besides accepting unconditionally, the offeree must avoid one other pitfall in order to effect a valid acceptance: an offer must be accepted in exactly the mode specified by the offeror in the offer. Thus, should the offeror say that acceptance must occur by a telegram, a letter would not be an effective acceptance. Similarly, if the offer says, "Acceptance required by return mail," an acceptance placed in the mail two days later would be invalid. Lastly, when the

Manner and Time of Acceptance

offer says, "Acceptance effective when received," a contract will not arise until the offeror receives the acceptance.

Nevertheless, the offeror may not care to stipulate the mode necessary for a valid acceptance. In such cases the offeree can use any reasonable medium of communication as long as he or she acts within a reasonable time. Usually the same medium as is used by the offeror is a reasonable, or authorized, mode of communication. Hence, in the absence of a stipulated method of acceptance, if the offeror makes the offer via the mails, mailing an acceptance should also be reasonable and thus valid. Another medium — even the telephone — may be reasonable, and therefore authorized, if this medium has been used in the parties' prior dealings or is sanctioned by local or industry custom.

Use of an authorized mode takes on particular significance because in most states acceptance is effective at the time of dispatch (mailing, wiring, and the like). This is called the *mailbox* or *implied agency rule* because the post office or telegraph office is deemed the agent of the offeror. To illustrate, assume that the offeror has not stipulated the mode of acceptance in the mailed offer sent to the offeree on 28 September. If the offeror subsequently attempts to revoke the offer on 1 October, and a valid acceptance has been mailed by the offeree on 30 September, there is a contract as of 30 September, even though the offeror does not receive the acceptance until 1 October. The law treats the post office as the offeror's agent and thus concludes that the offeror "received" the acceptance on 30 September, the offeree's mailing date. Because letters sometimes never arrive, it will be advisable for the offeree to secure postal or telegraphic receipts in order to prove after the fact the date on which the acceptance actually has been dispatched. In contrast, where an unauthorized mode has been used, the strict rule states that the offeror must receive the acceptance in order for it to be effective; the mailbox rule will be inapplicable. Some courts will enforce the agreement if the acceptance, though via an unauthorized mode, is timely, especially if the offeror's language about the mode to be used can be construed as a suggestion rather than a stipulation or condition. The Uniform Commercial Code lends credence to such decisions by sanctioning acceptances "in any manner and by any medium reasonable in the circumstances" (Section 2–206[1][a]).

As you can see, the time of contract formation becomes crucial. The mailbox rule allows acceptance, and hence a contract, to occur even before the offeror knows of the acceptance. Such acceptances cut off the offeror's otherwise almost unlimited right to revoke, because revocation must occur before acceptance in order for an attempted revocation to be effective. Offerors can curtail the effect of the mailbox rule by stipulating that acceptances will not be effective until received by them. Note, too, that in any event, the mailbox rule applies only to acceptances: revocations and rejections do not take effect until they are communicated to (that is, are received by) the offeree and offeror, respectively. Revocations and rejections do not become legally binding upon dispatch, as acceptances sometimes do.

1. What does a court mean by *mutual assent*?
2. Explain the phrase *objective theory of contracts.*
3. Briefly state the common law rules surrounding a valid offer.
4. Name and define the ways in which an offer can terminate.
5. Is an advertisement a bona fide offer? Why or why not?
6. In what situations will lapse occur by operation of law?
7. Discuss the common law rules of revocation.
8. Name and list the elements for each of the methods available for terminating the offeror's power of revocation.
9. What are counteroffers, and how do they arise?
10. Explain the term *mailbox rule* and its significance.

1. Sandra Speckel was injured when a car driven by Laurri Perkins collided with a truck in which Sandra was a passenger. In December, 1983, Speckel's attorney, Stephen Eckman, demanded the insurance policy limits of $50,000 to settle the case. In January, 1984, Perkins's attorney, Donald Wheat, informed Eckman that he had sent Eckman's demand to Perkins's insurance company for consideration even though he himself thought Wheat's settlement demand was too high. There was no more correspondence between the parties until about a week before the scheduled trial, when Wheat sent the following letter, dated 14 April 1984, to Eckman:

Dear Mr. Eckman:

In reviewing my file concerning this claim and the upcoming trial, I note that we have a demand in our file for policy limits of $50,000.00. While I agree that the case has some value, I cannot agree that this is a limits case.

At this point in time I have authority to offer you $50,000.00 in settlement of your claim against my client and her mother. I would appreciate hearing from you at your earliest convenience and would be pleased to carry any offer you may wish to make back to my client's insurance company for their consideration.

Very truly yours,
/s/Donald A. Wheat/cjh

Wheat never saw this letter, which his secretary had signed, and was unaware that his secretary had erroneously typed $50,000 rather than $15,000 as he had dictated. Eckman accepted the offer of $50,000 on behalf of his client on 17 April 1984. Eckman argued that the letter was a valid offer, enforceable as a contract upon Eckman's acceptance of it, because Wheat's subjective intention was irrelevant. Wheat contended that the internal inconsistency in the wording of his letter imposed a duty of inquiry on the offeree when factors raising a presumption of error existed. Who should win? (*Speckel by Speckel v. Perkins,* 364 N.W.2d 890 [Minn. App. 1985].)

2. Kern's Bakery decided to change the wrapping material used to package its products and discussed the proposed changes with R-P Packaging's representatives. On 28 December 1977, Kern's plant manager gave R-P's representative a verbal "order" for cellophane wrap. R-P's 4 January 1978 order acknowledgment form contained specifications, delivery instructions, an order date, and quantity. "Later" was typed in the space for the contract price; "W/A" was written in the space entitled "acknowledgment date." At the bottom of the acknowledgment form was typed: "Produce printing plates per artwork sent to Frank Tarpley, but first send photostats with color stripe to customers for approval before etching." R-P's representative testified that "W/A" stood for "will advise," which meant R-P did not have the customer's approval to proceed. R-P did not proceed with the artwork because Kern never approved it. In the meantime, on 3 January 1978, Kern's was purchased by Flowers Baking Company. As part of the contract for sale, Kern's represented that all pending contracts of more than $5000 to which it was a party were listed in the agreement. Kern's further agreed to indemnify Flowers (make up any losses suffered by Flowers) against all liability arising from any misrepresentation by Kern's. The order for cellophane from R-P was not listed. R-P's order acknowledgment arrived after Flowers had assumed control and was never received by Kern's. Flowers ultimately agreed to buy some wrapping material from R-P, accepted it, but then rejected it when the material was too short for the bakery trays. R-P sued Kern's and Flowers for $13,357.11, the purchase price of the packaging material. The court ruled there was no contract between R-P and Kern's under the UCC. Flowers argued there was sufficient evidence under UCC Section 2–204 to prove a contract existed between R-P and Kern's. Who was correct? (*Flowers Baking Co. of Lynchburg, Incorporated* v. *R-P Packaging Incorporated,* 329 S.E.2d 462 [Va. 1985].)

3. The Geremias bought a car through a credit union. Their contract with this institution obligated them to keep fire and collision insurance on the car. The contract further provided that if the Geremias were unable to maintain this insurance, the credit union could pay the premium and could apply this payment to the Geremias' loan. In October the Geremias were financially unable to pay their premium when due. Mrs. Geremia notified the treasurer of the credit union of this fact and told the treasurer to go ahead and pay the premium. When the Geremias' car was demolished, they discovered that the overdue premium had not been paid and that the insurance company would not indemnify them for their loss. The Geremias claimed they should not have to pay the credit union for the balance owed on the car because of the credit union's failure to pay the insurance premium. Should the court apply the doctrine of promissory estoppel to prevent the credit union from recovering on its loan contract with the Geremias? (*East Providence Credit Union v. Geremia*, 239 A.2d 725 [R.I. 1968].)

4. A contractor and supplier entered into a contract for carpeting being placed in condominiums by the contractor. Some of the orders involved carpeting of a higher quality in response to requests from certain condominium owners. The supplier sent nine bills of lading for upgraded carpeting to the contractor, and these bills of lading were signed by the contractor's employees. The contractor did not object to the supplier until nearly a year after the last shipment had been installed in the condominiums. The contractor, however, later asserted that he had a contractual obligation to pay only for basic carpeting and that he was not liable for the upgraded carpeting. Was the contractor correct? (*Barwick Pacific Carpet Co. v. Kam Hawaii Construction, Inc.*, 630 P.2d 638 [Haw. App. 1981].)

5. Klein, a construction equipment wholesaler, sued Pitman Manufacturing for breach of contract on its alleged failure to sell Klein certain fully assembled truck bodies. Pitman responded that Klein's second purchase order to purchase unassembled bodies was rejected by a Pitman counteroffer to sell the unassembled truck bodies at a reduced rate if Klein would first satisfy the balance owed from the first purchase order. Pitman argued that since Klein had not accepted this counteroffer, Pitman had the right to cancel the original contract. Who was right? (*Edward Klein Truck and Heavy Equipment Company, Inc. v. Pitman Manufacturing Company*, 512 F. Supp. 101 [W.D. Pa. 1981].)

6. In 1984, Koch had enrolled in a group insurance policy that provided $100,000 in accidental death benefits. In 1985, American Heritage Life Insurance Company (American Heritage) sent Koch a premium notice that included an application for increasing the death benefits under the policy to $150,000. The application provided that this increased coverage would "become effective upon the first day of the month following the receipt of [Koch's] premium payment." Koch signed that application on 26 March 1985, and on 29 March 1985, mailed the application and the check for the additional premium to American Heritage's agent, Orsdel. Orsdel received the application and additional premium on 3 April 1985. Koch subsequently died in an automobile accident on 16 April 1985. When American Heritage paid Mrs. Koch only $100,000, she argued that the mailbox rule made the post office the agent of American Heritage and that her husband's mailing the letter on 29 March 1985, constituted the company's "receipt" of the premium payment so as to validate the additional coverage as of 1 April 1985, prior to Mr. Koch's death. Should a court find this argument persuasive? (*American Heritage Life Insurance Company v. Koch*, 721 S.W.2d 611 [Tex. App. 1986].)

7. The Simses had sought the assistance of a Baton Rouge store owner, Betty

Lou Stokes, in opening a retail women's lingerie shop in Metairie, Louisiana. The agreement between the parties set out Stokes's responsibilities which included, among other things, that Stokes be present for a minimum number of days at the Metairie Store "unless both parties agree otherwise." The Simses ultimately sued for a $7500 payment they had made to Stokes on the ground that she had only worked in the Metairie store for one day and thus had breached their agreement. Stokes argued that the Simses knew that the language "unless both parties agree otherwise" was an escape clause insisted upon by Stokes because she knew her daughter's complications from a pregnancy might make Stokes's traveling to Metairie difficult. The Simses contended that Stokes had asked for the clause "in case things came up," and they denied that they knew specifically what Stokes had meant by this phrase. The Simses further stated that it was their understanding that if something did come up, the parties would mutually agree that Stokes could be absent. Was there a contract between the Simses and Stokes? (*Sims-Smith, Ltd.* v. *Stokes,* 466 So.2d 480 [La. App. 1985].)

8. Wheeler made an offer on property owned by Ronald D. Woods and Debra Woods Lane. The offer required the sellers to accept the offer in writing on or before midnight on 11 March 1984, in order for the offer to become binding. Woods and Land ultimately attempted to accept Wheeler's offer by calling Western Union and sending two mailgrams indicating their acceptance on March 12. Wheeler received these mailgrams on March 13. When Wheeler found out that Woods and Land had sold the property to another purchaser, he sued the sellers owing to his belief that he had an enforceable contract with them. Was his reasoning correct? (*Wheeler* v. *Woods,* 723 P.2d 1224 [Wyo. 1986].)

9. W.E. Gilbert & Associates (Gilbert) sued South Carolina National Bank for breach of an alleged contract for construction management services. In early 1981 the bank had developed a construction plan that it tentatively planned to implement over the ensuing year and a half. The bank had solicited applications from firms that desired to be the construction manager for the bank's projects and selected Gilbert. However, three months later, the bank terminated its relationship with Gilbert. Gilbert then sued the bank, arguing that a Gilbert brochure, a letter from the bank that lacked information about either the number of projects for which the bank would need management services or the compensation to be paid, and a letter from Gilbert that proposed a fee schedule but left for future reference the compensation to be paid for smaller projects established a contract. Would you agree with Gilbert? (*W. E. Gilbert & Associates* v. *South Carolina National Bank,* 330 S.E.2d 307 [S.C. App. 1985].)

10. On 16 July 1982, while serving as an inmate at the Essex County Jail, Caldwell Williams set himself on fire. As a result, county personnel transported Williams to the Saint Barnabas Medical Center (St. Barnabas),

where he remained a patient until 2 September 1982. St. Barnabas had no express agreement with the county because it was not the hospital county officials ordinarily used for the treatment of inmates; county personnel had taken Williams there solely because of St. Barnabas's burn unit. When St. Barnabas contacted a county official about Williams's bill on July 19, the official initially agreed that the county was liable for the bill. But on July 20, the official called St. Barnabas to inform the medical center that Williams's sentence had been suspended as of July 19 and that the county would accept liability only for charges incurred through 19 July 1982. Williams remained in St. Barnabas's through 2 September 1982; and his medical bills totaled almost $54,000. When neither Williams nor the county had paid the amount due, St. Barnabas sued the county. Should a court accept the county's contention that its obligation to pay for Williams's care terminated on the suspension of his sentence on 19 July 1982? (*St. Barnabas Medical Center* v. *Essex County,* 543 A.2d 34 [N.J. 1988].)

CHAPTER 10

Consideration:
The Basis
of the Bargain

THE BARGAIN AS A CONTRACT THEORY

Despite the rather checkered history that surrounds its principles, no doctrine of common law is as firmly entrenched today as the concept of *consideration*. Though it is shrouded in historical traditions, we nevertheless must come to grips with its tenets if we are to understand modern contract law.

Remember that early in the history of contracts the parties underwent elaborate rituals, such as sealing their contracts with wax and placing their insignia in the wax, in order to demonstrate their willingness to be bound to the terms embodied in the agreement. Although few contracts are under seal today, owing largely to the inconvenience of formalizing every contract, the idea that the parties ought to be actually bargaining and exchanging something of value rather than merely making empty promises has lingered. Filling this ideological gap was the evolution of the notion that the presence of consideration indicates an exchange of something of value by the parties, resulting in an agreement between the parties. Thus, consideration shows that some obligation or duty worthy of a court's protection actually exists. It also establishes that the parties are acting deliberately and intend to bind themselves to the terms of the agreement. Because it rids contracts of excessive formality while encouraging exchanges between people, the doctrine of consideration initially appears well suited to commercial and economic activity and hence to our study of business law. Nevertheless, some of the legal results under this doctrine seem quite harsh. For this reason, theories have emerged that permit an agreement to be binding in some cases despite the lack of consideration. Your overall comprehension will increase, however, if you try to remember the historical context surrounding this quaint doctrine.

Among the many definitions of the term *consideration,* one of the most common states that consideration is *a* **waiver,** *or promised waiver, of rights bargained for in exchange for a promise.* It always consists of either a benefit to the promisor or a detriment to the promisee, bargained for and given in exchange for a promise. You should not be surprised to see the words *bargain, promise,* and *exchange* playing such a prominent role in this definition, given what we have discussed previously. Consideration usually takes the form of money, but it may consist of an intangible, noneconomic benefit or detriment or anything of "value" to the parties.

DEFINITION

Waiver The voluntary surrender of a legal right; the intentional surrender of a right

Consideration as an Act or a Forbearance

Implicit in this doctrine is the necessity of the parties' bargaining over some present event or object and exchanging something of value in order to bind themselves to do (or to refrain from doing) something. It is important, then, to check the parties' language closely. Words that sound like promises may actually be **illusory** ones because the parties have not really committed themselves in any manner to the bargain. If one party never really agrees to do anything (for example, if Sharon Hall says, "I will sell you my car for $8000 *if I feel like it*"), the promise is illusory and unenforceable because no consideration is present.

Illusory Fallacious; nominal as opposed to substantial; of false appearance

In unilateral contracts, consideration manifests itself in an act or a forbearance to act (the consideration comes from refraining from engaging in a legal act). For example, suppose your parents promise you a new car if you will earn straight As in school. If you do, the agreement is supported by consideration and will be enforceable in a court of law, assuming you live in a state where family members can sue each other if they breach (that is, fail to perform) this agreement.

Let us apply our definition of consideration to see why the agreement is enforceable. You waived your right to unlimited leisure time in exchange for your parents' promise. You all bargained, or "dickered," about the straight As, so the car is not a gift to you. You must do something (study more than you

Promisors Those who make a promise or commitment

Promisee One to whom a promise or commitment has been made

would like) or refrain from doing something (watching television and engaging in other leisure activities) to earn it. Furthermore, your parents, the **promisors,** received a benefit (the satisfaction of knowing you are an honor student) while you, the **promisee,** suffered a detriment (studying hard all year) as a result of this bargain. Your act of making perfect grades has therefore been given in exchange for your parents' promise to buy you a car. Note that the benefit they have received has no dollars-and-cents economic value, yet the benefit is sufficient consideration to support their side of the bargain. They will receive what they asked to receive.

Consideration as a Promise to Act or to Forbear

The example we have just used is a unilateral contract. The analysis would be the same, however, if you had *promised* to earn straight As in exchange for your parents' promise to buy the car. A bilateral contract would have been created, with the respective promises constituting the consideration to support the agreement, as long as the promises are genuine, not illusory.

Taking our example one step further, if your parents breach this contract and you want to sue them, they may bargain with you about dropping the suit. If they promise to pay you $1000 if you do not sue, in exchange for your promise to forgo legal action, you will have made another enforceable contract. You know the reason: a promise to act or to forbear from a certain action, bargained for and given in exchange for another promise, is consideration. Therefore, you should be able to convince a court to force your parents to pay, should they refuse to do so.

However, as the following case indicates, forbearance alone may be insufficient to constitute consideration if the party's forbearance is based on a worthless claim.

State ex rel Ludwick v. Bryant
697 P.2d 858 (Kan. 1985)

FACTS   Virginia Bryant owned and operated a day-care service called Tender Loving Care, Inc. (TLC). On 31 July 1981, the check written on TLC's account by Bryant as part of the corporation's second-quarter wage report to the Kansas Department of Human Resources (Human Resources) was returned for insufficient funds. TLC stopped all operations in August, 1981. In October, 1981, Bryant individually filed a petition in bankruptcy and listed Human Resources as a creditor. On 29 April 1982, Bryant received a discharge in bankruptcy, but the debt owed by TLC to Human Resources was not allowed in the bankruptcy action because the bankruptcy court held Bryant was not personally liable for the taxes owed by TLC to the state. On 12 July 1982, a representative of Human Resources asked Bryant to come to its offices. While there, she was told she needed to pay the $231.79 debt of TLC. When she mentioned she had received a discharge in bankruptcy, department officials told her that she needed to pay the debt, since state unemployment taxes could not be discharged in bankruptcy. She eventually signed a personal guarantee to pay off TLC's debt on an installment basis. Bryant later contacted her attorney, who informed the department that the debt covered by the personal guarantee had been discharged in bankruptcy and that, further, the guarantee lacked consideration. Human Resources argued that consideration was present, since both Bryant and TLC had benefited from the guarantee's provisions relating to mode of payment and from the department's resultant forbearance from suit on the debt.

Was Bryant's guarantee to pay TLC's debt supported by consideration so as to create a valid contract between Bryant and Human Resources?

ISSUE

No. There was no consideration present in Bryant's guarantee because Human Resources' forbearance to sue Bryant and TLC was based on a worthless claim and as such provided no consideration to support the contract.

HOLDING

Kansas follows the traditional rule that any forbearance to prosecute or defend a claim or action, or to do an act that one is not legally bound to perform, is usually a sufficient consideration for a contract based thereon, unless the claim or defense is obviously invalid, worthless, or frivolous. Here, the debt owed by TLC was incapable of either enforcement or collection, making Human Resources' agreement to forbear without value. Hence, there was no consideration to support Bryant's execution of the guarantee.

REASONING

Going back to our earlier example, can your parents win if they try to argue that $8000 for a new car is too much, or that you are really doing nothing (that is, becoming an honor student is hardly a detriment to you) to secure your side of the bargain? They can try, but courts generally will not be receptive to such arguments. The classic rule states that courts will not inquire into the adequacy of the consideration. Courts instead will assume that the parties themselves are the best judges of how much their bargain is worth and whether their performances are substantially equivalent. Courts ordinarily will not "second guess" the parties after the fact. The following case illustrates this important principle.

Adequacy of Consideration

Buckingham v. Wray
366 N.W.2d 753 (Neb. 1985)

In November, 1979, John C. Wray II, an Omaha, Nebraska, auto parts dealer, and C. Norris Buckingham entered into a written agreement whereby Wray agreed to stock and maintain an inventory for an auto parts store, K-B Auto, owned by Buckingham in Carson, Iowa. The contract also required Wray to purchase the K-B inventory at 90 percent of the inventory's original cost. The contract provided that in addition Wray would be reimbursed for his travel to and from Buckingham's Iowa store but

FACTS

would not receive any compensation for his services to K-B Auto. Wray, moreover, could receive discounts from wholesale suppliers on purchases of inventory for K-B Auto under the terms of the contract. Unfortunately, K-B Auto eventually went out of business; and Buckingham sought performance of the contract provision relating to Wray's purchase of the K-B Auto inventory. Unable to locate Wray, Buckingham brought suit against Wray concerning the inventory that Buckingham had been unable to liquidate when K-B Auto had closed. Wray argued there was no valid contract between him and Buckingham because the consideration to support their agreement had been inadequate.

ISSUE   Was the parties' agreement supported by consideration, even though by its terms Wray was to receive no compensation for any services he rendered to K-B Auto?

HOLDING   Yes. There was sufficient value in the promises made by the parties to constitute adequate consideration to support the agreement between Wray and Buckingham.

REASONING   The general rule is that consideration will be deemed sufficient to support a contract if there is any detriment to the promisee or benefit to the promisor. Moreover, courts generally will not inquire into the adequacy of the consideration for a contract, which fact is left instead to the personal judgment of the parties, unless the inadequacy is so great as to suggest fraud. The lack of compensation for Wray's services did not in itself negate the existence of consideration, since compensation and consideration are neither identical nor synonymous. Valuable consideration to support a contract need not be translatable into dollars and cents. If consideration consists of performance or a promise of performance, which the promisor treats and considers as having value to the promisor, there is sufficient consideration for a contract. The promises of the parties and Wray's ability to receive discounts on purchases for his own stores as a result of the increased wholesale purchases made possible by Buckingham's purchases constituted adequate consideration to support the Buckingham–Wray contract.

There are, however, exceptions to the general rule that courts will not inquire into the adequacy of the consideration. If there is evidence that fraud, duress, undue influence, mistake, or other similar situations may have been present in the formation of the contract, adequacy of consideration becomes a much more significant issue. Courts in these situations may permit one or more of the litigants to back out of the deal. The doctrine of unconscionability (see Section 2–302 of the UCC), which holds that a court may refuse to enforce a contract if it is shockingly unfair or oppressive, can in some circumstances also form a further basis for overturning bargains where the consideration appears to be grossly inadequate. But remember that courts do not routinely use this rationale to overturn bargaining between parties.

CONSIDERATION IN SPECIAL CONTEXTS   Let us now look at the doctrine of consideration in the special contexts of contracts for the sale of goods, suretyship contracts, liquidated and unliquidated debt situations, and composition agreements.

As we learned in Chapter 9, the "firm offer" provision of the Uniform Commercial Code (Section 2–205) states that an offer to buy or sell goods by a merchant who gives assurance in writing that the offer will be held open may be irrevocable for a period of up to three months even if no consideration has been paid to the offeror. Intended to encourage commercial activity that is free from hagglings about "options," this provision dramatically changes the common law rules about consideration. Thus, even in the absence of consideration, courts will enforce a UCC "firm offer." The same is true of modifications under the UCC: they, too, are enforceable without consideration (Section 2–209[1]). In this context, we should refer again to output and requirements contracts, two types of sales contracts mentioned earlier in Chapter 9. Unless the language of these contracts indicates otherwise, courts ordinarily enforce output and requirements contracts as being supported by consideration. These courts reason that consideration is present in the form of the respective detriments suffered by the buyer and seller in obligating themselves to deal exclusively with the other party in these circumstances. The promises undergirding such contracts, then, are nonillusory, making the bargains enforceable.

Contracts for the Sale of Goods

In contrast to some situations in the UCC in which the requirement of consideration is relaxed, consideration is definitely required in suretyship contracts. Such contracts always involve three parties: a principal debtor, a creditor, and a surety. the surety agrees to be liable to the creditor in the event of the principal debtor's **default.** This is a typical commercial transaction. To illustrate, let us assume that Chan Wai (the principal debtor) wishes to buy a new car. She may seek financing from a credit union (the creditor), which in turn may require that she bolster her credit (and decrease its risk) by having another person (such as her father or mother) sign the note as a surety.

    If the principal debtor and surety simultaneously promise to pay the promissory note, these promises will be supported by a single consideration (the loan of money to Chan Wai by the credit union). Both promises will be supported by consideration and hence will be enforceable. If, in contrast, the credit union loans the money for the car to Chan Wai and *later* asks a surety to promise to pay in the event of her default, this second promise must be supported by new consideration before the surety's promise is legally binding. As we shall learn, Chan Wai's preexisting obligation to the credit union (because the loan has already been made) does not constitute consideration for enforcing the surety's subsequent promise to pay the credit union.

Suretyship Contracts

Default A failure to do what should be done, especially in the performance of a contractual obligation, without legal excuse or justification for the nonperformance

On the same rationale, if one owes a debt to another person, part payment of that debt is not consideration for full discharge of the debt. For instance, assume Jim Hays has his dentist perform a root canal treatment on him. At the outset, the dentist tells Jim the treatment will cost $190, and Jim agrees that this is a fair price. If Jim pays $150, he cannot successfully argue that this part payment is consideration for full discharge of the debt. Put in legal terms, the dentist will be able to argue that Jim is under a preexisting duty to pay the

Liquidated Debts

entire $190. Since neither party has waived any rights and since no bargaining has been done in exchange for this promise to pay $150, there is, by definition, an absence of consideration here. Hence, by the settled rule, Jim is liable for the entire bill, or $190. Central to this discussion is the fact that the debt is *liquidated;* that is, *the amount owed is not disputed.* Jim has agreed to pay $190, and he should not, after the fact, be allowed to escape this obligation. If he could, commercial dealings would be thrown into shambles!

If the dentist has any indication that Jim does not agree that the sum owed is $190 (presumably Jim would argue that he owes a lesser amount), in order to protect her rights fully, she should not cash Jim's check of $150. Instead, she should return it with a note saying she is not agreeing to accept the money as full payment of the debt. If the dentist is strapped for cash, she can cash the check and preserve her rights by endorsing it "with full reservation of all rights." Ideally, though, she should refrain from cashing the check. We shall see why this is true in the next section.

Unliquidated Debts

Contrast the situation in which Jim absolutely agrees that the debt owed to the dentist is $190 with this one. Jim has again agreed to pay $190 for the root canal treatment. He has paid half the fee but continues to have soreness around the gums, and the treated tooth is still sensitive to thermal changes. Although he wants to live up to his obligation to pay his debt, he does not believe he should pay the dentist the entire amount because he is not completely satisfied with the results. At this point, the debt is *unliquidated;* that is, *the precise amount owed is in dispute.* If Jim and the dentist ultimately *agree* on another figure — say $150 — Jim's payment of the $150 is consideration for full discharge of the debt. Once the dentist accepts this payment (for example, by cashing the check), Jim no longer owes her any money.

The difference between this situation and the earlier one in which Jim agreed he was liable for the entire $190 is probably clear. In the latter situation, the parties have waived rights bargained for in exchange for a promise. By so doing, each receives a benefit (Jim, by paying $40 less than he thought he would have to pay; the dentist, by getting most of the $190), and each suffers a detriment (Jim, by believing $150 is still too much; the dentist, by thinking she has lost $40) as a result of the bargained-for promise to pay. This notion of an exchange of rights is a hallmark of consideration.

One last note is appropriate. When Jim and the dentist agree on the $150 sum, technically there is a compromise (of the unliquidated debt) that subsequently has led to a satisfaction and an accord. A *compromise* is the settlement of a disputed claim by the mutual agreement of the parties. That agreement as to the amount is an *accord,* and the fulfillment of the agreement (the payment of the agreed-upon amount) is a *satisfaction.*

Composition Agreements

Unliquidated debt situations form the basis for a court's enforcement of a *composition agreement,* or *an agreement between a debtor and a creditor to accept a smaller percentage of the debt owed in full satisfaction of the claim,* as consideration for full discharge of the debt. Even though we shall not discuss **bankruptcy** until Chapter 31, you probably are aware that the bankruptcy of the debtor poses grave financial risks for the creditor, because in bankruptcy proceedings a creditor ordinarily realizes only a few cents on every dollar owed. Consequently, it is often in the creditor's best interest to give the debtor more time to pay (before the creditor forces the debtor into bankruptcy) or to agree to accept a smaller sum in full cancellation of larger claims through a composition agreement. By way of example, suppose the debtor owes creditors A, B, and C $6000, $4000, and $2000, respectively. The creditors may each agree to accept 50 percent of the respective debts as full satisfaction of their claims against the debtor. Thus, if the debtor pays creditor A $3000, creditor B $2000, and creditor C $1000, none of the three will be able to sue for the remaining amount. Courts analogize the result here to settlements of unliquidated debt situations, where the resultant compromise represents a satisfaction and accord for the debts. Similarly, in composition agreements, payments accepted by the creditors are supported by consideration and thus constitute full discharge of the debts.

Some courts would instead characterize the sums owed to the three creditors as liquidated debts and would find insufficient consideration in the subsequent agreement to justify full discharge of the debts. Ironically, these same courts in the next breath might sanction such agreements on public policy grounds (the debtor's avoidance of bankruptcy and the creditors' realization of partial payment). Whatever the rationale, courts clearly favor composition agreements and therefore enforce them.

Under certain circumstances courts will find a total absence of consideration and will not enforce the agreement that the parties have shaped.

As mentioned earlier, a promise that does not bind the promisor to a commitment is an *illusory promise*. Such promises can be performed without any benefit to the promisor or without any detriment to the promisee and hence are not supported by consideration. A promise "to order such goods as we may wish" or "as we may want from time to time" is not a genuine promise at all; it only appears to set up a binding commitment. Instead, it actually allows the promisor to order nothing. Such "will, wish, or want contracts," as they are often called, are void because they lack consideration. Contracts that purport to reserve an immediate right of arbitrary **cancellation** fall into this category of contracts as well. Because of the potential unfairness of allowing one side to free itself from an agreement to which the other side considers itself bound by merely giving notice of cancellation, courts are hostile to attempted exercises of a right of arbitrary cancellation. Courts therefore try to find some actual or implied limitations on the purported immediate right of arbitrary cancellation so as to make it a nonillusory, or binding, promise. Since consideration would exist for such promises, the agreement would be enforceable.

Bankruptcy An area of law designed to give an "honest debtor" a fresh start; the proceedings undertaken against a person or a firm under the bankruptcy laws

ABSENCE OF CONSIDERATION

Illusory Promises

Cancellation Any action shown on the face of a contract that indicates an intent to destroy the obligation of the contract

Preexisting Duty

As already mentioned briefly, if one performs an act (or refrains from doing something) that one has a preexisting obligation to do (or refrain from doing), settled law holds that such a person has suffered no detriment. Consequently, no consideration is present to support the underlying promise or performance.

Classic examples of these results come from cases involving law enforcement officers. Assume you live next door to a policewoman. Now imagine your neighbor coming to you with this proposition: for a mere $50 she will patrol around your house while you are gone on a trip. Since this sounds like a good deal to you, you agree. But you have second thoughts later and do not pay her. When she sues you in small claims court, she will probably lose because she has a preexisting duty (imposed by law) to try to keep your home free from burglaries. She has suffered no detriment in patrolling around your house, so there is no consideration to support her promise to you.

The following case illustrates the concept that there is no consideration to support a bargain in which one party is only promising to do what he or she already has an obligation to do.

Hurley v. Hurley
615 P.2d 256 (N.M. 1980)

FACTS

On 26 April 1977, the wife filed suit for divorce but later dismissed that lawsuit pursuant to a reconciliation and an alleged contract. In December, 1977, the husband filed for divorce. On appeal of the judgment for divorce, the wife argued that the judge had erred in not finding that she had a cause of action for breach of contract against the husband. She asserted that in return for her forbearance from prosecution of a divorce action in April, 1977, her husband had promised to refrain from infidelity, to be a faithful and providing husband, and to submit to counseling. She contended that these promises exceeded the scope of any existing marital obligations and that the husband's failure to keep these promises constituted a breach of contract for which she was entitled to damages.

ISSUE

Were the husband's promises supported by consideration so as to bring about a binding agreement?

HOLDING

No. The promises were not adequate consideration to create an enforceable contract.

REASONING

The wife's statement of the principle that forbearance from suit is adequate consideration for a contract is correct. However, a promise to do what a party is already obligated by contract or law to do is not sufficient consideration for a promise made in return. In this case, the husband had promised to do no more than what he was legally obligated to do; hence there was no consideration and therefore no breach. Furthermore, New Mexico law prohibits such promises. Indeed, this court itself had previously held that **nuptial** contracts that attempt to alter the legal relations of the parties "are generally held to be void for want of consideration, or against public policy," because it is the policy of this state to foster and protect the marital institution.

Nuptial Pertaining to marriage

Besides obligations or duties imposed by law, preexisting duties may stem from contractual agreements. There are numerous cases dealing with these situations. To use a simple example, suppose G & H Painting Service has contracted with you to paint your basement for $900. Halfway through the job, the crew boss tells you he will dismiss the crew unless you agree to pay him $200 more (he has just seen the latest consumer price index and knows inflation is winning against him). Because you are planning a party two days hence, you grudgingly say yes. The question, of course, is do you have to pay $900 or $1100? based on the doctrine of preexisting obligations, you will generally have to pay only $900, since the firm already owed you the duty of finishing the basement. But if you subsequently want G & H to lay a concrete patio for you, your promise to pay $500 in return for G & H's work on the patio is supported by new consideration—G & H was not obligated to construct the patio as part of your original agreement—and you must pay $500 more for this additional work.

To return to our earlier example, assume now that in the middle of winter there is a freakish humid spell that causes a paint-resistant fungus to grow in your basement. As a result, G & H has to paint the walls three times to cover them. If this condition arose after the firm began the work, most courts would characterize this as an unforeseen or unforeseeable difficulty and would obligate you to pay the higher price. The same would hold true if you and the firm had canceled the original contract and had started anew with different promises and obligations. In both situations, consideration would support the new promises. Strikes, inflation in the prices of raw materials, and lack of access to raw materials do not meet the test of "unforeseen or unforeseeable difficulties"; and new promises extracted on these bases would ordinarily lack consideration and thus be unenforceable.

In the next case, the court upheld the added consideration.

Brian Construction and Development Company, Inc. v. Brighenti
405 A.2d 72 (Conn. 1978)

Brian Construction and Development Company (Brian), a general contractor, subcontracted with Brighenti for excavation of a construction site. Brighenti had relied on test borings taken by Brian at the excavation site in formulating the subcontract price. When Brighenti began excavation, he discovered walls, slab floors, and other

FACTS

debris located beneath the surface, all of which were part of the basement of a factory previously located on the site. Brian agreed to pay Brighenti his costs for removing the unanticipated rubble, plus 10 percent. Brighenti never completed the job, so Brian sued for the damages allegedly suffered from this alleged breach of contract.

ISSUE   Was the subsequent agreement supported by consideration so as to create a binding contract?

HOLDING   Yes. There was a binding contract between the parties obligating Brighenti to remove the unexpected rubble.

REASONING   Brian's promise of additional compensation in return for a promise that the additional, required work would be undertaken constituted a separate, valid agreement. The unforeseen difficulties posed by the rubble became the subject of a separate, oral agreement that was binding as a new, distinct contract supported by valid consideration.

Moral Consideration

We have noted that harsh outcomes sometimes result from the application of the doctrine of consideration. Promises made from a so-called *moral obligation* embody one such subcategory of consideration and are generally not enforced. An example should indicate the strictness with which courts adhere to the requirement of consideration in these contexts.

Human nature is such that we are usually grateful if someone treats us kindly. This is especially true if we are the beneficiaries of truly humanitarian gestures. Conjure up in your mind the following circumstance. Your child has been saved from the jaws of a snarling Doberman pinscher and suffers nary a scratch because of the efforts of a passerby. The person who saved your child unfortunately suffers deep cuts that eventually require cosmetic surgery. Faced with such generosity, who among us would not promise this person the world? You are only human, so you offer to pay this Good Samaritan's lost wages while she is in the hospital. As time passes, however, you grow less willing to pay; and finally you cease paying her altogether. If she sues you, you will usually win because a court will conclude that she has bestowed a gift on you — that is, saving the child. Consequently, no consideration is present (note, too, that there was no bargaining *before* the humanitarian gesture in exchange for your promise to pay). Because of your self-interest, *you* may not think this particular result under this doctrine is harsh; but almost anyone else reading about this situation would. Therefore, in a few jurisdictions, courts would reject the settled rule by holding that the Good Samaritan could win. Note, though, that this would be the position taken by a minority of courts. The next case follows the majority rule.

In re Estate of Voight
624 P.2d 1022 (N.M. App. 1981)

Four months before he died, Mr. Voight gave two promissory notes for $13,500 each to his stepsons, John and Thomas Kapsa, for debts owed to the stepsons by their mother, Voight's deceased wife. When Mr. Voight died, the Kapsas sued Voight's estate to collect on the promissory notes.

FACTS

Were the promissory notes supported by consideration so as to be valid contracts?

ISSUE

No. Moral consideration does not constitute legal consideration.

HOLDING

Under Illinois law a person has no legal obligation to assume the debt of his or her deceased spouse. Furthermore, a moral obligation alone is not valid consideration for a promise to pay. Since Mr. Voight never had a legal duty to pay the Kapsas the money his wife owed them, the only consideration for the promissory notes was the moral duty he had felt. This was not sufficient to make the notes valid and enforceable in Illinois.

REASONING

Related to this doctrine of moral consideration is the doctrine of *past consideration*. This issue typically arises when a person retires and the former boss agrees to pay the employee a small **stipend** "in consideration of twenty-five years of faithful service." Since the old services are executed (completed or finished), they cannot form the basis for a new promise. The same is true of a promise to pay a relative based on the promisor's "love and affection" for the promisee. Notice that in both cases there is no bargaining and no *exchange* of anything of value. Accordingly, neither of the promises is supported by consideration and neither would be enforceable. As is often said, "Past consideration is *no* consideration."

Past Consideration

Stipend A fixed sum of money paid periodically for services or to defray expenses

As should now be apparent, whether or not the parties have bargained with a resulting exchange of value appears to be of crucial importance under the common law rules surrounding consideration. Still, courts will enforce agreements despite a lack of consideration in the following four situations: (1) promissory estoppel, (2) charitable subscriptions, (3) promises made after the statute of limitations has run, and (4) promises to repay debts after a discharge of bankruptcy.

EXCEPTIONS TO THE BARGAINING THEORY OF CONSIDERATION

In Chapter 9, we discussed promissory estoppel in the context of preventing an offeror's revocation of the offer. To recapitulate, we said that courts apply this

Promissory Estoppel

equitable doctrine in order to avoid injustice. Essentially the elements are the same whether we are dealing with offers or with consideration. In both, the promisor makes a definite promise that he or she expects, or should reasonably expect, will induce the plaintiff/promisee to act (or refrain from acting) in a manner that may be detrimental to the latter person; accordingly, the promisor will be held to his or her promise to avoid injustice. Simply put, the promisor will be prevented from asserting a defense (here, that there is no consideration) normally available.

In the earlier example where an employer offered to pay his employee "in consideration of twenty-five years of faithful service," promissory estoppel might be used as a substitute for consideration to enable the employee to win. In other words, if the employer has in fact paid the former employee $100 a month for ten years, and the employee has given up opportunities for part-time employment owing to an expectation of continued stipends, some courts will conclude that the payments must be continued despite the absence of bargaining or of an exchange of anything of value.

Charitable Subscriptions

Likewise, promissory estoppel may help promisees win in the next category, *charitable subscriptions,* which comprises another exception to the requirement of consideration. You can probably guess how this legal issue — *the promise to pay a certain sum to a nonprofit charity* — arises.

Typically, a generous person wishes to donate a sizable amount to a worthy charity and promises to do so. Later this humanitarian zeal wanes; the person no longer wishes to live up to the agreement. If you were the donor, what would you argue? In all likelihood, you would try to argue that you intended to bestow a gift. Since consideration is by definition lacking in a gift (there is no bargaining and no exchange of value), you could not be held liable on this promise.

Ordinarily, though, a would-be donor will have to live up to the agreement because charitable institutions rely on the belief that the amount pledged in subscriptions will be forthcoming and because people make pledges based on the knowledge that other people will be making similar pledges. Courts, of course, believe that charitable institutions (like universities, hospitals, or churches) serve noble purposes. Thus, in addition to resorting to promissory estoppel as a substitute for consideration as shown above, courts may alternatively enforce the promise on public policy grounds.

Promises Made After Expiration of the Statute of Limitations

State statutes of limitations set time limits on when creditors can bring suit against debtors for sums owed to them. Ordinarily this period is from two to six years, after which the creditor cannot maintain suit against the debtor. Sometimes the debtor wants to repay the debt even if this time limit has passed. As we have already learned, there seems to be no consideration present in such a circumstance; there is no bargaining, and it may be argued that the debtor's promise represents moral consideration at best.

But our analysis would be wrong under most state statutes and decisions, because the debtor's new promise to pay will be enforced if it is in writing. The public policy of encouraging people to pay their debts probably forms the basis for this exception to the bargaining theory of consideration.

As the next case shows, the written promise must be specific.

Curry v. Winnfield
398 So.2d 97 (La. App. 1981)

Curry was the holder of a promissory note executed by Winnfield on 26 June 1973. The note was secured by a real estate mortgage and was payable in thirty-six monthly installments commencing on 26 July 1973. Winnfield made no payments on the note. The statute of limitations for suing on such notes in Louisiana is five years. However, Curry did not file suit until 24 March 1980, more than five years after the default. On 9 April 1980, Winnfield wrote to Curry's attorney, "Please write me if I could work out some kind of agreement with the note." **FACTS**

Was the letter of April 9 a sufficient promise to pay to eliminate the running of the statute of limitations? **ISSUE**

No. This acknowledgment of debt was not a sufficient promise to allow Curry to sue despite the running of the statute of limitations. **HOLDING**

At the time the letter was written, the statute of limitations had already been exceeded. Yet, a natural obligation to pay the note still existed even where the time period for filing suit had passed. Nevertheless, for a natural obligation to be sufficient consideration for a new contract, there must be a new promise to pay the debt in order to eliminate Curry's bar to recovery posed by the running of the statute of limitations. The language contained in the letter did not amount to a new promise to pay the debt and therefore did not constitute a renunciation by Winnfield of the running of the statute of limitations. **REASONING**

The same policy is in play and the result is similar when a debtor subsequently promises to pay a debt after he or she has received a discharge in bankruptcy. Here again there is no consideration for this new promise, but most states will allow the enforcement of the promise, provided that the promise to pay is given in open court with a full understanding of its significance, as required by the Bankruptcy Reform Act of 1978. (Bankruptcy is covered in detail in Chapters 31 and 32.) **Promises to Pay Debts After Bankruptcy Discharges**

Consideration is a firmly entrenched doctrine in modern law. A common definition states that consideration consists of any waiver or promised waiver of rights bargained for in exchange for a promise. It exists when there is a **SUMMARY** benefit to the promisor or a detriment to the promisee bargained for and given in exchange for a promise. In unilateral contracts, consideration may take the form of an act or a forbearance to act. Conversely, the respective promises constitute consideration in bilateral contracts. In the absence of fraud, duress, undue influence, or unconscionability, courts will generally not inquire into the adequacy of the consideration. Although no consideration is necessary under the UCC provisions about firm offers and modifications of sales contracts, consideration will be necessary to hold a surety liable.

The doctrine of preexisting obligations mandates that one pay a liquidated debt in full; part payment is not consideration for full discharge of the debt. In contrast, part payment of an unliquidated debt, if accepted as full payment, represents a compromise of the debt and is supported by consideration. Such satisfaction and accord completely cancel the debt. The same rationale validates composition agreements.

Agreements based on illusory promises or promises grounded in either preexisting legal duties or preexisting contractual relationships lack consideration. The same is true of promises based on moral obligations, or past consideration. The four exceptions to the "bargaining" theory of consideration are (1) promissory estoppel, (2) charitable subscriptions, (3) promises made after the statute of limitations has run, and (4) promises to repay debts after discharges in bankruptcy. Agreements without consideration will be enforced in these situations.

DISCUSSION QUESTIONS

1. How did the concept of consideration develop historically?

2. Define *consideration.*

3. Can "doing nothing" ever be consideration to support a promise?

4. Why do courts refuse to inquire into the adequacy of consideration?

5. Discuss how the UCC treats consideration in contracts for the sale of goods.

6. Explain why part payment of a liquidated debt is not consideration for full discharge of the debt, but part payment accepted as full payment for an unliquidated debt is.

7. What are composition agreements, and how are they related to the doctrine of consideration?

8. When will courts enforce new promises made about the subject matter of an earlier contract?

9. Why has it been said that the doctrine of moral or past consideration permits harsh results?

10. Explain the four situations in which agreements will be enforced despite a lack of bargaining and hence consideration.

1. Nancy and Gerald Harrington were divorced in 1981. As part of their property settlement, Gerald was to retain the Harrington's farm. In return for the farm, Gerald signed a promissory note in which he agreed to pay Nancy $150,000 over a period of fifteen years. To secure this note, Nancy took two mortgages on the farm. Shortly thereafter, Gerald began experiencing financial difficulties and found that he would be unable to refinance previous bank loans unless Nancy were willing to release him from the note and mortgages and thus free the land from these encumbrances. At that time, the Harringtons' son, Ronn, was farming the land with his father. Because Gerald had remarried and his second wife had become pregnant, Nancy was concerned that Ronn would not inherit the farm. Therefore, she told Gerald that she was willing to satisfy the two mortgages and release him from liability on the promissory note if Gerald would execute a will leaving the farm to Ronn. An agreement to this effect was signed on 30 December 1981, subject to certain conditions; and on 1 April 1982, Gerald made a will in which he left the farm to Ronn on the condition that Nancy comply with the provisions of the 30 December 1981 agreement. Gerald subsequently obtained the needed refinancing and continued farming the land with Ronn. However, Nancy did not execute satisfactions of the two mortgages but instead instituted a foreclosure action against Gerald on the two mortgages. When a lower court concluded that the 30 December 1981 agreement was legally binding on Nancy, she argued she did not have to satisfy the two mortgages and release Gerald from the promissory note because his promise was illusory in that the 30 December 1981 agreement gave Gerald the unlimited right to encumber the farm in the event "future economic exigencies" so required. Was Nancy correct, or was there consideration to support the 30 December 1981 agreement. (*Harrington* v. *Harrington*, 365 N.W.2d 552 [N.D. 1985].)

2. Mr. Craig agreed to sell Sims property owned by Craig and his wife for $55,000. When Mrs. Craig returned from Europe, she refused to sell the property unless Sims paid $65,000. Both the Craigs had been involved with the negotiations relating to the sale of the realty for several months before Mrs. Craig's return. In addition, Sims had spent considerable sums in architectural fees and a nonrefundable option check that was to be applied to the purchase price. Thus, Sims felt economically compelled to execute the new contract. Was consideration present to support the new contract for a sale of $65,000? (*Sims* v. *Craig*, 627 P.2d 875 [N.M. 1981].)

3. Price worked as a salesperson for Mercury Supply Company (Mercury), a cleaning materials and janitorial supplies company, near Nashville. Weil, the owner of the company, gave Price several promotions over the years, and in March, 1975, changed Price's title to vice-president for sales. There was no change in Price's compensation at that time, and his duties re-

mained the same as they had been in his earlier positions of sales manager and sales coordinator. According to Price, Weil at this time orally promised him that he would never have to worry about employment because of the service he had rendered to the company in the past. Price also stated that Weil told him he had been hired as the vice-president for sales of Mercury for the rest of his life or until he retired. Unfortunately, over the years, the relationship between Price and Weil cooled; and Weil discharged Price on 2 March 1981. Price later argued that in March, 1975, the parties had entered into a valid oral employment contract in which he was hired as the vice-president for sales of Mercury for the rest of his life or until his retirement. Was there consideration present to support this alleged agreement? (*Price* v. *Mercury Supply Company, Inc.,* 682 S.W.2d 924 [Tenn. App. 1984].)

4. Leiter was an associate in a law firm with Parkhurst, Fraser, and Newlin. Because of Leiter's alleged conflict of interest in a sale of property that had resulted in damages to the law firm, on 24 July 1974, Leiter agreed to pay his three associates $4500 each within five years. Leiter died after making this agreement, and his estate later refused to pay the lawyers by arguing that there was no consideration to support Leiter's agreement with them. Was the agreement a valid compromise of Parkhurst, Fraser, and Newlin's claims? (*In re Estate of Leiter,* 409 N.E.2d 91 [Ill. App. 1980].)

5. In July of 1975, Pennsylvania Blue Shield (Blue Shield), the trade name of Medical Services Association of Pennsylvania, solicited bids for the lease of a computer. These bids were to be received by Blue Shield no later than 12:00 noon on 18 August 1975. Universal Computer Systems, Inc. (Universal), through its president, Warren Wilson, contacted Joel Gebert, the sole Blue Shield contact for the request for bids, and obtained Gebert's assurance that he would have the bid proposal picked up at the Allegheny Airlines ticket counter in Harrisburg on the morning of 18 August 1975, in time for the 12:00 noon deadline. Pursuant to Gebert's promise, Wilson dispatched his bid proposal by Allegheny Airlines' PDQ Service on 18 August 1975, at approximately 8:30 A.M. When Wilson called Gebert to give him the waybill number so that the proposal could be picked up, Gebert informed Wilson that he had changed his mind regarding his promise to pick up the bid proposal and would not do so. After many difficulties, Wilson finally persuaded Allegheny Airlines to release the package to a courier other than the addressee, Blue Shield; but the package arrived at Blue Shield after 12:00 noon and was rejected as untimely. Wilson argued that if the proposal had arrived in a timely fashion, Universal's bid would have been the lowest and that the firm should therefore receive damages in the amount of the expected profit on the contract. Was either Gebert or Wilson's promise illusory? If either was illusory, could Universal use promissory estoppel as a substitute for consideration? (*Universal Computer Systems, Inc.* v. *Medical Services Association of Pennsylvania,* 474 F. Supp. 472 [M.D. Pa. 1979], *modified* 628 Fed.2d 820 [3d Cir. 1980].)

6. Lenaxa State Bank had loaned Thurston approximately $34,000 for use in his lawn care business. Since Thurston had not paid the notes as they had become due, Lenaxa notified Thurston it would foreclose on the security agreements and repossess the collateral on the notes if Thurston did not take some action on the notes. Thurston and the bank subsequently agreed to execute a $20,000 second mortgage on Thurston's home. The bank further promised not to file this mortgage for two weeks so that Thurston could collect $23,000 in accounts receivable. If Thurston brought in the monies, Lenaxa promised it would destroy the mortgage. Thurston did not pay, so the bank filed the mortgage. Thurston argued there was no consideration to support the second mortgage because the bank had foreclosed; hence, there had been no forbearance. But the bank asserted there had been forbearance to sue for a time sufficient to constitute consideration. What should a court decide? (*Safety Federal Savings and Loan Association* v. *Thurston*, 648 P.2d 267 [Kan. App. 1982].)

7. Thomas was injured in March, 1981, while working for Rooks Transit Lines, Inc. On 9 November 1981, Thomas filed to collect insurance benefits from Michigan Mutual Insurance Company, Rooks's insurer. On 3 December 1981, the insurance company's adjuster contacted Thomas's attorney and offered to settle the claim for $664. On 29 December 1981, Thomas's attorney called the adjuster and informed him that Thomas had agreed to accept this settlement. The adjuster told the attorney that he would issue a check for $664 when Thomas had signed a voluntary dismissal and had mailed it to his attention. On 27 January 1981, Thomas's attorney informed the insurance company that Thomas had had a "change of heart" and that Thomas no longer wished to accept the $664. The insurance company argued that a valid settlement or compromise of the claim had occurred and that Thomas was obligated to accept the $664. Was the company correct? (*Thomas* v. *Michigan Mutual Insurance Company*, 358 N.W.2d 902 [Mich. App. 1984].)

8. Hamilton Bancshares, Inc. (Hamilton) entered into a "stock purchase option" with the Leroys whereby Hamilton could buy bank stock from the Leroys within an eighty-day period if it chose to do so. Each option was purportedly granted "in consideration of the sum of one dollar . . . it had paid. . . ." Hamilton also gave the Leroys $5000 in earnest money, "to be applied to the purchase price of the shares subject to the option in the event that the option is exercised and to be refunded to [Hamilton] in the event that this option is not exercised." Five weeks later, the Leroys attempted to withdraw the option, at which point Hamilton rejected this attempted withdrawal and exercised the option. The Leroys contended that since the $1 had not in fact been paid to them as recited in the option agreement, there was no consideration and hence no contract. The Leroys thus characterized the option agreement as an offer that could be withdrawn any time prior to acceptance. The Leroys further argued that since the $5000 was to be refunded to Hamilton if the option were not exer-

cised, the $5000 was of no benefit to them and therefore did not constitute consideration either. Hamilton admitted that the $1 had not in fact been paid but asserted that the Leroys' use of the earnest money for the period of the option constituted consideration sufficient to support the option. Who had the better argument, the Leroys or Hamilton? (*Hamilton Bancshares, Inc.* v. *Leroy,* 476 N.E.2d 788 [Ill. App. 1985].)

9. William B. Marty, Jr. became an employee of Cubic Corporation (Cubic) in December, 1976. At that time, he signed an invention and secrecy agreement in which he agreed to disclose to the company any ideas or inventions he conceived on company time, to assign to the company all rights in any such discoveries, to cooperate in obtaining patents on these inventions, and to refrain from disclosing any of Cubic's secret inventions or processes. Under the agreement, Cubic promised to pay the expenses of obtaining a patent; $75 upon the employee's execution of the patent application; and $75 if the patent were obtained. In mid-May, 1977, Marty thought of an idea for an electronic warfare simulator (EWS), a device for training pilots in electronic warfare. Cubic personnel viewed the idea favorably, funded an internal project to study Marty's concept, and submitted the EWS proposal to the Navy. In June, 1978, Marty, without Cubic's knowledge, applied for a patent on his invention and received the patent in 1979. When Marty offered to license the EWS to Cubic, Cubic insisted that the patent belonged to it and that Marty should assign the patent to the company. Cubic ultimately made Marty's continued employment contingent on this assignment. After Marty steadfastly refused to make the requested assignment, Cubic terminated his employment in 1980. When Cubic sued Marty for breach of contract, he argued that the agreement was unenforceable because the "token" bonus of $150 constituted consideration too inadequate to support a promise to convey the invention to Cubic. He also contended that his employment could not serve as the consideration for the agreement because Cubic had hired him before he had signed it. Should a court accept Marty's reasoning? (*Cubic Corporation* v. *Marty,* 229 Cal. Rptr. 828 [Cal. App. 1986].)

10. In 1982, First Interstate Bank financed a tractor and trailer for C. H. Betterton. From the outset, Betterton had difficulty making the loan payments. On 15 February 1984, Betterton met with a bank official, Stiles, who allegedly warned him that unless he paid off all the arrearages on his loans, the bank would immediately take measures to collect the debt. Betterton first told her the truck was in a Tucson repair shop. He then allegedly suggested to Stiles that he could bring the loan up-to-date and keep his payments current by having the broker for whom he worked (i.e., a person who secures contracts for transportation services and sees that they are paid for) take the payments out of his paycheck and transfer them directly to the bank. The broker agreed to make such payments in Betterton's behalf. Betterton, the broker, and the garage owner who was

repairing Betterton's truck all believed Stiles had promised to forgo repossession of the truck if the repairs were completed and the payments were made by the broker directly to the bank. However, Stiles had not told Betterton and the others that she had ordered Auto Recovery Bureau (ARB) to repossess the tractor-trailer rig. More importantly, she had not canceled this order after reaching the new agreement with Betterton. The very next day, ARB repossessed the truck while Betterton was making a delivery in Phoenix. When Betterton sued Stiles for breach of contract, the trial court held that no consideration underlay Betterton's agreement with Stiles because he was already under a preexisting duty to keep the truck in good repair pursuant to the terms of the security agreement he had signed with the bank. The lower court did not discuss at all the effect of Betterton's promise to have his broker make the payments directly to the bank. Should the appellate court uphold the lower court's decision? (*Betterton* v. *First Interstate Bank,* 800 F.2d 732 [8th Cir. 1986].)

CHAPTER 11

Contractual Capacity:
The Ability to Agree

LEGAL CAPACITY

Our examination of contract law thus far has stressed the importance of *the parties' mutual assent* to an agreement and some *evidence of their commitment* to be bound to the duties and obligations set out in that agreement. In learning about the legal requisites for agreement and consideration, objective factors like the words uttered or the value exchanged have merited most of our attention. We now place these matters aside and begin instead to concentrate on who the parties to the contract are and their *capacity*, or legal ability, to form a valid contract. Capacity, the third requirement for a valid contract, requires that the parties to the contract have *the legal ability to bind themselves to the contract and to enforce any promises made to them.* However, incapacity, or lack of such capacity, is the exception, not the rule. Hence, the burden of proof regarding incapacity falls on the party raising it as a defense to enforcement of the contract or as a basis for **rescission** of the contract.

Rescission An annulment or cancellation; a termination of the contract through restoration of the parties to the status quo

To determine *contractual capacity*, the law looks at the relative bargaining power of the parties involved. Historically, older persons have taken care of the younger members of society; so, too, the law attempts to protect children, who are not as adept at bargaining, from overreaching by those who are more experienced bargainers by allowing children under a certain age to disaffirm (or withdraw from) the contract. The same is true of persons who lack mental capacity, such as insane persons: contracts made by these persons may be absolutely void, voidable (the insane person can disaffirm the contract), or even valid (if, for example, the contract is made during a lucid period). Thus, the existence or absence of legal capacity and the consequences of proving incapacity depend heavily on the facts and on a given person's status. Indeed, the law often uses the status of a person as a basis for making legal distinctions and may in fact **circumscribe** the legal rights of any persons falling within these classifications. For this reason many jurisdictions limit the contractual rights of minors, insane persons, intoxicated persons, aliens, and convicts. In earlier times, the common law also curtailed the rights of married women to contract through laws called Married Women's Property Acts. Most states have eliminated these statutory restrictions, but some vestiges of these acts may remain in a few states. The extent of the legal disability placed on such classes of individuals comprises the central thrust of this chapter.

Circumscribe Limit the range of activity associated with something

MINORS

Most jurisdictions no longer follow the earlier common law rule that any person of either sex under twenty-one years of age is a *minor* (or an *infant*). Most states have changed this rule by statute to allow for achievement of *majority status* (that is, adult status) as early as age eighteen for almost all purposes. (A common exception involves the purchasing of alcoholic beverages.) Other states allow for termination of infancy status upon marriage or **emancipation.**

Emancipation Freedom from the control or power of another; release from parental care and the attainment of legal independence

Disaffirmance/ Rescission

To protect minors in their dealings with adults, the law allows minors to disaffirm (or avoid) their contracts with adults except in certain specialized cases, such as contracts involving necessaries. When the minor decides not to perform the legal obligations contemplated in the agreement by *disaffirming* the contract, this action results in a voidable contract. The minor has the option of performing the contract, but it is usually voidable on his or her part. The converse is not true: the adult who has contracted with a minor will ordinarily be unable to use the infancy of the minor to avoid the contract unless the minor allows the adult to disaffirm the contract. Simply put, do not contract with minors! Or, if you do, realize that the minor's powers may, in a given instance, be quite pervasive. Practically speaking, besides refusing to deal with minors, you can curtail their powers of avoidance by insisting that a parent or other adult cosign the contract with them. In this fashion you will have effectively limited the minor's power of *rescission, the ability to have the contract set aside.* This is true because even if the minor disaffirms the contract, the adult cosigner will still be liable on it.

Misrepresentation of Age

What if the minor intentionally misrepresents his or her age? For example, suppose seventeen-year-old Marcie tells the salesperson at Ace Used Cars that she is twenty-one and pulls out a falsified driver's license to "prove it." If Marcie later tries to avoid the contract with Ace, can Ace argue that this intentional misrepresentation prevents rescission? Under the law of most jurisdictions, the minor can still disaffirm the contract. (But in these circumstances, many times the adult will be able to disaffirm as well, despite the usual rule to the contrary.) Some states, though, hold that such a misrepresentation cuts off the minor's power of disaffirmance. Alternatively, some states allow rescission but force the minor to put the adult back in the position he or she would have been in but for the contract. In other words, assuming the same facts as above, some states will allow Marcie to disaffirm the contract but will either force her to return the car or will hold her liable in quasi contract for the reasonable value of the benefit Ace has conferred on her by furnishing her with the car. Also, Marcie will probably have to pay for any damage done to the car while it has been in her custody.

This result follows the usual rule that upon disaffirmance, the minor must return to the adult the property or other consideration that was the object of the contract, if possible. Strong policy reasons exist for this rule, called the *duty of restoration.* It clearly seems unfair to let the minor "have it both ways" — that is, get out of the contract and yet retain the consideration. The law therefore says that if the minor wants to avoid a contract, he or she must *totally* avoid it.

Sometimes, however, the minor cannot return the property or other consideration because it has been damaged or destroyed. Ace will be very upset if Marcie asks for the money that she has already paid on the car as well as total release from the contract and in exchange for all this presents Ace with a demolished car. In most states the minor will get exactly what he or she wishes because merely giving the car back fulfills the minor's duty of restoration. But in some states, Ace will be able to set off any payments received from the seventeen-year-old due to the damaged condition of the car. These states add to the duty of restoration, the *duty of restitution.* In short, these jurisdictions require the minor to give the adult consideration sufficient to put the adult back in the economic position the adult enjoyed at the beginning of the transaction between the parties. But as the case that follows illustrates, not all courts are willing to impose the duty of restitution on the minor in similar situations.

Weisbrook v. *Clyde C. Netzley, Inc.*
374 N.E.2d 1102 (III. App. 1978)

FACTS   Ronald Weisbrook bought a 1969 Chevrolet from Clyde C. Netzley, Inc. (Netzley, Inc.), in April, 1975. Weisbrook was seventeen at the time of the sale and had told the firm's salesperson of this fact. Shortly after the sale, a rod bearing gave out, causing substantial damage to the car's engine. When Weisbrook asked the Netzley firm to repair the damages, the firm refused by saying the car had been sold "as is." Soon thereafter, Weisbrook elected to rescind the contract; so he returned the car and asked for the purchase price back. When Netzley, Inc., refused to rescind the contract, Weisbrook sued for rescission based on his minority. Netzley, Inc., then asked for recoupment of the damages to the car that had occurred while it had been in Weisbrook's possession.

Where a minor had disaffirmed a contract, could the seller recoup the damages incurred while the property had been in the minor's possession?

ISSUE

No. *Recoupment* was not available as a remedy.

HOLDING

Weisbrook had not misrepresented his age at the time of the sale, had tried to disaffirm the contract, and had asked for the return of the purchase price only when Netzley, Inc., had refused to repair the car. Given these circumstances, rescission by the minor was appropriate; and the seller would not be entitled to recoup the damages Netzley, Inc., believed it had suffered thereby (the cost of repairs to the car, value of the use by Weisbrook while it was in his possession, and the amount of depreciation during that period).

REASONING

Changing the circumstances of our previous example a bit, let us assume Marcie had traded in another car when she had purchased the now-demolished one from Ace. When she avoids the contract, Ace has to return this trade-in to the minor as well in order to fulfill the adult's corresponding duty of restitution. If Ace has already sold this car to a **bona fide purchaser,** the minor cannot get the car back but can recover the price paid by the third party to Ace.

Bona fide purchaser A person who purchases in good faith, for value, and without notice of any defects or defenses affecting the sale or transaction

When minors like Marcie attempt to disaffirm transactions with adults, no special words or acts are required to effect an avoidance. Disaffirmances may be done orally or in writing, formally (by a lawsuit) or informally, directly or indirectly (the minor's conveying the car to someone else when the minor reaches majoritarian age is an avoidance of the contract with Ace Used Cars).

The minor's power of disaffirmance, whether the contract is executory or executed, ordinarily extends through his or her minority and for a reasonable time after achieving majority. As we have seen before, and as shown in the following case, how long a reasonable time is becomes a question of fact for a judge or jury to decide in light of all the circumstances.

Bobby Floars Toyota, Inc. v. *Smith*
269 S.E.2d 320 (N.C. App. 1980)

Charles Edward Smith, Jr., purchased an automobile from Bobby Floars Toyota, Inc. (Floars) on 15 August 1973. On that date the defendant was seventeen years old; he would have his eighteenth birthday on 25 September 1973. Smith executed a pur-

FACTS

chase money security agreement to finance $2362.00, the balance due on the purchase price of the automobile, payable in thirty installments of $99.05 each. After having made eleven monthly payments, ten of which were made after his eighteenth birthday, Smith voluntarily returned the automobile to Floars and defaulted on his payment obligations. The automobile was sold for $700.00, leaving a deficiency of $821.52. Floars brought this action to recover damages in the amount of the deficiency.

ISSUE Was Smith's voluntary relinquishment of the automobile ten months after attaining the age of majority a timely disaffirmance of his contract with Floars?

HOLDING No. Ten months was an unreasonable time within which to elect between disaffirmance and ratification, and Smith was therefore liable to Floars.

REASONING The settled rule is that the conventional contracts of an infant (that is, a minor), except those for necessaries and those authorized by statute, are voidable at the election of the infant and may be disaffirmed by the infant during minority or within a reasonable time after reaching majority. The definition of a reasonable time depends on the circumstances of each case; defining a hard-and-fast rule regarding precise time limits is impossible. Nevertheless, Smith's attempted disaffirmance in this case was untimely.

Ratification

Ratification means that the minor has in some fashion indicated (1) *approval of the contract made while he or she is an infant* and (2) *an intention to be bound to the provisions of that contract.* Ratification, then, is the opposite of disaffirmance and cuts off any right to disaffirm. Ratification takes two separate forms: express and implied. Even with express ratifications, or those situations in which the minor explicitly and definitely agrees to accept the obligations of the contract, the policy of protecting minors is so strong that many states require express ratifications to be in writing. The more common type of ratification occurs through indirect means, such as conduct that shows approval of the contract, even though the minor has said nothing specifically about agreeing to be bound to it. To illustrate, failure to make a timely disaffirmance constitutes an implied ratification of an executed contract. Thus, a minor who is not diligent in disaffirming within a reasonable time after attaining majority will have impliedly ratified the contract. Such lack of action does not ordinarily bring about ratification of an executory contract, however. Some courts, moreover, would hold that by itself, partial payment of a debt is usually not tantamount to ratification, unless payment is coupled to the minor's express intention to be bound to the contract. In any event, ratification cannot occur until the minor achieves majoritarian status. If ratification *were* possible beforehand, the law's protection of minors would be meaningless. The *Floars* case that we just cited provides a good illustration of these principles as well.

Bobby Floars Toyota, Inc. v. *Smith*
269 S.E.2d 320 (N.C. App. 1980)

Same as in the earlier citation.   **FACTS**

Had Smith impliedly ratified the contract?   **ISSUE**

Yes. Smith's acceptance of the benefits and continuation of payments under the   **HOLDING**
contract constituted a ratification of it and prevented a later disaffirmance.

Affirmation, or conduct showing ratification, would be sufficient to bind the infant,   **REASONING**
regardless of whether a reasonable time for disaffirmance had passed. The facts
here demonstrated that Smith's continued possession and operation of the car after
his eighteenth birthday and his making of ten monthly payments after he turned
eighteen were tantamount to ratification and precluded Smith's subsequent attempt at disaffirmance.

Even in the absence of ratification, minors will be liable for transactions   Necessaries
whereby they have been furnished "necessaries." *Necessaries* formerly encom-
passed only food, clothing, and shelter; but we shall see that the rule has been
broadened to cover other *things that directly foster the minor's well-being*. The basis
for the minor's liability is *quasi* contract, which you learned about in Chapter 8. (There can be no liability in *contract* law owing to the lack of capacity,
remember?) If an adult has supplied necessaries to the minor, the law will
imply liability for the reasonable value of those necessaries. Often, though, the
law will not impose liability on the minor for the cost of necessaries unless the
minor's parents are unable to discharge their obligation to support their child
and pay for such essentials.

The definition of necessaries depends on the minor's circumstances, or
social and economic station in life. In this sense, the rule is applied somewhat
subjectively. Although food, clothing, and shelter are covered, is a fur coat a
necessary for which the minor is liable? It may be, depending on the minor's
social station. Similarly, loans for medical or dental services or education may
also be necessaries in a given situation. There are numerous cases involving
cars, and many courts hold that a car, especially if it is used for coming and
going to work, is a necessary for which the minor is liable. Clearly, the definition of what constitutes a necessary changes as community values and mores
change.

The following case illustrates the point that a minor may not be held liable
for the cost of necessaries if the minor's parents are able to discharge their
obligation to support the child.

Greenville Hospital System v. Smith
239 S.E.2d 657 (S.C. 1977)

FACTS   Kenneth Smith, a minor, was admitted to Greenville General Hospital for emergency treatment for head injuries. He was hospitalized for eighty-seven days and received $9039.25 worth of services. Kenneth recovered an unspecified amount of damages for injuries sustained in the accident that caused his hospitalization. This sum was placed under the supervision of the probate court, and Kenneth's mother was appointed guardian for Kenneth's estate. After the hospital had billed Kenneth's father for the services and had received no payments, the hospital sued Kenneth's estate for the $9039.25.

ISSUE   Was Kenneth liable for these medical services?

HOLDING   Kenneth's liability for such necessaries would turn on whether his parents were able to discharge their obligation to pay his hospital expenses.

REASONING   A minor or his estate may be bound on an implied contract for such necessaries as medical treatment. However, a minor or his estate cannot be held liable for such costs unless the parents are unable to discharge their obligations to support. It was not clear whether the Smiths were able to pay, so that issue must be determined. If they were able to pay, they would be liable; if they were not, the minor's estate would be liable.

Special Statutes

Legislatures in many states have passed special statutes making minors liable in a variety of circumstances. Under such laws, minors may be responsible for educational loans, medical or dental expenses, insurance policies, banking account contracts, transportation by common carrier (for example, airline tickets), and the like. These statutes protect the interests of those persons who have dealt with minors who, despite their age, are exhibiting the skills and maturity of adults.

Torts and Crimes

The law similarly protects the interests of adults when an adult has suffered losses owing to a minor's torts and crimes. Thus, minors generally are unable to disaffirm liability for torts and crimes, areas of the law we discussed in Chapters 3 and 4, unless the minor is of "tender years," or too young to understand the consequences of his or her acts. Minors may also escape liability in these areas if the imposition of tort liability would bring about the enforcement of a contract the minor has previously disaffirmed. Note how, in this latter context, the law has chosen once again to protect minors at the expense of adults.

Like minors, insane persons may lack the capacity to make a binding contract. However, we shall see that the law in this area is somewhat more complicated.

To be *insane,* a person must be *so mentally infirm or deranged as to be unable to understand what he or she is agreeing to or the consequences attendant upon that agreement.* The causes of such disability — lunacy, mental retardation, senility, or alcohol or drug abuse — are irrelevant.

The contracts of persons who have been adjudged insane through court proceedings are absolutely void. Only their **guardians** have the legal capacity to contract on their behalf. However, the contracts of other insane persons are voidable. To disaffirm a contract, the person using insanity as a defense must prove that he or she was actually insane at the time of contracting. If the person were instead lucid and understood the nature and consequences of the contract, that person would be bound to the contract.

This power of an insane person to avoid contracts also extends to the heirs or personal representative of a deceased insane person. A living insane person's guardian possesses similar powers. Upon regaining sanity, a formerly insane person may nonetheless ratify a contract made during the period of insanity.

Determining whether a transaction by an insane person is void, voidable, or enforceable depends heavily on the facts, as the following case illustrates.

INSANE PERSONS

Effects of Transactions by Insane Persons

Guardians Persons legally responsible for taking care of the affairs of another who lacks the legal capacity to do

---

G.A.S. v. S.I.S.
407 A.2d 253 (Del. Fam. Ct. 1978)

FACTS

G. was the husband of S. In 1970, after thirteen years of marriage to S., G. began suffering mental problems and was diagnosed as a paranoid schizophrenic and a manic depressive. In 1974, after G. had suffered several recurrences of illness, S. sued him for divorce. On 20 February 1975, G. signed a separation agreement while he was an outpatient at Delaware State Hospital. In this agreement G. gave S. $750 per month in child support, beach property, and the marital home. He was released from the hospital six days after signing this agreement.

ISSUE

Did G. have legal capacity to contract on 20 February 1975, when he signed the separation agreement?

HOLDING

The court did not decide this issue because even if G.'s mental weakness had not risen to the level of contractual incapacity, such weakness in conjunction with the evidence of unfairness and undue influence that was present here made the contract voidable.

REASONING

The settled rule is that only competent persons can make a contract, and that where there is no capacity to understand or agree, there can be no contract. Here, because G. had not been adjudged mentally incompetent by a court, the agreement was not void but voidable. It fell to the court, then, to determine whether G.'s mental faculties had been impaired to such an extent that his ability to preserve his property rights intelligently and fairly was absent. The drugs G. had been taking probably had adversely affected his reasoning ability. However, the presence of unfairness and the wife's undue influence made the contract voidable at G.'s option anyway, which in turn made it unnecessary for the court to reach the issue of whether G. was incapable of comprehending the separation agreement.

Necessaries

By analogy to the rules covering minors, the law makes insane persons liable for necessaries in quasi contract. The categories of goods and services deemed necessaries for minors in addition generally extend to insane persons. In the context of insanity, fewer controversies should arise regarding whether medical or legal services are necessaries, as they probably are necessaries for which the insane person is liable.

INTOXICATED PERSONS

If a person is so thoroughly intoxicated that he or she does not understand the nature or consequences of the agreement being made, this mental disability approaches that of an insane person. Hence, under certain circumstances such a person can disaffirm any such agreement. However, this power of possible disaffirmance depends on the degree of intoxication involved, which in turn is a question of fact. As you would expect, slight degrees of intoxication do not constitute cause for disaffirmance of a contract.

Whether the intoxication was involuntary or voluntary may somewhat bear on the result, too. If a plaintiff has plied the defendant with liquor, that intoxication may be a factor in a finding of incapacity, fraud, or overreaching that will release the defendant from the agreement. Even voluntary intoxication can sometimes result in a voidable contract if the facts support this conclusion.

Upon regaining sobriety, the formerly intoxicated person may either avoid or ratify the contract. The rules about acting within a reasonable time apply here as well, and if the person does not quickly disaffirm the contract, an implied ratification will be found. Courts are generally hostile to avoiding contracts on the basis of intoxication except in unusual circumstances. Still, in the next case a judge invalidated part of an agreement owing to one party's chronic intoxication.

Galloway v. Galloway
281 N.W.2d 804 (N.D. 1979)

FACTS   Henry Galloway had sued his wife Betty for divorce. Betty was an alcoholic; but her husband testified that at the time she agreed to the divorce, she was lucid, sober, and fully capable of entering into the agreement, which had been presented to the court in September. Five days after the judge accepted the agreement and granted the divorce, Betty asked that this judgment be set aside.

Did Betty's alcoholism render her incapable of contracting? **ISSUE**

The evidence raised many doubts as to Betty's capacity to contract at the time she had entered the agreement and for an extended period afterward. Therefore, the court set aside the part of the agreement that dealt with the property settlement but upheld the divorce. **HOLDING**

Parties capable of contracting are essential to the existence of any contract. Although Betty had not been declared judicially incompetent until four months after signing the agreement, some evidence indicated that her judgment was impaired and that she had been drinking just days prior to signing the agreement. Since some evidence showed that Betty may have been incompetent to judge her rights and interests in relation to the agreement, the provisions of the agreement relating to the property settlement were set aside. **REASONING**

An *alien* is *a citizen of a foreign country.* Most of the disabilities to which an alien was formerly subject have been removed, usually through treaties. Thus, a *legal* alien can ordinarily enter contracts and pursue gainful employment without legal disabilities, just as any United States citizen can. Some states make distinctions based on the alien's right to hold or convey personal property (generally authorized under such statutes) and the right to hold, convey, or inherit real property (some restrictions may apply here). *Enemy* aliens, or those who are residents of countries with whom we are officially at war, cannot enforce contracts during the period of hostility but sometimes can after the war is over. **ALIENS**

Given the large numbers of illegal aliens in the United States, this area of the law promises to be ripe for future developments.

In many states, conviction of a felony or treason carries with it certain contractual disabilities. For instance, convicts may be prohibited from conveying property during their periods of incarceration. Such disabilities, if applicable, exist only during imprisonment. Upon release from prison, these persons have full rights to contract. **CONVICTS**

Believe it or not, under early common law married women's contracts were void. Women were viewed as their husband's property and as otherwise lacking in capacity to make contracts. This common law disability, reflected in Married Women's Property Acts, has been eliminated by statute or by judicial decision in almost all states. **MARRIED WOMEN**

SUMMARY

Minors, insane persons, intoxicated persons, aliens, and convicts may lack contractual capacity. Previously these restrictions applied to married women, too. In other words, these classes of people may lack the legal ability to bind themselves to an agreement and to enforce any promises made to them.

The contracts of a minor, usually defined as a person under age eighteen, are often voidable, even when the minor has misrepresented his or her age, at the option of the minor. This power of disaffirmance ordinarily extends through the person's minority and for a reasonable time after attaining majority. However, after reaching majority, a minor may ratify, or approve, the contract. Ratification may be express or implied. Even in the absence of ratification, a minor will be liable for necessaries in quasi contract. The definition of necessaries depends on the minor's station in life and the parents' ability to provide for the minor. Sometimes special statutes broaden a minor's areas of liability. A minor will almost always be liable for any tort and crime unless the minor is very young or the imposition of tort liability would bring about the enforcement of a contract previously disaffirmed by the minor.

The contracts of insane persons may be void, voidable, or enforceable. To be insane, a person must be sufficiently mentally deranged to be unable to understand what he or she is agreeing to or the consequences attendant upon that agreement. Such agreements are void, but contracts entered into during periods of lucidity are enforceable. Upon regaining sanity, a person may either ratify the contract or avoid it. Insane persons are liable for necessaries, just as minors are.

Total intoxication may render a person incapable of entering into a binding contract, but slight intoxication will not. Upon gaining sobriety, the person may either disaffirm or ratify the contract. However, courts are generally hostile to avoiding contracts on the basis of intoxication except in unusual circumstances.

Aliens, or persons who are citizens of foreign countries, may face legal disabilities with regard to contractual capacity. This is especially true of enemy aliens, residents of countries with whom our country is officially at war. Convicts and even married women may have limited rights to contract as well. State statutes should be consulted to determine the degree of disability, if any, that exists for these persons.

DISCUSSION
QUESTIONS

1. Why is the law concerned with the concept of capacity to contract?

2. Why do smart businesspersons say, "Don't deal with minors"?

3. Can minors disaffirm contracts if they have misrepresented their ages at the time of contracting?

4. How long does an infant's power to rescind a contract last?

5. What is ratification, and how can it occur?

6. Define *necessaries*.

7. Can an insane person's contracts ever be enforceable? Why or why not?

8. Explain the law as it relates to intoxication as a basis for contractual capacity.

9. How can alienage become a basis for contractual disability?

10. Discuss the current state of the law regarding the legal disabilities of convicts and married women.

1. The Bundys had contracted with Dalton to put vinyl siding on the house in which they resided. Dalton had assumed the house belonged to them. However, when Dalton attempted to collect for the work he had performed after the Bundys had not paid him, Dalton discovered that the house belonged to the Bundys' daughter, Janet, who was twelve years old. Was the vinyl a "necessary" for which Janet could have been held liable despite her minority? (*Dalton* v. *Bundy,* 666 S.W.2d 443 [Mo. App. 1984].)

2. Rogers, a nineteen-year-old, secured the services of a professional employment agency and did not pay the agency's service charge. In North Carolina at this time, twenty-one was the age of majority. Were such services a necessary so as to make Rogers liable to the agency despite his infancy? (*Gastonia Personnel Corporation* v. *Rogers,* 172 S.E.2d 19 [N.C. 1970].)

3. George Ferling, on 6 April 1981, drove his friend, Vivian Abernathy, and her daughter to the Mercantile Bank, where he added Abernathy's name to his bank account as a joint tenant. The bank employee testified that she had explained to Ferling the effect of this change and that Ferling appeared to understand what she was telling him. Some months before, on 16 December 1980, Ferling had been hospitalized with lung cancer. The doctors at that time believed that Ferling's cancer had spread to his brain because he was disoriented as to time and place. However, by January, 1981, he became oriented as to time and place and seemed to be improving. Ferling had stayed at Abernathy's home during his illness; she had taken care of him; and he had said he wanted to marry her. Upon Ferling's death, $20,401.89, the amount in Ferling's checking account, passed to Abernathy as the joint tenant. Ferling's estate sued Abernathy for this money on the ground that Ferling had been mentally incompetent on 6 April 1981 when he had added Abernathy's name to his account. Should the estate prevail in this lawsuit? (*Estate of Ferling* v. *Abernathy,* 670 S.W.2d 109 [Mo. App. 1984].)

4. Debra Hughes, an unwed mother, had her baby at age sixteen. Two months later, Debra and the father of the child, Bruce Haack, were married. When Debra's parents did not pay for her hospital bills, the hospital sued both Debra and her husband. Was Debra liable? Could Bruce be held liable even though the marriage had taken place after the birth of the baby? (*Madison General Hospital* v. *Haack,* 369 N.W.2d 663 [Wis. 1985].)

CASE PROBLEMS

5. Webster Street Partnership, Ltd. (Webster Street), had entered into a lease agreement with Sheridan and Wilwerding, who were both minors. Webster Street was aware of this fact. Both boys had left home voluntarily, with the understanding that they could return to their parents' residence whenever they desired. The boys disaffirmed the contract with Webster Street on 12 November 1982 when they were behind on the rent. Sheridan achieved majoritarian status on 5 November 1982, but Wilwerding never achieved his majority during the time period in question. Webster Street argued that the rental property was a "necessary" for which the boys were liable. Was Webster Street correct? Was Sheridan's disaffirmance valid, since he had become an adult legally on 5 November 1982? (*Webster Street Partnership, Ltd. v. Sheridan*, 368 N.W.2d 439 [Neb. 1985].)

6. The junior class of Springfield High School on 19 November 1980 signed a contract with the "Music Machine," a sound system operated by Michael Hebert, to provide music for their junior prom in May, 1981. The contract was signed by Wayne Howes, one of the class sponsors, and was approved by the principal of the school. In February of 1981, the school learned that the "Music Machine" was not a live band but a disc jockey sound system using tapes and records. Since the principal deemed such a nonlive sound system inappropriate for the prom, both he and Howes wrote to Hebert and informed Hebert the services of the "Music Machine" would not be required. When Hebert sued the school board, the principal, and Howes for breach of contract, the trial court held that only the members of the junior class were parties to the contract. Was the trial court correct in its conclusion that the junior class could be sued? (*Hebert* v. *Livingston Parish School Board*, 438 So.2d 1141 [La. App. 1983].)

7. Scherer and his wife got an uncontested divorce in the Dominican Republic. Scherer later argued that he had been drinking and taking Valium when he had signed the divorce agreement. Was intoxication sufficient to render Scherer legally incapable of contracting? (*Scherer* v. *Scherer*, 405 N.E.2d 40 [Ind. App. 1980].)

8. Farrar was seventeen when she entered into a contract with the Oak Park Swedish Health Spa. She used her father's Master Charge to pay for this membership, and her father paid the amount due to Master Charge. Farrar later attempted to disaffirm the contract on the grounds of infancy. Did Farrar's father ratify her contract with the spa by paying Master Charge? (*Farrar* v. *Swedish Health Spa*, 337 So.2d 911 [La. App. 1976].)

9. Halbman, a minor, contracted with Lemke for a 1968 Oldsmobile. A connecting rod broke, resulting in a garage repair bill of $637.40. Halbman never paid this bill and later attempted to disaffirm his contract with Lemke. Lemke sought to recoup the damages to the car up to the time of disaffirmance. The damages, Lemke stated, are represented by the garage bill. Did Halbman, upon successfully disaffirming the contract, owe

Lemke a duty of restitution for the damages to the car? (*Halbman* v. *Lemke,* 298 N.W.2d 562 [Wis. 1980].)

10. Tara Simmons, a minor, suffered personal injuries as a result of negligence on the part of the Parkette National Gymnastic Training Center (Parkette). When she sued Parkette, it defended with a "release" which Tara and her mother had signed and which had purported to relieve the organization from future liability for damages that Tara might suffer in connection with gymnastics. Did Tara's mother and her own signing of the "release" prohibit Tara from disaffirming the contract on the basis of minority? (*Simmons* v. *Parkette National Gymnastic Training Center,* 670 F. Supp. 140 [E.D. Pa. 1987].)

Legal Agreements

REQUIREMENT OF LEGALITY

By this time, you are undoubtedly aware of the emphasis of American contract law on bargaining and contract formation through the agreement of the parties. Yet, as with most human activities, the permissible boundaries for such conduct are not unlimited. Society at large also may have a stake in the agreement the parties have forged. An agreement to bribe public officials or to murder someone, for instance, has definite repercussions for society that extend beyond the parties who initiated the bargain. The law, then, imposes a requirement that the subject matter and purpose of the bargain be legal in order for the bargain to be recognized as a valid contract. In this sense, the term *illegal contract* is probably a misnomer; a bargain in general cannot attain the status of "contract" if it is tainted with illegality. Hence, such "contracts" are void. To be sure, the vast majority of business transactions are perfectly legal. But the prudent businessperson and citizen will be sensitive to the possibility that a bargain, however innocent it outwardly seems, may nevertheless involve a violation of a statute, common law, or public policy. In such cases, the bargain is illegal. An understanding of the types of bargains that are typically illegal and the effect of these transactions therefore seems desirable. An examination of these and similar concepts forms the focus of this chapter.

COMPONENTS OF ILLEGALITY

The most widely accepted definition of *illegality,* taken from the *Restatement (Second) of Contracts,* Section 512, states that *a bargain is illegal if its performance is criminal, tortious, or otherwise opposed to public policy.*

Both the subject matter of the bargain and the realization of its objectives must be permissible under state and federal statutes. Sometimes these statutes impose criminal penalties for their violation (for example, you may be imprisoned for *arson,* or malicious burning, if you bargain with someone about setting fire to your home or your business for the insurance proceeds). Other statutes may prohibit certain kinds of bargains without imposing criminal penalties if these statutes are violated. For example, to protect the public from unqualified tradespeople, a city ordinance may require all plumbers to be licensed. If Sue Weiss hires Logan Plumbing to fix her kitchen sink and later refuses to pay because Logan does not have the necessary license, in many jurisdictions Sue will win the case in court. Her bargain with Logan will be viewed as illegal, and the plumbing company will be unable to collect for its work.

The desire to protect the public also undergirds the prohibition of bargains involving **tortious** conduct (for instance, an agreement between two parties for the purpose of defrauding a third).

Tortious Relating to private or civil wrongs or injuries

Similarly, even in the absence of an agreement that violates a statute or one that requires the commission of a tort, courts may declare any bargain that will be detrimental to the public at large illegal on public policy grounds. Although the concept of *public policy* may fluctuate as different courts apply different standards, courts have increasingly used this rationale in a variety of contexts in which there appears to be no other basis for protecting the peace, health, or morals of the community. For example, a bank may offer a rather one-sided night depository agreement in which it refuses to accept liability for a deposit placed in its after-hours slot, even if the loss is due to the negligence of its own employee and the depositor can prove that he or she actually deposited the amount in question with the bank. It is difficult to characterize the bank's conduct as either criminal or tortious. Yet its treatment of consumers seems exceedingly unfair or shocking. The concept of public policy — here, the protection of depositors' expectations that the bank will take proper care of their deposits and the protection of consumers against one-sided agreements — will permit a court to invalidate such agreements on the grounds of illegality. Such agreements may be characterized as **exculpatory clauses** or **contracts of adhesion** (depositors may have had no choice but to accept the bank's terms).

Exculpatory clause A part of an agreement in which a prospective plaintiff agrees in advance not to seek to hold the prospective defendant liable for certain things for which that person would otherwise be liable

Contracts of adhesion Contracts whose terms are not open to negotiation — the offeree must "take it or leave it"

In general, an illegal bargain is void and hence unenforceable. This is ordinarily true whether the agreement is executory or fully executed. Usually a court merely leaves the parties where it finds them. Neither party, then, can sue the other. There are, however, exceptions to the general rule that courts will not give relief to parties who have created an illegal bargain. But, as the following case shows, when there are no public policy bases for suspending the usual rule, a court will refuse to give effect to a bargain tainted with illegality.

Wagner v. *State*
364 N.W.2d 246 (Iowa 1985).

FACTS

Wagner was an inmate at the Iowa State Penitentiary on 2 September 1981 when a riot occurred at the prison. During the riot, fires and other property damage ensued, and inmates held staff members hostage. As part of the negotiations to end the riot, the warden promised in writing that no reprisals would be taken against certain inmates, including Wagner. However, on September 9, Wagner was charged with disciplinary violations for his actions during the disturbance. He was the only individual on the list of those to whom the warden had promised no reprisals who, nonetheless, received sanctions. As a result, his "good time" was forfeited, which led to the revocation of his scheduled parole on 18 September 1981. In his **petition for post-conviction relief,** Wagner argued that the State had breached the no-reprisals agreement when he was disciplined for his conduct during the riot.

Petition for post-conviction relief A legal challenge to the constitutionality of a sentence handed down by a federal or state judge in which a prisoner asks for the sentence imposed to be set aside

ISSUE

Was the no-reprisals agreement, made by the warden under duress and in a violent situation, enforceable?

HOLDING

No. Such an agreement was illegal and void.

REASONING

Any agreement for immunity or amnesty that is produced by unlawful threats, such as the hostage situation in this case, is contrary to public policy and void. Promises extorted through violence and coercion are not promises at all; instead, they are void from the beginning and unenforceable as a matter of public policy. The State could have lived up to such an agreement if it had decided there were valid reasons for doing so. But a court will refuse to uphold such an agreement in circumstances such as these when the State has decided not to abide by its earlier agreement.

MALA IN SE AND *MALA PROHIBITA* BARGAINS

Early on, many courts were dissatisfied with the rule that illegal contracts are absolutely void. Some of these courts therefore distinguished between *bargains that violate statutes because they are evil in themselves (mala in se)* and *bargains that have been merely forbidden by statute (mala prohibita)*. The first type (for instance, an agreement to murder someone) fell within the general rule and was void.

However, some courts were prepared to view bargains included within the second type as voidable rather than void, depending on the nature and effect of the act prohibited by the statute. To illustrate, one case involved the sale of cattle in violation of a law stating that all cattle sold must be tested for brucellosis (a serious disease in cattle) sometime within the thirty-day period preceding the sale. The court clearly could have used this statutory violation as a basis for holding the agreement void. Yet the court concluded that this bargain was *mala prohibita,* not *mala in se,* because the contract was neither in bad faith nor contrary to public policy, and therefore enforced the contract.[1]

You may disagree with the court's interpretation of this infraction of the law. But you should know that in deciding the legality of an agreement, some courts have continued to distinguish between *mala in se* and *mala prohibita* bargains. More recent commentators have criticized these distinctions as invalid by arguing that any bargain that violates a statute is absolutely void no matter what the rationale behind the prohibition is. This represents the position most widely accepted today. Nevertheless, the continued use of these terms demonstrates the tendency of courts to weigh differences in the degree of evil and to determine the availability of judicial relief accordingly. We shall see further examples of this tendency later in the chapter. Two categories of bargains, however, are almost universally recognized as *mala in se:* agreements to commit a crime and agreements to commit a tort.

AGREEMENTS TO COMMIT A CRIME

The agreement we mentioned earlier involving arson could be called a *mala in se* bargain because the subject matter of the agreement itself, the commission of a crime, is morally bad. The same would be true of an agreement to kill someone, a so-called murder contract. Neither party could enforce such agreements; they would be absolutely void.

AGREEMENTS TO COMMIT A TORT

Likewise, an agreement that involves the commission of a tort is illegal and void. Besides fraud, which was mentioned earlier, such bargains may involve agreements to damage the good name of a competitor, to inflict mental distress on a third party, or to trespass against another's **chattels** or property in order to cause injury to the property.

Chattels Articles of personal (as opposed to real) property; any interests in property that are less than a freehold or a fee interest in land

AGREEMENTS VIOLATIVE OF STATUTES

As you know, statutes prohibit many activities. Determining whether a particular activity violates a statute (assuming that the activity is not *mala in se*) requires that courts resort first to the words of the underlying statute. Then

---

[1] First National Bank of Shreveport v. Williams, 346 So.2d 257, 264 (La. App. 1977).

courts must assess the legislative intent and, lastly, examine the social effects of giving or refusing a remedy in the particular situation. The next case is instructive.

Quinn v. Gulf & Western Corporation
644 F.2d 89 (2nd Cir. 1981)

FACTS   Quinn sued Gulf & Western Corporation, which was doing business as Mal Tool, for a 10 percent commission that Quinn had alleged Mal Tool owed him as compensation for his services in helping to procure a Tennessee Valley Authority (TVA) contract for Mal Tool. Mal Tool argued that any sales commission to Quinn was a "contingent fee" barred by a federal procurement statute and regulations.

ISSUE   Did the promised commission violate federal law?

HOLDING   Yes. The agreement was illegal and therefore void.

REASONING   Quinn's agreement was clearly an arrangement for a fee contingent on Mal Tool's contracting with TVA. To enforce such an agreement would encourage the peddling of government influence or access and would thus be contrary to the legislative intent of the procurement statute and regulations. A court of law cannot enforce an agreement that is illegal for the parties to make.

It is worthwhile to explore some categories of activities that courts ordinarily find violative of statutes. Among them are price-fixing agreements, performance of services without a license, Sunday laws, and wagering and usury statutes.

Price-Fixing Agreements

Monopolies The power of firms to carry on a business or a trade to the exclusion of all competitors

Oligopolies Economic conditions in which a small number of firms dominates the market but no one firm controls it

One category of activities that runs afoul of statutes involves price-fixing agreements. The purpose of such agreements generally is to restrain competition so as to create **monopolies** or **oligopolies** in order to control price fluctuations. The Sherman Antitrust Act, the Clayton Act, and the Federal Trade Commission Act, discussed in Chapter 46, comprise the major federal legislative enactments that make such bargains illegal. These agreements may also violate state statutes or alternatively may be invalidated on public policy grounds.

Performance of Services Without a License

Agreements relating to the performance of services without a license may constitute another type of statutory violation. Recall our earlier example involving Sue Weiss and Logan Plumbing Company. To protect the public from unqualified persons, state statutes often require the licensing of such professions as law, medicine, and public accountancy and such trades as electrical work, contracting, and plumbing. Before the state grants a license, the would-be practitioner usually must demonstrate minimal competency, after achieving the required educational qualifications, by successfully passing an examination. In such cases, the absence of a license prevents the professional or tradesperson from enforcing the bargain. Thus, if Sue's state requires Logan Plumbing to use professionally licensed plumbers, and the plumbers are not professionally licensed, Logan cannot force Sue to pay, because this bargain is illegal and void. However, assuming that Logan botches Sue's work and causes flooding in her kitchen, in most jurisdictions Sue will be able to recover her damages from Logan despite the absence of a license.

In contrast to a regulatory licensing scheme such as the one just mentioned, some states require licensing primarily as a revenue-producing mechanism rather than as a device for protecting the health and welfare of its citizens. If the primary intent of the licensing requirement is to produce revenue, the lack of a license will not affect the contract between the parties. If that were the case, Sue would have to compensate Logan.

It pays to remember that courts have fairly wide discretion in these matters and may take into account such factors as the absence of harm resulting from failure to obtain the license, the extent of the knowledge of the persons involved, and the relative "guilt" of the respective parties. If, for example, a court deems the amount forfeited by the unlicensed professional large enough to constitute a penalty, the professional ordinarily will be able to sue for the fee despite the lack of a license. As mentioned before, even in statutes assigning criminal sanctions, courts will look closely at the legislative intent of the statute in deciding whether to give or to withhold remedies.

Sunday laws, so named because they *prohibit the formation or performance of contracts on Sundays,* are troublesome because the terms of such statutes vary widely from state to state. The most common type of statute prohibits the conducting of secular business, or one's "ordinary calling" (such as selling merchandise), on Sunday. (You may be familiar with Sunday laws that forbid the sale of certain alcoholic beverages.) Exceptions usually involve works of charity or necessity, which can be accomplished on Sunday without fear of sanctions.

Sunday Laws

A violation of a Sunday statute in some jurisdictions voids the contract, unless the party asking for recovery can show, for instance, that he or she had no knowledge that the contract was executed on Sunday or that the agreement, though initiated on Sunday, was not accepted (and thus did not ripen into a contract) until later in the week.

Litigants in some jurisdictions have challenged the constitutionality of such statutes. These laws, by singling out Sunday as a "day of rest" from mercantile activity, may violate the First Amendment's prohibition against a governmentally established religion. In other words, Sunday is not the "Sabbath'' for all Americans; yet state governments' enactments of such laws arguably put the interests of one religious group ahead of the interests of others.

Wagering Statutes

Wagering contracts and lotteries are illegal in most states because of statutes prohibiting gambling, betting, and other games of chance. The underlying rationale for these laws is the protection of the public from the crime and familial discord often associated with gambling. To constitute illegal wagering, the activity must involve a person's paying consideration or value in the hope of receiving a prize or other property by chance. Wagering in the legal sense always involves a scheme in which risk has been *artificially* created; hence, insurance contracts or stock transactions in which risk is an inherent feature are not situations that implicate illegal wagering. On the other hand, raffles may be treated as unlawful wagering. For instance, because of relatively soft demand in the housing market, some enterprising couples in various parts of the country have recently attempted to raffle off their homes. The conduct of these people has violated the wagering statutes of some of these jurisdictions. It should be noted, however, that public lotteries are perfectly legal in many states. Additionally, if the participant is not required to give something of value in order to take part in the activity, it is probably not a lottery and consequently is probably legal.

Usury Statutes

Usurious contracts occur when *money is loaned at a greater profit (or rate of interest) than state law permits.* For usury to exist, there must be a loan of money (or an agreement to extend the maturity of a monetary debt) for which the debtor agrees to repay the principal at a rate that exceeds the legal rate of interest. In addition, the lender must intend to violate the usury laws. If these elements are present, the resultant contract is illegal. In most states, a usurious lender will be unable to collect any interest and may also be subject to criminal penalties. In others, only the amount of excess interest is denied; the lender can recover the remaining interest and principal. In a few states, the agreement is void; the lender receives no interest, no principal.

Acceleration clauses
Clauses in contracts that advance the date for payment on the occurrence of a condition or the breach of a duty

Prepayment clauses
Contract clauses that allow the debtor to pay the debt before it is due without penalty

Conditional sales contracts Sales contracts in which the transfer of title to the buyer is subject to a condition, most commonly the payment of the full purchase price by the buyer

Because there are wide variations among state usury laws, it is difficult to generalize. Loans to corporations may be exempt from a jurisdiction's usury statutes, as may short-term loans, especially if the lender will be incurring large risks in making the loans. **Acceleration clauses** and **prepayment clauses** are generally not usurious. The same is true of service fees that reflect the incidental costs of making a loan — filing and recording fees, for example. Sales under revolving charge accounts (open-ended credit accounts) or **conditional sales contracts** ordinarily are not usurious even if a higher-than-lawful rate is charged. Two reasons have been forwarded in justification of this position: (1) a bona fide conditional sale on a deferred-payment basis is not a loan of money; (2) the finance charge is merely a part of an increased purchase price reflective of the seller's risk in giving up possession of personal property (clothes, refrigerators, blenders, and the like) that depreciates quickly in value.

Time-price differential sales contracts may or may not be usurious, depending on applicable state law and/or special consumer protection statutes. Time-price differential sales contracts involve an offer to sell at a designated price for cash (say $6000 for an automobile) or at a higher price on credit (say $7500). Even though the maximum legal rate of interest in this state may be 18 percent, the 25 percent actual rate represented by the credit price will not be usurious as long as the final price reflects the credit nature of the sale rather than an intent to evade the usury laws.

The trend today is to raise the maximum interest rate and to increase the exceptions to the usury laws. Moreover, federally guaranteed loans allow interest rates that would otherwise violate state law. These factors have seriously eroded the original purpose of usury laws — the protection of debtors from excessive rates of interest. But, as mentioned earlier, little uniformity exists in the various states' usury statutes; so it is wise to consult these statutes if you are in doubt about the legality of a particular transaction. The case that follows illustrates a typical situation implicating the possible application of usury laws.

Time-price differential sales contracts
Contracts with a difference in price based on the date of payment, with one price for an immediate payment and another price if the payment is at a later date

Title & Trust Company of Florida v. Parker
468 So.2d 520 (Fla. App. 1985)

FACTS

The Parkers, California residents, were approached in May, 1980, by representatives of a California corporation known as EAC, Inc. (EAC), who proposed that the Parkers loan EAC $200,000. EAC was to repay the Parkers $305,000 ninety days later in exchange for this loan. As security for the loan, the Parkers received a mortgage on a parcel of real estate in Jacksonville, Florida, that EAC allegedly owned. Although the loan was evidenced by a note with a stated principal of $305,000 and a per annum interest rate of 18 percent, the true principal involved was $200,000, of which amount only $175,000 was eventually distributed to EAC. Thus, the actual interest rate involved in the transaction was 52 percent per annum and was in excess of 200 percent for the ninety days. Prior to the distribution of the loan proceeds, the Parkers received a title insurance commitment covering the mortgaged Jacksonville property from Title & Trust. Subsequently, Title & Trust discovered that the deed under which EAC allegedly held title to the property was a forgery. Thus, Title & Trust refused to issue a title insurance policy covering the Jacksonville parcel. In the meantime, before Title & Trust had given notice to Mr. Parker of EAC's defective title, the Parkers had already given the loan principal to the EAC officers. The Parkers sued Title & Trust for breach of commitment to provide title insurance when Title & Trust refused to reimburse the Parkers for their "loss." The Parkers asked for $305,000, the face value of the insurance commitment. Title & Trust argued that the Parkers had sustained no "loss" under the policy when their interest in the Florida property was declared null and void in the true owners' quiet title suit against the Parkers and EAC because under the Florida usury statute the Parkers' note and mortgage were unenforceable.

ISSUE

Could the Parkers recover from Title & Trust the face value of the title insurance commitment issued by Title & Trust even though the agreement in which the Florida property had been given as security for the loan was usurious?

HOLDING

No. Although the Parkers had sustained a loss, to award the Parkers the face value of the policy would give effect to the usurious part of the agreement and thus violate the public policy of the state.

REASONING

Courts, in general, have an affirmative duty to avoid allowing a party who violates public policy to receive any substantial benefits from his or her wrongdoing. Florida's statutes evidenced a clear legislative declaration of a public policy against usury, including both the forfeiture of usurious interest and the nonenforcement of a criminally usurious debt. Accordingly, the trial judge properly disallowed that portion of the damages predicated on the usurious interest rate by awarding the Parkers $175,000 in damages rather than $305,000, the face amount of the policy, or the total coverage afforded by the commitment issued by Title & Trust.

AGREEMENTS VIOLATIVE OF PUBLIC POLICY

As we saw in the *Wagner* case, judges more and more are using public policy as a basis for invalidating agreements. In holding that a contract is void on public policy grounds, a court is deciding the legality of the agreement before it in light of the public interests involved. Public policy frequently becomes an alternative ground for finding illegality. A court may strike down a contract to fix prices because it violates statutes, but it may also invalidate the same agreement because of the damage to the public that such a covenant poses. The *Quinn* decision indicates the law's use of this dual-edged sword, since one basis for the statute at issue in that case was a public policy: prevention of injury to the public interest that otherwise may result from public servants' succumbing to bribes or "kickbacks." However, because *public policy* is such a far-ranging term, courts often have to juggle competing interests in judging the legality of certain types of bargains.

In what is unquestionably one of the most controversial cases of the decade, the New Jersey Supreme Court had to balance such statutory directives and public policies in disposing of the widely publicized "Baby M" case.

In re Baby M
537 A.2d 1227 (N.J. 1988)

FACTS

In February, 1985, William Stern and Mrs. Mary Beth Whitehead entered into a surrogacy contract in which Mrs. Whitehead agreed to bear a child for Stern and his infertile wife. The contract provided that through artificial insemination using Mr. Stern's sperm, Mrs. Whitehead would become pregnant, bear the child, deliver it to Mr. Stern, and terminate her maternal rights so that Mr. Stern could adopt the baby. Mr. Stern, for his part, agreed to attempt the artificial insemination and to pay $10,000 to Mrs. Whitehead upon the delivery of the child to him after its birth. In a separate contract, Mr. Stern agreed to pay $7,500 to the Infertility Center of New York, which had brought the parties together. Mrs. Whitehead gave birth to a healthy baby girl on 27 March 1986. The Sterns named her Melissa; Mrs. Whitehead named her Sara. When the Sterns visited the hospital, Mrs. Whitehead told them she was not sure if she could give up the baby. But on 30 March 1986, she did so. Later that evening, however, she went to the Sterns' house and pleaded with them to let her have a week with the baby because she was suffering greatly about giving up the child. Concerned about the possibility of Mrs. Whitehead's committing suicide, the Sterns agreed, believing Mrs. Whitehead would keep her word. When it became apparent that Mrs. Whitehead would not return the child to the Sterns, Mr. Stern filed suit, seeking enforcement of the surrogacy contract and permanent custody of the child. Mrs. Whitehead, in the meantime, had fled the state; and the Sterns were unable to reacquire possession of Melissa for over four months.

Was such a surrogacy contract legal and enforceable in New Jersey?   **ISSUE**

No. Such a contract violated both New Jersey statutory law and the public policies of the state.   **HOLDING**

The trial court was wrong in enforcing the contract, terminating Mrs. Whitehead's   **REASONING**
parental rights, and allowing Mrs. Stern to adopt the child. Specifically, the surrogacy contract conflicted with laws prohibiting the use of money in connection with adoptions, laws requiring proof of parental unfitness or abandonment before courts could order termination of parental rights or grant adoptions, and laws making surrender of custody and consent to adoption revocable in private placement adoptions. Besides violating statutory law, the surrogacy contract also contravened several public policies of the state: that children should remain with and be brought up by both of the natural parents; that the rights of natural parents are equal concerning their child, with a father's right being no greater than a mother's; that consent to surrender of a child must be voluntary; and that the best interests of the child be taken into account in determining the fitness of the custodial father, the effect on the child of not living with her natural mother, and so forth. Hence, this surrogacy contract created and was based on principles directly contrary to New Jersey laws. Simply put, it guaranteed the separation of a child from its mother; it permitted adoption regardless of the adoptive parent's suitability; it totally ignored the child; it took the child from the mother regardless of her wishes and her maternal fitness; and it did all of this and accomplished all of its goals through the use of money. Moreover, the potential degradation of some women that might result from this arrangement had not been considered either. In sum, the harmful consequences of this surrogacy arrangement, particularly the arrangement's irrevocability and the money that purported to form the consideration for it, infected the entire contract. Therefore, in New Jersey, a surrogate mother's agreement to sell her child was void.

Covenants not to compete, also called *restrictive covenants,* are *express promises that a seller of a business or an employee who leaves a company will not engage in the same or a similar business or occupation for a period of time in a certain geographic area.* Such bargains may or may not be legal. If the purpose of these "noncompete   **Covenants Not to Compete** clauses" is to protect the buyer of a business from the possibility that the seller will set up shop two blocks from the original business establishment, or the former employer from the possibility that the ex-employee will sign on with a competitor, the restrictions on the seller or former employee, if reasonable in *time* and in *geographic scope,* will ordinarily be upheld as legal. But, as mentioned earlier, these situations are fraught with competing policies. It is clearly unfair to shackle unduly the employment opportunities of the seller (or former employee), who has to make a living. Similarly, if we curtail this person's business activities or occupational activities, we are in effect insulating the buyer (or former employer) from competition and may thereby unwittingly bring about higher prices. For this reason, many courts use public policy considerations in scrutinizing these restrictive covenants and in arriving at their decisions.

Usually such covenants are incidental to the sale of a business or to an employment contract. (Agreements not to compete that have no other purpose than the curtailing of competition are illegal as restraints on trade and are violations of antitrust law.) If, however, under the facts and circumstances, a particular covenant not to compete is unreasonably restrictive in time or geographic scope, it is within a court's power to rewrite the covenant so that it is less restrictive (a process called *blue-penciling*) and hence reasonable. But, as you have been cautioned in the past, do not expect courts to save you from bad (or illegal) bargains. Blue-penciling is comparatively rare. In fact, most courts would reject this approach, void the restrictive covenant, and construe the agreement without any reference to the covenant not to compete.

The next case shows how the question of the legality of a restrictive covenant can become the basis for a lawsuit.

Koger Properties, Inc. v. Adams-Cates Company
274 S.E.2d 329 (Ga. 1981)

FACTS   Koger Properties, Inc., a developer of office parks in Atlanta and other southern cities, sued Adams-Cates, the employer of John Heagy. Heagy, a former employee of Koger, had signed a restrictive covenant in which he had promised not to compete with Koger in any metropolitan area where Koger was engaged in its business at the time of Heagy's termination of employment with the company. When Heagy began working for Adams-Cates, managers of an office complex, Koger sued. Koger argued that if Heagy were allowed to work for a competitor in any of the cities where Koger did business, Heagy could lure away actual and potential tenants by using information developed at Koger's expense.

ISSUE   Was this restrictive covenant illegal?

HOLDING   Yes. It was illegal owing to the indefiniteness and unreasonableness of its terms.

A territorial restriction that could not be determined until the date of the employee's termination was too indefinite to be enforced. The covenant was also unreasonably broad in prohibiting Heagy from working in any metropolitan area where Koger was conducting business at the time of Heagy's termination. Such an indefinite and unreasonable restriction was void and unenforceable.

REASONING

Agreements to commit torts are illegal. Indeed, there seems to be little justification for a court's validating an agreement that has as its purpose an intentional breach of the duty of reasonable care to others. On the other hand, is there anything illegal about a bargain in which one party tries in advance to limit its liability in a particular set of circumstances? There unfortunately is no clear-cut answer to this question. Courts judge the legality of such *exculpatory clauses,* or bargains in which one person agrees to exonerate another person's activities from liability, on a case-by-case basis. You are probably familiar with many such attempts at exculpation. For example, a certain dry cleaner always writes on his customers' tickets, "Not responsible for elastic and buttons." When customers sign the tickets, the dry cleaner can argue that the customers have agreed to hold him harmless for any damages to those parts of their clothing. Restaurants that have signs saying "Not responsible for belongings left in booths" are attempting to achieve the same end. In general, these and other agreements in which one party promises not to hold the other liable for negligence are legal. In many jurisdictions, statutes covering workers' compensation, innkeepers, and landlord-tenant relationships make the issue of liability for these particular areas moot. However, in the absence of statutes or clear precedents, courts look closely to see whether the party who agrees to assume the risk of tortious conduct without any recovery has done so voluntarily. Another way of putting this issue is to ask whether the party who has initiated the exculpatory clause has superior bargaining power (or superior knowledge) over the other person. (Recall the bank deposit example earlier in this chapter.) If so, courts may strike the exculpatory clause down as being contrary to public policy. Courts often bandy about words like *oppressive, unconscionable,* and *unfair* when invalidating such clauses.

If the court believes an *adhesion contract* exists — that is, a contract drafted by the stronger party in order to force unfavorable terms on the weaker party — the court will probably find the clause contrary to public policy and thus illegal. This finding is by no means an easy task, however. Courts will necessarily weigh a variety of factors — the age of the parties, their respective degrees of expertise, their mental condition at the time they signed the clause (was the injured party drunk when he signed the exculpatory clause just before climbing onto the "mechanical bull" in Joe's Pub?), whether the language of the clause was in fine print, and the like. After analyzing these and other facts and policies, the court decides the legality of such clauses.

The *Porubiansky* case illustrates one court's disposition of such an issue.

Exculpatory
Clauses

Porubiansky v. Emory University
275 S.E.2d 163 (Ga. App. 1980)
Affirmed, 282 S.E.2d 903 (Ga. 1981)

FACTS   Porubiansky was accepted as a patient at Emory University's School of Dentistry Clinic. Before becoming a patient, she was told that all treatment would be administered by dental students and employees under the direction of a licensed dentist or by a licensed dentist. Porubiansky signed a consent form in which she agreed to hold the clinic and its personnel harmless for any injuries arising out of any dental treatment rendered. After about five months of care, she had a clinic dentist remove an impacted tooth. During this procedure, the dentist noticed that her jaw was broken and told her so. She sued Emory, alleging that her jaw was broken during the negligent removal of her tooth. The clinic denied this and pleaded the exculpatory clause in the consent form as a defense.

ISSUE   Was the exculpatory clause legal and hence a valid defense?

HOLDING   No. The clause was illegal.

REASONING   The exculpatory clause was void as against public policy, since the law requires that dentists possess and exercise a reasonable amount of care and skill. Thus, the public interest of the state of Georgia would not be served if dentists, or dental clinics vested with the responsibility of training future dentists, were permitted to relieve themselves from liability for their own negligence.

EXCEPTIONS: UPHOLDING ILLEGAL AGREEMENTS

As mentioned earlier, the general rule is that an illegal bargain is void; the court leaves the parties where they are as a result of the bargain. Despite this general rule, there are some situations in which a party may bring a successful suit based on an illegal agreement. Usually one cannot sue for enforcement of an illegal executory agreement, but in certain circumstances one may sue if the performance called for in the bargain has been rendered.

Parties Not *in Pari Delicto*

When one of the parties is less guilty than the other, the law states that the parties are not *in pari delicto (they are not equally at fault or equally wrong)*. The less guilty person may recover if recovery would serve the public interest in some way. For instance, the less guilty party may be a member of the class of persons a regulatory statute was designed to protect. If, in our earlier example, the statute requiring plumbers to be licensed were a regulatory as opposed to a revenue-raising statute, Sue would not be *in pari delicto* ("in equal wrong") with the plumber who had failed to comply with the statute. If she had given him $100 as a down payment on a garbage disposal, she could recover this money.

A policy of protecting the public from unlicensed tradespeople would be advanced by allowing her recovery. Such results, then, focus on the conduct of the less guilty party rather than on the illegality of the subject matter of the contract. Similarly, if Joanne works for a photographer who does not have a license as required by a local ordinance, she can still recover the wages due her if she does not know about her boss's noncompliance. The illegality here may be termed *incidental,* or **collateral.**

Collateral Secondary

Even if the parties are *in pari delicto,* the law will allow recovery by the person who shows repentance of the illegal bargain by rescinding it before it is consummated. For example, let us assume that a partnership attempts to bribe a state senator for favorable legislation. This agreement would be illegal because it is harmful to the public. If one of the partners attempts to rescind the transaction before the money is delivered to the senator, he or she can do so. This act is called *repentance.* Courts justify the partner's recovery of the money because such a result furthers the public interest of deterring illegal schemes.

Repentance

Agreements may consist of several different promises supported by different considerations. The parts of the bargain that involve legal promises and legal consideration will be enforced if they can be severed from the illegal parts. If, instead, either the illegal promise or the illegal consideration wholly taints the agreement, the entire agreement is void. Cases involving a restrictive covenant are good examples of *partial illegality.* If a court finds the restrictive covenant to be unreasonable in scope, the judge may sever it from the rest of the agreement because it is illegal. The remainder of the contract — a sale of a business, for example — will ordinarily be enforced because it is perfectly legal; it is divisible from the illegal portion.

Partial Illegality

The law imposes a requirement that the subject matter and purpose of a bargain be legal in order for the bargain to be recognized as a valid contract. A bargain is illegal if its performance is criminal, tortious, or otherwise opposed to public policy. Some courts distinguish between bargains that violate statutes because they are evil in themselves *(mala in se)* and bargains that have merely been forbidden by statute *(mala prohibita).* Many types of bargains violate statutes, such as price-fixing agreements, bargains in contravention of Sunday laws, wagering agreements, and usurious transactions. Performance of services without a license may make the agreement void if the statute is regulatory. In contrast, if the statute requires licensing as a revenue-enhancing measure, lack of a license will not void the bargain. Judges today look increasingly to public policy factors when deciding cases. Covenants not to compete (promises not to engage in the same or a similar business for a period of time in a certain geographic area) and exculpatory clauses (attempts to disclaim liability for negligence or other torts), if too restrictive or one-sided, may be struck down on public policy grounds.

SUMMARY

There are some exceptions to the rule that illegal bargains are void. Among these exceptions are agreements in which the parties are not *in pari delicto,* or of equal guilt; agreements in which one party repents of the illegal bargain before its consummation; and agreements in which the legal portions can be severed from the illegal segments.

DISCUSSION QUESTIONS

1. What is the difference between a *mala in se* and a *mala prohibita* bargain?

2. What is an exculpatory clause? Is it always legal? Why or why not?

3. What are covenants not to compete? What standards do courts use to judge their legality?

4. Describe the difference between a regulatory statute and a revenue-producing statute. What relief will courts give for the violation of these statutes?

5. What is a Sunday law?

6. Why are wagering and lotteries illegal in most jurisdictions?

7. What is a usurious contract?

8. What kinds of common financing devices are not considered usurious?

9. Describe the three most important exceptions to the general rule that an illegal bargain is void.

10. What is an adhesion contract?

CASE PROBLEMS

1. Under the terms of the National Bituminous Coal Wage Agreement of 1974, members of the Bituminous Coal Operators Association (BCOA) agreed to contribute to the United Mine Workers' health and retirement fund at a rate based on the amount of coal produced by the employer and on the amount of coal purchased from other producers who were not BCOA members. Kaiser, a BCOA member, complied with the first clause but refused to pay contributions on nonunion coal purchased. When the trustees of the United Mine Workers sued to compel Kaiser to make these contributions, Kaiser defended by saying that the clauses were illegal in that they violated Sections 1 and 2 of the Sherman Act (particularly the antimonopoly provisions) and a section of the National Labor Relations Act that prevents unions from bargaining for secondary boycotts of non-union goods. What would be the result, and why? (*Kaiser Steel Corp.* v. *Mullins,* 455 U.S. 72 [1982].)

2. A school district imposed a tax on the value of the occupations "of all persons residing in Central Dauphin School District . . . who are eighteen years (18) or older." A court later struck down this levy insofar as it sought to impose an occupations tax on "retired persons, housewives, and others who have not or do not engage in a gainful occupation" and

directed $529,000 in payment of refunds. The school district returned the $529,000 in tax payments but then claimed these refunds as "losses" under its insurance policy. The insurance carrier refused to pay because the money in question had been collected illegally and was an amount "deemed uninsurable." Should the school district collect? Why or why not? (*Central Dauphin School District* v. *American Casualty Company*, 426 A.2d 94 [Pa. 1981].)

3. William "Rick" Malecha sued the St. Croix Valley Skydiving Club, Inc., for damages arising from injuries he had suffered from a skydiving accident. On 27 August 1983, Malecha and two friends had taken a skydiving course of five hours' duration. He had paid for the training that morning and at some point during the day had signed a waiver of liability form. Among other things, the agreement specified that the club could not be "held responsible or liable for any negligence implied or otherwise." Malecha was seriously injured when his parachute failed to open as he made his first jump late in the afternoon of the 27th. When Malecha sued the club for negligence, it contended that his signing the agreement had released it from liability. What arguments should Malecha make in his own behalf? (*Malecha* v. *St. Croix Valley Skydiving Club*, 392 N.W.2d 727 [Minn. App. 1986].)

4. Vitality Centers, Inc. (Vitality), had leased an automatic telephone system from Potomac Leasing Company (Potomac). Potomac had bought the equipment from Leads Unlimited, Inc., the manufacturer, and had then entered into a lease agreement with Vitality. In essence, Potomac served an intermediary function after the manufacturer had located a would-be customer; but Potomac itself had no knowledge of the equipment. Indeed, the lease that Vitality had signed recited that fact. After it had made a few payments on the noncancellable, forty-eight-month lease, Vitality sent the equipment back to Potomac. When Potomac sued to enforce the lease, Vitality asserted that the subject matter of the lease was illegal and that the contract was therefore void. Unknown to Potomac, Vitality had used the equipment to dial phone numbers randomly to leave advertising messages and to record the responses of the persons answering the calls. Arkansas statutes prohibited all such activities. Should a court allow Vitality to raise the alleged illegality of the lease as a defense to Potomac's enforcement of the lease? (*Potomac Leasing Company* v. *Vitality Centers, Inc.*, 718 S.W.2d 928 [Ark. 1986].)

5. Richard Zientara had asked his friend and coworker, Chester Kaszuba, to have his wife, Bernice, purchase an Illinois lottery ticket for Zientara at her place of work in Illinois. Zientara and the Kaszubas were all Indiana residents. Kaszuba agreed, and Zientara therefore gave him an envelope containing the purchase price and the numbers selected for the ticket. Although Zientara's number won a lottery worth $1,696,800, Kaszuba refused to give Zientara the ticket and even made an effort to claim the

ticket for himself. As a result, Zientara filed suit against the Kaszubas on several theories, including breach of contract. The Kaszubas argued that the transaction with Zientara was an illegal and therefore an unenforceable transaction because the Indiana Constitution prohibits lotteries. Would a court find this assertion persuasive? (*Kaszuba* v. *Zientara,* 506 N.E.2d 1 [Ind. 1987].)

6. Brandau had signed a covenant not to compete in which he had agreed not to engage in the fertilizer business for one year following the termination of his employment with Evco. In exchange, Evco had agreed to pay Brandau $40,500 in three installments. After some wranglings about the second installment, a new covenant was accepted, and the second installment was paid. Several weeks later, Brandau began working for Lor-Al Corporation, Evco's competitor. Evco therefore no longer was willing to pay the final installment, and Brandau wanted his last month's wages from Evco. In the resultant lawsuit, what was the result? Why? (*Evco Distributing, Inc.* v. *Brandau,* 626 P.2d 1192 [Kan. App. 1981].)

7. Anabas Export Ltd. (Anabas) sold and delivered stickers featuring Michael Jackson's portrait to Alper Industries, Inc. (Alper), for resale and distribution by Alper. Anabas had not obtained Jackson's written permission to use his picture as required by New York law. When Anabas sued Alper for the contract price, Alper argued that the sale of the stickers was void and unenforceable. Was Alper right? Why or why not? (*Anabas Export, Ltd.* v. *Alper Industries, Inc.* 603 F.Supp. 1275 [S.D.N.Y. 1985].)

8. Kimbrough and Fox had been partners in a business known as ARA Rental and were also the equal owners of a corporation called C & G Inc., which consisted primarily of pieces of real property and equipment. When they decided to end their business relationship with each other, they divided these assets into two parcels. On 21 December 1979, Kimbrough and Fox tossed a coin to determine who would get each parcel. As a result of this coin toss, Kimbrough received what he deemed to be the less desirable parcel of property. Kimbrough later sued to have this agreement set aside on the ground that the coin toss violated the state's wagering statute and thus was void. How would you rule in this case if you were the judge? (*Kimbrough* v. *Fox,* 631 S.W.2d 606 (Tex. App. 1982].)

9. Wheeler was an industrial engineer who had performed industrial engineering services for Bucksteel Co. (Bucksteel). Oregon law provided that no one could practice engineering in the state unless he or she were registered and had obtained the required certificate to practice engineering. When Wheeler sued Bucksteel for services rendered, Bucksteel argued that the company owed Wheeler nothing because his failure to register as an engineer had made the contract for his services illegal. Was Bucksteel correct? (*Wheeler* v. *Bucksteel Co.,* 698 P.2d 995 [Or. App. 1985].)

10. San Benito Bank sued Rio Grande Music Company (RG Music) on a promissory note signed by Paco Betancourt, the founder of RG Music. Part of the company's "business" involved the smuggling of electronic equipment into Mexico. The bank had agreed to treat incoming checks drawn against Mexican banks in payment for the smuggled goods as "cash collections." When several of these checks were dishonored, Betancourt signed the promissory note that was at issue in the case to make up the deficiencies owed to the bank. When the bank sued to collect on this promissory note, RG Music contended that the bank's knowledge that the company was using the funds in illegal transactions made the note unenforceable. Was RG Music absolved from liability owing to this underlying illegality? (*San Benito Bank & Trust Company* v. *Rio Grande Music Company*, 686 S.W.2d 635 [Tex. App. 1985].)

CHAPTER 13

Genuineness of the Contractual Assent

REALITY OF CONSENT

We have already briefly discussed the proposition that a valid offer and acceptance form the heart of all contracts. We have also seen that an agreement supported by consideration, made by parties having the ability to contract, and based on a subject that is legal should issue into a valid contract. But appearances can be deceptive. Before we check to see whether the agreement necessitates proper form (that is, whether the contract must be in writing), a topic we will take up in the next chapter, we first have to ascertain whether the parties have *genuinely* assented to the contract. Put another way, is the consent given by the parties real, or are the facts actually different from those to which they have outwardly agreed? The existence of fraud, misrepresentation, mistake, duress, undue influence, or unconscionability precludes the mutual assent that is the foundation of modern contract law. Since these matters are of some consequence in our private and business dealings, we shall now turn our attention to a discussion of them and their legal effect.

FRAUD

Fraud is a word we all use fairly loosely, mainly because it lends itself to many definitions. At base, it consists of deception or hoodwinking, and it seems to involve a communication of some sort. But as one ancient case notes, "[a] nod or a wink, or a shake of the head or a smile" will do.[1] Sometimes even silence will suffice.

Hard though it is to pin down the essence of fraud, one common definition states that fraud is *a deliberate misrepresentation of a material fact with the intent to induce another person to enter into a contract that will be injurious to that person.* The essence of fraud becomes clearer as we break this definition down into smaller components.

To constitute fraud, the misrepresentation or misstatement must concern a *fact.* A fact is something reasonably subject to exact knowledge. Thus, a statement about the size of a car engine or the dimensions of a lot are probably factual.

Elements of Fraud

To show this first element of fraud, then, the plaintiff will have to prove that the defendant misstated a fact. Predictions, statements of value, and expressions of opinions do not generally equate with misrepresentations of fact.

Actually, in any given situation, it may be difficult to distinguish a fact from an opinion. Suppose a car salesperson says to you, "This little dandy will get you down the road at a pretty good clip. It has a great engine. It's a V-6, and those engines have been very serviceable." The first two remarks are probably opinions, also known as "puffs" or "dealer's talk." The statement about the type of engine probably is a fact. You may be unhappy, for instance, if you find a V-8 engine in the car after you purchase it; or if you find out V-6s have many problems and the salesperson knew this. In such a case, you may want to argue that you have been a victim of misrepresentation. However, courts tend to discount statements of value because of genuine differences in the way people assess things. When Joe says, "That ring is worth a thousand dollars," unless Joe is a jewelry dealer or an expert regarding the matter at hand and the other person is not, most courts will refuse to call Joe's statement a fact. Joe may indeed believe that his wedding ring is that dear, due to sentimentality. Such statements of value, because they are not factual, ordinarily do not constitute this first element of a showing of fraud.

The second element that a plaintiff must prove to recover in fraud is the *materiality* of the fact that was allegedly misstated. A fact is not material unless the plaintiff considers it of some importance when making the decision to enter the contract. To use our earlier example, you may not care one whit if the engine is a V-6. If you do not, the lack of a V-6 in the car you buy will not be a material fact. A court will enforce the bargain despite your protestations. The mileage of the car, the number of previous owners, the extent of the **warranties** given — all these will ordinarily be material to you. Misstatements about these facts may therefore lead to liability if you prove the other elements of fraud.

Warranties Representations that become part of the contract and that are made by a seller of goods at the time of the sale as to the character, quality, or nature of the goods

---

[1] Walters v. Morgan, 3 DeF., F. & J. 718, 724 (1861).

Scienter Guilty
knowledge; specifically,
one party's prior knowledge
of the cause of a subse-
quent injury to another
person

The element of fraud that is most unpleasant, as well as most difficult to prove, is the defendant's *knowledge of the falsity of his or her statement.* Sometimes called *scienter,* this means an evil intent. In other words, the defendant knew, or should have known, that he or she was misstating an important fact at the time of making the statement. Outright lies would, of course, meet this third requirement. Interestingly, the defendant may also be liable for reckless use of the truth or for a statement made without verifying its accuracy when verification was possible. To illustrate, assume that a prospective buyer says to the homeowner, "I guess the property line extends to that fence, doesn't it?" The homeowner nods yes, even though the line actually does not extend that far. What the homeowner may later call laziness may nevertheless be circumstantial evidence of the existence of *scienter* because that person presumably can ascertain fairly easily the boundaries of the property by checking the title. If the buyer purchases in reliance on this statement, a cause of action in fraud may be possible.

Closely related to the requirement of knowledge of the falsity of the statement is an *intent to deceive.* As noted earlier, deception is the hallmark of fraud. This element is difficult to disprove if the first three elements have been established, because courts can usually find no satisfactory reason for a defendant's misstatements except an intent to induce the plaintiff into accepting a sharp bargain.

The plaintiff must also prove that he or she *relied on the deception.* This showing will not be particularly burdensome, assuming the plaintiff's reliance is reasonable. For example, if Tom inspects a lakefront cottage with a front porch that is on the verge of caving into the lake, a court will not allow him to cry "foul" (or "fraud") if the porch crumbles into the water one month after Tom buys the cottage. The same will be true even if the owner has said the cottage is structurally sound. Clearly, Tom should have been aware of such a *patent* (obvious) defect. Since his reliance is unreasonable, he will not win if he sues for fraud. Changing the facts to involve carpenter ant infestation rather than a sagging porch, if we assume the insect damage is a *latent* defect (hidden/unobservable by the human eye), Tom may win unless the court thinks Tom's refraining from ordering a pest inspection is in itself unreasonable.

The final element of a plaintiff's proof, *detriment,* or injury, normally is not difficult to show. In our last example, Tom can argue that his damages amount to the sum needed to rid the cottage of carpenter ants and to repair the substructure of the dwelling. Alternatively, Tom may ask for rescission of the contract. If granted by a court, he will turn the cottage over to the original owner, and the owner will make restitution of the price Tom has paid for the property.

The following case illustrates what happens when a plaintiff is unsuccessful in proving all the elements of fraud.

Dement v. *Atkins & Ash*
631 P.2d 606 (Haw. App. 1981)

Dement owned thirteen lots, most of which were leased to Hirahara until 1979. **FACTS**
Wanting to develop the land, she signed an agreement with Atkins & Ash that
obligated her to pay the firm fees of $3000 per month for their services. She also
agreed to pay for architectural, soil, and structural services needed to develop the
property. Dement glanced at the agreement but did not read it. The next day she put
$20,000 in an account from which either she or Atkins & Ash could draw. After
$18,097.13 had been spent without the project's materializing (owing to Hirahara's
refusal to sell his lease or to participate in the project), Dement sued Atkins & Ash for
fraud and misrepresentation.

Were the elements of fraud present so as to justify an award of damages to Dement? **ISSUE**

No. She had failed to prove fraud. **HOLDING**

There was no evidence to show that Atkins & Ash had made any representations to **REASONING**
Dement before she had signed the agreement. Because there were no representations, she certainly could show no reliance either. Since fraud involves a representation of a material fact made for the purpose of inducing the other party to act,
known to be false by one party but reasonably believed true by the other party, and
on which the other party relies and acts to her damage, it was impossible for Dement
to establish all the elements necessary to prove fraud.

Successful proof of a cause of action in fraud usually justifies *rescission,* or the
setting aside of the contract. Hence, such contracts are voidable at the option of
the injured party (Tom, in the example we used earlier). As mentioned, an
alternative to rescission is recovery of damages sufficient to restore Tom to the
status quo, or the position he would have been in had the facts of the transaction
mirrored his conception of them at the time of his acceptance. Tom, as plaintiff, faces one final pitfall: he must act as quickly as possible, or he may waive
his cause of action, as will be explained later.

No discussion of fraud is complete without a reference to *silence* and its effect on Silence
whether a court will grant relief. The common law steadfastly held that "mere
silence is not fraud." This conclusion was predicated on the belief that fraud
necessitates some sort of overt communication. Since by definition silence
denotes the total absence of any statement, the rule arose that one could not be
liable for fraud unless one had said or done something (remember our first
element requiring a misstatement or misrepresentation of a fact). Many jurisdictions now reject this rule and hold, for instance, that the seller should

voluntarily tell Tom of any drainage problems, ventilation problems, or the like in order to encourage nonconcealment and honesty in business transactions. Similarly, if the buyer asks a question, the seller must answer truthfully and correct any wrong assumptions under which the buyer may be operating. A seller's silence in such instances today may not save the seller from possible legal liability. Still, the strict rule is that there is generally no duty to speak.

Even the common law, however, deemed some situations so fraught with the possibility of injury or detriment that it imposed a duty to speak on the party possessing the information. We have already examined one of these situations, that of latent defects. There is also a duty to speak in situations in which the parties owe each other **fiduciary** duties, or duties that arise from a relationship of trust. For example, an investment advisor should inform her client of her part ownership in ABC Corporation if the client asks her whether ABC stock is a "good deal." Similarly, if you are applying for insurance coverage, you cannot be silent if you are asked questions about your medical history. To avoid fraud, you must, for example, disclose the existence of a heart condition. Finally, a statement made in preliminary negotiations (such as, "This car has never been in a wreck") that is no longer true at the time of the execution of the contract (the car was hit from behind in the meantime) must be disclosed in order to escape a possible lawsuit based on fraud.

These are a few examples of situations in which there is an absolute duty to speak. Failure to speak is tantamount to fraud. In other situations, there may or may not be a duty to speak, as the next case shows.

Fiduciary   One who holds a special position of trust or confidence and who is thereby expected to act with the utmost good faith and loyalty

---

Hauben v. Harmon
605 F.2d 920 (5th Cir. 1979)

FACTS   Hauben sued Harmon for fraud and misrepresentation and sought rescission of a land sale contract he had entered into with Harmon. The land Hauben had purchased lies in a district where land is subject to **condemnation** by the state of Florida for flood control purposes. Harmon had not disclosed the state's possible condemnation to Hauben prior to the sale. Some months after the execution of the contract, the state filed a condemnation suit, and Hauben sued for rescission of the contract based on fraud.

Condemnation   The process by which privately held land is taken for a public use despite the owner's objection and lack of consent

ISSUE   Did Harmon's nondisclosure to Hauben of the fact of possible condemnation constitute fraud?

HOLDING   No. The nondisclosure was not tantamount to fraud.

REASONING   Before signing the contract, Hauben had inspected the property on two occasions, and Harmon's broker had even encouraged Hauben to call the local zoning board if he had any questions about the property. Even though Harmon had been in contact with the supervisors of the flood control project regarding the possible condemnation of this land, whether the piece of land sold to Hauben would be condemned remained purely speculative. Although nondisclosure of a material fact may justify a finding of fraud, a failure to disclose mere possibilities could not amount to a failure to disclose material facts. Moreover, here the buyer and seller apparently had equivalent access to information concerning the property; so it was not fraud that the seller knew facts unknown to the buyer yet refrained from telling the buyer of those facts.

MISREPRESEN-TATION

We have spoken at length about fraud. We can handle the subject of *misrepresentation* much more summarily. Basically, everything we have previously noted about fraud is true of a cause of action involving misrepresentation, with one notable exception: misrepresentation lacks the elements of *scienter* and intent to deceive. Nevertheless, misrepresentation (often called *innocent misrepresentation* to differentiate it from fraud) can lead to the imposition of legal remedies. The property owner's statement about the property boundaries may amount to innocent misrepresentation if *scienter* cannot be proved. Misrepresentation, or *the innocent misstatement of a material fact that is relied on with resultant injury,* makes the contract voidable at the option of the injured party. Rescission thus remains a possible (and in many jurisdictions the exclusive) remedy. Again, the plaintiff must act in a timely manner so as not to waive the cause of action.

Practically speaking, most plaintiffs allege both fraud and misrepresentation in the same suit. Fraud is harder to prove but is a more desirable theory from the plaintiff's point of view because successful proof of fraud brings with it the possibility of recovery under the tort of deceit. The elements of deceit are identical to those of fraud and upon a showing of deceit, a court may award *punitive* damages (damages beyond the actual losses suffered) in addition to the actual damages normally recoverable for fraud. But even if the plaintiff fails to prove fraud (and its twin, deceit), recovery on grounds of misrepresentation is possible. At the very least, a showing of fraud or misrepresentation will be grounds for rescission.

MISTAKE

Human nature is such that people often try to unravel transactions because they have made an error about some facet of the deal. Imagine the havoc that would arise if courts readily accepted these hindsight arguments. The upshot would be a decrease in contracts, since people would be wary of dealing with each other. As you no doubt realize, such unpredictability would unduly hamper commercial pacts. On the other hand, we have repeatedly stressed the importance of mutual assent in contract law. Thus, the law, on policy grounds, wishes to set the contract aside if the error is so great that it has tainted the parties' consent to the agreement.

The legal doctrine of *mistake* tries to balance these competing interests. Mistake occurs when *the parties are wrong about the existence or absence of a fact that is material to their transaction.* Note that the parties must be wrong about material *facts.* Thus, legal mistake is not synonymous with ignorance, inability, or inaccurate judgments relating to value or quality. Courts will rescind contracts on the ground of mistake *only* if the error is so fundamental that it cannot be said that the parties' states of mind were in agreement about the essential facts of the transaction. Mistakes as to law, in contrast, will oftentimes not form grounds for rescission of the contract. There are two different kinds of mistake: unilateral and bilateral (or mutual) mistake.

Unilateral Mistake

As the term implies, in a *unilateral mistake, only one party is mistaken about a material fact.* The general rule, with some exceptions, is that the courts will not rescind such contracts. The parties are held to their bargains as forged.

Unilateral mistakes often occur because of misplaced expectations of value. Let us suppose that Jacques goes to an antique store to look for a Duncan Phyfe table. He finds a table that he believes to be a Duncan Phyfe, and without mentioning his belief to the store owner, pays a hefty price for it. Later that evening, a friend informs him the table is not a Duncan Phyfe. If Jacques tries to avoid the contract, he will not be successful because only he was mistaken about a material fact — that is, that the table was a Duncan Phyfe. He was also mistaken as to value. In such unilateral mistake situations, courts take a "hands off" approach and leave the parties with the bargains they have made. Rescission of the contract is not granted.

The result here could be different if the store owner knew (or should have known) of Jacques's error or in some other fashion acted fraudulently or unconscionably. But the facts do not support such a conclusion; if they did, courts might allow rescission of the contract.

Likewise, courts will suspend the general rule of refusing to grant relief for unilateral mistakes in situations in which the mistake is a result of business computations. As the next decision illustrates, certain requirements must be met; but, in general, courts will grant rescission in such circumstances if the rescission will not injure any third parties. Note that rescission was the remedy given in the following case even though only Dick was in error (that is, the mistake was unilateral).

Dick Corporation v. Associated Electric Cooperative, Inc.
475 F. Supp. 15 (W.D. Mo. 1979)

FACTS Dick Corporation was a construction firm. In submitting a bid for the construction of a power plant, Dick made a mistake of $1,000,000. Dick bid $13,600,000 when it meant to bid $14,600,000. This occurred because the number $100,000 was placed on the summary sheet instead of the correct figure of $1,100,000. Dick was the lowest bidder on the project; but because of the discrepancy between its bid and the next lowest bid ($15,674,000), the engineering firm to which Dick had sent the bid had asked Dick to recheck its figures. The next morning, Dick called to say it had discovered its error. Dick wanted to perform the contract at the corrected price; and the Cooperative wanted it to do so, since even at the corrected price Dick was the lowest bidder.

Did Dick's unilateral mistake merit a court's giving the remedy of **reformation?**

ISSUE

Yes. The court reformed the contract to the correct sum of $14,600,000.

HOLDING

When a bidder for a public contract makes a unilateral mistake in preparing the bid owing to incorrect business computations, and the mistake is otherwise remediable, the bidder may obtain equitable relief by rescission or cancellation of the contract. Such relief will not be granted unless the error were made in good faith, prompt notice of the error were given, and the offeree had not altered its position because of the bid so as to suffer a hardship if relief were given. Put another way, the prerequisites for obtaining appropriate equitable relief are (1) the mistake must be of such consequence that enforcement would be unconscionable; (2) the mistake must relate to the substance of the matter under consideration; (3) the mistake must have occurred in good faith and regardless of the exercise of ordinary care; (4) it must be possible to return the other party to the status quo; and (5) there must exist no other circumstances that would make it inequitable to grant relief. Since both parties wanted the contract to continue, the court therefore ordered reformation and corrected the bid to $14,600,000.

REASONING

Reformation Equitable remedy whereby a court corrects a written instrument in order to remove a mistake and to make the agreement conform to the terms to which the parties originally agreed

---

If *both parties are in error about the essence of the agreement, bilateral* (or mutual) *mistake* exists. Courts will rescind such agreements on the rationale that, owing to a mistake about the existence, identity, or nature of the subject matter of the contract, a valid agreement has not occurred. If a mutual mistake of fact is present, either party may disaffirm this voidable contract unless rescission will cause injuries to innocent third parties. This is so because the parties' minds have not met on the salient facts of the transaction. For example, assume an American company contracts with a foreign company (headquartered in New York) for hand-loomed rugs. The firms contract in April, but, unknown to both parties, a warehouse fire had destroyed the rugs in March. The destruction of the subject matter makes the contract voidable on the grounds of bilateral mistake: the parties have made an error regarding a significant fact — that is, that the rugs existed at the time of contract formation. Lastly, **ambiguities** may bring about mutual mistake as well. If the American buyer believes that the term *rugs* means room-sized carpets, but, because of language difficulties, the foreign seller envisions rugs as identical in size to wall hangings, this ambiguity may constitute mutual mistake. If so, rescission will be justifiable.

Bilateral Mistake

Ambiguities Uncertainties regarding the meanings of expressions used in contractual agreements

If a court can easily remedy the mistake, a court may *reform* the contract, or *rewrite it to reflect the parties' actual intentions* (as the *Dick Corporation* court did). In

Reformation

our last example, assuming the rugs were obtainable, once the ambiguity comes to light, reformation would permit a court to make the subject matter of the contract room-sized rugs. After resort to a court's equitable powers of reformation, the contract would be fully enforceable. Be aware, though, that large backlogs of court cases form a substantial impediment to the availability of reformation as a practical remedy. As we have discussed throughout this unit on contracts, take pains to ascertain exactly what your agreement means beforehand. You will thereby avoid a great many frustrations (and expenses).

DURESS

There can be no genuine assent to the terms of an agreement where one person has assented while under duress. The person who has so assented can ask for rescission of the contract on the ground of duress.

Asserting the defense of *duress* means alleging that *one has been forced into the contract against one's will.* To constitute duress, the coercion must be so extreme that the victim has lost all ability to assent freely and voluntarily to the transaction. Given this definition, courts look for evidence of physical threats or threats that, if carried out, would cause intense mental anguish. Forcing a person to sign a contract at gunpoint would, of course, represent duress. To most courts, so would a spouse's threat to tell the parties' children that the other spouse has committed adultery. If, as a result of this intimidation, the spouse signs over a disproportionate share of the marital property, courts could rescind this agreement on the basis of duress. Similarly, courts generally view threats to institute criminal actions (even if there is a basis for these) in order to extract a contractual agreement as duress. Courts, however, ordinarily do not see threats of civil suits as equaling duress. Note how the court construed the threat involved in the case that follows.

Germantown Manufacturing Co. v. Rawlinson
491 A.2d 138 (Pa. Super. 1985)

FACTS Robert Rawlinson was the assistant controller at the Germantown Manufacturing Company. As such, he had embezzled over $327,000 from the company. When this misappropriation of funds was discovered, a representative of the company's insurer came to the Rawlinsons' house to have Mr. and Mrs. Rawlinson sign two **confession of judgment notes** to cover the embezzled funds. The first note was for $160,000—the amount Mr. Rawlinson admitted having taken. The second was for all amounts in excess of $160,000 that Rawlinson subsequently was determined to have embezzled. The insurance company representative allegedly indicated to Mrs. Rawlinson that since the Rawlinsons had $160,000 readily available, the judgment was, in effect, already satisfied. He also stated that there would be no criminal prosecution of Mr. Rawlinson if the Rawlinsons cooperated. Mrs. Rawlinson understood this to mean that if she signed the confession of judgment notes, her husband would not go to jail. During this meeting, she was crying

Confession of judgment notes
Promissory notes in which the defendant has given the plaintiff written permission to enter a judgment in favor of the plaintiff against the defendant in the event of a lawsuit

and visibly upset about what her husband had done. She had also recently suffered a miscarriage. The first note was ultimately satisfied, but the total amount owed on the second note turned out to be over $212,000. Mrs. Rawlinson asked the court to open judgment on the second note so that she could assert the defenses of fraud, misrepresentation, and duress to avoid her obligation on the second note.

Was Mrs. Rawlinson's signature on the second note procured by fraud, misrepresentation, and/or duress so as to permit the court to open judgment on that note?

ISSUE

Yes. Mrs. Rawlinson's signature had been obtained by fraudulent misrepresentations, and she had agreed to be liable on the note while under duress.

HOLDING

The representative of the insurance company had made fraudulent misrepresentations when he stated that the judgment was in effect satisfied while asking her to sign *both* notes. The misrepresentations were also material because they had induced her to sign the second note. Had she known the true terms of the second note, she would not have signed it. Hence, Mrs. Rawlinson had presented sufficient evidence of duress to constitute a meritorious defense and thus render the contract voidable. Moreover, the representative's statements included a threat to instigate a criminal prosecution of Mrs. Rawlinson's spouse. Thus, the "choice" available to Mrs. Rawlinson smacked of impermissible coercion. Her only alternative was to refuse to sign and thus place an unbearable stress on her marriage. This lack of meaningful choice represented the epitome of duress and unconscionability as well. Given the presence of fraud, misrepresentation, duress, and unconscionability, Mrs. Rawlinson should be allowed to open judgment on the note and to avoid its application to her.

REASONING

Our discussion to this point has focused on personal duress. Recently, the doctrine of *economic duress* has gained currency. Economic duress occurs when *one party is forced to agree to a further demand (usually an increase in price) as a consequence of receiving the commodities or services to which he or she is entitled under the contract.* In most instances, the injured party cannot obtain the goods elsewhere — hence, the wrongfulness of the leverage exerted over that person. We can use our earlier example of the hand-loomed rugs to illustrate this concept. Assume the New York-based rug company has the only hand-loomed rugs around, and the American buyer has agreed to pay $2500 per rug. Economic duress exists if the seller tells the American buyer (who has orders waiting to be filled) that he can have the rugs only if he is willing to pay $4000 apiece for them. Given the compulsion and the lack of alternate sources owing to the uniqueness of the goods, a court may well force the foreign company to sell the rugs at $2500 or allow the American to recover, after the fact, the difference in the contract prices.

Yet whether a court will grant a recovery to a plaintiff who alleges economic duress (or business compulsion) depends heavily on the particular facts of a given situation. For a good example of this proposition, read the next case.

Clearwater Construction & Engineering, Inc. v. Wickes Forest Industries
697 P.2d 1146 (Idaho 1985)

FACTS Clearwater Construction & Engineering, Inc. (Clearwater), and Wickes Forest Industries (Wickes) entered into a contract for the construction of several forest service roads called the Van Buren project. This contract extended through 31 December 1976. Clearwater did not complete the contract by this date, however, because logging operations had hampered its excavation work. On 1 February 1977 the parties executed a second contract that extended the completion date on the Van Buren project until 31 December 1977. Clearwater nonetheless experienced similar difficulties in completing the project by the 1977 date, owing, in Clearwater's view, to Wickes's failure to remove the right-of-way logs. Clearwater later filed suit for damages for Wickes's failure to pay Clearwater the contract price. At trial, Clearwater argued that the 1977 contract was either a valid, binding agreement which Wickes had breached or that, alternatively, it was invalid as the product of unlawful economic duress. Clearwater asserted the existence of economic duress as deriving from Wickes's alleged breaches of the 1975 contract, which breaches placed Clearwater in so precarious a financial condition that Clearwater was forced to sign the 1977 contract, against its will, in order to save itself from financial ruin. Wickes contended that Clearwater had an adequate remedy at law for the alleged breach of the 1975 contract and thus no economic duress was present. Wickes alternatively maintained that whether economic duress existed was irrelevant anyway, since Clearwater by its conduct had ratified the 1977 contract.

ISSUE Did the evidence show Clearwater had entered the 1977 contract as a result of economic duress? Alternatively, had Clearwater ratified the 1977 contract?

HOLDING Because Clearwater had ratified the 1977 contract, the trial court had committed reversible error by submitting the issue of economic duress to the jury.

REASONING The prerequisites for establishing the defense of economic duress, or business compulsion, are (1) that one side involuntarily accepted the terms of the other; (2) that the circumstances permitted no other alternative; and (3) that the circumstances resulted from the coercive acts of the opposite party. The precedents in this jurisdiction require the plaintiff to show more than a mere reluctance to accept or financial embarrassment in order to substantiate an allegation of economic duress. Rather, there must be a showing of acts on the part of the defendant that produced these two factors. In short, there must be proof that the duress resulted from the *defendant's* wrongful and oppressive conduct and not from the *plaintiff's* necessities. However, Clearwater's clear ratification of the 1977 contract made it unnecessary for the court to decide whether economic duress had been present. The general rule is that a contract entered into under duress is not void, but merely voidable, and may be ratified by subsequent acts of the party claiming duress. Ratification results where the party entering into the contract under duress intentionally accepts its benefits, remains silent, or acquiesces in it after an opportunity to avoid it, or recognizes its validity by acting upon it. The evidence indicated that Clearwater and Wickes had dealt with each other for over three years before Clearwater had first contended that the 1977 contract was invalid as a product of economic duress. In view of this undisputed evidence, the trial court was wrong in submitting the issue of economic duress to the jury. Instead, the judge should have determined the ratification issue as a matter of law.

As has been true of most reality-of-consent situations discussed in this chapter, contracts made under duress are ordinarily voidable. Hence, rescission may be effected at the option of the injured party *unless* the injured party ratifies the contract by acquiescing in the coercive conduct for an unreasonably long time. However, sometimes in such cases the conduct exemplifying duress is so extreme that a court will find the contract void. Threats directed at third parties (such as a relative) may give rise to duress of this sort if one party enters into the contract to protect the innocent third party.

UNDUE INFLUENCE

Closely related to duress is the concept of undue influence. Indeed, many courts view it as a subcategory of duress. Like duress, its existence depends heavily on the facts.

Undue influence is the use of a relationship of trust and confidence to extract contractual advantages. Newspapers are full of examples of such situations. Recall the allegations of undue influence that surround nurses who have been named beneficiaries of their patients' sizable estates or lawyers who have enormously benefited from their clients' **testamentary** dispositions. Since the favored nurse or lawyer has the ability to dominate or overreach the other party, the law often allows the rescission of such contracts. Because of the domination by another, the contracting party has actually not exerted his or her free will in entering into the contract but instead has given effect to the will or wishes of the other party.

Testamentary
Pertaining to a will

The law will presume undue influence in certain circumstances, notably in fiduciary relationships. In the example of the lawyer that we just cited, the mere existence of the relationship will require the lawyer to prove that the client made the disposition free from the lawyer's coercion. The law will demand that the lawyer, as a fiduciary, act with utmost good faith in dealing with persons who will be predisposed to follow whatever the lawyer advises. Like lawyers, parents may enjoy fiduciary relationships with their children, doctors with their patients, accountants with their clients, and so on. It is sometimes difficult for courts to determine when the persuasiveness of the fiduciary has become so intense that the other party has lost all vestiges of free will. But when they are convinced that this has occurred, they permit rescission of the challenged contract.

UNCONSCION-ABILITY

You may have noted some similarities between the concept of unconscionability, which we discussed in Chapter 10, and the ideas we have been considering in this chapter. Especially in the context of consumer law, some courts have set contracts aside when they have found the bargaining power of the parties so unequal as to be commercially shocking or unreasonably oppressive. In Chapter 12, we learned that some courts call such agreements contracts of adhesion, meaning that one party to the contract is able to impose its will on the other party through overreaching. The Uniform Commercial Code validates this approach in Section 2–302, but not all states have adopted this section of the UCC. Nevertheless, unconscionability may signal a lack of meaningful assent to a contract and may justify a court's subsequent intervention in behalf of the injured party.

SUMMARY

To have a valid contract, the assent of the parties must be genuine. The existence of fraud, misrepresentation, mistake, duress, undue influence, or unconscionability precludes the reality of consent that is the foundation of modern contract law. Fraud is a deliberate misrepresentation of a material fact with the intent to induce another person to enter a contract that will be injurious to that person. Predictions, statements of value, and opinions do not constitute fraud. Probably the most difficult element to prove is the defendant's knowledge of the falsity of the statement, or *scienter*. The plaintiff's reliance on the deception must be reasonable, or the plaintiff will be precluded from recovering. Successful proof of fraud makes the contract voidable and justifies rescission. Although the common law held that mere silence is not fraud, there were exceptions to this doctrine even in early common law times. Today, the judicial trend is to force disclosure of material facts if their concealment may injure the other party. Innocent misrepresentation may also result in legal liability.

Mistake occurs when the parties are wrong about the existence or absence of a fact that is material to their transactions. There are two types of mistake: unilateral (one person is in error) and bilateral, or mutual (both parties are in error). Courts will generally not rescind unilateral mistakes unless the other party knows, or should have known, of the mistaken party's error or uses it to take unconscionable advantage of the injured party. In these cases, as in situations involving errors in business computations, courts will allow rescission. If a mutual or bilateral mistake of fact is present, either party can disaffirm the contract. Ambiguity, for example, may lead to rescission. The equitable remedy of reformation allows a court to rewrite a contract to reflect the parties' actual intentions, but courts will not always permit reformation.

Duress exists when a person's will has been overridden as a result of another person's threats. Duress may be either personal or economic, the latter occurring when a seller withholds scarce commodities or services in order to extract a higher contract price. Undue influence is the use of a relationship of trust and confidence to gain contractual advantages. In certain relationships, the law will presume undue influence. The existence of unconscionability may signal a lack of meaningful assent to a contract and thus constitute grounds for a court's setting the contract aside.

<table>
<tr><td>

1. Can an opinion be equivalent to fraud?
2. When is a fact material?
3. What sorts of conduct may indicate the defendant's knowledge of a statement's falsity?
4. Discuss the requirement of a plaintiff's reliance when alleging fraud. What are the implications of this requirement?
5. How does silence relate to the legal theory of fraud?
6. In what situations is there a legal duty to speak?
7. Name, define, and explain the remedies for the two types of mistakes.
8. Define *duress.*
9. Discuss the recently emerging doctrine of economic duress.
10. In what circumstances will the law presume undue influence? Why?

</td><td>

DISCUSSION QUESTIONS

</td></tr>
</table>

<table>
<tr><td>

1. The Jacobses sued the Gallery of Homes and its agent, Howard Wolfley, for damages resulting from Wolfley's alleged misrepresentations. During negotiations between the Jacobses, who were represented by Wolfley, and the Phillippis, the sellers of the real estate in question, the Phillippis offered to sell the house at an interest rate of 12 percent with a balloon payment (the entire balance of the unpaid mortgage) due and payable within one year. Wolfley conveyed this offer to the Jacobses, who instructed Wolfley to make a further counteroffer of 10 percent for the first six months and 12 percent for the second six months. However, Wolfley did not inform the Phillippis of the further counteroffer by the Jacobses. Thus, the Phillippis believed that their offer of 12 percent interest had been accepted. The parties subsequently signed a real estate contract that provided for an interest rate of 12 percent and for a balloon payment of the balance plus interest within twelve months. The terms of this contract were complete and visible for review by the Jacobses. The Jacobses ultimately defaulted on this contract when they were unable to make the scheduled balloon payment. The Jacobses then sued to have the real estate contract rescinded on the ground of mutual mistake owing to their belief that the interest rate for the first six months should have been 10

</td><td>

CASE PROBLEMS

</td></tr>
</table>

percent, not 12 percent. Should a court grant rescission in these circumstances? (*Jacobs* v. *Phillippi,* 697 P.2d 132 [N.M. 1985].)

2. A mother put her infant daughter up for adoption on July 23 with an adoption agency. Four days later the mother asked for rescission of the agreement on the grounds of fraud and duress. Should her suit be successful? (*In re the Adoption of Baby Girl K.,* 615 P.2d 1310 [Wash. App. 1980].)

3. Clyde and Joni Joaquin were divorced in June, 1981. The terms of the divorce decree were based upon an agreement detailing the custody and property arrangements and upon an "appearance and waiver" document that permitted the court to grant the relief requested in the complaint for divorce. Clyde had signed both of these documents in late May, 1981. In 1982, Clyde nevertheless filed a motion to set aside the 1981 divorce decree on the rationale that he had not read either of these documents and had erroneously understood them to relate only to the dissolution of the marital bond with Joni, nothing more. Should the legal doctrine of mistake be applied to this situation? If so, would its application lead to a rescission of the divorce decree? (*Joaquin* v. *Joaquin,* 698 P.2d 298 [Haw. App. 1985].)

4. Rich & Whillock, Inc. (R & W), had contracted with Bob Britton, Inc. (Britton), a general contractor, to provide grading and excavation services for an Ashton Development, Inc. (Ashton), building project. R & W ultimately had to incur extra expenses owing to the presence of unexpected rock at the site. Britton and the developer at all times agreed to pay for the extra costs associated with the rock work. However, when R & W presented its final bill for $72,286.45, Britton and Ashton refused to pay. R & W told Britton the company would go broke if it were not paid because R & W was a new company; it had rented most of its equipment, and it had numerous subcontractors waiting to be paid. Britton eventually said R & W would be paid $50,000 or nothing. R & W officials complained that accepting this sum and the accompanying release from liability constituted "blackmail" to which R & W was acceding in order to survive. Could R & W later sue for the remaining $22,286.45 on the basis of economic duress? (*Rich & Whillock* v. *Ashton Development, Inc.,* 204 Cal. Rptr. 86 [Cal. App. 1984].)

5. Michael La Fleur suffered a work-related injury in January, 1975, when a forklift blade fell on his right foot. The company doctor thought the injury was superficial, even though La Fleur had continued to experience pain. A physician from the employer's insurance company diagnosed the injury as a sprain. In August, 1976, after the termination of his employment, La Fleur accepted a lump-sum settlement of $4,000 from the insurer in which he agreed as part of the release that the settlement represented the total amount of workers' compensation due him. However, after entering into this agreement, La Fleur experienced increasing discomfort in his right foot and was diagnosed as having arterial occlusive disease. As a

result, he underwent several operations, and eventually had both legs amputated above the knees. Hence, La Fleur was permanently confined to a wheelchair. An expert witness testified that the disease had existed at the time of the accident but had escaped diagnosis because it is difficult to detect. This expert also concluded that the forklift accident had aggravated this preexisting arterial disease and had led to the amputation of right leg. The added stress to the left leg that had resulted from the amputation of the right leg in turn caused the amputation of the left leg. La Fleur sued the employer and its insurer for rescission of the lump-sum agreement on the ground of mutual mistake. Should a court grant this requested remedy? (*La Fleur* v. *C. C. Pierce Co., Inc.*, 496 N.E. 2d 827 [Mass. 1986].)

6. Life Investors Insurance Company (Life Investors) sued Citizens National Bank of Wisner (Citizens) and the personal representative of Merle Gralheer's estate for the alleged overpayment of insurance proceeds to Citizens. Gralheer had borrowed money from Citizens, which had required him to purchase life insurance each time he had signed a note with the bank. When he had died of cancer, Life Investors had paid the entire claim — $38,000 — because Citizens's other insurance carrier, United Life Insurance Company (United Life), had denied liability. Under United Life's policies, debtors who have cancer or heart disease were not eligible for coverage. Life Investors therefore sued Citizens for $19,000, the amount of overpayment, claiming fraudulent misrepresentation and mutual mistake. On appeal, Citizens argued that the trial court had committed reversible error in failing to require Life Investors to elect between these two theories before presenting its case. Were these theories so inconsistent that the insurer should have chosen one or the other? (*Life Investors Insurance Company of America* v. *Citizens National Bank of Wisner*, 392 N.W.2d 771 [Neb. 1986].)

7. Four children of Delphine Wagner attempted to have the court appoint a conservator to manage Mrs. Wagner's estate because of her advanced age and the undue influence of two of her daughters, Clarinda and Clara Mae. Specifically, Mrs. Wagner had leased land previously farmed by some of the petitioners to another concern, resulting in a 160 percent greater income to Mrs. Wagner. At the time of the conservatorship hearing, Mrs. Wagner was seventy-nine years old and recently widowed. The doctors who examined Mrs. Wagner testified that she was oriented as to time and place, in good health, and neat and clean. The doctors also characterized Mrs. Wagner as strong-willed, feisty, and opinionated. The children asking for the conservator also described their mother as bull-headed and stubborn. The evidence as to one of the siblings' alleged undue influence was a statement by another sibling that Clarinda was with her mother all the time, that Clarinda was opinionated, and that Clarinda was probably telling her mother how to do everything. Should a court in these circum-

stances find that Mrs. Wagner had been subject to undue influence? (*In re Estate of Wagner,* 367 N.W.2d 736 [Neb. 1985].)

8. Orlandi leased approximately 3000 acres of West Virginia land to Goodell under a minimum royalty lease. Under the lease, Goodell was obligated to pay certain specified sums in advance for each of the first four years. No relationship existed between the payment schedule and any given quantity of coal that might be mined. After signing the lease, Goodell hired a contract miner who, based on May, 1979, drillings, concluded that the site contained too much rock to be profitably mined. Goodell made no further attempts to exploit his rights under the lease. When Goodell failed to make the first scheduled royalty payment, Orlandi sued. Goodell countered that the contract had been signed under a mutual mistake of fact as to the presence of merchantable and mineable coal on the property. Since no such coal was available, Goodell argued, the contract should be rescinded. How should the judge decide this case? (*Orlandi* v. *Goodell,* 760 F.2d 78 [4th Cir. 1985].)

9. Linda Chapman agreed to buy real estate from the Hoseks. About a month after she had signed the purchase agreement, the institution through which she had planned to finance the purchase informed her that the land was located in a flood-hazard area and that she would have to buy flood insurance as a prerequisite to obtaining the mortgage. Chapman, in addition, allegedly learned that during heavy rains the Hoseks' property had been damaged from flooding and had been made inaccessible. Therefore, some seven weeks after signing the purchase agreement, Chapman sued the Hoseks and the listing and selling brokers for rescission of the contract on the ground of fraud. Chapman contended that the defendants had concealed facts material to the transaction—the requirement of flood insurance and the propensity of the area to flood during heavy rains—and that these misrepresentations constituted fraud. Was Chapman correct? Could the defendants argue in defense that the information cited by Chapman was a matter of public record and that she was negligent in failing to discover the truth? (*Chapman* v. *Hosek,* 475 N.E.2d 593 [Ill. App. 1985].)

10. Lester Barrer's home had been sold at a tax sale to satisfy tax liabilities owed to the Internal Revenue Service (IRS). Because the Internal Revenue Code provides for the redemption of real property within 120 days of the sale of the property, the IRS informed Barrer that he could redeem his home by paying $17,400 to the IRS or to Curtis, the purchaser of the property, by 22 October 1981. On 20 October 1981, Barrer spoke with Emily Womack, the president of Women's National Bank (WNB), with whom Barrer was professionally acquainted, about a loan. Barrer and Womack later disputed several key points of information Barrer provided in his loan application, including, among other things, the fact that Columbia First Federal Savings and Loan Association (Columbia), the holder

of the principal mortgage on the home, had begun foreclosure proceedings on his home because he was six months behind in his mortgage payments. Barrer testified that he had said he ''thought'' he was two months behind; Womack, in contrast, testified that Barrer had said he was current on his payments. Barrer had disclosed the $30,000 tax liability that had forced the tax sale but had not indicated a contingent liability for an additional $11,000 owed by his corporation but which, at that time, had not been asserted against him personally. Although Barrer had not shown on the loan application that he had approximately $1,500 in unsatisfied debts pending against him, he had answered yes to a question asking whether he were the subject of any pending lawsuits. Without securing a credit report on Barrer, the bank had loaned him the $17,400 needed to redeem his home. Barrer had given the check to the IRS on 22 October 1981, believing that his home had been saved. That afternoon, Curtis, the tax sale purchaser, phoned WBN and spoke to an official there. Curtis provided the official with information about Barrer's arrearages with Columbia and the fact that the IRS was planning to hold another tax sale as soon as the $17,400 was paid. Based on this information and a credit report that was belatedly run on Barrer, the bank stopped payment on the $17,400 check it had given to Barrer. Barrer therefore was unable to redeem his home, and Curtis became the owner of it. When Barrer sued the bank for damages to compensate him for the loss of equity in his home, the bank alleged that Barrer's innocent misrepresentations provided it with grounds for rescinding the contract with him. Would you agree with the bank's asserted defense? (*Barrer* v. *Women's National Bank*, 761 F.2d 752 [D.C. Cir. 1985].)

CHAPTER 14

Interpretation and Proper Form of Contracts

THE IMPORTANCE OF FORM

In the preceding chapters, we discussed in detail the six requirements for a contract: offer, acceptance, consideration, capacity, legality, and reality of consent. Since we now understand the essentials of contract formation, we are ready to tackle some of the issues that may arise out of the contract itself. For instance, although the parties may have tried to be as precise as possible, questions about what the contract "really says" and whether certain conditions have been met may crop up as the parties begin their performance. One classic case involved a dispute over the word *chicken*. A Swiss buyer thought *chicken* meant broilers and fryers, or tender, juicy chicken. The New York seller, however, shipped stewing chicken to fulfill part of the contract; the Swiss buyer was not amused. As these parties found out, much to the disappointment of the buyer, contract **interpretation** often becomes an extremely important matter.

Interpretation The process of discovering the meaning of a contract; the defining, discovering, and explaining of unclear language

If the parties cannot resolve their differences, a court will be called on to decide what the disputed terms mean. To aid them in this task, courts have certain standards they can apply to unravel even the most ambiguous terms and phrases. However, other rules of law may limit these interpretive capacities. Judges are necessarily wary of tampering with a writing that was seemingly meant to be the final expression of the parties' intentions. For this reason, the **parol evidence** rule states that oral testimony ordinarily is not admissible to add to, alter, or vary the terms of a written agreement. In certain situations, parol evidence will be admissible to clear up ambiguities (such as the meaning of the word *chicken* mentioned earlier). Reference to the trade usages and customs of a particular industry may dispose of these types of ambiguity. Simply put, writing a contract does not guarantee that the subsequent performance of the contract will be free from semantic wranglings. But the alternative of contracting orally makes little sense because oral transactions multiply the potential interpretive problems.

Parol evidence Oral statements

In addition, according to the **Statute of Frauds,** certain categories of contracts must be in writing to be enforceable. The contract involving chickens, a type of goods, is one example, assuming the contract price is over $500. Others include contracts not to be completed within one year from the date of their making, contracts involving interests in land, contracts to answer for the debt of another, promises of **executors** and **administrators** to pay a claim against the estate of the deceased out of their own funds, and contracts made in consideration of marriage. The writing in these situations provides evidence that the parties really did contract about the matters in dispute, and it avoids the **perjuries** that were traditionally associated with these categories of contracts. In most other situations, the parties are free to contract orally, even though it is unwise to do so. This interplay among contract interpretation, the parol evidence rule, and the Statute of Frauds forms the subject of this chapter.

Statute of Frauds A statute requiring that specified types of contracts must be in writing in order to be enforceable

Executors The persons named and appointed in a will by the testator to carry out the administration of the estate as established by the will

Administrators The persons who have been empowered by an appropriate court to handle the estate of a deceased person

Perjuries False statements made under oath during court proceedings

JUDICIAL INTERPRETATION

In previous chapters, we dwelled on the importance of a *meeting of the minds* of the parties to the contract. Imprecise though this phrase is, it highlights one of the essential elements of a contract: the parties of necessity must have indicated, by their words or conduct, an intention to agree about some matter. Yet because language is an imprecise vehicle of expression, it may subsequently become apparent that the parties were not binding themselves to identical terms and courses of action (witness our "chicken" controversy). When this variance in expectations surfaces, disputes arise. If the parties cannot resolve these disputes, courts inherit the task of interpreting what the contract "really says."

Interpretation is *the process of determining the meaning of the words and other manifestations of intent that the parties have used in forging their agreement when the language of the agreement is not clear.* Ascertaining the parties' intent in order to enforce the contract as the parties wished is no mean feat. Problems arise primarily because words are symbols of expression and can take on an almost infinite number of meanings. Moreover, words do not exist in a vacuum. Determining how a certain party intended to use words or actions therefore becomes a factual issue. A court must examine one party's understanding and conduct in the situation, but it must also be conscious of how other reasonable persons would have understood these same words and actions under similar circumstances. In deciding between two competing views, courts often must consider the intentions of the parties through a frame of reference that has been called the "reasonable person," or objective, approach. This perspective allows the court to choose the interpretation that would be most consonant with the expectations of a prudent person in the same circumstances. Though not a perfect method, it at least ensures that the interpretation the court chooses is not so divergent from normality that it is nonsensical.

Standards

Because interpretation involves comparing the parties' words and conduct from some other perspective, certain standards of interpretation have evolved over the years. Probably the most common one is the standard of *general usage,* or the meaning that a reasonably prudent person who was aware of all operative uses and who was acquainted with the circumstances at play prior to and during the making of the agreement would attach to the agreement. For example, assume a relative of yours signed an agreement in which he gave $10,000 as a life membership fee for admission to a nursing home. Assume further that the agreement stated that for a trial period of two months, either your relative or the nursing home could suspend the agreement. On the occurrence of that event, the $10,000 (minus $200 per month) would be returned. What if your relative unfortunately dies after one month in the home? Can your relative's estate recover the $9800, or has the life membership fee been paid irrevocably?

By resorting to the standard of general usage, a court in a similar case decided that a reasonable person in your relative's place at the time of the execution of the contract would have understood the provision to mean that unless and until life membership status were obtained, the nursing home should return the money (less the amounts specified) to him. The court also asserted that if the nursing home had intended to retain the money in the event of a probationary member's death, it should have expressly stated this fact in the contract. Had the facts been different, the court might have applied the standard of *limited usage* (the meaning given to language in a particular locale) instead of the standard of general usage. There are several other standards that courts may apply in interpreting ambiguous contractual or statutory language; we shall discuss these in the following sections.

The standards employed in contract interpretation may turn on whether the contract is totally integrated. A *totally integrated contract* is one that *represents the parties' final and complete statement of their agreement.* Such a contract may be neither contradicted nor supplemented by evidence of prior agreements or expressions. The law assumes that the writing supersedes terms set out earlier in preliminary negotiations.

Total Integration

If a *writing is intended to be the final statement* of the parties' agreement *but is incomplete,* it is a *partially integrated contract.* Such a writing may not be contradicted by evidence of earlier agreements or expressions, but it may be supplemented by evidence of additional, consistent terms. Perhaps your relative and the nursing home orally agreed that his personal physician (rather than the nursing home's) would provide needed medical care. If the parties had left this provision out, the contract would represent a partially integrated writing. Since this provision does not appear to contradict the original agreement, it could be added later.

Partial Integration

In general, the more formal and complete the instrument, the more likely a court will find it to be a totally integrated agreement. According to the rules of integration, exchanges of letters, telegrams, and memoranda may indicate the formation of a contract; but they may not represent the final intentions of the parties. Rather, these communications may show only tentative and preliminary agreement. Some judges employ different standards of interpretation, depending on whether there has been integration. Where there is no integration, some would use the standard of reasonable expectation—that is, the meaning one party would reasonably expect the other to attribute to a term, given what the first party has said or done. If John is trying to buy a "fully equipped" car and a dispute later arises as to whether an air conditioner is included, a court will need to scrutinize the car salesperson's representations. If the agreement is integrated, a judge may instead apply the standard of limited usage—the meaning of the term as understood locally and in the trade—to see whether "fully equipped" cars ordinarily include air conditioners.

Rules of Integration

To supplement the appropriate standard of interpretation, courts also use rules of interpretation. Although authorities disagree as to the relative importance of these rules, you should be aware of the following common ones:

Rules of Interpretation

1. Courts should attempt to give effect to the manifested intentions of the parties.
2. Courts should examine the contract as a whole in order to ascertain the intentions of the parties.
3. Ordinary words should be given their ordinary meanings, and technical words should be given their technical meanings, unless the circumstances indicate otherwise.

4. Subject to the requirements of the parol evidence rule (discussed later in this chapter), all the circumstances surrounding the transaction should be taken into account.

Other rules state that reasonable constructions are favored where unreasonable alternative constructions are possible; that the main purpose of the agreement and all parts of the instrument will be given effect if possible; that special and specific words or provisions control general ones; that written words control printed ones; that words will be construed most strictly against the party who drafts the agreement; and that contracts affecting the public interest will be construed in favor of the public.

The case that follows demonstrates how vital interpretation is in determining what the wording of a contract means when disagreements subsequently develop.

Bache Halsey Stuart Shields, Incorporated
v. Alamo Savings Association of Texas
611 S.W.2d 706 (Tex. App. 1980)

FACTS

Bache, a securities broker, rented office space from Alamo in the Alamo Savings Tower. Bache had moved to the Alamo Savings Tower in order to get away from Merrill, Lynch, Pierce, Fenner & Smith, one of Bache's competitors, whose place of business was in close proximity to Bache's previous office. Bache's lease with Alamo granted Bache the right to exclude other securities brokers from the Alamo Savings Tower. Three years later, Alamo built a second tower 100 feet from the first tower and rented space in this tower to Merrill Lynch. Bache sued, alleging the lease to Merrill Lynch had violated its exclusionary clause with Alamo. Alamo filed a motion for a **summary judgment,** asserting that the plain language of the clause showed that the exclusionary clause applied only to office space in the building occupied by Bache, not to that in the second tower.

Summary judgment A judgment entered by a court when there is no substantial issue of fact present

ISSUE

Did Alamo's contract with Bache prohibit Alamo from leasing office space to a competing securities broker?

HOLDING

The trial court's granting of summary judgment for Alamo was incorrect.

REASONING

The language of the clause clearly restricted the excluded space to the first building. Yet a court must consider the wording of the instrument in light of all the circumstances in order to ascertain the intentions of the parties. The surrounding circumstances in this case were that Bache desired to "get away from" its competitor, Merrill Lynch, which had offices in "close proximity to" Bache's former offices in the Gunter Hotel. Clearly, one purpose of the clause in question was to allow Bache to achieve this purpose. At the time the Bache lease was being negotiated, Alamo had made known to Bache its intention to build a second tower on the same lot. But whether the parties intended that Alamo would be free to lease space in the second building to Bache's competitor, thereby restoring the condition which Bache was trying to escape — the "close proximity" of such competitor — was unclear. Since there was an issue of fact as to whether the parties intended that Alamo would be free to lease space to Bache's competitor in the second building, granting summary judgment was inappropriate.

The conduct of the parties often aids in contract interpretation. If the court is in doubt, the interpretation placed on the agreement by the parties themselves will be followed. For example, when one party has accepted a grade of wool inferior to the contract specifications for years, evidence of this conduct will be admissible in determining how the specifications should be interpreted. As you will learn in Chapter 18, Uniform Commercial Code Section 2–208, on course of performance, course of dealing, usage of trade, and contract construction, incorporates this rule of interpretation. You should therefore note its importance to the concept of contract interpretation and the courts' increasing reliance on it in Code transactions.

Conduct and Usages of Trade

Problems of interpretation may arise because of difficulties in distinguishing a promise from a condition. A promise is a vow or an agreement that places on the promisor a duty to do something or to refrain from doing something. A *condition,* in contrast, is *an act or event that limits or qualifies a promise.* The condition must occur before the promisor has a duty to perform or to refrain from performing.

CONDITIONS

Authorities classify conditions in two ways. The first category emphasizes the *timing* of the qualifying occurrence (the condition) in relation to the promised performance. Three subsets of this category include conditions precedent, concurrent conditions, and conditions subsequent. The second category stems from the *manner* in which the condition arises. Conditions created by the parties themselves are called *express conditions.* Conditions created by law are called *constructive* (or *implied*) *conditions.*

An agreement may explicitly state that *a certain act or event must occur before the other party has a duty to perform or before a contract exists.* If so, a *condition precedent* exists. For example, a person may promise (for consideration) to buy a car if the seller can deliver the car within ten days. A duty to buy the car does not arise unless and until the seller fulfills the condition. As mentioned, then, the timing of the condition and any later duty to perform go hand-in-hand. To be a condition precedent rather than a mere promise, the parties must indicate that the condition is an essential, vital aspect of the transaction. The buyer in our example will have to prove that delivery within ten days is essential to the transaction if the buyer later wishes to sue for rescission of the contract or

Conditions Precedent

damages on the ground that the seller has not delivered the car on time. A common condition precedent involves a buyer's signing a contract for the purchase of a new house subject to the sale of the buyer's current residence. You are undoubtedly familiar with such conditions precedent and can understand that the buyer will view this provision as an important consideration regarding his or her willingness to enter into the contract. The next case deals with the issue of a condition precedent.

Landscape Design and Construction, Inc. v. Harold Thomas Excavating, Inc.
604 S.W.2d 374 (Tex. App. 1980)

FACTS Thomas is a general contractor who hired Landscape, a subcontractor, to excavate a lake. The contract stated in Article III that "time is of the essence and the subcontractor agrees to complete the work . . . within ten working days of commencement." Landscape completed the excavation, but not within the ten days called for by the written agreement. Thomas asserted that it was not obligated to pay Landscape because the ten-day requirement was a condition precedent with which Landscape had not complied. Landscape argued that the provision was a covenant or promise, not a condition precedent, and that Thomas must pay.

ISSUE Did Article III of the contract constitute a condition precedent?

HOLDING No. Landscape was correct.

REASONING Normally a term such as *if* or *provided that* or some other phrase of conditional language must be present for a provision to be a condition precedent; otherwise, the provision is deemed a promise. Also, language will not be construed as a condition precedent when another reading of the contract is possible. Article V of the contract stated that full payment would be due when the work described in the contract was fully completed and performed consistent with Articles II and IV, not Article III. Therefore, Article III represented a promise, the breach of which would allow a recovery for damages (if damages could be proved); but it was not a condition precedent to Landscape's right to receive payment.

Concurrent Conditions

Concurrent conditions are a subset of conditions precedent. A *concurrent condition* obligates the parties *to perform at the same time.* Concurrent conditions (for instance, the transfer of goods in exchange for payment) underlie most commercial sales.

Conditions Subsequent

A *condition subsequent* is *any occurrence that the parties have agreed will cut off an existing legal duty.* It may also be a contingency, the happening or performance of which will defeat a contract already in effect. When a sales contract involving grain storage states that the contract will be of no effect if fire destroys the grain, a condition subsequent exists. Genuine conditions subsequent are rare. What may sound like a condition subsequent — for example, "Acme insurance will not pay for casualty losses if premises are unoccupied" — will be construed by many courts as a condition precedent. Courts that would characterize the provision as a condition subsequent would interpret the clause as stating that the occurrence of the condition (vacant premises) will cut off an existing legal duty (payment of the casualty loss). Other courts would say it is a condition precedent (premises must be *kept* occupied) that merely sounds like a condition subsequent because of its phrasing. Procedurally, this distinction can be significant. If it is a condition precedent, the insured has the burden of proof; if it is a condition subsequent, the insurer does. This distinction may be important because when the evidence is conflicting, the party who has the burden of proof often loses.

Express conditions — for example, "this sale can be consummated only by a payment of cash" — are those *spelled out* by the parties, either *explicitly* or *impliedly in fact*, within "the four corners of the instrument" (that is, they are contained within the document). However, as mentioned earlier and as the *Landscape Design* case shows, it is often difficult to distinguish a promise from a condition.

Express Conditions

A *constructive condition* is one *not expressed* by the parties *but read into the contract in order to serve justice* (that is, the condition is implied in law). It is difficult to differentiate between an express condition implied in fact and a constructive condition. For example, a provision as to the place of delivery normally is a condition precedent in a contract involving grain, but if such a condition is lacking, and in the absence of clear intent, a court may imply that the place for delivery is the seller's place of business (see UCC Section 2 – 308). This distinction takes on added importance with regard to discharging the contract. Strict compliance is necessary to discharge an express condition, while substantial compliance will suffice for constructive conditions.

Constructive Conditions

The relationship between conditions and contract discharges will be discussed more fully in Chapter 16.

Thus far, we have explored some of the concepts and rules dealing with contract interpretation. In so doing, we have stressed the importance of ascertaining the parties' intentions. We now turn to another important facet of contract law that is closely related to interpretation, the *parol evidence rule*. This rule is predicated on the belief that *oral evidence should not be admissible to alter, add to, or vary the terms of an integrated, written contract*. If the parties appear to have intended the writing as the final expression of their agreement, to allow later oral or written evidence that contradicts that writing would call into question the whole process of reducing one's agreement to writing. For instance, assume that Larry and Lynn sign a contract for the sale of a used car.

PAROL EVIDENCE RULE

They both agree — in a completed writing — that the price of the car is $6000. If one of the parties later tries to argue that the price is higher or lower, the parol evidence rule will preclude oral testimony to this effect, should litigation ensue as a result of this dispute. Imagine the havoc a contrary rule would cause. Courts therefore uphold the sanctity of totally integrated contracts by applying the parol evidence rule.

Because the parol evidence rule is designed to uphold a policy of protecting writings — those instruments representing the final intentions and terms of the parties — it is actually a rule of **substantive law** rather than a rule of evidence.

Substantive law The portion of the law that regulates rights, in contrast to law that grants remedies or enforces rights

For a good example of how the parol evidence rule can become an issue, read the following case.

Snow v. Winn
607 P.2d 678 (Okla. 1980)

FACTS A landlord sued his tenant in order to terminate the tenant's lease. The landlord claimed the tenant had breached the lease agreement by using the premises for a convenience grocery store in violation of the "purpose clause" of the agreement. This clause stated that the tenant would use the premises for a gasoline service station, car wash, and "associated activities." The landlord alleged he had an oral understanding with the tenant that the premises would not be used as a convenience store.

ISSUE Was this oral testimony admissible under the parol evidence rule?

HOLDING No. The court held this testimony was inadmissible.

REASONING The parol evidence rule prohibits oral testimony about an integrated, written instrument. Furthermore, even if the phrase *associated activities* may be viewed as a latent ambiguity (in which case oral testimony would be admissible to explain the meaning of such words), there was ample support for the trial court's conclusion that retail gasoline operations are commonly associated with convenience store facilities and that the parties intended to have food items sold on the premises.

EXCEPTIONS TO THE PAROL EVIDENCE RULE

The parol evidence rule will be disregarded, and parol evidence will be admissible, in certain circumstances. Among the more important of these are the following.

Partially Integrated Contracts

The policy base that underlies the parol evidence rule is not as compelling in situations in which the contract is partially integrated (that is, incomplete). In such cases, although the writing may not be contradicted by evidence of earlier terms, it may be supplemented by evidence of additional, consistent terms. (Recall our earlier example of your relative's medical care in the nursing home.)

Parol evidence is admissible to show mistake, fraud, duress, and failure of consideration, the kinds of situations we covered in Chapter 13. Since the existence of these situations casts doubt on the validity of the integrated writing, there is no overwhelmingly persuasive policy reason to justify exclusion of contradictory oral statements.

Mistake, Fraud, and Other "Reality-of-Consent" Situations

Parol evidence will also be allowed in order to clear up ambiguities (remember our "chicken" example) and to show that the agreement was not to become binding on the parties until a condition precedent was met, such as reduction of the agreement to writing or approval of the contract by a party's attorney. However, courts may allow evidence about a condition precedent only if this evidence does not contradict the written terms of the contract at issue.

Ambiguities and Conditions Precedent

Sections 2–202 and 2–208 of the Uniform Commercial Code deal with the parol evidence rule. Basically, the Code recognizes the rule but then reduces its impact by stating that evidence of course of dealing (conduct), usage of trade, and course of performance is admissible. Courts can also admit evidence of consistent, additional terms unless they find that the parties intended the writing as a complete and exclusive statement of the terms of the agreement. Moreover, the Code sets up priorities among these types of evidence: the express terms of the agreement control course of performance, course of dealing, and usage of trade. Evidence relating to course of performance in turn controls admissions about course of dealing and usage of trade.

Uniform Commercial Code

The historical ancestor for the parol evidence rule's policy of upholding the terms expressed in the parties' integrated writings is the original Statute of Frauds. Called An Act for the Prevention of Frauds and Perjuries, the English Parliament passed this law in 1677. Because perjury was so widespread in lawsuits involving oral contracts, Parliament decreed that certain classes of contracts must be *in writing* to be enforceable. Thus, the term *Statute of Frauds* is somewhat misleading, since such statutes deal with the requirement of a writing rather than with reality-of-consent situations like fraud. (The term *frauds* refers to the wholesale misrepresentations or perjured statements made to early English courts.) Every state has a statute of frauds modeled on the original one.

STATUTE OF FRAUDS

The Statute of Frauds requires that certain types of contracts be in writing before courts will enforce them. If the subject matter of the contract involves a type of contract thus enumerated in the Statute of Frauds, the agreement generally cannot be oral but instead must be in writing before a court will give it effect. The Statute of Frauds never arises as a legal issue unless a valid contract exists.

Affirmative defense A defense to a cause of action that must be raised by the defendant

The Statute of Frauds is also an **affirmative defense** that may be used by persons who do not want contracts to be enforced against them. A defendant who wishes to assert this defense must expressly plead it, or else the defendant will have waived the defense, and an oral contract that would otherwise violate the Statute of Frauds will be enforced against the defendant. The courts have been somewhat hostile to Statute of Frauds claims because of the injustice such statutes can cause. Consequently, some courts construe these statutes broadly and find various rationales for removing the contract from the statutes' coverage so as to enforce oral contracts.

Types of Contracts Covered

We will examine six categories of contracts covered by the Statute of Frauds: contracts to answer for the debt of another, contracts for interests in land, contracts not to be performed within one year of the date of their making, promises of executors and administrators of estates, contracts made in consideration of marriage, and contracts for sales of goods priced at $500 or more.

Contracts to Answer for the Debt of Another

Ordinarily, oral promises between two persons may be perfectly valid and enforceable in courts. When Linda orally promises to pay George $200 for a used cash register and he orally promises to sell it to her, there is a contract between the two parties. We call such promises *original* promises because both parties have promised to be *primarily* liable in all events if something should go awry in the transaction.

Sometimes the parties wish to avoid the primary liability that results from original promises. Rather, they want to be liable secondarily — that is, only in the event someone else defaults. Such agreements, called *collateral contracts,* are promises to answer for the debt or default of another. Collateral contracts typically involve three persons: the debtor (original promisor), the creditor (the promisee), and the third party, who is generally called a **guarantor** or **surety.** Notice that a collateral contract exhibits definite characteristics:

Guarantor One who promises to answer for the payment of a debt or the performance of an obligation if the person liable in the first instance fails to make payment or to perform

Surety A person who promises to pay or to perform in the event that the principal debtor fails to do so

Novations Substitutions by mutual agreement of new contracts in place of preexisting ones, whether between the same parties or with new parties replacing one or more of the original ones

1. There are three parties (but not all three-party transactions are collateral contracts — **novations,** for example, are not collateral contracts).

2. There are two promises, one original (debtor to creditor), and the other collateral (third party to creditor).

3. The second promise is a promise to accept only collateral, or secondary, liability resulting from the default of another.

Since such collateral promises are somewhat unusual (we generally assume people will be responsible for their own debts but not for another person's), the purpose of this provision of the Statute of Frauds is to require evidence — through a writing — of this undertaking of possible secondary liability.

The *intent of the parties* determines whether a three-party transaction involves a collateral contract, which must be in writing to be enforceable, or an original contract, which may be enforceable even if oral. For example, if Stein wants his grandson to have a car, he may cosign a note at a bank for the child. This is a three-party situation (Stein, his grandson, and the bank), but it is *not* a collateral contract. Stein and his grandson are joint, original promisors to the bank. As such, Stein is accepting liability in all events. The bank can sue *either* him or his grandson if the grandson defaults on his car payments.

If, however, Stein wishes to be only secondarily liable and the note is phrased so that he is, the contract is a collateral one. In the event of default, the bank must sue the grandson *without success before* Stein can be held liable. Note that the intent of the parties is crucial in determining the type of contract — original or collateral — that is involved. If it is deemed a collateral contract, the bank is protecting itself from a defense based on the Statute of Frauds by requiring the transaction to be in writing.

Because courts are generally hostile to the Statute of Frauds, there is an exception to the rule that a collateral contract must be in writing to be enforceable. This is called the *leading-object* or *main-purpose exception*: when the third party agrees to be liable chiefly for the purpose of obtaining an economic benefit, the second promise, even if oral, will be enforceable. Change our earlier example to one in which Stein *orally* tells the bank he will pay *if* his grandson defaults. When the grandson does not pay and the bank sues Stein, Stein will use the Statute of Frauds as his defense: there is no writing, and the contract appears to be a collateral one. If, however, the bank can prove that before Stein agreed to be liable, Stein knew that the institution was about to force the grandson into bankruptcy, which in turn would mean that Stein might lose sizable loans he had made to his grandson, the bank may be able to show that Stein's leading object in making the promise was to prevent economic loss to himself. Proving this, the bank can argue that Stein's conduct indicates he was the equivalent of an original promisor — he was willing to pay and to assume liability in all events, not just secondarily — in order to protect his economic position vis-à-vis his grandson's impending bankruptcy. The wise businessperson avoids such potential legal problems by requiring all promises to be in writing rather than relying on oral ones.

The next case illustrates many of these concepts.

Bassett Furniture Industries of North Carolina, Inc. v. *Griggs*
266 S.E.2d 702 (N.C. App. 1980)

Bassett sued Griggs on Griggs's alleged oral guarantees that he would pay the $30,000 loaned to Big Jim's, a corporation in which he was the major stockholder. The trial court had granted summary judgment because the oral guarantee did not satisfy the Statute of Frauds.

FACTS

Was an oral guarantee in these circumstances enforceable?

ISSUE

HOLDING   Yes. The oral guarantee was enforceable despite the Statute of Frauds.

REASONING   The evidence showed that Griggs, because of his position with the corporation and his own articulated goal of being a millionaire before he was forty, believed that he had a substantial personal interest in the extension of additional credit to Big Jim's. Since this conduct could well have satisfied the leading-object exception to the Statute of Frauds, summary judgment should not have been granted.

Contracts for Interests in Land

Mortgages Conditional transfers of property as security for a debt

Leases Contracts that grant the right to use and occupy realty

Easements Limited rights to use and enjoy the land of another

Any agreement that involves buying, selling, or transferring interests in land must be in writing to be enforceable. **Mortgages, leases, easements,** and sales agreements about standing timber and buildings attached to the land should also be in writing to satisfy the Statute of Frauds. Thus, if you orally offer to buy someone's house and the seller accepts your offer, this contract will be unenforceable because it does not comply with the Statute of Frauds.

Courts will nevertheless enforce oral contracts for the sale of land if the purchaser has paid part of the purchase price; and, with the seller's consent, the purchaser takes possession of the land and makes valuable improvements on it. This equitable remedy is called the *doctrine of part performance.* For example, assume Green moves onto Berry's land and, with Berry's oral permission, tears down an old garage, repaints the entire house, and rebuilds a barn, all at Green's expense. Green also has paid $5000 to Berry before undertaking these actions. When Berry later tries to claim there was no enforceable contract of sale between the two, a court can nonetheless order specific performance of the contract despite noncompliance with the Statute of Frauds. Courts justify such an exception to the requirement of a writing on the ground that the conduct of the parties prior to litigation shows the existence of a contract. Courts in such cases conclude that the parties' conduct can be explained only by the actual presence of such a contract. Equity will also give remedies in such situations to avoid the unjust enrichment of the seller.

Contracts Not to Be Performed Within One Year of the Date of Their Making

According to the Statute of Frauds, a promise in a contract that cannot be performed within one year from the date of the making of the agreement must be in writing to be enforceable. To illustrate, an oral promise to haul milk for a dairy producer during a one-year period cannot be valid under the Statute of Frauds in situations where it would be impossible to haul the gallonage of milk contracted for in less than one year. This would be the case if the parties had entered into the contract on December 15 with the term of the contract stated as running from January 1 to December 31 of the next year. Such a contract is one *not to be performed within one year of the date of its making* (December 15); therefore under the Statute of Frauds, to be enforceable, it must be in writing.

Courts have reacted hostilely to this section of the statute because of its harsh effects on the person who may suffer losses as a result of the rule's application. Thus, courts have often limited the coverage of this proviso to situations in which performance cannot *possibly* occur within one year's time (as in our example above). This limitation has led to rather strained results. For example, a bilateral contract in which an employee promises to work for an employer "for the employer's lifetime" sounds as if it invariably cannot be performed within one year. Some courts, however, interpret such language to mean that since it is *possible* — though not *probable* — that the employer might die within a year, an oral contract would be enforceable despite the Statute of Frauds. Under this approach, if the contract in our earlier example had obligated the hauler to transport the milk for "as long as the dairy farmer produces milk," such courts would reason that the dairy farmer could possibly cease operations within one year, thereby making the contract capable of being performed within one year from the date of the making of the contract. However remote this possibility, the fact that such a contingency *could* happen makes the oral contract enforceable and this section of the Statute of Frauds inapplicable. Other courts, though, would adopt the stricter approach and hold that the contracts at issue in both cases must be in writing to be enforceable. For one court's view of this matter, see the following case.

D & N Boening, Inc. v. Kirsch Beverages, Inc.
472 N.E.2d 992 (N.Y. 1984)

FACTS

D & N Boening, Inc. (Boening), was the exclusive subdistributor of "Yoo Hoo" Chocolate beverages in Nassau and Suffolk Counties, New York. Although there was no written contract between Boening and American Beverage Corp. (American), the prime distributor of "Yoo Hoo," American had agreed verbally to continue the franchise arrangement as long as Boening performed satisfactorily, exerted its best efforts, and acted in good faith. In 1982, Kirsch Beverage purchased American and shortly thereafter terminated Boening's subdistributorship. Boening then sued Kirsch for breach of contract. Kirsch, in turn, asserted that, under New York law, the agreement was void because it was barred by the Statute of Frauds.

ISSUE

Did this agreement have to be in writing under the Statute of Frauds because it is one that cannot be performed within one year from the date of its making?

HOLDING

Yes. The oral agreement between the parties called for performance of an indefinite duration and could only be terminated within one year by a breach of the agreement during that year. As such, the agreement fell within the coverage of the Statute of Frauds and was void under New York law.

REASONING

The underlying rationale for the Statute of Frauds' requirement of a signed writing for a contract not to be performed within one year from the date of its making was the mistrust of witnesses' memories regarding matters involving time periods longer than one year. In addition, courts have historically shrunk from giving too broad an interpretation to this provision of the Statute. Their tendency instead has been to limit its application to those contracts that by their very terms have absolutely no possibility in fact and law of full performance within one year. Under New York case precedents, the mere possibility of a breach within the first year of an agreement does not take the agreement out of the Statute. These cases' reasoning is applicable to this particular agreement, since according to its terms, the agreement required American to continue the Boening subdistributorship indefinitely: there was no expiration date and no options to terminate the agreement were reserved to either party. Indeed, the agreement could have continued in perpetuity unless Boening had failed to perform its subdistributorship satisfactorily, to exert its best efforts, and to act in good faith. Such a failure would not have constituted a permitted manner of performance; rather, it would have been a breach of the agreement. Being terminable only by Boening's breach, the agreement was not one that by its terms could be performed within one year. As such, it came within the coverage of the Statute of Frauds and was void under New York law because it was unwritten.

Some jurisdictions allow recovery for oral contracts that would otherwise be unenforceable because they extend for periods longer than one year when one party to the contract will be able to complete its performance within one year, even though the other party will be unable to do so. Courts may also apply promissory estoppel, which we learned about in earlier chapters, to allow recovery for otherwise unenforceable contracts.

Promises by Executors and Administrators of Estates

Promises by executors and administrators of estates to pay estate claims out of their own personal funds must be in writing to be enforceable. Since such agreements would be relatively unusual, the courts require a writing as evidence that the parties actually reached such an agreement.

Promises Made in Consideration of Marriage

Like the previous category, unilateral promises to pay money or to transfer property in consideration of a promise to marry are so uncommon that the law requires that such promises also be in writing in order to be enforceable. If the Benson family promises to pay $20,000 and to transfer the ownership of their condominium in Florida to Jim Lloyd if Jim promises to marry their daughter, Celie, the Bensons' promise must be in writing according to the Statute of Frauds. By analogy, antenuptial (or prenuptial) agreements, which we have seen in other contexts in earlier chapters, must also be in writing if they are to be enforceable.

Contracts for Sales of Goods Priced at $500 or More

In addition to the five common law categories of contracts that have to be in writing to be enforceable under the Statute of Frauds that we have just discussed, the Uniform Commercial Code also has several provisions that implicate the Statute of Frauds. The most important of these is UCC section 2–201, which states that contracts for sales of goods priced at $500 or more are not enforceable unless there is a writing sufficient to indicate that a contract for sale has been made between the parties and the writing is signed by the person against whom enforcement of the contract is sought. Therefore, according to the Statute of Frauds, a contract for a sale of produce — since the Code would classify produce as *goods* (i.e., identifiable, movable, personal property) — priced at $500 or more must be in writing. The Code further states that a writing is *not* insufficient if it omits or incorrectly states a term agreed on, but the agreement will not be enforced beyond the quantity of goods mentioned in such writing.

Under Section 2–201, however, oral contracts will be enforced if (1) the goods are to be specially manufactured for the buyer and are not suitable for sale to others in the ordinary course of the seller's business; (2) the buyer makes a partial payment or a partial acceptance (although the contract will be enforced only for the portion of goods paid for or accepted); or (3) the party being sued admits in court (or in court documents) that a contract was made for a certain quantity of goods.

The Statute of Frauds section in the Code also contains a novel provision that may trap the unaware merchant. A *merchant* who receives a signed written confirmation (for example, "This is to confirm our sale to you of 2000 bushels of apples, #6 grade, at $1.25/bushel, delivery Tuesday, /s/ Seller") and does not object to it in writing within ten days is bound to the contract. The policy underlying this result is a familiar one: a valid oral contract on the terms stated must exist if the other party (who, as a merchant, is considered a "pro") does not object to the confirmation. The moral of this section of the Code is: answer your mail, merchants!

Writing

As we have seen in other contexts, the writing required to satisfy the Statute of Frauds may be rather minimal. It may take the form of letters, telegrams, receipts, or memoranda. The writing must — at minimum — identify the parties to the agreement, the subject matter of the agreement, and all material terms and conditions. Several writings may be pieced together as long as they all refer to the same transaction.

Signature

Similarly, anything intended by the parties as a signature will suffice to satisfy the Statute of Frauds. This would, of course, include written signatures; but stamped signatures or even stationery letterheads have been held to be sufficient. The memorandum need not be signed by both parties as long as the party against whom enforcement is sought (or the party's authorized agent) has signed.

Notice how the court utilized many of these principles in deciding the following case.

Barber & Ross Co. v. Lifetime Doors, Inc.
810 F.2d 1276 (4th Cir. 1987), *cert. denied* 108 S.Ct. 86 (1987)

FACTS Barber & Ross (B & R) purchases millwork products, including doors, from manufacturers, prepares them for installation in new homes, and sells them to new home builders. Lifetime Doors, Inc. (Lifetime), is a large manufacturer of doors. In 1982, B & R began to buy various types of doors from Lifetime. In early 1983, Lifetime supplied B & R with sales literature that promised new purchasers "continuous production availability . . . in full proportion to monthly needs" that would ensure that purchasers could "order flexible quantities" in shipments of a "desired number" if they joined Lifetime's VIP Club. B & R's president therefore entered into an oral agreement with Lifetime whereby Lifetime promised to supply B & R's requirements of four truckloads of six-panel doors each month, in return for which B & R would purchase doors exclusively from Lifetime. From the middle of March to the middle of May of that year, B & R purchased both flush and six-panel doors exclusively from Lifetime under this agreement. However, in May, Lifetime suggested that B & R should purchase the six-panel doors from other manufacturers owing to Lifetime's shortages of these types of doors. In July, Lifetime instituted an "allocation system" that tied purchases of the more popular six-panel doors with sales of the less desirable flush doors. This system caused B & R to buy more flush doors than it needed and simultaneously resulted in B & R's receiving fewer six-panel doors. B & R in September finally terminated its contractual relationship with Lifetime owing to the negative effects on B & R's business caused by Lifetime's policy. B & R then sued Lifetime, claiming that Lifetime's allocation system had violated the antitrust laws and that Lifetime had breached the requirements contract between the parties. The trial court awarded B & R $2.1 million on these claims. On appeal, Lifetime argued that there could be no breach of contract because the alleged requirements contract was unenforceable under the Statute of Frauds.

ISSUE Was the alleged contract unenforceable under the Statute of Frauds?

HOLDING No. There was sufficient writing to indicate that the parties had formed a contract for the sale of goods; and this writing had been signed by the party against whom enforcement was sought.

REASONING The written sales brochures Lifetime had given to B & R met the requirements of the Statute of Frauds's signature requirement because the Lifetime Doors trademark that appeared on the documents was sufficient to authenticate the brochures. The writings also stated a sufficiently definite quantity for purposes of the statute because they referred to meeting the purchaser's needs. To be enforceable under this category of the Statute of Frauds, a writing must provide a basis for believing that the offered oral evidence rests on a real transaction. The writing need not, however, conclusively establish the existence of a contract to fulfill the requirements of the Statute of Frauds. Because the writings in this case had promised that Lifetime would meet the monthly needs of B & R, they were sufficient to support B & R's claim that an oral agreement had been reached to form a requirements contract.

SUMMARY

Interpretation is the process of determining the meaning of words and other manifestations of intent that the parties have used in forging their agreement. Over the years, certain standards and rules of interpretation, based on whether the contract is totally integrated or partially integrated, have evolved. A totally integrated contract represents the parties' final and complete statement of their agreement and cannot be contradicted. Similarly, a partially integrated contract is intended to be the parties' final statement, but it is incomplete. It may be supplemented with consistent, additional terms. The conduct of the parties and usages of trade may also aid in contract interpretation.

Conditions may pose special problems of interpretation. The different categories of conditions include conditions precedent, concurrent conditions, conditions subsequent, express conditions, and constructive conditions.

The parol evidence rule states that oral evidence is not admissible to alter, add to, or vary the terms of an integrated, written contract. However, the parol evidence rule will not be applied in some circumstances: partially integrated contracts; agreements suggesting mistake, duress, or fraud; ambiguity; conditions precedent; or in some commercial contexts.

In accordance with the Statute of Frauds, certain types of contracts must be in writing to be enforceable. These include collateral contracts, contracts for sales or transfers of interests in land, contracts not to be performed within one year from the date of their making, contracts for sales of goods of $500 or more, promises of executors and administrators of estates, and promises made in consideration of marriage. However, very little in the way of a memorandum or signature is necessary to satisfy the Statute of Frauds.

DISCUSSION QUESTIONS

1. What is the process of contract interpretation?
2. What is the legal difference between a totally integrated contract and a partially integrated contract?
3. Name any three rules of interpretation.
4. How are conduct and usages of trade important in contract interpretation?
5. Give an original example of a condition precedent and a condition subsequent.
6. What is the parol evidence rule?

7. Name and discuss the exceptions to the parol evidence rule.

8. Explain the basis for the Statute of Frauds, historically and currently.

9. What are the most important characteristics of a collateral contract, or a contract to guarantee the debt of another? Also, explain the exception to the rule that collateral contracts must be in writing.

10. Describe the exceptions to the rule that a contract for a sale of goods priced at $500 or more must be in writing.

CASE PROBLEMS

1. Marvin Mann had an insurance contract with State Farm Mutual Automobile Insurance Company (State Farm) whereby the company insured Mann against "losses" to his car, including "theft." The insurance policy specifically excluded coverage for losses to the auto occurring while the auto was in the possession of another under a conditional sale or purchase agreement. Mann had transferred possession to another individual in exchange for a personal check for the purchase price in the course of what Mann believed was a sale of the auto. However, the check was returned to Mann owing to insufficient funds. The "buyer" later admitted he knew the check would be dishonored and that he had intended to defraud Mann into parting with possession of the auto. The auto was never recovered. State Farm denied liability under the two provisions noted. Would you agree with State Farm's interpretation of the contract? (*Mann* v. *State Farm Mutual Automobile Insurance Company*, 698 P.2d 925 [Okla. 1985].)

2. Olde Village Hall negotiated with the Raouls about purchasing real property. The contract was oral, and the defendants did not plead this as a defense in the lower court. Could the defendants use this defense on appeal, or had they waived it by their inaction? (*Raoul* v. *Olde Village Hall, Inc.*, 430 N.Y.S.2d 214 [N.Y. App. Div. 1980].)

3. Pine Tree Electric Company, Inc. (Pine Tree), an electrical contractor, had for years bought electrical equipment and supplies from Graybar Electric Co., Inc. (Graybar), an electrical equipment and parts supplier. In 1978, however, Graybar cut off credit sales to Pine Tree because of Pine Tree's failure to pay its bills on time. In order to help Pine Tree's cash flow problems, the company solicited investors. Hollis Sawyer, a relative of one of Pine Tree's employees, advanced about $300,000 to Pine Tree. Sawyer effected a reorganization of the company in which he wound up with all the voting power as the sole preferred stockholder and as vice-president of the firm. Pine Tree shortly thereafter resumed its relationship with Graybar but soon missed two monthly payments owed to Graybar. At a meeting of Pine Tree and Graybar executives devoted to straightening out these credit problems, Sawyer allegedly told the Graybar representatives that if Pine Tree did not pay its account, he would. Graybar allegedly wrote a letter five days later memorializing the outcome of these discussions. Following this meeting, Graybar reopened Pine Tree's line of

credit. When Pine Tree was later forced into involuntary bankruptcy, Graybar sued Sawyer on the basis of this alleged guarantee. Sawyer argued that no contract of guarantee had been formed and that if one had been formed, the Statute of Frauds barred Graybar's suit. Who was correct? (*Graybar Electric Co., Inc.* v. *Sawyer,* 485 A.2d 1384 [Me. 1985].)

4. The City of Yonkers sued Otis Elevator Company (Otis) for breaking an alleged promise to remain in the city. The city argued that it, in 1976, had obtained approximately $12 million of urban renewal funding to allow the company to expand and modernize its plant. The city asserted that Otis's receipt of these funds imposed on Otis an obligation to remain in Yonkers for a "reasonable period of time, i.e., not less than 60 years." Thus, when Otis attempted to leave Yonkers for New Jersey in 1981, the city brought suit against the company. The city at trial ultimately conceded that no written contract imposed that obligation on Otis, nor had Otis made any express oral promise to that effect. Could a court nonetheless impose such an obligation on Otis, or would such a result violate the Statute of Frauds? (*City of Yonkers* v. *Otis Elevator Company,* 649 F. Supp. 716 [S.D. N.Y. 1986].)

5. Since 1940, Jacob Heller had occupied two suites of law offices at 51 Chamber Street, New York City. In 1965, New York City acquired title to the building in a condemnation proceeding. From 1965 to 1980, Heller was a month-to-month tenant. In 1980, Heller and George Croucher, then Director of the Bureau of Property Management for New York City, entered into an oral agreement whereby Heller agreed to relinquish Suite 1409 on the condition that the monthly rent for Suite 1425 remain at $201 and that the term of the tenancy last until Heller died. The city nevertheless attempted to terminate the lease in 1984 when Heller was eighty years old. Heller argued that his tenancy was protected by the oral lease, but the city contended that the Statute of Frauds barred any oral contract that by its terms could not be performed within one year from the date of its making. Who would win? Why? (*City of New York* v. *Heller,* 487 N.Y.S.2d 288 [N.Y. Civ. Ct. 1985].)

6. Mr. and Mrs. George Christou had resided at Rose Hill with George's brother, James, for years and had been paying half of the mortgage and real estate taxes during that time. When James moved out, the Christous began paying the entire mortgage and the full amount of the taxes, even though James's name appeared as owner on the deed to Rose Hill. Mrs. Christou contended these payments had resulted from an oral agreement whereby George had given up his interest in the family bakery in exchange for James's giving up his interest in Rose Hill. Mrs. Christou argued these payments constituted part performance of such magnitude as to take the alleged oral contract to convey real property out of the Statute of Frauds. Was she correct? (*Christou* v. *Christou,* 487 N.Y.S.2d 192 [N.Y. App. Div. 1985].)

7. Pando, a sixteen-year-old youth, alleged that Mrs. Fernandez had promised him that she would share a lottery prize equally with Pando if he would take her $4, purchase four tickets, select the numbers, and pray to "St. Eleggua" so that the saint would make his selections win. One of the tickets Pando purchased for Fernandez won $2.8 million. When Pando sued, alleging breach of a "partnership agreement," Fernandez denied the existence of any agreement and argued alternatively that if such an agreement did exist, it would run afoul of the Statute of Frauds because the prize was to be paid out in annual installments over a ten-year period. Was she correct? Also, had Pando complied with the conditions precedent that Fernandez's alleged agreement had set out? (*Pando by Pando* v. *Fernandez*, 485 N.Y.S.2d 162 [N.Y. Sup. Ct. 1984].)

8. Claude Chinn, a sales representative with Harris, had contacted American Web Press, Inc. (American Web), about a used M-1000 press it had for sale for $20,000. After Hansen, an American Web representative, had seen the machine in operation, Chinn tried to close the sale; but Hansen refused to sign any order forms. Hansen, however, did ask Chinn to prepare a list of contract terms Hansen could present to his attorney and banker. Chinn prepared this memorandum on a piece of roll-stock paper, and Hansen added two provisions. Chinn signed this document, but Hansen refused even to initial it. The parties agreed to meet early the next week to negotiate further the sale of the press. Harris ultimately sold the press to another party one day before its scheduled meeting with American Web executives. American Web then sued Harris for breach of contract. Was there a contract between the parties? If so, was this contract enforceable under the Statute of Frauds? (*American Web Press, Inc.* v. *Harris Corporation*, 596 F. Supp. 1089 [D. Colo. 1983].)

9. Attorney Thomas Drake had entered into an oral contract with Perry Skundor by which Drake had agreed to represent Skundor's adult son, David, in a felony case. Although Skundor had paid Drake a $350 retainer, had secured Drake as his son's counsel, had paid for his son's polygraph examination, and had investigated drug rehabilitation centers for his son, he refused at the time of the trial—some seven months later—to sign a promissory note guaranteeing the payment of his son's legal fees. Rather, Skundor insisted that his son was responsible for paying them. Drake, however, never received any payment from David. Could Perry Skundor, the father, successfully assert the Statute of Frauds as his defense when Drake sued him for the unpaid attorneys' fees? (*Drake, Phillips, Kuenzli & Clark* v. *Skundor*, 501 N.E.2d 88 [Ohio App. 1986].)

10. Richard Gillman began negotiating with Horn & Hardart Company about becoming a franchisee with the company's subsidiary, "Bojangles' Famous Chicken 'N Biscuits" (Bojangles). To this end, Gillman formed a corporation, R. G. Group, Inc., in the expectation he would get a Bojangles franchise. During one of his meetings with Bojangles' personnel,

Gillman received a copy of Bojangles' standard form development franchise agreement. Three other letters explaining the territory involved and confirming the areas left open for discussion (the development schedule and the exact territory boundaries, for example) also were sent to Gillman. However, no agreement was ever signed. Ultimately, Bojangles refused Gillman's application for a franchise; and Gillman sued Bojangles. Was there a contract between the parties? If there was, were the four documents mentioned, taken together, a sufficient memorandum to satisfy the Statute of Frauds? Alternatively, should promissory estoppel have been applied to keep Bojangles' offer open in these circumstances? (*R. G. Group, Inc.* v. *Horn & Hardart Company,* 751 F.2d 69 [2d Cir. 1984].)

CHAPTER 15

The Rights of Third Parties

ADDITION OF THIRD PARTIES TO THE RELATIONSHIP

A contract will influence the legal rights of the two parties who enter it. It may also influence the financial position of other people. In some situations, these other people are so significant in the contract that they too have legal rights under the contract and can even file a lawsuit to enforce these contractual rights. This chapter deals with whether these other people have enforceable legal rights.

THIRD-PARTY BENEFICIARY CONTRACTS

Persons and corporations that receive rights in a contract that they have not signed are called *beneficiaries*. It is really more appropriate to call this kind of beneficiary a third *person* because the additional person is not a *party* to the contract. However, we shall use the common terminology and refer to this person as a third party.

256

The two people who enter into the contract are commonly called the promisor and the promisee. The *promisor* is the party who promised to perform; the party to whom that promise was made is the *promisee*. Often in third-party beneficiary contracts, the promise is to deliver goods to or perform a service directly for a third party. For example, Jane was very busy; to save time in shopping for a Father's Day present and mailing it to her father in St. Cloud, Minnesota, she ordered an expensive shirt from the Neiman-Marcus catalog to be gift wrapped and delivered to her father. This arrangement is a third-party beneficiary contract. Her father is the third-party beneficiary. A beneficiary does not need to know about the contract in order for it to be valid.

Because these third parties are called beneficiaries, it is generally assumed that they receive something beneficial and good, but this is not always the case. The legal requirement for an intended beneficiary is that at least one of the contracting parties, usually the promisee, intended to have goods delivered to or services performed for that third party. The third party may not necessarily desire them. The beneficiary may, in fact, be very displeased upon receipt of the goods or services, as when a company offered to throw a cream pie in the face of any third-party beneficiary that the promisee designated.

An Incidental Beneficiary

Probably the most important factor in determining the rights of a third party is whether or not the third party is an intended or an incidental beneficiary. When the original parties to the contract, or at least one of them, *meant* to affect a noncontracting person by establishing the contract, the noncontracting person is an *intended beneficiary*. Intended beneficiaries have legal rights. If the benefit or action to the noncontracting party was *accidental*, or *not intended*, this party is an *incidental beneficiary*.

As an example of an incidental beneficiary, suppose an owner of a vacant city lot decides to build a high-rise garage on it. The owner enters into a contract with a builder to construct the garage. The neighboring lot has a high-rise office building on it, so the owner of that office building will benefit financially by the construction of the garage. This person is an incidental beneficiary, because neither the builder nor the original owner intended to benefit that person.

An Intended Beneficiary

An intended beneficiary does not have to be mentioned by name in the contract. It is sufficient for the parties to *clearly intend* to give the beneficiary rights under the agreement. In the absence of a clear expression of such an intent, the contracting parties are presumed to act for themselves. Sometimes the intended beneficiary may be one person from a group of people for whose benefit the contract was established. Automobile insurance, for example, is a contract between an insurance company and a driver, but it is also partially for the benefit of other drivers and pedestrians who share the road.

The distinction between intended and incidental beneficiaries is discussed in the case that follows; the legal relationships in the case are diagrammed in Figure 15.1.

Figure 15.1   Legal Relationships in *Allan* v. *Bekins Archival Services, Inc.*

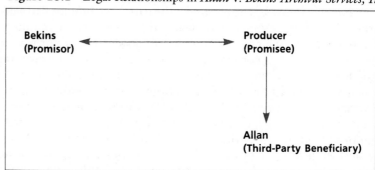

Allan v. Bekins Archival Service, Inc.
154 Cal. Rptr. 458 (Cal. App. 1979)

FACTS

Allan was the announcer and master of ceremonies in the television series called "Celebrity Bowling." He also had a partnership interest in the show, which was produced from 1970 to 1976. The producer of the show entered into a contract with Bekins Archival Service to store, inventory, and ship the videotapes of the series as authorized by the producer. Bekins was to receive a monthly fee for this service. The producer deposited 114 tapes with Bekins.

Bekins shipped tapes 1 through 26, as authorized. The tapes were never returned but Bekins's monthly inventory indicated that the tapes had been returned so the producer destroyed the duplicates of these tapes. Due to the loss of these tapes, the producer was unable to perform an agreement to have the series rebroadcast. If the series had been rebroadcast, Allan would have been entitled to royalty payments. Bekins had solicited business by representing that it had a specialized facility and that it recognized the high monetary value of the tapes.

ISSUE

Was Allan an intended third-party beneficiary of the contract between the producer and Bekins?

HOLDING

Yes. It can be inferred that the contract was made for Allan's benefit.

REASONING

To be an intended (express) beneficiary a person need not be named in the contract. If Allan can show that he is a person or member of a class for whose benefit the contract was made, he should recover. The intent to benefit the third party need not be manifested by the promisor (Bekins). It is sufficient if the promisor realizes that the promisee (the producer) has this intent. The decision may not extend to bit actors in a series, who have a smaller financial interest in the tapes.

The rights of an intended third-party beneficiary in a contract may be affected by the relationship between the promisee and the third party. If the promisee *meant to make a gift to the third party,* the third party is a *donee beneficiary.* Life insurance policies are excellent examples of third-party beneficiary contracts. If a husband purchases a $100,000 life insurance policy from Prudential Insurance Company of America and names his wife as the beneficiary, she is a donee beneficiary. The husband had no legal obligation to purchase this insurance. (He might be under a legal obligation to purchase life insurance under some marital contracts or divorce decrees, but this is uncommon.) He was, in effect, planning a gift to his wife that would take effect at his death. She would be a donee beneficiary. This example is shown in Figure 15.2.

> A Donee
> Beneficiary

Prudential Insurance Company, the promisor, promised to deliver $100,000 to the promisee's wife if he died under the terms of the policy. If Prudential refused to pay, the wife could sue the company directly as an intended third party. Prudential (the promisor) could use the same legal defenses against the wife (third party) as it could against the husband (promisee). These defenses might include lack of capacity to enter into a contract; lack of mutual assent; illegality in the contract; mistake in contract formation; fraudulent statements about the promisee's health; an improperly formed contract; or cancellation of the policy. There would also be no payment if the cause of death was excluded by the terms of the contract. Usually the courts disallow recovery by the beneficiary if the promisee has not performed his or her duty under the contract.[1]

According to the law in some states, the donee beneficiary's rights cannot be terminated after the contract is made. However, the promisee can still defeat the rights of the donee by not performing his or her contractual obligations.[2] In other states, the beneficiary's right is limited to situations in which

Figure 15.2   Donee Beneficiary

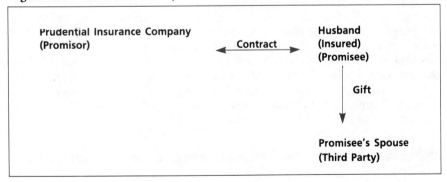

[1] 2 Williston on Contracts, 3rd ed., Section 395 (1959), p. 1066.
[2] Ibid., Section 396, pp. 1067, 1070.

the beneficiary knows about the contract and has accepted it verbally or by reliance on its terms. If the beneficiary has accepted the contract, then the beneficiary has a *vested* interest in it. In these states, a beneficiary with a vested interest must consent before there can be a rescission of the contract. This rule applies to both donee and **creditor beneficiaries.** Even so, a donee beneficiary cannot prevent the promisee from taking some action that will defeat the rights of the donee beneficiary — for example, if the promisee breached the contract by refusing to pay for the goods or services.

Creditor beneficiary A person who is entitled to performance by the promisee

Oman was a donee beneficiary in the case that follows. Rheims was a friend of hers who promised to give her a house. The court discussed her legal rights.

Oman v. *Yates*
422 P.2d 489 (Wash. 1967)

FACTS The Sundays agreed to sell a house to Oman. Oman signed the contract, but under the agreement she was not going to pay for the property; Rheims was going to pay the *complete* purchase price to the Sundays, in cash. Rheims wrote a check for the down payment, but there were not sufficient funds in his bank account to cover the check. The Sundays did not receive any payment on the contract. Rheims died, and Yates was named the executor of Rheims's estate.

ISSUE Is Oman entitled to the house?

HOLDING No. The Sundays did not receive payment.

REASONING Oman is not entitled to specific performance. She was a donee beneficiary and could not require Rheims or his estate to complete the gift. Delivery is necessary to complete the gift, and the property was never delivered to Oman. Promises to make gifts in the future are not enforceable. Rheims had no contractual obligation to deliver the property to Oman. In a suit against the promisor, third-party beneficiaries have the same rights as the promisee. Oman could not require the Sundays to transfer the property to her, as they were not paid. Defenses that are valid against the promisee are valid against the third-party beneficiary.

The Sundays could have requested specific performance, but they requested monetary damages instead. A settlement was worked out and they received monetary damages from Rheims's estate.

A Creditor Beneficiary

If the promisee owed a legal duty to the third party, the third party is a *creditor beneficiary.* Again, a life insurance policy is an excellent example. A working couple wished to purchase a house with a $100,000 mortgage. The bank was willing to lend them $100,000 based on the value of the home and both of their salaries. Since the bank felt that the husband could not afford the monthly payments without his wife's salary, the bank made the loan contingent on the purchase of **mortgage insurance** on her life. She agreed to purchase $100,000 of mortgage insurance from Connecticut Mutual Life Insurance Company. The bank is a creditor beneficiary. Examine Figure 15.3, where this arrangement is diagrammed.

Mortgage insurance
Insurance that will pay off a mortgage on a home if a contingency occurs

If the wife dies during the term of the mortgage, the bank can sue Connecticut Mutual directly on the insurance contract. Connecticut Mutual can use any defenses that it had against the wife as defenses against the bank.

If the wife tries to cancel the policy, the bank could successfully sue the wife, because canceling the insurance policy and not replacing it would be a breach of the contract between the bank and the wife. The bank, however, would probably allow her to substitute another insurance policy from a different company if the coverage was essentially the same. In reality, if the bank did not trust the wife to make the premium payments, they would require her to make the payments through the bank; then the bank would be assured that the payments were being made.

The differences between donee and creditor beneficiaries are not great. They both have basically the same rights against the promisor. Although many states say that the rights of a creditor beneficiary are directly derived from the promisee, courts usually provide the same type of protection for the creditor beneficiary as they do for the donee beneficiary. The only real differences are their rights against the promisee, and even these differences are becoming less pronounced. The distinction between creditor and donee beneficiaries was completely dropped by the *Restatement (Second) of Contracts*.[3] It is also beginning to disappear in some states, such as California.[4]

Figure 15.3   Creditor Beneficiary

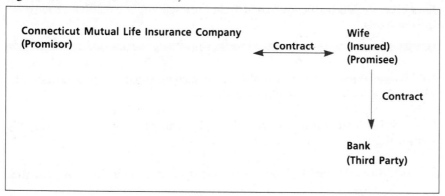

---

[3] *Restatement (Second) of Contracts*, Section 302.
[4] Allan v. Bekins Archival Service, Inc., 154 Cal. Rptr. 458, at 463, footnote 8.

A third party cannot successfully claim any better rights than those provided in the contract. The next case examines the importance of the underlying legal rights.

Harris v. Superior Court (Mirsaidi)
233 Cal. Rptr. 186 (Cal. App. 1986)

FACTS   Tiffany and Lisa Harris claimed that Dr. Mirsaidi was negligent in the birth of their daughter. They wished to have the dispute settled by arbitration. The Harrises received medical care from Dr. Mirsaidi and Hawthorne Community Medical Group, Inc., under a prepaid health services program provided through Mr. Harris's employer. The enrollment form signed by Mr. Harris stated "I agree that any claim asserted by a Member . . . against Maxicare, Hawthorne Community Medical Group, Inc., [three other entities], their employees or other contracting health professionals, pharmacies, or their employees for bodily injury to or death of a member, is subject to binding **arbitration.**"

Arbitration Submission of claim to people (arbitrators) who will determine rights

ISSUE   Did Dr. Mirsaidi have the right to choose either arbitration or litigation?

HOLDING   No. He was a third-party beneficiary of the contract entered into by Mr. Harris and Hawthorne Community Medical Group.

REASONING   The contract clause clearly provided that Hawthorne Community Medical Group was a party to the agreement. Hawthorne Community Medical Group could only provide medical care through its employees, like Dr. Mirsaidi. Dr. Mirsaidi could not accept patients and payments under the terms of the contract *and* deny the arbitration clause. He knew or should have known of the existence of the clause. Third parties cannot gain greater rights under the contract than the contracting parties already have. If Dr. Mirsaidi had been allowed to choose litigation, he would have been given greater rights.

In this case, the mother and daughter were also third-party beneficiaries under the insurance contract the father signed.

Analysis of Third-Party Beneficiary Contracts

In analyzing a situation involving a potential third party, it is important to answer the following questions:

1. Was the additional person involved from the beginning, or was that person added later?
2. Did the promisee intend to benefit the third party, or was it an accident?
3. Was the promisee making a gift to the third party, or was the promisee fulfilling a contract obligation to the third party?

If the additional party became involved later, there may have been an assignment or a delegation.

If the third person becomes involved after the initial contract formation, then that person is not a third-party beneficiary. Instead, there may have been either an assignment or a delegation. To understand the distinction between assignments and delegations, it is essential to remember the distinction between rights and duties. Contractual *rights* are the parts of the contract that a person is entitled to *receive.* Examples would be delivery of goods, payment for work completed, and discounts for early payment. Contractual *duties* are the parts of the contract that a person is obligated to *give.* These could include working an eight-hour day, paying 20 percent interest on credit card charges, and providing repair services. Rights can be assigned, and duties can be delegated. Although even judges and lawyers may be careless in their terminology, duties cannot be assigned. The rules of law dealing with delegation will always be applied to duties.

DEFINING
ASSIGNMENTS
AND
DELEGATIONS

An *assignment* occurs *when a person transfers a contractual right to someone else.* The transferor is called the *assignor,* and the recipient is called the *assignee.* After the assignment occurs, the assignor has completely lost all contractual rights. The assignor's right has been extinguished, and it now belongs exclusively to the assignee. The other party to the original contract, the promisor, now has to deliver the promised goods or services to the assignee. The assignee is the only one entitled to them.

ASSIGNMENTS

For example, a tenant is renting a house from a landlord. Under the lease, the tenant must pay $400 per month for rent. The landlord is in default on a personal loan obtained from the bank. The landlord assigns the $400 per month rent payment to the bank. The landlord, the assignor, has given up the legal right to the money. That right now belongs exclusively to the assignee, the bank. This situation is diagrammed in Figure 15.4.

Figure 15.4 Assignment

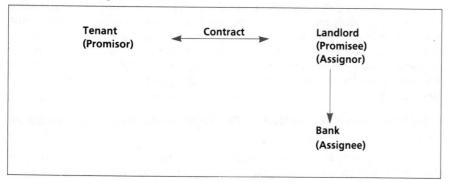

Formalities
Required for
Assignments

Generally, an assignment does not have to follow any particular format. Assignors must use words that indicate an intent to vest a present right in the contract to the assignee. This means that the assignor intends to transfer the right immediately, not at some time in the future. A writing is not required unless the state Statute of Frauds applies. This includes the Statute of Frauds provisions in the Uniform Commercial Code as adopted by the state. As with other contract provisions, it is preferable to reduce the assignment to writing. The assignment must contain an adequate description of the rights that are being assigned. In the following case, the judge analyzed the requirements for an assignment.

Mission Valley East, Inc. v. County of Kern
174 Cal. Rptr. 300 (Cal. App. 1981)

FACTS

The county tax collector arranged for seven parcels of land to be sold at a public tax sale. Under applicable California law, the owners could file a claim to receive any excess proceeds received by the tax collector for one year after the sale. (Excess proceeds are the amounts the tax collector receives minus the taxes owed and the tax collector's costs.) Neal, the attorney for Mission Valley East, Inc., wrote the owners and offered them $100 each for their remaining interests in the parcels. He led them to believe that their interests were almost worthless and that his client had purchased the property at the tax sale and needed a quitclaim deed and an assignment to obtain title insurance. Mission Valley East, Inc., had not purchased the parcels. After buying the quitclaim deeds and assignments, Mission Valley East filed a claim for the excess proceeds. The assignors were not aware that they had the right to excess proceeds.

ISSUE

Did the assignments transfer to Mission Valley East, Inc., the right to the excess proceeds?

HOLDING

No. There was no showing of intent to make such an assignment.

REASONING

Personal rights to claim money are freely assignable, but proof of the intention to assign any rights must be clear and positive. The assignment must describe the subject matter with sufficient particularity to identify the rights assigned. In this case, the deeds limited the assignment to the assignor's rights in real property and did not include personal rights, such as the right to excess proceeds. The rights to the excess proceeds were not specifically mentioned in the assignment.

Consideration is not required in order to have a valid assignment. Although the assignee need not give up consideration in exchange for the contract right, consideration is generally present. This factor affects the legal relationship between the assignor and the assignee. That relationship can be either a contract or a gift, but it is generally a contract, especially in business settings. In our earlier example, the landlord assigned the payments to the bank so that the bank would not sue the landlord or take other action to collect. People in business are not in the habit of making gifts to other businesspeople. A gift assignment would occur, for example, if a sales representative for a concrete company assigned the 10 percent Christmas bonus he earned to his eldest daughter for her college education fund.

Since the assignment extinguishes the assignor's rights and creates rights for the assignee, one would assume that the promisor must be told about the assignment. Surprisingly, this is not a legal requirement: an assignment is perfectly valid even though the promisor is never informed. There are a number of reasons why an assignee would want to give notice to the promisor, particularly if the assignor may be unethical or dishonest.

Notice of the Assignment

If the promisor *has* received notice of the assignment and then pays the promisee or delivers performance to the promisee, the promisor will still be obligated to pay or deliver performance to the assignee. In many instances, the promisor is not told about the assignment, and the promisee receives the performance and transfers it to the assignee. If the assignor does not transfer the performance to the assignee and the promisor has not been given notice, the assignee would have to take action against the assignor, who may have absconded with the funds.

In some cases, dishonest assignors have benefited by selling the *same* contract right to more than one assignee. Of course, if the second assignee has notice or knowledge of the prior assignment, that person will take subject to the rights of the first assignee. This usually is not the case. Dishonest assignors generally disappear with the funds and leave the innocent assignees to resolve their conflicting claims. Two theories are widely used by the courts to resolve these problems. One theory is that the first assignee to receive the assignment received all the rights; the assignor had nothing to assign to later assignees. This theory, commonly referred to as the *first-in-time approach* or the *American Rule,* is applied in some states. For example, if Anita, the promisee, assigned her right to Joel on January 1 and then assigned her right to Larry on January 15, Joel would receive the right according to this rule.

Other states apply the rule that the first assignee to actually give notice to the promisor receives the better right. This is called the *first-to-give-notice approach* or the *English Rule.* It is followed in California, Florida, and a few other states. In the prior example, if Larry had given notice to the promisor first, he would have prevailed under the English Rule. One of the policies underlying this rule is that a prudent assignee who is about to pay value for the assignment would check with the promisor. A promisor who had notice of earlier assignments would tell the prospective purchaser, and this step would prevent additional assignments. The advantage of giving notice should be obvious.

Under either rule of law, the assignor would be liable for fraud if he or she can be located with the money. However, there is nothing wrong with a promisee dividing up the contract rights and assigning *different* contract rights to different assignees.

Nonassignable Rights

Assignments have become an important aspect of our business and financial structure. They are important techniques for selling goods and obtaining cash. A common business practice among retail outlets is to sell expensive items on time. The retailer assigns the monthly payments to a credit corporation in exchange for cash. The retailer then uses the cash to buy more merchandise. A common example of this practice occurs when a buyer buys an automobile financed through a car dealership. Because of the importance of assignments in commercial transactions, courts are now predisposed to allow assignments. This favorable perspective is obvious in the courts' treatment of contract assignments. Assignments do not require the approval of the promisor. Even when the promisor vehemently opposes the assignment, the courts generally will allow it.

To prevent the assignment, the promisor must prove to the court that one of the following conditions exists:

1. The assignment would *materially* change the duty of the promisor.
2. The assignment would *materially* impair the chance of return performance.
3. The assignment would *materially* increase the burden or risk imposed by the contract.

The promisor must convince the court that he or she would be in a substantially worse position if the assignment were allowed. These requirements are included in Section 2–210(2) of the Uniform Commercial Code. These requirements are applicable unless the contract contains other provisions; they are discussed more fully in the following paragraph.

When the assignment materially changes the promisor's duty, then the promisor must perform a substantially different type or degree of work. Many assignments involve assigning monthly payments. As this simply requires that the promisor change the address on the monthly envelopes, the promisor's duty is not substantially different. As an example of a substantially different duty, suppose a promisor promised to paint the exterior of any one house and that this promise was made to Lynda, who owns a 1000-square-foot single-level house. Lynda assigns the right to Joanne, who owns a 2500-square-foot two-story house. The promisor could convince the court that this assignment materially affects his duty.

If the assignment impairs the chance of return performance, it increases the chance that the promisor will not receive consideration from the promisee.

For example, Chris wanted to have her portrait painted. She located a talented but struggling artist, John, who would paint the portrait for $200. John explained that he needed the money to buy canvas and quality oil paint before he started. Chris agreed to pay him the money on the first of the month. John was to start the portrait on the fifteenth. Now John wants to assign that payment to his landlord for unpaid rent. Chris could convince the court that this assignment would impair her chance of receiving the portrait.

An assignment will not be allowed if it increases the risk or burden of the contract. If John, the artist, tries to assign only $150 of the payment to his landlord, Chris may be able to convince the court that this assignment increases the burden or risk imposed by their contract, as John might purchase very cheap materials.

The proassignment attitude of the courts is also evidenced by their interpretation of the promisor-promisee contract. Even if the contract states that "no assignment shall be made" or that "there shall be no assignment without the prior consent of the promisor," most courts will still allow the assignment. Courts interpret these clauses as promises or covenants not to assign the rights. The assignor is then held legally responsible for making the assignment and must pay the promisor for any loss caused by the assignment. Often the promisor cannot prove the loss in court, so this is a rather hollow right. If the contracting parties really want to prevent assignments, they must use clauses like "all assignments shall be void" or "any attempt at assignment shall be null and void." Most courts will interpret this language as actually removing the power to make assignments.

The law has not always favored assignments. Some states still limit certain types of assignments. Common examples are prohibitions or limitations on the assignment of wages. Statutes in Alabama, California, Connecticut, District of Columbia, Missouri, and Ohio generally prohibit the assignment of future wages. In addition, California and Connecticut and many other states have special rules that apply to assignments of wages as security for small loans.[5]

An assignee obtains the same legal rights in the contract that the assignor had. If the assignee sues the promisor, the promisor may generally use the same defenses against the assignee that were available against the assignor. Examples of these defenses would include fraud, duress, undue influence, and breach of this contract by the assignor. The promisor will not, though, be able to use *every* conceivable defense against an assignee. The assignee's rights against the promisor were at issue in *Hefley* v. *Jones.*

Rights Created by the Assignment

---

[5] *Restatement (Second) of Contracts,* Introductory Note to Chapter 15 at pages 15 and 16.

Hefley v. Jones
687 F.2d 1383 (10th Cir. 1982)

FACTS   Jones contracted to sell a number of heifers and steers to Bonnett in two different contracts entered into on 2 March and 16 March 1978. On March 6 Bonnett agreed to sell to Hefley and Martin the heifers he had just bought from Jones; on March 24 he agreed to sell to Hefley and Martin steers he had bought from Jones. Bonnett and Jones contracted with each other again on 9 March and 10 April. Bonnett breached these latter contracts and disappeared with the $81,500 down payment he had received. Jones refused to deliver the steers and heifers to Hefley and Martin.

ISSUE   Had Bonnett made a valid, enforceable assignment of his contract rights to Hefley and Martin?

HOLDING   Yes. A valid assignment had been made.

REASONING   The Oklahoma Commercial Code applies because cattle are goods. The Code does not require any particular language to create an assignment. Contractual language may be interpreted in light of the course of dealing between the parties and the usage in the trade or business. Cattle are often sold many times between the original sale by the rancher and the ultimate purchase by a feedlot. The rancher delivers the cattle to the final purchaser and collects the remaining amount due on the purchase price. Commissions are settled through the chain of purchases. Bonnett had sold Jones's cattle contracts in the past. Jones's counterclaim against Bonnett on the other contracts had not matured at the time of the assignment, so it could not be used as a setoff against the assignee.

Warranties Implied by the Assignor

An assignor who makes an assignment implies that certain things are true about the assigned rights, namely, that (1) the right is a valid legal right, and (2) there are no valid defenses to the assigned right. These warranties need not be expressly stated but can instead be implied. If the assignor breaches the warranties, the assignee can successfully sue.

Waiver of Defenses Clause

A *waiver of defenses clause* in a contract attempts to give the assignee better legal rights than the assignor had. Often it is part of a standard printed contract prepared by the assignee or assignor and signed by the promisor. In it, *the promisor promises to give up legal defenses in any later lawsuit by the assignee.* In the contract, the promisor agrees not to exert defenses like fraud in the inducement or breach of warranty against any subsequent assignees. Often the consumer (promisor) is not aware that the contract contains a waiver of defenses clause or does not understand what it means. If effective, the clause reduces the promisor's bargaining power. For example, if a purchaser buys a product on time and the product is defective, a common reaction is to stop making payments. A waiver of defenses clause means that the buyer must keep on making payments. Consumer groups and government agencies have opposed waiver of defenses clauses because they reduce a consumer's bargaining power. Such a clause *is* enforceable under Section 9-206(1) of the Uniform Commercial Code, unless there is a different rule under statute or court decision for buyers or lessees of consumer goods. Some states with statutes forbidding or limiting these clauses include Alaska, District of Columbia, Missouri, Ohio, and Washington.[6] The Federal Trade Commission enacted a regulation barring these agreements in contracts by consumers.[7]

DELEGATIONS

Assignments and delegations may occur simultaneously. Initially, however, it will be easier to understand delegations if they are analyzed as a completely separate concept. In a *delegation, the promisor locates a new promisor to perform the duties under the contract.* The original promisor is called the *delegator,* and the new promisor is called the *delegatee.* For example, suppose a purchaser buys a new automobile from a car dealer. One of the terms of that contract is that the dealer promises to provide certain warranty work on the car for three years. The mechanic employed by the car dealer quits, so the dealer contracts with a garage to do the warranty work. This particular delegation is illustrated in Figure 15.5. As with assignments, there may be consideration for the delegation, but that is not necessary. If there is no consideration, the delegation is really a gift from the new promisor to the old promisor.

Figure 15.5   Delegation

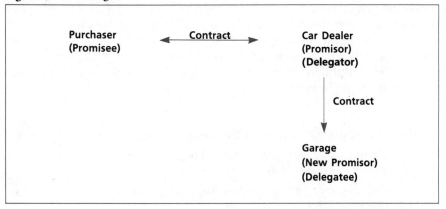

[6] *Restatement (Second of Contracts),* Introductory Note to Chapter 15 at page 10.
[7] 16 C.F.R. Section 433.1 – .3 (1975).

The purchaser of the car, the promisee, can sue the car dealer who made the promise if the warranty work is not performed. The purchaser can also generally sue the delegatee for failure to perform. In many states the purchaser can sue both the delegator and the delegatee at the same time, but the purchaser cannot collect twice.

The relationship between the delegator and the delegatee may be that of a contract or of a gift. If it is a contract relationship, the delegator has the right to sue the delegatee for nonperformance. If it is a gift relationship, the court would hold that the delegatee promised to make a gift in the future but failed to deliver it. Promises to make gifts in the future are not enforceable without promissory estoppel.

Delegations do not occur unless the delegatee assumes the contract duties. This assumption can be either expressly stated or implied. The trend of court decisions is to imply the assumption of the duties, especially when there is an assignment and a delegation. An example would occur when the parties state that there is an "assignment of the contract" or an "assignment of all my rights under the contract." Such statements are *generally* interpreted as indicating an assignment and a delegation of the duties by the delegator and an acceptance of the duties by the delegatee unless there is a clear indication of a contrary intention. This position is followed by the Uniform Commercial Code, Section 2–210(4), and the *Restatement (Second) of Contracts,* Section 328.

Delegations do not have the preferred status in the eyes of the law that assignments do. Courts are more inclined to deny a delegation. If the contract between the promisor and the promisee states that "there shall be no delegations," the courts will prevent delegations. The same is true if the contract calls for personal performance. Courts are also more likely to decide that a delegation is unfair to the promisee. Under the Uniform Commercial Code, Section 2–210(1), duties cannot be delegated if the agreement states that there will be no delegation or the promisor has a substantial interest in having the delegator perform the contract. Section 2–210(3) indicates that a contract clause that prohibits the assignment of "the contract" is to be construed as preventing only a delegation of the contract duties to the assignee.

To characterize an assignment or a delegation situation, one should answer the following questions:

1. Was the additional person involved from the beginning or added later?

2. Did the additional person undertake to perform a contract duty or become entitled to a contract right? Or both?

3. Did the language of the original contract prevent this transfer to an additional person?

4. Did the type of rights or duties prevent this transfer to an additional person?

When the Uniform Commercial Code is applicable, businesspeople need to review its assignment and delegation provisions. Some questions concerning assignments are not resolved in Article 9 of the Code. Certain types of assignments are excluded from Article 9 by Section 9–104. Some examples are: claims for wages, interests under an insurance policy, **liens** on real estate, and deposits in banks. Under Sections 9–201 and 9–203, provisions of Article 9 may be subordinated to state statutes regulating installment sales to consumers. Section 2–210 of the Code covers assignments and delegations under contracts for the sale of goods. This is only a brief overview.

UNIFORM COMMERCIAL CODE PROVISIONS

Lien A claim against property allowed by law

SUMMARY

An additional person who is involved in a contract from the beginning may be a third-party beneficiary. If the promisor or promisee meant to affect the third person under the contract, that person will be an intended beneficiary and will have enforceable rights. Intended beneficiaries can file lawsuits to protect their own legal rights. If they sue the promisor, the promisor can use against them the same defenses that are valid against the promisee. Creditor beneficiaries can sue a promisee who tries to cancel the contract. Donee beneficiaries will generally not be successful in a suit against the promisee because the donee beneficiary did not receive the gift.

An additional party who becomes involved after the contract is formed may be an assignee or a delegatee. A delegatee assumes the transferor's obligation to perform under the contract. The delegator will still be obligated to perform if the delegatee does not. An assignee receives a contract right from the transferor. An assignment extinguishes the contract right of the assignor and sets up this contract right exclusively in the assignee.

DISCUSSION QUESTIONS

1. Julia promised to buy her son, Jonathan, a car from Ted McNare's Volkswagen if Jonathan graduated from college. Does Ted McNare have any rights in the contract? Why or why not?

2. Monkey Business provides an unusual service. They employ costumed personnel who dress like apes, belly dancers, and clowns to deliver singing telegrams. If you hired Monkey Business to deliver a birthday greeting to your boss, what are the legal rights of Monkey Business, you, and your boss?

3. Some states have statutes prohibiting or limiting assignment of wages. What public policies might the state legislatures have been trying to promote with these statutes?

4. Should waiver of defenses clauses be enforced? What are the advantages and disadvantages of these clauses?

5. Is there any reason why an assignment of the Jones-Bonnett contract should not be allowed in *Hefley* v. *Jones,* 687 F.2d 1383 (10th Cir. 1982)?

6. What are the differences between assignees and third-party beneficiaries? In what ways are they similar?

7. Why do American courts favor assignments?

8. When will an assignment be allowed if the contract does not mention assignments?

9. What happens if the assignor assigns the identical contract right to three assignees? Who should recover from whom?

10. How do assignments and delegations differ from each other?

CASE
PROBLEMS

1. Stevens Air Systems contracted with Health Care Services Corporation (HCS) to provide health care to employees. HCS contracted with Omaha Indemnity to cover the catastrophic illnesses of these employees. The insurer signed the contract with the knowledge that HCS intended to benefit the Stevens employees who participated in the health plan. Were these employees intended third-party beneficiaries? Should contrary language in the HCS-Omaha contract influence this decision? (*Gilmore* v. *Omaha Indemnity*, 158 Cal. Rptr. 229 [Cal. App. 1979].)

2. Mrs. Murphy's nineteen-year-old son was killed in an accident caused by Pollard, who was insured by Allstate. Allstate already paid her the amount of money specified by the policy limits. Mrs. Murphy seeks to enforce a state law that requires insurance companies to use good faith and fair dealing in settling claims. Is Mrs. Murphy entitled to sue Allstate as a third-party beneficiary for failing to settle the claim fairly? (*Murphy* v. *Allstate Insurance Company*, 132 Cal. Rptr. 424 [Cal. 1976], 553 P.2d 584.)

3. Mr. Raymond Robson, Sr. and Mr. Raymond Robson, Jr. modified their contract two days before Mr. Robson, Jr. died. This modification removed the father-in-law's obligation to make payments to the widow from the proceeds of the company. Under the *original* contract the father-in-law was to receive all of his son's shares in their company when the son died, but the father-in-law was to pay $500 per month from the company proceeds to the wife for five years following the son's death or until she remarried, whichever occurred first. Mrs. Birthe Robson and Mr. Robson, Jr. were separated at the time of his death and a divorce action was pending. Is Mrs. Birthe Robson a third-party beneficiary of the contract between her husband and her father-in-law? Does she have enforceable rights? (*Robson* v. *Robson*, 514 F. Supp. 99 [N.D. Ill. 1981].)

4. A general release was negotiated and signed between the general contractor, Robbins, Inc., and the subcontractor, Hirsch. (The release was given for $34,000 and indicated that Hirsch would not be responsible for any difficulties arising from the project.) The owner of the premises sued to recover the amount that the owner had to pay to Sears, a tenant, who suffered damages allegedly due to the defective work performed by the

subcontractor. A substantial part of the building had collapsed. Is the owner an intended third party of the general release and consequently bound by the release? (*Sears, Roebuck and Co.* v. *Jardel Co.,* 421 F.2d 1048 [3rd Cir. 1970].)

5. Mr. Beaty, a professional basketball player, signed a contract to play for Kirst. General Insurance Company posted a security bond for his salary. Beaty's "contract" was sold to Daniels, then to the Stars, and then to the Spirits of St. Louis. Under the last contract, the Spirits were supposed to pay Beaty, but they have not been doing so. Can Beaty enforce the Stars-Spirits contract? Can Kirst or General Insurance Company enforce the Stars-Spirits contract? Why or why not? (*Kirst* v. *Silna,* 163 Cal. Rptr. 230 [Cal. App. 1980].)

6. Mr. Williams was injured while working on a drilling rig at Amchitka Island, Alaska. He was working for Parco, Inc. Parco had contracted with the Atomic Energy Commission (AEC) to drill certain test holes at Amchitka. Fenix & Scisson had a contract with the AEC to furnish engineering services in conjunction with drilling and mining operations there. Under this contract, Fenix & Scisson was required to inspect drilling operations and to recommend any improvements to the AEC. The firm was also required to take reasonable safety precautions in the performance of its work. This contract was supplemented by provisions that Fenix & Scisson had responsibility for overall industrial safety at the site. At the time of the accident, there were seven Parco employees on the job and one Fenix & Scisson employee on the job. Does Fenix & Scisson have a contractual duty to Williams? Is he an intended third-party beneficiary of their contract with AEC? (*Williams* v. *Fenix & Scisson, Inc.,* 608 F.2d 1205 [9th Cir. 1979].)

7. Patrick Puccia sold his restaurant to two buyers. He took back a note and second mortgage. Patrick transferred the note to the Bank of Palatine for collateral on other loans. The purported assignment dated 10 March 1981 provided as follows:

For value received, I hereby assign all my rights, title, and interest in and to: That certain note and trust dated 3-9-81 from the Bank & Trust Company of Arlington Heights, Trustee under trust no. 2635 dated 11-15-80 in the amount of $225,000 payable to Patrick Puccia [illegible] [to] the Bank of Palatine.

Did the purported assignment adequately describe the item to be assigned, even though the word "deed" was omitted from the term "trust deed"? (*Klehm* v. *Grecian Chalet, Ltd.,* 518 N.E.2d 187 [Ill. App. 1987].)

8. Mrs. Lara entered Kern County General Hospital to give birth. After the child was born, Mrs. Lara died. The hospital was not paid for medical services provided to the child. Under the state law, Mr. Lara, a seasonal farmworker, was billed for the services. The hospital assigned their claim

to Kern County Collection Service, a private organization. Should this assignment be allowed? What defenses may be available against the assignee? (*Lara* v. *Kern County Board of Supervisors,* 130 Cal. Rptr. 668 [Cal. App. 1976].)

9. Mr. and Mrs. Owen signed a contract to purchase a Motorola stereo record player and 140 albums from Universal. The contract said that the record player would be "free." The Owens could pay $698.00 cash or $849.72 if they paid over time. They agreed to pay over time. They signed the contract and a note. The printed terms on the back of the note indicated that the note would be assigned to Unico, and it was. Unico controlled numerous aspects of Universal's business. The contract stated, "Buyer agrees not to set up any claim against such seller as a defense, counterclaim, or offset to any action by an assignee for any unpaid balance of the purchase price or for possession of the property." The Owens were to make payments for 3 years; Universal was to make periodic deliveries of the albums for 5 1/3 years. Universal became insolvent, and the Owens did not receive most of their albums. Do the Owens have to pay Unico on the note? Should they have to make payment? Why or why not? (*Unico* v. *Owen,* 232 A.2d 405 [N.J. 1967].)

10. Mr. Milford owned a stud horse that he sold to Mr. Stewart. Under the terms of the written contract, Stewart was to allow Milford two breedings a year from the horse as long as the horse lived. This agreement stated that it was valid "regardless [of] to whom the horse may be sold," and the agreement was filed with the county clerk. Stewart sold the horse to McKinnie, who had read and understood the Milford-Stewart contract. McKinnie refused to honor the terms of the Milford-Stewart contract. Is McKinnie bound by the contract? Why or why not? (*McKinnie* v. *Milford,* 597 S.W.2d 953 [Tex. App. 1980].)

Methods of Discharging the Contract

When parties contract with each other, they naturally assume that each party will perform according to the terms of the agreement. Consequently, whenever the parties do what the contract calls for, we say that their duties under the contract have been discharged. *Discharge of a contract* involves *the legally valid termination of a contractual duty.* Upon discharge, the agreement between the parties has been fulfilled; the parties' duties and obligations to each other end at this time. As you might expect, there are numerous methods for discharging contracts, but they can be grouped into four main categories: discharge by performance, agreement of the parties, operation of law, and nonperformance.

Complete performance is one method of discharging a contract; but the law will, in certain circumstances, allow *degrees* of performance — *substantial performance*, for instance. Discharge may also result from the *agreement of the parties* — that is, through release, rescission, accord and satisfaction, novation, and the like. Similarly, a contract discharge will occur by *operation of law* in

TERMINATION OF THE CONTRACT

275

cases involving bankruptcy decrees, the expiration of the statute of limitations' period, and material alterations of contracts. Discharge by nonperformance comes about if the doctrine of impossibility and commercial frustration can be invoked. Breach of the contract—whether actual or anticipatory— also discharges the contract, as will noncompliance with the contract's conditions. We will study these various methods of discharging contracts in this chapter.

DISCHARGE BY PERFORMANCE

Complete Performance

The simplest, most common, and most satisfactory method of discharge is *complete performance.* (Yet, as we will see later, rendering complete performance may be easier said than done.) If Johnson has agreed to deliver five carloads of grain, and Kreczewski has agreed to pay $2000 per carload, complete performance will occur when Johnson makes the deliveries to Kreczewski and Kreczewski pays Johnson. The *parties' exact fulfillment of the terms of the contract* satisfies the intent of their agreement and their reason for contracting. Complete performance also extinguishes all the legal duties and rights that the contract originally set up. (Note, too, that performance would be complete if one of the parties *tenders* either the grain or the payment—that is, unconditionally offers to perform his contractual obligation and can so perform. That person would have completely performed the contract even if the other person does not accept the grain or the payment.)

As long as Johnson is fulfilling Kreczewski's reasonable expectations under the contract, discharge by complete performance will ensue once the parties have met their respective obligations under the agreement. However, if Johnson during the course of the deliveries does not live up to the letter of the agreement as to the quality of the grain sent to Kreczewski, Kreczewski should give Johnson prompt notice of these defects and should state formally that he expects complete performance. Kreczewski's failure to take such actions may allow Johnson to argue after the fact that Kreczewski has waived his right to expect complete performance.

Obviously, there are circumstances in which one party's performance does not mirror precisely the rights and obligations enumerated in the agreement. In such cases, the other party may question whether this degree of performance adequately fulfills the requisites of the contract.

Substantial Performance

The issue raised by such a question involves the legal sufficiency of less-than-complete performance. The law does not always require exact performance of a contract; hence, *minor deviations* from the performance contemplated in the contract may not preclude the discharge of the contract. This type of performance is called *substantial performance.* A party who has substantially performed may receive the payment agreed to by the parties. However, because substantial performance nevertheless represents a type of contract breach in that performance was not perfect and was instead a notch below the parties' reasonable expectations under the contract, the other party may sue for the damages occasioned by substantial, as opposed to complete, performance.

Before the doctrine of substantial performance is available to discharge the responsibilities of a performing party, two criteria must be met. First, the breach must not have been material; in other words, the defective performance must not destroy the value or purpose of the contract.[1] Second, the breach cannot be willful; that is, the deviations must not result from bad-faith conduct.

It should be noted that contracts that require one party to perform "to the satisfaction" of the other party may be held to a higher standard of "substantiality." In fact, in certain cases, such as those involving custom tailoring, some courts hold that the personal, subjective expectations of the dissatisfied party must be met in order to discharge the contract. Other courts hold that performance is substantial if the performance rendered would satisfy our old friend, "the reasonably prudent person under the same or similar circumstances." Courts will generally apply this latter test where performance is not based on personal tastes or aesthetic preferences (as may be involved in our custom tailoring example) but rather on satisfaction as to merchantability or mechanical utility (as in the purchase of a car).

Usually, however, the concept of substantial performance is more appropriately applied to construction contracts than to sales contracts. This is so because a disgruntled buyer has a duty to return or to reject a defective suit, whereas a dissatisfied occupier of land necessarily must keep the defective house or garage. The possibility of the unjust enrichment of the landowner makes the doctrine of substantial performance more attractive to courts in construction situations than in most other commercial contexts.

The next case illustrates some of these principles.

F. A. Gray, Inc. v. Weiss
519 A.2d 716 (Me. 1986)

FACTS At Weiss's invitation, F. A. Gray, Inc. (Gray), submitted a written and signed $3,895 proposal to Weiss for the preparation and painting of Weiss's house and barn. After discussions with Gray, Weiss asked Gray to do the job using stain instead of paint. After changing the word "paint" to "stain," Weiss signed and returned Gray's written proposal. Gray then began work on Weiss's house and barn. Before the work was completed, however, Weiss became dissatisfied with the appearance of the buildings and insisted that Gray stop. When Weiss refused to pay Gray for the work it had completed, Gray sought to recover the full contract price. Weiss argued that

---

[1] A material breach, as we shall see in later sections of this chapter, occurs when the performance rendered falls appreciably below the level of performance the parties reasonably expected under the terms of the contract. Such a breach discharges the other party from the contract.

Gray had breached the contract by proceeding to do the job with an inappropriate covering material that Gray, by virtue of its expertise, should have refused to use.

ISSUE   Could Gray recover for its work pursuant to the contract?

HOLDING   Yes. Gray's use of the oil stain did not preclude a court's finding that it had substantially performed the contract.

REASONING   There is no ready formula for determining what, in any particular case, amounts to "substantial performance" sufficient to justify a judgment for the contract price, lessened by deductions for asserted claims of defects or omissions. Such a determination is always a question of fact or a matter of degree. The factors courts take into account include: the work called for by the contract; the extent to which there has been compliance; the ratio of the cost of curing the defects and omissions to the total contract price; and the importance of any defects or omissions to the purpose of the contract. When a contractor has in good faith completed substantial performance of the terms of the contract, with only slight omissions and defects that can be readily remedied, the contractor may recover the contract price, less the damages resulting from these omissions. Deficient workmanship may constitute the difference between substantial and full performance, but such faulty workmanship will not necessarily bar recovery on the contract. The contract at issue required that Gray "thoroughly scrape, prime all bare wood, caulk loose joints, putty loose sash[es], and apply one coat [of] oil-base house stain." The contract further provided that "all work [should] be completed in a workmanlike manner according to standard practice." The records revealed that Weiss had selected stain as the material to be used after a discussion with Gray and that Gray had advised Weiss against the use of stain. In fact, Gray had finally agreed to use the stain only on the condition that Weiss approve a test patch before Gray would proceed. Weiss then approved the test patch Gray had stained. Because the contract specifically required stain rather than paint, Gray's use of an oil-based stain could not completely preclude his recovery under the contract.

DISCHARGE BY AGREEMENT OF THE PARTIES

The parties themselves can specifically agree to discharge the contract. Provisions to that effect may be part of the original contract between the parties or part of a new contract drafted expressly to discharge the initial contract.

Release

Release is a common method for discharging the legal rights one party has against another. To be valid, a *release* should be in *writing,* should be supported by *consideration,* and should effect an *immediate relinquishment* of rights or claims owed to another. For example, a landowner may sign a release in which he or she agrees to discharge the builder from the original contractual obligations, usually in exchange for money. Insurance companies commonly execute similar releases to be signed by the insured parties when the insurers pay for the insured parties' injuries.

Sometimes the parties may find it advantageous to call off their deal. This
process is called *rescission*. A contract of *rescission* is a *voluntary, mutual surrender
and discharge of contractual rights and duties whereby the parties are returned to the
original status quo.* A valid rescission is legally binding. In general, rescission
may be either in writing or oral (subject, you will recall, to the Statute of
Frauds' requirements under Section 2–209 of the UCC—moreover, rescis-
sions of realty contracts oftentimes must be written as well); formal or informal; express or implied.

The simplest method of rescission involves the termination of executory
bilateral contracts. If Johnson and Kreczewski in our earlier example *mutually
agree to cancel* their transaction, *express rescission* has occurred. On the other
hand, they may subsequently agree that seven boxcars of grain will be delivered instead of five. *Substituting this later agreement* for the old one brings about
an *implied rescission* of the earlier agreement. However, problems often ensue if
the parties attempt rescission of a unilateral contract (or a bilateral contract
where one party has fully executed his or her duties). In these situations, some
courts will infer a promise to pay for the performance rendered or require that
consideration be paid to the party who has performed before rescission will be
granted. Courts ordinarily resolve these issues by trying to ascertain the intent
of the parties; but as we have learned, this task is often a difficult one.

Note how the court applied these concepts in the case that follows.

Rescission

Ennis v. Interstate Distributors, Inc.
598 S.W.2d 903 (Tex. App. 1980)

Ennis, the former president of Interstate, signed a restrictive covenant in which he
agreed not to compete with Interstate in the sale and distribution of ice machines
(especially Frigidaires) and related products for a three-year period in a four-state
area after termination of his employment with Interstate. Upon Ennis's violation of
the covenant, Interstate sought rescission of it and restitution of the money the firm
had paid Ennis for signing the convenant. Ennis argued that rescission was not
appropriate because, owing to his partial performance, the status quo could not be
restored.

FACTS

Was a return to the status quo required as a condition of granting rescission?

ISSUE

No. Such a condition was unnecessary, and rescission was a proper remedy.

HOLDING

Rescission is authorized if there is a breach of contract in a material part. The breach
need not be total; a partial breach may be sufficient if it goes to the essence of the
contract. Similarly, restitution may be granted if a party to a contract has paid money
and the other party has wholly failed to perform. Ennis's employment violated the
covenant for all but three months of the time period and was a material breach.

REASONING

Ennis's failure to perform the obligations of the covenant warranted rescission and required restitution of the consideration Interstate had paid to Ennis.

<hr>

Accord and Satisfaction

As we learned in Chapter 10 when we discussed consideration in unliquidated debt situations, the parties may agree to *accept performance different from that required by their original bargain.* An agreement of this sort is called an *accord. When the parties comply with the accord, satisfaction* occurs, and discharge of the original claim by accord and satisfaction (that is, substituted performance) has resulted. The process of accord and satisfaction requires evidence of assent. Moreover, an accord will not be legally binding unless and until the performance required in the accord (that is, the "satisfaction") is rendered.

Using the *Ennis* case as an example, let us assume that Interstate asks Ennis for restitution of the $50,000 paid to him as part of the covenant not to compete. Ennis, of course, does not want to pay any of this money back. When the parties ultimately agree on a compromise figure — say $30,000 — an accord exists, and upon Ennis's paying the $30,000, satisfaction has occurred.

Novation

Just as the parties may agree to substituted performances, so they may agree to substituted parties. A *novation* is a contract that effects an *immediate discharge of a previously existing contractual obligation, creates a new contractual obligation or duty, and includes as a party to this new agreement one who was neither owed a duty nor obligated to perform in the original contract.* A novation, then, is a contract in which a new party is substituted for one of the parties in the previous contract. It differs from an accord in that the novation immediately discharges an obligation, whereas an accord is not executed until performance occurs. As you would expect, both the assent of the person to whom the obligation is owed (usually the creditor) and the assent of the new obligor (third party) are required for a valid novation. The assent of the previous debtor is usually not required, although that party can disclaim the benefit of the discharge if desired. The novation, in addition, must be supported by valid consideration.

To illustrate a novation, assume that Mary has leased an apartment for twelve months. After six months, Mary is going to be reassigned to a job in another state. If Mary can find a new tenant who is willing to take over the balance of her lease and if Mary's landlord will agree to substitute this new tenant in place of Mary, thereby releasing Mary from her lease obligations, a novation will exist. The old contract has been changed by a substitution of a new party for one of the old parties, with the consent of the remaining "old" party.

DISCHARGE BY OPERATION OF LAW

We have seen in other contexts that the law itself can mandate the discharge of certain contracts. As you will learn in Chapter 31, bankruptcy decrees discharge contractual obligations by operation of law. Most of the time a creditor will not receive the total owed, and yet the discharge in bankruptcy prevents the creditor from later suing the debtor for nonperformance (usually non-payment). Most states, however, allow the debtor to revive the obligation by a later promise to pay the creditor, subject to the Bankruptcy Act's provisions.

Statutes of limitation in all jurisdictions set up time periods within which lawsuits for certain claims must be brought. Noncompliance with these statutes may therefore discharge contractual claims. If the relevant state statute says that claims must be brought within six years of the time of the contract's formation, claims asserted in lawsuits brought after this time are unenforceable. When the transaction involves a sale of goods, Section 2 – 725 of the UCC states that the injured party must ordinarily file suit within four years of the occurrence of the breach. The underlying claim is therefore discharged by operation of law if a suit is not brought within this period. Each state's statutes should be checked as to the period of limitations because these differ from jurisdiction to jurisdiction.

The law will, moreover, discharge any contract that has been materially altered by one of the parties to the agreement. The alteration must be done intentionally and without the consent of the other party. Thus, if Johnson changes the carload price of the grain on the written contract from $2000 to $5000, Kreczewski can obtain discharge of this contract through operation of law.

Just as performance will discharge a contract, so too, under certain circumstances, will the nonperformance of the contract. Still, as we have discussed before, do not expect courts to apply these doctrines in order to save you from a bad bargain.

DISCHARGE BY NONPERFORMANCE

Until the middle of the last century, courts rejected outright the doctrine of impossibility as a method of discharging contracts. *Impossibility* as a legal concept refers to *an unforeseen event or condition that precludes the possibility of the party's performing as promised.* For instance, such events as the destruction of the subject matter of the contract without the fault of either party (Johnson's wheat burns before being loaded); supervening illegality (after the contract's formation, a law is passed that makes it illegal for trains to carry agricultural products into certain states); or conduct by one party that makes performance by the other party impossible (Kreczewski contracts for every possible car in carrying out other deals so that Johnson cannot procure the necessary cars for their transaction) generally discharge contracts. These examples involve *objective impossibility* (nonperformance of the contract is unavoidable; *no one* can perform the contract in these circumstances).

Impossibility

Another instance of objective impossibility that may also constitute grounds for discharging the contract is the death or disability of either party to a personal services contract (Johnson hires Pollock to paint his portrait, and

Pollock has a debilitating heart attack). This is an exception to the general rule that a contract will be binding and thus not dischargeable except through performance despite the death or disability of either party, unless the parties have agreed otherwise. The contract would not be discharged, however, if another painter is acceptable to Johnson.

On the other hand, courts have held that circumstances involving subjective impossibility (as opposed to objective impossibility like destruction of the subject matter) will not discharge contractual obligations. *Subjective impossibility* denotes nonperformance owing to personal, as contrasted to external, impossibility. In such cases, the contract *can* be performed, but *this particular person* is unable to fulfill the obligations contemplated in the contract. For this reason, nonperformance due to insolvency, shortages of materials, strikes, riots, droughts, and price increases will ordinarily not discharge contracts. However, some courts will temporarily suspend the duty to perform until the conditions causing the inability to perform have passed. More liberal courts may even discharge the contract if later performance will place an appreciably greater burden on the one obligated to perform. Given this division of opinion, the parties often will try to protect their rights by including express provisions covering the types of contingencies just described. Still, it is up to the courts to decide the validity of any such clauses.

The court in the next case applied the general rule about subjective impossibility in refusing to allow it as a method of discharging this particular contract.

Board of Education of the City of Chicago
v. *Chicago Teachers Union, Local 1*
412 N.E.2d 587 (Ill. App. 1980)

FACTS
In June, 1977, the Chicago Board of Education closed all schools and laid off all employees one day early for economic reasons. The union alleged that the one-day, end-of-school layoff was a breach of its collective bargaining agreement with the board. The board argued that its actions were justified because of deficits in the board's budget. The trial court ordered that all teachers be paid for this one-day layoff.

ISSUE
Were the deficits an unforeseen event that rendered the contract incapable of being performed?

HOLDING
No. The doctrine of impossibility was inapplicable to the facts of this case.

REASONING
The board, once it makes an appropriation for teachers' salaries in its budget, thereby implementing the salary provisions of the collective bargaining agreement, is contractually obligated to pay teachers for the period specified. Since the Educa-

tion Fund showed an operating surplus, there was insufficient evidence of a lack of funds to justify personnel layoffs. Moreover, impossibility of performance will not discharge a contract where the event causing the impossibility can be foreseen and guarded against in the contract. The contingency of lack of funds was foreseeable in light of the board's accumulated deficit and could have been expressly provided for in the agreement. Furthermore, even the insolvency of a promisor will not discharge one from one's duty to perform. For these reasons, the board's obligation to its teachers could not be excused on the ground of impossibility of performance.[2]

Because of the harshness of the general rule that impossibility will ordinarily not discharge the performance called for by a contract, the *doctrine of commercial frustration* has recently emerged as a basis for nonperformance. The doctrine will not be applied to excuse performance, however, unless *the essential purpose and value of the contract have been frustrated.* If the frustration could have been reasonably foreseen, the nonperforming party will be held to the bargain. Hence, courts will not utilize this doctrine to release parties from bad bargains. It is important to understand that in these cases performance is possible; but the value of the contract has been frustrated or destroyed by a supervening event not reasonably anticipated at the contract's formation. The Uniform Commercial Code uses the term *commercially impracticable* (Section 2 – 615) in a similar manner to excuse nonperformance in cases of severe shortages of raw materials due to war, embargo, local crop failure, and the like. These factors must either have caused a marked increase in price or have totally precluded the seller from obtaining the supplies necessary to his or her performance before courts will allow discharge.

   The next case, in which the court refused to accept the doctrine of commercial frustration as a defense, is instructive.

Commercial Frustration

Denali Seafoods, Inc. v. *Western Pioneer, Inc.*
492 F. Supp. 580 (W.D. Wash. 1980)

Denali had leased an ocean-going vessel to Western. Western had agreed to pay Denali $180,000 in four installments for the use of the vessel. The vessel was to be used for transporting frozen crab between Seattle and Alaska. Denali did not receive the installment payments as promised and sued Western. Western defended with the doctrine of commercial frustration because the vessel had run aground and been damaged.

FACTS

[2] On appeal, the Supreme Court of Illinois held that the board had discretionary power to impose a layoff for economic reasons, that it had exercised this power reasonably, and that this power could not be restricted by contract. (Board of Education of the City of Chicago v. Chicago Teachers Union, Local 1, 430 N.E.2d 1111 [Ill. 1981].)

ISSUE   Would commercial frustration be an appropriate defense in this case?

HOLDING   No. It was not a valid defense.

REASONING   The court stated that commercial frustration requires (1) an unexpected contingency; (2) no allocation of risk, either express or implied; and (3) commercial impracticability of performance. Grounding was not an unexpected contingency on voyages between Alaska and Seattle. Also, the contract spoke of redelivery of the vessel, maintenance, repair, damage, and insurance, all of which indicated an awareness of possible risks. Having assumed such risks, a party should not be allowed to escape liability for every "bad bargain" on the basis of commercial frustration.

Actual Breach

Breach of contract occurs when one or more of the contracting parties *fails to perform* the obligations set up by the contract. That there are different *degrees* of breach somewhat complicates the issue. A *complete* or *actual* breach of contract involves the nonperformance of a duty that is so *material* and essential to the agreement that the other party is justified in treating the agreement as at an end. The Uniform Commercial Code in Sections 2–703 and 2–711 embraces this common law principle. Actual breach generally discharges the other party's obligation to perform under the terms of the contract. However, rather than canceling the contract upon breach, the injured (or nonbreaching) party may elect instead to hold the nonperforming party to the contract through various types of remedies, which we will discuss in Chapter 17.

Anticipatory Breach

Sometimes one of the contracting parties will indicate in advance — through words or conduct — that he or she does not intend to abide by the terms of the contract. To illustrate, if Johnson unequivocally tells Kreczewski before the time performance is due that he will not send the grain as scheduled, Johnson will have wrongfully repudiated the contract. Johnson's action in legal terms is called *anticipatory breach*. In this situation, as in actual breaches, the injured party's potential responses are not limited merely to discharge of the contract.

The Uniform Commercial Code sanctions a kind of anticipatory repudiation in circumstances less definite than those allowable under the common law. Section 2–609 of the Code states that when reasonable grounds for insecurity arise with respect to one party's performance, the other party may demand adequate assurances of due performance and suspend performance until such assurances are forthcoming. If thirty days pass without reply, the party who has demanded the assurances may deem the contract repudiated. Kreczewski's actual or apparent **insolvency,** for example, may cause Johnson to invoke the provisions of Section 2–609. If Kreczewski does not respond within thirty days, Johnson may then treat the contract as repudiated. (See Section 2–610.)

Insolvency   Inability to pay one's debts as they become due

The following case deals with issues of assurances and breach.

Carfield & Sons, Inc. v. *Cowling*
616 P.2d 1008 (Colo. App. 1980)

Schmoll leased property owned by Alda Cowling and contracted on 19 June 1978 with Carfield to have Carfield erect a steel building by 1 September 1978 on Cowling's property. As required by the agreement, Schmoll made an initial payment of $5870 to Carfield. On 4 August 1978, Schmoll requested a refund of this 10 percent down payment because Carfield had not begun work on the project. Shortly thereafter, however, Carfield began the work, and Schmoll paid Carfield an additional $15,000. Carfield subsequently engaged Krug to pour the concrete floor for the building. Krug poured the floor on August 18, and three days later Krug's employee drove a gravel truck onto the floor. Schmoll, present when this occurred, ordered the truck off the concrete because he feared it would damage the floor. All parties agreed that a concrete floor should cure for seven days before any heavy weight is placed on it. Schmoll stopped payment on the $15,000 check because he believed the work could not be completed by September 1 and because he wanted portions of the concrete floor replaced, since he feared damage to the floor. In response, Carfield removed his work crew and sold the steel building on August 26 because he believed Schmoll was in breach. Later tests showed that the truck had not damaged the floor. The trial court determined that both Schmoll and Carfield had rescinded the contract and ordered Schmoll to pay Carfield for the floor but not for lost profits.

FACTS

Had Schmoll breached this contract?

ISSUE

The court **remanded** the case to the trial court for findings of fact because the evidence was unclear on one crucial point.

HOLDING

Carfield's breach of contract in permitting Krug's driver to come onto the concrete floor was not a material breach because the concrete was not damaged. Schmoll, nevertheless, reasonably believing the action was a breach, was obligated to ask for adequate assurances of performance in order to avoid liability on the contract. If Carfield refused to provide such assurances, Schmoll could treat the contract as terminated. Since the evidence was in conflict as to whether these assurances were actually asked for, the court remanded the case to the trial court for findings of fact on this matter.

REASONING

Remanded Returned the case to the same court from which it came in order to have some action taken on the case in that court

We have just discussed certain types of prospective nonperformance that will justify discharge of the contract. *Conditions,* or *limitations or qualifications placed on a promise,* may also bring about contract discharges. As we learned in Chapter 14, *express conditions* — those in which the parties *explicitly* or *impliedly in fact* set out the limitations to which their promises will be subject — are the most common type of conditions. (*Constructive* conditions, those read into the

Conditions

contract or *implied in law* in order to serve justice, are decidedly rarer.) When parties specifically agree that performance is contingent on the happening of a *future* event, an express condition *precedent* exists. Nonperformance of an express condition precedent (such as posting a performance bond) causes a failure of condition that nullifies the other party's duty to perform and discharges the contract. Similarly, the presence of an express condition *subsequent* (meaning that the occurrence of a particular event cuts off all ongoing contractual duties) discharges the obligations of both parties. For example, the buyer's returning goods before payment is due under the terms of a contract in which the buyer had reserved this right would constitute discharge of the contract. But, as noted in Chapter 14, to avoid a breach of an express condition, courts ordinarily require strict compliance. In contrast, substantial compliance generally avoids a breach of a constructive condition.

SUMMARY

Discharge of a contract refers to the legally valid termination of a contractual duty. Performance may be either complete or substantial. Both degrees of performance ordinarily discharge the contract. The parties may themselves agree to discharge the contract. Release, rescission, accord and satisfaction, and novation are examples of this method of discharging contracts. Bankruptcy decrees, the running of statutes of limitation, and material alterations of the contract will justify discharge of a contract by operation of law. In some circumstances, the nonperformance of one of the parties will discharge a contract. Courts that find evidence of destruction of the subject matter, intervening illegality, or conduct by one party that makes performance by the other impossible will excuse the resultant nonperformance. This is the doctrine of impossibility. However, in many other situations, impossibility will not justify discharge of the contract. The doctrine of commercial frustration has consequently arisen to mitigate the harshness of the common law's rejection of impossibility as a defense to nonperformance. Breach, whether actual or anticipatory, may also bring about discharge of the contract. The nonoccurrence of express conditions precedent and the occurrence of express conditions subsequent, in addition to constructive conditions, may cause discharge of a contract, as well.

DISCUSSION QUESTIONS

1. What are the four main methods of contract discharge?
2. What conditions must be met before substantial performance is legally possible? Does substantial performance always constitute a breach of the contract?
3. What characteristics must be present before a release is valid?
4. What is rescission?
5. Describe how accord and satisfaction occur.
6. How are accord and satisfaction different from a novation?

7. Explain fully the doctrine of impossibility and the doctrine of commercial frustration as they relate to discharge of contracts.

8. What sorts of situations will discharge a contract by operation of law?

9. Define and explain the legal consequences of anticipatory breach under the common law and the Uniform Commercial Code.

10. What is a complete, or material, breach of contract? What are the injured party's options when a complete breach occurs?

CASE PROBLEMS

1. Richard Au became a Gulf Oil dealer in 1971. His contract obligated him to sell Gulf products at carwash centers owned by Au in Ohio for ten years. Gulf agreed to loan Au money for structural improvements and construction of the carwash centers and to provide Au with special allowances and subsidies that permitted Au to sell Gulf products at competitive prices. The contract stated that Au had to pay the outstanding balance of any such loans if Au ever breached the contract. In case of a breach, Gulf had the option of terminating all contracts with Au by giving him ten days' notice of its decision. The oil crisis of 1973 led to Gulf's discontinuing its special allowances and subsidies with a resultant decline in Au's profit margins. Au purchased less gasoline each year as a consequence. In 1980, Gulf terminated Au without notice for Au's failure to pay $7000 for a shipment of gasoline. Au filed suit against Gulf, contending that Gulf's failure to pay him the special allowances and thereby to keep him and other Gulf dealers competitive constituted a breach of contract. Gulf had failed to perform substantially under the contract and had prevented him from so performing, Au asserted. He additionally argued that Gulf could not recover the $7000 because Gulf had failed to satisfy the condition precedent requiring ten days' written notice prior to termination of the contract. Were Au's arguments valid? (*Au Rustproofing Center* v. *Gulf Oil Corporation*, 755 F.2d 1231 [6th Cir. 1985].)

2. C. B. Dodge Company (Dodge) owned some land in Seattle on the shore of Lake Washington. In 1908, the Dodge Company had executed a quitclaim deed concerning a narrow strip of that property which bordered the lake so that the city could construct what is now Lake Washington Boulevard. The deed contained three conditions, one of which reserved the right, for Dodge itself and for its successors and assigns, to build and maintain a boathouse along the shore of Lake Washington. The city was responsible for acquiring the land necessary for the boathouse, as well as for allowing the building and use of it. Breach of this condition allowed the grantor, Dodge, or its successors to forfeit the grant. In 1983, Jack M. Martin, one of the successors to the Dodge land, and others asked the city for permission to build a boathouse. The Martins then attempted to exercise their right to forfeit the city's interest in the land along which Lake Washington is located. The city admitted that the language in the deed created a

condition subsequent, but argued that the condition subsequent was no longer enforceable owing to the passage of time. The city also maintained that the subsequent lowering of Lake Washington had made compliance with the condition subsequent legally impossible. The city claimed that because the state had given the newly uncovered shore land to the city on the condition that the land be used as a park, the city could not allow the construction of a private boathouse on this site. Would you accept these arguments if you were a judge? (*Martin* v. *City of Seattle,* 728 P.2d 1091 [Wash. App. 1986].)

3. Ben Lindsey was head basketball coach at Grand Canyon College for seventeen years. After winning two National Association of Intercollegiate Athletics (NAIA) championships, the University of Arizona hired him as its head coach in April, 1982. Although he had never been offered endorsement contracts while at Grand Canyon College, Lindsey's contract with Arizona, a National Collegiate Athletic Association (NCAA) member, made him attractive to shoe manufacturers and distributors. One such distributor, Classco, offered Lindsey a shoe endorsement contract worth $30,000 and seventy-five pairs of Adidas shoes if Lindsey would encourage his basketball players to wear Adidas brand basketball shoes during the season. Throughout the 1982–1983 basketball season, the players—with a few exceptions—wore Adidas brand shoes. When the university fired Lindsey as head coach in March, 1983, Classco refused to fulfill its second-year agreement with him. Classco argued that Lindsey's termination as head coach operated as a condition subsequent that extinguished Classco's obligation to perform. Should a court accept Classco's assertion? (*Lindsey* v. *Classco,* 642 F. Supp. 250 [D. Ariz. 1986].)

4. Annie Pooler had a baby out of wedlock in 1980. In January, 1981, the father of the child, James Taylor, agreed to support the child by paying Pooler $45 per week. About a year-and-a-half later, Pooler filed criminal abandonment proceedings against Taylor because he had not paid the agreed-upon support. The trial court held that Taylor's failure to make payments from November, 1981 to March, 1983, effected a rescission of the January, 1981 agreement and that Pooler's filing charges of abandonment amounted to a breach of the January agreement, as well. Was the court correct? (*Pooler* v. *Taylor,* 328 S.E.2d 749 [Ga. App. 1985].)

5. Jake Adams was seriously injured while racing a motorcycle at the Cherokee Dragway. Adams had signed a document entitled "RELEASE AND WAIVER OF LIABILITY AND INDEMNITY AGREEMENT" in which Adams had agreed not to sue the dragway for injuries. Embossed in red and beneath the signature of Jake Adams was the statement, "I HAVE READ THIS RELEASE." Adams argued that the release was not binding on him because he had not read it prior to signing, had not known it was a release from liability, and instead had assumed it was merely the registration form for the race. Did Adams's failure to read the release invalidate its legal effect? (*Adams* v. *Roark,* 686 S.W.2d 73 [Tenn. 1985].)

6. Mularz was to render basic architectural services to Park City for a fee of $125,000. The contract set up a schedule for the payment of fees. Upon the completion of the third phase, 80 percent of the total was due; at the completion of the bidding and negotiations stage, the remaining $25,000 would be paid. Park City abandoned the project before its completion. Park City argued that Mularz's fulfillment of the bidding and negotiation stage was a condition precedent to payment of the last $25,000. Mularz countered that the $125,000 was a fixed fee and that he was merely to serve as a consultant during the negotiations stage. Since he was willing and able to supply these consulting services, Mularz argued he should be paid. Who should win and why? (*Mularz* v. *Greater Park City Co.*, 623 F.2d 139 [10th Cir. 1980].)

7. A housing association assessed a $27-to-$75 yearly charge on the Tentindos for maintenance of the housing development. The Tentindos, as nonmembers of the association, argued that they should not have to pay this assessment in the absence of a novation and also because it was not in writing as required by the Statute of Frauds. The Tentindos, however, participated and voted in several of the association's meetings. Would this contract be enforceable against them? (*Tentindo* v. *Locke Lake Colony Association*, 419 A.2d 1097 [N.H. 1980].)

8. Alcoa had a long-term agreement to deliver molten lead to Essex. Alcoa's nonlabor production costs unforeseeably rose so that Alcoa stood to lose $75 million if held to the contract. Should Alcoa be allowed reformation of the contract on the grounds of impossibility or commercial frustration? (*Aluminum Company of America* v. *Essex Group, Inc.*, 499 F. Supp. 53 [W.D. Pa. 1980].)

9. On 17 July 1979, buyers contracted to purchase two apartment complexes in Tucson, Arizona. The buyers exercised their right to extend the closing date on three separate occasions, each time depositing $50,000 in escrow as consideration for the extensions. Although the parties had agreed that the closing would occur on 21 January 1980, the sellers learned on 18 January 1980 that the buyers would be unable to finance the remaining $3,900,000 that was due at the closing. The sellers brought suit on that date, requesting that the escrow amounts be awarded as damages for breach of contract. The buyers contended that the filing of the lawsuit by the sellers amounted to an anticipatory repudiation of the contract and thus relieved the buyers of any further obligation to perform. Were the buyers correct? (*Esplendido Apartments* v. *Olsson*, 697 P.2d 1105 [Ariz. App. 1984].)

10. W. E. Erickson Construction Company (Erickson) sued Congress-Kenilworth Corporation (C-K) for sums due for the construction of a concrete water slide known as "Thunder Mountain Rapids." Erickson argued that a corporate resolution that authorized the transfer of the land upon which the slide was being built to Erickson as security for payment and a subsequent letter acknowledging C-K's indebtedness of $550,000 to

Erickson represented an accord and satisfaction that made C-K liable to Erickson. Did the correspondence between the parties indicate that the terms of the original contract and the amount of fees due under this contract were sufficiently in dispute to constitute an accord and satisfaction? (*W. E. Erickson Construction, Inc.* v. *Congress-Kenilworth Corporation*, 477 N.E.2d 513 [Ill. App. 1985].)

Contractual Remedies

TYPES OF REMEDIES

Despite the parties' original intentions, the possibility exists that one party will fail to live up to the contractual obligations. As we have already learned, such nonperformance constitutes a breach of the contract and entitles the injured party to certain remedies, assuming the injured party does not wish to waive (or ignore) the breach. A *remedy* is *a cause of action resulting from breach of a contract*. After the occurrence of a breach, remedies attempt to satisfy the parties' expectations as of the time of the contract's formation. Remedies fall into two main categories: those resulting from a court's exercise of its powers "at law" (*legal* remedies) and those arising from a court's use of its powers of equity (**equitable** remedies). Although you as a layperson have probably always used the term *legal remedies* to encompass both types of relief, in this chapter you will learn to identify the sorts of situations in which it is appropriate for a court to order one kind of relief or the other. You will also become aware of the fact that these types of remedies are usually mutually exclusive.

The most common legal remedy sought is *damages,* or the amount of money that will put the injured party in the same position he or she would

Equitable Arising from the branch of the legal system designed to provide a remedy where no remedy existed at common law; a system designed to provide "fairness" when there was no suitable remedy "at law"

have been in had the other party performed. The injured party must *mitigate,* or minimize, these damages; but having fulfilled this legal duty, the injured party should be able at the very least to receive *compensatory damages,* those that will put the party in the same economic position that would have been enjoyed had the agreement been performed. If the facts permit, the injured party moreover may receive *consequential damages,* those indirect or special damages springing from the effects or aftermath of the breach itself; *punitive damages,* those damages over and above the actual damages that a court may award in order to deter the defendant from future malicious conduct; and *liquidated damages,* those agreed on by the parties in advance in the event of breach. A court may also give *nominal damages* (a small amount of compensation) for minor, technical contractual breaches that cause no actual losses.

In some situations, money damages will inadequately compensate the injured party for the loss of the bargain occasioned by the breach. Injured persons in these cases ordinarily resort to *equitable* remedies. These possible modes of relief include *rescission,* the cancellation or termination of the contract through the restoration of the parties to the status quo. Restoration is accomplished by *restitution,* the return of the goods, money, or property involved in the contract or the recovery of the reasonable value of the services rendered. *Specific performance,* or the court-ordered enforcement of the contract according to its exact terms, is an alternative type of equitable remedy, as is *quasi contract,* which we discussed in Chapter 8. *Quasi contract,* you may remember, refers to the situation in which a court creates a contract for the parties, despite their wishes and intentions, in order to prevent the unjust enrichment of one party. *Reformation,* or the court's rewriting of a contract in order to remove a mistake and to make the agreement conform to the terms to which the parties originally agreed, a topic discussed in Chapter 13, and *injunctions,* or court-ordered writs directing a person to do or to refrain from doing some specified act, sound in equity, as well. Courts' powers to award equitable remedies are **discretionary;** hence, courts will not normally give equitable remedies if the injured party has "unclean hands" (that is, has shown bad faith or dishonesty); if the injured party has unduly delayed bringing the lawsuit; if a **forfeiture** of property will result from the conferring of an equitable decree; if the court itself will necessarily have to supervise the implementation of the remedy granted; or if the remedy at law (ordinarily money damages, as you will recall) is available, determinable, and adequate.

Discretionary Having the freedom to make certain decisions

Forfeiture The loss of a right or privilege as a penalty for certain conduct

The parties may in advance attempt to limit the remedies available to the injured party. We previously discussed such efforts in the context of exculpatory clauses in Chapter 12. The UCC restricts this common law right to limit remedies in Section 2–719 by sanctioning contracts containing exclusive remedies' provisions unless the exclusive remedy fails in its essential purpose (as in a contract involving a computer printer that limits the exclusive remedy to repair and replacement of faulty parts where the printer turns out to be a "lemon" that cannot be fixed satisfactorily). The Code, in Section 2–719, also forbids contractual limitations of consequential damages for personal injuries from the use of consumer goods (the UCC dubs limitations on these sorts of damages **prima facie unconscionable** but notes that limitations of damages in purely commercial settings are not).

Prima facie   At first sight; on its face; something presumed to be true because of its appearance unless disproved by evidence to the contrary

It has been said that for every legal wrong there is a legal remedy. We shall explore in this chapter some of the contractual remedies that are obtainable.

DAMAGES

When one party breaches a contract, the other party is entitled to payment for lost expectations. The injured party therefore can bring an action for *damages, or the sum of money that will place the party in the same economic position that would have been enjoyed had the contract been performed.*

Unconscionable
Blatantly unfair and one-sided; so unfair as to shock the conscience

It is not necessary that the injured party be able to compute exactly what the damages were, as long as the losses were the natural and proximate consequences of the breach. In computing damages, courts ask whether the breaching party, as a reasonable person, should have foreseen at the time of contracting that these injuries would result from breach. If the nonperforming party should have foreseen the losses, courts will award damages to the injured party. The amount of damages awarded will of course depend heavily on the facts of the case.

The most common type of damages is *compensatory damages,* or those *sums of money that will place the injured party in the same economic position that would have been attained had the contract been performed.* Such damages are also called *actual* damages. Compensatory damages include all damages directly attributable to the loss of the bargain previously agreed upon by the parties, including lost profits and any incidental expenses incurred as a result of the breach. In a sale of goods, courts usually compute the difference between the contract price and the market price in formulating the actual damages. The same is ordinarily true of land contracts. Thus, if Miranda Construction Company, a developer of real estate for its own particular purposes, orders three bulldozers from Welling Machinery Company and, unfortunately, none of the bulldozers functions properly under such circumstances, Miranda should be able to recover the general or *direct damages* or losses occasioned by the defective equipment. Miranda's costs of repairing the machines constitute one type of direct loss. Alternatively, if Miranda has to buy new bulldozers at higher prices, Miranda will be able to recover the costs associated with obtaining this substitute performance. Assuming that Miranda's bad luck continues and a seller with whom Miranda has contracted to buy land for investment purposes fails to go through with this realty contract, Miranda can sue the reneging seller for the difference between the price of this piece of land and the one Miranda eventually purchases to take its place. Miranda can furthermore sue for such expenses as the additional brokers' fees or commissions attendant upon obtaining the second parcel of real estate, since these losses flow directly from the seller's breach as well. However, Miranda in both cases must deduct any expenses saved as a result of the breaches.

Compensatory
Damages

The following case deals with many of the concepts we have just discussed and illustrates how complex the computation of damages may be in a given case.

Snyder v. *Bio-Lab, Inc.*
405 N.Y.S.2d 596 (N.Y. Sup.Ct. 1978)

FACTS Snyder had used a teat dip manufactured by Bio-Lab on his dairy cows in order to prevent infectious mastitis, an inflammation of the udder that destroys milk-producing cells. The use of the dip severely burned the udders and teats of 59 of Snyder's 130 milking cows. Of these 59 cows, 39 were rendered useless as milk producers and were sent to slaughter; 9 were sold for beef; and the remaining 11, not as seriously injured as the others, were kept in the herd.

ISSUE Could Snyder recover as compensatory damages lost profits, including the market value of the slaughtered animals and the loss in milk production occasioned by the incident?

HOLDING Yes. Snyder received damages, subject to some offsets, for these losses.

REASONING The usual measure of damages for injury to, or destruction of, personal property is the amount that will return the owner, monetarily, to the status he or she enjoyed before the loss. The market value at the time of the loss, or the difference in market value before and after the injury, will generally be the measure applied. Any special value, particular qualities, or capabilities — such as a high rate of milk production or registration — are generally considered as factors making up market value. Thus, Snyder could recover the fair market value of the 48 slaughtered cows ($43,742), but must offset the salvage value of the animals ($10,441), for a loss of $33,301. Furthermore, Snyder could recover the loss of profits for a three-month period following the injury, during which time Snyder had attempted to replace the slaughtered cows with cows of equal quality ($7,512.44). He could also receive damages for the lost profits attributable to the introduction of the replacement animals into the herd, since experts had testified that the remaining cows produced significantly less milk when the replacement cows were added to the herd. To determine the time period for which these damages were recoverable, it was necessary to compare the earlier production rates of the cows with the production rates after the incident, taking into account the damaged and slaughtered cows, the unaffected cows, and the replacement cows. Hence, the loss attributable to the incident's impact on the remaining cows was $13,010.13 for the relevant five-month period. Given the $1,306.00 in special damages that were undisputed, Snyder was awarded $55,129.57 in damages.

Consequential Damages

Besides compensatory damages, it is also possible for plaintiffs like Snyder and Miranda to receive *consequential damages*. Consequential damages are those indirect or special damages springing from the effects or aftermath (i.e., the consequences) of the breach itself. Assume that in addition to the contracts mentioned, Miranda moreover loses a grading contract with the city because the bulldozers will not work and several rental contracts from retailers who wished to be part of a mall Miranda was planning to develop on the real estate he had tried to purchase from the seller. Can Miranda sue Welling and the seller for the losses accruing from these special circumstances and not just from the direct breach? To determine liability or the lack thereof, a court will apply the "reasonable person" test to see whether such lost contracts were a foreseeable result of Welling and the seller's breach. A judge will not award purely speculative or conjectural damages; but if a court finds Welling and the seller knew, or should have known, at the time of contract formation, of Miranda's circumstances and the potential effect of their breaches on Miranda, it may award incidental or consequential damages. The Uniform Commercial Code also recognizes this doctrine in Sections 2 – 715 and 2 – 710.

The following case indicates some of the factors a court will take into account before awarding consequential damages.

Redgrave v. Boston Symphony Orchestra, Inc.
855 F.2d 888 (1st Cir. 1988)

Vanessa Redgrave, the noted actress, sued the Boston Symphony Orchestra, Inc. (BSO), for breach of contract. Redgrave alleged that BSO had cancelled its Boston and New York performances of *Oedipus Rex,* in which Redgrave was to appear as a narrator, in retaliation for Redgrave's public expressions of support for the Palestinian Liberation Organization (PLO). BSO contended that the performances were cancelled owing to its concern for physical security and the risk of disruptions that would impair the artistic integrity of the performances. Redgrave argued she should receive as actual damages her performance fee of $31,000 and, in addition, consequential damages for the harm to her professional career caused by BSO's cancellation of her contract.

FACTS

Should BSO be liable for consequential damages arising from the loss of professional opportunities?

ISSUE

Yes. BSO was liable for the consequential damages represented by Redgrave's loss of one Broadway offer.

HOLDING

The district court jury found that the BSO's cancellation of the "Oedipus Rex" concerts had caused consequential harm to Redgrave's professional career and that this harm had been a foreseeable consequence within the contemplation of the parties at the time they had entered into the contract. However, the district court judge overturned the jury's verdict of $100,000 because of the court's belief that Redgrave had not met the strict standards required by the First Amendment for the

REASONING

recovery of such damages involving communicative activity. According to the district court, any statements of opinion by the BSO as reflected in the BSO cancellation and subsequent press release would be protected absolutely under the First Amendment and would bar the recovery of consequential damages. However, the district court had erroneously confused communication *about* BSO's contract cancellation with the notion of an implied communication of a particular message *by* BSO regarding Redgrave. Furthermore, under the district court's ruling, the cancellation of almost any contract with a notable figure could effectively be transformed into a statement protected by the First Amendment, thereby unnecessarily diluting the protections intended by contract law. Thus, although Redgrave would have to meet the strict contract requirements for finding consequential damages, no additional requirements would have to be imposed in this case because of the strictures of the First Amendment. In order for Redgrave to prove that BSO's cancellation had resulted in the loss of other professional opportunities, it would be necessary for her to present sufficient facts for a jury reasonably to infer that Redgrave had lost wages and professional opportunities subsequent to April, 1982; that such losses had been the natural and probable result of BSO's cancellation rather than the result of other, independent factors; that this harm had been a foreseeable consequence within the contemplation of the parties to the contract when it had been made; and that damages for such losses were capable of being ascertained by reference to some definite standard. The BSO had introduced evidence that Redgrave's political activities and statements had generated widespread media attention prior to the incident with the BSO. Therefore, to the extent that Redgrave might have experienced a decline in the quality of film offers received subsequent to April 1982, that decline could have resulted from Redgrave's political views and not the BSO's cancellation. Thus, it had been Redgrave's burden to introduce enough facts for a jury reasonably to infer that any decline in film and Broadway offers had been proximately caused by the BSO cancellation and not by the fact that producers independently had been concerned with the same factors that had motivated the BSO. The testimony of one Broadway producer who had considered hiring Redgrave had revealed that he had been affected by the BSO cancellation because the BSO was a premier arts organization dependent on the same type of support his theater was. From this testimony, a jury reasonably could have inferred that the BSO's cancellation had not just highlighted for this producer the potential problems that hiring Redgrave would cause but had actually been a cause of his decision. Hence, Redgrave had presented sufficient evidence to prove consequential damages of $12,000, the fee arrangement contemplated by him for Redgrave's appearance in his production, minus the expenses she personally would have incurred had she appeared in the play. Because she had been unable to prove the other allegations of lost professional opportunities, the court overturned the jury's $100,000 consequential damages award to Redgrave as erroneous.

Duty of Mitigation

In determining whether to give damages and, if so, how to measure them, courts place on the injured party the duty to *mitigate* (or minimize) these damages if possible. In other words, the injured party must *take affirmative steps to prevent escalation of the losses brought about by the breaching party.* In our bulldozer example, courts will expect Miranda to attempt to procure substitute bulldozers, assuming this is possible without undue risk or expense. If Miranda does not undertake such reasonable steps, his failure to mitigate damages will preclude his receiving consequential damages. Rather, the court will limit his losses to those accruing directly from the breach. But if Miranda can prove it was impossible to obtain substitute bulldozers, most courts will excuse his failure to mitigate. The duty of mitigation does not require the injured party to go to superhuman lengths. If the risks or expenses in mitigation attempts are unreasonably great, there is no duty to mitigate.

Punitive Damages

In contrast to their willingness to make compensatory and consequential damages available to injured parties, courts generally will not allow the recovery of punitive damages in breach of contract situations. *Punitive,* or *exemplary, damages* are imposed *not to compensate the injured party but to punish the wrongdoer in order to deter future conduct of this sort.* The old common law rule was that punitive damages were never appropriate for breaches of contract. Though still rare, some statutes now permit the imposition of punitive damages in contractual situations (such as **treble damages** under the antitrust laws). Furthermore, some courts have been willing to grant punitive damages in situations in which one party has acted willfully. An insurance company that unduly delays paying off legitimate contractual claims against it may be subject to punitive damages in order to discourage this type of conduct. Consumer transactions may also form the basis for an award of punitive damages if the circumstances so warrant.

Treble damages A statutory remedy in antitrust actions that allows the successful plaintiff to recover three times the damages suffered as a result of the antitrust violation

In the following case, the court refused to award punitive damages in a contract action involving an insurance company owing to the absence of any especially malicious conduct.

Kocse v. *Liberty Mutual Insurance Company*
377 A.2d 1234 (N.J. Super. 1977)

While driving his fiancée's car, Kocse had an accident that injured several persons. His fiancée's insurance firm was primarily liable. Liberty Mutual was the Kocse family's insurer. At first, Liberty Mutual believed Kocse was covered by his parents' policy and therefore paid some of his medical expenses. Later, when the fiancée's insurance carrier approached Liberty Mutual because of the belief that Liberty Mutual, which was secondarily liable, might have to pay some of the injured persons' claims, Liberty Mutual began scrutinizing Kocse's conduct more closely. Based on some statements Kocse had given Liberty Mutual, the company began to doubt that he was validly covered under his family's insurance plan. Liberty Mutual therefore subsequently declined to cover Kocse. Kocse, in turn, sued Liberty Mutual for breach of contract and punitive damages.

FACTS

Was Kocse entitled to punitive damages?

ISSUE

HOLDING   No. He was not so entitled.

REASONING   Punitive damages are not generally available in contract actions but instead are more appropriately granted in tort actions, especially where the conduct is fraudulent, malicious, or wanton. The question is whether this general prohibition against punitive damages in contract actions applies to disputes involving automobile insurance. Here, Liberty Mutual was clearly wrong in declining coverage. Moreover, Kocse's asserting that Liberty Mutual had spent more time trying to decline coverage than in defending Kocse from impending negligence suits had some merit. Yet Liberty Mutual's conduct was not so malicious as to warrant the extraordinary remedy of punitive damages.

Liquidated Damages

The parties may agree *in advance* that *upon breach a certain sum of money will be paid* to the injured party. This remedy is called *liquidated damages*. The amount agreed to by the parties fully satisfies the liability attendant on the breach that has occurred. Courts will enforce such provisions if (1) the amount agreed on is reasonable and not out of proportion to the apparent injury resulting from the breach; and (2) it would be difficult if not impossible to calculate accurately the damage in question. UCC Section 2–718 takes a similar approach in the context of sales contracts.

As a contractor, Miranda may well find himself subject to such a clause. Construction contracts typically have clauses assessing a per-day charge for delays in completing a building on time. As long as the per-day charge is reasonable, courts generally uphold these clauses because of the difficulty of ascertaining the amount of damages that breach of such a contract would cause.

Courts will not enforce *penalties,* however. Penalties consist of amounts unrelated to the possible damages that may occur and are usually excessively large. Such an arbitrary lump sum, even if the parties have agreed to it as satisfaction of a breach, will be void. The case that follows illustrates this very point.

Cook v. *King Manor and Convalescent Hospital*
115 Cal. Rptr. 471 (Cal. App. 1974)

FACTS   The Cooks entered into a land sale contract with King Manor. At the time of contracting to buy the hospital, the Cooks agreed to a clause that allowed King Manor to retain $25,000 as liquidated damages.

ISSUE   Was this provision a valid liquidated damages clause?

No. The clause was illegal because it was a penalty.

By statute, California law sanctions liquidated damages in situations where it would be impracticable or extremely difficult to fix the actual damage. The amount of liquidated damages must also represent a reasonable endeavor by the parties to estimate a fair average compensation for any loss that may have been sustained. King Manor had to prove these two points; and since King Manor could not prove them, the clause in question was a penalty and therefore void.

We have noted that for every breach of contract, an action for damages may be possible. However, in certain cases, especially those involving a minor, or technical, breach, the injured party sustains no actual losses or damages. A court may nevertheless award *a small amount of compensation* (say $10) for the breach. This type of remedy is called *nominal damages.* Sometimes a court or jury awards nominal damages because the injured party has not been able to prove the substantial damages that he or she claims to have suffered. Upon proof of a breach, the injured party is therefore entitled only to nominal damages, the token sum that a court will require the defendant to pay as an acknowledgment of the wrongful conduct in which he or she has engaged.

Nominal Damages

When the "at law" remedy of damages is unavailable, indeterminable, or inadequate, courts in the exercise of their powers of equity may award certain remedies. The plaintiff's eligibility to receive such fairness-oriented relief will depend on the absence of bad faith on the plaintiff's part and similar factors. Simply put, a plaintiff will not necessarily receive equitable remedies just because he or she asks for them. When they are available, the most significant types of equitable relief include rescission and restitution, specific performance, quasi contract, reformation, and injunction.

EQUITABLE REMEDIES

As we learned in the last chapter, the parties may voluntarily agree to rescind, or to set aside, their contract before rendering performance. This type of rescission discharges the contract. But rescission may also occur as a result of a material breach of the agreement. *Rescission* in this context refers to the cancellation or termination of the contract through the restoration of the parties to the status quo. Upon such rescission, the injured party may ask for restitution. *Restitution,* or the return of the goods, money, or property involved in the contract or the recovery of the reasonable value of the services rendered, is the legal term that describes the process by which the parties are returned to their original positions at the time of contract formation. In essence, then, restitution relies on quasi-contractual principles rather than on the original agreement, because once rescission has occurred, the original contract no longer exists. To avoid the unjust enrichment of the breaching party, the law permits

Rescission and Restitution

restitution by allowing the plaintiff to sue in quasi contract in order to recover. For this reason, in most jurisdictions, one cannot sue for both damages and restitution. This is true because in a suit for damages, the injured party sues on the contract. In contrast, in a suit for restitution, as we have just learned, rescission destroys the existence of the contract; and the injured party must sue in quasi contract. Hence most jurisdictions treat damages and restitution as mutually exclusive remedies; the injured party must elect to pursue one remedy or the other. If Miranda has paid Welling for the bulldozers, upon Welling's breach he can treat the contract as at an end (that is, rescind it) and then recover the money (consideration) already paid to Welling in order to avoid the unjust enrichment of Welling. Or, alternatively, he can sue for damages. The "election of remedies" doctrine prevents Miranda from recovering twice at common law. The UCC explicitly rejects this principle in Sections 2–703 and 2–711, demonstrating yet another way in which the Code has changed the common law.

Specific Performance

Whenever the remedy in damages or restitution would be inadequate or unjust, the injured party may ask a court to order *specific performance*. In these cases, *a court compels the breaching party to perform according to the exact terms of the agreement.*

Courts rely on uniqueness as one factor in deciding whether to grant specific performance. Since land is by definition unique, courts ordinarily grant specific performance for breaches of land contracts. For example, should you try to buy a prairie-style home on the river, money damages for breach of that contract are unfulfilling: money can buy a house similar to the one in the contract, but not *that* particular house. The inherent uniqueness of real estate may therefore convince a court to order the breaching party to convey the house to you — that is, give you specific performance — in order that justice may be done. The same may be said of contracts involving unique goods or chattels (articles of movable property). If Bogan breaches a contract to sell a Rembrandt painting, in the absence of fraud or illegality a court can compel Bogan to convey the painting to the buyer. But when the injured party can easily obtain the personal property or chattels, specific performance is an inappropriate remedy: money damages will be adequate in these cases.

Money damages ordinarily will not satisfy the parties in situations involving personal services contracts either. If these contracts are at issue, courts are reluctant to force the parties into a relationship in which at least one of the parties will be unhappy. How can the Oakland A's be sure Reggie Jackson will give his best efforts if he really wants to play for the Yankees? For this reason, and because courts are loath to force a party into what one party may characterize as "involuntary servitude," courts ordinarily do not grant specific performance. The A's instead can sue Reggie and the Yankees for money damages.

The court wrangled with these same issues in the following case.

American Broadcasting Companies, Inc. v. *Wolf*
420 N.E.2d 363 (N.Y. 1981)

Wolf was a sportscaster whom ABC had employed since 1976. In 1978, the parties entered into an agreement whereby Wolf agreed to negotiate in good faith and to give ABC the right of first refusal before he accepted employment with anyone other than ABC. After Wolf nonetheless accepted employment with CBS following the ninety-day negotiating period mentioned in the agreement, ABC then sued for specific performance of its agreement with Wolf.

FACTS

Should the court order specific performance of the contract?

ISSUE

No. This remedy is inappropriate.

HOLDING

Courts of equity have historically refused to order an individual to perform a contract for personal services. Especially after a personal services contract terminates, the availability of equitable relief against the former employee diminishes appreciably. In the absence of a **restrictive covenant,** since Wolf's employment had ended with ABC, he could work for whomever he pleased. Although equity will not decree specific performance in such a situation, ABC was free to pursue monetary damages for Wolf's violation of the part of the agreement mandating good-faith negotiation before he left ABC's employ.

REASONING

Restrictive covenant
A promise in which one person agrees to refrain from some activity for a certain time period in a given area

Just as damages and restitution generally are mutually exclusive remedies, so too, are damages and specific performance. The following case illustrates this principle.

Gulf Oil Corp. v. *Spriggs Enterprises, Inc.*
388 So.2d 518 (Ala. 1980)

Spriggs had bought land from Diamondhead after Diamondhead had promised it would not sell any of its property located between this land and Interstate 10 if that property were to be used for a service station. Four years later, Diamondhead nevertheless sold property to Gulf Oil, which intended to construct a service station on this property in spite of a restriction on the property that said it could be used only for a convenience store with no more than two gasoline pumps. Spriggs sued for fraud and breach of contract based on Diamondhead's refusal to live up to the restrictive covenant. The jury awarded Spriggs $250,000 in actual damages and $1,000,000 in punitive damages. In addition, the court ordered specific performance of the original agreement.

FACTS

ISSUE   Could Spriggs receive both damages and specific performance in the same suit?

HOLDING   No. These remedies were mutually exclusive, so Spriggs would have to elect one remedy or the other.

REASONING   In assessing damages of $1,250,000 against Gulf while at the same time ordering specific performance, the lower court had committed reversible error. Because damages and specific performance are inconsistent remedies for suits arising out of the same contract, Spriggs, the injured party, must accordingly elect his remedy.

Quasi Contract/ Reformation/ Injunction

Two concepts that we have discussed on several occasions in the contracts section, *quasi contract* and *reformation,* bear mentioning again before we leave the topic of equitable remedies. The other, an *injunction,* or a writ issued by a court of equity ordering a person to do or refrain from doing some specified act, does not arise as often in the context of contracts. But you should nonetheless be aware that it is a type of equitable remedy, as well. Quasi contract involves the situation in which a court creates a contract for the parties, despite their wishes and intentions, in order to prevent the unjust enrichment of one party. (For an extended discussion of this topic, see Chapter 8.) Reformation, on the other hand, concerns a court's rewriting a contract in order to remove a mistake and to make the agreement conform to the terms to which the parties originally agreed. (We discussed reformation in Chapter 13.)

WAIVER OF BREACH

Waiver The voluntary, intentional surrender of a legal right

Even though we have spent a great deal of this chapter studying the various remedies available to an injured party when the other party breaches the contract, we noted in the very beginning of the chapter that the injured party may be willing to accept less than complete performance. The law terms the injured party's giving up the right to receive the performance set out in the contract a **waiver** of breach. Once a waiver of breach occurs, the waiver in effect eliminates the breach, and the performance required under the contract continues as if the breach had never happened. In essence, waiver of breach precludes the termination or rescission of the contract; it serves as a method of keeping the contract operative between the parties. As usual, though, the nonbreaching party can later recover damages for anything that constitutes less than complete performance. Thus, if only one of the bulldozers delivered to Miranda were slightly defective or if Welling had been only slightly late in making what was otherwise a satisfactory delivery, Miranda may choose to waive such breaches in order to receive Welling's performance under the rest of the contract.

A waiver of breach ordinarily applies only to the matter waived and not inevitably to the rest of the contract. The same is true of subsequent breaches of the contract: normally the first waiver will not cover additional, later breaches, especially when the later breaches bear no relation to the first one.

However, the waiving party may want to stand on his or her rights after the first waiver and indicate in no uncertain terms that he or she will not tolerate future breaches. This course of action will eliminate the possibility of the breaching party's arguing that the waivers were so numerous and systematic that the breaching party believed less than complete performance was acceptable for the duration of the contract. Still, waiver remains a common business response in those circumstances in which the injured party's interests would be furthered by the continuation of the contract.

SUMMARY

Upon one party's breach of a contract, the other party is free to pursue several kinds of remedies unless the injured party waives the breach. Remedies fall into two main categories, legal ("at law") and equitable remedies. Usually a party sues for compensatory damages, or the amount of money that will place the party in the same economic position that he or she would have enjoyed had the contract been performed. Because the breaching party is liable for the foreseeable consequences of the breach, courts may award these actual losses and may even grant consequential losses or special damages if the facts so warrant. The injured party must mitigate the damages unless doing so will cause unreasonable expense or unreasonable risk. Failure to mitigate will limit the injured party to the recovery of direct losses.

Punitive damages are imposed to punish the wrongdoer in order to deter future malicious conduct. Some modern courts and statutes reject the old common law rule that punitive damages are never appropriate remedies for breaches of contract. The parties may also agree in advance on the sum of money to be paid for breaches of certain types. Such liquidated damages clauses are enforceable unless a court construes them as penalties. If the party sustains no actual damages, nominal damages may be awarded.

When the "at law" remedy of damages is unavailable, indeterminable, or inadequate, courts may order equitable remedies. Rescission and restitution constitute one such remedy and involve the termination of the contract through the restoration of the parties to the status quo. Damages and restitution are mutually exclusive remedies, so the injured party must elect (or choose) one remedy or the other.

If either damages or restitution will be inadequate, a court may order specific performance. This is an equitable remedy that compels the breaching party to perform according to the terms of the agreement. Courts usually grant specific performance when the subject matter of the contract is unique, but they are reluctant to grant specific performance in suits involving nonunique goods or personal services contracts.

Quasi contract, reformation, and injunctions, or writs ordering a person to do or refrain from doing some specified act, represent other types of equitable relief.

The injured party may choose to waive the breach in order to keep the contract going between the parties. Waiver of breach, or the injured party's giving up the right to receive the performance set out in the contract, does not preclude the injured party's seeking recovery for damages resulting from the breach, however.

DISCUSSION QUESTIONS

1. What is a remedy?
2. Name and define the two main types of remedies.
3. Explain how courts assess the existence of compensatory and consequential damages.
4. Define the duty of mitigation.
5. What is the relationship of punitive damages to contractual breaches?
6. Describe what liquidated damages are and under what conditions courts will enforce liquidated damages clauses.
7. Why does the remedy of restitution differ from an action in damages?
8. Under what circumstances is specific performance an appropriate remedy?
9. What is the legal consequence of waiving a breach of contract?
10. Define the term *injunction*.

CASE PROBLEMS

1. Dean Van Horn Consulting Associates, Inc. (Van Horn), employed Charles Wold, whom Van Horn trained in business consulting, including accounting, tax preparation, and advising clients, who were primarily doctors and dentists. When he became a full-time employee, Wold signed an employment contract that contained a restrictive covenant that obligated Wold to pay Van Horn as damages a set percentage of any billings Wold made to clients for services rendered if Wold, within three years of leaving Van Horn's employ, set up a competing corporation in violation of the noncompete clause contained in the employment contract. Wold formed a corporation called Professional Consulting Group, Inc. (PCG), immediately after he left Van Horn's. When Van Horn sued Wold on the basis of the restrictive covenant, Wold argued that Van Horn must be able to prove specific amounts of actual damages suffered in order to receive liquidated damages under a contract. Was Wold correct? (*Dean Van Horn Consulting Associates* v. *Wold*, 367 N.W.2d 556 [Minn. Ct. App. 1985].)

2. The Woodfins contracted with Briggs about the construction of a house. At the closing, the Woodfins questioned such things as the absence of a retaining wall for a dirt bank at the rear of the house and the lack of bathroom vinyl, attic insulation, and air conditioning thermostats. If the Woodfins want to receive "loss of bargain" damages (that is, the difference between the contract price and the actual value of the house at the time of the breach), would they have to prove that the fair market value of

the house, if completed, would be $45,000 rather than the $39,900 they paid? (*Briggs* v. *Woodfin,* 388 So.2d 1221 [Ala. Civ. App. 1980].)

3. Koenings was a staff attorney with the Joseph Schlitz Brewing Company (Schlitz). When Schlitz became the target of a friendly takeover attempt by G. Heileman Brewing Company in 1981, Schlitz's board of directors offered so-called golden parachute contracts, which allowed for a continuation of salary for a stated time period after termination of employment, to seventy key management employees as a method of making the takeover of the company less attractive to Heileman. In one provision of this contract, Schlitz promised to allow employees to treat any reduction in the employee's level of responsibilities as a termination. If the employee elected to take advantage of the termination procedure, the company promised to pay the balance of the employee's salary for the time period stated in the contract. Even though Heileman's attempt to take over Schlitz failed, Schlitz soon thereafter merged with Stroh's. As a result of this merger, Koenings argued, his responsibilities were substantially reduced. Thus, he took a job with another company and sued Schlitz for the thirteen months' salary remaining under the "golden parachute" contract. Did the failure of Schlitz to include a clause wherein Koenings agreed that any salary earned from another firm would be used to mitigate these liquidated damages make the termination provision of the contract unreasonable and therefore void on public policy grounds as a penalty? (*Koenings* v. *Joseph Schlitz Brewing Co.,* 377 N.W.2d 593 [Wis. 1985].)

4. In August, 1980, Camel Investments, Inc. (Camel), purchased Webber Oil Company from Orval and Vivian Webber. Camel paid the Webbers $250,000 in cash as a down payment and gave the Webbers a note for the balance of $1,075,000. The purchase agreement provided that Camel could offset sums due by Camel to the Webbers under the note by amounts due by the Webbers to Camel under the agreement. As part of the agreement, the Webbers retained one retail station known as WOCO #3. They promised to purchase all their gasoline from Camel and agreed not to compete with Camel in Okaloosa County in any way for a three-year period except by operating WOCO #3. In March, 1981, the Webbers' son, Ronald, began a petroleum distribution business, SAV-A-TON Petroleum, Inc., that directly competed with Camel in the county. The Webbers had provided some of the initial capital for this corporation. Because the Webbers began purchasing a substantial amount of gasoline from SAV-A-TON, Camel began offsetting $3000 per month on the note payment, the amount Camel calculated to be its lost profits. From this point on, the Webbers purchased almost all their gasoline from SAV-A-TON. In the subsequent lawsuit involving the parties, could Camel recover damages in the form of lost profits for both the Webbers' breach of the gasoline purchase provision and the covenant not to compete? (*Camel Investments, Inc.* v. *Webber,* 468 So.2d 340 [Fla. Dist. Ct. App. 1985].)

5. Transamerica Productions, Inc. (Transamerica), a film distributor, sued Kelly for removing from distribution a film about the rich and powerful that starred Carl Betz and Dina Merrill. Transamerica argued that this removal represented a breach of its motion picture distribution contract with Kelly. Transamerica therefore demanded $50,000 in damages for its lost profits. Kelly submitted that the marketing of a new film was such a speculative venture that there would be insufficient evidence on which a court could compute the alleged damages. Should a court accept Kelly's argument? (*Southwestern Financial Corp.* v. *Kelly,* 233 Cal.Rptr. 639 [Cal. App. 1987].)

6. In October, 1980, Gary and Deborah Rymer (the Rymers) contracted with Lou Menchio, Inc. (Menchio), for the construction of a home in an area that obligated the contractor to modify the lot so as to lower the groundwater table. Menchio thus undertook several types of ground work in preparation for the installation of a septic tank system. After the Rymers had moved into the house in March, 1981, the septic tank system failed in February, 1982. Menchio claimed that the installed system had been functional and that it had failed through no fault of his but, rather, because the groundwater table had become too high. When authorities declared the Rymers' home a public nuisance, the Rymers sued Menchio for breach of contract and negligence. A jury awarded the Rymers $23,000 in actual damages and $25,000 as punitive damages on the breach of contract claim. The jury also indicated that it had found for the plaintiffs on the negligence claim but had awarded no damages on this tort claim. Menchio therefore argued that the jury's award of punitive damages was improper, since the Rymers' recovery was based on the contract and not on the tort claim. Should the appellate court uphold this punitive damages award? (*Menchio* v. *Rymer,* 348 S.E.2d 76 [Ga. App. 1986].)

7. The Reuben H. Donnelley Corporation (Donnelley) had omitted the Midland Hotel (Midland) from its 1981 *Chicago Visitors Guide's* listing for ''Hotels'' (although it had mentioned the hotel under ''Banquet Rooms''). Midland was the only downtown business so omitted. Midland filed suit against Donnelley to recover the lost net profits allegedly caused by this breach of contract, and a jury awarded the hotel $500,000 on this theory. On appeal, Donnelley asserted that the award had been improper because the hotel had made few efforts to mitigate its damages and because the trial judge had failed to instruct the jury that lost profits would be allowed only if their loss was reasonably within the contemplation of the defaulting party at the time the contract was formed. How should the appellate court rule on this appeal? (*Midland Hotel Corporation* v. *Reuben H. Donnelley Corporation,* 501 N.E.2d 1280 [Ill. App. 1986], mod. 515 N.E.2d 61 [Ill. 1987].)

8. Gowing contracted with Blue Lakes Apartments, Ltd. (Blue Lakes), to purchase two condominiums for $54,000 each. This purchase contract allowed Blue Lakes to recommend the institution from which Gowing would seek financing for the purchase. Blue Lakes interpreted this clause to mean that if Gowing could not get financing from this source, Blue Lakes could reject Gowing as a purchaser so long as Blue Lakes returned Gowing's $5400 deposit. The bank that Blue Lakes had recommended approved Gowing's application for one unit but denied his application for the other. Although the bank failed to notify Gowing of this denial, the bank did notify Blue Lakes, which returned Gowing's deposit. Because the condominiums had appreciated in value to $60,000 and because Gowing had purchased the condominiums for resale purposes, Gowing sued the bank for specific performance, even though Blue Lakes had sold the second unit to a third party prior to the trial. Assuming the court found that Blue Lakes' interpretation of the financing clause was incorrect, that is, that Gowing did not have to rely on Blue Lakes' recommendation as to financing exclusively, could the court award Gowing compensatory damages rather than specific performance? Should the court award Gowing punitive damages? (*Blue Lakes Apartments, Ltd.* v. *Gowing,* 464 So.2d 705 [Fla. Dist. Ct. App. 1985].)

9. Morhlang agreed to purchase a lot from Draper, a developer, for $14,875. As part of the purchase agreement, Draper promised to bear the cost of relocating a gas company line and paving a street that abutted the lot. When Draper discovered that the cost of relocating the gas line would be $10,050, Draper offered to substitute another lot for the one Morhlang had chosen. Morhlang, who had obtained financing for the lot, sued Draper for specific performance of the agreement. Should a court award Morhlang his requested remedy? (*Mohrlang* v. *Draper,* 365 N.W.2d 443 [Neb. 1985].)

10. Copenhaver operated laundry facilities in apartment complexes in Texas. Berryman owned an apartment complex and had long-term contracts with Copenhaver for laundry facilities but terminated these contracts four years before their expiration date. Copenhaver alleged he had lost $13,886.58 as a result of this early termination; that is, he had lost the profits of the forty-seven months remaining under the contract. Berryman argued that the removal of the equipment had caused Copenhaver no damages because Copenhaver had ultimately placed the equipment in use in other laundry facilities. Copenhaver argued that because he had not placed the machines elsewhere for over six months, he should receive damages for the entire forty-seven months. Could Copenhaver recover these lost profits as part of his damages for breach of contract? Or, alternatively, should a court limit his damages to six months' worth of lost profits? (*Copenhaver* v. *Berryman,* 602 S.W.2d 540 [Tex. Civ. App. 1980].)

PART 3

The Law of Sales

The early common law of contracts was adequate for the society in which it developed, but it was inappropriate — if not inadequate — for a commercial society. As commerce developed and became more widespread, it became obvious that changes in the law were needed. A more modern set of rules than the common law was necessary to govern the business environment. Out of this need the law merchant was developed.

The sociological and technological advances of the twentieth century made the law merchant as outmoded for this era as the common law had been for the industrial revolution. Once again, new rules were needed. And once again, new rules were developed. This time the new legal area was called the Uniform Commercial Code (UCC).

One of the areas governed by the UCC is the law of sales. This area involves transactions in *goods* — tangible personal property. When a person buys groceries at the supermarket, goods are being purchased. An automobile is considered goods. So are major appliances, furniture, and clothing, among other things. An average American consumer will buy thousands of goods over his or her lifetime. Each of these transactions is governed by the UCC, Article 2, Sales. However, few consumers know or understand the laws that govern such transactions.

CHAPTER 18

Formation of the Sales Contract

THE SCOPE OF ARTICLE 2

The common law coverage of contracts provides a good framework for studying agreements between people. However, as society progressed and developed in England and in the United States, some elements of the common law became outdated. When this occurred, the law-making bodies often stepped in to try to resolve the problems presented by a changing society. One result of this intervention is the Statute of Frauds, which requires that certain types of contracts be in writing in order to be enforceable. Another example of legislative intervention to help the law keep pace with society is Article 2 of the Uniform Commercial Code. Article 2 governs the *sale* of *goods*.

Goods

Goods are defined in Section 2–105(1) of the Code. According to that section, *goods* mean *all things that are movable at the time they are identified to the contract.* The Code lists several things that are specifically included as goods, such as specially manufactured items; the unborn young of animals; growing crops;

Money A legally recognized medium of exchange

Things in action A personal right; an intangible claim not yet reduced to possession

and things attached to land, if they are to be separated from the land for their sale. The Code also specifically excludes some things, declaring them not to be goods. Examples are **money** when used as payment for a sale; investment securities; and **things in action,** such as rights under a contract yet to be performed. (Things in action are also sometimes referred to as *choses in action.*)

Sales

Article 2 also covers the *sale* of goods. Goods have already been defined, but what is a sale? According to Section 2 – 106(1), *a sale* is *the passing of title from the seller to the buyer for a price.* This is the only definition of a sale in Article 2, but there are several related and similar terms. For example, the words *contract* and *agreement,* when used in Article 2, refer to either the present or the future sale of goods. *Contract for sale* covers both a present sale and a contract to sell goods in the future. And a *present sale* is a sale made at the time the contract is made.

Transactions under Article 2 must involve two persons. One person is the *buyer.* A buyer is the person who purchases, or agrees to purchase, the goods. The other person is the *seller.* A seller is the person who provides, or agrees to provide, the goods covered by the contract.

The law of sales is very broad. It covers every sale of goods, whether made by a seller who is a merchant or by one who is a nonmerchant, and whether made to a buyer who is a merchant or to one who is a nonmerchant. Regardless of the status of the parties, Article 2 controls the sale. However, the status of the parties may affect how strictly the sale is regulated by the Code; the key factor here is the status of the parties as merchants or nonmerchants.

Expert A person with a high degree of skill or with a specialized knowledge

Employee A person working for salary or wages and who is subject to control by the employer

A *merchant* is defined as a person who deals in the type of goods involved, or who claims to be an **expert** in the type of goods involved, or who has an **employee** who is an expert in the type of goods involved.[1] Any other persons would be considered nonmerchants under the Code.

If neither party to the contract is a merchant, the Code requires that they act in *good faith.* This means that both parties must perform in an honest manner. If both parties to the contract are merchants, the Code requires that they act in good faith and in a *commercially reasonable manner.* This means they both must act honestly and that they must follow the normal fair dealings of their trades. If one party is a merchant and the other is a nonmerchant, each must meet the standards that go with the status occupied. The merchant must act in good faith and in a commercially reasonable manner. The nonmerchant must act in good faith.

The following case shows how one court decided whether a party was a merchant. Similar reasoning is likely to be followed by other courts facing the question of whether a party in a transaction is a merchant.

[1] Uniform Commercial Code, Section 2 – 104(1).

Decatur Cooperative Association v. *Urban*
547 P.2d 323 (Kan. S.Ct., 1976)

Urban had been a wheat farmer for twenty years and was a member of the Decatur Cooperative Association (Decatur). Early in 1973, a representative of Decatur had a telephone conversation with Urban in which Decatur alleged that an oral contract was entered into calling for Urban to sell 10,000 bushels of wheat to Decatur at a price of $2.86 per bushel. The assistant manager of Decatur prepared a written confirmation of this agreement and sent it to Urban. Urban received this confirmation and read it but did not give Decatur any written objection to its terms.

In August, 1973, Urban notified Decatur that he would not deliver any wheat to Decatur as called for in the confirmation. At that time the price of wheat stood at $4.50 per bushel. Decatur sued Urban for breach of contract.

FACTS

Was Urban a merchant in the wheat industry, so that the written confirmation sent to him by Decatur was sufficient to satisfy the Statute of Frauds and therefore make the oral agreement binding?

ISSUE

Urban was not a merchant under the UCC and was therefore not bound by the written confirmation sent by Decatur.

HOLDING

The court felt that "professionalism, special knowledge, and commercial experience" should be used to determine if a person is a merchant within the meaning of that term in Article 2. The Code virtually equates professionals with merchants, but it allows the casual or inexperienced person to operate at a less demanding level than is required of professionals in any business. Urban, as a wheat farmer, had expertise and special knowledge in the *raising* of wheat, but that does not mean that he had any special knowledge in the *sale* of wheat. The evidence showed that Urban only sold the wheat he grew, and that those sales were cash sales to local grain elevators. Such transactions do not provide the expertise needed to become a merchant as defined in the Code. Since Urban was not a merchant, the exception to the Statute of Frauds provided for in the Code is not applicable in this case.

REASONING

A contract for the sale of goods is normally formed in the same manner as a contract formed at common law. The Code recognizes that a contract exists whenever the parties act as if they have an agreement.[2] But the Code also goes beyond the common law. In an effort to reflect commercial reality, the Code will sometimes recognize a contract that would not be considered binding at common law.

Thus, in Section 2–204(2), the Code recognizes a contract when the time

FORMING THE CONTRACT

---

[2] Ibid., Section 2–204(1).

of the agreement is uncertain. And in Section 2–204(3), the Code permits a contract to stand even though some terms, such as price or quantity, are omitted from the agreement. At common law, the omission of any of these terms negated the existence of a contract. The courts would rule that the attempted contract failed owing to "indefiniteness of the terms." Under the UCC, if the parties *intend* to have a contract, and if remedies can be found in case there is a breach, the mere lack of some terms is held to be unimportant. A contract will be found to exist, and the missing terms will be supplied under other provisions of the Code.

Offer and Acceptance

As in regular contract law, a contract for the sale of goods needs both an offer and an acceptance. These technical requirements are covered by UCC Section 2–206. This section states that unless an offer obviously requires otherwise, the offer can be accepted in any reasonable manner under the circumstances.

It should be remembered that at common law the acceptance had to comply exactly with all the terms of the offer. Any variation was treated as a *counteroffer* (an attempt to vary the terms of the original offer) rather than as an acceptance. The Code has attempted to change this requirement.

Suppose the seller received an offer that included the following clause: "Acceptance should be made by sending a white pigeon carrying your note of acceptance tied to its left leg." At common law, a seller could *only* accept by tying a note to the left leg of a white pigeon. If the message was tied to the right leg, or if the pigeon was gray, the seller was deemed to have made a counteroffer.

Under the Code, the seller can accept by complying, or by nearly complying, or by using any other method of accepting that is reasonable. Thus, under some circumstances, the Code even permits the acceptance of an offer by performing rather than by communicating.

Conforming goods
Goods that fit the description contained in the contract; goods that people in the industry would recognize as the goods described

Nonconforming goods
Goods that do not fit the description contained in the contract

For example, an offer to buy goods may call for prompt shipment of the goods. In this case, the seller can accept by promptly shipping **conforming goods** to the buyer. Or the offer could be accepted if the seller notified the buyer that the goods would be shipped promptly. Or the seller could accept by promptly shipping **nonconforming goods** to the buyer. However, in the last case, the seller would not only have accepted the offer but would also (possibly) have breached the contract that was entered by the shipment-as-acceptance. (Probable breach will be treated more fully in Chapter 19.)

The seller who accepts by means of a prompt or current shipment must be careful. Assume the seller accepts by shipping but does not notify the buyer. If the buyer neither receives the goods nor hears from the seller within a reasonable time, the buyer may treat the offer as lapsed before acceptance.[3] When this happens, the buyer has no duty to pay for the goods when they finally

---

[3] Ibid., Section 2–206(2).

arrive. This leaves the seller with unsold goods at some distant point and no contract remedies to fall back on.

The next case dealt with shipment as acceptance; note that the shipment was treated as an acceptance *despite* the various written forms involved.

Nations Enterprise, Inc. v. *Process Equipment Co.*
579 P.2d 655 (Colo. App. 1978)

Nations sued Process for breach of contract, alleging that Process had failed to supply pumps to Nations for placement in a government installation. Process filed a counterclaim against Nations for the price of nine pumps shipped by Process and retained by Nations. Both parties agreed that a contract existed.

FACTS

Was the written purchase order prepared by Nations the complete contract?

ISSUE

No. The conduct of the parties showed a contract existed; Process is entitled to payment.

HOLDING

Although Process never executed the "acceptance copy" of the purchase order, it did ship the nine pumps, and Nations accepted and installed those pumps. The continuing negotiations between the parties that culminated in the shipment of acceptable pumps showed an *intent* to enter a contract. This, plus the acceptance by Nations of the shipped pumps, requires a finding that a contract was entered. No writing was needed. Process is entitled to payment.

REASONING

Very often both parties to the contract are merchants. When this situation occurs, it is also common to have the offer made on a standard form from the offeror, and the acceptance made on a standard form prepared by the offeree/ acceptor. A *standard form* is a *preprinted contract form,* with blanks left in certain places for later completion as the final contract terms are agreed to by the parties. Use of a standard form contract would normally have negated the contract at common law, but the Code makes allowance for it.

Standard Form Contracts

Under Section 2–207(1), an acceptance that is made within a reasonable time is effective, even if it includes terms that add to or differ from the terms of the original offer. The only exception is when the acceptance is *expressly* made subject to an agreement to the new or different terms.

If the purported acceptance includes new or different terms, the Code provides a solution.[4] The new terms are treated as *proposed additions* to the contract. If the contract is between merchants, the new terms become a part of the contract unless one of the following conditions exists:

---

4 Ibid., Section 2–207(2).

Figure 18.1   A "Conflict of Forms" Resolution

If the Offer Says and	If the Acceptance Says	The Contract Will Say
Include "A"	Nothing on "A"	Include "A"
Include "A"	Include "A"	Include "A"
Nothing on "A"	Include "A"	Include "A" (Maybe)
Nothing on "A"	Exclude "A"	Exclude "A" (Maybe)
Include "A"	Exclude "A"	Nothing on "A" (Maybe)
Exclude "A"	Include "A"	Nothing on "A" (Maybe)
Exclude "A"	Exclude "A"	Exclude "A"
Exclude "A"	Nothing on "A"	Exclude "A"

1. The contract will include "A" unless: including "A" will materially alter the duties of the parties; the offeror objects to the inclusion of "A"; or the offer specifically limits acceptance to the offer's original terms.

2. The contract will exclude "A" unless: excluding "A" will materially alter the duties of the parties; the offeror objects to the exclusion of "A"; or the offer specifically limits acceptance to the offer's original terms.

3. The contract will not mention "A" unless: the exclusion of "A" will materially alter the duties of the parties; the offeror objects to the exclusion of "A"; or the offer specifically limits acceptance to the offer's original terms.

4. The contract will not mention "A" unless: the inclusion of "A" will materially alter the duties of the parties; the offeror objects to the inclusion of "A"; or the offer specifically limits acceptance to the offer's original terms.

1.   The offer explicitly limits acceptance to the terms of the offer.

2.   The new terms materially alter the contract.

3.   The offeror objects to the new terms within a reasonable time.

If the contract is not between merchants, the courts will not normally uphold the new terms unless it can be shown that both parties accepted them.

If the offeree proposes different terms, Section 2–207(3) controls. This section states that when the parties *act* as if they have a contract, they *have* a contract. And if they have writings, the writings will be construed so that an agreement exists. The written contract will consist of the terms on which the parties agree, as well as of the terms included by one party without any objection by the other party. But it will *not* include any terms that contradict other terms, that have been objected to by one of the parties, or that materially alter the basic agreement.

Figure 18.1 shows how a "conflict of forms" problem would be resolved.

The following case shows one way in which the courts may resolve a "battle of the forms" between merchants. Compare the court's results with the chart in Figure 18.1.

Application of Doughboy Industries, Inc.
17 A.D.2d 216, 233 N.Y.S.2d 488 (1962)

The parties began doing business together in February 1960, performing two contracts. In each contract, each party used its own "standard form" to offer and/or to accept. On 6 May 1960, the buyer sent its purchase order to the seller in New York, ordering 20,000 pounds of film and asking for more film on a "hold basis," subject to change. The seller accepted and sent its written acknowledgment form, which included an arbitration clause, to the buyer in Wisconsin. The buyer subsequently wanted to reduce the goods placed on "hold basis," and the seller then refused to reduce the quantity.

FACTS

Should the controversy be settled by arbitration in New York, in accordance with the seller's form, or by litigation in Wisconsin, the buyer's location?

ISSUE

The controversy is to be settled by litigation.

HOLDING

The arbitration clause can be viewed as a material alteration or as a term nullified by a conflicting provision in the buyer's form. In either case, it will not be included as a part of the ultimate contract. Many prior New York cases had held that an agreement to arbitrate is material and not to be included by implication. In addition, the buyer's form (the first form issued) required the buyer to sign any later terms proposed by the other party. The buyer never signed such an agreement to arbitrate.

REASONING

Another area that gets special treatment for merchants under the Code is the area of firm offers.[5] At common law, an offer could be freely revoked by the offeror at any time before its acceptance. This right to revoke existed even though the offeror might have "promised" to keep the offer open for some given time period. Such a situation makes it very difficult for the offeree to make detailed plans.

The Code recognizes that the offeree may have to make plans and explore options before accepting an offer. The offeree may not be able to use promissory estoppel (see Chapter 9), but he or she may still be harmed if an offer is revoked. To eliminate this potential problem, the Code guarantees that firm offers cannot be freely revoked before acceptance. If a merchant *promises in writing* to keep an offer open and unmodified for some specified time, and *signs* the writing, a *firm offer* exists. The offer cannot be revoked by the offeror during the time the offeror agreed to keep the offer open. And if no time was

Firm Offers

[5] Ibid., Section 2–205.

specified, it cannot be revoked for a "reasonable time." But the reasonable time cannot exceed three months.

Statute of Frauds

So far, the discussion has focused on the intent to have a contract. However, there are some technical rules that will override intent. One of these involves the *Statute of Frauds*. This statute requires that a contract for the sale of goods for $500 or more must be in writing to be enforceable.[6] An oral agreement in this area is normally unenforceable.

Again, the Code attempts to recognize modern commercial reality in this area. If the parties have *any* writing signed by the party being sued, that writing is sufficient to satisfy the statute. Omitted terms or incorrectly stated terms will not defeat the proof of the contract.[7]

When both parties are merchants, a different rule applies. Suppose one merchant sends a written **confirmation** that would be binding on the sender. The other merchant will also be bound by the confirmation unless he or she objects to its contents *in writing* within ten days after receiving it.[8] This rule forces merchants to read their forms and to cooperate with other merchants. You will recall that this rule was asserted in the case of *Decatur Cooperative Association* v. *Urban*, discussed earlier in this chapter.

Finally, Section 2–201(3) of the Code lists three exceptions to the general provisions of the Statute of Frauds:

Confirmation A written memorandum of the agreement; a notation that provides written evidence that an agreement was made

1. No writing is needed where the goods are to be *specially* manufactured for the buyer and are of such a nature that they cannot be resold by the seller in the ordinary course of his business, and where the seller has made a substantial start in performing the contract.

2. No writing is needed if the party being sued admits in court or in the legal proceedings that the contract existed.

3. No writing is needed for any portion of the goods already delivered and accepted *or* already paid for and accepted.

Parol evidence rule A rule stating that when contracts are in writing, only the writing can be used to show the terms of the contract

In those areas where the parties have a written agreement, the **parol evidence rule** applies; that is, when there is a written agreement, and this writing is meant to be the final agreement, the writing cannot be contradicted by any oral agreement made at the same time as or before the writing.[9] But the writing can be explained or supplemented by additional evidence. Either party may show that course of dealings, usage of trade, or course of performance gives special meanings to certain terms of the writing. And either party may introduce evidence of additional, consistent terms to fill out any apparent gaps in the written agreement.

---

[6] Ibid., Section 2–201(1).
[7] Ibid.
[8] Ibid., Section 2–201(2).
[9] Ibid., Section 2–202.

Course of dealings refers to any prior conduct between the parties. Prior conduct sets up a pattern that may reasonably be followed in the present setting.[10] *Usage of trade* refers to a widely recognized and accepted industry practice. When usage of trade is proved, it is expected to be followed by the parties.[11] *Course of performance* involves repeated performance between the parties. If neither party objects to the performance, it is considered appropriate to continue so performing.[12]

In the following case, the court had to decide whether to admit evidence concerning course of dealings and usage of trade to interpret a written contract.

Celebrity, Inc. v. *Kemper*
632 P.2d 743 (N.M. 1981)

FACTS

Kemper, a retailer, had been doing business with Celebrity, a wholesaler, for some five years. During this period, whenever Kemper received a shipment of goods from Celebrity that contained any defective goods, Kemper would set the defective goods aside. The Celebrity salesman would later verify that the goods set aside were defective and would adjust Kemper's account to reflect the rejected merchandise.

When the delivery in controversy occurred, Kemper had once again set aside those goods he had felt were defective so that an adjustment could be made. The Celebrity salesman refused to make any adjustment, however, since the invoice for the shipment specified that any returns were to be made only upon prior written authorization and within five days of delivery. Despite the salesman's refusal to adjust the account, Kemper did nothing further until Celebrity demanded payment in full for the shipment. Upon Celebrity's demand, Kemper returned all the goods remaining from the shipment in question whether the goods were defective or not.

ISSUE

May Kemper rely on a course of dealing to return defective or nonconforming goods despite any contrary language in the invoice or the contract?

HOLDING

No. Kemper has acted unreasonably under the circumstances.

REASONING

When Kemper attempted to reject the defective goods as per the normal course of dealing between the two firms, the salesman for Celebrity pointed out that the invoice specified a different method for making returns. When a course of dealing is in conflict with the express terms of a contract, the express terms must control. Kemper had a duty to act in a reasonable and proper manner and to follow the express terms of the contract when they were pointed out to him. If there had been

[10] Ibid., Section 1–205(1).
[11] Ibid., Section 1–205(2).
[12] Ibid., Section 2–208(1).

no express contract terms to follow, Kemper's reliance on the course of dealings would have been appropriate. Since there were conflicting terms, the course of dealings was overridden by those terms.

Courses of dealings and courses of performance are normally based on current or prior conduct of the parties with one another. As such, both are readily apparent, and difficult to deny. Some trade usage patterns are less obvious, especially since the usage of trade may be applicable to situations in which one — or even both — of the parties are not merchants. For example, in California it is a standard usage of trade to use a formal bill of sale to transfer an automobile, truck, or boat by contract (see Figure 18.2).

It is generally the obligation of the parties to acquaint themselves with the usages of trade that apply and to comply with them if necessary.

Figure 18.2 Bill of Sale

BILL OF SALE

VEHICLE LICENSE NO OR VESSEL CF NO

VEHICLE OR HULL IDENTIFICATION NO	MAKE	BODY TYPE	MODEL	YEAR

FOR MOTOR-CYCLES ONLY: ENGINE NO ______

For the sum of ______ Dollars

($ ______) and/or other valuable consideration in the amount of

$ ______ , the receipt of which is hereby acknowledged, I/we did sell,

transfer and deliver to ______
(BUYER)

______
ADDRESS CITY STATE ZIP CODE

on the ______ day of ______ 19 ___ , my/our right, title and interest in and to the above described vehicle or vessel.

I/We certify under penalty of perjury that: (1) I/We are the lawful owner(s) of the vehicle/vessel and (2) I/We have the right to sell it, and (3) I/We guarantee and will defend the title to the vehicle/vessel against the claims and demands of any and all persons arising prior to this date and (4) the vehicle/vessel is free of all liens and encumbrances.

Signature of Seller X ______ Date ______

______
ADDRESS CITY STATE ZIP CODE

Courtesy of Bingham Toyota, Clovis, California.

As a broad general statement, the parties to a sales contract are to act in *good faith.* In addition, any merchant who is a party to a sales contract is obligated to act in a *commercially reasonable manner.* These two standards are broad enough that they adequately regulate the basic sales contract. The drafters of the Code decided, however, that more specific provisions were needed to supplement these rules and standards.

The most basic and obvious obligation is spelled out in Section 2–301. Under that section, the seller is to transfer and deliver conforming goods to the buyer. The buyer is then to accept and pay for the goods so delivered. Both parties are to perform in accordance with the terms of the contract. Conforming goods are goods that are within the description of the goods as set out in the contract.[13] (Delivery will be covered in Chapter 19, under "Seller's Duties.") Payment by the buyer will normally be in money. However, Section 2–304 permits payment in money, goods, realty, or "other." The manner of payment, whatever the form, will normally be spelled out in the contract.

So now we have both parties acting in good faith, with the seller selling and the buyer buying. And, of course, all is being done according to the terms of the contract. If that was all that Article 2 said, the rules of contracts from common law would be more than adequate to cover sales. The true value of the Code's coverage of sales is what it provides if, or when, the contract is defective in some area.

GENERAL OBLIGATIONS

Unconscionability

For example, Section 2–302 makes provisions for *unconscionable* contracts or contract clauses. Unconscionability means so unfair or so one-sided as to shock the conscience. Unlike the common law, which presumed that equal bargaining power existed, the Code realized that some parties can "force a bargain" on the other party. If the court feels that a contract is unconscionable, it may refuse to enforce the contract. If the court feels that only a clause of the contract is unconscionable, it will normally enforce all of the contract except the challenged clause.

The following case illustrates one way in which the court has attacked unconscionability.

Jones v. *Star Credit Corp.*
298 N.Y.S.2d 264 (Sup. Ct. N.Y. 1969)

FACTS

Mr. and Mrs. Jones, who were on welfare, agreed to buy a freezer from a salesman representing Your Shop At Home Service. The freezer had a base price of $900. After the addition of finance charges, insurance, and sales tax, the total purchase price was $1234.80. (Various damages and costs added in the case brought the total to $1439.69.) The Joneses had paid $619.88 when this

---

[13] Ibid., Section 2–106(2).

suit was filed. Star Credit Corp. claimed that the Joneses still owed $819.81. The court determined that the freezer had a maximum value *at retail* of $300 when it was purchased.

ISSUE   Is this contract unconscionable under the provision of the UCC?

HOLDINGS   Yes. Charging $1439.69 for a $300 freezer is unconscionable as a matter of law.

REASONING   The limited financial resources of the buyers were known to the seller, leading to the conclusion that advantage was taken of the buyers. The parties were grossly unequal in bargaining power. Since the buyers have already paid more than $600 for a $300 freezer, the creditor has been adequately compensated. No further payments are due.

Open Terms   The Code also recognizes that the parties may intend to have a contract even though the contract may omit some elements. In an effort to give the parties the "benefit of their bargain," the Code allows the omitted terms to be filled in by the court. (Remember, the court will *complete* a contract for the parties, but it will not write a contract for the parties.)

What happens when the parties intend to create a contract but fail to set a price? In such a case, Section 2–305 controls. Under this section, the price can be set by either of the parties or by some external factor. If nothing is said about price, the price is a *reasonable* price at the time of delivery of the goods. If the price is to be set by one of the parties, that party must set the price in good faith. A bad-faith price may be treated by the other party as a cancellation of the contract, or the other party may set a reasonable price and perform the contract.

In the following case, the court demonstrated the flexibility provided by the Code in interpreting a contract that would have failed at common law.

North Central Airlines, Inc. v. *Continental Oil Co.*
574 F.2d 582 (D.C. Cir. 1978)

FACTS   The parties had entered a contract for the sale of oil. The price of the oil was to be determined by averaging the posted prices of a particular type of oil. After the contract was entered, the federal government began to regulate the price of oil and introduced a new "two-tier" pricing system. Under the new federal price regulation, the contract method of pricing could not be followed.

ISSUE   If the agreed method of setting prices cannot be used, what price will be charged?

A reasonable price will be substituted for the contract price-setting mechanism.

According to UCC Section 2–305(1), when the agreed price standard fails, a reasonable price will be substituted, leaving the rest of the contract according to its original terms.

Sometimes the parties set a price and otherwise agree to contract terms except for *delivery*. Again, the Code provides a method to save the contract and to resolve the problem. Three different delivery sections may be utilized.

First, under Section 2 – 307 the seller is to make a complete delivery in one shipment unless the contract allows for several shipments. However, if the seller tenders a partial delivery and the buyer does not object, the seller can continue to make partial shipments *until* the buyer objects.

Second, Section 2 – 308 covers the place for delivery. If the contract is silent as to the place of delivery, delivery is at the *seller's* place of business. (Law students often miss this point. At first glance, it seems illogical. In reality, it is very logical. When a person buys a toaster or a can of beans, that person takes delivery at the store — the seller's place of business.) If the seller has no place of business, delivery is at the seller's residence. If the goods are known by both parties to be at some other place, the other place is the proper place for the delivery.

Third, Section 2 – 309 covers the time for delivery. If the contract is silent as to when delivery is to occur, delivery is to be within a reasonable time. Reasonable time here means reasonable in both clock time and in calendar time. The seller is to make delivery during normal business hours (clock time), and the seller is not allowed to delay unduly in the number of days before delivery (calendar time).

In addition to these rules, the Code resolves several other potential problems. Under Section 2 – 306, the Code specifically allows requirement contracts and output contracts. In a *requirement contract,* the seller provides all of a certain good that the buyer *needs.* In an *output contract,* the buyer purchases all of a certain good that the seller *produces.* Both types of contract were often declared unenforceable at common law since they were too indefinite in terms.

The Code also deals with *options.* If a contract calls for an unspecified product mix, the assortment of goods is at the *buyer's* option.[14] If the contract is silent as to how the goods are to be shipped, the shipping arrangements are at the *seller's* option.[15] However, if a party having an option delays unduly, the other party may act. The other party may elect to wait until hearing what is being done by the other party, or he may proceed on his own. Thus, if the buyer does not   Options

[14] Ibid., Section 2 – 311(2).
[15] Ibid.

notify the seller as to the product mix desired, the seller may delay shipping any goods, and the delay is excused.[16] Or the seller may select his own assortment and ship them, providing he acts in good faith.[17] Or the seller may treat the delay as a breach of contract by the buyer and seek remedies for the breach. (Remedies for breach of a sales contract are covered in Chapter 22.)[18]

Cooperation

As a final and overriding obligation, the parties are required to cooperate with one another in the performance of their duties. Any failure to cooperate or any interference with the performance of the other party can be treated as a breach of contract or as an excuse for a delayed performance.

SUMMARY

This chapter introduced the law of sales and Article 2 of the Uniform Commercial Code. It is important to distinguish sales contracts from other types of contracts. Article 2 attempts to deal with "commercial reality" in the sale of goods, whereas common law developed strict and rigid rules for the treatment of contracts. Article 2 also recognizes the difference between a merchant—a person who "specializes" in dealing with a particular type of goods—and a nonmerchant—a "casual dealer" in the goods.

The Code provides built-in flexibility in the formation of sales contracts. *Intent* is the key element in sales, rather than form. Offers and acceptances are likely to be found if the parties act as if they have an agreement. The Code even provides methods to supply missing terms, if it seems appropriate to do so in order to carry out the wishes and intentions of the parties.

The Statute of Frauds remains operative under Article 2, but its provisions are again less restrictive than they were under common law. There are three exceptions to the Statute of Frauds built into the Code, and the past dealings of the parties may also be taken into consideration in deciding what the parties have agreed to do.

Some general obligations are imposed on the parties to prevent or minimize abuses of the less rigid rules of Article 2. The parties are required to act in good faith; they may not act unconscionably; and they must cooperate with one another. Performance options are available to either party if the other party fails to cooperate fully or properly.

DISCUSSION QUESTIONS

1. How does the UCC define goods?
2. What is a sale, according to Article 2?
3. What are the three separate conditions that will qualify a person as a merchant?

---

[16] Ibid., Section 2–311(3)(a).
[17] Ibid., Section 2–311(3)(b).
[18] Ibid.

4. How can an offer be accepted under the law of sales?

5. The seller sent the buyer a form offering to sell certain goods. The buyer returned a form accepting the offer. The forms did not agree on every point. Do the parties have a contract? If so, what are its terms? If not, why?

6. What are the exceptions to the Statute of Frauds under Article 2 of the law of sales?

7. What constitutes a sufficient writing between merchants?

8. What are the basic duties of a merchant seller? Of a merchant buyer?

9. If the contract is silent as to the place of delivery, where should delivery take place?

10. When should delivery be tendered? Explain fully.

CASE PROBLEMS

1. Bunge Corp. was a major purchaser of corn. Bunge signed three contracts with Toppert, each calling for the delivery of 10,000 bushels of corn to Bunge. Bunge offered Toppert a fourth contract, but Toppert did not accept. Bunge was to pay for each contract as it was performed. Toppert delivered the corn for the first contract and began delivery on the second. Bunge refused to pay for the first. Bunge's reason for refusing to pay was that he wanted to force Toppert and Toppert's family to sign additional contracts. Is this a valid defense? (*Toppert* v. *Bunge Corp.*, 377 N.E.2d 324 [Ill. 1978].)

2. Campbell owned and operated a grain elevator. He orally agreed with a number of farmers to buy 7000 bushels of soybeans at $5.30 per bushel. Campbell then signed and mailed to the farmers a written confirmation of the agreement. The farmers denied that they were bound by the agreement because of the Statute of Frauds. Is their contention sound? (*Campbell* v. *Yokel*, 313 N.E.2d 628 [Ill. 1974].)

3. John, a candy manufacturer, purchased gelatin from Stein. John normally telephoned his orders to Stein and then sent a written purchase order later. Stein would send John a sales agreement with the shipment of gelatin. Stein's sales agreement included an arbitration clause. John felt one order of gelatin was unfit for his use, and he sued Stein. Stein asked the court to remove the case to arbitration. What should the court decide? (*Just Born, Inc.* v. *Stein, Hall & Co.*, 13 UCC Rep. 431 [Pa. Ct. Com. Pleas 1971].)

4. REMC supplied 135 volts of electricity to each of the rural homes that it serviced in Indiana. One of its customers, Helvey, alleged that this voltage damaged his home appliances, which were rated at 110 volts. Helvey sued REMC for the damages, but he filed the lawsuit more than four years after the damages were suffered. REMC claims that the UCC statute of limita-

tions precludes the lawsuit because it sells "goods." Helvey argues that REMC provides "services," so that the suit may still be filed. What will be the result? (*Helvey* v. *Wabash County REMC*, 278 N.E.2d 608 [Ind. 1972].)

5. LTV was manufacturing all-terrain vehicles for use in Asia. The vehicles had to be crated in order to be shipped. LTV entered an oral agreement with Bateman, calling for Bateman to produce packing crates for the vehicles, the crates to be built to LTV's specifications. LTV later refused to accept the crates prepared by Bateman. When Bateman sued, LTV raised the Statute of Frauds as a defense to the enforceability of the contract. Does Bateman need a writing in order to enforce this contract? (*LTV Aerospace Corp.* v. *Bateman*, 492 S.W.2d 703 [Tex. 1973].)

6. Preston needed to purchase a set of dentures. She visited Dr. Thompson, a denture specialist she found through an advertisement. Dr. Thompson spent six appointments making impressions and fitting Preston for her dentures, which were finally delivered two months later. Preston complained of pain when she ate with the new dentures. Dr. Thompson tried to correct the problem for seven months. When he could not correct the problem, Preston sued him for breach of warranty under the UCC. Dr. Thompson denied that he had participated in a sale of goods, and therefore asserted that he had not given any warranties to Preston. What result should occur? (*Preston* v. *Thompson*, 280 S.E.2d 780 [N.C. 1981].)

7. Casual Slacks entered into a written contract to sell clothing to Warren's, with delivery to be made during "June–August." Casual shipped the clothes in three roughly equal shipments, one a month. After the shipments, Casual received a check from Warren's for a substantially lesser amount than the contract called for. Casual refused to accept this check, and sued Warren's for the full contract price. Warren's defended against the lawsuit by alleging that Casual had breached the contract by improper shipment. According to Warren's, the clothing industry had a particular meaning for the term "June–August" that Casual had not followed. As a result, Warren's had suffered substantial losses, and the lesser amount of the check was to reflect those losses. How should the court treat this parol evidence of a usage of trade in conjunction with the written contract? Explain fully. (*Warren's Kiddie Shoppe, Inc.* v. *Casual Slacks, Inc.*, 171 S.E.2d 643 [Ga. App. 1969].)

8. Nicole owned and operated a "pony cart" amusement ride that had been purchased from Jones. Jones had originally purchased the ride from the manufacturer and had operated the ride for about two months before selling it to Nicole. Allen was injured while getting off of the ride. Allen's guardian sued Nicole for negligence and also sued both Nicole and Jones for breach of warranty and for strict liability. Is Jones a "merchant" and therefore liable for breach of warranty in this case? Why? (*Allen* v. *Nicole, Inc.*, 412 A.2d 824 [N.J. 1980].)

9. Castle and Pettibone entered into a contract that called for Pettibone to deliver to Castle an "880 Crusher." Instead, Pettibone sent Castle a "Pitmaster Crusher." Castle accepted delivery of the "Pitmaster" and used it for some time without objection. When Pettibone demanded payment of the purchase price, Castle refused to pay, arguing that Pettibone had breached the contract by sending the wrong type of crusher. Pettibone is now suing for the purchase price. What result should occur? (*Pettibone Minnesota Corp.* v. *Castle,* 247 N.W.2d 52 [Minn. 1976].)

10. Osterholt hired the Charles Drilling Co. to install a well and water system. By the terms of the contract, the drilling company was to drill a well at a preselected site, install a 315-gallon tank, and to lay the lines at least 36 inches below ground throughout the development. Charles Drilling Co. instead drilled the well in a different location, installed two 120-gallon tanks, and failed to lay the pipe the required 36 inches deep. Osterholt filed suit for breach of contract under the provisions of Article 2 of the UCC, and Charles Drilling Co. argued that this case was outside the UCC, being a service contract rather than a sale of goods. Should the contract be governed by the UCC or by common law contract provisions? (*Osterholt* v. *St. Charles Drilling Co.,* 500 F. Supp. 529 [D.C. Mo. 1980].)

Performance of the Sales Contract

SELLERS' DUTIES

The seller in a contract for the sale of goods has a very simple basic duty. The seller is to *tender delivery* of *conforming goods* according to the terms of the contract. The parties can agree to make delivery in any manner they desire. If they do not agree, or if they simply fail to consider how delivery is to occur, the Uniform Commercial Code covers the topic for them. Section 2–503 explains tender of delivery.

The seller has properly tendered delivery by putting and holding conforming goods at the buyer's disposition and then notifying the buyer that the goods are available. Normally the contract will tell the seller when and where to make the goods "available." When it does not, the seller must make his or her tender at a reasonable time and place, and the buyer must provide facilities suitable for receiving the goods.

This all sounds technical and confusing, but in reality delivery is fairly simple. There are five possible ways delivery can occur:

1. The buyer personally takes the goods from the seller.

2. The seller personally takes the goods to the buyer.

3. The seller ships the goods to the buyer by means of a **common carrier.**

4. The goods are in the hands of a third person **(bailee)**, and no documents of title are to be involved.

5. The goods are in the hands of a third person, and the seller is to deliver some **document of title** to the buyer.

If the seller properly tenders delivery under any of these situations and the goods are conforming, the seller has performed. Tender entitles the seller to have the buyer accept the goods, and it entitles the seller to receive payment for the goods.[1]

If the buyer and the seller make the delivery personally and directly (possibilities 1 and 2), proper tender is obvious. The seller will provide properly packaged goods to the buyer. The buyer will accept the goods and pay for them. Very neat, and very simple.

If the goods are in the hands of a third person, referred to as a bailee, delivery becomes somewhat more complicated. The seller in these cases must either provide the buyer with a **negotiable** document of title covering the goods (possibility 5) or get some acknowledgment from the bailee that the goods now belong to the buyer (possibility 4). If the buyer objects to anything less than a negotiable document of title, the seller must provide a negotiable document in order to prove that a proper tender of delivery was made.[2]

The UCC treats the topic of documents of title in Article 7. This article, entitled "Article 7: Warehouse Receipts, Bills of Lading, and Other Documents of Title," specifies the rights and the duties of all relevant parties in the handling of documents of title, whether those documents are negotiable or nonnegotiable. In addition to the coverage of a document of title by Parts 1 and 2 (for a warehouse receipt) or Parts 1 and 3 (for a bill of lading), both Parts 4 and 5 of this article deal with warehouse receipts and bills of lading if the document of title in question is negotiable. However, only Part 4 is also involved if the document of title is nonnegotiable. In order to reduce the amount of statutory coverage involved, and to avoid the problems of determining whether there has been a "due negotiation" of the document making the holder a "holder by due negotiation" most commercial warehousemen and common carriers simply issue nonnegotiable documents of title.

Most carriers prefer to use a nonnegotiable document of title to protect themselves. Figure 19.1 shows the first page of such a document. Figure 19.2 shows the provisions listed on the back of the same document.

None of the methods of delivery that we have described is very troublesome. The problems in understanding delivery normally arise when a com-

Common carrier A company in the business of transporting people or goods for a fee and holding itself out as serving the general public

Bailee One to whom goods are delivered with the understanding that they will be returned at a future time

Document of title A written evidence of ownership or of rights to something

Negotiable Transferable either by an endorsement and delivery or by delivery alone

---

[1] Uniform Commercial Code, Section 2–507(1).
[2] Ibid., Section 2–503(4)(a), (b).

Figure 19.1 A Nonnegotiable Warehouse Receipt (Front)

BEKINS

NON-NEGOTIABLE WAREHOUSE RECEIPT AND CONTRACT

I. ACCEPTANCE OF WAREHOUSE RECEIPT CONTRACT AND SIGNATURE IDENTIFICATION

BEKINS MOVING & STORAGE CO.   Date _____ 19 _____

Gentlemen:

I hereby acknowledge receiving your warehouse receipt and contract, Storage Lot Number _____ , and I have read the provisions, limitations, terms and conditions on the reverse side of this agreement. I hereby accept its terms and conditions, and affix my official signature hereto for your files.

A. _____
(PRINT YOUR NAME IN FULL)

_____
(STREET)   (CITY)   (STATE)   (ZIP)

Home Phone: _____   _____
Work Phone: _____   (SIGNATURE)

B. You are also authorized to accept orders for access, delivery or removal of my goods from:

_____
(IN YOUR OWN HANDWRITING PRINT IN AUTHORIZED PERSON'S NAME)

_____
(STREET)   (CITY)   (STATE)   (ZIP)

_____
(SIGNATURE OF PERSON AUTHORIZED ABOVE)

C. As Depositor, I understand that value protection in the amount of $ _____ at an additional monthly charge of $ _____ per month has been ordered for my account. I acknowledge that the amount of value protection represents the actual cash value of the property placed into storage. If value protection is not desired or Depositor wants to declare a higher value, please indicate below. Depositor agrees and understands that if value protection is not desired then the value of the property placed into storage, and the Company's liability in case of loss or damage arising out of Company's negligence or for any cause for which it may be liable for each or any article or the contents of any package or container stored hereunder or later received does not exceed and is limited to sixty (60¢) cents per pound per article, upon which agreed value the rates are based, the Depositor having been given the opportunity to declare a higher amount of value and to pay an additional charge and having elected not to do so.

Value Protection is not Desired _____ Please Initial and Date

Value Protection in the amount of $ _____ is Desired. _____ Please Initial and Date

D. In the event that the actual cash value of the entire lot of property stored on which the Depositor has declared a lump sum value is in excess of the lump sum amount so declared by the Depositor, it is agreed that the Depositor shall be regarded as being his own insurer to the extent of the difference, and the Depositor shall bear that proportion of any loss which the undeclared amount bears to the actual cash value of the property.

CUSTOMER'S COPY — RETAIN IN SAFE PLACE

II. NON-NEGOTIABLE WAREHOUSE RECEIPT AND CONTRACT

RECEIVED FOR THE ACCOUNT OF _____ _____ (hereinafter called the

Depositor) whose latest known address is _____

_____ the goods described on the inventory attached and by this reference made a part hereof (contents and condition of contents unknown) to be handled on monthly storage in warehouse situated at _____ at the monthly storage charge of _____ dollars subject to the provisions, limitations, terms and conditions herein printed on the face and reverse side hereof, all of which are agreed and assented to by the Depositor for himself and his heirs; and to be delivered to said Depositor upon payment of all charges. Storage rate herein is based on declared value of sixty (60¢) cents per pound per article, unless the Depositor has declared a higher value and agreed to the rate for higher value.

Storage Lot No. _____   Date _____ 19 _____

BEKINS MOVING & STORAGE CO.

SEE PROVISIONS, LIMITATIONS, TERMS AND
CONDITIONS OF CONTRACT ON REVERSE SIDE   By _____

W 15/1282   © THE BEKINS COMPANY 1977

Courtesy of Bekins Moving and Storage, Fresno, California.

Figure 19.2 A Nonnegotiable Warehouse Receipt (Back)

III. PROVISIONS, LIMITATIONS, TERMS AND CONDITIONS OF WAREHOUSE RECEIPT AND CONTRACT

1. OWNERSHIP OF GOODS: The Depositor has represented to the Company that the Depositor has the lawful possession of and legal right and authority to store all of the property herein described, and upon the provisions, limitations, terms and conditions herein set forth, and if there be any controversy or litigation concerning the property, the Depositor agrees to pay all storage and other charges which this Company may incur or become liable for or by judgment be compelled to pay in connection therewith, and this Company shall have a lien on said property for all storage and other charges.

2. TERMS OF PAYMENT: Payments for storage and other charges are due and payable upon the date of this receipt and on the same date of each succeeding month thereafter. Delinquent accounts shall incur interest at the maximum amount permitted by law commencing on the 61st day after payment is due.

3. ADDITIONS TO STORAGE LOT: Any additional goods hereafter delivered by the Depositor to the Company for storage as a part of this lot while this receipt is outstanding shall be subject to the terms and conditions hereof.

4. CORRECTION OF ERRORS: Unless notice is given in writing to the Company within thirty (30) days after either the mailing of this receipt to the Depositor or the delivery of this receipt personally to the Depositor, the attached inventory will be deemed to be correct, complete, and the terms and conditions accepted and shall likewise be binding on any future additions made to this lot.

5. LIABILITY OF COMPANY: A. Except as set forth in paragraphs B through D the Company agrees to indemnify the Depositor for all physical loss or damage to property while in the care, custody and control of the Company within a 50 mile radius of the warehouse. The total liability of the company for physical loss or damage shall in no event exceed: (1) the amount of the value declared by the Depositor or sixty (60¢) cents per pound per article; (2) the cost of repairing damaged property; (3) the cost of replacing lost or destroyed property with material of like kind and quality; (4) the actual cash value of such property at time and place of loss.

B. The Company shall not be liable for any loss, damage or delay caused by or resulting from:

    (1) An act, omission or order of Depositor or owner, or the agent thereof;

    (2) Depreciation, deteriorization, obsolescence and ordinary wear and tear;

    (3) The nature of the article or any defect, characteristic or inherent vice thereof including susceptibility to damage because of atmospheric conditions such as temperature and humidity;

    (4) Earthquake, flood, rising waters, acts of God or any other cause beyond the control of the Company.

    (5) Strikes, lockouts, labor disturbances, riots, civil commotions, or the act of any person or persons taking part in such occurrence or disorder;

    (6) Hostile or warlike action in time of peace or war by any authority maintaining or using military forces, nuclear reaction, nuclear radiation or radioactive contamination; insurrection, rebellion, revolution, civil war, usurped power, or any action taken by government authority against such occurrence.

    (7) Breakage of glass, chinaware or similar articles of a brittle or fragile nature unless packed and unpacked by the Company.

    (8) Insects, moth, vermin, or rodent unless the Depositor can establish that said insects, moth, vermin or rodent were not in his articles when delivered to the Company.

C. The Company shall not be liable for consequential damages from negligent delay or proximately caused by the physical loss or damage to any property unless they are specifically set forth in writing stating the nature and extent of the consequential damages that may be incurred in the event of either negligent delay or physical loss or damage to the property stored and the company acknowledges to the depositor in writing that it agrees to be liable for such consequential damages.

D. The Company shall not assume liability for loss or damage to articles of extraordinary value unless: (1) the depositor, in writing, specifically lists each such article specifically designating it as an article of extraordinary value; (2) the value of each such article is clearly indicated, and (3) the company is afforded the opportunity prior to acceptance of the property into storage to pack and otherwise provide adequate protection to such article (at company's pub-

lished charges) if in the estimation of the company, the depositor's packing or packaging is determined to be inadequate for the protection of such article.

As used herein, the term "articles of extraordinary value" refers to those articles which because of uniqueness or rarity have a value substantially in excess of the cost of newly manufactured items of substantially the same type and quality apart from such uniqueness or rarity, such as, but not limited to: (1) musical instruments of rare quality, or (2) historical significance, (3) original manuscripts, (4) first editions, or (5) autographed copies of books, (6) antique furniture, (7) heirlooms, (8) paintings, (9) sculptures, (10) other works of art, (11) hobby collections, and (12) exhibits.

6. SERVICE TO STORED GOODS: Many instruments and articles by their nature, frequently require attention and adjustment both during storage and after removal. The Company will not furnish any such attention or adjustment as part of its service. The services of this Company are limited to storage, packing, moving and shipping, and it does not accept liability in respect to such attention or adjustment. Should the Company, at its discretion, determine that moth-treating all or a portion of the goods stored hereunder is necessary for the protection of the goods of other persons stored in the warehouse, it may moth-treat same and add its charges therefor to the amount payable by the Depositor hereunder.

7. BUILDING — WATCHMAN: It is understood that the building is of fire-resistant contruction, but no guarantee is given that the contents of same cannot be destroyed by fire. No night watchman shall be required.

8. DELIVERY AND ACCESS TO GOODS: The goods deposited hereunder will be ready for delivery or access during regular working days, on 24 hours' notice, from the Depositor or any other specified person on his or her behalf on presentation of written authority executed by said Depositor and providing that all storage and other charges owing to the Company are paid in full. No transfer of this receipt will be recognized unless all charges are paid and transfer is entered on the books of the Company and a charge paid therefor. A warehouse labor charge will be made for placing goods in storage and for removing to platform for delivery. An additional charge will be made for all access to or part delivery of goods.

9. CHANGE OF ADDRESS: Notice of any change of address of the Depositor must be given by the Depositor to the Company, in writing and acknowledged in writing by the Company on the following monthly statement, and no notice of any change of address shall be valid or binding against the Company, if given in any other manner, and it is hereby expressly understood and agreed that all notices of any nature to the Depositor shall be sent to the latest known address as shown on the face of this warehouse receipt until such written notice of change is received by said Company, and acknowledged by it in writing on the following monthly statement.

10. SATISFACTION OF WAREHOUSEMAN'S LIEN: This Company shall have a lien upon any and all property deposited with it by Depositor, or on the proceeds thereof in its hand, for all lawful charges for storage and preservation of same or any part thereof, also for all lawful claims for money advanced, interest, transportation, labor, wrapping, weighing, coopering, and all other charges and expenses in relation to such property, or any part thereof, and also for all reasonable charges and expenses for notice and advertisement of sale and for the sale of the property where default has been made in satisfying this Company's lien. This lien may be enforced by the Company at any time either by public or private sale of the goods with or without a judicial hearing.

11. TIME FOR FILING CLAIM: As a condition precedent to recovery, a claim for any loss, damage, injury, overcharge or delay must be filed in writing with the Company within 60 days after delivery to depositor, or in the case of failure to make delivery, then within 60 days after a reasonable time for delivery has elapsed, and suit must be instituted against company within two years and one day from the date when notice in writing is given by the company to the claimant that company has disallowed the claim or any part or parts thereof specified in the notice. Where a claim is not filed or suit is not instituted thereon in accordance with the foregoing provisions, company shall not be liable and such claim shall not be paid.

DO NOT LOSE OR MISPLACE THIS RECEIPT

PRESENT THIS WAREHOUSE RECEIPT AND A WRITTEN ORDER WHEN ANY GOODS ARE TO BE WITHDRAWN. GOODS WILL BE DELIVERED ONLY UPON RECEIPT OF A WRITTEN ORDER SIGNED BY THE PERSON IN WHOSE NAME THEY ARE STORED.

THIS WAREHOUSE RECEIPT MUST BE RETURNED WHEN ALL THE GOODS ENUMERATED IN THE INVENTORY ARE WITHDRAWN.

TITLE TO PACKING MATERIALS PASSES TO CUSTOMER IMMEDIATELY UPON DELIVERY AT POINT OF ORIGIN.

Courtesy of Bekins Moving and Storage, Fresno, California.

mon carrier enters the picture (possibility 3). Now the seller must give the goods to the carrier, the carrier must transport the goods to the buyer, and the buyer must accept the transported goods and make payment for them. As one might expect, the more parties involved in a transaction, the more likely problems and confusion will enter the picture.

The seller must provide for reasonable carriage of the goods, taking into account the nature of the goods, the need for speed, and any other factors that will affect the delivery. The seller must then obtain and deliver to the buyer any necessary documents concerning the carriage, and the seller must promptly notify the buyer of the shipment.[3] Again, all these steps seem obvious, and none should cause any undue problems or hardships. The problems crop up when the parties use technical and/or legal terms without understanding their meaning.

Figure 19.3 A Nonnegotiable Airbill (Bill of Lading)

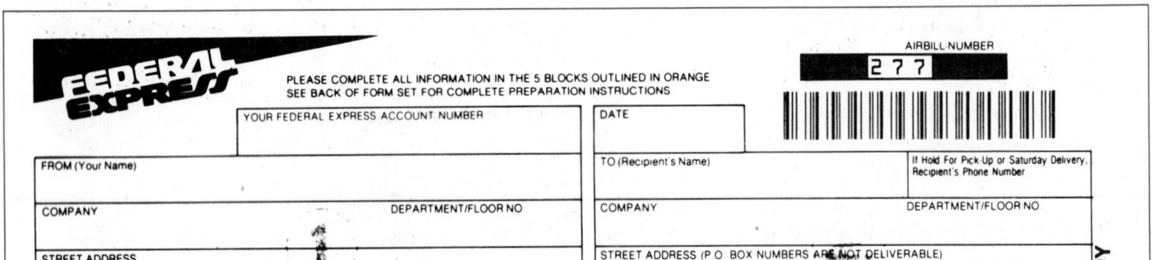

FEDERAL EXPRESS

PLEASE COMPLETE ALL INFORMATION IN THE 5 BLOCKS OUTLINED IN ORANGE
SEE BACK OF FORM SET FOR COMPLETE PREPARATION INSTRUCTIONS

AIRBILL NUMBER 277

YOUR FEDERAL EXPRESS ACCOUNT NUMBER

DATE

FROM (Your Name)

TO (Recipient's Name)

If Hold For Pick-Up or Saturday Delivery, Recipient's Phone Number

COMPANY | DEPARTMENT/FLOOR NO

COMPANY | DEPARTMENT/FLOOR NO

STREET ADDRESS

STREET ADDRESS (P O BOX NUMBERS ARE NOT DELIVERABLE)

CITY | STATE

CITY | STATE

AIRBILL NO. 681277100

ZIP ACCURATE ZIP CODE REQUIRED FOR CORRECT INVOICING

IN TENDERING THIS SHIPMENT, SHIPPER AGREES THAT F.E.C. SHALL NOT BE LIABLE FOR SPECIAL, INCIDENTAL OR CONSEQUENTIAL DAMAGES ARISING FROM CARRIAGE HEREOF. F.E.C. DISCLAIMS ALL WARRANTIES, EXPRESS OR IMPLIED, WITH RESPECT TO THIS SHIPMENT. THIS IS A NON-NEGOTIABLE AIRBILL SUBJECT TO CONDITIONS OF CONTRACT SET FORTH ON REVERSE OF SHIPPER'S COPY. UNLESS YOU DECLARE A HIGHER VALUE, THE LIABILITY OF FEDERAL EXPRESS CORPORATION IS LIMITED TO $100.00. FEDERAL EXPRESS DOES NOT CARRY CARGO LIABILITY INSURANCE.

ZIP ACCURATE ZIP CODE REQUIRED FOR OVERNIGHT DELIVERY

YOUR NOTES/REFERENCE NUMBERS (FIRST 12 CHARACTERS WILL ALSO APPEAR ON INVOICE)

PAYMENT ☐ Bill Shipper ☐ Bill Recipient's F.E.C. Acct. ☐ Bill 3rd Party F.E.C. Acct. ☐ Bill Credit Card
☐ Cash In Advance Account Number/Credit Card Number

SERVICES CHECK ONLY ONE BOX

PRIORITY 1
1 ☐ (OVERNIGHT PACKAGES) (Up to 70 LBS.)
COURIER PAK
2 ☐ OVERNIGHT ENVELOPE (Up to 2 LBS.)
3 ☐ OVERNIGHT BOX (Up to 5 LBS.)
4 ☐ OVERNIGHT TUBE (Up to 5 LBS.)
STANDARD AIR
5 ☐ DELIVERY 2ND BUSINESS DAY FOLLOWING PICK UP (Up to 70 LBS.)

OVERNIGHT LETTER
6 ☐ (Up to 2 OZ.)
7 ☐
8 ☐
9 ☐

"OVERNIGHT" IS NEXT BUSINESS DAY (MONDAY THROUGH FRIDAY); TWO DAYS FROM ALASKA/HAWAII. SATURDAY DELIVERY AVAILABLE IN CONTINENTAL U.S. SEE "SPECIAL HANDLING."

DELIVERY AND SPECIAL HANDLING CHECK SERVICES REQUIRED
1 ☐ HOLD FOR PICK UP AT FOLLOWING FEDERAL EXPRESS LOCATION SHOWN IN SERVICE GUIDE. RECIPIENT'S PHONE NUMBER REQUIRED
2 ☐ DELIVER
3 ☐ SATURDAY SERVICE REQUIRED See Reverse (Extra charge applies for delivery.)
4 ☐ RESTRICTED ARTICLES SERVICE (P-1 and Standard Air Packages only, extra charge)
5 ☐ SSS (Signature Security Service required, extra charge applies)
6 ☐ DRY ICE ______ LBS.
7 ☐ OTHER SPECIAL SERVICE ______
8 ☐ ______
9 ☐

PACKAGES	WEIGHT	DECLARED VALUE	O/S
TOTAL	TOTAL	TOTAL	

RECEIVED AT
SHIPPER'S DOOR
☐ REGULAR STOP
☐ ON-CALL STOP
☐ F.E.C. LOC. ______

Federal Express Corporation Employee No.

DATE/TIME For Federal Express Use

AGT/PRO

AGT/PRO

FEDERAL EXPRESS USE
FREIGHT CHARGES
DECLARED VALUE CHARGE
ADVANCE ORIGIN
ADVANCE DESTINATION
OTHER
TOTAL CHARGES

PART# 2041730750
FEC-S-0750 D/O/W
REVISION DATE
7-82 GBF
PRINTED USA

ORIGIN ACCOUNTING COPY

Courtesy of Federal Express Corporation, Memphis, Tennessee.

[3] Ibid., Section 2–504.

Figure 19.3 illustrates the type of contract a seller may have to enter in order to send the goods by means of a common carrier.

Every shipping contract must take one of two positions: it is either a *shipment* contract or a *destination* contract. In a shipment contract, once the seller makes a proper contract for the carriage and surrenders the goods to the care of the carrier, the goods belong to the buyer. The buyer has title and **risk of loss.** The seller has performed his or her part of the contract. In contrast, in a destination contract, the seller retains title and all risk of loss until the carrier gets the goods to the buyer or wherever the goods are supposed to go under the contract. The seller has not performed until the goods reach their destination. (Title and risk of loss are covered in detail in Chapter 20.)

Risk of loss Financial responsibility in case of injury, harm, or destruction of the subject matter

Under UCC Section 2–303, the parties can agree to allocate or share the risk of loss during transit. However, this sort of arrangement seems to be the exception rather than the rule. Most parties seem to ignore the problem of loss during shipment until a loss occurs. And, at that point, it is too late to begin negotiating about what to do if a loss occurs. Because of this normal oversight, and because so many shipments use standard terms, the UCC has allocated risk of loss and a number of other things when the parties to a contract use any of these standard shipping terms.

Free on board at a named place may be either a shipment contract term or a destination contract term, depending on the place named. If the contract terms are F.O.B. and the named place is the place of shipment (the *seller's* location), the contract is a *shipment contract. Once the seller has the goods loaded by the carrier, the seller has fully performed.* If the contract terms are F.O.B. and the named place is the destination (the *buyer's* location), the contract is a *destination contract. The seller has not performed until the goods arrive at the final point,* and thus the seller has the risk of damages during transit.[4]

F.O.B.

Free along side is a standard shipping term for seagoing transportation. Here *the seller is required to get the goods to the named vessel and port.* Having done so, the seller has performed. The buyer then has all the risks of loading, transporting, and unloading the goods. The buyer is responsible from the dock of shipment to the buyer's location.[5]

F.A.S.

There is a recent trend to treat F.A.S. as a seagoing F.O.B. term, with the term being either a shipment contract or a destination contract, depending on the named port. This current usage is gradually replacing the more traditional and more correct treatment of F.A.S. as a shipment contract term, with *ex-ship* being the more traditional and more correct term for a destination contract.

[4] Ibid., Section 2–319(1)(a), (b).
[5] Ibid., Section 2–319(2).

Ex-Ship

Like F.A.S., *ex-ship* indicates that the transportation is by sea. However, now *the seller is responsible for getting the goods both to the named vessel and port and unloaded from the vessel.* Here the seller has the risks of loading, transport, and unloading the goods. Until the goods reach the destination dock, they are the seller's responsibility.[6]

C.I.F. and C & F

C.I.F. means cost, insurance, freight. *C & F* means cost and freight. When either of these terms is used, *the seller quotes a lump-sum price to the buyer.* That single price will include the cost of the goods, the freight to get the goods to the buyer, and possibly the cost of the insurance to cover the goods during the carriage.[7] Both terms are deemed to be shipment contracts, with the buyer assuming all the risks associated with the transportation.

No Arrival,
No Sale

Under a *no arrival, no sale contract, the seller is facing the risk of loss if the goods are damaged or destroyed during transit.* However, even if the goods are damaged or destroyed, the seller may not be responsible to the buyer to perform the contract. If it can be shown that the seller shipped conforming goods, and it is not shown that the seller caused the loss or damage, the seller is released from the duty to perform.[8] However, if the goods shipped were not conforming or if the seller caused the loss, the seller is still obligated to ship conforming goods.

C.O.D.

Collect on delivery is a destination contract with a special feature: *the buyer is required to pay for the goods upon tender by the carrier, but is not permitted to inspect the goods until payment has been made.* If the buyer is unable or unwilling to pay upon tender, the goods are returned to the seller.

INTERVENING
RIGHTS

Once the seller's single duty has been performed, the focus of the sales contract shifts. The seller has performed, but it is not yet time for the buyer to perform. First, the buyer had an intervening right, the right to inspect the goods. If this inspection results in a discovery of some nonconformity, the seller *may* have a right to cure the defective performance so as to avoid a breach. Only after these intervening rights have been exercised—or waived—does the duty of the buyer to perform arise.

Inspection

The right of the buyer to inspect the goods is covered in UCC Section 2–513. This section empowers the buyer to inspect the goods in any reasonable manner and at any reasonable time and place. This includes inspection after the goods arrive at their destination, if the seller ships the goods.

The buyer bears the expense of inspection. This serves two functions: (1) it encourages the buyer to use a more reasonable method of inspection since the

[6] Ibid., Section 2–322.
[7] Ibid., Section 2–320.
[8] Ibid., Section 2–324.

buyer must pay for it, and (2) it eliminates "phantom" inspections, with the expenses billed to the other person. If the inspection reveals that the goods do not conform to the contract, the buyer is entitled to recover the expenses of the inspection from the seller, along with any other damages the buyer may be entitled to recover. (This and other remedies will be discussed in Chapter 22.)

There are two circumstances in which the buyer is required to pay for the goods before being allowed to inspect them. If the contract calls for *payment against documents* or if it is *C.O.D.*, inspection before payment is not allowed. However, such a preinspection payment is not treated as an acceptance under the code.[9] In contrast, if the right to inspect the goods before payment exists, a preinspection payment is treated as an acceptance.

If the buyer fails to inspect, or refuses to inspect, or inspects poorly, the buyer may waive some rights. Any defects that should be noticed or discovered by a reasonable inspection may not be argued after an unreasonable inspection. The one exception is when the seller promises to correct, or *cure,* the problem and then fails to do so. In other words, unless the defect is hidden (so that a reasonable inspection would not reveal it), the buyer must "speak now, or forever hold his peace."

Often the buyer will discover, on inspection, that the goods do not conform exactly to the description in the contract. When this happens, the buyer must make a decision: either (1) the nonconformity is minor, or of little or no consequence, in which case the buyer will normally accept the goods despite the nonconformity, or (2) the goods are too different from those described in the contract to be acceptable. When this happens, the buyer must promptly notify the seller, specifying in detail the problems with the goods that result in nonconformity.

Cure

If the time for performance has not yet expired, the Code gives the seller a chance to avoid being held in breach. The seller may *cure* the defect in the goods, *putting the goods into conformity with the contract.*[10] However, the cure must be completed within the time period in which the original contract was to be performed. No extension of time is permitted here.

Occasionally, a seller ships nonconforming goods and reasonably expects the buyer to accept them despite the nonconformity. Such an expectation may be realistically based on typical past dealings between the parties. In such a case, if the buyer decides to stand by the literal terms of the contract and refuses to accept the nonconforming goods, and so informs the seller, the UCC gives the seller a right to cure *even if* the time for performance is past.[11] If the seller informs the buyer of an intention to cure the defect, the seller is given a reasonable time to cure by substituting conforming goods so that the seller's performance is in compliance with the contract.

---

[9] Ibid., Sections 2–512, 2–513(3).
[10] Ibid., Section 2–508(1).
[11] Ibid., Section 2–508(2).

In the following case, the seller showed a willingness to cure defective performance, but the buyers refused to allow the seller a chance to cure. As a result, the buyers waived their right to rescind the contract.

Stephenson v. *Frazier*
399 N.E.2d 794 (Ind. App. 1980)

FACTS   The Stephensons purchased a modular mobile home from Frazier in 1974 for a total purchase price of $22,500. This price included the installation of a septic system and the construction of a foundation by Frazier on the Stephensons' property. The Stephensons objected to the quality of Frazier's work, and when they were still not satisfied, they sued for rescission of the entire contract. Frazier argued that the Stephensons interfered with his attempts to perform, in that they refused to allow him or his crew onto their property, and thus that they could not rescind.

ISSUE   Were the Stephensons entitled to a rescission of the sales contract?

HOLDING   No. They must perform the contract with Frazier.

REASONING   The sale of a modular home is covered by the UCC law of sales. According to the Code, the seller has the right to cure nonconformities if he informs the buyers that he intends to do so. Frazier did inform the Stephensons of his intent to cure, but they denied him the opportunity to do so. By denying Frazier this opportunity, the Stephensons waived their right to rescind based on nonconformity.

BUYERS' DUTIES   The buyer's duties on the sales contract only arise after the seller's duties have been completed and the intervening rights of the parties have been exercised, if these intervening rights in fact exist in the contract. Since the buyer is not required to inspect the goods, a failure to inspect operates as a waiver, and the buyer's duty to perform arises. If the buyer inspects and discovers a defect, the seller may have a right to cure. If the seller does in fact cure, the duty of the buyer arises.

Acceptance   The UCC states that the buyer can accept the goods, and thus be obligated to pay for them, in a number of ways.[12] After having had a reasonable time to inspect the goods, the buyer is deemed to have accepted them in one of the following ways:

---

[12] Ibid., Section 2–606(1).

1. by signifying that the goods are conforming to the contract

2. by signifying that the goods do not conform, but that they will be retained and accepted despite the nonconformity

3. by failing to make a proper **rejection** of the goods if they are nonconforming

    Rejection A refusal to accept upon proper tender

4. by doing anything that is not consistent with the seller's ownership of the goods

As mentioned earlier, acceptance obligates the buyer to pay for the goods at the contract price. It also prevents rejection of the accepted goods unless the defect was hidden or the seller promised to cure the defect and then failed to do so. Also, the acceptance of any part of a **commercial unit** is treated as an acceptance of the entire commercial unit.[13]

Commercial unit The normal "package" size for the industry involved and the type of goods being sold; an unbroken "unit"

The following case dealt with the issue of a hidden defect.

Hummel v. Skyline Dodge, Inc.
589 P.2d 73 (Colo. App. 1978)

Hummel was a used car dealer; Skyline Dodge was a new and used car dealer. A customer went to Hummel wanting to trade a used Dodge Dart for one of Hummel's cars. Hummel took the Dart to Skyline to see whether they would buy it from Hummel if Hummel took it in trade. Skyline's sales manager took the car for a test drive, looked it over, and agreed to buy it from Hummel. Hummel then traded with the owner, delivered the Dart to Skyline, and received payment for the car. Several days later, Skyline discovered that the Dart had a bent frame and was in very bad condition. Skyline asked Hummel to take the car back. When Hummel refused, Skyline stopped payment on its check. Hummel sued on the check, and Skyline countersued for damages.

FACTS

Had Skyline Dodge accepted the car when it took possession from Hummel? Were the defects in the car hidden, so that the acceptance, if it occurred, could be revoked on discovery of the defects?

ISSUES

Yes, Skyline had accepted the car; no, the defects were not hidden.

HOLDINGS

An acceptance was found because Skyline had examined the car and issued a check "without reservation." Payment following a cursory inspection is a valid acceptance. The defect was not hidden because Skyline had both the equipment and the expert personnel to examine the car thoroughly. It failed to do so through its own fault, not due to any action by Hummel.

REASONING

[13] Ibid., Sections 2–606(2), 2–607.

In the following case, the court found that the buyer had accepted the goods by failing to properly reject them despite an apparent nonconformity.

Plateq Corp. v. *Machlett Laboratories, Inc.*
456 A.2d 786 (Conn. 1983)

FACTS   Machlett Laboratories placed an order with Plateq for two lead-covered steel tanks. These tanks were to be used for the testing of x-ray tubes. According to the contract, delivery of the tanks was to occur at the Plateq plant, but the tanks were to be inspected for any possible radiation leaks after they were installed at the Machlett location. When the tanks were nearly completed, a Machlett engineer conducted a preliminary inspection. During this inspection he noticed some deviations from the specifications and pointed these problems out to Plateq. Plateq promised to have the problems corrected by the following day in time for the tanks to be delivered. The Machlett engineer agreed, and said that a truck would be sent to pick up the tanks shortly. Instead, Machlett sent a note of cancellation to Plateq and refused to accept the tanks.

ISSUE   Did Machlett properly reject the goods?

HOLDING   No. The conduct of Machlett and its engineer did not constitute a proper rejection.

REASONING   Plateq had substantially completed its performance under the contract when the Machlett engineer made his preliminary inspection. When the engineer pointed out some deviations, Plateq agreed to correct the problems. At this time the performance period had not yet expired, and Plateq had the right and the opportunity to cure the defect. Machlett's attempt to cancel the contract was an improper rejection which prevented Plateq from completing its performance as scheduled. An improper rejection is treated as an acceptance, and Plateq is entitled to the contract price.

Payment

Once the seller tenders delivery and the buyer accepts, or fails to reject properly, the buyer has a duty to tender payment. Likewise, in the case of a C.O.D. contract or a payment against documents, the buyer has a duty to tender payment. The buyer is allowed to tender payment in any manner that is normal in the ordinary course of business — typically by check or draft. A seller who is not satisfied with this can demand **cash.** But in so doing, the seller must allow the buyer a reasonable extension of time to obtain cash.[14] This would normally be viewed as one banking day.

Cash Money, an officially recognized medium of exchange

Once the buyer tenders payment, the normal contract for the sale of goods is fully performed. Each of the parties received what it wanted, and nothing

---

[14] Ibid., Section 2–511(1), (2).

further is required. However, there are some special problems, which will be discussed next, and some special circumstances, which will be discussed in Chapter 22, on remedies.

The commercial world is crowded with businesses trying to get "a foot in the door," or trying to keep "a foot in the door," or just looking for a new gimmick that will give them an edge. As a result, some new forms of business dealings have arisen. The UCC has attempted to deal with two of these new areas — sale on approval and sale or return — that resemble an old area — consignments. The Code deals with these new areas in Sections 2–326 and 2–327.

SPECIAL PROBLEMS

A *sale on approval* exists if *the buyer "purchases" goods primarily for personal use with the understanding that the goods can be returned, even if they conform to the contract.* The buyer is given a reasonable time to examine, inspect, and try the goods at the seller's risk. Neither title nor risk of loss passes to the buyer until and unless the buyer accepts the goods. The buyer is deemed to have accepted the goods if one of the following occurs:

Sale on Approval

1. The buyer signifies acceptance.
2. The buyer does not return the goods.
3. The buyer subjects the goods to unreasonable usage.

The following example involves a contract for sale on approval.

Sam "purchases" a new lawn mower with a thirty-day "free home trial." He uses the mower six times in three weeks, cutting his lawn and in no way abusing the product. After the third week Sam returns the mower and refuses to pay the purchase price. Since this was a sale on approval and Sam never approved, he is not responsible for the price.

A *sale or return* exists if *the buyer "purchases" goods primarily for resale with the understanding that the unsold goods may be returned to the seller even if they conform to the contract.* In this situation, both title and risk of loss lie with the goods. Goods stolen from the buyer cannot be returned, so they are "sold" to the buyer. The seller must be paid for them.

Sale or Return

The following example indicates how the purpose of a sale or return differs from the purpose of a sale on approval.

Sam "purchases" some automobile stereo systems from Smooth Sounds, Inc., on a sale-or-return contract. Sam displays the stereo in his service station. If a customer wants an auto stereo system, Sam will sell it and install it. Sam can return any unsold units to Smooth Sounds for a refund or for credit on future goods. However, a thief breaks into Sam's station and steals the stereos. Sam must pay Smooth Sounds for the stereos since he cannot return them.

Consignment

In a *consignment, the owner of the goods allows a consignee to display and sell the goods for the owner/consignor.* The UCC treats such an arrangement as a sale or return unless one of the following occurs:

1.   The consignor ensures that signs are posted specifying that the goods on display are consigned goods.
2.   The consignor proves that the creditors of the consignee were generally aware of the consignments.
3.   The consignor complies with the rules for secured transactions under Article 9 (see Chapters 28 and 29).

Obviously, the Code has limited, if not eliminated, consignment in the modern business world. Most such arrangements today are merely treated as sale-or-return contracts. The importance of such a distinction is shown in the following case.

Collier v. *B & B Sales, Inc.*
471 S.W.2d 151 (Tex. 1971)

FACTS   B & B Sales was a supplier of stereo equipment. B & B entered into a contract with Collier that called for B & B to deliver stereo equipment to Collier. The invoice called for the equipment to be picked up from Collier if it had not been sold within ninety days. After the goods were delivered, but before the ninety days had expired, Collier's store was burglarized and all the equipment purchased from B & B was stolen. B & B demanded payment for the goods from Collier. Collier argued that the transaction had been a consignment, and that B & B had risk of loss.

ISSUE   Was this a consignment, so that B & B had risk of loss, or was this a sale or return so that Collier had risk of loss?

HOLDING   This transaction was a sale or return, so that Collier had risk of loss.

REASONING   The agreement between Collier and B & B treated the transaction as a sale, and the invoice sent to Collier indicated that this was a sale but that any unsold goods would be taken back by B & B after ninety days. This meant that the goods belonged to Collier for the ninety-day period. According to UCC Section 2–326, this was a sale or return, in which title and risk of loss run with possession. Collier had possession, and therefore he had risk of loss.

An auction gets special mention under UCC Section 2–328. In an *auction, the auctioneer, on behalf of the seller, sells the goods to the highest bidder.* The auctioneer does not give the same warranties to a buyer that other sellers of goods give.

A sale at auction is not complete until the auctioneer accepts a bid. Even then, if a bid is made while the auctioneer is in the process of **"knocking down,"** the auctioneer may elect to reopen bidding.

The goods at an auction are presumed to be put up "with reserve." An auction will be deemed "without reserve" only if by its terms it is specifically and expressly stated to be "without reserve." *With reserve* means that the auctioneer may declare all the bids to be too low and may refuse to accept any bids or to make any sale. In contrast, if the auction is *without reserve,* the highest bid made must be accepted, and a sale made.

What if the *seller* enters a bid, directly or indirectly, in an effort to drive up the bidding? The winning bidder in such a case may choose to renounce his or her bidding and to avoid the sale or may elect to take the goods at the last good-faith bid before the seller entered the bidding.

Auctions

"Knocking down" The acceptance of a bid by an auctioneer, signified by the fall of the gavel after the announcement that the goods are "Going, going, gone!"

In the performance of a sales contract, each party has some duty or duties to perform, and each has some right that may be asserted. The seller is to tender delivery of conforming goods as per the contract. The buyer is to accept and pay for the goods so tendered. The buyer normally has the right to inspect the goods before accepting or paying. If the inspection discloses any defects, the seller frequently has the right to cure, correcting the defect in the goods or in the performance.

The parties to a sale often use standard shipping terms. These terms have been defined by the UCC as forming either a shipment contract or a destination contract. In a shipment contract, the buyer bears the risks of loss or damage during transportation. In a destination contract, the seller bears the risks of loss or damage during transportation.

Some special problems have developed from modern business practices. Before the adoption of the UCC, consignments were frequently used to sell goods. Today, consignments have virtually been replaced by sale-on-approval and sale-or-return contracts. Each area is specially treated under Article 2, as are auctions.

SUMMARY

---

1. According to the UCC, what constitutes a proper tender of delivery?
2. What is the legal effect of a shipment contract as compared with that of a destination contract?

DISCUSSION QUESTIONS

3. How may the buyer inspect goods?

4. What must the seller do to get payment in legal currency rather than by check?

5. How may an owner/consignor prove that the goods are "on consignment" rather than a sale or return?

6. Acme Corp., a Boston business, entered a contract to sell goods to Zephyr. The contract called for Zephyr to pay $10,000 for the goods "F.O.B. Chicago." Under this contract, which party is responsible for the risk of shipping the goods, and why?

7. Biltless Mfg. sent goods to Smart Set Co. under a no arrival, no sale contract. After the goods were sent but before they arrived, Biltless learned it could double its profit in another market. If Biltless recovers the goods from the carrier, what rights can Smart Set assert?

8. Scott, a merchant, sent Roy some goods under a contract. Roy was to receive the goods by December 18. On December 12, Roy received nonconforming goods from Scott, and Roy promptly called Scott to inform him. What should Scott do to minimize his losses?

9. Mary and Agnes are merchants. Mary sent goods to Agnes under a contract. Agnes glanced at the boxes and paid Mary for the goods. Agnes later discovered that the goods were of inferior quality and design. What rights does Agnes have against Mary, and why? What, if anything, should Agnes have done differently?

10. Farm Goods, Inc., sold Ralph a tractor under a sale-on-approval contract. After Ralph plowed twenty acres, he loaned the tractor to his neighbor Ben. Once Ben had plowed another forty acres, Ralph informed Farm Goods that he was returning the tractor, since it did not meet with his approval. Farm Goods sues Ralph. What will be the result, and why?

CASE PROBLEMS

1. The Giffees purchased a mobile home from Fegett in 1970. In 1971, Mrs. Giffee became ill, and the Giffees had the mobile home moved back to Fegett's lot so that it could be displayed and offered for resale. Fegett agreed to relay any offers he received on the mobile home to the Giffees. One of Fegett's creditors attached and removed a number of mobile homes from Fegett's lot, including the one owned by the Giffees. The Giffees are now suing Fegett for the value of the mobile home, alleging that the arrangement was a sale or return and that Fegett had risk of loss on the mobile home. What should the court rule in this case? (*Founders Investment Corp.* v. *Fegett* [Ky. App. 1978].)

2. Church purchased three mobile homes from Southland Corp. As part of the contract, Southland was to supply a crew to install gas and electric lines and to "hook up" the mobile homes. During the installation, Church smelled gas and asked the work crew to check for leaks. A few days later, one of the mobile homes exploded and burned because of a gas leak. Southland denied liability, arguing that risk of loss had already passed to Church. What was the result? (*Southland Mobile Home Corp.* v. *Chyrchel,* 500 S.W.2d 778 [Ark. 1973].)

3. The plaintiff, a wholesale jeweler, delivered two diamonds to the defendant, a retail jeweler, so that the defendant could display the diamonds and attempt to sell them for the plaintiff. Some ten days after the defendant received the diamonds, they were stolen from his store. There was no showing of any fault on the part of the defendant for the theft of the diamonds. Is the defendant liable to the plaintiff for the value of the diamonds stolen from the store? On what legal theory would you decide the question? (*Harold Klein & Co., Inc.* v. *Lapardo,* 308 A.2d 538 [N.H. 1973].)

4. Scampoli purchased a new color television set from Wilson, paying cash for the purchase. Wilson guaranteed ninety days free service and a one-year warranty on all parts. The set was delivered to Scampoli, but when it was turned on it did not perform properly. The delivery man promised to send a repairman to correct the problem. Two days later a service representative arrived and attempted to correct the problem. After working on the set for some time, the service representative told the buyer he would have to take the set back to the shop to adjust it properly. The buyer refused to allow the removal of the set for repair, insisting that she was entitled to a "new" set and not one that had been "repaired." The buyer retained the set but demanded a refund of the purchase price. Can the dealer properly perform this contract by making adjustments or minor repairs, or must he substitute a new television for the one delivered? Explain fully. (*Wilson* v. *Scampoli,* 228 A.2d 848 [D.C. App. 1967].)

5. In January, the Murrays bought a motor home from Holiday Rambler, paying $11,000 for it. From the very beginning, the Murrays had problems with the motor home, and by July it had been returned to Holiday Rambler for repairs and adjustments nine times. Holiday Rambler paid for all of these repairs and adjustments. In July, the Murrays took a trip in the motor home in which they encountered numerous difficulties. The motor home stalled while climbing a mountain, the brakes failed while descending a mountain, the electric system caught on fire, and gas fumes became so bad the Murrays were forced to evacuate the vehicle. Despite all these problems, the Murrays managed to get the motor home back to their home and then back to the dealer. Holiday Rambler offered to provide additional free repairs, but the Murrays declined, and instead demanded a rescission of the contract. Does Holiday Rambler have the right to cure the defects in this situation, or can the Murrays revoke their acceptance of the product? (*Murray* v. *Holiday Rambler, Inc.,* 265 N.W.2d 513 [Wis. 1978].)

6. Lumber Sales contracted to deliver five boxcars of lumber to Brown. Brown admitted receiving four carloads but denied receiving the fifth and refused to pay for the fifth carload of lumber. The evidence established that the fifth boxcar was delivered to the railroad siding as called for in the contract but that the lumber was apparently stolen from the car before Brown inspected it or took possession of it. Under these circumstances, who should bear the risk of loss? (*Lumber Sales, Inc.* v. *Brown,* 469 S.W.2d 888 [Tenn. 1971].)

7. Farm Supply delivered a tractor and a plow to Crosby on a sale on approval contract. Crosby used the tractor and plow in a reasonable and proper manner for nearly eight weeks. At that time a representative of Farm Supply asked when Crosby would pay for the tractor, and Crosby replied that he had no money at the time but was expecting some income shortly. The tractor and plow were destroyed in a fire a short time later. Crosby alleges that he never "approved" the sale and is thus not liable for the value of the equipment. What result should occur? (*Lane Farm Supply, Inc.* v. *Crosby,* 243 N.Y.S.2d 725 [1963].)

8. Karinol entered into a contract with Pestana that called for Karinol to send a shipment of watches to Pestana. There were no provisions in this contract for allocating the risk of loss, and no standard shipping terms were used in the agreement. Karinol made appropriate arrangements for sending the goods to Pestana, delivered the goods to the carrier, and notified Pestana that the goods were en route. Unfortunately, the goods never arrived at the Pestana warehouse. Each party asserts that the other party had risk of loss in this contract. Which party should bear the risk of loss and why? (*Pestana* v. *Karinol Corp.,* 367 So.2d 1096 [Fla. 1979].)

9. Brown agreed to sell Price two barges of coal. The coal was tendered to Price at Mining City, as per the contract. Price then transported the coal to Bowling Green as was his custom. Brown was never paid for the coal, and he sued Price for the contract amount. Price contended that since he never inspected the coal, he never accepted it, and that since he never accepted it he was not liable for the contract price. What result should occur in this case? (*Brown* v. *Price,* 268 S.W. 590 [Ky. 1925].)

10. Smith bought a new Chevrolet from the local Chevrolet dealer. While driving the new automobile home, it broke down owing to mechanical failure. Smith thereupon notified the dealer that he was cancelling the contract and stopped payment on the check he had issued to pay for the auto. The Chevrolet dealer argues that he had the right to cure the defective performance and that Smith acted improperly. Which party should prevail and why? (*Zabriskie Chevrolet, Inc.* v. *Smith,* 240 A.2d 195 [N.J. 1968].)

CHAPTER 20

Title, Risk of Loss, and Bulk Sales

TITLE TO GOODS

When the term *title* is used, it refers to *legal ownership*. The legal owner of goods is said to have title. When goods are sold, title passes from the seller to the buyer. Title is a very important concept, but in some respects it is not as important today as it was in the past.

Historic Importance

Under common law, title was of paramount importance. Nearly all aspects of the contract hinged on title and its location. Risk of loss was placed on the party having title. The outcome of many lawsuits depended on who had title, so the courts spent a great deal of time and energy on this issue.

Modern Rule

The UCC specifically states that all the rights, duties, and remedies of any party apply without regard to title unless title is specifically required.[1] However, in recognition of the importance of title, some provisions have been made to help in locating title in the sale of goods.

Under the Code, title passes from the seller to the buyer when the seller completes performance of *delivery*. Thus, the type of delivery contract becomes important in determining which party has title. If the delivery contract is a

---

[1] Uniform Commercial Code, Section 2–401.

345

Reservation of title An attempt by the seller to retain title until such time as the buyer has fully performed the contract; a denial by the seller that the buyer owns the goods

shipment contract, title passes to the buyer at the time and place of shipment. If the contract is a destination contract, title passes to the buyer when delivery is tendered at the destination. These rules apply even though the seller may claim to have "reserved title." The Code states that a **reservation of title** is, in reality, only the reservation of a security interest.

In the following case, the seller claimed to retain title to the goods. When the buyer subsequently resold the goods, the seller brought criminal charges against the buyer. Notice how the court used the UCC to resolve the criminal case.

Commonwealth v. Jett
326 A.2d 508 (Pa. 1974)

FACTS　　The Jetts purchased an organ from Menchey Music. The organ was delivered to the Jetts, but Menchey claimed that it "retained title" until the installment sales contract had been fully paid. The Jetts made several payments on the contract, and then defaulted in their payments. Menchey tried on several occasions to collect the payments that had been missed, and finally obtained a writ of replevin in order to recover the organ. Unfortunately, when the writ was served, it was discovered that the Jetts had sold the organ. Menchey then brought criminal charges against the Jetts for fraudulent conversion of its (Menchey's) property, the organ.

ISSUE　　Did Menchey Music have title to the organ at the time the Jetts sold it, so that the sale represented a criminal conversion?

HOLDING　　No. Under the provisions of the UCC, title had passed to the Jetts so that their sale of the organ was not criminal.

REASONING　　Even though this was a criminal case, its resolution depended on the commercial law that controlled the transaction, the UCC. Article 2 permits the parties to choose the time and the manner in which title will vest in the buyer, but such a choice requires explicit agreement. If the parties do not explicitly agree, title will pass as provided in Section 2–401. A seller is not permitted to retain title in an installment sales contract because such a retention would negate the provisions of Article 9 on Secured Transactions. In order to carry out the policies of the UCC, an attempt to reserve or retain title by the seller must be treated as a reservation of a security interest. Thus, title had passed to the Jetts, and since the Jetts had title at the time they sold the organ, they could not have committed a fraudulent conversion.

In some sales contracts, the goods are *not to be delivered.* Again, the Code specifies how title is to pass. If the goods are not to be moved and the seller is to deliver a document of title, title passes when and where the document is given to the buyer. If no documents are to be delivered, title passes at the time and place the contract is made.

Of course, under any set of circumstances, title cannot pass unless the goods are in *existence* and *identified* to the contract. The existence of the goods presents no problem: either the goods exist or they do not exist. However, identification can present a problem. Goods are identified to a contract when they are shipped, marked, or otherwise designated by the seller as the goods that will satisfy the contract.[2]

Occasionally title will pass from the buyer back to the seller. If the buyer *rejects* the goods, or refuses to accept, receive, or retain them, title **revests** in (passes back to) the seller.[3] This is true even if the buyer is acting improperly by refusing the goods. Likewise, if the buyer properly revokes an acceptance, title revests in the seller.

Revests Is vested again; is acquired a second time

The location of title is still important in the area of *creditor rights*. A creditor of one of the parties may be able to **attach** any goods that belong to that party. Thus, creditors are very anxious to know where title lies. This also helps to explain the UCC's treatment of consignments, discussed in Chapter 19. The Code is very careful in spelling out the rights of each party when creditors are involved. Section 2–402 deals with the rights of creditors of the seller when goods are sold. The rights of an **unsecured creditor** of the seller are limited by the rights of the buyer to recover the goods once the goods are identified to the contract. In a legal tug-of-war between the buyer and a creditor of the seller, the buyer will normally win if the goods have been identified as the goods covered by the sales contract.

Attach To tie, bind, fasten, or connect; to seize property under court order

Unsecured creditor A general creditor; a creditor whose claim is not "covered" by collateral

Another problem arises when, as sometimes happens, the seller "sells" goods but *retains possession.* In such a case, the seller's creditors can treat the sale as *void* if the retention by the seller is fraudulent under state law. The seller's only defense is that of being a merchant who retained the goods in good faith in the ordinary course of business for a commercially reasonable time. Thus, a seller who holds identified goods in "lay-away" would have a valid defense to the fraudulent retention charge. But a seller who holds the goods without a valid reason could be in trouble.

The following hypothetical case illustrates a fraudulent retention by the seller.

John, a blacksmith deeply in debt, feared his creditors would sue him and take his equipment to pay the debts. To prevent this, he "sold" his equipment to Lil, who let John retain possession of "her" equipment. When John's creditors tried to attach the

---

[2] Ibid., Section 2–501(1)(b).
[3] Ibid., Section 2–401(4).

equipment to satisfy the debts, John denied he owned it. He produced the bill of sale as proof. The sale would be fraudulent since John retained the goods after the sale in bad faith. The creditors could thus treat the sale as void and attach the equipment.

Conclusive presumption An inference of the truth or the falsity of a fact from which a result *must* follow as a matter of law

Different states treat the issue of fraudulent retention differently. There are three possible rules. Some states say that such a retention is a **conclusive presumption** of fraud; the seller automatically loses. Other states say such a retention is prima facie proof of fraud; the seller loses unless able to show good cause for the retention. In yet other states, the retention is just one bit of evidence to be viewed along with all other evidence in deciding whether a fraud occurred.

Entrustment The delivery of goods to a merchant in goods of that type

The issue of **entrustment** can also present problems regarding title.[4] A purchaser of goods has the power to transfer any rights to the goods that his or her transferor had; in addition, a person who has a *voidable* title can transfer full and valid title to a good-faith purchaser for value (of course, that person has to make such a transfer before the voidable title is avoided). But sometimes the seller may not have purchased the goods. Even then, the seller may be able to transfer good title: if the seller is a merchant who regularly deals in the type of goods that the owner has entrusted to him, the merchant can transfer good title to those goods to a buyer in the ordinary course of business. Of course, the entruster does have remedies against the merchant to whom the goods were entrusted. The following two examples show the difference between an entrustment and a mere **bailment.**

Bailment The transfer of the possession of goods with the understanding that the goods will be returned later

---

Betty took her watch to Roger's Jewelry to have it repaired. Roger's sells new and used watches in its normal business dealings. If a customer comes into the store and "purchases" Betty's watch, that customer will own the watch. Betty's only recourse will be to sue Roger's for her loss. By entrusting the watch to Roger's, she gave Roger's the legal power to transfer good title.

Roger took his watch to Betty's Radio Shop to have it repaired. Although Betty's does not deal in watches, Betty sometimes repairs watches for her friends, and she agrees to do this for Roger. If a customer comes into Betty's and "purchases" Roger's watch, Roger can recover the watch from the customer. Since Betty does not deal in watches, the transaction with Roger was not an entrustment, and Betty's could not legally transfer title to the customer.

---

[4] Ibid., Section 2–403.

The following case deals with the issue of entrustment of goods to a merchant and also with the requirement that the buyer of the entrusted goods must act in good faith in the ordinary course of business in order to acquire good title.

Mattek v. Malofsky
165 N.W.2d 406 (Wis. 1969)

FACTS

Frakes, an automobile dealer, was in lawful possession of an automobile that had been entrusted to him by Mattek, the owner. Malofsky, another automobile dealer, purchased the car in question from Frakes without the knowledge or the consent of Mattek. Mattek sued Malofsky to recover the car, and Malofsky raised the defense of having obtained good title from Frakes.

ISSUE

Does Malofsky qualify as a buyer of an entrusted item in the ordinary course of business and thus possess good title?

HOLDING

No. Malofsky was not a buyer in the ordinary course of business and therefore did not acquire good title to the car.

REASONING

Although the dealing between Mattek and Frakes qualified as an entrustment, giving Frakes voidable title, the sale to Malofsky did not qualify as a sale in the ordinary course of business. As a merchant, Malofsky was aware that Frakes was required by law to provide a certificate of title to the buyer (Malofsky) at the time of the sale. When Frakes did not provide such a certificate of title, Malofsky was on notice of an irregularity in the sale, and his failure to procure such a certificate was unreasonable as a matter of law. This set of circumstances removes the sale from the ordinary course of business and thus defeats the alleged title of Malofsky.

Insurable Interest

The term *insurable interest* refers to *the right to purchase insurance on goods to protect one's property rights and interests in the goods.*[5] The buyer gains an insurable interest when existing goods are identified to the contract even if the goods are nonconforming. If the goods are not identified, the buyer gains an insurable interest once identification occurs. Likewise, if the goods are not yet in existence, the buyer gains an insurable interest as soon as the goods come into existence.

The seller has an insurable interest in the goods for as long as the seller retains title or any security interest in the goods; and either party has an

[5] Ibid., Section 2–501.

Figure 20.1 The Movement of Risk of Loss and Title

Form of Delivery	Circumstances in Which Title Passes to Buyer (Section 2–401)	Circumstances in Which Risk of Loss Shifts to Buyer (Section 2–509)
1. Delivery by carrier		
a. With shipment contract	At the time and place of shipment	When carrier receives the goods
b. With destination contract	Upon tender of delivery	When delivery is tendered at destination
2. Delivery by warehouseman		
a. Via negotiable document of title	Upon delivery of document to buyer	When buyer receives the document
b. Via nonnegotiable document of title	Upon delivery of document to buyer	After the buyer has a reasonable time to notify the bailee
c. With no document of title	At the time and place of contract	Upon bailee's acknowledgment of buyer's right to goods
3. Personal delivery		
a. By merchant seller	At the time and place of contract	Upon delivery of goods to buyer
b. By nonmerchant seller	At the time and place of contract	Upon tender of goods to buyer

insurable interest if that party also has a risk of loss. Notice that title is not necessary for an insurable interest to exist.

Figure 20.1 outlines the circumstances in which title and risk of loss are transferred from the seller to the buyer in the different types of sales contracts we have discussed. We will take up the subject of risk of loss in the next section.

RISK OF LOSS

The term *risk of loss* refers to *the financial responsibility between the parties if the goods are lost, damaged, or destroyed before the buyer has accepted them.* Notice that risk of loss refers to the relationship between the *buyer* and the *seller*. It does not refer to the possibility that an independent carrier of the goods may be liable. Nor does it refer to the possible liability of any insurer of the goods or of their delivery. The allocation of risk of loss often depends on the method of the performance.

A buyer who has risk of loss must pay the seller for the goods if the goods were properly shipped. This situation arises most commonly in a shipment contract: if the seller shipped conforming goods, but during the journey the goods were damaged, destroyed, or lost, the buyer is liable and must perform the contract as agreed. Of course, the buyer may have recourse against the carrier or against an insurer for the loss, but such recourse involves a separate contract or relationship.

If the contract involved is a destination contract, the seller bears the risk of loss. In this situation, any lost, damaged, or destroyed goods are the responsibility of the seller. The seller will be required to ship more goods or to make up the loss to the buyer in some other manner. And the seller will then have to proceed against the carrier or the insurer for any remedies that may be available.

In the following case, the court found that a shipment contract was involved, so risk of loss had passed to the buyer when the carrier received the goods from the seller.

Ninth Street East, Ltd. v. Harrison
5 Conn. Cir. 597, 259 A.2d 772 (1968)

Harrison ordered clothes from Ninth Street East in November 1966. Ninth Street East delivered the goods to a common carrier in Los Angeles, forwarding the invoices to Harrison at his store in Connecticut. The invoices all read "F.O.B. Los Angeles" and all stated: "Goods Shipped at Purchaser's Risk." The shipments were made collect. The carrier attempted to deliver the goods at Harrison's store on 12 December 1966. The store manager demanded that the goods be delivered inside the store. The carrier refused to do so. Harrison objected to Ninth Street East. During the controversy, the goods were lost by the carrier. Ninth Street East sued Harrison for the goods.

FACTS

Who had risk of loss on this shipment of goods?

ISSUE

Harrison. The delivery was a shipment contract.

HOLDING

The use of the term *F.O.B. Los Angeles* was a controlling factor on risk of loss. Title to the goods and risk of loss passed to Harrison when Ninth Street East gave the carrier possession in Los Angeles. The controversy about delivery was between Harrison and the carrier and has no effect on the rights of the seller to collect.

REASONING

Notice that in the preceding case, a shipment contract was *specified*. In the next case, a shipment contract was *presumed*. Any time a destination contract is not specified, the court treats the contract as a shipment contract.

Dana Debs, Inc. v. Lady Rose Stores, Inc.
319 N.Y.S.2d 111 (1971)

FACTS   Lady Rose sent a written order to Dana Debs for the purchase of 288 garments. The purchase order called for Dana Debs to "ship via Stuart, 453 W. 57th St." Stuart picked up the goods and gave Dana Debs a receipt for the merchandise. Four days later, Stuart informed Dana Debs that it (Stuart) had lost the entire shipment. Dana Debs then informed Lady Rose of the loss and sent Lady Rose a bill for the goods.

ISSUE   Which party had the risk of loss when the goods were lost by Stuart?

HOLDING   Lady Rose had the risk of loss and must pay for the shipment.

REASONING   The carrier arrangements established a shipment contract. Dana Debs was instructed to "ship via Stuart." Once Stuart took possession of the goods, Dana Debs had done everything called for in the contract, and the title and risk of loss had passed to Lady Rose Stores.

In contracts that do not involve the use of an independent carrier, the risk of loss will frequently depend on how adequately the parties have performed. Several possibilities are explored next.

Breach of Contract

If the seller breaches the contract by sending nonconforming goods, risk of loss remains with the seller until either the seller cures the defect or the buyer accepts the goods despite the nonconformity.[6] In order for this provision to apply, the goods must be so nonconforming that the buyer may properly reject the tender of delivery.

Sometimes the buyer accepts the goods that the seller sent but later finds them to be nonconforming. When this occurs, the buyer often has the right to revoke acceptance (see Chapter 22). When accepting the goods, the buyer assumed risk of loss. When the nonconformity is discovered and the acceptance is revoked, what happens? The buyer retains risk of loss, *but only to the extent* of the buyer's insurance coverage. Any loss in excess of the insurance rests on the seller.

Repudiation Rejection of an offered or available right or privilege, or of a duty or relation

Sometimes the buyer breaches a contract, usually by **repudiation,** after the goods are identified but before they are delivered. In such a case, risk of loss has not yet shifted from the seller to the buyer. As a result, the risk still rests on the seller. However, since the buyer is in breach, any loss in excess of the

---

[6] Ibid., Section 2–510.

seller's insurance coverage rests on the buyer. Of course, the buyer will face this possible loss only for a commercially reasonable time.

If the contract is *not* breached, risk of loss is much more technical. It is difficult to determine where risk of loss resides until the entire contract is reviewed. The UCC recognizes four distinct contract possibilities to allocate risk of loss when the contract has not been breached.[7] In addition, the parties can by contract agree to allocate the risk.

No Breach of Contract

The first situation arises in a contract whereby the seller sends the goods by means of a *carrier*. If the goods are sent by means of a *shipment* contract, risk of loss passes to the buyer when the goods are delivered to the carrier. This is true even if the seller reserves rights in the goods pending payment.

In contrast, the seller may enter into a *destination* contract with the carrier. Risk of loss then does not pass to the buyer until the goods are properly tendered at the point of destination. Once the goods are made available to the buyer, the buyer has risk of loss.

The second situation arises when the goods are in the hands of a *bailee* and they are not to be physically delivered. When the bailee is holding the goods, the contract must be very carefully analyzed. The contract may call for the seller to deliver a negotiable document of title to the buyer. If so, risk of loss passes when the buyer receives the document from the seller. If the seller is not to use a negotiable document of title but does use a nonnegotiable document, risk of loss passes only after the buyer has a reasonable opportunity to present the document to the bailee. And sometimes no document at all is used. In such cases, risk of loss passes to the buyer when the bailee acknowledges the rights of the buyer in the goods.

The third situation arises when the goods are in the possession of the *seller* and a carrier is not to be used. Under these circumstances, the *status* of the seller is the key. If the seller is a merchant, risk of loss does not pass to the buyer until the buyer takes possession of the goods. If the seller is not a merchant, risk of loss passes upon *tender* of delivery to the buyer. The following two examples show how risk of loss varies with the status of the seller.

Joan is a used car dealer. She enters a contract with Bob to sell him a car. She tells Bob that the keys are in the car and to go pick it up at any time. Before Bob gets there, the car is destroyed by a fire. Since Joan is a merchant, she still has risk of loss. She will have to provide Bob with another car or refund his money.

Jack is *not* a car dealer of any sort. He enters a contract to sell his car to Marie. He tells her the keys are in the car, and she can pick it up at any time. This is a tender of delivery.

---

[7] Ibid., Section 2–509.

Before Marie gets the car, it is destroyed by a fire. She must bear the loss since Jack was a nonmerchant.

The fourth set of circumstances applies to a *sale on approval.* Here risk of loss remains with the seller until the buyer accepts the goods by approval of the sale. Of course, the various ways the buyer can "accept" should be kept in mind.

Finally, the parties can *agree* to allocate risk of loss in any way they wish. Risk of loss can be divided in any manner the parties feel is proper. Such an agreement must be very explicit or else the Code provisions just discussed will be applied.

BULK SALES

A few years ago, some owners of troubled businesses began following a questionable business practice. Finding themselves in a bind, with business off, assets depleted, and their creditors demanding payment, these owners elected to take a less than ethical way out of their dilemma. They sold their businesses — lock, stock, and barrel — for cash and disappeared before their creditors knew what had happened. Faced with a new owner, an unsecured creditor could not assert a claim against the business assets.

In an effort to prevent such occurrences, the drafters of the UCC included Article 6, "Bulk Transfers." Article 6 outlines the only proper and protected method for selling businesses that fall under its coverage. A failure to follow the rules may result in some very substantial losses for the buyer.

Article 6 begins its coverage by defining a *bulk transfer* as "any transfer in bulk and not in the ordinary course of the transferor's business of a major part of the materials, supplies, merchandise or other inventory."[8] In addition, if the seller transfers a *substantial* part of the equipment in connection with a bulk transfer of inventory, the equipment is also part of the bulk transfer and is thus covered by Article 6.[9] Finally, Article 6 is restricted in coverage to businesses that have the sale of merchandise from stock as their principal business function. Service enterprises such as a barber shop are not covered; however, a bakery would be covered.

Notice that no figures are used in the "definitions." A *major part* of the materials, supplies, or merchandise probably means *over half,* and a *substantial part* of the equipment probably means *less than half.* The final determination lies with the courts. The absence of an absolute figure allows a case-by-case analysis, but, more important, it does not leave the room for maneuvering that a definitely stated percentage would. Any businessperson in doubt as to whether the sale is a bulk transfer would be well advised to comply with Article 6.

[8] Ibid., Section 6–102(1).
[9] Ibid., Section 6–102(2).

If the sale is a bulk transfer, the buyer and the seller need to show they have taken four separate steps. If these steps are properly taken, the buyer obtains the goods free of any claims by the seller's creditors. If the parties fail to properly satisfy any step, the seller's creditors may assert their claims against the *buyer* as well as the seller.

The first step is taken by the seller. The seller must prepare a list of creditors, in writing and under oath. The list must include the name and address of every creditor and the amount of each creditor's claim. The *seller* is responsible for the accuracy of this list. Any errors or omissions cannot be held against the buyer unless the buyer knew of the error and ignored it.[10]

The second step is taken by both the buyer and the seller. The two parties must prepare a list of all items being transferred. The list must include sufficient identification to inform an interested party of what was sold. The buyer must retain the property list and the list of creditors for six months following the sale or must file them with a designated public office.[11]

The third step is taken by the buyer. The buyer must notify every creditor on the creditor list of the sale and when it will occur. This notice must be given at least ten days before the buyer pays for the goods *or* receives them, whichever happens first. Any creditor who is on the list and who is not notified may ignore the sale and proceed against the goods even after the sale. This rule does not apply if the bulk transfer is made by auction.[12]

The fourth step is also taken by the buyer. The buyer is responsible for seeing that the payments that he or she makes are applied to the seller's debts. It is the duty of the buyer to distribute the money to the listed creditors first, with any surplus going to the seller. And if the money will not cover all the debts, the buyer must pay the creditors **pro rata**.[13]

Pro rata Proportionately; according to percentages

These steps seem to impose a heavy duty on the buyer, but the rationale underlying them is one of public policy: the buyer of a business or its assets should know that the seller has debts, and the buyer is thus in a position to prevent losses by the creditor; the creditor is seldom in the same position; and the seller cannot always be trusted to perform properly. However, the law does protect a buyer who follows the rules, as the next case illustrates.

Adrian Tabin Corp. v. *Climax Boutique, Inc.*
338 N.Y.S.2d 59 (Sup. Ct. N.Y. 1972)

L.D.J. Dresses made a bulk sale of its business to Climax Boutique through Paul Warman, a principal in Climax Boutique. L.D.J. Dresses provided an **affidavit** to

FACTS

[10] Ibid., Section 6–104(2), (3).
[11] Ibid., Section 6–103.
[12] Ibid., Section 6–105.
[13] Ibid., Section 6–106.

Affidavit A written statement made under oath

the buyers that it had no debts and that there were no creditors. The buyers ran a lien search and discovered no liens outstanding against L.D.J. At the time of the bulk sale, Adrian Tabin Corp. was a creditor of L.D.J. Adrian Tabin claimed that since it was not notified of the sale, the sale was void as to its claim.

ISSUE

Is the claim of the creditor valid against a buyer in bulk who was unaware of the creditor?

HOLDING

No. The good faith of the buyer in bulk cuts off the claim of the creditor.

REASONING

The UCC bulk sale provisions place the responsibility for the accuracy of a creditor list on the seller. The buyer is not liable for any errors or omissions on the creditor list unless the buyer *knows* of the error. Here the purchaser had no knowledge of the creditor, and the purchaser had conducted an inquiry. The creditor's claim in the sold assets is cut off.

SUMMARY

In this chapter, we examined the concept and importance of title to goods. Under the UCC, title passes at any time the parties agree. If the parties do not agree, title passes when the seller completes his or her performance. Title can revest in the seller if the buyer refuses to accept the goods, rejects them, or revokes the acceptance. The primary area in which title is important today is that of creditor rights.

The concept of risk of loss is much more important under the Code than it was under common law. Risk of loss refers to the party — buyer or seller — who must bear the burden of lost, damaged, or destroyed goods when the loss occurs during the performance stage of the contract.

A bulk sale is any sale of a major part of the seller's business that is not made in the ordinary course of business. The Code's provisions on bulk sales are designed to protect the seller's creditors.

DISCUSSION QUESTIONS

1. Under the Uniform Commercial Code, when does title pass from the seller to the buyer?

2. What does it mean when the seller "reserves title" to the goods?

3. What is an insurable interest? Can more than one party have an insurable interest in goods?

4. What does the term *risk of loss* mean?

5. In a bulk sale, what are the four steps required under Article 6?

6. George sells some goods to Harry. Harry leaves the goods in George's possession. Some of George's creditors attempt to attach the goods, alleging that the sale is void as far as their rights are concerned since George

retained possession. If George is not a merchant, what should the result be?

7. Harvey takes his watch to Ralph's Repair Shop and asks Ralph to fix it. Ralph repairs all sorts of things but does not sell anything regularly. One of Ralph's employees sells Harvey's watch to a customer. What should Harvey do?

8. Scott shipped nonconforming goods to Ellen under a sales contract. The goods were shipped under a shipment contract. When the goods arrived, they had been damaged. Who bears the risk of loss, and why?

9. Jim, a merchant, sold goods to Dennis. Dennis was to pick them up later that day. When Dennis arrived to pick up the goods, he discovered they were damaged. Jim insisted that since Dennis had paid for them, they were his. Was Jim correct or not? Explain.

10. Acme's owner has decided to go out of business. He has offered to sell all of his inventory and equipment to Stan if Stan will pay cash. Stan suspects that Acme is in financial trouble, and he asks you what he should do to protect himself. What advice would you give?

CASE PROBLEMS

1. Bowman purchased a Cessna airplane in 1969. He purchased an insurance policy on the plane from American Home Assurance, with the policy to run from 23 December 1969 through 23 December 1970. On 12 December 1970, Bowman agreed to sell the airplane to Hemmer. The plane was destroyed before Hemmer took possession. Bowman submitted a claim to his insurance company, but they denied liability, alleging that Bowman had no insurable interest in the plane as of 12 December 1970. Bowman sued American Home Assurance. What should the result be? (*Bowman* v. *American Home Assurance Co.,* 213 N.W.2d 446 [Neb. 1973].)

2. Medico owned a used Buick. It delivered the car to Smith, a used car dealer, so that Smith could sell it. Smith sold the car to Wessel Buick. Wessel Buick sold it to Country Cousin Motors. Country Cousin sold the car to Carter. Smith never paid Medico for the car. Medico sued Carter to recover the car. Who should prevail? (*Medico Leasing Co.* v. *Smith,* 457 P.2d 548 [Okla. 1969].)

3. Ramos purchased a new motorcycle from Wheel Sports, paying the full purchase price. Ramos received all the necessary papers to register and insure the motorcycle. However, Ramos left the motorcycle with Wheel Sports until he returned from his vacation. While Ramos was on vacation, the motorcycle was stolen from Wheel Sports. Who must bear the risk of loss? (*Ramos* v. *Wheel Sports Center,* 409 N.Y.S.2d 505 [1978].)

4. Martin agreed to purchase a truck and a haystack mover from Melland's, trading in his old truck and haystack mover as part of the deal. Martin transferred the title on the trade-in to Melland immediately but retained

possession and continued to use the old truck and mover until the new ones were ready. While Martin was still using his old truck and haystack mover, they were destroyed by a fire. Who must bear the risk of loss? (*Martin v. Melland's, Inc.,* 283 N.W.2d 76 [N.D. 1979].)

5. Halifax was a licensed loan company. It borrowed money from several sources and then loaned those funds to its customers. Halifax sold its business to Credithrift and used the proceeds of the sale to repay Commercial Bank, one of its creditors. No notice of the sale, nor any proceeds from the sale, were given to Guggenheim, another creditor of Halifax. Halifax is not available, and Guggenheim has sued Credithrift for the amount owed by Halifax, alleging that the sale was made in violation of the Bulk Sales Act so that the buyer is liable for the preexisting debts of the bulk seller. Who should prevail? (*Credithrift Financial Corporation v. Guggenheim,* 232 So.2d 400 [Fla. 1970].)

6. Chatham agreed to buy a boat from Clark and paid the full purchase price for the boat. When Chatham went to take delivery of the boat from Clark there was a storm, and delivery could not be made. When Chatham later returned for the boat, he was informed by Clark that his boat had sunk. Chatham has sued for damages, alleging that there was not identification of the boat that he had purchased and that therefore neither title nor risk of loss ever passed to him. Assuming that Chatham is correct in his assertion regarding identification, what result should occur? (*Chatham v. Clark's Food Fair, Inc.,* 127 S.E.2d 868 [Ga. 1962].)

7. Brooks was a judgment creditor of Lambert. Lambert entered into a contract with Weinberg that transferred the personal property, equipment, and fixtures — but not the liquor license — of the Delaware Athletic Club. Brooks is seeking to set aside the sale from Lambert to Weinberg on the ground that the sale was not made in accordance with the Bulk Sales provisions of the UCC. Should the sale be treated as a Bulk Sale, or was the sale made properly without regard to the Bulk Sales Act? (*Brooks v. Lambert,* 10 D.&C.2d 237 [Pa. 1957].)

8. Eberhard and Brown entered into a contract for the sale of goods. The contract called for Eberhard to "ship the goods to" Brown's location. Nearly 10 percent of the goods were apparently lost in transit, and Brown refused to accept or pay for the shipment as it arrived. Eberhard has sued for the contract price, and Brown has countersued for losses owing to a breach of contract. Which party should bear the risk of loss in this contract and thus should lose the lawsuit? (*Eberhard Manufacturing Company v. Brown,* 232 N.W.2d 378 [Mich. 1975].)

9. Hayward entered into a contract to purchase a boat from Postma. By the terms of the contract, Postma was to receive the boat from the manufacturer, install a number of options, and deliver the boat to Lake Macatawa. Hayward issued a promissory note to Postma to pay for the boat, and granted Postma a security interest in the boat. One clause of the security

agreement called for Hayward to maintain adequate insurance on the boat. After Postma received the boat from the manufacturer, but before the boat had been delivered to the Lake, a fire at Postma's destroyed the boat. Hayward asked Postma to pay off the note covering the boat, and Postma refused. Hayward argues that Postma has risk of loss, and Postma argues that Hayward should have been carrying insurance to protect against any loss to the boat. Which party is correct? (*Hayward* v. *Postma*, 188 N.W.2d 31 [Mich. 1971].)

10. LeConte and Silver entered into a contract that called for LeConte to build a sloop for Silver. The sloop was to be constructed in Holland, and then brought to New York for delivery to Silver. The contract included a clause that specified "title to the vessel hereby ordered shall not pass to the purchaser until the entire purchase price and any extra charges have been paid in full . . . and builder has delivered its bill of sale." When LeConte tendered the sloop in New York, a dispute arose as to whether the sloop had been constructed properly. Silver refused to pay the entire price LeConte quoted, LeConte refused to turn over the bill of sale, and Silver sued to obtain possession. Silver alleged that under the UCC, title passed to him when delivery was tendered by LeConte in New York. What result should occur in this case? (*Silver* v. *Sloop Silver Cloud*, 259 F. Supp. 187 [S.D.N.Y. 1966].)

CHAPTER 21

Warranties and Product Liability

THE CONCEPT OF WARRANTIES

Express Actually stated; communicated from one party to the other

Implied Imposed by operation of law; presumed to be present under the circumstances

Statutory Created by statute; imposed by law

A *warranty* is "a promise that a proposition of fact is true."[1] Since a warranty is a promise, it becomes *a part of the contract* in the sale of goods. Warranty protection is very often the best protection that a buyer can have in a sale. Warranties are of three types: **express, implied,** and **statutory.** The fact that one type of warranty is present does not mean that the other types are absent. In fact, all three types may be present in one contract.

At common law, the courts presumed that the parties to a contract had equal bargaining power. They also strongly believed in "freedom of contract." Thus, the courts were reluctant to interfere in the contractual relationship. The rule of *caveat emptor* — let the buyer beware — was regularly followed. As the commercial world matured, the positions of the parties to a sales contract began to change. It became less likely that the parties would truly have equal bargaining power — and less likely that the seller of the goods had also manufactured them. The courts and legislatures began to seek means of protecting the consumer. Implied and statutory warranties and product liability provided

---

[1] *Black's Law Dictionary*, rev. 4th ed., 1968.

those means. The consumer has now become so protected that many people feel the rule is *caveat venditor* — let the seller beware!

An *express warranty* can only be given by the *seller*. Such a warranty is said by the UCC to be a part of "the basis of the bargain." Section 2 – 313 mentions three different ways in which the seller creates an express warranty:

1. Any *affirmation* of a fact or a promise that relates to the goods creates an express warranty that the goods will match the fact or the promise.
2. Any *description* of the goods creates an express warranty that the goods will match the description.
3. Any *sample* or *model* of the goods creates an express warranty that the goods will conform to the sample or the model.

Any of these three methods creates an express warranty if it is "the basis of the bargain." It is not necessary for the seller to use such words as *warrant* or *guarantee.* It is not even necessary for the seller to *intend* to create an express warranty. All that is necessary is that the seller employ one of these methods in a manner that causes the buyer to believe that a warranty is given.

The Uniform Sales Act, which preceded the UCC, required the buyer to show *reliance* before an express warranty was found. The UCC seems to have removed the requirement of proving reliance. Instead, reliance appears to be presumed. The rule under the Code is that the seller must *disprove the existence of an express warranty.* In other words, if the buyer can prove the seller affirmed a fact, described the goods, or used a model or a sample, an express warranty is presumed. To disprove the existence of the warranty, the seller must show proof that the conduct described by the buyer was *not* the basis of the bargain. If such proof cannot be shown, the express warranty will be included in the contract.

Express warranties focus on *facts.* Mere opinions of the seller are not taken to be warranties. The seller is also allowed a certain amount of "puffing." However, there is often a fine line between opinion and fact, and the seller should be extremely careful. If a statement is **quantifiable,** it is likely to be treated as a fact. If the statement is **relative,** it will normally be treated as opinion. Thus, the statement that "this car gets thirty miles per gallon" would normally be treated as a warranty. But "this is a good car" would normally not be a warranty.

The seller also needs to be careful in advertising. Advertisements that depict a product as having certain characteristics may very well be treated by the courts as affirmations of fact and thus as express warranties.

Finally, the Code views the timing of the statement or conduct from the buyer's perspective. Under Section 2 – 209(1), a modification of a sales contract is valid without consideration. This means that the seller can create an express

Quantifiable Capable of exact statement; measurable, normally in numbers

Relative Not capable of exact statement; as compared to some other standard or model or system; also known as comparative

warranty before the contract is formed, while forming the contract, or after the contract is formed.

Sellers would be well advised to remember two things. If they *know* a fact, they should state it honestly. If they do *not* know, they should not speculate! It is too easy to give an express warranty without realizing it.

The following is one of the landmark cases in express warranty law. Notice how the court viewed the relative knowledge of the parties and the special circumstances of the case in reaching its finding of fact.

Wat Henry Pontiac Co. v. Bradley
210 P.2d 348 (Sup. Ct. Okla. 1949)

FACTS　　On 22 October 1944, Mrs. Bradley went to Wat Henry Pontiac to purchase a used car. She dealt with the used car sales manager. Mrs. Bradley testified that she asked many questions, and the seller assured her the car was in good condition. He allegedly said: "This is a car I can recommend," and "It is in A-1 shape." Mrs. Bradley stated that she had to travel to Camp Shelby, Mississippi, with her seven-month-old child to see her husband, and she asked for a test drive. The sales manager replied that the car was mechanically perfect, but that because of gas rationing she could not give it a test drive. She bought the car and drove it home. Several days later, after she had set out for Camp Shelby, the car broke down and required extensive repairs. The sales manager, a former mechanic, testified that he gave no warranties and that he explained to Mrs. Bradley that there were no warranties on the car.

ISSUE　　Did the seller give any express warranties on the car in this sale?

HOLDING　　Yes. Under the circumstances of this case, the seller did give express warranties.

REASONING　　Mrs. Bradley was ignorant of the facts in this case. The defects in the car were hidden, and the buyer was not allowed a test drive. The seller was an expert in automobiles. He had served a long time as a mechanic and so stated to the buyer. His statements as to the condition of the car constituted a warranty and not mere opinion.

IMPLIED WARRANTIES

As pointed out in the preceding section, express warranties are a part of the contract. They are not present unless given by the seller. The court will not find an express warranty unless it is created by the seller as a basis of the bargain. In contrast, *implied warranties are imposed by law.* Implied warranties are present unless voluntarily surrendered by the buyer or excluded by the seller.

The UCC recognizes four possible types of implied warranties: title, infringement, merchantability, and fitness for a particular purpose. Some, all, or none of the warranties may be present in any given contract, depending on the circumstances surrounding the transaction.

Every contract for the sale of goods carries a warranty of title by the seller *unless* such a warranty is excluded by specific language warning the buyer that title is not guaranteed or *unless* the sale is made under circumstances that put the buyer on notice that title is not guaranteed.[2] If neither of these conditions is present, warranty of title exists. A warranty of title ensures the buyer of the following:

Warranty of Title

1. The transfer of the goods is proper.
2. The buyer is receiving good title.
3. The goods are free of hidden security interests, encumbrances, or liens.

In other words, the buyer is assured that no one may assert a claim to the goods superior to that of the buyer.

In the following case, an apparently innocent seller of goods was found to have breached the warranty of title in his sale.

Ricklefs v. *Clemens*
531 P.2d 94 (Kan. 1975)

In March, 1971, Clemens sold a Corvette Stingray to Ricklefs for $1500 plus Ricklefs' 1969 Pontiac trade-in. At the time of the sale, Clemens delivered to Ricklefs a certificate of title for the car. According to the title certificate, the car was a 1969 Corvette, and the title was free of all liens and encumbrances not specifically noted on the certificate. In December, 1971, Ricklefs was informed by an FBI agent that the car was stolen and that if he (Ricklefs) continued to operate the car he was likely to be arrested. Ricklefs subsequently contacted Clemens and demanded restitution.

FACTS

Do the facts show a breach of the implied warranty of title in this case?

ISSUE

Yes. According to the Official Comments of the UCC, a disturbance of quiet possession is one method of establishing a breach of warranty of title.

HOLDING

The warranty of title that a seller gives to a buyer should allow the buyer to rely on the fact that he will not be drawn into any later contests to establish ownership of the goods. Any facts that subsequently come to light that cast a substantial shadow over title are sufficient to constitute a breach of the warranty of title. In this case,

REASONING

[2] Uniform Commercial Code, Section 2–312.

the warning from the FBI agent that Ricklefs might be arrested for the continued operation of the automobile that had allegedly been stolen was sufficient to cast such a shadow over his title, and thus to constitute a breach of the warranty of title. The fact that Clemens may have been innocent of any wrongdoing is irrelevant.

Warranty Against Infringement

A warranty against infringement can be given by either the buyer or the seller, although it is normally given by the seller.[3] No other implied warranty can be given by either party. The *infringement* protected against is the *rightful claim of any third person. Patent* infringement is probably the most common type of problem dealt with under this warranty.

To give this warranty, the seller must be a merchant who regularly deals in the type of goods involved. The buyer who warrants against infringement need not be a merchant. Any buyer who furnishes specifications to the seller for a special manufacture of goods must warrant against infringement if the seller complies with the specifications.

Warranty of Merchantability

Probably the most commonly breached, and the most commonly asserted, implied warranty is the warranty of merchantability. A warranty of merchantability is given whenever a merchant of goods, including a merchant of food or drink, makes a sale. Failure to satisfy any of the following six criteria means that the goods are not merchantable and that the warranty has been breached:[4]

1. Goods must pass without objection in the trade, under the description in the contract.

2. If goods are **fungible,** they must be of fair average quality within the description.

Fungible Virtually identical and interchangeable; not different from other goods of the same description

3. Goods must be suitable for their ordinary purpose and use.

4. Goods must be of even kind, quality, and quantity.

5. Goods must be adequately contained, packaged, and labeled as required under the agreement.

6. Goods must conform to the promises and facts contained on the label, if any.

Under this warranty, merchant sellers have been found liable because of bobby pins in soft drink containers, worms in canned peas, a decomposing mouse in a soda bottle, and a hair dye that caused the buyer's hair to fall out.

Because numerous merchantability cases have involved disputes over food and drink, the courts have developed special rules to determine mer-

---

[3] Ibid., Section 2–312(3).
[4] Ibid., Section 2–314(2).

chantability in these cases. Some states follow the "foreign–natural" test; others follow the "reasonable expectations" test. Under the foreign–natural test, a chicken bone in a chicken salad sandwich would not involve a breach since chicken bones are "natural" to chicken. But a cherry pit in a chicken salad would be "foreign" and thus would establish a breach. Under the reasonable expectations test, the court attempts to establish what a reasonable person would expect to find in the food. Any foreign object would show a breach, but so would some natural objects. Thus, a chicken bone in a chicken salad sandwich might show a breach if it is unreasonable to expect to find a bone in such a sandwich.

The following case illustrates the approach a court might take in a merchantability-of-food case.

Webster v. Blue Ship Tea Room
347 Mass. 421, 198 N.E.2d 309 (1964)

Webster ordered a cup of fish chowder at the Blue Ship Tea Room. As she was eating the chowder, a fish bone became lodged in her throat. She underwent two esophagoscopies at Massachusetts General Hospital because of the presence of the bone in her throat. **FACTS**

Did the fish bone in the chowder constitute a breach of the warranty of merchantability? **ISSUE**

No. The fish chowder as served was fit to be eaten and merchantable. **HOLDING**

A person eating fish chowder in Massachusetts must expect to encounter some fish bones. The court felt that both the foreign-natural test and the reasonable expectations test would yield the same result. **REASONING**

Any seller, whether a merchant or a nonmerchant, may give the implied warranty of fitness for a particular purpose. In order for this warranty to come into existence, the following conditions must be present:[5]

Warranty of Fitness for a Particular Purpose

1. The seller must know that the buyer is contemplating a particular use for the goods.
2. The seller must know that the buyer is relying on the seller's skill, judgment, or knowledge in selecting the proper goods for the purpose.

[5] Ibid., Section 2–315.

3. The buyer must not restrict the seller's range of choices to a particular brand or price range or otherwise limit the scope of the seller's expert judgment.

Notice that the warranty here is for a *particular* purpose. Also note that merchantability covers *normal* purpose or use. Thus, even if the warranty of fitness for a particular purpose is not found, the warranty of merchantability will normally be available to protect the buyer. However, if the seller is not a merchant, the buyer may have to prove the warranty of fitness for a particular purpose in order to have any implied warranty protection.

Occasionally a case will involve allegations that the warranties of merchantability and fitness for a particular purpose have both been breached. With the courts' growing tendency to protect the buyer, the seller in such a case is quite likely to lose on at least one of the warranties. And the seller may lose on both counts, as the seller in the following case discovered.

Vlases v. *Montgomery Ward & Co.*
377 F.2d 846 (3d Cir. 1967)

FACTS   Vlases purchased 2000 chickens from Montgomery Ward to start a chicken business. After receiving the birds, Vlases discovered that they were afflicted with avian leukosis, a bird cancer. Vlases sued Montgomery Ward for breach of its implied warranties of merchantability and fitness for a particular purpose. Montgomery Ward claimed that the disease is not detectable in baby chicks, and that the chickens could have become ill after the sale.

ISSUE   Did this sale violate the implied warranties of merchantability and fitness for a particular purpose?

HOLDING   Yes. The seller is responsible for breach of warranty when inferior goods are sold.

REASONING   The purpose of implied warranties is to make the seller responsible for selling inferior goods. That the defect was difficult to discover is not an adequate defense. The law does not care what precautions the seller took. The issue is merely the quality of the goods provided to the buyer. The quality was inferior. No exclusions of the warranties were present. The warranties were therefore breached.

STATUTORY WARRANTIES   Before 1975, many consumers faced certain problems in the area of warranty law: many manufacturers disclaimed warranty protection, leaving the consumer with little or no protection; and most manufacturers put the warranty terms inside a sealed package so the consumer did not know what warranty provisions were involved until after the sale. As a result of these problems, the Magnuson-Moss Act – Consumer Product Warranty Act became law in 1975.[6] This law covers any consumer good manufactured after 3 January 1975. The manufacturer must provide the consumer with presale warranty information. The manufacturer should also set up informal settlement procedures to benefit the consumer.

The manufacturer does not have to give any express warranties. However, according to the law, a manufacturer who does give a warranty must designate it as either *full* or *limited.* To qualify as a full warranty, the warranty must meet at least four requirements:

1. It must warrant that defects will be remedied within a reasonable time.

2. It must conspicuously display any exclusions or limitations of consequential damages.

3. An implied warranty must not be limited in time.

4. It must warrant that if attempts to remedy defects fail, the consumer will be allowed to select either a refund or a replacement.

Any warranty that is not full is limited. In a limited warranty, implied warranties may be limited to a reasonable time.

WARRANTY EXCLUSIONS

The seller can modify or exclude warranties. The simplest way to exclude an *express* warranty is not to give one. If the seller is careful, no express warranties will exist. Sometimes a seller will create an express warranty orally but will attempt to exclude any express warranties in writing. In this case, the court will turn to UCC Section 2 – 316(1). The court will take the warranty and the exclusion as consistent with one another if possible; otherwise, the warranty will stand.

Excluding or modifying *implied* warranties is not so easy. To exclude or modify a warranty of mechantability, either orally or in writing, the word *merchantability* must be used. If the exclusion is written, the exclusion must be conspicuous. To exclude or modify a warranty of fitness for a particular purpose, the exclusion must be written, and it must be conspicuous; no oral exclusions of fitness are allowed.[7]

Under Section 2 – 316(3), it is possible to exclude all implied warranties under three sets of circumstances:

1. If language such as "as is" or "with all faults" is used properly so that the buyer is duly informed that no implied warranties are given.

2. If the buyer has thoroughly examined the goods or has refused to examine

6 15 USCA, Sections 2301 – 2312.
7 UCC, Section 2 – 316(2).

them before the sale, no implied warranty is given for defects that the examination should have revealed.

3.   Under course of dealings, course of performance, or usage of trade, implied warranties are not given as a matter of common practice.

In the following case, the court was faced with the question of whether a written disclaimer of warranty was properly given so that the buyer was aware of the disclaimer.

Fairchild Industries v. *Maritime Air Services, Ltd.*
333 A.2d 313 (Md. 1975)

FACTS   In 1969, the parties entered into a contract for the lease of a helicopter from Fairchild to Maritime. The lease contained an option to buy, which was exercised by Maritime in 1969. Accordingly, the parties entered into a purchase agreement. This agreement consisted of a printed form furnished by Fairchild, and with all relevant provisions being typed on the form. Among the provisions typed into the agreement was a paragraph that asserted that the sale was to be made "as is" and that the seller was giving no warranties, express or implied, except the warranty of title.

When Maritime encountered problems with the helicopter, it asserted that the helicopter was not merchantable, and that Fairchild was liable for breach of the implied warranties of the sale. Fairchild alleged that no implied warranties were present in the sale.

ISSUE   Did the inclusion of the paragraph in the sales agreement operate as an effective disclaimer of the implied warranties in this sale?

HOLDING   No. The attempt to disclaim the warranties was not conspicuous, and was therefore ineffective as a disclaimer.

REASONING   Section 2–316 of the UCC is designed to protect buyers from unexpected and unbargained disclaimers of warranty protections. The Code requires that such disclaimers be conspicuous if they are in writing so that a buyer will not be taken unaware after the sale is consummated. A seller may not claim, after the fact, that a writing was intended to be conspicuous. Fairchild could have typed the alleged disclaimer in uppercase letters rather than in the lowercase that were actually used. Unless a written disclaimer is properly communicated, it is of no effect. Since Fairchild did not properly disclaim the implied warranties, the implied warranties are present.

If warranties do exist, the next question is, *whom* do they protect? At common law, the answer was simple but unsatisfactory. Since the warranty was a part of the contract, it extended only to a party to the contract. Thus, the buyer was covered, but no one else. The UCC has changed this. Section 2–318 has the following three alternative provisions, and each state has selected *one* of the alternatives:

1. Warranties extend to any member of the buyer's family or household or any guest in the buyer's home if it is reasonable to expect that person to use or consume the goods.

2. Warranties extend to *any natural person* (human being) who could reasonably be expected to use or consume the goods.

3. Warranties extend to *any person* (remember, a corporation is a *legal person*) who could reasonably be expected to use or consume the goods.

The seller may not exclude or modify the extension of the warranties to those third-party beneficiaries.

PRODUCT LIABILITY

Occasionally, a situation arises in which a person is injured by goods and no warranty provisions are available to protect the injured party. When such a situation occurs, the injured party is not without remedy. He or she may discover that although warranty protections are lacking, potential remedies are available under tort law. The injured party may be able to assert *negligence* or even *strict tort liability*.

At common law, negligence could be used only in two circumstances. The injured party could recover damages on the ground of negligence by showing that he or she was in privity of contract with the negligent party. Because in most instances the injured party was in contact only with an innocent intermediate party, and not with the negligent manufacturer, this requirement effectively removed the possibility of suing for negligence. The other circumstance ignored the privity requirement. If the goods were found to be *imminently* or *inherently dangerous*, privity was not required. A product is imminently dangerous if it is reasonably certain to threaten death or severe bodily harm. An item is inherently dangerous if it is dangerous by its nature. Imminent danger is commonly found in negligent production; inherent danger, in negligent use.

In 1916, the American courts effectively laid the privity defense to rest. In the landmark case of *MacPherson* v. *Buick Motor Co.*, the court allowed an injured plaintiff to sue a manufacturer and to recover damages despite a lack of privity. Other courts quickly adopted the *MacPherson* rule, and, as a result, privity of contract is seldom asserted as a negligence defense today.

In the following case, the plaintiff's lack of privity was raised as a defense to the lawsuit. The court rejected the lack of privity defense and allowed the case to proceed on its merits.

Embs v. *Pepsi-Cola Bottling Co. of Lexington, Kentucky, Inc.*
528 S.W.2d 703 (Ky. 1975)

FACTS   Embs was shopping at Stamper's Cash Market. She went to an upright soft drink cooler and removed several bottles from the cooler and placed them in her basket. As she turned away from the cooler, she heard a sound like a shotgun. She looked and saw a gash in her leg, broken glass on the floor, and soda pop on her dress. Embs was taken to the hospital by Mrs. Stamper, who told her that a Seven-Up bottle had exploded and that several other Seven-Up bottles had similarly exploded that week.

Pepsi-Cola Bottling Company was the local bottler of the Seven-Up and loaded all the Seven-Up bottles delivered to the Stamper's Cash Market. Arnold Vice was the local distributor of Seven-Up, and he delivered and unloaded all the Seven-Up in stock at the store. Mrs. Embs sued all three for strict product liability owing to the explosion of the bottle. The defense asserted by all three was lack of privity of contract with Mrs. Embs.

ISSUE   Were the defendents liable to Mrs. Embs despite a lack of privity of contract between her and any of the three defendants?

HOLDING   Yes. The lack of privity of contract is irrelevant in a case such as this.

REASONING   The public policy of the state is furthered by minimizing the risk of personal injury and property damage, and this can best be done by charging the costs against the manufacturers and retailers who can procure liability insurance, spreading the cost of such insurance to their customers. Given this public policy objective, it makes no sense to protect one class of persons from injury but not another. The imposition of strict liability without regard to privity of contract effectively discourages the distribution of defective products and imposes no unreasonable burden on the businesses. The injured third party should be compensated, and the multiple defendants should trace the defect for allocation to one of them. The burden should not be placed on the innocent party.

The other basis for recovery for an injured party is *strict tort liability*. This theory is set out in *Restatement (Second) of Torts,* Section 402A. Section 402A is widely followed by the courts of the United States. The section states:

(1)   One who sells any product in a defective condition unreasonably dangerous to the user or consumer or to his property is subject to liability for physical harm thereby caused to the ultimate user or consumer, or to his property, if

(a)   the seller is engaged in the business of selling such a product, and

(b)   it is expected to and does reach the user or consumer without substantial change in the condition in which it is sold.

(2)   The rule stated in subsection (1) applies although

(a)　the seller has exercised all possible care in the preparation and sale of his product, and

(b)　the user or consumer has not bought the product from or entered into any contractual relation with the seller.

The following case shows how the theory of strict tort liability is currently being applied. Notice that the injured plaintiff is asserting a defect in design and also that he should recover for injuries that were *increased,* as opposed to *caused,* by the allegedly defective design. Such rulings will apparently continue to be the thrust of strict tort liability for some time to come.

Larsen v. *General Motors Corp.*
391 F.2d 495 (8th Cir. 1968)

FACTS

Larsen was driving a 1963 Chevrolet Corvair, with the permission of its owner. While operating the car, Larsen was involved in an accident. The impact occurred on the left front corner of the Corvair, causing a severe rear thrust of the steering column into Larsen's head. Larsen alleged that the Corvair was negligently designed and that a design defect increased his injuries. He alleged (1) negligence in design, (2) negligent failure to warn drivers, and (3) breach of the warranty of merchantability. General Motors based its defense on a lack of duty to make cars safe during a collision.

ISSUE

Is the manufacturer liable for negligent design of the product?

HOLDING

Yes. This defect led to a readily foreseeable zone of danger for the operator of the car.

REASONING

The manufacturer has a duty to use reasonable care in designing its product so that the article is safe for its intended use. The product must be reasonably fit and free of hidden defects. For an automobile, the probability of an accident is very high. Injuries from such accidents are readily foreseeable. It is irrational to limit the liability of the manufacturer to those situations in which the defect causes the accident. Where the injury to the occupant is enhanced by the manufacturer's lack of reasonable care, the manufacturer is liable.

SUMMARY

Warranty law and product liability are two major areas of consumer protection — a subject that has been receiving an increasing amount of attention for some years.

　Warranty protection comes in three broad forms: express warranties, which are given by the seller; implied warranties, which are imposed by law;

and statutory warranties, which are primarily concerned with disclosures to consumer-purchasers. Warranties are considered a part of the contract covering the sale of goods.

Warranties may be excluded by the seller or surrendered by the buyer. The method of exclusion depends on the type of warranty involved.

Under product liability, the manufacturer or the seller may be held liable because of negligence in making, designing, or packaging the product. The manufacturer may also be held strictly liable, despite any lack of due care. This is true if the product, in its normal use, is imminently or inherently dangerous.

DISCUSSION QUESTIONS

1. George is negotiating with Steve for the sale of a boat. George tells Steve the boat will easily pull three water-skiers. Steve buys the boat and discovers that if there are three skiers, the boat will not move fast enough to allow them to get up on their skis. What will result if Steve attempts to sue George? Explain.

2. Carl saw an advertisement on television in which a person used a Leather-mate pen to open a tin can by stabbing the pen into the can. The announcer then said: "Leather-mate. For $1.29, not *just* a fine pen." Carl got out his Leather-mate and attempted to open a can with it. The pen shattered and seriously cut Carl's hand. (The can was unharmed.) Could Carl successfully argue that the commercial created a warranty? Explain.

3. Bob is buying a stereo from Earl. Bob asks Earl about the distortion figures for the stereo. Earl does not know the correct answer, but he does not want Bob to realize his lack of knowledge. What will happen if Earl answers, and his answer is incorrect? How should Earl answer?

4. Sue bought some goods from Perry. About two weeks later, one of Perry's creditors attempted to enforce a lien against the goods. If the creditor succeeds in taking the goods from Sue, what steps should Sue take against Perry?

5. Herb bought a chicken salad sandwich from a vending machine. While eating the sandwich, Herb bit into a chicken bone and as a result broke two of his teeth. The state imposes the foreign–natural test. What will result if Herb sues the vending machine company? Explain.

6. Lynn was enjoying happy hour at a local tavern. She ordered a martini with an olive. When she bit the olive, she broke her teeth on the olive pit. The state imposes the reasonable expectations test. What will result if Lynn sues the olive supplier? Explain.

7. Scott, a 280-pound painter, went to a hardware store to buy a stepladder. The ladder had a warning that it was unsafe for more than 250 pounds. The clerk told Scott not to worry; the ladder was safe for up to 400 pounds. Scott bought the ladder, and when it later collapsed under him, he was injured. What should the result be if Scott sues the hardware store? Explain.

8. Explain the difference between a full warranty and a limited warranty under the Magnuson-Moss Warranty Act.

9. A manufacturer negligently built a door so that the lock would not hold properly. Debbie bought the door for her home. The lock did not hold, and a burglar robbed Debbie because of the improperly functioning lock. May Debbie sue the manufacturer for negligence?

10. Rayex sold sunglasses advertised as safe for baseball. A high school athlete was using the baseball sunglasses when he misplayed a fly ball. The ball hit the glasses and they shattered, blinding the athlete in one eye. It was subsequently discovered that the lenses of the sunglasses were unreasonably thin and not impact resistant. How should the athlete argue to establish strict tort liability?

CASE PROBLEMS

1. Williams, a commercial tomato grower, purchased tomato seeds from Brown Seed Store. Brown had purchased the seeds from Green Seed Co., a commercial distributor of tomato seeds. Green Seed had sold the seeds as a "Pink Shipper" variety to Brown. Brown in turn had sold the seeds to Williams as "Pink Shipper" seeds. In fact, the seeds were not "Pink Shipper" but some unknown and inferior variety of tomato. Because of the difference in quality, Williams was unable to market his tomato crop, and it spoiled in the field. Williams sued Green Seed Co. for breach of warranty. What should be the result? (*L. A. Green Seed Company of Arkansas* v. *Williams*, 438 S.W.2d 717 [Ark. 1969].)

2. Dunham was using a hammer to fit a pin into a tractor accessory. While he was "tapping" the pin into place, the hammer broke and a chip from the hammer struck him in the eye. As a result, he lost his vision in the injured eye. Dunham sued both the manufacturer, V & B, and the distributor, Belknap, alleging strict liability in tort. The manufacturer and the distributor based their defense on the fact that the hammer contained no defect in construction. What should be the result? (*Dunham* v. *Vaughan & Bushnell Mfg. Co.*, 42 Ill.2d 339, 247 N.E.2d 401 [1969].)

3. Gates ordered a quantity of pipe from Northern Plumbing. Gates was using the pipe to manufacture harrow attachments, and Northern was aware of this planned use. Gates had supplied a sample of the pipe he wanted to purchase from Northern when he placed the order. The sample had a wall thickness of 0.133 inches. Northern supplied pipe with a wall thinner than that ordered. The pipe supplied was not satisfactory for Gate's purpose. Did Northern breach the implied warranty of fitness for a particular purpose? (*Northern Plumbing Supply, Inc.* v. *Gates*, 196 N.W.2d 70 [N.D. 1972].)

4. Anderson, the owner of a casino-hotel, special-ordered carpeting from Mohasco. The carpet was to be installed in the hotel lobby and in the casino. Mohasco produced the carpet to the specifications of Anderson

and installed it as requested. After installation, Anderson refused to pay. He alleged that the carpet was "shaded" and appeared water stained even though it was not. Mohasco sued for its $18,500 under the contract. What should be the result? (*Mohasco Industries, Inc.* v. *Anderson Halverson Corp.,* 520 P.2d 234 [Nev. 1974].)

5. Sheeskin was carrying a six-pack of Coca-Cola to his shopping cart in a supermarket when one of the bottles exploded. As a result of the explosion, Sheeskin lost his balance, fell to the floor, and suffered multiple injuries. He sued both the supermarket and Coca-Cola Bottling, alleging breach of warranties of merchantability and negligence. What should be the result? (*Sheeskin* v. *Giant Foods, Inc.,* 318 A.2d 874 [Md. 1974].)

6. Tarulli purchased an exotic bird from Birds in Paradise. At the time of the sale, Birds in Paradise asked Tarulli to have the bird examined by a veterinarian. Tarulli declined to have the bird examined. Subsequently, the bird Tarulli had purchased died. It appeared that the bird was ill at the time of the sale. Tarulli sued Birds in Paradise for breach of the implied warranty of merchantability. Birds in Paradise denied that Tarulli received the warranty due to his failure to "inspect" the bird. How should the case be decided? (*Tarulli* v. *Birds in Paradise,* 26 U.C.C. 872 [N.Y. 1979].)

7. Klages was employed as a night auditor at Conley's Motel. While working as a night auditor, Klages had been the victim of an armed robbery at the motel. In order to protect himself in the event of another robbery, Klages purchased a mace pen from General Ordinance. The pen was advertised as causing "instantaneous incapacitation" so that an attacker was "subdued—instantly." The mace pen was also advertised as being as effective as a gun without the permanent injury from using a gun. Shortly after purchasing the pen, Klages was again held up by an armed robber. He squirted the robber with the mace, hitting him in the face with the mace discharge. The robber was not instantaneously incapacitated, however, and he shot Klages in the head. As a result of the gunshot wound, Klages lost all sight in his right eye. Klages has sued the manufacturer of the mace pen for misrepresentation. What should be the result in this case? (*Klages* v. *General Ordinance Equipment Corporation,* 367 A.2d 207 [Pa. 1976].)

8. Heckman was using a power press manufactured by Federal Press. While operating the press, Heckman's hand was caught in the mechanism and severely injured. The press as manufactured did not have a "guarding device" to prevent injuries such as the one suffered by Heckman. As a result, Heckman sued Federal for defective design and for producing an unreasonably dangerous product. What result should occur in this case? (*Heckman* v. *Federal Press Co.,* 587 F.2d 612 [3rd Cir. 1978].)

9. Catania went to Brown, a retail paint dealer, and asked Brown to recommend a paint to cover exterior stucco walls on his home. Brown recommended a specific brand of paint and also told Catania how to prepare the

walls prior to the painting. Catania followed all the instructions carefully, but the paint peeled soon after it was applied. Catania is suing Brown. What theories should Catania rely on in the lawsuit, and what results should occur? (*Catania* v. *Brown,* 231 A.2d 668 [Conn. 1967].)

10. Swenson was a corn farmer. He planted 300 acres of corn in 1972 and treated his crop with a rootworm insecticide. He applied Bux to 225 acres and Thimet to the remaining 75 acres. In July Swenson discovered severe rootworm damage to the corn treated with Bux but no rootworm damage to the crops treated with Thimet. As a result, Swenson has sued the manufacturer of Bux for breach of the implied warranty of merchantability. What result should occur? (*Swenson* v. *Chevron Chemical Co.,* 234 N.W.2d 38 [S.D. 1975].)

CHAPTER 22

Remedies for Breach of the Sales Contract

THE REASON FOR REMEDIES

The overwhelming majority of sales contracts are performed by the parties as expected. The seller will tender conforming goods to the buyer at the time and place of delivery. The buyer will then inspect the goods, accept them, and pay the seller the price agreed to in the contract. Of course, not every tender is letter perfect. But when the tender of delivery is flawed, the seller will normally cure the defect. Again, the parties are left with their bargain as agreed.

However, in some cases the tender is never made, or it is made in so insubstantial a manner that it is treated as a breach of contract. Also, some sellers refuse to cure a defective performance or lack the time to do so. And some buyers refuse to pay the agreed price or are unable to do so. Under these circumstances, the other party must look to *remedies* to minimize the effect of the breach.

This chapter will examine remedies from the seller's viewpoint, and then from the buyer's viewpoint. In either case, certain remedies will be available at some times; other remedies, at other times. The last part of the chapter will explore some technical rules that affect how and when remedies may be sought or established.

If the buyer wrongfully rejects goods, refuses to pay for the goods, or otherwise breaches the contract, the seller is entitled to remedies. The possible remedies available to the seller depend on *when* the buyer breaches. The seller has six possible remedies if the breach is *before* acceptance. If the breach is *after* acceptance, the seller has two possible remedies. Figure 22.1 summarizes the types of preacceptance and postacceptance remedies available to the seller. We shall discuss each of these in turn.

If the buyer breaches the contract *before* accepting the goods, the seller may seek up to six different remedies. The seller does not have to choose just one possible remedy: as many of the six can be used as are needed in the particular case.

The first possible remedy is to *withhold delivery of the goods.* The seller does not have to deliver or to continue delivering goods to a buyer who is not willing to perform the contract properly. In addition, if the seller discovers that the buyer is insolvent, the seller may withhold delivery unless the buyer pays in cash all prior charges *and* the cost of the current shipment.

The second possible seller's remedy is a little more complicated. It is known as *stoppage of delivery in transit.*[1] To use this remedy, the goods must be in

Figure 22.1 Sellers' Remedies

1. **Preacceptance Remedies**
   If, before accepting the goods, the buyer repudiates or breaches the contract or becomes insolvent, the seller may do any, or all, of the following:
   a. Withhold delivery of goods still in the seller's possession
   b. Stop delivery of goods in transit (subject to some size-of-shipment limitations)
   c. Identify goods to the contract in order to establish the amount of damages (which includes the right to decide to complete construction or to terminate work in process)
   d. Resell any goods, or any work in process, in the seller's possession
   e. Sue for damages based on the resale or on lost profits, or sue for the performance of the contract
   f. Cancel all future performance owed to the buyer under the contract

2. **Postacceptance Remedies**
   If the buyer accepts delivery of the goods and then fails or refuses to pay for them, the seller may do one or both of the following:
   a. Sue for the amount due under the contract
   b. Reclaim the goods, provided the buyer is insolvent *and* the seller can assert the claim within ten days of the delivery (a written misrepresentation of solvency waives the ten-day limit)

[1] Uniform Commercial Code, Section 2–705.

Carrier A third party hired to deliver the goods from the seller to the buyer

the possession of a third person — a **carrier** or a bailee. If the seller discovers that the buyer is *insolvent,* the seller may stop delivery of any goods in the possession of a third person. If the buyer *breaches* the contract, the seller may also be able to stop the delivery; however, before the seller can stop delivery because of a breach, the delivery must be of a *carload, truckload, planeload,* or larger shipment.

The seller must also make provisions to protect the carrier or the bailee before a stoppage is permitted. The seller must notify the carrier or bailee in enough time to reasonably allow a stoppage and must indemnify that carrier or bailee for any charges or damages suffered because of the stoppage.

The third remedy for the seller allows the seller to exercise some discretion in the treatment of unidentified goods.[2] If the buyer breaches the contract, the seller may *identify goods* to the contract that were unidentified before the breach, thus helping to establish damages. Also, the seller may decide either to *complete goods* that were incomplete or to *stop production* and *resell* the goods for scrap. Either of these options may be used provided that the seller is exercising reasonable business judgment.

The fourth seller's remedy gives the seller the right to *resell* those goods that are still in the seller's possession.[3] A seller who does resell the goods, and who does so in good faith in a commercially reasonable manner, may also be able to collect damages from the buyer. If so, the damages are figured by taking the resale price from the contract price, adding consequential damages, and subtracting any expenses saved.

The seller may elect to resell in a public sale or in a private sale and may resell the entire lot of goods as a unit or by individual units. All the seller has to do is establish that the resale was totally commercially reasonable. This means that the method, time, place, and terms must all be shown to be reasonable. And the seller must give the breaching buyer notice of the sale, if possible.

Normally, the issue of reasonableness will be raised in a private sale, but if given notice, the buyer has little opportunity to defeat the resale. In a public resale, reasonableness is well defined. Except for recognized futures, the resale can be made only on *identified* goods. It must occur at a normal place for a public sale unless the goods are perishable. The breaching buyer must be given notice of the time and place of the resale. Notice must be given as to where the goods are located so prospective bidders can inspect them. If the seller fails to meet any of these criteria, the resale is not commercially reasonable, and therefore the seller cannot recover any damages.

If the seller resells the goods for more than the contract price, an interesting situation arises. If the buyer breached, the seller may keep the excess. If the buyer rightfully rejected the goods, the seller may still keep the excess, but now the excess is defined as anything above the buyer's security interest.

The fifth option available to the seller is to *sue the buyer.* The seller may

[2] Ibid., Section 2–704.
[3] Ibid., Section 2–706.

elect to sue for damages, for lost profits, or for the contract price.[4] If the seller has not yet completed the goods or has not yet identified the goods, the seller will normally sue for damages. Damages are determined by taking the difference between the contract price and the market price at the time and place of breach, adding any incidental damages, and subtracting any expenses saved.

The seller may discover that the damages computed do not put him or her in as good a position as performance of the contract would have. If so, the seller may elect to sue for lost profits. The seller will show the profits that full performance would have netted and sue for this amount plus the recovery of any expenses reasonably incurred. In the following case, the seller properly utilized the remedy of suing for lost profits as a measure of damages.

Anchorage Centennial Development Co. v. *Van Wormer & Rodrigues* 443 P.2d 596 (Alaska 1968)

FACTS

In connection with the centennial of the purchase of Alaska from Russia, the Centennial Development Co. hired Van Wormer & Rodrigues to mint 50,000 anniversary coins. Later the commission canceled the contract before performance was completed. Van Wormer & Rodrigues sued the commission for damages and for lost profits of 3¢ per coin.

ISSUE

Is Van Wormer & Rodrigues entitled to lost profits?

HOLDING

Yes. Lost profits are a proper remedy in this type of case.

REASONING

The UCC tries to place an injured party in as good a position as would have been enjoyed with performance. If the goods are useless to any other party, as are these commemorative coins, lost profits are the only practical remedy available.

If the seller is unable to resell the goods, and the goods have been identified to the contract, the seller may elect to sue for the contract price. However, an election to sue for the contract price places a burden on the seller. The seller must hold the goods for the buyer and deliver them to the buyer when the buyer pays for them.

The final preacceptance seller's remedy is the right to *cancel.* Upon giving notice to the buyer, the seller can cancel all future performance due to the buyer under the contract. Cancellation does not discharge the buyer or hinder the seller in collecting or enforcing any other rights or remedies resulting from the breach.

[4] Ibid., Sections 2–708, 2–709.

Postacceptance

Once the goods have been *accepted* by the buyer, and the buyer has breached the contract, the seller may select either or both of two remedies.

The first of these remedies is by far the more common. The seller may *sue the buyer* for the price of the goods. Since the buyer has accepted, the buyer's duty to pay is established. Thus, winning the case is almost a certainty. However, many buyers who do not pay are *unable* to pay. They are insolvent. In such a situation, winning the case is a Pyrrhic victory—the winner suffers nearly as much as the loser.

If the buyer has accepted goods, and the buyer is insolvent, the seller will probably rely on the second available postacceptance remedy: the seller will attempt to *reclaim* the goods.[5] To do so, the seller must prove that the following two situations occurred:

1. The buyer received the goods on credit *while insolvent.*
2. The seller demanded the return of the goods within ten days of delivery to the buyer.

This remedy is obviously of limited value, since many credit terms are for thirty days or longer and the seller has only ten days in which to act. But there is one exception. If the buyer *misrepresented* his or her solvency *in writing* to the seller within three months before delivery, the ten-day limit does not apply.

BUYERS' REMEDIES

In much the same manner as the seller, the buyer also has a range of possible remedies. And like the seller, the buyer's remedy options depend on the timing of the breach. The buyer has six preacceptance and three postacceptance remedies available. These remedies are summarized in Figure 22.2.

Preacceptance

Before the buyer accepts, the seller may breach by nondelivery, or by delivery of nonconforming goods. Under either circumstance, the buyer may elect any or all of the following remedies.

The first buyer's remedy is to *sue for damages.*[6] The buyer is allowed to recover the excess of market price over contract price at the time of breach and at the place of delivery. To this amount are added any additional damages. This amount is then reduced by any expenses the buyer might have saved because of the breach.

The second remedy available to the buyer is that of *cover.*[7] The buyer covers by buying *substitute* goods from another source within a reasonable time of the breach. If the goods obtained through cover cost more than the contract

---

[5] Ibid., Section 2–702(2).
[6] Ibid., Section 2–713.
[7] Ibid., Section 2–712.

Figure 22.2   Buyers' Remedies

1.   **Preacceptance Remedies**
     If the seller fails to tender delivery of conforming goods, the buyer may do any, or all, of the following:
     a.   Sue for damages for the breach of contract
     b.   Cover and sue for any damages resulting from the cost of cover
     c.   Seek specific performance if the goods are unique or replevin if the goods are not unique but cover could not be obtained
     d.   Claim any identified goods still in the possession of the seller, provided the seller has become insolvent within ten days of receiving a payment from the buyer
     e.   Resell any nonconforming goods shipped by the seller in order to minimize the overall losses involved
     f.   Cancel any future duties under the contract, without surrendering any present rights

2.   **Postacceptance Remedies**
     If the seller delivers nonconforming goods, with a nonconformity that is hidden or that was not cured despite the seller's assurance that cure would be effected, the buyer may do the following:
     a.   Revoke the acceptance *if* the nonconformity substantially impairs the value of the contract, which then allows the buyer to seek any preacceptance remedies
     b.   Sue for damages *if* the nonconformity is not sufficient to allow for revocation
     c.   Seek recoupment by deducting the damages suffered from the amount owed the seller under the contract

price, the buyer may collect the excess costs from the breaching seller, plus other expenses incurred in effecting cover.

The third remedy is available if the goods cannot be obtained by cover. The buyer may seek *specific performance* or *replevin*.[8] If the goods are unique, the court may order specific performance, and the seller will have to deliver the goods in accordance with the contract. If the goods are not unique but are unavailable from other sources at the time, replevin is available. Once the buyer shows an inability to cover, the court will order replevin.

The fourth remedy is probably rare in actual practice. *If* the seller has identified the goods to the contract, and *if* the buyer has paid some or all of the contract price, and *if* the seller becomes insolvent within ten days of receipt of the payment, the buyer can *claim the identified goods*.[9] The likelihood of this chain of events occurring is not very high. But if it does occur, the buyer is protected.

The fifth remedy available to the buyer frequently baffles and amazes students: under appropriate circumstances, the *buyer* may *resell* the goods. This

---

[8] Ibid., Section 2–716.
[9] Ibid., Section 2–502.

remedy becomes available when the seller ships nonconforming goods to the buyer. Upon receipt of the nonconforming goods, the buyer must notify the seller of the nonconformity. Furthermore, if the buyer is a merchant, the buyer must request instructions from the seller as to disposal of the goods. If no instructions are given, the buyer must attempt to resell the goods for the seller. The resale must be reasonable. A buyer who does resell may deduct an appropriate amount for expenses and commissions and then apply the balance to the damages resulting from the breach. Any excess must be returned to the seller.

The final preacceptance remedy available to the buyer is the right to *cancel.* Upon discovery of a breach by the seller, the buyer may notify the seller that all future obligations of the buyer are canceled. Cancellation will not affect any other rights or remedies of the buyer under contract.

Postacceptance

Once the buyer has accepted the goods, the focus shifts. A buyer who accepts *cannot* reject the goods. However, the buyer *may* be able to *revoke* the acceptance. Revocation is permitted if the defect is hidden, or if the defect was to be *cured* by the seller and no cure occurred.[10] Revocation is available only if the defect **substantially impairs** the value of the goods to the buyer. If the buyer properly revokes acceptance, the buyer is treated as having rejected the initial delivery and is permitted to assert preacceptance remedies.

Substantially impairs
Makes worth a great deal less, seriously harms or injures, or reduces in value

The buyer may accept the goods and later discover a defect or other breach that is not sufficient to permit a revocation. When this happens, the buyer will select the second possible remedy, *suit for damages.*[11]

Notice in each of the following cases how revocation can be used by an innocent buyer of defective goods. Also notice how the buyer who wishes to revoke must act in a reasonable and timely manner in order to exercise this remedy.

Schumaker v. *Ivers*
238 N.W.2d 284 (S.D. 1976)

FACTS In November, the Schumakers visited a music store owned by Ivers to look at electric organs. Ivers recommended a particular model to the Schumakers and suggested that they allow him to deliver it to them on a trial basis. In December, the organ was delivered to the Schumakers. The Schumakers noticed nothing wrong with the organ and the next week they paid the full purchase price for it. At that time they also discussed warranty protections and service with Ivers. About two weeks later, the organ began to malfunction. The Schumakers called Ivers to complain, and he promised to have a serviceman come by to repair the organ. Nearly three months later the serviceman arrived. His efforts to repair the organ failed, and in May, the Schumakers

---

[10] Ibid., Section 2–608.
[11] Ibid., Section 2–607.

demanded a refund for the purchase. Instead Ivers delivered a replacement organ. This organ also proved defective, and again the Schumakers demanded a refund. In June, Ivers attempted to redeliver the original organ, allegedly repaired and in good working order, but the Schumakers refused. Finally, in August, the Schumakers filed suit to revoke their acceptance and to recover the purchase price.

Can the Schumakers revoke their acceptance of the organ nine months after it was delivered?

ISSUE

Yes. The Schumakers acted properly throughout the transaction, and their revocation was timely in these circumstances.

HOLDING

The Schumakers had informed Ivers that they wanted to revoke their acceptance and receive a refund of their payment in May, after numerous attempts to repair the original organ had failed. When they accepted the second organ, it was clearly with the understanding that this organ would work properly. When it failed to so operate, the Schumakers notified Ivers of their intent to revoke in a timely manner. The Schumakers had cooperated with Ivers throughout the transaction, and they had notified Ivers properly, so they were allowed to revoke.

REASONING

In the following case, the court ruled that holding the goods was not retaining them, and so the right of the buyer to revoke still existed.

Garfinkel v. Lehman Floor Covering Co.
60 Misc.2d 72, 302 N.Y.S.2d 167 (1969)

Garfinkel purchased carpeting from Lehman and had it installed. Upon installation, Garfinkel noted an unsightly condition in the carpet. The defect was immediately called to the attention of Lehman. Lehman sent representatives who twice tried to correct the problem without success. Garfinkel thereupon notified Lehman that he was rejecting the carpet, asked that it be removed, and demanded his money back.

FACTS

Did Garfinkel lose his right to revoke by "retaining" the carpet on his floor?

ISSUE

No. Garfinkel acted in a proper manner in this case.

HOLDING

The UCC requires a buyer who rejects defective goods to hold them for the seller's disposition for a reasonable time. The buyer has no further duty if the goods are rightfully rejected. This means that the buyer may retain the goods at his home while awaiting the removal of those goods by the seller. To hold otherwise would place the buyer in an untenable position. The goods here are bulky. To require the buyer to remove them and return them to the seller at

REASONING

the buyer's expense would be unduly burdensome. The burden should be on the merchant seller in this type of transaction. The seller delivered the goods; it is only fair that he should also remove them.

━━━━━━━━━━━━━━━━━━━━━━━━━━━━━━━━━

The third remedy available to the buyer is *recoupment.* Normally this third remedy will be used together with the second. The buyer will notify the seller that the buyer is recouping by deducting damages from the contract price owed to the seller. If the seller does not object, recoupment is used. If the seller objects, the buyer may not recoup. But the buyer can still sue for damages.

MODIFICA-TIONS

The parties to the contract are allowed to tailor their remedies to fit the particular contract. The parties may, by *expressly including* it in the contract, provide for remedies *in addition to* the remedies provided by the Uniform Commercial Code.[12] Or they may provide for remedies *instead of* those provided by the Code. Or they may place a *limit* on the remedies that may be used.

If the parties so desire, they can select one remedy that is to be used as the exclusive remedy for their particular contract. Such an exclusive remedy must be followed unless circumstances change so that the remedy no longer adequately covers the damages.

Consequential dam-ages Damages or losses that occur as a result of the initial wrong but that are not *direct* and *immediate*

Liquidated damages An amount expressly stipulated by the parties to the contract as the measure of damages if a breach occurs

Consequential damages may be excluded or limited by the parties in the contract. Such an agreement will be enforced unless the court finds it to be unconscionable.

The parties may also provide for **liquidated damages** if the provision is reasonable, the difficulty of setting the loss is substantial, and establishing actual loss would be inconvenient, if not impossible.[13] Of course, if the amount designated as liquidated damages is found unreasonable, the clause is void.

Sometimes the seller justifiably withholds delivery from the buyer when the buyer has paid part of the contract price. In such a case, the *buyer,* even though in breach, can recover any payments made *in excess of* any liquidated damages called for in the contract or, if there is no liquidated-damages amount, the *lesser* of 20 percent of the total contract value or $500.

SPECIAL PROBLEMS

In determining *when* remedies may be obtained and *what* remedies to seek, several special problems may arise. The courts need to know whether a breach has occurred. If there has been a breach, the courts need to know when it occurred. And the courts need to know if any legal excuses are involved. Some of these problems will be analyzed next.

---

[12] Ibid., Section 2–719
[13] Ibid., Section 2–718

Occasionally one of the parties to a contract will **repudiate** his or her obligations *before* performance is due.[14] If such a repudiation will substantially reduce the value to be received by the other party, the other party may choose *one* of three courses of conduct:

1. He or she may await performance for a commercially reasonable time *despite* the repudiation.

2. Or this party may treat the repudiation as an *immediate* breach and seek any available remedies.

3. Or the party may suspend his or her own performance under the contract.

A repudiating party is allowed to *retract* the repudiation at any time up to and including the date performance is due, if the other party permits a retraction.[15] No retraction is allowed if the nonrepudiating party has canceled the contract or has *materially* changed position in reliance on the repudiation. A retraction reestablishes the contract rights and duties of each party.

When the parties enter a contract for the sale of goods, each expects to receive the benefit of the bargain made. If, before performance is due, either party feels *insecure* in expecting performance, the insecure party may demand assurances of performance.[16] The insecure party must make a *written* demand for assurance that performance will be tendered when due. Until the assurances are given, the requesting party may **suspend** performance. If no assurance is given within thirty days of request, it is treated as repudiation of the contract.

Adequate
Assurances

Suspend To cause to cease for a time; to become inoperative for a time; to stop temporarily

Sometimes a seller may be *forced* into a delay in making delivery, may not be able to make delivery, or may have to make only a partial delivery. Normally this would be treated as a breach. However, some of these situations fall into the area of *excused performance* and hence are *not* treated as a breach.[17]

Excused
Performance

Performance is excused, in whole or in part, if performance has become *impracticable* because of the occurrence of some event whose *nonoccurrence* was a basic assumption of the contract. Also, performance is excused if the seller's delay or lack of performance is based on compliance with a *governmental order or regulation.*

If the seller has an excuse for less than full performance, the seller must notify the buyer **seasonably.** If performance will be reduced but not eliminated, the seller is allowed to *allocate* deliveries among customers in a reasonable manner. Upon receiving notice of a planned allocation due to some excuse, the buyer must elect whether to terminate the contract or to modify

Seasonably Timely; being done in the right time; occurring within a reasonable, prompt time period

---

[14] Ibid., Section 2–610.
[15] Ibid., Section 2–611.
[16] Ibid., Section 2–609.
[17] Ibid., Section 2–615.

it.[18] Modifying it means accepting the partial delivery as a substitute performance. A failure to modify within thirty days will be treated as a termination.

Duty to Particularize

When the buyer rightfully rejects goods, the buyer must do so properly.[19] If the goods are rejected owing to a *curable* defect, the buyer may reject only by stating *exactly* what the defect is. A failure to do so will preclude the use of that defect in court to prove breach. And if the buyer cannot prove breach, the seller will be deemed to have performed properly. Thus, a *failure to particularize* will result in the buyer's being required to pay for the goods or in liability to the seller.

STATUTE OF LIMITATIONS

Any lawsuit for breach of a sales contract must be started within four years of the breach, unless the contract itself sets a shorter time period. (The time period cannot be less than one year.) The fact that a breach is not discovered when it occurred is not material. The time limitation begins at *breach*, not at *discovery*. This reemphasizes the need for a buyer to inspect the goods carefully and completely in order to protect his or her interests.

SUMMARY

Although most sales contracts are fully performed and the performance is normally satisfactory, sometimes a nonperformance occurs. When nonperformance is found, the innocent party usually seeks remedies for breach of contract.

When the buyer fails to perform, the seller will seek remedies. The available remedies depend on when the buyer breached. If the buyer breached before acceptance, the seller will seek one or more of six preacceptance remedies. If the buyer accepts the goods and then breaches, the seller will seek one or both of two postacceptance remedies. By the same token, if the seller breaches, the buyer will seek remedies. Again, the buyer's available remedies will depend on when the seller breached. If the seller breached before the buyer accepted the goods, the buyer may seek one or more of six remedies. If the seller breaches after the buyer accepts, the buyer has three available remedies.

Occasionally a nonperformance turns out not to be a breach. It may involve a special problem that excuses performance. Or it may involve a special problem that affects the rights of the innocent party. Great care must be exercised by both parties in these special problem areas.

DISCUSSION QUESTIONS

1. Ace Mfg. agreed to produce and sell some goods to Sampson. The contract called for ten shipments of twenty-five units each. After satisfactorily

---

[18] Ibid., Section 2–616.
[19] Ibid., Section 2–605.

completing five shipments, Ace sent the sixth shipment. Order number 7 was then in process. Sampson wrongfully rejected shipment number 6. Ace decided to complete the work on number 7 and to sue Sampson for the price on shipments 6 and 7 and for lost profits on the others. Sampson argued that Ace could not complete number 7 at his (Sampson's) expense. Who is correct? Explain.

2. Tom shipped goods to Martin via Allied Parcel Service. After the goods were shipped, Tom discovered that Martin was insolvent. What should Tom do to protect himself and Allied?

3. Robert, the seller, was in possession of goods that Suzanne had wrongfully rejected. Robert sold the goods to Bart for one-half the contract price without telling anyone about the sale. May Robert collect the unpaid balance of the contract price from Suzanne? Explain.

4. Helen sold goods to Earl on credit, with delivery made on September 9. On September 12 Helen discovered Earl was insolvent. What postacceptance remedies may Helen assert? Explain.

5. Paul ordered goods from Jim, with delivery due October 12. On October 1 Jim notified Paul that he (Jim) was unable to deliver. Paul buys substitute goods within three weeks but has to pay twice the price Jim was to have charged. What rights does Paul have against Jim? Explain.

6. Bob and Sam entered into a contract that called for Sam to deliver goods to Bob, and for Bob to pay $1500. Bob gave Sam a $500 deposit on the goods. During the contract period, Sam discovered that Bob was insolvent, and Sam decided to withhold delivery of the goods to Bob. While Sam admits that he is in breach, he also asserts that he is entitled to restitution for his deposit on the goods. Is Bob entitled to restitution, and if so, how much is he to recover from Sam?

7. Martha entered into a contract with Amy that called for Amy to manufacture and deliver goods to Martha, with delivery to occur in six months. Three months later, Martha phoned Amy and repudiated the contract. At the time, Martha thought she could obtain the goods from another source at a substantially lower price. When Martha realized that her repudiation would operate as a breach, she immediately called Amy, apologized for her conduct, and attempted to retract her repudiation. What are Amy's rights in this case?

8. Bert ships nonconforming goods to Ernie. Ernie rejects the goods, but Bert does not instruct Ernie as to disposition of the goods. What should Ernie do?

9. Ruth signs a contract to buy goods from Mike, with delivery in three months. One month later Ruth repudiates. What may Mike do?

10. Bob is to deliver some very expensive merchandise to Carol. Bob hears that Carol is having financial problems, and he is afraid he will not be paid. What can Bob do to minimize his worries? What will Carol be required to do?

CASE
PROBLEMS

1. The Detroit Screwdriver Co. agreed to specially manufacture a stud-driving machine for Ladney. Before Detroit completed the machine, Ladney called and canceled. Detroit immediately stopped working on the machine and sued Ladney for breach of contract. Ladney argued that by halting production, Detroit had acted in bad faith and could therefore collect no damages. What should be the result? (*Detroit Power Screwdriver Co. v. Ladney,* 25 Mich. App. 478, 181 N.W.2d 828 [1979].)

2. Gray shipped three reels of cable to Shook under a contract that they had formed. Two of the three reels were not satisfactory, and Shook rejected them. Gray was notified of the rejection. The two rejected reels were left at the construction site. Four months later the reels were stolen. Gray then sued Shook for the price of the two reels, alleging improper rejection. What should be the result? (*Graybar Electric Co. v. Shook,* 283 N.C. 213, 195 S.E.2d 514 [1973].)

3. Barnes purchased a car from Burnham on credit. Later Barnes requested some free repairs on the car, which Burnham refused to supply. After nine months, Barnes returned the car to Burnham and stopped making payments. When Burnham sued Barnes for the unpaid balance, Barnes claimed to have rescinded the sale and canceled the contract. Who should prevail? (*Barnes v. Chester Burnham Chevrolet,* 217 So.2d 630 [Miss. 1969].)

4. Eastern ordered 150 lawnmowers from Turf Man Sales and accepted delivery of the mowers on March 28. At the time of the order, Eastern was insolvent, was unable to pay for the mowers, and had no intention of paying for them. On April 4, Turf Man learned of the financial condition of Eastern and made a demand by telephone for the return of the mowers. On April 8, Turf Man made demand on the court-appointed receivers of Eastern for return of the mowers. Is Turf Man within its rights under the UCC to recover the mowers, or does Turf Man have to exert physical control over the goods in order to recover them? Discuss fully. (*Metropolitan Distributors v. Eastern Supply Co.,* 21 D.&C.2d 128 [Pa. 1959].)

5. Neri ordered a boat from Retail Sales, paying $4250 as a deposit and obtaining a promise from Retail Sales to have immediate delivery, as opposed to the normal six weeks for delivery. After Retail Sales received the boat from the manufacturer but before Neri took possession, Neri's attorney wrote a letter to Retail Sales attempting to rescind the sale and to recover the deposit made by Neri. Retail Sales refused to refund the deposit and sued Neri for breach of contract. What result should occur? What are the rights of each party to this contract? Explain fully. (*Neri v. Retail Marine Corp.,* 30 N.Y.2d 393, 334 N.Y.S.2d 165 [1972].)

6. Purdon contracted with Birkner for the purchase of some 3500 Christmas trees. The trees were to be "Number One" grade trees, being over 5½ feet tall and of good shape and form. When the trees were delivered, Purdon objected that the trees were inferior. Birkner, a wholesaler with thirty-two years of experience in the industry, assured Purdon that the trees

were as described. Purdon believed Birkner, retained the trees, and attempted to sell them. At the close of the Christmas season, Purdon had sold only 600 trees, and he refused to pay for them as per the contract. Birkner sued for breach of contract, and Purdon counterclaimed that he had revoked his acceptance of the trees and was not liable. What result should occur? (*Birkner* v. *Purdon*, 183 N.W.2d 598 [Mich. 1970].)

7. Mott had a contract to purchase 4000 bushels of grain from Svihovec, with delivery to occur in March. Mott refused to accept delivery in March owing to an alleged shortage of boxcars. Mott similarly refused delivery in April or in May. Finally, in June, Svihovec sold the grain to another party. In September Mott demanded delivery from Svihovec, and when delivery was refused, Mott sued for breach of contract. What result should occur? (*Mott Equity Elevator* v. *Svihovec*, 236 N.W.2d 900 [N.D. 1975].)

8. Wegematic advertised that is had produced a revolutionary new type of digital computer. On the basis of these advertisements, the United States agreed to purchase one of the new computers. Wegematic failed to deliver the computer as agreed, alleging that the delay was due to unforeseen technological difficulties. Is this a valid excuse for nondelivery? (*United States* v. *Wegematic*, 360 F.2d 674 [2d Cir. 1966].)

9. In June, Maple Farms signed a contract to supply milk to City School District for the coming school year at a fixed price. By December, the price of milk had increased 25 percent over the price in June when the contract had been signed. Maple Farms asked the court to declare the contract terminated because of impracticability. What should the court rule? (*Maple Farms, Inc.* v. *City School District*, 352 N.Y.S.2d 784 [1974].)

10. Belcher purchased an irrigation machine from Irrigation Motor. The machine was installed in January. The machine failed to work properly, and Belcher so informed the seller. The seller made numerous unsuccessful attempts to correct the problem, and in July Belcher informed Irrigation Motor that he was rescinding the contract. May Belcher revoke his acceptance and rescind the contract? (*Irrigation Motor & Pump Co.* v. *Belcher*, 483 P.2d 980 [Colo. 1971].)

PART 4

The Law of Commercial Paper

Commercial paper takes many forms. In its most familiar form, we know it as the check that we look forward to on payday and that our creditors look forward to on their paydays. If you have ever taken a loan from a bank, you have signed some type of promissory note, which is another form of commercial paper.

Merriam-Webster defines commercial paper as "short-term negotiable instruments arising out of commercial transactions." Millions of such instruments are signed each day, not only because they are a safe and convenient means of doing business that eliminates the risk of dealing in cash, but also because they are acceptable in the commercial world as a credit instrument — a substitute for money.

This part of the text explores how and why commercial paper is so widely used and so readily accepted in the modern commercial world.

CHAPTER 23

An Introduction to Commercial Paper

HISTORIC OVERVIEW

Commercial paper of some type has been present in nearly every society that has developed a substantial commercial system. Documents very similar to the contemporary **promissory note** have been dated back to about 2100 B.C. The merchants of Europe were using negotiable documents on a broad scale by the thirteenth century. In fact, the use of **drafts** was so widespread that a substantial portion of the law merchant was devoted to their proper treatment.

Commercial paper had become so pervasive by the late nineteenth century that the English Parliament began to enact special statutes to govern its use. Following the example of the English, the National Conference of Commissioners on Uniform State Laws drafted the *Uniform Negotiable Instruments Law* (NIL) for the United States in 1896. Each of these statutes merely attempted to cover the common law rules that had been developed over the years.

The NIL was designed to unify and codify the rules and laws of each

Promissory note A written promise to pay a sum of money at a future time unconditionally

Drafts Orders for the payment of money drawn by one person on another

jurisdiction regarding all negotiable commercial documents. However, the breadth of the topical coverage made the NIL unwieldy and difficult to apply to the commercial world of the twentieth century.

Thus, the *Uniform Commercial Code* (UCC) was written to comply more readily with the demands of the modern business world. It has been adopted by every state in the union except Louisiana, and Louisiana has adopted some portions, including Articles 3 and 4. The UCC, or "the Code" as it is frequently called, has retained most of the traditional rules and views of commercial paper. But it has used its codification to standardize and to clarify the topic rather than to change it. The codification of commercial paper is located in Article 3 of the Code.

THE SCOPE OF ARTICLE 3

The Uniform Commercial Code is divided into eleven articles. Each article has a different purpose and is designed to do a different thing. For example, Article 1 deals with general concepts and definitions, among other things. Articles 10 and 11 deal with the effective dates of coverage and some technical details. The remaining eight articles (Article 2 through Article 9) are each devoted to a particular topic of commercial law. The article dedicated to commercial paper is Article 3, cited as "Article 3: Uniform Commercial Code — Commercial Paper."

Negotiable instruments Written promises or orders for the payment of a sum certain of money to order or to bearer

Subject to Liable, subordinate, subservient, inferior, obedient to; governed or affected by

Documents Instruments on which are recorded matter that may be used as evidence; written instruments used to prove a fact

The Code's coverage of commercial paper is restricted to **negotiable instruments,** as defined in Section 3 – 103, and it is limited to these instruments. Section 3 – 103(1) states that Article 3 governs neither money, nor documents of title, nor investment securities. Moreover, Section 3 – 103(2) cross-references to the coverages of Articles 4 (bank collections and deposits) and 9 (secured transactions), stating that Article 3 is **subject to** these referenced articles.

Thus, one finds that Article 3 covers negotiable instruments but not other types of commercial or negotiable documents and that two other articles of the Code may supplement, complement, or override the provisions of Article 3.

FUNCTIONS AND FORMS

Commercial paper has two major *functions:* it is designed to serve as a substitute for money, and it is designed to serve as a credit instrument. In satisfying either use, it carries certain contract rights, certain property rights, and some special rights due exclusively to its nature as commercial paper.

Every negotiable instrument is presumed to be a contract, but not every contract is a negotiable instrument. The difference between a contract and a negotiable instrument is one of *form.* To be negotiable, an instrument must be (1) current in trade and (2) payable in money. These criteria are obviously too broad and too vague to be of much practical significance. Accordingly, Article 3 has more fully defined the requirements an instrument must meet in order to be negotiable. (These requirements will be dealt with in detail in Chapter 24.)

UCC Section 3–104 lists the four forms a negotiable instrument may take. Every negotiable instrument must be in one of these forms:

1. promissory note
2. certificate of deposit
3. draft
4. check

The first two forms, promissory notes (referred to as notes) and certificates of deposit (referred to as CDs), are one class of negotiable instruments; this class is known as promise paper. Drafts and checks constitute the other class, which is known as order paper.

The distinctive features of order paper, or three-party paper, are that each instrument contains an *order* to pay money and that at least *three parties* are necessary to fill the legal roles involved. The order element will be pointed out in the following sections, and the rules governing this class of negotiable instrument will be explained in the final portion of the chapter. The three parties are the drawer, the drawee, and the payee. As noted, this class consists of drafts and checks.

ORDER PAPER ("THREE-PARTY" PAPER)

A *draft* is *an instrument in which one party, the drawer, issues an instrument to a second party, the payee.* The draft is accepted by the payee as a substitute for money. The payee expects to receive money at some time from the third party, the drawee. The reason the payee expects to receive money from the drawee is contained in the basic form of the instrument. As will be pointed out, the drawer issues an order to the drawee to pay a sum of money. This order, coupled with the three roles involved, distinguishes drafts from promise paper. The components of a draft are illustrated in Figure 23.1.

Drafts

The most common type of order paper is a *check*. Checks are special types of drafts. Like a draft, a check necessitates the involvement of three parties, but there are two differences. A check is, by definition, a **demand instrument;** in contrast, a draft may be a demand instrument or a **time instrument.** And on a check, *the drawee must be a bank;* in contrast, anyone may be the drawee on a draft. Figure 23.2 illustrates the various elements of a check.

In both a check and a draft, the drawee is obligated to the drawer. This obligation is normally a debt owed to the drawer. When the drawer *orders* the drawee to pay, the drawer is directing the drawee as to how the debt should be discharged or partially discharged. The order to the drawee to pay, coupled with the obligation to pay, assures the payee that payment will probably be made by the drawee at the appropriate time.

Checks

Demand instrument An instrument that is due at once; a present debt or obligation

Time instrument An instrument that is due at a future, determinable time or date

Figure 23.1 A Bank Draft

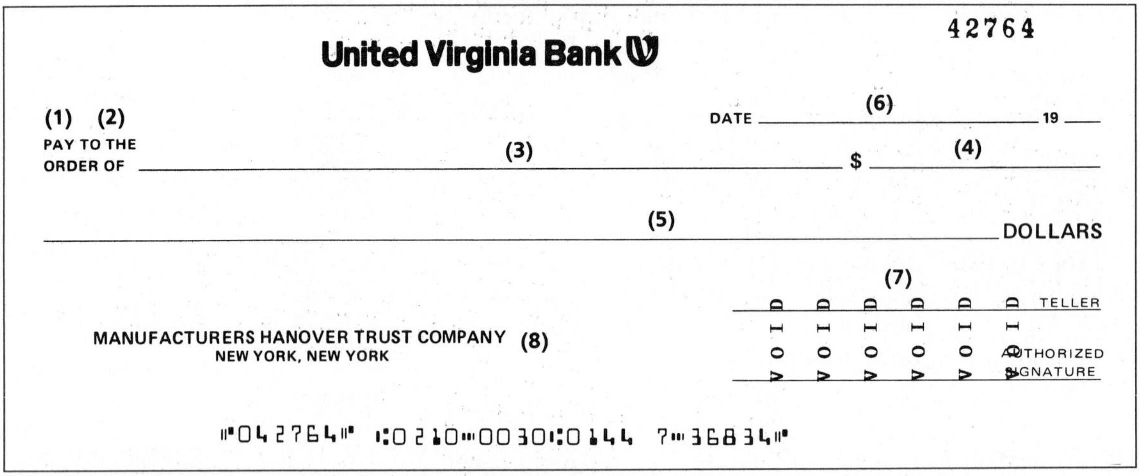
42764

United Virginia Bank

(1) (2)
PAY TO THE ORDER OF (3)

DATE (6) 19

$ (4)

(5) DOLLARS

(7)

VOID VOID VOID VOID VOID TELLER

AUTHORIZED SIGNATURE

MANUFACTURERS HANOVER TRUST COMPANY (8)
NEW YORK, NEW YORK

⑈042764⑈ ⑆0210⑉0030⑆0144 7⑉36834⑈

Courtesy of Crestar Bank (formerly United Virginia Bank) of Radford, Virginia.

(1) The order. **(2)** Words of negotiability. **(3)** The payee. **(4)** The amount, in numbers. **(5)** The amount, in words. **(6)** The date of issue. **(7)** The drawer's signature. **(8)** The drawee.

The Order

Both a check and a draft contain an order. The drawer orders the drawee to pay the instrument. The language used is not a request. The drawer does not "ask," or "hope," or even "expect" the drawee to pay. The drawer *demands* that payment be made. If you look at Figure 23.1 or 23.2, you will see that the drawer tells the drawee to: "*Pay* to the order of ___(Payee)___." It should also

Figure 23.2 A Check

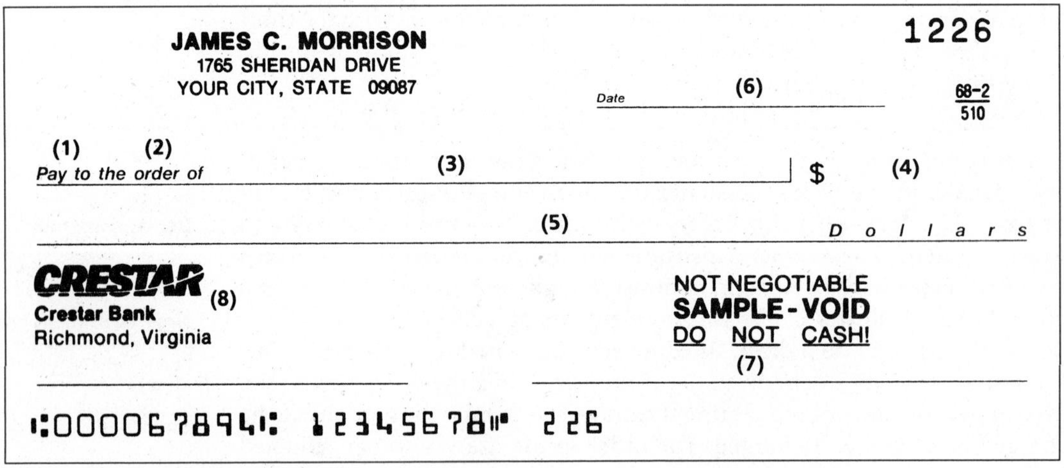
JAMES C. MORRISON
1765 SHERIDAN DRIVE
YOUR CITY, STATE 09087

1226

Date (6)

68-2
510

(1) (2)
Pay to the order of (3) $ (4)

(5) *Dollars*

CRESTAR (8)
Crestar Bank
Richmond, Virginia

NOT NEGOTIABLE
SAMPLE-VOID
DO NOT CASH!
(7)

⑆000067894⑆ 12345678⑈ 226

Courtesy of Crestar Bank, Radford, Virginia.

(1) The order. **(2)** Words of negotiability. **(3)** The payee. **(4)** The amount, in numbers. **(5)** The amount, in words. **(6)** The date of issue. **(7)** The drawer's signature. **(8)** The drawee.

be noted that the *order* is the word *pay;* the phrase "to the order of" is *not* the order. This phrase is a term of negotiability. Its meaning will be explained in the next chapter, which deals with negotiability.

The Drawer

The person who *draws* an order instrument, who *gives* the order to the drawee, and who **issues** the instrument to the payee is known as the *drawer.* This person originates the check or the draft. The drawer does not pay the payee directly. The drawee is expected to pay the payee or the **holder,** upon proper **presentment.** That is why the drawer gives the drawee the order. The drawer expects the order to be obeyed because of a prior agreement or relationship between the drawer and the drawee. If the order is obeyed, the drawee pays the payee or holder, and the drawer has performed.

Issues Puts into circulation

Holder One legally in possession of a negotiable instrument by negotiation

Presentment The act of giving a negotiable instrument to the drawee or maker for acceptance and/or payment

The Drawee

The party to whom the order on the check or draft is *directed* is the *drawee.* The drawee is told by the drawer to "pay to the order of" the payee. It is the drawee who is expected to make payment to the presenting party. However, the drawee has no duty to the payee or to the holder to pay, despite the order. The only duty the drawee has is a duty owed to the drawer. The duty of the drawee is to **accept** the instrument. Before acceptance, there is only the prospect that the drawee will pay when the time for payment arrives. Once the drawee accepts, the drawee has a contractual obligation to pay the presenter. This relationship is illustrated in Figure 23.3.

Accept Make an engagement to pay the negotiable instrument in money when due

The Payee

The *payee* is the person to whom the instrument is *originally issued.* The payee may be specifically designated, as in "Pay to the order of *Jane Doe*"; the payee

Figure 23.3 The Parties on Order Paper

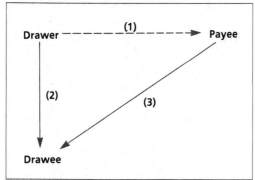

(1) The drawer is *presumed* to have a contract with the payee since the instrument was issued. (2) The drawer is *presumed* to have a contract or an understanding with the drawee which will cause the drawee to obey the *order.* (3) The payee and the drawee have *no* contract, and *no* understanding on the instrument in question until *presentment* and *acceptance* occur.

may be an office or title, as in "Pay to the order of *Treasurer of Truro County*"; or the particular payee may be unspecified, as in "Pay to the order of *bearer*." The payee may decide to seek payment personally, or the payee may decide to further negotiate the instrument. The words "to the order of" allow the payee to order the drawee to make payment to some other party.

PROMISE PAPER ("TWO-PARTY" PAPER)

Maker One who makes or executes a promise-paper negotiable instrument

The class of negotiable instruments covering notes and CDs is promise paper, or two-party paper. The distinctive features of this class are that each instrument contains a *promise* to pay (or to repay) money and that only *two parties* are necessary to fill the legal roles involved. These two parties are known as the **maker** and the payee.

The term *two-party* is confusing to many people. Many stores have signs prominently posted stating that they do not accept "two-party checks." These so-called two-party checks are, in reality, checks that are being negotiated by the payee to a later holder. The store does not want to accept a check unless it receives it *directly* from the drawer. But there is no such legal creature as a *check* that is "two-party paper."

The promise element of promise paper will be pointed out in the following sections, and the rules governing this class of negotiable instrument will be explained in the final portion of the chapter.

Promissory Notes

The promissory note is the oldest known form of negotiable instrument. It is normally used as a credit instrument, executed either at the time credit is extended or as evidence of a preexisting debt not yet repaid.

In a note, one party (the maker) *promises* to pay the other party (the payee) a sum of money at some future time. The promise may call for a lump-sum payment, or it may call for installment payments over time. The note may specify the payment of interest in addition to the principal; it may have the interest included in the principal; or it may be interest free. The note may recite details about **collateral.** Despite any or all of these possibilities, the basic form is constant. Such an instrument is illustrated in Figure 23.4.

Collateral A security given in addition to the direct security, intended to guaranty its validity or ensure its performance

Certificates of Deposit

A *certificate of deposit* (or a CD, as it is commonly called) is a special type of note issued by a *bank* as an acknowledgment of money *received,* with a *promise* to repay the money at some future date. Many people think of a CD as a time savings account, in contrast to a passbook savings account. In reality, though, a CD is not a savings account at all. It is most commonly a time deposit of money with a bank.

A CD normally pays higher interest than a savings account, with the interest varying according to the amount of time the certificate is to run. Most certificates run for some multiple of six months, and they come in some multiple of $1000. However, a number of banks offer CDs for shorter time periods, such as ninety days. And some banks are beginning to offer CDs for multiples of $100. One type of CD is illustrated in Figure 23.5.

Figure 23.4   A Promissory Note

Great American Federal
Savings Bank

PROMISSORY NOTE

Loan No.

Borrower(s)
Name(s) _____ and _____
          first   middle   last   first   middle   last

(1) (2) Address **(3)   (2)**
Borrower (jointly and severally if more than one) promises to pay to Great American Federal Savings Bank ("Lender"), or order, in U.S. money, at its office in San Diego, California, or elsewhere Lender designates, principal and interest on unpaid principal from the date advanced until paid, in amount, annual rate and consecutive monthly installments as follows:

Principal	$ **(4)**	Annual Interest Rate	%
Installments	$	on the same day of month beginning	
Minimum Interest	$ 100.00		

Interest will be computed on the basis of a 12 month year and 30 day month. The date of payment, whether early or late, will be disregarded for purposes of allocating the payment between principal and interest; each payment will be treated for this purpose as though made on its due date.

PREPAYMENT: Full or partial prepayment may be made without penalty except Borrower will pay any minimum interest amount specified. Borrower will tell Lender in writing that Borrower is making a prepayment. Lender will use all prepayments to reduce the principal subject to its right to first apply payments received to any past due interest or other charges. Partial prepayments will not delay the due dates nor change the amount of monthly payments unless Lender agrees in writing to those delays or changes. Full prepayment may be made at any time. Lender may require that partial prepayment be made on the same day as monthly payments are due. Lender may also require that the amount of any partial prepayment be equal to the amount of principal that would have been part of the next one or more monthly payments.

LATE CHARGE: Borrower will pay a late charge of 5% of each installment not paid within 15 days of its due date, or $5.00, whichever is greater.

DEFAULT AND ACCELERATION: If Borrower fails to timely pay any installment when due or to perform any provision contained in any document securing this Note, Lender may, at Lender's option, declare all sums owed hereunder immediately due and payable. Borrower will pay all reasonable expenses and attorney's fees of Lender in any action relating to Borrower's obligations.

SELLER, IF ANY: Borrower intends to use some or all of the loan proceeds to pay _____,
as Seller, amounts due Seller under a contract between Seller and Borrower, dated _____.
Borrower represents that a true and correct copy of the contract has been furnished to Lender and that it contains the entire agreement between Seller and Borrower. The following notice applies only to the named Seller, if any, and to the proceeds hereof paid to said Seller under the described contract.

NOTICE: ANY HOLDER OF THIS CONSUMER CREDIT CONTRACT IS SUBJECT TO ALL CLAIMS AND DEFENSES WHICH THE DEBTOR COULD ASSERT AGAINST THE SELLER OF GOODS OR SERVICES OBTAINED WITH THE PROCEEDS HEREOF. RECOVERY HEREUNDER BY THE DEBTOR SHALL NOT EXCEED AMOUNTS PAID BY THE DEBTOR HEREUNDER.

NON-WAIVER: By accepting payment after its due date or after notice of default, Lender will not waive its right to prompt payment when due of other sums, or to declare a default, or to proceed with any remedy it has. Without affecting the liability of anyone else, Lender may release anyone liable, may change payment terms, and add, alter, substitute, or release security.

☐ This Note is secured by a Security Agreement.
☐ This Note is unsecured.

BEFORE SIGNING ORIGINAL, WE RECEIVED AND READ A COMPLETED COPY HEREOF.

(5)
_____   _____   _____   _____
Borrower's Signature   Date   Borrower's Signature   Date

_____   _____   _____   _____
Borrower's Signature   Date   Borrower's Signature   Date

(Sign Original Only)

C-1-424 (Rev. 6/83)

Courtesy of Great American Federal Savings Bank of San Diego and Fresno, California.
(1) The *promise.* **(2)** Words of negotiability. **(3)** The *payee.* **(4)** The amount borrowed. **(5)** The signature of the *maker.*

Figure 23.5 A Negotiable Certificate of Deposit

Courtesy of Great American Federal Savings Bank (formerly San Diego Federal) of San Diego and Fresno, California.
(1) The date of issue. **(2)** The amount of the "deposit," in words. **(3)** The amount of the "deposit," in numbers.
(4) The *payee*. **(5)** The maturity date. **(6)** The amount to be paid. **(7)** The signature of the *maker*.

Many banks today offer some variation of a "saver's certificate" rather than a negotiable certificate of deposit. It appears that the CD is becoming extinct. However, some CDs still exist, so the topic at least needs to be raised. But the widespread replacement of CDs with other forms of certificates makes this primarily an area of historic interest.

The Promise

Promise paper is so called because it contains a promise. The maker of the instrument *promises* to pay an amount of money to the payee or to a holder. The instrument does not say that the maker "might" pay, or will "probably" pay, or will "agree" to pay. The instrument says that the maker promises to pay an amount of money to the payee or to the order of the payee.

The Maker

The duties performed by the drawer and the drawee on order paper are effectively combined in promise paper: both duties fall to the *maker*. The maker *makes the promise* ("I promise to pay to the order of [the payee]"); the maker *issues the instrument to the payee;* and the maker *pays the instrument upon proper presentment.* However, there is one important difference from order paper. While the drawee is not obligated to any holder until acceptance, the maker *is* liable to a holder from the date of original issue. This is illustrated in Figure 23.6.

Figure 23.6 The Parties on Promise Paper

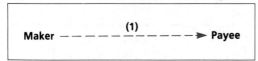

(1) The maker is *presumed* to have a contract with the payee since an instrument has been issued, and the maker is obligated to accept and to pay the instrument upon proper presentment by the maker or by a holder.

Negotiable instruments are widely used in our economy. They are used as a substitute for money. They are used for convenience. They are used as credit instruments. They are used to pay bills, to buy things, and to borrow. Some of the most important uses of each type are set out in the following sections.

The most commonly used type of negotiable instrument is a check. Many people use checks rather than cash for regular daily purchases. Checks are regularly written to the supermarket for groceries, to the utility companies to pay bills, to the landlord to pay the rent, and to the bank to make loan payments. In addition, many working people receive their salaries or wages in periodic paychecks from their employers.

Checks are widely used because they are easily written, easily carried, and widely accepted. Carrying and using checks is safer than carrying and using cash. If a person loses a blank, unsigned check, no harm is done. All that was lost was a piece of paper. If a person loses cash, the money is gone. The bank will not take an unsigned check, but it will take lost money. Great care should be taken with checks. A signed check, otherwise blank, is as good as cash. Anyone finding such a check can complete the blanks and receive cash for it as completed.

Businesses often use drafts to pay for merchandise ordered, especially when the buyer and the seller are in different states. Drafts may be payable "at sight" (that is, on demand), or they may be "time drafts" (that is, they are payable at a future date). Often a seller of goods will send a draft to the buyer for acceptance. If the buyer accepts, he or she has agreed to pay any holder who makes proper presentment. Such a draft is called a *trade acceptance.*

With the recent liberalization of federal and state banking laws and regulations, a number of changes have occurred in the area of commercial paper. One of these changes has been in the area of drafts. Today many credit unions offer accounts similar to the checking accounts offered by banks and savings and loan institutions. These drafting accounts offer the same uses for credit union depositors as are available to depositors of banks. Technically, however, these are *not* checking accounts, and there are some minor differences. A sample "share draft" is illustrated in Figure 23.7.

USES OF NEGOTIABLE INSTRUMENTS

Checks

Drafts

Figure 23.7   A Share Draft

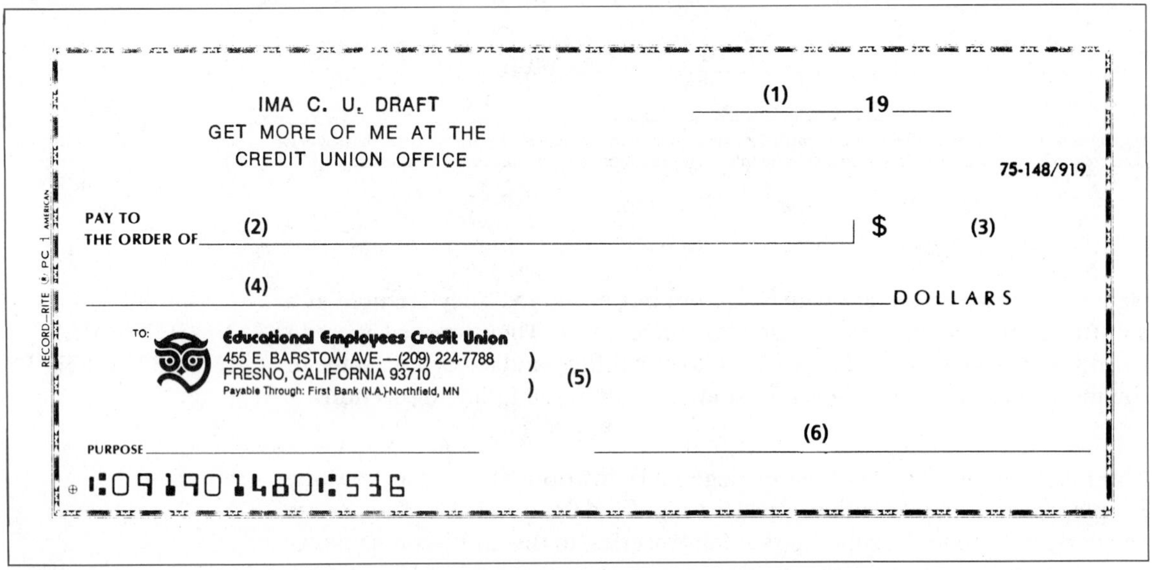

IMA C. U. DRAFT
GET MORE OF ME AT THE
CREDIT UNION OFFICE

(1)   19_____

75-148/919

PAY TO
THE ORDER OF_____ (2) _____ $ (3)

(4)

DOLLARS

TO: **Educational Employees Credit Union**
455 E. BARSTOW AVE.—(209) 224-7788
FRESNO, CALIFORNIA 93710   )
Payable Through: First Bank (N.A.)-Northfield, MN   )   (5)

PURPOSE _____   (6)

⑂ ⑈091901480⑈536

Courtesy of Educational Employees Credit Union of Fresno, California.
(1) The date of issue. **(2)** The payee. **(3)** The amount, in numbers. **(4)** The amount, in words. **(5)** The drawee.
(6) The signature of the drawer.

Promissory Notes

Mortgage note A contract binding all of a property to secure payment of a promissory note

Installment note A promissory note calling for periodic payments at predetermined times

Promissory notes are used as instruments of credit. They are also used as evidence to show a preexisting debt. Any time a customer borrows money from a bank, the borrower must sign a promissory note. This signed note proves the existence of the debt, the amount owed, the manner of repayment, and any other terms important to the loan agreement. Notes are so widely used that special types of notes have developed. Real estate loans normally involve a **mortgage note.** Automobile loans usually involve an **installment note.** Many banks also use a device called a commercial loan note or a signature note for short-term unsecured loans (loans made without collateral).

Certificates of Deposit

A certificate of deposit is an instrument issued by a bank evidencing a debt owed to a depositor. These instruments commonly call for the bank to pay to a proper presenter the amount deposited plus interest at a stated future date. Although regularly thought of as a type of special savings account, CDs are really credit instruments. They recognize money "borrowed" by the bank from its depositor.

SUMMARY

Article 3 of the Uniform Commercial Code involves negotiable instruments, also known as commercial paper. These negotiable instruments serve two major functions: they operate as a substitute for money, and they are used as credit instruments. All negotiable instruments are "current in trade" and are payable in money.

There are two major classes of commercial paper, and two types of negotiable instrument are included in each class. The first class, order paper, is primarily used as a substitute for money. This class consists of checks and drafts. The necessary parties involved in this class of instrument are the drawer, the drawee, and the payee. The other class, promise paper, is primarily a credit instrument. It consists of promissory notes and certificates of deposit. The necessary parties involved are the maker and the payee.

DISCUSSION QUESTIONS

1. The person who promises to pay money on a promissory note has a particular role. What is this role called?

2. On a check, a particular institution must be the drawee. What type of institution is the drawee on a check?

3. What special requirement other than the drawee requirement distinguishes a check from a draft?

4. A check or a draft must contain a communication from the drawer to the drawee. What form does this communication take?

5. One type of negotiable instrument is frequently referred to as a time deposit or as a time savings account. What is the proper legal name of this type of instrument?

6. Commercial paper has two major functions. What are these functions?

7. The Uniform Commercial Code supplanted the Uniform Negotiable Instruments Law in covering commercial paper. How was the UCC able to simplify this area, when the NIL could not do so?

8. What two sets of duties on order paper are performed by the maker of promise paper?

9. On order paper such as a check, what must occur before the drawee is obligated to make payment?

10. Every type of commercial paper has a role for the person receiving the instrument initially. What is the proper name of this role?

CHAPTER 24

Negotiability

FORMAL REQUIREMENTS

Defenses Arguments offered by the defendant as reasons in law or fact why the plaintiff should not recover

Unconditional Not limited or affected by any condition

Commercial paper has a special place in business law. Under certain circumstances, the holder of a negotiable instrument is permitted to collect the money despite any **defenses.** The instrument, if correctly made or drawn, will move easily through the commercial world. However, the law is very jealous of these potential benefits. To carry the benefits of negotiability, an instrument must meet the formal requirements of negotiability. These requirements are set out in Section 3 – 104(1) of the UCC:

Any writing to be a negotiable instrument within this Article must

(a) be signed by the maker or drawer; and
(b) contain an **unconditional** promise or order to pay a sum certain in money and no other promise, order, obligation or power given by the maker or drawer except as authorized by this Article; and,
(c) be payable on demand or at a definite time; and
(d) be payable to order or to bearer.

These elements are pictured in Figure 24.1. Notice that *every* element must be present. The absence of any element negates negotiability. This does not mean that the paper becomes worthless. It only means that the paper is no longer negotiable under the law. And that means no holder would have the protec-

Figure 24.1 The Elements of Negotiability

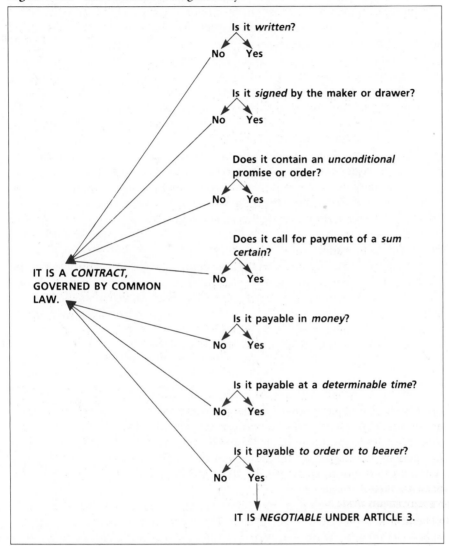

Is it *written*?
No   Yes

Is it *signed* by the maker or drawer?
No   Yes

Does it contain an *unconditional promise or order*?
No   Yes

Does it call for payment of a *sum certain*?
No   Yes

IT IS A *CONTRACT*, GOVERNED BY COMMON LAW.

Is it payable in *money*?
No   Yes

Is it payable at a *determinable time*?
No   Yes

Is it payable *to order* or *to bearer*?
No   Yes

IT IS *NEGOTIABLE* UNDER ARTICLE 3.

tions afforded by Article 3. The person holding the paper would still have potential contract rights, however.

Commercial paper represents an **intangible right,** the right to collect money at some future time. However, to satisfy the requirements of Article 3, the proof of this right must be tangible. The simplest way to prove that the right exists is to put it in writing. As defined in Section 1–201 (46), a writing includes "printing, typewriting or any other intentional reduction to tangible form."

Writing Requirement

Intangible right A right that has no physical existence of its own

For many people, the type of negotiable instrument most frequently encountered is the check. Most checks are in a standard form, preprinted on paper. Similarly, many drafts are preprinted, in standard form, on paper. Also, most certificates of deposit are preprinted on paper. And many notes are preprinted in a form readily adaptable to the needs of the lender/preparer. These preprinted, standardized forms are familiar, and they contain blanks at all the appropriate places to streamline their completion. However, such convenience is just that — a convenience. It is *not* a necessity.

Commercial paper is equally valid when prepared by handwriting on a scratch pad. Or on a matchbook cover. Or on virtually any other relatively permanent thing. For example, several years ago, on a television series entitled "Love American Style," a couple was marooned on a desert island. The only thing they had for entertainment was a deck of cards. According to the plot, they spent their time playing gin. When they were rescued, the young lady had won $1 million. As evidence, she had a check . . . written on her stomach! Despite the comedy implications so heavily emphasized, such a check would be valid.

On April 15, a disgruntled taxpayer completed his tax return. When he mailed in his return, he included a check for the taxes due and a note. The note said: "You've been trying to get it for years, and you've finally succeeded. Here's the shirt off my back." The note was pinned to his check, which was written on his undershirt.

However, the joke was on him. The IRS cashed it!

Signature Requirement

On a check or a draft, an order is given by the drawer. On a note or a CD, a promise is given by the maker. Given the widespread use of preprinted forms as negotiable instruments, some protection is needed from fraud or trickery. The UCC tries to minimize the potential for fakery. It does this by requiring a *signature* by the maker or the drawer. Most people think of a signature as a manual subscription, an autograph. That is a signature, but it is not the only possible type of signature.

A corporation, being an inanimate creature, cannot sign its own name. Yet corporations need to "sign" checks. The checks can, of course, be signed by agents of the corporation. But even this is impractical. Some corporations issue thousands of checks each month. An authorized signer would spend nearly an entire career "autographing" checks for the corporation.

Fortunately, the UCC solved this problem. The solution is found in Section 1–201 (39), which defines a signature as *any mark or symbol executed with the present intent to authenticate a writing.* Thus, a corporation can use a stamp to sign checks. Likewise, a negotiable instrument can be signed by affixing an *X*, or a thumbprint, or any other intentionally affixed symbol.

There are problems with unusual types of signatures. They may be so strange that people will be hesitant to accept them or the instrument containing them. And the unusual signature must be proved by the person trying to claim the instrument.[1]

It makes no difference where the instrument is signed. Although it is normal to sign in the lower right-hand corner of the face of the instrument, the signature can be anywhere. For example, in a note beginning "I, Mary Smith, promise to pay," Mary Smith's signature following the word *I* would be sufficient.

One of the ways in which a signature can be made on a negotiable instrument was shown in the following case.

First Security Bank of Brookfield v. Fastwich, Inc.
612 S.W.2d 799 (Mo. 1981)

FACTS

The Smiths were the officers and directors of Fastwich. As officers of the corporation, they were authorized to borrow money on behalf of the firm. Fastwich needed funds, and the Smiths approached First Security Bank for a loan. First Security loaned the firm $10,000 and prepared a promissory note as evidence of the debt. In the upper left hand corner of the note was typed "Fastwich, Inc." In the lower right hand corner of the note was the following:

[Typed]FASTWICH, INC.
[Signed]John J. Smith, Jr. [s]Carolyn Smith
[s]   Gary D. Smith   [s]Cheryl J. Smith

Fastwich subsequently defaulted on the loan, and the bank attempted to collect the money owed. Fastwich denied that it was liable to the bank because the bank failed to establish the validity of its signature on the note.

ISSUE

Was Fastwich's signature on the note? If so, was the signature valid?

HOLDING

Yes. Fastwich's signature was on the note, and the presence of the signature carries a presumption of validity.

REASONING

Section 3–307 of the Code presumes that all signatures are genuine or authorized unless the action involves an obligation of a person who has died or who has become incompetent. Absent one of those circumstances, the defendant must introduce evidence that the signature is a forgery or was not authorized. In this case, Fastwich failed to introduce any evidence that called the validity of the signature into question, so the signature must be presumed to be genuine. The Code permits a signature by typing, and it permits a signature by authorized representatives. Both appear to be present in this case. Fastwich's signature was, therefore, on the instrument, and the signature must be presumed to be valid until it is shown to be otherwise.

---

[1] Uniform Commercial Code, Section 3–307(1)(a).

Unconditional Promise or Order Requirement

Negotiable instruments are designed to move easily through the commercial world. To serve effectively as a substitute for money, a negotiable instrument must be freely transferable. It also needs to be in a form that people can accept. These needs are met by the requirement that the promise made, or the order given, be *unconditional.* A person taking possession of a negotiable instrument wants to know that payment can be reasonably expected under *every* circumstance. A prospective holder would not be eager to accept an instrument that says payment *might* be made, or will be made *only if* something happens. The holder wants an unconditional promise that the money will be paid.

The Code has gone to great lengths to define *unconditional.* Section 3 – 105 lists ten different things that do *not* make the promise or order conditional. However, a reading of this section by the uninitiated may be confusing. As a result, the courts frequently rely on the so-called four-corner rule. The four-corner rule requires that every necessary bit of information to determine rights on an instrument be contained within its four corners; that is, the information must be found *on the instrument itself.* If the holder must look to some source of information other than the instrument in order to determine rights, the instrument is not negotiable. (The four-corner rule also applies to *time of payment* and *sum certain* requirements.)

Several standard statements frequently found on a negotiable instrument are deemed to be *not* conditional. Some of the more important of these follow:[2]

1.   A statement of consideration as the basis for the instrument is not a condition to payment. This is true whether the consideration has been performed or has merely been promised. And it is true if the instrument says it was issued "as per agreement," or uses words of similar meaning. Since the instrument is presumed to be issued because of an agreement, a statement that this is true does not make payment conditional.

2.   A statement that the instrument arose from a separate agreement or that it refers to a separate agreement does not make payment conditional. This is true even if the separate agreement sets out the rights for acceleration of payment.

3.   A statement concerning security interests or collateral connected to the instrument will not make payment conditional. This is true even if the holder may, at various times, demand that additional collateral be put forward to protect the interests of any holders involved.

4.   A statement indicating that a particular *account* is to be debited or that a particular fund is expected to provide reimbursement is not conditional. Nor is it conditional if the entire assets of a partnership, unincorporated association, trust, or estate are listed as the sole source of payment.

However, it is deemed conditional, and therefore a denial of negotiability,

[2] Ibid., Section 3 – 105(1).

if payment is restricted to a particular source of funds other than those just mentioned.[3]

Thus, a statement that a particular note is to be paid from the proceeds from selling a car is conditional. No holder would be able to rely on payment in such a note unless it was known that (1) the car had been sold, and (2) the selling price was at least as great as the note amount.

It is also deemed a condition if the instrument is *subject to* or *governed by* a separate agreement or document.[4] This means that an instrument drafted "as per our contract" is negotiable. But an instrument "subject to our contract" is *not* negotiable.

In the following case, a note was treated as nonnegotiable because of its reference to a separate contract that was to be treated as a part of the "note."

Holly Hill Acres, Ltd. v. *Charter Bank of Gainesville*
314 So.2d 209 (Fla. 1975)

Holly Hill Acres, Ltd., executed and delivered a promissory note and a mortgage to Rogers and Blythe. Rogers and Blythe subsequently transferred the note and the mortgage to Charter Bank of Gainesville as security on another note. Eventually Holly Hill dishonored the note. The bank sued both Holly Hill and Rogers and Blythe.

FACTS

Was the note negotiable, so that Charter Bank could be a holder in due course?

ISSUE

No. The note was conditional and therefore not negotiable.

HOLDING

The note in question contained the following clause: "This note with interest is secured by a mortgage on real estate, of even date herewith, made by the maker [Holly Hill Acres] here of in favor of the said payee. . . . The terms of said mortgage are by this reference made a part hereof." Because of this reference, the court ruled that the instrument was conditional and thus not negotiable. Holly Hill could assert its defense and avoid paying the Charter Bank of Gainesville. A holder in due course can exist, and override defenses, only on a negotiable instrument.

REASONING

A holder of a negotiable instrument must know how much money is to be received when the instrument is paid. The amount is commonly specified exactly, which makes the determination simple, but this is not necessary to satisfy the *sum certain* requirement. To meet the requirement of a sum certain,

Sum Certain
Requirement

---

[3] Ibid., Section 3 – 105(2)(b).
[4] Ibid., Section 3 – 105(2)(a).

the amount must be calculable from the face of the instrument. This once again raises the four-corner rule. All the necessary information must be on the instrument for the calculation of the total amount due, even if the calculation has not been done.

Under Section 3–106(1), the sum is certain even if it is to be paid under any of the following conditions:

1.   with stated interest or by stated installments
2.   with stated different rates of interest before and after default or a specified date
3.   with a stated discount or addition if paid before or after the date fixed for payment
4.   "with **exchange**" or "less exchange," whether at a fixed rate or at the current rate
5.   with costs of collection or an attorney's fee, or both, upon default

As if these provisions are not enough, Section 3–118(d) provides that a statement that the instrument is payable "with interest" still carries a sum certain. The rationale is that "with interest" means interest at the **judgment rate,** and the holder has *constructive notice* of what the judgment is for the jurisdiction. However, payment of interest at the **current rate** is not a sum certain. The current rate varies, and the holder would need to look beyond the four corners to determine the amount due.

Money Requirement

Since commercial paper serves as a substitute for money, payment must ultimately be made in *money.* Money is defined as *a medium of exchange authorized or adopted by a domestic or foreign government as part of its currency.*[5] Thus, gold and silver are *not* money, but pounds sterling, lira, drachmas, and the like are.

There are really only two problems with payment "in money." The first problem arises when payment is stated in a foreign currency. The second problem involves alternatives for payment. The UCC resolves the first problem, and a number of cases decided under the NIL apparently resolved the second.

Under Section 3–107(2), when foreign currency is called for, the instrument must be read carefully. If the instrument *specifies* the foreign currency, payment must be made in that currency. But if the foreign currency is merely *stated,* payment may be made either in the foreign currency or in U.S. dollars at the exchange rate on the payable date.

To understand the second problem, suppose that an instrument calls for the payment of $2000 or ten ounces of gold; is this instrument negotiable? The answer depends on who has the option. If the *maker* or *drawer* can decide which medium to offer at the due date, the instrument is *not* negotiable. However, if

Exchange Interchange or conversion of the money of two countries or of current and uncurrent monies with an allowance for differences in value

Judgment rate Rate of interest prescribed by the laws of the particular state or country, which must be paid in all cases where the law allows interest regardless of the debtor's consent

Current rate Rate of interest currently being charged by financial institutions and recognized as the "going rate" or the "market rate"

[5] Ibid., Section 1–201(24).

the *holder* has the option of choosing the money or the alternative, the instrument *is* negotiable. The reasoning behind this rule is that if the holder has the option, the money *must* be available, thus satisfying the requirement of payment in money. The alternative payment form gives the holder a hedge against inflation, thus making the instrument more enticing and increasing its marketability.

Not only does a holder want to know how much money will be paid (sum certain), and in what medium (money), but also *when* payment can be expected. The question of when will depend on the instrument, but it must be payable either *on demand* (Section 3 – 108) or at a *definite time* (Section 3 – 109).

An instrument is payable on demand when payment is to be made *at sight,* or *at presentment,* or when no time for payment is stated. Any form of instrument may be payable on demand, but promise paper (notes and CDs) is normally not payable on demand. A check *must* be payable on demand, by definition. Thus, a **postdated check** is technically no longer a check; rather, it is a draft.

The payee or holder must be able to tell when the instrument is payable by looking at the face of the instrument. Unless the instrument *specifies* that it is to be paid at some future date (payable at a definite time), it is payable on demand. On demand means whenever the holder presents it to the drawee or maker. A check has no time provisions (see Figure 23.2). It will normally be dated *when* issued with the date of issue. It is payable from that date forward. If a drawer issues a check on June 1 but dates it June 15, the check is not payable on demand. The check has therefore become a *time draft.*

An instrument is payable at a definite time if, by its terms, it is payable at a time that can be determined from its face. This definite time will frequently be some stated future date, as "24 September 19XX." Or it may be at some time after a stated date, such as "90 days after 3 March 19XX." Either of these dates would be definite even if some provision was made for accelerating the payment date. And they would be definite with a provision for extending the time, if the holder has the option of extension, or even if the maker or **acceptor** has the option of extending the time. However, in this last situation the extension must be a predetermined definite period, not to exceed the original term.

The UCC also stipulates that payment is at a definite time if payment is a stated period after sight (that is, after presentment). Thus, an instrument calling for payment "60 days after sight" is payable at a definite time. Although the holder must act (present the instrument to establish the date of sight), once the act is done, the date is definite.

However, one must be careful in this area. According to Section 3 – 109(2), payment is *not* at a definite time if it is to occur only upon an act or occurrence that is of uncertain date. This is true even if the event has already occurred. For example, an instrument payable "30 days after Uncle Charlie dies" is not negotiable, even if Uncle Charlie has already died. The holder would have to go outside the instrument to determine the time of occurrence

Determinable Time Requirement

Postdated check   Check delivered before its date, generally payable at sight or on presentment on or after the day of its date

Acceptor   The person who accepts a negotiable instrument (generally the drawee) or who engages to be primarily liable for its payment

before the time to pay the instrument could be set. The following case illustrates the point.

Barton v. *Scott Hudgens Realty & Mortgage, Inc.*
222 S.E.2d 126 (Ga. App. 1975)

FACTS   Barton executed and issued an instrument to Scott Hudgens Realty & Mortgage (Hudgens). The instrument promised to pay $3000 to the order of Hudgens "upon evidence of an acceptable permanent loan of $290,000 for Barton, and Barton's acceptance of the commitment." Hudgens obtained a loan commitment for Barton, but Barton did not accept the loan. Hudgens then sued Barton on the "promissory note."

ISSUE   Is the instrument in question a negotiable promissory note?

HOLDING   No. This instrument was not payable on demand or at a definite time. Therefore, it was not negotiable.

REASONING   This instrument was payable "upon evidence of an acceptable permanent loan ... and ... acceptance of the [loan] commitment." The UCC requires that an instrument be payable at a determinable time in order to be negotiable. The time here was not determinable from the face of the instrument, so it was not negotiable. (Under contract law provisions, Hudgens was awarded a verdict on the agreement.)

Words of Negotiability Requirement

To be negotiable, even if every other element is present, an instrument must contain words of negotiability. The words are "Pay to order" or "Pay to bearer." The reason these words are so important is that the law reads them as authorizing the free transfer of the instrument. Omitting to use one of these terms is a denial of free transferability and therefore a denial of negotiability.

If an instrument that is otherwise negotiable calls for payment by stating "Pay to Pete Jones," it is not negotiable. By its terms, *only* Pete Jones is authorized to receive payment. However, an endorsement that says "Pay to Pete Jones" would not affect negotiability. Endorsements cannot negate negotiability once it exists.

To be payable *to order*, the terms of the instrument must state that it is payable *to the order or assigns of a specified individual* or to a *specified individual or to the individual's order.*[6] The designated individual may be a *person,* as in "Pay to Paula Lopez or order"; an *office,* as in "Pay to the order of the Treasurer of

---

[6] Ibid., Section 3–110(1).

Washington County''; an *estate* or *trust,* as in ''Pay to the order of the Johnson Estate''; or an unincorporated association, as in ''Pay to the XYZ Partnership or order.'' An instrument payable to order requires an endorsement to be negotiated (see Chapter 25 on negotiation and endorsements).

If no particular individual is designated, the instrument must be payable *to bearer* to be negotiable. An instrument is payable to bearer when, by its terms, it is payable to bearer or to the order of bearer; or to ''cash'' or the order of ''cash''; or to a named person or bearer, as in ''Pay to Joe Jakes or bearer'' or ''Pay to the Order of Joe Jakes or bearer'' (Section 3 – 111). No endorsement is needed to negotiate an instrument payable to bearer.

Despite the detailed elements covered so far in this chapter, some problems still arise. In an effort to minimize these problems and to reduce the number of lawsuits involving commercial paper, the drafters of the UCC added some special sections. These sections deal with recurring problem areas and define how they are to be treated.

The first of these sections is 3 – 112, which covers certain *terms* and *omissions* that do not affect negotiability. Most of the coverage is devoted to terms. Subsection (b) says that a statement that collateral has been given as security, or that such collateral may be sold in case of default, has no effect on negotiability. Similarly, subsection (c) says that a promise to maintain or to protect any collateral given will not affect negotiability. And subsections (d) and (e) allow provisions covering **confession of judgment** or the waiver of other legal rights without affecting negotiability. However, these subsections do require that no rights be waived before the due date of the instrument. A blanket waiver, especially by confession of judgment, without regard to the due date will effectively destroy negotiability.

The omission area is covered in subsection (1). Here the Code says that omitting any statement of consideration as a reason for issuing an instrument has no effect. Nor does the omission of a stated place for payment or drawing deny negotiability.

More commonly, problems arise as to meaning rather than as to negotiability. For this reason, Section 3 – 118 covers several standard ambiguities. The rules set forth in this section apply to *every* instrument.

If there is a reasonable doubt whether the instrument is a draft or a note, the *holder* may treat it as either. Further, a draft that names the drawer as the drawee is treated as a note.

If an instrument has internal contradictions, the Code says that *handwritten* terms control over typewritten or printed (that is, typeset) terms. If the conflict is between typewritten and printed terms, typewritten ones control. And if the ambiguity is between words and numbers, the words control *if they are clear.* However, if the words are ambiguous, the numbers control. This means that if a check read:

CONSTRUC-TION AND INTERPRETA-TION

Confession of judgment A judgment in which the defendant, instead of entering a plea, confesses the action; a written commitment whereby the defendant consents to allowing the plaintiff to confess a judgment against the defendant.

$7.85

Seventy-Eight & $\frac{05}{100}$ _____ dollars

the check would be for seventy-eight and 05/100 dollars ($78.05). But if the check read:

$7.85

Seven & Eighty-Five dollars

the check would be for seven and 85/100 dollars ($7.85). The next case dealt with just such an issue of ambiguity.

Wall v. *East Texas Teachers Credit Union*
533 S.W.2d 918 (Tex. 1976)

FACTS   Wall issued a promissory note to the East Texas Teachers Credit Union, using 170 head of cattle as collateral. The note was for $19,896.01 in numbers, and for "Nineteen hundred eight hundred Ninety six and 01/100 Dollars" in words. The note obviously contained an ambiguity concerning the amount of the debt. Wall sued to have the amount determined.

ISSUE   In case of an ambiguity, should the words control over the numbers?

HOLDING   In this particular case, no. The words themselves are ambiguous, so the numbers control.

REASONING   The words here were grammatically incorrect or unorthodox for expressing a monetary amount. The words conflict with both the numbers and the repayment terms. Accordingly, the numbers control. Wall owes $19,896.01.

Finally, unless the instrument specifies, a provision for interest is interpreted as meaning interest at the judgment rate for the jurisdiction where the instrument is to be payed. Also, interest is considered to run from the date of the instrument, unless a different period is specified. If the instrument bears interest but is not dated, interest runs from the date of issue.

SUMMARY

This chapter examined the technical requirements for negotiability of an instrument under Article 3. The first requirement is that the instrument be written, or reduced to tangible form. Next, the instrument must be signed by the maker or the drawer. The promise (for notes or CDs) or the order (for checks or drafts) must be unconditional. All of the terms must be included on the face of the instrument.

The instrument must be payable in money, a recognized governmental currency. The amount of the payment must be a sum certain, which means the amount can be computed from the face of the instrument. In addition, the time of payment must be determinable from the face of the instrument, or it must be payable on demand. Finally, the instrument must contain "words of negotiability." This means it must be payable "to order" or "to bearer."

In case the instrument contains ambiguities, the code provides a method of interpretation. Handwriting controls over typing and over printing. Typing controls over printing. Words control over numbers if the words make sense. If the words do not make sense, the numbers control.

DISCUSSION QUESTIONS

1. How can a negotiable instrument be "signed" by a nonhuman entity?

2. Normally any attempt to restrict payment to a certain source of funds makes the instrument conditional. Why is this considered a condition on payment?

3. What is meant by the phrase *sum certain in money?*

4. Why is an instrument payable "30 days after sight" payable at a definite time?

5. Would the following instrument be considered negotiable?

> I promise to pay to the order of Chris Jamison four thousand dollars ($4000.00) plus 8% interest. Interest is to be figured from 9-1-90.
>
> *Donald McDonald*

6. The courts have consistently held that an I.O.U. is not negotiable. The following is a typical I.O.U.:

> I.O.U. $300
>
> (s) *Donald McDonald*

Why would such a document be deemed nonnegotiable?

7. Glenda issued a promissory note to Ralph. Ralph transferred the note to Phil. When Phil tried to collect from Glenda, she refused to pay. The note stated that interest was payable "at the prime rate." Assume the case hinges on the negotiability of the note, and that all other elements are satisfactory. Is this note a negotiable instrument?

8. Don drew a draft to the order of Pam. The draft called for the payment of $750 for an oak dining room suite. How could this payment be worded so that it would be a negotiable instrument?

9. Marvella issued a time draft to Herman, with payment "6 months to the day after our marriage." He married her on January 4; she divorced him on May 11; and he demanded payment on July 4, all of the same year. Was the draft a negotiable instrument? Discuss fully.

10. Bob issued a note to Larry. The note had the following terms included in its body:

> Interest at 14% per annum. [This term was printed.]
> Interest at 14 ¼%. [This term was typewritten.]
> Plus interest. [This term was handwritten.]

How will interest be calculated on the note, and why?

CASE PROBLEMS

1. Schleider arranged with his dentist to have certain dental work performed. In order to pay for the dental work, Schleider issued an instrument to the dentist. The instrument contained a promise by Schleider to pay to the order of the dentist $480. The instrument also contained the following clause: "In case of death of maker, all payments not due at death are cancelled." The dentist transferred the instrument to Reserve Plan two days later. Schleider claims that the dental work was never performed, and refuses to pay Reserve Plan. Reserve Plan asserts that it is a holder in due course and is entitled to payment despite the adequacy of the dental work. Is the instrument a negotiable instrument, so that Schleider has to pay Reserve Plan? (*Reserve Plan, Inc.* v. *Schleider*, 145 N.Y.S.2d 122 [1955].)

2. Stickler, an employee of Glass Lake House, was authorized to sign checks drawn on the Glass Lake House account. Stickler signed and issued two checks drawn on the Glass Lake House account. Both checks were made payable to William Payne. Payne subsequently endorsed both checks and delivered them to Jenkins, a holder in due course. The drawee bank dishonored both checks upon presentment, and Jenkins sued Evans, the owner of Glass Lake House to recover the face amount of the checks. Evans denies that he or Glass Lake House is liable since neither his name nor the name Glass Lake House appears on the signature line of either check. Who should prevail in this case? (*Jenkins* v. *Evans*, 295 N.Y.S.2d 226 [1968].)

3. Hellman hired Evenson to sell an apartment complex that Hellman

owned. Evenson located a buyer, and the buyer and Hellman worked out the details for the sale of the complex. Upon the conclusion of the negotiations, Hellman issued a promissory note to Evenson for $12,500 as payment for Evenson's work in selling the apartment complex. The buyer later defaulted on the sales contract, and Hellman refused to honor the promissory note he had issued to Evenson. When Evenson sued to collect the note, Hellman argued that there was a condition attached to payment of the note, namely that the buyer complete the sale as agreed. Since the buyer did not complete the sale, Hellman argues that he is not liable to Evenson for the note. Assuming that the note is in every other respect negotiable, should the court admit Hellman's parol evidence concerning conditions for payment? (*Evenson* v. *Hlebechuk,* 305 N.W.2d 13 [N.D. 1981].)

4. Yost executed and delivered to Appliances, Inc., an undated ninety-day promissory note payable to the order of Appliances, Inc. When ninety days had elapsed, Appliances, Inc., demanded payment and Yost refused to honor the note. Yost asserts that the note was not a negotiable instrument and that he is therefore not liable to Appliances, Inc., for the money allegedly owed on the note. Is the note negotiable? What rights, if any, belong to Appliances, Inc., in this case? (*Appliances, Inc.* v. *Yost,* 29 UCC Rep. Serv. 560 [Conn. 1980].)

5. Briggs signed and issued the following note:

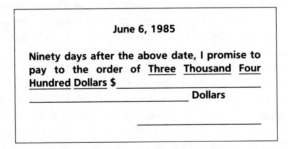

June 6, 1985

Ninety days after the above date, I promise to pay to the order of Three Thousand Four Hundred Dollars $_____

_____ Dollars

The party in possession of this note argues that the note is a bearer-negotiable instrument. Briggs argues that the note is not negotiable. Who is correct and why? (*Broadway Management Corp.* v. *Briggs,* 332 N.E.2d 131 [Ill. 1975].)

6. The Glendora Bank sued Davis to collect on a promissory note that Davis had issued. The only issue in the case was whether the note was negotiable. The note contained the following clause:

> This note is given in payment of merchandise and is
> to be liquidated by payments received on account of
> sale of such merchandise.

Is this a negotiable promissory note? Explain. (*Glendora Bank* v. *Davis,* 267 P. 311 [Cal. 1928].)

7. Paddock signed the following document:

> **August 9, 1958**
>
> For value received, I, we, or either of us promise to pay to Harper Realty, or order, the sum of Twelve Thousand Three Hundred Dollars, said amount to be paid in equal installments of Seventy-Five Dollars each, payable monthly after date beginning _____1, 1958, and on the first day of each month thereafter until the full amount first named herein shall be paid in full.

Paddock asserts that this document is not negotiable since it is not payable at a definite time. Is this document a negotiable instrument? (*McLean* v. *Paddock,* 430 P.2d 392 [N.M. 1967].)

8. Williams gave Cooper a promissory note that was payable "at the earliest possible date." Williams claimed that this made the note payable on demand. Cooper claimed that it was not negotiable. Who is correct? (*Williams* v. *Cooper,* 504 S.W.2d 564 [Tex. App. 1973].)

9. Horne issued a note to Clark. The note, by its terms, prohibited Clark from transferring, assigning, or pledging the note without the prior written permission of Horne. Is this note a negotiable instrument under Article 3 of the UCC? (*First State Bank at Gallup* v. *Clark,* 570 P.2d 1144 [N.M. 1977].)

10. McDonald stole numerous money orders from the United States Post Office, along with an imprinting machine. McDonald used the machine to prepare a number of money orders for the maximum amount of $100, endorsed them, and cashed them at First Bank. First Bank then presented the money orders to the government and was paid for them. The government is now suing First Bank to recover the money paid to the bank on the money orders. The bank argues that the money orders are negotiable instruments, so the bank is protected by the UCC. The government argues that a money order is not a negotiable instrument. Which side is correct on this issue? Which party should prevail? (*United States* v. *The First National Bank of Boston,* 263 F. Supp. 298 [D.C. Mass. 1967].)

Negotiation and Holders in Due Course

TRANSFER

Negotiable instruments are intended to flow through the commercial world. In order to "flow," the instrument needs to be transferred from person to person. The form these transfers take determines the rights that can be asserted by each person gaining possession of the instrument.

The entire process begins with a transfer known as an *issue*. UCC Section 3–102(1)(a) defines an issue as the first delivery of an instrument to a holder or a **remitter.** Either the maker or the drawer causes the instrument to be prepared and initially placed into one of the streams of commerce.

A negotiable instrument, once issued, is presumed to support an underlying contract. It also contains all the necessary elements to be a contract, and as such it can be *assigned*. As was explained in Chapter 15, an assignment is the voluntary transfer of one's legal rights. In an assignment, one party, the assignor, transfers his or her rights under a contract to another party, the

Remitter A person who sends or transmits money to another, especially by purchasing a cashier's check or bank draft

Setoffs Rights that exist between two parties, each of whom owes an ascertained amount to the other, to set off their respective debts by way of mutual reduction so that only the net amount will be paid

assignee. The assignee takes these rights *subject to* any and all claims, defenses, and **setoffs** available to the obligor (the party expected to perform the contract). This means the assignee may very well be unable to enforce the rights transferred because of some defense or defect the obligor can assert on the contract.

These same rights and defenses apply to the transfer of a negotiable instrument by means of an assignment.[1] This presents a problem when dealing with negotiable instruments. Since assignees can have no greater rights than those of their assignors, very few people would be willing to accept a negotiable instrument by such a transfer. The possibility of collecting the money due would be too speculative. The assignee could seldom be certain that the promise would be kept or that the order would be obeyed at the due date, since some defense might exist that would override the original obligation. Obviously, something more is needed to protect the possessor of the commercial paper and to facilitate the free flow of commercial paper through commercial channels. That something more is provided by the UCC, and it is known as *negotiation.*

A negotiation is the transfer of a negotiable instrument *in such a manner* that the transferee becomes a *holder.*[2] To determine the "manner" needed, one must examine the form of the instrument. If the instrument is payable *to order,* it must be properly **endorsed** and **delivered** to be negotiated. If the instrument is payable *to bearer,* delivery alone is sufficient to constitute negotiation.

Endorsed Signed with one's name so that the endorser's rights in the negotiable instrument are transferred to another

Delivered Placed within the actual or constructive possession or control of another

For example, a check that says "Pay to the order of *Ollie Oliver*" must be endorsed by Ollie Oliver before it can be negotiated. If Ollie simply delivers the check to another person without endorsing it, the transfer would be an assignment. The terms imposed by the drawer — pay to the order of Ollie Oliver — require that Ollie *prove* he is transferring his rights. His endorsement provides that proof.

In contrast, a check that says "Pay to the order of *bearer*" does not need to be endorsed in order to be negotiated. Delivery alone is enough to show negotiation. The terms imposed by the drawer at the time of issue — pay to the order of bearer — tell the drawee that anyone in possession is entitled to payment.

If the instrument requires an endorsement, the endorsement must be written on the instrument itself or on an *allonge,* a paper so firmly affixed to the instrument as to become a part of the instrument. Also, to be a negotiation, the endorsement must transfer the entire instrument or the entire unpaid balance. Any attempt to transfer less than the entire balance of the instrument is treated as a partial assignment, not as a negotiation.[3]

The following case illustrates the concept of a transfer as an assignment and not as a negotiation.

---

[1] Uniform Commercial Code, Section 3–201.
[2] Ibid., Section 3–201(1).
[3] Ibid., Section 3–202(2), (3).

Waters v. *Waters*
498 S.W.2d 236 (Tex. App. 1973)

Jerry Waters and his ex-wife, Patsy Waters, entered a property settlement as part of their divorce. Part of the property settlement agreement was that a note Jerry had issued to Patsy's father should be paid to Patsy. The note, payable to Jim Still, was delivered to Patsy, but it was not endorsed by the payee. Some time later Jim Still died. Patsy sued Jerry on the note, and Jerry denied that Patsy was entitled to enforce the note.

FACTS

Was Patsy entitled to enforce the promissory note?

ISSUE

Yes. The evidence established that Patsy was the owner of the note, and as such she was permitted to seek collection on it from the maker.

HOLDING

The lack of any endorsement by Jim Still does not preclude Patsy's rights. The owner of a promissory note may transfer it without any endorsement or without any written assignment. The lack of any endorsements prevented Patsy from attaining the status of holder. But she can still seek to collect as an assignee or as a donee in a gift.

REASONING

ENDORSE-MENTS

An *endorsement* must be placed on a negotiable instrument that is payable to *order* before it can be effectively negotiated. In addition, an endorsement on an instrument *creates a contract* between the endorser and the transferee. For this reason, many people will not accept the transfer of a *bearer* instrument unless the transferor endorses it. Even though bearer paper may be effectively negotiated by delivery alone, the transferee usually demands the added security of the endorsement contract. To further emphasize the importance of endorsements, the UCC states in Section 3–402 that "unless the instrument clearly indicates that a signature is made in some other capacity it is an endorsement."

There are two reasons for endorsing an instrument. One reason is to affect *negotiation*. The other is to affect *liability*. The endorsements that affect negotiation tell the holder that another endorsement is needed to negotiate the instrument further (a *special* endorsement); that no further endorsements are needed in order to negotiate the instrument further (a *blank* endorsement); or that the instrument has been restricted to some special channel of commerce, such as banking (a *restrictive* endorsement). The endorsements that affect liability either (1) admit and/or agree to honor the contract of endorsement (an *unqualified* endorsement) or (2) expressly deny any liability on the contract the endorsement represents (a *qualified* endorsement). Every endorsement must affect negotiation as well as liability.

There are three types of endorsements affect negotiation: special, blank, and restrictive. Two types affect liability: unqualified and qualified. Every endorsement must affect both negotiation and liability. Thus, each endorsement must fit one of the boxes in the matrix shown in Figure 25.1.

Notice that each box is numbered. We will use these numbers to refer back to the matrix as we discuss some examples of the various types of endorsements. Throughout the examples, we will be using the check shown in Figure 25.2.

**Special
Endorsement**

A *special* endorsement *specifies the party to whom the instrument is to be paid or to whose order it is to be paid.*[4] This means that a special endorsement makes the instrument *order* paper. Even if it was issued as bearer paper, a special endorsement will turn it into order paper. The party specified will have to endorse it before it can be negotiated further. Figure 25.3 shows an example of a special endorsement.

Figure 25.1 The Endorsement Matrix

	Unqualified	Qualified
Special	1	2
Blank	3	4
Restrictive	5	6

Figure 25.2 The Check as Issued

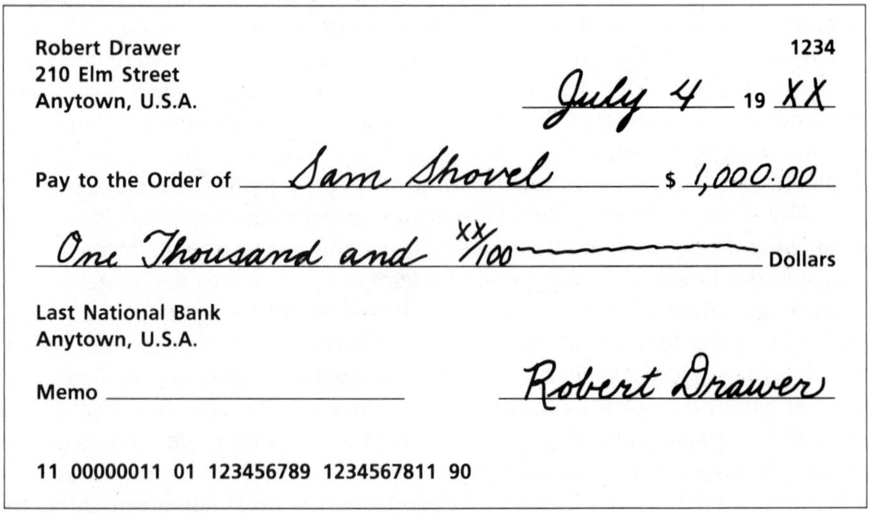

Robert Drawer
210 Elm Street
Anytown, U.S.A.

1234

July 4 19 *XX*

Pay to the Order of ___*Sam Shovel*___ $ *1,000.00*

One Thousand and ^XX/100^ ——————— Dollars

Last National Bank
Anytown, U.S.A.

Memo _____

Robert Drawer

11 00000011 01 123456789 1234567811 90

---

4 Ibid., Section 3–204(1).

Figure 25.3   A Special Endorsement

Figure 25.4   A Blank Endorsement

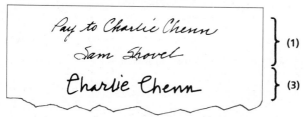

A *blank* endorsement *does not specify the party to whom the instrument is to be paid.* The normal form of a blank endorsement is a mere signature. Such an endorsement makes the instrument *bearer* paper.[5] As such it is negotiable by delivery alone, without any need for further endorsements. In Figure 25.4,(3) would be a blank endorsement.

    Notice that at this point the check has every endorsement that is necessary for negotiation. Should the check now be lost or stolen, the finder or the thief could effectively negotiate it. To protect against such an occurrence, Section 3–204(3) empowers any holder to **convert** a blank endorsement into a special endorsement. This is done by writing appropriate words above the blank endorsement, as is shown in Figure 25.5. Here a holder added the words "Pay to Mata Harry, or order" above Charlie Chenn's endorsement. This phrase could have been added by Charlie Chenn when he negotiated the check to Mata Harry. More likely, Mata Harry added the phrase after she received the check from Charlie Chenn. By adding the phrase, she has protected herself against losing the check or having it stolen.

A *restrictive* endorsement purports to prohibit any further negotiation of the instrument. Or it is conditional. Or it contains words that indicate it is to be deposited or collected, such as "for deposit," "for collection," or "pay any bank." Or it has some other restriction specified as to its use.[6]

    However, once an instrument as issued satisfies all the tests of negotiability, no endorsement can remove its negotiable status.[7] Even with a restrictive endorsement, further negotiation and transfer is permitted. In Figure 25.6, (5) shows a restrictive endorsement.

Blank Endorsement

Convert   To change from one form or function to another

Restrictive Endorsement

[5] Ibid., Section 3–204(2).
[6] Ibid., Section 3–205(1), (2), (3), (4).
[7] Ibid., Section 3–206(1).

Figure 25.5 A Blank Endorsement Converted
to a Special Endorsement

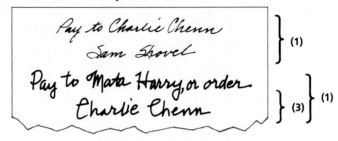

Figure 25.6 A Restrictive Endorsement

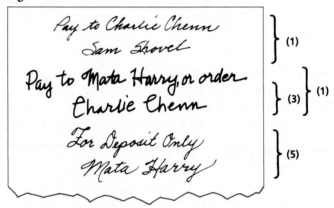

It should be noted that each of these sample endorsements refers to the *unqualified* endorsement column of the matrix set out in Figure 25.1. The reason for this is contained in UCC Section 3–414. Under this section, an endorsement is presumed to be unqualified. To be *qualified,* the endorsement must contain specific words of qualification.

Unqualified Endorsement

Dishonored Refused for acceptance or payment upon proper presentment

Notice Information; knowledge of a fact or a state of affairs

An *unqualified* endorsement *carries with it a contract.* The endorser is committed to the *endorsee* (the person to whom the instrument is transferred by endorsement) or to any later endorser if the instrument is **dishonored,** and proper **notice** is given. The normal order of payment among the endorsers is the reverse of the order in which they endorse.[8] Thus, endorser number 4 would collect from number 3; number 3 would collect from number 2; and number 2 would collect from number 1. This is known as the secondary chain of liability, and it will be covered in more detail in Chapter 26.

[8] Ibid., Section 3–414(1), (2).

A *qualified* endorsement is one that *denies contract liability*. The endorser includes words such as "without recourse" in the endorsement. These words have the legal effect of telling later endorsers that the qualifying endorser will *not* repay them if the instrument is dishonored. By accepting a qualified endorsement in a negotiation, the later endorsers also agree to the contract terms of the qualified endorsement. In Figure 25.7, each of the earlier endorsements is shown as unqualified; in Figure 25.8, each is shown as qualified. Note the

**Qualified
Endorsement**

Figure 2.57   Unqualified Endorsements

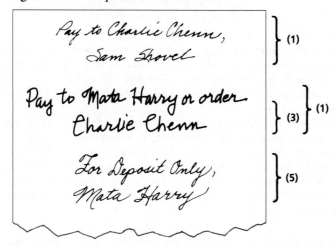

Figure 25.8   Qualified Endorsements

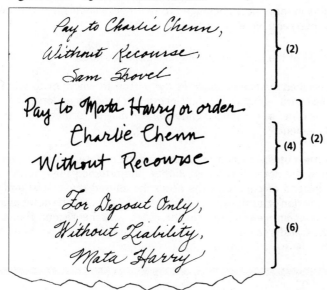

specific language necessary to change an endorsement from the presumed unqualified endorsement to a qualified endorsement.

In the following case, the court had to deal with the issue of a special endorsement and its effect on subsequent negotiations. Notice the effect that the endorsement had on an attempt to further negotiate the notes in question.

Klomann v. *Sol K. Graff & Sons*
317 N.E.2d 608 (Ill. 1974)

FACTS Sol K. Graff & Sons were real estate brokers. They were involved in the sale and exchange of a number of properties on behalf of Fred Klomann. As a result of these transactions, Sol K. Graff & Sons owed Klomann $13,000. The firm issued three promissory notes payable to the order of Klomann and totalling $13,000 as payment of the account.

Fred Klomann later negotiated these notes to his daughter by special endorsement. His daughter examined the notes and returned them to her father for collection without endorsing them. Some time later Fred Klomann scratched out the name of his daughter in the special endorsements, substituted the name of his wife, and transferred possession of the notes to his wife. The following month Fred's wife demanded payment on the notes from Sol K. Graff & Sons. Payment was refused, and she filed suit on the notes.

ISSUE Does Georgia Klomann (Fred's wife) have sufficient rights in the notes to collect them from the maker?

HOLDING No. The rights in these notes belonged to the special endorsee, Candace Klomann (Fred's daughter) and were never transferred by her.

REASONING Section 3–204 of the Uniform Commercial Code provides:

(1) A special endorsement specifies the person to whom or to whose order it makes the instrument payable. Any instrument specially endorsed becomes payable to the order of the special endorsee and may be further negotiated only by his endorsement.

In this case, the notes were specially endorsed to Candace, and she never endorsed or negotiated the notes thereafter. Rather, she returned them to her father for collection. Instead of collecting the notes, he altered the special endorsements without permission or authority and attempted to negotiate the notes again. At that time, Fred Klomann had no rights in the notes, and this second transfer by Fred vested in the transferee only such rights as were held by the transferor. Since Fred had no rights, he transferred no rights to Georgia.

At the beginning of this chapter, we examined the transfer of negotiable instruments. It was pointed out that a transfer leaves the transferee in the role of assignee. And it was stated that a *negotiation* leaves the transferee in the role of a *holder*.

HOLDER

The role of holder is important in negotiable instruments. It normally carries contractual rights against several parties involved with the instrument. It also normally carries **warranty rights** against some parties involved with the instrument. And it is an essential element before a party can become a *holder in due course*, perhaps the most favored position in the law of commercial paper.

Warranty rights Rights to enforce implied promises that certain facts in relation to the negotiable instrument are, or shall be, as they were stated or promised to be

A holder is *a person in possession of a negotiable instrument drawn, issued, or endorsed to him, to his order, to bearer, or in blank*. Thus, the holder either receives the original issue from the maker or drawer or receives a negotiation through endorsement and/or delivery. A holder has the right to transfer, negotiate, discharge, or enforce the instrument in the holder's own name.[9] However, a holder is subject to any defenses on the instrument that a maker or drawer can assert.

HOLDER IN DUE COURSE

To overcome even one of the defenses on the instrument that may be available to the maker or drawer, the holder needs to acquire holder in due course status. Great care needs to be exercised here. The **burden of proof** of having holder in due course status lies with the person claiming the status.[10] A holder must prove he or she is a holder in due course; such status is not presumed. A holder or an assignee is subject to any defense the drawer or maker can assert. A holder in due course is subject only to some defenses of the maker or drawer. The holder in due course prevails over most available defenses.

Burden of proof The legal necessity of affirmatively proving a fact or facts on an issue raised between the parties in a cause of action

The Code defines a *holder in due course* as a holder who takes an instrument *for value, in good faith*, and *without notice* of any defenses or defects affecting the instrument.[11] The issues of value and good faith are relatively simple to establish. However, the "without notice" issue can be difficult to prove at times.

Section 3–303 sets out three methods of *giving value* for an instrument. Notice that each method involves performance by the holder, not just a commitment to perform in the future. The first method is either to perform the agreed consideration or to acquire a security interest in the instrument. *Doing* something is a giving of value here, but *promising* to do something is not. The second method is to take the instrument as payment for, or as security on, a preexisting debt or obligation. This method is valid even if the claim is not yet due. The third method is to give a negotiable instrument in exchange for the one received or to make an irrevocable commitment to a third person (not the

---

[9] Ibid., Sections 1–201(20), 3–301.
[10] Ibid., Section 3–307(3).
[11] Ibid., Section 3–302(1).

transferor) as the basis for the transfer. Once the holder can prove that value was given, the holder goes on to the next test.

In the following case, the question of whether a party was a holder in due course (HDC) hinged on the presence of value.

Saka v. *Mann Theatres*
575 P.2d 1335 (Nev. 1978)

FACTS   Affinity Pictures wanted to rent a theatre to exhibit one of its films. Affinity approached the Mann Theatre chain and arranged to rent the Boulevard Theatre for two weeks at a rental of $5,442 per week. Saka, one of the film's producers, delivered two checks to the Mann Theatre chain as payment for the rental price. Mann promptly presented both checks to the bank. One of the checks was honored, and the other was dishonored. Mann contacted Saka about the dishonored check during the first week of the rental period. Saka assured Mann that the check would be honored the following week, and Mann permitted the second week of occupancy by Affinity. When the check was again dishonored, Mann initiated an action against Saka.

ISSUE   Was the Mann Theatre chain a holder in due course on the check?

HOLDING   Yes. Mann was a holder, took in good faith, gave value, and had no notice of any defects at the time it acquired the check.

REASONING   At the time that the check was initially dishonored, Mann had already begun performance of the agreement, so that the contract was no longer executory. Since performance of the rental agreement had already begun, Mann had given value within the meaning of the UCC. The other elements required to be a holder in due course were either established or were not at issue in the case. Since Mann had given value, Mann was an HDC, and was entitled to collect the instrument from Saka.

The next requirement is that the holder take the instrument in *good faith*. Good faith is defined as honesty in fact in the transaction.[12] This requirement is actually measured by a negative test. The holder acted with good faith if bad faith is not present. To show lack of good faith, it must be proved that the holder either had *actual knowledge* of a defect in the instrument or *ignored* facts that would show the defect. Usually, all the holder needs to do is to allege good faith. The burden of proof will then shift to the maker or drawer. It will be up to the maker or drawer to prove bad faith, or actual knowledge of some defect, by the holder. Very few cases involve bad faith.

---

[12] Ibid., Section 1–301(19).

The final requirement to establish holder in due course status is that the holder take the instrument *without notice* of any defenses or defects on the instrument. Section 3–304 of the Code lists certain areas that affect the notice provision. Each of these areas is examined in the following sections.

A purchaser of a negotiable instrument has notice of a defect if the instrument is incomplete in some material respect. Thus, a missing signature or a missing amount would be notice. So would a missing date on a *time* instrument. But a missing date on a *demand* instrument, such as a check, is not notice since it is not material. It is not material because a demand instrument is payable at issue, and even if it is not dated, it has been issued. The simple fact of its existence proves that it has been issued.

Facts That Are Notice

Notice of a defect also exists if the instrument is visibly altered or bears visible evidence of a forgery. And it is notice if the instrument is irregular on its face. This means that an erasure of an obligation of a party or of an amount is notice of a defect.

A holder who takes an instrument stamped "NSF" (not sufficient funds), or "Payment Stopped," or "Paid" would have notice of a defense or defect on the instrument. It has been presented, and it has been dishonored or paid. The holder knows this by looking at the face of the instrument. Taking an **overdue** instrument is also considered notice. An instrument is overdue if the holder has reason to know that any payment is overdue, or is in default, or that acceleration has occurred. And a demand instrument is overdue after demand has been made *or* after an unreasonable time lapse following issue. While *unreasonable time* is ambiguous, some guidelines are available. A reasonable time for a draft would normally be longer than that for a check but shorter than that for a demand note. And a reasonable time on a non-interest-bearing note would be shorter than on an interest-bearing note. A reasonable time on a check is presumed to be thirty days. Reasonable times on other instruments would depend on the instrument itself, the community it is circulated in, and any other relevant factors. Each case must be handled differently.

Overdue Unpaid beyond its maturity date

In the following case, a drawer of a check argued that a holder had notice of a defense so that the holder could not be a holder in due course.

Jaeger & Branch, Inc. v. *Pappas*
433 P.2d 605 (Utah 1967)

FACTS

Pappas was building a hotel in Park City, Utah. He had been purchasing a number of materials from Allo Distributing Company of North Hollywood, California. Pappas had ordered a shipment of carpeting from Allo, and Allo had arranged to purchase and ship the carpeting to Pappas. The carpeting had been ordered from Jaeger & Branch. Jaeger & Branch had the shipment delayed pending payment from Allo. When Pappas called Allo to find out where the carpet was, Allo asked Pappas to call

Jaeger to try to straighten things out. Pappas called Jaeger and gave Jaeger assurance that the carpeting would be paid for promptly. Pappas sent a check payable to the order of Allo, Allo promptly endorsed the check and delivered it to Jaeger, and Jaeger deposited the check with his bank. In the meantime, the carpeting shipment had been released and delivered to Pappas.

After the conversation with Jaeger, Pappas called Allo again, and informed Allo that unless Allo sent "everything you say you're going to" Pappas would place a stop payment order on the check. Pappas did, in fact, place a stop payment order on the check so that the check was returned to Jaeger. Jaeger sued Pappas for the amount of the check, and Pappas denied that Jaeger was a holder in due course.

ISSUE   Did Jaeger have notice of any defenses on the check issued by Pappas?

HOLDING   No. Nothing in the facts would provide Jaeger with notice of any defenses on this check.

REASONING   From a review of the facts and the evidence of the case, the court could find nothing that would have placed Jaeger on notice of any defenses on the check. The mere fact that Pappas had called Jaeger before issuing the check to Allo is not sufficient to provide notice. While it is true that a holder must act in reasonable manner and should make inquiry if the facts indicate the possibility of a defense on the instrument, the reverse is also true. If there is nothing to indicate a defense exists, the holder need not make inordinate inquiries. In this case, there was nothing to indicate that the check was subject to any defenses, and Jaeger acted properly. He qualified as a holder in due course and is entitled to collect the check.

Facts That Are Not Notice

Antedated Affixed with an earlier date; dated before the instrument was written

Accommodation party One who has signed an instrument without receiving value and for the purpose of lending his or her name to some other person as a means of securing credit

The UCC, in Section 3–304(4), states that the following facts, standing alone, are not notice even if the holder has knowledge of the fact:

1.   The instrument was **antedated** or postdated.

2.   The instrument was issued or negotiated for an executory promise, *unless* the holder has notice of defenses to the promise.

3.   Any party has signed as an **accommodation party.**

4.   A formerly incomplete instrument was completed.

5.   Any person negotiating the instrument is or was a fiduciary.

6.   There was a default on an interest payment on the instrument.

It is also not treated as notice if any party has filed or recorded a document, if the holder would otherwise qualify as a holder in due course. And before notice is effective, it must be received in a time and a manner that give a reasonable opportunity to act on the information.[13] Notice must be received

---

[13] Ibid., Section 3–304(5),(6).

before the holder receives the instrument. Once the holder has received the instrument, later notice is irrelevant.

The status of holder in due course is a preferred legal position. The holder in due course takes an instrument free of *personal defenses.* Although the holder in due course is subject to *real defenses,* he or she will be able to enforce the instrument against any other defense or defect. This position is far superior to that of a mere holder or an assignee. A holder or an assignee is subject to any and every defense or defect in the instrument.

A mere holder, an assignee, or a transferee takes possession of a negotiable instrument subject to every available defense. In contrast, a holder in due course takes the instrument subject only to *real* defenses. The HDC is not subject to personal (sometimes referred to as limited) defenses. A *personal defense* is one that affects the *agreement* for which the instrument was issued. It does *not* affect the *validity* of the instrument. The validity of the instrument is not in question; it is acknowledged to be valid. The underlying agreement is the point of contention. A real defense, on the other hand, questions the legal validity of the instrument.

The most common types of personal defenses are those available on a simple contract. The most common of these contract defenses are failure of consideration, fraud, duress, and breach of warranty. In addition, the holder may frequently be faced with the personal defenses of nondelivery, theft, payment, or any other cancellation.

Most of the simple contract defenses were covered in Part II ("The Law of Contracts") and need no further review here. However, fraud does need some added coverage because negotiable instrument law recognizes two types of fraud. One type, fraud in the *inducement,* is a personal defense. The other type, fraud in the *execution,* is a real defense.

Fraud in the inducement is a personal defense because the fraud committed is a fraud related to the *agreement.* The maker or drawer *intentionally* and *knowingly* issues a negotiable instrument to the payee. However, this issue is made to support an underlying agreement, and the agreement is based on fraudulent representations. The underlying contract is voidable because of the fraud, but the instrument is valid, subject only to a personal defense.

Of the other personal defenses not based on simple contract defenses, only one will be covered here. Nondelivery of the instrument needs special treatment. (The rest are covered in Chapter 26, in the section on discharge.) To issue an instrument, the maker or drawer must *deliver* the instrument to the payee or to an authorized representative of the payee. If the payee gains possession of the instrument without the knowledge or consent of the maker or drawer, the defense of nondelivery is available against a mere holder. Another type of nondelivery occurs when the maker or drawer gives the payee possession, but with a condition attached before delivery is effective. The

EFFECT OF HOLDER IN DUE COURSE STATUS

Personal Defenses

condition may be that the payee perform some act, which is then not performed. Technically, delivery never occurred because the condition was never satisfied, and the defense of nondelivery can be raised as a personal defense.

Real Defenses

A *real defense,* sometimes referred to as a universal defense, *challenges the validity of the instrument itself.* If a real defense can be established, the negotiable instrument is voided by operation of law, and no one can enforce the instrument. Thus, even a holder in due course will lose to a real defense. It should be kept in mind that if a maker or drawer alleges a real defense, the maker or drawer must establish the defense as real. A failure to do so will normally still leave a valid personal defense, but such a defense will not prevail against a holder in due course.

Section 3–305 of the UCC lists five potential types of real defenses. Each of the five is covered in the following sections.

Infancy

The first real defense is infancy, "to the extent that it is a defense to a simple contract."[14] To determine whether infancy is a real defense, state law must be examined. If the statutes in the state where the instrument is issued allow infancy to be asserted as a defense to the underlying contract, the infancy may also be raised as a real defense on the instrument. Even if state law does not give such a broad defense, it is still useful as a personal defense; however, a holder in due course can override that defense.

Other Incapacity, Duress, or Illegality

The second real defense is "such other incapacity, or duress, or illegality of the transactions, as renders the obligation of the party a nullity."[15] Again, the relevant state law will be controlling. If the state statutes void the transaction, the instrument is also voided. If not, the defense is personal in nature. An example would be the issuance of a check to pay a gambling debt. If gambling is illegal in the state, a defense exists on the instrument, but it is probably only a personal defense. However, if the check contains a notation that it is meant as payment for a gambling debt, the defense becomes real. The instrument itself now reflects the illegality.

Other types of illegality that might affect a negotiable instrument, and hence operate as a real defense on the instrument include usury, agreements that violate public policy, and attempting to do business in a state when not licensed to do so. In the following case, a merchant was conducting business in a state where the merchant was not licensed. Notice how the court handles the defense in the case.

---

[14] Ibid., Section 3–305(2)(a).
[15] Ibid., Section 3–305(2)(b).

Pacific National Bank v. Hernreich
398 S.W.2d 221 (Ark. 1966)

FACTS

Hernreich operated a jewelry store in Fort Smith, Arkansas. He would periodically purchase diamonds from salesmen of the Sebel Company, a foreign corporation that was not licensed to do business in the state of Arkansas. Sebel would then discount the notes Hernreich signed when he purchased the diamonds, selling them to Pacific National Bank.

Hernreich executed three notes in early 1963, payable to the order of Sebel. Sebel then sold the notes to the bank. Shortly thereafter Sebel died, and the company was dissolved. When the notes came due, Hernreich refused to pay them.

ISSUE

Can a holder in due course of promissory notes collect the notes from the maker despite the illegality of the execution of the notes?

HOLDING

No. The illegality affecting these notes was a real defense and as such will defeat the claims of a holder in due course.

REASONING

An Arkansas statute states that any foreign corporation that fails to properly register to do business within the state of Arkansas cannot make any contracts in the state, and any alleged contracts so entered cannot be enforced in either law or equity. The promissory notes Hernreich signed were contracts entered into with an unregistered corporation — Sebel Company. As such these notes were void ab initio, and the status of the bank as a holder in due course is irrelevant.

Fraud

The third real defense is fraud in the *execution*. In this defense, the maker or drawer must prove two things: (1) lack of knowledge of the instrument signed and (2) no reasonable opportunity to discover the nature or terms of the instrument.[16] To establish this defense, the maker or drawer must *prove* that discovering the nature of the signed instrument was not reasonable at the time of signing. Such proof will be virtually impossible unless the signing person is either illiterate or is involved in a strange set of circumstances. The following hypothetical case illustrates such a setting.

Freddy Hornet, a famous rock musician, was signing autographs outside a theater after a performance. Sonya Smith, among others, shoved a paper in front of Freddy for him

---

[16] Ibid., Section 3–305(2)(c).

to sign. However, the paper she shoved was a promissory note, payable to her order, for $50,000. Freddy signed it without reading it, and Sonya left the theater area. Sonya later sued Freddy to collect the money called for in the note.

If Freddy can prove these facts, he will have a real defense and will not have to pay the note.

Discharge in Insolvency

The fourth real defense is a "discharge in insolvency proceedings."[17] This area basically refers to a discharge in bankruptcy proceedings. Bankruptcy is a federally guaranteed *privilege,* and federal law prevails over conflicting state law. The federal bankruptcy law discharges the enforceability of the instrument, creating a statutory real defense on the instrument. (Bankruptcy is covered in Chapter 31.)

Other Discharges

The final real defense is "any other discharge of which the holder has notice when he takes the instrument."[18] This defense is misleading. Referring to it as a real defense is probably improper in theory, if not in fact. To be a holder in due course, a holder cannot have notice of any problems, defenses, or defects in the instrument. If the holder has notice, the holder cannot qualify as an HDC. Thus, the notice referred to in the Code defeats HDC status. Having this notice has the same effect as a real defense, but it is really a denial of holder in due course protection. This means that since the holder has notice, he cannot be an HDC; but *if* he were an HDC, he would lose since he faces a real defense.

In addition to the real defenses, a maker or drawer can avoid liability on an instrument against an HDC under two other circumstances. One circumstance may afford total avoidance: Section 4–404 states that an *unauthorized* signature is wholly inoperative against the person whose name is signed unless that person ratifies the signing or is not allowed to deny its validity. Thus, a forgery is a possible defense against even a holder in due course.

The other circumstance may afford partial avoidance: Section 4–407 states that if an instrument is materially *altered* through no fault of the maker or drawer, an HDC may enforce it as originally issued (the alteration is a real defense to the extent altered). If the alteration is due to the fault of the maker or drawer, the defense is merely personal and cannot be asserted against a holder in due course.

STATUTORY LIMITATIONS

The protected status given to holders in due course makes abuses possible. If a payee obtains an instrument by wrongful means and then negotiates it to an

---

[17] Ibid., Section 3–305(2)(d).
[18] Ibid., Section 3–305(2)(e).

HDC, the maker or drawer will nearly always be obliged to pay the instrument. As will be seen in the next chapter, the maker or drawer can sue the payee to recover the money paid. However, the payer must be *found* to be sued. And the finding may not be easy. If the payee and the "HDC" are working together, the maker or drawer is easily taken, usually with no chance of recovering.

Because of this potential, the Federal Trade Commission (FTC) passed a regulation in 1976. This regulation, designed to protect *consumers,* modifies the holder in due course rules in some circumstances. If a consumer credit transaction is involved, the instrument used must contain the following notice, printed prominently:

> ANY HOLDER OF THIS CONSUMER CREDIT CONTRACT IS SUBJECT TO ALL CLAIMS AND DEFENSES WHICH THE DEBTOR COULD ASSERT AGAINST THE SELLER OF GOODS OR SERVICES OBTAINED PURSUANT HERETO OR WITH THE PROCEEDS HEREOF. RECOVERY HEREUNDER BY THE DEBTOR SHALL NOT EXCEED AMOUNTS PAID BY THE DEBTOR HEREUNDER.

The effect of the rule is to make even an HDC subject to any defenses available against the payee, which is a tremendous protection for the consumer. This rule may have a great impact on the use of consumer credit contracts in the future.

If the notice is present in a consumer credit transaction, any holder of the instrument has agreed *by the terms of the instrument* to remain subject to any defenses of the maker or drawer. This means that a consumer could avoid payment to any HDC in possession of the instrument if the consumer could avoid payment to the payee.

If the notice is not included in a consumer credit transaction, an **unfair trade practice** is involved. The consumer can file suit against any holders who are deemed to have committed an unfair trade practice for all damages involved.

The following case is one the consumer probably would have lost before the passage of this FTC rule.

Unfair trade practice
Conduct not previously considered improper under the law but now prohibited by the Federal Trade Commission in the interest of the general public.

Jefferson Bank & Trust Co. v. Stamatiou
384 So.2d 388 (La. 1980)

Stamatiou purchased a truck from Key Dodge, signing a chattel mortgage and sale agreement. The agreement included a promissory note and the FTC clause that preserves the consumer debtor's rights against subsequent holders in due course. The agreement also specified that the note was to be assigned to Jefferson Bank & Trust Co. Shortly after the sale, Stamatiou alleged that the truck had become inoperable. As a result, he notified Key Dodge and Jefferson Bank that he wanted to rescind the contract. Jefferson Bank later instituted

FACTS

this lawsuit against Stamatiou for the unpaid loan amount, alleging that Stamatiou used the truck as business equipment and not as a consumer good.

ISSUE   Is the FTC clause preserving defenses in consumer credit sales valid in a non-consumer credit transaction?

HOLDING   Yes. If the clause is included in the agreement, it is a part of the contract despite the debtor's status.

REASONING   Freedom of contract is a right of the parties. They can include any contractual clauses they desire. The mere fact that Jefferson Bank later argued that the clause was not meant to apply except for consumer credit contracts is immaterial. They put it in; they must honor it. The defenses that could be asserted against Key Dodge can also be asserted against Jefferson Bank. The bank was put on notice by the terms of the contract that any defenses good against Key Dodge were also good against the Bank.

SUMMARY

A negotiable instrument can be transferred in a number of ways. The original transfer from the maker or the drawer is an issue. Once issued, it can be further transferred by assignment or by negotiation. An assignment gives the assignee no special rights or protections. In contrast, a negotiation may confer some individual rights on the recipient. When a negotiation occurs, the transferee becomes a holder.

Most negotiations involve the use of an endorsement. Endorsements may affect further negotiation, and they may affect liability of the parties. Special, blank, and restrictive endorsements affect negotiations. Qualified and unqualified endorsements affect liability.

Once a negotiation occurs, the holder has the opportunity to achieve the most favored status in commercial paper: he or she may become a holder in due course. A holder in due course is a holder who takes an instrument in good faith, for value, and without notice of any defenses or defects on the instrument. A holder in due course can defeat a personal defense. A real defense will defeat a holder in due course.

The Federal Trade Commission enacted a special rule in 1976 to protect consumers. The rule denies any protection against any defenses, even for an HDC, on a consumer credit instrument.

DISCUSSION QUESTIONS

1. Why is the distinction between assignments and negotiations so important?

2. How can a holder endorse an instrument to minimize his or her potential secondary liability?

3. Arnita issued Carol a check payable to the order of Carol. Carol sold the

check to Lynn, but neglected to endorse it. At this point, what is Lynn's legal status?

4. Assume the same facts as in question 3. What legal rights does Lynn have against Carol?

5. Ann is in possession of a check that Dan issued to her. She would like to mail the check to her bank, to be deposited to her checking account. How should she endorse the check to give herself maximum protection, and why does such an endorsement give maximum protection?

6. Lloyd has a promissory note originally issued by Randy. However, Lloyd is afraid Randy might default on the note when it comes due. Jim is willing to buy the note from Lloyd. Is there a way for Lloyd to endorse the note to minimize his potential loss if Randy dishonors the note?

7. Denise issued the following check to Bill:

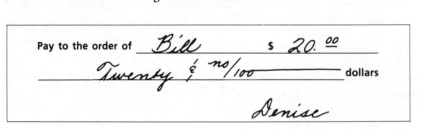

Bill adds the number 2 before the "20.00" and adds the words *Two Hundred* before the "Twenty." He then negotiates the check to Sarah, an HDC. How much will Denise have to pay Sarah, and why?

8. Charles has a note issued by David. He discovers that David is about to go through a bankruptcy, so he negotiates the note to Richard. Richard qualifies as a holder in due course. What are Richard's rights against David?

9. Sam calls on Brenda, asking to demonstrate a new carpet cleaner. After the demonstration, he makes his sales pitch, but Brenda refuses to buy. Sam then pulls out a pad of paper and asks Brenda to sign so that Sam "can get paid by the boss for the demonstration." Brenda signs a promissory note. What defense, if any, can Brenda later assert on the note?

10. Assume the same facts as in question 9. If an HDC has the note, what would Brenda need to prove to avoid paying the note?

1. Higgins executed a promissory note payable to the order of Westerly Hospital. The hospital endorsed the note in blank and negotiated it to a bank, with the hospital guaranteeing payment if Higgins defaulted. Higgins defaulted, the hospital paid the note as guaranteed, and the bank delivered the note to the hospital. The hospital sued Higgins to collect. Higgins contended that the hospital is not a holder and therefore may not

CASE PROBLEMS

sue. Is Higgins correct? (*Westerly Hospital* v. *Higgins,* 256 A.2d 506 [R.I. 1969].)

2. Vanotti agreed to purchase some land in Arizona from a developer. He signed a promissory note for $4400 to cover the purchase. The note gave Vanotti the right to rescind the sale for six months. The developer negotiated the note to Salter. Three months after signing the note, Vanotti decided to rescind the contract. Salter sued Vanotti on the note, claiming that he (Salter) was entitled to payment as a holder in due course. Is Salter correct? (*Salter* v. *Vanotti,* 599 P.2d 962 [Colo. App. 1979].)

3. Wesley issued a check to the payee for $1400. The payee deposited the check at his bank and then withdrew $140 from the account. In the interim, Wesley had issued a stop payment order against the check, which the drawee bank honored. The payee's bank argued that it was a holder in due course on the check. Wesley argued that the bank was not a holder in due course. Is the bank an HDC? Explain. (*Falls Church Bank* v. *Wesley Heights Realty, Inc.,* 256 A.2d 915 [D.C. App. 1969].)

4. Blackburn issued a check to Vanella as payment for an automobile. Vanella then deposited the check at Midland Bank, receiving credit and cash for the check. Blackburn stopped payment on the check, and Midland Bank sued Blackburn to collect the amount of the check. Blackburn alleges that Vanella misrepresented the condition of the automobile at the time of the sale, and due to this misrepresentation Blackburn is not liable on the check. What result should occur? (*Marine Midland Trust Company of Rochester* v. *Blackburn,* 271 N.Y.S.2d 388 [1966].)

5. Drexler, an agent of Eldon's, Inc., purchased stocks through the firm of Merrill, Lynch, Pierce, Fenner & Smith, Inc., by means of a check drawn by Eldon's, Inc., to the order of Merrill, Lynch. Eldon's had not authorized the issuance of the check and was unaware that Drexler was using the corporation's checks for his personal benefit. When Eldon's discovered what Drexler was doing. Eldon's attempted to recover the monies from Merrill, Lynch. Merrill, Lynch asserts that it is a holder in due course and as such is not subject to Eldon's defenses against Drexler for improper delivery. Eldon's argues that a payee cannot be a holder in due course. What result should occur in this case? (*Eldon's Super Fresh Stores, Inc.* v. *Merrill, Lynch, Pierce, Fenner & Smith, Inc.,* 207 N.W.2d 282 [Minn. 1973].)

6. Dental Supply had an employee who endorsed checks payable to the order of Dental Supply by means of a rubber stamp. The stamp did not restrictively endorse the checks, rather endorsing them in blank. The employee cashed thirty-five of the checks that she had stamped rather than deposit them and retained the money for her personal use. When Dental Supply learned what had happened, it sued the bank for conversion of its funds. Is the bank liable to the firm for conversion of the funds? Is the bank liable on any other grounds? Discuss fully. (*Palmer & Ray Dental Supply of Abilene, Inc.,* v. *First National Bank,* 477 S.W.2d 954 [Tex. Civ. App. 1972].)

7. Haar drew two checks payable to the order of Western Aircraft. Western took the checks to Peoples Bank where Western kept its accounts. Peoples Bank called City Bank, the drawee, to confirm that the checks were good. Following this call, Peoples Bank allowed Western to cash one check and to deposit the other. Peoples Bank subsequently learned that Haar had issued stop payment orders against both checks. Peoples Bank then sued Haar to recover on the checks. Is Peoples Bank a holder in due course on these two checks? (*Peoples Bank of Aurora* v. *Haar*, 421 P.2d 817 [Okla. 1966].)

8. Murphy issued a check payable to the order of Brownsworth. Brownsworth took the check to Manufacturers Bank seeking a cashier's check to replace the check given to him by Murphy. Manufacturers Bank called the drawee bank to ascertain that the check issued by Murphy was good, received a positive reply, and took the check issued by Murphy as payment for the cashier's check requested by Brownsworth. Murphy subsequently issued a stop payment order on the check. When Manufacturers Bank sued to collect the amount of the check, Murphy asserted that Manufacturers could not be a holder in due course since it lacked good faith in the transaction. As evidence of this lack of good faith, Murphy asserted that Brownsworth was not a regular customer of the bank, so the bank should not have issued a cashier's check in this situation. Does the argument advanced by Murphy establish a lack of good faith? Explain. (*Manufacturers & Traders Trust Co.* v. *Murphy*, 369 F. Supp 11 [Penn. 1974].)

9. Favor issued a promissory note to Cochise Park as payment for land that Favor was purchasing. As a part of the deal, Cochise Park gave Favor a "Money Back Guarantee and Exchange Agreement" as a separate document. This separate document granted Favor the right to withdraw from the transaction and to receive his promissory note back if he was not satisfied with the sale. Two weeks later Cochise Park sold the note to Yaffe, and then Cochise Park filed for bankruptcy. Favor inspected the land, was dissatisfied with it, and demanded the return of his promissory note as per the separate document's provisions. Yaffe, who knew nothing of the separate document, refused to return the note and sued Favor for the note. What result should occur? Explain. (*Favor* v. *Yaffe*, 605 S.W.2d 342 [Tex. 1980].)

10. Sardou executed and delivered a promissory note to Harvey. Harvey then endorsed the note with the following language: "For valuable consideration, we hereby assign all of our rights title and interest in the within installment note to W.O. Stewart. /s/ Harvey." The note was defaulted on by Sardou, and Stewart sued Harvey as the endorser of the note. Harvey alleges that the endorsement he used was a qualified endorsement, so he is not liable to Stewart for the default on the note by Sardou. Is the endorsement a qualified endorsement? What are the rights of Stewart and of Harvey in this case? (*Coulter* v. *Stewart*, 379 P.2d 910 [Ariz. 1963].)

CHAPTER 26 ▮

Liability and Discharge

BASIC CONCEPTS

Commercial paper is used as a substitute for money. However, at some point, the holder of the paper is going to want the money for which the paper was substituted. This desire will normally lead to a presentment to the maker or drawee. In most cases, the maker or drawee will then pay the money as provided; the instrument will be canceled; and its commercial life will terminate. Unfortunately, such a series of events does not happen every time. Some makers or drawees refuse to pay the presented instrument. When this occurs, the issue of *liability* arises. And some holders inadvertently fail to make a proper presentment. When this occurs, the concept of *discharge* arises.

THE CHAINS OF LIABILITY

The term *liability* refers to an obligation to pay the negotiable instrument involved. There are several possible types of liability in commercial paper. The obligation to pay may be based either on **primary liability** or on **secondary**

liability. The liability may also be based on contract principles, warranty principles, or the admissions of one of the parties.

The *maker* of a note is the primary party on that note. It is the maker to whom the holder will first look for payment, and the maker is expected to pay. The *drawee* is the primary party on a check or a draft. It is the drawee to whom the holder will first look for payment, and the drawee is expected to pay.

There is, however, a substantial difference between the position of the primary party on a note and that of a primary party on a draft or a check. The maker is primarily liable on the note as soon as the note is issued. The drawee is not primarily liable until such time as the drawee accepts the check or the draft. Thus, a check or a draft does not have a party primarily liable when it is issued; rather, it has an *expectation* that primary liability will exist at a later time.

The *drawer* of a check or a draft and the *endorsers* of any negotiable instrument are secondary parties on that instrument. Secondary parties face potential secondary liability on an instrument. A secondary party agrees, by acting either as the drawer or as the endorser, to pay the instrument *if certain conditions are met.* To hold a secondary party liable, a person holding the instrument must prove three things: (1) *presentment* was properly made; (2) the primary party *dishonored* the instrument; and (3) *notice* of the dishonor was properly given to the secondary party. In addition, each secondary party faces certain warranty liabilities by virtue of being a secondary party. These will be discussed later in this chapter.

Presentment is *a demand for acceptance or for payment* of a negotiable instrument. The demand is made on the maker, the drawee, or the acceptor of the instrument. The presentment can be made through a **clearinghouse** or at a place specified in the instrument. If the presentment is made through the mail, presentment occurs when the mail is *received.* This puts the danger of postal delay on the presenting party. If the presentment is to be made at a specified place and if the person who is to receive it is not there at the proper time, presentment is excused. This removes the danger of drawee or maker absence from the presenter. If a note is payable at a bank in the United States or a draft is to be accepted at such a bank, the note or draft must be presented at that bank.[1]

The rules of presentment are very important, because presentment must be made before a dishonor can be shown. And dishonor must be shown before any secondary party (except the drawer) can be held on his or her liability. The only exception to this rule is if presentment is *excused.*

The rules that govern presentment are fairly straightforward. Section 3–503 of the UCC explains the *time* for presentment: the holder must

---

[1] Uniform Commercial Code, Section 3–504(1), (2), (4).

Primary liability Liability of the party to be looked to first for payment

Primary Parties

Secondary liability Liability of parties on a negotiable instrument upon default by the primary party

Secondary Parties

Presentment

Clearinghouse Device or association for the adjustment and payment of daily balances between banks in a city

make presentment within a reasonable time, or else the presentment is improper. The reasonable time concept has two components: the time must be reasonable in both a *clock* sense (time of day) and a *calendar* sense (day of the week).

In every case, presentment must be made at a reasonable time of day — that is, during normal working hours. An alleged presentment made at a bank or business address at three o'clock in the morning would be improper and would not be effective to prove a dishonor.

The clock concept is obvious, but the calendar one is a little confusing. If the instrument is *not* a check, the proper time for presentment is determined by the language of the instrument. According to UCC Section 3 – 503(1):

1. If the instrument is payable at, or a specific time after, a stated date, presentment for acceptance must be made *on* or *before* the date set for payment.

2. If the instrument is payable after sight, it must be presented for acceptance within a reasonable time of its date or its issue, whichever is later.

3. If a date for payment is specified, presentment must be made on *that date*.

4. If the instrument is accelerated, presentment is due within a reasonable time after the acceleration.

Certified Assured in writing that the instrument has been accepted by the bank and that payment will be made on proper presentment

In contrast, the holder of a check must abide by different rules, unless the check has been **certified.** The holder must present the check to the drawee bank within thirty days of its date or its issue, whichever is later, to hold the drawer liable *on that check.* A delay beyond this thirty-day period will not excuse the drawer from liability. Such a delay will merely excuse the liability on that particular check. The drawer may be forced to redeem the check by paying cash or by issuing a new negotiable instrument to replace the original check. A second time limit is also involved with an uncertified check: the check must be presented within seven days of an endorsement to retain the liability of the endorser. Thus, a check presented within thirty days of its issue but more than seven days after an endorsement could be enforced against the drawer, but not against the endorser.

Once presentment is made, the focus shifts to the maker, drawee, or acceptor. If the presentment is made for *acceptance,* the drawee has until the close of business the next business day to accept the instrument. And if the holder agrees in good faith, another business day may be granted to the drawee to decide whether to accept the instrument.[2] If the presentment is made for *payment,* the drawee, acceptor, or maker may delay paying the instrument until an investigation is made to decide that payment would be proper. However, payment must be made *before* the close of the business day on which the presentment was made.[3] Any delay beyond these time limits is treated as a dishonor of the instrument presented.

---

[2] Ibid., Section 3 – 506(1).
[3] Ibid., Section 3 – 506(2).

Persons receiving a presentment do have some protection. They can require some proof from the presenter of the presenter's right to have the check; and requesting these proofs is *not* treated as a dishonor. They can require the presenter to show them the instrument. They can demand reasonable identification of the presenter. They can require a showing of authority to make the presentment. They can demand the surrender of the instrument upon payment in full. If the presenter fails or refuses to comply with any of these requests, the presentment is considered improper. However, the presenter is allowed a reasonable time to comply with any of the requests.[4]

The importance of presentment is illustrated in the following case.

Kirby v. *Bergfeld*
186 Neb. 242, 182 N.W.2d 205 (1970)

Kirby agreed to buy some land from Bergfeld, giving Bergfeld a check for $20,000 at the time of closing. Bergfeld took the check to his bank and asked that the cashier telephone Kirby's bank to verify that sufficient funds were on deposit to cover the check. The bookkeeper at Kirby's bank stated that sufficient funds were on deposit. Bergfeld continued to hold the check, never presenting it to Kirby's bank. Later, Bergfeld ordered his attorney to tear his signature off the contract and refused to sell the land to Kirby. Kirby sued for specific performance. Bergfeld claimed that Kirby was in breach.   **FACTS**

Should specific performance be granted to Kirby? Had Bergfeld made a proper presentment of the check, so that it was dishonored by nonpayment?   **ISSUES**

An inquiry by telephone is not a proper presentment. The check was not dishonored, so specific performance should be granted.   **HOLDINGS**

Under the UCC, presentment may be made by mail, through a clearinghouse, or in person. Presentment by telephone is not authorized or contemplated. Since there was never a presentment, there was never a dishonor. Accordingly, Kirby was not in breach. Specific performance is ordered.   **REASONING**

When the drawee decides to accept an instrument, the drawee must sign the instrument. *By signing the draft or check, the drawee agrees to honor the instrument as presented.* This act of *acceptance* fixes the primary liability of the drawee. (An order instrument has no primary liability until it has been accepted by the drawee.)   Acceptance

[4] Ibid., Section 3–505.

Draft-varying acceptance A purported acceptance, valid only if the presenter will agree to terms not included in the instrument itself

The acceptance can be made even if the instrument is incomplete, but it must be made for the instrument as presented. Suppose the drawee tries to change the terms of the draft in the acceptance. The presenter can treat this as a dishonor. But if this **draft-varying acceptance** is agreed to by the presenter, the drawer and every endorser are discharged from secondary liability.

Dishonor

An instrument is *dishonored* when *proper presentment is made, and acceptance and/or payment is refused.* A dishonor also occurs when presentment is excused and the instrument is not accepted or paid.[5] (Under UCC Section 3–507[3], the return of an instrument for lack of a proper endorsement is *not* a dishonor.) The failure of the primary party to accept the instrument within the proper time is also a dishonor. A check returned because of insufficient funds or because of a stop payment order is dishonored. A refusal by the primary party is a dishonor. Dishonor is a *denial* of primary liability, and it activates the secondary liability of endorsers and of the drawer (see Figure 26.1). Remember that before dishonor, the secondary parties faced only *potential* secondary liability. The act of dishonor may, and usually will, move this liability from potential to actual.

Protest

Once an instrument is dishonored, the holder is thrown into the secondary chain of liability (see Figure 26.1). Following the secondary chain involves

Figure 26.1 The Chains of Liability

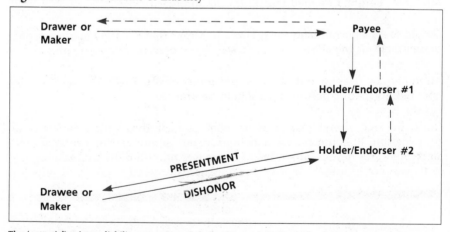

The (potential) primary liability moves in a *clockwise* manner, following the solid lines. Upon dishonor, the holder is thrown into the secondary chain of liability. Secondary liability moves in a *counterclockwise* manner, following the dotted lines. It should be remembered that this is only an illustration and that there could be more or fewer holders/endorsers than are shown here. It should also be noted that the *maker* occupies the positions of both the drawer and the drawee.

[5] Ibid., Section 3–507.

going back to prior holders to recover the amount of the instrument. However, in order to follow the secondary chain, the holder must follow certain steps.

One of these steps involves *protest,* although this particular step is fairly rare. A protest is a *certificate* of dishonor. The certificate is made by a United States consul or vice-consul or by a notary public.[6] The certificate states that the named instrument was properly presented (or that presentment was excused) and that it was dishonored. It also may state that notice has been given and, if so, to whom it was given. Protest is not needed in every case of dishonor. Protest is necessary only if there is a dishonor on a draft drawn or payable outside the United States or its territories. These drafts are commonly referred to as **foreign bills.** Protest may be used on any other instruments that are dishonored, but it is not necessary on any other dishonored instruments.

Foreign bills Bills drawn in one state or country on a foreign state or country

If protest is necessary, it must be made within the proper time (discussed in the following section). Should the holder fail to give protest within the time limit, *all* secondary parties are excused from liability. This includes the drawer. The holder who fails to make a proper protest on a foreign bill will lose all secondary claims and will end up collecting nothing on the instrument.

When the dishonored instrument is drawn and payable in the United States or its territories and possessions, no protest is required. However, the holder still has an obligation. The holder must give *notice* to prior parties in order to establish their secondary liabilities. The notice may be given to any or all persons who may be liable on the instrument. And it may be given *by* any person who has received notice, in addition to the holder.[7]

Notice

The notice may be given in any reasonable manner. It may be written or oral. It may be given in any terms or in any form, so long as it adequately *identifies the instrument* and *states that it was dishonored.*[8] The UCC is concerned with the rights of the holder. Allowance is even made for an error in the description of the instrument in the notice. A **misdescription** will not affect the validity of the notice unless it misleads the person being notified.

Misdescription Error or falsity in the description of the subject matter that is misleading on a material point

The notice must be given in a timely manner. A bank must give notice before its **midnight deadline.** That is, it must give notice before midnight of the banking day *after* the banking day on which the bank learns of the dishonor. The holder of a dishonored instrument must give notice by midnight of the third business day following dishonor. Finally, a prior party who has received notice has three business days after receiving notice to give notice to holders prior to his or her possession.[9]

Midnight deadline Midnight of the next banking day following the banking day on which the relevant item or notice is received

The following case shows what can happen to a bank that fails to act within its time limits.

[6] Ibid., Section 3–509(1).
[7] Ibid., Section 3–508(1).
[8] Ibid., Section 3–508(3).
[9] Ibid., Section 3–508(2).

First Wyoming Bank v. Cabinet Craft Distributors, Inc.
624 P.2d 227 (Wyo. 1981)

FACTS   Quality Kitchens delivered a $10,000 check to Cabinet Craft as payment on account. Cabinet Craft deposited the check with Security Bank in Billings, Montana. Security Bank then placed the check in the bank collection system. The check moved through the system to First Wyoming Bank, the drawee. First Wyoming then sent the check by courier to the computer center for processing. The courier arrived at the computer center with the check, but decided not to await the processing due to flooding of the main road back to First Wyoming's locale. The check was returned to First Wyoming three days later, and First Wyoming dishonored the check due to insufficient funds in the drawer's account. Cabinet Craft sued the bank for the check due to its delay in the processing stages.

ISSUE   Did First Wyoming dishonor the check in a timely manner? If it did not, was its delay in dishonoring the check excused?

HOLDING   No to both issues. The check's dishonor was unduly delayed, and the delay was not excused under the Code.

REASONING The UCC allows a bank to delay its dishonor under some circumstances, providing the bank acts with due diligence. However, the bank bears the burden of proving its due diligence in order to take advantage of the excuse. In this case, the bank failed to establish its due diligence for two reasons. First, when the checks were not promptly returned from the computer center, the bank did not make any inquiries as to the location of the checks that had been sent there for processing. Second, the courier could have taken a secondary route back from the computer center to the bank even if the main road was indeed flooded. By choosing to have the checks flown back by commercial airline rather than having the courier wait for them and then drive them back as was normally done, the bank acted in a less than diligent manner. The bank's delay was unexcused, and the bank is liable for the check.

It is normal for each party to give notice to his or her immediate transferor. However, sometimes the transferor cannot be found or, when found, cannot pay. For that reason, a holder should give notice to every prior party who can be located. This increases the chances that the holder will eventually recover on the dishonored instrument.

A failure to give proper or timely notice will operate as a release from liability for all the secondary parties *except* the drawer. It should be observed that this is different from the rule on protests. An improper protest releases the drawer along with the other parties, but improper notice does not release the drawer.

Normally, the duty to make presentment or to give protest or notice is *waived* or *excused.* When these situations arise, Section 3–511 of the Code controls. Under these situations, delay is excused when the party is unaware that action is needed or when the delay is due to circumstances beyond the control of the holder. However, in the second case, the holder must act with reasonable *diligence* once the cause of the delay passes. This section of the Code may also excuse presentment, protest, or notice completely. A complete excuse will arise under any of the following three circumstances.[10]

1.   The party to be charged has expressly or impliedly waived the right.

2.   The party to be charged has dishonored the instrument or has no right to expect or to require acceptance or payment.

3.   The presentment, protest, or notice cannot be made with reasonable diligence.

A negotiable instrument is a *contract,* although it is a contract with special treatment under the law. One recognition of contract law principles is found in UCC Section 3–401. This section states that "no person is liable on an instrument unless his signature appears thereon." However, once the signature is found, the signing party faces potential liability. The type of liability depends on the capacity in which it was signed. Again, the Code helps. According to Section 3–402, every signature is *presumed* to be an endorsement unless the instrument clearly indicates some other capacity.

LIABILITY

The maker of promise paper and the acceptor of order paper give a contract. Each agrees to pay the instrument according to the terms of the instrument at the time of his or her engagement or *as completed* if it was incomplete. The drawer of order paper promises to pay any holder or any endorser the amount of the instrument if it is dishonored.[11]

The endorsers of commercial paper also give a contract by the act of endorsing, unless the endorsement is qualified. By the act of endorsing, the endorser promises that upon dishonor and *proper* notice, he or she will pay the instrument *as endorsed* to any subsequent holder. The endorsers are presumed to be liable to one another on a dishonored instrument in the order endorsed, moving from bottom to top.[12]

Two other parties *may* be involved in contractual liability on commercial paper: the accommodation party and the guarantor. Each of these parties has special potential contract liability. An *accommodation party* is a person who signs an instrument to "lend his name," or his credit, to another party. He signs as a favor, usually without getting anything out of the transaction. The accommodation party is liable to subsequent parties in the capacity in which

---

[10] Ibid., Section 3–511(2).
[11] Ibid., Section 3–413(1), (2).
[12] Ibid., Section 3–414.

he signed.[13] If required to pay because of his secondary liability, he is entitled to recover from the accommodated party.

A *guarantor* is a person who adds the words "payment guaranteed," or their equivalent, to a signature on an instrument. A guarantor waives the need for presentment, protest, or notice. Likewise, a guarantor waives any protection under the Statute of Frauds. And a guarantor promises to pay the holder for a dishonored instrument without the need to go to any other party.[14]

In addition to the basic contract liabilities just discussed, persons who present or transfer negotiable instruments make certain *warranties*. These warranties carry with them the possibility of liabilities also, and warranty liabilities cannot be disclaimed as contract ones can. An endorser may deny contract liability by the use of a qualified endorsement. But warranty liability is still present even if the endorsement is qualified, unless the qualified endorsement specifically excludes warranties. An endorser could qualify the endorsement so that warranties are also excluded, even though endorsing with such a qualification to later holders makes the endorsement highly unusual. The endorser who would use such an endorsement would be well protected, but the instrument would be very difficult to transfer since few subsequent holders would be willing to accept such a negotiation.

The warranties involved in commercial paper are set out in Section 3–417 of the UCC. There are two major categories of warranties: *presentment* warranties and *transfer* warranties. Presentment warranties are fairly simple. Any person who obtains acceptance or payment, and any prior transferor, warrants the following facts to the acceptor or payor:.[15]

1. The person has good title, or is authorized to act by a person with good title, to obtain acceptance or payment.

2. The person has no *knowledge* that the signature of the maker or of the drawer is unauthorized.

3. The instrument has not been materially altered.

In transfer warranties, any person who transfers an instrument *for consideration* warrants the following facts to the transferee.[16]

1. The person has good title, or is authorized by a person having good title, to make the transfer.

2. All signatures are genuine or authorized.

3. The instrument has not been materially altered.

4. No defenses of any party are good against the transferor.

---

[13] Ibid., Section 3–415.
[14] Ibid., Section 3–416.
[15] Ibid., Section 3–417(1).
[16] Ibid., Section 3–417(2).

5. The person has no knowledge of any insolvency proceedings that affect
the instrument.

In addition, if the transfer is made by means of an endorsement, the
endorser gives the transfer warranties to any and all subsequent good-faith
holders. The only variation in the transfer warranties arises when the transfer
is made by means of a qualified endorsement. In that case, the qualified
endorser gives all the same warranties *except* for the one that concerns defenses
(item 4). Qualified endorsers warrant only that they have no knowledge of any
defenses that are good against them, not that there are no defenses.[17]

As was pointed out earlier, a person's signature must appear on an instrument
before that person can be held liable on the instrument. Thus, a forgery or an
unauthorized signature is normally of no legal effect. However, an unauthorized signature can be *ratified* by the named person, and it then becomes fully
effective.[18] In some circumstances, **imposters** can sign, and the signature is
fully effective. Under Section 3–405, an imposter may sign the name of the
payee if he induced the maker or drawer to issue the instrument to him thinking
he was the payee. This is known as the *imposter rule.* A similar set of facts leads
to the *fictitious-payee rule.* Under this rule, the maker or drawer is induced to
issue a check or a note to a named payee. However, the payee who is named
has no right to the instrument and did not know of its issuance. The person
who induced the issuance may sign for the "fictitious payee," and the signature is fully effective.[19] The following hypothetical cases illustrate these two
special problem areas.

**SPECIAL
PROBLEMS**

Imposters Persons who
assume the identity or title
of another for the purpose
of deception

Fred stole a radio from Herb. Fred then approached Thelma, told her that he was Herb,
and offered to sell the radio to her. Thelma wrote a check payable to the order of Herb to
pay for the radio. Under the imposter rule, Fred may effectively endorse the check by
writing Herb's name, UCC Section 3–404 on unauthorized signatures notwithstanding.

Steve worked for Acme. Part of his job was preparing checks to be used in paying bills
and then taking those checks to Mr. Burton to be signed for the company. Steve slipped
a check payable to Hall and Associates in among the other checks for Mr. Burton to
sign. In fact, no money was owed to Hall and Associates. If Steve later removes the
phony check and endorses it "Hall and Associates," the endorsement is valid under the
fictitious-payee rule, UCC Section 3–404 notwithstanding.

---

[17] Ibid., Section 3–417(3).
[18] Ibid., Section 3–404(2).
[19] Ibid., Section 3–405(1)(b).

In the following case, the court was faced with an imposter-endorsed check and had to use the imposter rule to resolve the issues.

Philadelphia Title Insurance Co. v. *Fidelity-Philadelphia Trust Co.*
419 Pa. 78, 212 A.2d 222 (1965)

FACTS Edmund Jezemski and his wife, Paula, were separated and living apart. Edmund was the executor and sole heir of the estate of his mother. Included in the estate was a parcel of real estate in Philadelphia. Paula arranged for a mortgage on this property without the knowledge or the consent of Edmund. Paula arrived at the office of an attorney with a man she introduced as her husband, Edmund. She then executed a deed conveying the property from the estate of Edmund's mother to Paula and Edmund as tenants by the entireties, executed a mortgage from the Title Company, and took a check payable to the order of Paula and Edmund Jezemski from the Title Company. Paula and "Edmund" endorsed the check, and Paula cashed the check, which was eventually paid by Fidelity-Philadelphia Trust Company.

When Edmund learned what had happened, he brought an action to have the mortgage set aside as well as the deed. The Title Company then sued the bank to recover the amount of the check.

ISSUE Is the bank liable for paying a check made payable to an imposter and then endorsed by that imposter and presented to the bank in an otherwise proper manner?

HOLDING No. The issuance of a check to an imposter by the drawer makes the forged endorsement of the imposter effective against the drawer.

REASONING Normally, a forgery is wholly inoperative against the party whose signature is forged unless ratified by that person. However, an exception exists when the forgery is the result of an imposter who induces the drawer to issue the instrument to the imposter in the name of the person whose signature is forged. The UCC specifically deals with this type of situation so that, in a situation where one of two innocent parties must bear the loss, the loss is placed on the party better able to have prevented the loss. The drawer who issues an instrument to an imposter is in a better position to prevent the loss than is the innocent bank, which merely honors the endorsement of the imposter.

DISCHARGE The term *discharge* means *to remove liability or potential liability on a negotiable instrument.* A discharge can take place in a number of ways. Some methods discharge all the parties, while others discharge only a few. The most important and most common types of discharge are explained in the following sections.

The most common type of discharge is the payment or other satisfaction of the instrument.[20] In the vast majority of cases, the primary party pays the instrument on presentment and cancels it (or otherwise marks it as paid). Were this not so, negotiable instruments would not be so readily accepted in the commercial world.

There are only two exceptions to payment operating as a discharge. A payment will not operate as a discharge when it is made in bad faith to a thief or to a person holding through or after a thief. And it will not operate as a discharge if the paying party makes a payment that violates a restrictive endorsement. (*Note:* An intermediary bank or a nondepository bank *may* be discharged even though it ignores the restrictive endorsement, provided it acts in good faith.) In these examples, the bad faith of the payor does not remove liability. The proper party, the person who should have received payment, is still entitled to payment, and the liability of the wrongfully paying party remains.

If a party *tenders payment* in full to a holder *when an instrument is due* or later, and the holder *refuses* the payment, a discharge occurs.[21] The party tendering payment is discharged to a limited extent. No additional interest can be added to the instrument after the date of the tender, nor can any other costs or attorney's fees be added to the instrument. Any other parties on the instrument (endorsers, drawers, and the like) are *totally* discharged if, to collect on the instrument, they could theoretically have sued the party who made the tender of payment.

A holder may discharge a party by canceling that party's signature on the instrument or by canceling the instrument itself.[22] Cancellation may be shown either by striking out a portion, such as one signature, or by striking out the entire instrument. It can also be shown by destroying or mutilating a signature or the entire instrument. To be effective, the cancellation must be done intentionally.

Renunciation operates as a discharge whenever the holder *delivers* a *written* and *signed* statement to the discharged party that renounces (gives up) any rights against that person.[23] Such a discharge is good against the renouncing party but not against any later holders, unless they were aware of the renunciation.

Under the UCC Section on impairment, a holder may elect to release some party from liability on the instrument.[24] Or a holder may decide to release some *collateral* that is being used to secure payment of the instrument. How-

[20] Ibid., Section 3–603.
[21] Ibid., Section 3–604.
[22] Ibid., Section 3–605.
[23] Ibid.
[24] Ibid., Section 3–606.

ever, in so doing, the holder will also discharge some or even all of the secondary parties on the instrument. When the holder releases a particular prior party, the holder also releases any *other* prior party who might have had recourse against the originally released party. And when a holder releases collateral, the holder releases *every* prior party, since each prior party might have had recourse against the collateral. There are only two exceptions to these rules:

1. If a prior party agrees to the release of another party or to a release of the collateral, the agreeing party is not discharged by the release.

2. If the holder *expressly* reserves rights against a party, then that party is not released or discharged. However, the releases by the holder are also *not* effective as far as the nondischarged party is concerned. In other words, the party who was expressly not discharged does not have any change in his or her position.

Other Discharges

If a party is a former holder of an instrument and later *reacquires* the instrument, a partial discharge occurs.[25] Any person who held the note *between* the two holdings of the reacquiring party is discharged from liability to the reacquiring party. And if the reacquiring party *strikes out* the endorsements of the intervening persons, they are totally discharged on the instrument. For example, if George holds a note, endorses it to Betty, and then buys it back from Betty, Betty is discharged from liability to George.

A fraudulent material alteration also acts as a discharge.[26] If the alteration is fraudulent and material, any party who does not consent to the alteration is totally discharged from liability under most circumstances. A holder in due course may still enforce the instrument as it was originally issued even though it has been materially altered.

Finally, any undue delay in presentment operates as a discharge for all prior endorsers. An undue delay in giving notice of a dishonor will operate as a discharge of all prior endorsers and *may* discharge a drawer or maker. And an undue delay in a *necessary* protest will operate as a discharge of all the prior parties, both endorsers and drawer.[27]

When the delay involves notice, and payment was to be made at a named bank, the drawer or maker may be discharged. However, to be discharged, the following facts must be shown:

1. The bank became insolvent *during the undue delay.*

2. The maker or drawer lost funds held by the bank that were intended to cover the instrument.

---

[25] Ibid., Section 3–208.
[26] Ibid., Section 3–407.
[27] Ibid., Section 3–502.

3.   The maker or drawer assigned in writing his or her rights against the bank for the lost funds to the holder.

SUMMARY

Negotiable instruments are formal contracts. As such, they carry certain contract responsibilities and liabilities. The maker of promise paper has primary liability. The drawee of order paper faces potential primary liability. Once the drawee accepts an instrument, the drawee has primary liability. If the primary liability is denied or refused, every prior holder is secondarily liable. In addition, the drawer of order paper is secondarily liable on a dishonored instrument.

In order for the holder to enforce the primary liability of the instrument, proper presentment must be made on the maker or drawee. At that point, the primary party will either accept the instrument or dishonor it. If dishonor occurs, the holder will give notice to prior parties to establish their secondary liability. The holder may also be required to give protest, especially on foreign bills.

Negotiable instruments carry both contract liability and warranty liability. The warranty liability may be transfer warranty liability or presentment warranty liability.

The final stage for most instruments is discharge. Discharge can be, and normally is, based on payment or satisfaction. Some discharges are partial, either discharging a portion of the liability or just a few of the parties. Tender of payment is a partial discharge. Cancellation, renunciation, and impairment are all discharges of some of the secondary parties.

DISCUSSION QUESTIONS

1.   How does a holder prove that a drawee has accepted a draft or a check?

2.   In order to show proper presentment, what must the presenting party establish?

3.   There are five transfer warranties. How do they differ when qualified and unqualified endorsements are used?

4.   Why does the UCC grant a discharge when collateral is impaired?

5.   Why is a renunciation less advantageous for a prior party than a cancellation?

6.   Bernie was the holder of a time draft payable on 7 September 19XX. When Bernie looked at his calendar, he saw that September 7 fell on a Sunday. What should Bernie do to establish proper presentment?

7.   Bill issued a check to Sarah on 1 June 19XX. Sarah endorsed it over to Mike on June 6, and Mike endorsed it over to Pete on June 10. Pete took the check to the bank on 8 July 19XX, and the bank dishonored the check. What rights can Pete assert against *each* of the other parties? How should he proceed?

8. Amy transferred a note to Jim by delivery alone. At the time of the transfer, the maker of the note was involved in an insolvency proceeding. Jim was unable to collect the note from the maker. What are his rights against Amy?

9. Joe issued an interest-bearing demand note to Jane. Jane negotiated the note to Larry. Larry in turn negotiated it to Tom. Joe offered to pay Tom, but Tom refused the payment. What effect does Tom's refusal have on each of the other parties?

10. Dan issued a check to Ron. Ron fraudulently raised the amount payable from $100 to $400. He then negotiated the check to Sam, a holder in due course. If the bank dishonors the check, what are Sam's rights against Ron? Against Dan? Explain.

CASE
PROBLEMS

1. Robinson endorsed and delivered two checks to Dluge. Dluge presented the checks to the bank, and the bank dishonored them. Dluge then returned the checks to Robinson. Several months later, Dluge died. His estate sued Robinson for the value of the two checks based on his secondary liability as an endorser. What should be the result? (*Dluge* v. *Robinson,* 204 A.2d 279 [Pa. 1964].)

2. Cotton issued a negotiable promissory note to Jones in 1955. Over the next twelve years, until the death of Jones in 1967, Cotton made regular payments on the note. After Jones died, a paper was found among his personal effects. The paper called for the cancellation of any unpaid balance on the note Cotton had issued if Jones died before Cotton. Cotton alleged that this paper was a valid renunciation. Jones's estate argued that is was not valid. What should be the result? Explain. (*Greene* v. *Cotton,* 457 S.W.2d 493 [Ky. 1970].)

3. American Music and Disneyland Records entered into a series of contracts. After the contracts were performed, American Music owed Disneyland Records $93,000. To cover this debt, ten promissory notes were issued, payable to Disneyland. Each note was signed by Irv Schwartz individually, with no mention in the notes of American Music. When the notes were not paid, Disneyland sued Schwartz. Schwartz argued that Disneyland should have sued American Music, and not Schwartz. What should be the result? (*Schwartz* v. *Disneyland Vista Records,* 383 So.2d 117 [Fla. 1980].)

4. An employee of May Department Store forged the endorsements on checks drawn to the order of fictitious payees and then cashed the checks at National Bank. The bank charged the checks so honored to the account of May Department Store. When May discovered what had occurred, it sued the bank to recover the monies charged to its account on the forged endorsements. Is the bank liable to May Department Store on these forged endorsements? (*May Department Store* v. *Pittsburgh National Bank,* 374 F.2d 109 [3rd Cir. 1967].)

5. Shea applied to Franklin Bank for a loan so that he could purchase an automobile from his father-in-law, MacMurray. Franklin Bank approved the loan application and issued a check payable to the order of Shea and MacMurray. Shea later presented the check to the Chase Manhattan Bank, and Chase Manhattan paid Shea the face amount of the check in cash. The check as accepted by Chase Manhattan had a forged endorsement purportedly by MacMurray. Chase Manhattan alleges that MacMurray's "endorsement" falls within the imposter rule, while Franklin Bank argues that it is an inoperative forgery. Which bank is correct, and why? (*Franklin National Bank* v. *Chase Manhattan Bank, N.A.*, 328 N.Y.S.2d 25 [1972].)

6. Mobilla endorsed a promissory note "without recourse" and discounted the note to Union Bank. The signature of the maker on the note was a forgery, and the bank was unable to collect from the maker named on the note. When the bank then sued Mobilla, he raised the qualified endorsement as a defense to the bank's action. Should the qualified endorsement of the payee preclude the bank's claim against the payee? (*The Union Bank* v. *Mobilla*, 43 Erie Co. Leg. J. 45 [Pa. 1959].)

7. Theta issued a note to Thompson. The note was subsequently negotiated from Thompson to Exten, and then from Exten to Hane. The note contained an acceleration clause that called for payment on demand in the event of a default by Theta. Theta defaulted on the note in 1965, but Hane did not demand payment as per the acceleration clause until 1967. When Theta refused to pay Hane despite his demand, Hane sued Exten on his endorsement. Is Exten liable to Hane based on his endorsement of the note? Explain fully. (*Hane* v. *Exten*, 259 A.2d 290 [Md. 1969].)

8. Rock Island sold some cattle to Empire, receiving a check from Empire as payment for the cattle. Rock Island deposited the check with its bank, and the check moved through the normal banking channels to the drawee bank. At the time the check arrived at the drawee bank, Empire did not have sufficient funds on deposit to cover the check. Rather than dishonor the check immediately, the drawee bank held the check for six days to give Empire an opportunity to make a deposit. When no deposit was made, the check was returned unpaid due to insufficient funds. Shortly thereafter, Empire filed a petition in bankruptcy. Rock Island is now attempting to collect the check from the drawee bank. Is the bank liable to Rock Island in this situation? Why? (*Rock Island Auction Sales* v. *Empire Packing Co.*, 204 N.E.2d 721 [Ill. 1965].)

9. Kaiser entered into a lease agreement with Northwest that called for Kaiser to make monthly payments to Northwest for rent, taxes, and maintenance. A controversy arose over the terms of the lease, but Kaiser continued to send Northwest his checks every month. Northwest held these checks without making presentment for some time. Finally, some ten months later, Northwest presented all ten checks to the bank. A number of the checks were refused by the bank since the checks were

considered "stale" and due to insufficient funds on deposit at the time. Northwest has demanded payment from Kaiser for these dishonored checks, and Kaiser has asserted that he was discharged from liability due to the undue delay in making presentment. Who should prevail and why? (*Kaiser* v. *Northwest Shopping Center, Inc.,* 544 S.W.2d 785 [Tex. 1976].)

10. Progressive Management issued a demand note payable to the order of New Haven Bank for $10,000. Clarke had endorsed the note as follows: "Presentment for payment and notice of nonpayment are hereby waived. Further the endorser consents without further notice or assent (a) to the terms and conditions of this note or any renewal or extension thereof, (b) to the exchange or surrender of the collateral, and (c) to extension of time for payment, or change of interest rate, of this note or of the collateral." Progressive Management defaulted on the note, and New Haven Bank proceeded against Clarke for the balance due on the note. Clarke argues that the endorsement is not a guarantee and that he is not liable. Is Clarke liable to New Haven Bank? Is Clarke entitled to demand notice after proper presentment and dishonor? (*First New Haven National Bank* v. *Clarke,* 368 A.2d 613 [Conn. 1976].)

Bank – Customer Relations

BASIC CONCEPTS

In the United States today, nearly every business organization has a checking account. In addition, many, if not most, of the adults in this country have checking accounts. Workers receive their pay by check. Checking account information is normally required on credit and loan applications. Millions of checks move through the economic system each day. Yet very few people actually understand this checking system they are using.

A new customer walking into a bank follows the signs that lead to the "New Accounts" desk. Upon sitting down at this desk, the novice depositor is inundated with trivial information and details. Several different types of accounts — interest plus checking, free checking, ready-reserve checking, and so on — are briefly mentioned in passing; multiple colors and styles of checks are displayed; a "signature card" is handed to the customer with instructions to "sign at the X"; a deposit ticket is prepared; and a deposit is made in the customer's name in this new account. Before *really* knowing what has happened, the new customer is back on the street, the proud possessor of a personal checking account. And more likely than not, the customer has no idea of what all this legally means.

By signing a signature card, the customer has entered a multirole legal relationship with the bank. The signature card represents a *contract* that the customer accepts on signing the signature card, even though he or she probably is unaware of any of its terms or conditions. In addition, the customer is now governed by Part 4 of Article 4 of the Uniform Commercial Code, which governs the bank–customer relationship. And the customer has entered into an *agency* relationship and has agreed to a *debtor–creditor* relationship, as well.

The contract that the customer entered is relatively simple. It covers such things as **service charges** that can be imposed, minimum balance requirements for the customer's account, and technical terms and conditions. Likewise, the coverage afforded by Article 4 of the Code is fairly simple. Basically, it spells out the *mandatory* rights and duties of each of the parties. These will be dealt with later in the chapter.

The agency portion of the agreement is a complete surprise to most depositors. (Agency is covered in Chapters 33 through 35.) To put it simply, the bank is the *agent* and the depositor is the *principal.* An agent is required to obey any *lawful order* of the principal that deals with the agency. This explains in part the language used on a check. The depositor/principal is *ordering* the agent/ bank to "Pay to the order of" someone. The check does not say "Please pay." Nor does it say "I would appreciate it if you would pay." It says "PAY!" This language is an *order,* and the order is usually lawful. Therefore, the bank must obey that order or face possible liability to the depositor for the disobedience.

The final relationship is variable. Normally, the customer will have a positive balance in the checking account. As a result, the customer is a *creditor* of the bank, and the bank is a *debtor* of the customer. Occasionally the bank will pay an **overdraft** on the customer's account. When this happens, the customer has a negative balance in the account, and the roles reverse. Now the bank is a creditor of the customer, and the customer is a debtor to the bank.

THE CUSTOMER: RIGHTS AND DUTIES

The first and main duty of a customer is to act with due care and diligence. Whether writing a check, inspecting a monthly **statement,** or endorsing a check; whether making a deposit or cashing a check—the customer is required to act in a careful and reasonable manner. If customers remember that it is their money being handled, and that carelessness could cause them to *lose* that money, they are more likely to be careful.

Customers have several rights that they may exercise. They may **stop payment** on a previously issued check, and they may collect damages from the bank if the bank errs in the handling of the account. But before they can exercise these rights, customers must show that they have acted properly and/or that the bank has acted improperly.

For example, suppose that Louis issues a check to pay for some merchandise. The merchant presents the check to the bank for payment, and the bank dishonors the check. Louis is now likely to have some problems with the merchant. He may have to pay the merchant a "handling fee" or a "service charge" for the returned check. He may face a lawsuit filed by the merchant to

---

Service charges Charges imposed by the bank on the customer for the rendering of certain specified services in handling the customer's account

Overdraft The act of checking out more money than one has on deposit in a bank, which is in the nature of a loan, implying a promise to pay

Statement A summation of the customer's activities with the account for the period, accompanied by the items paid by the bank in good faith to support the debit entries on the statement

Stop payment An order issued by the drawer to the drawee that a specified check or draft *not* be paid on proper presentment

collect the amount of the check plus costs and interest. And in many states he *may* face a *criminal* charge for passing *hot* (bad) checks.

But what if the dishonor was due to an error by the bank, not to any carelessness or wrongdoing on Louis's part? Louis will still have to settle his own problems with the merchant, but the criminal action will be dropped. And Louis will be able to proceed against the bank for collection of any and all damages he might have suffered in this ordeal.

According to UCC Section 4–402, the bank is liable to its customer for any damages *proximately caused* by a *wrongful* dishonor of the customer's check. The damages expressly covered in the section include the following:

1. damages due to an arrest

2. damages due to a prosecution

3. any other consequential damages that can actually be proved

From this language, it sounds as if the customer will end up in a reasonably good position: the customer will recover the "handling fees," the interest, and any other costs paid to the merchant; the customer will recover any damages related to the arrest; and the bank will end up taking all the losses on this case. But sounds, like looks, can be deceiving.

In seeking damages from the bank, the customer must prove that the bank's conduct was the **proximate cause** of the losses suffered by the customer. Such proof is often difficult. If the bank can show that the customer contributed to the loss, the bank will probably owe nothing, and the customer will collect nothing. The hypothetical case that follows represents the type of problem that might prevent the customer's victory.

Proximate cause That which, in a natural and continuous sequence, produces the injury, and without which the injury would not have occurred

---

Bob had a balance in his checking account of $120.15. He made a deposit on Friday for $900, using a blank deposit slip provided by the bank. In completing the deposit slip, Bob accidentally wrote his account number incorrectly. The following Tuesday, Bob wrote a $500 check to Sam's Stereo to purchase a turntable. Sam took the check to the bank on Wednesday, and the bank returned it unpaid due to insufficient funds. Sam assessed Bob with a $10 service charge and demanded that Bob repurchase the check, along with a 10 percent "interest fee." Sam also filed criminal charges for the "hot check."

Bob paid $100 bail to get out of jail after his arrest, and he paid Sam the $560 in cash to get the proceedings dropped. If Bob now sues the bank, he will learn a shocking lesson. Bob's negligence caused the loss, so the bank is not liable. If Bob had used his own *personalized, precoded* deposit slips, he would probably have won. He didn't, and he will definitely lose.

The customer also has a right to issue *stop payment* orders to the bank. If done properly, the bank must obey this order to stop payment, or it will face liability to the customer for any damages caused by disobeying the order. To be effective and to be properly made, the order must be given to the bank in a reasonable manner. That is, the bank must receive a *complete* description of the check (number, payee, amount, date, reason) with enough "lead time" to allow the bank to react to the order.[1] A minimum of a few hours will normally be required, and it may take as long as a full banking day to get the word out to the bank's various branch offices.

The customer can give either an *oral* or a *written* stop payment order. If made orally, the order is valid for fourteen calendar days. After fourteen days it expires unless it has been put into writing. A written order is good for six months, and it can be renewed for additional six-month periods.[2] Of course, every renewal will entail another service charge.

If the customer properly gives the bank a stop payment order, and the bank pays the check despite the order, the customer *may* be able to collect damages from the bank. To do so, the customer will have to *prove* that she suffered damages because the check was paid.[3] To prove this, she will have to show that the presenter could not have collected from her (the customer) *if* payment had been stopped as ordered. If the customer would have lost a case to the presenter, she will not be able to collect any damages from the bank.

The following case shows one area in which no stop payment order may be given.

National Newark & Essex Bank v. Giordano
268 A.2d 327 (N.J. 1970)

FACTS

Giordano borrowed $9500 from the bank in order to purchase two trucks. The bank issued a **cashier's check** payable to the order of Fiero, the seller of the trucks. Giordano delivered the check to Fiero and took possession of the trucks. He then discovered that the trucks were defective and asked the bank to stop payment on the check. The bank refused to stop payment and sued Giordano for the amount due on the loan.

Cashier's check A check drawn by a bank against its own funds

ISSUE

May a bank stop payment on its own cashier's check?

HOLDING

No. A cashier's check may not have payment stopped as a matter of law.

REASONING

A cashier's check has been "accepted" by the bank on issue. Once a check has been accepted by the drawee, payment must be made on proper presentment.

---

[1] Uniform Commercial Code, Section 4–403(1).
[2] Ibid., Section 4–403(2).
[3] Ibid., Section 4–403(3).

To permit a bank to accept a check and to then dishonor it at the request of a customer would negate the rules governing acceptance. Thus, the court ruled in favor of the bank.

The bank periodically must send statements to its customers. The customer has a duty to examine and to **reconcile** this statement. A failure to do so will result in a waiver of rights in favor of the bank. And the reconciliation must be made *promptly,* since undue delay also operates as a waiver of rights and claims against the bank.[4] The bank satisfies its duty to provide a statement to the customer by mailing it or by holding it available for the customer, if the customer so requests. The customer satisfies his duty by promptly and carefully examining and balancing the statement when it is received.

Reconcile To make consistent or compatible; to bring into harmony or agreement

By failing to make a prompt examination, the customer cannot assert against the bank

1. an unauthorized customer signature,
2. a material alteration of the check, or
3. any other unauthorized signatures or alterations made *by the same person,*

provided that the customer had a reasonable time to examine the statement and to notify the bank of any problems or irregularities. The "reasonable time" available to the customer may not exceed fourteen calendar days.[5]

To complete the statement inspection duty, the customer must report any unauthorized signatures and/or any material alterations within one year of the statement date or lose the right to raise these issues. And any unauthorized endorsements must be reported to the bank within three years of the statement date, or the right to raise this issue is lost.[6]

What does all this technical jargon mean? When a customer receives a statement, he must inspect it promptly. *Promptly* means within fourteen days. If there are any unauthorized signatures or any material alterations, the bank must be notified by the customer. If the customer notifies the bank *within* fourteen days of receiving the statement, he or she gets *all* the money back on the unauthorized signatures, and the alteration amount back on the alterations. If notice is given to the bank after fourteen days but within one year, the customer recovers the amount of the *first* signature or the *first* alteration by *each* signer or alterer. And the customer puts the bank on notice for any future signings or alterations. However, the customer cannot recover on any of the checks between the first one and the date of notice. If notice is over one year after the statement date, the customer cannot recover anything from the bank.

---

[4] Ibid., Section 4–406(1).
[5] Ibid., Section 4–406(2).
[6] Ibid., Section 4–406(4).

If there is an unauthorized endorsement, it must be reported to the bank within three years, or the customer cannot recover anything from the bank.

The following case illustrates the duty of a customer to reconcile the statement.

K & K Manufacturing, Inc. v. *Union Bank*
628 P.2d 44 (Ariz. 1981)

FACTS Knight was the president and majority stockholder of K & K Manufacturing. The only two employees of K & K were Knight and Garza, the bookkeeper. Garza's duties included preparing checks for Knight to sign, and reconciling the bank statements for the K & K account and for Knight's personal account. From March, 1977, through January, 1978, Garza forged Knight's signature on nearly seventy checks. The forged checks were worth over $60,000, with nearly $50,000 from K & K's accounts and over $11,000 from Knight's personal account. The bank informed Knight numerous times during this period that his personal account was overdrawn, but Knight never investigated or questioned this fact. An audit of the company's books revealed Garza's actions, and Knight sued the bank for the losses, alleging that the bank had breached its contract by honoring the forgeries.

ISSUE Is the bank liable for the losses suffered by Knight due to the forgeries by Garza?

HOLDING No. The bank had done nothing improper in this case, and had not breached its contract.

REASONING A bank customer has a duty to reconcile his statements and to notify the bank of any alterations, forgeries, or irregularities. A customer is not excused from his duty to act in a careful and prudent manner because the customer has erroneously placed his trust in a dishonest employee. A bank's depositors are chargeable with the knowledge of any facts that an honest employee would have discovered by acting in a reasonable and prudent manner. In this case, a reasonable and prudent examination of the bank statements would have revealed the forgeries in the bank statement of May, 1977, and would have given the bank notice at that time. By waiting until after January, 1978, Knight has acted improperly.

THE BANK: RIGHTS AND DUTIES Since the bank is the agent of the customer, it must obey any lawful orders of the customer. This duty to obey gives the bank a very important right: it can charge to the customer's account *any* item that is properly payable from the customer's account. The bank can pay the check even if payment creates an overdraft.[7] The bank can also pay a check that was incomplete when issued

[7] Ibid., Section 4–401(1).

and then completed by some later holder. The bank may even know that a holder completed the check and still pay it as completed. The only exception is when the bank has notice that the completion was improper or was done in bad faith.[8]

In accordance with the rules that govern timely presentment, the bank may refuse to honor any *stale checks*. A stale check is one that is more than six months old and has not been certified. If the bank dishonors a stale check, it is not liable to the customer for any damages. However, the bank may, at its option, honor a stale check. Again, the bank will not be liable for any damages suffered by the customer if it honors the check in good faith.[9] It should be remembered that a written stop payment is good for six months, the period after which a check becomes stale. Suppose a customer issues a written stop payment order. Six months elapse without the check's ever being presented, and the customer does not renew the stop payment order. The payee now presents the check to the bank. The check is stale. A stop payment order had been in effect on that check. The bank honors the check. If the bank can prove that it acted in good faith, it will face no liability for its payment of the stale, once-stopped check.

Under normal agency rules, if the principal dies or becomes incompetent, the agency terminates by operation of law. After this termination, if the agent continues to perform its agency duties, the agent becomes personally liable, and the principal has no liability. This rule would be impractical in commercial paper, so the UCC expressly changes it. As applied to the bank–customer relationship, agencies do not automatically end at the instant of the principal's death or incompetence.

Under Section 4–405(1), the bank is fully authorized to perform its banking functions on the account of a customer who has died or has become incompetent until the bank *knows* of the occurrence and has had adequate time to react to the news. Even if the bank knows of the customer's death, its power to act is not terminated. Section 4–405(2) permits the bank to continue to honor checks drawn on the account for ten days after the date of a death unless a stop payment is placed on the account by an interested party.

Sometimes banks make mistakes. A bank may honor an instrument that had a stop payment order covering it, or it may do something else that allows the customer to recover damages from the bank. When this happens, the bank has some protection: it is entitled to **subrogation.** Subrogation means that the bank is given the rights that some other parties could have raised if the bank had not made improper payment. UCC Section 4–407 gives the bank three different sets of rights to assert through subrogation:

Subrogation The substitution of one person in the place of another with reference to a lawful claim, demand, or right

1. the rights of a holder in due course against the maker or drawer
2. the rights of the payee or any other holder against the maker or drawer

---

[8] Ibid., Section 4–401(2).
[9] Ibid., Section 4–404.

3.   the rights of the drawer or maker against the payee or any other holders

Thus, the bank has the rights of both sides and of every interested party. From this buffet of rights, the bank can select the set of rights that give it the greatest likelihood of winning the case.

The bank has the right to enforce the terms of its contract with the customer. Among other things, this allows the bank to impose certain service charges and fees against many of its customers each month. The bank may be able to collect a specific amount every month; it may be able to collect a specific amount in any month the customer's account balance falls below a certain amount; or it may be able to charge a specific amount for every check written by the customer. The bank will impose a service charge for handling a stop payment order. Likewise, it may charge a customer when it pays an overdraft or when it dishonors a check, if honoring it would have created an overdraft.

The duties of the bank are simple. The bank is required to honor the terms and conditions of its contract. It is required to obey the rules of agency. And it is required to act in good faith in a commercially reasonable manner.

SPECIAL PROBLEMS

Two areas deserve further mention: certified checks and unauthorized signatures.

Certified Checks

A *certified check is one that has already been accepted by the drawee bank.*[10] In other words, the bank has assumed primary liability and agreed to pay the check on a later presentment. Certification can be done at the request of the drawer or of any holder. A refusal by the bank to certify the check is *not* a dishonor.

How does certification occur? Either the drawer or a holder presents the check to the bank and requests certification. If the bank agrees to certify, it follows certain steps. First, it *charges* the account of the customer and *credits* its own "Certified Check Account." Thus, the money is held by the bank in the bank's own account, and the customer has already "paid" the amount of the check. Second, the bank punches a hole in the encoded account number of the check to ensure that the check will not be paid a second time on a later presentment. Third, a stamp is made on the face of the check, and the terms of the certification are written into the stamped form.

If the drawer seeks and receives the certification, the drawer remains secondarily liable until final payment. However, if a holder seeks and receives the certification, the drawer and all prior endorsers are discharged from liability.

Unauthorized Signatures

Under UCC Section 1–201(43), an *unauthorized signature is one made without any authority express or implied,* and it includes a forgery. An unauthorized signature

---

[10] Ibid., Section 3–411.

is wholly inoperative against the person whose name was signed unless that person later ratifies the signing. It cannot be used to impose liability on the purported signer. However, in some circumstances, an unauthorized and unratified signature is still binding on the purported signer. According to Section 3–406, if a person contributes to the unauthorized signing through *negligence*, he or she will be held liable to any good-faith holder of the instrument.

Many businesses "sign" checks by means of a stamp. The business may leave the stamp and its checks in a place where they are easily reached by a nonauthorized person (most likely a thief). Such conduct on the part of the business is negligent, and the negligence leads to the unauthorized "signing." In such circumstances, the business may not later assert the defense that the signing was unauthorized if the holder is a holder in good faith. Notice that the holder does *not* have to be a holder in due course; the fact that the holder is in good faith is sufficient. The *negligence* of the wronged party is the key: the wronged party must be negligent, and the negligence must cause the loss. Otherwise, the unauthorized signature cannot be used against the person whose name was signed.

CREDIT UNION SHARE DRAFT ACCOUNTS

There has been a recent increase in the use of share draft accounts through credit unions. Many individuals are selecting an account with a credit union rather than with a bank due to more personalized treatment by the credit union, or lower charges and fees, or for a number of other reasons. These share draft accounts operate in most respects like a checking account opened at a bank, but there are a few differences. A credit union does not return the customer's cancelled checks in a monthly bank statement. Rather, the credit union will send the customer a synopsis of the activities on the account for the period, normally a month. This synopsis will list the drafts that were presented and accepted, but it will not include the cancelled drafts. The customer must reconcile the statement on the basis of the summation and then go to the credit union office to straighten out any problems, examine drafts for alterations, or look for unauthorized signatures.

The drawer of a share draft has the same right to stop payment on the draft as the drawer on a check possesses. And the same time limits—fourteen days for an oral order, six months for a written order—operate on the stop payment order directed to the credit union/drawee.

These share draft accounts also have instruments that are payable on demand, the same as a check. Further, the drawer can postdate, or antedate, the share draft. The treatment in nearly every respect is the same as the treatment given to checks. The differences tend to be minor and technical and have little impact on the customer or the customer's use of the account.

ELECTRONIC FUND TRANSFERS

Recent technological advances have provided banking with a new method of doing business and with a new type of service to provide for its customers. This new method of doing business is the *electronic fund transfer*, which allows for computerization of checking accounts and for faster, (theoretically) more accurate banking transactions. The Electronic Fund Transfer Act, which became effective in 1980, provides the basic legal framework for this method of doing business. In addition, the UCC's Permanent Editorial Board is considering revisions to the Code to reflect the advent of electronic banking. This method of financial dealing may eventually make the current checking or drafting account obsolete, or nearly so, due to the delays and expenses of handling checks or drafts when compared to electronic banking.

While electronic fund transfers can be initiated in a number of ways, four methods have already become widely used. One method is the Point of Sale (POS) terminal and the "debit" card. In a POS transaction, the customer will present the merchant with a debit card, the merchant will imprint the card and have the customer sign, and the funds will be automatically transferred from the customer's account to the merchant's account. The transaction is similar in format to the use of a credit card, but there is no delay for the merchant in receiving the money from the sale.

A second, and more familiar, method is the use of Automated Teller Machine (ATM) transfers. The bank customer inserts his or her card in the machine, enters his or her personal identification number (PIN), and selects a transaction. The customer can make a deposit, a withdrawal, a transfer from one account to another, a payment, or do any of a number of other banking transactions.

If the bank is a participant in a network, the customer may be able to authorize payments to predetermined accounts by phone. Here, the customer calls the bank and, using the buttons on a Touch-Tone®phone, can designate preselected "payees" who will be paid an amount determined by punching in the amount of the "electronic check" so that the funds are automatically transferred.

Finally, there are preauthorized automatic payments, and preauthorized direct deposits. In both cases, regular amounts are deducted from, or added to, the customer's account balance on designated dates to ensure that payment (or credit) is received without any worries about forgetting to send in the check or drive to the bank to make the deposit.

As the public becomes more familiar and more comfortable with electronic fund transfers, the use of this form will grow and develop. And as that happens, the use of checks will begin to decline. The decline will be gradual at first, but by the next century we may do virtually all of our "banking" electronically.

SUMMARY

The most frequently used negotiable instrument is the check. As a result, special attention must be paid to the bank—customer relationship. When a customer opens a checking account, a multirole relationship is created. The bank and the customer have a contract; they are involved in an agency; they have a debtor—creditor relationship; and they are controlled by Article 4 of the UCC.

Customers have a duty to exercise due care in their dealings with their accounts. They are required to inspect their statements carefully and promptly for any irregularities, alterations, or unauthorized signings. They may also issue stop payment orders to the bank. Since the bank is the agent of its customers, it is obligated to obey such orders.

The bank is required to abide by the terms of its contract with the customer. It must pay properly drawn checks if the customer has sufficient funds. And it must act in good faith.

Certified checks and unauthorized signatures can present special problems. A certified check is one that has been accepted by the bank and then circulated through the normal channels of commerce. Unauthorized signings are sometimes caused by the negligence of the customer; in such a case, the bank is not liable for honoring the unauthorized signing.

Credit unions have begun to get actively involved in the business of providing accounts to customers. Credit union share draft accounts, similar to checking accounts in virtually every aspect, have become a common alternative to the traditional checking accounts offered by banks. The credit unions tend to have lower minimum balance requirements and lower fees and charges for their credit union members who elect to open share draft accounts.

Electronic fund transfers are the probable wave of the future. By using the capacity and speed of computers and by eliminating the paper required by traditional checking accounts, funds can be moved more quickly, more accurately, more efficiently, and more inexpensively than is possible with checking accounts. This is a developmental area that will grow rapidly over the next several years.

DISCUSSION QUESTIONS

1. Where do the terms and conditions of the contract between the bank and the customer originate?

2. What should a stop payment order include?

3. Why should a customer examine a bank statement within fourteen days?

4. How does certification of a check take place?

5. Denise made a deposit at her bank on a personalized deposit slip. She was not aware that the deposit was mistakenly credited to the account of another customer. She wrote a check that would have been good if the deposit had been properly credited to her account, but it was dishonored due to insufficient funds. What are her rights in this situation?

6. Vicki issued a stop payment order on a check she had issued to a gas station. The bank paid the check over the stop payment order. What must Vicki do to recover her money on this check from the bank?

7. James received his bank statement August 1. He examined it and discovered a forgery on August 14. He notified the bank on August 18. A second forgery by the same person was presented to the bank and honored by the bank on August 16. What are the rights of James and of the bank on the second forged check?

8. Bob issued a check to Carl. Carl negotiated it to Dave. Dave negotiated it to Edna. Edna went to the bank seeking certification of the check. The bank refused to certify the check. What are Edna's rights against each of the parties?

9. Freddy's Fenders pays all of its bills by check. The checks are signed by means of a rubber stamp. A thief breaks into the office of Freddy's Fenders, breaks open the locked desk, and steals some checks. He then opens the safe and steals the rubber signature stamp. The bank unknowingly cashes several of these stolen checks when they are presented. What are the rights of Freddy's Fenders against the bank in this case?

10. What is an electronic fund transfer? What are the current methods for transferring funds electronically?

CASE
PROBLEMS

1. C.I.T. issued two checks totaling $11,000 to McCarthy. McCarthy endorsed and deposited the checks in his account, to be collected. C.I.T. placed a stop payment order on the checks with its bank before the checks were presented. Upon presentment, the bank accidentally honored the checks despite the stop payment. The bank then charged C.I.T.'s account for the $11,000. C.I.T. sued to have its account credited for the $11,000. If the only defense C.I.T. has is personal in nature, what should be the result? (*Universal C.I.T. Credit Corp.* v. *Guaranty Bank & Trust Co.,* 161 F. Supp. 790 [Mass. 1958].)

2. A church opened a checking account with First National Bank. The checks had to be signed by Jordan and Jackson, two elders of the congregation. Bank statements were to be mailed to Jordan. Over the span of one year, fifty checks were issued by Jordan, with Jordan forging Jackson's signature on each of the checks. The church sued the bank to recover on the fifty forged checks. What should be the result? (*Jackson* v. *First National Bank of Memphis,* 403 S.W.2d 109 [Tenn. App. 1966].)

3. Kendall discovered that his business was in trouble and that he had too little money to continue operating the business until things improved. He then received an agreement from his bank whereby the bank agreed to cover any overdrafts on Kendall's checking account until the business became profitable. The bank then dishonored several checks drawn by Kendall due to insufficient funds. Kendall sued the bank for the damages caused by these dishonors. What should be the result? (*Kendall Yacht Corp.* v. *United California Bank,* 50 Cal.3d 949, 123 Cal. Rptr. 848 [Cal. App. 1975].)

4. Vickrey fired Sanford from his job, giving Sanford one check for his wages and a second check as payment for some stock Sanford had purchased from Vickrey. Sanford deposited the checks in his bank, and then he returned to the business and verbally threatened Vickrey. As a result,

Vickrey issued a stop payment order on the second check. Sanford sued Vickrey to collect on the check. What should be the result? (*Vickrey v. Sanford,* 506 S.W.2d 270 [Tex. App. 1974].)

5. Harvey made reservations at a resort hotel that had advertised in a national magazine. The hotel required advance payment by cashier's check, which Harvey sent to the hotel just before his arrival. When Harvey arrived at the hotel, he found that the advertisements were misleading and that he had been cheated. He immediately checked out and called the bank to try to stop payment on the cashier's check. Must the bank honor the stop payment order that Harvey placed? (*Moon Over the Mountains, Ltd. v. Marine Midland Bank,* 87 Misc.2d 918, 386 N.Y.S.2d 974 [1976].)

6. Cicci issued a check to Santo for $3000. The check was issued as the proceeds of a loan Cicci had agreed to make to Santo. Several days later Santo presented the check to the drawee bank, the check was accepted by the bank, and the $3000 in cash paid to Santo. Unfortunately, Cicci had given the bank a stop payment on the check prior to the presentment by Santo. Cicci is now suing the bank for paying the check despite the stop payment order. The bank alleges that Cicci suffered no loss and, thus, that the bank is not liable even though it ignored the stop payment order. Which party should prevail in this case? (*Cicci v. Lincoln National Bank & Trust Co. of Central New York,* 260 N.Y.S.2d 100 [1965].)

7. Ralph and Bertha Huber were the only parties authorized to sign the checks issued by the Huber Glass Company. The Hubers hired Miller as a bookkeeper in 1960. Over the next three years Miller forged the signature of Ralph Huber on some thirty-eight checks, endorsed the checks, and deposited the money to his personal account. Ralph Huber discovered this pattern of embezzlement in late 1963 and sued the bank to recover the $24,000 paid out to Miller on the forgeries. The bank denies liability. What should be the key issue in this case, and which party should prevail? (*Huber Glass Co.* v. *First National Bank of Kenosha,* 138 N.W.2d 157 [Wis. 1965].)

8. Tenn was approached by Hawley with a proposed business opportunity. Tenn was interested but wanted additional time to think the deal over. However, he did give Hawley a check for $6000, which Hawley was "to hold" until Tenn made a decision. Hawley deposited the check in his bank, and the bank presented the check to the drawee. The drawee accepted the check even though Tenn did not have sufficient funds on deposit to cover the check. When Tenn learned what had occurred, he tried to recover from Hawley but was unable to do so. Tenn now denies the authority of the bank to pay the overdraft on his account and refuses to repay the bank. The bank has sued Tenn for the monies advanced in excess of Tenn's balance. Is Tenn correct, or is the bank entitled to recover the overdraft from Tenn? Explain fully. (*City Bank of Honolulu* v. *Tenn,* 469 P.2d 816 [Haw. 1970].)

9. Sims deposited a check with her bank. The drawee bank was located in another city, and the depository bank had a policy of "holding" the deposit credit for three days to allow the check to "clear." One of the tellers at the depository bank mistakenly placed a ten-day hold on the funds, so several small checks written by Sims after the three-day period but before the ten-day period had expired were dishonored by the bank. Sims is suing the bank for wrongful dishonor of these checks, seeking the following damages: $1.50 for a long-distance phone call to clarify the acceptance of the check; $130 for lost wages, since Sims took a week off owing to her embarassment; and $500 for mental suffering and inconvenience. What should Sims collect from the bank? (*Bank of Louisville Royal* v. *Sims,* 435 S.W.2d 57 [Ky. 1968].)

10. Thomas entered into a contract with Gallo for the purchase of two rugs, giving Gallo a postdated check for $2500 and agreeing to pay the $8000 balance by the end of the month. On December 10, Thomas went to the drawee bank and placed a stop-payment order on the check. (The check was accurately described in the stop-payment order.) The following day, Gallo presented the check at the bank and the bank accepted and cashed it despite the stop-payment order. Thomas, being unaware that the check had been paid by his bank, called Gallo, told him that the deal was cancelled, and asked Gallo to pick up the rugs. Two days later, Gallo picked up the rugs from Thomas. When Thomas received his statement he learned for the first time that the check had been paid by the bank. Thomas demanded his money back from the bank. What result should occur? (*Thomas* v. *Marine Midland Tinkers National Bank,* 381 N.Y.S.2d 797 [1976].)

PART 5

Debtor – Creditor Relations

At one time, lending money was considered a dishonorable occupation. Under canon law, moneylenders were not allowed to charge interest on loans. To do so was to commit a sin. Moreover, people did not often borrow in those days; when they wanted to buy something, they usually saved until they could pay cash for the purchase.

With the arrival of the industrial revolution, things began to change. Borrowing, and the use of credit, became an important aspect of good business management. If a business could borrow the money to buy equipment and then use that equipment to generate income over and above the cost of the loan, the business was ahead. Unfortunately, some businesses did not generate enough profits to repay the loan. When this happened, defaults occurred.

Eventually, legal methods were developed to protect the parties to credit transactions. Creditors were allowed to *secure* the debt by taking legal rights on certain assets of the debtor. And debtors were sometimes allowed to escape onerous debt burdens and start over with a clean slate. This part of the text deals with the rights — and the duties — of debtors and creditors, an especially important topic in our consumer-oriented American economy.

CHAPTER 28

Secured Transactions: Security Interests and Perfection

Credit is an extremely important aspect of current American business practices. Without it, many successful firms would never have gotten started. Yet the person who extends credit (the creditor) undertakes the risk that the person to whom he or she has given credit (the debtor) will not be able to repay the debt in full. Understandably, the creditor wishes to be protected against such losses before they occur. The Uniform Commercial Code's methods of creating protection for the creditor form the basis of this chapter's discussion.

We have already seen that a commercial transaction in one of its simplest forms may involve a sale of goods in which the buyer pays cash. Alternatively, the buyer may use a check or draft to pay for all (or a portion of) the goods. In this chapter, we shall examine a third method of closing a commercial transaction: the buyer may give the owner of the goods a *security interest*. The portion of the Uniform Commercial Code that deals with these matters is Article 9, entitled "Secured Transactions; Sales of **Accounts** and **Chattel Paper**."

Despite the availability of several methods of structuring a commercial transaction, use of secured transactions is very common in business today; hence, an understanding of Article 9 is crucial. To illustrate, let us assume that

CREDIT FINANCING AND ARTICLE 9

Accounts Rights to payments for goods sold or leased or for services rendered that are not evidenced by an instrument or chattel paper

Chattel paper A writing that evidences both a monetary obligation and a security interest in specific goods

475

Bart Brown wishes to buy a meat freezer and a cash register for his new restaurant business. He may pay for part of the sale in cash and receive possession of the items in exchange for giving the seller of the goods a security interest in this equipment. Such a security interest "secures" or ensures payment by the buyer so that if Bart does not pay the seller, the latter can repossess the goods. Thus, a secured transaction allows buyers to receive goods sooner than they would have if they had been forced to pay cash; and, at the same time, it permits sellers to protect themselves by retaining the right of repossession in the event of a buyer's nonpayment. As we shall see, sellers must comply with several additional rules under Article 9 relating to perfection and priorities to ensure that they will have first rights to the equipment in the event of Bart's **default.** We shall discuss these concepts further in this chapter and Chapter 29.

Default A failure to do what should be done, especially in the performance of a contractual obligation, without legal excuse or justification for the nonperformance

Using the terminology adopted by the Code, we can further characterize the seller as the *secured party* ("a lender, seller, or other person in whose favor there is a security interest, including a person to whom accounts or chattel paper have been sold").[1] Bart is of course the *debtor* ("the person who owes payment or other performance of the obligation secured, whether or not he owns or has rights in the collateral, and includes the seller of accounts or chattel paper").[2] Bart and the seller have presumably entered into a *security agreement* ("the agreement which creates or provides for a security interest").[3] Lastly, the freezer and cash register constitute *collateral* ("the property subject to a security interest").[4] Article 9's applications are very broad, since it may cover relatively simple business transactions like the one we have described, or it may extend to highly complex forms of business financing, such as accounts receivable financing.[5]

The 1972 Official Text of Article 9 differs substantially from the 1962 Official Text. A majority of states have adopted the 1972 version, but since some states still follow the 1962 rules, you should check your jurisdiction to see which version applies. We shall use the 1972 Official Text of Article 9 in Chapters 28–30.

Part of the richness of Article 9 stems from its unified approach to secured financing. Before the UCC came into being, there existed a wide variety of security devices that had arisen rather haphazardly in response to perceived security financing needs. These devices—known by such strange names as "pledges," "chattel mortgages," "conditional sales," "trust receipts," and "factor's liens"— were very technical. Hence, a seller who had mistakenly

---

[1] Uniform Commercial Code, Section 9–105(m).

[2] Ibid., Section 9–105(d). This section further states that "[w]here the debtor and the owner of the collateral are not the same person, the term 'debtor' means the owner of the collateral in any provision of the Article dealing with the collateral, the obligor in any provision dealing with the obligation, and may include both where the context so requires. . . ."

[3] Ibid., Section 9–105(1).

[4] Ibid., Section 9–105(c). Collateral also includes accounts and chattel paper that have been sold.

[5] Uniform Commercial Code, Section 9–106.

chosen the wrong device or who had not complied with the ticklish requirements of a particular device might later find that he or she had no valid security interest. Moreover, these devices were limited in scope; they could not reach **general intangibles**—such as television or motion picture rights or the goodwill of a business or service—which most of us today would recognize as important sources of commercial collateral. Lastly, these devices placed great emphasis on who held title during the course of the parties' dealings.

> **General intangibles**
> Personal property other than goods, accounts, chattel paper, instruments, documents, or money; for example, goodwill, literary rights, patents, or copyrights

The Code's creation of a single device, the Article 9 security interest, as a substitute for the numerous devices that had grown up as a result of a hundred years' worth of common law and statutory developments was welcome indeed. Article 9's rejection of the older devices' distinctions based on form (and concepts of "title")[6] has led to a simplified structure. This format more accurately reflects the wide variety of present-day secured financing transactions and allows for commercial recognition of new forms of financing without passing new statutes or changing old ones. This chapter will focus on some of the provisions of Article 9 that illustrate the Code's breadth and flexibility.

In general, according to Section 9–102, Article 9

> applies (a) to any transaction (regardless of its form) which is intended to create a security interest in personal property or fixtures including goods, documents, instruments, general intangibles, chattel paper or accounts and also (b) to any sale of accounts or chattel paper.

SCOPE OF ARTICLE 9

By a "security interest," Article 9 means "an interest in personal property or fixtures which secures payment or performance of an obligation."[7] The personal property or collateral that will be subject to a security interest takes many forms. Moreover, the Code categorizes collateral according to either (1) the *nature* of the collateral or (2) its *use*. Thus, *documents* (warehouse receipts, bills of lading, and other documents of title), *instruments* (drafts, certificates of deposit, stocks, and bonds), *proceeds* (whatever is received upon the sale, exchange, collection, or other disposition of collateral or proceeds), and three kinds of collateral defined earlier, *accounts, chattel paper,* and *general intangibles,* represent the types of collateral that the Code classifies primarily on the basis of their *nature.*

Goods are the most common type of collateral, and a more detailed discussion of this category illustrates how the Code classifies collateral on the basis of the debtor's *use.* According to the Code, "goods" include all things that are movable at the time the security interest attaches or that are fixtures.[8] The

---

[6] Section 9–202 makes the concept of title, that is, whether the secured party or the debtor has title to the collateral, immaterial under the Code.

[7] Uniform Commercial Code, Section 1–201(37).

[8] Ibid., Section 9–105(h). Goods may also include such things as standing timber, growing crops, and the unborn young of animals.

Code then further distinguishes goods with regard to the debtor's use of them. *Consumer goods* are those used or bought for use primarily for personal, family, or household purposes. Thus, a debtor may give a security interest in his or her furniture or car to a secured party. *Equipment* includes goods used or bought for use primarily in business. Bart's freezer and cash register are equipment collateral, as a truck would be for the electric company. *Farm products* are also a type of goods. The Code defines farm products as crops, livestock, or supplies used or produced in farming operations. Interestingly, then, a farmer may give a security interest in wheat, corn, and cows, or even in milk, since the Code covers the products of crops or livestock in their unmanufactured states, as well.[9] *Inventory*, defined as goods held by a person for sale or lease or raw materials used or consumed in a business, is another type of goods. Inventory differs from consumer goods and equipment because inventory is held for sale rather than use.[10] Such things as coal or packages for goods are therefore inventory, as is a dealer's supply of cars or a merchant's supply of tires, paint, clothing, or toys. The last type of goods that the Code delineates is *fixtures*. Goods are fixtures when they become so related to particular real estate that an interest in them arises under real estate law.[11] Furnaces and central air-conditioning units are fixtures.

Given these differences in definition, it is not surprising that the Code makes these classes of goods mutually exclusive. In other words, the same property cannot at the same time and to the same person be both equipment and inventory. In borderline cases — for example, a social worker's car or a farmer's pickup — the principal use to which the property has been put determines the type of collateral involved.[12] Because the Code's rules regarding perfection, priorities, and default often turn on the type of collateral involved (as we shall see further in Chapters 29 and 30), you should be aware of the importance of knowing which category of collateral is present in a given transaction.

Whatever the kind of collateral that is subject to the security interest, it is apparent that the Code drafters meant Article 9 to apply to all *consensual* security interests in personal property and fixtures as well as to certain sales of accounts and chattel paper (often called "assignments").[13] In our earlier example, we can say that Bart Brown and the seller of the meat freezer and the cash register have freely agreed to enter into this commercial transaction. Since personal property is involved (the freezer and register are "goods"), Bart has agreed to let the seller retain an interest in the goods until Bart pays for them — a method of ensuring the performance of Bart's obligations — and the seller, in turn, has agreed to give the goods to Bart now (even though the seller

---

[9] Ibid., Section 9 – 109(1), (2), (3).
[10] Ibid., Section 9 – 109(4), Official Comment 3.
[11] Ibid., Section 9 – 313(1)(a).
[12] Ibid., Section 9 – 109, Official Comment 2.
[13] Ibid., Section 9 – 104(c).

has not received the total price for them) in exchange for the right to repossess the freezer and register if Bart does not pay. This transaction therefore fulfills all the requirements of an enforceable security interest.

Given the necessity for consent between the parties, Article 9 accordingly does not apply to a "security interest" that arises by **operation of law** rather than through the agreement of the parties. Examples of such situations include a **mechanic's lien** on Bart's restaurant that an unpaid contractor obtains as a result of renovating Bart's place of business. The lien represents the money Bart owes for the labor and materials involved in the construction of the restaurant. Since Bart and the contractor have not agreed in advance that the contractor will have an interest in Bart's restaurant, this is a nonconsensual arrangement that arises as a consequence of the parties' *status* (the contractor is a creditor who now is using the restaurant as security for the debt Bart owes) rather than as a result of *mutual consent*. It is therefore not an Article 9 security interest.

This result also stems from the fact that Article 9 in general does not apply to real property, or real estate. Instead, as mentioned, it applies only to security interests in *personal* property. Hence, Article 9 has no bearing on land mortgages or on landlords' liens either. And while it specifically includes within its scope the old methods of creating security interests (for example, pledges, chattel mortgages, and factor's liens),[14] it specifically exempts from its coverage security interests that are subject to any federal statute and certain other categories of transactions, including wage and salary claims and claims resulting from court judgments.[15]

In some cases, a transaction, although covered by Article 9, may also be subject to any local statutes governing usury, retail installment sales, and the like (for example, the Uniform Consumer Credit Code). In those situations, in the event of a conflict, the provisions of any such statute, and not Article 9, are controlling.[16]

One test to use in deciding whether Article 9 applies is to ask whether the transaction *is intended* to have effect as security. If the answer is yes, Article 9 probably covers the transaction.

Operation of law
Certain automatic results that must occur following certain actions or facts because of established legal principles and not as the result of any voluntary choice by the parties involved

Mechanic's lien A statutory protection given to certain builders, artisans, and providers of material that grants a lien on the building and the land improved by such persons

SECURITY INTEREST

As we have just noted, Article 9 broadly defines *security interest* as *an interest in personal property or fixtures that secures payment or performance of an obligation.* One of the assets of the Code, as previously discussed, is the flexibility attendant on such sweeping definitions. And, in fact, courts have had few problems in recognizing a security interest. Despite this seeming simplicity of definition, one area — that of leases "intended as security" in contrast to "true" leases — has caused businesspersons and courts some difficulties.

[14] Ibid., Section 9–102(2).
[15] Ibid., Section 9–104.
[16] Ibid., Sections 9–201, 9–203(4).

The Code states definitively that Article 9 applies to "a lease intended as security."[17] It also notes that whether a lease is intended as security must be determined by the facts of each case and that the inclusion of an option to purchase does not in and of itself make the lease one intended for security. On the other hand, a provision that on the expiration of the lease the person who is leasing (called the "lessee") becomes the owner, or has the option of buying the property for very little money, makes the lease one intended as security.[18] In this latter situation, the transaction more closely resembles an installment sales contract, especially when, as is often the case, the "rental" payments equal the selling price of the property subject to the "lease." The "lessor" (the person leasing the personal property to another) is actually a secured party who is using the monthly leasing payments as monthly installments on a conditional sales agreement. This transaction *would* be subject to the Code's provisions because it would be a lease intended as security, not a true lease.

Why, one may ask, is this an important distinction anyway? The answer will become clear when we discuss the process of "perfection." If such a lease is intended as security, it will be subject to Article 9's filing requirements. A true lease will not be because in general Article 9 does not apply to situations in which one pays merely for the right to use the goods for a specified period of time without ever becoming the owner of the leased property. Debtors in Article 9 transactions are trying to buy the property that is the object of the security interest. At the same time, secured parties are retaining an interest in the property until this transfer of ownership is accomplished by the debtor's paying all that is owed. In a true lease, the parties never contemplate such an eventual transfer of ownership.

Given this, if we change the facts of our earlier hypothetical case to have Bart lease the freezer and cash register, assuming this is a true lease, Article 9 does not govern. However, if in effect the owner of the freezer and register is retaining *title* to the goods to ensure that Bart will pay for the goods, we have a *lease intended as security*; and the parties must follow Article 9's rules. This means, as we shall see later, that if Bart goes bankrupt, the **trustee in bankruptcy** will be able to get the equipment because Bart will be deemed the owner of the equipment. He has in effect been *paying* for the items on an installment sales basis, even though the parties have called the transaction a "lease." By not filing, the original owner of the equipment has not perfected his or her interest in the equipment and will not be able to repossess the equipment (or any other type of collateral). Since the law in these circumstances treats the bankruptcy trustee as a **lien creditor,** the trustee will have superior rights to those of our unperfected original owner.

While the following case does not involve the trustee in bankruptcy, it illustrates the necessity of following the Code's rules if a court later characterizes the transaction at issue as a lease intended as security.

Trustee in bankruptcy The person appointed by the bankruptcy court to act as trustee of the debtor's property for the benefit and protection of the creditors

Lien creditor One whose debt is secured by a claim on specific property

---

[17] Ibid., Section 9–102(2).
[18] Ibid., Section 1–201(37).

In re Chisholm
54 Bankr. 52 (M.D. Fla. 1985)

Chisholm, the president of A&B Grading and Trucking Service, Inc. (A&B), in October, 1980, had contacted Rozier Machinery, Inc. (Rozier), to inquire about leasing equipment needed by A&B to complete a construction excavation job in Brandon, Florida. After securing Chisholm's personal guarantee as to the obligations of A&B, Rozier had leased several pieces of heavy equipment to A&B. Under the terms of the leases, A&B was to pay $95,700.60 plus state sales taxes over a three-year period. In addition, A&B was responsible for the care and maintenance of the equipment, was required to insure the equipment as well as to bear the risk of loss, and was obligated to make rental payments roughly equal to the purchase price plus interest. The option to purchase in the leases provided for the rental payments to be deducted from the original cash purchase price of $87,845.00, but the amount equivalent to an annual interest rate of 18 percent was then added to the purchase price. Chisholm and A&B argued that as the transaction was a lease intended as security (and as such a secured transaction), he and A&B had been entitled to notice before Rozier had disposed of the collateral upon A&B's failure to pay. Rozier claimed that the leases were not disguised secured sales but true leases and that no notice had been required.

FACTS

Were the leases secured transactions so that Rozier had been obligated to give the debtors notice before it had disposed of the collateral?

ISSUE

Yes. The leases were ones intended as security, not true leases. Rozier's failure to give notice to the debtors therefore prevented Rozier from later suing for a **deficiency judgment.**

HOLDING

The lease agreements were in fact secured transactions. The principal test in determining whether a transaction is a lease intended as security or a true lease is the intent of the parties. In assessing intent, a court must consider such factors as whether the lessee or the lessor bears the risk of loss, the payment of taxes, maintenance, and repair costs; whether warranties are excluded; and whether the rental payments are roughly equal to the purchase price plus interest.

    Applying these factors to the case at hand, it was clear that A&B as "lessee" had been responsible for insurance and the care and maintenance of the collateral. Moreover, the risk of loss had been on A&B; and Rozier had disclaimed the most important warranties under sales law. The total rental payments over a three-year period amounted to $95,700.60 plus state sales tax, a sum the court deemed roughly equal to the purchase price of the equipment ($87,845.00) plus interest. The terms of the purchase option, involving as they had, a deduction of rental payments from the purchase price and an attendant increase in the price paid to reflect an annual interest rate of 18 percent, constituted further evidence that the leases at issue had not been true leases but secured transactions. As such, A&B and Chisholm had been entitled to notice of Rozier's sale of the equipment.

REASONING

Deficiency judgment
A court judgment for that part of a secured debt not realized from the sale of the property used as security

CREATION AND ENFORCE-ABILITY OF THE SECURITY INTEREST

A security interest is of negligible value unless it is valid and enforceable. It therefore behooves the owner of the freezer and the register in our earlier hypothetical case to attain the status of a *secured creditor* (or secured party). In this way, if Bart, the debtor, later cannot — or will not — pay for the equipment, the secured party will be able to repossess the goods and, if perfected, enjoy priority over the claims that other third parties, like the bankruptcy trustee, may assert regarding the property. However, before the secured party has an enforceable security interest in the collateral, the security interest must "attach."[19] *Attachment* concerns the process by which the secured party and the debtor create the security interest and thereby confer on the secured party certain enforceable rights to the collateral vis-à-vis the debtor. Attachment does not give the secured party rights necessarily superior to those obtained by other creditors (an additional step called perfection is necessary to accomplish this). Nevertheless, as the first step in the creation and enforceability of a security interest, attachment remains extemely important.

According to the UCC, attachment occurs when a prospective secured party does all of the following:

1. enters into a *security agreement* whereby the prospective secured party and the debtor agree that a security interest will attach

2. possesses a security agreement signed by the debtor or, alternatively, retains possession of the collateral

3. ascertains that the debtor has rights in the collateral

4. gives value

As the next case shows, the omission of any of the requirements just listed invalidates the security interest.

Manger v. Davis
619 P.2d 687 (Utah 1980)

FACTS   Manger had asked Davis to sell her 9.72 carat ring for her. Davis, however, had pledged the ring (valued at $140,000) to W.M.P. Corporation in order to further his own business interests in a company called CD & M. Using the ring as collateral, W.M.P. had advanced a loan of $20,000 to the promoters of CD & M and had appointed its bank as its agent for holding possession of the ring as a means of perfecting its security interest. When the CD & M promoters had not paid the loan, W.M.P. had paid the bank and had taken possession of the ring. Manger sued for its return.

[19] Ibid., Section 9–203.

Was W.M.P.'s security interest valid?

No. It was not valid because attachment had not occurred.

A security interest cannot attach until the debtor has rights in the collateral. Unless Davis had had rights in the collateral (the ring), he could not have authorized the pledge, and the security interest of W.M.P. could not have attached. The relationship between Manger and Davis had been a consignment whereby Davis had given possession with authority to sell only on the express consent of Manger. Therefore, the authority conferred by Manger on Davis had not given him the right or power to pledge it in his own interests. Consequently, since Davis had had no authority to pledge the ring, W.M.P. had not acquired a valid security interest in the ring, and Manger could recover possession of the ring.

Most would-be secured parties are more careful than their counterparts in the *Manger* case when attempting attachment by possession. A simple **pledge** of a coin collection in which the owner of the collection insists, in accordance with the agreement, on keeping it until the debtor pays for it ordinarily will be enforceable because attachment will have occurred. In most cases, however, as in our situation involving Bart, the debtor will not agree to the secured party's retaining possession of the collateral (without his meat freezer "on site," Bart will presumably have few customers!). Thus, in lieu of possession, a signed security agreement will be necessary before the security interest is valid.

To comply with the Code, security agreements must

Pledge A debtor's delivery of collateral to a creditor, the collateral to be possessed by the creditor until the debt is paid

1. be in writing
2. create or provide for a security interest
3. reasonably identify the collateral
4. be signed by the debtor[20]

Although these requirements seem simple, a great deal of litigation has resulted from a creditor's failure to use forms that include this minimal information or from a failure to fill out these forms correctly. A security agreement may contain many other terms as well, such as the amount of the indebtedness and the terms of payment; liability in the event of risk of loss or damage to the collateral; a requirement of insurance on and the maintenance and repair of the collateral; a warranty by the debtor that he or she owns the collateral free from liens or security interests; a statement of the debtor's rights (if any) regarding removal of the collateral to another location; and a description of

---

[20] Ibid., Sections 9–203(1), 9–110.

events that constitute default by the debtor. The security agreement shown in Figure 28.1 includes some of these terms.

A security agreement may also extend the security interest of the secured party to all collateral of the kind that is the subject of the agreement, which the debtor may acquire *after* entering into this agreement. Thus, if Bart, after entering into a security agreement with the seller of the freezer, obtains an industrial grade bread-making machine, use of an *after-acquired property clause* in the original security agreement means that the seller may also get the bread-making machine if Bart ultimately fails to pay for the freezer and the cash register. Or, alternatively, assume Bart is a seller of radios and that he gives a security interest to a creditor who has provided him with an inventory of radios. Every time Bart sells one of the original radios and uses the money from this sale to purchase another radio to replenish his inventory, the creditor's security interest in the original inventory of radios leaves the first radio,

Figure 28.1   Security Agreement Form

SECURITY AGREEMENT USED WITH
LOAN ON
GOODS, FIXTURES, OR EQUIPMENT

_____, 19 _____

_____
(NAME)

_____
(NO. AND STREET)   (CITY)   (COUNTY)   (STATE)

(Hereinafter called "Debtor") hereby grants to St. Joseph Bank and Trust Company, South Bend, Indiana (Hereinafter called "Bank"), a security interest in the following property together with all tools, accessories, parts, equipment and accessions now attached to or which may hereafter at any time be placed in or added to the property; also any replacements of such property herein described (hereinafter called "Collateral"):

_____

_____

_____

The security interest granted hereby is to secure payment and performance of the liabilities and obligations of debtor to Bank of every kind and description, direct or indirect, absolute or contingent, due or to become due, now existing or hereafter arising (hereinafter called "Obligations").

Debtor hereby warrants and covenants:

1. The collateral is being acquired for the following primary uses:____ personal, or family use,____business use, or ____farming operations

2. The Collateral_____will_____ will not be acquired with the proceeds of the loan provided for in this Agreement. (In the event the Collateral will be acquired with the proceeds of the loan, the Bank may disburse such proceeds to the seller of the Collateral.)

3. In the event the Collateral will be attached to real estate, the description of such real estate and the known owner of record of such real estate are set forth hereafter. If the Collateral is attached to such real estate prior to the perfection of the security interest granted herein, the Debtor will, on demand, furnish the Bank with a disclaimer or disclaimers executed by persons having an interest in such real estate. Real estate described;_____

_____

_____

4. The Collateral will be kept at the address of the Debtor set out below, which in the case of a business is the address of the principal office of such business within this state. Debtor will not remove the Collateral from the state without the prior written consent of the Bank. If the Collateral is being acquired for farming use and the Debtor is not a resident of Indiana, the Collateral will be kept at the address set forth in the description of

Figure 28.1   *(Continued)*

the Collateral. Debtor will immediately give written notice to the Bank of any change of address and in the case of a business, any change in its principal place of business and if the Collateral consists of equipment normally used in more than one state, any use of the Collateral in any jurisdiction other than a state in which the Debtor shall have previously advised the Bank such Collateral will be used.

5. Debtor has, or will acquire, full and clear title to the Collateral and except for the security interest granted herein, will at all times keep the Collateral free from any adverse lien, security interest or encumbrance.

6. No financing statement covering all or any portion of the Collateral is on file in any public office.

7. Debtor authorizes the Bank at the expense of the Debtor to execute and file on its behalf a financing statement or statements in those public offices deemed necessary by the Bank to protect its security interest in the Collateral. Debtor will deliver or cause to be delivered to the Bank any certificates of titles to the Collateral with the security interest of the Bank noted thereon.

8. Debtor will not sell or offer to sell or otherwise transfer the Collateral or any interest therein without the prior written consent of the Bank.

9. Debtor will at all times keep the Collateral insured against loss, damage, theft and other risks in such amounts, under such policies and with such companies as shall be satisfactory to the Bank, which policies shall provide that any loss thereunder shall be payable to the Bank as its interest may appear and the Bank may apply the proceeds of the insurance against the outstanding indebtedness of the Debtor, regardless of whether all or any portion of such indebtedness is due or owing. All policies of insurance so required shall be placed in the possession of the Bank.

Upon failure of the Debtor to procure such insurance or to remove any encumbrance upon the Collateral or if such insurance is concelled, the indebtedness secured hereby shall become immediately due and payable at the option of the Bank, without notice or demand, or the Bank may procure such insurance or remove any encumbrance on the Collateral and the amount so paid by the Bank shall be immediately repayable and shall be added to and become a part of the indebtedness secured hereby and shall bear interest at the same note rate as the indebtedness secured hereby until paid.

10. Debtor will keep the Collateral in good order and repair and will not waste or destroy the Collateral or any portion thereof. Debtor will not use the Collateral in violation of any statute or ordinance or any policy of insurance thereon and the Bank may examine and inspect such Collateral at any reasonable time or times wherever located.

11. Debtor will pay promptly when due all taxes and assessments upon the Collateral or for its use or operation.

12. The occurrence of any one of the following events shall constitute default under this Security Agreement: (a) nonpayment when due of any installment of the indebtedness hereby secured or failure to perform any agreement contained herein; (b) any statement, representation, or warranty at any time furnished the Bank is untrue in any material respect as of the date made; (c) Debtor becomes insolvent or unable to pay debts as they mature or makes an assignment for the benefit of creditors or any proceeding is instituted by or against the Debtor alleging that such Debtor is insolvent or unable to pay debts as they mature; (d) entry of judgment against the Debtor; (e) loss, theft, substantial damage, destruction, sale or encumbrance to or of all or any portion the Collateral, or the making of any levy, seizure or attachment, thereof or thereon; (f) death of the Debtor who is a natural person or of any partner of the Debtor which is a partnership; (g) dissolution, merger or consolidation or transfer of a substantial portion of the property of the Debtor which is a corporation or partnership; or (h) the Bank deems itself insecure for any other reason whatsoever.

When an event of default shall be existing, the note or notes and any other liabilities may at the option of the Bank and without notice or demand be declared and thereupon immediately shall become due and payable and the Bank may exercise from time to time any rights and remedies of a secured party under the Uniform Commercial Code or other applicable law. Debtor agrees in the event of default to make the Collateral available to the Bank at a place acceptable to the Bank which is convenient to the Debtor. If any notification or disposition of all or any portion of the Collateral is required by law, such notification shall be deemed reasonable and properly given if mailed at least ten (10) days prior to such disposition, postage prepaid to the Debtor at its latest address appearing on the records of the Bank. Expenses of retaking, holding, repairing, preparing for sale and selling, shall include the Bank's reasonable attorneys' fees and expenses. Any proceeds of the disposition of the Collateral will be applied by the Bank to the payment of expenses of retaking, holding, repairing, preparing for sale and selling the Collateral, including reasonable attorneys' fees and legal expenses and any balance of such proceeds will be applied by the Bank to the payment of the indebtedness then owing the Bank.

No delay on the part of the Bank in the exercise of any right or remedy shall operate as a waiver thereof, and no single or partial exercise by the Bank of any right or remedy shall preclude other or further exercise thereof or the exercise of any other right or remedy. If more than one party shall execute this Agreement, the term "Debtor" shall mean all parties signing this Agreement and each of them, and such parties shall be jointly and severally obligated hereunder. The neuter pronoun, when used herein, shall include the masculine and the feminine and also the plural. If this Agreement is not dated when executed by the Debtor, the Bank is authorized, without notice to the Debtor, to date this Agreement.

This Agreement has been delivered at South Bend, Indiana, and shall be construed in accordance with the laws of the State of Indiana. Wherever possible each provision of this Agreement shall be interpreted in such manner as to be effective and valid under applicable law, but if any provision of this Agreement shall be prohibited by or invalid under applicable law, such provision shall be ineffective to the extent of such prohibition or invalidity, without invalidating the remainder of such provision or the remaining provisions of this Agreement.

This Agreement shall be binding upon the heirs, administrators and executors of the Debtor and the rights and privileges of the Bank hereunder shall inure to the benefit of its successors and assigns.

_____

Address: _____

_____   _____

F1025

Courtesy of Trustcorp Bank, South Bend, Indiana (formerly St. Joseph Bank and Trust Company, South Bend, Indiana).

affixes to the proceeds, follows the proceeds through Bart's bank account, and affixes to the radio purchased to restock the inventory. Such after-acquired property clauses are common in secured transactions.

In the following case, one party disputed whether the financing statement adequately described the after-acquired property in question. (Financing statements, which we shall discuss in some detail shortly, are forms placed in the public records that indicate a secured party's retention of a security interest in certain collateral.)

Consolidated Equipment Sales, Inc. v. *First Bank & Trust Company of Guthrie* 627 P.2d 432 (Okla. 1981)

FACTS

McBride, an asphalt and paving contractor, had acquired an Allis-Chalmers wheel loader from Consolidated in 1973. The facts were unclear as to whether Consolidated had sold or leased the wheel loader to McBride. Both a sales contract and a lease contract existed. Earlier that same year, McBride and the bank had negotiated two loans, for which the bank had filed financing statements that had listed as security "all paving equipment and grading equipment, now owned [or] hereafter acquired." McBride had filed for bankruptcy in 1975. Shortly thereafter, the wheel loader had been found missing from McBride's business site and later had been located at Consolidated's shop. Consolidated had repaired the equipment and later had sold it for $28,400. After it had won judgments against McBride for his default on earlier loans, the bank sued Consolidated for **conversion** of the wheel loader. The bank contended its financing statement covered the wheel loader, but Consolidated claimed it was the true owner of the wheel loader because the bank's language had inadequately described the after-acquired property.

Conversion The unauthorized and wrongful exercise of dominion and control over the personal property of another to the harm of that other person

ISSUE

Was the description of the financing statement sufficient to give the bank priority over Consolidated?

HOLDING

Yes. It was a sufficient description of the collateral.

REASONING

Consolidated's argument that the description "all machinery, paving equipment and concrete equipment" had been insufficient to include the wheel loader was incorrect. Section 9–110 of the Code states that a "description" of personal property is sufficient "whether or not it is specific if it *reasonably identifies* what is described" (emphasis added). Thus, notice sufficient to cause the other party to inquire further about the collateral subject to the secured interest is all that is needed in the financing statement; it need not describe the collateral in exacting detail. McBride's ownership of a paving business should have put Consolidated on notice to inquire further about the bank statement's reference to after-acquired property. Hence, the description was sufficient to give the bank priority over Consolidated with regard to ownership of the wheel loader.

The need for evidence of the parties' intentions forms the basis for requiring such information on the security agreement. If the parties have spelled out their respective rights and duties in advance, there should be fewer disputes as to the terms of the agreement and as to the property that represents the collateral for the obligation secured.

PERFECTION

Thus far, we have primarily focused on the relationship between the creditor and the debtor and how the creditor may protect his or her interest in the collateral by becoming a secured party. Yet in that earlier discussion we noted that the processes leading to the creation and enforceability of a secured interest only give the secured party rights greater than those of the debtor; on the other hand, they do not necessarily confer on the secured party superior rights to the collateral vis-à-vis other creditors and the bankruptcy trustee. Now we turn to a discussion of how secured parties can protect themselves against such third parties who also may be claiming rights in the collateral. In other words, how can the seller/secured party in our earlier example protect the freezer and register from Bart's other business creditors (say produce suppliers) if Bart's financial situation deteriorates to the point that either the produce suppliers or—if Bart is on the verge of insolvency—the trustee in bankruptcy is trying to get all of Bart's equipment to satisfy creditors' claims against him?

Perfection is the process by which secured parties protect their collateral from the clutches of later creditors who have also given value when the debtor has used the same pieces of equipment as collateral for loans from them. The date of perfection, in turn, is the date from which the law measures priorities if there are competing claims among other perfected creditors. The topic of priorities among secured parties will be addressed in Chapter 29.

In general, perfection occurs in one of three ways: by the creditor's filing a financing statement, by the creditor's taking possession of the collateral, or by the creditor's doing nothing beyond attachment. This last type is called *automatic perfection* (or perfection by attachment); and, as we shall learn, it is the method sellers of high-volume, relatively inexpensive items like televisions or stereos ordinarily choose. Rather than filing a financing statement or taking possession of the collateral, such creditors instead rely solely on their security agreement with the debtor to perfect their interests in the collateral.

The policy underlying the first two methods involves giving public notice of the existence of the security interest. In other words, the drafters of the Code believed that to deserve the status of a perfected secured creditor, the would-be secured party ought to undertake some affirmative action. And by either filing or possessing, the secured party is doing something that will give anyone looking for a security interest in the collateral notice of the secured party's claim. In the third situation, the nature of the collateral makes the costs of providing public notice higher than the benefits to be gained from filing; for this reason, the Code does not place any affirmative duties on the secured creditor in these situations beyond attachment.

Figure 28.2   Methods of Perfecting a Security Interest

Type of Collateral	Perfection Method (Generally)
Consumer goods (excluding motor vehicles and fixtures)	Automatic (if a purchase money security interest) Possession Filing
Equipment	Filing Possession
Farm products	Filing Possession
Inventory (including motor vehicles)	Filing Possession
Fixtures	Filing Automatic (if a purchase money security interest) Possession (in theory)
Proceeds	Filing Automatic (if security interest in original collateral perfected)
Documents (negotiable)	Filing Possession Automatic (for 21 days)
Instruments	Possession Automatic (for 21 days)
Chattel paper	Filing Possession
Accounts	Filing Automatic (in some instances)
General intangibles	Filing
Letters of credit	Possession
Motor vehicles	Filing Compliance with state certificate of title statutes
Aircraft, copyrights, and the like	Filing (under applicable federal statutes, not under the UCC)

Figure 28.2 summarizes the methods of perfecting a security interest in various types of collateral.

Filing

Whether it is necessary to file in order to be perfected depends on the type of collateral involved. If the collateral is accounts or general intangibles, filing is ordinarily the only method of perfection.[21] For goods (including fixtures), chattel paper, and negotiable documents, the secured party may file but is not obligated to do so. Because of their negotiability, interests in money, instruments, and **letters of credit** can never be perfected by filing (possession is the usual method).[22] If filing is necessary, Section 9–403 of the UCC states that the

---

[21] Ibid., Sections 9–302, 9–401.
[22] Ibid., Section 9–304(1).

presentation of a financing statement and the required fees to the appropriate state or local filing officer and that officer's acceptance of the statement constitutes filing. Hence, the device that the Code uses to give notice of the security interest is a *financing statement.* (An alternative method of filing, which we shall not discuss in detail, involves registering the security interest according to the requirements of statutes other than the UCC, like state acts covering the certification of title for automobiles, trailers, mobile homes, and boats.) According to Section 9–402, to be legally effective, a financing statement must contain certain information: the names of the debtor and secured party; their addresses; a statement indicating the types, or describing the items, of collateral. It must also show the signature of the debtor. Figure 28.3 represents

Letters of credit
Agreements made at the request of a customer that the bank will honor drafts or other demands for payment on compliance with the conditions specified in the credit

Figure 28.3   Financing Statement Form

Courtesy of Trustcorp Bank, South Bend, Indiana (formerly St. Joseph Bank and Trust Company, South Bend, Indiana).

a typical financing statement. The filing of such a document allows third parties to obtain information about the security interest from either the secured party or the debtor. Thus, if Bart wants credit from a wholesaler, and the latter wants to take a security interest in Bart's equipment before extending credit, the wholesaler will check the public records for financing statements to see which of Bart's equipment is already subject to security interests held by other creditors. This will help the wholesaler make its decision about extending Bart credit or not.

The question of whether a copy of the security agreement, if filed, is the legal equivalent of a financing statement has arisen repeatedly. The Code notes that the security agreement will constitute an effective filing if it contains the information required for a financing statement and if it has been signed by the debtor.[23] But because the description of the collateral in the security agreement serves to create enforceable rights in the collateral for the secured party, it must necessarily be more detailed than the information set out in the financing statement, which only provides public notice of a claimed interest in the collateral. Given these differing rationales, it is therefore probably wise not to treat security agreements and financing statements interchangeably for filing purposes, as the following case demonstrates.

Sommers v. International Business Machines
640 F.2d 686 (5th Cir. 1981)

FACTS   Sommers, the trustee in bankruptcy, sued International Business Machines (IBM) and West Publishing Company (West) for certain personal property in the debtor's estate, even though IBM and West had claimed perfected interests in this property. West had sold $20,875 worth of law books to Legal Cooperatives, Inc. (LCI). Thereafter, West had filed a financing statement with the secretary of state of the state of Texas. The financing statement had contained the names and addresses of LCI as the debtor and West as the secured party. It had been signed by West, but not by the debtor, LCI. Also, it had not described the collateral; instead, it had contained the following notation: "LAW BOOKS SEE ATTACHED SECURITY AGREEMENT." A photostatic reproduction of the purchase order had been attached to the financing statement. The trustee in bankruptcy had tried to avoid LCI's obligation to West on the grounds that the purchase order did not qualify as a security agreement under the UCC since it did not contain language granting the vendor a security interest in the goods, or, alternatively, on the grounds that the financing statement did not meet the requirements of Section 9–402 of the UCC, since it was not signed by the debtor and did not contain an adequate description of the collateral.

ISSUES   Was the purchase order signed by an LCI officer a security agreement? If so, was it properly perfected?

[23] Ibid., Section 9–402(1).

Yes. It was a security agreement. No. It had not been properly perfected.

The language in the purchase order to the effect that West had retained title to the books until they had been paid for was sufficient to reserve a security interest in the books to West. But a copy of the security agreement was not effective as a financing statement even if it had fulfilled all but one of the requirements of a financing statement (that is, the debtor had not signed the financing statement). The statutory requirements for a financing statement had to be met if a security agreement were filed as a financing statement. In addition, to call the omission of a formal requisite—here the signature of one of the secured parties—a "minor error which was not seriously misleading" was unpersuasive. Therefore, because West's security interest in the collateral was unperfected, the trustee in bankruptcy could claim the books.

As implied in the *Sommers* case, a financing statement that substantially complies with the Code's requirements will be effective even though it contains *minor* errors that are not seriously misleading.[24] This provision of the Code is indicative of one policy of Article 9, which is to simplify the filing requirements and "to discourage the fanatical and impossibly refined reading of such statutory requirements in which courts have occasionally indulged themselves."[25] Nevertheless, as the next case shows, failure to provide an address may preclude perfection of the security interest.

In re L & K Transportation Co., Inc.
8 Bankr. 921 (D. Mass. 1981)

The debtor had bought a trucking business and had given the seller a security interest in, among other things, a **common carrier** certificate. The debtor had become bankrupt, and the trustee in bankruptcy had challenged the security interest. The financing statement had not included the debtor's address.

FACTS

Common carrier A person or firm offering to the public, for compensation, the service of transporting people or goods

Did the omission of the debtor's address on the financing statement invalidate the legal effectiveness of the filed statement?

Yes. This financing statement did not legally perfect the seller's security interest because of the omitted information.

The trustee was correct. Although the Code should be liberally construed and applied in order to promote its underlying purposes and policies of simplifying and

---

[24] Ibid., Section 9–402(8).
[25] Ibid., Section 9–402, Official Comment 9.

clarifying commercial transactions and despite the fact that a financing statement is to be upheld "even though it contains minor errors which are not seriously misleading," this was not such a minor error. Unless it could be shown that the debtor was so well known that there would be no question of its identity, this financing statement would not perfect the seller's interest. In fact, the evidence had shown that the debtor was clearly not so well known that mail could be delivered to it by utilizing its name alone as an address. Thus, the absence of the debtor's address on the financing statement had precluded the establishment of a valid security interest.

Yet, as the next case illustrates, the financing statement will ordinarily be effective if it contains enough information to enable the party searching the records to look further.

In re Glasco, Inc.
642 F.2d 793 (5th Cir. 1981)

FACTS Citizens Bank of Perry had financed marine engines for Glasco, Inc., which operated its business solely under the name "Elite Boats, Division of Glasco, Inc." To perfect its security interest, the bank had filed a financing statement listing the debtor as "Elite Boats, Division of Glasco, Inc." A filing clerk in the secretary of state's office had indexed the financing statement under the name listed but had not cross-indexed it under "Glasco, Inc." In 1977, the debtor had filed for bankruptcy. The trustee in bankruptcy had asked the secretary of state whether any financing statements had been filed under "Glasco, Inc." Since the trustee had not requested a search under "Elite Boats" or "Elite Boats, Division of Glasco, Inc.," the bank's financing statement had not been disclosed. Without notice to the bank, the trustee had sold the marine engines; and the bank sued the trustee for the sale proceeds.

ISSUE Was the financing statement sufficient to perfect the bank's interest in the marine engines?

HOLDING Yes. It was sufficient even though it had listed the debtor by its business name rather than its legal corporate name.

REASONING To perfect a security interest in collateral, a creditor must file a financing statement that contains sufficient information to cause one searching the records to inquire further about what collateral is subject to the secured interest. Noteworthy, too, is the fact that the Code emphasizes commercial realities rather than corporate technicalities. If a financing statement substantially complies, it will be effective even though it contains minor errors that are not seriously misleading. Here, it was undisputed that the debtor had held itself out to the community and to creditors as "Elite Boats, Division of Glasco, Inc." in its checks, stationery, bank accounts, bills, telephone listings, and contracts. Thus, listing the debtor by the sole name in which it did business — it apparently never used just "Glasco, Inc." — was not seriously misleading because any reasonably prudent creditor would have requested the secretary of state to search under "Elite Boats" in addition to "Glasco, Inc." Therefore, the financing statement was in substantial compliance with the filing requirements under Florida law and was sufficient to perfect the bank's security interest.

Despite the result in the *Glasco* case, other courts have held that the creditor's filing of a financing statement that lists the debtor's trade or business name rather than its legal name constitutes an insufficient filing to perfect a security interest under Section 9 – 402. In short, because the law differs among the various jurisdictions on this point, the creditor's precision in filing the appropriate information often determines whether the courts deem the security interest at issue perfected or unperfected.

You should in addition be aware that sometimes a creditor will file a financing statement even before the completion of the security agreement. But even though a financing statement may be filed before a security agreement is made or a security interest otherwise attaches,[26] filing before attachment does not constitute perfection.[27] Without attachment at some later time, there is no perfection.

The Code's flexibility is nowhere more apparent than in its handling of the proper place for filing the financing statement. The Code does not take a stance on whether filings should be local or statewide, issues that had caused a great many pre-Code problems. Instead, in Section 9 – 401(1), it provides three different options that depend on the type of collateral involved, thus allowing the respective states to choose the method they believe is most conducive to giving notice of claims.

A financing statement generally is effective for a period of five years from the date of filing, at which time the security interest lapses (or becomes unperfected) unless a continuation statement is filed before this lapse.[28] The secured party may file such a statement within six months prior to the expiration of the financing statement. The secured party must sign the continuation statement, identify the original statement by file number, and state that the original statement is still in effect.[29] The filing of a continuation statement prolongs the effectiveness of the original financing statement for five years, and the Code does not limit the number of such statements that a secured party can ultimately file.

Assuming that the secured party has neither released all or part of the collateral described in the financing statement[30] nor assigned its security

---

[26] Ibid., Section 9–402(1).
[27] Ibid., Section 9–303(1).
[28] Ibid., Section 9–403(2), (3).
[29] Ibid.
[30] Ibid., Section 9–406.

interest to another,[31] the Code imposes certain additional duties on the secured party. For example, the secured party must comply within two weeks whenever the debtor requests a statement of account or a list of collateral from the secured party. (Presumably the debtor will request such information owing to lack of certainty as to the total amount owed.) Failure to comply may make the secured party liable for losses to the debtor caused by the noncompliance and may, in rare cases, even cost the secured party its security interest. This will be true as to any security interests reflected in the lists written up by the debtor should any persons be misled by the secured party's failure to comply (as, for instance, by failing to correct the list).[32] On the other hand, the Code protects the secured party from burdensome requests by limiting the debtor to one such list or statement every six months. The secured party may charge ten dollars for each additional request within this time period.[33]

Once there are no outstanding obligations under the financing statement, the Code sets out a procedure that may require the secured party to file a termination statement noting discharge of the obligations and/or termination of the financing agreement. Where consumer goods are concerned, the Code places an affirmative duty on the secured party to file a termination statement within one month or within ten days following written demand by the debtor once the debtor has completely paid for the goods. In all other cases, however, the secured party need not file a termination statement unless the debtor requests such a filing.[34] But when compliance is necessary, the Code subjects noncomplying secured parties to certain penalties. Termination statements, which refer to the appropriate financing statement by file number, clear the public records so that the presence of old, irrelevant financing statements will not leave a would-be creditor with an unrealistic picture of a credit applicant's creditworthiness and reliability.

Possession

As mentioned earlier, the secured party's possession of the collateral is in some cases the method used for perfecting the security interest.[35] Historically, when financing arrangements were more primitive, possession of the personal property was the surest sign of ownership; hence, perfection by possession was the most popular method. Even today secured parties ordinarily must perfect security interests in letters of credit, money, and instruments in this manner and may perfect goods, negotiable documents, or chattel paper in this fashion as well. For instance, a bank may require a debtor to give it possession of the debtor's stocks and bonds as collateral for securing a loan. As noted earlier, this is called a pledge.

As we shall discuss in more detail later, the type of collateral involved is

---

[31] Ibid., Section 9–405(2).
[32] Ibid., Section 9–208(2).
[33] Ibid., Section 9–208(3).
[34] Ibid., Section 9–404(1).
[35] Ibid., Section 9–305.

relevant to whether perfection can occur by possession. If the creditor's possession of collateral (and the debtor's resultant *lack* of possession) is to serve as public notice of the security interest to other parties, the collateral must be tangible; that is, one must be able to see, touch, or move it. All the types of collateral mentioned in the preceding paragraph as perfectible by possession have this attribute. On the other hand, contract rights, accounts that constitute a significant portion of the debtor's business, and general intangibles merely represent rights and have no physical embodiment. Thus, they can never be perfected by possession; filing is necessary.

Automatic perfection is the method used for perfecting *purchase money security interests* in consumer goods.[36] As mentioned earlier, in these situations, *perfection occurs on attachment alone.* A look at the nature of these transactions shows why filing is unnecessary. The Code defines a purchase money security interest as one retained by the seller of the collateral to secure all or part of its price or taken by a person who by making advances or incurring an obligation gives value to enable the debtor to acquire rights in the collateral.[37]

Automatic Perfection

Typically, a seller will retain a purchase money security interest in the collateral, whether it be a stove, refrigerator, washing machine, or stereo. This means that the seller will usually sell to the buyer, on an installment basis, goods that the buyer will use for personal purposes. The seller will in turn retain a security interest in the consumer goods — for instance, a stereo — to secure the unpaid purchase price. If the buyer misses any installment payments, the seller can repossess the collateral. The secured party's purchase money security interest is perfectible the moment the transaction has occurred because there is a written security agreement signed by the debtor, the secured party has given value, and the debtor has rights in the collateral (that is, attachment has occurred). All of this will have happened (thanks to the modern wonder of "form contracts") a short time before the debtor walks out with the stereo in hand.

Given the type of collateral involved — consumer goods — and the frequency with which such transactions occur, the UCC has commonsensibly followed pre-Code law in eliminating the filing requirement for these types of commercial deals. It would make little sense to require a merchant to pay the filing fees and other administrative costs associated with filing for every $100 item sold. Moreover, there would be few benefits from filing in such situations, since consumer goods — already low in price and prone to rapid deterioration — are not the types of property later secured parties would want as collateral anyway. Therefore, the public notice to such creditors afforded by filing would have little value and would only clutter the filing offices. The same rationale underlies the availability of automatic perfection as a method for perfecting certain transfers of accounts, documents, and instruments, as well.

[36] Ibid., Section 9–302(1)(d).
[37] Ibid., Section 9–107.

RELATED TOPICS

Two other topics deserve consideration before we leave the issues covered in this chapter: multistate transactions and proceeds.

Multistate Transactions

A related aspect of perfection involves the problem of collateral, such as equipment, that the debtor can move across state or county lines. The Code's rules for such situations, expressed in Section 9–103, are very complex. In general, the Code says that with respect to ordinary goods, the secured party should perfect its interest by filing or by some other method in the state where the collateral is located. On removal, the secured party should file in the new jurisdiction.

If a *purchase money security interest* is involved and both parties at the time of the creation of the security interest understand that the debtor will move the collateral to another jurisdiction, the law of the new jurisdiction controls perfection for thirty days after the debtor receives possession, assuming the collateral is moved in that time. To avoid losing priority of perfection, the secured party ought to file in both jurisdictions. If collateral has been perfected in one jurisdiction and then is moved to another, it remains perfected for its period of original perfection or for four months, whichever expires first. Thus, the secured party should file in the new jurisdiction before four months are up.

The removal of motor vehicles from jurisdiction to jurisdiction is covered by state certificate of title laws and by the Code.[38] Because these laws are very complicated, a wise secured creditor will keep abreast of the debtor's removal of these vehicles in order to do everything possible to retain a perfected security interest in them. Generally speaking, a secured party will need to reperfect (usually by filing) within four months of the collateral's being removed to the new jurisdiction if the new jurisdiction is a non-title certificate state. If, in contrast, the jurisdiction to which the debtor has removed the motor vehicle requires perfection by notation of the security interest on the title, reperfection in this situation will not occur by filing in the new jurisdiction but rather by the secured party's noting its interest on the motor vehicle's certificate of title. In such circumstances, the secured party may have longer than four months in which to reperfect, since reperfection will be necessary only when the debtor requests the surrender of the vehicle's title in order to receive new registration papers in the new state. At that time, the prudent secured party will note its interest again on the new certificate of title and thus remain perfected.

Proceeds

The final point to be made about security interests and perfection is that the Code allows a secured party's interest to reach the proceeds of the debtor's disposition of the collateral.[39] In other words, the secured party has a "lien" (similar to that which we just discussed in the context of multistate transactions) that "floats" over the collateral and includes as "proceeds" whatever is

---

[38] Ibid., Sections 9–103(1)(a), (2); 9–302(3)(b), (4).
[39] Ibid., Section 9–204.

received on the sale, exchange, collection, or other disposition of the collateral.[40] If Bart were to sell the freezer and cash register to another person, the secured party's interest in the collateral would extend even to the cash proceeds realized from this sale. Thus, the issue of proceeds, and the Code's treatment of it, implicates not only perfection rules but also priority rules (especially when, as is often the case, the trustee in bankruptcy is involved as well).

SUMMARY

A secured transaction assures payment by the buyer: if the buyer does not pay the seller, the seller's security interest will allow the seller to repossess the property. A secured transaction typically involves a secured party, a debtor, a security agreement, and collateral. The Code categorizes collateral according to its nature or its use. One type of collateral is goods; the different classes of goods are mutually exclusive. Collateral may also consist of documents, instruments, letters of credit, proceeds, accounts, chattel paper, and general intangibles. Article 9 applies to consensual security interests in personal property or fixtures but not to those arising by operation of law. It covers leases meant as security but not "true" leases. Attachment is the process by which the secured party gets an enforceable security interest in the collateral. A signed security agreement is evidence that attachment has occurred.

Perfection is the method by which secured parties protect themselves against later creditors of the debtor. Perfection can take place in one of three ways: (1) by the creditor's filing a valid financing statement, (2) by the creditor's possession of the collateral, and (3) by automatic perfection. The method of perfection that the secured party should use often depends on the type of collateral involved. If filing is the applicable method, a legally effective financing statement must be used.

The Code's rules regarding multistate transactions are very complex, but the secured party should check them whenever the debtor moves the collateral from one jurisdiction to another in order to ensure continuation of perfection. The secured party generally can reach the proceeds of the debtor's later disposition of the collateral if he or she has met certain requirements under the Code.

DISCUSSION QUESTIONS

1. What is a secured transaction?
2. Define a security interest.
3. Name and define the various types of property recognized by the Code as collateral.
4. If I do not pay the mechanic who fixes my car and he or she gets a judgment against me, does the mechanic have an Article 9 security interest in my car? Why or why not?

---

[40] Ibid., Section 9–306.

5. What is the difference between a "true lease" and a "lease intended as security"?

6. What is attachment, and what are the requirements for it?

7. Name the criteria necessary for a valid security agreement.

8. Define perfection and discuss *in detail* the three methods by which perfection occurs.

9. What kinds of things will cause a financing statement to be ineffective?

10. What problems can arise if Debbie Dunn has given her bank a security interest in bulldozers, and she moves the bulldozers from Indiana to Michigan?

CASE PROBLEMS

1. A farmer had granted a security interest in his chickens to a bank and a government agency. Upon the farmer's bankruptcy, both creditors claimed the chickens. The bank had taken a security interest in all of the debtor's "inventory." The agency argued chickens are livestock and therefore farm products, not inventory, under the Code. Did the bank's security interest cover the chickens? (*In re Northeast Chick Services* v. *Collins*, 43 Bankr. 326 [D. Mass. 1985].)

2. Clark had rented a television set from Rent-It Corporation for $17 per week. The lease also had provided that if Clark chose to rent the equipment for seventy-eight consecutive weeks at this same rate, title would pass to Clark. Was this arrangement a true lease or a disguised credit sale? (*Clark* v. *Rent-It Corporation*, 511 F. Supp. 796 [S.D. Iowa 1981], reversed on other grounds, 685 F.2d 245 [8th Cir. 1982], cert. denied 459 U.S. 1225 [1982].)

3. Bufkin Brothers, Inc. (Bufkin), was an appliance and television dealer. Appliance Buyers Credit Corporation (Appliance) was Bufkin's inventory financier and, in 1974, had filed financing statements covering Bufkin's current and after-acquired inventory. Prior to the expiration of these statements, Appliance had filed continuation statements in order to maintain its perfected interest in the Bufkin inventory. On one of these statements, no signature by any of Appliance's employees had appeared in the space designated for the secured party's signature. However, Appliance's corporate name had been typewritten in the space designated for the secured party's name immediately above the space for the signature. Appliance had acknowledged that the secured party must sign a continuation statement in order for it to be valid under the UCC but had argued that the typewritten name satisfied this signature requirement. Was Appliance correct? (*In the Matter of Bufkin Brothers Inc.* v. *Appliance Buyers Credit Corporation*, 757 F.2d 1573 [5th Cir. 1985].)

4. Bellman had offered to buy cattle from Rohweder at $625 per head. Because Bellman could not obtain financing to complete the purchase,

Rohweder had entered a "share agreement"—not uncommon in the cattle business—under which Bellman would breed the Rohweder cows and care for all the cows and calves. For these services, Bellman would receive 40 percent of the calf crop. Rohweder would remain the owner and receive the rest of the calves. Pursuant to this arrangement, Rohweder had delivered 710 cows to pastures Bellman had rented in Nebraska. Later, Bellman had begun to experience financial difficulties and had filed for bankruptcy. Aberdeen Production Credit Association (PCA) had security agreements with Bellman, and upon his bankruptcy, argued that the after-acquired property clauses in these agreements covered Rohweder's livestock, as well. Rohweder contended that he at all times had remained the owner of the cattle and had only relinquished possession to Bellman. Rohweder asserted that PCA's alleged security interest was invalid because Bellman's mere possession of the livestock and Bellman's unexercised option to purchase had not given the debtor sufficient rights in the collateral for a security interest to attach. Who had the better argument? (*Rohweder* v. *Aberdeen Production Credit Association,* 765 F.2d 109 [8th Cir. 1985].)

5. The Renslows, the debtors, had granted Prairie State Bank (the Bank) a security interest in twelve guns. The Bank had perfected its interest as of 13 April 1981 by filing a financing statement in Illinois and by taking possession of the guns in November, 1981. The Renslows had then moved to Arizona and in August, 1982, had regained the guns from the Bank, which had been holding them. The Internal Revenue Service (IRS) had obtained tax liens against the debtors in June and October, 1982. In September, 1982, the guns had been stolen. Although the guns had been insured, the insurer did not know to whom to pay the insurance proceeds, since both the IRS and the Bank had claimed them. The evidence showed that the Bank had failed to reperfect its interest within a four-month period after the guns had been sent to the debtors' new location in Arizona and that the IRS's lien had been obtained after that four months' time. Who had priority as to the insurance proceeds, the Bank or the IRS? (*Prairie State Bank* v. *Internal Revenue Service,* 745 P.2d 966 [Ariz. App. 1987].)

6. A.A.A. Lift Truck, Inc. had merged with A.A.A. Lift Truck Leasing, Inc. A.A.A. Lift Truck, Inc., thereby had lost its "corporate existence." Would a security agreement signed by A.A.A. Lift Truck, Inc., as the debtor be enforceable against A.A.A. Lift Truck Leasing, Inc.? (*White Motor Credit Corp.* v. *Euclid National Bank,* 409 N.E.2d 1063 [Ohio Com. Pl. 1978].)

7. A 1974 "Inventory Loan and Security Agreement" had given Northwest Acceptance Corporation (Northwest) a security interest in the following collateral: "All inventory of Borrower (wherever located), whether now owned or hereafter acquired, of the following general description or type: Miscellaneous new and used construction and logging equipment." The

description of the collateral in the financing statement had been even more limited; it had covered "all new and used inventory and equipment evidenced by [the] Trust Receipt held by [the] secured party." Lynnwood Equipment, Inc. (Lynnwood), which was a guarantor of the loan, argued that the extent of the security interest had to be determined by reading the security agreement and the financing statement together. Northwest, the creditor, in contrast, submitted that the security agreement alone defined the extent of the security interest. Whose reasoning was most persuasive? (*Northwest Acceptance Corporation* v. *Lynnwood Equipment, Inc.*, 834 F.2d 823 [9th Cir. 1988].)

8. Essex was in the business of selling yachts at retail. Hartford National Bank (HNB) had provided Essex's initial capital of $60,000 in exchange for which Essex had given HNB a security interest in all its present and after-acquired inventory. First Pennsylvania Bank (Pennsylvania) had earlier become a purchase money secured party and as such had also retained a security interest in Essex's after-acquired property. HBN had perfected by filing before Pennsylvania. Thus, when Essex had defaulted on its obligations to HNB, HNB had repossessed nine boats (all of Essex's inventory) that had been in Essex's possession, at which time Pennsylvania had asserted its security interest in the boats, as well. At trial, the evidence had shown that under Pennsylvania's arrangement with Essex and the manufacturer of seven of the nine boats in question, Pennsylvania had held title and would transfer the title to any boat sold directly to the purchaser. Essex at no time had held title to the boats. The court therefore concluded that as to the seven boats, Essex had never acquired any rights in them and that HBN's security interest had not attached to them. Should the appellate court overturn this result? (*Hartford National Bank and Trust Company* v. *Essex Yacht Sales, Inc.*, 492 A.2d 230 [Conn. App. 1985].)

9. The Findleys had raised catfish on a so-called catfish "farm." Sunburst Bank (the Bank), the secured party, had filed a financing statement in the county where the Findleys resided but had not filed any such statement in the country in which the catfish ponds were located. In contesting the Bank's security interest, the Findleys had argued that since "crops" are included within the definition of "farm products," their catfish were therefore crops. As such, according to the Findleys, in order to create a security interest and then to perfect a lien on catfish under Section 9–203, a reasonable description of the location of the catfish ponds should have been an integral part of the security agreement and financing statement. Were the Findleys correct? (*In re Findley*, 76 Bankr. 547 [N.D. Miss. 1987].)

10. Valley Bank and Rockwell International Credit Corporation (Rockwell) were creditors of Curtis Press. Valley Bank held a security interest in "all of the equipment" of Curtis Press, while Rockwell held a purchase money security interest in a particular piece of Curtis's equipment. Both secured

parties had duly perfected their interests in the state of Idaho. However, Curtis had later moved the equipment to Wyoming and then had defaulted on the obligations owed to both creditors. In this case, a Wyoming UCC statute required Rockwell and Valley Bank to reperfect their security interests within four months after the collateral had entered that state, but neither creditor had done so. After this period had expired, Valley Bank had located the equipment and had reperfected its security interest by taking possession of the collateral. Rockwell then had belatedly reperfected its security interest by filing a continuation statement with the Wyoming Secretary of State. When Rockwell had asked Valley Bank to relinquish the equipment, the bank had declined. Rockwell then sued the bank, arguing that its interest in the collateral was superior. Which party would prevail in the lawsuit for the collateral? (*Rockwell International Credit Corporation* v. *Valley Bank,* 707 P.2d 517 [Idaho App. 1985].)

CHAPTER 29

Secured Transactions: Priorities

THE CODE AND COMPETING CLAIMS FOR THE SAME COLLATERAL

In Chapter 28, we examined the process of attachment and perfection, the methods by which secured parties protect their respective interests in the collateral against the debtor and against later creditors of the debtor, especially the trustee in bankruptcy, who, under the bankruptcy laws, occupies the status of a lien creditor. As mentioned, the date of perfection becomes particularly significant when, as is sometimes the case, on the debtor's default, several secured parties claim a perfected security interest in the same collateral. The Uniform Commercial Code's system for deciding which competing claim is superior — that is, which claim has priority — is the focus of this chapter.

PRIORITIES

A secured party's having priority over other creditors is of enormous practical importance. The one catastrophe every creditor fears most is the bankruptcy of the debtor. The reason for this is simple: in the event of bankruptcy, each creditor runs the risk of receiving only a few cents of every dollar loaned to the debtor. Yet, as we have previously discussed, a creditor can maximize the chances of recovering the money owed by attaining the status of a perfected secured party. This means that the creditor will have first claims to the collateral and thus will have the best chance (generally by selling the collateral) of realizing most, if not all, of the debt. A perfected secured party, then, will have priority over general (or unsecured) creditors and lien creditors, including the trustee in bankruptcy. After the secured party has disposed of the collateral, any money in excess of that owed to the secured party may be applied to the claims of these other creditors. In many instances, however, no money will be available to satisfy these latter claims. Thus, we cannot overemphasize the importance of becoming a secured party.

Not surprisingly, given the advantages attendant on being a secured party, most creditors strive to achieve this status. This fact in turn leads to the possibility that several secured parties will claim a security interest in the same collateral. How, then, can we determine who among this class of favored parties has priority? Or, to use informal lingo, who has "first dibs" on the collateral?

The UCC's rules on priorities, contained in Section 9–312, are difficult to unravel and understand. In general, the Code validates a "first-in-time, first-in-right" approach whereby those who have perfected their claims first will have priority. For example, if both competing security interests have been perfected by filing, the first to be filed has priority, whether the security interest attached before or after filing.[1] For this reason, it makes sense for a creditor/lender to file a financing statement covering the transaction even *before* all the requirements for attachment have been met, because it is the date of filing that will control who has priority in the collateral. Thus, the time of attachment is often less important than the time of perfection (here, by filing), even though there can be no perfection without attachment.

For example, suppose that Third Bank files a financing statement covering the inventory in Penny Pope's Sporting Goods store on 10 December 1987, and Fourth Bank files such a statement on the same inventory on 1 February 1988. Third Bank will have priority over Fourth Bank, even though Fourth Bank may have given value first and thus have attached its interest before Third Bank did. However, note that neither Third Bank nor Fourth Bank can have a perfected interest until attachment occurs. Simply put, Third Bank's earlier filing gives it a superior interest in the inventory under the UCC's "first-to-file" rules. Because the Code determines priorities from the time of filing—if all secured parties have filed—it behooves a would-be secured party to file as soon as possible.

The Code's drafters have justified this "race to the recording office" as a necessary protection of the public filing system. In the drafters' view, Fourth Bank, though it has attached its interest first, cannot complain, because it

---

[1] Uniform Commercial Code, Section 9–312(5)(a).

could have checked the public records and thus have learned of Third Bank's claimed interest before taking its security interest. According to the drafters, lenders like Third Bank who plan to make a series of subsequent advances and who have filed first should be able to make those later advances without having, as a condition of protection, to check each time for filings *later* than theirs.[2] Hence, in our hypothetical case, Third Bank will have priority because it has filed first.

The following case illustrates these and other aspects of the Code's priorities rules.

Genoa National Bank v. *Sorensen*
304 N.W.2d 659 (Neb. 1981)

FACTS

Sorensen, a farmer, had granted security interests in his growing crops to two different persons, Fichtl and Nelson. Both creditors had filed financing statements locally, but they had not filed until 3 November and 17 November 1978, respectively, with the Public Service Commission, as required by a Nebraska law that had become effective on 2 September 1977. In the meantime, on 11 October 1978, Genoa National Bank had obtained a judgment against Sorensen based on promissory notes that Sorensen owed to the bank. On 19 October 1978, the bank had caused the sheriff to **levy execution** on the grain that had been harvested from the land covered by Fichtl and Nelson's security agreements. Fichtl and Nelson argued that their liens were prior and superior to the bank's.

Levy execution To seize and sell property to satisfy a judgment

ISSUE

Were Fichtl and Nelson perfected secured parties so that their interests would take priority over that of a **judgment creditor?**

HOLDING

Yes. Their liens were perfected before the bank had acquired its judgment lien and thus were superior to the bank's lien.

REASONING

Judgment creditor A creditor who has obtained a court verdict that allows the enforcement of an execution, or seizure and sale of property

While central filing was required for growing crops, it was not required for harvested crops. Thus, when the crops had been harvested, the locally filed financing statements became sufficient to perfect the security interests and therefore had priority over the judgment lien, which had not been obtained until after the crops had been harvested. The evidence was clear beyond contradiction that if the crops had remained "unharvested" until such time as the judgment creditor had obtained its judgment and levied execution, it would clearly have priority over the security creditors who had failed to file their financing statements in the offices of both the county clerk and the Public Service Commission. But in this case, long before the judgment creditor had acquired any interest on which levy could have been executed, the crops had been harvested and taken to an elevator. The bank's argument that if a filing is improperly made at the outset, it may never be corrected or made

[2] Ibid., Section 9–312, Official Comment 5.

valid was incorrect because the purpose of filing is to give **constructive notice** to the world and actual notice to those who would take the trouble to look. Thus, if at any time after 21 October 1977, the date on which the crops had been harvested, and 11 October 1978, the date on which the bank had acquired its judgment lien, Fichtl or Nelson had wished to take further action to perfect their liens on harvested crops, they would have been required simply to refile their financing statement in the office of the county clerk where it was already on file. Acceptance of the bank's position would mean that even though there was a financing statement on file in the office of the county clerk before the bank had acquired its judgment and levied execution, and it was proper in all respects as to harvested crops, the court should nevertheless ignore that financing statement because the security holders had not had a second stamp placed on the document after the crops had been harvested. To make such a requirement would be simply to ignore the Code's clearly stated position that if a filing was properly perfected when made, a change in status will not deprive the holder of its lien interest and that a financing statement may be filed before the security interest attaches. Therefore, Fichtl and Nelson's filings had been made in advance of their acquiring their interest in the harvested crops and attaching at such time as the crops were harvested, thereby eliminating the requirement of a duplicate filing. Hence, the better rule, and the one supported both by the language of the Uniform Commercial Code and logic, required that if an otherwise unperfected lien is not filed at all the proper places at the time of filing, but through the passage of time or change in character of the property becomes a proper filing under the provisions of the Uniform Commercial Code, the lien also becomes properly perfected and is superior to all other liens not otherwise perfected prior to the time that the previous security lien had been perfected.

Constructive notice
Information that a person is treated as knowing, whether actually known or not

---

Order of Perfection

As we learned in Chapter 28, filing is just one of three alternative methods of perfection. With purchase money security interests in consumer goods, for instance, one may rely on automatic perfection; or one may perfect by taking possession of the collateral. In all such cases (that is, where there has been no filing by any of the parties), the first to perfect takes priority.

Order of Attachment

If for some reason none of the parties has perfected its security interest, the first interest to attach enjoys priority. However, be aware that it is definitely not advisable to rely on attachment alone as a vehicle for attaining priority, because an *unperfected* secured creditor will not enjoy a preferred status in bankruptcy proceedings. Simply stated, to gain priority over other secured parties and over the trustee in bankruptcy, it is imperative to file as soon as possible if filing is an acceptable mode for perfecting a security interest in the type of collateral involved, or, if filing is not appropriate, to perfect one's interest as soon as possible in the appropriate manner.

The seller in the following case unfortunately learned this rule the hard way.

Berga v. *Amit International Trade, Ltd.*
511 F. Supp. 432 (E.D. Pa. 1981)

FACTS   Amit had bought $138,515.79 worth of clothes on credit from Berga, an Italian corporation, on 6 June 1978. Earlier, in April, 1976, Fidelity Bank had loaned money to Amit and had retained a security interest in the goods, including after-acquired property and proceeds. Fidelity had filed financing statements to this effect both locally and centrally. When Amit had not paid Berga, Berga had demanded, in October, 1979, that Amit return the clothes. In November, 1979, Fidelity had sold the clothes to satisfy part of Amit's indebtedness to it. Berga admitted that it had not retained a security interest in the goods but argued that for Fidelity to enjoy priority, Fidelity would have to have been unaware of Berga's interest in the clothes.

ISSUE   Is absence of knowledge a requirement for a secured party to defeat an unsecured party?

HOLDING   No. Absence of such knowledge is not necessary under the UCC.

REASONING   Section 9–312 of the Code states that an unperfected security interest is subordinate to that of a secured party who has filed. While Berga had not perfected by either filing or possession, Fidelity had perfected its interest by filing two financing statements. The basic scheme of Section 9–312's priorities permits one to rely on the filing system's record rather than on one's knowledge of a prior security interest. Therefore, the Code apparently has made any "knowledge requirement" irrelevant. Under Section 9–312, Fidelity, because it had filed, was a secured party with priority over an unsecured party like Berga.

EXCEPTIONS   We will now turn our attention to some very important exceptions to the general rules of priorities. The first of these deals with a purchase money security interest that is held by a purchase money secured party.

Purchase Money Security Interests   For reasons that will soon become clear, a purchase money secured party enjoys priority over interests that precede his or her interest in time, provided the party complies with certain provisions of the Code. In other words, a purchase money security interest contradicts our previously described "first-to-file-or-to-perfect" rules on priorities. An analysis of the types of commercial situations that involve purchase money security interests and purchase money secured parties will explain why the Code sanctions a special status for these interests.

As we learned in Chapter 28, a security interest is a purchase money security interest to the extent that it is "(a) taken or retained by the seller of the collateral to secure all or part of its price; or (b) taken by a person who by making advances or incurring an obligation gives value to enable the debtor to acquire rights in or the use of collateral if such value is in fact so used."[3] As should be apparent from this definition, purchase money secured parties typically are sellers or lenders who, by their extensions of credit, permit the debtor to acquire rights in the collateral. But not all sellers or lenders qualify for purchase money secured party status. We will be able to understand how purchase money secured parties differ from other secured parties if we reexamine our earlier example involving Third Bank and Penny Pope.

This time let us assume that Third Bank has agreed to finance Penny's inventory. As her inventory financier, Third Bank agrees to give Penny letters of credit (or a line of credit) upon which Penny can draw at irregular intervals and from which the bank can issue future advances of funds to her as she needs them. To protect itself, Third Bank creates and perfects a security interest in all present and after-acquired property of Penny's and all proceeds thereof. In such situations, Third Bank has a so-called floating lien over Penny's inventory, since the lien covers the items of inventory as they stand on the shelf and even "floats" over other inventory and property that Penny acquires through subsequent advances or loans from Third Bank. Third Bank's "lien" also covers the proceeds of any items that Penny sells. Generally speaking, Third Bank will compel Penny to maintain a certain ratio of inventory and will gauge her repayment of the loans and its later advances with reference to this ratio. Typically, Third Bank will ask Penny to promise to refrain from *double financing,* or using this same inventory as collateral for a subsequent loan from another creditor, say Fourth Bank.

We can understand Third Bank's reasons for protecting its security interest in the inventory: it is well aware that, should Penny's business go bankrupt, it will need to have priority if it is going to realize any money from its extension of credit. Hence, on the one hand, the law wants to protect secured parties like Third Bank so that they will be willing to extend credit to businesspeople like Penny. One way to accomplish this is to give them priority if they are the first to file or to perfect.

But, on the other hand, it seems unfair for Third Bank to have the ability to restrict unduly Penny's access to credit. Potential subsequent creditors may see Third Bank's previously filed financing statement on the inventory and may refuse to extend Penny credit because of Third Bank's seeming priority based on its compliance with the first-to-file-or-to-perfect rules. Where will she get credit if, for some reason, Third Bank refuses to give her more loans or advances?

The UCC attempts to balance both Penny's and Third Bank's interests by giving priority to purchase money security interests. In other words, if Fourth Bank advances money (say $10,000) to enable Penny to acquire additional inventory, Fourth Bank will have priority over Third Bank to the extent of the value given, here $10,000, because the law characterizes Fourth Bank as a

---

[3] Ibid., Section 9–107.

purchase money secured party in these circumstances. (Third Bank, as the inventory financier and the holder of an after-acquired property and future advances clauses, is a nonpurchase money secured party here.) However, to earn this priority, Fourth Bank will have to fulfill certain requirements, depending on the type of collateral involved.

If the collateral is inventory, Fourth Bank enjoys priority over Third Bank's conflicting security interest in the same inventory (and in identifiable cash proceeds) received on or before the delivery of the inventory to a buyer (here, Penny). This will be true provided that the purchase money security interest has been perfected by filing at the time the debtor receives possession of the inventory, and the purchase money secured party notifies *in writing* any persons who have previously filed financing statements covering inventory of the same types that he or she (the purchase money secured party) has or expects to acquire a purchase money security interest in the inventory of the debtor. The purchase money secured party must also describe the inventory by item or type. To acquire priority over Third Bank, Fourth Bank must meet these requirements.[4]

To those who feel this "superpriority" for purchase money secured parties is unfair to inventory financiers like Third Bank, the drafters of the Code offer the following policy justifications. The notification procedures required by the Code will tip off Third Bank that Penny is "double financing." At this point, if it believes itself vulnerable, Third Bank may curtail future advances to Penny and may, assuming that the security agreement so provides and that it gives notice, demand payment from Penny (by arguing that such double financing constitutes a condition of default). Third Bank thus has ways of protecting itself from Penny if it so desires, and in the meantime Penny has acquired new avenues of credit. Third Bank also has the added protection of knowing that it will still have priority with regard to the inventory if Fourth Bank does not comply with the Code's requirements.

If the security interest covers noninventory collateral (such as equipment or consumer goods), Fourth Bank, as a purchase money secured party, will have priority over Third Bank, as a holder of a conflicting security interest in the same collateral or its proceeds, if the purchase money security interest is perfected at the time the debtor receives possession of the collateral or within ten days thereafter.[5] Hence, it is clear that the type of collateral involved dictates what a creditor must do to achieve purchase money secured party status. Why is less required (a ten-day "grace period" for filing and no need to give notice to holders of previously filed security interests) of one who wishes to attain priority in noninventory collateral? Apparently, the drafters of the Code believed that arrangements for periodic advances against incoming property are unusual outside the inventory field; thus, they did not think there was a need to notify noninventory secured parties, because, in fact, only in rare

---

[4] Ibid., Section 9–312(3).
[5] Ibid., Section 9–312(4).

instances would such a previous financier even exist. Simply put, equipment and consumer goods are not usually valuable enough for several creditors to have taken security interests in them. To illustrate, if Penny buys a new refrigerator to preserve the "bounce" of the tennis balls she is selling, the refrigerator will be equipment because she uses it in her business. Should Fourth Bank lend her the money to buy the refrigerator, it will become a purchase money secured party if it files a financing statement within ten days of Penny's receiving the refrigerator. It will have priority over Third Bank, despite lack of notice to the latter, even if Third Bank has filed a financing statement indicating an interest in "all inventory, *equipment,* and after-acquired property of Penny Pope's Sporting Goods Store." If Fourth Bank does *not* file within ten days, Third Bank will have a priority claim to the refrigerator under the usual first-to-file-or-to-perfect rules.

If there are two or more competing purchase money security interests in the same type of collateral, the Code applies the usual first-to-file-or-to-perfect rule in determining priority in this situation. Thus, the purchase money secured party who files first will have superior rights.

The following case illustrates the types of legal issues that crop up in the context of purchase money security interests.

Davis Bros., Inc. v. *United Bank of Littleton*
701 P.2d 642 (Colo. App. 1985)

United Bank of Littleton (the Bank) and Davis Bros., Inc. (Davis Bros.) were creditors of Drug Fair, a retail drug store and pharmacy. On 14 November 1975, the Bank filed a financing statement covering all the debtor's inventory, furniture, fixtures, equipment, accounts receivable, and all after-acquired property. On 27 September 1976, Davis Bros. filed a financing statement to secure payment of a $62,822.28 note and which listed as collateral Drug Fair's inventory, prescription records, and all "drug and sundry inventory of debtor which debtor has purchased or may purchase from secured party and in which secured party has taken or will take a purchase money security interest." Davis Bros. subsequently supplied Drug Fair with merchandise for sale in its business on a weekly credit basis. The Bank learned of Davis Bros.' financing statement on 16 February 1977 as the result of a lien search. However, Davis Bros. did not give the Bank any other notice that it had or expected to acquire a purchase money interest in debtor's inventory. During April, 1979, the Bank took possession of and sold debtor's inventory and prescription records without giving Davis Bros. notice of the sale. At the time of the sale, Drug Fair owed Davis Bros. $7,951.84 on an open account for drugs and sundries purchased from Davis Bros. after the filing of Davis Bros.' financing statement. This amount was over and above the amount due on the note. Davis Bros. then brought suit for an accounting of the proceeds of the sale and for damages for conversion of the items in which it had priority. The trial court granted summary judgment as to Davis Bros.' claim for conversion of the debtor's prescription records and the drugs and sundries for which

FACTS

Davis Bros. had a purchase money security interest. Following trial on the issue of damages, the court entered judgment for $25,000 for conversion of the prescription records and $7,951.84 plus interest at the rate of 18 percent per annum for conversion of the drugs and sundries.

ISSUE

Did the judge err in granting damages to Davis Bros. for conversion of the drugs and sundries owing to the Bank's priority as to these items?

HOLDING

Yes. Although the evidence showed that the Bank had converted the prescription records, the Bank nonetheless enjoyed priority as to the inventory items allegedly converted, since Davis Bros. had not complied with the statutory requirements for gaining priority in these circumstances.

REASONING

Colorado's UCC statute requires a purchase money secured party in inventory to perfect its interest by the time the debtor receives possession of the collateral and to give notice to the holder of a conflicting security interest who has previously filed a financing statement covering the same types of inventory in order to enjoy priority vis-à-vis other creditors in inventory. This notice should state that the person giving the notice has or expects to acquire a purchase money security interest in the inventory of the debtor and should describe the inventory by item or type. Davis Bros.' failure to send written notice to the Bank made it ineligible to attain priority as a purchase money secured party. Therefore, the Bank, as the result of its previously filed financing statement, enjoyed priority as to the inventory in question and by definition could not be liable for conversion of the inventory.

Bona Fide Purchaser of Consumer Goods

Besides purchase money secured parties, another class of persons who may have priority over a previously perfected security interest is the bona fide purchaser of consumer goods.[6] Recall from Chapter 28 that "consumer goods" are goods that have been used or bought for use primarily for personal, family, or household purposes.[7] Thus, this section of the Code limits priority to the purchase of this type of collateral. Examination of this Code provision shows further limitations, since to enjoy priority over a previously perfected security interest, a buyer must be ignorant of the security interest, must pay value, and must use the goods for personal, family, or household purposes.

To illustrate, assume that Henry Smith wishes to sell his refrigerator to Margaret Hernandez. Margaret does not know it, but Handley, the owner of the appliance store where Henry bought the refrigerator, has a perfected security interest in this consumer good (Handley is relying on automatic perfection — that is, the mere attachment of the security interest.) If Margaret pays value and uses the refrigerator in her home, she will have priority; in other words, she will retain the refrigerator even if Handley tries to repossess it from her, should Henry default in his payments. However, if Margaret plans to

[6] Ibid., Section 9–307(2).
[7] Ibid., Section 9–109(1).

use the refrigerator in her dental office for the purpose of keeping anesthetics cold, Handley will win because Margaret does not fit Section 9–307(2)'s definition of a bona fide purchaser (because of her nonpersonal use of the collateral).

So far, we have been assuming that Handley will rely on automatic perfection, which, as discussed in Chapter 28, is the mode generally preferred by the Handleys of the world because they can thereby avoid the expense and inconvenience of filing. However, under Section 9–307(2), if Handley files a financing statement covering a consumer good before a buyer purchases it, Handley, not the bona fide purchaser, will have a priority claim to it. Handley, then, must decide whether the possibility that a refrigerator will be sold to a bona fide purchaser outweighs the inconvenience of filing. If he thinks it does, he should file in order to attain priority; if not, he can rely on automatic perfection to keep him secure from the claims of everyone except this specialized type of bona fide purchaser.

The secured party in the next case undoubtedly regretted its failure to file a financing statement on the fixture that was in dispute.

Kibbe v. *Rohde*
427 A.2d 1163 (Pa. Super. 1981)

FACTS

The Patz Company had retained a security interest in the barn cleaner that it had sold to the Bulls but had neglected to file a financing statement on this fixture. The Kibbes later bought the land on which the barn cleaner had been installed. Some time after the sale, Rohde, an employee of Patz, removed the barn cleaner because Patz had not been paid for it. The Kibbes sued Rohde and Patz for trespass and for the value of the barn cleaner, asserting that they were bona fide purchasers for value of the farm and its fixtures.

ISSUE

Did the Kibbes merit the status of bona fide purchasers for value because they had bought the farm and the barn cleaner without knowledge of Patz's security interest in the barn cleaner?

HOLDING

Yes. They were bona fide purchasers for value.

REASONING

A lawyer had searched the appropriate records for the Kibbes before the sale and had found no liens on the property. Since this was the only knowledge available to the Kibbes at the time they had become purchasers, there was no evidence showing that the Kibbes had any knowledge or notice of Patz's security claim. Accordingly, the jury verdict against Patz for trespass and for conversion of the barn cleaner was correct.

Buyer in the Ordinary Course of Business

A buyer in the ordinary course of business may, according to Section 9-307(1), have priority over a perfected security interest. To use our earlier example, when Henry Smith buys the refrigerator from Handley's Appliance Store, he is a buyer in the ordinary course of business. *Anyone who buys goods from a merchant seller in a standard (as opposed to an extraordinary) transaction is a buyer in the ordinary course of business.* As such, Henry will take the refrigerator free of a security interest created by his seller (Handley may have given a security interest in his inventory of appliances to Third Bank), even though the security interest is perfected and even if Henry (as a savvy business law student) knows of Third Bank's security interest. The policy reasons for such a result are probably obvious: will the Henrys across our country buy refrigerators (or stereos or garden tractors) if the Third Banks of our nation can repossess them? Hardly. Therefore, buyers in the ordinary course of business — by definition those who may know of the existence of a perfected security interest but who buy in good faith and without knowledge that the sale of them is in violation of the ownership rights or security interest of a third party — have priority in such competing claims situations. Although many people use the terms *bona fide purchaser* and *buyer in the ordinary course of business* interchangeably, they are distinct concepts. We more appropriately term one *consumer* who has bought goods from another consumer in an occasional sale a bona fide purchaser. Buyers in the ordinary course of business, in contrast, are purchasers who are buying from a seller who routinely sells from inventory or otherwise regularly engages in such transactions.

But, as the next case indicates, if the buyer engages in a nonroutine business transaction, he or she will not enjoy priority as a buyer in the ordinary course of business would.

Bank of Illinois v. Dye
517 N.E.2d 38 (Ill. App. 1987)

FACTS   Bank of Illinois (the Bank) was a "floor-plan" financier of Gordon McGrath, who did business as McGrath Auto Sales (McGrath). The Bank, on 16 July 1984, filed a financing statement that covered "new and used motor vehicles" acquired by McGrath and that authorized McGrath to sell, lease, and consume its inventory in the ordinary course of business. In July, 1985, McGrath pledged a 1985 Buick Riviera to R. Edward Dye, delivered a duplicate Indiana certificate of title to the vehicle, and received in return a $15,300 advance. Although the parties later disputed the date that the vehicle had come into Dye's possession, they did agree that the Bank's security interest was created, under the floor-plan financing, prior to Dye's taking possession of the car. Dye also testified that he and Gordon McGrath had been close friends for over thirty years. He said that, from the early 1980s through 1985, he had bought and sold eight or ten cars through McGrath at a dealers' auction in Indianapolis. McGrath subsequently had suggested to Dye that he could cut costs by allowing

McGrath to keep the "paperwork" including the certificates of title, while he, Dye, used a set of dealer's license plates on the cars. Dye admitted that, as a result, he had had no proof of ownership of any of the vehicles; but he had not found that unusual, because he and Gordon had been "very good friends." He indicated further that he was "sure" Gordon McGrath had handled the transactions involving the vehicles he had bought and sold in a manner different from those for other people who had purchased cars from the dealership. As to the "purchase" of the 1985 Buick Riviera, Dye testified that he had paid the same price for the car as McGrath had paid for it; he had paid no taxes on it until December 1985; he had received no certificate of title until December 1985; he had always used McGrath's dealer's plates; he had signed a document representing to the state that the sale had occurred in December rather than June; and he had returned the car to McGrath's lot whenever McGrath had needed to show the car to "prospective clients." Apparently, McGrath had never informed Dye of the Bank's security interest. Dye argued that he had been a buyer in the ordinary course of business who could take the car free of the Bank's security interest.

Was Dye a buyer in the ordinary course of business?   **ISSUE**

No. He was not a buyer in the ordinary course of business. Therefore, the Bank could recover the Buick from him.   **HOLDING**

Although Dye had argued that McGrath's sale to him was "in the ordinary course of business," owing to the fact that he and McGrath had engaged in other similar transactions, the crucial questions centered around whether the transaction between the buyer and seller was "customary in the business" and whether the buyer was "a typical buyer in an ordinary business transaction with the seller." Here, the incidents surrounding Dye's purchase of the vehicle from McGrath had indicated that the sale was not in the ordinary course of business. For example, McGrath had sold the vehicle at the same price at which he had purchased it. Furthermore, McGrath had added no sum to the sales price that represented the required Illinois tax payments. Indeed, McGrath had never paid such a tax, and, eventually, Dye himself had paid the tax in December, 1985. No certificate of title had been assigned to Dye or requested until December, 1985, when Dye purportedly had learned for the first time that McGrath was having difficulties. McGrath had also allowed Dye to use McGrath's dealer's license plates, and Dye had thus participated in a fraud upon the state of Illinois, which had been entitled to a registration fee for the vehicle. Moreover, Dye had participated with McGrath in sending a false document to the secretary of state representing the date of the sale as December, 1985, rather than June, 1985. Lastly, the vehicle had been made available to McGrath after the sale so that it had always been present on the seller's floor when a check of the "floor-planned" vehicles was made by the Bank, including one occasion when the Bank had made an unannounced check. Most of the foregoing unusual aspects of the transaction had given the impression to the outside world and to Dye that McGrath had not parted with his ownership of the automobile. In total, these factors were so atypical and uncustomary as to negate any argument that the sale had been in the ordinary course of business.   **REASONING**

Common Law and Statutory Liens

Under Section 9–310 of the Code, certain liens that arise by operation of law have priority over a perfected security interest in the collateral. For instance, if Monty Moore takes his car to Avenue Auto Repair (AAR) and does not pay Harry, the owner of AAR, Harry will have a common law or statutory lien on the car to the extent of the money owed him for his services or materials. Harry can retain possession of the car; and, in the event of Monty's default, he can force Westside Savings and Loan, the secured party for Monty's car, to pay him for his repairs before Westside realizes any proceeds from the sale of Monty's car.

Fixtures

As discussed in Chapter 28, generally Article 9 does not cover security interests in real estate. However, as you may remember, in addition to covering personal property, Article 9 also encompasses fixtures (goods that have become so related to real estate that an interest in them arises under real estate law). In many parts of the country, factories, schools, and homes almost invariably have a fixture called a furnace. In most cases, a mortgagee (the party who loaned the money for the purchase of the land) has a security interest in the real property, while a secured party may have retained an interest in the furnace. Knock-down, drag-out fights over priority sometimes occur as a result of this dovetailing of real property and personal property interests if the seller of the furnace wishes to repossess the furnace but confronts the mortgagee of the land, who claims the furnace as part of his or her real estate security interest.

Section 9–313 of the Code sets out rules for settling these problems. According to the Code, a perfected security interest in fixtures has priority over the conflicting interest of an **encumbrancer** or owner of real estate when (1) the security interest is a purchase money security interest; (2) the security interest is perfected by a fixture filing — that is, filing in the office where a real estate mortgage would be filed or recorded — before the goods become fixtures (or within ten days thereafter); and (3) the debtor has an interest of record in the real estate or is in possession of it. Thus, if Fire Power Furnace Company sells Earl LePage, the lessee of Port-Hole Pub, a furnace on an installment basis and retains a security interest in the furnace until it is paid for, Fire Power will have priority over Earl's lessor (or the mortgagee of the Pub) if (1) it is a purchase money secured party and (2) it perfects its security interest before the furnace is installed (or within ten days of that time).[8]

Similarly, a perfected security interest in fixtures will have priority if (1) the fixtures are readily removable factory or office machines or readily removable replacements of domestic appliances that are consumer goods and (2) before the goods become fixtures, the security interest is perfected by any method permitted under Article 9.[9] Therefore, if Don Dunn's garbage disposal disintegrates and he buys one from Hosinski's Appliance Store through a

Encumbrancer The holder of a claim relating to real or personal property

---

[8] Ibid., Section 9–313(4)(a).
[9] Ibid., Section 9–313(4)(c).

conditional sales contract, Hosinski's will have priority over Don's mortgagee (whose mortgage covers not only the real property but the plumbing and appliances) if it perfects its security interest before it installs the disposal in Don's home. Since you no doubt remember that perfection of such consumer goods may occur through attachment, Hosinski's will have priority as of the moment Don signs the security agreement.

It may, however, be in Hosinski's best interests to perfect by resorting to a fixture filing, because such a filing will ensure its priority over subsequent encumbrancers or purchasers whose interests arise after Hosinski's.

Lastly, when the secured party has priority over all owners and encumbrancers of the real estate, that party may, on default, sever and remove the collateral (such as the furnace) from the real estate. A secured party who elects to do this has a duty to reimburse any encumbrancer or owner of the real estate who is not the debtor for any physical injury caused to the property by the removal. Correspondingly, a person entitled to reimbursement may refuse permission to remove until the secured party gives adequate security for the performance of this obligation.[10]

SUMMARY

The rules on priorities represent the Code's attempt to decide who, among validly perfected secured parties, has superior rights to the collateral. In general, the Code validates a "first-in-time, first-in-right" approach. Thus, if competing security interests have been perfected by filing, the first to be filed has priority, whether the security interest attached before or after filing. If neither party has filed, the first party to perfect has priority. And if no one has perfected, the first interest to attach has superior rights to the collateral. There are some exceptions to these priority rules. For instance, a purchase money secured party may prevail over earlier, perfected creditors if the party follows certain Code provisions that make distinctions according to the type of collateral involved. Similarly, bona fide purchasers of consumer goods and buyers in the ordinary course of business may defeat prior perfected interests in some situations. Likewise, certain liens that arise by operation of law have priority over perfected security interests in the collateral. Moreover, a secured party holding a security interest in fixtures will defeat a real property claimant if, for example, the secured party follows the requirements of the Code for a "fixture filing," or a filing in an office where real property interests are recorded.

DISCUSSION QUESTIONS

1. Why is the issue of priority important?
2. Why should a lender file a financing statement even before the deal is completed?
3. Enumerate the rules regarding priorities in the absence of filing.

---

[10] Ibid., Section 9–313(8).

4. Explain the importance of purchase money secured parties and why they merit priority.

5. List the rules for becoming a purchase money secured party in inventory collateral.

6. List the rules for becoming a purchase money secured party in noninventory collateral.

7. What is a bona fide purchaser? Does such a purchaser always have priority? How does this person differ from a buyer in the ordinary course of business?

8. Does a secured party have priority over the holder of a common law lien? Explain why or why not.

9. What steps should a secured party in fixtures take to protect his or her interest?

10. Why does a secured party in fixtures have to reimburse the owner of the land (when that person is not the debtor) upon removing the collateral from the real property?

CASE PROBLEMS

1. Sarah Jean Jackson purchased furniture from Easy Living Furniture (Easy Living) in November, 1983. Easy Living financed the purchase price and retained a purchase money security interest in the furniture but never filed a financing statement covering this transaction. When Jackson filed for bankruptcy, the trustee contended that its interest in the furniture was superior to Easy Living's. Would you agree? (*Ledford* v. *Easy Living Furniture*, 52 Bankr. 706 [S.D. Ohio 1985].)

2. Garris purchased a Kenworth truck from Peterbilt Southern, Inc., which, for consideration, then assigned the note and security agreement covering the truck to Paccar Financial Corporation. Thereafter, Garris "lease-purchased" the truck to Hard Times in exchange for a pickup truck. Although the written agreement between Garris and Hard Times did not specify that Hard Times was assuming the obligation to pay the installments to Paccar as they came due, Hard Times specifically agreed to pay for all repairs and costs of operation. Hard Times, in fact, made four installment payments to Paccar but refused to make any subsequent payments because of a bill of $12,638.56 owed to Harnett Transfer for repairs to the truck. When Paccar called Hodges, a director, shareholder, and chief executive officer of both Hard Times and Harnett Transfer, to threaten repossession because of Hard Times's missed payments, Hodges said he would put a mechanic's lien for $12,000 on the truck and that Paccar would never get the truck back. Harnett Transfer later sold the truck at a foreclosure sale in order to satisfy its mechanic's lien, and Hard Times was the purchaser at this sale. When Paccar subsequently tried to repossess the truck, Hard Times asserted that Harnett Transfer, as the

possessor of a mechanic's lien, had priority over Paccar's security interest and that because Hard Times had been a purchaser for value at the sale conducted to satisfy Harnett Transfer's lien, it had acquired title free of any interests over which Harnett Transfer had been entitled to priority, including Paccar's interest. Should Hard Times have priority over Paccar? (*Paccar Financial Corporation* v. *Harnett Transfer, Inc.,* 275 S.E.2d 243 [N.C. App. 1981].)

3. Computer Accounting Incorporated (CAI) had been providing accounting services to Pacific Mountain Corporation (PMC). PMC had been in the market for a computer to perform its accounting work. Eventually, the parties had agreed to purchase a Honeywell, Inc. (Honeywell), computer system. On 26 May 1978, CAI entered into an "Original Equipment Manufacturer" (OEM) contract with Honeywell to sell the latter's computers. This document provided that a security interest would be retained in any equipment Honeywell delivered to CAI until CAI's "obligations [had been] paid in full." CAI then confirmed existing orders with Honeywell for two computer systems, one for PMC and one for CAI. In June, 1978, CAI prepared and forwarded a written purchase agreement to PMC that provided that most of the equipment would remain in the possession of CAI and would be used by CAI when not in use by PMC. In late September or early October, 1978, CAI and PMC agreed that a subsidiary of PMC, Consolidated Commercial Investors Corporation (CCIC), would be substituted as purchaser. The equipment was then leased to CAI, apparently for tax advantages. On 9 October 1978, to finance this transaction, CCIC executed a loan agreement with Puget Sound National Bank whereby CCIC granted the bank a security interest in the computer. On 20 October 1978, the bank filed its financing statement. The computer was delivered to CAI but did not function properly. Although CCIC paid CAI in full for the system, the computer was never delivered to CCIC. CAI then refused to pay Honeywell; CCIC defaulted on its loan; and the bank brought and won an action to acquire possession of the collateral. When Honeywell argued that its interest in the computer was superior to the bank's, the court held CCIC was a buyer in the ordinary course of business and thus took the computer free of Honeywell's security interest. Honeywell then countered with the argument that CCIC could not be a buyer in the ordinary course of business because the goods had never been delivered to CCIC. Was possession of the goods a prerequisite for becoming a buyer in the ordinary course of business? (*Puget Sound National Bank* v. *Honeywell, Inc.,* 698 P.2d 584 [Wash. App. 1985].)

4. Between February and May, 1982, Mark Products U.S., Inc. (Mark Products), sold seismic exploration equipment to a consortium called the Vibrosearch companies. The equipment was sold on an open account, unsecured basis, with payment due thirty days following delivery. Mark Products shipped the goods to the various states in which the Vibrosearch

companies operated. By May, all deliveries had been made and received. In June, 1982, InterFirst Bank Houston, N.A. (InterFirst), loaned the parent company, Vibrosearch, Inc., $9,000,000 and established a $2,500,000 line of credit. These loans were evidenced by two promissory notes, both dated 30 June 1982, and secured by guaranty agreements and security agreements in favor of InterFirst. The security agreements covered all of the Vibrosearch companies' assets, including all the seismic exploration equipment sold by Mark Products. In early July, InterFirst filed the required financing statements in the appropriate states and in Texas, the principal place of business of Vibrosearch, Inc. As of 16 July 1982, the amount of indebtedness owed by the Vibrosearch companies to InterFirst was $8,314,003.60. By that time, Mark Products had become concerned over the Vibrosearch companies' outstanding indebtedness and had sought additional security. Hence, on 16 July 1982, Vibrosearch, Inc., executed a promissory note in favor of Mark Products in the principal amount of $772,854.03, representing the balance of the unpaid purchase price of the equipment. Simultaneously, Vibrosearch, Inc., also signed a financing statement and a security agreement, the latter of which provided that Vibrosearch, Inc., would not sell, lease, rent, or otherwise dispose of the equipment without the written consent of Mark Products. In addition, it purported to grant Mark Products a first priority security interest in the seismic exploration equipment. On 1 September 1982, Mark Products filed a financing statement with the state of Texas, but did not file financing statements in any other states. Mark Products argued that it had held a purchase money security interest as of 3 September 1982 that took priority over InterFirst's secured claim. It further asserted that the Vibrosearch companies had not become a "debtor" and the goods had not become "collateral" for purposes of Section 9–107 until the security agreement had come into existence. Moreover, Mark Products asserted, the grace period for filing under the purchase money security interest provision would start to run only after there was a "debtor" in possession of "collateral." Should a court agree with Mark Products's claim and find that it had priority over InterFirst? (*Mark Products U.S., Inc.* v. *InterFirst Bank Houston, N.A.,* 737 S.W.2d. 389 [Tex. App. 1987].)

5. Northwestern Sales, Inc. (Northwestern), sold its inventory to Prairie Distributors (Prairie) in March, 1978, with Northwestern retaining a security interest in Prairie's inventory, after-acquired property, proceeds, and accounts receivable for the unpaid balance of the purchase price. On 19 April 1978, Northwestern filed a financing statement with the Morton County Register of Deeds and with the secretary of state on 21 June 1978. Mandan Security Bank (MSB), which had financed part of Prairie's purchase and had taken a security interest in Prairie's accounts receivable and inventory, filed a financing statement with the secretary of state on 10 May 1978. On 2 March 1979, Northwestern assigned to Ruben Elhard, its sole shareholder, all of its rights and interests, including the $125,000

promissory note and "all security interests and financing statements" executed by Prairie in favor of Northwestern. In May, 1979, Prairie began doing business with Tappan and entered into a security agreement on 11 May 1979 with Tappan. Tappan notified MSB in writing that it had or expected to acquire a purchase money security interest in Prairie's inventory but had not so notified Elhard or Northwestern. However, Tappan had called Northwestern's president to inquire about details in Northwestern's filing that Tappan had found confusing. Tappan filed a financing statement with the secretary of state on 19 June 1979. When Elhard ultimately sued Prairie to recover on his unpaid promissory note, he claimed priority over Tappan, the purchase money secured party, on the ground that Tappan's telephone conversation with Northwestern's president had been insufficient to satisfy the notification procedures placed on purchase money secured parties under the Code. Was Elhard right? (*Elhard* v. *Prairie Distributors, Inc.,* 366 N.W.2d 465 [N.D. 1985].)

6. Hamilton Bank (the Bank) and ITT Corporation (ITT) were secured creditors of Diaconx Corporation (Diaconx). Upon Diaconx's bankruptcy, a dispute developed regarding the status of ITT's security interest vis-à-vis the Bank's. All the parties agreed that in April, 1984, the Bank had obtained a perfected security interest in the property of the debtor, including after-acquired inventory, and that ITT later had obtained a perfected purchase money security interest in certain inventory thereafter obtained by the debtor. They further agreed that ITT had given notice to the Bank of its security interest before Diaconx had received the property at issue here, but only after ITT had perfected the security interest by filing. Diaconx argued that ITT's failure to give notice of the lien claim to the Bank, prior to perfection, had subordinated ITT's security interest to that of the Bank. ITT responded that its providing notice prior to Diaconx's obtaining the relevant inventory had been sufficient to establish its priority over the Bank. Under Section 9–312, who had the better argument? (*In re Diaconx Corporation,* 79 Bankr. 602 [E.D. Pa. 1987].)

7. National Bank of Commerce of Mississippi (the Bank) perfected a purchase money security interest in a John Deere tractor purchased by Lexie Williams, Jr. in March, 1979, with a loan from the Bank. The Farmers Home Administration (FmHA) subsequently obtained a second lien on the tractor as security for a 1982 loan to Williams. On 9 March 1984, the Bank's 1979 financing statement expired without the Bank's having filed a continuation statement within six months before the statement had lapsed. When Williams defaulted on his loan with the Bank, the Bank repossessed the tractor and sold it. After retaining the amount due it on the loan, the Bank forwarded the remainder to the FmHA. The FmHA, however, contended that the Bank should have paid it the entire sales price because its lien had priority over the Bank's owing to the lapsed financing statement. The Bank argued that it had reperfected its purchase

money security interest (by possession) upon its repossessing of the tractor in 1986 and thus still enjoyed priority over the FmHA. Would this argument persuade a court to rule in the Bank's favor? (*In re Williams,* 82 Bankr. 430 [Bankr. N.D. Miss. 1988].)

8. On 3 August 1978, Citizens and Southern Bank (C&S) filed a financing statement covering all equipment, inventory, accounts receivable, chattel paper, instruments, proceeds, and all after-acquired property of its debtor Randall Helton d/b/a United TV. On 27 November 1978, Helton entered into an "inventory financing agreement" with Appliance Buyers Credit Corporation (ABCC) to finance the occasional acquisition of inventory from King's Appliance. On 24 November 1978, ABCC filed a financing statement listing itself as the secured party and Helton as the debtor and covering all television sets, stereos, radios, organs, pianos, and other equipment. On 1 December 1978, ABCC sent notification to C&S that it had or expected to acquire a purchase money security interest in Helton's inventory and described the inventory by item or type. ABCC eventually assigned the security interest in the inventory so financed to King's Appliance, which had shipped merchandise to Helton. When Helton defaulted on his obligations both to C&S and to King's Appliance, C&S took possession of all Helton's inventory and gave notice of its intention to sell the inventory to satisfy Helton's indebtedness to it. King's Appliance argued that as ABCC's assignee it held a perfected security interest in part of the inventory that was prior to that of C&S. C&S asked for and got a summary judgment on the ground that the UCC absolutely requires the purchase money secured party to give notification in writing to the holder of the conflicting security interest *before* the date on which the purchase money secured party files its financing statement. Would you agree with the court's interpretation of Section 9–312(3)(b)? (*King's Appliance & Electronics, Inc.* v. *Citizens & Southern Bank of Dublin,* 278 S.E.2d 733 [Ga. App. 1981].)

9. ITT Industrial Credit Company (ITT) had a perfected interest in a 1973 trencher (a large piece of equipment). The financing statement covering the trencher had been filed in the correct place. Under its terms, Hogan, the debtor, was to have paid for the trencher in full by September, 1977. Nothing in the financing statement indicated that the trencher might be used as security for future advances by ITT. In December, 1975, Hogan purchased a 1976 trencher with funds obtained from Union Bank and Trust Company (the Bank). He gave the Bank a security interest in the 1976 trencher and listed the 1973 trencher as additional collateral. The 1973 loan was paid on schedule in September, 1977, but ITT filed no termination statement on it. On 13 October 1977, Hogan purchased two trucks and trailers with a loan from ITT. ITT at that time retained a security interest in both the new equipment and the 1973 trencher, which it listed on the new separate agreement as "additional collateral." ITT

filed this new agreement on 19 October 1977. When Hogan ultimately defaulted on obligations owed to his creditors, ITT argued it had priority with regard to the 1973 trencher owing to the fact that the original financing statement was filed before the Bank had filed its interest in the 1973 trencher and the original financing statement had not yet expired at the time of its new loan. Was ITT right? (*ITT Industrial Credit Company* v. *Union Bank and Trust Company,* 615 S.W.2d 2 [Ky. App. 1981].)

10. Courtright first leased and then exercised an option to purchase from Dolsen a clarifier, a piece of equipment that treats waste from potato-processing plants. The clarifier sits in a steel tank twenty-four feet in diameter and is connected by pipes to the processing plant itself. It is embedded in a concrete slab, and the plant cannot be operated without the clarifier. The agreement that Dolsen and Courtright had signed in 1972 required the latter to lease the clarifier for sixty months at a monthly rental rate of $550. It also had contained an option whereby Courtright could purchase the clarifier at the end of the lease's term for $2500. Under the lease, Courtright had assumed the full responsibility for injury, damage, or destruction of the clarifier and had agreed to pay all taxes assessed against it. At the end of the lease, the clarifier would be worth $33,000. Dolsen had purchased the clarifier from Warden, another plant operator, but the clarifier had remained attached to Warden's potato-processing plant. In 1974, Warden had filed for bankruptcy and, in 1975, Cotten had bought Warden's plant. Cotten had searched all the available records and had discovered no notice of Courtright's or Dolsen's interest in the equipment. A Washington UCC provision stated that security interests in fixtures do not take priority over a subsequent bona fide purchaser for value of any interest in the real estate. In 1977, Courtright exercised its option and bought the clarifier from Dolsen. Courtright, claiming he was the true owner of the clarifier, sued Cotten for it. Who had superior ownership interest in the clarifier, Courtright or Cotten? (*Courtright Cattle Company* v. *Dolsen Company,* 619 P.2d 344 [Wash. 1980].)

Secured Transactions: Default

THE CODE AND DEFAULT

The previous chapters dealing with secured transactions considered the methods by which secured parties can protect their interests in the collateral. Neither the debtor nor the secured party, however, wants to speak the unspeakable: the possibility that the debtor will *default,* or fail to meet the obligations set out in the security agreement. Still, this unspeakable moment sometimes occurs.

The default of the debtor is a bittersweet moment for the secured party. On the one hand, default distresses the secured party because it reveals that the debtor may be unable or unwilling to pay the debt to the secured party. But on the other hand, the secured party has worked hard to preserve his or her status as one superior to an unsecured lender and as one who thus has rights to the collateral on default. In brief, Part 5 of Article 9 allows the secured party, on the debtor's default, to take possession of the collateral and to dispose of it in satisfaction of the secured party's claim. Yet, in so doing, the Code provides the debtor with certain protections and makes the secured party liable for any noncompliance with applicable Code provisions.

Interestingly, the Code does not define the term *default.* Basically, the parties decide what will constitute default, and the security agreement embodies these conclusions. Nonpayment by the debtor is perhaps the easiest definition of default. But as Figure 28.1 showed, default clauses are often broad and lengthy. Security agreements also often include acceleration clauses by which the secured party demands that all payments be made immediately. In the absence of bad faith and unconscionability, courts routinely uphold these clauses.

On default, the secured party may resort to various alternative remedies. Using non-Code remedies, the secured party may become a judgment creditor, may **garnish** the debtor's wages, or may **replevy** the goods. Code remedies include strict foreclosure (retention of the collateral in satisfaction of the debt) and resale of the collateral. In Section 9 – 501(1), the UCC further provides that non-Code and Code rights and remedies on default are cumulative. Yet it is clear that secured parties must be unsuccessful in enforcing their rights by one method before they can utilize another method against the debtor. Neither the Code nor case law sanctions an approach whereby a secured creditor may employ non-Code and Code remedies simultaneously against the debtor.

Garnish Receive assets of the debtor that are in the hands of a third party in order to satisfy a debt owed

Replevy Acquire possession of goods unlawfully held by another

The Code says that on default, secured parties may seek a court judgment, may **foreclose,** or may otherwise enforce the security agreement by any available judicial procedure.[1] Accordingly, secured parties can use their Code remedies of repossession and resale with the possibility of a deficiency judgment for which the debtor is liable, or they can follow the non-Code remedy of becoming judgment creditors by filing suit, obtaining a judgment, and having the sheriff use a **writ of execution** to levy on the goods and then sell them at a public sale. The proceeds of this sale are paid to the secured party. Another non-Code alternative to levying on the goods involves **garnishment** of a set percentage of the debtor's wages. Although there are certain advantages to following these non-Code remedies (in cases where the value of the collateral has decreased so far that the possibility of reaching assets beyond the collateral would be desirable), in practice most creditors elect the tidier and speedier remedies of repossession and resale that the UCC allows.

The following case involved a creditor who chose to pursue non-Code remedies.

NON-CODE REMEDIES

Foreclose Cut off an existing ownership right in property

Writ of execution A writing, issued by a court, enforcing a judgment or decree

Garnishment A legal proceeding in which assets of a debtor that are in the hands of a third person are ordered held by the third person or turned over to the creditor in full or partial satisfaction of the debt

---

Rug Mart, Inc. v. *Pellicci*
384 So.2d 1325 (Fla. Dist. Ct. App. 1980)

Rug Mart installed a carpet in the Pelliccis' new home and retained a security interest in the carpet. When the Pelliccis did not pay, Rug Mart sought to foreclose a me-

FACTS

---

[1] Uniform Commercial Code, Section 9 – 501(1).

chanic's lien on the home. The Pelliccis argued that Rug Mart's taking of a security interest in the carpet limited it to the remedies of a secured party under the Uniform Commercial Code.

ISSUE   Was Rug Mart entitled to pursue only Code remedies?

HOLDING   No. Rug Mart's remedies were not limited solely to those set out in the Code.

REASONING   Rug Mart could elect between Code and non-Code remedies such as foreclosures on liens. In choosing a non-Code remedy, however, Rug Mart had elected to treat the installed carpeting as realty and had abandoned its right to pursue contractual remedies under the written security agreement.

RIGHT OF REPOSSESSION

Unless already in possession of the collateral, a secured party has the right to take possession of the collateral upon the debtor's default. In so doing, that party may employ "self-help" measures; that is, secured parties can repossess the collateral themselves without judicial procedures *if* they can do so without breaching the peace.[2] Repossession carries with it inherent dangers, however. Besides risking possible tort liability if the repossession is not accomplished without a breach of the peace, the secured party also risks UCC liability[3] and the loss of the right to a deficiency judgment. Needless to say, this aspect of the Code has spawned numerous lawsuits. In general, the courts assess such factors as whether the secured party entered the debtor's home or driveway without permission and whether the debtor agreed to the repossession. Although it is difficult to make generalizations in this area, if the creditor repossesses an automobile from a public street and the debtor is not there to object to this procedure, most courts will hold there has been no breach of the peace. Nevertheless, in recent years, some questions have arisen as to the constitutionality of this "self-help" provision of the Code on the ground that repossession without notice to the debtor may deprive the debtor of due process rights.[4] Statutes authorizing replevin may be subject to the same constitutional argument.

The next case illustrates one court's disposition of this constitutional question.

Jefferds v. *Ellis*
522 N.Y.S.2d 398 (N.Y. App. Div. 1987)

FACTS   Jefferds had "leased" a tractor truck from Ellis under a "home drafted" agreement that had said nothing about default or Ellis's right of repossession. After Jefferds had

---

[2] Ibid., Section 9–503.
[3] Ibid., Section 9–507.
[4] Fuentes v. Shevin, 407 U.S. 67 (1972); Mitchell v. W. T. Grant Co., 416 U.S. 600 (1974).

paid nine monthly installments of $460.00 each without default, Ellis seized the vehicle in question without prior notice and without any judicial process. Ellis had seized the truck when the vehicle had been temporarily parked by Jefferds on the land of a third party with the keys left in the vehicle. Ellis's reasons for seizing the truck had been based on his subjective view that Jefferds had not been taking satisfactory care of it and that, as a result, the vehicle was becoming unsafe. When Jefferds sought the return of the truck, Ellis argued that Section 9–503 of the Code permitted self-help repossessions and that his actions were legal since the "lease" was actually a secured transaction and thus subject to the UCC's provisions.

Was Ellis's unilateral act of repossessing the truck under an agreement which had made no mention of repossession and which had occurred in circumstances in which the "lessee"/buyer was current with regard to payments owed permissible under the UCC and constitutional under New York law?   **ISSUE**

Yes. The court held that Section 9–503 was constitutional in the circumstances of this case.   **HOLDING**

The lower court had been incorrect in holding that the rights afforded to a secured party upon default under Section 9–503 unconstitutionally deprived Jefferds of his constitutional right to due process under the Constitution of the State of New York because he had not been given a judicial hearing prior to the repossession. No logical reason had been advanced as to why a repossession under a conditional sales contract, such as the one in this case, should be treated differently from repossession under a chattel mortgage pursuant to UCC Sections 9–503 and 9–504, the latter of which New York courts previously had determined to be constitutionally permissible. Hence, the holdings by New York courts, that peaceable self-help remedies by secured creditors do not involve "state action" but rather constitute private action not governed by the Fourteenth Amendment, were consonant with the holdings of the courts of many other states and clearly applied to the repossession of Jefferd's truck, as well.   **REASONING**

Besides repossession by self-help, the Code also sanctions the secured party's requiring the debtor to assemble the collateral at a reasonably convenient place to be designated by the secured party if the security agreement provides for this.[5] Moreover, when the collateral consists of heavy equipment that makes physical removal burdensome or expensive, the Code permits the secured party to render the equipment unusable and to dispose of the collateral on the debtor's premises, thus eliminating the need for physically removing the collateral.

These rules do not cover accounts and general intangibles, because one cannot possess purely intangible collateral. When the debtor is in default with regard to these types of collateral, the secured party may notify the person who is obligated on the intangibles to make payments directly to him or her. The

[5] Uniform Commercial Code, Section 9–503.

secured party may also take control of any proceeds to which he or she is entitled under the UCC.[6]

STRICT FORECLOSURE

After default and repossession, the secured party may decide *to retain the collateral in complete satisfaction of the debt.*[7] This remedy is called the secured party's right of *strict foreclosure.* Strict foreclosure may be attractive to the secured party for several reasons: (1) the value of the collateral may be approximately equal to the debt; (2) the expenses of court actions are avoided; (3) there can be no subsequent controversies about whether the resale price was fair; and (4) the UCC sets out matter-of-factly the requirements for effecting strict foreclosure.

However, to effect strict foreclosure, the secured party must comply with certain requirements, which include the following:

1. The secured party must send written notice of his or her intention to retain the collateral to
   a. the debtor, unless the debtor has signed *after* default a statement renouncing his or her right to force a sale of the collateral (in the case of consumer goods, no other notice need be sent);
   b. any other secured parties who have in writing notified the secured party who is foreclosing that they claim an interest in the collateral.
2. The secured party must wait twenty-one days after sending notice in order to receive objections in writing to the secured party's proposed retention of the collateral.[8]

If the secured party receives no such objections, he or she can utilize the remedy of strict foreclosure, but the secured party will thereby give up any claims to a deficiency judgment.

In contrast, strict foreclosure is not permissible in certain situations:

1. Whenever the secured party actually receives written objections from those entitled to notification within twenty-one days, the secured party must sell the collateral.
2. If the collateral consists of consumer goods and the debtor has paid 60 percent of the cash price of a purchase money security interest or 60 percent of the loan in all other cases, the secured party must sell the collateral unless the debtor has, *after* default, renounced in writing the right to require a sale of the collateral.[9]

---

[6] Ibid., Section 9–502.
[7] Ibid., Section 9–505(2).
[8] Ibid.
[9] Ibid., Section 9–505(1).

The policy behind this UCC provision recognizes the debtor's substantial equity in the collateral and the fact that resale may result in a surplus that would by right belong to the debtor. Therefore, in the absence of the debtor's renunciation of the right to demand resale, the secured party cannot retain the collateral. This section also contains penalties for noncompliance: when the secured party is obligated to sell the collateral, failure to do so within ninety days makes the secured party liable in either **conversion** or damages (under a statutory formula enumerated in the Code).[10]

Conversion The unauthorized and wrongful exercise of dominion and control over the personal property of another to the harm of that other person

RESALE OF REPOSSESSED COLLATERAL

On the other hand, the secured party may choose initially to satisfy the debtor's obligation by reselling, leasing, or otherwise disposing of the collateral.[11] In fact, secured parties use this remedy of foreclosure by sale much more frequently than strict foreclosure. The liberality of the Code's provision for resale allows the secured party to realize the highest resale price possible and at the same time to reduce the possibility of a deficiency judgment. In this way, both the secured party and the debtor benefit.

The sale may be either public or private, subject always to the requirement that the method, manner, time, place, and terms of such sale be commercially reasonable.[12] A public sale, or auction, is the more ordinary occurrence; but the Code encourages private sales when, as is often the case, a private sale through commercial channels will increase the chances for a higher resale price.

Secured parties must usually notify debtors of the time and place of any public or private sale. When the collateral consists of nonconsumer goods, foreclosing secured parties must in addition notify any other secured party who has notified them in writing of a claimed interest in the collateral. A secured party who claims an interest must notify the foreclosing secured party before the latter sends notification to the debtor or before the debtor renounces his or her rights. Thus, the burden is on the claimant secured parties to notify the foreclosing secured party of their interest before a corresponding duty to notify them of sale ever arises. In certain circumstances, the secured party may nonetheless dispense with notification if the collateral is perishable, threatens to decline speedily in value, or is of a type customarily sold on a recognized market.[13] The policy reason for notification stems from a belief that those who have an interest in the collateral — the debtor and **junior secured parties** — may want to bid on the collateral or send their friends to do so.

By the same token, a debtor may agree contractually to waive this required notice. The case that follows illustrates how a court may treat such a waiver.

Notice

Junior secured parties Any secured parties whose security interests are subordinate to that of the priority secured party

---

10 Ibid.
11 Ibid., Section 9–504.
12 Ibid., Section 9–504(3).
13 Ibid.

Van Bibber v. Norris
419 N.E.2d 115 (Ind. 1981)

FACTS   Norris sued Van Bibber and American Fletcher National Bank (AFNB) for damages for the wrongful repossession of his mobile home and the loss of its contents. One of the provisions in the security agreement Norris had signed allowed AFNB to accelerate the amount due and to repossess without notice on Norris's default. Norris argued that since AFNB had routinely accepted late payments without declaring a default, a duty had arisen to notify him of AFNB's intention to repossess.

ISSUE   Did AFNB have a duty to notify Norris of repossession despite the waiver of notice stated in the acceleration clause?

HOLDING   No. There was no such duty.

REASONING   A security agreement in general is to be enforced according to its terms. Hence, an agreement containing a nonwaiver and a nonmodification clause would give the secured party the right to take possession of the collateral without notice on default.

Commercially Reasonable Sale

A great deal of litigation has arisen from the Code provision stating that the sale itself must be commercially reasonable. According to the UCC, the fact that a better price might have been obtained at a different time or by a different method does not in itself make the sale commercially unreasonable. Similarly, sales in conformity with the commercial practices of dealers in the type of collateral sold or sales made in the usual manner on recognized markets demonstrate commercial reasonableness as well. Lastly, a court's approval of a sale or the sanctioning of a sale by a creditors' committee also makes the sale commercially reasonable.[14] In these cases, the debtor's arguing that the resale price is insufficient will not constitute grounds for a court's denying the secured party a deficiency judgment. But, in some circumstances, a court may deny a secured party its right to a deficiency judgment. The following case illustrates one such circumstance.

Liberty National Bank of Fremont v. Greiner
405 N.E.2d 317 (Ohio App. 1978)

FACTS   Liberty National Bank foreclosed by sale on eleven used trucks that Greiner had used to secure business loans from the bank when Greiner defaulted on these loans. Greiner argued that he should not be liable for the resultant deficiency judgment

[14] Ibid., Section 9–507(2).

because the bank had not carried out its disposition of the collateral in a commercially reasonable manner. Specifically, Greiner asserted that he had received insufficient notice of the sale.

Was the notice received by Greiner sufficient under UCC provisions relating to foreclosure by sale?   **ISSUE**

No. The notice was insufficient to satisfy the requirements of the Code.   **HOLDING**

The notice had not made clear what type of sale (public or private) was contemplated and had specified the site of the sale only as Fremont, Ohio. In addition, it had not specified the time of the sale. This lack of precision thus had not constituted notice to Greiner of the time, place, and date of sale. Consequently, even though the other aspects of the sale had met the requirement of commercial reasonableness, the absence of effective notice precluded the bank's obtaining a deficiency judgment.   **REASONING**

The Code even sets out the order for applying the proceeds of the sale.[15] According to the Code, the secured party must apply the proceeds realized from the disposition of the collateral in this order: Proceeds

1. payment of the reasonable expenses of retaking and disposing of the collateral, including reasonable attorneys' fees if provided by the security agreement
2. satisfaction of the debt owed to the secured party
3. payment of remaining proceeds to eligible junior secured parties in the same collateral
4. payment to the debtor of any surplus, and corresponding liability on the debtor's part for any deficiency, unless the parties have otherwise agreed

It is nevertheless possible that no sale will ever occur because the debtor has the right to redeem the collateral at any time before the secured party has disposed of it. *Redemption* consists of the debtor's extinguishing the secured party's security interest by tendering payment of all obligations due, including expenses incurred by the secured party in retaking and preparing the collateral for disposition (usually resale) and in arranging for the resale. Such expenses may also include attorneys' fees and legal expenses. A debtor who can accomplish redemption before sale or strict foreclosure can retain the collateral. This fact notwithstanding, a debtor may, after default, agree to waive the right to redeem.[16] The debtor presumably could not waive such rights in the original security agreement; rather, default must precede such waivers.   **DEBTORS' RIGHTS**

[15] Ibid., Section 9–504(1),(2).
[16] Ibid., Section 9–501(3), 9–506.

SECURED PARTIES' DUTIES

Besides having to observe the previously mentioned duties regarding disposition of the collateral, secured parties also have the duty of taking reasonable care of the collateral while it is in their possession—either before or after default. They are liable for any losses caused by their failure to meet this obligation, but they do not lose their security interests if such a loss occurs.[17] Unless the parties have otherwise agreed, the secured party can charge to the debtor payment of reasonable expenses, such as insurance and taxes, incurred in the custody, preservation, or use of the collateral. Moreover, the Code places the risk of accidental loss or damage on the debtor to the extent of any deficiency in insurance coverage. The secured party may also hold as additional security any increase or profits (except money) received from the collateral, but the secured party should either turn over any money so received to the debtor or apply it to reduce the secured obligation. There is a duty to keep the collateral identifiable except for **fungible** collateral that may be commingled. Lastly, the secured party may either repledge the collateral on terms that do not violate the debtor's right to redeem it or use the collateral if this will help to preserve it or its value (for example, in an ongoing business, the operation of equipment that has been given as security).[18]

Fungible Virtually identical; interchangeable; descriptive of things that belong to a class and that are not identifiable individually

Once the expenses of holding the collateral have been defrayed, as mentioned, the secured party must turn over any remaining proceeds to the debtor. On the other hand, the debtor remains liable for any deficiency—the difference between the available proceeds and the amount of indebtedness and expenses that remain—unless the parties have agreed otherwise or state law eliminates this obligation.[19]

Debtors sometimes try to argue that the amount received from the sale of the collateral (the usual basis for computing deficiencies or surpluses), if lower than the collateral's market value, makes the sale commercially unreasonable. But courts ordinarily do not respond favorably to such arguments as long as fraud is not present and the secured party has attempted in good faith to attract buyers. Similarly, these arguments will generally not affect the rights of the purchaser at the sale: the purchaser takes the collateral free and clear of such claims if the purchase is made in good faith.[20]

However, a secured party's failure to comply with the duties regarding disposition of the collateral may subject the secured party to statutory liability under Section 9–507 for losses by debtors or junior secured parties and, if consumer goods are involved, to a damages formula that sets up a statutory penalty. As we saw in the *Liberty National Bank of Fremont* v. *Greiner* case, some courts will also deny the secured party the right to a deficiency judgment as a consequence of noncompliance or misbehavior.

[17] Ibid., Section 9–207(3).
[18] Ibid., Section 9–207(2).
[19] Ibid., Section 9–504(2).
[20] Ibid., Section 9–504(4).

When a debtor defaults, the secured party may pursue either non-Code or Code remedies. Under the Code, the secured party may take possession of the collateral and either retain it in complete satisfaction of the debt (strict foreclosure) or dispose of it by public or private sale (foreclosure by sale). In either case, notification of the debtor and perhaps other parties as well must take place if the secured party is to escape Code liability. The secured party's right of strict foreclosure may be limited by such things as the debtor's paying 60 percent of the price of collateral consisting of consumer goods.

If a sale is undertaken, it must be conducted in a commercially reasonable manner. The Code also enumerates the order in which the proceeds of a sale should be applied, assuming a sale has occurred. However, the debtor may cut off the secured party's right to foreclosure by sale or strict foreclosure by redeeming the collateral before the secured party disposes of it by resale or retention. When the secured party is in possession of the collateral either before or after default, the party must take reasonable care of the collateral. Failure to live up to this and other duties subjects the secured party to liability for any losses caused thereby, to possible damages under a statutory formula, and to possible denial of the right to a deficiency judgment. By the same token, debtors ordinarily are liable for any deficiency that still remains after the sale or other disposition of the collateral.

SUMMARY

DISCUSSION QUESTIONS

1. What is default?
2. What kinds of non-Code remedies can the secured party pursue?
3. Describe fully the UCC's treatment of the right of repossession.
4. Explain the requirements necessary for effecting strict foreclosure.
5. Name the situations in which strict foreclosure is not permissible.
6. Discuss the rules relating to foreclosure by sale or resale of the repossessed collateral.
7. How can one tell whether a sale has been conducted in a "commercially reasonable" manner?
8. Enumerate the order in which proceeds are applied after a sale.
9. What is redemption?
10. List the secured party's duties of reasonable care of the collateral and the liabilities that may result from a secured party's failure to observe his or her applicable duties.

CASE PROBLEMS

1. Schmode's, Inc. (Schmode's), sold to Harco Leasing Company (Harco) a 1978 International tractor truck and a 1970 Hobbs trailer. Harco and the Wilkinsons entered into a conditional sales agreement with respect to the truck and the trailer. Schmode's guaranteed to Harco that if the Wilkinsons defaulted on their obligations so as to result in Harco's reclaiming the

truck and trailer from the Wilkinsons, that Schmode's would repurchase them from Harco. The Wilkinsons defaulted and on 19 December 1979 they delivered the truck and trailer to Schmode's. Schmode's repaired the collateral and tried to sell it. When these efforts failed, Schmode's began leasing it to others through mid-April of 1983, during which time the collateral was operated a minimum of 204,000 miles. Schmode's honored its agreement with Harco and paid the sum due Harco from the Wilkinsons. The collateral was publicly sold on 28 April 1983. The Wilkinsons argued that Schmode's retention and use of the collateral for almost three years amounted to strict foreclosure and that the Wilkinsons therefore could not be held liable for any deficiency judgment. Were the Wilkinsons correct? (*Schmode's, Inc.* v. *Wilkinson,* 361 N.W. 2d 557 [Neb. 1985].)

2. First National Bank of Pulaski, Tennessee (First National), was the secured creditor of Gary and Katie Jones. When the Joneses became unable to make the payments on their loan, First National repossessed the farm equipment that the Joneses had used as security for their indebtedness and sold the property at a sale. The Joneses argued that First National's sale had violated Section 9–504 because First National's notification to the Joneses of the sale a few days prior to it had been oral. Must a secured party give written notice of the sale in order to comply with the Code's resale provision? (*Jones* v. *First National Bank of Pulaski,* 505 So.2d 352 [Ala. 1987].)

3. Jackson County Bank was a secured party for Vinson Ford's purchase of cars. Ford Motor Credit Company (Ford Credit) also held a security interest in some of Vinson's cars. After several checks from Vinson Ford had been returned for insufficient funds, Ford Credit, during a meeting with bank representatives, orally advised the bank that it planned to dispose of some of the cars by selling them as soon as possible to some Ford dealers. No specific dates were mentioned, and no written notice of any intent to sell was sent to the bank. When the bank argued that Ford Credit had not conducted the sales in a commercially reasonable manner, Ford Credit's defense was that the sale was in a recognized market, and therefore no notice was needed. Who was correct? (*Jackson County Bank* v. *Ford Motor Credit Company,* 488 F. Supp. 1001 [M.D. Tenn. 1980], vacated and remanded, 698 F.2d 1220 [M.D. Tenn. 1982].)

4. The Backeses sold a restaurant to the Carlisles and the Martins, who began business as Village Corner, Inc., in July, 1984. By December, 1984, the debtors had ceased making payments; and by 1 February 1985, they had defaulted on the promissory note they had signed with the Backeses. On March 29 the Backeses took possession of the premises; and on April 1 they sold the collateral to new tenants without notifying the Carlisles and Martins of the sale. The Backeses argued that the sale fell within one of the exceptions to the Code's notice requirement, since on March 29 they

had had only two options: to sell the collateral to the new tenant for whatever the new tenant offered, or to remove the collateral and sell it for a possibly lesser amount. At that point, the Backeses asserted, they had been confronted with a take-it-or-leave-it proposition. Because the new tenant had planned to move in on April 1, they contended, there had been insufficient time for notice. Thus, because the property had threatened to decline speedily in value, the Backeses had justifiably dispensed with notice to the Carlisles and Martins. Should a court accept this argument? (*Backes* v. *Village Corner, Inc.,* 242 Cal. Rptr. 716 [Cal. App. 1987].)

5. Would a secured creditor be guilty of breaching the peace and therefore illegally repossessing a vehicle if it had unauthorizedly entered the driveway of the debtor's residence to remove the vehicle? Would a repossession be illegal if the secured party had broken into the debtor's place of business and replaced the locks with new ones? (*Butler* v. *Ford Motor Credit Company,* 829 F.2d 568 [5th Cir. 1987] and *Riley State Bank of Riley* v. *Spillman,* 750 P.2d 1024 [Kan. 1988].)

6. The Wipperts operated a cattle ranch east of Browning, Montana, on the Blackfeet Indian Reservation. The Wipperts had borrowed $44,729.97 from the Blackfeet Tribal Credit Program and had used "all cattle now owned or hereafter owned by [them]" as collateral for the loan. When the Wipperts defaulted, the tribe informed them by letter that it planned to sell the collateral. However, the letter said nothing about the time and place of the proposed sale, even though the security agreement between the Wipperts and the tribe had required the tribe to give the Wipperts five days' prior written notice of the time and place of the sale. The cattle were sold at public auction, leaving a deficiency of $17,698. The Wipperts maintained that the tribe's failure to give them notice as required by the security agreement and Montana's UCC statute precluded the tribe's receiving a deficiency judgment. The tribe argued that since this collateral was of a type customarily sold on a recognized market, i.e., cattle sold at auction, notice of sale was not required. Who had the better argument? (*Wippert* v. *Blackfeet Tribe,* 695 P.2d 461 [Mont. 1985].)

7. Toomey had sold farming equipment to Bohannon under a purchase money security agreement and had retained a security interest in the equipment. Toomey immediately had assigned the agreement to CCEC for value. Bohannon was to make all payments to CCEC. Under the agreement between Toomey and CCEC, Toomey was to purchase the equipment from CCEC if Bohannon should happen to default. Toomey would then sue Bohannon for any deficiency that Toomey had suffered. Bohannon defaulted, and CCEC repossessed the equipment; but CCEC failed to inform Toomey of Bohannon's death in time for Toomey to enter a claim against the Bohannon estate. When CCEC sued Toomey for its deficiency, Toomey defended that CCEC had failed to protect his rights against prior

parties, and that he was therefore not liable to CCEC. Who was correct? (*Toomey Equipment Company, Inc.* v. *Commercial Credit Equipment Corporation,* 386 So.2d 1155 [Ala. Civ. App. 1980].)

8. Burk sold 950 steers to Emmick Cattle Company. Burk agreed to accept a draft drawn on Northwest Bank for the purchase of the cattle when the bank told Burk (orally) that the funds were available to cover the draft. Burk delivered the cattle to Emmick, but the bank refused to honor the draft. Burk then reclaimed the cattle and sold them, but for less than Emmick was to have paid. Burk later sued Emmick for the deficiency. Emmick argued that once Burk had reclaimed the cattle, he could no longer sue for any deficiency. Was reclamation the only remedy Burk could pursue? (*Burk* v. *Emmick,* 637 F.2d 1172 [8th Cir. 1980].)

9. Ford Motor Credit Company (FMCC) was the floor plan inventory financier for Suburban Ford. The security agreement between the parties permitted FMCC to take immediate possession of the collateral without legal process upon Suburban's default. As a result of an audit on 11 March 1981, FMCC realized Suburban Ford was in default and demanded payment. The business closed on 13 March 1981. The owners of Suburban Ford argued that FMCC was liable to them in tort because FMCC's actions had caused the collapse of the agency. They also contended that the sale of the cars had not been commercially reasonable, since FMCC had sold the cars in bulk rather than leaving the vehicles with the dealership, which could have sold them at retail for higher prices. Were Suburban Ford's contentions persuasive? (*Ford Motor Credit Company* v. *Suburban Ford,* 699 P.2d 992, cert. denied, 474 U.S. 995 [1985].)

10. United Missouri Bank of Kirkwood (the Bank) loaned David Goodman $7,306.03 for the purchase of a Ford van and retained a security interest in the van. The Bank repossessed the van on 5 December 1980 when Goodman had become two months behind in his payments. On December 8, the Bank notified Mann that he would have ten days to redeem the collateral or it would be offered for sale. Goodman also was informed he could redeem the van any time prior to the actual disposition. The approximate amount in question was $2,078.77. The Bank advertised the sale on 17 December 1980 and, on December 22, received a written bid for $1,200.00, which was later accepted. Other lower bids were received and rejected. The buyer took possession on either December 22 or 5 or 6 January 1981, and after the first application was denied, owing to technical deficiencies, a repossession title was issued on January 28. Goodman also advertised the van for sale at $3,200.00, a price at which he received some inquiries but no offers. On 21 January 1981, Goodman's attorney attempted to redeem the collateral but, since the van had already been sold, was refused. Goodman argued the Bank had converted the van in selling the van and refusing Goodman's offer to redeem the van. Would you agree? (*Mann* v. *United Missouri Bank of Kirkwood,* 689 S.W.2d 830 [Mo. App. 1985].)

CHAPTER 31

Straight Bankruptcy

HISTORIC BACKGROUND

When the colonists broke away from England to set up the United States of America, they had a strong desire to avoid problems that they had encountered under the English system of government. The United States Constitution and the Bill of Rights were drafted specifically to prevent some of these problems. One problem area was the treatment of debtors.

In England, persons unable or unwilling to pay their debts were very commonly thrown into debtors' prison. Once in prison, a debtor might remain there for years waiting for friends or family to raise funds to repay the debt or until the creditors agreed to the debtor's release. Less commonly, the debtor would agree to some form of indentured servitude. Under such an agreement, the debtor had to work for a preset number of years at little or no salary to repay the debt.

To prevent such treatment of debtors in this country, the founding fathers made provisions in the Constitution for bankruptcy. Article I, Section 8, of the United States Constitution says: "The Congress shall have the Power . . . to establish . . . uniform Laws on the subject of Bankruptcies throughout the United States."

For much of the history of the United States, there has been some form of federal bankruptcy regulation. Although the Constitution seemingly calls for exclusive federal control of this area, the bankruptcy laws have tended to coexist with state law in many areas. In fact, state law is often used to define problems or to provide solutions to bankruptcy problems.

Until very recently, bankruptcy was governed by the federal Bankruptcy Act, enacted in 1898. This act was quite technical, and many people found it confusing. In 1978, Congress passed a new law, the Bankruptcy Reform Act, which took effect 1 October 1979. The Bankruptcy Reform Act had two major purposes. It was designed to provide for fair and equitable treatment of the creditors in the distribution of the debtor's property. But, more important, it was designed to give an "honest debtor" a "fresh start."

Unfortunately, the Bankruptcy Reform Act had some technical problems (discussed below) that resulted in its being declared unconstitutional. As a result, the Bankruptcy Amendments and Federal Judgeship Act of 1984[1] was enacted. This new act was intended to clarify the jurisdiction of the bankruptcy courts and to resolve the constitutional problems presented by the Bankruptcy Reform Act. At the same time, Congress made the new bankruptcy coverage more sensitive to the needs of the creditors and made some effort to reduce or eliminate the problem of debtor abuses of the former bankruptcy laws.

THE BANKRUPTCY REFORM ACT

Adjunct Added or joined to another

The Bankruptcy Reform Act called for a whole new adjudicative system of bankruptcies. Under the act, each United States district court was to contain a separate, **adjunct** bankruptcy court. These bankruptcy courts were to be staffed by bankruptcy *judges,* each of whom was to serve a fourteen-year term. The bankruptcy judges were to be appointed by the president, subject to approval by the Senate. It was hoped that this new system, which replaced the "referees" acting through the district courts, would simplify and speed up bankruptcy proceedings.

The new bankruptcy court–bankruptcy judge system encountered a major roadblock when, on 28 June 1982, the United States Supreme Court declared it unconstitutional. As a result, the entire area of bankruptcy jurisdiction was in doubt. The case that raised the challenge to the Bankruptcy Reform Act involved the Northern Pipeline Company, which filed a petition in bankruptcy in January, 1980. As a part of the petition, Northern Pipeline sued Marathon Pipe Line Company for breach of contract in the bankruptcy court. Marathon sought dismissal of the suit on the basis of the unconstitutional nature of the bankruptcy courts established by the Bankruptcy Reform Act.

The United States Supreme Court handed down its opinion in the *Northern*

---

[1] P.L. 98–353.

Pipeline Construction Co. v. *Marathon Pipe Line Co.*[2] case on 28 June 1982. This opinion totally confused the validity of the Bankruptcy Reform Act. Article III of the Constitution requires that the judicial power of the United States must be exercised by judges who have life tenure during good behavior and who are not subject to salary diminution. Bankruptcy judges, established by Congress under Article I powers, lacked both of these protections. They were to serve for fourteen years, not for life; and their salaries were to be set by statute, subject to adjustment. The Court also ruled that Congress had improperly given the bankruptcy courts too much power, allowing them to exercise jurisdiction over *all matters* arising under bankruptcy laws; bankruptcy courts may not exercise Article III powers over constitutional or state-created areas of law.

The Supreme Court granted Congress an extension to 4 October 1982 to reconstitute the bankruptcy courts or to limit their jurisdiction. Congress did not react to the Court's opinion by the deadline, but President Reagan requested an additional extension to 24 December 1982 so the matter could be studied further. This deadline also passed with no solution presented by Congress.

For nearly two years, Congress did nothing to resolve the problem. During this period the bankruptcy courts continued to operate under an "emergency rule" suggested by the Judicial Conference of the United States and accepted by the United States Courts of Appeals. This emergency rule, approved in some form by nearly all of the U.S. District Courts, allowed the bankruptcy courts to hear all bankruptcy cases in their entirety unless one of the parties to the action requested the District Court to remove the case due to improper jurisdiction. The orders of the bankruptcy court could be appealed to the District Courts, and the District Courts, at their discretion, could either accept the findings of the bankruptcy court or hold a new hearing on the matter.

Thus the Bankruptcy Reform Act was implemented under this emergency rule until Congress finally moved to resolve the problems presented by the opinion in *Northern Pipeline.* Since the substantive aspects of the Bankruptcy Reform Act had not been challenged in that opinion, they were still followed under the emergency rules.

The act has four major operative sections, called chapters. These chapters are Chapter 7, "Liquidation"; Chapter 9, "Adjustment of Debts of a Municipality"; Chapter 11, "Reorganization"; and Chapter 13, "Adjustments of Debts of an Individual with Regular Income." In a Chapter 7 proceeding, the debtor's **nonexempt assets** are sold, the proceeds are distributed to the creditors, and a discharge is normally granted. Under Chapters 9, 11, and 13, the debtor *restructures* and *rearranges* things so that the creditors will (normally) be paid in full. In this chapter, we will examine a straight bankruptcy proceeding — that is, a Chapter 7 liquidation. In the next chapter, we will look at other bankruptcy proceedings available under Chapters 11 and 13 and at alternatives to bankruptcy.

Nonexempt assets
Those assets available under the law for the payment and satisfaction of the debtor's creditors

[2] 458 U.S. 50 (1982).

BANKRUPTCY AMENDMENTS AND FEDERAL JUDGESHIP ACT OF 1984

President Reagan signed the Bankruptcy Amendments and Federal Judgeship Act of 1984 into law 10 July 1984. This act addresses the problems presented by *Northern Pipeline* by restructuring and redefining the bankruptcy court system and its jurisdiction. In addition, it makes a number of substantive changes to the Bankruptcy Reform Act and its coverage.

Under the new law, bankruptcy judges are still to be appointed for a term of fourteen years at an (initial) salary of $66,100* per year. (Since the tenure and the salary are both established by statute and are subject to changes by the legislature, the bankruptcy judges are still not Article III judges, the original problem addressed by the court in *Northern Pipeline*.) The appointments are to be made by the U.S. Court of Appeals in which the District Court is located. These appointments are to be made from a slate of nominees recommended to the Circuit Court by the judicial councils of each circuit. Only persons who apply to the judicial council for a judgeship may be considered for recommendation by the Court of Appeals. The judicial council is to submit a list of three nominees for each judgeship. The Court of Appeals will then either select one of the nominees or reject all of them and request a new submission.

Since these new bankruptcy judges are not Article III judges, the bankruptcy courts will have limited jurisdiction under the new law. The 1984 Amendments grant exclusive and original jurisdiction in all bankruptcy matters to the U.S. District Court. The District Court *may* then refer any or all such cases to the bankruptcy court for adjudication. However, after referral to the bankruptcy court, the case may be withdrawn by the District Court, either on its own motion or on the motion of any party to the proceedings, "for cause shown." Since the law is so new, the final determination of the jurisdiction to be exercised by these new bankruptcy courts is unknown. Additionally, the meaning of "for cause shown" will need to be defined by the courts in a number of cases before the limits imposed by that phrase are known. It will probably be several years before the parameters have been established and the new court system is fully understood.

STRAIGHT BANKRUPTCY

To many people, the term *bankruptcy* means just one thing — a *liquidation of the debtor's assets in order to obtain a discharge from debts.* This form of bankruptcy carries some very negative connotations to a great many people. These people view a *straight* bankruptcy — or a Chapter 7 proceeding — as an admission of failure. Rather than viewing this as a "fresh start" for an "honest debtor," they feel that it is a "cop-out" by a "deadbeat." However, times are changing. More and more people are beginning to realize that a liquidation is a financial and legal option designed to help a person who has been flooded by debt. The stigma of failure is being removed, and the number of Chapter 7 proceedings is increasing annually. There are two types of Chapter 7 bankruptcies: voluntary and involuntary.

Any person, firm, or corporation may file a voluntary bankruptcy petition, with *five* exceptions:

1. railroads
2. government units
3. banks
4. savings and loan associations
5. insurance companies

The debtor who files a voluntary petition does not even need to be **insolvent.** If a debtor desires to eliminate the debts, the debtor can file the petition, consent to the court's jurisdiction, and receive a discharge. In theory, a debtor with $1 million in cash and *total* debts of $250 could file for bankruptcy. In practice, such an event is extremely unlikely.

Insolvent The condition of being unable to pay one's debts; lacking the means or property to pay one's debts

The 1984 Bankruptcy Amendments have made one major substantive change in this area. Prior to the 1984 Act, bankruptcy was viewed as a *right* of the debtor, and the *needs* of the debtor were not considered by the court. As a result, a number of debtors were apparently abusing the bankruptcy system, using Chapter 7 proceedings to eliminate unsecured debts they could have repaid in full.[3] The new law permits the bankruptcy judge to hold a hearing designed to determine the need of the debtor for the relief being sought. If the judge feels that granting the relief would be a "substantial abuse" of Chapter 7, the petition is dismissed.

In addition, the new law requires that all debtors be made aware of the alternative provisions of Chapter 13 repayment plans before they are allowed to file a Chapter 7 petition. By so doing, it is hoped that more debtors will elect a repayment plan rather than a liquidation procedure. This will work to the benefit of the creditors, and may also help a number of debtors by allowing them to retain more of their assets than they would under a Chapter 7 liquidation.

Often a debtor will get deeply in debt and try to avoid bankruptcy. When this happens, the creditors will frequently decide to petition the debtor into bankruptcy against his will. They do so by initiating an involuntary bankruptcy proceeding.

An *involuntary* petition may be filed against any person, firm, or corporation that meets certain criteria, with *seven* exceptions:

1. the *five* debtors who may *not* file a voluntary petition (see above)
2. farmers
3. charitable corporations

---

[3] *Monograph #23, Consumer Bankruptcy Study; Consumers' Right to Bankruptcy,* Credit Research Center, 1982.

A *farmer* is defined as an individual who received more than 80 percent of gross income in the prior year from the operation of a farm that he or she owns and operates.

If a debtor does not fall within one of these exceptions, the debtor is potentially subject to an involuntary petition. The vast majority of debtors in this country do not fit into one of these exceptions. However, the creditors who file the petition must show that all the criteria are satisfied before they may file. There are three criteria: one related to conduct, one to numbers, and one to debt.

Conduct

Creditors must allege, and prove, that the debtor is "guilty" of one of two acts: either the debtor is not paying debts as they become due, *or* the debtor appointed a receiver or made a general assignment for the benefit of the creditors within the 120 days that preceded the filing of the petition. Under the latter test, the receiver or assignee must have taken possession of the debtor's property.

Number

The proper number of creditors for the particular debtor must join in the petition. If the debtor has a *total* of twelve creditors or more, *at least* three of them must sign the petition. If the debtor has fewer than twelve creditors, one or more creditors must file.

Debt

Contingent Possible, but not assured; doubtful or uncertain; dependent on the occurrence of some future event that is itself uncertain or questionable

The creditors who file the petition must have an aggregate claim against the debtor of *at least* $5000 that is neither secured nor **contingent.** A debtor with less than $5000 in general unsecured debts may not be involuntarily petitioned into bankruptcy.

The following example shows one problem that petitioning creditors may face.

Bob has seven creditors. He has made no payments for four months to any of them. He owes Ralph, one of the creditors, $6000. Ralph has $2000 in collateral. Unless another creditor, with at least $1000 in unsecured debt, will join Ralph on a petition, Ralph cannot institute an involuntary petition.

If a debtor is involuntarily petitioned into bankruptcy, the debtor may deny that he is bankrupt and request a trial. A debtor who wins a trial can collect damages from the creditors who signed the petition.

Once a petition is filed, the judge will issue an **order for relief** (unless the debtor files an answer denying bankruptcy and demands a trial). At this point, the proceeding is in motion, and it will continue until the final orders are entered. Upon entering the order for relief, the judge promptly appoints an *interim trustee.* The interim trustee takes possession of the debtor's property until a permanent trustee can be selected.

The filing of a petition in bankruptcy operates as an *automatic stay* against creditors who are involved in any legal actions against the debtor. The creditors must suspend any legal actions already commenced, and must delay filing any new actions, pending the outcome of the bankruptcy proceedings. Similarly, the creditors may not initiate any repossession actions against the assets of the debtor. This automatic stay provision is designed to ensure that all the creditors are afforded equitable treatment under the bankruptcy proceedings by preventing any one creditor from gaining an advantage through his actions at the expense of the other creditors.

The court will call for a meeting of the creditors within a reasonable time of the order for relief. The debtor, the interim trustee, and the creditors — but not the judge — will all attend this meeting. The debtor is expected to submit to an examination by the creditors concerning the debtor's assets, liabilities, and anything else the creditors feel is important. Although the debtor may not like it, it is best to cooperate fully: a refusal to cooperate may result in a denial of **discharge.** The creditors may also elect a permanent trustee at this meeting. If no trustee is elected, the interim trustee becomes the permanent trustee by court appointment.

The permanent trustee is the key figure in the bankruptcy proceeding. The trustee is the representative of the *debtor's* estate, and the trustee will attempt to preserve this estate to protect the interests of the *unsecured creditors.* The estate that the trustee preserves is made up of all the property the debtor has when the case is begun and any property the debtor acquires within the 180 days following the petition-filing date. The trustee must gather all of these assets, liquidate the *nonexempt* assets, and generally handle the creditors' claims. The trustee also raises objections to the granting of a discharge if the debtor gives cause to do so. The trustee may be helped by a *creditors' committee,* a group of at least three and at most eleven unsecured creditors who consult with the trustee as needed.

The debtor has certain duties to perform, as well. The debtor must file a relatively detailed series of schedules that are intended to reveal his or her financial position so that the bankruptcy court can properly evaluate the need for relief, and so that the interests of the various creditors can be protected. The debtor must provide a list of creditors, both secured and unsecured, the address of each creditor, and the amount of debt owed to each. The debtor must also provide a schedule of his financial affairs and a listing of all property owned, even if that property will be claimed as an exempt asset. Finally, the debtor must provide a list of current income and expenses. This list may well show that the debtor should be in a Chapter 13 repayment plan rather than a Chap-

**THE
BANKRUPTCY
PROCEEDING**

Order for relief A transferral of jurisdiction over the debtor's estate to the bankruptcy court

Discharge The release of the debtor from the obligation of all debts that were proved in the proceedings so that they are no longer a charge against the debtor

ter 7 liquidation proceeding. If it does, the court may, on its own motion, dismiss the Chapter 7 proceeding following a hearing, and can then encourage the debtor to refile under Chapter 13. However, the law also carries with it a presumption in favor of the debtor. The debtor is presumed to be entitled to receive the order of relief for whatever chapter was chosen by the debtor. The schedules are to be prepared by the debtor under oath and signed. Knowingly submitting false information in these schedules is a crime under the bankruptcy law.

The debtor also must cooperate fully with the trustee and surrender all property to the trustee. Finally, the debtor must attend any and all hearings and comply with all orders of the court. If this is done, a discharge will normally result.

The debtor can also *exempt* some assets from the trustee's liquidation. This exemption is, surprisingly, governed by *state* statutes. If state law permits, the debtor may elect to take either the state exemptions or the federal exemptions. If no such choice is allowed by state law, the debtor must take the state exemptions. Under no circumstances may the debtor take both sets of exemptions.

Over thirty states have elected the override provision, requiring the debtor to take the state exemptions. And even if the debtor is in a state that allows the choice of either the federal or the state exemptions, another limitation has been imposed by the 1984 Amendments. In a joint filing, both the husband and the wife must select the same exemptions — either state or federal. They will no longer be allowed to select the exemptions individually, which allowed one to take the federal exemptions while the other took the state exemptions.

The Bankruptcy Reform Act exempts the following property from the proceeding:

1. equity in the debtor's home of up to $7500

2. if there is no equity in the home or if the equity is less than $7500, the unused portion of the $7500 in a joint petition or $3750 in an individual petition

3. equity in one automobile of up to $1200

4. household goods and clothing, up to $200 per item and up to $4000 aggregate

5. jewelry up to $500

6. tools of the debtor's trade, including books, up to $750

7. any unmatured life insurance policies owned by the debtor

The act also permits a debtor to convert goods from nonexempt classes to exempt classes before filing the bankruptcy petition. And if there is a lien on, or security interest attached to, otherwise exempt property, the debtor can redeem it — which automatically exempts it — by paying off the lien-holding creditor.

Once the permanent trustee has assumed control of the estate and the exempt property has been removed from the estate, the serious business of bankruptcy begins. Those claims of creditors that are *allowable* must be filed. Only allowable debts may participate in the distribution of the estate. Allowable claims may be filed by the debtor, by the creditor, or even by the trustee. But they *must* be filed within six months of the first creditors' meeting.

Nearly every debt that existed before the order for relief will be allowable. There are four major exceptions to this statement. The following four debts are not allowable, or at least are not *fully* allowable:

1. claims that would be unenforceable against the debtor, such as contracts based on fraud or duress
2. claims for interest that are figured beyond the petition date, since interest may no longer accrue once a petition is filed
3. damages based on a lease violation or termination, to some extent (the landlord can prove a debt only up to the greater of one year's rent *or* 15 percent of the balance of the lease [with a 3-year maximum] plus any unpaid rent already due and payable)
4. damages based on breach of an employment contract, if those damages *exceed* one year's compensation, plus unpaid wages due and payable

The following example shows how allowable claims are used.

Nancy filed a voluntary bankruptcy petition on August 1. At that time, she was three months behind on her rent, and she still had ten years remaining on her lease. She was also two weeks behind on her payroll. Both of her employees had two years remaining on their employment contracts.

Nancy's landlord can assert a claim only for twenty-one months of rent (three months already due plus 15 percent of ten years remaining on the lease, or eighteen months). Each of Nancy's employees can claim only fifty-four weeks of wages (two weeks already earned plus one year — or fifty-two weeks — for breach of the employment contract).

The landlord's claim for the other eight and a half years and each employee's claim for the other year will not be allowed.

While administering a debtor's estate, a trustee may discover that the debtor committed certain improper actions. A trustee who discovers such conduct is obligated to recover the transferred property for the benefit of the unsecured

Allowable Claims

Recovery of Property

creditor. These improper acts fall into two major categories: *voidable preferences* and *fraudulent conveyances.*

Voidable Preferences

A *voidable preference* is a *payment made by a debtor to one or a few creditors at the expense of the other creditors in that particular creditor class.* This is not as complicated as it may seem at first glance.

A transfer is deemed a *preference,* and therefore voidable, if all the following five conditions are met:

1. The transfer benefits a creditor.
2. The transfer covers a preexisting debt.
3. The debtor is insolvent at the time of the transfer. (A debtor is *presumed* to be insolvent during the ninety days preceding the date of the petition; this presumption is rebuttable by the debtor.)
4. The transfer is made during the ninety days preceding the petition date.
5. The transfer gave the creditor who received it a greater percentage of the creditor's claim than fellow creditors will receive as a result of the transfer.

A transfer is not deemed a preference if it fits *any* one of the following tests:

1. The transfer is for a new obligation, as opposed to a preexisting debt.
2. The transfer is made in the ordinary course of business.
3. The transfer involves a purchase money security interest (see Chapter 28).
4. The transfer is a payment on a *fully* secured claim.
5. The transfer is for normal payments made to creditors within ninety days prior to the petition, if the payments *total* less than $600 per creditor.

The following case illustrates the importance of timing in bankruptcy proceedings.

Matter of Duffy
3 B.R. 263 (1980)

FACTS   Duffy entered a long-term lease agreement with Avis Rent-a-Car but made no rental payments until 30 July 1979. On July 30, Duffy sent Avis a check for $400 *postdated* 3 August 1979. The check was paid by Duffy's bank on 6 August

1979. Duffy filed a petition for relief in bankruptcy eighty-eight days after the check was paid by the bank. The trustee in bankruptcy challenged the payment to Avis as a voidable preference since it was paid within ninety days of the petition.

Was this payment to Avis a voidable preference under the Bankruptcy Act? And if the payment was a voidable preference, was Avis entitled to an exception by the giving of new value as of the payment date?

ISSUES

Yes, it was a voidable preference since payment was received within ninety days of the petition; but Avis gave no "new value" when it elected not to repossess the leased automobile.

HOLDINGS

Under the law of commercial paper, a check is not "paid until accepted and honored by the bank." This acceptance occurred within the ninety-day period, so the voidable preference rules are applicable. Avis did not give new value by forbearance from repossession of the car. Avis substituted an obligation for a preexisting obligation; it did not give new value. The forbearance by Avis did not enhance the estate of the debtor, and the conduct of Avis in no way aided the other creditors. The payment is a voidable preference, and the trustee can recover the $400 for the debtor's estate.

REASONING

Fraudulent Conveyance

A *fraudulent conveyance* is a *transfer by a debtor that involves actual or constructive fraud.* Actual fraud is involved if the debtor *intended* to hinder or delay a creditor in recovering a debt. An example of such a transfer would be a sale by the debtor to a relative so a creditor could not foreclose on the asset. Constructive fraud is involved when the debtor sells an asset for *inadequate* consideration and as a result of the sale becomes insolvent, or if the debtor is already insolvent at the time of the unreasonable sale. It is also deemed constructive fraud to engage in a business that is undercapitalized. Any fraudulent conveyance made during the one year preceding the petition may be set aside by the trustee under federal law. And some *state* statutes permit the avoidance of such conveyances during the preceding two to five years. The trustee uses the time period that most strongly favors the creditors.

Once the trustee has gathered and liquidated all available assets and allowed all provable claims, the estate is distributed to the creditors. The Bankruptcy Reform Act contains a mandatory priority list of debts. Each class of creditors takes its turn, and no class may receive any payments until all higher-priority classes are paid in full. All creditors *within* a given class will be paid on a pro rata basis until either the claims are paid in full or the estate is exhausted.

Distribution of Proceeds

The highest priority of claims is the expense of handling the estate. All of the costs incurred by the trustee in preserving and administering the bankruptcy must be paid first.

The next class of claims involves debts that arise in the ordinary course of business *between* the date the petition is filed and the date the trustee is appointed.

The third and fourth priorities are interrelated. Priority 3 is wages earned by employees of the debtor during the ninety days preceding the petition, up to a maximum of $2000 per employee. Priority 4 is unpaid contributions by an employer to employee benefit plans, if they arise during the 180 days before the petition, up to $2,000 per employee. However, these claims are reduced by any claims paid in priority 3. Thus, the maximum priority for each employee is a total of $2000. Any claims in excess of this amount go to the bottom of the list.

The fifth priority is given to grain farmers who have a claim against the owner or operator of a grain storage facility, and to United States fishermen against individuals who operate a fish produce storage or processing facility. In either case, the priority is limited to $2,000 per individual creditor.

The sixth priority is claims by consumers for goods or services paid for but not received. The mazimum here is $900 per person as a priority, with any surplus claim going to the bottom of the list.

The final priority claim is in favor of debts owed to government units. This class is basically made up of taxes due during the three years preceding the petition.

After all priority claims are paid, the balance of the estate is used to pay general unsecured creditors. When all unsecured creditors have been paid in full, any monies left are paid to the debtor. Normally the funds will not cover the general creditor claims, and a pro rata distribution is necessary. This leaves the creditors with less money than they were owed. The debtor must then hope for a *discharge* to make the balance of the claims uncollectible.

Discharge

A discharge can be granted only to an *individual.* And a discharge can be granted to an individual only if he or she is an honest debtor. A discharge will be denied if the debtor made a fraudulent conveyance or does not have adequate books and records. In addition, a debtor will be denied a discharge if he or she refuses to cooperate with the court during the proceedings. And no discharge will be granted if a discharge was received during the previous six years. A denial of discharge means that the unpaid portions of any debts continue and are fully enforceable after the proceedings end.

Even if a discharge is granted, some claims are not affected. Under the Bankruptcy Reform Act, certain debts continue to be fully enforceable against the debtor even though the debtor received a discharge. The following ten major classes of debts are not affected by a discharge:

1. taxes due to any government unit
2. debts that arose because of fraud by the debtor concerning his financial condition

3. claims not listed by the creditors or by the debtor in time for treatment in the proceedings

4. debts where the debtor embezzled or stole the money

5. alimony

6. child support

7. liabilities due to malicious torts of the debtor

8. fines imposed by a government unit

9. claims that were raised in a previous case in which the debtor did not receive a discharge

10. student loans, unless the loan is at least five years in arrears

In addition to these ten classes of debts, the 1984 Amendments addressed the problem of debtors who "load up" with debts just prior to filing a petition, knowing the proceedings will discharge these recently incurred debts. Under the new law, any debtor purchases from one creditor of $500 or more in "luxury" goods or services that are incurred within forty days of the petition are presumed to be nondischargeable. Similarly, any cash advances of $1000 or more that are received from one creditor within the twenty days prior to the petition are presumed to be nondischargeable. The debtor will have the burden of proof and will have to convince the court that these debts were not fraudulently incurred with the intent of receiving a discharge in order to have these debts discharged. Notice that a discharge is possible but that the debtor has the burden of proof!

Finally, even if a discharge is granted, it may be revoked. If the trustee or a creditor requests a revocation of the discharge, the request may be granted. The request must be made within one year of the discharge, and the debtor must have committed some wrongful act, such as fraud during the proceedings. The possibility of revocation encourages the debtor to remain honest. In the following case, the court denied a discharge to the debtor.

In re Mazzola
4 B.R. 179 (1980)

FACTS

Mazzola was the sole stockholder of Dennis M. Construction Co., Inc., a firm engaged in constructing homes. One home built by the company was sold to LaVangie. LaVangie claimed that the home was defective, and he obtained an attachment on some land owned by Mazzola in August 1979. Mazzola managed to get the attachment released in September 1979, immediately sold the land, deposited the money, and used the money to pay several creditors of the corporation. On 15 October 1979, Mazzola filed a voluntary petition in bankruptcy. One of the debts from which Mazzola sought a discharge was the claim brought by LaVangie.

ISSUE   Should Mazzola be denied a discharge in bankruptcy because of his conduct in concealing property during the year preceding the petition?

HOLDING   Yes. Mazzola was guilty of bankruptcy offenses and should be denied a discharge.

REASONING   Discharges are granted only to honest debtors. In this case, Mazzola had acted fraudulently before he filed the petition. The petition that he prepared contained numerous false statements, most of which were made with reckless disregard for the truth. Mazzola's explanations for his erroneous answers fell far short of credibility. The answers that he gave were too self-serving to be deemed coincidence or innocent mistake.

On some occasions, a debtor who has been granted a discharge in bankruptcy may decide that he would like to repay the creditor despite the discharge. If the debtor truly wants to repay the debt, he may voluntarily *reaffirm* the debt and then repay it. However, the requirements for a reaffirmation were substantially increased by the 1984 Amendments. Prior to the 1984 Amendments, a debtor could reaffirm any debts at virtually any time. Too often this led to a debtor reaffirming debts out of a sense of guilt following the discharge, and putting himself in the same sort of financial position as had originally led to the petition. As a result, the 1984 Amendments require that any reaffirmations be made in writing, and be filed with the court. In addition, the written agreement must be filed before the debtor is granted a discharge. If the debtor has an attorney, the attorney must file a declaration that the debtor was fully informed of his rights, voluntarily agreed to the reaffirmation, and that the agreement will not impose an undue hardship on the debtor or his dependents. If the debtor does not have an attorney, the court must approve the reaffirmation, and the court will not grant approval unless the repayment is in the best interests of the debtor.

SUMMARY   Federal law governs the topic of bankruptcy, which is designed to give an honest debtor a fresh start. A new law, the Bankruptcy Reform Act, took effect in October, 1979. The act provided for the establishment of bankruptcy courts as a separate branch of the United States district court system. These courts are presided over by bankruptcy judges who specialize in handling bankruptcy petitions.

Under Chapter 7 ("Liquidation"), bankruptcy can be initiated by the debtor or by the creditors. The debtor initiates the proceedings by filing a voluntary petition. The creditors initiate the proceedings by filing an involuntary petition against the debtor. Five "public interest" corporations are prohibited from filing a voluntary petition; any other debtor may file such a petition, even if solvent. Creditors may file an involuntary petition against most debtors, but only if the debtor has acted improperly, *and* the proper number of creditors join the petition, *and* the proper amount of unsecured debts is involved.

Once the petition is filed, a judge appoints a trustee to administer the bankrupt's estate. The trustee is to preserve the estate for the protection of the unsecured creditors. The debtor is allowed some exemptions so that a fresh start is possible. The rest of the estate is available for settling debts.

Once the exempt property is removed, the balance of the estate is liquidated and the proceeds are applied to the allowable claims of the creditors.

The proceeds are applied first to priority classes as set up by the Bankruptcy Reform Act. After all priority classes are paid in full, the balance of the proceeds is applied to the claims of the unsecured creditors. The debtor will then seek a discharge. If the debtor has been honest and has cooperated, a discharge will probably be granted. If not, the debts will continue.

DISCUSSION QUESTIONS

1. What are the two major purposes of the Bankruptcy Reform Act?

2. A liquidation of the debtor's estate is referred to as what type of bankruptcy?

3. What three "tests" must the creditors meet in order to petition a debtor into bankruptcy involuntarily?

4. Ronald is involved in a bankruptcy. The state in which he lives allows the debtor to select either the federal or the state exemptions. The state exemptions completely exempt the debtor's homestead. Ronald does not own a home. What should he do? Why?

5. Martha has filed a bankruptcy petition, dated August 1. She has as one of her debts a $30,000 loan dated June 1 that had 18 percent interest and was due on December 1. How much of this total indebtedness is provable in the bankruptcy proceeding?

6. How does the new bankruptcy coverage deal with the problem of a debtor "loading up" with debts just prior to the filing of the petition? Is this treatment an appropriate solution to the problem of a debtor who "loads up" with debts?

7. What does the new bankruptcy coverage provide for credit card companies and other unsecured creditors to improve their position over the position they enjoyed under the Bankruptcy Reform Act? Does this new treatment make a substantial difference? Should this have been done, or should the old treatment have been retained?

8. Herb was having financial problems. In a desperate attempt to save his business, he ordered a new product line from Ace Equipment. Herb paid for the new goods on delivery by Ace. Herb's creditors filed a bankruptcy petition five weeks later. If the trustee challenges the payment to Ace as a voidable preference, what will happen? Explain fully.

9. Sam knew he was about to go bankrupt. Just days before he filed his

petition, he sold his new Lincoln to his secretary for $300. What must the secretary prove in order to keep the Lincoln? Explain.

10. Sharon ordered a new washing machine and drier from Honest Al's Appliances. She paid the full $1300 at the time. Before receiving the machines, Sharon was notified that Honest Al had gone bankrupt. What are Sharon's rights? Explain.

CASE PROBLEMS

1. While insolvent, and within the ninety days preceding the filing of a petition, the debtor transferred property to a creditor as payment of a preexisting debt. The creditor had a security interest, and the collateral was worth more than the debt. Was this a voidable preference?(*In re Conn,* 9 Bankr. 431 [1981].)

2. In May, a debtor granted a security interest to a creditor. In August, the debtor filed a bankruptcy petition. At the time the security interest was created, the debtor was insolvent and the creditor was aware of the insolvency. Is this a fraudulent conveyance? (*In re Peoria Braumeister Co.,* 138 F.2d 520 [7th Cir. 1943].)

3. Moureau entered into a lease with Leaseamatic. Later Moureau defaulted on the lease, and Leaseamatic obtained a judgment against Moureau for the total amount due. Moureau filed a voluntary petition in bankruptcy shortly thereafter, but in the petition he never mentioned Leaseamatic nor the claims they were asserting nor the judgment they had obtained. Moureau was granted a discharge in the bankruptcy proceedings and then denied the right of Leaseamatic to any payments, citing the discharge as proof. Is Leaseamatic still entitled to its judgment, or has its right been cut off by the discharge? (*Moureau* v. *Leaseamatic,* 542 F.2d 251 [5th Cir., 1976].)

4. The Karachi Cab Company borrowed money from Wapnick, using its taxi licenses as security for the loan. Wapnick attempted to perfect the security interest, but filed her financing statement in the wrong office so that the security interest was improperly perfected. Karachi Cab went bankrupt shortly thereafter, and the trustee in bankruptcy attempted to avoid the security interest of Wapnick. Can the trustee in bankruptcy defeat the security interest of Wapnick in this case? (*In re Karachi Cab Co.,* 21 Bankr. 822 [1982].)

5. Baker has filed for a discharge in bankruptcy under Chapter 7. She has monthly take-home pay of $650, and monthly expenses of $925. Among the debts listed by Baker in her petition are three student educational loans totalling some $6,600. She can establish that she has special circumstances, and that the repayment of the three loans would cause her an undue hardship. In this situation can the court grant a discharge from the student educational loans? (*Baker* v. *University of Tennessee at Chattanooga,* 10 Bankr. 870 [1981].)

6. Collomb transferred the proceeds from a life insurance policy to Wyatt in exchange for Wyatt's promise to support her. Wyatt used the money to purchase a residence in which Collomb lived for some time. Title to the residence was retained by Wyatt. Collomb eventually filed suit, claiming that Wyatt had not supported her as he had promised, and claiming that the real estate belonged to her. She argued that the realty was held by Wyatt in a constructive trust, and should be deeded over to her. The court granted Collomb a judgment against Wyatt, and Wyatt filed a bankruptcy petition before Collomb could foreclose on the land. Should Collomb be allowed to terminate the automatic stay provision and foreclose on the real estate? (*Collomb* v. *Wyatt*, 6 Bankr. 947 [1980].)

7. Jenkins owed Friedman some $225,000 in losses arising from trading in commodities futures. Friedman attempted to involuntarily petition Jenkins into bankruptcy and to have the trustee recover some properties and assets that Jenkins had transferred to other creditors. Friedman argued that these transfers were voidable preferences under bankruptcy law. Jenkins resisted the involuntary petition, arguing that he was a farmer, and as such was immune from an involuntary petition. Jenkins, admittedly, was engaged in operating a farm, and had received gross income of $60,000 from his farming operations. He had also received $3,000 from the sale of insurance. But Friedman asserted that a $330,000 loan Jenkins received should also be counted as income so that Jenkins could not receive the necessary percentage of income from farming operations to be classified as a farmer. Is Jenkins a farmer under the standards of the bankruptcy laws? (*Jenkins* v. *Petitioning Creditor Ray E. Friedman*, 664 F.2d 184 [8th Cir. 1981].)

8. Turpin filed a petition in bankruptcy, and filed all the necessary schedules and information. However, he did not include his interests in a pension fund or a profit-sharing plan to which he was entitled under his employment. The trustee in bankruptcy argued that these assets also had to be included and had to be transferred to the trustee. Turpin argued that these were more similar to future wages, to which he was not yet entitled, and thus should not be included or transferred to the trustee. Who should prevail? (*Matter of Turpin*, 644 F.2d 472 [5th Cir. 1981].)

9. The Belchers filed a voluntary bankruptcy petition, and listed their exempt assets as provided for under the state exemptions. One of the assets the Belchers claimed as exempt was a duplex they owned. The Belchers occupied one half of the duplex and rented the other half. The bankruptcy trustee urged that only one half of the duplex was exempt since only one half was the homestead of the debtors. The Belchers argued that since the primary purpose of the duplex was to provide them with a home, the rental of half of it was incidental, and should not be excluded from the exemption. How should the duplex be treated? (*Belcher* v. *Turner*, 579 F.2d 73 [10th Cir. 1978].)

10. Kaiser purchased a home in Miami for $300,000. He had the house put in his wife's name rather than in his name or in their names. He paid all expenses and maintenances from his corporate funds rather than from personal funds. Two years later, Kaiser filed a Chapter 7 bankruptcy petition, and did not list the Miami house as one of his assets. The trustee in bankruptcy argued that Kaiser had committed a fraudulent transfer of assets by placing the house in his wife's name and asked the court to include the house in the debtor's estate. What should the court do in this case? (*In re Kaiser*, 722 F.2d 1580 [2d Cir. 1983].)

Alternatives to Straight Bankruptcy

In the last chapter, we examined a Chapter 7 liquidation proceeding, commonly referred to as a straight bankruptcy. Many people have the mistaken idea that Chapter 7 proceedings are all the Bankruptcy Reform Act covers. In reality, several other types of proceedings are also available under the Bankruptcy Reform Act. The first sections of this chapter will discuss two of these proceedings: a corporate reorganization under Chapter 11 of the Bankruptcy Reform Act and a wage earner's repayment plan under Chapter 13 of the act. Neither of these plans calls for a liquidation of the debtor's assets in order to cover the debts, and under both plans, the creditors can reasonably expect to be paid in full by the debtor. In the last sections of the chapter, we shall discuss alternatives to bankruptcy. These nonbankruptcy alternatives are normally available under state statutes, in contrast to the federal statutes that provide for bankruptcy.

OTHER BANKRUPTCY PLANS

Chapter 11 bankruptcy proceedings, known as *reorganizations,* are designed to allow the debtor to adjust his or her financial situation. Chapter 11 is used by

Reorganizations

debtors to avoid liquidations. Although reorganizations are designed primarily for use by corporate debtors, individuals are also allowed to use the reorganization format.

The major advantages of a reorganization are that it allows a business to continue, and it forces creditors who object to go along with the plan despite their objections. In addition, the creditors will normally receive more than they would have in a liquidation under Chapter 7.

Any debtor who could use Chapter 7, *except* stockbrokers and commodity brokers, may also use Chapter 11. Like a liquidation proceeding, a reorganization may be either voluntary or involuntary. And the same limitations apply here as apply to a liquidation petition (refer to page 539 for a detailed description of how petitions may be initiated).

The Proceedings

Once the petition has been filed, the court will do three things:

1. It will enter an order for relief.
2. It will appoint a trustee, if requested to do so by any interested party.
3. It will appoint creditor committees to represent creditors. Equity security holders will be represented by a separate committee.

If no interested party asks for the appointment of a trustee, the *debtor* is permitted to retain possession and control of the assets and/or the business. The committees appointed by the court will meet with the trustee if one is appointed, or with the **debtor in possession** if no trustee is appointed, to discuss the treatment of the proceedings. The committees will also investigate the debtor's finances and financial potential, and they will help prepare a plan for reorganizing that will benefit all the interested parties.

In the event that no one asks for the appointment of a trustee, the court may appoint an **examiner.** The examiner or the trustee will investigate the debtor and the debtor's business activities and business potential. On the basis of this investigation, a recommendation will be made to the court. The recommendation may be a reorganization plan, or it may be a suggestion that the proceedings be transferred from Chapter 11 to Chapter 7 (liquidation) or to Chapter 13 (wage earner plan). The court will normally follow such a recommendation unless a good reason not to follow it is presented.

Debtor in possession A debtor who does not turn possession of his or her assets over to the trustee

Examiner A person appointed by the court to investigate the financial position and condition of the debtor

The Plan

The purpose of a reorganization is to develop a *plan* under which the debtor can avoid liquidation while somehow managing to satisfy the claims of the creditors. Obviously, the right to propose a plan can be very important. If the debtor remains in possession (that is, no trustee is appointed), *only* the debtor may propose a plan during the first 120 days after the order for relief. *Any* interested party (debtor, creditor, stockholder, or trustee) may propose a plan under any of three conditions:

1. if a trustee is appointed
2. if the debtor fails to propose a plan within the 120-day period
3. if the debtor proposes a plan within 120 days, but it is not accepted by all affected **classes of creditors** within 180 days of the order for relief

Classes of creditors Categories of creditors based on the nature of the obligation that gives rise to the debt

For a plan to be confirmed, it must designate all claims by class as well as specify which classes will be **impaired** and which will *not* be impaired. It must also show how the plan can be implemented successfully. Among factors that the court will examine are the following:

Impaired Rendered less valuable or less enforceable

1. plans to sell any assets
2. plans to merge, consolidate, or divest
3. plans to satisfy, or modify, any liens or claims
4. plans to issue new stock to generate funds

If new stock is to be issued, it *must* have voting rights. No new nonvoting stock may be issued under a reorganization plan.

Each class of creditors that is impaired is allowed to vote on the plan. A class is deemed to have accepted the plan if creditors having at least two-thirds of the dollar amount involved *and* more than one-half of the total number of creditors approve it. If a creditor class is not impaired by the plan, it does not need to approve the plan.

Despite the vote, no plan can be accepted or rejected by the creditors. The final word is left to the court. The court will hold a hearing on the plan, and the court may then confirm or reject it. The court may confirm a plan if it was accepted by at least one class of creditors. If all the creditor classes approve the plan, the court will normally confirm it. Similarly, if all the creditor classes reject the plan, the court will normally reject it. But final word is with the court alone. The vote of the creditor classes simply provides the court with guidance.

Once the court approves a plan, it becomes binding on everyone affected by it. The court will look at the plan's fairness to each interested group, especially those creditors impaired by the plan. And the court will look at the viability of the plan. Finally, if the court feels the plan will not work or is not fair, the court can order the proceedings converted to a Chapter 7 liquidation. This last-ditch power encourages everyone involved to act in good faith, since Chapter 11 is normally better than Chapter 7 for all concerned.

In the following case, the court rejected a plan that the debtor proposed.

Matter of Landmark at Plaza Park, Ltd.
7 Bankr. 653 (1980)

FACTS   Landmark at Plaza Park, Ltd., has as its only substantial asset an apartment complex. City Federal, the only creditor in its class, held a first mortgage on the property. The mortgage was for $2,250,000 at $9\frac{1}{2}$ percent. Landmark proposed a reorganization under Chapter 11 of the Bankruptcy Reform Act. The proposed plan was acceptable to every creditor class except City Federal, which objected to the original plan and to the modified plan. The plan proposed by Landmark as it related to City Federal provided the following:

1. Landmark would pay City Federal monthly, *interest only*, $12\frac{1}{2}$ percent interest on the mortgage beginning in the sixteenth month and running through the thirty-sixth month.

2. Landmark would issue a new note payable in three years in exchange for all current liabilities owed City Federal.

3. Landmark would reassume operation of the apartment complex.

City federal was impaired by the proposed reorganization.

ISSUE   Could City Federal be subjected to the plan despite its objections?

HOLDING   No. The court held that the proposed plan was not feasible, and therefore City Federal could not be forced to accept it.

REASONING   The plan as proposed by Landmark did not comply with the requirements of the Bankruptcy Reform Act for overriding the objections of a creditor class. The plan would have required City Federal to make a 100 percent loan at a rate below what other borrowers under similar circumstances would have had to pay. A minimum rate of 15 percent on the loan would have been necessary for approval of the plan. Even with a 15 percent interest rate, the plan could not have been approved unless it was likely to be carried out by the debtor. Landmark had not realistically projected its income and expense figures. It was very unlikely that Landmark could meet its obligation to City Federal under the plan, so the plan was denied.

Repayment Plans

Chapter 13 of the Bankruptcy Reform Act is designed to allow a debtor with a regular source of income to adjust the debts and to repay all creditors. Chapter 13 plans are available only to individual debtors; they cannot be used by corporations. They are also available only to debtors who have less than $100,000 in unsecured debts and less than $350,000 in secured debts. Chapter 13 is unavailable to a debtor who exceeds either maximum. In such a case, the debtor will have to use Chapter 7, Chapter 11, or some non-bankruptcy alternative.

The Proceedings

In many respects, a repayment plan is the simplest bankruptcy proceeding for an individual debtor. The court will again issue an order for relief, and a trustee will be appointed. The trustee will perform the investigation duties that would be followed under a reorganization, but only if the debtor operates a business. And the trustee will carry out the plan proposed by the debtor, if the plan is approved by the court.

The Plan

The debtor must file a proposed repayment plan with the court. The plan must provide equal treatment to each creditor claim within any given class. This does *not* mean that each class must be treated equally — only that *within* each class, every creditor must be treated equally. The plan must also make some provision for clearing up any defaulted debts or defaulted payments on debts. And the plan must not call for payments beyond a three-year period, unless the court feels that a longer period is necessary. Even then, the plan must be carried out within five years.

The court will approve the plan if the following conditions are met:

1. The plan appears to be fair to all parties.
2. The plan is in the best interests of the creditors.
3. It appears that the debtor can conform to the plan.
4. The plan proposes to pay at least as much as would have been paid under Chapter 7.

Once approved, the plan is binding on all parties, with or without their consent. At that point, the debtor must turn over to the trustee enough of the debtor's income to make the payments called for under the plan.

If the debtor performs the plan as approved, the court will grant a discharge. The discharge terminates all debts provided for in the plan — if they are dischargeable in a liquidation — that received their full share under the plan. In addition, the court can intercede and grant a discharge *during* the plan, even though the plan has not been completely carried out. The court will do so *only* if the following three factors are present:

1. The debtor cannot complete the plan owing to circumstances beyond the debtor's control.
2. The general (lowest-priority) creditors have received at least as much as they would have received in a liquidation.
3. The court does not feel it would be practical to alter the plan.

The likelihood of such a court intervention during the plan is not very high, but the option is there. And, once again, the desire to provide a fresh start for an honest debtor is obvious.

In the next case, because the court did not feel the debtor was being honest, it denied him a "fresh start."

In re Yee
7 Bankr. 747 (1980)

FACTS Yee was a financial analyst. His annual pay was $16,800. He had total debts of nearly $13,000, including debts of $2600 on a National Direct Student Loan and $380 in parking tickets. He proposed a repayment plan under Chapter 13 whereby he would pay $30 a month for thirty-six months and have all his debts discharged. He had no assets not subject to exemption, so that in a liquidation his creditors would receive nothing. The court denied his repayment plan on the grounds that it was not filed in good faith.

ISSUE Can the court deny a repayment plan that proposes token payments and that would result in the discharge of substantial debts after minimal payments?

HOLDING Yes. If the court finds a lack of good faith, it may deny a Chapter 13 repayment plan.

REASONING Unlike a Chapter 7 proceeding, in which the court has virtually no role, a Chapter 13 plan must meet with judicial approval. Here Mr. Yee had proposed a plan that would permit him to escape his debts rather than repay them. After expenses, his plan would pay only about 7 percent of his debt. Such minimal payments would constitute an abuse of Chapter 13. The plan is denied owing to an absence of good faith.

1984 Amendments

The Bankruptcy Amendments of 1984 have tightened the requirements for a Chapter 13 repayment plan. The new standards also reduce the burden on the courts, since the good faith of the debtor, as in *Yee,* is not an issue. Rather, a more tangible standard than the apparent good faith of the debtor has been substituted.

The new law allows any unsecured creditor to block the debtor's proposed repayment plan if the plan does not meet one of two criteria:

1. The plan calls for the payment of 100 percent of the creditor's claim; or
2. the plan calls for the debtor to pay 100 percent of all income not necessary to support the debtor's immediate family for at least three years.

Unless the debtor shows that the plan satisfies one of these two criteria, the Chapter 13 repayment plan will be rejected by the court. The debtor will then have to file a new plan, change over to a Chapter 7 proceeding, or withdraw the petition.

Under the 1978 Bankruptcy Reform Act, debtor payments under a repayment plan did not begin until the plan was confirmed by the court. This gave many debtors a four- to six-month "grace period" in which the debtor retained all his or her assets, but no payments were made, to the detriment of the creditors. The 1984 Amendments call for payments to begin *within* thirty days of the filing of the plan, subject to confirmation of the plan by the court. The debtor makes these payments to the trustee, who holds the monies paid until confirmation of the plan by the court and then distributes them to the various creditors. If the debtor fails to make payments to the trustee in a timely manner, the plan can be dismissed by the court.

Finally, the 1984 Amendments provide for modification of the plan after it is confirmed. The trustee, the debtor, or any creditor may petition the court to increase or decrease the debtor's payments whenever the debtor's circumstances or income warrant such a modification. Prior to the 1984 Amendments decreases were possible, but increases were not permitted.

NON-BANKRUPTCY ALTERNATIVES

In many other cases, a debtor or creditor will object to undergoing a bankruptcy, perhaps because of a distaste for the stigma of bankruptcy or for a number of other reasons. But a wish to avoid bankruptcy does not remove the financial problems of the debtor. Often the debtor or creditor will select a nonbankruptcy alternative to "get out from under." Whether such a decision will work depends on a number of factors.

Prejudgment Remedies

The creditors of a troubled debtor will frequently use some *prejudgment procedure* in an effort either to get paid or to force the debtor into acting before a judicial verdict is issued. Three major prejudgment procedures are available to creditors.

The first remedy is **attachment.** A creditor may go to the clerk of the court and obtain a writ of attachment on the basis of the creditor's word that the debtor has not satisfied some claim. The creditor must normally post a bond to cover any potential liability in case the attachment is not made in good faith.

Attachment The act or process of taking, apprehending, or seizing persons or property by virtue of a writ, summons, or other judicial order and bringing the same into the custody of the law

The creditor will then have the sheriff levy on as much of the debtor's estate as is needed to satisfy the claim of the attaching creditor. The sheriff will take control over these assets until the proceedings terminate.

Once the attachment occurs, the creditor must proceed to get a judgment against the debtor. If a judgment is obtained, the assets may be sold to cover the judgment unless the debtor pays outright in order to have the assets released. If the creditor fails to get a judgment within some preset time period, the attachment and lien will expire.

Attachments frequently lead to bankruptcy petitions. The creditors who did not seek an attachment will file an involuntary petition, alleging that the attaching creditor has received a preference. If they petition within four months of the attachment, the courts will normally overturn the attachment.

The second major prejudgment remedy is a *garnishment*. (A garnishment can also be used as a postjudgment remedy under some circumstances.) In a garnishment, the targeted assets are in the hands of some third person, and not in the hands of the debtor. The assets that the third person controls belong to the debtor or are owed to the debtor. For example, a checking account balance *belongs* to the debtor but is "held" by the bank. The debtor's wages are *owed* to the debtor but are "held" by the employer.

The creditor will officially notify the third person to hold, or retain, the assets pending a judgment. A third person who ignores this notification will become *personally* liable to the creditor when a judgment is entered. Normally, the freezing of the debtor's checking account or paycheck will "encourage" the debtor to resolve the dispute rapidly.

The third major prejudgment remedy is *receivership*. This remedy is not a favored prejudgment choice today, unless it is initiated by the debtor, because of the ready availability of bankruptcy relief. In a receivership, the court appoints some disinterested third person to manage the affairs of the debtor. This receiver is responsible for preserving the debtor's estate until a judgment is reached. Liens on the property of the debtor continue under a receivership, but the property affected cannot be bothered without permission of the court.

Postjudgment Remedies

Unless the debtor pays the debt or the creditor cancels it, the parties must eventually resolve the case by some other means. This is normally done by the entry of a judgment by the court. A creditor who wins the case and receives a judgment will probably seek one of three major postjudgment remedies to satisfy his or her claim.

The first of these is an *execution*. In an execution, the creditor will attempt to seize and sell as many of the debtor's assets as are needed to cover the judgment. This is done by procuring a writ of execution from the court and then having the sheriff levy on the debtor's assets. After the sheriff levies, the assets seized are appraised, a notice of sale is made, and the goods are sold. (The sale is usually at a public auction, commonly referred to as a judicial sale.) The proceeds of the sale or a predetermined percentage of the appraised value, whichever is higher, will be applied to the debts owed to the creditor. (The percentage varies from state to state, since this is a state remedy.)

Redeem To buy back; to liberate an estate or article from mortgage or pledge by paying the debt for which it stood as security

The debtor is usually allowed to **redeem** any real property and some personal property within a fixed period after the sale by paying the purchaser the necessary amount. A purchaser should also be aware that only the debtor's interest in the asset has been purchased. There may very well be other liens or claims or other problems to be confronted later. Thus, the selling price is usually fairly low.

The second major postjudgment remedy is a *supplementary proceeding*. A supplementary proceeding can be used only if the writ of execution is unsatisfied. In a supplementary proceeding, the creditors attempt to discover any assets of the debtor by examining and questioning any interested parties. If assets are discovered, the creditors can have a receiver appointed to preserve the assets or they can have the court order a sale of the assets.

The third major postjudgment remedy is a *garnishment*. Garnishments were already discussed as a prejudgment remedy, but there is a slight difference here. *Before* a judgment is entered, the third person is instructed to *hold the assets. After* a judgment is entered, the third person is told to *turn the assets over* to cover the debts owed. If wages are garnished, some amount must be left to allow the debtor to subsist until the debt is paid.

The next case shows one limitation of a garnishment.

Peterson v. *Peterson*
571 P.2d 1369 (Utah 1977)

The plaintiff and the defendant were divorced. As part of the divorce decree, the plaintiff was to receive child support payments. The defendant fell behind in these payments, and the plaintiff sought a writ of garnishment against the defendant's checking account to obtain the delinquent payments. The defendant objected to the writ, arguing that the money in the account belonged to his second wife, and not to him.

FACTS

Are funds in a checking account subject to garnishment if the garnishee did not earn the funds?

ISSUE

No. A garnishment can be used only against monies of the garnishee.

HOLDING

The defendant in this case had not worked in over a year. The funds in the checking account were almost entirely derived from the earnings of the defendant's current spouse. Both parties considered the funds on deposit to belong to the spouse. None of the money "belonged" to the defendant. Since the garnishment was improper, it was set aside.

REASONING

Debtors often decide to get out from under on their own by initiating remedies under state law rather than seeking a discharge in bankruptcy. A debtor who so decides will usually choose one of two options.

The first option is an *assignment for the benefit of creditors*. Here the debtor freely and voluntarily transfers property to a third person, in trust, to pay the creditors. Creditor consent is not needed, and once the transfer is made, the property is beyond the reach of the creditors. Unfortunately for the debtor,

Debtor-Initiated Remedies

such a transfer does not result in an automatic discharge. Not only that, it may result in the filing of a bankruptcy petition by the creditors.

To avoid these problems, many debtors prefer to reach a *contractual agreement* with the creditors. Such an agreement *does* require creditor consent, but it will also result in discharge. The debtor may seek a composition or an extension, or both.

In a *composition,* each creditor who is involved agrees to take *less* money than is owed, if the money is paid immediately, as full satisfaction of the debt. Such an arrangement is a contract between the debtor and the creditors as well as among the creditors. Thus, at least two creditors must join before the composition is valid. Otherwise, it would be invalid because of lack of consideration (see Chapter 10).

In an *extension,* the creditors agree to a longer repayment period in order to receive full payment. Again, the courts view it as a dual contract between debtor and creditors and among the creditors.

In either a composition or an extension, the contract among the creditors is based on their acceptance of a change in performance in exchange for an agreement by each not to file suit to collect the original contract. Thus, both a composition and an extension are supported by consideration. Each is a contract. And the court will enforce either as it would enforce any other contract.

SUMMARY

An embattled debtor need not always go through liquidation in order to make a fresh start. There are other bankruptcy and nonbankruptcy remedies that may work equally well.

Under bankruptcy, the debtor may seek a reorganization under Chapter 11 or a repayment plan under Chapter 13. Each of these requires court approval of the plan, and each requires the debtor to propose the plan in good faith. In a reorganization, the debtor adjusts his or her financial position to allow a business to continue. In a repayment plan, the debtor proposes a method of repaying debts over a three-to-five year period. Good faith and fairness are essential in both plans.

Some creditors seek nonbankruptcy remedies under state law. The creditor may seek either prejudgment remedies to force the debtor to act or postjudgment remedies in order to collect. Either type of action may result in a bankruptcy proceeding. The debtor may also seek a nonbankruptcy remedy under state law. This will normally involve a contract with the creditors. And, again, it will frequently result in a bankruptcy proceeding.

DISCUSSION QUESTIONS

1. What role does the examiner or the trustee play in a reorganization under Chapter 11?

2. What does the court look at in deciding whether to approve a repayment plan under Chapter 13?

3. What will happen to the debtor under a repayment plan if, owing to a change in circumstances, he or she cannot complete the plan as approved by the court?

4. What new rights have been given to an unsecured creditor in a Chapter 13 repayment proceeding by the 1984 Amendments that substantially increase the creditor's position over that enjoyed under prior bankruptcy law? How will these new rights help the creditor?

5. Under the Bankruptcy Reform Act, a Chapter 13 proceeding was often judged by the good faith of the debtor in proposing the plan. The 1984 Amendments have replaced the debtor's good faith criterion with a new test. How can this test be used to successfully determine whether the debtor is allowed to use a repayment plan or will be subjected to a liquidation proceeding instead?

6. What is the difference between a prejudgment and a postjudgment garnishment proceeding?

7. Why does the law specify that a minimum percentage of appraised value must be applied to debts in an execution? Does this rule reflect more of a public policy concern for the debtor or for the creditor?

8. Why would a debtor make an assignment for the benefit of his or her creditors?

9. Why would a creditor be willing to agree to a composition agreement? Why would a composition agreement occasionally be better for the creditor than a bankruptcy proceeding?

10. How is an extension plan similar to a Chapter 13 repayment plan? How is it different from a Chapter 13 repayment plan? Which seems to be better for the debtor?

CASE PROBLEMS

1. Miller and Fox entered a contract for the sale of some horses. When Miller failed to produce papers on one of the horses as required by the contract, Fox refused to pay for the horse. Miller then obtained a writ of attachment against Fox for the unpaid balance. Fox objected to the attachment since Miller had breached the contract. Can Miller enforce the attachment when he (Miller) is in breach? (*Miller* v. *Fox,* 571 P.2d 804 [Mont. 1977].)

2. Satterwhite filed a Chapter 13 repayment plan with the court. Under the plan, Satterwhite listed monthly debts of $2072 and a monthly income of $1500. He alleged that all of his assets were exempt and proposed to pay each of his creditors the sum of $1.00, which is more than they would receive in a liquidation. He requested that this plan be approved and a discharge granted to him. What should the bankruptcy court do? (*In re Satterwhite,* 7 Bankr. 39 [Tex. 1980].)

3. Telemart, a retail grocer, filed a Chapter 11 petition on September 13.

Lewis, one of Telemart's suppliers, had delivered some $60,000 worth of merchandise on credit to Telemart between August 27 and September 25. When Lewis learned of the Telemart petition, Lewis demanded a return of all the goods as provided by the UCC, Article 2. Is Lewis entitled to a return of the goods under the UCC, or do the goods remain with the bankrupt's estate for treatment and distribution under the bankruptcy laws? (*In the Matter of Telemart Enterprises, Inc.,* 524 F.2d 761 [1975].)

4. Whitman filed a petition for a repayment plan under Chapter 13 of the Bankruptcy Code. One of her debts was an automobile loan from Memphis Bank. The loan carried an interest rate of 21 percent. The bankruptcy court felt that this rate was too high, and ordered Whitman to repay the bank the loan at an interest rate of 10 percent. The bank has appealed this ruling of the bankruptcy court. Should the loan be repaid at the 21 percent called for by the loan agreement, at the 10 percent established by the bankruptcy court, or some other rate? Explain your reasoning. (*Memphis Bank & Trust Co.* v. *Whitman,* 692 F.2d 427 [6th Cir. 1982].)

5. Jones filed a petition for a repayment plan under Chapter 13. She listed total debts of $28,300, all unsecured. Included in this amount was a debt of $18,300 to the state Department of Public Aid for their overpayments of public aid. Jones proposed a plan that called for her to pay $210 a month for 36 months. Such a payment schedule left her $80 a month for her living expenses for herself and her four children. The plan was objected to by the Department of Public Aid, which asserted that the plan called for the repayment of only 10 percent of her total debt, and was therefore not a good faith repayment plan. Should this plan be approved by the court under Chapter 13? (*In re Jones,* 31 Bankr. 485 [1983].)

6. Johns-Manville was a major producer of asbestos products. Asbestos exposure to its customers had led to some 16,000 lawsuits being filed against Johns-Manville, with many more lawsuits expected in the future. As a result of the potential liabilities faced by the company due to these lawsuits, Johns-Manville filed for a Chapter 11 reorganization. Several creditors of Johns-Manville asserted that the filing was not in good faith, and should be dismissed by the court. Among the grounds asserted for this challenge was the fact that Johns-Manville was a very successful corporation and was not insolvent or close to insolvency. Should the court dismiss the petition? (*In re Johns-Manville Corporation,* 36 Bankr. 727 [1984].)

7. Tracy, Inc., filed a petition to reorganize its business under Chapter 11 of the Bankruptcy Code. One of Tracey's creditors objected to the Chapter 11 proceeding, and asked the court to convert the proceeding to Chapter 7. The court, in its preliminary investigation, discovered that Tracey had no place of business, no business telephone, no inventory, no equipment, and no employees. What should the court do in this situation? (*In re Tracey Service Co., Inc.,* 17 Bankr. 405 [1982].)

8. Barnes has filed a petition seeking approval of a repayment plan under Chapter 13. His plan calls for the payment of 100 percent of his income in excess of the amount necessary to support his family. The plan also calls for the repayment of his total debt to his secured creditors, and the payment of approximately 1 percent of the debt he owes to his unsecured creditors. Should the court approve this repayment plan? Explain. (*In re Barnes*, 5 Bankr. 376 [1980].)

9. Iacovoni filed a petition for approval of a repayment plan under Chapter 13. In the plan, Iacovoni asserted that he had no income in excess of the amount necessary to support his family. As a result, he proposed to pay nothing to his creditors. He has asserted that since all of his assets are exempt, the creditors are in as good a position as they would be in under a Chapter 7 proceeding, and thus that the court should approve his repayment plan. How should the court treat this petition? (*In re Iacovoni*, 2 Bankr. 256 [1980].)

10. Young received a traffic ticket in 1979. In 1980, Young filed a petition for relief under Chapter 13 of the Bankruptcy Code. In her plan, she proposed the payment of 100 percent of all of the debts she owed, including the traffic ticket. The court approved her plan. Before the plan was fully performed, though, Young's driver's license expired. The state refused to renew her license until such time as the traffic ticket was paid in full. Young has asked the bankruptcy court to order the state to issue her license. Should Young be given her license in this case? (*In re Young*, 10 Bankr. 17 [1980].)

PART 6

The Law of Agency

One of humanity's fondest dreams is to be able to be in more than one place at the same time. This is obviously a physical impossibility. Fortunately, though, the law has found a way to do *legally* what cannot be done *physically*. By using an agent, a person can be in more than one place simultaneously—at least legally.

An *agent* is a person empowered to "be you," within the scope of the agency. Whatever the agent hears, you "heard." Whatever an agent says, you "said." Whatever an agent does, you "did." In other words, you are legally responsible for your agent's conduct—within the scope of the agency.

There are obvious benefits to be derived from "being" in many places at one time, but there are also many potential problems if your various "selves" do not conduct themselves properly. Part 6 explores these benefits and potential problems.

CHAPTER 33

The Creation and Termination of an Agency

Agency law deals with the relationships between workers and the people who hire workers. It includes their duties and responsibilities both to each other and to the public at large. No one can really avoid agency law. Almost everyone at some time works as an employee or hires an employee. Moreover, agency relationships arise not only in business situations but also in nonbusiness situations, as, for example, when someone returns books to the library for a friend.

AGENCY LAW AND AGENCY RELATION-SHIPS

Most agency relationships do not require litigation because they run smoothly. To resolve the legal problems that do arise, one must look to agency law, contract law, and tort law. In most of these subject areas, the court will rely heavily on state law. Much of the law of agency has been studied by the American Law Institute and is discussed in their publication, *Restatement (Second) of Agency*, which states:

1. Agency is the fiduciary relation which results from the manifestation of consent by one person to another that the other shall act on his behalf and subject to his control, and consent by the other so to act.
2. The one for whom action is to be taken is the principal.
3. The one who is to act is the agent.[1]

An agency relationship is consensual in nature. It is based on the concept that the parties mutually agree that (1) the agent will act on behalf of the principal, and (2) the agent will be subject to the principal's direction and control. In addition, the parties must be competent to act as principal and agent.

RESTRICTIONS ON CREATING AN AGENCY RELATIONSHIP

A broad range of situations are affected by agency law, from a small partnership with two partners to a corporation with thousands of employees, and from a highly skilled petroleum engineer to a sixteen-year-old babysitter. In fact, everything a corporation does, it does through agents. There are very few restrictions on who can form agency relationships and what can be done through agency relationships.

Capacity to Be a Principal

With the exception of minors and incompetents, any person can appoint an agent. It is generally true that any person having capacity to *contract* has capacity to employ an employee (servant) agent or a nonemployee (nonservant) agent. (The distinction between these two agents is that a principal has more control over the actions of the former than over those of the latter.) Since agency is a consensual relationship, the principal must have capacity to give a legally operative consent.[2]

Some states have determined that a minor lacks capacity to be a principal. In other states, a minor has the capacity to enter into an agency relationship, but the agency relationship is voidable. (The *Restatement [Second] of Agency*, Section 20, takes the second position.) In these states, the agreements entered into by the minor's agent would also be voidable to the same extent that the minor's own contracts would be voidable. The key is that the contract is really entered into by the principal.

---

[1] *Restatement (Second) of Agency* (Philadelphia: American Law Institute, 1958), Section 1.
[2] Ibid., Section 20, Comment b.

Generally, anyone can be an agent. Even persons who do not have capacity to act for themselves—for example, minors or insane persons—can act as agents for someone else. It is the capacity of the *principal* that is controlling, not that of the agent. Obviously, however, principals should exercise care to appoint agents who are able to make sound decisions.

Capacity to Be an Agent

Generally, an agent can be assigned to do almost any task. There are, however, some nondelegable duties, such as the following:

Duties an Agent Can Perform

1. an employer's duty to provide safe working conditions[3]
2. a person's duty under some contract terms
3. a landlord's duty to tenants
4. a common carrier's duty to passengers
5. a person's duty under a license issued to that person
6. the duty of a person engaged in inherently dangerous work to take adequate precautions to avoid harm

Other nondelegable duties are defined by various state statutes. These may consist of many different types. If the duty is nondelegable and the principal attempts to delegate the duty to someone else, the principal will be personally liable if the task is not properly completed. *Nondelegable duties* really mean that the *task* can be delegated, but the *responsibility for its proper completion* cannot.

A person who hires another to engage in ultrahazardous activities will be liable for any injury that results. This rule applies whether the person who is hired is an employee or an **independent contractor.**

Independent Contractor Person hired to perform a task but not subject to the control of the employer

The distinction between general and special agents is a matter of degree. A *special agent* is *employed to complete one transaction or a simple series of transactions.* The relationship covers a relatively limited period and is not continuous. A *general agent* is *hired to conduct a series of transactions over time.* The amount of **discretion** the agent has is immaterial in making the distinction between general and special agents.

In deciding whether an agent is a general agent or a special agent, courts should look at all the following factors:

TYPES OF AGENCY RELATION-SHIPS

General and Special Agents

Discretion The right to use one's own judgment in making a decision between the alternatives

1. the number of acts that will be completed to achieve the authorized result
2. the number of people who will be dealt with before achieving the desired result
3. the length of time that will be necessary to achieve the desired result[4]

[3] Ibid., Section 492, Comment a.
[4] Ibid., Section 3, Comment a.

The manager of a card shop is a general agent. In contrast, a person who delivers a package to a customer of the store on a one-time basis is a special agent. It is sometimes difficult to categorize an agent who is between these two extremes.

Gratuitous Agents

Payment is not necessary in a principal-agent relationship. If a person volunteers services without an agreement or an expectation of payment, that person may still be an agent. The requirements for a *gratuitous agency* are that *one person volunteered to help another, and the person being helped accepted this assistance.* For instance, Susie was visiting Joel, who had some yard work to do. Susie offered to help. While she was pruning a tree, she carelessly sawed off a limb, which fell on a car belonging to Joel's neighbor. The courts could find that Susie was Joel's agent, in which case Joel would be liable for the damage that Susie caused.

EMPLOYEES AND INDEPENDENT CONTRACTORS

Most workers are either employees or independent contractors. The distinction among the terms *agent, employee,* and *independent contractor* is confusing, partly because authors and judges apply differing definitions to these terms, and partly because common usage differs from legal usage. This text uses the definitions of the *Restatement (Second) of Agency.*

Employees

An employer is a special type of principal who has the right to tell his or her agent both what to do and how to do it. The agent then falls into a special class of agents called employees or servants. The more modern term is *employees.* An employer (a master) has a right to control *how* the task is done by the employee (the servant). The actual exercise of this control is not necessary. It is sufficient that the employer has the *right* to control. Thus, interns in hospitals, airline pilots, sales clerks, and officers of a corporation are employees.

The distinction between employees and independent contractors is important because a principal is rarely liable for the unauthorized physical acts of an agent who is not an employee. Consequently, a principal will not generally be liable for the torts of an independent contractor. Principals sometimes label someone an independent conractor to escape liability, but the courts will look behind the label and make a judgment about the true nature of the relationship. The distinction between employees and independent contractors is also important in determining rights and benefits under unemployment insurance laws, workers' compensation laws, and similar statutes.

Independent Contractors

An *independent contractor* is hired to complete a task for someone else. The physical acts of the independent contractor are not controlled or subject to the control of the hiring party. The independent contractor *relies on his or her own expertise to determine the best way to complete the job.* Anyone who contracts to do work for another is either an employee or an independent contractor. Courts look at many factors in distinguishing between the two, as illustrated by the next case.

F.A.S. International, Inc. v. Reilly
427 A.2d 392 (Conn. 1980)

F.A.S. operated three correspondence schools — Famous Artists School, Famous Writers School, and Famous Photographers School. F.A.S. used practicing professionals to analyze and critique their students' correspondence lessons. The professionals had no regular office hours. They took the work to their homes, offices, or studios and returned it to F.A.S. when completed. F.A.S. did not supply office space or equipment, but they did supply stationery. The professionals were given only one or two assignments at a time. They were not expected to complete a certain number of assignments per day. F.A.S. did not guarantee that they would receive a minimum amount of work to do. The professionals were paid only for the lessons that they completed. They had no paid vacations, holidays, sick leave, overtime pay, or fringe benefits. F.A.S. did not withhold social security or federal income tax from their pay. Most of the professionals also had independent businesses or worked for others.

FACTS

Were the professionals working for F.A.S. as employees?

ISSUE

No. The court held that they were independent contractors.

HOLDING

This case arose because of a complaint from the administrator of the state unemployment compensation fund. Under Connecticut law, the court stated, the term *employees* should be defined more liberally in reference to unemployment compensation than in reference to other situations. However, it should not be construed unrealistically. Nonetheless, the court held that the common law relationship of master and servant did not exist in this case. The fundamental distinction between an employee and an independent contractor depends on the existence of the right to control the means and the methods of work. Some states require very little supervision in order to find control. Connecticut applies the common law rule. The state supreme court has adopted this definition: "[a]n independent contractor is one who, exercising an independent employment, contracts to do a piece of work according to his own methods and without being subject to the control of his employer, except as to the result of his work." The basic principles of this definition have not been modified. Even with a liberal interpretation of the terms, these professionals were not employees.

REASONING

Independent contractors may be agents, but that is not a necessary condition of being an independent contractor. If an independent contractor agrees to complete a job and the hiring party retains *no* direction over how the work is completed, then the independent contractor is not an agent, and the hiring party is not a principal. In this case, the independent contractor owes no fiduciary duties to the hiring party, and the independent contractor cannot bind the hiring party to a contract. For example, a nonagent independent contractor who is building a house on an owner's lot cannot bind the owner to a contract.

Independent contractors who are agents (1) have fiduciary duties and (2) can bind their principals to contracts. For example, attorneys owe their clients fiduciary duties when they work out a settlement and then agree to it. On the other hand, attorneys are not employees. Legal clients cannot control when their attorneys come to work in the morning or how long a lunch they take.

The following case addressed the issue of whether an independent contractor was an agent.

Canton Lutheran Church v. Sovik, Mathre, Sathrum & Quanbeck
507 F. Supp. 873 (D. S.D. 1981)

FACTS   A church wanted to build an addition to its principal structure. It entered into a contract with Sovik, Mathre, Sathrum & Quanbeck for professional services as an architect. Later, it entered into a contract with a builder to construct the building that the architect had designed. The architect agreed to be responsible for supervision of the work. The architect signed a certificate that the addition was substantially completed in accordance with the specifications. The building addition cracked because the concrete contained calcium chloride. The building specifications did not call for the use of calcium chloride, and its use was not authorized.

ISSUE   Did the architect have a fiduciary duty to the church?

HOLDING   Yes. The architect was an agent and as such owed a fiduciary duty to the principal.

REASONING   An architect preparing a plan for a land owner generally acts as an independent contractor. With respect to the architect's duty to supervise the builder, the architect generally acts as an agent, thus serving as a representative of the party for whom the job is being completed. In such a case, there is a fiduciary duty. This is especially true when the architect has agreed to guard against deficiencies in the work of the builder by supervising the builder's work. The relationship, then, is one of trust and confidence. South Dakota law defines a fiduciary, in part, as an agent. In this case, there was sufficient evidence that the architect breached its fiduciary duty. It appeared that the architect had fraudulently concealed the builder's breach of contract. This issue was returned to the trial court.

Responsibility for an Independent Contractor   A person who hires an independent contractor is usually not responsible for the independent contractor's wrongdoings. Courts make exceptions when the independent contractor was hired to engage in ultrahazardous activities or to commit a crime. The hiring party will also be responsible if the hiring party actually directs the independent contractor to do something careless or wrong or if the hiring party sees the independent contractor do something wrong and does not stop it. Recently, courts have also held hiring parties liable for their failure to adequately supervise independent contractors and for carelessly selecting their independent contractors.

In many states, the trend has been to increase the number of situations in which a person who hires an independent contractor may be held liable. In the following case, a person is held liable for the acts of his independent contractor.

Henderson Brothers Stores, Inc. v. Smiley
174 Cal. Rptr. 875 (Cal. App. 1981)

FACTS

Smiley, a licensed roofing contractor, was hired to reroof MacDonald's building with asphalt. The asphalt must be heated to the melting point in a large tar kettle. Smiley was using such a kettle. He had placed it in a passageway between MacDonald's building and Henderson's warehouse. The kettle suddenly erupted and shot flames ten to twenty feet in the air. This set fire to the Hendersons' building. This type of eruption is very common in the use of a tar kettle. The normal operation of tar kettles in roofing work presents a significant, recognizable danger of fire. Setting the thermostat too high, allowing the tar level in the kettle to be too low, and allowing carbon to build up increases this risk. There is evidence that all three occurred in this case.

ISSUE

Did the hot roofing operation involve a special danger of fire so that MacDonald should be liable for the acts of its independent contractor, Smiley?

HOLDING

Yes. MacDonald should be liable for the acts of its independent contractor.

REASONING

The general rule is that there is no vicarious liability for the person who hires an independent contractor. American courts recognize a number of exceptions to this rule. One such exception to the general rule of nonliability is where the contractor is engaged in the performance of "inherently dangerous" work. This is also called the "peculiar risk" doctrine. Under the *Restatement (Second) of Torts*, the hiring party is directly liable for failing to provide in the agreement with the independent contractor for the independent contractor to take appropriate precautions in cases of "peculiar risk." It is not necessary for the application of this rule that the work be of the type that cannot be done without a risk of harm to others. The rule is based on the negligent failure of the employer or the contractor to take appropriate special precautions.

| DUTIES OF THE AGENT TO THE PRINCIPAL | In all respects, the agent must protect the interests of the principal. This is clearly evidenced by the specific duties discussed in the following sections. |

Duty of Good Faith

The duty of good faith is also called the fiduciary duty, and the rule is that every agent owes the principal the obligation of faithful service. The most common violations of this duty include concealing essential facts that are relevant to the agency, obtaining secret profits, and self-dealing. Suppose the principal was looking for a parcel of agricultural land, and the agent located a suitable parcel. The agent arranged for its sale to the principal without first informing the principal that the agent owned a one-third interest in the parcel. This would be a violation of the agent's fiduciary duty to the principal.

Duty of Loyalty

An agent has a duty to be loyal to the principal and to look out for the principal's best interests. Thus, an agent must not compete with the principal, work for someone who is competing with the principal, or act to further the agent's own interests. For example, suppose Lucy, the principal, has asked her agent to purchase a parcel of land that would be a good location for a shopping center. The agent discovers a good parcel at an excellent price. The agent has a duty not to buy it for himself unless he specifically asks Lucy for permission to disregard these rules and she grants that permission.

In the following case, we see another type of breach of the duty of loyalty. Here the agent did not provide loyal service because he concealed essential facts and did not perform the purpose of the agency.

Black v. Dahl
625 P.2d 876 (Alaska 1981)

FACTS Dahl rented and operated Illiamna Lake Lodge on a long-term lease. Dahl was behind in his lease payments and was in danger of losing his entire investment. He contacted Black, a real estate salesman, about finding a purchaser for Dahl's interest. They entered into an agreement under which Black would receive a 10 percent commission if he located a buyer. Black located two partners who were interested in the premises. These partners wanted to see the financial records and to make a physical inspection. Dahl was not informed of these requests. Black also told the partners that if they delayed ten to fifteen days, they could acquire the lease for $10,000 less. When Dahl asked Black about the progress on the negotiations, Black indicated that he guessed the partners were not interested. Dahl lost his financial interest because he defaulted on the lease. After the default, the partners purchased the lease from others. Dahl did not share in this money.

ISSUE Did Black violate his duty of loyalty as an agent?

Yes. Black did not protect Dahl's interest.

Black owed Dahl a duty to try to find a buyer for Dahl's interest in the premises. Once a buyer was located, Black had a duty to use due diligence to close the transaction. Black violated his duty. In fact, he discouraged the buyers from completing the purchase until after Dahl had lost his interest by default.

The agent also has a duty not to divulge secret information that gives the principal an advantage over the competition. These are commonly called trade secrets. The duties of loyalty and good faith are very similar. If an agent has violated one, there is a good chance the agent has violated them both.

Agents must follow all *lawful* instructions as long as doing so does not subject them to an unreasonable risk of injury, even if they think the instructions are capricious or unwise. They need not follow instructions that are outside the course and scope of the agency relationship. They must repay their principals for damages suffered because they failed to follow instructions.

Duty to Obey All Lawful Instructions

An agent has a duty to act as a reasonably careful agent would under the same circumstances. Again, if the agent fails to live up to this obligation and it causes the principal a loss, the agent will be obliged to reimburse the principal.

Duty to Act with Reasonable Care

The agent has a duty to keep personal funds separate from the principal's funds. If the agent wrongfully uses the principal's funds to purchase something, the court may impose a **trust** and treat the matter as though the purchase were originally made for the benefit of the principal. Such a trust — that is, a trust imposed by a court for the purpose of preventing unjust enrichment — is called a *constructive trust*.

Duty to Segregate Funds

Trust Arrangement whereby one person holds legal title for another person with equitable title

An agent has a duty to account for money received. This is really a combined function of delivery of the funds and record keeping. The funds must usually be delivered to the principal (or an authorized third party). If the money was received while the agent was not in the course and scope of the employment, the agent has a duty to turn it over to the third party.

Duty to Account for Funds

The duty to give notice requires that an agent will inform the principal about crucial facts that are discovered in the scope of the agent's employment. For example, if a tenant gives an apartment manager notice that the tenant will move out at the end of the month, it is assumed that the manager will inform the owner. In fact, the principal may be bound by this notice even though the agent failed to inform the principal. It is said that the notice is "imputed" to the principal.

Duty to Give Notice

DUTIES OF THE PRINCIPAL TO THE AGENT

A principal has an obligation to compensate the agent under the terms of their agreement. Recall that some agents are not entitled to compensation. Other types of agents are entitled to compensation under special arrangements that developed under common law. These unique situations are also generally included in the written contract. For example, real estate brokers are entitled to their commissions in some states if they find a buyer who is ready, willing, and able to buy the parcel. This may be true even if the sale later falls through because of destruction of the building, the buyer's inability to obtain a loan, or some other circumstance. Some states follow a different rule, whereby a sale must close before a commission is earned.

A principal also has an obligation to provide the agent with a reasonably safe place to work and safe equipment to use.

TERMINATION

Agreement of the Parties

An agency relationship is governed in the first instance by the agreement between the principal and the agent. It is usually based on a contract that is established for a set period. For example, if a real estate agent has a listing to sell a house according to certain terms, one of the terms is generally the period for which the contract is going to run, say ninety days; that agreement will terminate at the end of ninety days.

The parties can agree to amend the agency agreement to terminate the agency relationship early. They can also agree to extend the agency agreement. For example, if the house that we just referred to was not sold in ninety days, the owner and agent could specifically extend the agency agreement for another sixty days.

If the parties consent to the continuation of the agency relationship beyond the period originally stated, it may be implied as a renewal of the original contract for the same period and under the same conditions *if* the parties have not specifically altered the terms and conditions of the original agreement.

Agency at Will

If the agency agreement does not specify a set date, a set period, or a set occurrence that will terminate it, then the relationship is an *agency at will*. *Either party can terminate the relationship by giving notice to the other.* This is consistent with the theory that agency is a voluntary relationship between the parties.

The concept of an agency at will is changing, and some states are holding an employer liable if an employee is fired for the wrong reason.[5] The court dealt with such an issue in the following case.

---

[5] See Savodnik v. Korvettes, Inc., 488 F. Supp. 822 (E.D. N.Y. 1980), p. 825, fn. 3, for a listing of states that recognize abusive discharge.

Savodnik v. *Korvettes, Inc.*
488 F. Supp. 822 (E.D. N.Y. 1980)

Morton Savodnik was employed by Korvettes from 7 October 1963 to 26 January 1977, when he received his termination notice. During that period, he received frequent promotions and annual increases in pay. He was never fined, demoted, or warned about his job performance. Savodnik claimed that he suffered a heart attack because of his termination. He had participated in Korvettes' retirement plan and would have been entitled to the money Korvettes contributed to the plan in his name after he worked for them for fifteen years. Savodnik alleged that Korvettes fired him to prevent him from receiving their contribution. Korvettes did not deny this.

FACTS

Did Korvettes lawfully fire Savodnik?

ISSUE

No. Korvettes needs a valid reason to fire Savodnik.

HOLDING

Under the traditional doctrine of employment at will, the employer or the employee could terminate the contract at will and without reason. However, this doctrine is undergoing dynamic development. In many states, the courts are rewriting the traditional doctrine because of careful assessments of what would benefit the economic system and the public good. Courts are allowing an employee to recover when the firing is based on retaliation, bad faith, or an attempt to avoid paying an employee's commissions. Since this is an issue governed by state law, the court in this case was bound by New York law. New York courts have not yet recognized a cause of action for wrongful firing or abusive discharge. New York **precedents** indicate a willingness to recognize this tort cause of action. The court found that Mr. Savodnik was a model employee for over thirteen years and that Korvettes had no justification for firing him; in addition, Korvettes had a pattern of firing employees to avoid giving them rights in the company retirement plan.

REASONING

Precedents Prior court cases that control the decision at hand

   (These parties were also involved in a trial on related issues, which was reported at 489 F. Supp. 1010 [E.D. N.Y. 1980].)

   There are other prohibitions on firing agents at will. If the agent was fired on the basis of sex, race, religion, or national origin or some other violation of civil rights, then the courts may decide that the principal may not terminate the relationship.

Logically, an agency relationship will terminate when the purpose for which it was created has been fulfilled. There would be no sense in continuing the relationship beyond that point.

Fulfillment of the Agency Purpose

Revocation

Principals can revoke or terminate the authority of their agents to act for the principal. They should directly notify their agents of termination. The notice that the agency relationship is being terminated should be clear and unequivocal. Indirect notice will sometimes be sufficient — for example, hiring a second agent to complete all the duties of the first agent. Because an agent owes the principal a duty to obey, the principal can terminate the agency at any time, even if there was an agreement that the agency relationship should continue longer. Even a statement in the agreement that the agency cannot be terminated would not affect the principal's ability to terminate it. Although the principal may have the *ability* to terminate the agency, he or she may not have the legal *right* to do so; in such a case, the agency would be terminated, but the principal would be liable for damages if this termination was a breach of contract.

Renunciation

Renunciation occurs when the agent notifies the principal that he or she will no longer serve as agent. In other words, the agent resigns. Since an agency relationship is voluntary, an agent may renounce. However, the agent may be liable to the principal if the renunciation is a breach of their contract.

Operation of Law

Operation of law denotes an automatic occurrence that does not require the action of any person. Operation of law will generally terminate an agency relationship under any one of the following circumstances:

1. when the agent dies
2. when either party becomes insane
3. when the principal becomes bankrupt
4. when the agent becomes bankrupt, if the bankruptcy affects the agency
5. when the agency cannot possibly be performed (for example, when the subject matter of the agency is destroyed)
6. when there is an unusual and unanticipated change in circumstances that destroys the purpose of the agency relationship
7. when a change in law makes it illegal to complete the agency relationship

The traditional rule was that the death of the principal would also terminate the agency relationship immediately. Because this rule can cause hardship, many states modified their law to take a more liberal approach. Under this more liberal rule, the death of the principal will not immediately terminate the agency relationship if immediate termination would cause a hardship.

When the relationship is terminated by the operation of law, it is usually not necessary to give notice to the other party or to the public at large. This rule is discretionary, and a court may decide not to apply it if it would cause a great hardship.

When an agent or a principal terminates the agency relationship early, the agent or principal has a duty to notify the other party so that the other party does not waste effort on a relationship that no longer exists.

It may be crucial to notify third parties even if it is not required, as in termination by operation of law. The agent may find it advantageous to do so, but the principal will find it even more important. If the principal fails to notify a third party, the third party may transfer money, like a rent payment, to the agent with the expectation that the agent will forward the funds to the principal. If the agent is unhappy with the termination, the agent may unlawfully abscond with the money.

The notice may take various forms. The preferred method is to personally notify the third person by mail, telephone, or telegram. Personal notice is generally required for all third parties who have had dealings with the agent. The advantage of using the telephone is that it is fast, but there is no written proof of the notification; the third party may deny receiving the notice. Notice should be given promptly, since one of its purposes is to prevent losses caused by a disgruntled agent who feels that the termination was unjust.

The law also accepts notice by publication (also called constructive notice). Usually such notice is published in the legal notices in the newspaper.

The principal will be protected if the third party actually knows that the agency relationship has been terminated even if the third party did not receive notice from the principal (that is, the third party may have heard about the termination from the agent or from someone else).

If the principal revokes the agent's authority wrongfully, then the agent can sue for breach of contract. If there is an anticipatory breach and the principal notifies the agent in advance of the breach, the agent can sue the principal immediately for the anticipated damages. The agent, at his or her election, may decide to wait until after the contract period and then sue for actual damages. In either case, the agent has an obligation to mitigate damages or to keep them as low as possible by searching for another similar position with another principal in the same locality.

Most agency relationships are formed for the benefit of the principal, but some are formed for the protection and benefit of the agent. The latter most commonly occur when the agent has loaned money to the principal, and the principal is securing the loan with collateral.

The statement in a contract that an agency is irrevocable will not make it true. Courts will analyze the facts to make sure that the agent has an *interest* in the collateral itself. Many court cases of this type arise because the principal wishes to terminate the agency relationship and the agent wishes to prevent it. Two special situations do restrict the principal's *ability* to terminate the agency relationship: (1) agency coupled with an obligation and (2) power coupled with an interest.

Agency Coupled with an Obligation

Suppose Paula needed cash for an investment. Since the banks would not lend Paula the money, she decided to borrow the $50,000 from Angela for two years. Angela insisted on having collateral, so Paula gave Angela the right to sell her apartment building if Paula did not repay her in two years. Angela was entitled to take her $50,000 and her expenses out of the sale, but she had to give the rest of the money to Paula. In this situation, Paula, the principal, had an *obligation* to her agent, Angela, to repay the $50,000. Angela could, if necessary, sell the property to obtain payment. Although a principal cannot terminate such an arrangement at will, the death of a party or a bankruptcy that affects the agency could terminate it.

Power Coupled with an Interest

Power coupled with an interest is similar to an agency coupled with an obligation, but it is more formal and the "agent's" rights are better protected. The parties have a power coupled with an interest if the "agent's" interest is taken through some formal document — for example, if Angela's interest had been taken through a mortgage on Paula's property. It also differs from an agency coupled with an obligation in that the death or bankruptcy of a party would not terminate it. As the name implies, it is not actually an agency relationship.

SUMMARY

Agency relationships center on the agreement between a principal and an agent that the agent shall act for the benefit of the principal. The principal must have capacity to consent to the relationship. The agent need not have contractual capacity. An agent who does not receive compensation is a gratuitous agent.

In determining the legal rights of the parties, it is important to determine whether the worker is an employee or an independent contractor. An independent contractor is hired to complete a job. The hiring party does not direct how the independent contractor does the task. In contrast, a principal can exert a lot of control over an employee and how the employee performs assigned duties. Because the principal can control the employee, the principal is more likely to be held financially responsible for the employee's acts.

An agent has a duty to act in good faith, to act loyally, to obey all lawful instructions, to act with reasonable care, to segregate funds, to account for all funds, and to give notice.

An agency relationship may terminate at a specified time agreed upon by the parties, at the will of the parties, or after the purpose of the agency has been fulfilled. It may be revoked or renunciated by one of the parties. It may also be terminated by operation of law. The method of termination will depend, at least in part, on the terms of the agreement.

A principal generally has the power to terminate an agency relationship even if the termination is wrongful. The principal does not have the power to terminate either an agency coupled with an obligation or a power coupled with an interest.

1. Tom purchased a new home through Gary, his realtor. The house needed a lot of work, so Tom arranged for George to paint the interior, for Harry to repair the furnace, for his own sons to plant grass in the back yard, and for Martha to clean the interior. Based on normal hiring relationships, who are agents, employees, or independent contractors, and why? Are the agents special agents or general agents, and why?

2. Tommy hired Jack to deliver one cord of pine wood for the fireplace in the house he rented. Jack usually just dumped the wood in the driveway—a practice known as a driveway delivery. However, this time he decided to help Tommy stack the wood in the garage. Tommy was standing in the garage as Jack backed the truck into position. Jack backed the truck too far, damaging both the truck and the garage wall. Was Jack an employee or an independent contractor? Who is liable to the injured third person (the landlord), and why? Who would have been liable if the truck had injured Tommy? Why?

3. Kurt was going to Lake Tahoe for a week's vacation. His friend Karen gave him $5 to bet on a particular football game while he was there. Kurt forgot all about placing the bet. If he had placed the bet, Karen would have won $15,000. What rights does Karen have? Suppose Karen's team had lost, what rights would Karen have then?

4. Ronnie worked for Acme Grocery Store. One day while Ronnie was unloading produce from a truck, Jimmy stopped to talk to him. Jimmy got in the truck, and as he was handing the boxes to Ronnie, Jimmy carelessly dropped a box on a person walking down the alley. Who is responsible for the injury, and why? Is it relevant that Jimmy was not being paid? If so, why?

5. Peter hired Andy to purchase some goods for him on the open market. While Andy was shopping, Ted offered Andy a $100 rebate if Andy purchased the goods from him. Andy did and kept the $100 for himself. What are the rights of the parties? Why?

6. Elaine worked as a travel agent for Travel Enterprises, Inc. As an incentive, a cruise ship line offered travel agents one free passage on a cruise for every twenty-five paying passengers they book on the line. The cruise ship line felt that this practice is good public relations. Elaine has earned two free passages. Who is entitled to these passages, and why?

7. After nine years of marriage, Jill and John have decided to get a divorce. Their neighbor Charlie, who is an attorney, is going to do the legal work for both parties and handle the property settlement. Are there any problems with this arrangement? Why?

8. Brad called Marty, his stockbroker, to tell him that Ellen, Brad's girlfriend, was going to purchase some stock from Marty. Brad directed Marty to charge the purchases against the brokerage account of Brad and his wife, Sue. What is the broker's responsibility to Brad and his wife? What advice would you give Marty?

9. Steve managed a 200-unit apartment complex. The owners wanted to convert the apartments to condominiums. The city council was going to have a hearing on the issue. Instead of sending the notice to the owners, the council sent the notice to Steve. What are the rights and obligations of the parties? Why?

10. Sarah signed a written contract stating that her agency relationship would last for four years and that she would have the irrevocable right to take orders from homemakers for aluminum pots and pans for her principal. In an attempt to economize, her principal fired her. What rights does Sarah have?

CASE PROBLEMS

1. Resnik worked for Day Realty as a licensed real estate salesperson. Resnik claimed that Day did not pay him the commission to which he was entitled. Resnik filed a complaint with the state labor commissioner. Since the state labor commissioner had jurisdiction only over employees, it was important to determine whether Resnik was an employee or an independent contractor. Under the applicable state law, a real estate salesperson cannot contract in his or her own name; can be employed only by a licensed real estate broker; can work under only one broker; and must allow his or her license to remain with the broker. If the broker fails to supervise the salesperson adequately, the broker's own license may be revoked or suspended. The Resnik–Day contract specifically said that Resnik was an independent contractor. Is Resnik an employee or an independent contractor? Why? (*Resnik* v. *Anderson and Miles*, 167 Cal. Rptr. 340 [Cal. App. 1980].)

2. Grace Hill purchased some furniture from Grant's. The furniture was defective so Hill contacted the seller, who assured her that they would send someone to repair the furniture. The repairman, Newman, identified himself as being from Grant's. Shortly after Newman left, an explosion and fire started in Hill's apartment and burned her severely. It was allegedly caused by the negligence of the repairman. Was Newman an independent contractor? Is Grant Furniture Company liable for Newman's actions? (*Hill* v. *Newman*, 316 A.2d 8 [N.J. Super. 1973].)

3. The attendant at a service station fatally shot Mrs. Giles's son. Under the lease agreement and the dealer contract, the oil company did not have the right to control the day-to-day operations of the service station and its employees. It was not in the custom of exercising such control. Was the attendant an employee of the oil company? Should the oil company be held liable? (*Giles* v. *Shell Oil Corporation*, 487 A.2d 610 [D.C. App. 1985].)

4. The cable splicers established their own work schedules and hired their own employees. They were highly skilled specialists who provided their own tools and trucks. They did not need routine supervision. The splicers bid for the jobs on a flat sum and were paid each week for the work that had been satisfactorily completed. Twenty percent of the contract price was held back until the job was completed. The splicers did not work on the contractor's premises. The splicers could work for several contractors simultaneously. Were the cable splicers employees of the contractor and so covered by the state unemployment compensation law? (*D. O. Creasman Electronics, Inc.* v. *State Department of Labor,* 458 So.2d 894 [Fla. App. 1984].)

5. Personnel employed by an independent security agency committed intentional torts. The security agency had been hired by the owners of the property for the purpose of protecting their premises and their invitees. Under these circumstances should the owner be liable for the acts of the security personnel? (*Peachtree-Cain Co.* v. *McBee,* 327 S.E.2d 188 [Ga. 1985].)

6. Anthony hired Jo'Dee to excavate a swimming pool site. Jo'Dee did not have the necessary state license to do excavation work. Anthony exercised the right to control Jo'Dee's work. A truck owned by one of the partners of Jo'Dee and driven by David Zaugg struck a motorcycle ridden by Harry Foss. Zaugg, an employee of Jo'Dee, was returning to the construction site after dumping a load of debris from the excavation. Zaugg turned left across Foss's lane without signaling or seeing Foss. Foss was killed in the accident. The truck driver had been instructed not to drive the truck. Were Zaugg and Jo'Dee independent contractors of Anthony at the time of the accident? (*Foss* v. *Anthony Industries,* 189 Cal. Rptr. 31 [Cal. App. 1983].)

7. The Silvas wanted to sell a parcel of real estate, and they listed it for sale with Bisbee, who worked for Midkiff Realty. A joint venture was formed for the purpose of purchasing this property. Bisbee was to manage this joint venture and in exchange was to receive 10 percent of the profits. The buyers and sellers agreed on a purchase price of $100,000 and terms. The Silvas were never informed that the purchaser was part of a joint venture or that Bisbee had an interest in the joint venture. There was substantial evidence that Bisbee believed that the property was worth more than $100,000 at the time of the sale. Did Bisbee breach her fiduciary duty to the Silvas? (*Silva* v. *Bisbee,* 628 P.2d 214 [Haw. App. 1981].)

8. The Wilsons borrowed money from Household Finance Corporation (HFC). At the time of the loan HFC sold the Wilsons a group creditor's disability policy. HFC was a major beneficiary under the insurance. West Coast Life Insurance Company provided the insurance. Claims were supposed to be made through HFC. Mr. Wilson became permanently disabled and so notified HFC. West Coast Life Insurance failed to make the payments under the policy, so HFC brought legal action against the Wilsons in Small Claims Court for the unpaid payments. Did HFC owe a duty of

good faith and fair dealing to the Wilsons? Did HFC breach its fiduciary duty to the Wilsons? (*Wilson* v. *Household Finance Corporation,* 182 Cal. Rptr. 590 [Cal. App. 1982].)

9. Kinmon contracted with the auctioneer to sell some real estate. The auction contract did not state that a minimum price would be realized. It indicated that the property would be sold for the highest price obtainable. Kinmon told the auctioneer that he expected to receive $103,500 for the property. The auctioneer indicated that the property would sell for its highest price on the date of sale. During the bidding, Kinmon went up to the auctioneer and stated that if the property brought less than $70,000, "I will take you to [the] Supreme Court." King went on with the auction and sold the property to the highest bidder for $35,000. Did Kinmon effectively revoke the agency relationship? (*Kinmon* v. *J. P. King Auction Company, Inc.,* 276 So.2d 569 [Ala. 1973].)

10. From 1953 until July, 1967, Geary worked as a sales representative for United States Steel Corporation (USS). Geary, an employee at will, sold tubular products to the oil and gas industry. USS designed a new product for use under high pressure. Geary believed that this new product had not been adequately tested and created a serious danger to users. He voiced his concerns to his superiors and was told to sell the product. He then contacted the vice-president in charge of the product to get action. The product was withdrawn from the market. Geary was fired. Under the circumstances, was Geary entitled to protection from being fired? Should he be protected from being fired? (*Geary* v. *United States Steel Corporation,* 319 A.2d 174 [Pa. 1974].)

Agency: Liability for Contracts

An agent may have many and varied duties, all or part of which may consist of forming contracts for the principal. This chapter deals with the liability of the agent, the principal, and the third party for the proper performance of these contracts. In applying rules of law, the court is often influenced by the reasonable expectations of the third party — that is, how the third party perceives the situation. The distinction between employees and nonemployees is not significant when the agent has entered into a contract; the courts will treat them the same. (The distinction *is* significant if the agent commits a tort.) Both classes of workers may enter into contracts for their principals. For the purpose of simplification, the term *agents* in this chapter will include both employee and

A FRAMEWORK
FOR CONTRAC-
TUAL
LIABILITY

587

nonemployee agents. The prime issue for consideration is whether the principal authorized the agent to enter into the contract. Another important factor is whether the principal is a disclosed, an undisclosed, or a partially disclosed principal. The status of the principal in this regard is determined when the agent and the third party enter the contract; the legal relationships are fixed at that time.

IMPOSING LIABILITY ON THE PRINCIPAL

A principal of any type will not be liable for every act committed by his or her agent. Nor will a principal be liable for every contract signed by the agent. To determine whether the principal should be held liable, the court will examine whether the agent was authorized to enter into this type of contract. Authority can be established in a number of different ways. They are commonly referred to as types of authority, and often they overlap in a given situation. For the third party to recover a judgment, all that needs to be proved is that one type of authority exists. Generally, authority to act as an agent includes authority to act only for the benefit, not the detriment, of the principal.

Express Authority

Express authority occurs when *the principal tells the agent that the agent has authority to engage in a specific act or to do a particular task,* as when a principal says to her secretary, "Please order some more stationery." Courts often strictly construe the words the principal uses when giving the authority. If the principal says to the agent, "Locate premises for another card shop," usually the court will interpret this to mean that the agent was not authorized to *buy* a store for the card shop. Therefore, an agent should also interpret the instructions narrowly or should ask for clarification.

Ratification

Ratification occurs when *the agent does something that was unauthorized at the time, and the principal approves it later.* It is approval by the principal after the contract was formed by the agent and after the principal has knowledge of the material facts.

When a principal ratifies a contract, the principal must ratify the whole agreement. The principal cannot elect to ratify parts of the contract and disregard the less advantageous parts.

The principal does not need to communicate the ratification verbally to anyone.[1] Generally, ratification may occur by an express statement or it may be implied by the principal clearly indicating through his or her conduct an intent not to disaffirm. An example of the latter would be if the principal retained and used the goods received under the agreement after learning of the contract and its terms. The ratification needs to follow the same form that the original authorization would have required. In a limited number of situations, the ratification will have to be in writing. If the agent–third-party contract

---

[1] *Restatement (Second) of Agency* (Philadelphia: American Law Institute, 1958), Section 97.

must be in writing under the Statute of Frauds, then the ratification must be written too.

Courts have imposed additional limitations on the doctrine of ratification. Both the principal and the agent must have been capable of forming a contract when the original contract occurred *and* when it was ratified. The relation-back doctrine is applied to ratified contracts. It states that if the contract is properly ratified, it is as if the contract were valid the whole time. Modern courts will not apply this doctrine if it would harm an innocent party who obtained rights in the contract during the time between the original contract formation and the ratification. Ratification cannot occur if important contract terms are concealed from the principal. Ratification will be effective only if the principal knows all the relevant facts. Also, the agent must have **purported** to act for the principal when the agent entered into the contract. If the agent did not reveal his or her agency capacity or if the agent was working for an undisclosed principal, there can be no ratification.

Purported Gave the impression that; reputed

Incidental authority reasonably and necessarily arises in order to enable the agent to complete his or her assigned duties. Suppose an agent is provided with merchandise that is to be sold door to door. The agent will reasonably and necessarily have incidental authority to deliver the merchandise and to collect the purchase price. As another example, take a builder who is hired as an on-site supervisor for a construction job. To complete the job, the supervisor would have incidental authority to hire, fire, and direct other employees on the site. No one realistically expects the supervisor to construct the building alone. The supervisor would also have incidental authority to purchase supplies.

Incidental Authority

Although in its reasoning the court in the following case referred to "implied" authority, which we shall discuss next, the case really centered on the issue of incidental authority.

St. Ann's Home for the Aged v. Daniels
420 N.E.2d 478 (Ill. App. 1981)

Daniels arranged to have his mother hospitalized in 1977. Dr. Smith, the physician in charge of the case, told Daniels that his mother was ready to be released from the hospital but should not return to her own apartment. Dr. Smith suggested that she be placed in St. Ann's and said that he could arrange this. Daniels agreed. Dr. Smith was a neighbor of the Danielses as well as their family physician. When Daniels returned from a business trip, he found that his mother had been admitted to St. Ann's, and he indicated that this arrangement was satisfactory.

FACTS

Did Dr. Smith have authority to bind Daniels to pay for his mother's care?

ISSUE

Yes. He did have this authority.

HOLDING

REASONING Dr. Smith was acting as Daniel's agent. An agency relationship does not depend only on an express statement, it may also be implied from the facts. It may be shown by reference to the situation of the parties, their acts, and other relevant circumstances. Daniels admitted that he had told Dr. Smith to go ahead and make the arrangements to have his mother placed in St. Ann's. Daniels did not have to expressly say that he would be responsible for the costs. A principal is bound for the acts he or she expressly authorizes the agent to do. A principal is also bound by the agent's normal acts that are necessary to complete performance.

Implied Authority

Implied authority is based on the agent's position or on past dealings between the agent and the third party. One type of implied authority arises when an agent is given a title and a position. It will be implied that the agent can enter into the same type of contracts that people with this title normally can. A vice-president of sales and marketing will have implied authority to purchase advertising in newspapers and on radio and to contract with an advertising agency for a new ad campaign. The agent will have this authority because *most* vice-presidents of sales and marketing have such authority. When the principal gave the agent the title, the agent received the implied power that goes with it.

Implied authority may also exist because of a series of similar dealings in the past between the agent and the third party. If the principal did not object to the past transactions, it is assumed that the principal authorized the earlier contracts and that this type of transaction is within the agent's power. For example, if a secretary customarily orders office supplies for a business on a monthly basis, the secretary has implied authority to continue to order office supplies in this manner.

Implied authority may exceed actual expressed authority. If the third party reasonably believed that the agent had this particular authority and did not know that the agent lacked it, the third party can recover on the basis of this implied authority.

Emergency Authority

Emergency authority is inherent in all agency relationships. It need not be expressed. *It provides the agent with authority to respond to emergencies even though the principal and agent never discussed the type of emergency or how to respond to it.* Suppose the owner of a jewelry shop leaves his manager in charge and goes out for supper. While the owner is absent, a fire starts in the stock room. In an effort to contain the fire, the manager rushes to the hardware store next door and charges four fire extinguishers. The principal—the owner—will have to pay for the fire extinguishers. The manager had emergency authority to purchase them.

Emergency authority will be found when all the following circumstances exist:

1. when an emergency or unexpected situation occurs that requires prompt action

2. when the principal cannot be reached in sufficient time for response

3. when the action taken by the agent was reasonable in that situation and it was expected to benefit the principal

Apparent Authority

Apparent authority occurs when *the principal creates the appearance that an agency exists or that the agent has broader powers than he or she actually has.* It is different from actual authority (express or implied) in that here the representation of authority is made to the third party rather than to the agent.[2] Apparent authority is based on the conduct of the principal; the conduct must cause a reasonable third party to believe that a particular person has authority to act as the principal's agent. An agent with apparent authority may or may not have actual authority.

Apparent authority may be created by intentional or careless acts of the principal and reasonable reliance by the third party. However, if the third party knew the agent did not have this authority, the reliance would not be reasonable.

In some cases, apparent authority exists even though there is no real agent. The person acting in the agent's role may be considered a "purported agent" (that is, one who claims to be an agent). Sometimes this purported agent is no longer an agent, and sometimes the person never was an agent. For example, suppose a company fires a sales representative but neglects to collect its samples, displays, and order forms from the representative. The ex-representative then takes a number of customer orders and disappears with the cash deposits. The company will have to return the deposits or credit the deposits to the customers' orders, because the ex-representative still had apparent authority to take orders. To prevent this situation, the company should have required the ex-representative to return all its sales materials.

When an agency relationship is terminated, a principal should take certain steps to terminate apparent authority. The principal should inform the agent that the relationship is terminated, call or send notices to people who have dealt with that agent, and sometimes advertise in newspapers and journals that the relationship is terminated. The principal should collect all identification tags, samples, displays, and order forms, as well as any other materials that could be used as evidence of the agency relationship.

Sometimes the purported agent never was employed by the principal, and yet the principal's conduct may cause the principal to be liable for the "agent's" actions. For example, a large and often understaffed department store does not require its clerks to wear identifying jackets or vests or even name tags. A customer selects some merchandise and walks toward a cash register. Another customer steps behind the cash register, rings up the sale, puts the merchandise in the bag, and pockets the payment. The store cannot charge the customer again for the merchandise. It is bound by the acts of the purported agent.

[2] Warren A. Seavey, *Handbook of the Law of Agency* (St. Paul, Minn.: West, 1964), Section 8D, p. 19.

Before they apply apparent authority, some courts require that the principal's actions give rise to a reasonable belief in the agent's authority and that there be detrimental reliance on the part of the third party.[3] A number of factors need to be considered, but the existence of apparent authority is a factual issue to be determined in each case.

A third party must act reasonably or the court will not apply the concept of apparent authority. The third party must take into consideration the facts and circumstances surrounding the transaction and the type of authority involved. Sometimes, based on the information available, the third party must investigate further before reasonably relying on apparent authority. In the following case, the court examined the reasonableness of the third party's behavior.

General Overseas Films, Ltd. v. Robin International, Inc.
542 F. Supp. 684 (S.D. N.Y. 1982)

FACTS General Overseas Films, Ltd. (GOF), acting through Robert Haggiag, agreed to lend $500,000 to Robin International, Inc. (Robin). Robin was owned and controlled by Nicholas Reisini. Reisini asked whether Haggiag would extend the payment dates if Reisini could provide a guarantee from Anaconda. Reisini introduced Haggiag to Charles Kraft, vice-president and treasurer of Anaconda. Kraft told Haggiag that Anaconda would guarantee Robin's debt to GOF up to the amount of $1 million. After some partial payments and numerous extensions, Robin was unable to pay and GOF filed suit on the guarantee.

ISSUE Did Kraft have the authority to bind Anaconda on the loan guarantee?

HOLDING No. Kraft did not have such authority.

REASONING Kraft did not have express authority to guarantee a loan. Article 9 of Anaconda's by-laws authorized the treasurer to borrow money for Anaconda; it did not authorize the treasurer to guarantee loans to another corporation. Moreover, Kraft did not have apparent authority to guarantee a loan. Guaranteeing a loan to another corporation is an extraordinary power and is not normally inferred from an agency relationship. Usually it must be specifically stated, especially in a case such as this one, where there was no logical business connection between Anaconda, Robin, and the loan. Apparent authority is based on the principal's action or inaction that allows the agent to mislead others. Article 9 of Anaconda's by-laws did not manifest the authority to guarantee the debt of another corporation, and Anaconda did not clothe Kraft with this type of authority. Haggiag did not exercise due care in relying on the guarantee. He should have realized that Anaconda's guarantee was unusual, and he should

---

[3] General Overseas Films, Ltd. v. Robin International, Inc., 542 F. Supp. 684 (S.D. N.Y. 1982), p. 688, fn. 2.

have required additional information about Anaconda and Robin's business relationship and about Kraft's authority to make the guarantee. Haggiag knew that his bank would not accept Kraft's guarantee without additional proof of Kraft's authority. A third party who deals with an agent must make a reasonable effort to discover the actual scope of authority. Haggiag did not.

Apparent authority may be used to hold a principal liable on contracts entered into by the agent. It ordinarily will not be used to make a principal liable for physical harm caused by the agent through negligence, assault, trespass, and similar torts.

Authority by estoppel prevents a principal who has misled a third party from denying the agent's authority. It is also called ostensible authority. It occurs when the principal *allows* the purported agent to pass himself or herself off as an agent and does not take steps to prevent the purported agent's representation.

Authority by Estoppel

Estoppel authority may occur by itself or in conjunction with other types of authority. When there is no express, incidental, implied, emergency, apparent, or ratification authority, then estoppel authority will be used only to protect the third party. It will not constitute the basis of a successful lawsuit by the principal against the third party. It creates rights for the third party and liabilities for the principal. It protects the third party or allows the third party to be reimbursed for injuries. As with other doctrines of agency law, the courts are weighing the respective rights of two relatively innocent people — the third party and the principal. The purported agent could be sued for fraud, but generally that person cannot be located or has insufficient funds to cover the losses caused.

Authority by estoppel is illustrated in the following example.

Roy was walking to class one Wednesday when he passed Grace and David, who were standing next to Roy's car. He overheard Grace pointing out all the car's features to David. It was evident that Grace was trying to sell the car to David on Roy's behalf. Roy thought this amusing and did not stop to clarify the situation. He went to class instead. He later learned that David made a $200 down payment on the car and that Grace disappeared with the money.

In a lawsuit between David and Roy, David would prevail. The court would apply agency by estoppel and decide that Roy is estopped (prevented) from denying that Grace was his agent, and Roy could have easily denied this. Roy's failure to speak helped to cause David's loss. The court would protect David from a loss by allowing him to recover.

The types of authority are summarized in Figure 34.1.

Figure 34.1 Rights of a Principal

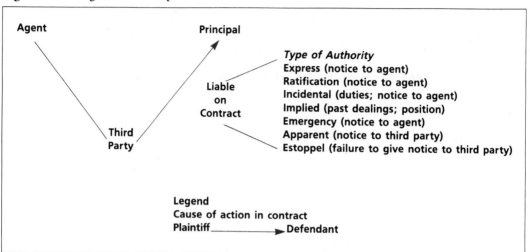

Imputing the Agent's Knowledge to the Principal

A principal may be held responsible for information known to the agent but not actually known by the principal. This concept is called *imputing knowledge.* Because an agent has a duty to inform the principal about important facts that relate to the agency, it will be assumed that the agent has performed that duty.

If the agent failed to perform this duty and the failure caused a loss, the principal, not the third party, should suffer the loss, because the principal selected the agent, placed the agent in a position of authority, and had control over the agent.

Knowledge of the agent is not always imputed to the principal. The information received by the agent must relate to the subject matter of the agency. If the principal owns a real estate firm, a movie theater, and a hardware store, and the agent works at the hardware store, knowledge that the agent obtains about the real estate firm will not be imputed. The knowledge must be within the scope of the agency. The court examined such an issue in the following case.

Ford Motor Credit Company v. Weaver
680 F.2d 451 (6th Cir. 1982)

FACTS   Weaver Farms purchased two Ford tractors and other farm equipment from Cleveland Ford Tractor (CFT), Inc., on an installment sale. One provision of the installment sale contract was that the contract would be assigned to Ford Motor Credit Company (FMCC), and it was. CFT and FMCC have the same parent corporation. FMCC frequently purchases commercial paper from CFT. FMCC has the right of first refusal on commercial paper that CFT creates, and customers leave contracts and payments at CFT for FMCC. Weaver Farms filed a petition for a Chapter 11 bankruptcy. FMCC was listed as a creditor, but their notice was delivered to CFT.

Should notice delivered to CFT be imputed to FMCC? **ISSUE**

No. It should not. **HOLDING**

Notice or knowledge of an agent may be imputed to the principal in certain **REASONING** situations. It is imputed when the agent acquired the notice or knowledge while acting within the scope of his or her authority, and when the knowledge pertains to matters within the scope of that authority. Just because an agent can collect payments for another, it does not follow that the agent can accept legal notice. This general rule is applicable in bankruptcy cases. CFT did not have actual or implied authority to collect the outstanding balance, receive legal notices for FMCC, or represent FMCC in any bankruptcy proceeding. CFT could act as a repository and accept individual payments, but that is a different type of authority. There was no apparent authority to accept legal notice in this case.

Before a principal will be bound by knowledge received by the agent, the agent must generally have actual or apparent authority to receive this type of knowledge.

When an agent clearly discloses that he or she is representing a principal and **DISCLOSED** identifies the principal, the principal is *disclosed*. In these situations, the princi- **PRINCIPAL** pal may be bound to the contract by any of the types of authority that have been discussed.

Normally when an agent indicates that he or she is entering into a contract on **Liability of the** behalf of the disclosed principal, the agent will not be liable on the contract. It **Agent** is clearly understood that the third party should look to the principal alone for performance. As with most legal rules, there are exceptions. If the agent fails to represent his or her capacity as such, the agent will be personally bound. The agent will also be bound if he or she intended to be bound. For example, the agent may say, "You can rely on me," or "You have my word on it." Why would an agent want to be liable on the principal's contract? Why would an agent want to undertake additional liability? An agent might do this if it is necessary to make a sale. The prospective buyer is unsure about the principal and his or her reputation or financial backing. Perhaps the prospect has a long working relationship with the agent, so the prospect is persuaded by the agent's guarantee of performance. If the agent indicates an intent to be bound on the contract, he or she will be bound. The agent doesn't really have valid grounds to complain if he or she is accepted at his or her word. The third party would generally prefer to sue the principal on the contract instead of the agent since the principal often has more assets.

Warranty of Authority

Whenever an agent of a disclosed principal enters into a contract, the agent makes all the following implied warranties. These warranties are not stated by the agent; they are implied by the situation.

1. The disclosed principal exists and is competent.
2. The agent is an agent for the principal.
3. The agent is authorized to enter into this type of contract for the principal.

The third party can sue the agent to recover for losses that were caused by the breach of warranty of authority. Perhaps the third party had losses because she did not receive the goods that were covered by the contract. Further, suppose the principal is not responsible for the losses because the agent was not authorized to enter into this type of contract. The third party can sue the agent.

If the agent fears that he does not have the authority to enter into this type of contract, he may be concerned about the warranties of authority. He would be wise, then, to negate the warranties. This can be accomplished by stating that there is no warranty or by specifically stating to the third party the limitations on the agent's actual authority. For example, Rhoda hires Beth as an agent and tells her to locate a parcel of agricultural real estate. Beth locates a parcel that meets Rhoda's specifications. The owner of the parcel wants Beth to sign the purchase contract, but Beth is not sure whether she has authority to sign. If she fully and truthfully discloses the situation surrounding her authority, Beth would negate the warranty of authority. If the owner still wished to sign the contract with Beth, the owner would assume the responsibility and loss if the contract were not authorized. Here the owner would be relying on his own judgment.

The agent may also be liable for fraud if he intentionally misrepresented his authority.

Liability of the Third Party

Lawsuit by the Principal

When a principal has been disclosed from the beginning, the third party realizes, or should realize, that the principal has an interest in the contract. The principal can successfully sue the third party on the contract if the agent was authorized to enter into this type of contract for the principal. In other words, the third party will be liable if there is express, implied, incidental, emergency, apparent, or ratification authority.

Lawsuit by the Agent

Normally the agent has no right to sue the third party on a contract. An agent *may* successfully sue the third party if the agent can show that she has an interest in the contract. The most common type of interest would be one in which the agent was entitled to a commission on the sale. For example, a real estate broker, the agent, entered into a contract on behalf of a homeowner, the principal. The agent was entitled to a 6 percent commission payable from the proceeds of the sale. The third party, the buyer, breached the contract. The agent could sue to recover the lost commission. (In this type of case, the principal may decide that it is not worth suing, but the agent may feel that it is.)

An agent may also successfully sue the third party when the agent intended to be bound. This rule is based on equitable principles. If the agent is liable to the third party, then the third party should be liable to the agent, too. In some cases, a principal may assign to the agent the right to file the lawsuit. In these cases, also, the agent could sue on the contract.

UNDISCLOSED PRINCIPAL

An *undisclosed* principal is one whose existence and identity are unknown to the third party. There are many reasons why a principal would want to be undisclosed—to negotiate a better deal or simply to negotiate a deal, or to conceal an investment in a project or a donation to a charity. For example, Thomas, a politician, wants to invest in a racetrack. He is aware that racetracks and betting on the horses have an unsavory reputation; so he hires an agent to negotiate the investment for him. Thomas buys the investment through his agent and thus remains anonymous.

Liability of the Agent

When the principal is completely undisclosed, the third party believes that she is contracting with the agent and that the agent is dealing for himself. Based on her knowledge, that assumption is reasonable. If there is a default on the contract, the third party can sue the agent. As far as the third party is concerned, there were only two parties to the contract: the third party and the agent. The court dealt with such an issue in the case that follows.

Murphy v. *Dell Corporation*
440 A.2d 223 (Conn. 1981)

DeLisa, an agent for Dell Corporation, entered into a contract with Murphy. There was conflicting testimony over whether DeLisa indicated his role as Dell Corporation's agent. The lawsuit was originally filed against Dell Corporation and DeLisa. Murphy withdrew the complaint against Dell Corporation.

FACTS

Is DeLisa personally liable for the balance due on the contract?

ISSUE

Yes. He is personally liable.

HOLDING

REASONING   The trial court concluded that Murphy did not "notice" that the contract was with Dell Corporation and that DeLisa failed to disclose his representative capacity. "The law is settled that where an agent contracts in his own name, without disclosing his representative capacity, the agent is personally liable on the contract." The trial court decided the questions of fact in favor of Murphy. Their decision must be upheld unless it is clearly erroneous.

Liability of the Principal

If the third party discovers the identity of the principal, the third party can sue the principal. The principal will be held liable if the agent was authorized to enter into this type of contract for the principal.

The third party, then, has legal rights against both the agent and the principal. This does not mean that the third party can collect twice. The third party must make an *election* to sue either the agent *or* the principal. Obviously, an important factor in this decision is who has the funds to pay a judgment. If the third party sues the principal and loses, he or she will be barred from then suing the agent. The reverse is also true. There is one exception, and that is if the third party sues the agent and loses *before* discovering the principal. In that case, the third party is not considered to have made an election and will be permitted to sue the principal later.

Liability of the Third Party

The third party may not be the one who suffers damages because of a breach of contract but may, in fact, be the one who committed the breach. Since the third party thought he was liable to the agent, it is reasonable to allow the agent to sue him. The law allows this action.

Under some circumstances, the undisclosed principal may, in her own name, also be able to sue the third party. There are some limitations, however. The principal can file a lawsuit by herself only if the contract is **assignable.** (See Chapter 15 for a discussion of assignable contracts.) If it is assignable, the position of the third party would not be jeopardized by either the assignment or the suit by the principal. The agent could assign the contract to someone else; so the agent should be able to "transfer" the contract rights to the

Assignable rights
Contract rights that may be transferred legally

Figure 34.2   Rights of an Undisclosed Principal

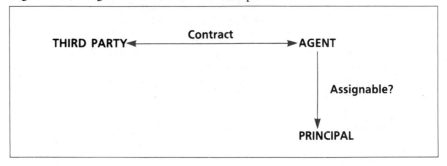

principal. This relationship is shown in Figure 34.2. The third party will have to pay for the damages only once.

The principal may not be able to sue in her own name because the contract is not assignable, or the principal may still wish to keep her identity secret. Then the principal can arrange for her agent to file the lawsuit in the agent's name.

A *partially disclosed principal* is one whose existence is known to the third party but whose identity is not. In other words, the agency is disclosed, but the principal is undisclosed. An example would be Robert Smith's signing a contract as "Robert Smith, agent." The rules that are applied to partially disclosed principals are similar to those applied to undisclosed principals. The principal may be sued if the contract is breached, and the suit will be successful if the principal authorized the actions of the agent. The principal can sue the third party. The contract need not be assignable because, in this case, the third party knew that another party in interest was involved.

The general rule is that when an agent is working for a partially disclosed principal, the agent will be personally liable on the contract. The third party is probably relying on the agent's reputation and credit. It is unlikely that the third person is relying on the reputation and credit of the unrevealed principal. The exception would be if the contracting parties agreed that the agent would not be held liable. This may occur if the agent indicated that he or she would not be bound and the third person did not object to this limitation.

PARTIALLY DISCLOSED PRINCIPAL

The agency relationship is contractual in nature. It will actually be a contract if the principal and agent both give up consideration, which is generally the case. As with other contracts, the Statute of Frauds may apply and require written evidence of the contract. The provisions of the Statute of Frauds that are most likely to apply are those relating to contracts that cannot possibly be performed within one year and contracts involving the sale of real estate. Even if the Statute of Frauds does not apply, it is wise to write the contractual provisions.

The equal dignities rule also requires that some agency agreements be in writing. This rule states that the agent-principal contract deserves (requires) the same dignity as the agent–third-party contract. This is shown in Figure 34.3: if contract A must be written, then contract B must be written. If the agent was hired to locate and purchase goods costing over $500, then the UCC Statute of Frauds requires that the agent–third-party contract be in writing. The equal dignities rule will require that the agent–principal contract also be in writing.

CONTRACT BETWEEN THE PRINCIPAL AND THE AGENT

The Need for a Writing

Some employment contracts contain *covenants* (promises) that the agent will not work for a competing firm. It may provide that (1) the agent will not "moonlight" with the competition or (2) the agent will not compete with the

Covenants Not to Compete

Figure 34.3 Equal Dignities Rule

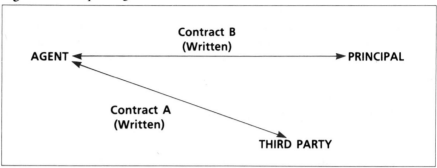

principal after this employment relationship is terminated. Some contracts do both. The second provision is usually applicable if the agent either quits or is fired. It also specifies a time period for which the competition is to be restricted and the area in which the competition is not allowed — for example: "If this employment is terminated by the employee or the employer, then the employee shall not establish or obtain employment with another cable television company in Chicago, Illinois." This restriction may seem harsh if the agent's skills are valuable only to a cable television company.

There are competing legal considerations in disputes about these covenants. On the one hand, the agent did agree not to compete. Perhaps he was desperate for the position and felt that he would not get it without signing the covenant. The agent may not have had equal bargaining power with the principal. Generally, parties *are* bound by their contract provisions. On the other hand, it would be a hardship on the agent to unduly restrict his ability to locate another job. In addition, it would be harmful to society if people were not allowed to seek the positions for which they are most highly qualified. For these reasons, courts scrutinize covenants not to compete to determine whether the covenant is legal. Courts do not favor covenants not to compete. The covenant will be illegal if it is against public policy.

To determine whether the covenant is against public policy, the court will examine its reasonableness. It will look at the situation surrounding the employment to see whether the principal has a legitimate interest in preventing the competition.

Covenants not to compete are also prevalent in another type of contract — one in which the owner of a business sells the business to a buyer and the buyer obtains a promise that the previous owner will not compete with him. In such cases, the buyer has an interest in not having competition from the seller. Generally, the buyer pays a larger purchase price so that the seller will sell the **goodwill** of the business *and* sign a covenant not to compete with the buyer. Courts are more inclined to enforce covenants not to compete in these contexts.

There are additional requirements for a valid covenant not to compete. The time and area specifications of the covenant must be reasonable. What is

Goodwill The good name and reputation of a business and thereby the ability to attract clients

reasonable depends on the type of employment. Covenants containing time periods of two to five years are generally acceptable to the courts. The limitation is really the time period for which the agent would be able to draw contacts away from the principal or the time period in which these contacts would still have value. The covenant also must be reasonable in the area specified. The standard is: if the agent moved, how far could she still attract the contacts? The answer will depend on the field of the agent's expertise. For example, a patient might travel halfway across the country to see a world-famous heart transplant specialist, but many patients will not even go across town to see a general practitioner.

If the principal has a legitimate business interest and the covenant is reasonable, the principal could sue the breaching agent or former agent for an injunction or contract damages. However, a principal may structure a covenant not to compete that is too broad. The courts apply one of two approaches in such cases. One is to declare the covenant void and to ignore it. The agent can then do whatever he wishes with impunity. Another approach is for the court to reform (modify) the contract to make its restrictions reasonable.

Courts may examine the following criteria in determining whether to enforce a covenant not to compete in an employment contract:

1. Is the restraint reasonable in the amount of protection it affords, or is it excessive?

2. Is the restraint unreasonable because it is unduly harsh on the agent?

3. If the agent worked for a competitor, would that threaten irreparable injury to the principal?

4. Is the agency relationship of a unique and unusual type?

Some state statutes hold that a principal cannot prevent an ordinary employee from engaging in competition once the employment is over.[4]

A covenant not to compete is not necessary to prevent an agent from divulging trade secrets or customer lists after the employment is terminated. Under common law, this behavior is a violation of the agent's duties of loyalty.

The following case dealt with the issue of a covenant not to compete.

Holiday Food Co., Inc. v. Munroe
426 A.2d 814 (Conn. Super. 1981)

Munroe worked as a salesperson for Holiday Food, a company that sold and   **FACTS**
delivered frozen foods. Munroe never examined or used the customer list that
the company made available to its sales staff. His supervisor provided him with
the names and addresses of contacts, which he kept in a personal notebook.

---

[4] See, for example, California Business and Professions Code, Section 16600.

During his employment with Holiday Food, Munroe expressly refused to sign a covenant not to compete. When he left to start a competing frozen-food business, Munroe took his notebook with him and started to call on his old contacts.

ISSUE   Did Munroe violate his duties when he solicited orders from his old customers?

HOLDING   No. Munroe did not violate his duties to Holiday Food.

REASONING   Unless the name of a customer is a trade secret, former employees can contact customers who used to order from them. A trade secret may include any formula, device, pattern or compilation of information that people use to get an edge over their competitors. Unless there is a covenant not to compete, agents may compete with principals after the agency is terminated. They may not use trade secrets revealed to them or surreptitiously discovered by them. Customer lists may or may not be trade secrets depending on the facts of a particular case. Courts may examine the extent to which the employee-employer relationship was a confidential one; how the employee acquired the information; the former employee's personal relationship with the customers; and the unfair advantage obtained by the former employee. An appellate court should not overturn a trial court's decision unless it is clearly erroneous. The trial court's decision that the customer list was not a trade secret was upheld in this case.

SUMMARY   A disclosed principal is one whose identity and existence are known to the third party. A partially disclosed principal is one whose existence is known but whose identity is not. When the principal is undisclosed, the third party thinks he or she is dealing only with the agent. In this case, the agent will be bound on the contract because the agent is a "party" to it. The type of principal affects the rights and obligations of the agent, the principal, and the third party.

When the principal has been disclosed, the principal can sue and be sued on the contract if there is express, implied, incidental, emergency, apparent, or ratification authority. These types of authority often overlap. If only authority by estoppel exists, courts will apply it to protect a third party but not to protect the principal. Information received by the agent in the course and scope of the job will generally be imputed to the principal. Usually the agent of a disclosed principal would not be bound on the contract itself; but the agent may be responsible for breach of warranty of authority. The third party will be liable to the principal on the contract and to the agent if the agent had an interest or intended to be bound.

The agency agreement needs to be in writing if this is required by either the Statute of Frauds or the equal dignities rule. Covenants not to compete may be valid if the principal has a legitimate interest in preventing the competition, provided that the limitation is reasonable in the length of time and the area specified.

1. What is a partially disclosed principal? How might partial disclosure occur?

2. Ted farmed 200 acres of cotton. His neighbor had an additional 100 acres of cotton, which was for sale. Since Ted and his neighbor had been feuding for twelve years, the neighbor would not sell the land to Ted. Ted hired Rose to act as his undisclosed agent. Rose bought the land and started to transfer it to Ted. The neighbor tried to stop the transfer. What would be the legal rights of the parties in this situation?

3. How do the rights and liabilities of an agent to a partially disclosed principal differ from those of an agent to an undisclosed principal?

4. Sally, a secretary, ordered four reams of erasable typing paper and had it delivered to her home. Sally had the bill sent to her employer. Based on the information provided, did Sally have authority to do this? Why or why not? What additional information would be helpful? Why?

5. What is the difference between implied authority and implied ratification?

6. Besides collecting samples, displays, and order forms, what else should a principal do to terminate the apparent authority of an agent?

7. Bonnie was buying a house through Angie, who was a real estate agent. Angie recommended that they have an appliance inspector inspect the house before the sale was completed. Angie made the arrangements. Joe, the inspector, said that all the major appliances were in proper working order. The sale went through, and Bonnie is now living in the house. Joe has not been paid yet. By whom is he entitled to be paid? Why?

8. Why are warranties of authority applicable only when there is a disclosed principal?

9. Would it be reasonable if a fast-food chain required all new employees to sign an agreement that they would not work for another fast-food restaurant for six months after leaving the chain? Would it be legal? Could an ex-employee legally reveal the recipe for the chain's special blend of eleven herbs and spices? Why or why not?

10. Lisa had some charges on her telephone bill that she did not understand. The bill stated that billing inquiries should be made by calling (412) 312-2941. She called the number and spoke with Janet. Janet said that she would remove the charges. The charges have not been removed. Is Lisa entitled to have them removed? Do you think Janet had authority for her statement? Why or why not?

1. Leonard Taylor, a district manager for Pargas, Inc., diverted checks into his personal account at Rapides Bank. The payee on these checks was his employer. He endorsed the checks with a rubber stamp that had Pargas's name and address on it. Rapides Bank never obtained a corporation reso-

lution authorizing Taylor to endorse the checks. There was no authorization for Taylor to deposit these checks to his personal account. Should Rapides Bank or Pargas suffer the loss? (*Pargas, Inc.* v. *Estate of Taylor,* 416 So.2d 1358 [La. App. 1982].)

2. Carol Horowytz opened a checking account with Bank of America. The account documents indicated that Horowytz was doing business under the trade name of E.D.S. The signature card indicated that J. Pearl, Horowytz's father, had power of attorney. The card stated that Pearl had authority to sign and endorse checks, notes, and drafts and transact all business with the bank. It did not specifically state that Pearl had authority to borrow money on Horowytz's credit. Did Pearl have authority to borrow money that Horowytz would have to repay? (*Bank of America, National Trust and Savings Association* v. *Horowytz,* 248 A.2d 446 [N.J. County Ct. 1968].)

3. Grace Hill purchased some furniture from Grant's. The furniture was defective so Hill contacted the seller, who assured her that they would send someone to repair the furniture. The repairman, Newman, identified himself as being from Grant's. Shortly after Newman left, an explosion and fire started in Hill's apartment and burned her severely. It was allegedly caused by the negligence of the repairman. Did Newman have apparent authority? Was he an apparent agent for Grant's? Is Grant Furniture Company liable for Newman's actions? (*Hill* v. *Newman,* 316 A.2d 8 [N.J. Super. 1973].)

4. The defendant owned two farms and he hired David Berry to operate them. Berry and his family lived in the house on the main farm. In 1953, Berry asked the plaintiff to bale the hay "on the hill." Plaintiff did so and then made out a bill for the defendant. This bill was paid about a month later. In 1954, Berry asked the plaintiff if he would "bale the hay on the hill the same as last year." The plaintiff baled the hay and presented the bill as he had done before. When defendant returned from a trip, he refused to pay. The defendant claimed that he was leasing the farms to Berry in 1954 and selling some of the crops and livestock to him. Berry was the owner of the hay in 1954. The defendant did not give the plaintiff any notice that there was a new business arrangement with Berry; there was no apparent change in the operation of the farm. Should the defendant be liable to the plaintiff for the bill? (*Record* v. *Wagner,* 128 A.2d 921 [N.H. 1957].)

5. Walker left his trailer at the Pacific Mobile Homes, Inc. lot to be sold on consignment. Walker dealt with Robert Stewart, who was seen on the lot on numerous occasions. There was a sign on the lot that indicated that the whole business was an enterprise of Pacific Mobile Homes, Inc. Stewart used the principal's forms and stationery to write up a consignment agreement. Stewart seemed to be the only person present on the lot and seemed to be in control of the office. Later, a Robert Henderson telephoned Walker in Oregon and asked him if he had left his trailer on

consignment. Henderson explained that Stewart was no longer at Pacific Mobile Homes but that Henderson was now the manager. Walker was informed that his trailer had been sold and he received a few payments. Henderson absconded with the rest of the funds. Henry Shelly, president of Pacific Mobile Homes, testified that neither salesman had authority to complete a sale; Shelly had to sign all sales documents. Shelly said that his company forbade its salesmen to take trailers on consignment and that he did not know anything about Walker's trailer. Would a reasonable person assume that Stewart and Henderson had authority from the mobile home company to buy, sell, and deliver trailers for cash, on credit, consignment, or in exchange? (*Walker* v. *Pacific Mobile Homes, Inc.,* 413 P.2d 3 [Wash. 1966].)

6. Morrow was planning a business trip to Honduras in a private plane and wanted flight insurance. He discussed the matter with Bennett, who was the attendant at the insurance counter in the airport and who sold insurance from a number of different companies. Bennett selected an insurance policy for him and completed the application. In the space provided for flight information, Bennett wrote "private air." The printed policy stated that it covered only travel on an aircraft operated by a scheduled air carrier. It also stated that the insurance agent could not vary the terms of the policy. Morrow died when the private plane crashed. Did Bennett have implied or apparent authority to issue insurance coverage to Morrow? Why or why not? (*Travelers Insurance Company* v. *Morrow,* 645 F.2d 41 [10th Cir. 1981].)

7. James Cecka instructed the account representatives to sell short seven contracts for April cattle. He told them to sell out the contracts before any loss occurred in excess of $2100. He then told them to buy seven contracts of April cattle and "to maintain my same relative position" by selling short contracts for October cattle. A cattle contract is the trading unit used on the Chicago Mercantile Exchange; cattle are traded on a "contract basis," not by total poundage; a "contract" represents a standard poundage that is set by the Chicago Mercantile Exchange. Between April and October, there was an increase in poundage and margin requirements for the type of cattle contracts in which Cecka had invested. Poundage was increased from 25,000 to 40,000. The account representatives failed to inform Cecka about this change. Cecka did not tell the account representatives to maintain the same dollar or poundage position. Cecka did not tell the representatives how many contracts to buy. Did the account representatives violate their duty to Cecka? Were they obligated to tell him about this change? (*Cecka* v. *Beckman & Co., Inc.,* 104 Cal. Rptr. 374 [Cal. App. 1972].)

8. At the suggestion of Petrich, a real estate broker, Chapple decided to build a movie theater on an unimproved lot that she owned and to rent the theater to Rodriques. When the construction bids were in, Chapple felt the lowest bid was still too high, and she asked Petrich to negotiate with

Big Bear (the lowest bidder) to obtain a lower price. Big Bear prepared a list of modifications and presented them at a meeting attended by Petrich, Rodriques, and the architect. Those present at the meeting agreed to reduce the capacity of the air conditioner from a twenty-ton capacity to an eight-ton capacity. Chapple was not informed of this agreement. She signed a written contract to have Big Bear construct a movie theater that would have a twenty-ton-capacity air-conditioning unit. Rodriques signed an addendum to the contract calling for a reduction to an eight-ton air conditioner. No one asked Chapple to sign the addendum. An eight-ton unit was used. Could Chapple successfully sue for breach of contract, or did someone, acting as her agent, authorize the change of plans? What type of authority did the agent have? Should knowledge about this change be imputed to Chapple? (*Chapple* v. *Big Bear Super Market No. 3*, 167 Cal. Rptr. 103 [Cal. App. 1980].)

9. Snelling and Snelling, Inc., licensed PPS to operate an employment agency in Pittsburgh. The contract between them stated, in part, that it was a license agreement; that the licensee was not authorized to act for or on behalf of Snelling in any matter whatsoever; that the licensee could not change location without Snelling's written approval; that the licensee could not use any name or service mark other than that of Snelling and Snelling; that the licensee had to use Snelling's training manuals and procedures; that the licensee had to advertise in the Yellow Pages following a form required by Snelling; that the licensee had to obtain insurance naming Snelling as an additional insured; and that the licensee had to promptly notify Snelling of any claims under the insurance. When a dispute arose over PPS's placement practices, the plaintiff filed suit against PPS and Snelling and Snelling. Process for both defendants was served at the PPS office. Was this adequate service of process on Snelling and Snelling, or should the lawsuit against Snelling and Snelling be dismissed? Did PPS have the authority to act as Snelling's agent in accepting service of process? (*Sauers* v. *Pancoast Personnel, Inc.*, 439 A.2d 1214 [Pa. Super. 1982].)

10. Continental sued Eugene Grovijohn and his new employer, Amoco Chemicals, to enforce a covenant not to compete. Grovijohn was a plant manager in the plastic beverage bottle division of Continental. He was never employed there as an engineer or a technician. Grovijohn had agreed not to disclose, "directly or indirectly," or "use outside of the Continental organization during or after [his] employment, any confidential information" without Continental's consent. Amoco hired Grovijohn as a plant manager. There was no evidence that Grovijohn intended to reveal confidential information or that Amoco intended to use confidential information. Should Amoco be prevented from employing Grovijohn in this capacity? (*Continental Group, Inc.* v. *Amoco Chemicals Corp.*, 614 F.2d 351 [3rd Cir. 1980].)

CHAPTER 35

Agency: Liability for Wrongs and Losses

AGENT'S LIABILITY

Agents often engage in physical activities or labor on behalf of the principal. These activities bring the agent into close contact with the general public. When the agent is careless or overly aggressive, there is a good chance that some members of the public will be injured. This chapter deals with the agent's and the principal's responsibility to the public for these injuries when they occur.

Vicarious liability for torts involves different policy considerations from those surrounding an agent's ability to bind the principal in business dealings with third persons. In contract matters, there is a conscious desire to interact with the public and a conscious decision to enter into business arrangements with the public by means of the agent. In most tort situations, neither the principal nor the agent desires that the tort occur. But once the tort has occurred, someone has to suffer the financial burden, even if that someone is the innocent victim. Who should pay? The principal? The agent? Or the third person?

The general rule of tort law is that everyone is liable for his or her own

Vicarious liability Legal responsibility for the wrong committed by another person

607

torts. This general rule is followed in agency law. Since the agent committed the tort, the agent is liable for the harm that occurs. The fact that the agent is working for the principal at the time of the tort does not alter the general rule.

PRINCIPAL'S LIABILITY:
RESPONDEAT SUPERIOR

When the agent commits a tort that harms a third person, the agent should be responsible for the harm. However, in agency law, there are some circumstances in which the principal is also held liable for the torts committed by the agent. Notice that in these situations the *principal* is being held liable for the conduct of the *agent*. Since the agent is also liable for the tortious conduct, the liability is said to be *joint and several.* This means that either party may be held liable (several liability), or that both parties may be held liable (joint liability).

The theory under which *principals are held liable for the torts of their agents* even though the principals are not personally at fault is known as *respondeat superior.* Literally, it means "let the master answer." It is also referred to as a "deep-pockets" theory, based on the belief that the principal's pockets are deeper (that is, they hold more money) than those of the agent. The law generally involves an attempt to balance competing interests, which can clearly be seen in the application of the *respondeat superior* doctrine. If, for example, the victim has suffered $175,000 in injuries from an automobile accident caused by the negligence of an agent, and the agent has a total net worth of only $50,000, the victim cannot be fully compensated by the agent. However, if the principal is a multimillion-dollar corporation, the principal could fully compensate the victim. In these circumstances, the court must evaluate all the facts and determine whether *respondeat superior* should be applied in this particular case.

Respondeat superior is not based on the idea that the principal did anything wrong. Rather, it involves a special application of the doctrine of **strict liability.** Simply put, the principal hired the agent; the agent did something wrong; the principal should pay. "But for" the existence of the agency, no harm would have resulted. Someone should pay; the principal is best able to pay and afford the loss; therefore, the principal will have to pay. However, *respondeat superior* does require a *wrongful act* by an agent for which the principal can be held liable. The following case dealt with such an issue.

Strict liability Liability for an action simply because it occurred, not because it is the fault of the person who must pay

---

Morrison v. Concord Kiwanis Club
279 S.E.2d 96 (N.C. App. 1981)

FACTS   Barbara Ann Morrison and her sister were attending the Kiwanis Camp for handicapped children. Barbara had had physical disabilities resulting from cerebral palsy since birth. She was generally confined to a wheelchair. Her mother described Barbara's balance control problem to Westbrook, a camp counselor, when she brought the children to the camp. It was not camp policy to require a completed camp registration form or a doctor's medical statement. Barbara's mother was told that the children would be active and play ball, go canoeing, and swim. Later that day Barbara wanted to swing on a little stagecoachlike glider. The counselors tried to dissuade her, but she was insistent. Wilson, the camp director, asked if she had been on a swing glider before. Barbara said she had, and this was confirmed by her sister. Wilson carried Barbara over and put her on the swing. She held onto the seat. She seemed secure, so Wilson pulled the swing back a few inches and let it go. Wilson and Westbrook were standing at opposite sides of the swing. Barbara fell off the seat and onto the floor of the swing. No one was able to catch her in time. She suffered injuries and was taken to the hospital.

Is the Kiwanis Club responsible based on *respondeat superior?*   **ISSUE**

No. The Kiwanis Club is not responsible.   **HOLDING**

Respondeat superior is based on the concept that the employer is liable for the   **REASONING**
torts of its employees. Here there was no evidence that the employees accidentally or intentionally committed a tort. The jury specifically found that the employees — the camp director and the camp counselor — were not negligent. The Kiwanis Club might have been responsible because of its own negligence in hiring employees, in training employees, or in not establishing admissions procedures. This would be true if the Kiwanis Club's negligence had been the proximate cause of the injury. The plaintiff did not prove that theory of recovery.

Respondeat superior does not make the principal an insurer for all acts of the agent. The principal is liable only for those actions that are in the *course* and *scope* of the employment. Consequently, the issue in most cases in which the agent committed the tort, but the suit is against the principal, involves a decision as to whether the agent was in the course and scope of employment when the tort was committed. To resolve this question, it is important to know the agent's duties, working hours, state of mind, deviation from route, assigned location, and the principal's right to control the agent. It does not matter if the principal fails to exert actual control over how the agent completes the tasks as long as the principal has the right to use this control. The principal's *right to control* is really what distinguishes "servant" and "nonservant" agents. A principal who has the right to control may be called a *master,* and the agent may be called a *servant. Respondeat superior* applies only to servant agents. It does not apply to nonservant agents because the principal lacks control and thus is not a master. This chapter will use the general terms *principal* and *agent.* (For the purposes of this chapter, the term *agent* will imply a servant type of agent, and the term *principal,* a master.)

In the following case, the court examined the course and scope of an agent's employment.

Bowers v. *Potts*
617 S.W.2d 149 (Tenn. App. 1981)

FACTS

Potts was employed as foreman for J. W. Petty Construction Company, which was laying an underground conduit for South Central Bell. The job required the extraction of dirt, which was stored at two locations so that it could later be replaced in the trenches. Petty had promised any excess dirt to South Central Bell and to Smyrna Hardware and Lumber Company. Terrell knew that Potts was supplying dirt and contacted Potts about hauling some to Terrell's property. Potts agreed to do this in his spare time for $10 or $15 per load. Potts was hauling the dirt to Terrell's on a Saturday, his day off, using his own truck to do so, when he had an accident with another vehicle. Weatherly, the driver of the other vehicle, died at the scene. Bowers, Weatherly's **personal representative,** filed this suit for wrongful death.

Personal representative A person who handles the financial affairs of someone who has died

ISSUE

Was Potts in the course and scope of his employment for Petty?

HOLDING

No. Potts was acting for himself, not for Petty.

REASONING

Potts was being paid by Terrell and not by Petty. Potts worked for Petty on weekdays and not on Saturday. Potts was not at the location where he conducted work for Petty. There is no evidence that this activity helped Petty or was strongly motivated by an intent to help Petty. Potts did it to help himself and Terrell. There is no competent testimony to support the idea that Potts's activities were authorized, permitted, known, or ratified by Petty, nor did Potts's actions benefit Petty. At the end of the job, Petty had to correct the dirt stockpile deficiency. The deficiency was caused, at least in part, by Potts's activities. Potts was held liable for his negligence, but Petty was not.

Factors Listed in the *Restatement of Agency*

The *Restatement (Second) of Agency* indicates the factors that should affect the determination of whether an agent is in the scope of his or her employment. The factors include the following:

General Statement

(1) Conduct of a servant is within the scope of employment if, but only if:
  (a) it is of the kind he is employed to perform;
  (b) it occurs substantially within the authorized time and space limits;
  (c) it is actuated, at least in part, by a purpose to serve the master; and
  (d) if force is intentionally used by the servant against another, the use of force is not unexpectable by the master. . . .[1]

---

[1] *Restatement (Second) of Agency* (Philadelphia: American Law Institute, 1958), Section 228(1). Copyright 1958 by The American Law Institute. Reprinted with the permission of The American Law Institute.

Kind of Conduct Within Scope of Employment . . .

(2) In determining whether or not the conduct, although not authorized, is nevertheless so similar to or incidental to the conduct authorized as to be within the scope of employment, the following matters of fact are to be considered:
   (a) whether or not the act is one commonly done by such servants;
   (b) the time, place and purpose of the act;
   (c) the previous relations between the master and the servant;
   (d) the extent to which the business of the master is apportioned between different servants;
   (e) whether or not the act is outside the enterprise of the master or, if within the enterprise, has not been entrusted to any servant;
   (f) whether or not the master has reason to expect that such an act will be done;
   (g) the similarity in quality of the act done to the act authorized;
   (h) whether or not the instrumentality by which the harm is done has been furnished by the master to the servant;
   (i) the extent of departure from the normal method of accomplishing an authorized result; and
   (j) whether or not the act is seriously criminal.[2]

No one or two of these factors are controlling. The judge or jury should weigh all the factors involved and reach a decision. Since the triers of fact exercise a lot of discretion in these cases, fact situations that seem very similar may result in different decisions by the court.

Two of the factors analyzed by the courts in determining course and scope of employment are whether the tort occurred on the work premises and whether it occurred during work hours. These factors were influential in the following case.

Time and Place of Occurrence

Chastain v. Litton Systems, Inc.
694 F.2d 957 (4th Cir. 1982)

Beck was an employee of Litton Systems, Inc. On the day in question, Litton Systems was having its annual pre-Christmas party. Employees were to clock in and out that day in order to be paid for a full day of work, but they did not have to perform any actual work. Litton provided music, food, and beverages. Beck became intoxicated at the party. About one hour and twenty minutes after he left, while driving his van, Beck ran through a red light and hit another car. He killed the occupants of that car, and their husbands filed this suit.

FACTS

Is Litton responsible for the accident based on *respondeat superior*?

ISSUE

[2] Ibid., Section 229(2).

HOLDING   Perhaps. The case should be returned to the trial court for a decision on the facts.

REASONING   Litton would be responsible for the negligent or willful acts of its employees in the scope of their employment. North Carolina courts have not decided whether an employer who provides alcoholic beverages is liable to innocent victims who are injured. State law imposes liability on businesses that serve and charge for alcoholic beverages, but not on social hosts. This situation is similar to that of a business that serves drinks. Whether Litton was advancing a business purpose is a question of fact to be decided by a jury. Beck's activities may have been within the course and scope of his employment. The time that should be examined is the time during which he became intoxicated.

The United States Supreme Court denied Litton's petition for writ of certiorari. (462 U.S. 1106 [1983].)

Failure to Follow Instructions

A principal can be held liable for an agent's acts even though the principal instructed the agent not to commit torts generally or not to perform a specific act. The disobedience of the agent does not necessarily exempt the principal from liability, as illustrated in the following example.

Larry worked as a dock worker. According to the contract, he was paid on an hourly basis. During idle hours, when there were no ships to load or unload, the dock workers commonly sat at their cranes, swinging the loading hooks around above the dock. On one such occasion, a stranger, unfamiliar with operations there, walked down the dock and was hit by the hook attached to Larry's crane. The stranger was hospitalized with serious injuries. Is the principal liable for the injuries?

Yes. Larry was at work during normal working hours. He was using a crane supplied by his principal. The principal was aware of the dock workers' habit of swinging the loading hooks and had told them to stop it. However, he had not enforced that rule.

Failure to Act

A principal can also be held liable under *respondeat superior* when the agent fails to act as directed. For example, a railroad switch operator was supposed to throw a switch on the track at the same time every day. One day he carelessly failed to do so, a train derailed, and passengers on the train were injured. The principal is liable for the agent's negligence.

Respondeat superior does not decrease the agent's liability for wrongdoing, but it makes an additional party, the principal, also liable. There are many legal situations, such as the one just described, in which multiple parties are liable.

Another issue that sometimes arises is *who* the principal is. Who controls the manner in which the agent shall do the work? The principal, or employer, is the one who not only can order the work but also can order how it shall be done.

One would not expect a problem in determining who the principal is, but resolution of the problem is not simple when there is a borrowed agent. In such a case, who is the principal? The lending principal, the borrowing principal, or both? Again, the important factors are the course of the employment and the ability to control the agent. Consider the following example.

Jerry worked for Typewriter, Inc. Typewriter, Inc., was having its office remodeled by Interiors Redone. Since the contractors doing the work were a little short-handed, Jerry's supervisor told him to help them. After painting the walls in the main lobby, Jerry negligently failed to put up Wet Paint signs. A customer leaned against the wall and ruined his clothes. Who was Jerry's principal at the time of his negligent act?

Some courts would decide that both Typewriter, Inc., and Interiors Redone are liable. Jerry was subject to the control of both, and his actions benefited both. Other courts would conclude that Interiors Redone is liable because Jerry was working *primarily* in their business at the time of the negligence. Still other courts would hold Typewriter, Inc., liable because ultimately Jerry was subject to their control and they supplied his paycheck.

The following case involved the issue of which principal employed Eberling.

Krzywicki v. *Tidewater Equipment Co., Inc.*
600 F. Supp. 629 (D. Maryland 1985)

A longshoreman, Henry Krzywicki, suffered extensive injuries when a crane operator dropped a 2 1/2-ton load of cargo directly on him. Krzywicki was a member of a gang of longshoremen supplied to Prudential Lines by Atlantic and Gulf Stevedores, Inc. The barge was owned by Prudential Lines, Inc. The crane was owned by Tidewater and was furnished to Prudential under a written lease. The crane operator, George Eberling, was loading the barge at the time. Jocelyn Taylor, the signalman, was employed as a longshoreman by Atlantic and Gulf. Eberling and Taylor were working under a system where Eberling would move a load of cargo over the barge and lower it unless he observed a signal to stop. In this case he did not observe a signal to stop, since Taylor temporarily left his station to go to the restroom. Taylor was determined not to have been negligent in causing the accident. Krzywicki was determined not to have been negligent in moving across the barge when he knew that a signalman was on duty who would alert the crane operator if men were under the load. Krzywicki had a right to reasonably assume that a warning would be given if he were in a danger zone and

FACTS

that the load would not be lowered. Krzywicki is now permanently disabled and unable to return to work.

ISSUE

Who was the employer of Eberling, the crane operator?

HOLDING

He was the servant of the crane owner, Tidewater.

REASONING

Eberling knew that there were longshoremen working in the barge who he could not see. It was negligent to load the barge unless there was a negative signal that it was unsafe to lower the load. The court concluded that this was true whether or not this was the practice in this port. Affirmative signals should have been used. Standard crane signal procedures called for affirmative signals if it was okay to lower the load.

If Eberling had been paying attention, he would have noticed that the signalman was not in position. He had a duty to find out who was acting as signalman. Taylor was not in position. Eberling wrongly assumed that some other longshoremen standing on the pier were acting as signalmen even though neither one of them had given him a signal.

Under the borrowed servant doctrine, the parties may allocate between themselves the risk of any loss caused by the employee's negligent acts. One of the factors to be considered was whether there was a meeting of the minds between the parties as to the status of the employee in question. One factor that is important is whose work is being performed. This is usually decided by who had the power to direct and control the servant. One factor to be considered is whether one or both parties carried liability insurance that would cover the risk of loss. Eberling was the servant of his general employer, Tidewater. He was paid by Tidewater; Tidewater had the right to discharge him; Tidewater selected him for this job; Tidewater had employed him for a considerable period of time; Tidewater owned the crane; and the benefit to Prudential was for only a short period of time. The work was for the benefit of Prudential, but Prudential did not have control over the crane operations. Eberling, a skilled crane operator, was free to operate the crane in accordance with his own judgment. Both Prudential and Tidewater had liability insurance; they agreed that Eberling should remain the servant of Tidewater. Eberling was not a borrowed servant of the barge owner at the time of the accident.

A shipowner has no duty to be present during the complete loading operation or to inspect the equipment. It is reasonable for him to rely on the harbor workers to avoid unreasonable risks.

Crimes and Intentional Torts

Assault A threat to touch someone in an undesired manner

Battery Unauthorized touching of another person without legal excuse or that person's consent

Courts are more reluctant to hold a principal liable under *respondeat superior* for intentional wrongs like **assault** and **battery** than they are for negligence on the part of the agent. Still, principals can be held liable for intentional acts such as slander, libel, invasion of privacy, and assault and battery. Many criminal acts are also torts, and the principal may be held civilly liable for the financial loss under *respondeat superior*. *Respondeat superior* is not used to impose criminal liability on the principal. The issue in the following case was whether the principal could be held civilly liable for an intentional act by a baseball player.

Manning v. *Grimsley*
643 F.2d 20 (1st Cir. 1981)

Manning attended a professional baseball game at Fenway Park in Boston. As Grimsley, a pitcher for the Baltimore Orioles in that game, was warming up in the right-field bull pen, the spectators in the nearby stands continuously heckled him. Grimsley periodically turned to stare at them. His catcher left and walked over to the bench. Grimsley wound up and threw the ball, which went toward the stands, through the fence, and hit Manning.

FACTS

Could the Baltimore Orioles be held liable for Grimsley's conduct?

ISSUE

Yes. The Baltimore Orioles could be financially liable for his conduct.

HOLDING

Under Massachusetts law, an employer can be liable for damages resulting from an assault by an employee. It must be proved that the employee's assault was in response to the plaintiff's conduct, which at the time was interfering with the employee's ability to perform his duties successfully. Here there was sufficient evidence that Grimsley was responding to the heckling, which might have annoyed him and interfered with his ability to perform his duties successfully. The court held that Manning was entitled to a jury trial on the factual issue and returned the case to the trial court for a decision on the facts.

REASONING

Courts will hold a principal liable for some of an agent's serious wrongdoings, but not for others. The question is often one of degree. How serious was the tort or crime? Should the principal have expected it? Is there much variance between the assigned tasks and the wrongdoing?

Principals may be held *directly* responsible, as well as strictly liable, for the wrongs committed by their agents. Examples include situations in which the principal instructed the agent to commit the wrong; did not properly supervise the agent; ratified or approved the agent's tort; or was negligent in the selection of the agent. The following example illustrates a principal's negligence in the selection of an agent.

Direct Liability of
the Principal

The Great Escape, a neighborhood bar, hired Barry to work as a bouncer in the evenings. Barry was 6'4" and weighed 280 lbs. One evening the bartender noticed that Carl, a customer, was drunk and was becoming loud and obnoxious. The bartender, who was Barry's supervisor, asked Barry to evict him. When Barry asked him to leave, Carl swung at Barry but was so drunk that he missed. Barry swung back and continued to hit Carl until Carl collapsed. Carl later died from the injuries received. Is the Great Escape civilly liable for Carl's death?

Yes. The court held that even though Barry had never beaten a customer, the owner of the bar knew that Barry had a hot temper and was often involved in fights. Barry did not have the proper disposition for this job, and the owner should have realized that.

Conspiracy A situation in which two or more people plan to engage in an illegal activity

Solicitation A situation in which one person convinces another to engage in criminal activity

Agency is not the only area of law that may be involved when an agent commits a crime. Often a principal will be liable based on his or her own fault. If a principal directs or encourages an agent to engage in criminal activity, the principal will probably be held personally liable for such acts as **conspiracy, solicitation,** or accessory to the crime. In addition, some criminal statutes create liability for the principal even though the principal does not intend to violate the statute or does not know of the illegal act or condition. For example, state liquor laws often state that tavern or restaurant owners are liable if minors are served alcohol in their bars. In most states, this is true whether or not the owner approved of such action or even knew that it had occurred. Other examples include statutes that prohibit the sale of impure food or beverages no matter who is at fault. The purpose of these statutes is to stimulate principals' interest so that they *care* whether these things occur in their establishments.

INDEMNIFICATION

When a principal pays a third person under *respondeat superior* for injuries caused by the agent, the principal is entitled to *indemnification*, or *the right to be repaid*, from the agent. Unlike most other theories, *respondeat superior* is not based on the fault of the principal; here the principal is only providing "deep pockets" for the agent's fault. The principal should be entitled to recover from the person who caused the loss — the agent — so the law allows the principal to recover. As a practical matter, the principal will generally have insurance that will cover the payment. Also, the agent will not normally have sufficient funds to make the payment. If the agent is still employed by the principal, the principal may be able to withhold part of the reimbursement from each paycheck until the principal is completely repaid.

Sometimes an *agent* may be entitled to indemnification from the *principal* if the agent paid the third person who was injured by the agent's tort. It would depend on the particular facts of the case. Such cases are based either on contract law or on the law of restitution.[3] Courts are influenced by what they believe to be just, considering the business and the nature of the particular relationship.[4] Under the *Restatement (Second) of Agency*, an agent is entitled to indemnification if the agent, at the direction of the principal, commits an act that constitutes a tort, but the agent believes that it is not tortious.[5] Obviously if

---

[3] Warren A. Seavey, *Handbook of the Law of Agency* (St. Paul, Minn.: West, 1964), Section 168, p. 265.

[4] *Restatement (Second) of Agency*, Section 438(2)(b).

[5] Ibid., Section 439(c) and Comment on Clause (c).

an agent completes a task that he or she knows to be illegal or tortious, the agent is not entitled to indemnification. An illustration follows.

John, a junior in high school, worked for Cutter's Appliance store. Willy had not been making the monthly payments on a color television that he had bought at the store. Mr. Cutter told John to go to Willy's home to repossess the television. He also told John that the store still owned the television and that any amount of force was allowed in retaking possession. When Willy resisted, John shoved the door open, pushed Willy out of the way, and took the television. Under state law, these acts constituted trespass, assault and battery, and use of unlawful force to repossess goods. If John pays Willy for his injury, then John has a right to indemnification, if the trier of fact believes that John was, in *good faith,* following Mr. Cutter's instructions.

As another example, suppose Peggy, a principal, told Simon, her agent, that she had obtained permission to drive trucks across land owned by someone else, in order to commence her mining operation. In fact, she had not obtained permission. Simon would unintentionally commit trespass if he drove his truck across the other person's property. If Simon were required to pay that person for the trespass, he would be entitled to indemnification from Peggy, as he was following her instructions in good faith.

Figure 35.1 illustrates the relationships between the primary parties when the agent commits a tort. The agent's right to indemnification is questionable because the courts require that the agent follow the principal's instructions in good faith before receiving indemnification. The principal's right to indemnification is questionable because many agents cannot afford to reimburse the principal.

Figure 35.1 Liability for Tortious Injury to a Third Person

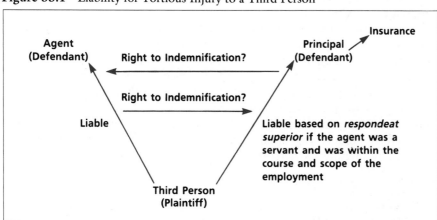

INJURY ON THE JOB

A principal has a duty to provide employees with a reasonably safe place to work and reasonably safe equipment to use at work, considering the nature of the employment. If this is not possible, the principal should warn employees about unsafe conditions that they may not discover even if they are reasonably careful.[6]

Although courts *sometimes* apply similar rules to employees and independent contractors, there are distinct differences in their legal relationships. Nevertheless, courts have on occasion allowed independent contractors to recover for injuries sustained on the job.[7]

If an employee is hurt at work, the employer could utilize a number of defenses to avoid reimbursing the employee for the injury and for any medical bills. Negligence by the employee or the employee's assumption of the known risk would be two such defenses. For example, the employee might have been driving a truck too fast for icy road conditions or might not have been wearing safety goggles provided by the employer.

Workers' compensation Payments to injured workers based on the state statute

In some cases, the injured employee would be covered by **workers' compensation.** Usually workers' compensation claims are not barred by contributory negligence or by assumption of the risk. In some states, particular types of workers are not covered under the workers' compensation statute. For example, in New Mexico, agricultural workers are not covered under the state statute.

At common law, the *fellow servant doctrine* also acted to bar recovery by the agent. A servant could not recover for work-related injuries if they were caused by another servant of the same master. Like assumption of the risk, this doctrine acts as a complete bar to recovery. This rule is applicable to many work-site accidents. Most of the time when an employee is injured on the job, that injury is caused not by the employer but by another employee at the job site. One justification suggested for this doctrine is that the master is often remote from the work site. The agent, on the other hand, is likely to know of hazards at work and to know of careless fellow employees. Another justification used to support the doctrine is that an agent "assumed the risk" of being injured by co-workers.

The existence of the fellow servant doctrine encouraged the spread of state workers' compensation statutes. These statutes may seem to be the opposite extreme from the fellow servant doctrine. They are not based on the fault of the employer, and the employer's negligence need not be shown in court. The worker needs only to show that his or her injury was caused in the course and scope of the job. These statutes exist in most states and provide for fixed amounts of compensation. The worker can easily determine how much he or she is entitled to receive; this allows the quick settlement of claims and discourages many lawsuits. When workers' compensation statutes are applicable,

---

6 Ibid., Section 492.

7 Rodney v. U.S., 77-4028 (9th Cir. 1980); Cioll v. Bechtel Corp., No. 733794 (San Francisco City Super. Ct., 23 April 1981).

legal action against the employer based on common law theories is generally prohibited.

The state statutes vary in format. Some have organized a fund to which the employers contribute, and injured employees collect from the fund. Some states allow employers to purchase insurance or to establish their own funds. In most states, the employee is allowed to recover even if he or she was negligent in causing the injury or if he or she assumed the risk. The injured employee generally receives compensation according to a schedule of payments depending on the type of disability and how long the employee was out of work.

Workers' compensation statutes vary in the following respects:

1. Some cover only major industrial occupations.

2. Some exclude small shops with few employees.

3. Some exclude injuries caused intentionally by the employer or other workers.

Because of the variety, it is important to examine the particular statute at issue.

If the workers' compensation statute does not apply, generally the employee will be permitted to sue based on common law theories.

SUMMARY

An agent is liable for his or her own tortious and criminal acts. The fact that the agent was working at the time is immaterial. The fact that the principal may also be liable to the third party is immaterial too.

A principal may be liable for the acts of his or her agents. Much of this liability is based on the doctrine of *respondeat superior*. A principal is liable for the torts committed by an agent if the agent was acting in the course and scope of the employment. Many factors are used in analyzing what activity is in the course and scope of the employment. A principal may also be held liable if he or she commits a tort or a crime. This liability is not based on *respondeat superior*. It would include situations in which a principal is negligent in selecting an agent or directs an agent to commit a crime.

Even though a court holds a principal liable to the third party, this does not mean that the principal will necessarily bear the loss. The principal will generally be entitled to indemnification from the agent, although such indemnification may not be practicable.

The principal has a duty to provide a reasonably safe place to work.

DISCUSSION QUESTIONS

1. David hired Annabelle as a housekeeper. Her main duties were to remain in the house and clean, prepare meals, and do the laundry. One afternoon, Annabelle received a call from One-Day Drycleaners. David's suit was ready to be picked up. Annabelle decided to go and get the suit in her car.

On the way home, she ran a red light and hit Julie's car. The police officer who came to the scene said that Annabelle's intoxication was the main cause of the accident. Annabelle had had a few drinks with her lunch. David knew that Annabelle had a drinking problem when he hired her and that she was trying to reform. Who is responsible for the damage to Julie's car, and why?

2. Cindy had just started working as an accountant for Big Eight Accounting Firm. On her first audit, Cindy's supervisor sent her to get the coffee and doughnuts every morning. One morning on the way to get the doughnuts, Cindy did not notice that the traffic had stopped in front of her, and she collided with Claudia's car. Who is responsible for the damage to Claudia's car, and why?

3. Cindy prepared a joint tax return for Sammy and Lenora Johnson during her first year at Big Eight. She did not prepare the return correctly, and the IRS assessed $4000 more in taxes and penalties. What rights do the Johnsons have? Why?

4. The employees at an Atlantic City casino "helped" a compulsive gambler lose millions of dollars that the gambler had embezzled from his employer. This was in violation of the state gambling regulations pertaining to credit regulations and cash procedures. Should the casino be held liable for the acts of its employees? Why or why not? Should the employees be held liable? Why or why not?

5. After class in the afternoon, Jim had a job delivering floral arrangements for Flowers by Flo. Flo often told Jim not to take friends in the truck when he made deliveries. One day Jim saw Nanci, a classmate, waiting for the bus. He was going toward her home, so he gave her a lift. Jim carelessly drove off the side of the road, and Nanci was injured. Who is liable to Nanci for her injuries, and why?

6. Janet works as Bill's secretary at Waincoat, Inc. Bill forgot to buy his wife a birthday present, so he sent Janet out to buy one at lunch. While Janet was looking in the jewelry store for a present, she carelessly burned another customer's suit with her cigarette. Who is liable for the damage to the suit, and why?

7. Randy worked as a stock boy in the produce department of May Fair Market. The store prided itself on having the best produce in town. Caroline, a customer, came into the grocery store and started to complain about the quality of the produce generally and of the lettuce specifically. When Randy could not stand her tirade any more, he pushed Caroline, and she fell and broke her ankle. Who is liable to Caroline, and why?

8. Saul worked for Central Cable Co. installing cable television in residential areas. The company needed water to repave the street after the cable was installed. Without permission, Saul used water from Rosemary's tap. When Rosemary got home from work and saw this, she was furious. Her

water bill was based on usage, and Saul had been using her water all day. Who is liable to Rosemary, and why?

9. Jeff made deliveries for Superior Meat Packing Company. On Wednesday, he complained to the company mechanic that his truck was not braking correctly. The mechanic said he would check it out immediately. On Thursday afternoon, the brakes failed, and Jeff was unable to stop the truck. He collided with a telephone pole and suffered neck and back injuries. Who is liable? Why?

10. Neal was stationed on the aircraft carrier USS Archer. One night in August, they were having night maneuvers so the pilots and crew could practice night takeoffs and landings. One of the planes crashed on the deck, injuring a number of people and killing Neal. The investigation revealed that some of the crew were suffering from fatigue and some were under the influence of narcotics. Can Neal's wife and children recover? From whom and why?

CASE PROBLEMS

1. Roland had an interview with the personnel department of the sawmill. They discussed working hours, benefits, and the required physical examination. The physical would be completed at the company's expense. On his way to Western Clinic for the physical, Roland negligently allowed the car he was driving to roll backward, and it crushed McLean against a building. Who should be liable to McLean, and why? (*McLean* v. *St. Regis Paper Company*, 496 P.2d 571 [Wash. App. 1972].)

2. Anthony hired Jo'Dee to excavate a swimming pool site. Jo'Dee did not have the necessary state license to do excavation work. A truck owned by one of the partners of Jo'Dee and driven by David Zaugg struck a motorcycle ridden by Harry Foss. Zaugg was returning to the construction site after dumping a load of debris from the excavation. This task was necessary to the completion of the job. Zaugg turned left across Foss's lane without signaling or seeing Foss. Foss was killed in the accident. The truck driver had been instructed not to drive the truck. Should Anthony be held responsible under *respondeat superior?* Should Jo'Dee be held responsible under *respondeat superior?* Was Zaugg acting outside his scope of employment? (*Foss* v. *Anthony Industries*, 189 Cal. Rptr. 31 [Cal. App. 1983].)

3. A car driven by Appling, a lawyer employed by Richman and Garrett, collided with the car in which Michael and Georgette Wank were riding. Appling had gone to lunch with a representative of one of the firm's clients and a number of other business contacts. At the lunch Appling had several alcoholic drinks. Between 3:30 and 4:00 that afternoon, Appling called the office and spoke to one of the partners to advise him that he would not be coming back to the office. The partner asked Appling to stay where he was and someone would come to get him. Appling rejected that suggestion and drove himself in his own automobile. The accident oc-

curred between 6:30 and 6:45 P.M. Appling does not remember where he was going at the time of the accident. There was evidence at the time of trial that Appling had another accident earlier that afternoon in the parking lot of another restaurant. Is the law firm liable for the alleged negligent driving of Appling? (*Wank* v. *Richman and Garrett,* 211 Cal. Rptr. 919 [Cal. App. 1985].)

4. Sams was a pastor of a church and Calhoun was a member of his congregation. Calhoun often mowed the lawns of Sams's rental properties without charge as a favor to Sams. Calhoun's lawn mower was defective because it was missing a protective guard. One day when Calhoun operated the lawn mower on Sams's rental property, it threw up a projectile into Michael Burns's eye. Michael, a six-year-old, had been playing on the sidewalk. Is Sams liable for the injury caused to Michael Burns? (*Burns* v. *Sams,* 458 So.2d 359 [Fla. App. 1984].)

5. Thomas Brown had severe mental retardation, which was evidenced by mumbled speech and a nervous, fidgety manner. He was arrested for stealing a money order. Officers Pool and Polidori interrogated Brown and his accomplice. The officers pointed their guns at the two suspects and played with their guns and ammunitions during the interrogation. Pool pointed his police revolver at Brown and shot him. Brown died of the wound. Should the doctrine of *respondeat superior* be applied to Pool's behavior? (*Wagstaff* v. *City of Maplewood,* 615 S.W.2d 608 [Mo. App. 1981].)

6. Williams, an employee of Harrison Electrical Constructors, contended that he was injured by an explosion. The explosion allegedly occurred when an AMC (Arkansas Mechanical Contractors, Inc.) welder stuffed paper in the end of a pipe that was being welded. This caused the buildup of acetylene gas and the resulting explosion. Williams contended that this was done as a practical joke or to harass Williams because he was not a union member. AMC employees were not authorized to use acetylene gas for any purpose other than cutting steel for welding. All employees were strictly prohibited from using acetylene gas to produce an explosion or for practical jokes. Could AMC be held liable for the act of its employee? (*Williams* v. *Natkin & Co.,* 508 F. Supp. 1017 [E.D. Ark. 1981].)

7. Thompson, a laborer for Seaman Plumbing Company, received injuries when he was buried alive while trying to connect Seafood Haven's sewage line to the municipality's sewer system. It is necessary to slope deep ditches to prevent cave-ins. The ditch in which Thompson was working was not sloped. Thompson was not on the municipality's property and the municipality had not contracted for the work. Who, if anyone, is liable to Thompson for his injuries? (*Thompson* v. *City of Bayou La Batre,* 399 So.2d 292 [Ala. 1981].)

8. Wallace drowned in a swimming pond located on the premises of Sunnyside Beach and Campground. The campground was operated by Wilgus. Wallace was employed by Consolidated Cigar Corporation as a summer

worker at a youth farm work camp called Camp Clark. Camp Clark was leased by Consolidated from Clark Brothers and was operated by the Shade Tobacco Growers Agricultural Association in association with Consolidated and others. His employer had a verbal agreement with Wilgus to allow its workers to use the swimming pond. Wallace was not being paid at the time of the drowning. Wallace and two other boys were at the swimming pond under the supervision of two Camp Clark employees at the time. The employer provided supervisors, transportation, and equipment for its employees to use the swimming pond. The purpose was to improve the morale of its workers and to increase productivity. Did the drowning occur during the course of Wallace's employment within the meaning of the Massachusetts Workmen's Compensation Act? (*Wallace* v. *Shade Tobacco Growers, Etc.,* 642 F.2d 17 [1st Cir. 1981].)

9. Karl Cox, Jr., had operated a cotton stripper for at least twenty years of his life, and he had been working for Karl Cox, Sr., for a number of years. He had been operating a cotton stripper in short cotton for a few days before he was hurt. Cotton strippers have a tendency to become clogged, especially in short cotton. Cox, Jr., was operating the stripper when it became clogged. He got off the machine, left it running, and tried to kick the clog loose with his foot. His foot got caught in the machine and became severed. Is the employer liable for the injury to the employee? Are any defenses available to the employer? (*Cox* v. *Cox,* 555 P.2d 378 [N.M. App. 1976].)

10. Nealey was instructed to haul a load of furniture from North Carolina to Texas. Nealey stopped in Mobile, Alabama and picked up Bryant, a hitchhiker. Bryant and Nealey struck up a friendship and Nealey bought meals for Bryant and let Bryant sleep in the cab of the truck in exchange for Bryant's help in unloading the furniture. Nealey stated that he might be able to find work for Bryant in North Carolina, so Bryant returned with Nealey instead of getting off at his original destination. One tire blew out on the truck and Nealey elected to drive on to a larger town with only one tire on that axle. Bryant realized that this was dangerous. Bryant was injured when the second tire blew out and the truck rolled over. Under Mississippi law the assumption of risk defense cannot be used in employment relationships. Did an employment relationship exist between Nealey and Bryant? (*Bryant* v. *Nealey,* 599 F. Supp. 248 [N.D. Miss. 1984].)

PART 7

Business Organizations

The owner — or owners — of every business must select some form of business organization. The selection may be made after long and careful deliberation, or it may be made by circumstances and conduct. But it must be made. All too frequently the selection is made in a haphazard and reckless manner, without due regard for the legal and economic ramifications of the organizational form that has been selected.

Should the entrepreneur "go it alone" in a proprietorship? If so, the entrepreneur will have absolute authority — and no one to help with the really difficult decisions. Should a partnership be formed? For many businesses, the simplicity of a partnership makes it an ideal form, but the entrepreneur should be aware that a partnership entails the sharing of management powers and duties. Should a corporation be formed? The corporation offers many advantages, including the possibility of franchising, but the entrepreneur should be aware of the heavy federal regulation such an organizational form faces.

This part of the text cannot, and will not, tell any businessperson which type of organization should be chosen. No one form is ideal for any — or every — business. However, after studying Part 7, a person who is considering the formation of a business should be able to evaluate the advantages and disadvantages of the alternative forms available. Such an evaluation should lead to a carefully considered and intelligent selection, one that is right for *that* person and for *that* particular business.

▌

Formation of a Partnership

HISTORIC OVERVIEW

The partnership as a business form is very old. It can be traced back to ancient Babylon, and perhaps even further. It was known to, and widely used by, the Romans during the height of the Roman Empire. In fact, Roman merchants introduced the partnership throughout Europe as they conducted trade with the peoples conquered by the Roman legions.

Among the nations that "discovered" the Roman partnership was England. Later, the English common law modified this form of organization somewhat and used it in the development of the British Empire. Among the places the English utilized the partnership was the United States — although the area was at that time known as "the Colonies."

The United States followed the English common law of partnerships for quite some time. However, partnership law in the United States has now been *codified.* The controlling law today is found in the *Uniform Partnership Act* (UPA) for general partnerships, and in either the *Uniform Limited Partnership Act* (ULPA) or the *Revised Uniform Limited Partnership Act* (RULPA) for limited partnerships. The UPA has now been adopted in every state except Georgia and Louisiana, and is also followed in Guam, the Virgin Islands, and the District of Columbia. Either the ULPA or the RULPA is followed in every state except Louisiana. The RULPA is currently followed in twenty-two states, with the ULPA followed in the remaining twenty-seven states that have adopted one or the other of the two uniform acts.

Partnerships are formed for a variety of reasons. For example, many **professionals** enter partnerships because they are not allowed to incorporate under some state laws. (The so-called Big 8 CPA firms are all partnerships, so they can conduct business in every state.) Some people enter partnerships to avoid the technical steps required to form a **corporation,** not to mention the expense. And some people form partnerships because it seems like the thing to do.

A partnership has many of the best features of the other major types of business organizations, but it also has some of the worst features of the other types. The various features of proprietorships, partnerships, limited partnerships, and corporations are compared in Figure 36.1. A partnership is relatively easy to form, and the formation is normally informal — very much as is the case with a **proprietorship.** Like a corporation, a partnership has a wider potential financial base than a proprietorship. And like a corporation, the partnership has more expertise to draw from.

However, a partnership is not *perpetual,* as a corporation may be. A partnership will eventually dissolve. Also, the partners face unlimited liability for business-related conduct, as does a proprietor. In contrast, the shareholders in a corporation have limited liability.

No one business form is perfect. Each has some advantages that the others lack; each has some drawbacks the others avoid. The decision as to the type of business organization one should choose should never be made lightly. Nor should it be made automatically. The "pros" and "cons" of each available alternative should be carefully weighed. Only then should a decision be made.

Professionals In the sense used here, a member of a "learned profession," such as a doctor, a lawyer, or an accountant

Corporation An artificial person or legal entity created by or under the authority of a state or nation, composed by a group of persons known as stockholders or shareholders

Proprietorship A business with legal rights or exclusive title vested in one individual; a solely owned business

PARTNERSHIPS DEFINED

Uniform Partnership Act

Section 6(1) of the Uniform Partnership Act defines a partnership. According to this section, a partnership has five characteristics. It is

1. an association
2. of two or more persons
3. to carry on a business
4. as co-owners
5. for profit.

The sixteen words set out in this list are deceptively simple. In fact, a tremendous amount of interpretation is often involved in fitting an organization into

Figure 36.1 A Comparison of Different Types of Business Organizations

	Proprietorship	Partnership	Limited Partnership	Corporation
Creation:	Proprietor opens the business, subject to state and local licensing laws, etc.	Partners enter into an agreement, either orally or in writing; no formalities are required.	Partners enter into a partnership agreement and file a written form designating the limited partners and the general partners.	Parties prepare and file *formal* legal documents known as articles of incorporation with the state of incorporation; they must comply with any relevant state or federal security statutes or regulations.
Termination:	Proprietor closes the business; death, insanity, or bankruptcy of the owner also terminates the business.	Partners agree to dissolve the partnership; death, bankruptcy, or withdrawal of any partner also dissolves the partnership. The terms of the agreement or a court order may dissolve the partnership. Liquidation of the assets after a dissolution winds up the business.	Partners follow same procedure as for a partnership, but with a difference in the order of distributing assets in case of a winding up.	Parties close the business, liquidate all business assets, surrender the corporate charter, and distribute the assets as per state law; termination may also be due to state action revoking the charter.
Taxation:	All business profits are taxed as regular income of the owner; there are no federal income taxes on the business, per se.	The business must file a federal tax return, but it is for information only. The income of the business is taxed as regular income to the partners.	The same procedure is followed as for a regular, general partnership.	Normal corporations are taxed as a separate taxable entity; any dividends are taxed to the stockholders. A sub-Chapter S corporation, created by IRS, is taxed as if it were a general partnership despite its corporate status. A sub-Chapter S corporation is treated differently only for federal tax purposes.

(Continued)

Figure 36.1 *(Continued)*

	Proprietorship	Partnership	Limited Partnership	Corporation
Liability:	Proprietor is liable for all business assets, and then all personal assets of the owner (unlimited personal liability).	Partners are liable for all business assets, and then all personal assets of the partners, jointly and severally (unlimited personal liability).	Partners are liable for all business assets, and then all the personal assets of the *general* partners, jointly and severally; limited partners have limited liability — they are liable only to the extent of their contribution.	Parties are liable for all business assets; stockholders are *not* personally liable for debts of the corporation (limited liability).
Advantages:	Simplicity of creation; complete ownership and control of the firm.	Informality of creation; greater potential for expertise and capital in management (because there is more than one manager).	Somewhat greater flexibility than a general partnership; much greater potential access to capital.	Longevity — potential for perpetual existence; potentially unlimited access to capital and to expertise; freely transferable ownership; limited personal liability of the owners.
Disadvantages:	Limited capital; limited expertise; limited existence (when the owner dies, the business terminates).	Limited existence; lack of flexibility; potential liability.	Some rigidity in ownership and decision making; personal liability of general partners; limited existence.	"Double taxation" (except for sub-Chapter S); much more federal regulation; considerably more state regulation; formality and rigidity of the organization.

the definition of a partnership. To illustrate the potential problem, we shall discuss the terms in the order listed.

An Association

The courts have consistently held that a partnership must be entered *voluntarily;* that is, no one can be forced to be a partner against his or her will. Thus, "an association" has been interpreted as being "a voluntarily entered association." Being realistic, the courts also realize that people occasionally disagree. The measure of voluntariness is the willingness to associate *at the creation* of the relationship. Later disagreements will not automatically destroy the partnership. Thus, "an association" means a mutual unanimous assent to be partners jointly and severally at the time of agreement.

Of Two or More Persons

Persons here is interpreted broadly. It means persons in the biological sense, *or* persons in the legal sense, *or* persons in any other sense — in other words, two or more identifiable entities that elect to associate. Thus, each partner may be a human being, a corporation, a partnership, or even a joint venture.

To Carry on a Business

The third element of the definition has two separate segments. First, it must be determined whether there is a business. A business is defined as any trade, occupation, or profession; so most associations meet this test. However, it must then be determined whether the business is being "carried on." Carrying on implies some continuity. A business must be fairly permanent and long range in order to be carried on. If a business appears to be short term, it is quite possible that the courts will rule that no partnership exists. However, if the other elements of a partnership are present, the short-term business may well qualify as a joint venture.

As Co-Owners

The fourth element is probably the most important and the most confusing one. Co-ownership is like pornography: it is hard to define, but you know it when you see it.

Co-ownership does not refer to a sharing of title on the assets used in the business. Instead, it refers to a sharing of ownership of the business itself. The business is an intangible asset. A business often *uses* assets of a tangible nature, but it need not *own* any tangible assets. For example, several lawyers may enter a partnership. The partnership owns a business that provides services, and services are intangible. The lawyers may lease an office; they may rent furniture. They may not own a single tangible asset, yet they co-own a business.

How, then, is one to know if people involved in a business are co-owners? The simplest way is to look at the agreement the people made when the business was started. If the agreement states that they are partners, or co-owners, of the business, they are co-owners of the business. But all too often the agreement is ambiguous, unclear, or oral. In such a situation, the agreement is of no help in resolving the co-ownership question. Then the courts must look beyond the agreement.

Profits The gain made in the sale of produce or manufactures, after deducting the value of the labor, materials, rents, and all expenses, together with the interest of the capital expended

The courts will normally look at how the parties treat **profits.** If the parties share profits, or net returns, there is prima facie evidence that a partnership exists — that is, the partnership is presumed to exist unless disproved by evidence to the contrary. The sharing of profits creates a **rebuttable presumption** that a partnership was formed. The burden then shifts to the parties to *disprove,* or to rebut, the presumption.

Rebuttable presumption An inference of law that holds good until it is invalidated by proof or a stronger presumption

The UPA recognizes five rebuttals.[1] If one of the parties can prove that profits were shared for one of the reasons listed below, no partnership exists. If such proof is not made, the sharing of profits establishes that a partnership *did* exist. The rebuttal is valid if profits are shared for one of the following purposes:

1. as payment of a debt, by installments or otherwise (a promissory note or a judgment note should be produced as evidence)

2. as payment of wages to an employee or of rent to a landlord

3. as payment of an annuity to the representatives of a deceased partner

4. as payment of interest on a loan (again, some *document* will probably be necessary)

5. as payment of consideration in the sale of goodwill or other property, whether by installment payments or otherwise

For Profit

The final element of the definition is probably the easiest to show. All that is needed is a profit *motive.* If the business was created to return profits, this test of a partnership is met. Thus, nonprofit associations cannot, by definition, be partnerships.

In the following case, the sharing of profits established the existence of a partnership.

Stuart v. Overland Medical Center
510 S.W.2d 494 (Mo. 1978)

FACTS   Dr. Stuart, a physician, withdrew from the Overland Medical Center. Upon his withdrawal, he claimed that the medical center was a professional partnership in which he had been a partner prior to his withdrawal and that he wanted to receive his share of the partnership.

[1] Uniform Partnership Act, Section 7(4).

The Overland Medical Center argued that the arrangement was an expense-sharing operation rather than a partnership, so that Dr. Stuart was not a partner and was not entitled to any share of the business enterprise.

Each physician at the Center was paid based on that doctor's billings for services rendered less a percentage of those billings applied to the expenses of the Center.

Was there a partnership agreement involved in the operation of the Overland Medical Center?

ISSUE

Yes. The Overland Medical Center was a partnership, and Dr. Stuart was a partner in that partnership.

HOLDING

A partnership agreement need not be written in order to be valid and enforceable. The sharing of profits operates as prima facie evidence of the existence of a partnership, and in this case the doctors were sharing "profits," albeit in a strange manner. The share of income each doctor allocated to expenses was in no way related to the expenses that doctor had actually incurred. Thus, any one doctor's contribution toward expenses could actually help to defray the expenses of another of the doctors. In this manner, there was a sharing of profits. Since the medical center presented no evidence to rebut this presumption, the center is deemed to be a partnership, and Dr. Stuart is entitled to a share of the assets of the business.

REASONING

A limited partnership is set up under the Uniform Limited Partnership Act (ULPA). Under Section 1 of the ULPA, a limited partnership can be created by two or more persons, so long as at least one person is designated as a **limited partner.** With this one exception — the classification of partners — a limited partnership has the same characteristics as a general partnership set up under the UPA. However, a limited partnership is more formal than a general partnership. In order to set up a limited partnership, the partners must sign and swear to a written certificate that details all the important elements of the partnership agreement. This certificate must then be officially filed with the correct public official, as specified in the statutes of the state where the limited partnership is created.

A limited partner is so called because that partner has *limited liability.* A limited partner is not personally liable for any obligations of the partnership. However, there is a price to pay for this protection. A limited partner is precluded from management of the business. A limited partner who takes part in management automatically loses the limited status[2] and becomes a *general* partner, subject to unlimited personal liability. Any partner who is not limited is a general partner.

Uniform Limited Partnership Act

Limited partner A limited-partnership member who furnishes certain funds to the common stock and whose liability extends no further than the funds furnished

---

[2] Ibid., Section 303.

Revised Uniform
Limited
Partnership Act

In 1976, the National Conference of Commissioners on Uniform State Laws approved a Revised Uniform Limited Partnership Act (RULPA). This Revised Act was made available to the states as of 1977, and by the end of 1985 had been adopted by twenty-two states. While most of the topical coverage is essentially the same, there are some technical differences between the ULPA and the RULPA. For example, under RULPA, the certificate of agreement forming the limited partnership must be filed with the secretary of state for the state in which the limited partnership is formed; the Revised Act calls for profits and losses to be shared on the basis of capital contributions unless the agreement specifies some other distribution; and the distribution of assets upon termination of the entity and the liquidation of its assets is treated differently under the Revised Act from the way it is treated under the ULPA. One of the interesting aspects of RULPA is found in Section 1105. In this section, RULPA specifies that any cases not provided for in the Revised Act are to be governed by the provisions of the ULPA.

Throughout the three chapters on partnerships, 36, 37, and 38, any major differences between the ULPA and the RULPA will be discussed. If the coverage is essentially the same, no distinction between the two acts will be mentioned.

PARTNERSHIP PROPERTY

Although a partnership is not required to own property, most partnerships do in fact own some property. Even if the partnership chooses not to own property, it must have access to possession and use of some physical assets. And this access and use *may* lead to ownership, at least under the UPA and in the eyes of the court.

Partnership property is defined in Section 8 of the UPA. Under this section, the following kinds of property are deemed to be *partnership* property (owned by the partnership):

1. all property originally contributed to the partnership as a partner's capital contributions
2. all property acquired *on account of* the partnership
3. all property acquired with partnership funds, unless a contrary intention is shown
4. any interest in real property that is acquired in the partnership name
5. any conveyance to a partnership in the partnership name, unless a contrary intention is shown

If an individual partner wants to retain personal ownership but *allows* the partnership to *use* property, that partner should be extremely cautious. Unless the intention is made obvious, the property he thought he still owned may legally belong to the partnership. (The reason this is so important will be discussed in length in Chapter 38, on dissolution.)

A partnership is created by *agreement* of the partners. The agreement is a contract. Unless it falls within the Statute of Frauds, it may be oral. In other words, no formality is required in setting up a general partnership. (Note, however, the formal requirements for creating a limited partnership, which we have already discussed.)

THE PARTNERSHIP AGREEMENT

A reasonably prudent, cautious person would be expected to take great care in negotiating the basic partnership agreement and then reducing the agreement to written form. Yet all too often a partnership is begun with little or no detailed negotiation. And even if the parties are very careful, situations may arise that were never considered and are therefore not covered by the agreement. To minimize the harm such situations could create, the UPA imposes certain rules to be followed *unless* the agreement provides otherwise and specifies certain areas that the agreement must cover.

Unless the agreement between the parties says otherwise, the following rules are imposed by operation of law:

Imposed Rules

1. Each partner is entitled to an equal voice in the management of the business.
2. Each partner is entitled to an equal share of profits, without regard to capital contributions.
3. Each partner is expected to share any losses suffered by the business in the same proportion as profits are to be shared.
4. The books of the partnership are to be kept at the central office of the business.

In addition, some rules are imposed and *must be followed* by the partners, no matter what the agreement says. Any attempt to modify these rules in the agreement is contrary to public policy, so that the modification would be deemed *void*. Among these rules are the following:

1. Each partner is deemed to be an *agent* for the partnership and for each copartner, so long as the partner is acting in a business-related matter.
2. Each partner is personally, *unlimitedly liable* for torts or contracts for which the partnership has too few assets to cover the debt or liability.
3. Each partner is expected to devote service to the partnership only, and not to any competing business ventures.

In addition to those terms imposed by law, the partnership agreement should cover some other areas. For instance, the agreement should designate the *name* of the business. This name cannot be deceptively similar to the name of any other company or business, and it cannot mislead the public as to the nature of the business.

Express Terms

The agreement should cover the *duration* of the business. How long will the partnership last? Such an understanding in the beginning can avoid serious disagreements later. It should also cover the *purpose* of the business. Knowing what you are trying to do not only makes it easier to operate a business but also helps to avoid any controversies later.

Finally, the agreement should discuss in detail how, or if, a partner *can withdraw* from the business. In this area, the rights of a withdrawing partner should be very carefully spelled out so that no one, including a court, will misconstrue the agreement's terms.

Of course, any other items the partners feel should be included can be discussed, agreed on, and included. In fact, the more detailed the original agreement, the better. A carefully drawn, well-thought-out agreement cannot be anything but helpful to all partners.

TAXATION

For taxation purposes, the partnership form of business is neither an advantage nor a disadvantage. Basically, the partnership is not taxed, but the individual partners are taxed on the receipts of the firm. The federal income tax rules and regulations do not recognize the partnership as a taxable entity. The firm must file a federal tax return, but the return is for information purposes only. Each partner is taxed on his or her share of the firm's profits for the year, whether these profits are distributed to the partners or not. Each partner is also taxed on the capital gains — or allowed to take the deductions for capital losses — the firm experiences during the tax year.

Many states also treat the partnership as a mere conduit for the transfer of income to the partners. In these states, the partnership is not taxed, but the partners are taxed on the firm's income whether distributed or retained by the firm for reinvestment or expansion.

OTHER AREAS

Estoppel A person's own act or acceptance that stops or closes that person's mouth to allege or plead the truth; a bar or impediment that precludes allegation or denial of a certain fact or state of facts

Technically, no partnership can exist without an agreement. However, a third person who is dealing with someone who *claims* to be a partner may be able to proceed against the partnership and/or the alleged partners. Such a situation raises the issue of a partnership by **estoppel.**

Suppose person D calls on person X. D tells X that he (D) is a partner in firm ABC. In fact, D is *not* a partner. Suppose further that X signs a contract, expecting ABC to perform the contract as signed. Is X entitled to performance from ABC?

On the basis of these facts, the answer would be a resounding NO! Since the firm, ABC, did nothing to cause X to believe that D was a partner, ABC is not estopped from denying that D is a partner, nor is it estopped from refusing the contract.

But what if X telephoned the firm, and the firm claimed that D was a partner? Now X could hold ABC to the contract. ABC would be estopped to deny that D was a partner. To use estoppel, three facts must be shown:

1.   that someone who is not a partner was *held out* to be a partner
2.   that the third person justifiably relied on the holding out
3.   that the person will be harmed if no liability is imposed

In the following case, estoppel was used to hold the partnership liable.

Anderson Hay & Grain Co. v. Dunn
467 P.2d 5 (N.M. 1970)

Anderson Hay & Grain Co. extended credit to Ruidoso Downs Feed Concession, a business apparently being operated by Dunn and Welch. The credit was extended on the basis of Dunn's financial responsibility, and Dunn was the person contacted for payments on the account. On at least one prior occasion, Dunn and Welch had entered a contract in which each had been designated the "party of the second part." Dunn denied that he and Welch were partners and that he was liable to Anderson on the account.   **FACTS**

Was Dunn a partner by estoppel of the Ruidoso Downs Feed Concession?   **ISSUE**

Yes. Dunn's public conduct toward Welch amounted to a holding out of himself as a partner.   **HOLDING**

By his own admission, Dunn thought of himself as a partner to Welch. When a person represents himself to be a partner, or allows himself to be represented as a partner, he is liable to any persons who extend credit in reliance on that representation. Dunn, by his conduct, actions, and words, furnished substantial evidence to Anderson that he and Welch were partners. If Dunn did not want to be treated as a partner, he should not have consented to being held out as a partner. Before this lawsuit, Dunn never denied he was a partner. He always mailed payments as if he were a partner. His conduct induced Anderson to believe he was a partner. The court therefore held that Dunn was a partner *by estoppel.*   **REASONING**

Notice the difference in the conduct of the purported partner in the following case, and how the court found that a partnership by estoppel was not present due to that difference in conduct.

Cox Enterprises, Inc. v. *Filip*
538 S.W.2d 836 (1976)

FACTS Trans Texas Properties, a business owned and operated by Filip, wanted to place some advertisements in the *Austin-American-Statesman,* a newspaper owned by Cox Enterprises. One of the employees of Trans Texas told the newspaper that Elliot was a co-owner of Trans Texas. The employee had no authority to make such a representation concerning Elliot, and Elliot was not aware that such claims were being made. The newspaper relied on Elliot's "status" as an owner of the business, and on Elliot's financial condition in agreeing to run the advertisements for Trans Texas on credit. The newspaper made no effort to verify the relationship between Elliot and Trans Texas. The advertisements were run in the newspaper, but Trans Texas never paid for the ads. Cox sued Filip and Elliot for the debt, alleging that they were doing business as Trans Texas. Elliot denied liability since he was not an owner of the business or in any way involved with the business.

ISSUE Did the facts justify treating Elliot as a partner by estoppel?

HOLDING No. Elliot did not consent to being held out as a partner of the firm.

REASONING Cox Enterprises argued that it had relied on Elliot's status as a co-owner in extending the credit to Trans Texas, and that it was harmed as a result of its reliance. Cox also asserted that Elliot was negligent in not discovering that he was being represented as a partner in the firm, and that Elliot had an affirmative duty to seek out the third parties to whom he had been represented as a partner. Cox felt that by acting in this "negligent" manner, Elliot was estopped to deny his status as a partner. The court disagreed with the positions put forward by Cox. Elliot never consented to being held out as a partner, Elliot was not aware of this particular situation, and had no duty to seek out any and every third person who might think he was a partner, and Cox had acted improperly by merely accepting the fact that Elliot was a partner without any efforts to verify this information.

Two other business relationships look like partnerships but do not qualify as partnerships under either the UPA or the ULPA. The first of these is a joint venture; the other is a mining partnership.

A **joint venture** has all the characteristics of a partnership except one. It is *not* set up to "carry on a business." A joint venture, by definition, is *set up to carry out a limited number of transactions, very commonly a single deal.* As soon as that deal (or those transactions) are completed, the joint venture terminates. The reason this form is important is that the agency power of the joint venture is limited; thus, a member of the venture is not as likely to be held responsible for the conduct of the other members of the venture. In all other respects, partnership law is applied.

Joint Venture A commercial or maritime enterprise undertaken by several persons jointly; an association of two or more persons to carry out a single business enterprise for profit

A **mining partnership** is a uniquely American creation. A mining partnership *is* a partnership, but it has special characteristics not found in a non-mining partnership. In a regular partnership, no partner can sell his interest or leave his interest to his heirs in a will. In a mining partnership, the sale of an interest or the bequeathing of an interest by will is permitted.

One theory about how this special treatment evolved is that during the California gold rush, after partners discovered gold, one partner would suddenly and "mysteriously" have a fatal accident, which left the mine to the surviving partner. In an effort to extend the life span of successful miners, the mining partnership laws were developed. The death of a partner merely brought *another* partner, the deceased partner's heir, into the business. Thus, no advantage was gained by the death of a partner.

Mining partnership
An association of several owners of a mine for cooperation in working the mine

SUMMARY

Every business enterprise must have an organizational form. Partnerships fall between the two extremes of organizational form — that is, proprietorships and corporations. A partnership has the advantages of being easily formed and of having multiple contributors, whose different opinions and expertise are always available. A partnership has the disadvantages of somewhat limited existence and unlimited personal liability for each partner.

A partnership is defined in the UPA as an association of two or more persons carrying on a business as co-owners for profit. This definition requires that the partners voluntarily agree to enter the business and that the business be somewhat permanent in nature. Co-ownership is the key element of the definition. This element is so important that a sharing of profits by the people involved creates a presumption of co-ownership, which in turn creates a presumption that a partnership exists.

A limited partnership is similar to a regular, or general, partnership with two major exceptions: there must be at least one limited partner who may not participate in the management of the business, and somewhat formal documents must be prepared and correctly filed in order to establish the limited partnership.

Partnership property is a confusing area. Any property owned by the business belongs to the partners together, not to any one partner individually. Five different tests are applied by the courts to decide whether any particular asset belongs to the partnership.

Partners are expected to comply with the basic partnership agreement at all times. However, the law imposes some duties on the partners in the event the agreement does not cover certain areas of responsibility. Some of these rules are followed unless the partners agree otherwise. Some of the rules *must* be followed as a matter of law.

In some areas, no regular partnership agreement is involved, but it appears that a partnership exists. The first of these is a partnership by estoppel: there is no partnership agreement, but the parties act as if there were an agreement, to the detriment of some third party. The other two areas are joint ventures and mining partnerships. Both have special rules applied to separate them from ordinary general partnerships.

DISCUSSION QUESTIONS

1. Why are so many "professional businesses" (law offices, doctors' offices, and the like) partnerships rather than corporations?

2. List some of the advantages and disadvantages of the partnership form of business organization.

3. Under Section 6 of the UPA, what are the five characteristics of a partnership?

4. How do the courts decide whether the people involved in a business are co-owners of that business?

5. How is a mining partnership different from a general partnership?

6. Bob, Carol, and Ted set up a partnership. Later, Bob and Ted wanted to bring in Alice as a fourth partner. Carol objected to allowing Alice to enter. A vote was taken, and Alice got two votes of approval and one of disapproval. What should be the result, and why?

7. Ed, Tim, and Dennis had a business concept they were sure would be successful if they could establish it properly. Unfortunately, they were short of capital and could not afford to begin the business without financial support. Marge was willing to put up the necessary capital, but she was unwilling to face the liability of a general partner. Marge has agreed to be a limited partner in the business. What must the parties do to establish a limited partnership under the ULPA? Must they do anything differently under the RULPA?

8. Larry and Darrin formed a partnership. Darrin contributed $10,000. Larry let the partnership use an office building he owned, rent free. Three years later, the business dissolved. Darrin claims the building is partnership property. Larry claims he still owns the building personally. Who is correct, and why?

9. Sam and Ruth enter a partnership. Sam does not want Ruth to be his agent or to participate in managing the business. What should he do to see that his wishes are carried out?

10. Tim and Margie are partners. In order to get a loan, they tell the bank Denise is also a partner. Relying on Denise's credit, the bank makes the loan. Tim and Margie default, and the bank sues Denise. What must the bank prove in order to hold Denise liable for the loan?

CASE PROBLEMS

1. Herbst owned a farm that was operated by Parzych. Parzych operated the farm to pay off a debt of $6000 he owed Herbst. The debt was to be repaid by an equal share of profits from the farming operation. Parzych purchased some supplies from Rosenberger on credit. When Parzych did not

pay the bill, Rosenberger sued Herbst for the debt. Rosenberger contended that since Parzych and Herbst shared profits, they must be partners. Is this contention correct? (*Rosenberger* v. *Herbst,* 232 A.2d 634 [Pa. 1967].)

2. Travis and St. John agreed to buy some land as an investment. They agreed to share all expenses, profits, and losses equally. A mortgage was taken out in St. John's name, and the deed was put in St. John's name. For five years St. John kept up all payments, receiving nothing from Travis during this period. Finally, St. John notified Travis that the venture was terminated, and that he would return Travis's investment if he was able to sell the land for a profit. When St. John eventually sold the property for a profit, Travis sued for his share of the gain. Are Travis and St. John partners in this transaction? Is Travis entitled to half of the profit from the sale of the land? Explain. (*Travis* v. *St. John,* 404 A.2d 885 [Conn. 1978].)

3. Bowen was the owner of a tavern and all its supplies. He hired Cutler to manage the tavern, giving Cutler complete managerial control. Bowen and Cutler divided the profits equally. The Salt Lake City Redevelopment Agency disrupted the tavern's business in carrying out a project, and it paid Bowen $10,000 for losses incurred. Cutler sued for her share of the $10,000, alleging that since she and Bowen split the profits equally, they were partners. Is her contention correct? Explain. (*Cutler* v. *Bowen,* 543 P.2d 1349 [Utah 1975].)

4. Young Lumber Co. and Altman entered into an agreement whereby Altman was to supervise a job Young Lumber was obligated to perform. Altman was to receive one-half of the profits from the job. All bills were to be paid by Young Lumber. Does this agreement create a partnership? Explain. (*United States* v. *Young Lumber Co.,* 376 F. Supp. 1290 [S.C. 1974].)

5. Harber, Pittman, and Calvert orally agreed to build and sell houses as partners. Harber then withdrew $6000 from the partnership account to purchase three lots on which to construct houses. The deeds to the lots were listed in Harber's name alone, as were the titles to the three houses when they were built. Harber then sold the properties at a profit. Is Harber entitled to keep all the profits for himself? (*Davis* v. *Pioneer Bank & Trust Co.,* 272 So.2d 430 [La. 1973].)

6. Elwood Grissum and his sister Nora operated a farm for many years. Over that period Elwood told many people that Nora was his partner, and the farm had signs reading "Elwood and Nora Grissum Farms." The Grissums also regularly shared the profits received by the farm over the years. However, there was no formal agreement between the two as to the existence of a partnership. Upon Elwood's death, the state tax department declared that the entire farm had belonged to Elwood as a sole proprietor and assessed the estate taxes accordingly. Nora challenged this assessment, alleging that a partnership had existed and that she owned the farms as the surviving partner. Was there a partnership between the Grissums? (*Grissum* v. *Reesman,* 505 S.W.2d 81 [Mo. 1974].)

7. Adams and Wolff were partners in an automobile body and repair shop. The partnership failed to pay social security taxes or unemployment insurance contributions that had been withheld from the pay of the shop's employees. According to the terms of the partnership, Wolff was responsible for collecting and paying these federal taxes. The government obtained a tax lien on the assets of the business and levied the lien against a bank account owned by Adams. Adams claimed that the tax liability was one owed by Wolff alone, without regard to the partnership, due to the language of the partnership agreement. Is Adams correct in his assertion? (*Adams v. United States,* 328 F. Supp. 228 [D.C. Neb. 1971].)

8. Kelley and Galloway were accountants. They formed a partnership to conduct their business. Eventually they hired Smith as an employee of the firm. Although Smith was only an employee, Kelley and Galloway held Smith out to the public as a partner, and Smith consented to this holding out. Smith resigned from the firm and filed suit against the partnership, claiming that he was a partner by estoppel and entitled to a share of the assets of the business. Is Smith entitled to a share of the firm? Explain fully. (*Smith v. Kelley,* 465 S.W.2d 39 [Ky. 1971].)

9. Robert owned and operated a successful lawn mower company. His son, Robert, Jr., opened a clothing store in some excess space in the father's building. The father and son agreed that Robert, Jr., would pay rent and operate the business himself, once it became a viable enterprise. To further help the son, the father signed a bank loan for the son's business, and both the father and the son were authorized to sign checks for the clothing store. Robert, Jr., ordered some clothing from Van Heusen on account. Van Heusen called the father and asked about the new clothing store. Robert assured them that the business was going well. No mention was made that Robert, Jr., was the sole owner of the store or that Robert, Jr., was to be solely liable for the bills. Shortly after Van Heusen shipped the clothing to the store, Robert, Jr., closed the business. Van Heusen is now suing the father for the unpaid shipment. The father denies that he was a partner or that he is liable to Van Heusen. What result should occur? (*Phillip Van Heusen, Inc. v. Korn,* 460 P.2d 549 [Kan. 1969].)

10. The Millers were married in 1959. After the marriage, Mrs. Miller gave up her job, moved to Jackson with Mr. Miller, and began to help him run his nursery business. There was no agreement between the Millers, and no capital contribution was ever made by Mrs. Miller. She did keep the company books and was responsible for hiring and firing employees. When Mr. Miller died, Mrs. Miller alleged that the nursery was a partnership and that she was the surviving partner. Is there a partnership here between the Millers? (*Miller v. City Bank & Trust Co.,* 266 N.W.2d 687 [Mich. 1978].)

CHAPTER 37

Operation of a Partnership

RIGHTS OF THE PARTNERS

A person who enters a partnership acquires certain rights. Some of these rights are gained through the agreement, and some are gained through the terms of the UPA. This book cannot cover all the rights that the partners might decide to cover in the agreement, but it can examine those rights imposed by operation of law.

Management

By virtue of status as a partner, each partner is entitled to an equal voice in management. In conducting ordinary business of the partnership, a majority vote controls. In order to conduct any extraordinary business, a unanimous vote is required.[1] A matter is considered extraordinary if it changes the basic *nature* or the basic *risk* of the business.

While the UPA requires that each partner be given an equal voice in managing the business, the partners are allowed to agree on the definition of equal. Such an agreement can be beneficial to a dynamic business. If the

[1] Uniform Partnership Act, Section 18(h).

643

partnership is forced to conduct its business by majority vote, opportunities could be lost because a vote might not be taken quickly enough.

To avoid this problem, many partnership agreements *define* the management voice of each partner. It should be remembered that such a definition must be included in the agreement to be valid. For instance, a partnership composed of A, B, C, and D might provide the following management divisions:

1. A is in charge of purchasing.
2. B is in charge of marketing.
3. C is in charge of accounting and personnel.
4. D is in charge of paper clips and office neatness.
5. Any other areas are governed by a vote.

Under such an agreement, B could make marketing decisions *immediately*, without the necessity of a meeting among the partners to vote on some marketing question. Likewise, A could decide matters concerning purchasing; C could make personnel decisions; and D could dust the furniture without consulting with the other partners.

Reimbursement

Each partner is entitled to repayment by the partnership for any money spent to further the interests of the partnership. In addition, each partner is entitled to interest on the advances or payments made, unless the agreement says otherwise. Each partner is also entitled to a return of his or her **capital contribution** at the close of the partnership, provided enough money is present to repay each partner after all liabilities have been satisfied.[2]

Capital contribution
Money expended in acquiring, equipping, and promoting an enterprise

Profits and Losses

Unless the agreement says otherwise, each partner is entitled to an *equal* share of the profits of the business. The profits are *not* automatically divided in the same percentage as capital contributed. Nor are they automatically divided in any other unequal manner. This is the *only* remuneration to which any partner is always entitled.[3] No partner is automatically permitted to draw a salary from the business even if that partner devotes extra time to running the business. However, the agreement can be worded in such a manner that a partner receives a salary from the business, with the remaining profits then divided in some predetermined manner. But such a salary provision must be expressly set out in the agreement. Losses are divided among the partners in the same ratio as profits would have been shared.

Books and Records

Each partner is entitled to free access to the books and records of the business. This includes the right to inspect the records and to copy them as the partner

---

[2] Ibid., Section 18(a), (b), (c).
[3] Ibid., Section 18(f).

sees fit. Along a related line, each partner is expected to give, and entitled to receive, detailed information on any matter that affects the partnership.[4]

Each partner is a co-owner of partnership property with the other partners. The ownership is defined as **tenancy in partnership.**[5] This tenancy *entitles the partner to possess the property for partnership purposes,* but *not* to possess it for nonpartnership purposes. However, if all the partners *agree* to a nonpartnership usage, such a usage is allowed.

    This tenancy also carries with it a right of survivorship. This means that if a partner dies, the *other partners* own the property. It is *not* inherited by the heirs of the deceased partner if any other partners are still surviving. Thus, the last surviving partner will own the partnership individually. The heirs of the last partner may not possess the property except for partnership purposes.

Partnership Property

Tenancy in partnership A special form of ownership of property, found only in partnerships, in which each partner has an equal right to possess and to use partnership assets for partnership purposes, and which carries a right of survivorship

Any partner is entitled to a formal *account* — that is, a statement or record of business transactions or dealings — if he or she feels mistreated in the partnership.[6] Specifically, any partner who is excluded from the business or from use of business properties is entitled to an account. And the UPA provides for an account in any other circumstances that render it just and reasonable. In effect, at any time there is an internal argument or disagreement about the business operation, the courts will say an account is just and reasonable.

    Each partner is a fiduciary for every other partner, and is expected to account to the other partners and to the partnership for any benefits received or any profits derived without the knowledge and consent of the other partners.[7] In the following case, a partner was accused of violating his fiduciary duty and of deriving a secret profit from partnership affairs.

Right to an Account

Marsh v. *Gentry*
642 S.W.2d 574 (Ky. 1982)

Marsh and Gentry formed a partnership with the purpose of buying and selling race horses. During the course of their partnership, they purchased a mare, Champagne Woman, and her foal, Excitable Lady. Two years later, the partners put Excitable Lady up for sale in an auction. Gentry then bought Excitable Lady at the auction, without telling Marsh that he intended to bid on the filly. The following year, Marsh learned that Gentry had purchased the filly, but Gentry claimed to have sold her in the interim. Marsh learned that Gentry still owned the horse only when Excitable Lady won the Debutante Stakes at Churchill Downs the following summer. Marsh then filed suit against Gentry.

FACTS

---

    [4] Ibid., Sections 19, 20.
    [5] Ibid., Section 25.
    [6] Ibid., Section 22.
    [7] Ibid., Section 21.

ISSUES   Did Gentry violate his fiduciary duty to Marsh? Is Marsh entitled to an accounting?

HOLDINGS   Yes, to both issues. Gentry violated his duty to his partner, and his partner is entitled to an accounting to discover the extent of the damages.

REASONING   A partner must act as a fiduciary toward his other partners and must account for any benefits derived or profits earned without the consent of the other partners. Here, Gentry purchased a horse being sold by the partnership without telling his partner that he intended to bid on the horse, which was a violation of his fiduciary duty. He then retained ownership of the horse after claiming that he had sold her and raced her in stakes races without revealing his ownership or sharing any of the profits from the racing successes of the horse. Marsh is entitled to an accounting and to a division of profits from the transactions.

DUTIES OF THE PARTNERS

Agency Duties

Each partner is an *agent* of the partnership and of every other partner. Thus, any conduct by a partner that is *apparently* authorized is binding on the partnership. And since each partner is *personally* liable for partnership debts, such an act makes each partner at least *potentially* personally liable.

This is obviously a possible financial hazard to the partners. To reduce somewhat the danger that could be presented by a reckless partner, the UPA restricts *some* agency power. Under Section 9(3), there is no apparent authority to do any of five specific acts unless *unanimously* approved. These five acts are as follows:

Assignment for the benefit of creditors An assignment in trust made by debtors for the payment of their debts

Goodwill The fixed and favorable consideration of customers arising from established and well-conducted business

1. making an **assignment for the benefit of creditors** by transferring partnership property to a trust for the creditors of the business
2. selling or otherwise disposing of the **goodwill** of the business
3. performing any act that would make it impossible to carry on the business
4. confessing a judgment against the partnership
5. submitting a partnership claim to arbitration

Notice the scope of these acts. The first three frustrate business, and the last two remove the partners' right to their "day in court." With these five exceptions, any other act of a partner that is within the scope of apparent authority is binding.

For example, a partner may sell and convey real property owned in the partnership name.[8] The conveyance may be made in the business name *or in the name of the partner.* In either case, the conveyance is valid, even if unauthorized, if the grantee has passed title on to an innocent third party in a subse-

---

[8] Ibid., Section 10.

quent sale. If the grantee is still in possession of the property, the other partners can recover the property, provided the sale was not authorized.

Also, if a partner makes an **admission** about partnership affairs, and the admission is within the partner's authority, the partnership is bound.[9] The firm will have to honor the admission and uphold it if it was within the admitting partner's authority, even if it harms the business.

Since each partner is an agent, *notice* given to any partner on a partnership matter is as good as notice given to each of the partners.[10] This is simply the application of basic agency law to a partnership/agency situation. Similarly, knowledge gained, or *remembered,* while one is a partner is imputed to each copartner.

If a partner acts, or fails to act, in the course and scope of the business, and the act or omission causes harm to a third person, each partner is as liable to the third person as the partner who committed the tort.[11] The partners face joint and several liability. They can be sued together or separately for the harm. Thus, the injured party might be harmed by partner A but sue only partners B and C and win the suit. In such a case, B and C would have to pay for the harm caused by A even though A was not named as a defendant. Again, this is merely an application of agency law principles to the partnership setting.

Likewise, if a partner *misapplies* money or property of a third person that is in the possession of the partnership, the partnership is liable. All the partners, or each of them, may have to answer for the breach of trust of one of them.[12] Again the liability is joint and several.

It should be obvious by now that being a partner *may* be hazardous to your financial health. Even if you are a careful, painstaking, and cautious person, you face potential financial liability, maybe even disaster, from the conduct of your partners. What rights do you have that protect you? What rights are available for the protection of *any* partner from the excesses of another member of the partnership?

One right protects the other partners and the partnership from a creditor of a partner. Suppose that Al, Bill, and Cindi are partners. The business is very profitable, and Bill and Cindi are solvent. However, Al is in deep financial trouble. Several of Al's creditors sue Al to collect their claims. They win the suit, only to discover that Al cannot pay the judgment from his personal assets. Can these creditors foreclose on Al's share of the partnership assets? No. All the creditors can do is to get a **charging order** from a court.[13] Under a charging order, the debtor/partner's *profits* are paid to the creditors until the claims are fully paid. Thus, the partnership can continue, and Bill and Cindi are

Admission A statement that will be accepted in court as evidence

Charging order An order granted to a judgment creditor that the property of the judgment debtor shall stand charged with the payment of the amount for which judgment shall have been recovered, with interest

[9] Ibid., Section 11.
[10] Ibid., Section 12.
[11] Ibid., Section 13.
[12] Ibid., Section 14.
[13] Ibid., Section 28.

protected. Only Al suffers — but only Al was the debtor, and only Al should suffer.

By the same token, suppose that the partnership is in financial difficulty, but that some of the partners are solvent. Can the partnership's creditors proceed directly against the individual partners, bypassing or ignoring the assets of the firm? No. The creditors of the firm must first proceed against the assets of the firm. The following case illustrates this point.

Horn's Crane Service v. Prior
152 N.W.2d 421 (Neb. 1967)

FACTS   Prior and Cook were two of three partners in a partnership. The business entered a written contract with Horn's Crane Service and received supplies and services from Horn. When the firm failed to pay Horn's, Horn's immediately sued Prior and Cook individually and personally on the debt. Prior and Cook defended on the basis that Horn's must first proceed against the business assets before it can proceed against the personal assets of the individual partners.

ISSUE   May a partnership creditor proceed directly against the partners as individuals if the firm defaults on its obligations?

HOLDING   No. The creditor must first proceed against the partnership assets or allege that the partnership has too few assets to permit a recovery.

REASONING   The creditor extended credit to the partnership, so that the partners are entitled to expect that business assets will be used to cover the obligation so far as possible. To permit the creditor to bypass the firm and to proceed directly against the individual partners is unfair. Such conduct benefits the unsued partners disproportionately and harms the sued partners disproportionately. The case was dismissed for failure to state a proper cause of action.

Fiduciary Duties   Another protection given to the partners is the legal status assigned to each partner. Each member of a partnership is a *fiduciary* of the other partners and of the business itself.[14] The fiduciary position carries with it certain responsibilities and certain duties. As was shown in *Marsh* v. *Gentry, supra,* each partner is required to account for, and to surrender to the firm, any profits derived from the business or from the use of business assets. No partner is allowed to have a conflict of interest with the partnership. And each partner is entitled to indem-

---

14 Ibid., Section 21.

nification from a partner who causes a loss or liability from misconduct in the course and scope of employment.

While the partners are dealing internally, they are each aware of the rights and duties of one another. Each partner should know the terms of the basic agreement. And each should know the limits of his or her authority. However, a third person who deals with the partnership has no such advantage. Any nonpartner who deals with the firm must rely on *appearances*. As a result, a third person who deals with the partnership may be given certain rights by the court that are specifically denied by the basic partnership agreement.

RIGHTS OF THIRD PERSONS

As noted earlier, each partner is an agent of the partnership. Thus, if a partner negotiates a contract on behalf of the partnership, that partner is negotiating as an agent. From agency law, we know that if the agent has the *apparent authority* to perform an act, the principal is bound by the act. The same rule applies here. If the partner has the apparent authority to enter the contract, the partnership is bound to honor the contract.

Contracts

In many instances, the partner has the *actual* authority to enter the contract. If so, the partnership is obviously bound, and the partner who negotiated the contract is no more liable than the other partners.

In some cases, the partner has the apparent authority to enter the contract but lacks the actual authority. Under these circumstances, the partnership will still have to honor the contract with the third person. But the partner who negotiated the contract will be liable to the partnership for any losses that arise because the partner exceeded his or her authority.

In still other cases, the partner does not have even apparent authority; if a contract is negotiated, the negotiating partner is personally obligated to perform, but the firm is *not* liable on the agreement.

When the court examines these agreements, the apparent authority of the partner is of overriding importance. To help in deciding the scope of authority, courts often look at the type of business the firm is conducting. If the partnership buys and sells as its primary business purpose, the court views the partnership (unofficially) as a *trading* partnership. If the primary business purpose is to provide services, the court views it (unofficially) as a *nontrading* partnership. In a trading partnership, the partners are presumed to have broad powers. In a nontrading partnership, partners are deemed to have much narrower powers. A partner in a trading partnership is presumably authorized to perform *any* management-related duties. In contrast, a partner in a nontrading business is apparently authorized to do only those things reasonably necessary to further the main business purpose of the partnership.

In the following case, one partner signed a contract on behalf of the partnership, and the other partner attempted to rescind the contract at a later date.

Ball v. *Carlson*
641 P.2d 303 (Col. 1981)

FACTS   Carlson and Teegardin were partners in C.I.T., a real estate developing firm. Carlson entered into a contract with the Balls to sell them a house in a C.I.T. development, with the sale "contingent upon approval of the subdivision by county commissioners." The original closing date for the sale could not be met by C.I.T., due to its inability to get approval by the supervisors. Carlson asked the Balls to extend the time for closing the sale, and they agreed. Soon thereafter, Teegardin informed the Balls that they would have to pay an additional $8,000 in order to buy the house. The Balls did not agree to this added cost. The following month the Balls were informed by C.I.T.'s real estate agent that the contract had been terminated by C.I.T., and their deposit on the house was returned to them.

ISSUE   Was C.I.T. bound by the contract with the Balls even though only Carlson signed the agreement?

HOLDING   Yes. Carlson had the apparent authority to bind the partnership to this contract.

REASONING   The UPA designates each partner as an agent of the partnership for carrying out the purpose of the business. C.I.T. was in the business of developing and selling real estate, and Carlson had the apparent authority to enter into contracts for either of these purposes. Thus, Carlson's signature on the contract with the Balls was binding on the partnership and Teegardin must also abide by the terms of the contract. Even if there was a limitation on the authority of Carlson, that limitation was not made known to the Balls, and they were entitled to rely on the apparent authority that a partner in such a business would normally be expected to possess.

Borrowing in the Partnership Name

Perhaps the most important area in which the court applies the trading-versus-nontrading distinction is in the borrowing of money. In a trading partnership, the firm deals from inventory. Inventory must be purchased. Purchases require money. Thus, a partner has the apparent authority to borrow money in the firm name.

In a nontrading partnership, money is not as obviously needed. As a result, the courts are less apt to impose liability on the firm for a loan that was made to a single partner even though that partner borrowed the money in the partnership name. The following case involves the trading/nontrading partnership distinction.

Torts and Crimes

Tort feasor A wrong-doer; one who commits or is guilty of a tort

Again, it must be pointed out that each partner is an agent for every other partner. Under agency law, a *tort* committed by an agent leaves the agent liable as the **tort feasor.** And it may leave the principal liable, jointly and severally with the agent, under the theory of *respondeat superior*. If the injured person can establish that the partner was performing in "the course and scope of employ-ment," the firm and each of the partners are liable for the tort. If the tort is willful and malicious, the firm is normally not liable. The following hypotheti-cal cases help to illustrate these points.

Mary, Ned, and Oscar are partners. Ned is driving to a business meeting to represent the firm in some negotiations. On the way to the meeting, Ned runs a stop sign and hits Sam. Since Ned was on a job-related errand, all three partners are liable to Sam, as is the partnership itself.

Mary, Ned, and Oscar are still partners. Oscar is now driving to a business meeting to represent the firm. On the way, Oscar sees Tom crossing the street. Oscar is still angry at Tom for an insult from long ago. Oscar accelerates the car and *intentionally* runs over Tom. Since the tort was willful and malicious, neither Mary nor Ned nor the firm is liable to Tom.

If the willful and malicious tort is also a tort that furthers any business interests of the firm, the other partners may well be liable. If the intentional tort is not related to the business purpose, the other partners may still be held liable, provided that they assent to or ratify the conduct. Otherwise, the other partners face no liability for intentional torts. The following case illustrates this concept.

Vrabel v. *Acri*
103 N.E.2d 564 (Ohio 1952)

Florence and Michael Acri owned and operated a restaurant and bar as partners. **FACTS**
They worked together in the cafe for some time before marital problems led to a separation. After the separation, Michael operated the cafe alone, with no help from Florence. Vrabel and a friend stopped at the bar for a drink in February 1947. While they were seated at the bar, Michael Acri shot and killed Vrabel's companion, and then assaulted and injured Vrabel. Michael was sent to prison, and Vrabel sued Florence for damages, alleging that since she was still Michael's partner, she was liable for Michael's tort.

Is Florence liable for a malicious tort committed by her partner that was not **ISSUE**
within the scope of normal partnership business?

No. Since Florence neither assented to nor ratified the conduct, she is not liable. **HOLDING**

REASONING   Michael's attack against Vrabel and his friend was not within the scope of operating a cafe. Such conduct was a clear departure from his employment and from his business purpose. It would be improper in this case to hold that the principal or partner ratified the conduct. Florence never assented to, participated in, or ratified the assaults. Thus, she was not liable.

_____

If a partner commits a crime, what liability do the noncriminal partners face? For most crimes, the other partners are *not* liable. Most crimes require **mens rea** *(criminal intent)*. To be convicted of such a crime, a person must commit it or **aid and abet** in its commission. Unless evidence of involvement is shown, only the partner who committed the criminal act will be liable.

However, some crimes can be committed *without* criminal intent. Such crimes are normally *regulatory* in nature; these crimes involve violations of administrative areas rather than violations in traditional criminal areas. If one of these crimes is committed, *all* the partners are criminally liable.

Mens rea A guilty mind; a guilty or wrongful purpose; a criminal intent

Aid and abet To help, assist, or facilitate the commission of a crime; to promote the accomplishment of a crime

SUMMARY   Each partner has certain rights in the business by virtue of his or her status as a partner. These rights may be limited or defined by the agreement. If there is no agreement to limit the rights, each partner has an equal voice in management, a right to an equal share of profits or losses, equal access to books and records of the firm, and an equal right to use partnership property for partnership purposes. They also have a right to be reimbursed for expenditures and a right to an account.

Each partner is an agent for every other partner and is a principal of every other partner. As a result, all the regular rules of agency apply. And each partner is a fiduciary of the other partners.

When a partner deals with some third party, the firm is bound by the conduct if it was apparently or actually authorized. Again, agency principles apply to the torts of a partner. If the tort is in the course and scope of employment, the partners are jointly and severally liable. If it is beyond the scope of employment, only the tort feasor is liable, unless the other partners ratify the conduct.

Any liability for crimes committed by a partner is not imposed on the nonacting partners unless they ratify the conduct.

DISCUSSION
QUESTIONS

1. What is a partner's management right in a partnership?

2. If a partner advances money to further the partnership, what is the partner entitled to receive?

3. The partnership agreement is silent as to profits and losses. Bob put up 50 percent of the money for the business, and Sam and Sue each put up 25 percent. The firm netted $12,000. How much should each partner receive? Explain.

4. Scott felt Mel and Nancy were cheating him in their partnership. He asked to see the books and records to determine whether he was being cheated. Mel and Nancy refused to allow Scott to examine the books. What rights can Scott assert?

5. Denise and Vicki formed a partnership. Two years later, Vicki bought herself a new car, paying for it with a partnership check. If the partnership dissolves, what are Denise's rights in the car? Explain.

6. Tim and Ed were partners. Tim got tired of the business and sold it to Dan. Ed objected to the sale and sued to have it declared void. Dan claims Tim had the apparent authority to sell. How should the court rule, and why?

7. Margaret and Barbara are partners. Barbara called a customer and said the firm would not be able to deliver certain goods on time. The customer immediately sued for anticipatory breach. Margaret objects to the suit, saying the customer has no grounds to expect a breach. Do you agree? Explain.

8. Terry is a partner with Debbie and Donna. Terry learns of a fact that affects the business but does not tell Debbie or Donna. Terry dies, and Debbie and Donna are sued on the basis of the information Terry had received. Can Debbie and Donna successfully assert their ignorance of the fact?

9. April, Jim, and Dan were partners in a retail business. Dan went to the bank and borrowed $10,000 to "buy more goods." The loan was made in the partnership name. Dan took the money to Las Vegas and lost it all at the roulette table. If the bank sues April and Jim on the loan, what should be the result? Explain.

10. Paul and Alma are partners. Paul commits a fraud in negotiating a contract for the firm. If the defrauded party sues Alma, who should win, and why?

1. Waagen and Gerde were partners in the management of a fishing vessel. Gerde invented a new type of fishing net for catching sharks. He felt he should be entitled to some money for the development of the net, and so he withheld some earnings to pay himself. Waagen sued for an accounting of these withheld funds. What should be the result? Explain. (*Waagen v. Gerde et ux.,* 36 Wash.2d 563 [1950].)

2. Phillips and Harris were partners in a used car dealership. Rather than drive their own personal cars, both partners regularly drove cars the business was trying to sell. While driving a car the business had for sale, Phillips was involved in an accident. The passengers in the other car sued the partnership as well as Phillips. Harris contended that the accident was not within the course of employment and that the business should not be liable. Is this contention correct? (*Phillips v. Cook,* 210 A.2d 743 [Md. 1965].)

CASE PROBLEMS

3. Summers and Dooley were partners in a trash collection business. Summers asked Dooley, who was retired, if Summers could hire another employee. Dooley refused to agree to the hiring, and Summers hired the employee despite the lack of consent. Summers then sued Dooley for $6000, one-half the wages paid to the new employee, as reimbursement of a business expense. Is Summers entitled to the money? (*Summers* v. *Dooley* 481 P.2d 318 [Idaho 1971].)

4. Two brothers, Perry and Eli, were partners in a ranching operation. They orally agreed to sell the ranch. Perry was to handle the negotiations for the sale. Eli was to be consulted before any sale was finalized. Perry found a buyer and told Eli about the terms. Eli did not object at that time, and a contract was drawn up with the buyer. Later, Eli decided that he did not want to sell. If Eli has not signed the contract, must he carry out the sale? (*Ellis* v. *Mihelis,* 384 P.2d 7 [Cal. 1963].)

5. Lyle, Peters, and Barton were the partners in a firm that built packing crates and wood products. Barton, without the knowledge of the other partners, entered into a contract with Bole that called for the firm to sell lumber to Bole. In exchange, Bole paid Barton in advance for the lumber to be delivered. Bole never received the lumber, and Barton never accounted to the firm for the money Bole had paid. Bole sued the partnership for the lumber, or for the damages suffered due to nondelivery. Lyle and Peters deny any liability. What result should occur and why? (*Bole* v. *Lyle,* 287 S.W.2d 931 [Tenn. 1956].)

6. Amerco filed a lawsuit against Bohonus, a member of a partnership, for a personal, nonbusiness claim. Amerco won the lawsuit, obtaining a judgment against Bohonus. The judgment was not satisfied, and Amerco then sought to enforce the judgment against the partnership property of Bohonus. The trial court ordered the sale of partnership property to satisfy the debt Bohonus owed Amerco. The remaining partners objected to this judicial sale, claiming that the court lacked the authority to sell the partnership assets for a personal liability of a partner. What should the appellate court do? What are the rights of the partners, the firm, and Amerco? (*Bohonus* v. *Amerco,* 602 P.2d 469 [Ariz. 1979].)

7. Mr. and Mrs. Soden were partners in the operation of an apartment building. Starkman, one of the tenants, refused to pay her rent for July until Mr. Soden made some repairs to her apartment as he had promised. While Mr. Soden was out of town, Mrs. Soden once again asked for the July rent, and was again refused. At that point, Mrs. Soden took a broom and beat Starkman with it. Starkman has sued both Mr. and Mrs. Soden for the tort. Was Mrs. Soden acting within the course and scope of her authority so that the partnership and each partner is bound for her tort? Explain. (*Soden* v. *Starkman,* 212 So.2d 763 [Fla. 1969].)

8. Maclay, his wife, and his children were all patients of the Kelsey Clinic. Maclay felt that Dr. Brewer, one of the partners in the clinic, was attempt-

ing to alienate the affections of Mrs. Maclay. Maclay went to see Dr. Kelsey, a senior partner in the clinic, with his suspicions, but Dr. Kelsey did nothing about the matter. Alleging that the affair between his wife and Dr. Brewer still continued after his discussion with Dr. Kelsey, Maclay sued Dr. Brewer and the clinic for the tort of alienation of affections. Assuming that Dr. Brewer was, in fact, guilty of the tort, should the clinic be held liable due to the status of Dr. Brewer as a partner? Explain fully. (*Kelsey-Seybold Clinic* v. *Maclay*, 466 S.W.2d 716 [Tex. 1971].)

9. Smith and Jones were partners in a real estate business. By the terms of the agreement, each partner was to share profits and losses equally. In 1972, Jones purchased a piece of rental property in his own name and then reimbursed himself from the partnership account. The property was carried on the books of the firm, but Jones retained all the rents and paid all expenses himself. The firm dissolved in 1975, and Smith demanded that Jones turn over half of the rents and profits from the rental property. Jones alleges that the property is his alone and that he owes nothing to Smith. What should the court do in this case? (*Stauth* v. *Stauth*, 582 P.2d 1160 [Kan. 1978].)

10. William and Charlotte operated the Davis Nursing Home as a partnership. William entered into a contract with Feingold to sell Feingold the nursing home, its assets, and its goodwill. Charlotte was unaware of the contract and refused to consent to the sale when she learned of it. Feingold has sued for specific performance of the contract. Who will prevail? (*Feingold* v. *Davis*, 282 A.2d 291 [Pa. 1971].)

CHAPTER 38

Termination of a Partnership

TYPES OF TERMINATIONS

Partnerships, like all good—and many bad—things, must eventually end. However, the ending of a partnership is different from what most people expect. The partnership may end while the business enterprise continues. If so, a dissolution occurs. Or the partnership and the business enterprise may both end. If so, a dissolution and a winding up occur. These variations in the termination of a partnership are the focus of this chapter.

DISSOLUTION

Technically, a *dissolution* "is the change in the relation of the partners caused by any partner ceasing to be associated in the carrying on as distinguished from the winding up of the business."[1] This means that *any time a partner leaves the business, the partnership is dissolved.* The change in the relations of the partners changes the partnership.

    The fact that a partner "leaves" the business does not mean that the

---

[1] Uniform Partnership Act. Section 29.

business must cease to exist. The remaining partners may be allowed to continue the business. Or they may be required to terminate the business. What they may, or may not, do depends on the method and manner of dissolution.

Section 31 of the UPA lists several different causes of dissolution. Any of these events will cause a dissolution of the partnership, but they may not require a **winding up** of the business. We shall examine these causes of dissolution next.

Winding up Settling the accounts and liquidating the assets of a partnership or corporation for the purpose of making distribution and dissolving the concern

A dissolution may be caused by the terms of the partnership agreement. For example, the time period set up in the agreement may expire, or the original purpose of the partnership may be fulfilled. If a partnership was established to operate for two years, and two years have elapsed, the partnership is dissolved. If a partnership was established to sell 100 parcels of land, and all the land has been sold, the partnership is dissolved. Of course, a new agreement could be made to extend the time or to modify the purpose, if the partners so desire.

Without Violation of the Agreement

If the agreement does not specify a particular time period or a particular, limited purpose, a partner may simply decide to quit. Unless the agreement denies this right to withdraw, such a decision operates as a dissolution without violation of the agreement.

All the partners may decide to terminate the partnership. If they do so, the partnership is dissolved without violating the agreement. This is true *even if* a definite time period was set and that time has not yet expired. And it is true even if a particular purpose was declared and the purpose has not yet been achieved.

Finally, a partnership is dissolved without violation of the agreement if any partner is expelled from the partnership by the other partners, *provided that* the expulsion is permitted by the agreement. Thus, if X, Y, and Z vote to remove Q from the firm, *and the agreement permits such a vote,* the partnership is dissolved without violation of the agreement.

Normally, a dissolution that does not violate the agreement will lead to a winding up *unless* the agreement itself provides for a continuation of the business. If the agreement does not specify that a continuation is permitted, the partner who causes the dissolution may demand that a winding up take place. Such a demand must be obeyed, even though it will normally harm the remaining partners, who may very well wish to continue the business. Thus, every partnership agreement should contain some provisions for continuing the business. (Of course, an *expelled* partner cannot demand a winding up of the business if the expulsion was done in good faith by the other partners.)

No one can be forced to be a partner against his or her will. This means that any partner has the *power* to withdraw from any partnership at any time. But it does *not* mean that a partner has the *right* to withdraw at any time. A withdrawing partner may very well be violating the terms of the partnership agreement by withdrawing. If so, the remaining partners may continue the business if they so desire, even though the partnership has been (technically) dissolved. The

In Violation of the Agreement

partner who withdrew in violation of the agreement has no right to demand or require a winding up.

Similarly, the partner who withdraws in violation of the agreement does not have the right to demand that the business be continued. Once a partner withdraws in violation of the agreement, the remaining innocent partners may decide to do whatever they feel is most appropriate. In the following case, a partner who withdrew in violation of the agreement learned that, upon his withdrawal, all the options belonged to the remaining partners.

Ohlendorf v. *Feinstein*
636 S.W.2d 687 (Mo. 1982)

FACTS   The Missouri State Highway Commission was accepting bids on seven tracts of land. Feinstein submitted a bid of just over $568,000 that was accepted by the Commission. Upon learning that his bid had been accepted, Feinstein entered into a partnership with Ohlendorf and Whaley to sell the land. Several months later Ohlendorf notified the other partners that he was withdrawing from the partnership due to differences of opinion. Ohlendorf also informed the Commission that the partnership would not close the sale of the seven tracts of land. After this, Ohlendorf sued the other two partners to recover his capital contributions. The other partners refused to return his capital, and countersued Ohlendorf for damages and for lost profits from the aborted purchase so that they could wind up the partnership affairs.

ISSUE   Did the remaining partners have a duty to continue the business so as to mitigate the damages faced by Ohlendorf?

HOLDING   No. Ohlendorf's withdrawal in violation of the agreement permitted the remaining partners to either continue the business or to wind it up at their option.

REASONING   The UPA specifically allows the remaining partners to elect their remedies when a partner withdraws in violation of the partnership agreement. They may continue the business if they so desire and seek damages from the withdrawing partner. Or they may elect to wind up the business and sue the withdrawing partner for damages caused by the wrongful withdrawal. The mere fact that continuing the business would likely result in profits to the remaining partners is irrelevant. When Ohlendorf withdrew, he placed the other partners in a position to decide how to proceed. They chose to sue for damages, as was their right under the law. Their selection must be sustained under the provisions of the UPA.

By Operation of Law   A partnership may also be dissolved by operation of law, if any one of the following three events occurs:

1.   Something happens that makes it unlawful for the business to continue or

for the partners to continue the business. Thus, a law that prohibited anyone from selling rabbits would terminate a partnership in the rabbit-selling business. And a partnership that lost its import license would be dissolved even though importing itself was still legal.

2. A partner dies.

3. A partner or the partnership goes bankrupt.

The final method for dissolving a partnership is by court order. As explained in Section 32 of the UPA, a court will order a dissolution only if *asked* to do so. The person who wants to dissolve the partnership must petition the court; the court will not go out looking for partnerships that need to be dissolved.

   Most commonly, the petitioning person is one of the partners or a representative of one of the partners. Even if a petition is filed, dissolution is not automatic. The court must have *grounds* to grant the request. The following grounds will justify a dissolution by court decree:

By Court Order

1. insanity of any partner

2. incapacity, other than insanity, of a partner that prevents that partner from performing the contractual duties called for in the agreement

3. misconduct by any partner that will make it difficult to continue operating the business

4. intentional or repeated breach of the agreement by a partner, or any behavior that makes the continuation of the business impossible or impractical

5. evidence that the business can be continued only at a loss with no prospect of a profit turnaround in the near future

6. any other circumstances that make a dissolution equitable in the eyes of the court

It should be noted that insanity does *not* automatically dissolve the partnership; a petition must be filed seeking dissolution. If the remaining partners wish to continue the business with an insane partner, they have the right to do so.

   It is also possible that some person may "purchase" the interest of a partner and then decide to seek a court-ordered dissolution.[2] Such a court order may be granted only if one of two sets of circumstances can be shown:

1. The agreement had a specific term, or a particular purpose, and it has been fulfilled or satisfied.

At will Having no specific date or circumstances that would bring about a dissolution

2. The partnership was a partnership **at will** at the time of the purchase.

---

[2] Ibid., Sections 27, 28.

CONTINUA-TION OF THE BUSINESS

Once a dissolution occurs, a very important decision must be made. Will the business terminate through a winding up, or will the business continue? In most cases, an ongoing business is more valuable than the assets that make up the business; the sum is greater than its parts. Thus, the remaining partners will normally want to continue operating the business if they can possibly do so. However, this may not be satisfactory to a withdrawing partner. For this reason, the partners should consider the problem of a continuation when they draw up the original agreement, and they should make provisions for the problem at that time.

The remaining partners have the *right* to elect to continue the business under any one of the following circumstances:

1. The withdrawing partner withdraws in violation of the agreement.

2. The withdrawing partner consents to the continuation when he or she could have demanded a termination and winding up.

3. The agreement permits a continuation following a dissolution.

Unless one of these circumstances occurs, a dissolution will be followed by a winding up.

Withdrawing Partners

Any time the business is continued following a withdrawal, the continuing partners have a duty to the withdrawing partner. The withdrawing partner must be both indemnified (that is, secured against anticipated losses) and bought out. The purpose of the indemnification is to protect the withdrawing partner from any claims of creditors of the partnership. The withdrawing partner is still liable for any debts owed that arose during membership in the partnership and association with the business. Without an indemnification agreement, a withdrawing partner might be tempted to force a winding up in order to minimize potential liability. But the indemnification agreement is assurance that the continuing partners will repay for any losses the withdrawing partner may suffer on account of partnership obligations.

Withdrawing partners are also entitled to payment for their interest in the business, including any undistributed profits, at the time of withdrawal. However, if a withdrawal is in violation of the partnership agreement, the continuing partners may deduct *damages*, based on breach of contract theories, from the payment to adequately cover the harm caused by the breach. The following case illustrates this point.

━━━━━━━━━━━━━━━━━━━━━━━━

Grund v. Wood
490 P.2d 955 (Colo. 1971)

FACTS   Grund was one of several partners in a medical partnership. The written partnership agreement included a covenant not to compete by practicing medicine within five miles of the partnership clinic for two years following withdrawal. It further provided for liquidated damages of up to $15,600 for violating the restrictive covenant. Grund had signed the agreement. He withdrew from the firm and began practicing medicine within five miles of the clinic within two years of his withdrawal. Grund sued to recover his share of the assets, and the partnership paid him his share less the $15,600 stipulated in the agreement. Grund then sued to recover the $15,600.

Was Grund entitled to the $15,600 the partnership had withheld?   **ISSUE**

No. The partnership was merely enforcing its rights under the agreement for a withdrawal in violation of the agreement.   **HOLDING**

The covenant not to compete was an entirely proper contract provision, and the liquidated damages clause was based on a reasonable method of establishing damages where the proof of damages would be very difficult to ascertain. Grund signed the agreement, he knew the terms, and he violated the agreement. The court held that he could not recover the $15,600.   **REASONING**

The continuing partners may pay former partners in a lump sum and settle the matter. If they do not, or cannot, make a lump-sum payment, the withdrawing partners are allowed to elect how payment will be made. They can either receive interest on the unpaid portion until they receive payment in full, or they can elect to receive a portion of profits that corresponds to their unpaid portion of the value of their share until they are paid in full. However, this election must be made at the time of withdrawal, and once made, it cannot be changed unless the continuing partners agree to the change.

Occasionally, a new partner is brought into the business. When this happens, a continuation obviously occurs. No one would want to enter a business in order to see it go through a winding up. The continuation is treated slightly differently when a new partner enters the firm. As a partner, the new entrant is liable for the debts of the partnership. But the existing creditors did not rely on the new partner's credit when they decided to extend credit. As a result, it seems unfair to impose unlimited liability on the new partner. UPA Section 41(7) resolves this problem by specifying that the new partner is liable to preexisting creditors only up to the amount of his or her capital contribution. In other words, an entering partner has limited liability to preexisting creditors but still faces unlimited personal liability with respect to future creditors.   **Entering Partners**

Winding up is *the termination of the business enterprise.* In winding up, one must **marshal** and **liquidate** the assets of the business and then distribute the proceeds of this process to the proper parties.   **WINDING UP**

General Partnerships

Marshal To arrange assets or claims in such a way as to secure the proper application of the assets to the claims

Liquidate To assemble and mobilize assets, settle with creditors and debtors, and apportion the remaining assets, if any, among stockholders or owners

The priority for distributing the proceeds is set out in UPA Section 40. The first priority is claims owed to creditors who are not partners. If the proceeds are sufficient to pay this class entirely, they will be so paid. Any surplus carries over to the next priority class. Any deficit will cause two things to happen: a pro rata distribution of the proceeds within the class, and a collection of the balance from the personal assets of the partners, jointly and severally.

The second priority to receive the proceeds is claims owed to the partners *as creditors* of the business. Again, any surplus will be applied to the next priority class. And again, any deficit will be made up from the personal assets of the partners. It should be noted that a partner who wishes to be treated as a creditor of the firm will need to present clear and convincing evidence of the debt. It is normally presumed that any monies advanced to the firm were advanced as a capital contribution, not as a loan. The court will normally demand some written proof, such as a promissory note, that the funds were meant as a loan. Without such proof, the partner is likely to find that what he or she thought was a loan was, in the eyes of the court, a capital contribution.

The third priority is return of the capital contributions of the partners. Any surplus will be carried over to the fourth and final priority. Any deficit will be allocated among the partners pro rata. The fourth and final priority category is profits. Any monies left over after all the other classes have been satisfied will be distributed as profits, according to the terms of the partnership agreements. There can be no deficit here.

The creditors of the partnership have first claim on any partnership assets, as well as a secondary claim on the partnership assets that reflect the interest of the indebted partner in the business. However, the claims by individual creditors against partnership shares are limited by UPA Section 28. The individual creditor is normally given a charging order by the court while the business is in operation in order to minimize the disruption of normal business operations.

The examples that follow illustrate how the various interested parties may be treated in a dissolution of a partnership and a winding up of the business. In each example, there are three partners — X, Y, and Z — whose net worths are shown immediately below. In addition, each partner has made the capital contributions specified, and X has made a loan to the firm. Notice the effect the different asset positions of the partners have on the partners individually.

Partners	Personal Assets	Personal Liabilities	Net Worth
X	$100,000	$ 20,000	$80,000
Y	80,000	40,000	40,000
Z	40,000	100,000	(60,000)

Each partner contributed $50,000 to the partnership; profits and losses are to be shared equally. X loaned the firm $30,000 (there is a signed promissory note for this loan).

The partnership has $200,000 in proceeds and $290,000 in liabilities to regular creditors, plus the $30,000 owed to X.

Step 1. Partnership proceeds are distributed to regular creditors (priority 1), leaving a deficit of $90,000.

Step 2. Each partner *owes* an additional $30,000 to priority 1 creditors. However, Z has no money, and so X and Y will have to pay the full $90,000 between them (X will pay $50,000 and Y will pay $40,000) and hold claims against Z (X for $20,000, and Y for $10,000). Both Y and Z are now insolvent.

Step 3. Under priority 3, X, Y, and Z each owe X $10,000. X "pays" himself, and Y and Z each owe X $10,000.

The partnership has $309,000 in proceeds and $300,000 in regular liabilities, plus the $30,000 owed to X.

Step 1. The priority 1 debts are paid in full, and the $9000 surplus is carried over.

Step 2. Priority 2 debts are paid until the money runs out. Thus, X receives the $9000 left from priority 1 and is still owed $21,000. X "pays" himself $7000; Y pays X $7000; Z owes $7000. Z is insolvent, and X will probably not collect.

The partnership has $500,000 in proceeds, $200,000 in regular liabilities, and the $30,000 owed to X.

Step 1. Priority 1 debts are paid in full, with a surplus left of $300,000.

Step 2. Priority 2 debts are then paid in full (X gets his $30,000), leaving a $270,000 surplus.

Step 3. Priority 3 is taken care of next. Each partner receives a full return of his capital contribution, leaving a surplus of $120,000.

Step 4. The final priority is satisfied; the $120,000 is distributed as profits, with $40,000 going to each of the partners.

In addition, the regular individual creditors will also be paid in full in this case, as follows. X received:

```
$ 30,000 loan payment
  50,000 return of capital
  40,000 profits
  80,000 net worth
$200,000 net worth
```

X and Z received:

```
$ 50,000 return of capital
  40,000 profits
$ 90,000 distribution
```

Y had a net worth of $40,000, which has increased to $130,000. Z had a net worth of ($60,000), which has increased to $30,000.

The following case dealt with the claims of partners as creditors of the partnership.

In re Hess
1 F.2d 342 (D.C. Pa. 1923)

FACTS   Weir, Ligo, Hess, and Hanna were partners. Weir withdrew from the firm, selling his interest to the remaining partners. Later Ligo withdrew, again selling his interest to the remaining partners. Neither Weir nor Ligo was paid in cash; instead, both took promissory notes. Hess and Hanna later went bankrupt, and Weir and Ligo sought payment along with the regular creditors of the business.

ISSUE   Were the claims of Weir and Ligo properly filed against the partnership?

HOLDING   Yes. However, they were not on an equal standing with the creditors who had not been partners.

REASONING   Although both Weir and Ligo have provable, valid claims, they will not be permitted to compete with the regular creditors of the firm. Weir, having withdrawn first, takes precedence over Ligo, but Weir must wait until all the creditors with claims predating his retirement have been paid. Ligo must wait until Weir has been paid and until all creditors whose claims arose after Weir retired, but before Ligo withdrew, have been paid. Subject to these restrictions, Weir and Ligo are entitled to assert their respective claims against the partnership.

Limited Partnerships   The distribution of assets in a limited partnership is substantially different from that in a normal general partnership. Under ULPA Section 23, the assets are distributed in the following order:

1. claims of creditors who are not partners
2. income owed to limited partners
3. capital contributions of the limited partners
4. loans made to the firm by any partners
5. profits owed to general partners
6. capital contributions of the general partners

As in the liquidation of a general partnership, no category receives any proceeds until each higher-priority category has been paid in full.

Under the Revised Uniform Limited Partnership Act, the distribution of proceeds is treated differently. The Revised Act calls for distribution in the following order:

1. claims of nonpartner creditors and claims of partners as creditors;
2. any amounts owed to former partners prior to their withdrawal from the firm;
3. return of capital contributions of all partners;
4. the remainder distributed as profits to all the partners.

SUMMARY

When a partnership undergoes a change in the relationship among the partners, a dissolution occurs. Thus, a withdrawal by any partner is a dissolution, whether the agreement allows such conduct or not. Likewise, a dissolution will occur when the purpose of the agreement has been carried out, or when its time has expired. A dissolution will occur by operation of law if a partner dies, if any partner goes bankrupt, or if the purpose becomes illegal. Finally, a dissolution can occur by court order.

When a dissolution occurs, the remaining partners may be allowed to continue the business. If the business is continued, the withdrawing partner must be bought out and indemnified.

Often the partnership must be wound up if a dissolution occurs. In a winding up, the assets of the firm must be marshaled and liquidated, and the proceeds must be distributed according to law. The proceeds must be used first to pay debts that the partners owe to nonpartner creditors. Next, the creditors who are also partners must be paid. After that, the partners recover their capital contributions. Anything left is then distributed as profits.

DISCUSSION QUESTIONS

1. A, B, and C agreed to be partners for five years. After the five years had elapsed, B and C wanted to continue the business. A wanted to withdraw. May A withdraw and dissolve the partnership within the terms of the agreement? Explain.

2. X, Y, and Z formed a partnership for the purpose of selling 500 mobile homes. After selling 200 of the homes, all three partners decided that things were not working out. If all three agree to dissolve, is the dissolution in violation of the agreement? Explain.

3. Ruth, Sam, and Tom formed a partnership. Sam refused to abide by the rules and terms of the agreement. After repeated efforts to persuade Sam to change his attitude, Ruth and Tom agreed to expel Sam from the firm. What rights may Sam assert at this time?

4. Abner, Bert, and Lois were partners in a bakery. Abner suffered a nervous breakdown and was placed in a mental institution. Abner's wife demanded Abner's share of the business, alleging that Abner's insanity had dissolved the partnership. Discuss her allegation.

5. Scott was in a partnership. He was also heavily in debt. One of his creditors went to court and got a charging order against Scott's share of the business. Under what circumstances can this creditor seek a court-ordered dissolution of the business?

6. Maria entered an existing partnership as a new partner in 1979. She contributed $20,000 at that time. By 1983, her share had grown to $50,000. How much can creditors who had claims predating Maria's entry into the firm collect from Maria's share of the business? From her personal assets?

7. In winding up of a partnership, how can the creditors of individual partners gain access to partnership assets? Explain fully.

8. Robin was one of two members of a partnership. The partnership and Robin's partner both became bankrupt. Robin had $100,000 above her total personal liabilities. The partnership still owed $40,000, the other partner still owed $40,000, and both had been totally wiped out of assets. What will happen to Robin's $100,000? What rights will this give to Robin?

9. Given the following figures, work out the final financial position of each of the partners (net worth, cash, amounts owed, amounts receivable) following a winding up of their business:

	Bill	Charles	Larry	BCL Partnership
Assets	$70,000	$50,000	$50,000	$200,000
Liabilities	20,000	45,000	85,000	190,000
Capital contribution	50,000	25,000	25,000	
Profits	50%	25%	25%	

10. Given the following figures, work out the final financial position of each of the partners (net worth, amounts owed, amounts receivable) following a winding up of their business under both the ULPA and the RULPA.

	Beth	Cheryl	Linda	B & C
	(General Partners)		(Limited Partner)	(The Firm)
Assets	$67,500	$123,250	$ 87,900	$350,000
Liabilities	24,000	101,000	86,400	200,000
Capital contribution	50,000	50,000	100,000	
Loans to firm	0	5,000	7,000	
Share of profits	35%	35%	30%	

1. Cooper and Isaacs were partners in a janitorial supply business. They each signed a written agreement that, among other things, specified the acceptable methods for dissolution of the partnership. Some five years later, Cooper sought a court-ordered dissolution and winding up under the UPA. Isaacs argued that by seeking a court-ordered dissolution, Cooper had committed a wrongful dissolution in violation of the agreement. Isaacs then claimed the right to continue the business as a proprietor. Is Isaacs correct? (*Cooper* v. *Isaacs*, 448 F.2d 1202 [D.C. Cir. 1971].)

2. Davis and Shipman entered a partnership in 1954. The following year, the partnership dissolved, with Shipman continuing the business under its original name. Shipman agreed with Davis that Shipman would pay all existing debts. However, Shipman defaulted on some of the loans, and the creditors sued Shipman and Davis. Davis contended that he was not liable for any of the debts after his withdrawal from the firm. Is Davis correct? (*Credit Bureau of Merced County* v. *Shipman*, 334 P.2d 1036 [Cal. 1959].)

3. Three people formed a partnership to operate a loan company. Two of the three died, and the surviving partner reached an agreement with the estates of the two deceased partners that allowed a continuation of the business. The surviving partner then contended that she was the sole proprietor of the firm. Is the loan company now the sole property of the surviving partner? (*Miller* v. *Sabales*, 169 A.2d 671 [Md. 1961].)

4. The State House Inn was built and operated as the sole asset of a partnership that consisted of forty-nine partners. One of the partners was Polikoff. After several years of operation, the people who originally planned the inn and created the partnership formed a corporation and attempted to transfer the partnership assets to the new corporation. Polikoff objected to the incorporation and sought a court-ordered winding up of the business. What should the court do in this case? (*Polikoff* v. *Levy*, 270 N.E.2d 540 [Ill. 1971].)

5. Barclay and Barrie were partners. Their partnership agreement provided that the firm was to operate for five years and that each partner was to give reasonable time and attention to the operation of the business. During the first year of the business, Barrie suffered a stroke that left him paralyzed on one side and therefore unable to devote any time or energy to the business. Barrie's mental abilities were unimpaired, and the doctors forecast a full physical recovery within the term of the agreement. Nonetheless, Barclay sought a court-ordered dissolution of the partnership owing to Barrie's inability to perform as agreed. Should the court grant the dissolution? Explain your answer fully. (*Barclay* v. *Barrie*, 102 N.E. 602 [N.Y. 1913].)

6. William formed a hatchery business and operated the business as its sole owner. Some time later, William's son Donald joined William in the business, and they agreed to form a partnership. William contributed his

already-successful business to the partnership, with a total fair market value of $41,000. Donald contributed nothing to the business, but instead he took over the management of the business, allowing William to semi-retire. All expenses were subsequently paid from the partnership accounts, and all profits were divided equally between William and Donald. Several years later, Donald died. William claims that he is entitled to a return of his investment before any assets may be distributed to Donald's estate. Donald's widow insists that the assets of the firm be divided evenly between herself as Donald's heir and William. How should the court treat the assets of the business? (*Petersen* v. *Petersen,* 169 N.W.2d 228 [Minn. 1969].)

7. A husband and wife operated a business as partners. The wife suspected her husband of having committed adultery. As a result she filed a divorce action and also sued for a court-ordered dissolution of the partnership. In her dissolution petition, she stated that she had filed for a divorce and that her husband had refused to distribute her share of the assets to her upon demand. Is the wife entitled to a dissolution and winding up of the partnership on these grounds? (*Jones* v. *Jones,* 179 N.Y.S.2d 480 [1956].)

8. Williams and Burrus desired to begin a restaurant and bar as partners. Under state law, Williams was not allowed to own a liquor license, so Burrus obtained the required license in his own name, with no mention of Williams or his interest in the business. Once the business began, Burrus refused to give Williams his share of the profits as per their agreement or to buy Williams out and then to operate the business as a proprietorship. As a result, Williams filed suit for a court-ordered dissolution and for an accounting. Discuss the rights of the two parties to this partnership. (*Williams* v. *Burrus,* 581 P.2d 164 [Wash. 1978].)

9. Homer Ramseyer and his two sons, Donald and Duane, operated a cattle business as partners for ten years. The partnership owned two separate cattle ranches. Homer decided to leave the ranching business, and reached an oral agreement with his sons for the termination of their business. Homer deeded his rights in one of the ranches to his sons, and they deeded their rights in the other ranch to Homer. Homer also sold all his rights in the cattle to his sons in exchange for a promise by the sons to pay $20,000 and to assume all partnership debts. Four years later, Homer filed suit against his sons for an accounting for all transactions during the four-year period, and for a judicial dissolution and liquidation of the business. Was the oral termination of the partnership and the continuation of the business by Donald and Duane legally enforceable, or should Homer be granted his dissolution and liquidation? (*Ramseyer* v. *Ramseyer,* 558 P.2d 76 [Idaho 1976].)

10. Taylor and Bryan were partners. The partnership had no debts and had a bulldozer as its only remaining asset. Each partner filed suit seeking a dissolution and damages. The judge denied the damage claims asserted by

each of the partners, awarded the bulldozer to Taylor, and ordered Taylor to pay Bryan one half the fair market value of the bulldozer. Taylor objected to the judge's ruling, arguing that the bulldozer should be sold, and the proceeds divided between the partners. What should the appellate court rule? (*Taylor* v. *Bryan*, 664 S.W.2d 52 [Mo. 1984].)

CHAPTER 39

Formation of a Corporation

IMPORTANCE OF CORPORATIONS

In 1987, corporations in the United States produced $2,674.1 billion worth of products and services. This production, coupled with the fact that corporations made $273.3 billion in profits before taxes in 1987, graphically illustrates that corporations currently represent a vitally important form of business organization in the United States.[1] An understanding of the essentials of the formation of a corporation therefore seems warranted.

We define a *corporation* as an *artificial person created under the statutes of a state or a nation, organized for the purpose set out in the application for corporate existence.* United States corporations, while subject to applicable federal statutes, primarily are entities derived from state law and thus enjoy certain powers granted to them by state law. One of a corporation's unique features stems

---

[1] U.S. Department of Commerce, Bureau of Economic Analysis, *Survey of Current Business* (Washington, D.C.: U.S. Government Printing Office, March, 1988).

from its separateness from the people who own it. That is, a corporation exists in its own right as a legal person distinct from the shareholders. Even though it exists only in contemplation of law, as a legal person it possesses certain attributes and powers that have led to its increasing popularity as a form of business organization. This chapter will explore how and why this growth has occurred.

HISTORY

No exact moment of recorded history pinpoints the existence of the first corporation. But some evidence suggests that people recognized the concept of corporate personality to some extent as early as the time of Hammurabi (about 2083 B.C.). Certainly by Roman times, vestiges of corporateness had appeared through imperial **fiat.** From its very origins, then, the concept of corporateness depended on legislative grant. Canon law, borrowing from the Romans, distinguished between the "corporation sole" (composed of a single person, usually a high-ranking church officeholder) and the "corporation aggregate" (composed of several persons). The *fiction theory* — that a corporation is an artificial legal person separate from its shareholders — probably developed from the papacy's desire to accommodate priests who had taken vows of poverty forbidding them to hold property. Since controlling the activities and finances of these clergymen was very lucrative, the church devised ways (the corporation) to allow church officers to own property. This separation of the artificial person from the natural persons associated with it spawned the modern view that the corporation, not the shareholders, owns the corporate property and that shareholders are ordinarily not liable for debts incurred by the corporation. The development of the law merchant, the forerunner of modern commercial law, mirrored these and similar views of corporateness.

Fiat An order issued by legal authority

By the seventeenth century, English monarchs had tightened control over corporations, which were deemed to exist by virtue of "concessionary grants" of power from the state. Not surprisingly, the *concession theory* was part of the common law heritage that remained with American colonists after they had asserted their independence from Britain. At first, Americans viewed corporations with suspicion because several well-known, unsavory schemes had been perpetrated through use of the corporate form. But such suspicions gradually relaxed as the advantages of corporations, such as the potential to raise **capital,** became apparent. However, as the corporate form developed, each state jealously guarded its power over these artificial creatures. This careful regulation of corporations, augmented now by federal securities statutes, remains an essential characteristic of the law of corporations.

Capital Corporate assets or property of a fixed or permanent nature used in carrying on a business

ADVANTAGES

The popularity of the corporation as a business form results from its comparative advantages over other types of business organizations. One advantage is the insulation from liability provided by the corporate form. As mentioned earlier, corporate debts are the responsibility of the corporation. Since the shareholders' liability ordinarily is limited to the amount of their investment, creditors of the corporation normally cannot reach the shareholders' personal assets to pay for corporate debts.

Related to the idea of insulation from liability is the second advantage, the centralization of management functions. In other business forms such as partnerships, *all* the general partners have an equal voice in the management of the firm's affairs. Centralizing the management functions in a small group of persons possessing management expertise avoids some of the friction that may, in a given case, plague partnerships.

Continuity of existence is viewed as a third advantage. The corporation continues to exist in the eyes of the law even on the death of the officers, directors, or shareholders or the withdrawal of their shares. This potential for perpetual existence provides stability.

Correlating with this factor is the fourth advantage, free transferability of shares, which in turn opens up new possibilities for access to outside capital. These attributes unquestionably convince many large and small businesses to employ the corporate form. However, in a given situation, a sole proprietorship (a business enterprise owned and run by one person) or a partnership (discussed in Chapters 36–38) may better suit the business's needs. You therefore should seek the advice of a lawyer, an accountant, or another investment adviser before deciding which form of business enterprise you should use.

One reason for this caution derives from the fact that distinct disadvantages may result from choosing the corporate form. The tax treatment of corporations stemming from the law's recognition of corporations as separate entities for federal income tax purposes represents one such negative aspect. The corporation pays taxes on all its income as earned; and this income, when distributed to shareholders in the form of dividends, also produces taxable income for the shareholders. This structure in effect brings about so-called double taxation. Moreover, because corporate losses are not passed through to the shareholders, shareholders do not receive the tax advantages that would otherwise accompany such losses. Yet the creation of what the Internal Revenue Code terms an "S" corporation (regular corporations are dubbed "C" corporations) may offset these tax drawbacks and thereby give relief from these burdensome results. Subchapter S of the Internal Revenue Code permits certain corporations to avoid corporate income taxes and, at the same time, to pass operating losses on to their shareholders. In this sense, federal tax laws covering S corporations are analogous to the laws covering partnerships but are uniquely corporate at the same time. Attaining S corporation status involves an elective procedure and the necessity of strict compliance with statutory dictates in order to achieve this status.

The federal tax laws limit eligibility for Subchapter S election to domestic small business corporations having no more than thirty-five shareholders (individuals, estates, and certain trusts qualify as shareholders, but partnerships, corporations, and nonqualifying trusts do not) and no more than one class of stock issued and outstanding. Moreover, the presence of even one nonresident alien shareholder makes the corporation ineligible for S status, as will the corporation's exceeding the passive investment income limitations set out in the statute. In order to make a proper election, all shareholders must consent to the election, and the filing must be timely and proper. Once an election occurs, renewals are unnecessary; S status remains in effect so long as none of the events that can trigger loss of the election (an excessive number of shareholders or passive investment income, for example) occurs.

As mentioned, the corporation is an invisible, intangible, artificial person. **CORPORATE** Therefore, it ordinarily enjoys most of the rights that natural (flesh-and-blood) **NATURE** persons possess. For example, it is a citizen and a resident of the state in which it has been incorporated. Thus, under the Fourth Amendment, it cannot be the object of unreasonable searches or seizures. Similarly, under the Fourteenth Amendment, it must be afforded its rights of due process and equal protection. In addition, a corporation takes on the nationality of either the nationality and/or residence of the persons controlling it (called the "aggregate test") or the nation in which it was incorporated or where it has its principal place of business (dubbed the "entity" test).

A landmark case illustrating some of these concepts follows.

Petrogradsky Mejdunarodny Kommerchesky Bank
v. National City Bank of New York
170 N.E. 479 (N.Y. 1930)
Cert. Denied, 282 U.S. 878 (1930)

Petrogradsky, a Russian bank, sued a New York bank for a $66,749.45 balance **FACTS** standing to its credit. In 1917, as a result of the Bolshevik Revolution, the Russian bank's assets had been confiscated and its stock canceled. On this basis, the New York bank had said the Russian bank as a corporation had been dissolved and no longer was a juristic (legal) person. Therefore, the New York bank had refused to pay the credit balance.

Had the Russian bank ceased to exist as a legal person? **ISSUE**

No. It continued to exist. Hence, the American bank would have to pay the Russian **HOLDING** bank the amount in dispute.

The Russian bank had not ceased to exist as a legal person. Indeed, the law presumes **REASONING** that a corporation continues perpetually. If assets remain either in the domicile or elsewhere, there is no dissolution, either virtual or legal. Since there is no indication that pre-Bolshevik Russian law regarding juristic personality differs from American law, the presumption of continuance of corporate personality must tilt the balanced scales. Therefore, the corporation survives in such a sense and to such a degree that it can still be dealt with as a person in lands which do not recognize the decrees of the Bolsheviks.

FORMATION

The process of forming a corporation involves complicated issues that demand the attention of well-versed professionals. One of these considerations consists of choosing the most desirable type of corporation for the particular circumstances.

Types of Corporations

The *public-issue private corporation* is the best-known type of private corporation. We are all familiar with American Telephone & Telegraph (AT&T), General Motors (GM), International Business Machines (IBM), General Electric (GE), and other large public-issue corporations. The central advantage of public-issue corporations is their access to capital in the form of new shares. Yet the shareholder has very little say in the management of such giant concerns. For this reason, there is another type of private corporation, the *close corporation.* This limits the management of the firm to a select few shareholders and restricts the transferability of shares in order to consolidate control. Close corporations allow a firm to enjoy many of the advantages of the corporate form (such as favorable tax treatment) without giving up the day-to-day control more appropriately associated with sole proprietorships or partnerships. An inherent disadvantage of close corporations, on the other hand, stems from a lack of free transferability of shares; these shares are often not as liquid or salable as those of public-issue corporations. Private corporations may also include *professional corporations,* those organized for conducting a particular occupation or profession. Doctors, lawyers, dentists, and accountants may find it advantageous financially (because of tax and pension benefits, for example) to form such corporations. Most states have special statutes regulating professional corporations. Typically, these statutes limit share ownership in such corporations to duly-licensed professional persons. Despite the limited liability offered by the corporate form, under these statutes the professional is ordinarily personally liable for his or her own malpractice or similar torts as well as for any such acts performed by others who are under the professional's supervision.

A city is an example of a *public* or *municipal corporation.* We often call public utilities *quasi-public corporations* because they are private corporations that nevertheless furnish public services like electricity, gas, or water.

Corporations such as the ones we have described are generally for profit. But nonprofit corporations, or those organized for charitable purposes, also exist. Special statutes in some jurisdictions regulate educational institutions, charities, private hospitals, fraternal orders, religious organizations, and other types of nonprofit corporations.

Despite the negative connotation of the word, *promoters* may be vital to the formation of the corporation, practically speaking. Although the law does not require the services of promoters as a precondition to incorporating, promoters *begin the process of forming a corporation by procuring subscribers for the stock or by taking other affirmative steps toward incorporating.* Thus, promoters facilitate the creation of the corporation by bringing interested parties together and by "midwifing" the venture until the corporation is formed. We can also label promoters *preincorporators.*

Promoters' activities bring up a host of legal issues. Since the promoter is working on behalf of an entity not yet created, questions arise as to who is liable on contracts made on the corporation's behalf before its inception: the promoter or the corporation? The general rule is that the promoter will be liable for goods and services rendered to him or her before the corporation's formation. However, the corporation may become liable for the promoter's contracts (and possibly torts) after formation by adoption or **ratification** of the promoter's contract, novation, or release. In most cases, this liability is joint and does not (except for novations and express releases of liability) eliminate the promoter's personal liability.

The possibility of double-dealing inheres in the process of promotion. For this reason, the law treats promoters as owing fiduciary duties to the corporation. Therefore, the promoter must act in good faith, deal fairly, and make full disclosure to the corporation. Despite several older, complicated cases, the liability of promoters as fiduciaries is not as pervasive a problem today as in the past because of the disclosures mandated by the Securities Act of 1933. But, in occasional cases, the promoter has to give back to the corporation secret profits, embezzled funds, and other damages. Therefore, anyone desiring to act as a promoter should seek professional advice beforehand.

We call the document that signals the official existence of the corporation the *articles of incorporation.* State statutes prescribe the contents of the articles; but, as Figure 39.1 (pages 676–678) illustrates, typically the articles include the name of the corporation, its purpose, its duration, the location of its principal office or **registered agent** (also called *resident agent*), its powers, its capital structure (that is, the number of shares and minimum **stated capital**), its directors and their names (these people are usually the incorporators), and the signatures of the incorporators (in most jurisdictions they do not have to be shareholders). Once the incorporators file the articles with the appropriate state official (ordinarily the secretary of state) and pay all the required filing fees, the state issues a formal certificate of incorporation, or license.

In most states, corporate existence begins at the issuance of the certificate of incorporation by the secretary of state in the state of incorporation. After it issues such a certificate, the state will normally not interfere with this grant of power. Unless the corporation by its conduct poses a definite and serious danger to the welfare of the state's citizens (for example, by engaging in

Promoters

Ratification The acceptance of and the binding to an act that was unauthorized when committed and that was voidable before the ratification

Articles of Incorporation

Registered agent Person designated by a corporation to receive service of process within the state

Stated capital The amount of consideration received by the corporation for all shares of the corporation

Certificate of Incorporation

Figure 39.1   Articles of Incorporation

ARTICLES OF INCORPORATION
OF

_____

These Articles of Incorporation have been prepared in order to form a corporation in keeping with the provisions of the Indiana General Corporation Act, as amended (Act).

ARTICLE I

Name

The name of the corporation is _____ (Corporation).

ARTICLE II

Purposes

The Corporation shall engage in the business of _____ .
However, it shall also be able to transact any lawful business for which corporations may be incorporated under the Act.

ARTICLE III

Term of Existence

The Corporation shall have perpetual existence.

ARTICLE IV

Resident Agent and Principal Office

The post office address of the principal office of the Corporation is _____
_____ . The name and address of the Corporation's Resident Agent for service of process is _____ .

ARTICLE V

Authorized Shares of Stock

The Corporation shall have authority to issue one thousand shares of common stock having no par value. Owners of these shares of common stock shall have the right at every meeting of the shareholders to one vote for each share of stock listed in their name on the books of the Corporation. No shares of stock held in the name of the Corporation or not issued by the Corporation shall be entitled to any voting rights.

The Board of Directors shall be entitled to authorize the issuance of the stock of the Corporation in such a manner as to take advantage of Section 1244 of the Internal Revenue Code.

Subject to the provisions of ARTICLE XI, shares of the capital stock of the Corporation may be issued by the Corporation for such amount of consideration as may be fixed from time to time by the Board of Directors and may be paid in money, in other property, or in services already performed by the Corporation.

Figure 39.1 *(Continued)*

ARTICLE VI

Requirements Prior to Doing Business

The Corporation will not begin business until consideration having value of at least One Thousand Dollars ($1000) has been received for the issuance of shares of stock.

ARTICLE VII

Board of Directors

Section 1. Names and Post Office Addresses of the Initial Board of Directors. The names and post office addresses of the initial Board of Directors of the Corporation are as follows:

Name	Street No. or Building	City	State	Zip

Section 2. Qualifications of Directors.
None.

Section 3. Number and Election of Directors. The Board of Directors of the Corporation shall consist of not less than one nor more than ___ members. It shall initially consist of ___ member(s). The directors shall have the power to have the bylaws specify the exact number of directors. Directors shall be elected annually by a majority of the shares of stock represented at the annual meeting of shareholders. They shall hold office either until the next annual meeting of the shareholders or until their replacements are properly elected.

Any director or the entire Board of Directors may be removed at any time either at an annual or special meeting of the Corporation's shareholders called for that purpose. The removal shall be by the affirmative vote of the holders of the majority of the outstanding shares and shall be effective immediately even if a successor is not elected simultaneously. Any vacancy on the Board of Directors shall be filled only by the shareholders either at the annual meeting or a special meeting of the shareholders called for that purpose.

Directors need not be shareholders of the Corporation.

ARTICLE VIII

Name and Address of Incorporator

Name	Street No. or Building	City	State	Zip

ARTICLE IX

Provisions for Regulation of Business and Conduct of Affairs of Corporation

Meetings of shareholders and directors may be held outside the state of Indiana.

Any contract or other transaction between the Corporation and any of its directors shall be valid for all purposes, even though the director is present at the meeting of the Board of Directors which acts upon the contract or transaction and notwithstanding his participation, if the fact of his interest shall be disclosed or known to the Board of Directors.

Figure 39.1 *(Continued)*

ARTICLE X

Indemnification of Members of Board of Directors

In furtherance and not in limitation of the powers conferred by applicable law, the Board of Directors of the Corporation is expressly authorized to provide indemnification to directors, officers, and employees to the full extent permitted by Indiana law, it being the policy of the Corporation to safeguard its directors, officers, and employees from expense and liability for actions they take in good faith in furtherance of the interests of the Corporation and its shareholders.

ARTICLE XI

Requirement of Greater Than a Majority Vote

The affirmative vote of holders of ___ % of the outstanding shares entitled to vote shall be necessary for any of the following corporate actions:

1. an increase or decrease in the number of members of the Board of Directors
2. the classification of members of the Board of Directors into groups
3. the issuance of shares of common stock including treasury stock
4. the amendment of these Articles of Incorporation
5. merger or consolidation of the Corporation
6. reduction or increase of the stated capital of the Corporation
7. sale, lease, or exchange of the major portion of the assets of the Corporation
8. dissolution of the Corporation
9. the employment and compensation of any officers of the Corporation

As the Incorporator of this Corporation, I verify and affirm that subject to the penalties of perjury the facts contained herein are true and, in witness whereof, sign these Articles of Incorporation this ___ day of _____, 19__.

_____

This instrument prepared by _____ of Roemer and Mintz, Attorneys-at-Law, 1400 St. Joseph Bank Building, South Bend, Indiana 46601.

Courtesy of Charles Roemer, Roemer and Mintz, Attorneys-at-Law, South Bend, Indiana.

wholesale fraud), the state will honor the certificate and allow the corporation to conduct its usual business without impediment. Figure 39.2 represents a typical certificate of incorporation.

Organizational Meeting

In some jurisdictions, official corporate existence begins, not on the issuance of the certificate of incorporation, but after the first organizational meeting of the corporation. This is an important meeting because during it bylaws are adopted, the preincorporation agreements are approved, and officers are elected.

Bylaws

Bylaws are *the rules and regulations adopted by a corporation for the purpose of self-regulation, especially of day-to-day matters not covered by other documents.* These

Figure 39.2 Certificate of Incorporation

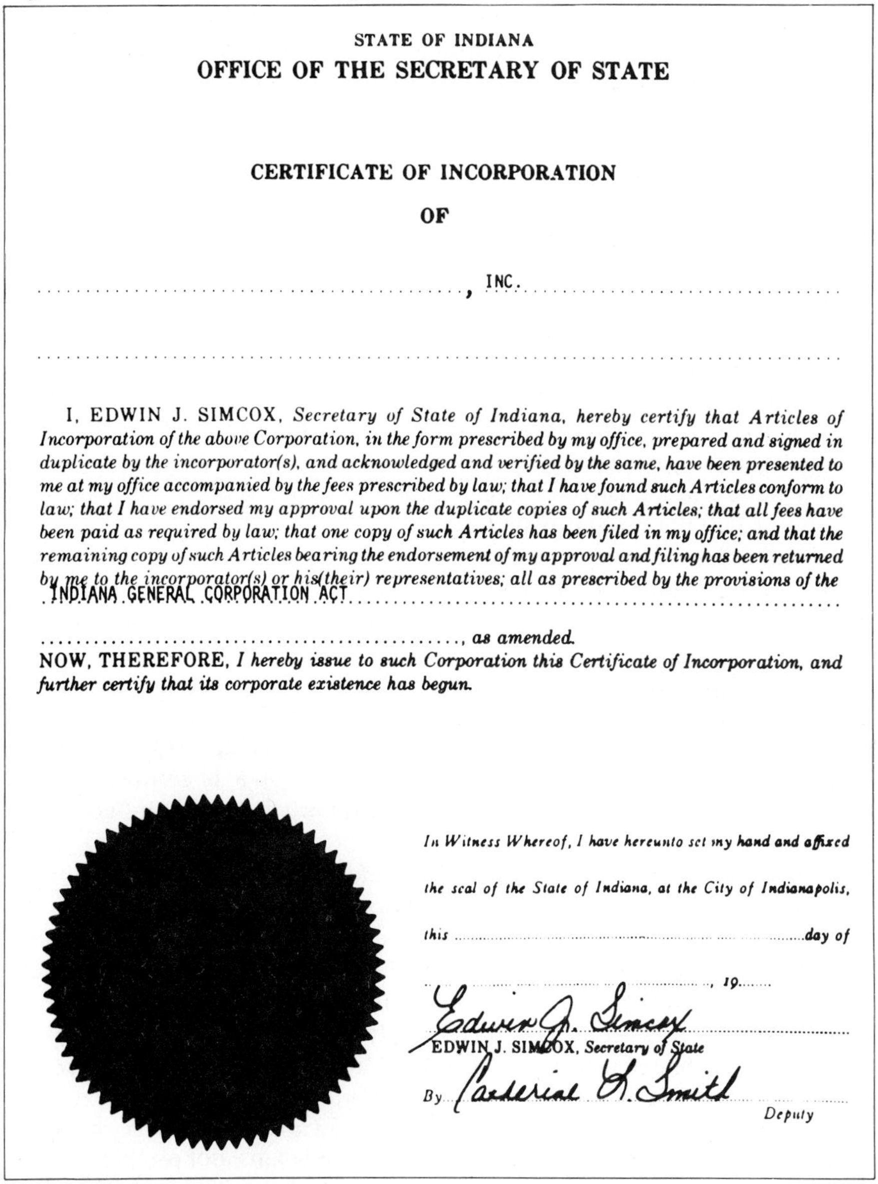

STATE OF INDIANA
OFFICE OF THE SECRETARY OF STATE

CERTIFICATE OF INCORPORATION

OF

...., INC. ....

....

I, EDWIN J. SIMCOX, *Secretary of State of Indiana, hereby certify that Articles of Incorporation of the above Corporation, in the form prescribed by my office, prepared and signed in duplicate by the incorporator(s), and acknowledged and verified by the same, have been presented to me at my office accompanied by the fees prescribed by law; that I have found such Articles conform to law; that I have endorsed my approval upon the duplicate copies of such Articles; that all fees have been paid as required by law; that one copy of such Articles has been filed in my office; and that the remaining copy of such Articles bearing the endorsement of my approval and filing has been returned by me to the incorporator(s) or his(their) representatives; all as prescribed by the provisions of the* INDIANA GENERAL CORPORATION ACT ....

...., *as amended.*
NOW, THEREFORE, *I hereby issue to such Corporation this Certificate of Incorporation, and further certify that its corporate existence has begun.*

In Witness Whereof, I have hereunto set my hand and affixed

the seal of the State of Indiana, at the City of Indianapolis,

this ....day of

....................................., 19........

Edwin J. Simcox
EDWIN J. SIMCOX, *Secretary of State*

By *Pacderial H. Smith*

Deputy

Courtesy of Douglas D. Germann, Sr., Attorney-at-Law, Mishawaka, Indiana.

are ordinarily not filed in a public place as are the articles of incorporation. Rather, they constitute the corporation's internal rules for the governance of its own affairs. They must, however, be consistent with the jurisdiction's corporate statute and the corporation's articles. Bylaws typically cover the location of the corporation's offices and records; describe the meetings of the shareholders and the directors; set out the powers and duties of the board of directors, officers, and executive committee; establish the capitalization of the corporation; and fix the methods for conducting the corporation's business, such as execution of contracts and deeds and notices of meetings.

DE JURE VERSUS DE FACTO CORPORATE STATUS

As we have seen, it is relatively easy to obtain corporate status if one carefully follows the required statutory procedures. Nevertheless, because ours is not a perfect world, it is still necessary to examine the consequences of failure to comply with such statutory requirements. *Defective incorporation,* as this concept is called, may be a matter of degree. If the defect in formation (or noncompliance with the incorporation statute) is slight, the law characterizes the corporation as *de jure (valid by law)*. The general rule is that where substantial compliance with all steps necessary for incorporation has occurred, the resultant entity is a *de jure corporation.* If an address is wrong in a provision mandating an address or a relatively insignificant provision has been overlooked, de jure status will not ordinarily be lost.

Sometimes, however, the defect involved is so serious that the law cannot consider the corporation a de jure one. Corporateness and all its attributes may still be retained, however, if certain conditions are met: (1) a law under which the business could have been incorporated exists; (2) there was a good-faith effort to comply with the statute; and (3) there was some use or exercise of corporate powers. Such entities are called *de facto corporations (corporations in fact if not in law)*. Only the state can attack the existence of a de facto corporation. Hence, if the state does not bring an action to dissolve its certificate (or its charter), the firm will enjoy all the powers and privileges that inhere in the corporate form.

This result is probably fair. Even if the defects in compliance are serious, if both the entity and third parties have previously dealt with each other in the belief that corporateness exists, fulfilling the expectations of the parties seems justifiable. Yet the law should scrutinize the parties' nonfulfillment of statutory dictates in order to avoid the frustration of legislative intent. In recent years, statutory provisions have increasingly reflected the view that the issuance of a certificate of incorporation will create a presumption that the corporation has been validly formed (that is, it has attained de jure status) except in actions brought by the state. If the state has taken no action and has issued no certificate, the presumption is that corporate status has not been attained. In this case, third parties can hold individual shareholders personally liable. These developments have greatly eroded the importance of the de facto doctrine; but, as the next case illustrates, some courts have continued to make distinctions between de jure and de facto corporations. It is therefore important to understand both the historical backdrop and the modern trends in this area of the law.

Bankers Trust Company of Western New York v. *Zecher*
426 N.Y.S.2d 960 (N.Y. Sup. Ct. 1980)

A bank sued for repossession of restaurant equipment that was security for an $11,136.31 loan made to Roseberry Inn. Zecher, one of the owners of the inn, countered with the assertion that the bank could have acquired no interest in the equipment because Roseberry Inn, Inc., was not a legally existing entity at the time the security agreement had been entered into, as it had not yet filed a certificate of incorporation with the secretary of state. The facts showed that the certificate of incorporation had been executed on 24 July 1975, the date of the security agreement, but had not been filed with the state until 30 July 1975.

FACTS

Was Roseberry Inn, Inc., a corporation at the time of the formation of the contract?

ISSUE

Yes. It was a corporation at that time.

HOLDING

To show the existence of a de facto corporation, it was necessary to show the existence of a law under which the corporation might have been organized, an attempt to organize the corporation, and an exercise of corporate powers thereafter. Because there had been a good-faith attempt to comply and numerous examples of use of the corporate name, the corporation was a de facto corporation as of 24 July 1975. The corporation was therefore liable to the bank.

REASONING

We have just seen that the law will sometimes recognize corporateness when incorporation has been defective. Now we will examine situations that call for disregarding the corporate entity even when compliance with the incorporation statute has been correct.

DISREGARDING THE CORPORATE ENTITY

The usual rule is that the shareholders in a corporation enjoy limited liability. Because the corporation is a separate entity from the shareholders, the law normally will not be interested in who owns or runs the corporation. Sometimes, though, it will be necessary to "pierce the corporate veil" (the shield that keeps the corporation and its shareholders' respective liabilities separate) in order to serve justice. For example, when the corporate form is being used to defraud others or for similar illegitimate purposes, courts may pierce the corporate veil to place liability on the shareholder who is using the corporate form impermissibly. If Roberts is the sole shareholder in an association that is so thinly capitalized initially that it cannot reasonably meet its obligations, or if Roberts is "draining off" the corporation's assets for his personal use, the law *may* fix personal liability for the obligations incurred on Roberts, despite the corporate form. If Roberts instead can reasonably meet his obligations and does not drain off corporate assets, his having as a goal the limitation of his liability is valid. In this case, there will be no personal liability. Courts therefore must examine the facts closely to see if a particular situation justifies disregard of corporateness or not. Put another way, if the corporation is a mere "shell" or "instrumentality" or in reality is the "alter ego" of the shareholder, courts can use their powers of equity to impose liability on the controlling shareholders.

This is not to say that close ("one-person") corporations are always candidates for disregard of the corporate entity — quite the contrary. The usual rule is that the law will not disregard corporateness if there has been no domination by the shareholder for an improper purpose (such as fraud or evasion of obligations) and resultant injury to the corporation (such as mismanagement), third parties, or the public at large. Courts will uphold corporateness as long as the controlling shareholder keeps corporate affairs and transactions separate from personal ones, adequately capitalizes the business initially and forgoes the draining off of corporate assets, incorporates for legitimate reasons (tax savings, limitation of liability, and so on), and directs the policies of the corporation toward its own interests, not personal ones. These same principles in general apply to situations involving parent-subsidiary (that is, affiliated) companies, another potentially troublesome area for deciding whether corporateness should be retained or disregarded.

Note how the court applied these concepts in the following case.

McKinney v. Gannett Co., Inc.
817 F.2d 659 (10th Cir. 1987)

FACTS   Robert McKinney had sold his corporation, The New Mexican, Inc., which published a daily newspaper called the *New Mexican*, to Gannett Co., Inc. (Gannett). At the time of the sale, McKinney had signed a ten-year employment contract with the *New Mexican* that allowed him to remain as the publisher and chief executive officer of the newspaper. Although Gannett had not been a signatory to this contract, it had been executed at the same time as the agreement and plan of reorganization that had made Gannett the parent company of the *New Mexican*. When a financial scandal and labor difficulties subsequently occurred at the *New Mexican*, McKinney was fired. He then sued Gannett for breaching the employment contract owing to his contention that Gannett was essentially the alter ego of the *New Mexican*.

ISSUE   Should a court pierce the corporate veil between Gannett and the *New Mexican* and impose liability on Gannett?

HOLDING   Yes. Gannett was the alter ego of the *New Mexican* and thus was liable to McKinney even though Gannett had not signed the employment contract at issue.

REASONING   Generally, the law will recognize the separate corporate status of a parent corporation and its subsidiary. This is true even where, as in this case, the parent corporation owns all the shares in the subsidiary and the two enterprises share common directors and officers. Nevertheless, courts have adopted the alter ego theory in those instances in which the idea of separate corporate status has been used to work an injustice. Piercing the corporate veil through the alter ego doctrine is therefore an equitable remedy by which courts will treat the two corporations as one. Here, numerous facts indicated that disregarding the separate corporate status of the companies was appropriate. First, Gannett completely owned the stock of the *New Mexican* and controlled its board of directors. Second, Gannett itself had disregarded the companies' separate corporate statuses and had treated its subsidiaries, including the *New Mexican*, as divisions of the whole. Third, all of the *New Mexican*'s revenues had gone to Gannett. Fourth, Gannett had approved all of the *New Mexican*'s capital expenditures. Fifth, Gannett had drafted the employment contract and had negotiated with McKinney as to the rights and duties of the parties. In sum, Gannett had used its dominion over the *New Mexican* for an improper purpose: to frustrate the contract rights of McKinney as the chief executive officer and publisher of the *New Mexican*. Hence, McKinney was justified in suing Gannett as the alter ego of the *New Mexican* and in asking a court to pierce the corporate veil between the two companies.

CORPORATE POWERS

As we learned earlier, the articles of incorporation may set forth the powers of the corporation. Such provisions may actually be redundant because state statutes normally set out what corporations can permissibly do. These are called *express powers* and include such things as the ability to conduct business, to exist perpetually (unless the articles define a shorter period or the state dissolves the corporation), to sue and be sued, to use the corporate name or seal, and to make bylaws.

In addition, corporations possess *implied powers* to do everything reasonably necessary for the conduct of the business. Typical implied powers consist of holding or transferring property, acquiring stock from other corporations, borrowing money, executing commercial paper, issuing bonds, effecting loans, reacquiring the corporation's own shares, and contributing to charity. Statutes may enumerate these and other implied powers.

ULTRA VIRES

As noted earlier, the powers of corporations were more heavily circumscribed years ago than they are today. Since the strict application of the concession theory had held that corporate status was a privilege (in contrast to a right), acts outside the boundaries established by law for the corporation were *ultra vires (beyond the scope or legal power of a corporation as established by the corporation's charter or by state statute)* and therefore void. When sued, corporations could use ultra vires as a defense to enforcement of a contract. With the advent of implied powers, and a consequent relaxation of the concession theory and a widening of permissible corporate purposes, a corporation's use of this doctrine for avoidance of contractual duties has become largely outmoded. Thus, the modern trend is to curtail application of the ultra vires doctrine as a defense and in general to uphold the validity of actions taken by the corporation unless the action is a public wrong or forbidden by statute. Sometimes, however, the result depends on whether the transaction is executory or executed.

Injunctive actions
Lawsuits asking a court of equity to order a person to do or to refrain from doing some specified act

Shareholder **injunctive actions** against the corporation, shareholder suits on behalf of the corporation to recover damages occasioned by an impermissible act, and proceedings by the state to dissolve the corporation because of repeated violations of applicable law constitute practically the only areas that remain possibilities for application of the doctrine. Not surprisingly, then, state statutes abolishing the defense of ultra vires usually exempt these three situations from the statute's coverage.

TORTS AND CRIMES

Older precedents had held that a corporation was not answerable for torts and crimes because these were ultra vires acts (so called because no corporation had the power to commit torts and crimes). Today, the rule is much different: corporations are vicariously liable for the torts of their employees by virtue of the doctrine of *respondeat superior*. They are also liable for the criminal acts of their directors, officers, and other agents. It is easy to understand why this would be so in nonintentional torts (such as negligence) or criminal statutes involving nonintent, *mala prohibita* situations (such as violations of environmental statutes or antitrust laws). But it is harder to accept the imposition of a corporation's liability for its agents' intentional torts that require showings of intent, such as **larceny.** In these cases, in contrast to situations in which the conduct is not willful, courts will generally not hold the corporation liable unless a high-ranking official (a "superior servant") has committed the acts and the corporation has intended to retain the benefits of or has participated in the tort or crime.

Larceny A felonious taking of the personal property of another person with the intent to deprive the owner of possession and to convert it to one's own use

The following case involved intentional or conscious disregard of one's duty to another.

Pendowski v. *Patent Scaffolding Company*
411 N.E.2d 910 (Ill. App. 1980)

FACTS

Punitive damages
Damages awarded to a plaintiff over and above those to which he or she would normally be entitled because of the excessive wrongfulness of the defendant's conduct

Pendowski was injured when a jack handle used in erecting scaffolding fell twenty stories and struck him on the foot. Doctors eventually amputated part of his foot. While the company had worked on the scaffolding, it had used no safety lines on tools and had placed no safety net under the scaffolding. The jury returned a verdict of willful and wanton negligence and awarded Pendowski $500,000 in compensatory damages and $200,000 in **punitive damages.** The company appealed on the ground that the evidence was insufficient to prove willful and wanton negligence.

Could the company be held liable for punitive damages? **ISSUE**

No. The jury's award of punitive damages may have resulted from an incorrect **HOLDING**
instruction.

When a corporate master is to be held vicariously liable for the actions of its em- **REASONING**
ployees, punitive damages for willful and wanton conduct will be available only if a
superior officer of the corporation ordered, participated in, or ratified the "outra-
geous misconduct" of the employee. Yet the judge's instruction to the jury would
impute liability to the company for *any* act committed by the employee. For this
reason, the jury's award of punitive damages must be reversed.

**FOREIGN COR-
PORATIONS**

A corporation will usually be incorporated in the state in which it will carry out
most of its business. However, the fact that some jurisdictions are more hospit-
able to corporations than others tempers this generalization.

For instance, some jurisdictions may allow favorable tax treatment of
corporations or may lower the minimum stated capital requirements. Delaware is one such jurisdiction. When the corporation is *operating within the state
of its incorporation,* it is called a *domestic corporation.* We have already seen how
the state can, through its incorporation laws, regulate the activities of its
domestic corporations.

A state can also require *foreign corporations (ones not incorporated in that
state)*[2] to "qualify" before "doing business" in that state. *Qualification* usually
involves filing required forms, paying fees and taxes, and appointing a resident
agent (for service of process). A state cannot require qualification of wholly
interstate corporations because such actions would conflict with the commerce clause of the Constitution. The amount of activity that will constitute
doing business has spawned a great deal of litigation, despite the fact that state
statutes generally try to define this term. The term most commonly means that
*a foreign corporation is transacting in the state a substantial portion of its ordinary
corporate business.* Maintaining bank accounts, conducting sales through independent contractors, holding meetings of directors or shareholders, or maintaining or defending court actions will not amount to "doing business" for
qualification (but may for jurisdiction or taxation) purposes.

Noncompliance with qualification statutes may bar a corporation from
maintaining (but not defending) court actions in the state or may result in
criminal penalties (fines). Moreover, lack of qualification may impose on the
directors, officers, and shareholders personal liability for corporate debts.

The following case illustrates some of the foregoing principles.

---

[2] Corporations incorporated under the laws of other nations are generally known as *alien*
corporations.

Davis & Dorand, Inc. v. Patient Care Medical Services, Inc.
506 A.2d 70 (N.J. Super. 1985)

FACTS   Patient Care Medical Services, Inc. (Patient Care), is a home health care agency incorporated and doing business in New Jersey. Davis & Dorand, Inc. (Davis & Dorand), a foreign corporation incorporated in the state of New York, is an advertising agency that came to Patient Care's office in West Orange, New Jersey, to make a sales presentation in order to procure business from Patient Care. Following that presentation in 1983, Davis & Dorand transacted business with Patient Care's New Jersey office on a continual basis concerning advertising that Davis & Dorand ultimately placed, on a regular basis, in New Jersey newspapers by telephone or mail from New York. Davis & Dorand maintained no offices or employees, bank accounts, mail drops, or telephones in New Jersey; nonetheless, when Patient Care failed to pay Davis & Doran for its services, it sued Patient Care in New Jersey.

ISSUE   Had Davis & Dorand, a foreign corporation, been "transacting business" in New Jersey so as to be subject to qualification in New Jersey as a prerequisite for bringing a lawsuit?

HOLDING   Yes. Davis & Dorand had been "transacting business" in New Jersey without being qualified, and this failure to obtain a certificate of authority from New Jersey prohibited its maintaining an action in the state's courts.

REASONING   The term "transacting business" requires that a foreign corporation be engaged in local activity within New Jersey. If a foreign corporation's activities in New Jersey are limited only to interstate sales, then the state cannot require the corporation to obtain a certificate of authority. However, Davis & Dorand's continuous activities in New Jersey for Patient Care over the past two years have been completely local activities and thus not a part of interstate commerce. For instance, Davis & Dorand's representatives came into New Jersey and offered its advertising services to a New Jersey corporation that desired to advertise only locally in New Jersey newspapers. Then, on a regular basis over a two-year period, Davis & Dorand worked with Patient Care and with various New Jersey newspapers to have the Patient Care advertisements placed in New Jersey media—a completely intrastate process. Therefore, Davis & Dorand, as a foreign corporation, was subject to the requirements of the New Jersey qualification statute. Because Davis & Dorand had failed to obtain the required certificate of authority, it was prohibited from maintaining the present action in New Jersey courts.

STATE AND FEDERAL SECURITIES LAWS

To protect the public from fraudulent schemes, states also regulate the issuance of corporate securities. Although the content of these statutes varies from state to state, these laws emphasize antifraud and registration provisions. Such statutes are called *blue sky* laws because the securities are often worth no more than pieces of the "blue sky."

states cannot regulate — that is, in
1933 and the Securities Exchange
rities and secondary distributions,
t federal statutes in the securities
al securities laws in detail in Chap-
because corporations may well be

SUMMARY

d by the state and endowed with
development of corporations illus-
'entity" theory) of corporations —
parate and distinct from its share-
s have the advantages of limited
ctions, continuity of existence, free
favorable tax treatment. There are
: public-issue private corporations,
ons, public corporations, and quasi-
ns exist in all jurisdictions, as well.
corporations. Although the corpora-
r's activities, in some cases it will be.
n signals the corporation's official
the issuance of a certificate of incor-
fore the corporation can attain cor-
will not be lost if substantial compli-
the courts will view the entity as a
ven grant de facto (in fact but not in
n the fulfillment of certain require-
incorporation will eliminate the need
e jurisdictions. This development in
resume de jure status in such circum-
state. At times, however, courts will
disregard corporate status even when complete compliance with the statute
has taken place. "Piercing the corporate veil" in order to impose personal
liability on a shareholder will occur when the corporate form becomes the
means for furthering illegitimate ends.

Corporations enjoy certain express and implied powers. Years ago courts
had held that corporations were not responsible for ultra vires acts (those
beyond the power of the corporation), but they now limit the application of
this doctrine to a few specialized situations. Corporations may be liable for the
torts and crimes of their agents and employees; but, when instituting corporate liability, courts often distinguish between torts and crimes that require
specific intent and those that do not.

States can require foreign corporations to "qualify" in their jurisdictions
if these corporations transact a substantial amount of business in those states.
State and federal securities laws represent additional methods of regulating
corporations.

Buslaw 2004
Test I: 76%
Concentrate on study guide,
Memorize BR for forms.

DISCUSSION QUESTIONS

1. What is a corporation? How did the concept of a corporation evolve?
2. Name five advantages of corporations as business associations.
3. Name and define the various types of corporations.
4. Discuss the rights and duties of promoters.
5. Enumerate in general the contents of articles of incorporation.
6. How does a de jure corporation differ from a de facto corporation? What requirements are necessary for a corporation to acquire de facto status?
7. Under what circumstances will a court or the state "pierce the corporate veil"?
8. Discuss the express and implied powers of corporations.
9. What is the ultra vires doctrine, and what are the circumstances in which it may be applied?
10. Discuss the concepts of "foreign" corporations and "qualification" in other jurisdictions.

CASE PROBLEMS

1. James E. McFadden, Inc. (McFadden), sued United States Fidelity and Guaranty Company (USF&G), a bonding firm, for monies owed to it for construction work McFadden had done for Baltimore Contractors, Inc. (Baltimore). Although USF&G had provided no bonding services for Baltimore on the project in question, McFadden sued USF&G on the theory that USF&G had so completely taken control of Baltimore in 1980 that Baltimore was a mere instrumentality or alter ego of USF&G. Among other things, USF&G's 1980 agreement with Baltimore contained provisions for: transferring all funds paid to Baltimore to USF&G in order to cover construction contracts bonded by USF&G; turning over all profits from joint ventures to USF&G to be applied to reducing Baltimore's line of credit; allowing USF&G to complete projects in Baltimore's name and at Baltimore's expense if Baltimore failed to complete them; installing an accounting system satisfactory to USF&G, including the sending of monthly financial statements to USF&G; and authorizing USF&G to have prompt access to all project sites bonded by it and to all of Baltimore's books, records, and other job accounts. Baltimore alleged that these provisions, plus the lack of a scheduled repayment plan, demonstrated that Baltimore had relinquished control to USF&G. USF&G, in contrast, argued that the provisions merely served as a vehicle by which it could minimize its losses if Baltimore failed to repay the $20,000,000 loan from USF&G that had been the subject of the 1980 agreement. Were the business affairs of Baltimore and USF&G so entwined that a court should pierce the corporate veil and impose liability on USF&G in these circumstances? (*James E. McFadden, Inc.* v. *Baltimore Contractors, Inc.,* 609 F. Supp. 1102 [E.D. Pa. 1985].)

2. Cross was a member in good standing of the Midtown Club, Inc. (Midtown), a Connecticut corporation in Stamford. The certificate of incorporation had stated that the sole purpose of the corporation was "to provide facilities for the serving of luncheon or other meals to members." Neither the certificate of incorporation nor the bylaws of the corporation had contained any qualifications for membership, nor had either contained any restrictions on the luncheon guests members could bring to the club. Cross sought to bring a female to lunch with him, and both he and his guest were refused seating at the luncheon facility. Cross then wrote twice to the president of the corporation to protest the action, but he received no reply to either letter. On three different occasions, Cross submitted applications for membership on behalf of a different female, and only on the third of those occasions did the board process the application, which it then rejected. Shortly after both of the above occurrences, the board of directors conducted two separate pollings of its members, one by mail, the other by a special meeting held to vote on four alternative proposals to amend the bylaws of the corporation concerning the admission of women members and guests. None of these proposed amendments to the bylaws received the required number of votes for adoption. Following that balloting, the plaintiff again wrote to the president of the corporation and asked that the directors stop interfering with his rights as a member to bring women guests to the luncheon facility and to propose women for membership. The president replied that "the existing bylaws, house rules, and customs continue in effect, and therefore [the board] consider[s] the matter closed." Cross sued the corporation on the rationale that Midtown had committed an ultra vires act in excluding women members. Should Cross win on this theory? (*Cross* v. *Midtown Club, Inc.,* 365 A.2d 1227 [Conn. Super. 1976].)

3. Mrs. Bannen was the bookkeeper in the professional association (corporation) formed by her husband, a medical doctor, in 1980. She had served as an unpaid secretary, receptionist, and bookkeeper for the sixteen years the practice was a partnership. In 1981, the Bannens separated. When they divorced, the court refused to award Mrs. Bannen an interest in Dr. Bannen's professional corporation because South Carolina law restricted ownership of shares in professional corporations to duly-licensed members of the profession concerned. Mrs. Bannen then argued that this statutory prohibition should not preclude the court's consideration of her husband's interest in the professional corporation in the court's decision regarding an equitable property settlement. Would you agree? (*Bannen* v. *Bannen,* 331 S.E.2d 379 [S.C. App. 1985].)

4. A federal district court issued two grand jury subpoenas, one addressed to a corporation calling for testimony and production of the corporation's business records, and the other addressed to the "Custodian of Records," also calling for testimony and production of the corporation's business

records. The custodian, who was the majority shareholder and sole operating officer and director of the corporation, which had only three shareholders, moved to quash (i.e., cancel) the subpoena for the corporation's records. He argued that the corporation was essentially a one-man operation much akin to a sole proprietorship, and thus to compel the corporation to produce its records would be to force the custodian to act to incriminate himself in violation of a recent Supreme Court precedent. According to this precedent, the custodian insisted, a sole proprietor could assert the Fifth Amendment privilege against self-incrimination because, although the contents of the subpoenaed records were not privileged, the testimonial character of the act of producing the records was. Was the shareholder's contention that this privilege applied when corporate records are subpoenaed persuasive? (*In re Two Grand Jury Subpoenae Duces Tecum,* 769 F.2d 52 [2nd Cir. 1985].)

5. Cranson wanted to incorporate a business called Real Estate Service Bureau. With the help of an attorney, he prepared articles of incorporation, which he thought the attorney sent to the appropriate state office on 1 May 1961. Cranson conducted all transactions on behalf of the corporation, including the purchase of eight typewriters from International Business Machines Corporation (IBM), between May and November 1961. At no time did Cranson assume any personal obligations regarding the typewriters. Unknown to Cranson, his attorney had not filed the articles of incorporation until 24 November 1961. In the meantime, Cranson's business began to fail, and IBM sued Cranson for the $4,333.40 due on the typewriters. Would only Real Estate Service Bureau be liable for this debt, or could IBM also sue Cranson personally? (*Cranson* v. *International Business Machines Corporation,* 200 A.2d 33 [Md. 1964].)

6. Morgan signed a promissory note in his capacity as president of Beefmastor, Inc., on 19 November 1970. The note represented partial payment for Smith's business, which was located in Georgia. Beefmastor, Inc., was subsequently incorporated on 31 December 1970. After making some payments, Beefmastor, Inc., defaulted on the note. Smith then sued Morgan. Could Morgan, the promoter, be held personally liable in these circumstances? (*Smith* v. *Morgan,* 272 S.E.2d 602 [N.C. App. 1980].)

7. First National Bank of Boston (First National) wished to spend money to publicize its views on a proposed constitutional amendment that would have permitted the Massachusetts legislature to impose a graduated tax on the income of individuals. A Massachusetts law prohibited banks and certain other associations from making contributions or expenditures "for the purpose of . . . influencing or affecting the vote on any question submitted to the voters, other than one materially affecting any of the property, business, or assets of the corporation." Another section of the statute stated that a question concerning tax matters was not a question that fell within the statutory exemption. Any corporation violating the

statute could receive a maximum fine of $50,000, and directors and officers violating it faced fines of $10,000, imprisonment for up to one year, or both. After First National made its wishes known to Bellotti, the Attorney General of Massachusetts, he informed the bank that he would enforce the statute against it if it attempted to disseminate its views in violation of the statute. First National sued, arguing that the statute unconstitutionally deprived it of its First Amendment right to express its views on issues of public importance. First National contended that it as a legal person possessed First Amendment rights just as natural persons do. Bellotti argued that Massachusetts had the right to limit commercial speech in this context because wealthy and powerful corporations had the resources to drown out other points of view, thereby undermining democratic processes. Who had the more persuasive viewpoint, First National or Bellotti? (*First National Bank of Boston* v. *Bellotti,* 435 U.S. 765 [1978].)

8. McElfish was the president and a primary stockholder of Gags Enterprises, Inc. (Gags). Gags owned the Sandspur Bar in Melbourne, Florida. The bar had a studio apartment attached to the back, which was occupied at various times by McElfish, who acted as the bar's manager. As he had done on other occasions, McElfish invited Schroeder to go with him to a party at another lounge in Melbourne to assist him in entertaining business clients. After the party, they returned to the apartment at the Sandspur. An argument arose between them which resulted in McElfish's inflicting numerous personal injuries on Schroeder. McElfish explained that he had been trying to remove Schroeder from the premises because she was rowdy and intoxicated, and that he had wanted to lock up the bar for the evening. Should Gags be liable for the $31,500 in compensatory damages and $30,000 in punitive damages awarded by the jury to Schroeder? (*Kent Insurance Company* v. *Schroeder,* 469 So.2d 209 [Fla. Dist. Ct. App. 1985].)

9. Velsicol had formed and capitalized Wood Ridge as its wholly owned subsidiary in 1960. Wood Ridge then purchased the assets of F.W. Berk & Company (Berk), including the 40-acre tract upon which Berk had operated a mercury processing plant. From 1960 to 1974 Wood Ridge operated this plant. In 1967, Wood Ridge declared a land dividend of 33 acres, subdivided from the 40-acre tract, to its parent corporation Velsicol. Velsicol remained the owner of the 33-acre tract. The adjoining 7.1-acre tract, on which the mercury processing plant was located, was owned by Wood Ridge until its merger into Ventron in 1974. Wood Ridge had been created for the sole purpose of Velsicol's acquiring the assets of Berk and continuing the business. Velsicol personnel, directors, and officers were constantly involved in the day-to-day operation of the business of Wood Ridge, and quality control of Wood Ridge was handled by Velsicol. In general, Wood Ridge was treated as a division of Velsicol. During the operation of the mercury processing plant by Berk and Wood Ridge,

mercury had flowed and drained into Berry's Creek from the industrial site, and mercury-contaminated waste had been dumped on both the 7.1-acre tract and the 33-acre tract. The New Jersey Department of Environmental Protection eventually sued Velsicol for the cleanup and removal of mercury pollution in Berry's Creek. Velsicol argued it could not be held liable for Wood Ridge's activities. Would you agree? (*State* v. *Ventron,* 468 A.2d 150 [N.J. 1983].)

10. The Associated Press (AP) is a New York corporation engaged in the business of gathering news. Briarcliff Communications Group, Inc. (Briarcliff), owed AP for news services and wirephotos AP had furnished it. Although AP provided news services both nationally and internationally, AP also operated a substantial news gathering service in Georgia that covered news particular to the state. Nonetheless, AP had not registered to do business in Georgia. Would AP's failure to qualify in Georgia preclude its bringing a lawsuit against Briarcliff in Georgia? (*Briarcliff Communications Group, Inc.* v. *Associated Press,* 268 S.E.2d 356 [Ga. App. 1980].)

CHAPTER 40

Operation of a Corporation

SHAREHOLDERS AS OWNERS OF THE CORPORATION

If you or someone in your family owns stock in a private or publicly held corporation, you already know that the shareholders are the "owners" of the corporation. Your holding share (stock) certificates, such as the one pictured in Figures 40.1 and 40.2 (pages 694 and 695), signifies that you own a portion of the corporate entity. Moreover, ownership of shares confers on the shareholder certain rights, which we shall discuss in this chapter. Interestingly, however, ownership of shares does not allow the shareholder to claim a specific asset of the corporation (say a building) as his or hers. You may recall from Chapter 39 that corporate property remains the corporation's; for this reason, shareholders cannot transfer title of such property to others. Thus, even though you could sell your car (assuming it belonged to you) to a friend, as a stockholder in PAK Corporation, you could not transfer the car to that same friend if it were a corporate asset. On the other hand, the portion of the

Figure 40.1   Stock Certificate (Front)

Courtesy of Charles Roemer, Roemer and Mintz, Attorneys-at-Law, South Bend, Indiana.

ownership of the corporation indicated by a share generally entitles the shareholder to vote on certain corporate issues, to receive dividends, and to obtain, on the corporation's liquidation, the percentage of corporate assets represented by the shares.

At the outset, then, you should be aware that the shareholders, although the ultimate "owners" of the corporation, exert only indirect control over the day-to-day operations and overall policies of the firm. As you shall see in Chapter 41, the officers and the board of directors, not the shareholders, bear the responsibilities for these functions. Shareholders, with the exception of controlling shareholders in a close corporation (a "one-person" or "family" corporation), ordinarily have no voice in the management of the corporation. Yet the shareholders form the bedrock of corporate structure because they select the directors, who in turn choose the officers. Additionally, the board of directors and officers are ultimately answerable to the shareholders.

Two other points deserve mention. First, as Figure 40.3 (page 696) indicates, proprietorships in 1984 outnumbered corporations about four to one.

Figure 40.2   Stock Certificate (Back)

Courtesy of Charles Roemer, Roemer and Mintz, Attorneys-at-Law, South Bend, Indiana.

Yet in terms of growth in sheer numbers between 1960 and 1984, the number of corporations almost tripled while the number of proprietorships increased by about one-fourth.[1] The percentages of total sales illustrated in Figure 40.4 (page 697) also reflect this phenomenal corporate growth, again at the expense of proprietorships. Since corporations are continuing to rise in popularity as a form of business organization, it behooves us to understand the basis of the operation of corporations from the shareholders' point of view.

Second, although we most often think of corporate America in terms of huge corporations like American Telephone & Telegraph (AT&T), General Motors (GM), or International Business Machines (IBM), government statistics show that about 20 percent of all corporations earn under $25,000 per year and 40 percent earn less than $100,000. Indeed, only about 16 percent earn

---

[1] U.S. Internal Revenue Service, *Statistics of Income, Business Income Tax Returns* and *Statistics of Income, Corporation Income Tax Returns* (Washington, D.C.: U.S. Government Printing Office, various years).

$1,000,000 or more.[2] From such statistics, we can deduce that relatively small corporations form the backbone of corporate America and that many of these are probably closely held rather than public-issue corporations, given their size.

In this chapter, we shall discuss the general operation of the corporation and the shareholders' rights and duties without differentiating between public-issue and close corporations, unless the concept under discussion seems especially well-suited to close corporations and the preservation of the special management functions associated with them.

RIGHTS AND DUTIES OF SHAREHOLDERS

Types of Stock Owned

Shareholders exert indirect control over the corporation by virtue of their ownership of shares; the more they own, the more power they wield. A shareholder may own *common stock,* which allows the shareholder to receive dividends, to vote on corporate issues, and to receive property upon the corporation's liquidation. Or the shareholder may own *preferred stock,* which, as its name suggests, confers priority with regard to dividends, voting, or liquidation rights. Furthermore, within the preferred stock, there may be several classes, or series, that set out different gradations of priority for each class. Under most state statutes, the corporate articles of incorporation must spell out the preferences; such preferences generally will not be implied.

Figure 40.3   Proprietorships, Partnerships, and Corporations by Numbers and Percentages, 1984

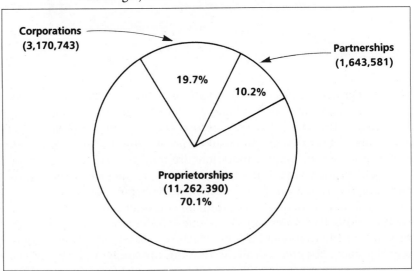

Source: U.S. Internal Revenue Service, *Statistics of Income, Business Income Tax Returns* and *Statistics of Income, Corporation Income Tax Returns* (Washington, D.C.: U.S. Government Printing Office, various years).

[2] Ibid.

Figure 40.4 A Comparison of Proprietorships, Partnerships, and Corporations: Percentage Breakdown of Sales Receipts, 1960–1984

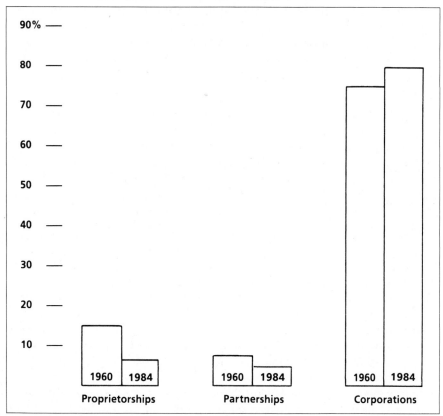

Source: U.S. Internal Revenue Service, *Statistics of Income, Business Income Tax Returns* and *Statistics of Income, Corporation Income Tax Returns* (Washington, D.C.: U.S. Government Printing Office, various years).

The most common preference right involves priority with regard to *dividends* (cash, property, or other shares that the board of directors declares as payment to shareholders). For example, preferred stockholders may receive dividends paid at a specified rate (for example, 7 percent) before any other classes of stock receive dividends. Should any dividends remain after payment to the various classes of preferred and common stockholders, preferred shareholders often have *participation* rights; that is, they can take part in this further distribution of dividends rather than having their dividend rights restricted to the preferred stock dividend. In addition to dividend and participation rights, preferred shareholders receive corporate assets before any other stockholders do upon the liquidation of the corporation. After the debts of the corporation are paid, preferred shareholders are the first to receive the **par value** of their stocks (plus any outstanding dividends); common stockholders receive assets only if sufficient assets to pay their stocks' par values remain. Should there

Par value The face value assigned to a stock and printed on the stock certificate

be additional assets after payment to the common stockholders, the preferred and common shareholders normally share this balance in proportion to the shares that each holds individually. Preferred shareholders may also enjoy *conversion* rights (the option to change preferred stock into common stock or corporate bonds) and/or *redemption* rights (the enforced repurchase of shares by the corporation in certain authorized circumstances).

Shareholders' Meetings

Notice

In general, shareholders' meetings may not occur unless the corporation has sent written notice of the meeting to all shareholders of record. Statutory and bylaw provisions often spell out the procedures for giving notice. Such notice ordinarily contains the time, date, and place of the meeting, as well as a statement of the purpose of the meeting. Most statutes require at least ten days' notice before a meeting can legitimately be conducted, but shareholders can expressly waive this requirement in writing before or after the meeting, or they can impliedly waive it by not protesting the lack of notice.

Quorum

Shareholder meetings cannot take place in the absence of a quorum. State statutes and corporate bylaws or articles usually state the percentage of outstanding shares, or shares entitled to vote, that will constitute a quorum. A majority of such votes will usually be necessary for a quorum; yet the Model Business Corporation Act sanctions articles that set the quorum requirement at a mere one-third of all outstanding shares.[3] *Dissident shareholders* (that is, those who disagree with the actions of management) may prevent a quorum by not attending meetings; but the law remains unsettled as to whether a subsequent walkout of dissident shareholders, once a quorum is present, will invalidate the meeting.

Election and Removal of Directors

One of the foremost powers held by shareholders comes from the shareholders' capacity to elect and to remove directors. Although the articles of incorporation usually designate the people who are to serve as the initial directors, these directors may serve only until the first annual meeting. At that time, the shareholders may elect some (or all) of them to the board of directors. If vacancies occur on the board because of deaths or resignations, the shareholders normally fill these vacancies. However, the articles of incorporation or bylaws may permit the directors to fill these posts. Directors usually serve

---

[3] The Model Business Corporation Act (1969) began as a drafting effort in 1943 by the American Bar Association's Section on Corporation, Banking, and Business Law; its intent was to modernize corporate law and to achieve greater uniformity among jurisdictions by creating a statute that balances the interests of the state, the corporation, the shareholders, and management. Most of the states follow either the older Model Business Corporation Act (MBCA) or the 1984 version, the Revised Model Business Corporation Act (RMBCA).

staggered terms. This means that only a certain proportion of directors (for example, one-third) will be up for reelection at any given meeting. Such staggered terms ensure continuity of leadership on the board. In recent years, there has been a trend toward adding **"outsiders"** on the board of directors.

Shareholders have *inherent* power (that is, power regardless of articles or bylaws) to remove a director for cause. Previous cases have upheld the exercise of such rights when directors have engaged in embezzlement or other misconduct, have failed to live up to their duties to the corporation, or have undertaken unauthorized acts. The director, of course, may appeal his or her removal to a court of law. Statutes, articles of incorporation, and bylaws may also allow removal without cause.

"Outsiders" Directors who are not shareholders or officers

Amendment of the Bylaws

Bylaws are provisions intended to regulate the corporation and its management. To be valid, bylaws must comply with state incorporation statutes and the articles of incorporation. Shareholders retain inherent power to amend (or repeal) bylaws, but they must do so in accordance with the proportion of outstanding shares mandated by state law.

Voting

The voting rights exercised by shareholders at meetings allow them indirect control of the corporation and the board of directors. All shareholders of record as of the date of the shareholders' meeting ordinarily appear on the voting list and can vote. Shareholders can either be present at the meeting and vote in person, or they can assign their voting rights to others, who then vote their shares for them by **proxy.** If distant shareholders in public-issue corporations do not want to participate personally in the meeting, they may sign a document called a proxy, giving the proxy holder authority to act as their agent. Figures 40.5 and 40.6 (page 700) show such a document. Whoever controls large blocs of proxies in a public-issue corporation may in effect thereby dictate the outcome of the election. For this reason, management (and sometimes dissident stockholders) in such corporations may solicit proxy votes in order to consolidate voting power. Not surprisingly, then, bloody proxy wars have occurred at various times in United States corporate history. Because of these high stakes and the accompanying possibilities for abuse, federal law now ensures that proxy solicitations will be carried out fairly. Chapter 44 discusses these provisions. Within the corporation, impartial parties called inspectors, judges, or tellers oversee the election to ensure fairness.

Proxy A person appointed and designated to act for another, especially at a public meeting, such as a meeting of the shareholders of a corporation; the document or instrument used to appoint someone to act in a representative capacity as a proxy

In most corporate matters, a shareholder can cast one vote for each share held. This is called *straight voting.* Unless the voting involves an extraordinary corporate matter (such as dissolution, merger, amendment of articles of incorporation, or sale of substantially all the assets), the decision made by a majority generally controls. Thus, votes of over 50 percent for any ordinary corporate matter usually become binding on the corporation; in extraordinary matters,

Figure 40.5 Proxy (Front)

ST. JOSEPH BANCORPORATION, INC.
COMMON STOCK PROXY SOLICITED ON BEHALF OF THE BOARD OF DIRECTORS

The undersigned Shareholder of ST. JOSEPH BANCORPORATION, INC., South Bend, Indiana, does hereby nominate, constitute and appoint Richard A. Rosenthal, Arthur H. McElwee, Jr., or either of them (with full power to act alone), my true and lawful attorney(s) and proxy(ies), with full power of substitution, for me and in my name, place and stead to vote all of the shares of common stock of said Bancorporation, standing in my name on its books, at the annual meeting of its shareholders to be held in the Center for Continuing Education at the University of Notre Dame, on April 19, 1983 at 7:30 o'clock p.m., and at any adjournments thereof, upon all subjects that may properly come before the meeting including the matter described in the proxy statement furnished herewith, subject to any directions indicated below, with all powers the undersigned would possess if personally present.

ELECTION OF DIRECTORS — Frederick K. Baer, Roy L. Beck, Edwin S. Ehlers, Jack E. Ellis, James W. Frick, Gerald Hammes, V. Robert Hepler, Gerald A. Hickey, William P. Johnson, Jr., Gerald A. Kamm, Edward A. Mangone, Daniel A. Manion, Arthur H. McElwee, Jr., Godfrey V. Miholich, Joseph C. Miller, Joseph H. Nash, Robert W. O'Connor, Samuel Raitzin, Richard A. Rosenthal, Frank E. Sullivan and Phillip A. Traub.

☐ VOTE FOR all nominees listed above, except vote withheld from (to withhold authority to vote for any individual nominee, write in the name on the line below):

_____

☐ VOTE WITHHELD from all nominees.

(continued on reverse side)

Courtesy of Trustcorp Bank, South Bend, Indiana (formerly St. Joseph Bank and Trust Company, South Bend, Indiana).

Figure 40.6 Proxy (Back)

IF NO DIRECTIONS ARE GIVEN, THE PROXIES WILL VOTE FOR THE ELECTION OF ALL LISTED NOMINEES. THE BOARD OF DIRECTORS RECOMMENDS A VOTE "FOR" ALL NOMINEES LISTED ON THE REVERSE SIDE. THE UNDERSIGNED HEREBY REVOKES ANY PROXY HERETOFORE GIVEN IN RESPECT OF THE SAME SHARES OF STOCK.

Dated: _____ , 1983   _____ (L.S.)

_____ (L.S.)

Please sign your name in the same manner as it appears on your stock certificate. When signing for a corporation or partnership or as agent, attorney or fiduciary, please state your full title as such. If your stock stands in the names of two or more persons, it is necessary that each sign this Proxy.

PLEASE DATE, SIGN AND MAIL THIS PROXY PROMPTLY IN THE ENCLOSED ENVELOPE.

Courtesy of Trustcorp Bank, South Bend, Indiana (formerly St. Joseph Bank and Trust Company, South Bend, Indiana).

statutes may require a higher proportion (say two-thirds) of votes for the action taken to be legally binding. In straight voting, therefore, unless otherwise indicated, a plurality of votes (or shares) cast determines the outcome of an issue.

To offset shareholders who own large blocs of votes and who may therefore be able to control appreciably the outcomes of elections, most state statutes today either permit or require *cumulative voting.* Cumulative voting applies only to the election of directors and becomes a method for ensuring some minority representation on the board. The following example illustrates the difference between straight and cumulative voting. Assume that at the annual shareholders' meeting, three directors will be elected from a field of six candidates — U, V, W, X, Y, and Z. Under straight voting, shareholder A, who owns 100 shares, can cast 100 votes for each of three directors, say U, V, and W. If instead cumulative voting is used, A can cast 300 votes for U or can divide 300 votes among any three candidates in any proportion he or she wishes (for example, 150 for U, 100 for V, and 50 for Y). In this fashion, A's votes "accumulate" — hence, the term *cumulative voting.* The ability of a minority shareholder to have an impact on the election of directors thus becomes more potent under cumulative voting than under straight voting. To dilute the "prominority" effects of cumulative voting, management may stagger the terms of directors, reduce or enlarge the size of the board, or remove directors elected by the minority. To counter such steps, lawmakers in many jurisdictions have passed statutory provisions that protect cumulative voting rights by making such steps illegal or by using statutorily enacted formulas that safeguard the beneficial effects of cumulative voting.

Voting trusts, like proxies and cumulative voting, are devices used to consolidate votes for control. A shareholder can create a voting trust by transferring to **trustees** the shares he or she owns. Once the shareholder has entered into such an agreement, or trust, the shareholder has no right to vote the shares until the trust terminates. However, the trustees issue a "voting trust certificate" to the shareholder to indicate that the shareholder retains all rights incidental to share ownership except voting. In contrast to proxies, which are generally revocable, voting trusts are normally irrevocable. State statutes, however, usually limit the duration of voting trusts to a specified time period, such as ten years (with possible extensions).

Trustees Persons in whom a power is vested under an express or implied agreement in order to exercise the power for the benefit of another

Pooling agreements are similar to voting trusts. In such agreements, shareholders agree to vote the shares each owns in a specified way. As we shall see in Chapter 41, both voting trusts and pooling agreements are valid and enforceable as long as they do not in effect preempt the directors' managerial functions. This may happen if the shareholders who enter into these arrangements are also directors. For example, it is legal for the shareholders to agree through voting trusts or pooling agreements to vote for director A at the annual meeting's election of directors (even if director A is also one of the shareholders who enters into the arrangement). But if the shareholders' agreements involve their pledging to bring about the dismissal of the current chief executive officer of the corporation, voting trusts or pooling arrangements to this effect will normally be unenforceable because selection of officers is ordinarily a function of the directors.

Shareholders of close corporations probably utilize voting trusts and pooling arrangements more than their counterparts in publicly held corporations. Because modern statutes recognize the unique status of close corporations—that is, that they are more similar to partnerships than are most corporate entities—some states will enforce agreements that bind the shareholders as if they were directors in those situations in which all the shareholders are parties to the agreement. Such statutory developments illustrate the law's ability to change whenever reality dictates such modifications.

The judge in the following case applied some of the principles just discussed in resolving the issue that was in dispute.

Adler v. Svingos
436 N.Y.S.2d 719 (N.Y. App. Div. 1981)

FACTS   Adler, Shaw, and Svingos owned an equal number of shares in 891 First Ave. Corp., a restaurant. They had entered into an agreement stating that all corporate operations, including changes in corporate structure, would require the unanimous consent of the parties. When Adler and Shaw tried to sell the business, Svingos objected, relying on the shareholders' agreement. Adler and Shaw brought a court action to declare the agreement void because it violated a statutory provision stating that only articles of incorporation can legally allow greater than normal voting requirements for shareholder action. The plaintiff shareholders thus alleged that the unanimous voting provision of the shareholders' agreement was void.

ISSUE   Was a unanimous voting provision that had not been included within the corporate articles but had instead been set out in a shareholders' agreement void and unenforceable?

HOLDING   No. The agreement was enforceable because the parties had intended to accomplish the purely ministerial act of amending the certificate of incorporation.

REASONING   Because the New York corporate statute allowed greater than normal voting requirements in the certificate of incorporation, the plaintiffs could be ordered to file the appropriate amendments necessary to reform the certificate of incorporation. In addition, since they had given their consent to the agreement, the plaintiffs could not now use the omission of the agreement's provisions from the certificate to justify the sale of the business without Svingos's consent. The fact that the parties had put the record of their undoubted agreement in the wrong place would permit the ordering of the purely ministerial act of amending the articles of incorporation. Accordingly, the shareholders' agreement was valid and binding on the parties.

We discussed earlier the various types of stock (preferred or common) that the corporation can issue. We also learned that preferred stock may be divided further into various classes or series. The right to receive *dividends — a portion of a corporation's profits paid out to its shareholders on a pro rata basis, as voted by the board of directors* — may ultimately hinge on the type of stock owned by the shareholders.

Most shareholders buy shares in "for-profit" public-issue corporations primarily to receive dividends. Such shareholders normally care less about the control functions their shares represent than about the financial aspects of their shares — namely, dividends. Thus far, we have spoken of a *right* to receive dividends, but that is a very loose use of the term. Actually, no "right" to receive dividends without fail exists. The power to declare dividends resides with the board of directors. In the absence of demonstrated bad faith on the directors' part, shareholders cannot compel the directors to declare dividends. The directors alone decide, first, *if* dividends will be distributed. If so, they also determine the timing, type, and amount of the dividend. Of course, shareholders hope to receive from their investment in the corporation the financial profits represented by dividends. *Cash dividends* are the most common type. However, the dividend may also take the form of *property* or *stocks.* For example, assume shareholder Barney of XYZ Corporation has received shares in Erstwhile Corporation, a subsidiary of XYZ, or, alternatively, shares in XYZ; this is called a *stock dividend.*

If cash dividends are involved, the directors must make certain that the dividends have been paid from a *lawful source.* In general, statutes limit the sources of dividends to *current net profits* (those earned in the preceding accounting period) or *earned surplus* (the sum of the net profits retained by the corporation during all previous years of existence). Any declaration of dividends that will impair the corporation's *original capital structure* (the number of shares originally issued times their stated value) is illegal and may subject the directors and shareholders to personal liability. Similarly, payment of dividends during the corporation's insolvency or any payment that will bring about insolvency is illegal.

As noted earlier, preferred stockholders enjoy priority with regard to distribution of dividends. They also receive protection from the rules that limit the source of dividends because directors normally cannot declare dividends if the declaration will thereby jeopardize the liquidation preferences of the preferred shareholders. Once a dividend is lawfully declared, preferred stockholders receive their dividends first. Common stockholders receive dividends only if adequate funds remain after the preferred stockholders have been paid. Sometimes preferred stockholders have *participating* preferred stock. This means they not only receive their original dividend but also share (or "participate") with the common stockholders in any dividends that are paid after the common stockholders receive their original dividends. In other words, participating preferred stockholders may be able to dip twice into the dividend fund. Usually preferred stock is nonparticipating, however.

We should note one last wrinkle in declaring preferred dividends. Preferred dividends may be *cumulative*, which means that the sum (or accumulation) of all preferred dividends that were not paid in a given year must be paid before common shareholders receive any dividends. In contrast, *noncumulative* preferred dividends permit the preferred stockholder to receive only the dividend preferences for the *current accounting period*, and the common stockholders then receive their dividends should any funds remain. Under this type of preference, the preferred shareholders lose all dividends for any years in which the directors have chosen not to declare a dividend.

Figure 40.7 sets out a flowchart that summarizes the various forms dividends may take.

Preemptive Stock Rights

Sometimes it is necessary for a corporation to increase its capital by issuing new shares. Since this is an extraordinary matter involving amendment of the articles of incorporation (the original number of shares and their par value would change with this new capitalization), shareholders must vote on the

Figure 40.7   Dividends: A Flowchart

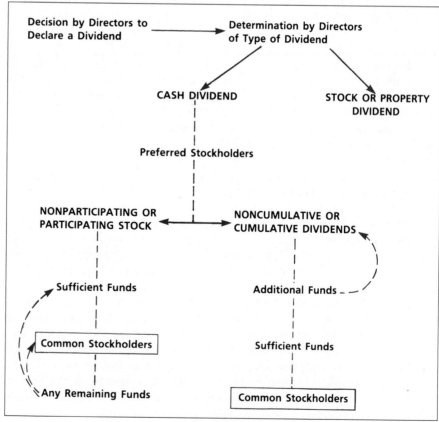

issuance of these new shares. But a shareholder's interest in this matter extends beyond voting rights. A simple example will illustrate this point. Assume Bonnie owns 10 shares of Samp Corporation. Samp's original capitalization involved 100 shares sold at $100 each ($10,000 stated capital). At that time, Bonnie owned 10 percent of Samp Corporation (10 shares/100 total shares). If Samp issues another 100 shares as a result of the amending of the articles, Bonnie will then own 5 percent of the corporation (10 shares/200 total shares). As a result of this new capitalization, her voting power has decreased proportionately; and so has her right to receive a higher amount of dividends and a higher proportion of corporate assets in the event of liquidation. Early on, common law courts, realizing the inherent unfairness of this sequence of events, began to protect the Bonnies of the corporate world by a doctrine called *preemptive rights.* These courts trumpeted the notion that the right of first refusal inheres in stock ownership; before the corporation can sell to anyone else, it must offer to sell to Bonnie the number of shares that will restore her total share of ownership to the proportion she held before this new issuance. Bonnie in effect can "preempt" the rights of other would-be purchasers of the stock because she can purchase before they get a chance to do so. Nevertheless, once the corporation has notified Bonnie of her preemptive rights, she has a limited time to exercise them. If she does not take advantage of the offer, she waives her rights of preemption.

Preemptive rights normally apply only to shares issued for cash and will not apply to shares issued in exchange for property (such as a commercial building) or services (such as shares issued to lure a chief executive officer to Samp), or to shares issued as share dividends, or to *treasury stock* (stock originally issued but subsequently reacquired by the corporation). In this last situation, there is no new issue and hence no reduction in Bonnie's proportionate interest in Samp Corporation. In the other situations in which Samp issues shares for consideration other than money, preemptive rights may cripple the corporation's financing efforts and obstruct the corporation's legitimate, profit-maximizing activities, such as acquiring property and recruiting top-flight executives. Because of the possible frustration of these worthwhile aims, courts and statutes alike dispense with protecting Bonnie's preemptive rights in these circumstances despite the dilution of her proportional ownership interests. If Samp were a publicly held corporation, judicial and statutory treatment of Bonnie's preemptive rights might well be different, too.

The rights of shareholders to inspect corporate records arise from both common law doctrines and express statutory provisions. In general, shareholders have access to such corporate materials as stockholder lists; minutes of shareholders' meetings; board or officers' meetings; financial records, such as books of account or other periodic summaries; and business documents, including tax returns, contracts, and office correspondence or memoranda.

At common law, inspection rights were qualified (rather than absolute) because shareholders had to demonstrate that the reason for inspection in-

Inspection of Corporate Records

volved a "proper purpose" — that is, that the motivation for the inspection related to his or her status as a shareholder. Seeking shareholder lists for communicating with shareholders about corporate matters or attempting to examine corporate financial records to determine the value of shares, the propriety of dividends, or possible mismanagement ordinarily signals requests that will qualify as proper purposes. On the other hand, a shareholder's asking for information to learn trade secrets for the benefit of the corporation's competitors or to bring "strike suits" (those without any real merit) in order to impede the management of the corporation will normally constitute improper purposes. Assuming the inspection is for a proper purpose, the shareholder generally can employ attorneys and accountants and other personnel to aid in the examination of the records, the making of copies or summaries, and the like.

Most statutes similarly require a showing of "proper purpose," but once the shareholder has alleged a proper purpose, they may shift the burden of proof to the corporation to show an "improper" purpose on the shareholder's part. Sometimes statutes make the burden of proof — or the party who has the burden — dependent on the type of record being requested. Statutes may also restrict inspection rights only to certain shareholders (for example, those who have held their shares for at least six months or who own at least 5 percent of the outstanding shares). However, these statutory restrictions do not eliminate the shareholder's common law inspection rights. But, as mentioned, the shareholder — not the corporation — will have the burden of proving proper purpose under these common law doctrines. Federal securities law and state statutes that mandate annual disclosure of profit and losses, officer compensation, and the like have made inspection rights somewhat less important: the information made available to the shareholder under these statutes encompasses the type of information that shareholders in the past could learn about only by exercising their rights of inspection.

The case that follows illustrates some of these concepts.

Hatleigh Corporation v. Lane Bryant, Inc.
428 A.2d 350 (Del. Ch. 1981)

FACTS   Hatleigh, a major stockholder in Lane Bryant, had requested a list of shareholders in order to solicit proxies regarding the election of the board of directors. Lane Bryant argued that Hatleigh's request was not bona fide because he had no intention of actually soliciting the proxies.

ISSUES   Was Hatleigh's request for inspection of corporate records for a proper purpose and thus valid? If so, what was the scope of that inspection right?

Yes. Hatleigh had shown a proper purpose for the inspection. Thus, he was entitled to a breakdown of all the brokerage firms holding Lane Bryant stock (so that he could learn the names of the true owners of the stock) and to other materials such as existing financial data and computer tapes.

HOLDINGS

Lane Bryant had conceded that Hatleigh's demand technically complied with the Delaware statute allowing inspection rights because solicitation of proxies would constitute a "proper purpose" under the statute. However, Lane Bryant contended that Hatleigh's purpose was nevertheless improper because he had not actually intended to solicit proxies. However, Hatleigh's failure to retain a proxy-soliciting firm until only two days before trial did not show that Hatleigh had failed to form a bona fide intention to solicit proxies at the time of his demand for a stockholder list. Hence, Hatleigh's inspection was for a proper purpose. Therefore, Lane Bryant would have to provide Hatleigh with a breakdown of the various brokerage firms that had held Lane Bryant stock for their clients. This and other computer tapes reflecting transfers of Lane Bryant shares, if in existence, would constitute the scope of the inspection right; Lane Bryant would not need to prepare information specially for Hatleigh. Furthermore, Hatleigh would bear the costs of reproducing such information and computer tapes.

REASONING

The next case shows an interesting twist to the issue of shareholder inspection rights. (The attorney–client privilege is discussed on page 94.)

In re LTV Securities Litigation
89 F.R.D. 595 (N.D. Tex. 1981)

A group of buyers and sellers of various securities of LTV and some of LTV's shareholders brought a **class action** alleging a conspiracy by LTV to defraud shareholders by overvaluing the inventories of Jones & Laughlin Steel Co., one of LTV's subsidiaries, through a series of accounting manipulations. LTV refused to disclose certain information, asserting the attorney–client privilege.

FACTS

Class action A lawsuit filed by some members of a group on behalf of all the members of the same group

Would the attorney–client privilege bar a shareholder's right to discover the minutes of board of directors and audit committee meetings, as well as other formal LTV records?

ISSUE

Yes. A valid attorney–client privilege would take precedence over a shareholder's statutory inspection rights.

HOLDING

The right of a shareholder to inspect a corporation's "stock ledger" or "list of stockholders" is nearly absolute. But when a shareholder asks to inspect other books and records, even assuming a proper purpose for such requests, the right to inspect

REASONING

must be balanced against the interests of the corporation in nondisclosure. If directors can confer in confidence with counsel and be protected under the attorney–client privilege, such a privilege should also cover the recording of those confidences, such as minutes of board meetings. In the absence of a showing of special need for the minutes or a lack of other means to obtain the underlying information sought, inspection rights under these circumstances should be denied.

Transfer of Shares

As discussed earlier, ownership of share (stock) certificates signifies ownership of a portion of the corporate entity. Thus, these shares are the shareholder's property. Like other owners of property who have the right to transfer the property (by gift or sale) to others, shareholders can generally transfer their shares to someone else. Figure 40.8 illustrates that a transfer of shares generally occurs through endorsement and delivery of the stock certificate in con-

Figure 40.8 Stock Certificate Record of Transfer

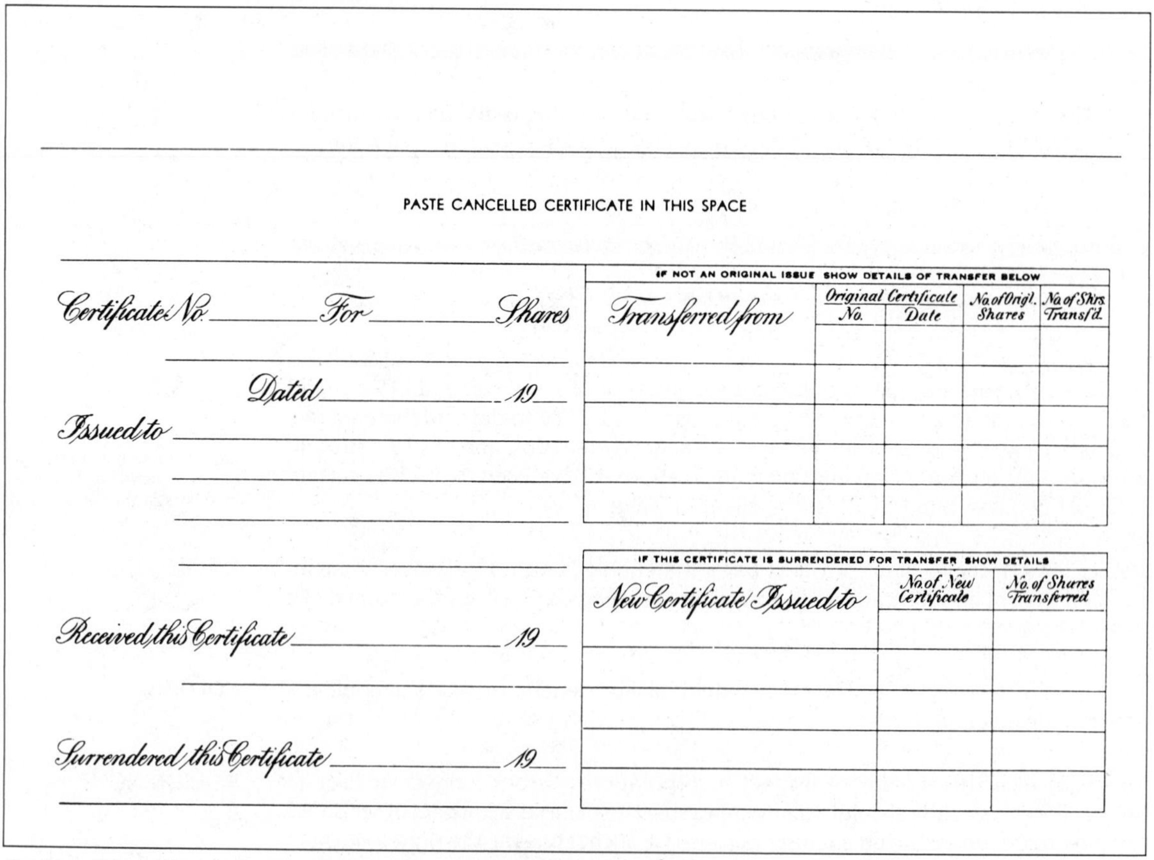
PASTE CANCELLED CERTIFICATE IN THIS SPACE

Certificate No. _____ For _____ Shares

Dated _____ 19__

Issued to _____

Received this Certificate _____ 19__

Surrendered this Certificate _____ 19__

IF NOT AN ORIGINAL ISSUE SHOW DETAILS OF TRANSFER BELOW

Transferred from	Original Certificate No.	Original Certificate Date	No. of Origl. Shares	No. of Shrs Transf'd.

IF THIS CERTIFICATE IS SURRENDERED FOR TRANSFER SHOW DETAILS

New Certificate Issued to	No. of New Certificate	No. of Shares Transferred

Courtesy of Charles Roemer, Roemer and Mintz, Attorneys-at-Law, South Bend, Indiana.

junction with a surrender of the certificate for subsequent reissue to the new owner by the corporation's secretary or, in a large corporation, by its transfer agent. Stock exchange rules regulate the conduct of transfer agents, who are professionals who help the corporate secretary with the myriad of details attendant on large-scale transfers (that is, the buying and selling) of stocks. Because of the administrative headaches associated with transfers of stock in these situations, including the cumbersomeness of actual physical transfers of stock certificates, present-day techniques (such as a brokerage firm's holding title to stock through bookkeeping entries rather than actual transfers of certificates) will probably lead ultimately to the abolition of stock certificates and their replacement by computer printouts.

Despite these new developments, the right to transfer stock in general remains otherwise unfettered. Restrictions placed on the stock, however, may limit this right of transferability.

It is not hard to understand why restrictions on the transferability of stock may be advisable. Such restrictions commonly occur in close corporations. We have already discussed the fact that close corporations are like partnerships in that the controlling shareholders actively take part in the day-to-day management of the corporation. Consequently, shareholders in close corporations often attempt to preserve their control over the affairs of the corporation through voting trusts and pooling arrangements. Such attempts at consolidation of power will be meaningless without restrictions on the stock's transferability. To illustrate, in the absence of such restrictions, stockholder A in Family Corporation can transfer his or her shares to another person and thereby force the original three stockholders of Family Corporation to include this previously unknown (and presumably unwanted) shareholder in corporate decisions about corporate affairs. Restrictions on stock transfers within close corporations help to avoid such unhappy results. Such restrictions result from shareholder agreements and are legal if the restrictions are reasonable. Courts try to balance the legitimate interests of the shareholders in limiting the corporation to a few congenial shareholders and the right of a shareholder to transfer his or her property (called the "right of alienation"), a right considered in our legal system as inherent in the ownership of property. A right of "first refusal" — that is, the shareholder who wishes to sell must first offer his or her shares to the corporation or to the other shareholders — is enforceable as a valid restriction on transfer because it is a reasonable restraint on **alienation.** In contrast, a restriction that states that "these shares are nontransferable" will probably be unreasonable and therefore unenforceable.

Alienation The transfer of ownership to another

It follows that even a reasonable restriction (such as "future sale or disposition of these shares shall take place in accordance with the shareholder agreement that controls them; and sale of them cannot take place until the holder of them offers them to the corporation or to each other shareholder, on the same terms") must appear conspicuously on the stock certificate if the restriction is to be valid. Such conspicuous notice is meant to protect any subsequent purchaser of the shares by informing him or her of the restricted nature of the stock. If this notice of restriction on transfer is missing, the purchaser will not have to abide by the restriction unless he or she otherwise has notice of the restriction. However, if the restriction is reasonable and appears on the face of the stock certificate, the corporation can refuse to transfer the shares to the purchaser. The purchaser's remedy will involve forcing shareholder A to give back the money paid to A for the shares.

If the transfer satisfies all legal requirements, including the applicable provisions of Article 8 of the UCC and state securities laws, the purchaser (transferee) pays the price asked, and shareholder A (transferor) endorses and delivers the stock to the purchaser. Then the corporation, when notified, must register the transfer and change corporate records to denote the new ownership in order to guarantee to the new owner the rights incidental to stock ownership in Family Corporation.

Liquidation

The process of *liquidation* consists of the *winding up of the affairs of a business in order to go out of business; that is, the marshaling of assets and the subsequent reduction of those assets to cash in order to pay the claims of creditors.* During this "winding up," the corporation pays all debts and creditors from the corporate assets and then distributes any remaining assets to the shareholders. The process of dissolution, which denotes the end of the corporation's legal existence, may immediately precede or follow liquidation. Though the terms *dissolution* and *liquidation* are often used together, they are not synonymous. We shall discuss dissolution in Chapter 42.

Throughout the liquidation period, the corporation has all the rights and powers reasonably necessary to effect liquidation. Moreover, during this period, the corporation can sue and be sued. Under most statutes, the board of directors continues the management of the corporation unless a court has ordered the dissolution and liquidation. In the latter case, the court may appoint a special person (called a **receiver**) to oversee the liquidation. If the directors unlawfully continue the business of the corporation after dissolution and beyond the time reasonably necessary to wind up the corporation's affairs, they may become personally liable for the corporation's debts. Caution among the directors (and controlling shareholders) is therefore in order during the liquidation process.

Receiver An unbiased person appointed by a court to receive, preserve, and manage the funds and property of a party

State statutes normally protect creditors during liquidation by requiring the corporation to notify creditors of dissolution and liquidation so that these creditors can file their claims against the corporation during this time period. A creditor who receives notice but does not file a claim may lose the right to sue later on this claim. Retention of this right, on the other hand, allows the creditor to recoup from shareholders any distributions of corporate assets that have occurred before payment of creditors' claims. To protect creditors, the law characterizes the illegal distributions as held "in trust" for the benefit of the creditors because the creditors have rights superior to those of the stockholders in these instances. The directors may also incur liability for distributions illegally declared up to the amount of claims that remain unpaid.

After the corporation has satisfied its debts to its creditors, the shareholders ordinarily receive the proportion of the remaining net assets represented by their respective share ownership. However, as discussed earlier, the articles of incorporation may set out one or more classes of shares as meriting liquidation preferences over another class or classes of shares. For instance, preferred stockholders usually receive their shares of the net assets before holders of common stock do. (Note, however, that preferred shareholders *never* receive payment before creditors do.) But if the preferred shareholders do not enjoy liquidation preferences, they will participate with the common shareholders on a share-for-share basis. Sometimes the articles give to the preferred shareholders both liquidation preferences and participation rights with the common shareholders. Because cash is the usual method for satisfying liquidation preferences, it may be necessary for the corporation to sell its assets to raise the amount necessary to take care of these preferences. Under most statutes, the corporation can distribute property instead of cash in satisfying liquidation preferences; but it will be illegal to favor some shareholders through grants of property (as when a corporation gives controlling shareholders valuable patents or trademarks) while doling out cash to minority shareholders.

LIABILITIES

As we learned in Chapter 39, one of the most significant advantages of the corporation as a type of business association is the limited liability afforded to shareholders. In other words, the shareholders risk only their investment. Except for situations in which courts can disregard the corporate entity, shareholders normally do not become personally liable for corporate debts. In this section, we shall look at some other circumstances that may cause a shareholder to be personally liable for obligations of the corporation.

Watered Stock

At the time of the formation of the corporation, the articles of incorporation spell out the *capital structure* of the corporation. In brief, the money to operate the corporation initially results from the issuance of securities to investors. The authorization for such securities ordinarily occurs early in the process of the corporation's formation, probably by board action at the organizational meeting. Most authorities classify securities into two main types: *debt securities* and *equity securities.* Bonds are examples of debt securities. Those investors who hold bond securities have lent money to the corporation and thus are creditors of the sort who will have claims on the corporate assets superior to the claims of shareholders in the event of liquidation. Bond holders normally do not enjoy ownership rights in the corporation but instead stand in a creditor–debtor relationship with the corporation. In contrast, equity securities create a shareholder relationship. The investor pays for the securities in exchange for shares (or stock) issued in the investor's name. As discussed previously, ownership of these shares confers on the equity holder (shareholder) certain ownership rights in the corporation. The consideration the corporation receives for these shares constitutes the stated capital of the corporation. The board of directors establishes a fixed value of each share of such capital stock (for example, $10 per share). This is called *par value* stock. The corporation may also issue *no-par value* stock, which has no fixed value but may be sold at whatever price the directors deem reasonable (called "stated value"). No-par value shares permit a corporation to issue stock in return for corporate assets that currently are worth little but have the possibility of high, though speculative, returns (such as corporate assets in the form of high-technology developments).

If no statutory provisions to the contrary exist, the corporation may issue shares in exchange for any lawful consideration, including cash received, property received, or services actually rendered. Just as the board of directors generally sets the price of the shares, so, too, the board normally fixes the value of the property received or services rendered. As long as the board makes these decisions in good faith and in the absence of fraud, courts will not use these decisions to impose legal liability on the directors.

However, the shareholder who receives *shares of a corporation that are issued as fully paid when in fact the full par or stated value has not been paid by the purchaser* owns *watered stock.* The shareholder is personally liable for the deficiency, that is, "the water." For example, if a shareholder pays $8 per share and the par value or stated value is $10 per share, the shareholder is liable to the corporation for "the water" — here, $2 per share. Watered stock problems normally arise in situations in which services have been rendered in exchange for stock. If the corporation issues $4000 worth of its shares in exchange for A's making a high-technology machine later found to be worth $2000, A will be liable for $2000 worth of watered stock. Usually A's liability is to the corporation, but some states will allow corporate creditors to impose liability on A when the corporation is insolvent and unable to meet its obligations as they come due. In some jurisdictions, such creditors can hold shareholders liable for the amounts by which their shares are watered. However, B, a later purchaser from A, will normally not be liable for watered stock because the rule regarding watered stock applies only to initial corporate issuances and purchases of stock, not to later transfers of the stock.

The use of no-par value stock and the impact of federal and state securities regulation have greatly reduced the incidence of suits alleging liability for watered stock. Still, shareholders should be aware of this legal doctrine.

Stock Subscriptions

Stock subscriptions are *"agreements" by investors ("subscribers") to purchase shares in a corporation.* The law views a subscription as an offer, and most state statutes make subscriptions irrevocable for a certain period unless the subscription itself provides otherwise. A subscriber may enter into such "agreements" either before or after the corporation's formation. If the stock subscription occurs before the corporation's formation (usually as a result of promoters' activities), some states treat the subscription as an offer that is automatically accepted by the corporation upon its formation. Other states require formal acceptance of the subscription/offer before a valid contract between the subscriber and the corporation arises.

Because an accepted stock subscription is a contract, various types of liabilities arise upon the breach of the subscription contract. Thus, the corporation can sue the subscriber for the subscription price if the subscriber refuses to pay the agreed price. In some cases, creditors of a corporation that has become insolvent may also force the subscriber to pay the amount owed on the subscription. (By the same token, the subscriber can sue the corporation if the corporation refuses to issue the shares that are the object of the subscription.)

As in the case of watered stock, securities laws have reduced the incidence of shareholder liability for stock subscriptions.

Illegal Dividends

We noted earlier that cash dividends must be paid from a lawful source. Any declaration of dividends that will impair the original capital structure of the corporation is illegal and may subject both the directors and the shareholders to personal liability. Shareholders who receive an illegal dividend are absolutely liable for its return if the corporation is insolvent when the dividend is paid. In such cases, the corporation's creditors can sue the shareholders directly for the amount of the illegal dividend. If the corporation is instead solvent when the illegal distribution takes place and remains solvent even after it, only shareholders who *knew* the dividend was illegal (for example, because it is from an improper source) must repay the dividends to the corporation. Innocent shareholders can retain the dividends. Directors who have been held liable for distributing illegal dividends can also force shareholders who knew of the illegal dividends to pay the amounts received back to the directors. The shareholders and directors thus share liability in such circumstances.

Dissolution

Dissolution signals the legal termination of the corporation's existence. It may occur voluntarily (by actions of the incorporators or shareholders) or involuntarily (by court actions initiated by the state or a shareholder). It is important to note that majority (or controlling) shareholders may incur liability if the purpose of the dissolution is to "freeze out" minority stockholders and to strip them of rights or profits they would otherwise enjoy. The basis of this liability is that controlling shareholders owe fiduciary duties to minority shareholders. Generally speaking, controlling shareholders must exert control for the benefit of *all* shareholders, not just for themselves. Dissolutions that prejudice minority shareholders' interests while greatly enhancing majority shareholders' interests may subject the latter to personal liability if minority shareholders sue.

In the following case, the controlling shareholders paid a steep price — personal liability — for failing to dissolve the corporation and for continuing the corporation's existence after the termination of the corporation's right to do business.

━━━

Nabakowski v. *5400 Corporation*
503 N.E.2d 218 (Ohio App. 1986)

FACTS   In 1981, G. John Harris and Marlene Harris (the Harrises) incorporated the 5400 Corporation (the Corporation) for the purpose of managing a building located at 4900 Euclid Avenue. Eventually, this closely held corporation became a lottery sales agent for the Ohio Lottery. As a result, a ticket issuing machine (TIM) was placed on the corporate premises so that the corporation could operate a daily game terminal there. G. John Harris hired his son, Mark, to run the daily lottery operations, including the TIM. On 4 November 1983, the state canceled the corporation's charter owing to the nonpayment of its franchise taxes. However, the corporation continued its daily operations. Indeed, on 3 September 1984, Mark Harris initiated a scheme whereby the TIM would spew tickets continuously and Mark would electronically place these bets in the group of tickets eligible to win the lottery. A computer repairman discovered this deception on 4 September 1984, while responding to a service call that had arisen from a blown fuse. He then notified the Lottery Commission (the Commission), which quickly deactivated the TIM and filed charges against Mark for his theft of $200,000 in tickets. Nabakowski, the Director of the Lottery Commission, also sued the Corporation and the Harrises for defrauding the Commission; and a jury found G. John Harris and Marlene Harris personally liable for $187,000.

ISSUE   Could the controlling shareholders and officers of a corporation that had continued to conduct business after the cancellation of the corporate charter be found personally liable for corporate obligations?

HOLDING   Yes. After the termination of the corporation's charter, the authority of the corporation to do business had ceased, and the principals were personally liable for the corporate obligations incurred.

REASONING   According to Ohio law, after the cancellation of a corporation's articles of incorporation, the corporation should cease to do business and should do only such acts as are required to wind up its business. Moreover, after such a cancellation of the corporate charter, the officers who carry on new business do so as individuals, lose the protection of the Ohio Corporation Act, and are personally responsible for the obligations they incur. In this instance, the Harrises, in their capacity as shareholders and officers of a corporation whose charter had been canceled, had hired Mark Harris to be in charge of the lottery terminal. They also had renewed their contract with the Lottery Commission knowing that their corporation was not in good standing with the state. Consequently, they had become liable for any obligations arising pursuant to their contract with the Lottery Commission. The Harrises could not claim the potential benefits that might flow to the corporation from Mark Harris's scheme to defraud the Lottery Commission while simultaneously disowning the consequences of the corporation's illegal operations. The Harrises as principals, with either passive or active knowledge of the scheme to defraud, therefore had become liable personally for their employee Mark's actions when they had elected to continue doing business with the Lottery Commission after their charter had been canceled.

SUMMARY

The shareholders of a corporation, although the ultimate owners of the corporation, exert only indirect control over the day-to-day operation and overall policies of the firm. Yet ownership of shares carries with it certain rights. The types of rights shareholders enjoy may vary depending on the type of stock involved. Ownership of common stock permits the shareholder to receive dividends without priority over other shares and to vote on corporate issues. In contrast, ownership of preferred stock confers priority as to dividends, voting, or liquidation rights. In addition, preferred stock may have participation rights, conversion rights, and/or redemption rights.

Shareholders' meetings provide the vehicle by which both common and preferred stockholders exercise their most significant control over the corporation. Corporate bylaws usually require an annual meeting (primarily for election of directors) and may authorize special meetings in appropriate circumstances. Such meetings ordinarily cannot occur in the absence of prior notice or a quorum. One of the shareholders' foremost powers involves the election and removal of directors. Shareholders have inherent power to remove a director for cause and may have power to remove a director without cause. Shareholders may also amend or repeal bylaws.

All shareholders of record as of the date of the shareholders' meeting customarily appear on the voting list and can vote. Shareholders can either cast their votes in person or by proxy. Federal securities laws now cover proxy solicitations. For most corporate matters, straight voting is used. However, for election of directors, many state statutes either permit or require cumulative voting. Cumulative voting protects the interests of minority shareholders but may be countered by such strategies as staggered terms for directors. Other devices used to consolidate control of corporate affairs through voting include voting trusts and pooling arrangements. These devices are especially useful in close corporations.

Dividends represent financial returns on shareholders' investments. Yet shareholders cannot compel directors to declare dividends; the directors alone have this power. The board must also make certain that dividends, if declared, have been paid from a lawful source. Dividends may be cumulative or noncumulative.

When a corporation increases its capital by issuing new shares, shareholder approval is necessary. To protect a shareholder's proportionate interest in the corporation when recapitalization occurs, the doctrine of preemptive rights is ordinarily applicable.

Shareholders' rights to inspect corporate records arise from both common law doctrines and express statutory provisions. Ordinarily, if a shareholder can demonstrate a "proper purpose" for requesting access to the records, the shareholder will be able to examine certain corporate documents.

Shares, because they are property, can generally be transferred by the shareholder. But in certain circumstances, restrictions on the transferability of shares seem warranted.

The process of liquidation (or "winding up") occurs when the corporation pays all debts and creditors from the corporate assets and then distributes any remaining assets to the shareholders. Directors may incur personal liability if they continue the business of the corporation beyond the time reasonably necessary to wind up the corporation's affairs. Creditors who have preserved their claims against the corporation can recoup from shareholders any distributions of assets that occurred prior to payment of creditors. Directors may also incur liability for the remaining unpaid claims. After creditors' claims have been satisfied, the shareholders normally receive the proportion of the remaining net assets represented by their respective share ownership, subject to any liquidation preferences that the corporation has authorized.

Shareholders may be liable to the corporation or creditors for "watered stock," and a subscriber may be liable to the corporation or to creditors if the subscriber breaches a stock subscription. Declaration and distribution of illegal dividends may subject both directors and shareholders to personal liability. Controlling shareholders may incur liability if the purpose of the corporation's dissolution is to "freeze out" minority stockholders and to strip these stockholders of rights or profits they would otherwise enjoy.

DISCUSSION QUESTIONS

1. Explain the boundaries of the rights conferred by ownership of shares. Then name and define the various types of stocks.

2. What is a *quorum*, and how does this term relate to shareholder meetings?

3. Describe shareholders' power to remove and elect directors.

4. Explain what the following have to do with shareholders' meetings: (a) proxies, (b) straight voting, (c) cumulative voting, (d) voting trusts, and (e) pooling agreements.

5. Describe the process by which dividends reach stockholders.

6. What are "preemptive rights"?

7. Explain how a shareholder secures the right to inspect corporate documents.

8. In what situations may transfers of shares be restricted?

9. Explain what *liquidation* of the corporation means.

10. How can liability arise for "watered stock," stock subscriptions, illegal dividends, and dissolution?

1. Harold L. Jones incorporated and operated Confection Products Corporation (CPC) as a candy manufacturing business. Jones also incorporated and operated Tom Sawyer Enterprises, Ltd. (TSE), as a sales arm of CPC. Jones owned 100 percent of TSE. During 1974, Mercantile Trust Company National Association (Mercantile) made several loans totaling $128,000 to CPC secured by liens on the inventory and accounts receivable of CPC and TSE. Jones signed a personal guarantee on these loans in his corporate capacity as owner of 78 percent of the stock of CPC and not individually. Also during 1974, CPC and TSE's candy operations encountered serious financial difficulties, and Jones therefore attempted to get a long-term loan guaranteed by the Small Business Administration (SBA). Jones forwarded to Mercantile a completed SBA loan application together with a chattel mortgage on all of the candy manufacturing equipment of TSE. When Mercentile could not obtain an SBA loan for the corporations, Janice Rennie, its loan officer, recorded the chattel mortgage as additional collateral for the previous Mercentile loans to CPC. Since Mercantile had failed to obtain a long-term SBA loan for CPC and TSE, Jones went to other banks and lending institutions in an attempt to obtain long-term financing. Jones claimed that he had been unable to obtain long-term financing owing to the wrongfully recorded chattel mortgage on TSE's candy manufacturing equipment. At trial, a jury found that the chattel mortgage on equipment of TSE tendered to Mercantile was to be used in connection with obtaining long-term financing and not as additional security for the original loans to CPC. CPC, TSE, and Jones in his individual capacity sued Rennie and Mercantile for misrepresentation, slander of title, interference with business relationships, and negligent handling of the lien papers. Could Jones, as a shareholder, successfully sue Mercantile in his individual capacity for damages done to CPC and TSE? (*Jones* v. *Rennie,* 690 S.W.2d 164 [Mo. App. 1985].)

2. The directors of Datapoint Corporation (Datapoint) adopted a bylaw that in effect limited the taking of corporate action by written shareholder consent in lieu of a shareholder meeting for sixty days. The bylaw furthermore deferred the effectiveness of any consent actions until the termination of any lawsuits brought to challenge such consent actions. A Delaware law conferred on shareholders the right to take corporate action through such consents in lieu of a meeting. Datapoint adopted this bylaw in order to repel hostile takeover attempts and thereby to give the corporation time to defeat any such shareholder action initiated by a hostile offeror through solicitations of Datapoint's own proxies or revocations of outstanding shareholder consents. Did the board have the power to pass

CASE PROBLEMS

this bylaw? (*Datapoint Corporation* v. *Plaza Securities Company*, 496 A.2d 1031 [Del. 1985].)

3. Pybus, a shareholder and director of Chavco Investment Company, Inc., wanted to inspect the corporate books to determine if the rental on a building, the principal asset of the corporation, was so low as to constitute corporate waste. The corporation refused to allow Pybus to inspect the corporate records. Pybus argued that as a shareholder he had shown a proper purpose and that, furthermore, as a director, his right to inspect such records was absolute. Was Pybus correct? (*Chavco Investment Company, Inc.* v. *Pybus*, 613 S.W.2d 806 [Tex. Civ. App. 1981].)

4. Henry Ford, the president and major shareholder of Ford Motor Co., in 1916 refused to pay special dividends even though special dividends had been paid in the past and the surplus on hand in 1916 was about $112 million. Ford's articulated reason for withholding dividends was his desire to employ more people and thus to spread the benefits of capitalism to the largest number of people possible. To accomplish this, Ford proposed to put the profits back into the business rather than to declare dividends. The Dodge Brothers, minority shareholders of approximately 10 percent of the stock, sued to compel the declaration of a dividend. Should a court force Ford to pay dividends in these circumstances? (*Dodge* v. *Ford Motor Co.*, 170 N.W. 668 [Mich. 1919].)

5. Saxon Industries, Inc. (Saxon), was a publicly held Delaware corporation in the paper distribution and converting business. Since April, 1982, it had operated as debtor-in-possession in a voluntary Chapter 11 bankruptcy reorganization. Saxon's last shareholders' meeting had occurred on 21 June 1981. After filing for Chapter 11 reorganization in April, 1982, new management, experienced in restoring financially troubled companies, was retained. Although no stockholders' meetings were held, the Saxon Board eventually elected five new directors. Under new management Saxon sold several unprofitable operations, and for the first six months of the 1984 fiscal year showed operating profits in excess of $4 million with annual sales of approximately $400 million. Despite such progress, Saxon's shareholders' deficit remained at approximately $200 million. When Alco Standard Corporation agreed to buy Saxon, NKFW Partners (NKFW) sued to compel an election of directors. By then, over thirty-one months had elapsed since Saxon's last annual meeting. Saxon argued that the shareholders should air their grievances in bankruptcy court rather than in a shareholders' meeting because NKFW's only purpose for requesting the meeting was to achieve for the stockholders a more substantial payment in the reorganization. Saxon further contended that allowing the shareholders' grievances to be aired in the bankruptcy forum, as opposed to a stockholders' meeting, would be more suitable because the bankruptcy court would consider and weigh the competing demands and relative equities of all the interested parties.

Delaware law called for annual stockholders' meetings and permitted courts to order such meetings if the directors failed to call the meetings. Would the insolvency of the corporation divest the corporation's stockholders of their right to elect directors at an annual meeting? (*Saxon Industries* v. *NKFW Partners*, 488 A.2d 1298 [Del. 1984].)

6. Wallace helped to pass a 100 percent quorum requirement in the bylaws in 1972, when he was the sole shareholder and one of the directors of Capital Credit and Collection Service, Inc. Four years later, the plaintiffs purchased 49 percent of the business. In 1979, a majority of the directors, including the plaintiffs, removed Wallace as president. Three months later, Wallace used his majority shares to remove the minority directors from the board, arguing that the prior action had been illegal because of the 100 percent quorum requirement in the bylaws. The plaintiffs asserted that the extraordinary quorum requirement, because it had been imposed by the bylaws rather than by the articles of incorporation, was invalid. Who was correct? (*Jones* v. *Wallace*, 628 P.2d 388 [Or. 1981].)

7. Hagerbaumer, a shareholder in a close corporation, sued to compel the corporation to buy her restricted shares in accordance with a 1976 buy-and-sell agreement. This agreement stated that the remaining shareholders had the right of first refusal and that if they refused to buy, the corporation had to purchase the stock. The remaining shareholders argued there was no duty to purchase her shares because the 1976 agreement had been rescinded by a 1977 agreement. Should Hagerbaumer win if the terms of the 1977 agreement, though different, are consistent with the possible sale to the corporation in the event of a refusal of the remaining shareholders to purchase her shares? (*Hagerbaumer* v. *Hagerbaumer Brothers, Inc.*, 305 N.W.2d 4 [Neb. 1981].)

8. As partial payment for Chrysler Corporation's (Chrysler's) sale to it of the assets of Chrysler's former Airtemp Division, Fedders Corporation (Fedders) transferred all of its Series B preferred stock to Chrysler. The sales agreement contained terms contemplating possible misstatements of the true value of assets and contained extensive provisions for remedies. Fedders' certificate of incorporation required that it pay dividends on its Series B stock ratably with any dividends paid to Series A preferred shareholders. Fedders had paid dividends on the Series A shares since the sale, but Fedders argued that it had no obligation to pay Chrysler dividends on the Series B shares because Chrysler had overstated the value of Airtemp's assets. On these facts, could Fedders avoid its obligation to pay dividends on the Series B shares? (*Chrysler Corporation* v. *Fedders Corporation*, 416 N.E.2d 1036 [N.Y. 1980].)

9. Dynamics Corporation of America (DCA) sued CTS Corporation (CTS) to compel CTS to afford it inspection rights as a shareholder of CTS. DCA had begun to acquire CTS stock in 1980, and litigation was still pending between the parties regarding this proposed acquisition. The information

requested by DCA included: (a) all records and minutes of the 1981 CTS annual meeting of shareholders; (b) books of account reflecting all expenditures for research and development since January, 1978 and all legal fees paid or incurred in connection with claims and suits asserted by CTS against DCA; (c) all fees paid or owed to Goldman, Sachs & Company since 11 August 1980; and (d) the minutes of all regular and special meetings of the Board of Directors of CTS since 11 August 1980. CTS through its CTS Knights subsidiary and DCA through its Reeves Hoffman Division were direct and substantial competitors in markets for the sale of quartz crystals and electronic quartz crystal products, and DCA was also a potential competitor of CTS in other lines of business. Indeed, DCA had previously hired away from CTS Knights one of its key engineering employees for the Reeves Hoffman Division. In addition, it had been established that CTS's books of account did not contain separate notations for research and development expenditures. That information was contained in work papers prepared by CTS accountants, including the names of CTS employees who were engaged in research and development, the salaries of each, and the activities upon which CTS was expending its research and development efforts. CTS considered this information confidential and protected it as such. Copies of the minutes of the 1981 meeting had been offered to all shareholders at the 1982 annual meeting, and DCA's president and general counsel had been in attendance at that meeting. CTS asserted that Goldman, Sachs & Company had been retained for litigation advice, including the DCA suit in federal court, and that the minutes of directors' meetings reflected legal advice received by CTS regarding the federal litigation with DCA, as well as tentative CTS business plans. Given these facts, how should the court rule on DCA's suit? (*Dynamics Corporation of America* v. *CTS Corporation,* 479 N.E.2d 1352 [Ind. App. 1985].)

10. On 8 April 1966, Phillip B. Ingle (Ingle), James H. Glamore (the sole stockholder of Glamore Motor Sales, Inc.), and the corporation entered into an agreement whereby Ingle, the corporation's general manager, was to purchase twenty-two of the one hundred outstanding shares of the corporation's common stock. The agreement also made Ingle a director and secretary of the corporation and gave him the option to purchase eighteen additional shares of the corporation's stock. The agreement provided that "in the event that INGLE shall cease to be an employee of the corporation for any reason [James H. Glamore] shall have the option, for a period of 30 days after such termination of employment, to purchase all of the shares of stock then owned by INGLE." Pursuant to the terms of the 1966 agreement, the plaintiff purchased an additional eighteen shares of stock. An agreement was drawn up in 1973 reflecting this change in circumstances by acknowledging that the plaintiff then owned forty of the one hundred outstanding shares of stock. The repurchase provision in the 1973 agreement was identical to that of the 1966 agreement. On 1 January 1982, the corporation issued sixty more shares of stock.

James H. Glamore purchased twenty-two shares and his two sons (defendants William B. Glamore and Robert L. Glamore) purchased nineteen shares each. An agreement dated 1 January 1982, between Ingle, James H. Glamore, William B. Glamore, Robert L. Glamore, and the corporation, reflected that change. Again, the agreement contained the identical repurchase provision language. On 9 May 1983, at a special meeting of the board of directors of the corporation, Ingle's employment with the corporation was terminated. On 1 June 1983, James H. Glamore notified Ingle that he was exercising his option to purchase all of Ingle's stock. Ingle then sued, arguing that the alleged breach of the 1982 agreement and his termination resulted from Glamore's desire to exercise the option to purchase Ingle's stock. Was Ingle's interpretation of the agreement — that Glamore could only repurchase the shares if the corporation had good cause for discharging Ingle — correct? (*Ingle* v. *Glamore Motor Sales, Inc.*, 490 N.Y.S.2d 240 [N.Y. App. Div. 1985].)

CHAPTER 41

Management of a Corporation

BOARD OF DIRECTORS

The right to manage the affairs of the corporation falls squarely on the board of directors. Although shareholders, the ultimate "owners" of the corporation, retain the power to elect and remove directors, this prerogative does not give shareholders a direct voice in management. Nor can shareholders compel the board to take any action: the directors are not agents of the shareholders; they owe loyalty primarily to the corporation. (As noted before, however, different rules may apply if the corporation is a close corporation.)

Rights and Duties

Number and Qualifications

The articles of incorporation usually name the initial directors. Older statutes required at least three directors, but the modern trend—owing, no doubt, in

722

part to the increased numbers of close corporations — is to permit as few as one or two directors. To avoid deadlocks, the articles or bylaws usually authorize an uneven number of directors.

Unless otherwise provided in the relevant statutes, articles, or bylaws, directors need not be either shareholders in the corporation or residents of the state where the corporation has its principal place of business. Where qualifications are necessary, the election of unqualified persons is voidable, not void. Until the corporation employs proper proceedings to displace the unqualified directors, the law considers them de facto directors (that is, directors in fact if not in law). Consequently, most of their acts as directors are effective; and de facto directors must live up to the same corporate duties and standards that qualified directors do. Directors generally have the right to appoint interim replacements on the board when vacancies arise owing to the death, resignation, or incapacity of a director.

Term of Office

Directors serve for the time specified in state statutes, unless the articles or bylaws limit the term to a shorter period. Directors usually serve for one year unless the corporation has set up a "classified board" (a board divided into classes of directors with staggered election dates — for example, three directors elected every year for three-year terms). Directors continue to hold office until the shareholders elect their successors and the latter take office. Thus, sitting directors do not automatically drop off the board at the end of their terms.

Sometimes shareholders will remove directors before their terms on the board end. As discussed in Chapter 40, shareholders may remove directors for cause (which was the only basis for removal at common law). Modern statutes relax this standard by permitting a majority of shareholders to remove directors at any time during their terms without cause. However, in those jurisdictions that require cumulative voting, directors cannot be removed if the number of votes cast against the removal would have elected those directors to the board. Directors who have been removed can ordinarily seek court review of the dismissal.

Meetings

Traditionally, the board could validly exercise its powers only when acting collectively, not individually. The law emphasized the value of decision making arrived at through collective debate, deliberation, and judgment. For this reason, statutes set out rules permitting the board to act only when it was formally convened. Moreover, directors traditionally had to be present to vote (they could not vote by proxy or send substitutes to deliberate for them) and could do so only at a duly announced and formalized meeting.

Today, most modern statutes dispense with the formalities previously required of directors' meetings. Thus, even though the bylaws usually fix the times for regular or special board meetings, statutes today allow meetings to occur even without prior notice. To be a valid meeting, however, either before or after the meeting each absent director — *in writing* — must waive the right to prior notice, consent to the meeting, or approve the minutes of the meeting. Similarly, some states even allow the board to act without a meeting, assuming the articles or bylaws permit informal action, as long as all directors consent and file their consents in the corporate minute book. In fact, telephone conference calls suffice in several states. Given this decided trend toward informality, the board can hold its meetings anywhere unless the articles or bylaws declare otherwise. Meetings outside the corporation's state of incorporation or principal place of business are, in general, perfectly legal.

Unless the articles or bylaws set a higher or lower percentage, a simple majority of the directors ordinarily constitutes a quorum. Actions taken by a quorum of directors are binding on the corporation. Yet two questions may still arise in any discussion about quorums. First, may directors who intentionally miss a meeting to prevent a quorum later question the validity of the action taken at the meeting? Since different cases have produced different results, it may be prudent to check the law on this matter for your particular jurisdiction. Second, may directors count toward the quorum (or vote) if the board will be voting on matters in which they are personally interested? Modern statutes generally allow directors to participate as long as compliance with statutory provisions meant to ensure fairness to the corporation (such as disclosure of the interest) has occurred. If there is no such statute, the case results vary from jurisdiction to jurisdiction. Some cases have allowed the interested directors to be counted; other cases have not.

Normally each director casts his or her own vote in person. Directors ordinarily cannot vote by proxy. Whether interested directors can vote depends on the relevant statutes and case law of the appropriate jurisdiction, as noted above. Directors usually cannot agree in advance about how they will vote on corporate matters. Such a formal agreement is not binding because it is void on public policy grounds; directors owe fiduciary duties to the corporation and must be free to exercise their judgment in a totally unrestricted fashion. Such agreements may be valid, however, among directors in a close corporation if all the shareholders/directors agree to the plan.

Delegation of Duties

Most statutes authorize the board of directors to delegate managerial authority to officers and executive (or other) committees. Such delegation of duties ensures the smooth running of the day-to-day affairs of the corporation and promotes efficiency by utilizing the expertise of the various committee members (as in a salary committee). You are probably familiar with such committee structures in noncorporate arenas. If no statutory provisions specifically allow delegation of duties, courts will interpret any attempts at delegation very strictly. Moreover, should the delegation become too broad and pervasive, such actions will probably be void, owing to this relinquishment of the board's management functions. Similarly, attempts to place control of the corporation in fewer persons than the entire board of directors will be illegal (even in close corporations), since the corporation deserves the best efforts of all its directors, who in turn owe fiduciary duties to the corporation. Delegation of authority to persons outside the directorial ranks (except for officers), such as **arbitrators** or management consultants, therefore becomes extremely difficult to justify legally.

Arbitrators Independent persons chosen by the parties or appointed by statute and to whom the issues are submitted for nonjudicial settlements of cases or controversies.

Compensation

In times past, the corporation had no duty to compensate directors for their services. Older cases had held that directors would not be paid for their services unless the articles or bylaws authorized the compensation before the directors had rendered the services. Even under these circumstances, however, directors could receive payment for extraordinary services taken at the board's request (such as recruitment of executive officers), despite the lack of a prearranged, specific agreement, on quasi-contractual grounds (see Chapter 8 for a discussion of quasi contract). Today, although many corporations still pay their directors little or no compensation for their services, an increasing number of corporations do pay rather hefty sums. Since directors today often are not substantial shareholders and since they are subject to ever-expanding duties and concomitant possibilities of liability, compensation seems defensible.

The directors normally determine the salaries of the officers of the corporation. Questions of possible conflicts of interest may arise when directors also serve as officers, because in effect the directors will be participating in the fixing of their own salaries. As noted earlier in our discussion of quorum requirements, statutes may empower interested directors to vote on these issues as long as disclosure of the interest has been made (the possible conflicts of interest here should be obvious) and the transaction is otherwise fair to the corporation. The board can hire officers to serve for periods longer than the board's tenure as long as the period involved is reasonable in length. Likewise, the amount of compensation paid to officers must also be reasonable. Otherwise, the compensation package (fixed salary, bonuses, share options, profit sharing, annuities, deferred compensation plans, and so on) may be attacked as a "waste" of corporate assets by the directors. Corporate salaries in the millions of dollars are not uncommon today. Moreover, it has become a relatively common strategy for the board to give "golden parachutes" — hefty, guaranteed salary packages — to their chief executive officers when the board's corporation is the target of a hostile takeover attempt. Since the acquirer will be obligated to pay these inflated salaries after the acquisition, "golden parachutes" become a strategy for fending off the would-be takeover. "Golden parachutes," as you would expect, raise controversial questions about possible conflicts of interest, possible waste of corporate assets, and the like, because the officers will be receiving money for doing no work upon their severance from the corporation. The emergence of such stratagems illustrates once again the ever-changing, dynamic nature of the legal institution and its attempts to answer new questions of law.

Liabilities

State corporation statutes, common law doctrines, and federal securities and antitrust laws may impose liability on a director for noncompliance with the duties or requirements set out in those doctrines and statutes. Directors, by the very nature of their positions, make numerous decisions—collectively and individually. Increasingly, the performance of these duties subjects directors to possible personal liability, either individually or with the other members of the board who have approved or engaged in the forbidden conduct. Directors must use great caution in order to avoid liability in the form of civil damages or criminal fines.

Although not always the case, today it is legal—indeed, common—for corporations to indemnify (pay back or reimburse) their directors for liabilities accruing from their corporate positions. Through indemnification, directors receive from the corporation the losses and expenses incurred from litigation brought against them personally for actions undertaken in behalf of the corporation in the directors' corporate capacities. Statutes may limit the right of indemnification in certain circumstances. For instance, indemnification for criminal fines may be unavailable when directors have engaged in unlawful activities that they knew at the time were illegal. Statutes often empower corporations to purchase "D and O liability insurance" for their directors, officers, and other employees to cover nonindemnifiable liabilities.

Other Rights

Because directors alone have the right to declare dividends, they (as well as the shareholders) may be personally liable for improper dividends.

Directors, like shareholders, may enter into agreements about how they will vote as directors. But if such agreements unduly fetter the board's managerial functions, the agreements will be void on public policy grounds. These agreement will ordinarily be valid, however, in close corporations in which all the shareholders/directors have assented to the terms.

The rights of directors to inspect corporate records are even more compelling than shareholders' rights because access to corporate records is essential if directors are to discharge their fiduciary duties and decision-making functions. Unlike shareholders' rights, many states characterize the directors' right of inspection as absolute. Yet this right would be unavailable in some states if directors abuse the right by attempting to use it for an improper purpose that damages the corporation, such as misappropriation of trade secrets or confidential trade information.

OFFICERS

The selection or removal of officers is an important managerial function of the board of directors. While directors are responsible for the overall policies of the corporation, officers conduct the day-to-day operations of the firm and execute the policies established by the board. These lines of authority are well established in American law. Nevertheless, you may have heard of a "rubber stamp" board—that is, a board that merely approves as corporate policy the directions suggested by the officers. Although such situations no doubt actually exist, it is important to understand that such management represents a perversion of the usual corporate roles: the directors should manage, and the officers should carry out the management goals delegated to them by the directors.

Who Really "Manages" the Corporation?

Qualifications

Rights and Duties

Officers are agents of the corporation and must therefore live up to the fiduciary duties placed on agents. Statutes often name the officers that a corporation must have, and either these statutes or the corporate bylaws usually spell out the respective officers' authority. Typical officers include president, vice-president, secretary, and treasurer (or comptroller). The top executive may also be called the chairman of the board, the chief executive officer, or the general manager. The same person ordinarily can serve as more than one officer, but some statutes prohibit the same person from serving as both president and secretary.

Term of Office

The board ordinarily appoints the officers, who serve at the will of the directors. (Some modern statutes, on the other hand, allow the shareholders to elect the officers.) Either the board or the president can appoint junior or senior officers. Officers usually serve at the pleasure of the board because the board in most jurisdictions can remove officers with or without cause, even when the officer has a valid employment contract. But after such removal without cause, the corporation may be liable in damages to the former officer for breach of the employment contract. As we shall see later, the directors normally escape personal liability if they have removed the officer in accordance with the "business judgment rule"; that is, they have exercised due care while making corporate decisions. In rare instances, the state, the courts, or the shareholders can remove officers. These instances will nearly always involve a removal "with cause."

Compensation

In earlier times, officers, like directors, traditionally served without pay because they usually were shareholders who could expect their investment in the corporation to multiply by virtue of their work on the corporation's behalf. Thus, there was no need to supplement these corporate profits with a salary. Today, since neither directors nor officers must also be shareholders, the corporation usually pays a prearranged, fixed salary (recall in this context the possible existence of so-called golden parachutes as well). In addition, the corporation commonly adds to this salary profit-sharing plans, bonuses, share options, deferred compensation plans, pensions, annuities, and other fringe benefits like health care and expense accounts. Such compensation packages often turn out to be substantial indeed. Compensation, to be lawful, should be reasonable and not represent waste of corporate assets. If waste is present, both directors and officers may be liable to the corporation for this waste. Courts have even ordered the officers to return to the corporation the amounts deemed excessive compensation.

Agency Law

Because officers are agents of the corporation, they have authority to bind the corporation. It would probably benefit you at this point to review the material on agency in Chapters 33–35. Briefly, an officer's authority may be actual (either express or implied) or apparent. *Express authority* derives from state statutes, the articles, or the bylaws. Any of these three sources may spell out the duties, responsibilities, and authority of the respective officers, although the bylaws are the most common source. In these situations, the corporation has determined the boundaries within which the officer shall act on behalf of the corporation. *Implied authority* is also known as *inherent authority.* By virtue of their office or title, presidents have inherent authority to direct corporate meetings and to act on behalf of the corporation with regard to transactions occurring in the ordinary and regular course of its business. For instance, it will normally be part of a president's authority to hire real estate brokers for the purpose of selling corporate property. Yet the president cannot validly sell or mortgage corporate assets without the approval of the board (and sometimes that of the shareholders). The president can have authority, however, to bind the corporation to sale or services contracts arising in the usual course of business (for instance, the president of a grain elevator can authorize purchases of wheat from local farmers). Courts sometimes uphold expansions of authority for presidents who are chief executive officers or general managers.

Vice-presidents normally possess no authority by virtue of their office but of course will enjoy the authority the president has if they succeed to the presidency owing to the president's absence, resignation, or death. Similarly, neither the treasurer nor the secretary can normally bind the corporation. The law ordinarily limits them to fairly ministerial intracorporate functions; but some jurisdictions give the treasurer authority to write, accept, endorse, and negotiate corporate checks and promissory notes.

Corporate officers may have *apparent authority* to bind the corporation. Apparent authority arises when the corporation by its actions indicates to a third party that an officer or agent is empowered to engage in certain transactions on behalf of the corporation. For example, if the corporation has customarily allowed the president to buy property on the corporation's behalf without prior board approval, the president in this instance will have apparent authority to bind the corporation to such a real estate transaction. The corporation cannot later allege lack of actual authority as a defense to consummation of the sale. Likewise, the seller of the property may use the theory of estoppel (the corporation is prevented from denying a defense otherwise available to it) to counter a defense of lack of actual authority. Estoppel may be used when the third party has been damaged because of the third party's good faith in and reasonable reliance on the corporation's creation of circumstances that appear to clothe the officer with apparent authority. In fact, estoppel may bind the corporation to transactions that result from unauthorized acts of the officer. Subsequent ratification (approval) of previously unauthorized acts will also bind the corporation. Even if the president had no authority to buy real estate, a later board resolution that approves the sale constitutes a ratification and binds the corporation to complete the transaction.

Liabilities

Officers who attempt to contract on behalf of the corporation without authority to do so may be personally liable to the other contracting party. Similarly, nondisclosure of the fact that the officer is acting on behalf of the corporation, even when the officer's actions are authorized, will lead to the personal liability of the officer. (The rules for an agent's signing commercial paper are discussed in Chapter 34.) Officers who commit torts may be personally liable to the injured party, although, as you may recall from Chapter 35, the corporation may also be liable for torts committed by the officer during the scope of his or her employment under the doctrine of *respondeat superior*. Thus, a bank president who converts funds to his or her own use may be liable to the depositor, as may the bank under *respondeat superior*. Yet, as the following case illustrates, if the officer actively participates in the tort, a court may impose liability solely on the officer.

National Acceptance Company of America v. *Pintura Corp.*
418 N.E.2d 1114 (Ill. App. 1981)

FACTS

Nieto, the president of and sole shareholder in Pintura Corporation, allegedly **converted** checks belonging to National Acceptance by endorsing them and placing them in Pintura's account instead of sending them to the rightful **assignee,** National Acceptance Company. The latter sued Pintura and also sued Nieto for personal liability.

Converted Tortiously exercised unlawful dominion over the property of another to the harm of that person

ISSUE

Was Nieto personally liable for the monies allegedly **converted** when he realized no personal benefits from the alleged conversion?

HOLDING

Yes. Because the evidence showed that Nieto as a corporate officer had converted five checks on behalf of the corporation, his active participation in this tort rendered him personally liable for those funds, even though there was no proof that he personally benefited from the funds.

REASONING   Corporate officers will not be liable for the corporation's torts simply by virtue of the office, but officers will be individually liable for the corporation's torts in which they actively participate. Moreover, liability for conversion generally does not require that the converter personally benefit from the conversion, since the essence of conversion is not the acquisition of property by the wrongdoer but the deprivation of the owner's property. Because the **assignee** corporation, National Acceptance, had not authorized Nieto's endorsement and deposit of checks into Pintura's account, Nieto was the proximate cause of National Acceptance's loss and could be held individually liable for the conversion carried out on behalf of Pintura Corporation.

Assignee The recipient of a legal transfer of one's legal rights under a contract

---

FIDUCIARY DUTIES OWED TO THE CORPORATION

Directors, officers, and controlling shareholders owe assorted duties to the corporation and sometimes to shareholders and creditors. These are called *fiduciary* duties because the directors, officers, and controlling shareholders occupy a position of trust and faith with regard to the corporation and other constituencies. Generally speaking, these obligations fall into three broad categories: the duty of obedience, the duty of diligence (or due care), and the duty of loyalty. These duties may arise from statute, but more often they issue from decisional law.

Obedience

Directors, officers, controlling shareholders, and other corporate managers must restrict their actions and those of the corporation to lawful pursuits. Any action taken beyond the scope of the corporation's power is an illegal, ultra vires act. Violation of a positive rule of law or statute by definition constitutes an illegal act. Any such actions by managers violate their duty of obedience and may subject them to personal liability.

Diligence

Because corporate managers act on behalf of the corporation, they are obligated to perform their duties with the amount of diligence or due care that a reasonably prudent person would exercise in the conduct of his or her own personal affairs or in the same or similar circumstances. You have probably noticed the familiar ring of this language. We talked about this kind of standard when we discussed negligence. Basically, the duty of due care obliges a corporate manager to perform his or her duties in a nonnegligent fashion. Note that the law does not expect a director, officer, or controlling shareholder to be perfect or all-knowing. Honest errors of judgment will not lead to liability for breach of the duty of diligence. If liability were imposed in such situations, who would ever consent to be a director or officer?

Instead, the law excuses the conduct if the manager has made the error in good faith and without being clearly and grossly negligent. This is called the "business judgment rule." Needless to say, whether the manager's decision satisfies the "business judgment rule" or, in contrast, is grossly negligent and hence unacceptable becomes a question of fact. Nonattendance at corporate meetings or inattention to corporate affairs leading to ill-preparedness may cause the manager to incur liability for breach of the duty of diligence or due care. Similarly, failure to fire an obviously unworthy employee, failure to obtain casualty insurance, failure to heed warning signs suggesting illegal conduct (such as embezzlement), or reliance on unreasonable statements by attorneys or accountants may lead to liability. The manager will nonetheless incur liability only for such losses as his or her own negligent conduct causes. Consequently, if a director formally dissents about a matter that is later held to be negligent, that director will avoid liability. It is usually no defense that the director was a "figurehead" or served without pay; but a manager's reliance on *reasonable* expert reports, such as those by accountants or attorneys, usually exonerates the manager from liability unless violations of securities acts are involved.

The following dispute centered on the possible application of the "business judgment rule" to a decision made by the directors.

Abella v. *Universal Leaf Tobacco Co., Inc.*
546 F. Supp. 795 (E.D. Va. 1982)

FACTS

Abella brought a **derivative action** on behalf of Universal Leaf Tobacco to recover $1.2 million expended by the directors and officers to fend off a takeover attempt by Congoleum Corporation. Universal argued that Abella's complaint should be dismissed because a specially appointed committee of Universal's board of directors had recommended abandonment of the lawsuit on the grounds that the claims in the suit were meritless.

Derivative action A suit filed by a shareholder on behalf of the corporation to enforce a corporate cause of action

ISSUE

Could a committee of disinterested directors terminate a shareholder's derivative suit under the business judgment rule?

HOLDING

Yes. Viginia law permits a directors' special litigation committee to effect the dismissal of a derivative suit against a corporation and its directors based on the directors' business judgment that the suit is contrary to the corporation's best interests.

REASONING

A decision to institute legal proceedings on behalf of the corporation normally is within the directors' discretionary power. Moreover, Virginia law allows the delegation of board authority to a committee of two or more directors. Yet a shareholder may bring a derivative action to show either that the directors are wrongdoers or that their refusal to bring suit to enforce a corporate right is an abuse of their discretionary power. Since, in these circumstances, any demand made on the corporation to enforce such a suit would have been futile, Abella was excused from this usual prerequisite for bringing a derivative action. For the committee permissibly to terminate Abella's suit, Universal had to prove both the independence and good faith of the special litigation committee and the existence of a reasonable investigation leading to reasonable conclusions before the business judgment rule could be satisfied. The fair, independent, exhaustive reconstruction of Universal's dealings with Congoleum by the directors' committee thus provided justification for the directors' dismissal of Abella's derivative suit against the corporation and its directors on the basis of their business judgment that the suit was contrary to the corporation's best interests.

Loyalty

Because directors, officers, and controlling shareholders enjoy positions of trust with the corporation, they must act in good faith and with loyalty toward the corporation and its shareholders. The undivided loyalty expected of fiduciaries means that managers must place the interests of the corporation above their own personal interests. Sometimes these corporate interests and personal interests collide, and it becomes necessary to resort to applicable statutes and decisional law. Usually such collisions involve (1) corporate opportunities or (2) conflicts of interest.

The *corporate opportunity* doctrine forbids directors, officers, and controlling shareholders from diverting to themselves business deals or chances that in fairness or in justice belong to the corporation. Personal gains at the expense of the corporation represent a breach of the manager's fiduciary duties.

A "corporate opportunity" commonly will be found if the manager discovers the opportunity in his or her capacity as director and it is reasonably foreseeable that the corporation would be interested in the opportunity because it relates closely to the corporation's line of business. For example, if Wanda is a director in a real estate development corporation (Real Property Corp.) and Ray offers to sell property to Wanda because he knows she is a director of Real Property, Wanda should not buy the property for herself, since to do so will violate her duty of loyalty. If the corporation would reasonably be interested in the land for its corporate development program, Wanda must disclose this opportunity to the corporation. Once she has given the corporation this "right of first refusal," Wanda can ordinarily purchase the property *if* the corporation refuses the opportunity or is financially unable to effect the purchase.

Upon Wanda's breach of the duty of loyalty, corporate remedies include damages (the profits Wanda makes as a result of the sale) or the imposition of a **constructive trust** (a court will treat Wanda as a trustee who is holding the property for the benefit of the corporation). A court can then force Wanda to convey the property to Real Property Corp. and to pay Real Property any profits realized on the transaction

In the case that follows, the court applied some of the foregoing principles.

Constructive trust
A trust imposed by law to prevent the unjust enrichment of the purported owner of the "trust" property

Southeast Consultants, Inc. v. McCrary Engineering Corporation
273 S.E.2d 112 (Ga. 1980)

McCrary was an engineering firm specializing in the construction of water and sewerage projects for municipalities. Hood was the former president of McCrary who had started Southeast Consultants, Inc. (Southeast) without McCrary's knowledge. In fact, Hood had used McCrary's Atlanta office and its equipment, supplies, and personnel in Southeast's engineering operations. McCrary also contended that Southeast had solicited its clients. Most important, McCrary argued that Hood and Southeast had usurped a corporate opportunity belonging to McCrary by bidding on the Danielsville project for which McCrary had prepared the preliminary study.

FACTS

Was the Danielsville contract a business opportunity properly belonging to McCrary so that the trial court was correct in prohibiting Southeast from bidding on it?

ISSUE

Yes. The Danielsville planning contract was an opportunity in which McCrary had an expectancy growing out of a preexisting relationship with the City of Danielsville, and Southeast thus had no right to bid on the contract.

HOLDING

The Danielsville planning contract fell within the scope and ability of McCrary's business as McCrary's interest and expectancy in that contract had resulted from the preliminary study conducted for Danielsville. Furthermore, since Hood had created and nurtured Southeast at McCrary's expense, Hood had violated his fiduciary duties of loyalty, good faith, and fair dealing to McCrary by creating and operating Southeast within McCrary but without McCrary's knowledge and by hiring McCrary's personnel en masse.

REASONING

Compare the court's reasoning in *Southeast Consultants, Inc.* with that of the court in the following case to see if you can understand why the respective courts arrived at different results.

Chemical Dynamics v. Newfeld
728 S.W.2d 590 (Mo. Ct. App. 1987)

Chemical Dynamics, Inc., which did business as The Schultz Co., was a close corporation with forty shares, twenty-three of which were held by the Schultz family. A. Y. (Abe) Schultz, Sol Schultz, and Lawrence Newfeld were the managing officers and directors of the corporation. On 6 December 1967, the corporation leased a building for use as its offices and its manufacturing facilities. The lease contained an option provision whereby the corporation could purchase the property for $300,000. In

FACTS

1970, when the corporation experienced financial difficulties and was unable to pay the rent as due, Sol Schultz assigned the lease and purchase option to Newfeld in exchange for Newfeld's advancing the corporation the $21,492.38 needed to avoid the firm's eviction from the building. The owners notified Newfeld in February, 1973, of their willingness to sell the building, even though the option to purchase had already expired. In October, 1973, Newfeld, with the help of Harry and Sol Schultz, purchased the property. In 1975, after all the creditors had been paid, Abe Schultz demanded the return of the property to the corporation. When Newfeld refused to do so, Abe, on behalf of the corporation, sued Newfeld for usurpation of the corporate opportunity represented by the purchase of the property.

ISSUE   Had Newfeld breached his fiduciary duty to the corporation by allegedly seizing for his own benefit the business opportunity of purchasing the building leased by the corporation?

HOLDING   No. Newfeld's purchase had not constituted a corporate opportunity.

REASONING   The corporate opportunity doctrine forbids a corporate director from acquiring for his or her own benefit an opportunity that would have been valuable and germane to the corporation's business, unless that opportunity is first offered to the corporation. If, however, a business opportunity is presented to an officer in his or her individual capacity, rather than in his or her official capacity as an officer or director, the opportunity is that of the officer and not that of the corporation. The test of whether a particular opportunity is an individual or corporate one is largely a question of fact. The pivotal question in this case centers on whether the option to purchase the building constituted a corporate opportunity. On 20 November 1970, the corporation had been in severe financial straits; eviction from its business quarters had been imminent. Yet the corporation had not had the money, the means, or the credit to come up with the money for the back rent. Thereupon, Newfeld had been willing to invest his own funds to save a corporation that was operating at a loss and unable to pay its creditors. Because Newfeld had risked his own money when other experienced businessmen had refused to do so, the assignment of the lease constituted consideration for the business risk Newfeld had been willing to take. Moreover, by A. Y. Schultz's own admission, the corporation had not been in the financial position to buy the building until 1975, two years after the purchase by Newfeld. Hence, Newfeld had not appropriated a business opportunity from the corporation. Rather, he had merely exercised his rights under the lease that the corporation had freely assigned to him. The fact that Sol Schultz and Harry Schultz had helped Newfeld in financing the purchase was also immaterial. Had Newfeld not funded the corporation in 1970, a real danger existed that the corporation could not have continued and that, by 1973, the investment of every shareholder would have been lost. Given these facts, Newfeld was under no duty to exercise the option for the benefit of the corporation. Because the option to purchase the building was an opportunity that had belonged to him in his individual capacity, rather than in his official capacity, Newfeld had not usurped a corporate opportunity so as to justify the imposition of a constructive trust.

The most common example of a possible *conflict of interest* occurs when a director, officer, or controlling shareholder personally contracts with the corporation. As an illustration, let us assume that George is a director of Real Property Corporation and that he is willing to sell a piece of his own property to the corporation. Because of his personal interests, George will undoubtedly hope to make as much money as possible on the transaction. Yet his position as a director of Real Property Corporation obligates him to accept as low a price as possible in order to benefit the company. George obviously faces a difficult dilemma. Most states will allow the transaction if George makes a full disclosure of his interest to the board of directors of Real Property Corporation before the board begins its deliberations on the proposed contract and if the resultant contract is fair and reasonable to the corporation. However, whenever George does not fully disclose his interest or if the terms of the contract are unfair or unreasonable, the contract will be voidable by the corporation.

An additional concern in these situations stems from whether George (who is called an "interested" director) should be allowed to vote on the contract. At common law, George could not vote — or even be counted toward the quorum — at the meeting where the matter was to be discussed. Although modern statutes (and articles or bylaws) vary, in general, George can vote and be counted toward the quorum if, as noted earlier, he discloses his interest and the resultant contract is fair to the corporation.

As mentioned in Chapter 40, the duty of loyalty also prohibits directors, officers, or controlling shareholders from prejudicing minority shareholders' rights by "freezing out" minority shareholders through such actions as forcing dissolution of the corporation or changing liquidation preferences.

In the context of corporate takeovers, allegations of breach of fiduciary duties commonly arise. As the sophistication of both the "raider" and the target corporation has increased, directors of the latter have responded creatively — and metaphorically — to mount a host of defensive moves meant to blunt the would-be acquiring firm's appetite for the target corporation. The development of exotic (but apt) terms such as *greenmail* and *poison pill* to describe these thrusts and countermeasures masks the more important issue of whether the law will approve of these deterrent efforts. The next case is illustrative of a typical "poison pill."

Greenmail A term describing the process by which a firm threatens a corporate takeover by buying a significant portion of a corporation's stock and then selling it back to the corporation at a premium when the corporation's directors and executives, fearing for their positions, agree to buy the firm out

Poison pill Any strategy adopted by the directors of a target firm in order to decrease their firm's attractiveness to an acquiring firm during an attempted hostile takeover

Unocal Corporation v. *Mesa Petroleum Company*
493 A.2d 946 (Del. 1985)

On 8 April 1985, Mesa Petroleum Company (Mesa) the owner of approximately 13 percent of Unocal Corporation's (Unocal's) stock, commenced a two-tier "front-loaded" cash tender offer for 64 million shares, or approximately 37 percent of Unocal's outstanding stock, at a price of $54 per share. The "back-end," or second

FACTS

tier of the offer, consisted of "junk bonds" that would change Unocal's capitalization significantly from its present structure. Unocal's board of directors met on 13 April 1985 to consider the Mesa tender offer. The next day the board passed a resolution providing that if Mesa acquired 64 million shares of Unocal stock through its own offer, Unocal would buy the remaining 49 percent outstanding for an exchange of debt securities having an aggregate par value of $72 per share. The board resolution also stated that the offer would be subject to other conditions, including the exclusion of Mesa from the proposal. When Unocal initiated its exchange offer on 17 April 1985, Mesa immediately filed suit. On April 22, the Unocal board met again and, upon the advice of its investment bankers, waived the Mesa exclusion as to 50 million shares. This fact notwithstanding, Mesa in its lawsuit contended that (1) Unocal's discriminatory exchange offer violated the fiduciary duties Unocal owed it, and (2) the directors' conduct fell outside the application of the business judgment rule because the directors, by tendering their own shares, would derive a financial benefit that was not available to all shareholders.

ISSUES   Did the Unocal board have the power and duty to adopt a defensive self-tender offer to oppose a takeover threat it had perceived to be harmful to the corporation? If so, was its action entitled to the protection of the business judgment rule?

HOLDING   Yes. Delaware law gives the board inherent power to deal selectively with its stockholders, provided that the directors have not acted solely to entrench themselves in office. Indeed, the board's power to act arises from its fundamental duty and obligation to protect the corporation's stockholders from perceived harm, irrespective of its source. Since the board's actions had been reasonable in relation to the threat posed and had been motivated by a good faith concern for the welfare of the corporation and its stockholders, the business judgment rule was available to the directors as a defense.

REASONING   The business judgment rule is a presumption that, in making a business decision, the directors of a corporation have acted on an informal basis, in good faith, and in the honest belief that the action taken was in the best interests of the company. In such circumstances, the judiciary should not substitute its judgment for that of the board if the latter's decision can be attributed to any rational business purpose. Here, the Unocal directors had concluded that the value of Unocal was substantially above the $54 per share, cash, "front-end" offer. Furthermore, they had determined that the subordinated securities to be exchanged in Mesa's announced squeeze-out of the remaining shareholders in the "back-end" tier of the merger were "junk bonds" worth far less than $54. Such a two-tier offer ordinarily represents a classic coercive measure designed to stampede shareholders into tendering at the first tier, even if the price is inadequate, out of fear of what they will receive at the back end of the transaction. Wholly beyond the coercive aspect of an inadequate two-tier tender offer, this threat had been posed by a corporate raider with a national reputation as a "greenmailer." Hence, in adopting the selective exchange offer, the board's stated objective had been either to defeat the inadequate Mesa offer or, should the offer still succeed, to provide the 49 percent of its stockholders, who would otherwise be forced to accept "junk bonds," with $72 worth of senior debt. Both purposes were valid, and such efforts would have been thwarted by Mesa's participation in the exchange offer in several respects. First, if Mesa could have tendered its shares, Unocal would have been effectively subsidizing the former's continuing effort to buy Unocal stock at $54 per share. Second, Mesa could not have, by definition, fit within the class of shareholders being protected from its own coercive and inadequate tender offer. Thus, the board's decision to offer what it had determined to be the fair value of the corporation to the 49 percent of its shareholders who would otherwise have been forced to accept highly subordinated "junk bonds" was reasonable and consistent with the directors' duty to ensure that the minority stockholders received equal value for their shares.

Thus, the Unocal directors possessed the power to oppose the Mesa tender offer and to undertake a self-tender offer made in good faith and upon a reasonable investigation pursuant to a clear duty to protect the corporate enterprise. Further, the selective stock repurchase plan chosen by Unocal was reasonable in relation to the threat that the board rationally and reasonably had believed was posed by Mesa's inadequate and coercive two-tier tender offer. Under those circumstances, the board's action was entitled to be measured by the standards of the business judgment rule. Thus, unless it were shown by a preponderance of the evidence that the directors' decisions had been primarily based on perpetuating themselves in office, or some other breach of fiduciary duty such as fraud, overreaching, lack of good faith, or being uninformed, a court should not have substituted its judgment for that of the board. Given the lower courts' findings that the exchange offer had been predicated on the board's good faith belief that the Mesa offer was inadequate, that the board's action had been informed and taken with due care, that Mesa's prior activities had justified a reasonable inference that its principal objective was greenmail, and, implicitly, that the substance of the offer itself had been reasonable and fair to the corporation and its stockholders if Mesa were included, it would have been inappropriate to hold that the Unocal directors had acted in such a manner as to have passed an unintelligent and unadvised judgment. Hence, the directors could rely upon the business judgment rule to justify their actions.

Corporate managers who violate the Securities Act of 1933 (the '33 Act) and the Securities Exchange Act of 1934 (the '34 Act) may incur liability as well. Because both acts will be discussed in Chapter 44, it is sufficient to note here the broad outlines of possible liability.

The '33 Act is basically a disclosure statute and thus requires that **registration statements** be filed with the Securities and Exchange Commission (SEC), the federal agency that oversees the enforcement of federal securities laws, whenever certain securities are initially offered to the public through the mails or through interstate commerce. The '33 Act also requires that any information that goes into the prospectus (the description of the securities that is given to every prospective purchaser of the securities) be true. False or misleading assertions in either the registration statement or the prospectus or any material omissions in these documents may subject a wide array of corporate personnel to liability. Directors, officers, attorneys, and auditors/

LIABILITY UNDER FEDERAL SECURITIES LAWS

Registration statements Formal statements about securities that are filed by corporations with the Securities and Exchange Commission before offering an issue of securities for sale to the public

accountants—indeed anyone who has signed the registration statement or provided expert information incorporated either in this statement or in the prospectus (such as investment bankers)—may incur liability.

The '34 Act augments the '33 Act by regulating securities after their initial issue. Congress designed this act to prohibit fraud in the national markets that trade stocks and to ensure the fairness of securities transactions generally. Section 10b of the '34 Act, and especially Rule 10b-5 of this section, prohibits deceitful and fraudulent purchases or sales of securities made on the basis of "material inside information." This prevents "insiders"—usually directors, officers, dominant shareholders, or other corporate personnel—from buying or selling stock on the basis of information that is not yet available to the investing public. "Insiders" must either disclose the "material inside information" or abstain from securities activity until the information reaches the investing public. Insiders (and "tippees," those who have learned material information from "insiders") face liability for violation of Section 10b and Rule 10b-5.

Directors, officers, and stockholders who own 10 percent or more of a corporation's stock may also incur liability for violations of Section 16b of the '34 Act. Section 16b forbids "short-swing profits," those profits realized by these three classes of insiders on any purchase and sale (or vice versa) of the corporation's stock within a six-month period. Insiders violating this section must return their profits to the corporation. This represents yet another method for protecting the investing public from market manipulations by those who *may*, by virtue of their positions, have access to material inside information.

As mentioned in Chapter 40, proxy solicitations also fall within the purview of the '34 Act. Section 14a requires that proxy solicitations sent to shareholders be accurate and truthful so that shareholders can make an informed decision about how they wish their proxies to be voted. False and misleading proxy statements ordinarily make corporate managers subject to personal liability.

These federal laws, supplementing as they do state securities law and state corporate and decisional law, round out our discussion of the various ways directors, officers, controlling shareholders, and other corporate personnel may incur liability. Corporate managers should tread warily in these areas.

SUMMARY

The right to manage the corporation falls squarely on the board of directors. Shareholders cannot compel directors to take any action, because the directors are not the agents of the shareholders but, rather, owe loyalty primarily to the corporation. The modern trend is to lower the number of directors and to lessen the traditionally stringent rules about directors' qualifications. Directors generally are qualified to appoint replacements on the board when vacancies arise owing to death, resignation, or incapacity. Directors usually serve for one year unless the corporation has established a "classified" board. In many jurisdictions, shareholders can remove a director with or without cause.

Today, most modern statutes dispense with the formalities required of directors' meetings in the past. Directors' meetings may even occur without prior notice if the directors subsequently manifest their consent to the meeting. Unless the articles or bylaws set a higher or lower percentage, a simple majority of the directors ordinarily constitutes a quorum. Actions taken by a quorum of directors are binding on the corporation. Normally, each director casts his or her vote in person. Except in close corporations, directors' agreements about how they will vote on corporate matters are void on public policy grounds.

Most statutes authorize the board of directors to delegate managerial authority to officers and executive committees. Broad delegations of authority to persons outside the directorial ranks are usually invalid.

Directors may or may not receive compensation from the corporation. The directors normally determine officers' compensation. Such compensation packages are usually legal if reasonable in amount. Otherwise, a shareholder can attack the compensation as a "waste" of corporate assets.

Performance of directorial duties may lead to personal liability for directors. Sometimes, though, the corporation will indemnify the directors for liabilities accruing from their corporate positions. Directors have the right to declare dividends, enter into agreements, and inspect corporate records.

Officers are agents of the corporation and thus must live up to the fiduciary duties placed on agents. The board ordinarily appoints the officers, who serve at the will of the directors. Officers may bind the corporation by express, implied, or apparent authority. But the unauthorized acts of officers may make them personally liable to the other contracting party.

Directors, officers, and controlling shareholders owe fiduciary duties to the corporation. Broadly speaking, these duties fall into three categories: the duty of obedience, the duty of diligence (or due care), and the duty of loyalty. The duty of obedience forbids ultra vires acts. The "business judgment rule" constitutes a defense to liability for violation of the duty of diligence. Under this rule, the manager will not be liable if he or she makes an erroneous decision in good faith and without clear and gross negligence. The duty of loyalty, among other things, precludes directors, officers, and controlling shareholders from usurping corporate opportunities or prejudicing the corporation because of undisclosed conflicts of interest.

Corporate managers may also be liable for violations of the federal securities laws' registration, antifraud, and proxy solicitation rules.

1. Describe the various powers vested in directors.
2. In what ways have statutes dispensed with the formalities previously required of directors' meetings?

DISCUSSION QUESTIONS

3. What are the boundaries of directors' delegations of authority to officers and corporate committees?

4. Explain briefly directors' responsibilities regarding officers' compensation and their own salaries.

5. Briefly enumerate the rights and liabilities of directors. How do officers' rights and liabilities differ from those of directors?

6. Name and define the three sources of an officer's authority to bind the corporation.

7. Explain the three broad categories of fiduciary duties owed to the corporation by directors, officers, and controlling shareholders.

8. What is the "business judgment rule"?

9. Explain how a corporate manager may "usurp a corporate opportunity."

10. In what ways can corporate managers prevent charges of conflicts of interest from being levied against them?

CASE PROBLEMS

1. Wilhite was the president of Growers Supply, Inc. (Growers Supply), a wholesale garden and lawn supply business. Panzico was a shareholder who had another business for which he made purchases from Growers Supply. In 1977 and 1978, Panzico approached Wilhite about withdrawing from the corporation. On 31 May 1978, Panzico allegedly surrendered his $8750 worth of stock to Wilhite as partial payment on his account with Growers Supply and paid the remaining balance of $5920.14 on 5 June 1978. Panzico continued to make purchases for his business after this date but otherwise had no connection with Growers Supply. After two years passed, the other corporate shareholder, McCarty, purchased the accounts receivable of the firm, which had gone bankrupt. McCarty then sued Panzico for $8750 on the rationale that he had been unaware of Wilhite's acceptance of the stock surrender and that Wilhite's authority as president had not extended to the acceptance of surrendered stock as partial payment of a debt. How should the court rule in this case? (*McCarty v. Panzico*, 467 So.2d 1229 [La. Ct. App. 1985].)

2. For several years, Horace Lowder had managed All Star Mills (Mills), a family business owned primarily by Horace, his brother, Malcolm, and their wives. Mills had mainly produced flour and animal feed. At Horace's suggestion, Mills had built a building used by All Star Hatcheries (Hatcheries) and All Star Foods (Foods). Horace had owned Hatcheries and had controlled Foods. He had also used Mills's funds to form and operate All Star Industries (Industries), a finance company owned by Horace; to finance the purchase of land for Foods; and to pay Hatcheries's and Foods's employees' salaries. As a result of Horace's actions, Mills, which at one time had engaged in the businesses of flour milling, cornmeal milling, feed production, raising broilers, and egg marketing, by 1975 was en-

gaged in no businesses except the leasing of its facilities to businesses owned or controlled by Horace Lowder. Malcolm eventually brought a derivative action on behalf of the corporation arguing that Horace, as a de facto officer or director, had breached certain fiduciary duties owed to the corporation and that liquidation of the corporation had become necessary because of the animosity the other shareholders had exhibited toward him as a result of his bringing suit. Should a court accept Malcolm's contentions? (*Lowder* v. *All Star Mills, Inc.*, 330 S.E.2d 649 [N.C. App. 1985].)

3. Leader and other former minority shareholders of Hycor, Inc. (Hycor) sued the majority shareholders for their actions in amending the articles of incorporation and the resultant recapitalization of the corporation from the original authorized capital stock of two million shares with a par value of $.01, to five hundred shares, with a par value of $40. Under the amended articles, each "old share" would be worth 1/4000 of a "new share." In addition, no capital shares would be recognized after the recapitalization (or "reverse stock split"); each holder of a fractional share would instead receive $5 upon the surrender of each "old" share certificate. The majority shareholders justified their action of "going private" as resulting from the poor market performance of the stock and the low dividends produced in the past. What legal theory should the minority shareholders have used in contesting these actions? (*Leader* v. *Hycor, Inc.*, 479 N.E.2d 173 [Mass. 1985].)

4. Shields was the president and a board member of Production Finishing Corporation (Production Finishing) from January, 1974, through August, 1981. Production Finishing at that time was responsible for most, if not all, of the polishing work in the Detroit area with the exception of the polishing work for Ford Motor Company (Ford), which had its own polishing plant in Monroe, Michigan. A longstanding objective of Production Finishing was to obtain the Ford business if Ford ever decided to cease its operations in that area. Shields, as a representative of Production Finishing approached Ford on a regular basis with proposals to let Production Finishing do its polishing work. When Shields learned that Ford was considering ceasing its polishing operations, he brought this information to the attention of Production Finishing's board of directors at a meeting on 29 April 1981. Pursuant to the board's request, Shields then contacted the manager of the Ford Motor Monroe Plant and arranged a meeting at which Production Finishing's proposal to obtain Ford's polishing business was discussed. The manager did not favor the proposal because, with the Ford business, Production Finishing would have a monopoly in the area. On the basis of this statement, at some point in the discussion, Shields asked the manager if Ford would let him do the work in his individual capacity. Shields subsequently incorporated Flat Rock Metal on 8 July 1981, with the intent that Flat Rock would perform the polish-

ing services for Ford. Shields, as the president and controlling stockholder of Flat Rock, throughout his dealings with Ford, did not inform the Production Finishing board of directors that Ford had refused to give its business to Production Finishing or that Shields was pursuing the Ford opportunity on his own account. However, Shields did disclose his intentions to Omer O'Neil and informed O'Neil of Ford's refusal in this regard when he asked O'Neil to leave Production Finishing and go with him to his new company. O'Neil was never a member of the board of directors and, in fact, reported to Shields at Production Finishing. Should a court hold Shields liable for breach of fiduciary duties for his failure to disclose Ford's refusal to Production Finishing, or did he satisfy this duty of disclosure by his informing O'Neil of this refusal? (*Production Finishing Corporation* v. *Shields,* 405 N.W.2d 171 [Mich. App. 1987].)

5. Eli W. Kaufman, a former vice-president and general sales manager in the radio division of CBS, Inc. (CBS), sought indemnification from CBS for his share of costs incurred in defending and settling a suit brought against him by a female employee. At a well-attended business dinner, in an apparent attempt to be humorous, he had grabbed a piece of the female subordinate's clothing and had made a lewd remark about her in public. The New York statute allowed indemnification whenever the corporate officer had acted in good faith for a purpose reasonably believed to be in the best interests of the corporation. Were Kaufman's actions within the scope of this statutory provision so as to warrant indemnification? (*Kaufman* v. *CBS, Inc.,* 514 N.Y.S.2d 620 [N.Y. Civ. Ct. 1987].)

6. Guth was a vice-president of Loft, a candy, syrup, and beverages manufacturer. While in this position, Guth bought a controlling interest in Pepsi-Cola, then a fledgling company. Guth used Loft's facilities and personnel to market and develop Pepsi and replaced Coca-Cola with Pepsi at all of Loft's stores at a substantial loss to Loft. Had Guth usurped a corporate opportunity from Loft? (*Guth* v. *Loft, Inc.,* 5 A.2d 503 [Del. Ch. 1939].)

7. In 1984, the directors of Household International, Inc. (Household), approved a preferred stock rights dividend plan (the "Rights Plan") in an attempt to prevent hostile takeovers. Although very complicated, the "Rights Plan" basically set out a process by which shareholders could both exchange a new series of preferred stock upon the payment of an exercise price of $10,000 per share and purchase the common stock of the acquiring corporation at a price reflecting a market value of twice the exercise price of the right. In other words, a Household shareholder could buy $200 worth of the acquiring corporation's common stock for $100. The exercise of these rights could occur only if a corporation gained control of 20 percent of Household's common shares or made a tender offer for 30 percent of Household's outstanding stock. Should neither of these "triggering events" occur, the rights could not be exercised. Moran, one of the two directors who had voted against the "Rights Plan," had

argued that it would cost the shareholders their ability to sell their shares to an acquiring company at a premium over market value and thus would deprive shareholders of significant property rights without their approval. Would the business judgment rule protect the directors' actions in these circumstances? (*Moran* v. *Household International, Inc.,* 490 A.2d 1059 [Del. Ch. 1985], aff'd 500 A.2d 1346 [Del. 1985].)

8. In June, 1984, the Steinberg Group, which had recently purchased about 12 percent of the shares of Walt Disney Products (Disney), advised the Disney directors that it was prepared to make a two-tier tender offer for 49 percent of the outstanding Disney shares at $67.50 per share and at a later date to pay $72.50 per share for the remaining shares. That same day, the Disney directors agreed to repurchase all the stock held by the Steinberg Group for about $77 per share. As a result, the Steinberg Group realized a profit of about $60 million. Disney borrowed the entire sum necessary to repurchase its shares and thereby increased its debt considerably, since it had earlier acquired another corporation in order to make itself, through this new indebtedness, unattractive to the Steinberg Group, who at that time had purchased sizable amounts of Disney stock. After the sale to the Steinberg Group, the price of Disney stock had dropped to below $50 per share. Thus, the Steinberg Group had received a price 50 percent above the market price following the transaction. The plaintiffs sued the Disney directors who had voted in favor of the purchase and the Steinberg Group to recover the $325 million paid to the latter. Should a court impose a constructive trust for this amount? (*Heckmann* v. *Ahmanson,* 214 Cal. Rptr. 177 [Cal. App. 1985].)

9. Richard Allison, the chief executive officer of Lehigh Valley Cooperative Farmers, Inc. (Lehigh), convinced Lokay to join Lehigh as a vice-president. After only two years, Lehigh dismissed Lokay as a result of staff reductions. Allison also was fired because an audit of Lehigh's finances had revealed that its 1970 and 1971 annual reports had greatly overstated the firm's financial health. Lokay sued Lehigh for breach of contract and fraudulent misrepresentation on the rationale that he had been induced to leave his former employer partly on the basis of the 1970 and 1971 reports. The corporation argued that because it had been as much a victim of Allison's fraud as Lokay had been, it should not be held liable for Allison's activities in these circumstances. Was the corporation's defense persuasive? (*Lokay* v. *Lehigh Valley Cooperative Farmers, Inc.,* 492 A.2d 405 [Pa. Super. 1985].)

10. PAF Corporation (PAF) had purchased property located at 527 South Green Road in South Euclid, Ohio. In September, 1967, PAF leased its property to Arrow Builders Supply Co. (Arrow) for five years at $400 per month. Arrow had an option to renew the five-year lease at an annual rental to be negotiated between the parties. Arrow remained on the property beginning in August, 1972, on a month-to-month basis at $500 per

month. Theodore Poulos and his wife owned Arrow and executed the original lease agreement on Arrow's behalf as president and secretary, respectively. Peter Apicella was an employee of Arrow until May, 1981. In June, 1968, Euclid Railroad Company (Euclid Railroad) leased the property to the rear of PAF's property to PAF. PAF agreed to sublet this land, collect the rent from the sublessees, and remit 50 percent of the gross rents collected to Euclid Railroad. The lease-management agreement further provided that the term of the lease could be extended to encompass the term of any of the subleases negotiated by PAF. The lease-management agreement was executed on behalf of Euclid Railroad by Lillian Fornaro, president, and Theodore Poulos, secretary-treasurer. When Lillian Fornaro died in 1975, her heirs terminated the lease-management agreement; but PAF was not formally notified of the termination. Although various parties used Euclid Railroad and PAF's property continuously, no rents were collected after 1975. On 16 February 1982, Apicella filed a shareholders' derivative action against PAF, Poulos, Fornaro, and Arrow, alleging that PAF had leased its property for an inadequate rental fee and that PAF had failed to obtain fees from sublessees for the use of PAF's property. What should Apicella use as his theory for imposing liability? (*Apicella* v. *PAF Corporation,* 479 N.E.2d 315 [Ohio App. 1984].)

CHAPTER 42

Dissolution, Merger, Consolidation, and Other Acquisitions

In Chapter 40, we briefly touched on the subject of dissolution when we discussed shareholders' rights in the event of liquidation of the corporation. Thus far, though, we have paid scant attention to fundamental changes in the corporate structure that may endanger the rights of shareholders and creditors. Actions bringing about some of these fundamental changes— dissolution, merger and consolidation, sale of substantially all the corporate assets, and stock acquisition—form the central focus of this chapter.

FUNDAMENTAL CHANGES IN CORPORATE STRUCTURE

As noted earlier, dissolution involves termination of the corporation as a legal entity, or juristic person. The term *dissolution* is not synonymous with *liquidation*, which refers to the winding up or termination of the corporation's busi-

DISSOLUTION

ness or affairs. To coin a metaphor, if the filing of the articles of incorporation represents the "alpha" of corporate existence, dissolution represents the "omega." Corporate existence is impervious to most events, including such unusual occurrences as bankruptcy or the cessation of business activities. Dissolution, then, because it represents an extraordinary circumstance, or an organic change in corporate structure, must occur formally in order to have legal effect. Dissolutions are of two types: voluntary and involuntary.

Voluntary Dissolution

As we learned in Chapter 39, corporations theoretically can exist perpetually. On the other hand, a corporation's articles may limit the period of corporate life to, say, ten years. Alternatively, the incorporators may decide at some point to end the corporation's existence, even though the articles specify the perpetual duration of the corporation. In both cases, such voluntary dissolutions must be carried out through formal procedures. Statutes ordinarily set out the requirements for these nonjudicial, voluntary dissolutions. Typically, these statutes mandate board action recommending dissolution, shareholder voting to approve the dissolution (usually by the holders of two-thirds of the outstanding shares), and/or filing of a notice to creditors prior to dissolution. On compliance with these and any other necessary procedures, a certificate of dissolution should be filed with the secretary of state or other designated state officer. At this time, the dissolution is legally effective. Remember, though, that liquidation may follow or precede dissolution, so it is possible that some limited corporate activity may occur after dissolution. On voluntary liquidation, the shareholders share proportionately — subject, of course, to any liquidation preferences — in the net assets of the corporation that remain after satisfaction of creditors' claims. As discussed in earlier chapters, courts will prohibit dissolutions that "freeze out" minority shareholders, especially if a controlling shareholder has initiated the dissolution. Also, be aware that the rules regarding dissolutions may vary when a close corporation, instead of a publicly held corporation, is involved.

Involuntary Dissolution

Occasionally, the state, the shareholders, or the corporation's creditors may request dissolution of the corporation. Such judicial proceedings are involuntary because this time the corporation itself is not asking for dissolution; rather, other constituents are requesting a court to terminate the corporation's existence because of corporate wrongdoings or prejudice to shareholders or creditors. Involuntary dissolutions by their very nature occur less frequently than voluntary ones.

Dissolution at the Request of the State

Because the corporation is a creation of the state, the state retains the power to rescind the corporation's certificate when the corporation's actions present a clear danger to the public. For instance, the state may ask for involuntary dissolution of a corporation that has engaged in systematic securities fraud.

More often, however, grounds for involuntary dissolution involve noncompliance with state requirements, such as failure to pay taxes or to file annual reports. In lieu of petitions for involuntary dissolution, the state may seek suspension of the corporation. Suspension works as a deprivation of the corporation's right to conduct its business and certain other powers, but it is not as drastic or as permanent a remedy as dissolution. On compliance with corporate statutes, the state can order a reinstatement of the corporation.

Dissolution at the Request of Shareholders

Shareholders can also petition the courts for dissolution of the corporation. We have already briefly touched on some of the situations that can precipitate such shareholder actions; examples include "freeze-outs" (or oppression) of minority shareholders' interests as well as allegations of corporate waste of assets. Statutes usually authorize judicial dissolution for these and other examples of corporate mismanagement, but courts will sometimes order dissolutions in similar circumstances even in the absence of express statutory provisions. Deadlock among directors or shareholders constitutes an additional ground for involuntary dissolution. Courts will intervene when a shareholder can show that the deadlock among directors or controlling shareholders has so paralyzed the corporation that it can no longer conduct its business advantageously. When corporate strife has reached these levels, courts may order involuntary dissolution. Alternatively, some state statutes permit the appointment of a provisional, or temporary, director who breaks the deadlock and thus allows the corporation to continue functioning. Other statutory methods for limiting a court's ordering involuntary dissolution in these circumstances consist of provisions allowing holders of a majority of the corporation's outstanding shares to purchase the shares owned by the shareholders who are requesting dissolution and/or provisions setting out a minimum number of shareholders (for example, one-third of the corporate shareholders) who must join in the petition for involuntary dissolution before it can be presented to a court. In contrast to these potential impediments to maintaining an action for involuntary dissolution, shareholders in close corporations frequently agree in advance that on the happening of a certain event, such as deadlock, each shareholder will be able to request dissolution. Courts ordinarily enforce such agreements.

Dissolution at the Request of Creditors

The theory of corporate personality normally prevents creditors from compelling involuntary dissolution of the corporation. But statutes requiring prior notice to creditors protect creditors' rights during dissolution and liquidation, as do statutes allowing the appointment of a receiver who takes over the corporation's business and conducts it for the benefit of the creditors. Possibly, creditors can also petition for the involuntary bankruptcy of the corporation to preserve their rights. Neither the appointment of a receiver nor the institution of involuntary bankruptcy proceedings results in the dissolution of the corporation, however. As we have seen, formal statutory procedures spell out the necessary steps for effecting this fundamental change in corporate structure.

As the following case shows, courts are reluctant to force dissolution and instead prefer to recognize alternative remedies based on their inherent equitable powers.

Alaska Plastics, Inc. v. *Coppock*
621 P.2d 270 (Alaska 1980)

FACTS Muir was a minority shareholder in a close corporation and the ex-wife of one of the original incorporators of Alaska Plastics. She had received a one-sixth interest in the corporation as part of the property settlement in her divorce. The three defendants were the remaining shareholders in Alaska Plastics. On several occasions, Muir had not been notified of shareholders' meetings and hence had taken no part in meetings in which the other shareholders had voted themselves annual directors' salaries and the like. The other shareholders had negotiated with Muir about purchasing her shares for over a year, but Muir had refused because she had believed the offer was too low. At the 1975 annual meeting, the shareholders ratified the acts of the directors of the previous year, including Alaska Plastics's purchase of Valley Plastics. Muir did not dissent from this shareholder vote. Shortly after this meeting, Alaska Plastics's Fairbanks plant, which was uninsured, burned to the ground. As a result, Valley Plastics took over all of Alaska Plastics's manufacturing and sales operations. Muir sued, arguing that the corporation should be involuntarily dissolved and liquidated because she, a minority shareholder, had been deprived of benefits accorded the other shareholders.

ISSUE Was the trial court's judgment that the majority shareholders should be forced to buy Muir's shares in exchange for a fair and equitable value supportable?

HOLDING Yes. The trial judge had the power to order an equitable remedy such as this, especially since it was less drastic than dissolution or liquidation. However, it would be necessary to remand the case so that Muir could establish a basis for such a remedy.

REASONING Four remedies exist for protecting minority shareholders in such situations: provisions in the articles of incorporation may permit the purchase of shares on the happening of some event; the shareholder may petition the court for involuntary dissolution; on some significant change in corporate structure, such as merger, the shareholder may demand appraisal rights; and a purchase of shares may be justified as an equitable remedy on a finding of breach of a fiduciary duty between directors and shareholders. Because the evidence showing the need for the first three remedies was lacking, the case had to be remanded to allow the trial court to determine whether Muir had established that the acts of the majority shareholders had been illegal, oppressive, or fraudulent, or, alternatively, that they had constituted waste or misapplication of corporate assets. Muir's proof of such a breach of fiduciary duty would justify the trial court's order as an equitable remedy less drastic than liquidation.

Like dissolutions, mergers and consolidations bring about fundamental, or organic, changes in the corporation's structure. Dissolution is also related to these two concepts because dissolution of a corporation (or corporations) occurs automatically on either a merger or a consolidation, and the procedures for carrying out a merger or consolidation are similar to dissolution procedures.

Technically, a *merger* differs from a consolidation. In a merger, *one corporation* (called the "acquirer" or "acquiring" firm) *purchases another firm* (called the "acquired" or "disappearing" firm) *and absorbs it into itself.* This new entity is called the *survivor corporation;* the "acquired" firm no longer exists.

A *consolidation* is similar, except that in a consolidation *two or more existing corporations combine to form a wholly new corporate entity.* Since most statutes treat the procedures for mergers and consolidations as if the two were identical transactions, this part of our discussion will focus only on mergers. But, as noted, they are analytically different ways of bringing about major changes in corporate structure, as Figures 42.1 and 42.2 illustrate.

MERGER AND CONSOLIDATION

Figure 42.1 Structural Changes as a Result of Merger

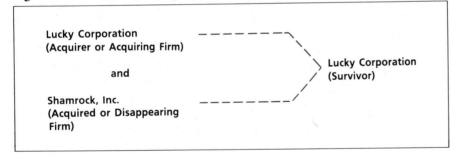

Figure 42.2 Structural Changes as a Result of Consolidation

Rationales for Merger

The last two decades have witnessed a phenomenal upsurge in the number of mergers — for reasons with which you, as business students, are no doubt familiar.

Economies of Scale

Economies of scale refer to reductions in per unit costs resulting from larger plant size. A merger may permit a firm to achieve economies of scale and thus to compete much more efficiently: the larger the firm, the easier it is for the firm to receive discounts on sales and advertising and thereby to achieve lower costs. Accumulation of resources resulting from merged firms also facilitates access to financing. Two beer producers who have just merged generally present a more attractive credit risk for lending institutions than you would if you were attempting to get capital for your wine business currently run from your basement. Bigness may also spawn more research and development. A merged firm ordinarily has more funds to spend on these activities and can utilize its capital in this manner. The capital in your struggling wine business, in contrast, typically goes for electricity, rent, and other overhead costs. You may want to invest in research on capping methods or grape hybrids, but economies of scale make such research and development much more feasible in large firms. Mergers between manufacturers and customers (called "vertical" mergers) may lessen transaction costs and bring about economies of scale in this fashion also. As you will learn in Chapter 46, a firm can use economies of scale to drive out smaller, less efficient firms because of the dominance it may achieve owing to its size and wealth ("deep pockets"). The antitrust laws serve to protect the process of competition from the retaliatory, abusive conduct in which large firms may engage. In the absence of antitrust concerns, mergers to effect economies of scale are legally sound, indeed customary.

Knowledge

A common merger scenario involves a larger company that attempts to merge with a smaller company because the latter possesses valuable technological information or "know how." An established computer firm, for instance, may find a merger with a software firm valuable if the software firm has made technological breakthroughs deemed valuable by the computer firm. Thinking back to economies of scale for a moment, in a given case it may well be cheaper for the computer firm to purchase this software firm and its patents, trademarks, and trade secrets than to expend the funds for the research and development that it would take to approximate the software. Furthermore, the merged firm may be able to retain the staff of the smaller firm and thereby realize further future gains from these persons' collective expertise and inventive capacities.

Diversification

The decade of the 1970s marked a large increase in the number of mergers undertaken for the purpose of diversification. Many firms jumped into areas previously unrelated to their principal lines of business through conglomerate mergers. Sears, Roebuck, long a retail merchandising mainstay, now sells insurance, stocks, and real estate because of its recent mergers. Many other firms have undergone similar expansions of their business interests. Diversification minimizes the risks that are inherent in a firm's restricting itself to one industry and the risks caused by economic cycles. Sears's diversification allows it to offset any losses in retail sales caused by seasonal buying with insurance and brokerage sales, which are not tied to the same cycles. Critics of diversification have argued, however, that diversification dilutes capital markets by making it easier for a diversified company to hide its actual profits and losses. These authorities maintain that lending institutions' abilities to assess the credit-riskiness of diversified companies are impaired by mergers aimed at diversification. This estimation, coupled with some experts' fears about the implications of the excessive concentrations of economic power represented by diversified companies, has led some to argue for heightened antitrust enforcement against conglomerate mergers. But the present enforcement posture appears to reject such fears.

Competition

Inherent in a great deal of what we have discussed so far is an underlying desire to control — if not curtail — competition. One firm clearly does not want to be at the mercy of another firm in times of scarcity. Therefore, a merger between a supplier of aluminum and a fabricator of aluminum, for instance, seems a viable strategy for cutting down on some of the supply side uncertainties. Naturally, though, antitrust concerns may also lurk in mergers designed to control the competitive process; so caution is warranted.

Other Rationales

Other rationales for mergers include tax savings, utilization of cash-rich assets to pump up concerns that need such assets for expansion and growth, and preservation of management prerogatives. Critics of the last rationale have argued that many mergers occur because of the egos of important management officials who want to become the executive officers of even bigger companies. Such "power trips," these critics assert, lead to such socially undesirable consequences as the possible sacrifice of shareholders' interests, personnel displacement, and the uprooting of smaller corporations from the local community of which they were an integral part. The previously mentioned controversies over hostile takeovers, "golden parachutes," "poison pills," and defensive mergers (that is, mergers in which corporation A merges with corporation C to avoid A's being taken over by corporation B) often surface in such criticisms, as well. You can probably recall the newspaper accounts of recent takeover attempts that have raised similar issues.

Board of Directors   Procedure

Whatever the rationale for the merger, once the firms have decided to merge, state statutes set out the steps that must be followed in bringing it about. Such statutes generally require that each corporation's board of directors adopt a merger plan that names each corporation and signifies the name of the surviving corporation; the appropriate terms and conditions of the merger; the method for converting the acquired firm's securities into the securities of the acquiring firm (stock for cash, stock for stock, and the like); and any amendments to the articles of the acquiring corporation that have resulted from the merger.

But as the following case illustrates, thorny problems can arise from these seemingly straightforward actions.

Jewel Companies v. *Pay Less Drug Stores Northwest, Inc.*
741 F.2d 1555 (9th Cir. 1984)

FACTS   In September, 1979, Pay Less Drug Stores (Pay Less) retained the investment banking firm of Goldman, Sachs & Co. to locate a merger partner. Jewel Companies (Jewel), a Chicago-based company engaged primarily in the retail grocery business, was included among the companies contacted. On 9 November 1979, Jewel and Pay Less agreed to a tax-free merger. The merger agreement was executed in writing, formally approved by both boards of directors, signed on behalf of each corporation by its respective president, and made public in a press release on 9 November 1979. Articles 9.9 and 10.5 of the Jewel–Pay Less merger agreement obligated the board of directors of each firm to "use its best efforts to fulfill those conditions . . . over which it has control or influence and to consummate the Merger." Pay Less further obligated itself under Article 9 to forbear from the sale or transfer of any of its properties or assets, and from entering into or terminating any contract other than in the ordinary course of business. The merger agreement moreover provided that Pay Less could not "agree to, or make any commitment to" effect any sale, transfer, or extraordinary action prohibited in Article 9. However, when the Jewel–Pay Less merger agreement was publicly announced, Pay Less Drug Stores Northwest, Inc.'s (Northwest's), management made public its intention to make a competing bid in a press release issued 31 December 1979. This release further noted that Northwest had conditioned its merger offer upon Pay Less's board's abandonment of the proposed merger with Jewel. When Pay Less ultimately merged with Northwest, Jewel then sued Northwest for damages arising from Northwest's allegedly tortious interference with contract and prospective commercial advantage. The district court granted Northwest's motion for a summary judgment.

ISSUE   Was an exclusive merger agreement, that is, one in which the board of directors had agreed to forbear from entering into competing and inconsistent agreements until the shareholders' vote occurred, lawful under California law?

HOLDING   Yes. California corporate statutes permitted a board's entering into an exclusive merger contract.

REASONING   An exclusive, board-negotiated merger agreement may confer considerable benefits upon the shareholders of a firm. For example, a potential merger partner might be reluctant to agree to a merger unless it was confident that its offer would not be used by the board simply to trigger an auction for the firm's assets. Therefore, an exclusive merger agreement might be necessary to secure the best offer for the shareholders of a firm. In that sense, permitting a board of directors to decide that a proposed merger transaction was in the best interests of its shareholders at a given point in time and to agree to refrain from entering into competing contracts until the shareholders had considered the proposal would not conflict in any way with the board's fiduciary obligations. Furthermore, in many ways, shareholders might have more safeguards from market losses in board-negotiated transactions than in others. According to the court, even after the merger agreement had been signed, a board could not, consistent with its fiduciary obligations to its shareholders, withhold information regarding a potentially more attractive competing offer. While the board could bind itself to exert its best efforts to consummate the merger under California law, it could only bind the corporation temporarily, and in limited areas, pending shareholder approval. Hence, the shareholders retained the ultimate control over the corporation's assets. They remained free to accept or reject the merger proposal presented by the board, to respond to a merger proposal or tender offer made by another firm subsequent to the board's execution of an exclusive merger agreement, or to hold out for a better offer. Given the benefits that might have accrued to shareholders from an exclusive merger agreement, such an agreement would not compromise their legal rights. Therefore, the district court's fears that exclusive merger agreements are anticompetitive and contrary to public policy because they subvert the welfare of shareholders were unfounded. Yet the conclusion that, under California law, the Pay Less board could lawfully commit itself to submit the Jewel proposal to its shareholders on an exclusive basis would not answer the question of whether such an exclusive arrangement was intended by the parties to the transaction at issue. Because the record had not demonstrated conclusively whether the parties had intended that the Jewel–Pay Less agreement would obligate the Pay Less board to abstain from negotiating or executing a competing merger agreement with the board of another firm, summary judgment was inappropriate. Finally, the district court's ruling—that even if the Jewel–Pay Less agreement were binding and valid, Northwest's interference with that agreement would have been justified—lacked legal authority because such a holding would be akin to the "law of the jungle." Indeed, the district court's ruling—that society's interests in promoting "healthy competition" among those seeking to take over existing companies would justify interference with an otherwise valid merger agreement between the boards of directors of two corporations—squarely conflicted with California law. On this alternative basis, the district court's granting of a summary judgment for Northwest was erroneous, as well.

The case that follows, one of the most well-publicized decisions in recent years, illustrates the financial and legal risks attendant upon a company's canceling its merger with one firm in order to unite with another. This case also underscores the federal courts' reluctance to usurp state courts' jurisdiction over issues important to the respective states unless there is a clear need to do so.

Pennzoil Company v. Texaco, Inc.
107 S.Ct. 1519 (1987)

FACTS Getty Oil Co. and Pennzoil Company (Pennzoil) negotiated an agreement under which Pennzoil was to purchase about three-sevenths of Getty's outstanding shares for $110 a share. However, Texaco, Inc. (Texaco) eventually purchased the shares for $128 a share. Pennzoil subsequently filed a complaint against Texaco alleging that Texaco had tortiously induced Getty to breach the contract to sell its shares to Pennzoil. In that suit, Pennzoil sought actual damages of $7.53 billion and punitive damages in the same amount. In 1985, a jury returned a verdict in favor of Pennzoil, finding actual damages of $7.53 billion and punitive damages of $3 billion. The parties anticipated that the judgment, including prejudgment interest, would exceed $11 billion. Moreover, this expected judgment would give Pennzoil, as a judgment creditor, the right to secure a lien on all of Texaco's real property located in any county in Texas and to obtain a writ of execution allowing it to take possession of Texaco's assets. To avoid the execution of such a judgment, under Texas law, Texaco could have filed a bond in the amount of the judgment. In this case, because the amount of the bond required by law would have been more than $13 billion, it was clear that Texaco would not have been able to post it. As a result of the business community's assessment that Pennzoil would be able, under the lien and bond provisions of Texas law, to commence enforcement of the judgment before Texaco's appeals had been resolved, Texaco began experiencing the negative effects of the jury's verdict almost immediately. Among other things, its stock prices dropped; it had difficulty obtaining credit; and its bond rating was lowered. Texaco therefore asked the federal courts to enjoin Pennzoil from taking any action to enforce the judgment. Pennzoil argued that, under the so-called abstention doctrine, the federal courts should abstain from enjoining the execution of its judgment pending state court proceedings.

ISSUE Could the federal courts lawfully enjoin Pennzoil, which had prevailed in a trial in state court, from executing the judgment in its favor pending appeal of that judgment to a state appellate court?

HOLDING No. The lower federal courts should have abstained from hearing the case under the abstention doctrine.

REASONING The courts below should have abstained under the principles of federalism enunciated in *Younger* v. *Harris*, 401 U.S. 37 (1971). Both the district court and the court of appeals had failed to recognize the significant interests harmed by their unprecedented intrusion into the Texas judicial system. Similarly, neither of those courts had applied the appropriate standard in determining whether adequate relief was available in the Texas courts. Abstention under *Younger* was therefore warranted whenever the state's interests in the proceeding were so important that exercise of the federal judicial power would have disregarded the **comity** between the states and the federal government. Another important reason for abstention was to avoid unwarranted determinations of federal constitutional questions. When federal

Comity The principle that obliges the federal government to give effect to the laws and decisions of a state out of respect for the state

courts interpret state statutes in a way that raises federal constitutional questions, "a constitutional determination is predicated on a reading of the statute that is not binding on state courts and may be discredited at any time — thus essentially rendering the federal court decision advisory and the litigation underlying it meaningless." *Moore* v. *Sims,* 442 U.S. 415, 428 (1979). Moreover, this concern had special significance in this case because Texaco had chosen not to present to the Texas courts the constitutional claims asserted in this suit. Thus, it was impossible to be certain that the governing Texas statutes and procedural rules actually raised these claims. Moreover, the Texas Constitution contains an "open courts" provision that appears to address Texaco's claims more specifically than the Due Process Clause of the Fourteenth Amendment does. Hence, upon this case's being filed in federal court, it was entirely possible that the Texas courts could have resolved it on state statutory or constitutional grounds, without reaching the federal constitutional questions Texaco raised in this case. Furthermore, the state had an important interest in enforcing the order and judgments of its courts; federal injunctions that interfered with the execution of state judgments would have challenged the very process by which those judgments had been obtained. So long as those challenges related to pending state proceedings, proper respect for the ability of state courts to resolve federal questions presented in state court litigation mandated that the federal courts stay their hand. Non-abstention, therefore, would have disregarded the comity between the states and the federal government. Lastly, abstention under *Younger* was appropriate because Texaco had presented no evidence to buttress its contention that Texas courts would have been unable to hear its constitutional claims within the limited time available to it. When a litigant has made no effort to present its claims in state court, federal courts should assume that state procedures will afford an adequate remedy, in the absence of unambiguous authority to the contrary, and thus should abstain under *Younger.*

Shareholders

After each of the boards of directors has adopted a merger plan, the shareholders of both corporations ordinarily must approve the merger. As with dissolutions, normally the holders of two-thirds of the outstanding shares must approve this fundamental change, although in some states approval by a bare majority of the holders of the outstanding stock will suffice. In some states, however, statutory provisions dispense with the necessity for shareholder approval in "short-form" mergers (those involving a merger between a subsidiary and a parent company that owns 90 to 100 percent of the subsidiary's stock). Since the parent's ownership interest is so high, a vote of approval would be a mere formality; requiring such a vote thus makes little practical sense. Once all the required steps have been followed, the directors file the plan with the appropriate state office. After the state approves this plan, the surviving corporation receives a "certificate of merger," and it can begin conducting business.

Effect of Merger

Once the state issues the certificate of merger, the acquired corporation ceases to exist; only one corporation survives. The survivor takes on all the assets, rights, and liabilities of the disappearing (acquired) corporation by operation of law. This means, among other things, that creditors of the acquired corporation are now the creditors of the survivor corporation. Similarly, pending damages suits (such as a products liability case) against the acquired corporation, if successful, will be paid by the survivor corporation.

Appraisal Rights

Thus far, we have discussed the positive side of a merger; that is, we have examined the merger only from the point of view of those who want it. However, in any given merger, there will be persons who object to, or dissent from, the merger. Because many people believe it is unfair to require someone to become a shareholder in a new corporation that may be totally different from the one in which he or she has originally invested, statutes in most states give dissenting shareholders **appraisal rights.** Appraisal rights *allow dissenters to sell their shares back to the corporation for cash for the fair **market value** of the shares.* In this way, a dissenting shareholder can avoid becoming a shareholder in the survivor corporation and can, at the same time, protect his or her original investment.

Appraisal rights The rights in certain extraordinary corporate activities to have a security evaluated and the appraisal value paid to the owner

Market value The current price the stock would sell for on a stock exchange

To be eligible for appraisal rights, a shareholder ordinarily must follow a set statutory procedure. Although the respective state statutes vary regarding the steps with which a dissenting shareholder must comply, in general such statutes require the dissenter to send a written notice of his or her objection to the merger before the meeting at which the merger will be considered. Next, the shareholder must make a written demand on the corporation for the fair value of the shares after the merger has been approved. The corporation must then make a written offer to purchase at a price it believes represents the fair value (or the fair market value) of the shares. If the corporation and the dissenting shareholder disagree about the fair value of the shares, either party may petition a court to determine the fair value of the shares in an appraisal proceeding. Valuation of shares is quite complicated, but this task becomes somewhat easier if the stock is traded on the New York or American Stock Exchange; in such cases, a court will place great importance on the market price of the stock when assigning a fair value to the stock. Otherwise, a court will usually arrive at its valuation determination by weighing a number of factors, including market price, investment value, net asset value, and dividends. Some jurisdictions deny appraisal rights for certain types of mergers (for example, shareholders of the parent company in a "short-form" merger may have no appraisal rights) and certain types of corporations (those with stock listed on a national securities exchange or those with more than 2000 shareholders). Since appraisal rights generally represent the exclusive remedy for a dissenting shareholder who opposes a merger, it is important for the shareholder to use vigilance in complying with the strict statutory provisions and short time periods involved.

In the following case, the court ordered an appraisal-like remedy.

Weinberger v. *UOP, Inc.*
457 A.2d 701 (Del. 1983)

Weinberger was a former shareholder of UOP, which, through a merger, had become a wholly owned subsidiary of Signal. UOP's minority shareholders at the time of the merger had been paid $21 per share for their former interests in UOP. Weinberger sued to set aside the merger on the grounds that the $21-per-share price paid to the UOP minority shareholders was grossly inadequate and rendered the merger unfair. Alternatively, Weinberger asked for damages.

FACTS

Was the merger fair to the UOP minority shareholders?

ISSUE

No. The merger was unfair to the UOP minority shareholders because the price paid for the shares was inadequate.

HOLDING

The evidence indicated that the inside directors had withheld information showing that payment of $24 per share would have been a good investment for Signal. Accordingly, the merger did not meet the fairness test due to this breach of the fiduciary duties owed by UOP's board (which had been substantially controlled by Signal) to UOP's minority shareholders. Therefore, on remand, the lower court should have conducted appraisal-like hearings in order to decide the damages necessary to compensate Weinberger and the other minority shareholders of UOP for the directors' unfair dealings and the unfair price paid by them.

REASONING

Despite a corporate offer to pay a certain price for stock, a court that believes the price is unfair can order an appraisal, as the court in the following case did.

Klurfeld v. *Equity Enterprises, Inc.*
436 N.Y.S.2d 303 (N.Y. App. Div. 1981)

Klurfeld, an Equity Enterprises (Equity) minority public shareholder, brought a class action to enjoin the merger of Equity with New Equity Corp. (Newco) on the ground that the purpose of the proposed merger—the elimination of the public shareholders—constituted a breach of fiduciary duties owed to the public shareholders by Gross and Moelis, the controlling shareholders, sole directors, and principal officers of Equity. As a result of the proposed reorganization, Gross and Moelis would own all the stock of Newco, and the public minority shareholders would be paid $2.00 per share. Before the merger had been approved by the two corporations, Klurfeld had entered into a settlement with the defendants whereby he had accepted on behalf of the class a price of $2.50 per share. When the merger was

FACTS

approved, Del Giorgio, another plaintiff, indicated that he objected to the settlement and would pursue his right to an appraisal because he believed the stock was worth $8 to $10 per share. The lower court ordered a hearing to determine whether the terms of the settlement were fair, reasonable, and adequate. The lower court ultimately accepted a settlement whereby the minority public shareholders received $2.60 per share.

ISSUE   Was the proof presented by the defendants sufficient to establish the fairness of the amended offer of $2.60 per share?

HOLDING   No. The price did not represent a fair settlement. Thus, the lower court should determine the fair value of the stocks by reference to the process employed in a statutory appraisal hearing.

REASONING   A court should strictly scrutinize the fiduciary duties owed by majority stockholders to minority stockholders when a freeze-out of minority stockholders has occurred as a result of a corporate reorganization. Similarly, appraisal would not be the exclusive remedy of a minority stockholder like Del Giorgio where the illegality of the merger had been alleged. Therefore, Del Giorgio, in claiming an illegal freeze-out, had not waived his right to challenge the settlement of Klurfeld's original class action by seeking an appraisal at the time the corporation had approved the merger. The expert who had given 70 percent weight to the market value of the shares when setting their value had thereby unfairly distorted the value of the shares. Since that

Book value The worth of a business, arrived at by deducting liabilities from assets

expert should have paid more attention to **book value,** the trial court should, if it wished to do so, appoint a disinterested expert to help it set the value of the shares in further proceedings in order to remedy the unfair settlement that had frozen out the minority shareholders.

SALE OF SUBSTANTIALLY ALL THE ASSETS

Rather than acquiring another firm through a merger, a corporation can instead buy all, or substantially all, of another firm's assets. For example, a shipping company may buy the ships of a rival company as an alternative to merging with it. This method of acquisition enjoys favor because it is procedurally simpler than a merger. Approval by the shareholders of the acquired firm ordinarily is necessary, but approval by the acquiring firm's shareholders is not. Even then, a sale of substantially all the assets made in the regular course of the corporation's business (as when a corporation is formed to build a tanker, and the tanker is then sold to an oil company) would not normally require shareholder approval. Shareholder approval thus becomes necessary only in the event of a fundamental change in the corporate structure—the disposal of operating assets in order to terminate the business activities of the corporation. Most states provide appraisal rights for dissenting shareholders in these circumstances as well. In addition, various methods of protecting creditors find expression in the statutes governing sales of substantially all the assets. In a merger, the acquiring firm takes on all the liabilities of the acquired firm by operation of law; but since this is not the case when all or substantially all the assets are sold, corporate statutory provisions, UCC Article 6's provisions on bulk transfers, and decisional law have developed to give creditors remedies if such sales prejudice their rights.

STOCK ACQUISITION

An alternative method for acquiring the business of another corporation involves stock acquisitions. Instead of buying substantially all the assets of a corporation, the acquiring corporation's directors may decide to buy the stock of the acquired corporation. Since the acquisition implicates only the latter corporation's individual shareholders, who can decide for themselves whether to sell at the price offered for the stock, the directors of the acquired corporation have no right to approve or disapprove the stock acquisition. Similarly, there are usually no requirements of shareholder approval or appraisal rights. However, the federal securities laws may apply to such corporate takeovers, as we shall see in Chapter 44.

Because sales of substantially all the assets and stock acquisitions may have the ultimate effect of mergers, some companies have characterized their acquisitions in one of these fashions in order to avoid the strict statutory procedures required of mergers. Transactions that take the *form* of sales of assets or stocks but nevertheless have the *effect* of mergers are called *de facto mergers*. Because shareholders and creditors can be injured through de facto mergers, courts in jurisdictions that recognize the doctrine can set the transactions aside and require compliance with the relevant merger statutes (shareholder approval, appraisal rights, and so on).

A famous case involving a de facto merger follows.

Farris v. Glen Alden Corp.
143 A.2d 25 (Pa. 1958)

FACTS

The officers of Glen Alden entered into a "reorganization agreement" with the officers of List Industries Corporation. Glen Alden was a coal company, and List was a more diversified company owning interests in textiles, theaters, real estate, and gas and oil. Glen Alden's shareholders approved the transaction. As a result of the reorganization agreement, Glen Alden acquired most of the assets and all the liabilities of List, and List was dissolved. Farris, a shareholder in Glen Alden, sought an injunction against the reorganization, stating that it was actually a merger and that it had not given appraisal rights to dissenting shareholders. Glen Alden argued that the transaction was a purchase of corporate assets with respect to which shareholders had no rights of dissent or appraisal.

ISSUE

Was the transaction a purchase of assets or instead a de facto merger?

HOLDING   The transaction was a de facto merger that should have followed the statutory procedures required of mergers in order to be legal.

REASONING   Farris would be a shareholder in a much different type of corporation once the transaction was consummated. The new company would be twice as large but would have seven times the long-term debt held by Glen Alden before the reorganization. Control of Glen Alden would also pass to the List directors, who would have a majority of the directorships on the new board of directors. Farris's proportionate interest in Glen Alden would be reduced to only two-fifths of what it was before the reorganization, and the value of his shares would be substantially reduced. Hence, the transaction was in reality a merger, and Glen Alden should have accorded Farris his statutorily required appraisal rights.

SUMMARY

Dissolution involves the termination of the corporation as a legal person. Dissolution is not synonymous with the term *liquidation,* which refers to the winding up of the corporation's business. Dissolutions may be either voluntary or involuntary. Statutes set out the formal requirements for a voluntary dissolution. Typically, voluntary dissolution involves board action, shareholder approval, and notice to creditors. On voluntary dissolution, the shareholders share proportionately in the net assets of the corporation that remain after satisfaction of creditors' claims. Involuntary dissolutions — those effected by judicial proceedings — occur less frequently than voluntary dissolutions.

The state can rescind or suspend the corporation's certificate when the corporation's actions present a clear danger to the public. On compliance with corporate statutes, the state often orders the corporation's reinstatement. Shareholders can also petition the courts for dissolution of the corporation because of corporate oppression, mismanagement, or deadlock among directors or shareholders. Statutes sometimes limit the conditions under which shareholders can petition for involuntary dissolution. Creditors normally cannot compel involuntary dissolution of the corporation. Neither the appointment of a receiver nor the institution of involuntary bankruptcy proceedings results in the dissolution of the corporation.

Mergers and consolidations can also bring about fundamental changes in the corporation's structure. Technically, mergers and consolidations differ, since in a merger one firm absorbs another, while in a consolidation both firms combine to produce a wholly new entity. The upsurge in mergers stems from a desire to effect economies of scale, to gain technical knowledge, to diversify, to control competition, and to avoid taxes. The negative aspects of mergers include the possible sacrifice of shareholders' interests, personnel displacement, and the uprooting of firms from the local community.

State statutes set out the procedures necessary for bringing about a merger. The directors ordinarily adopt a merger plan, which the shareholders of both firms must approve. Shareholder approval is not necessary in "short-form" mergers. After the state approves the filed merger plan, the surviving corporation receives a "certificate of merger" and can begin conducting business. At this time, the acquired corporation ceases to exist. The surviving corporation takes on all the assets, rights, and liabilities of the transferor corporation by operation of law.

Most state statutes permit appraisal rights for stockholders who object to the merger. Appraisal rights allow dissenters to sell their shares back to the corporation for cash equal to the shares' fair market value. To be eligible for appraisal rights, shareholders usually must follow a set statutory procedure. If the corporation and dissenting shareholders cannot agree about the fair market value of the shares, either party may petition a court to determine their value in an appraisal proceeding. Appraisal rights are normally not available for certain types of mergers and certain types of corporations.

Rather than merging, a corporation can instead buy all or substantially all the assets of another firm. This method of acquisition entails far fewer procedures than a merger. Nevertheless, most statutes in this area try to protect creditors' rights when such sales take place. Stock acquisitions are also simpler than mergers but may be subject to the federal securities laws.

Care must be taken to avoid de facto mergers, transactions taking the form of a sale of substantially all the assets or a stock acquisition but nevertheless having the effect of a merger. Because noncompliance with merger statutes can prejudice the rights of shareholders and creditors, courts may set such de facto mergers aside and order compliance with the procedures mandated by the merger statute.

DISCUSSION QUESTIONS

1. What is dissolution?
2. Who can bring about an involuntary dissolution, and how is this done?
3. Explain why creditors ordinarily cannot cause dissolution.
4. How does a merger differ from a consolidation?
5. List and explain four rationales for mergers.
6. What procedures must a corporation generally follow to merge with another company?
7. Explain the meaning and importance of appraisal rights.
8. Why in a given case would a sale of substantially all the corporate assets be preferable to a merger?
9. List one major drawback of a stock acquisition as a substitute for a merger.
10. Explain the legal significance of a de facto merger.

CASE PROBLEMS

1. Henry Neidorff and David Radom were the sole shareholders in a lithography firm. When Neidorff died, he bequeathed his shares to his wife, Anna,

who was Radom's sister. Thereafter, David and Anna were the sole shareholders in the corporation. They had been unfriendly before Henry's death, and that animosity had escalated to the point that Radom petitioned for dissolution on the ground of deadlock. Radom alleged that Anna would not sign his salary checks, had refused to cooperate in the election of directors, and so on. Anna, in turn, countered with the assertion that she had cooperated in all matters except for signing checks. She said she had refused to sign checks because of her pending lawsuit against Radom for corporate waste. Should the court order involuntary dissolution? (*In re Radom & Neidorff, Inc.,* 119 N.E.2d 563 [N.Y. 1954].)

2. Monahan Building Maintenance, Inc., provided commercial cleaning services. In 1977, Monahan Building Maintenance purchased substantially all the assets of Monahan Commercial Cleaners, Inc., including a cleaning contract with Sage Realty. Monahan Building hired over 90 percent of Monahan Cleaners' employees and assumed the collective bargaining agreement that covered these employees, including lobby attendants. Under this contract, Sage had dictated the job standards for the lobby attendant position, including the uniforms worn by the lobby attendants. Hasselman was a lobby attendant who, as part of the employment contract, had been made to wear a revealing outfit. She had been the object of sexual harassment as a result of this uniform, but neither Sage nor Monahan Cleaners had done anything about her complaints. After she had been discharged for not wearing the uniform, she had sued Sage and Monahan Cleaners for sexual discrimination. Could Monahan Building, the successor corporation, now be liable for Monahan Cleaners' discriminatory acts? (*Equal Employment Opportunity Commission* v. *Sage Realty Corporation,* 507 F. Supp. 599 [S.D. N.Y. 1981].)

3. Dayton sued Peck, Stow and Wilcox Co. (PSW-1) under products liability law for personal injuries he suffered in 1976 while operating a metal-shearing machine manufactured by the firm. PSW-1 had manufactured the machine in question in 1957. In 1963, PSW-1 had sold its assets for cash to Veeder-Root, which had never manufactured metal-shear machinery. The purchase agreement had expressly provided that Veeder-Root would not be liable for any claims based upon negligence or products liability. As part of the transaction, Veeder-Root had set up a new corporation, Peck, Stow and Wilcox Co. (PSW-2), to carry on the business of PSW-1. The shareholders, officers, and directors of PSW-1 had not become shareholders, officers, or directors of PSW-2; the purchase had also left the shareholders' relationship to their respective companies unchanged. In addition, PSW-1 had undergone no liquidation or dissolution at that time. In 1966, Veeder-Root had merged with PSW-2; the metal-shear business had been carried on by Veeder-Root's Peck, Stow and Wilcox Division. In the same year, Veeder-Root had changed its name to Veeder Industries, Inc. (Veeder). In 1975, Veeder had sold all the assets of

its Peck, Stow and Wilcox Division to P.S.&W. Co. (PSW-3), a corporation formed to make the purchase. As part of the sales agreement, Veeder had agreed to retain responsibility for liabilities arising from products manufactured or sold by its Peck, Stow & Wilcox Division before 1 December 1975. With this transaction, Veeder's involvement with the manufacture and sale of metal-shear machinery had ceased. Dayton argued Veeder should be liable for his injuries because the "purchase" of PSW-1 by Veeder had actually been a merger. Do you agree? (*Dayton* v. *Peck, Stow and Wilcox Company,* 739 F.2d 690 [1st Cir. 1984].)

4. On 28 August 1979, a man injured in the capsizing of a showboat sued Missouri Valley Steel, Inc., for his injuries and the death of his pregnant wife. Missouri Valley Steel, Inc., had been dissolved on 13 August 1976, but Kansas law permitted suits to be brought against dissolved corporations for three years after dissolution. Had the plaintiff, Patterson, lost his right to sue by filing suit fifteen days too late, or should the court allow him to sue by extending corporate life beyond the statutory period? (*Patterson* v. *Missouri Valley Steel, Inc.,* 625 P.2d 483 [Kan. 1981].)

5. McGowan was a shareholder in Grand Island Transit Corporation. The firm's merger with another firm was approved by its shareholders on 10 December 1979. McGowan appeared at this meeting, objected to the merger, and said he would exercise his right of dissent within the twenty-day period as required by statute. He received notice of approval of the merger on 12 December 1979, and his attorney notified the corporation of McGowan's electing to dissent on 10 January 1980. On 18 January 1980, the corporation returned McGowan's stock certificates and said his notice of dissent was untimely. Was the corporation right in its belief that it did not have to pay McGowan for his shares? (*McGowan* v. *Grand Island Transit Corporation,* 437 N.Y.S.2d 158 [N.Y. App. Div. 1981].)

6. Davis Aircraft Products Co., Inc. (Davis), was engaged in the business of designing, manufacturing, and selling restraints used in aircraft. Prior to November, 1984, Davis had conducted its manufacturing operations out of a building located in Northport, New York. When the Northport facility required extensive repairs, Davis commenced a search for a new building. Subsequently, it purchased a building in Bohemia, New York, that Davis's president viewed as a more efficient facility. After the purchase, Davis continued in the same business as before the move and did not discontinue any of its former operations. Dukas, a shareholder, alleged that the transaction was voidable because the corporation had not obtained the required authorization from its shareholders. Was Davis's purchase a sale of substantially all its assets such as to require shareholder approval of the transaction? (*Dukas* v. *Davis Aircraft Products Co., Inc.,* 516 N.Y.S.2d 781 [N.Y. App. Div. 1987].)

7. Piggly Wiggly Helms, Inc. (Piggly Wiggly), dissolved in 1976 after Bonsall had fallen in one of Piggly Wiggly's grocery stores. At the time of the

accident, Bonsall had reported the fall to store personnel and had later been contacted by Piggly Wiggly's insurance agent. Bonsall had then contacted an attorney, who had held numerous discussions with Piggly Wiggly's insurance agent. Sometime thereafter, Piggly Wiggly had initiated dissolution proceedings and, as required by law, had published notices in the newspaper concerning its intent to dissolve the corporation. By law, the corporation had had an obligation to notify every known creditor of this fact, as well. No specific notice had been sent to Bonsall. She later argued that the corporation's dissolution had not been effective as to her because of this lack of notice and that Piggly Wiggly should therefore be liable for her injuries. How should a court rule on her claim? (*Bonsall* v. *Piggly Wiggly Helms, Inc.,* 274 S.E.2d 298 [S.C. 1981].)

8. On 1 March 1983, Olin Corporation (Olin) acquired 63.4 percent of the outstanding stock of Philip A. Hunt Chemical Corporation (Hunt) for approximately $25 per share. In addition, Olin agreed that if it or an affiliate were to acquire all or substantially all of the remaining Hunt common stock within one year of the closing date, Olin would pay the equivalent of at least the net purchase price per share (approximately $25). The closing date was 1 March 1984. Although Olin had prepared computations based on the assumption that it would acquire 100 percent of Hunt, in September, 1983, a memorandum listing the pros and cons of such an acquisition noted that Olin would be obligated to pay $25 per share whereas after 1 March 1984 it could acquire the minority shares at a lower price. In the memorandum, the figure used as an example was $21.50 per share. Olin decided to do nothing at that time. Shortly before the expiration of the one-year commitment, Olin began taking steps to acquire the minority shareholders' interests in Hunt. On February 24, the two companies issued a press release announcing Olin's intention to acquire Hunt's publicly held minority stock through a $20 per share cash merger. Rabkin and other minority shareholders sued to block the merger on the grounds that the sole purpose of the merger was to obtain the minority interests for a fraudulently low and unfair price through Olin's intentional timing of the merger immediately after the expiration of the one-year commitment and that the absence of arms' length negotiations constituted a breach of fiduciary duty. It was also alleged that Hunt's improved earnings and general business prospects had estopped the corporation from paying a price lower than $25 because Olin had stated in required securities filings that the price paid for the minority stock would reflect these and other factors. Assuming that in this state, a minority shareholder's exclusive remedy is appraisal in the absence of fraud, had Rabkin shown fraud so as to avail himself of other equitable remedies? (*Rabkin* v. *Philip A. Hunt Chemical Corporation,* 498 A.2d 1099 [Del. 1985].)

9. Rosenblatt, a minority shareholder in Skelly Oil Company (Skelly), brought a class action against Getty Oil Company (Getty), challenging the

fairness of the merger of Getty and Skelly. Getty, prior to the merger, had been a major Skelly shareholder. The evidence showed that, prior to the initiation of merger negotiations, Getty had known that it would be sued. Thus, it had sought to structure the transaction to meet the standards imposed by Delaware law. At the initial meeting held on 16 July 1976, Getty and Skelly management had been given a legal research memorandum on valuation methods approved by Delaware courts. Moreover, Getty had been cognizant of the potential conflicts among the interlocking managements of both companies. Accordingly, at the 15 July 1976 meeting, when Getty had designated Kenneth Hill of Blyth Eastman as its chief negotiator, Hill had immediately resigned from Skelly's board, on which he had served for ten years. Similarly, a partner in the law firm Hays, Landsman & Head had resigned from the Skelly board because the law firm had been representing Getty. As to the structure of the actual negotiations, Getty and Skelly had agreed on 15 July 1976 to have Dolyer & McNaughton (D&M), a well-known petroleum engineering firm, estimate their respective reserves and analyze their future prospects. Getty and Skelly also had agreed to evaluate separately their respective surface assets and then negotiate those values. As a result of hard bargaining, the parties had accepted a stock exchange ratio of .5875 Getty shares for one share of Skelly, after Getty had advocated a .5 and Skelly a .7 ratio. On these facts, did Rosenblatt have a good cause of action? (*Rosenblatt* v. *Getty Oil Company*, 493 A.2d 929 [Del. 1985].)

10. Bowman and Bridges were shareholders, directors, and employees of State Bank of Keysville (the Bank). In 1979, the Bank proposed to merge with NB Corporation. After learning of Bowman and Bridges's opposition to the merger, the president of the Bank told them that their voting against the merger would have a definite adverse effect on their jobs. Both women executed their proxy cards in favor of the merger against their will, under duress, and out of fear of losing their jobs. At the special meeting on 26 June 1979, 2008 shares of the Bank's common stock, including their eleven shares, were voted in favor of the merger proposal. This was eight votes more than the number necessary to constitute the required two-thirds majority for approval of the plan. Two days after the special meeting, however, Bowman and Bridges wrote a joint letter to the Bank president stating that their proxies were invalid, illegally obtained, improper, and null and void. Accordingly, they wrote, only 1997 votes had been cast in favor of the merger, three less than the votes necessary for approval. On 6 July 1979, the Bank board voted to abandon the merger. The merger was aborted, according to Bowman's and Bridges's allegations, because the Bank feared that the illegal activities involved in obtaining the proxies of stockholders, including the plaintiffs, would be discovered. Six days later, the Bank's directors, by a five to four vote, decided to discharge the plaintiffs from their employment with the Bank.

The women sued, arguing that the Bank, in discharging employees who were also shareholders, had acted in violation of securities and corporation laws because the Bank had acted against employees who had been merely exercising their protected rights as shareholders in questioning the manner in which proxies had been obtained for a proposed merger. The Bank argued the women were employees-at-will who could be fired at any time. Should Bowman and Bridges receive damages? (*Bowman* v. *State Bank of Keysville,* 331 S.E.2d 797 [Va. 1985].)

CHAPTER 43 ▮▮▮▮▮▮▮▮▮▮▮▮▮▮▮▮▮▮▮▮▮▮▮▮▮▮▮▮

Franchising

Although franchising began in America over a century ago when breweries licensed beer gardens as a means of distributing their products, franchising did not become recognized as a distinct method of doing business until after World War II.[1] Since then, and especially in the last ten years, franchising has contributed significantly to the United States' achieving its position as the world's largest market. Presently more than 2000 U.S. companies encompassing over forty different economic sectors use the franchise method for distributing their goods or services both domestically and internationally.[2] Among the types of businesses that use franchise systems are the following: automobile dealerships; gasoline stations; restaurants; convenience stores; soft drink bottlers; nonfood merchandising businesses (such as drug, electronics, cosmetics, and

THE SIGNIFI-CANCE OF FRANCHISING AS A BUSINESS METHOD

---

[1] Harold Brown, *Franchising — Realities and Remedies,* 2nd ed. (New York: Law Journal Press, 1978), p. 1.

[2] International Trade Administration, U.S. Department of Commerce, *Franchising in the Economy 1985–1987* (Washington, D.C.: U.S. Government Printing Office, 1987), p. vi.

home furnishings companies); travel agencies; hotels, motels, and camp-grounds; automobile and truck rental services; printing and copying services; tax preparation firms; real estate businesses; accounting firms; cleaning services; lawn and garden services; laundry services; equipment rentals; early childhood education and daycare centers; and beauty salons.

According to an estimate of the U.S. Department of Commerce, franchises overall would sell $591 billion worth of such goods and services in 1987, an increase of 6 percent over the figures for 1986 and about 77 percent higher than the level of sales at the beginning of the 1980s; similarly, the number of persons employed in franchising systems would probably reach 7 million by the end of 1987.[3] Figure 43.1 shows that by 1987, franchises would account for approximately one-third of all retail sales in the United States ($515.2 billion of the $1,585 billion total in retail sales).

As these statistics demonstrate, franchising has developed into an impor-

Figure 43.1   Franchising as a Percentage of Retail Sales, 1987

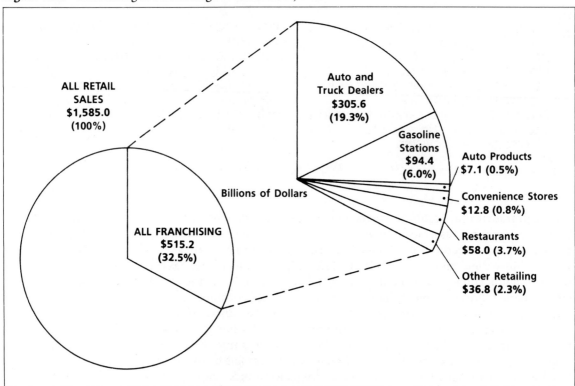

Source: International Trade Administration, U.S. Department of Commerce, *Franchising in the Economy 1985–1987* (Washington, D.C.: U.S. Government Printing Office, 1987), p. 15.

[3] Ibid., p.1.

tant and popular method of marketing and distribution. In this chapter, we shall examine why this has occurred.

No universally accepted definition of the word *franchise* exists. Nevertheless, the following definition, taken from the Washington Franchise Investment Protection Act, Section 19.100.010(4), is typical:

> "Franchise" means an oral or written contract or agreement, either expressed or implied, in which a person grants to another person a license to use a trade name, service mark, trade mark, logotype or related characteristic in which there is a community interest in the business of offering, selling, distributing goods or services at wholesale or retail, leasing or otherwise and in which the franchisee is required to pay, directly or indirectly, a franchise fee.

DEFINITION

Service marks, trademarks, and **logotypes** are symbols that identify the origins of goods and services. The person or firm that grants a franchise to another is called the *franchisor*. The person receiving the franchise is known as the *franchisee*. Franchises, or retail businesses involving sales of products or services to consumers, fall into two general categories:

Service marks Distinctive symbols designating the services offered by a particular business or individual

Trademarks Distinctive marks or symbols used to identify a particular company or its products

Logotypes Identifying symbols

1. *Distributorships* (also called *product* or *trade name franchises*), in which a manufacturer/franchisor licenses a franchisee to sell its product either exclusively or with other products. The franchisee often has the exclusive right to sell the product in a designated area or territory.

2. *Chain-style businesses* (also called *business format franchises*), in which a franchisee operates a business under the franchisor's trade name and is identified as a member of a select group of persons who deal in this particular business. In exchange for the franchise, the franchisee ordinarily must follow a standardized or prescribed format as to methods of operation and may be subject to the franchisor's control with regard to the materials used in making the product, site selection, the design of the facility, the hours of the business, the qualifications of personnel, and the like.[4]

Distributorships were estimated to account for 71 percent of all franchise sales in 1987, with total annual sales by this type of franchisors reaching $421 billion—an increase of more than 4 percent over the figures for 1986. However, the overall number of such establishments has decreased since 1972 owing to the closings of gasoline stations and automobile and truck dealerships.[5]

In contrast to the predicted decrease in distributorships, chain-style franchises were expected to increase in number to almost 353,000 in 1987, a 16.8

---

[4] Gladys Glickman, *Franchising*, Business Organizations, vol. 15 (New York: Matthew Bender, 1983), Section 2.02.

[5] International Trade Administration, *Franchising*, p. 1.

percent increase since 1985. Annual sales were expected to increase 20.8 percent over the figures for 1985, totaling $171 billion in 1987. Large franchisors — that is, those with 1000 or more units each — should continue to dominate this category of franchising; they accounted for 48 percent of total sales and 49 percent of all chain-style establishments in 1985. Most of these large franchisors engage either in restaurant businesses or in the retailing of automotive products and services.[6]

BENEFITS OF FRANCHISING

Whatever the form the particular franchise takes, the advantages of a franchise system as a method of doing business make it attractive to both potential franchisees and franchisors.

The benefits to franchisees include the following:

1.   the opportunity to commence a business despite limited capital and experience

2.   the goodwill that results from marketing a nationally known, high-quality trademark or service mark, which not only benefits the individual franchisees but also raises customer acceptance throughout the system

3.   the availability of the franchisor's business expertise in such areas as inventory control, warehousing, advertising, market research, and product innovation

4.   an assured supply of materials, the use of bulk buying techniques, and access to training and supervision

The benefits to franchisors include:

1.   the franchisee's investment of capital

2.   the goodwill and other advantages flowing from the franchisee's entrepreneurial abilities, including the enhanced value of the trademark or service mark

3.   the availability of an assured distribution network, which brings about economies of scale in labor costs, produces a more certain demand curve, and reduces wide fluctuations in sales

4.   a larger asset base, which makes the franchisor better able to secure credit, enhance profits, avoid financial risks, attract the best talent, lobby for favorable legislation, and defray litigation costs[7]

Thus, the franchisor and franchisee are generally able to accomplish more together than they can through individual effort. In an era of increasing vertical integration, some have seen franchising as the last bastion for the

[6] Ibid., pp. 3–5.
[7] Brown, *Franchising,* pp. 6–12.

independent businessperson: franchising provides independent businesspersons with the means of opening and operating their own businesses, and it allows small businesses to compete with mammoth corporations. In addition, franchising fosters the expansion of an established product or service. It may also bring about the rescue of an otherwise failing business.

By lowering barriers to entry, franchising as a type of business system furthers many of the antitrust policies you will learn about in Chapter 46. It thus provides societal and economic benefits to the public at large as well as to individual consumers. On the other hand, the franchisor's often extensive control over the franchisee's conduct of the business together with other aspects of the franchisor-franchisee relationship have spawned complicated legal questions. We shall consider some of these issues in the remainder of this chapter.

FRANCHISING COMPARED WITH OTHER BUSINESS RELATIONSHIPS

A franchise generally involves a form of marketing or distribution in which one party grants to another the right or privilege to do business in a specified manner in a particular place over a certain period of time. It has sometimes been difficult to distinguish such a relationship from other types of business relationships. The distinction may nonetheless be legally important, since in recent years about one-third of the states have passed laws dealing specifically with franchising, and the Federal Trade Commission has established regulations covering franchising. Until trouble develops, the two parties may consider the holder of the right to do business in a prescribed manner as an independent contractor. But when the grantor terminates its business relationship with the holder, the holder may try to characterize the relationship as a franchise in order to fall under the protection of such statutes. Even before the relationship between the two parties sours, government agencies tend to view the relationship as one of employment, not of independent contracting. If the holder of the privilege is an employee or agent rather than an independent contractor, the law requires the grantor to pay withholding and social security taxes, federal minimum wages, and workers' compensation. In addition, in such circumstances the grantor may be subject to the provisions of other labor laws and private antitrust suits.

It is especially difficult to classify the relationship if the holder of the privilege is a distributor. As we have already noted, a distributor may be a franchisee. Yet it is also possible that a distributor is instead an employee, a **consignee,** or an independent contractor, depending on the details surrounding the distributor's relationship with its supplier. As you would expect, courts delve deeply into the particular facts at issue (most notably evidence of the grantor's degree of control over the distributor) in making such determinations.

Still, the law is fairly well settled with regard to certain issues: **cooperatives, concessionaires,** joint ventures, general partnerships (although a partnership can act either as a franchisor or a franchisee), and sales agencies

Consignee A person to whom goods are shipped for sale

Cooperatives Groups of individuals, commonly laborers or farmers, who unite in a common enterprise and share the profits proportionately

Concessionaires Operators of refreshment centers

ordinarily are not deemed franchises. And, as you will learn in Chapter 44, a franchise agreement does not usually amount to a security under federal or state law because the distributors/franchisees invest their own efforts in the franchise and do not expect to obtain benefits solely from the efforts of others. In other words, the "passive investment" component generally associated with securities remains unsatisfied in the typical franchising arrangement.

In the following case, the court had to decide whether the business relationship in dispute involved a franchise arrangement or merely an employer-employee relationship.

Quirk v. Atlanta Stove Works, Inc.
537 F. Supp. 907 (E.D. Wis. 1982)

FACTS   Quirk entered into a written agreement with Atlanta Stove Works in which he agreed to be the firm's exclusive sales representative in a territory consisting of Wisconsin, Iowa, Illinois, and upper Michigan. Under the terms of the agreement, Quirk was paid on a commission basis for the purchase orders he solicited. Atlanta Stove Works also supplied Quirk with a car. Among other duties, Quirk promoted the firm's products by attending local trade and sales shows where he distributed catalogues and price lists and displayed samples of the stoves manufactured by Atlanta. When Atlanta attempted to terminate Quirk by giving him thirty days' notice as required by its agreement with him, Quirk argued that he should have been given ninety days' notice as required by the Wisconsin Fair Dealership Law because he was Atlanta's dealer (franchisee).

ISSUE   Was the business relationship in question a franchise arrangement, which would require compliance with the Wisconsin Fair Dealership Law?

HOLDING   No. The relationship in question was that of employer–employee and thus was not covered by this particular state law.

REASONING   The Wisconsin Fair Dealership Law had been intended to cover small businesspersons who, as franchisees, had made a substantial financial investment as part of their association with the grantor of the dealership or franchise. The Wisconsin legislature had meant to protect such persons from termination without good cause and adequate notice. Yet Quirk's relationship with Atlanta Stove Works had not fallen under this law. Quirk had never made any financial investment in inventory, physical facilities, or goodwill as part of his association with the firm. Instead, he had merely solicited orders and had not been required to extend credit or to assume the risk of nonpayment by Atlanta's customers. Atlanta also had set the price, discounts, and all other terms of sale. In addition, the firm had paid Quirk $1500 per month (repayable out of later commissions) in those months when his commissions on sales had not reached this amount. Besides supplying him with a company car, Atlanta also had withheld taxes on Quirk and had contributed to the state unemployment and workers' compensation systems on Quirk's behalf. Owing to all these factors, Quirk had been an employee of Atlanta, not a dealer or franchisee; and the Wisconsin Fair Dealership Law accordingly had not covered their relationship. For that reason, the court granted Atlanta Stove Works' motion for summary judgment.

SETTING UP THE FRANCHISING RELATIONSHIP

Franchisors usually recruit franchisees by advertising their particular business. The franchisor then sends "franchisee kits" to those who answer the advertisement. Typically, this franchise kit points out in glowing terms the potential for success in this particular industry. To the uninitiated layperson or the businessperson with little previous experience and limited capital — those who may be most inclined to enter a franchising arrangement — the franchisor's promotional documents, market studies, and statistics seem highly persuasive. Even at the outset, then, the franchisee relies heavily on the franchisor for guidance. The pervasiveness of the franchisor's control often leads to later legal difficulties, as we shall see.

Because of the large number of variables involved, it is difficult to come up with a brief, comprehensive description of the dynamics of consummating a franchising arrangement. But, in a nutshell, once the parties have established initial contact and have decided to enter into a franchising relationship, the parties usually first sign a detailed agreement. In this agreement, the franchisor grants to the franchisee the right to use the mark or standardized product or service in exchange for a franchise fee. The franchisor then uses its real estate expertise to designate a specific franchise location, designs and arranges for the standardized construction of the facility, and installs fixtures and equipment therein. The franchisor intensively advertises the product in exchange for an advertising fee (usually a percentage of gross sales) paid by the franchisee. In addition, the franchisor creates training programs, prepares training manuals, and sets out stringent guidelines — even as to the hiring of personnel, personnel's dress and grooming standards, and the like — for the day-to-day operation of the business. Once the franchise becomes operative, the franchisee must follow the procedures set out in the franchisor's confidential operating manual or risk termination of the franchise. This manual usually mandates strict accounting procedures and authorizes the franchisor to inspect the books and records at any time. The franchisee typically pays a set **royalty fee** (usually based on a certain percentage of the gross sales) on a monthly or semimonthly basis to the franchisor. The franchise agreement normally obligates the franchisee to secure liability insurance to protect the franchisee and franchisor against casualty losses and tort suits. The franchisee usually also has the responsibility of meeting state requirements regarding workers' compensation.

Royalty fee Payment made in exchange for the grant of a right or a license

The last two areas ordinarily covered in the franchise agreement — quality control and termination — pose most of the potential legal problems. It is easy to understand the franchisor's desire for quality control: only by maintaining uniform standards of quality and appearance can the franchisor preserve its reputation and foster the public's acceptance of its product. For this reason, franchisors typically obligate the franchisee to buy products and supplies from them at set prices or from suppliers who can meet the franchisor's exacting specifications and standards. Forcing franchisees to buy only from their own franchisors would probably constitute antitrust violations, a topic we shall discuss later in this chapter. (As the law currently stands, the same would be true if the franchisor set resale prices for the franchisee; nevertheless, the franchisor can within the law *suggest* resale prices.) Critics of franchising have argued that, practically speaking, the franchisee would have a difficult, if not impossible, time finding a supplier who would meet the franchisor's specifications, with the result that, under the guise of quality control, franchisees often must pay inflated prices for supplies.

The termination provisions of a franchising agreement, as noted, also constitute legal pitfalls for the unwary. The franchise agreement ordinarily sets out the duration of the franchise (say ten years) and usually contains provisions for renewals after this time period has passed. As part of the covenants, or promises, made about the term of the agreement, the franchisee usually agrees to a covenant not to compete for a set time period after the termination of the franchise. The conditions of default, such as a franchisee's insolvency or failure to pay monthly or semimonthly fees when due, that lead to termination are reproduced in the franchise agreement. In these and other "for cause" situations, the agreement normally calls for the franchisor to give the franchisee time (for example, ten days) to cure these instances of default. Most agreements provide for notice of termination, and the existing state laws on franchising generally set out a required notice period (say ninety days) before the franchisor can effect a termination.

When prospective franchisees lack business acumen, they are likely to accept without question the thirty-to-fifty page agreement that the franchisor typically offers. This disparity in bargaining power has led to the passage of state and federal laws and the promulgation of administrative regulations designed to protect franchisees when they enter their agreements (through mandated disclosures) and upon termination (through notice provisions). Courts, too, have increasingly tried to protect franchisees by closely scrutinizing franchise agreements. In the following case, the court dealt with the issue of deceptive practices surrounding a franchisee's entry into an agreement.

Bailey Employment System, Inc. v. Hahn
545 F. Supp. 62 (D. Conn. 1982)
Affirmed 723 F.2d 895 (2d Cir. 1983)

FACTS   Bailey Employment System, Inc. (Bailey), sold an employment service franchise to Hahn for a $10,000 franchising fee. In the course of making the sale, Bailey's representatives told Hahn that the volume from such a franchise for each employment counselor could go as high as $90,000 and that the average volume was $36,000 per year. Actually, only about 20 percent of Bailey's counselors earned $36,000. Bailey's representatives also stated in their promotional communications that Bailey's franchisees earned average incomes of $500 to $700 every week, even in recessions. Again, only a small percentage of Bailey franchisees actually earned these amounts. Bailey's representatives, in addition, stated that a new Bailey franchisee could earn a living wage after the first six months of operation, whereas, in reality, only one franchisee had achieved this feat. Statements in company brochures on "projected earnings" were similarly unreliable. Bailey also failed to disclose to Hahn that its franchise attrition rate was high and that it was involved in litigation with several of its franchisees.

Were Bailey's misrepresentations a deceptive practice prohibited by the Connecticut Unfair Trade Practices Act, which would allow Hahn to recover from Bailey?

ISSUE

Yes. Because the statements had had a tendency to deceive the franchisee, Hahn, Bailey was ordered to reimburse Hahn for the $10,000 franchise fee and the $3473 in royalty payments he had made to Bailey. An award of $26,946 in punitive damages was also made to Hahn.

HOLDING

All the promotional statements had been misleading and therefore actionable under the Connecticut statute. A franchisor should disclose any information, positive or negative, that would affect a buyer's decision about whether or not to purchase. Since the appropriate formula for damages was restitution, Hahn was entitled to recovery of $13,473 in actual damages. Because a measure of deterrence was warranted and because of Bailey's long history of using deceptive practices on prospective franchisees, Hahn was awarded $26,946 in punitive damages, as well.

REASONING

Most litigation involving franchises has centered on termination provisions in the franchising agreement. Because termination can leave the franchisee with little to show after years of effort and expense, courts, whenever possible, try to find a basis of relief so the franchisee is not without a remedy. The following case involved such an issue.

ABA Distributors, Inc. v. Adolph Coors Company, Inc.
542 F. Supp. 1272 (W.D. Mo. 1982)

ABA Distributors, Inc. (ABA), was a Missouri beer distributor authorized to distribute Adolph Coors Company, Inc. (Coors), beer. From 1 June 1973 to 21 March 1980, Coors had not sold beer in any states east of the Mississippi River, nor had it had any distributors in that territory. ABA had become a Coors distributor on 1 June 1978 for the territory in and around Kansas City, Missouri. ABA had invested over $1.4 million in order to obtain the Coors distributorship. In January, 1979 and 1980, Coors

FACTS

officials told the president of ABA that Coors believed ABA had been distributing Coors products outside its assigned geographic territory. ABA denied these allegations. In March, 1980, a Coors official orally announced to a group of distributors at a conference in Phoenix that any distributor selling outside its assigned geographic area would be terminated immediately and without notice once Coors discovered such a fact. From February, 1979, to March, 1980, a private investigator hired by Coors maintained surveillance on ABA's warehouse. On 8 March 1980, the investigator called Coors's counsel to report that three small trucks had left the ABA warehouse and had delivered beer to a large trailer truck parked several blocks away. The investigator had made no inquiries at ABA about this delivery and had not attempted to find out the destination of the trailer truck. Nevertheless, without any further investigation by Coors, Coors officials called the president of ABA to Golden, Colorado, on 19 March 1980 and terminated ABA's distributorship. At this meeting, Coors officials did not charge that ABA had sold Coors beer out of state but charged instead that ABA had been dishonest with regard to out-of-state sales. Coors temporarily divided ABA's distributorship between two other distributors. Coors sent ABA a letter of termination on 21 March 1980, effective immediately without notice. ABA's franchise agreement with Coors provided for termination upon thirty days' notice unless the franchisee had engaged in violations of law, dishonesty, or moral turpitude or had been convicted of a felony. In these "for cause" circumstances, termination could be immediate. ABA argued that since its conduct had not fallen into any of these categories, Coors's termination of its distributorship had breached the franchise agreement.

ISSUE   Had Coors wrongfully terminated ABA's distributorship by breaching the franchise agreement?

HOLDING   Yes. Coors's conduct had violated both Missouri common law and statutory law.

REASONING   Coors had breached the fiduciary duty of good faith and fair dealing that it owed ABA under Missouri law when it attempted, without actual knowledge of any facts to support the grounds stated in its letter of 21 March 1980, to terminate ABA without notice under the agreement. Both common law contract law and Missouri's UCC Section 1-203 imposed an obligation of good faith on Coors. Because Missouri's franchise law applied to beer distributorships, the ninety days' notice required under this statute would invalidate the thirty days' notice provision in Coors's agreement even if Coors had complied with the provisions of its agreement. Therefore, under applicable Missouri law, Coors's attempt to terminate ABA without notice had breached its fiduciary duty to ABA — the duty of fair dealing and good faith it owed to ABA — and the franchise statute's requirement of at least ninety days' notice before an attempted termination. For these reasons, the 21 March 1980 notice of termination was set aside, and Coors was ordered to give ABA the opportunity to sell its distributorship according to the provisions on transferability within the distributorship agreement. Furthermore, Coors must avoid any unreasonable withholding of approval of any prospective buyers ABA might find. Should a good-faith disagreement in this regard arise, however, either party could invoke the arbitration provision of the agreement. This disposition of the dispute represented a more effective remedy than money damages, which would have been inadequate in that, unlike a sale of the distributorship, such damages would not have allowed ABA to recoup its substantial investment in Coors products.

Although courts will, whenever possible, try to find a basis of relief for the franchisee, they will not force franchisors to stick with obviously inept franchisees. The following case illustrates this point.

Tappan Motors, Inc. v. Volvo of America Corporation
444 N.Y.S.2d 938 (N.Y. App. Div. 1981)
Affirmed 490 N.Y.S.2d 168 (N.Y. 1985)

FACTS

In November 1960, Tappan Motors, Inc. (Tappan), became a franchised Volvo dealer. The franchise agreement stated, among other things, that Tappan should use its best efforts to sell Volvo products in its area of responsibility and should keep an adequate inventory of parts for meeting customer demands. In July, 1979, Volvo informed Tappan by letter that it believed the dealership to be in default of various obligations under the agreement and that it had sixty days in which to cure these defaults. In September, 1979, Volvo told Tappan in writing that it was terminating Tappan as a franchisee because Tappan had not corrected these defects. Before the passage of the required thirty days' written notice, Tappan sought and got a permanent injunction to stop Volvo from terminating its franchise. Volvo appealed this order.

ISSUE

Was Volvo justified in terminating Tappan's franchise?

HOLDING

Yes. Volvo had had sufficient cause to terminate Tappan's franchise as required under New York law.

REASONING

New York law prevented Volvo from terminating a franchised dealer either in bad faith or in the absence of good cause shown. The evidence had showed that (1) Tappan had repeatedly experienced problems in servicing Volvo automobiles; (2) Tappan's facilities had been neither as large nor as clean as Volvo required; (3) some of the specialized tools required for servicing Volvos had been missing from Tappan's premises; (4) certain of Volvo's factory service manuals also had been missing; (5) Volvo customers at Tappan had been subjected to inconvenience and excessive waiting times for repairs; (6) Tappan had failed or refused to keep an adequate inventory of Volvo parts; (7) Tappan had delayed installation of a computer system for the control of its parts inventory until after its termination had been scheduled to take effect; and (8) Tappan had repeatedly complained about its allocation of automobiles and had threatened to dissuade customers from purchasing a Volvo elsewhere if Tappan could not supply them with the Volvo model of their choice. These factors, considered jointly, had more than sufficed to justify Volvo's decision to terminate Tappan's franchise pursuant to the contract and in accordance with the section of the law requiring good cause. Moreover, because there had been no indication that Volvo had acted other than in good faith in deciding to terminate the agreement, there was no reason to interfere with Volvo's decision to terminate Tappan.

DECISIONAL LAW AND STATUTES AFFECTING FRANCHISING

As the *Bailey Employment System* and *ABA Distributors* cases illustrate, courts have been sensitive to the issue of damages in the franchising context. This is particularly true in circumstances involving terminations, because on termination the franchisee may be left with nothing. Termination provisions, especially when coupled with transferability terms that allow the franchisor to reject potential buyers, may clothe the franchisor with an inordinate amount of power vis-à-vis the franchisee. As we have seen, courts can turn to common law, their own powers of equity, and/or applicable statutes in shaping relief. Some of the statutes mentioned earlier were designed by their drafters to correct perceived abuses and overreaching by franchisors; indeed, few regulations pertain to the conduct of franchisees. Clearly, such statutes have improved the bargaining position of franchisees, but some critics have argued that they also make franchise systems more rigid and encourage litigation. Some state legislatures have passed special laws to protect automobile dealers from excessive competition by requiring that notice be given to established automobile dealers and to the state motor vehicle regulatory agency before a franchisor can establish a new dealership or relocate an existing one. The notice provision allows established dealers to object to the granting of any additional dealership licenses and thereby to protect their economic stakes in a particular territory. In *New Motor Vehicle Board of California* v. *Orrin W. Fox Co.*,[8] the Supreme Court upheld a California statute of this type even though Fox had argued that the statute was violative of the antitrust laws and unconstitutional on grounds of due process.

On the federal level, the Automobile Dealers' Franchise Act, also known as the Automobile Dealers' Day in Court Act (15 U.S.C. Section 1221), in a similar vein allows a terminated dealer to bring an action in federal court asking for retention of the franchise if the dealer can prove that the franchisor has conducted the termination in bad faith and coercively. The federal Petroleum Marketing Practices Act (15 U.S.C. Section 2801) protects motor fuel distributors and dealers from arbitrary terminations as well. However, even with these statutes, courts have allowed franchisors to terminate franchisees for such reasons as misconduct or failure to meet sales quotas, to observe quality standards, to maintain appropriate investment levels, and the like.

[8] 439 U.S. 96 (1978).

Nevertheless, the presence of these laws helps to ensure that the bargaining power between franchisors and franchisees will be more commensurate and balanced.

The Federal Trade Commission has promulgated a trade regulation rule on franchise disclosure meant to satisfy the same aims. This 1979 rule, and state laws that mandate similar disclosure provisions, have helped to do away with the abuses associated with the sale of franchises. Continuing investigations of the franchise industry under the power to prohibit deceptive and unfair trade practices granted to the Federal Trade Commission by the Federal Trade Commission Act should effectively reinforce these other regulatory measures.

In addition, antitrust laws, such as the Sherman Antitrust Act and the Clayton Act, may apply to various aspects of the franchising relationship. We learned earlier that, as a condition of using their trademark or service mark, franchisors often attempt to impose on franchisees territorial restrictions and restrictions on supplies or prices that may run afoul of the antitrust laws. Consumer protection statutes may also affect the franchising relationship: franchises that extend credit on installments or through charge accounts may be subject to various truth-in-lending statutes. In addition to its requirement of good faith, the UCC's warranty provisions and its section on unconscionability may be applicable to franchising. Since the law on franchising at this time appears to be unsettled yet proliferating, a thoughtful examination of such laws by franchisors and franchisees alike seems warranted.

Some franchisors have bridled at the passage of such franchising statutes because they perceive them as serious limitations on their freedom to contract and to manage their businesses. Consequently, franchisors have raised constitutional arguments against these laws. The parts of the Constitution relied upon in these challenges include the following:

CHALLENGES TO FRANCHISING REGULATORY STATUTES

1. *Impairment of the obligation of contracts.* The Constitution prohibits a state from passing a law that makes substantive changes in contractual rights.

2. *Due process.* The Fourteenth Amendment bans vague, standardless laws.

3. *Federal supremacy.* Article VI of the Constitution makes federal law the supreme law of the land. Thus, a state franchising law that conflicts with a federal law (say the Lanham Act's regulation of trademarks) will be unconstitutional.

4. *Interstate commerce.* Article I, Section 8, of the Constitution prohibits the states from placing undue burdens on interstate commerce.

As the following case shows, such arguments can be successful.

Southland Corporation v. Keating
465 U.S. 1 (1984)

FACTS   The Southland Corporation (Southland) is the owner and franchisor of 7-Eleven convenience stores. Southland's standard franchise agreement provides each franchisee with a license to use certain registered trademarks, a lease or sublease of a convenience store owned or leased by Southland, inventory financing, and assistance in advertising and merchandising. The franchisees operate the stores, supply bookkeeping data, and pay Southland a fixed percentage of gross profits. The franchise agreement also contains the following provision requiring arbitration: "Any controversy or claim arising out of or relating to this Agreement or the breach thereof shall be settled by arbitration in accordance with the rules of the American Arbitration Association . . . and judgment upon any award rendered by the arbitrator may be entered in any court having jurisdiction thereof." Keating was a 7-Eleven franchisee. In May, 1977, he filed a class action against Southland on behalf of a class of 800 California franchisees, alleging, among other things, fraud, oral misrepresentation, breach of contract, breach of fiduciary duty, and violation of the disclosure requirements of the California Franchise Investment Law. Southland asserted as an affirmative defense to this suit the franchisee's failure to arbitrate and moved to compel arbitration. The trial court granted Southland's motion to compel arbitration of all claims except those based on the California Franchise Investment Law. This statute provides: "Any condition, stipulation or provision purporting to bind any person acquiring any franchise to waive compliance with any provision of this law or any rule or order hereunder is void." After a trial and appeals, the California Supreme Court interpreted this statute to require judicial consideration of claims brought under the state statute and accordingly refused to enforce the parties' contract to arbitrate such claims. In so doing, California's highest court rejected the state appellate court's holding that the California Franchise Investment Law did not invalidate arbitration agreements and that if it had rendered such agreements involving commerce unenforceable, such a result would conflict with Section 2 of the United States Arbitration Act.

ISSUE   Was the California Franchise Investment Law in conflict with federal law and thus unconstitutional?

HOLDING   Yes. This state law directly conflicted with the Federal Arbitration Act and thereby violated the Supremacy Clause.

REASONING   Congress's enactment of Section 2 of the Federal Arbitration Act represented a declaration of a national policy favoring arbitration and a withdrawal of the power of the states to require a judicial forum for the resolution of claims that the contracting parties agreed to resolve by arbitration. A portion of Section 2's language — "an agreement in writing to submit to arbitration an existing controversy arising out of such a contract, transaction, or refusal, shall be valid, irrevocable, and enforceable, save upon such grounds as exist at law or in equity for the revocation of any contract" — stood as clear evidence that Congress had mandated the enforcement of arbitration agreements and that such clauses should be revoked only upon "grounds as exist at law or in equity for the revocation of any contract." Nothing in the Act indicated that the broad principle of enforceability had been subject to any additional limitations under state law. Indeed, the legislative history revealed that Congress had meant to remedy two problems in enacting the Federal Arbitration Act: the old common law hostility toward arbitration and the failure of state arbitration statutes to mandate enforcement of arbitration agreements. To confine the scope of the Act to arbitrations sought to be enforced in federal courts would frustrate what Congress had intended as a broad enactment appropriate in scope to meet the large problems Congress was addressing. Justice O'Connor's interpretation of the Federal Arbitration Act as a procedural statute applicable only in federal courts was erroneous. Under her interpretation, claims brought under the California Franchise Investment Law would not be arbitrable when they had been raised in state court. But it was clear beyond question that if this suit had been brought as a diversity action in a federal district court, the arbitration clause would have been enforceable. Because the interpretation given to the Federal Arbitration Act by the California Supreme Court would therefore encourage and reward **forum shopping,** to attribute to Congress the intent, in drawing on the comprehensive powers of the Commerce Clause, to create a right to enforce an arbitration contract and yet make the right dependent for its enforcement on the particular forum in which it is asserted would be inappropriate. And since the overwhelming proportion of all civil litigation in this country is in the state courts, Congress apparently had not intended to limit the Arbitration Act to disputes subject only to *federal* court jurisdiction, since such an interpretation would frustrate Congressional intent to place "[a]n arbitration agreement . . . upon the same footing as other contracts, where it belongs." Rather, Congress, in creating a substantive rule applicable in state as well as federal courts, had intended to foreclose state legislative attempts to undercut the enforceability of arbitration agreements. Therefore, for these reasons, the California Franchise Investment Law violated the Supremacy Clause of the Constitution.

Forum shopping
Choosing the court or place of jurisdiction that will be most favorable to the litigant

THE FRANCHISING ENVIRONMENT

Ownership Trends

Since 1975, there has been a demonstrated increase in conversions of company-owned franchise units to franchisee-owned ones. According to industry sources, this increase has probably occurred because most of the units that companies have repurchased have represented temporary buy-backs for legitimate business reasons rather than the companies' desire to withdraw from the franchise system or to operate these units permanently themselves. The number of minority-owned franchises has increased, as well. Yet a record number of franchises — 78 — operating 5667 outlets failed in 1985, according to government statistics. However, industry sources minimize these figures by noting that the sales volume lost by these firms has remained minuscule. Recent surveys also indicate that 36 percent of all franchise agreements are for terms of twenty years or more. The rate for renewal in 1985 was 91 percent. Approximately one-fourth of the nonrenewals resulted from franchisors' objections; the remainder stemmed from the franchisees' decisions not to renew or from mutual agreement between the franchisor and franchisee. Franchisees initiated approximately 58 percent of the terminations in 1985, compared with approximately 36 percent initiated by the franchisors; about 6 percent resulted from mutual agreement. Franchisors approved all but 3 percent of the proposed sales of franchisees by franchises to other businesspersons.[9] Taken together, these statistics indicate overall stability in the field of franchising.

International Markets

Government studies suggest that U.S. franchisors will continue to pierce international markets, despite the numerous problems inherent in complying with the local laws of other nations. Canada continues to be the most important market for U.S. franchisors. As Figure 43.2 shows, Canada in 1985 represented about one-third of all U.S. international outlets, while Japan constituted the second-largest foreign outlet, and the United Kingdom ranked third. Interestingly, Canada, Mexico, Japan, the United Kingdom, and the continental European countries are, in a similar fashion, setting up an increasing number of franchises in the United States. The international ramifications of franchising thus should become even more significant as the growth of communication and transportation systems continues to narrow the gap among consumer preferences around the world and as the advantages of franchising become more apparent to our international neighbors. This is a development that promises to be well worth watching.

SUMMARY

Franchising has become a significant method of doing business both in the United States and abroad. A franchise is an agreement in which one person pays a fee in exchange for a license to use a trademark, service mark, or logotype while engaged in distributing goods or services. The person or firm granting the franchise is called the franchisor; the person receiving the franchise is known as the franchisee. Franchises fall into two general categories: distributorships or chain-style businesses. The advantages of franchising make it an attractive method of doing business for both franchisees and franchisors.

Courts have had some problems in distinguishing franchise relationships from other types of business relationships, such as independent contracting. Yet such a distinction may be important under state and federal franchising laws, tax laws, labor laws, and antitrust laws. Some areas of the law are settled: cooperatives, concessionaires, joint ventures, general partnerships, and sales agencies generally are not deemed the legal equivalent of a franchise; a franchise is not considered a security either.

The franchisor strictly controls the franchise relationship in order to assure product uniformity and to protect the goodwill associated with its trademark or service mark. Two areas ordinarily covered in the franchise agreement — quality control and termination — pose the most legal problems. State and federal laws may cover these two aspects of the agreement, and a

[9] International Trade Administration, *Franchising*, pp. 10–13.

Figure 43.2 International Franchising, 1985

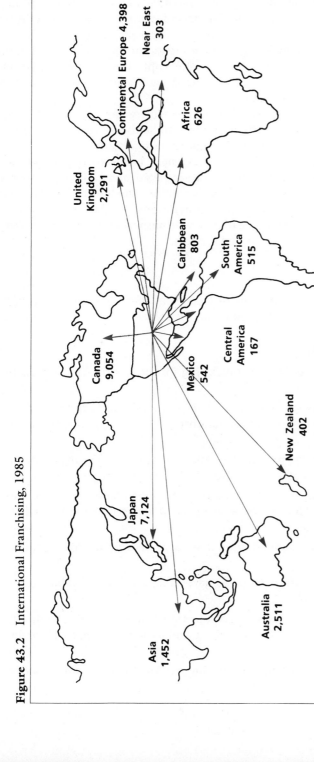

Source: International Trade Administration, U.S. Department of Commerce, *Franchising in the Economy*, *1985–1987* (Washington, D.C.: U.S. Government Printing Office, 1987), p. 7.
Number of franchising companies = 342; number of franchising outlets = 30,188.

wise franchisor should take care not to run afoul of these laws by pressing for unreasonable provisions or terms. Special industry laws at both the federal and state levels may also protect franchisees. The Federal Trade Commission's franchise disclosure regulations, antitrust laws, consumer protection statutes, and the UCC constitute further bases for controlling abusive behavior by franchisors. Franchisors have challenged such statutes on constitutional grounds, sometimes successfully.

For the last few years, the franchising industry has witnessed an increase in conversions of company-owned units to franchisee-owned ones. Although several franchisors failed in 1985, other industry statistics indicate overall stability in the franchising field—for example, leases are of a long-term nature; nonrenewals are usually franchisee-initiated; and franchisors' approvals of transfers in ownership are ordinarily routine. The international aspects of franchising should continue to gain in significance in the coming decades as more sophisticated communication and transportation systems allow for global dissemination of goods and services.

DISCUSSION QUESTIONS

1. Name eight different types of businesses that use franchising as their distributional method. Then list and describe the two main classifications of franchises.

2. Define the word *franchise.*

3. Describe four benefits of franchising for the franchisee and franchisor, respectively.

4. For what purposes does the law make distinctions between franchising and other types of business relationships, such as independent contracting?

5. Briefly explain the steps involved in setting up a franchising arrangement and describe what areas the franchising agreement normally covers.

6. Discuss why quality control and termination clauses are important to franchisors and how these same provisions nevertheless pose legal pitfalls for franchisors.

7. Enumerate the types of statutes that franchisees can use to curb the power of franchisors.

8. What four constitutional bases have franchisors used to challenge franchising statutes?

9. List some of the current trends in franchising regarding failure rates, renewal and termination decisions, and franchisors' approvals of ownership transfers.

10. Name the three most important international markets for United States franchisors.

1. The FTC in December, 1983, charged Royco Automobile Parts, Inc., of Jacksonville, Fla. (Royco), and Robert W. Sowerby, a director and president of Royco, with violating the FTC franchise rule by failing to furnish prospective franchise purchasers with specific documents. The FTC also claimed that the defendants had violated the FTC Act by representing, contrary to fact, that: a prospective franchisee could reasonably expect to gross over $164 and net over $45 per account per week; Royco franchises earned the highest rate of return in the auto parts industry, 300 percent per year; an investment in a Royco franchise was riskless because Royco agreed to reimburse the franchisee if his investment is unsuccessful; Royco provided its franchisees with experienced "locators" who in turn provided financially secure accounts, training and advice, advertising and other support, and special manufacturers' discounts; and Royco shipped initial parts inventories within three to ten days. Was the FTC correct? If so, should a court make the defendants pay $567,200 to franchisees victimized by these alleged misrepresentations and a $400,000 penalty for violating the franchise rule? (*U.S.* v. *Royco Automobile Parts, Inc.,* 49 *Antitrust & Trade Regulation Report* [BNA], 213, 25 July 1985 [M.D. Fla. 1985].)

2. A class action was instituted against Montgomery Ward Catalog Sales (Montgomery Ward) on the ground that its catalog sales agency program had stated that the business entities created under the program were franchises within the meaning of the Illinois Franchise Act. All the named class representatives operated franchises outside of Illinois; hence, Montgomery Ward argued that the provisions regarding termination and nonrenewal of the relationships were not applicable to causes of action asserted on behalf of agencies located outside of Illinois. However, the class representatives noted that the contracts with Montgomery Ward provided that the agreements would be governed by the laws of Illinois. Should a court give extraterritorial effect to the Illinois Act? (*In re Montgomery Ward Catalog Sales Litigation,* 680 F. Supp. 182 [E.D. Pa. 1987].)

3. Kolb became a Chrysler franchisee in 1969 under an agreement in which he contributed $30,000 to the creation of the dealership and Chrysler contributed $90,000. Because the dealership subsequently lost $30,000 in 1969 and $60,000 during the first six months of 1970, Chrysler bought out Kolb for a nominal consideration and sold the dealership to another person. Although the business prospered thereafter, Kolb had completely lost his investment in the project. In 1971, Kolb sued Chrysler under the state dealership law and the federal Automobile Dealers' Day in Court Act because Chrysler had failed to make an audit at the end of twelve months as required by the agreement and had instead begun an audit after ten months, in which it was determined that the business was losing money. A finding that Chrysler failed to act in good faith in terminating the

dealership would warrant Kolb's prevailing in the suit. What should the finding be? (*Kolb* v. *Chrysler Corporation*, 661 F.2d 1137 [7th Cir. 1981].)

4. In 1974, Ernst and Barbara Ann Larese entered into a ten-year franchise agreement with Creamland Dairies. The franchise agreement provided that the franchisee "shall not assign, transfer or sublet this franchise, or any of [the] rights under this agreement, without the prior written consent of [Creamland] and Baskin Robbins, any such unauthorized assignment, transfer or subletting being null and without effect." In February and August, 1979, the Lareses attempted to sell their franchise rights, but Creamland refused to consent to the sale. They subsequently charged Creamland with interfering with their contractual relations with the prospective buyers by unreasonably withholding consent to the sale. Should a court impose a "reasonableness" standard on this "consent to transfer" clause, or did the clause give Creamland an absolute, unqualified right to refuse to consent to proposed sales of the franchise rights? (*Larese* v. *Creamland Dairies, Inc.,* 767 F.2d 716 [10th Cir. 1985].)

5. Cullen sued BMW of North America, the franchisor, for damages resulting from the fraudulent conduct of its franchisee, Bavarian Auto Sales. Cullen had paid $18,000 for a new BMW but had received neither the car nor his money back. Cullen argued that BMW should be liable for the $18,000 because it had negligently created a situation that allowed its franchisee to defraud customers. Cullen alleged that BMW had allowed customers to rely on the good reputation of BMW in dealing with Bavarian Auto Sales, even though BMW knew of five prior incidents of the franchisee's failure to deliver cars that had been paid for and despite the franchisee's failure to make payments to BMW for over six months. Because BMW could have foreseen his ultimate injury at its franchisee's hands, Cullen argued that BMW was negligent and should be liable to him. Should this theory be successful? (*Cullen* v. *BMW of North America, Inc.,* 691 F.2d 1097 [2d Cir. 1982], cert. denied 460 U.S. 1070 [1983].)

6. Markim and Roseli were McDonald's franchisees for twenty years. At the end of this period, their franchises were not renewed. Markim and Roseli argued that their nonrenewals violated Nebraska's Franchise Practices Act because McDonald's had not complied with a provision in their agreement that obligated McDonald's to give them first consideration for an additional five-year period. Markim and Roseli argued that "first consideration" meant that they should be given preference over other would-be franchisees. McDonald's maintained that its top management personnel had met for over two hours to discuss these particular franchises and that they had thereby met their obligation to give the terminated franchisees "first consideration." Who was correct? (*McDonald's Corporation* v. *Markim, Inc.,* 306 N.W.2d 158 [Neb. 1981].)

7. In December, 1979, Gyp-Crete Corp. (Gyp-Crete) and McKeown Distributors, Inc. (McKeown), of Windsor, Connecticut, entered into a distributor-

ship agreement giving McKeown the nontransferable right to sell Gyp-Crete brand gypsum cement in New England and New York for ten years. John P. McKeown, Sr., was the company's sole owner and operator. Paragraph 14 of the agreement gave Gyp-Crete the right to terminate the agreement upon the transfer of a majority of the voting stock in McKeown or in the event "its ownership or control is in any way substantially changed. . . ." Paragraph 15 of the agreement barred assignment and delegation of the distributor's duties unless there was an assignment to John McKeown, Sr.'s, two sons and Gyp-Crete gave prior written consent. There were no provisions in the agreement relating to sales quotas, management training, and financial support from Gyp-Crete or to the hiring of employees. Paragraph 2(B) of McKeown's contracts with its three customers contained a clause providing that if McKeown sold the product to anyone else within the customer's assigned territory, McKeown would pay that customer 90 percent of the sales price less cost. Gyp-Crete ultimately became concerned about the quality of the product and the competence and experience of its distributors and applicators. John McKeown, Sr., who handled all technical and quality control aspects of applying Gyp-Crete flooring, died on 3 July 1981. On August 5, Gyp-Crete notified McKeown that it was terminating the agreement pursuant to paragraphs 14 and 15 and that the termination would take effect in thirty days. Gyp-Crete subsequently notified McKeown's customers that McKeown was no longer Gyp-Crete's distributor, offered to supply them and became the distributor of its product in McKeown's former territory, and charged McKeown's former customers about 20 percent less than they had been charged by McKeown. McKeown sued Gyp-Crete under the Connecticut Franchise Act, which defines a franchise in part as the operation of a business pursuant to "a marketing plan or system prescribed in substantial part by a franchisor" where such operation is "substantially associated" with the franchisor's trademark. Was McKeown a franchisee of Gyp-Crete? (*McKeown Distributors, Inc.,* v. *Gyp-Crete Corporation,* 618 F. Supp. 632 [D. Conn. 1985].)

8. Lippo operated a Mobil Oil Corp. (Mobil) service station in Schaumburg, Ill., from 1974 until 1982. The franchise was governed by a series of documents executed on 1 March 1979. Paragraph 6 of the retail dealer contract imposed a duty not to sell non-Mobil products through Mobil equipment or under Mobil signs and gave Mobil a right of immediate termination if the provisions of the paragraph were violated. Article 4A of a supplemental agreement provided that if either party defaulted in the performance of any obligation under the franchise relationship and if the default continued uncorrected for ten days after written notification of the default, then the aggrieved party could upon written notice terminate the franchise relationship. On 29 September 1980, Lippo purchased 7500 gallons of non-Mobil gasoline. This gasoline was delivered to the station at 2:00 p.m. and sold to the public through Mobil equipment and under

Mobil's signs until 4:00 p.m. on the following day. Under Mobil's direction, Lippo then covered Mobil's pumps and signs with plastic and masking tape. He continued to sell the remaining non-Mobil gasoline and sold Mobil gasoline that was delivered on October 1. On 12 November 1980, Mobil sent Lippo a notice of termination based on his sale of non-Mobil gasoline. The notice charged Lippo with violating the service station lease and the retail dealer contract. Lippo then sued Mobil, arguing that the attempted termination violated the Petroleum Marketing Practices Act (PMPA). Mobil argued that misbranding was such a serious violation of the agreement that it could not be cured and that, even if the default were cured, Mobil did not violate the PMPA. Who had the better argument? (*Lippo* v. *Mobil Oil Corporation,* 776 F.2d 706 [7th Cir. 1985].)

9. McDonald's System, Inc.'s (McDonald's), standard franchise agreement requires franchisees to purchase only "approved menu items," and the only approved sugar-sweetened cola is Coca-Cola. Although McDonald's neither sells Coca-Cola to its franchisees nor receives any rate or commission on Coca-Cola's sales to franchisees, Martino argued the restriction was nonetheless illegal because McDonald's has an economic interest in Coca-Cola syrup sales to franchisees in the form of payments of advertising allowances by Coca-Cola to be used in the promotion of McDonald's products. Until the end of 1972, the advertising allowances were paid directly to OPNAD, a national advertising fund separate from McDonald's. But since the beginning of 1973, Coca-Cola had paid the allowance directly to the franchisees, which they then used to defray OPNAD contributions or for cooperative regional advertising or individual advertising programs. Martino contended that because McDonald's controls OPNAD, the Coca-Cola requirement leads to advertising allowances that are funneled into advertising controlled by McDonald's, thus primarily benefiting McDonald's. In addition, Martino characterized the Coca-Cola requirement as a vertical restraint restricting the ability of a franchisee or a syrup seller other than Coca-Cola, or both, to compete. McDonald's showed that its purchases had no substantial effect on the rest of the cola syrup market. Was Martino correct in claiming that this contractual provision violates the antitrust laws? (*Martino* v. *McDonald's System, Inc.,* 625 F. Supp. 356 [N.D. Ill. 1985].)

10. Smothergill was licensed by Dunkin' Donuts of America, Inc. (Dunkin' Donuts), to operate two stores. Each agreement required Smothergill to keep accurate sales records, to pay a basic franchise fee of 4.9 percent of gross sales, and to pay an advertising fund fee of 2 percent of gross sales. Smothergill's right to continue in possession of those premises was expressly conditioned on his remaining as a franchisee in good standing under the related franchise agreements. In August, 1978, Dunkin' Donuts notified Smothergill it was terminating his franchise agreements owing to his intentional underreporting of gross sales. Dunkin' Donuts then

brought suit to enforce its claimed right of termination and to collect damages. The trial court found that Smothergill was "guilty of unconscionable cheating." The court concluded that Smothergill's delinquency in recordkeeping was part of a deliberate effort to underreport sales, which in turn would result in underpayment of franchise fees, advertising fund fees, rental override charges (7 percent of the amount by which gross sales exceeded $150,000 per year), and evasion of state and federal taxes. As the remedy for Smothergill's noncompliance with the franchise agreement, the contract provided that the agreement be terminated and that "the rights of the [franchisee] hereunder [should] cease." The trial court indicated that this phrase required that Smothergill lose the right to possess the stores, to operate the franchises, and to transfer them for value. The contract also provided that the breaching franchisee was obligated to pay as damages all amounts owed to Dunkin' Donuts as a result of the underreported sales, the full costs of investigating such underreporting, and reasonable attorneys' fees incurred as a result of the breach. However, the trial court fashioned its own remedy on the basis of equitable considerations to replace what it termed the "disproportionately harsh" remedies in the franchise agreement. Having determined that the combined value of Smothergill's two Dunkin' Donuts locations was at least $250,000, the court believed that the surrender of the stores by Smothergill in addition to payment of the other specified damages would result in an "inappropriate windfall" for Dunkin' Donuts. Therefore, the court provided that, although Smothergill would lose all rights to occupy and operate the stores, Dunkin' Donuts should pay him $115,000 upon his surrender of the franchises, a figure representing the full value of the franchises, less the substantial damages due to Dunkin' Donuts as a result of the franchisee's breach ($135,000). Should this decision be upheld on appeal? (*Dunkin' Donuts of America, Inc.* v. *Middletown Donut Corp.*, 495 A.2d 66 [N.J. 1985].)

Securities Regulation

FEDERAL LAWS

In Chapters 40 and 41, we briefly examined some provisions of the 1933 and 1934 Securities Acts. While it is not possible in one chapter to discuss fully the complex interplay of federal and state securities laws, we shall attempt in this chapter to understand the broad outlines of this complicated area of the regulation of business.

Securities regulation has come to be known as "federal corporate law." This label stems in large measure from the extensive federal laws and the rules set forth by the *Securities and Exchange Commission* (SEC), the federal agency charged with primary responsibility for the enforcement and administration of federal laws covering securities, public utility holding companies, trust indentures, investment companies, and investment advisers. The SEC consists of five members appointed by the president for five-year terms. To ensure impartiality, securities law requires that no more than three of the commissioners be members of the same political party. The SEC and its staff have generally enjoyed a high-quality reputation among those in the securities field.

The Securities Act of 1933 (the '33 Act) defines a *security* as "any note, stock, treasury stock, bond, debenture, evidence of indebtedness, . . . or participation in any profit-sharing agreement, . . . investment contract, . . . fractional undivided interest in oil, gas, or other mineral rights, or, in general, any interest or instrument commonly known as a 'security.'" Subsequent case decisions have made it clear that the essence of a security involves an investment in a common enterprise whereby the investor has no managerial functions but instead expects to profit solely from the efforts of others.[1] For this reason, court interpretations of what constitutes a security based upon this so-called economic reality test have been broad and far-reaching. Courts have construed investments in condominiums, citrus groves, and cattle, when others have been employed to manage such assets, as securities subject to federal securities laws.

 The '33 Act is basically a disclosure statute meant to protect the unsophisticated investing public. It ensures such protection by requiring the registration of most securities when they are initially offered and by enforcing various antifraud provisions.

The Securities Act of 1933

Procedures

Section 5 is the heart of the '33 Act. It provides that any security that is not exempt must be registered with the SEC before it can be sold through the mails or through any facility of interstate commerce, such as **securities exchanges.** The corporation issuing the security must file a *registration statement* with the SEC and provide investors and would-be investors with a *prospectus* — a document presented by a corporation or its agents announcing the issue of corporate securities, stating the nature of the securities and the financial status of the issuing firm, and asking the general public to purchase the securities covered. The registration statement contains detailed information about the plan for offering and distributing the security; the names and salaries of managers and others who control the corporation; a description of the security; and information about the issuer and its business, including detailed financial reports. The prospectus must contain similar information in summary form. The underlying purpose of both the registration statement and the prospectus is the protection of the unsophisticated investor. These documents purport to inform a prospective investor of everything he or she should know before purchasing a security. Some critics argue, however, that the SEC requires so much information that an unsophisticated investor can make little sense of the

Securities exchanges
Organized secondary markets in which investors buy and sell securities at central locations

---

[1] The Supreme Court in Gould v. Ruefenacht, 471 U.S. 701 (1985), held that where an instrument bears the label "stock" and possesses all the characteristics typically associated with stock, the instrument is a "security"; a court need not look beyond the character of the instrument to the economic substance of the transaction in such cases.

myriad details that appear in the statement and the prospectus. These commentators believe the SEC's "overregulation" has actually undercut the worthy purposes of the '33 Act.

Some activities can take place before the filing of the registration statement. For example, the *issuer* (the corporation selling the stock) itself can distribute the securities, or it can enter into preliminary negotiations with **underwriters,** who may agree to handle the stock offerings. The SEC has twenty days in which to examine the registration statement. If the registration statement is complete and accurate, it becomes effective at the end of this twenty-day waiting period. The securities can be sold at this time. During the waiting period, the issuer or underwriter can accept oral purchase orders, but the SEC limits written advertisements to "tombstone ads," so called because they are boxed in the shape of a tombstone, and preliminary "red herring" prospectuses, so dubbed because of red lettering on them to the effect that a registration statement has been filed but is not yet effective. After the registration statement becomes effective, the issuer or underwriter must provide every would-be investor with a prospectus before the sale; otherwise, the sale of the securities will not be legal. These rules reinforce the '33 Act's "truth-in-securities" policies.

Underwriters Persons or institutions that insure the sale of corporate securities by agreeing to sell securities to the public and to buy those not sold

Exemptions

The '33 Act exempts certain *classes* of securities from the registration and prospectus requirements discussed above. It is important to note, however, that there are *no* exemptions from the antifraud provisions, which we will examine in the next section. The exemptions include securities issued by federal and state governments and banks; short-term commercial paper; issues by nonprofit organizations; issues by savings and loan associations subject to state or federal regulation; issues by common carriers subject to the jurisdiction of the Interstate Commerce Commission; insurance policies and certain annuities subject to regulation by state and federal authorities; and intrastate issues of securities.

In addition, the '33 Act exempts certain *transactions:* private offerings (those that do not involve public offerings of securities, as is the usual case); and transactions by persons other than issuers, underwriters, or dealers; certain brokers' and dealers' transactions; and small public issues. The SEC has established prerequisites and complex rules that must be followed in order to secure exemption from the registration process for these and certain other transactions. For instance, in one famous case, Ralston Purina Co. had sold nearly $2 million of stock to its "key employees" without registration. The "key employees" who had purchased the stock had included shop and dock foremen, stenographers, copywriters, clerical assistants, and veterinarians. Ralston Purina had maintained these were "private offering" transactions because the offer had not been made to all its employees and hence had not been a public offering subject to registration under the '33 Act. Asserting that the aim of the '33 Act is to protect investors by promoting full disclosure of information thought necessary for informed investment decisions, the Supreme Court concluded that Ralston Purina had not shown that the employees involved here had access to the kind of information that registration would disclose. Thus, the Court held that this attempted private offering (or "private placement") was not a bona fide exempt transaction and that registration should have occurred.[2]

Antifraud Provisions

In addition to registration requirements, the '33 Act contains several antifraud provisions. Section 12 prohibits oral or written misstatements of material facts or omissions of material facts necessary to keep the statements from being misleading in the circumstances in which they were made. Section 17 is a general antifraud provision that makes it unlawful for any person to use the mails or interstate commerce to employ any device or scheme that will defraud another person or to engage in any transaction, practice, or course of business that defrauds or deceives the purchaser. Basically, then, Section 17 makes illegal any form of fraud, untrue statement of a material fact, or omission of a material fact involving the sale of any securities in interstate commerce or through the mail. Because of the complexities inherent in the issuance of securities, anyone who contemplates issuing securities should seek the counsel of professionals who specialize in the securities field.

Liabilities and Remedies

The potential liabilities spawned by the '33 Act also pose a significant reason for seeking competent advice. Section 11 imposes civil liability for any registration statement that contains untrue statements of a material fact or omissions of material facts that would make the registration statement misleading in the circumstances in which a purchaser buys the securities. Such a purchaser can receive as damages an amount not exceeding the price paid for the securities. Section 11 places liability on every person who signed the registration statement; on every person who was a director or was named in the registration statement as about to become a director; on every accountant, engineer, appraiser, or any other professional expert whose statement or report appears in the registration statement; and on every underwriter. All such persons, except the issuer, may escape liability by showing that they acted with "due diligence." This statutory defense of "due diligence" varies as to the type of defendant involved and whether the misrepresentations or omissions are found in the "expertised" or "nonexpertised" portions of the registration statement. The defense generally is available to anyone who, after reasonable investigation, had reasonable grounds to believe, and did believe, that the registration statement was accurate and did not omit material facts that were either required or necessary to make the statement not misleading. Additionally, Section 12 exacts civil liability from any person who sells securities through the mails or in interstate commerce by means of a prospectus or

---

[2] Securities and Exchange Commission v. Ralston Purina Co., 346 U.S. 119 (1953).

oral communication that includes misrepresentations or omissions of necessary material facts. Such persons can avoid liability if they can show that they did not know, and in the exercise of reasonable care could not have known, about the untruths or omissions. The injured party can sue only the person who actually sold the security but can recover the price paid for the security. Section 17's antifraud provisions may be used as a basis for criminal liability. Moreover, Section 24 sets up criminal sanctions for willful violations of the '33 Act.

The case that follows illustrates many of the principles that we have just discussed.

Escott v. BarChris Construction Corporation
283 F. Supp. 643 (S.D. N.Y. 1968)

FACTS The purchasers of certain securities of BarChris sued under Section 11 of the '33 Act, alleging that the registration statement filed with the SEC about these stocks contained materially false statements and material omissions. The defendants included the persons who had signed the registration statement (primarily directors and officers), the underwriters (investment bankers), and Peat, Marwick, Mitchell & Co. (BarChris's auditors).

ISSUES Had the registration statement included materially false statements and material omissions? If so, had the defendants successfully shown the statutory defense — that is, that they had acted with due diligence?

HOLDINGS Yes. The registration statement had included materially false statements and material omissions; furthermore, only the outside directors had been able to sustain even a part of their "due diligence" defense (and they could show due diligence only with respect to the "expertised" portion of the registration statement).

REASONING The registration statement had contained materially false statements and material omissions. A material fact is a fact that, had it been correctly stated or disclosed, would have deterred the average prudent investor from purchasing the securities in question. Therefore, BarChris's overstatement of its sales and gross profits and its understatement of its liabilities in 1961 had satisfied this definition. But the prospectus statements about BarChris's status in December 1960 had been rather minor errors and hence nonmaterial. However, the prospectus's 1961 balance sheet had contained material errors. Nonetheless, the "due diligence" statutory defense was available to all the defendants except the issuer, BarChris. However, none of the inside directors and officers had sustained the due diligence defense with respect either to the "expertised" (that is, the financial reports prepared by accountants) or "unexpertised" portions of the registration statement. The outside directors similarly had not sustained their due diligence defense with regard to the unexpertised part of the registration statement, primarily because they had neither familiarized themselves with its contents nor questioned its major points. On the other hand, the outside directors had shown due diligence regarding the "expertised" portion of the statement because of their confidence in the auditors, Peat, Marwick, Mitchell & Co. Like the inside directors and officers, the underwriters and the auditors had failed to establish the due diligence defense with respect to either portion of the registration statement.

While the 1933 Act deals with the initial issuance of securities, the Securities Exchange Act of 1934 (the '34 Act) regulates the secondary distribution of securities. As such, the '34 Act's jurisdiction extends to the registration and distribution of securities through national stock exchanges, national securities associations, brokers, and dealers. The '34 Act also supervises proxy solicitations of registered securities, regulates tender offers, limits insider trading, forbids short-swing profits, and in general tries to eliminate fraud and manipulative conduct with respect to the sale or purchase of securities. Thus, in many ways the '33 and '34 Acts are similar and supplement each other. But the reach of the '34 Act, with its supervision of national exchanges and over-the-counter sales of securities, is even broader than that of the '33 Act.

The Securities Exchange Act of 1934

Registration and Reporting

The '34 Act requires any issuer who trades securities on a national stock exchange to register with the SEC. In addition, any firm engaged in interstate commerce with total assets of over $5 million and at least 500 shareholders must comply with Section 12's registration provisions. For violations of Section 12, the SEC can revoke or suspend the registration of the security involved.

Like the '33 Act, the '34 Act tries to ensure that the investing public will have sufficient information about publicly traded securities when these investors make their decisions about whether to buy stocks. Hence, the '34 Act mandates certain disclosures by firms covered by the Act when the securities are listed with national exchanges or traded over the counter. Basically, these obligatory disclosures include detailed registration statements similar to the information required under the '33 Act as well as annual and quarterly reports. SEC Forms 8–A, 8–K, 10–K, and 10–Q, which companies use for compiling this information, are complex and contain substantial amounts of facts and figures relating to the companies' businesses. (Some companies may utilize EDGAR, the SEC's electronic data-gathering system, which it has employed experimentally for certain filings.) Other SEC provisions impose liability on the company for damages resulting from an investor's reliance on misleading statements contained in any such documents.

Proxy Solicitations

As discussed in Chapter 40, a proxy is an assignment by the shareholder of the right to vote the shares held by the shareholder. Since proxies become a device for consolidating corporate power and control, one cannot underestimate their importance both to management and to those who wish to oust the present management ("dissident" shareholders). Because of the high stakes involved for both competing factions, it is vitally important that the information provided to shareholders be accurate. If shareholders receive misleading information, they will make their decision regarding who should be given their proxies — management or dissidents — in ignorance of the true facts. To prevent such abuses, Section 14 of the '34 Act makes it illegal for a company registered under Section 12 to solicit proxies in a manner that would violate the SEC rules and regulations that protect the investing public. Section 14 also sets out rules mandating disclosure of pertinent information to shareholders at corporate meetings even when there will be no solicitation of proxies.

The disclosure required of proxy solicitations includes a proxy statement, which contains detailed information, and a proxy form, on which the shareholder can note his or her approval or disapproval of each proposal that will be voted on at the corporation's meeting. Before the corporation (or dissidents) sends proxies to shareholders, the SEC must approve the statement and the form. These preliminary proxies must be filed with the SEC at least ten days before they are sent to shareholders. If the meeting involves the election of directors, any proxy statement must also include an annual report detailing, among other things, the financial aspects of the company. Similarly, as mentioned earlier, any proxy contest requires full disclosure of all pertinent facts regarding the matters under consideration, such as the identity of all participants in the proxy contest and the reasons for the proxy solicitation.

Section 14 also authorizes the inclusion of shareholder proposals of no more than 500 words in any management-backed proxy solicitation. This SEC rule allows a shareholder to express an opinion regarding the recommendations management has made without incurring the significant costs involved in an independent proxy solicitation. This aspect of Section 14 thus attempts to preserve the balance of power between management and insurgents in order to safeguard the democratic aspects of the corporation. As you would expect, management usually opposes the inclusion of such proposals. SEC rules authorize exclusion of proposals that are not "proper subjects" for action by shareholders; proposals that center on personal claims or grievances; proposals that are not significantly related to the corporation's business or are beyond the corporation's power to bring about (that is, proposals that primarily promote economic, political, racial, religious, or social causes); and proposals that are substantially similar to a proposal submitted but not approved within the past five years. In disputes as to whether the corporation can exclude the proposal, the SEC normally decides who is correct. Management bears the burden of proof regarding why the proposal was properly excluded. Shareholder proposals have dealt with management compensation, company policies allegedly leading to discrimination or pollution, and even opposition to the Vietnam War. Shareholder proposals usually are unsuccessful.

The corporation ordinarily pays for the expenses incurred in proxy contests if either management or the insurgents win. The law is unsettled as to whether the corporation should pay the costs of a contest if management loses, but the trend is to make the corporation (not the managers themselves) pay even in those circumstances.

Liability for misleading proxy statements or those that omit a material fact necessary to make the statement true and not misleading is absolute. Any person who sells or buys securities in reliance on such statements can recover from the corporation.

Tender Offers

In addition to regulating proxies, since 1968, the Williams Act, codified in Sections 13 and 14, has also regulated *tender offers* or *takeover bids,* whether hostile or friendly, wherein *one publicly held corporation (the "tender offeror") attempts to acquire control of another publicly held company* (the "target"). Section 14, in conjunction with Section 13, sets forth filing and registration requirements for any person who becomes the owner of more than 5 percent of any class of securities registered under Section 12. In general, these provisions force the offeror to provide the target company's shareholders with the names of the offerors and their interests, the purpose of the takeover, the method of disposing of the target firm's stocks and assets, and so forth. Additionally, any statements the management of the target firm makes in opposition to the merger must also be filed with the SEC. Provisions for liability under this aspect of the '34 Act are similar to those instituted for violations of the proxy rules.

The Supreme Court recently answered the numerous questions that had arisen about the constitutionality of state regulation of tender offers or takeovers in a case involving Indiana's statute.

CTS Corporation v. *Dynamics Corporation of America*
107 S.Ct. 1637 (1987)

FACTS

The federal Williams Act and implementing regulations govern hostile corporate stock tender offers by requiring, among other things, that offers remain open for at least twenty business days. The Indiana Act concerning Control Share Acquisitions applies to certain business corporations chartered in Indiana that have specified levels of shares or shareholders within the state and that opt into the Act's protection. The Indiana Act provides that the acquisition of "control shares" in such a corporation — shares that, but for the Act, would bring the acquiring entity's voting power to or above certain threshold levels — does not include voting rights unless a majority of all preexisting disinterested shareholders so agree at their next regularly scheduled meeting. However, the stock acquiror can require a special meeting within fifty days by following specified procedures. Dynamics Corporation announced a tender offer that would have raised its ownership interest in CTS Corporation above the Indiana Act's threshold. At the same time, Dynamics also filed suit in federal court alleging federal securities violations by CTS. After CTS opted into the Indiana Act, Dynamics amended its complaint to challenge the Act's validity under the federal Williams Act and the Commerce Clause.

ISSUE

Was the Indiana takeover statute invalid owing to its **preemption** by the Williams Act or its unconstitutionality under the Commerce Clause?

HOLDING

No. The Indiana Act is consistent with the provisions and purposes of the Williams Act and is not preempted thereby. Furthermore, the Act does not violate the Commerce Clause.

REASONING

Preemption Doctrine providing that as to certain matters, federal law takes precedence over state laws

The Indiana Act is consistent with the provisions and purposes of the Williams Act and is not preempted by this federal law. Because the Indiana Act protects independent shareholders from the coercive aspects of tender offers by allowing them to vote as a group, it furthers the Williams Act's basic purpose of placing investors on an equal footing with takeover bidders. Moreover, the Indiana Act avoids the problems that had led to a finding of preemption for other state takeover statutes, since it neither gives management or the offeror an advantage in communicating with shareholders nor imposes an indefinite delay on offers. Moreover, the possibility that the Indiana Act will delay some tender offers does not mandate preemption. The state Act neither imposes an absolute fifty-day delay on the consummation of tender offers nor precludes offerors from purchasing shares as soon as federal law permits. Hence, it does not conflict with the shorter, twenty-day period established by federal law. If a tender offeror fears an adverse shareholder vote, it can condition the tender offer on the shares receiving voting rights within a specified period and thus avoid the fifty-day period. Furthermore, even assuming that the Indiana Act does impose some additional delay, only "unreasonable" delays conflict with the Williams Act. Here, it cannot be said that a fifty-day delay was unreasonable, since that period fell within the sixty-day maximum period Congress had established for tender offers. If the Williams Act were construed to preempt any state statute that causes delays, it would preempt a variety of state corporate laws of hitherto unquestioned validity. The longstanding prevalence of state regulation in this area suggests that, if Congress had intended to preempt all such state laws, it would have said so.

The Indiana Act likewise does not violate the Commerce Clause. The Act's limited effect on interstate commerce is justified by the state's interests in defining attributes of its corporations' shares and in protecting shareholders. Moreover, the Act does not discriminate against interstate commerce, as it has the same effect on tender offers whether or not the offeror is an Indiana resident. That the Act may apply most often to out-of-state entities who launch most hostile tender offers is irrelevant, since a claim of discrimination is not established by the mere fact that the burden of a state regulation falls on some interstate companies. Furthermore, the Act does not create an impermissible risk of inconsistent regulation of tender offers by different states. It simply and evenhandedly exercises the state's firmly established authority to define the voting rights of shareholders in Indiana corporations and thus subjects such corporations to the law of only one state.

The court of appeals' holding that the Act unconstitutionally hinders tender offers ignores the fact that a state, in its role as overseer of corporate governance, enacts laws that necessarily affect certain aspects of interstate commerce, particularly with respect to corporations with shareholders in other states. A state has interests in promoting stable relationships among parties involved in its corporations and in ensuring that investors have an effective voice in corporate affairs. The Indiana Act validly furthers these interests by allowing shareholders collectively to determine whether the takeover is advantageous to them. The argument that Indiana has no legitimate interest in protecting nonresident shareholders is unavailing, since the Act applies only to corporations incorporated in Indiana that have a substantial number of shareholders in the state. Even if the Act should decrease the number of successful tender offers for Indiana corporations, this would not offend the Commerce Clause. The Act does not prohibit any resident or nonresident from offering to purchase, or from purchasing shares in Indiana corporations, or from attempting thereby to gain control. Rather, it merely provides regulatory procedures designed for the better protection of the corporations' shareholders.

Thus, the Indiana Control Share Acquisitions provisions of the Act evenhandedly determine the voting rights of shares of Indiana corporations. As such, the Act does not conflict with the provisions or purposes of the Williams Act. To the limited extent that the Act affects interstate commerce, this is justified by the state's interests in defining the attributes of shares in its corporations and in protecting shareholders. Congress has never questioned the need for state regulation of these matters; nor does such regulation offend the Constitution.

Insider Trading

As mentioned in Chapter 41, directors, officers, and controlling shareholders may violate the federal securities laws if they engage in "insider trading." We noted then that the '34 Act makes such activities illegal and sets out possibilities of far-ranging liability. Section 10b of the '34 Act makes unlawful any manipulative or deceptive device used through the mails or in interstate commerce in connection with the purchase or sale of any security. SEC Rule 10b–5 augments Section 10b by providing for liability for any fraudulent or deceitful activity that involves misleading material facts or omissions of material facts that would make a statement misleading in the circumstances in which it was made.

When material inside information is involved, the insider must *either* publicly disclose the information to ensure that the investing public that does not have access to the information will not be prejudiced *or* abstain from trading in the securities. But it is nevertheless difficult to judge when information is important enough to be considered "material." The *Basic Incorporated* case, which follows, provides some guidelines in this important area.

Basic Incorporated v. Levinson
108 S.Ct. 978 (1988)

FACTS Basic Incorporated (Basic) was a public-issue corporation that provided materials for the manufacture of steel. In 1976, Basic held meetings with representatives of Combustion Engineering Co. (Combustion) regarding the possibility of a merger. During 1977 and 1978, Basic made three public statements denying that it was engaged in merger negotiations. Yet, on 18 December 1978, Basic asked the New York Stock Exchange to suspend trading in its shares and issued a release stating that it had been "approached" by another company concerning a merger. On December 19, Basic's board endorsed Combustion's offer of $46 per share for its common stock and on the following day publicly announced the company's approval of Combustion's tender offer for all the outstanding shares of Basic. Levinson and other Basic shareholders who had sold their stock after Basic's final public statement on 21 October 1977, and before the suspension of trading in December, 1978, sued Basic and its board of directors for violations of Section 10b of the 1934 Act and Rule 10b–5 allegedly stemming from Basic's denials of the merger negotiations prior to the official announcement.

ISSUE Did Basic's denials about the preliminary merger negotiations constitute material misrepresentations under Section 10b and Rule 10b–5?

HOLDING Yes. Information concerning the existence and the status of preliminary merger discussions would be significant to a reasonable investor's trading decision. Consequently, Basic's inaccurate and incomplete statements were material and thus violative of Section 10b and Rule 10b–5.

REASONING As the *SEC* v. *Texas Gulf Sulphur* case had shown, the materiality requirement of Rule 10b–5 with respect to contingent or speculative information or events depends on the facts. Whether merger discussions in a particular case are material therefore are similarly fact-specific. Generally, in order to assess the probability that the event will occur, a fact finder will need to look to indicia of interest in the transaction at the highest corporate levels. Board resolutions, instructions to investment bankers, and actual negotiations between principals or their intermediaries may serve as indicia of such interest. To assess the magnitude of the transaction to the issuer of the securities allegedly manipulated, a fact finder will need to consider such facts as the size of the two corporate entities and the stocks' potential premium over market value. No particular event or factor short of closing the transaction need be either necessary or sufficient by itself to render merger discussions material. Rather, materiality depends on the significance the reasonable investor would place on the withheld or misrepresented information. If, as noted in the *TSC Industries, Inc.* v. *Northway, Inc.*, case, there is a substantial likelihood that the disclosure of the omitted fact would have been viewed as significant by a reasonable investor, the information is material. Hence, there is no valid justification for artificially excluding from the definition of materiality information concerning merger discussions, which would otherwise be considered significant to the trading decision of a reasonable investor, merely because agreement-in-principle as to the price and structure had not yet been reached by the parties or their representatives. The courts above had accepted a presumption, created by the fraud-on-the-market theory and subject to rebuttal by Basic, that persons who had traded Basic shares had done so in reliance on the integrity of the price set by the market, but that because of Basic's material misrepresentations that price had been fraudulently depressed. Requiring plaintiffs to show a speculative state of facts — that is, how they would have acted if omitted material information had been disclosed, or if the misrepresentations had not been made — would place an unnecessarily unrealistic evidentiary burden on the Rule 10b–5 plaintiff who had traded on an impersonal market. Because most publicly available information is reflected in market price, an investor's reliance on any public material misrepresentations, therefore, may be presumed for purposes of a Rule 10b–5 action. Nevertheless, any showing that severs the link between the alleged misrepresentation and either the price received (or paid) by plaintiffs, or their decision to trade at a fair market price, will be sufficient to rebut the presumption of reliance. In summary, the standard of materiality set forth in *TSC Industries, Inc.* v. *Northway* will govern future Section 10b and Rule 10b–5 cases. Thus, materiality in the merger context depends on the probability that the transaction will be consummated and its significance to the issuer of the securities. Materiality therefore depends on the facts and must be determined on a case-by-case basis. Courts may apply a presumption of reliance supported by the fraud-on-the-market theory; that presumption, however, is rebuttable.

Although Section 10b does not expressly provide for civil liability, it, as a broad antifraud provision, applies to any manipulative or deceptive device used in connection with any purchase or sale of any security by any person; there are no exemptions from coverage. Similarly, Rule 10b–5 has been applied to the activities of corporate *insiders* — directors, officers, controlling shareholders, employees, lawyers, accountants, bankers, consultants, and anyone else who has access to material inside information that may affect the price of the stock. Before the *Chiarella* case, which follows, persons considered insiders included even those who purchased or sold stock based on tips provided directly or indirectly by directors, officers, and the like. Hence, the SEC would have considered a barber who buys stock on the basis of market information learned from overhearing a director's discussing with its spouse an upcoming business trip as an insider, as well. The *Chiarella* case has cast some doubt on whether such remote "tippees" will be liable in the future. The SEC nevertheless is continuing to prosecute such people as the barber for securities violations unless they either "disclose" or "abstain."

Chiarella v. *United States*
445 U.S. 222 (1980)

Chiarella was a printer who worked for a firm that printed takeover bids. Although   **FACTS**
the identities of the firms had been left blank, Chiarella was able to deduce the

names of the target companies from other information contained in the documents he was preparing for printing. Without disclosing his knowledge, Chiarella purchased stock in the target companies and sold the stock when the takeover attempts became public knowledge. Chiarella thereby gained $30,000 in fourteen months. The SEC indicted him on seventeen counts of violating Section 10b and Rule 10b–5 of the '34 Act.

ISSUE   Were Section 10b and Rule 10b–5 applicable to Chiarella, who had been neither an insider nor a "tippee" recipient of confidential information from the target company?

HOLDING   No. Section 10b and Rule 10b–5 were not applicable to Chiarella because he was not a corporate insider; rather, he was a complete stranger who had dealt with the sellers only through impersonal market transactions.

REASONING   The fraudulent conduct prohibited by Section 10b and Rule 10b–5 had not occurred here. Although past administrative and judicial interpretations had established that silence in connection with the purchase or sale of securities might operate as a fraud actionable under Section 10b, the element required to make silence fraudulent — a duty to disclose — was absent in this case. Chiarella had been a complete stranger to the sellers of the target company's securities and thus was not in a fiduciary relationship with them. Hence, affirming Chiarella's conviction would recognize a general duty between all participants in market transactions to forgo actions based on material, nonpublic information. The imposition of such a broad duty, departing as it would from the established doctrine that duty arises from a specific relationship between two parties, would be ill-advised.

The Supreme Court's decision in *Dirks* v. *Securities and Exchange Commission* appears to reinforce *Chiarella* by emphasizing the basic principle that only *some* persons, under *some* circumstances, will be barred from trading while in possession of material nonpublic information.

Dirks v. *Securities and Exchange Commission*
463 U.S. 646 (1983)

FACTS   In 1973, Raymond Dirks was an officer of a New York broker-dealer firm that specialized in providing investment analysis of insurance company securities to institutional investors. On March 6 Ronald Secrist, a former officer of Equity Funding of America, told Dirks that the assets of Equity Funding, a diversified corporation primarily engaged in selling life insurance and mutual funds, had been vastly overstated as the result of fraudulent corporate practices. Stressing that various regulatory agencies had failed to act on similar charges made by Equity Funding employees, Secrist urged Dirks to verify the fraud and disclose it publicly. Dirks then visited Equity Funding's headquarters in Los Angeles and interviewed officers and employees of Equity Funding. Although neither Dirks nor his firm owned or traded any Equity Funding stock, some of Equity Funding's clients and investors sold their holdings in Equity Funding as a result of information that Dirks had shared with them during his investigation. Dirks also urged *The Wall Street Journal* to write a story about the fraud allegations.

Eventually, the California insurance authorities uncovered evidence of the fraud, after which the SEC filed a complaint against Equity Funding. The SEC also investigated Dirks's involvement, finding that he repeated confidential corporate information in violation of securities rules. However, since he had played an important role in bringing Equity Funding's massive fraud to light, the SEC merely **censured** him.

Censured Formally reprimanded for specific conduct

Did the disclosure of material nonpublic information received from insiders of a corporation with whom Dirks had no connection to investors who had relied on the information in trading in the shares of the corporation violate the '33 and '34 Acts?

ISSUE

No. Dirks, as a tippee of inside material nonpublic information, in these circumstances had had no duty to abstain from use of the inside information where the tippers had been motivated by a desire to expose fraud rather than from a desire either to receive personal benefits or to bestow valuable information on him so that he could derive monetary benefits from what they had told him. Thus, Dirks's conduct had not violated the antifraud provisions of the '33 and '34 Acts.

HOLDING

Chiarella had held that a duty to disclose under Section 10b would not arise from the mere possession of nonpublic market information but rather from a relationship between the parties. Therefore, in determining whether a tippee had been under an obligation to disclose or abstain, it was necessary to ascertain whether the insider's "tip" had constituted a breach of the insider's fiduciary duty. In the absence of a personal gain to the insider, there would be no breach of duty to the stockholders. Similarly, in the absence of such a breach by the insider, there could be no derivative breach by someone like Dirks. Thus, tippees in Dirks's position had inherited no duty to disclose or abstain until a breach of the insider's fiduciary duty had occurred. The appellate court's affirmance of Dirks's censure by the SEC was therefore in error.

REASONING

The *Chiarella* and *Dirks* cases therefore appear to limit significantly the concept of who an "insider" is for Section 10b purposes. According to *Chiarella*, "outsiders" — those who are not in positions of trust or confidence within the companies involved in the litigation — are under no duties to abstain from trading on nonpublic material information, unless they are actual "tippees" of "insiders." Reinforcing *Chiarella*, *Dirks* holds that "tippees" of "insiders" who have divulged material inside information out of motives other than personal gain may avoid liability, as well. Because the "tippees'" potential liability derives from the "insiders'" fiduciary duties to the corporation, the absence of any breach of those duties by the "insiders" leads to a finding of no breach on the "tippees'" part either.

The SEC, however, is continuing to prosecute "outsiders" and their "tippees" on the theory that "outsiders'" misappropriation of nonpublic material information works a fraud on the securities market or constitutes fraud as to the employers of the persons being sued. As such, the SEC reasons, this fraudulent conduct violates the securities laws' insider trading prohibitions. The SEC's aggressive posture in this context is particularly noteworthy, given the absence of authoritative Supreme Court rulings or legislation regarding the legal validity of this theory (although Congress has considered legislation to amend the securities laws to reflect the SEC's position). The doctrinal development of these insider trading precedents and the resultant interplay among the Supreme Court, Congress, and the SEC regarding this area of the law underscore both the important public policy aspects of the law's treatment of insider trading and the significant interrelationships of the various components of our legal system that are empowered to address this issue.

The following case, which owes a large debt analytically to both *Chiarella* and *Dirks,* employs the common law doctrine of *in pari delicto,* a concept we discussed in Chapter 12, in the context of insider trading. It also shows that, *Chiarella* and *Dirks* notwithstanding, "tippees" of corporate insiders who have provided tips containing false and incomplete information may sue these insiders for their losses.

Bateman Eichler, Hill Richards, Inc. v. *Berner*
472 U.S. 299 (1985)

FACTS Berner and other investors sued Bateman Eichler, Hill Richards, Inc. (Bateman Eichler), for trading losses resulting from an alleged conspiracy between Lazzaro, a broker employed by Bateman Eichler, and Neadeau, the president of T.O.N.M. Oil & Gas Exploration Corporation (T.O.N.M.). Berner contended that Lazzaro and Neadeau had divulged false and incomplete information on the pretext that it was accurate inside information about a gold strike that T.O.N.M. would soon announce. Berner and the others, relying on this information, had bought T.O.N.M. stock, which had decreased substantially below the purchase price when the mining venture had fallen through. The district court dismissed Berner's suit and absolutely barred him and the others from any recovery because they had been *in pari delicto* with Lazzaro and Neadeau. However, the court of appeals refused to allow the *in pari delicto* doctrine to be used as a defense to shield the violators from the reach of the securities laws' sanctions.

ISSUE Did the common law *in pari delicto* defense bar a private damages action under the federal securities laws against corporate insiders and broker-dealers who had fraudulently induced investors to purchase securities by misrepresenting that they had been conveying material nonpublic information about the issuer?

HOLDING No. A private action for damages on the grounds of Berner's own culpability would be barred only where, as a direct result of his own actions, Berner bore at least substantially equal responsibility for the violations he had sought to redress and where preclusion of the suit would not significantly interfere with the effective enforcement of the securities laws and the protection of the investing public.

The common law defense at issue in this case derives from the Latin, *in pari delicto potior est conditio defendentis:* "In a case of equal or mutual fault . . . the position of the [defending] party . . . is the better one." This defense is grounded on two premises: first, that courts should not lend their good offices to mediating disputes among wrongdoers; and, second, that denying judicial relief to an admitted wrongdoer is an effective means of deterring illegality. Traditionally, the *in pari delicto* defense was narrowly limited to situations where the plaintiff truly bore at least substantially equal responsibility for his injury, because in such cases it did not always follow that the wrongdoers stood *in pari delicto,* for there might be, and often were, very different degrees of guilt. Notwithstanding these traditional limitations, many judges had given the *in pari delicto* defense a broad application to bar actions where plaintiffs simply had been involved generally in the same sort of wrongdoing as defendants. Using this latter rationale, Bateman Eichler had argued both that Berner was an ordinary tippee who had acted voluntarily in choosing to trade on inside information and that Section 10b and Rule 10b – 5 would apply to any violations without recognizing gradations of culpability in support of its contention that Berner's fault had been equal to that of Lazzaro and Neadeau. However, such precedents as *Chiarella* and *Dirks* mandate the rejection of this contention in the context of insider trading cases because a person whose liability is solely derivative cannot be said to be as culpable as one whose breach of duty gave rise to that liability in the first place. Moreover, insiders and broker-dealers who selectively disclose material nonpublic information commit a potentially broader range of violations than do tippees who trade on the basis of that information. Although a tippee trading on insider information will be, in many circumstances, guilty of fraud against individual shareholders, the insider in disclosing such information is not only guilty of fraud, but also frequently violates fiduciary duties toward the issuer itself. And in cases in which the tipper intentionally conveys false or materially incomplete information to the tippee, the tipper commits an additional violation: fraud against the tippee. Such conduct is particularly egregious when committed by a securities professional, who owes a duty of loyalty and fair dealing to his client. In the absence of other culpable actions by a tippee that can fairly be said to outweigh these violations by such insiders and broker-dealers, the tippee properly cannot be characterized as being of substantially equal culpability as his tippers. Nothing in the facts of this case shows anything to the contrary either. Finally, denying the *in pari delicto* defense in such circumstances will best promote the primary objective of the federal securities laws — protection of the investing public and the national economy through the promotion of a high standard of business ethics in every facet of the securities industry; the *in pari delicto* defense, by denying any incentive to a defrauded tippee to bring suit against his defrauding tipper, will significantly undermine this important goal. The deterrence of insider trading most frequently will be maximized by bringing enforcement pressures to bear on the sources of such information — corporate insiders and broker-dealers. Allowing tippees to sue broker-dealers without making the *in pari delicto* defense available to the latter will "nip in the bud" the first step in the chain of dissemination of material inside information. For these reasons, the public interest will most frequently be advanced if defrauded tippees

REASONING

are permitted to bring suit and to expose illegal practices by corporate insiders and broker-dealers to full public view for appropriate sanctions.

Short-Swing Profits

Section 16b is also aimed at gains by corporate insiders. This provision of the '34 Act requires everyone who is directly or indirectly the owner of more than 10 percent of any security registered under Section 12 or who is a director or officer in a so-called Section 12 corporation to make periodic filings with the SEC. In these SEC filings, they must disclose the number of shares owned and any changes in the amount of shares held. This section, designed to prevent unfair use of information obtained by virtue of an inside position in the corporation, forces insiders to disgorge or return to the corporation any profits they realize from the purchase or sale of any security that takes place in any time period of less than six months — that is, *short-swing profits*. Section 16b does not apply to any transaction in which the owner was not an owner at both the time of purchasing and the time of selling; on the other hand, directors and officers face liability if they held their positions at the time either of sale or of purchase. Interestingly, though, Section 16b covers transactions that fit the enumerated criteria even when the transactions were not actually based on inside information. It is, then, in essence a preventive section. Thus, if Director Wallis sells stock in Continuing Corp. for $5000 and five months later buys an equal number of shares for $3000, Wallis will have to pay to the corporation the $2000 in profits so realized.

Liabilities and Remedies

The '34 Act creates a private right of action for those who have dealt in securities on the basis of misleading registration statements (liability pursuant to Sections 12 and 18), tender offers (Section 13), and proxy solicitations (Section 14). Under Section 16b, the corporation or a shareholder suing in a derivative action for the benefit of the corporation may recover short-swing profits realized by officers, directors, and shareholders controlling at least 10 percent of the securities involved. Private actions under Section 10b and Rule 10b – 5, the catchall antifraud provision, may be brought by any purchasers or sellers of any securities against any person who has engaged in fraudulent conduct, including a corporation that has bought or sold its own shares. The early Section 10b cases, such as the *Texas Gulf Sulphur* case cited in the *Basic* decision, had expansively imposed liability under Section 10b and Rule 10b – 5. However, the Supreme Court, in *Ernst & Ernst* v. *Hochfelder*, has limited the reach of Section 10b by requiring a private person to prove that the securities law violator intended to deceive, manipulate, or defraud the injured party.[3] After *Hochfelder*, proof of negligent conduct alone will not constitute a violation of Section 10b. Similarly, the holding in the case that follows, *Santa*

---

[3] 425 U.S. 185 (1976); reh'g. denied, 425 U.S. 986 (1976).

Fe Industries, Inc. v. *Green,* which refused to extend Section 10b's prohibition against manipulative and deceptive conduct to management's alleged violations of fiduciary duties, signals somewhat of a retreat from the Court's prior, ever-expanding view of possible liability under Section 10b.

Yet the Court's recent opinion that apparently allows securities cases to be brought under the Racketeer Influenced and Corrupt Organizations Act (RICO)[4] and the SEC's ability to penalize inside traders up to three times the amount of the profit gained or the loss avoided as a result of the unlawful purchase or sale suggest the availability of potent remedies to discourage securities laws violations. To illustrate, some commentators argue that Drexel, Burnham, Lambert Inc.'s recent decision to plead guilty to six criminal counts and to pay a record-breaking $650 million in fines and restitutions for securities violations stemmed from its desire to avoid further indictments under RICO.

Santa Fe Industries, Inc. v. Green
430 U.S. 462 (1977)

FACTS

Green and other minority stockholders of Kirby Lumber Corp. argued that Santa Fe's "short-form merger" with Kirby had involved a fraudulent appraisal of the fair market value of Kirby's stock. Green asserted that the purpose of this fraudulent appraisal had been to freeze out the minority stockholders in violation of Section 10b and Rule 10b–5 of the Securities Exchange Act of 1934, whose provisions, respectively, make it "unlawful for any person . . . [t]o use or employ . . . any manipulative or deceptive device or contrivance in contravention of [SEC rules]" or to use any "artifice to defraud" or to act in a way "which operates or would operate as a fraud or deceit."

ISSUE

Would the term *fraud* in Section 10b and Rule 10b–5 of the 1934 Act encompass a breach of fiduciary duty in connection with a securities transaction?

HOLDING

No. Section 10b or Rule 10b–5 reaches only conduct involving manipulation or deception; so a breach of fiduciary duty by majority stockholders, without any deception, misrepresentation, or nondisclosure, would not violate the statute or the rule.

REASONING

The recent *Ernst & Ernst* v. *Hochfelder* case had made clear that the term *fraud* in Rule 10b–5 refers to manipulative or deceptive conduct. Thus, Green's attempt to bring within the reach of the rule all breaches of fiduciary duty in connection with a securities transaction would result in an impermissible interpretation of the securities laws. Such a breach of fiduciary duty would fall under the '34 Act's coverage only if the conduct were manipulative or deceptive. In contrast, any such breach of fiduciary duty by majority shareholders without deception, misrepresentation, or

[4] Sedima S.P.R.L. v. Imrex Co., Inc., 105 S.Ct. 3275 (1985).

nondisclosure would not violate the '34 Act. Moreover, private causes of action under the '34 Act should not be implied when what is at issue—here the fairness of the transaction—is at best a subsidiary concern of the federal legislation. This was especially true, when, as in this case, the cause of action is one traditionally relegated to state law. A decision in favor of Green would federalize corporate conduct customarily left to state regulation and would extend Section 10b and Rule 10b–5 to cover transactions involving internal corporate mismanagement.

Securities and Exchange Commission Actions

Consent decree An agreement sanctioned by a court that in effect is an admission by the parties that the decree represents a just determination of their rights based on the real facts of the case, if such facts had actually been proved

The '34 Act empowers the SEC to conduct investigations of possible violations of the securities laws. Many times such investigations lead to censure or, alternatively, culminate in a **consent decree** signed by the alleged wrongdoer in exchange for less stringent sanctions. But the SEC can also order an administrative hearing conducted by an administrative law judge to determine if penalties are in order with respect to any security, person, or firm registered with the SEC. As mentioned earlier, revocation of registration or suspension of distribution of the security (or the activities of the person or firm) are but two of the enforcement powers that the SEC possesses. The SEC itself may review the hearing officer's decision and, if necessary, modify the sanctions originally levied. A party adversely affected by a final SEC order can seek review of such orders in a circuit court of appeals. Besides administrative proceedings, the SEC can bring court actions to enjoin violations of the securities laws on a "proper showing" of a reasonable likelihood of further violations. The SEC can also refer cases to the Justice Department which then mounts criminal actions against willful violators of securities laws and rules. A crackdown on Wall Street insider-trading abuses led to successful cases against well-known traders Ivan Boesky and Dennis Levine.

STATE REGULATION

Because the assorted federal statutes preserve the states' power to regulate securities activities, any transactions involving securities may be subject to state law as well as federal law. Such state laws, often called "blue sky" laws, though varied, normally include three types of provisions: (1) antifraud stipulations, (2) registration requirements for brokers and dealers, and (3) registration prerequisites for the sale and purchase of securities. With respect to the last, three methods of securities registration ordinarily exist: notification (a streamlined method for securities with a stable earnings record); qualification (a formalized program similar to the procedures mandated by the '33 Act); and coordination (a regimen that directs the issuer to file with the state a copy of the prospectus filed with the SEC under the '33 Act). State laws frequently exempt from registration the same classes of securities exempted from the '33 Act and additionally often exempt stocks listed on major stock exchanges. Exempted transactions customarily include private placements, or limited offerings, and isolated nonissuer transactions. State laws generally provide for sanctions and liabilities similar to those imposed under federal law, but the small securities staffs in most states make the possibility of civil liability a more potent deterrent for violations. In 1956, the National Conference of Commissioners on Uniform State Laws drafted a Uniform Securities Act meant for adoption by the states. This attempt at uniformity for resolving securities questions among the various states has not been wholly successful, however.

One additional topic merits our attention before we leave the subject of the securities laws. On 19 December 1977, President Jimmy Carter signed into law the Foreign Corrupt Practices Act (FCPA). The FCPA resulted from post-Watergate congressional hearings about questionable payments made to foreign officials by hundreds of United States firms, including Exxon, Northrop Corporation, Lockheed Aircraft Company, Gulf Oil, and GTE Corp. Testimony revealed that such companies had given foreign officials large payments, or bribes, in order to land sizable contracts for themselves. In their own defense, these United States firms argued that foreign officials often demanded such payments as a condition of doing business and that without such "grease" payments, or sums paid to facilitate transactions by minor governmental functionaries, bureaucratic red tape would have brought all their business dealings to a complete halt.

Congressional investigators found that such questionable payments often took the form of secret slush funds, dubious transfers of funds or assets between subsidiaries and parent companies, improper invoicing procedures (for example, false payments for goods or services that were never received), and bookkeeping practices designed to camouflage improper payments or procedures. Indeed, these corrupt practices by United States corporations even extended to payments made to engineer the overthrow of foreign governments hostile to the business interests of the firms involved and to attempts to keep competitors out of certain foreign countries through bribery of the appropriate foreign officials. To compound the improprieties, these same firms often deducted such so-called business expenses from their tax returns. Since accounting irregularities, including secret funds and falsified or inadequate books, formed the vehicle by which firms most often effected these questionable payments and bribes, Congress attempted to put an end to these practices by enacting the FCPA, which contains both antibribery provisions and accounting standards.

The FCPA itself amends Sections 13a and 13b–2 of the Securities Exchange Act of 1934. The FCPA's antibribery sections provide criminal penalties for actions taken by issuers (that is, firms subject to the '34 Act) or any domestic concern (even those not subject to the '34 Act) when an officer, director, employee, agent, or stockholder acting on behalf of such businesses corruptly uses the mail or any instrumentality of interstate commerce either to offer or actually to pay money (or anything of value) to any foreign official for the purpose of influencing the foreign official to assist the firm "in obtaining or retaining business for or with, or directing business to, any person."[5] In

THE FOREIGN
CORRUPT
PRACTICES ACT

---

[5] 15 United States Code Section 78(dd–1), (dd–2).

addition, it is unlawful under the FCPA to offer or to give payments or gifts for similar purposes to any foreign political party (or officials or candidates thereof) or to any person who the United States concern knows will transmit the payment or thing of value to any of the classes of persons specifically prohibited from receiving such bribes.[6] Gifts or payments that are lawful under the written laws and regulations of the foreign country involved or that constitute bona fide reasonable expenditures (such as travel or lodging) incurred by such persons during the performance of a contract with the foreign government do not fall within the FCPA's proscriptions. Moreover, these antibribery provisions do not extend to payments made to these classes of persons when the payments' purpose is to expedite or facilitate the performance of routine governmental action. Hence, "grease" payments to obtain permits or licenses to do business in the foreign country, visas, work orders, phone service, police protection, or inspections are legal as long as the employee receiving them is not a person who is known as someone who is acting as a conduit for governmental officials to whom the FCPA forbids corrupt payments or gifts. However, decisions by foreign officials to award or continue business with a particular party are not included in the definition of "routine governmental action."[7] Purely commercial bribery of corporate officials who have no governmental connections and who do not act as conduits for governmental officials thus appears to be legal, but business records should reflect such payments in order to comply with the FCPA's accounting standards described below. Recent amendments to the FCPA empower the Attorney General, after consultation with the SEC and others, to issue guidelines describing specific types of conduct that would satisfy the strictures of the Act and, when requested by firms, to issue opinions as to whether certain specified prospective conduct by these firms would conform with the Act. Once promulgated, these regulations and advisory opinions should greatly facilitate U.S. firms' attempts to comply with the FCPA.

Although all individuals and domestic concerns (whether these latter be corporations, partnerships, sole proprietorships, or any other sort of association) are subject to the FCPA antibribery provisions, only issuers subject to SEC jurisdiction must comply with the FCPA's accounting standards. These record-keeping standards require issuers to do the following:

(A)   make and keep books, records, and accounts, which, in reasonable detail, accurately and fairly reflect the transactions and dispositions of the assets of the issuer; and

(B)   devise and maintain a system of internal accounting controls sufficient to provide reasonable assurances that —

   (i)   transactions are executed in accordance with management's general or specific authorization;

   (ii)   transactions are recorded as necessary (I) to permit preparation of

---

6 Ibid.
7 Ibid.

financial statements in conformity with generally accepted accounting principles or any other criteria applicable to such statements, and (II) to maintain accountability for assets;

(iii) access to assets is permitted only in accordance with management's general or specific authorization; and

(iv)   the recorded accountability for assets is compared with the existing assets at reasonable intervals and appropriate action is taken with respect to any differences.[8]

Because they largely eliminate the possibility of secret slush funds for bribing foreign officials, these provisions serve a beneficial purpose. Yet the statute gives no specific guidelines for setting up a particular internal control system. Rather, it leaves the choice of the particular system to the individual firm. The statute's vagueness has therefore created confusion on the part of some businesspersons as to what type of record-keeping system will suffice. Given the FCPA's criminal penalties for knowingly failing to comply, this is not an idle worry.

Further compounding such worries is the SEC's promulgation of far-ranging regulations designed to promote the reliability of the information requested in the FCPA's record-keeping provisions. These regulations prohibit both the falsification of accounting records and misleading statements made by an issuer's directors or officers to auditors or accountants during the preparation of required documents and reports.

The FCPA's imposition of criminal penalties — setting corporate fines of a maximum of $2 million for violations and a maximum of five years' imprisonment and/or $100,000 in fines for willful violations by corporate individuals — and individual civil penalties not to exceed $10,000 should adequately deter U.S. corporations and corporate personnel engaged in international business from such illegal activities. Adding further strength to the criminal penalties is the FCPA's prohibition of a corporation's indemnifying its employees against liability under this Act.[9] Other remedies available under the '34 Act, such as injunctions, may also be used in the enforcement of the FCPA by the Justice Department and the SEC, which share enforcement responsibilities under it.

Critics of the FCPA argue that its provisions and resultant regulations have greatly increased both American businesses' costs of doing business and the enforcement agencies' costs, all of which negatively affect the American public. On the other hand, such laws and supplementary regulations carry the attendant advantages of heightened investor information and decreased numbers of scandals involving American bribery of foreign officials.

Since the FCPA is of relatively recent vintage, case law interpreting it is sparse. And because of the legal, social, and ethical issues it represents, it promises to remain a controversial law for some time to come.

---

[8] Ibid., Section 78(m).
[9] Ibid., Section 78(ff).

SUMMARY

The Securities Act of 1933 and the Securities Exchange Act of 1934 extensively regulate securities. In essence, a "security" involves an investment in an enterprise whereby the investor has no managerial functions but instead expects to profit solely from the efforts of others. The '33 Act is basically a disclosure statute meant to protect the unsophisticated investing public. The '33 Act, in furtherance of this purpose, requires the filing of a detailed registration statement with the SEC and the furnishing of a prospectus to all potential investors. Until the registration statement becomes effective, selling and promotional activities remain limited. The '33 Act exempts certain classes of securities from the registration and prospectus requirements: small public offerings, distributions of close corporation securities, short-term commercial paper, intrastate issues, issues by nonprofit organizations, and securities issued by the federal and state governments. The '33 Act in addition exempts certain transactions, such as private offerings. The '33 Act also contains several antifraud provisions. Civil liability may attend violations of the '33 Act. One section places liability on everyone who signed the registration statement, was named as a director, contributed an expert opinion to the statement, or underwrote the issue. All such persons, except the issuer, may escape liability by showing they acted with "due diligence." Other sections establish civil and criminal liability.

The '34 Act regulates the secondary distribution of securities. Its reach is therefore even broader than that of the '33 Act: the '34 Act covers proxy solicitations and tender offers, limits insider trading, forbids short-swing profits, and in general tries to eliminate fraud and manipulative conduct with respect to the sale or purchase of securities. Any issuer who trades securities on a national stock exchange must register with the SEC, according to the '34 Act. Like the '33 Act, the '34 Act mandates certain disclosures by the firms that it covers when the securities are listed with the national stock exchanges or traded over the counter.

Regulation of proxy solicitations is an important facet of the '34 Act. The '34 Act authorizes the inclusion of shareholder proposals that involve "proper subjects" in management proxy solicitations in order to further the democratic aspects of corporations. Liability for misleading proxy statements is absolute, as is liability for misleading statements made during tender offers or takeover bids. The '34 Act also prohibits insider trading because of the injury to the investing public that may otherwise ensue. When material inside information is involved, the insider must either publicly disclose the information or refrain from trading in the securities. Directors, officers, and some shareholders in certain corporations must refrain from buying or selling securities within less than a six-month period under the '34 Act's section on short-swing profits. Possible liability under the '34 Act is far-reaching, despite the existence of some Supreme Court decisions suggesting less expansive impositions of liability in the future.

The Securities and Exchange Commission (SEC) can conduct administrative hearings with respect to securities violations and can seek injunctions to stop continued violations.

State securities laws — called "blue sky" laws — usually set up antifraud provisions and registration requirements for brokers and dealers and for the sale of securities. These laws vary greatly in form and reach. The Uniform Securities Act, meant to eliminate the lack of uniformity among state securities laws, has not been wholly successful.

Since 1977, the Foreign Corrupt Practices Act (FCPA) has forbidden American businesses to make corrupt payments to foreign officials for the purpose of obtaining foreign business. Noncompliance with the FCPA's anti-bribery provisions and record-keeping standards may subject individuals or corporations to criminal penalties.

DISCUSSION QUESTIONS

1. What, essentially, is a security?
2. Explain the primary purposes of the Securities Act of 1933 and the Securities Exchange Act of 1934.
3. List the types of information contained in the registration statement under the '33 Act.
4. What are "tombstone ads" and "red herring" prospectuses?
5. List the '33 Act's exempt classes of securities and transactions.
6. Explain what a proxy is and describe the SEC rules surrounding proxy solicitations.
7. What are the '34 Act's provisions regarding insider trading?
8. Discuss the laws regarding short-swing profits and discuss why the '34 Act prohibits these profits.
9. Enumerate the liabilities and remedies possible under both the '33 and the '34 Acts.
10. Explain the enforcement powers held by the Securities and Exchange Commission and how state regulation of securities differs from federal regulation.

CASE PROBLEMS

1. R. Foster Winans was a reporter for the *Wall Street Journal (WSJ)* and one of the writers of the "Heard on the Street" securities column. The government sued him and others for participating in a scheme to trade in securities based on information misappropriated from the *WSJ* in violation of its conflicts-of-interest policy. The information allegedly stolen from the paper had concerned the timing, content, and tenor of market-sensitive stories scheduled to appear in the column. Winans and others tipped by Winans had traded in the stocks featured in the column just before the column had appeared and had realized thousands of dollars of profits as a result. The government argued that Winans's misappropriation of this market-sensitive confidential information had operated as a fraud on the *WSJ* in connection with the purchase and sale of securities in the featured stocks. Winans contended that as a noninsider who had owed no duty to the corporations he had written about, and as a nontippee of any corpo-

rate inside information, the *Chiarella* and *Dirks* cases' holdings exonerated him from liability. Should a court use this "misappropriation of information" theory to impose securities laws and mail fraud liability on Winans? (*Carpenter* v. *U.S.*, 108 S.Ct. 316 [1987].)

2. The Securities and Exchange Commission (SEC), as part of its statutory authority to conduct nonpublic investigations of possible violations of the securities laws, often issues subpoenas to obtain relevant information under those investigative powers. When Jerry T. O'Brien learned that he was the target of an investigation involving the issuance of a subpoena to a third party, he argued that he must be given notice of this fact in order for the subpoena to comply with the Fifth Amendment Due Process Clause, the Sixth Amendment Confrontation Clause, the Fifth Amendment Self-Incrimination Clause, SEC statutes, and prior decisional law. Should the Court impose such a notice requirement on the SEC's subpoena power? (*Securities and Exchange Commission* v. *O'Brien*, 467 U.S. 735 [1984].)

3. Borak was a shareholder in J. I. Case Co. He sued for damages resulting from the merger of Case and American Tractor Company on the grounds of breach of fiduciary duties by directors and misrepresentations contained in management's proxies. Borak also sued to invalidate the merger. Case contended that Section 14 of the '34 Act did not authorize a private cause of action such as Borak's. Do federal courts have the power to order remedial relief of the type Borak sought? (*J. I. Case Co.* v. *Borak*, 377 U.S. 426 [1964].)

4. Blau, a stockholder in TideWater Associated Oil Company (TideWater), sued derivatively to recover short-swing profits allegedly realized by Lehman Brothers, an investment banking firm, and by Thomas, a member of Lehman Brothers and a TideWater director. Blau alleged that Lehman Brothers had "deputized" Thomas to represent its interests on TideWater's board and that, through this inside information, Lehman Brothers had purchased TideWater stock and had realized short-swing profits in violation of Section 16b. Could Lehman Brothers be held liable under Section 16b because Lehman Brothers had actually been functioning as a TideWater director through its "deputization" of Thomas to act for Lehman Brothers, not for himself? (*Blau* v. *Lehman*, 368 U.S. 403 [1962].)

5. In December, 1982, Burlington Northern, Inc. (Burlington), made a hostile tender offer for El Paso Gas Co. (El Paso) to which a majority of El Paso's shareholders ultimately subscribed. However, Burlington did not accept the tendered shares, and instead, in January, 1983, after negotiations with El Paso, announced a new and friendly takeover agreement. Pursuant to this agreement, Burlington, in January, rescinded the December tender offer and substituted a new one, which was soon oversubscribed. The rescission of the first tender offer caused a diminished payment to those shareholders who had tendered during the first offer,

because those shareholders who retendered were forced to sell fewer shares. Barbara R. Schreiber filed suit on behalf of herself and other similarly situated shareholders alleging that Burlington, El Paso, and members of El Paso's board violated Section 14(e)'s prohibition against "fraudulent, deceptive or manipulative acts or practices . . . in connection with any tender offer." Schreiber claimed that Burlington's withdrawal of the December tender offer, coupled with the substitution of the January tender offer, had constituted a "manipulative" distortion of the market for El Paso stock. Burlington argued that the term "manipulative" required acts involving misrepresentation or nondisclosure, neither of which had been present in the offer in dispute. In addition, Burlington contended that courts should not read the term "manipulative" as an invitation to oversee the substantive fairness or the quality of tender offers, a matter better left to the marketplace, according to the company. Who had the more persuasive argument, Schreiber or Burlington? (*Schreiber* v. *Burlington Northern, Inc.,* 472 U.S. 1 [1985].)

6. Manor Drug sued Blue Chip Stamps under Section 10b and Rule 10b–5 of the '34 Act for damages based on allegedly pessimistic statements in a prospectus once sent to Manor Drug. Relying on these statements, Manor Drug had not purchased Blue Chip stock. Could a nonpurchaser of stock sue under Rule 10b–5 for damages in a private suit, or was the rule's coverage limited only to actual buyers or sellers of securities? (*Blue Chip Stamps* v. *Manor Drug Stores,* 421 U.S. 723 [1975], reh'g. denied 423 U.S. 884 [1975].)

7. Ivan K. Landreth and his sons operated a lumber business in Washington. The Landreths offered their stock in the business for sale through both Washington and out-of-state brokers. Samuel Dennis bought the Landreths' business and with other investors formed Landreth Timber Co. (the Company). After the acquisition was completed, the sawmill did not live up to the purchasers' expectations because the rebuilding costs, about which Dennis had been given notice, had exceeded earlier estimates; and new components had turned out to be incompatible with existing equipment. Eventually, the Company sold the mill at a loss and went into receivership. The Company then filed this suit seeking rescission of the sale of stock and $2,500,000 in damages, alleging that the Landreths had widely offered and then had sold their stock without registering it as required by the '33 Act and that the Landreths had negligently or intentionally made misrepresentations and had failed to state material facts as to the worth and prospects of the lumber company, all in violation of the '34 Act. The Landreths defended with the proposition that the federal securities laws did not apply to the sale of 100 percent of the stock of a closely held corporation. How should the Court have ruled in this case? (*Landreth Timber Company* v. *Landreth,* 471 U.S. 681 [1985].)

8. Texas Gulf Sulphur Company (TGS) had discovered valuable mineral resources through an exploratory drill hole in Ontario, Canada. The defen-

dants, TGS officers and geologists, had attempted to keep this ore strike confidential. They and certain of the persons to whom they had given tips purchased shares of TGS during the drilling efforts. In response to a newspaper article that had speculated about a rich TGS strike, the defendants on 12 April 1964 issued a press release regarding the Canadian drilling operations. Some investors took the release to be optimistic; others thought it painted a gloomy picture of the drilling prospects. A few days later, an official TGS press statement trumpeted a 25-million-ton ore strike. The SEC maintained that the April 12 press release was materially false and misleading, that the defendants had realized that it was so, and that the issuance of the press release had violated Section 10b and Rule 10b–5 of the Securities Exchange Act of 1934. What was the standard for deciding whether the press release had violated Section 10b and Rule 10b–5 of the '34 Act? (*Securities and Exchange Commission* v. *Texas Gulf Sulphur Company*, 401 F.2d 833 [2d Cir. 1968], cert. denied, 404 U.S. 1005 [1971], reh'g. denied 404 U.S. 1064 [1972].)

9. The International Brotherhood of Teamsters, Chauffeurs, Warehousemen, and Helpers of America (Teamsters) set up a noncontributory, compulsory pension plan for employees represented by the Chicago local. Under this plan, employees therefore had no choice as to participation in it and did not have the option of demanding that the employer's contribution be paid directly to them as a substitute for pension eligibility. The employees paid nothing to the plan themselves. Daniel had been denied a pension upon his retirement because of a break in the twenty years of continuous service required for pension eligibility. He subsequently sued the Teamsters, arguing that the pension plan was a security and that certain misstatements and omissions by Teamsters' officials violated Section 10b of the '34 Act and Section 17 of the '33 Act. Was the pension plan in question a security? (*International Brotherhood of Teamsters, Chauffeurs, Warehousemen & Helpers of America* v. *Daniel*, 439 U.S. 551 [1979].)

10. Huddleston sued Herman & MacLean, the accounting firm, which had issued an opinion regarding the financial information contained in the registration statement of Texas International Speedway, Inc. (TIS), when TIS offered its securities for sale. Huddleston and other purchasers brought a class action under Section 10b of the '34 Act on the rationale that representations made in the registration statement and prospectus had defrauded them. Herman & MacLean argued that Huddleston was limited to the express remedy for misstatements in registration statements that Section 11 of the '33 Act enumerates. In other words, Herman & MacLean submitted that an action for fraud accruing from a registration should be exempt from liability under Section 10b because such conduct was actionable under Section 11. Were the remedies provided by Section 10b and Section 11 exclusive or cumulative? If they were cumulative, should a plaintiff have a higher burden of proof under a 10b action, since fraud actions at common law would impose a higher standard of proof? (*Herman & MacLean* v. *Huddleston*, 459 U.S. 375 [1983].)

PART 8

Government Regulations

As technology developed and businesses grew large and powerful, the operation of a business became less personal, and the scope of business operations expanded. Many people felt that the individual was being sacrificed on the altar of profits: the "Almighty Dollar" was becoming more important than the nation's people. As a result, government imposed its power and prestige on the business environment to balance the interests of society more evenly with the interests of business.

This part of the text explores some of the government regulations that have developed in response to social demands. The initial area of government regulation dealt with antitrust law, which endeavored to protect competition in the business setting. Once competition was attained and protected, social demands changed. Now society wanted to protect the consumer and to protect the environment, as well. Again government intervened, regulating these areas as business affected them. Society also called for labor regulations, protecting the worker from management, and management from the worker. Once again, government intervened with regulations designed to resolve these problems.

CHAPTER 45 ▰▰▰▰▰▰▰▰▰▰▰▰▰▰▰▰▰

An Introduction to Government Regulation

HISTORIC PERSPECTIVE

In the United States today, business is heavily regulated by government. Local regulations tell a business where it may do business; state regulations deal with the selling of securities, loan rates, and highway weight limits; federal regulations deal with pollution, the safety of employees, consumer protection, and labor negotiations. These are but a few of the regulated areas and topics. The influence of government regulations is pervasive: it covers nearly every aspect of the business situation. However, this has not always been the case.

As is often mentioned in American history texts, America was built on a **laissez-faire** economy. Business was run by businessmen, government was run by politicians, and the two groups left one another alone. Buyers were often ignored, with *caveat emptor* being the rule of the land. Workers were virtually unprotected. If they did not like their jobs, they could quit. If they did not work, they were fired. If they joined a union, they were fired—*and* they quite often faced criminal conspiracy charges. The nineteenth century was a great time to be an American entrepreneur, especially a wealthy one.

Unfortunately for business, these easy times came to an end. Too many "Captains of Industry" were viewed as "Robber Barons." Too many workers

Laissez-faire A term meaning "hands off"; a government attitude that business operates best when uninhibited by the government

Caveat emptor A term meaning "let the buyer beware"; a reference to the fact that the buyer had very few, if any, remedies if the product was defective

821

were abused or mistreated. Too little land was left for westward migration. By the end of the nineteenth century, the voice of the regulators was beginning to be heard.

SHOULD GOVERNMENT REGULATE BUSINESS?

The answer to the question of whether government should regulate business is yes. It is also no. It depends on who is being asked, what type of regulation is being discussed, and which level of government is involved.

History shows that some regulation or intervention is necessary. Unless some protections are provided against business excesses, society suffers. But too much intervention is probably as bad as too little. Government cannot run business effectively—only businesspeople can do so. Overregulated businesses will suffer financial problems; underregulated businesses tend to create social problems. Somewhere between these extremes a happy medium must exist, and this happy medium needs to be reached for the well-being of business, government, and society.

SOURCES OF GOVERNMENT POWER

The primary source of power for government regulation of business is found in the commerce clause of the United States Constitution. Article I, Section 8, Clause 3, of the Constitution states: "The Congress shall have power . . . to regulate commerce with foreign nations, and among the several states." In addition, Article I, Section 8, also gives Congress the power to levy taxes. These two powers, taken together, form the foundation of federal government regulation of business.

The history of the commerce clause has been checkered. The Supreme Court has interpreted it, expanded the interpretation, contracted the interpretation, and then expanded it again. In 1824, the Supreme Court had its first occasion to interpret the commerce clause. Chief Justice Marshall's opinion in *Gibbons* v. *Ogden* defined commerce as "the commercial intercourse between nations, in all its branches, . . . regulated by prescribing rules for carrying on that intercourse."[1] Marshall went on to note that the federal government could regulate commerce that *affected* other states, even if that commerce was local in nature.

As a result of this interpretation, federal power to regulate business was viewed as a broad power for nearly three-quarters of a century. The Interstate Commerce Act of 1887 permitted the Interstate Commerce Commission (ICC) to regulate local railroad rates and local railroad safety because interstate rates and safety were directly affected.[2] The federal government also was allowed to

[1] 9 Wheat (22 U.S.) 1 (1824).
[2] 24 Stat. 379 (1887).

regulate local grain and livestock exchanges since they were involved in transactions that affected the rest of the nation.

However, not all court opinions of the period were in favor of regulation. In 1873, the Supreme Court decided *In re State Freight Tax*.[3] The Court opinion stated that *among* (from the commerce clause) meant *between*. As a result, the opinion held that the federal government could regulate only **interstate** commerce. As an added contraction of the federal power to regulate business, the Supreme Court limited the definition of commerce. In its 1888 opinion in *Kidd v. Pearson,* the Court ruled that commerce meant **transportation**.[4] As a result of these two opinions, federal regulation of business was suddenly restricted to actual interstate transportation and did not reach business deals that *affected* interstate business but that were conducted entirely in one state. Such transactions were defined as **intrastate** and therefore beyond the scope of federal regulation.

Interstate Between two or more states; between a point in one state and a point in another state

Transportation Carrying or conveying from one place to another; the removal of goods or persons from one place to another

Intrastate Begun, carried on, and completed wholly within the boundaries of a single state

It was under this new, restricted definition that the Sherman Act was passed in 1890 (see Chapter 46 for a detailed treatment of this act). The Sherman Act and many later federal statutes were interpreted narrowly or were held unconstitutional under this new definition of the federal authority to regulate business.

This narrow view of federal power did not change again until 1937. In the opinion from *NLRB* v. *Jones & Laughlin Steel Corp.,* which overturned fifty years of narrow interpretation, Chief Justice Hughes said:

> When industries organize themselves on a national scale, making their relation to interstate commerce the dominant factor in their activities, how can it be maintained that their industrial relations constitute a forbidden field into which Congress may not enter when it is necessary to protect interstate commerce from the paralyzing consequences of industrial war?[5]

So the Court came full circle. Possibly the most picturesque definition of interstate commerce today, and of the federal power to regulate such commerce, was provided by Justice Jackson. In *United States* v. *Women's Sportswear Manufacturers Ass'n.,* a local price-fixing arrangement was challenged under the Sherman Act; in upholding the right of the government to regulate the case, Justice Jackson stated: "If it is interstate commerce that feels the pinch, it does not matter how local the operation which applies the squeeze."[6]

The following case illustrates the current Supreme Court view of interstate commerce.

[3] 15 Wall. (82 U.S.) 232 (1873).
[4] 128 U.S. 1 (1888).
[5] 301 U.S. 1 (1937).
[6] 336 U.S. 460, 464 (1949).

Heart of Atlanta Motel v. United States
379 U.S. 241, 85 S.Ct. 348 (1964)

FACTS   The Heart of Atlanta Motel had a policy of refusing service to blacks. The federal government challenged this policy, asserting a violation of the Civil Rights Act of 1964. The government argued that the motel was involved in interstate commerce and that federal intervention was therefore permitted by the commerce clause. The motel argued that it was purely intrastate and therefore exempt from federal regulation.

ISSUE   Was the motel involved in interstate commerce and therefore subject to federal regulation?

HOLDING   Yes. Because the motel served interstate travelers, it was involved in interstate commerce.

REASONING   The motel was readily accessible from two interstate highways. It advertised in national magazines, and it placed billboards on federal highways. Approximately 75 percent of its guests were from outside the state of Georgia. To allow such discrimination would discourage travel by the black community. The motel was set up to serve interstate travelers, it drew much of its business from interstate travelers, and it was involved in interstate commerce. The discriminatory practice in room rentals was prohibited.

SCOPE OF GOVERNMENT POWER

The preceding case, *Heart of Atlanta,* points out just how broadly the commerce clause can be interpreted. Using such a broad interpretation as a basis for regulation, the federal government can affect many activities. Under such an approach, virtually *any* aspect of commercial dealing can be brought under federal supervision and control. How much of this potential regulatory power has government decided to exercise? The next three chapters, while not exhausting the scope of federal regulatory coverage, should illustrate how widespread this power has become. The following topics are covered.

Business Dealings

Trusts Associations having the power or tendency to create a monopoly, to control production, or to interfere with free trade

Monopolize To get, have, or exploit a monopoly; to get full possession or control of; to dominate completely

Antitrust law is designed to regulate *business dealings.* The most important of the laws include the following:

1. the Sherman Act, dealing with **trusts** and attempts to **monopolize**
2. the Clayton Act, dealing with price discrimination, exclusive dealings, tying contracts, and interlocking directorates
3. the Federal Trade Commission Act, covering unfair trade practice

(These topics are discussed in Chapter 46.)

In the area of *consumer protection,* the federal government regulates such activities as the following:

1. labeling and packaging of products
2. consumer credit, through such provisions as the Truth-in-Lending Act
3. the reporting of the credit standing of consumers, through the Fair Credit Reporting Act
4. debt collection practices, through the Fair Debt Collection Practices Act

In the area of *environmental protection,* government regulations cover the following:

1. clean air, with such laws as the Clean Air Act and its amendments
2. water pollution, through the Clean Water Act and related statutes
3. noise pollution, with several noise control acts
4. pesticides, through laws like the Federal Insecticide, Fungicide, and Rodenticide Act

(Consumer and environmental protections are covered in Chapter 47.)

Chapter 48 discusses labor and employment in the context of such statutes as the Wagner Act and the Taft-Hartley Act. The chapter also looks at topics like Social Security and OSHA from the federal realm, and workers' compensation and unemployment provisions at the state level.

The area of government regulation of business is clearly broad and varied. These chapters are not designed to be exhaustive; they are intended as a mere introduction, an ''appetizer'' of sorts. Many books that treat these topics in much greater detail are available for the interested reader.

Much of the work of regulating business is conducted by administrative agencies. While most of us are familiar with the three official branches of American national government — the legislative, the executive, and the judicial — we may tend to overlook the *unofficial* fourth branch — the administrative. The administrative branch of government has been especially active since the 1930s. The Great Depression and the presidency of Franklin Delano Roosevelt saw a tremendous growth in the use of administrative agencies as a major means of regulation. A great deal of government intervention in the business sphere is conducted through administrative agencies. As a result, some understanding of administrative law is essential to an understanding of government regulation of business.

Administrative agencies are set up by Congress; and since Congress "creates" them, Congress can terminate them. Hence, they are not an independent branch of government. They have only as much authority as is **delegated** to them by the legislature, and as a result they must answer to Congress for their conduct. Congress establishes a basic policy or standard and then authorizes an agency to carry it out.

Delegated Assigned responsibility and/or authority by the person or group normally empowered to exercise the responsibility or authority

Once established, the agency will have certain **quasi-legislative** and **quasi-judicial** powers. The agency is allowed to pass rules and regulations within its area of authority and to hold hearings when it feels the rules and regulations have been violated. The power of the Congress to abolish the agency and the power of the courts to review the agency's conduct are considered a sufficient control device. It is believed that the agency will not exceed its authority or abuse its discretion so long as these two *official* branches of government are keeping a watchful eye on the agency's conduct.

Quasi-legislative Partly legislative; empowered to enact rules and regulations but not *laws*

Quasi-judicial Partly judicial; empowered to hold hearings but not trials

Some Constitutional provisions also limit the power of administrative agencies. Both the Fifth and the Fourteenth Amendments to the United States Constitution require that due process of law and equal protection under the law be given to each person. The courts hold that agency action must satisfy these criteria. Of special importance is due process, which has two elements: procedural and substantive.

Procedural Due Process

An agency must provide for *fairness* in its proceedings to ensure procedural due process. If a person is facing a proceeding that affects his or her rights, that person is entitled to a full due process hearing. This would include the right to present witnesses, the right to cross-examine witnesses, the right to an attorney, and possibly other rights, as well. If the agency is involved in a less personal proceeding, such as rule making or fact finding, fewer personal protections are needed. Notice of the time, place, and purpose of the meeting might be adequate for procedural due process if the agency's proceeding is not directed at personal conduct. However, as noted, as the conduct of the agency becomes more closely related to personal conduct, the amount of procedural due process required increases to the point where it may require a full adversarial proceeding with witnesses, evidence, and attorneys.

Substantive Due Process

Substantive due process normally refers to the *content* of the rules and regulations. The agency may enact only rules and regulations that bear a rational relationship to the agency's purpose or function. Furthermore, these rules and regulations must focus on the particular problem being treated. If the regulations are too broad, they violate the substantive due process provisions. Likewise, they are prohibited if they unfairly discriminate against one person or group. The rules and regulations must not be arbitrary or capricious.

The following case illustrates how the courts treat the topic of substantive due process. The case deals with a state statute rather than an administrative regulation, but a similar analysis would be used if administrative conduct were involved.

Griswold v. Connecticut
381 U.S. 479, 85 S.Ct. 1678 (1965)

The state of Connecticut passed a law prohibiting the use of contraceptives and also prohibiting the counseling of people on their use. Griswold was the executive director of Planned Parenthood, and Buxton was a doctor, a professor at Yale Medical School, and the medical director of Planned Parenthood. Both were arrested and convicted of violating the anticontraception statute. Both challenged the statute as unconstitutional because it violated the due process clause of the Fourteenth Amendment.

FACTS

May a state prohibit any and all use of contraceptives within the scope of the Fourteenth Amendment?

ISSUE

No. The statute as written denied substantive due process of law.

HOLDING

A married couple is entitled to certain realms of privacy, and this statute infringes on that realm. The statute had the maximum destructive effect on the couple's privacy and was unreasonably broad. The Court held that the statute was un-constitutional and reversed the convictions.

REASONING

If someone is dissatisfied with treatment received at the hands of an adminis-trative agency, that person may ask the court to review the proceedings. However, the court will review the proceedings only from the point of view of their legality. *Issues of fact* are normally not subject to judicial review. The court is required to follow the *substantial evidence rule,* which states that the agency's findings of fact must be followed if they are based on substantial evidence. This means that judicial review will normally focus on four possible areas of agency error:

Judicial Review

1. The agency violated procedural due process.
2. The agency violated substantive due process.
3. The agency violated the Constitution.
4. The agency exceeded its authority.

As a result of the restricted nature of judicial review and the pervasive nature of administrative agencies in the business world, this area of regulation has become very important today. A person who plans to advance very far in business would be well advised to study administrative law in some detail. This introductory coverage should serve to whet the appetite, but it hardly satisfies the need.

SUMMARY

Government regulation of business is a fact of life in the modern business environment. Whether regulation takes the form of local zoning ordinances, state income taxation, or federal antitrust regulation, businesses today must deal with it. And the only way to deal with government regulation is to recognize and understand it.

Federal regulation of business is based on both the commerce clause of the United States Constitution, which authorizes Congress to "regulate commerce among the several states," and the taxing power, also included in the Constitution. But most of the regulation is based on the commerce clause.

The commerce clause has been interpreted in such a way that federal regulation is permitted only if *interstate* commerce is involved. To qualify as interstate, the transaction must directly affect citizens of at least two different states or countries.

If an interstate connection is present, federal regulation may be applied. The federal government regulates many aspects of business, including business dealings in violation of the antitrust laws and aspects relating to consumer and environmental protection and labor and employment practices.

Much of the actual regulation of business is carried out by administrative agencies. Administrative agencies are created by Congress, and Congress then delegates to the agencies the authority to carry out certain duties. Agencies are involved in a large number of regulatory areas. These agencies are required to assure due process of law in carrying out their responsibilities, and they are subject to judicial review to ensure that they conduct themselves properly.

DISCUSSION
QUESTIONS

1. What is *commerce* according to the United States Supreme Court?

2. What is the current Court view of *interstate commerce?*

3. What powers do administrative agencies exercise?

4. Explain procedural due process.

5. Explain substantive due process.

6. Suppose that the federal government decides that too many narcotics are being smuggled into the country on small planes. In an effort to stop this drug traffic, the appropriate administrative agency prohibits "all small planes" from flying over the national borders. How could this rule be challenged? Explain.

7. How may judicial review be used to prevent the abuse of power by administrative agencies?

8. Assume that the Federal Trade Commission, the agency charged with regulating trade practices, felt that XYZ Corporation was involved in unfair trade practices. Could the commission publish a notice that it was holding hearings concerning XYZ and then prosecute XYZ for its alleged wrongful conduct? Explain your answer.

9. Assume that the Constitution did not contain a "Commerce Clause." How

might national business practices be different in the absence of this federal authority to regulate business?

10. What is to prevent any of the states from enacting tariffs and other barriers to trade to favor the business of that one state over the businesses of other states? What rights does a state have to regulate the trade within that state?

CASE PROBLEMS

1. An Oklahoma statute prohibited any person who was not a licensed optometrist or ophthalmologist from fitting eyeglass frames or replacing lenses in frames. Several opticians challenged this statute under the due process clause of the Constitution. What result should be reached by the court? (*Williamson* v. *Lee Optical Co.*, 348 U.S. 483 [1955].)

2. Darby operated a lumber mill in Georgia. He employed workers at less than the federally prescribed minimum wage and had them work more than the federally prescribed maximum number of hours per week. Both federal criteria were to be found in the Fair Labor Standards Act. Owing to these violations by Darby, Congress prohibited Darby from shipping his lumber to any other state unless he complied with the standards of the federal statute. Darby challenged this prohibition. How should the court resolve this case? (*United States* v. *Darby*, 312 U.S. 100 [1941].)

3. The Lake Nixon Club, near Little Rock, Arkansas, was an amusement and recreation area. The club operated as a private club, with a membership fee of $25 charged to prospective members when they joined the club. The club membership was restricted to Caucasian applicants. When the club was challenged for violation of the Civil Rights Act of 1964 under the *Heart of Atlanta Motel* precedent, the club defended its position by alleging that it was not a public accommodation nor did it cater to interstate travelers. What should the court consider in deciding this case? How should the court rule? (*Daniel* v. *Paul*, 395 U.S. 298 [1969].)

4. Ohio law provided that mayors had the authority to try bootlegging cases anywhere in the county the mayor desired. It further provided that one-half of any fines collected in these cases go into the municipal treasury. Tumey was arrested, tried, and convicted of bootlegging within the state of Ohio. He challenged the conviction, alleging that he was denied due process of law by the financial interest of the mayor who heard and decided the case against him. Has Tumey been denied due process in this case? (*Tumey* v. *Ohio*, 273 U.S. 510 [1927].)

5. Grubb borrowed $55.94 from Dollar Loan Company. The loan carried a specified interest rate of 65.46%. On the loan fee, Dollar Loan used the words "loan fee" rather than "prepaid finance charges" as required by the Truth-in-Lending Act. Does such wording by Dollar Loan violate the Truth-in-Lending Act? Is this the sort of transaction the federal government should be able to regulate as part of its concern with consumer

protection? (*Grubb* v. *Oliver Enterprises, Inc.,* 358 F.Supp. 970 [D.C. N.D. Ga. 1972].)

6. Sail'er Inn, the holder of an on-sale liquor license, hired several women to work as bartenders in its establishment. The state statute prohibited women from being hired as bartenders unless the women so hired were the licensees, the wives of licensees, or the sole shareholders of a licensee corporation. The state Department of Alcoholic Beverage Control attempted to revoke the license of Sail'er Inn due to the hiring of the women. Sail'er Inn filed suit to prevent the revocation of its license, and asserted that the Civil Rights Act of 1964 prohibited it from discriminating against women. In this conflict between federal and state regulation of a business, which regulation should be followed, and why? (*Sail'er Inn, Inc.* v. *Kirby,* 485 P.2d 529 [Cal. 1971].)

7. SCRAP filed suit against the Interstate Commerce Commission's decision to allow the railroads to increase the normal tariff on freight by 2.5%. SCRAP asserted that the increased charges added to the cost of shipping recyclable materials and, in doing so, posed a threat to the environment. Does this case fall within the environmental protection coverage of the federal government so that an environmental impact statement can be ordered from the ICC? Is this a proper case for federal action? (*Students Challenging Regulatory Agency Procedures* v. *United States,* 346 F.Supp. 189 [D.C. D.C. 1972].)

8. The NLRB included both professional and nonprofessional employees of a Westinghouse plant in an elected bargaining unit following a vote by the employees to select a bargaining unit. However, the NLRB did not provide a separate ballot for the professional employees covered by the total vote. Under the National Labor Relations Act, such a separate ballot of the professional workers is required. When the results of the collective bargaining vote were announced, some of the professional employees objected and filed suit. The NLRB contended that judicial review of the agency's conduct was not appropriate. Should judicial review be available in this case? (*Leedom* v. *Kyne,* 358 U.S. 184 [1958].)

9. The Virginia Highway Commissioner, without any prior notice or hearings, ordered the Southern Railway Company to eliminate the railroad crossing at Antlers, Virginia, and to build an overpass to replace the crossing. The order included plans and specifications for the overpass. Southern refused to obey the order and filed suit, alleging that the order constituted a denial of due process. Did the order, as issued, amount to a denial of due process? If so, what would be necessary in order to protect the due process rights of Southern? (*Southern Railway Co.* v. *Virginia,* 290 U.S. 190 [1933].)

10. Willner passed the New York Bar examination, but was denied admission to the Bar due to the adverse report of the Committee on Character and

Fitness. Willner asked for, and was given, a hearing by the committee to appeal its report. At that hearing, Willner was informed that a particular attorney had written a negative letter about Willner. Willner was not allowed to confront the author of the letter or to ascertain and contest the bases for the negative recommendation of the committee. Willner has challenged the committee's recommendation as a denial of due process. What result should occur? (*Willner* v. *Committee on Character and Fitness*, 373 U.S. 96 [1963].)

CHAPTER 46

Antitrust Legislation

THE BASIS OF REGULATORY REFORM

For the first 114 years of United States history, business had a fairly free field in which to work. There was little federal regulation and little effective state regulation. The courts and the federal government took a "hands off" attitude toward business. The rule of commercial law seemed to be: "You pays your money, and you takes your chances!" In such an environment, Cornelius Vanderbilt, buccaneering railroad tycoon of the 1800s, was able to crow, "What do I care about the law? Hain't I got the power?"

The tide began to turn in the late 1800s as the public tired of the irresponsible behavior of some of the so-called Robber Barons. The press began to call for reforms and for public protection from "big business." Finally, in 1890, a beachhead was established. The assault on business had begun. Government regulation of business was to become a major factor in the management of commercial affairs. All the regulations that affect business today, all the government inputs and interventions that confront the modern businessperson, can be traced back to *the* cornerstone of business regulation. The law that changed American business so dramatically was the Sherman Antitrust Act.

Congress passed the Sherman Antitrust Act in 1890. The purpose of the act was to preserve the economic ideal of a **pure-competition economy.** To reach this ideal, the Sherman Act prohibits combinations that *restrain trade,* and it prohibits attempts to *monopolize* any area of commerce. Violations of the act can result in fines, imprisonment, injunctive relief, and civil damages.

The Sherman Act is a fairly short statute, but its few words cover a great number of actions. Section 1 states:

> Every contract, combination in the form of trust or otherwise, or conspiracy, in restraint of trade or commerce among the several States, or with foreign nations, is hereby declared to be illegal.

Because nearly every contract can be viewed as a restraint of trade, if this section were to be interpreted literally, virtually all business dealings that affect interstate commerce would be prohibited. For example, a customer who contracts to buy some item from seller 1 will normally *not* buy the same type of item from any of the competitors of seller 1. As a result, the courts initially interpreted the Sherman Act very narrowly; this worked in such a way that the act was virtually negated.

The courts eventually found a comfortable middle ground. To give the act the scope that Congress had intended, the courts developed the "rule of reason" as a means of applying the provisions of Section 1. Under this test, not *every* "contract, combination, or conspiracy" is prohibited. Rather, only those "contracts, combinations, or conspiracies" that *unreasonably* restrain interstate commerce are prohibited. If a firm can show that its conduct was reasonable, it can avoid a prosecution under Section 1.

This defense provided business with an opportunity that it lost no time in using to its best advantage. Given a sufficient amount of time to prepare a defense, almost any business can show that its conduct was "reasonable" under the circumstances. Because of the results that the rule of reason produced, the courts had to reevaluate their approach. The amended approach retained the rule of reason but added a new category: the courts declared some conduct to be so lacking in social value as to be an automatic violation of Section 1. These actions, called *per se violations,* tend to directly contradict the economic model of pure competition.

The next case dealt with one type of per se violation, price fixing.

THE SHERMAN ACT

Section 1

Pure-competition economy An economy in which no single business has enough power to affect supply or demand and in which prices are set by the market in perfect equilibrium

---

Goldfarb et ux. v. *Virginia State Bar et al.*
95 S.Ct. 2004 (1975)

The Goldfarbs wanted to purchase a home in Fairfax County, Virginia. The financing agency required them to obtain title insurance, which required a title

FACTS

examination. By state law, only a member of the Virginia Bar Association could legally perform the title examination. When the Goldfarbs contacted a local attorney, he quoted them a fee as established by the county bar association, 1 percent of the value of the property, for a title examination. The Goldfarbs decided to shop around for a lower fee, but every attorney who quoted a fee to them quoted the same fee, that fee published by the Fairfax County Bar Association. The Goldfarbs then retained the first attorney to whom they had spoken, obtained their title examination, and then sued the state and county bar associations, alleging an illegal price-fixing arrangement in violation of Section 1 of the Sherman Act.

ISSUE   Is the imposition of a minimum fee schedule and the adherence to that fee schedule an illegal price-fixing agreement?

HOLDING   Yes. The habitual setting of prices at a fixed percentage without regard to the efforts required or any other variable constituted a price-fixing agreement in violation of the law.

REASONING   The Court found that the "suggested minimum fee schedule" resulted in a rigid price floor maintained by the state's attorneys, with each attorney adhering to the schedule both to comply with the announced professional norms and to avoid "fee wars" with the other members of the bar association. Further, since only a member of the Virginia Bar Association may provide the service of title examinations and since a title examination is required to purchase real property in the state of Virginia, a price-fixing scheme existed that no prospective purchaser of real property could escape or avoid. The provision of a title examination is a "service" and that service is performed for a fee, which places it within the definition of "commerce." This price fixing is an unreasonable restraint on commerce and constitutes a violation of the Sherman Act, Section 1.

The per se violations under the Sherman Act, Section 1, are as follows:

1.   *horizontal price fixing* (agreements on price among competitors)
2.   *vertical price fixing* (agreements on price among suppliers and customers)
3.   *horizontal market divisions* (agreements among competitors on who can sell in which region)
4.   *group boycotts* (agreements among competitors not to sell to a particular buyer or not to buy from a particular seller)

Clearly, few businesses would be careless (or stupid) enough to actually agree to such conduct. As a result, the courts have had to infer such agreements from the conduct of the parties. If the courts find such conduct to be **conscious parallelism,** a violation may occur. Conscious parallelism, by itself, is not conclusive proof of a violation of Section 1. However, it is to be weighed — and

Conscious parallelism
Intentional establishment of the price set by another; a form of *tacit* price fixing

weighed heavily — by the courts in determining whether a Section 1 violation is present. Generally, conscious parallelism coupled with some other *fact,* however slight, is sufficient to support a jury verdict of price fixing in violation of Section 1. But if the conduct is **price leadership,** no violation is present. And how can anyone distinguish conscious parallelism, from price leadership? There is no answer to such a problem. It poses a Gordian knot for the court every time it is raised.

Price leadership
Recognition of the power of a competitor and establishment of a price similar to that set by the competitor to avoid a price war

The two hypothetical cases that follow show the problem of deciding whether conduct is permitted or prohibited.

Alpha, Beta, and Gamma are concrete producers in Minnesota, Iowa, and Wisconsin, respectively. All three must compete with Omega, a concrete producer with plants in all three states. Alpha, Beta, and Gamma agree that each company will sell *only* in its home state, so that each can reduce expenses and thus compete more effectively with Omega. Before the agreement, each of the small companies had 10 percent of the market, and Omega had 70 percent. After the agreement, each of the small companies had 17 percent, and Omega had 49 percent.

Despite this apparent increase in competition, the conduct of Alpha, Beta, and Gamma is a per se violation of Section 1 of the Sherman Act because it is a horizontal market division.

Al, Bob, and Charlie are cement salesmen in Michigan, Ohio, and Indiana, respectively. They all work for Oscar Concrete, a cement producer with plants in all three states. Oscar tells them that Al is to sell cement only in Michigan, Bob is to sell only in Ohio, and Charlie is to sell only in Indiana. This is a horizontal market division, but since only one firm is involved, it is *not* a violation of Section 1.

Section 2 of the Sherman Act is as brief as Section 1, and it is equally as broad. Section 2 provides the following:

Section 2

> Every person who shall monopolize, or attempt to monopolize, or combine or conspire with any other person or persons, to monopolize any part of the trade or commerce among the several States, or with foreign nations, shall be deemed guilty of a misdemeanor.

It should be noted that Section 2 can be violated either by one person acting alone or by multiple parties acting in concert. In contrast, Section 1 can be violated only by multiple parties acting together. (To avoid confusion, remember that it takes *2* people to violate Section 1; it takes only *1* person to violate Section 2.)

Many people have the mistaken idea that monopolies are prohibited by Section 2. There is no law against having monopoly power. The prohibition in

Section 2 is against *monopolizing*. This means that it is illegal to seek a monopoly or to attempt to keep a monopoly once one is attained, but it is not illegal to have a monopoly.

In the following case, the court dealt with the monopolizing issue.

United States v. Aluminum Co. of America
148 F.2d 416 (2d Cir. 1945)

FACTS   From its founding in 1888 until 1909, Alcoa held a legal monopoly over the manufacture of aluminum owing to its possession of two patents. From 1909, when one of the patents expired, until 1912, Alcoa retained its monopoly position by illegal methods, which were eventually discontinued or forbidden.

In 1938 an action was commenced against Alcoa for continued monopolization of the aluminum market in violation of Section 2 of the Sherman Act. With a relevant product market of "virgin" ingot and a relevant geographic market of the United States, Alcoa controlled over 90 percent of the market and had only been below 80 percent three times in the years from 1912 through 1938. During these years, Alcoa had regularly increased its productive capacity and had anticipated the increased demand for aluminum, being always ready to meet these increases with its new and expanded capacity.

ISSUE   Was Alcoa guilty of monopolizing the aluminum industry, or had its monopoly been "thrust upon" it?

HOLDING   Alcoa was guilty of monopolization in violation of Section 2 of the Sherman Act.

REASONING   The Court felt that intent was irrelevant in this case, except that Alcoa meant to keep its share of the market and did keep that share, which it enjoyed through 1909. The fact that it kept that market by "innocent" procedures is irrelevant as well. Alcoa enjoyed a monopoly position, and it exercised its monopoly power to prevent competitors from entering the market. Such conduct is a violation of the monopolization restrictions of the Act.

Relevant market The area in which a product is sold, including geographic area and all competitive and substitute products

If a firm is found to dominate an industry, it is also found to possess monopoly power. As a rule of thumb, 70 percent of the **relevant market** is deemed to be monopoly power. When such power is present, there is a presumption that Section 2 was, or is, violated. However, a number of defenses exist to rebut this presumption. The dominant firm may argue that it is not attempting to retain its power, or that it acquired its position legally, or that its position was "thrust upon" it. Any of these defenses is sufficient to prevent a Section 2 prosecution.

The next hypothetical case shows how the defense can be applied.

Ralph developed a new product, Kleenzall, which does what any other soap or cleanser does, except that it does it better and is cheaper. Kleenzall is good for washing dishes, clothes, floors, walls, and even hair. Kleenzall was so good a product that Ralph soon had 95 percent of every cleanser and soap market. The major soap producers sued Ralph for monopolizing the industry in violation of the Sherman Act, Section 2.

Ralph is not guilty. He did nothing wrong in acquiring his market share. This monopoly was "thrust upon" him by sheer efficiency.

When a Sherman Act violation is shown, both criminal and civil remedies are available. An individual can be fined up to $100,000 and can receive up to three years in prison; a corporation that is convicted can be fined up to $1 million. Moreover, an injunction can be issued against the prohibited conduct. As a final disincentive, any harmed parties can recover treble damages plus attorney's fees. This means an injured firm can take its damages, multiply them by three, and then add attorney's fees. In at least one case, damages assessed exceeded $200 million. Needless to say, such damages strongly discourage prohibited conduct.

Sanctions

By 1914, Congress realized that the Sherman Act alone was not sufficient to solve the major business problems of the country. The Sherman Act was *remedial* in nature: if a problem existed, the Sherman Act could be used to help correct the problem. But nothing was available to *prevent* a problem from developing. In an effort to correct this regulatory deficiency, Congress decided to enact some preventive legislation. The result was the Clayton Act, which was designed to nip problems "in their incipiency." The Clayton Act has four major provisions, each dealing with a different potential problem.

THE CLAYTON ACT

The first regulating section of the Clayton Act, Section 2, prohibits **price discrimination.** The original Section 2 made it illegal for a seller to discriminate in price between different purchasers unless the price difference could be justified by a difference in costs. This provision soon placed a number of sellers in a terrible bind. Major purchasers often demanded special prices from sellers. If the sellers refused, they lost the business; if they agreed, they violated the law. As a result, Section 2 was amended in 1936 when the Robinson-Patman Act became law. Under the Robinson-Patman Act, buyers were prohibited from knowingly accepting a discriminatory price. In addition, the act prohibited such indirect benefits as dummy brokerage fees and promotional kickbacks.

A person accused of price discrimination can defend against the charge by showing that he or she is meeting, but *not* beating, the price being offered by a competitor. The accused can also defend by showing that the lower price is

Section 2

Price discrimination
The practice of discriminating among competing customers by offering them the same product at different prices

being offered because of obsolescence, seasonal variations, or damage to the goods being sold.

The following case involved a major price-discrimination scheme.

Utah Pie Co. v. Continental Baking Co.
386 U.S. 685 (1967)

FACTS   Utah Pie Co. was a local bakery operating in the Salt Lake City area. It began producing frozen pies in 1957, with immediate success. In 1958, Utah Pie built a new plant and gained a competitive edge over its three major competitors, Pet, Continental, and Carnation. The three major competitors each independently lowered their prices in the Utah market in an effort to cut into Utah Pie's market share. Utah Pie filed suit against all three, alleging violations of the Robinson-Patman Act.

ISSUE   Did the special prices offered by the three major producers in the Utah market amount to unlawful price discrimination?

HOLDING   Yes. Each of the three discriminated in price in violation of the Robinson-Patman Act.

REASONING   There was evidence that Pet's prices in Utah were lower than the prices it charged for the same products in California or in other western markets. Pet also had admitted to sending spies into Utah Pie so that it could gain information to use against Utah Pie. Moreover, Pet suffered losses on its sales in Salt Lake City during the entire challenged period. Continental's share of the market was small from 1957 through 1960. In 1961, Continental lowered its price in Salt Lake City to $2.85 per dozen on frozen pies. This price was below its cost and was offered only in Salt Lake City. Utah Pie was forced to lower its prices to their lowest point ever ($2.75 per dozen) to compete. Carnation also offered lower prices in Utah than in any other regional market. Its pies were sold below cost — as much as $0.50 per dozen less than in other western markets.

The Court held that sellers may not sell like goods to different buyers at different prices if the result harms competition. The fact that Utah Pie was expanding its sales volume was not enough to deny recovery. The Utah Pie market had a dramatically declining price during this period, and the decline was due to predatory price discrimination.

The Robinson-Patman Act also changed the standards needed to show a violation. Under the original Section 2, it had been necessary to show that *general competition* had been harmed, but under the Robinson-Patman Act, it is sufficient to prosecute on a showing that a *competitor* was injured.

The following example illustrates this point.

Bill's Bathtub Boutique is the largest customer of Paul's Porcelain Palace. Bill's biggest competitor is Dan's Discount Tub Store. Bill tells Paul that unless Paul gives him a 10 percent price reduction, he will take his business elsewhere. If Paul gives Bill this price reduction and does not give the same reduction to Dan, both Bill and Paul will be in violation of the Robinson-Patman Act.

The second major prohibition under the Clayton Act is found in Section 3. This section bans exclusive-dealing contracts and tying arrangements when their "effect may be to substantially lessen competition or tend to create a monopoly." Notice again the preventive intent of the act: actual harm need not be shown, merely the likelihood that harm will eventually occur.

    In an **exclusive-dealing contract,** one party requires the other party to deal with him, and him alone. For example, the seller tells the buyer that unless the buyer buys *only* from the seller, and not from the seller's competitors, the seller will not deal with the buyer. For such a demand to be effective, the seller must be in a very powerful market position.

    In a **tying arrangement,** one party — usually the seller — refuses to sell one product unless the buyer also takes a second product or service from the seller. For example, a manufacturer of cosmetics might refuse to sell a facial moisturizer unless the buyer agrees to purchase the manufacturer's soap. Usually, for this sort of arrangement to work, the seller needs a highly valued, unique product to which he or she can tie a commonly available product. As a defense to a charge that such an arrangement lessens competition or creates a monopoly, the seller may attempt to show that the tied product is tied for quality-control reasons. To do so, the seller must prove that no competitors produce a competing product that works adequately with the controlled product.

The third major section of the Clayton Act, Section 7, deals with mergers. As originally written, the only prohibited type of merger was one in which the stock of another firm was acquired if its effect might be "substantially to lessen competition, or [to] tend to create a monopoly." This prohibition was so narrow that it was rather easily evaded by merging firms.

    To broaden the scope of the law, Congress amended Section 7 in 1950 by passing the Cellar-Kefauver Act. The amended Section 7 prohibits the acquisition of stock *or assets* of another firm that may tend to have a negative effect on *any line of commerce.* As a result, firms are now subject to Section 7 in almost any type of merger — horizontal, vertical, or conglomerate. A *horizontal merger* is one between competing firms; a *vertical merger* is one between a firm and one of its major suppliers or customers; a *conglomerate merger* is one between firms in two noncompetitive industries.

    As a challenge to a merger, the government might argue that a "concentration trend" would be established, or that one of the firms was a "potential

Section 3

Exclusive-dealing contract An agreement between two parties in which one party agrees not to do business with the other party's competitors but to deal exclusively with that party

Tying arrangement An agreement between two parties in which one party's purchase of a product or service from the other party is contingent upon purchasing a second product or service from that other party

Section 7

entrant" into one of the industries affected by the merger. As a defense to a challenged merger, the merging firms might raise the "failing-company" doctrine, showing that without the merger one of the firms would have gone out of business.

The following case illustrates the potential-entrant doctrine.

United States v. Falstaff Brewing Corporation
410 U.S. 526 (1973)

FACTS Falstaff was the fourth largest brewer in the United States, but it did not sell any beer in New England. Falstaff decided to enter the New England beer market by merging with a strong regional brewer. After some investigation, Falstaff decided that a merger with Narragansett would be the best way to enter the market. Narragansett was the largest beer supplier in New England at the time of the merger with Falstaff. The United States challenged the merger as a violation of Section 7 of the Clayton Act.

ISSUE Was Falstaff a "potential entrant" into the New England market, so that its merger was improper?

HOLDING Yes. Falstaff was the nearest major brewer to New England that did not yet compete there. As such, it had to be considered a potential entrant.

REASONING The number of brewers in New England had decreased from thirty-two in 1935 to only six in 1964. Even though Falstaff alleged that it would never have entered the New England market unless it did so by acquisition, it was still a potential entrant and a potential competitor of the six breweries operating there at the time. The other brewers in New England could not know what Falstaff had decided. Falstaff was known to be interested in the New England market; its location on the very border of New England was certain to make the firms located there behave as if Falstaff might enter the market. Because of its size, its location, and its interest, Falstaff was a potential entrant into the market.

The following examples show the failing-company doctrine and the concentration trend.

Fred's Stereo is in severe financial difficulty. Irv's Interstate Sound Store, the largest stereo dealer in the region, buys Fred's. Under the failing-company doctrine, if Fred's would have gone bankrupt, the merger with Irv's is probably permissible.

The belt business is made up of many small producers of belts. The leather industry is made up of many small producers of leather. Bert's Belts, the tenth largest belt producer, wants to merge with Lanny's Leather, the fourth largest leather producer. Such a merger would not greatly alter the position of the other firms in either industry.

The government could probably successfully challenge this merger as a first step toward a concentration trend that would eventually harm competition in both industries by reducing the number of firms in each.

The final substantive section of the Clayton Act is Section 8. This section prohibits *interlocking directorates.* That is, no one may sit on the boards of directors of two or more competing corporations if either of the firms has capital and surplus in excess of $1 million, if a merger between them would violate any antitrust law.

Section 8

The year 1914 was a very busy one for antitrust regulation. Congress passed not only the Clayton Act but also the Federal Trade Commission Act. The Federal Trade Commission Act did two important things:

THE FEDERAL TRADE COMMISSION ACT

1. It created the Federal Trade Commission (FTC) to enforce antitrust laws, especially the Clayton Act.
2. In Section 5, it provided a broad area of prohibitions to close loopholes left by other statutes.

Section 5 of the FTC Act prohibits "unfair methods of competition" and "unfair and deceptive trade practices." This broad language permits the FTC to regulate conduct that might technically be beyond the reach of the other, more specific antitrust statutes.

The area of unfair and deceptive trade practices was intentionally made broad and somewhat vague to grant the FTC the leeway to proceed against any commercial practices that seem to be unfair or deceptive *under the circumstances.* If the statute had been specific, businesspeople could have found methods to circumvent it, methods that might be unfair or deceptive but within the technical limits of the law. The strength of the law has been its breadth, as well as the willingness of the FTC to attack practices that had been followed for many years.

To further strengthen the FTC position, a violation can be found without proof of any actual deception. A mere showing that there is a "fair possibility" that the public will be deceived is sufficient to establish that the conduct is unfair and deceptive. And if a representation made by a company is ambiguous, with one honest meaning and one deceptive meaning, the FTC will treat it as deceptive and as a material aspect of the transaction, so that remedies are available.

If the FTC opposes a business practice as unfair or deceptive, it issues a *cease-and-desist order*. The business must then stop the challenged conduct or face a fine for disobeying the order. The fine is $5000 per violation. This sounds small until it is realized that each *day* the order is ignored constitutes a separate violation. Thus, ignoring the order for one week would cost $35,000 in fines; for a month, $150,000 in fines; and so on.

In recent years, the FTC has become particularly concerned about two business practices: deceptive advertising and "bait-and-switch" advertising. In an effort to force truth in advertising, the FTC has been carefully studying the commercials run by corporations and ordering *corrective advertising* in many cases in which the advertising was deemed especially misleading. The case that follows is one of the best known in this area. In it, the FTC attacked Warner-Lambert for the ads it had run for one of its products, Listerine.

▆▆

Warner-Lambert Co. v. *FTC*
562 F.2d 749 (D.C. Cir. 1977)

FACTS   Warner-Lambert is the producer of Listerine mouthwash. Listerine has been produced, without a change in the formula, since 1879. And, from 1879 to 1972, it had been represented as a beneficial treatment for colds, cold symptoms, and sore throats. In 1972, the FTC issued a cease-and-desist order prohibiting such advertising claims in the future. In addition, the FTC ordered Warner-Lambert to run *corrective advertising* to remove any impression built up in the public that Listerine was a cold and sore throat medicine. Warner-Lambert agreed to stop the advertisements but objected to running the corrective advertisements.

ISSUE   May the FTC require corrective advertising to remedy the harm done by prior misleading or deceptive advertising?

HOLDING   Yes. The FTC may order corrective advertising in appropriate cases.

REASONING   The ingredients in Listerine are not of sufficient quantity to have any therapeutic effect. Even if the quantities were sufficient, gargling would not allow the ingredients to reach the affected areas. Moreover, the germs Listerine reputedly kills have no effect on either colds or sore throats.

The FTC has the power to shape remedies to fit the problem presented. Corrective advertising is an appropriate remedy to inform past *and* future consumers of prior deceptive advertisings and beliefs created by the advertiser. Corrective advertising is not a violation of the First Amendment. Rather, it is a necessary step to remove from the public mind a false belief placed there by the wrongdoer. The court ruled that Warner-Lambert would have to run corrective advertising. All Listerine ads would have to state: "Listerine will not help prevent colds or sore throats or lessen their severity." This correction had to appear in every advertisement until Warner-Lambert had run $10 million worth of advertisements.

Bait-and-switch advertising involves advertising a product at an especially enticing price to get the customer into the store — the "bait" — and then talking the customer into buying a more expensive model — the "switch" — because the advertised model is sold out or has some alleged defect. An advertiser who refuses to show the advertised item to the customer or who has insufficient quantities on hand is engaging in an unfair trade practice in violation of Section 5 of the FTC Act.

Some common law unfair trade practices should also be mentioned, such as palming off goods and violating trade secrets. *Palming off* involves advertising, designing, or selling goods as if they were the goods of another. Basically, the person who is palming off goods is fraudulently taking advantage of the goodwill and brand loyalty of the imitated producer. It will also frequently involve patent, copyright, or trademark infringements.

As we noted earlier in the text, *trade secrets* are special processes, formulas, and the like that are guarded and treated confidentially by the holder of the trade secret. Employees of a firm that has trade secrets must not betray their loyalty to the firm by revealing the trade secrets to others. To do so is a tort, and the employee can be held liable for any damages suffered by the employer. In addition, the firm or person who receives the information is guilty of appropriating the trade secret, and use of the secret can be stopped by injunctions; the recipient of the information will also be liable for damages suffered by the trade-secret holder.

As we just mentioned, palming off frequently involves the infringement of a patent, a copyright, or a trademark. These three areas, along with a few others such as service marks and trade names, are protected by federal statutes and are registered with the United States Patent Office.

A *patent* is a federally created and protected monopoly power given to inventors. If a person invents something that is new, useful, and not obvious to a person of ordinary skill in the industry, the inventor is entitled to a patent. In exchange for making the method of production public, the patent grants the inventor an exclusive right to use, make, or sell the product for seventeen years. If anyone violates this exclusive right, the patent holder can file an infringement suit. If the court upholds the patent, the infringer will be enjoined from further production and will be liable for damages to the holder of the patent.

A *copyright*, protected by the Copyright Office in the Library of Congress, is the protection given to writers, artists, and composers. The creator of a book, song, work of art, or similar item has the exclusive right to the profits from the creation for the life of the creator plus fifty years. Any infringement can result in an infringement action in federal court, with injunctive relief and damages being awarded to the holder of the copyright.

A *trademark* is a mark or symbol used to identify a particular brand name or product. Copying the trademark of a competitor or using a symbol deceptively similar to that of a competitor is a violation of the Lanham Act of 1946, and the violator is subject to an injunction and the imposition of damages.

EXEMPTIONS

Some conduct appears to violate various antitrust rules, and yet the actor is never challenged for the conduct. Many people are confused by this lack of action, asking why that party is allowed to do something when others are not allowed to do the same thing. The reason is probably that the particular party belongs to a group specifically exempted from antitrust coverage.

Labor unions are exempt from the provisions of the Sherman Act by the Norris-LaGuardia Act, passed in 1932. They are also exempt from the Clayton Act by Section 6 of the Clayton Act. The exemption applies only to "labor disputes" and normal union activities. Farm cooperatives are also exempt from antitrust coverage so long as they are engaged in the sale of farm produce. (There are a number of other exemptions, but they have little impact on business law.)

SUMMARY

Since 1890, the federal government has been attempting to regulate business to ensure competition. This legislative effort is referred to as antitrust law. The cornerstone of antitrust law is the Sherman Act, which prohibits joint conduct that unreasonably restricts competition, as well as attempts to monopolize any area of commerce. Some conduct is considered so lacking in social value that it constitutes a per se violation. Other questionable conduct is measured under the rule of reason. If a violation is found, injured parties are entitled to treble damages.

As the Sherman Act was found to be insufficient to prevent many violations, Congress enacted several other statutes to help protect the competitive ideal. One of these statutes is the Clayton Act, which prohibits price discrimination (by means of the Robinson-Patman Act), exclusive-dealing contracts and tying arrangements, a number of mergers (by means of the Cellar-Kefauver Act), and interlocking directorates.

As a means of protecting competition, Congress passed the Federal Trade Commission Act. This act has two major aspects: it created the Federal Trade Commission to act as a watchdog in the antitrust area, and it prohibits unfair and deceptive trade practices.

DISCUSSION QUESTIONS

1. What is the "rule of reason" as used in cases involving Section 1 of the Sherman Act?

2. What is "conscious parallelism," and how does it relate to the Sherman Act?

3. How can a firm totally dominate an industry and not be guilty of monopolizing in violation of Section 2 of the Sherman Act?

4. What were the major *new* prohibitions that the Robinson-Patman Act added to Section 2 of the Clayton Act?

5. What did the FTC Act prohibit in an effort to close the antitrust loopholes?

6. Which two groups are specifically exempt from antitrust regulation?

7. Anna and Bruce are competitors in the frozen quiche market. They agree to charge the same price for their products and to compete only in quality and advertising. What antitrust laws, if any, have they violated?

8. Samantha is a major shirt manufacturer. She sells shirts at one price but gives a quantity discount on orders of 5000 shirts or more. Only 2 of Samantha's customers, out of 600 customers, can take advantage of this quantity discount. Is Samantha in violation of any antitrust laws?

9. Mort is one of many producers of sugar cane. He developed a new machine for processing sugar cane that was much faster and much cheaper than any other machine. Mort would lease his machine to processors only if the processors would buy all their sugar cane from Mort. What antitrust questions are raised by Mort's conduct?

10. Arctic Airlines advertises that it "gets you there ON TIME more often than any other airline." In fact, Arctic has a very bad record of arriving on time. What might the FTC do to Arctic in regard to this advertising campaign?

CASE PROBLEMS

1. Klor's was a retail appliance store operating next door to Broadway-Hale, a department store. Broadway-Hale also sold appliances. Broadway-Hale convinced several national manufacturers of appliances not to sell their products to Klor's if they wanted to keep their accounts with Broadway-Hale. Klor's objected to this conduct, which Broadway-Hale characterized as "a private quarrel." Have any antitrust laws been broken? (*Klor's, Inc.* v. *Broadway-Hale Stores, Inc.*, 359 U.S. 207 [1959].)

2. Weinberg was on the boards of directors of Sears, Roebuck and of B. F. Goodrich. The government sued both companies, seeking a ruling that Weinberg could not sit on both boards under the Clayton Act. Both Sears and Goodrich sold major home appliances and automobile parts. Was this enough to classify them as competitors, so that they violated Section 8 of the Clayton Act? (*United States* v. *Sears, Roebuck & Co.*, 111 F. Supp. 614 [S.D. N.Y. 1953].)

3. An automobile rental company called itself Dollar-a-Day Car Rentals. The FTC challenged the name as deceptive and misleading to consumers. The company defended by pointing out that the customers were able to learn the true price by asking. Is this a sufficient defense? (*Resort Car Rental System, Inc.* v. *FTC*, 518 F.2d 962 [9th Cir. 1975].)

4. Fortner Enterprises needed capital for land acquisition and for the devel-

opment of the land once acquired. In exchange for a promise to purchase at least 210 prefabricated steel homes from U.S. Steel, U.S. Steel agreed to lend $2 million to Fortner through its wholly owned Credit Corporation subsidiary. Fortner later ran into some difficulties in its development, and it sued U.S. Steel for antitrust violations, alleging that the loan and purchase was an illegal tying arrangement and a violation of Section 1 of the Sherman Act. What should be the result? (*United States Steel Corp.* v. *Fortner Enterprises, Inc.*, 429 U.S. 610 [1977].)

5. The Fedders Corporation advertised that its air-conditioning equipment was unique, possessing "reserve cooling power." In fact, Fedders had no evidence that established its equipment as unique. The FTC issued a cease-and-desist order against the advertisements. Fedders challenged the issuance of the cease-and-desist order even though it admitted that its advertising was "misleading." Was the FTC conduct appropriate in this case? (*Fedders Corp.* v. *FTC*, 529 F.2d 1398 [2d Cir. 1976].)

6. Kodak controlled 82 percent of the film market, 61 percent of the camera market, and 67 percent of the color print market. Kodak then introduced a new camera, the "110 Instamatic," and the film that it required. Berkey filed suit against Kodak, alleging violations of the Sherman Act, Sections 1 and 2. Is Kodak guilty of a Section 2 violation, monopolization? Discuss fully. (*Berkey Photo, Inc.* v. *Eastman Kodak Co.*, 603 F.2d 263 [2d Cir. 1979].)

7. The regional beer distributors in central California decided among themselves to stop allowing the use of short-term trade credit without interest to the beer retailers of the region. The beer retailers objected to this decision, arguing that it constituted an illegal price-fixing agreement among the distributors in violation of Section 1 of the Sherman Act. Analyze the case and decide which side should prevail. (*Catalano, Inc.* v. *Target Sales*, 446 U.S. 635 [1980].)

8. A number of "discount houses" and "referral services" operated to sell new cars to the public at bargain prices. A number of Chevrolet dealers began to supply new Chevrolets to these discount houses without the permission of General Motors. G.M. received a promise from its dealers that they would no longer sell new cars to these outlets. To assure compliance, G.M. set up an investigation system using "professional buyers" who would purchase cars from the discount houses. The money used to make these purchases was contributed by the dealers. If a Chevrolet dealer delivered a car to the discount outlets, G.M. would call that dealer in and "persuade" the dealer to repurchase the car and to stop such dealings in the future. The federal government discovered this practice and initiated a lawsuit to stop the practice. What argument would the government use to prevent this practice, and how should the court resolve the case? (*United States* v. *General Motors Corp.*, 384 U.S. 127 [1966].)

9. All-State was an aluminum siding company. All-State sold two grades of aluminum siding, "ADV" and "PRO". Virtually all of the advertising and

promotional materials prepared by All-State concerned "ADV" siding, its lower priced product. The salesmen for All-State would get a customer to sign a contract to purchase the "ADV" siding, and would then point out defects in the product and encourage the customers to switch to "PRO", a higher priced and allegedly higher quality product. The salesmen received no commission for sales of "ADV" but were paid a commission for the sale of "PRO" siding. The FTC has challenged this sales technique as a prohibited "bait-and-switch" method, which is unfair and deceptive to the customer. Should the FTC be able to issue a cease and desist order to prevent this sales technique? (*All-State Industries of North Carolina, Inc. v. Federal Trade Commission*, 423 F.2d 423 [4th Cir. 1970].)

10. Brown Shoe Company wanted to merge with Kinney. At the time of the proposed merger, Brown was the number three shoe retailer in the country and the number four shoe manufacturer. Kinney was the number eight shoe retailer in the country and the number twelve manufacturer. Both companies were in good financial condition, and there were no indications that either was about to fail in the foreseeable future. The government challenged the merger as a violation of Section 7 of the Clayton Act. Brown responded that the merger would have little effect on the total shoe market in the United States, and also that the companies were not truly competitors since Kinney sold low-price shoes while Brown sold medium-price shoes. Do you find Brown's arguments persuasive? Should the merger be blocked? (*Brown Shoe Co. v. United States*, 370 U.S. 294 [1962].)

CHAPTER 47

Consumer and Environmental Protection

NEW AREAS FOR GOVERNMENT REGULATION

The second half of the twentieth century is witnessing a new revolution in business law. This revolution is not nearly as dramatic, or as obvious, as the antitrust revolution of the early part of the century. However, its ultimate effect may well be greater.

Two major areas of social reform legislation are affecting business today. The first, consumer protection, affects the relationship between a business and its customers. The second, environmental protection, affects the production process. Both are concerned with the ethereal concept known as "quality of life." And both have been hailed as a panacea by some, and condemned as a

Pandora's box by others. In reality, they are probably neither a cure-all for society's ills, nor a curse-all intent on destroying business.

The U.S. Administrative Procedure Act, 5 U.S.C. 553, provides, *inter alia:*

§553. Rule Making

(b)   General notice of proposed rule making shall be published in the Federal Register, unless persons subject thereto are named and either personally served or otherwise have actual notice thereof in accordance with law. . .

(d)   The required publication or service of a substantive rule shall be made not less than thirty days before its effective date, except —

   (3)   as otherwise provided by the agency for good cause found and published with the rule.

(Sept. 6, 1966, P.L. 89–554, §1, 80 Stat. 383.)

The following case discusses what constitutes "good cause" for making an agency ruling effective in less than thirty days.

United States Steel Corp. v. *U.S. Environmental Protection Agency*
605 F.2d 283 (7th Cir. 1979)

The EPA made an air quality regulation effective immediately instead of the usual thirty days after publication in the Federal Register. U.S. Steel attacked the agency for lacking the "good cause" required by law for bypassing the usual thirty-day waiting period.

FACTS

Did the EPA have "good cause" to bypass the thirty-day waiting period?

ISSUE

Yes. Numerous circumstances provide good cause to bypass the waiting period.

HOLDING

The Administrative Procedure Act, 5 U.S.C. 553, provides federal administrative agencies with broad power to determine what constitutes "good cause." The legislative history of the statute reflects that:

REASONING

Many rules . . . may be operative in less than thirty days because of inescapable or unavoidable limitations of time, because of demonstrable urgency of the conditions they are designed to correct, and because the parties subject to them may during the usually protracted hearing and decision procedures anticipate the regulation.

As indicated in our discussion of warranty and product liability in Chapter 21, concern for the consumer has a relatively long legal history. But that concern

CONSUMER PROTECTION

has been for an *injured* consumer, and *only* for an injured consumer. Over the past several years, the legislature, deciding that other consumer protections were also needed, has enacted a new wave of consumer protection statutes.

Consumer Credit

Consumer credit in the United States is a very big business. Many consumers rely on the use of credit to purchase various goods and appliances, from air conditioners to automobiles to televisions and stereos, and much more. For many years, such purchases were regulated only at the state level. This led to a great variety of regulation and to differing treatment in different states of consumers who had entered virtually identical transactions. While some variety still exists, several federal regulations now in effect have helped to level the treatment of consumers in different states in certain respects. We shall discuss some of the most important of these federal statutes.

Federal Consumer Credit Protection Act

In 1968, Congress enacted the Federal Consumer Credit Protection Act (FCCPA), 15 U.S.C. 1601 et seq. The FCCPA deals with the rights of consumers to know and understand the credit terms to which they are agreeing before they agree. Under this act, the creditor must inform the consumer of the finance charges involved in the transaction, and the information must be put in terms of an annual percentage rate (APR). In addition, the consumer must be made aware of *when* finance charges are imposed, *how* they are calculated, and any other relevant details of the credit arrangement.[1]

The following case shows how this statute can be applied.

Chapman v. Miller
575 S.W.2d 581 (Tex. App. 1978)

FACTS   Miller entered into a retail installment contract to purchase a used car from Chapman Motor Sales. The contract called for a $200 down payment, followed by six weekly payments of $25, and then by eighteen monthly payments of $70.47. Miller managed to make the payments until the sixth month. At that time, Miller defaulted, and Chapman repossessed the car, demanding the entire balance due from Miller. When Miller was unable to make the demanded payment, Chapman sold the car for the balance due from Miller, plus $19.69. Miller challenged the entire transaction, alleging that Chapman had violated the Federal Consumer Credit Protection Act.

ISSUE   Is an inadequate disclosure of the seller's security interest a violation of the Federal Consumer Credit Protection Act?

---

[1] For an excellent article exploring federal attempts to simplify this area, see Griffith, *Recent Developments in the Effort to Simplify Truth in Lending,* 19 Tulsa L.J. 30, Fall 1983.

Yes. The contract used by Chapman inadequately ensured full disclosure of all   **HOLDING**
terms to the customer.

The customer signed on the front of the contract form provided by Chapman   **REASONING**
and the signature did not follow "the full content of the document." Any
violation of the disclosure requirements, even a minor one, defeats the purpose
of the law. The penalty was twice the finance charges on the loan, plus court
costs and attorney fees. (*Note:* The law did not negate the repossession and
sale of the car by Chapman. It merely penalized him for inadequate disclosure.)

Fair Credit Billing Act

As a complement to the FCCPA, Congress enacted the Fair Credit Billing Act,
15 U.S.C. 1601 et seq., in 1975. This act specifies the rights of both the creditor
and the consumer/debtor if there is any dispute about a credit account or a
credit bill. The consumer is told *exactly* how to complain about any alleged
errors in the credit bill (these will normally be errors on a charge account), and
the creditor is required to respond to the complaint in a timely manner. The
creditor must either explain the error or correct it. The creditor may *not* do the
following:

1. try to collect the amount involved in the dispute until the dispute is settled
2. restrict the consumer's use of his or her credit account during the controversy, except for an unrelated but justifiable cause
3. report that the consumer is in arrears or that his or her bill is delinquent
   because of nonpayment of the disputed amount.

Once the controversy is resolved, the parties continue their dealings as they
had before the controversy arose.

Uniform Consumer Credit Code

The Uniform Consumer Credit Code (UCCC) was proposed in 1968. This code
was intended to do for consumer credit law what the Uniform Commercial
Code has done for commercial law. It was, and is, a codification of the major
consumer credit areas as well as the various court rulings and statutes that
have governed these areas. The intent was to establish a nationally recognized
set of laws so that consumer credit law could become uniform. To date, the
UCCC has not been widely adopted, although it is often referred to by legal
writers and legal practitioners.

Equal Credit Opportunity Act

In an effort to ensure civil rights in the consumer credit world, Congress passed
the Equal Credit Opportunity Act, 15 U.S.C. 1691 et seq. This act prohibits the

denial of credit by any business that regularly extends credit to any applicant on the basis of sex, marital status, race, color, religion, national origin, or age. When a customer applies for credit, the business has thirty days in which to reply to the application. If the company denies the application, it must specify the reasons for the denial. A California federal court has held that the statute applies to leases as well as sales.[2]

Fair Credit Reporting Act

When a person applies for credit, an investigation is usually conducted into the applicant's financial history and affairs. The accuracy of the information is obviously very important in the decision-making process. In an effort to protect the consumer from inaccurate records and from improper denials of credit, Congress passed the Fair Credit Reporting Act in 1970, 15 U.S.C. 1681 et seq. This act has very broad provisions designed to ensure that the person being investigated is being given the benefit of honest and accurate information, which can be used in a meaningful manner. The purpose of the statute is to protect the reputation of consumers. It gives consumers the right to fair treatment by businesses by respecting the confidentiality, accuracy, relevancy, and the proper utilization of credit information.

The act prohibits the use of obsolete material in any credit report. It also requires that the consumer be given written notice *beforehand* that an investigation will, or might, be conducted. The consumer has the right to discover the types of information in the credit record as well as the sources of the information, and to find out who has received the information during the previous six months (or the previous two years, if the information was received by a potential employer).

If the consumer disagrees with the information contained in the records, the consumer can notify the reporting company of the disagreement, and the reporting company must reinvestigate the challenged material. If the reinvestigation shows that the original information was not accurate, it must be changed to reflect the truth. If the reinvestigation supports the original information's accuracy, the consumer must be so notified; the consumer may then submit a written explanation of the information. This written statement *must* be included in the files and provided to any potential creditors.

Fair Debt Collection Practices Act

As a final protection of consumers in the consumer credit area, Congress passed the Fair Debt Collection Practices Act in 1977. This act is intended to eliminate the threatening, harassing, and abusive debt collection practices of days gone by. No longer may a collector make excessive numbers of phone calls or harassing phone calls to the debtor. No longer may a collector visit the

---

[2] See Brothers v. First Leasing, 724 F.2d 789 (9th Civ. 1984).

debtor's neighbors, telling them that the debtor is "a deadbeat" who fails to repay debts and obligations.

The act applies only to **debt collectors** (collection agencies), not to the actual creditor. Under the law, the debt collector may not bother the debtor at inconvenient times, such as during working hours or very late at night. If the debtor informs the collector that he or she has an attorney, the collector may communicate *only* with that attorney, not with the debtor; and the debt collector may not use any collection techniques deemed to be unfair, deceptive, or harassing. Should the collector violate these rules, the debtor can sue for damages and will normally collect a fairly substantial verdict. An Illinois court held that the following language was harassing, oppressing, and abusing because the tone of the language in the letter was designed to embarrass the debtor:

> Our field investigator has now been instructed to make an investigation in your neighborhood and to personally call on your employer. (*Rutyna* v. *Collection Accounts Terminal, Inc.*, 478 F. Supp. 980 [N.D. Ill. 1979].)

Debt collectors
Businesses that collect accounts due and payable but that do *not* extend the credit being collected

Product Safety

The area of product safety has become increasingly important. Consumers who are injured by defectively manufactured, designed, or packaged products have a number of different possible remedies to choose from — some at common law, some under the Uniform Commercial Code, and some under recently enacted federal statutes.

Magnuson-Moss Warranty Act – Consumer Product Warranty Act

The Magnuson-Moss Warranty Act – Consumer Product Warranty Act, discussed in Chapter 21, requires that the retailer disclose to the consumer the types of warranties provided in the sale of consumer goods. The disclosure must be made at the time of the sale. This statute has done a great deal to minimize, if not to eliminate, the use of hidden disclaimers of warranties.

Consumer Product Safety Act

In 1972, the Consumer Product Safety Act, 15 U.S.C. 2051 et seq., became law. This act was designed to protect consumers from injuries resulting from the use of dangerous consumer goods. The act also created the Consumer Product Safety Commission, which encourages the following endeavors:

1. research into the causes and the possible prevention of consumer product-related injuries
2. the development of uniform safety standards in consumer products
3. the development of comparison standards for consumers so that the relative safety of different products can be compared

Enforcement and Remedies	Each of these consumer protection statutes provides for different remedies or enforcement provisions. For example, the Federal Consumer Credit Protection Act has no provision for the consumer to collect damages if the creditor fails to comply with the provisions of the law. However, the creditor is subject to a penalty of twice the finance charge, with a minimum of $100 and a maximum of $1000, plus attorney's fees of the harmed consumer.

The Fair Debt Collection Practices Act is enforced by the Federal Trade Commission. If a debt collector violates the provisions of this act, the injured, harassed, or otherwise harmed consumer may recover damages plus attorney's fees. In addition, if the *collector* sues the consumer to collect on a debt, and the consumer can prove that the suit itself is harassing or otherwise improper, the consumer can recover attorney's fees, and the suit will be dismissed. The Commission has the power to ban consumer products that it determines to be hazardous. Using that power, the Commission has banned unstable refuse bins, extremely flammable contact adhesives, lead-containing paint, products containing asbestos, and certain all-terrain vehicles.

ENVIRONMEN-TAL PROTECTION	In many areas of the United States, the environment has taken a great deal of abuse. For many years, the sheer size of the country and the ease of migration contributed to the decline of the nation's environment. If an area became too dirty, crowded, or polluted for a comfortable life, the residents could simply pack up their belongings and move to a new, cleaner, less crowded area. As the population grew and the land began to fill up, such migration became less of an option. When all the free homestead lands were finally occupied, the ability to move west and then start afresh virtually ended. For the first time, people were forced to remain in an environment after it had become fouled.

Some of the horror stories about the environment are almost legendary. Los Angeles has been noted for its smog. Akron, Ohio, smells like burning rubber; when the wind is right, Akron can be smelled before it is seen from the highway. From about twenty miles away, Gary, Indiana, looks like a large gray mushroom on the horizon. Pittsburgh was once infamous for its soot and black skies. And Cleveland's *river* once caught on fire! However, the situation is far from hopeless. Any recent visitor to either Cleveland or Pittsburgh can attest to what is possible if the local citizens decide to recreate a pleasant environment.

Congress has "helped" to persuade businesses that they should cooperate with the citizenry in re-creating a livable environment. For the past several decades, federal environmental regulation has been growing tremendously as an area of governmental regulation of business. We shall discuss some of the more important of these laws next.

National Environmental Policy Act	The National Environmental Policy Act (NEPA) became law in 1970. This act has two major components. First, it established the Council on Environmental Quality (CEQ), an advisory council that operates under the president. The

purpose of the CEQ is to help ensure that the various environmental laws are obeyed. The CEQ has no actual powers of enforcement; rather, it advises the president on environmental policy. The actual task of enforcing federal environmental regulations falls to the Environmental Protection Agency (EPA), which was established by executive order in 1970. The EPA also sets national pollution standards.

The second major component of NEPA is the requirement that before any federal laws, recommendations, or activities that may affect the environment can be undertaken, an *environmental impact statement* must be prepared. At the very least, the environmental impact statement must do the following:

1. describe the anticipated impact the proposed conduct will have on the environment

2. describe any *unavoidable* consequences of the conduct

3. examine possible alternative methods of achieving the desired goals

4. distinguish between long-term and short-term environmental effects

5. describe resource commitments that could not be reversed by the conduct

Once the statement is prepared, the EPA must analyze and evaluate the proposed conduct from an environmental perspective. In addition, other interested parties (local governments, citizens' groups, and the like) can comment on the proposal and their feelings about it. Only after all this has been done and the plan has been approved can the federal proposal proceed.

In the following case, the lack of a proper environmental impact statement prevented federal action.

Natural Resources Defense Council, Inc. v. Morton
458 F.2d 827 (D.C. Cir. 1972)

The Department of the Interior planned to sell some offshore oil lands for development. In connection with the sale, an environmental impact statement was prepared by Morton, the Secretary of the Interior. The Natural Resources Defense Council, a citizens' group, objected to the environmental impact statement, arguing that the statement failed to adequately explore available alternatives.

FACTS

How fully must an environmental impact statement examine alternatives under NEPA?

ISSUE

Since the environmental impact statement is intended to be the environmental source material for decision making, it must fully examine obvious alternatives.

HOLDING

The statement prepared by the Department of the Interior discussed problems pre-

REASONING

sented by possible oil pollution, but that was the only thing discussed in detail. It failed to discuss the effect of the sale in meeting energy needs and its effect on market prices. It also failed to fully detail the alternatives raised within the report. The statement need not be exhaustive, but it must contain sufficient information to allow a reasonable weighing of the factors involved and a reasonable decision based on those factors. The court granted an injunction until the Department could prepare an adequate environmental impact statement.

Air

Pollution Impurities, dirt, or contamination

Clean Air Act and Amendments

Congress passed the Clean Air Act in 1963. This act was designed to provide federal assistance to the various states in combating multistate air **pollution.** The primary aim of the law was to control air pollution at its source, which was generally viewed as a *local* problem, although one with wide-ranging effects. Since the problem was local in nature, the solutions were to be developed by state and local governments. However, it quickly became apparent that the legislature had not gone far enough in the original law. As a result, various changes in the act were introduced over the years.

The act was first amended in 1963, in the Clean Air Act of 1963, and next in 1965 in the Motor Vehicle Air Pollution Control Act, followed by the Clean Air Act of 1966.

Still dissatisfied, Congress quickly followed with the Air Quality Act of 1967, the Clean Air Amendments of 1970, the Energy Supply and Environmental Coordination Act of 1974 (ESECA), and the 1977 amendments to the Clean Air Act.

The total coverage of the Clean Air Act and its various amendments is substantially beyond the scope of this book. A review of some of its major goals, however, is appropriate and relevant. For example, the 1970 amendments demanded that automobile emissions of carbon monoxide and hydrocarbons had to be reduced 90 percent by 1975. This was a direct effort to combat the increasingly prevalent smog problem in urban areas. The 1977 amendments were designed to *maintain* air quality that exceeded federal standards and to *improve* air quality that fell below federal standards in urban areas.

The following case shows one way in which these laws have been used.

Ethyl Corp. v. *Environmental Protection Agency*
541 F.2d 1 (D.C. Cir. 1976)

FACTS Under the Clean Air Act, the EPA is empowered to regulate gasoline additives that are considered a danger to public health. As one step in this direction, the EPA ordered annual reductions in the lead content in gasoline. Ethyl Corporation was a major producer of gasoline additives that increased octane rating. It objected to the reductions in lead ordered by the EPA.

Was the EPA's conduct in ordering a reduction in lead additives to gasoline an abuse of its discretion?

ISSUE

No. The EPA had acted in a proper manner and had obeyed all the procedural rules it needed to follow.

HOLDING

Environmental protection is a developing field. The agencies that must protect the environment are forced to decide on the basis of predictions based on less than complete evidence. Looking at both sides of the issue, the EPA had carefully examined the issue of public health with regard to lead additives to gasoline. On the basis of this examination, the EPA determined that lead additives endanger public health. The court had to *presume* that the agency acted properly unless contrary evidence was produced. After reviewing the evidence, the court could not say that the EPA acted improperly, and so the ruling was upheld.

REASONING

Other regulations deal with aircraft emissions, "stationary emission sources" (smokestacks and the like), and the use of lead and other additives in fuel; and various national standards exist for a number of major pollutants, as well as guidelines for the acceptable levels of each of them. In addition, the nation has been divided into a number of "atmospheric regions," each of which is expected to develop its own plan to attain the desired levels of compliance with these rules and regulations.

Noise Control Act

In 1972, Congress found that noise presents an increasing danger to the nation's health and welfare. Although the primary responsibility for noise control rests with the states, federal action was essential because of the need to deal with the problem uniformly. The Administrator of the Environmental Protection Agency has the power to set: noise emission standards for products distributed in interstate commerce; standards for railroad noise and motor carrier noise; and standards for the labeling of products that emit noise.

The following case demonstrates the reach of our nation's noise control law.

Recreation Vehicle Industry Association v. *E.P.A.*
653 F.2d 562 (D.C. Cir. 1981)

The EPA failed to include motor homes on its published list of major noise sources. When the EPA attempted to control the noise emissions of motor homes by classifying them as "medium and heavy trucks" the motor home association sued the EPA for attempting to regulate motor homes when they were not mentioned as a major source of noise.

FACTS

ISSUE   Could the EPA regulate motor home noise?

HOLDING   Yes.

REASONING   The EPA did list medium and heavy trucks as a major source of noise. Although motor homes were not specifically mentioned, neither were fire engines, trash-removal vehicles, cement-mixers, or many other kinds of specialized vehicles that could be considered under the broad category of "medium and heavy trucks." The vast majority of motor homes are built on a medium or heavy truck chasis; therefore, motor homes are included.

Water

Clean Water Act

Most people who are aware of federal regulations concerning water pollution seem to believe the Clean Water Act of 1972, 33 U.S.C. 1251 et seq., was the first federal water pollution law. In fact, Congress began to regulate water quality in 1886 with the River and Harbor Act. The River and Harbor Act required that anyone dumping refuse into any navigable waters had to have a permit, and the permit limited the refuse that could be dumped. The act was amended in 1899, and in 1965 Congress passed the Federal Water Pollution Control Act to further strengthen these previous laws by expanding the power of the federal government in limiting any dumpings in navigable waterways.

The 1972 Clean Water Act was designed to clean up America's waters. The act set timetables for compliance with its various goals. These timetables were pushed back by amendments to the act passed in 1977. The goals of the act include the following:

1.   to make the waters safe for swimming and recreational use
2.   to protect types of wildlife that rely on the waters
3.   to eliminate dumping in the waterways
4.   to mandate use of the "best available technology" by governmental and industrial groups that discharge pollutants into the waterways during the interim until all such dumpings and discharges are banned

To date, the goals have not been satisfactorily met, but some progress has been made. The statute was further amended in 1981 to include municipal waste water treatment construction grants.

Land

Public domain Lands that are open to public use

The protection and preservation of land has been the most obvious area of federal environmental regulation. As early as the presidency of Theodore Roosevelt, there was concern for some protection of the environment and for some preservation of America's natural resources. The **public domain,** land owned and/or controlled by the federal government, comprises nearly

725 million acres; to put this into some perspective, federally controlled land, national parks, and wildlife refuges occupy about as much land as is contained in the subcontinent of India.[3]

In addition to the obvious federal regulation and control of these federal lands, a number of federal statutes regulate how private land can be used and what can be used on private land. We shall discuss some of the more important of these regulations next.

Toxic Substances Control Act

Congress passed the Toxic Substances Control Act in 1976, 15 U.S.C. 2601 et seq. The act had two major goals. The first was to regulate the use of chemicals known to be toxic in nature. The second, and more important, goal was to create a method for testing new chemical compounds. Under this second aspect, the manufacturers of any new compounds were to determine what effect the compound might have on people or on the environment before the compound could be made available for public use. This portion of the act has done a great deal of good already. It has prevented the introduction of potentially toxic substances into the streams of commerce, and it has shown the harmlessness of some other new substances currently being used.

Federal Insecticide, Fungicide, and Rodenticide Act

In 1947, Congress passed a law, 7 U.S.C. 136, to regulate the use of insecticides, fungicides, and rodenticides — substances used to kill insects, fungi, and rodents, respectively. This act was amended and strengthened in 1972 when the Federal Environmental Pesticide Control Act was passed. These two laws are designed to regulate the production and use of insecticides and related products to protect the environment.

Solid Waste Disposal Act

Congress decided in 1965 to encourage recycling of solid wastes and at the same time to discourage their improper disposal. To this end, the Solid Waste Disposal Act, 42 U.S.C. 6901 et seq., became law. The three main aspects of this act are (1) federal encouragement of recycling and other uses of solid waste, (2) federal aid and control in setting up new technology for efficient disposal of unusable waste, and (3) prohibition of future open dumping on the land and elimination of present open dumps. Included in this area are the selection and treatment of landfills, the discovery of uses for waste products, and federal aid to local governments in handling waste products. The statute was amended in 1970, 1976, and 1978.

---

[3] J. Hanks, R. Tarlock, and E. Hanks, *Environmental Law and Policy*, abridged ed. (St. Paul, Minn.: West, 1975), p. 247.

Resource Conservation and Recovery Act

Congress was so pleased with the gains realized under the Solid Waste Disposal Act that in 1976 it enacted the Resource Conservation and Recovery Act, 42 U.S.C. 6901 et seq. Once again, the target was solid waste. Under this act, the EPA issues permits for solid waste disposal at federal facilities and also reviews state action in treating nonfederal solid waste disposal.

Enforcement and Remedies

The enforcement provisions of the federal environmental protection laws are somewhat varied. Under NEPA, interested groups can force compliance with the EPA. They can force the filing of an environmental impact statement and then a full public hearing before the objectionable conduct can be carried out. Injunctive relief until compliance is the basic remedy here.

Under the Clean Air Act and its amendments, the primary means of forcing compliance is through a suit filed by citizens or by a government agency. As a general rule, damages are recoverable only under a common law nuisance action, not under federal law.

Under the different water pollution statutes, citizens can enforce the law by suing to seek compliance, and a guilty firm can be fined; again, damages would normally have to be recovered under common law property right principles. However, the fines for noncompliance can be quite heavy. A first offense carries a minimum fine of $25,000. Subsequent convictions carry fines of *up to* $50,000 per day and up to two years in prison.

SUMMARY

Over the past several years, a growing body of law has been concerned with consumer protection. Laws protecting the environment have also grown tremendously. These two areas reflect a new trend in federal legislation—a move to improve the quality of life.

In the area of consumer protection, legislation has taken two major directions: consumer credit protection and product safety. The consumer credit protection area requires, among other things, that a full disclosure of credit and finance terms and charges be given to the consumer; that the consumer be told how to object to billing errors *without penalty;* that all consumers be treated fairly in credit applications, without regard to age, sex, race, or marital status; that the consumer be allowed to examine and explain a credit report; and that the consumer be protected from unfair debt collection practices. The area of product safety is addressed by the Magnuson-Moss Warranty Act and the Consumer Product Safety Act. Both are designed to protect consumers from defective products and to inform the consumer as to where and how defective products can be reported.

Environmental protection is aimed at preserving and protecting the nation's air, water, and land from pollution, waste, and abuse. The Clean Air Act is designed to ensure that we can continue to breathe in the future. The Clean Water Act is aimed at making our waterways suitable for recreational use and safe for fish and fowl. Land protection aims at reducing toxic substances and minimizing litter. To implement these protections, the Environmental Protection Agency was created to oversee the National Environmental Policy Act.

1. A credit card customer disagrees with the monthly bill received from the company and then takes the proper steps in objecting to it. What may the company do? What may the company not do?

2. Fred was denied credit with a local store. The denial was based on a poor credit report the store received from the local credit bureau. Fred believes that the information in the credit bureau files is inaccurate. What are Fred's available rights in this matter?

3. Bob is several months behind in his payments to Sam's Store. Sam's turns the account over to Debtor Collection Service (DCS) for collection. DCS calls Bob's employer asking for help in collecting the bill; it calls Bob late at night asking for payment; and it interviews Bob's neighbors about any money he may owe them. What may Bob do?

4. Paul received a loan the terms of which are in violation of the Federal Consumer Credit Protection Act. If Paul sues the creditor for these violations, what can he recover?

5. The Clean Air Act was amended in 1970. One of the amendments dealt with automobile exhaust emissions. What was the stated goal of this amendment?

6. Federal regulation of water pollution began with the River and Harbor Act of 1886. What did this act do in its efforts to minimize water pollution in federal waters?

7. What are the major goals of the Clean Water Act of 1972?

8. How has the Toxic Substances Control Act of 1976 been used to protect the environment from potentially toxic substances?

9. Under the provisions of the National Environmental Policy Act, an environmental impact statement must be filed with the Environmental Protection Agency before certain federal conduct is permitted. What must this environmental impact statement include?

10. If a firm is found guilty of violating the Clean Water Act, what possible penalties does it face for a first offense? For any subsequent offenses?

1. Representatives of Associates Discount made a number of telephone calls to Callarama, to Callarama's wife, and to several of Callarama's relatives in trying to collect an unpaid account owed to Associates Discount. The phone calls were threatening, harassing, and obscene. They were also malicious and damaging. Callarama sued Associates for damages, and Associates moved to dismiss, alleging that Callarama had no legal reme-

dies available. What should be the result? (*Callarama* v. *Associates Discount Corp. of Delaware, Inc.,* 329 N.Y.S.2d 711 [1972].)

2. The Tennessee Valley Authority was building a dam on the Little Tennessee River. If the dam were completed, an endangered species of fish would be irreparably injured. Several environmental agencies attempted to prevent the completion of the dam. Could the dam be halted by the courts once it was nearing completion? (*Tennessee Valley Authority* v. *Hill,* 437 U.S. 153 [1978].)

3. New York City enacted an ordinance regulating permissible levels of exhaust emissions for taxicabs. The taxi owners challenged the ordinance, arguing that the federal Clean Air Act had overridden the local ordinance. Is this contention correct? (*Allway Taxi, Inc.* v. *City of New York,* 340 F. Supp. 1120 [S.D. N.Y. 1973].)

4. The Consumer Product Safety Act calls for product safety to be specified in terms of performance requirements rather than design requirements. The Consumer Product Safety Commission (CPSC) ordered that all power lawn mowers produced after 1981 must have a "blade-control system" that prevents the blade from turning after the controls are released. Southland Mower Co. challenged this rule, alleging that it was a design requirement rather than a performance requirement and therefore beyond the authority of the CPSC. What should be the result? (*Southland Mower Co.* v. *Consumer Product Safety Commission,* 619 F.2d 499 [5th Cir. 1980].)

5. The Washington State Department of Highways and the United States Department of Transportation planned to construct a federally funded highway near Kimball Creek Marsh, a wildlife preserve in the state of Washington. The government filed an environmental impact statement but failed to consider the impact on Kimball Creek Marsh. Several residents of the area near the proposed highway sought to block construction of the highway, alleging that the environmental impact statement was inadequate. What should be the result? Explain. (*Daly* v. *Volpe,* 350 F. Supp. 252 [W.D. Wash. 1972].)

6. Perez was accused of loan sharking and was convicted of violating the Federal Consumer Credit Protection Act by engaging in his loan sharking activities. Perez challenged the constitutionality of the federal statute and the ability of the federal government to prosecute him for an activity that was purely local in nature and thus exempt from federal regulation. Can Perez be convicted of a violation of the Federal Consumer Credit Protection Act for a purely local activity? (*Perez* v. *United States,* 91 S.Ct. 1357 [1971].)

7. Charles entered into a contract with Drauss and signed the agreement at the appropriate place. The contract was printed on both the front and the back of the form that Charles signed, but the signature line was on the front. However, the text of the front incorporated the back side of the

document by reference. Charles later objected to the terms of the contract and sought relief under the Federal Consumer Credit Protection Act. Drauss defended by arguing that the terms on the back were incorporated by reference and further that Charles had read none of the contract, so Charles could not object to that portion on the back. How should this case be resolved? (*Charles* v. *Drauss Co., Ltd.,* 572 F.2d 544 [5th Cir. 1978].)

8. Arco suffered an accidental oil spill at an off-shore drilling site. Arco complied fully with the federal reporting and cleaning requirements for such a spill, but after this was done, the region was still polluted by the accidentally spilled oil. The federal government then assessed monetary damages against Arco, with the money to be used to pay for additional cleanup of the area. Arco objected to this assessment for damages when there was absolutely no showing of fault or negligence by Arco in relation to the spill. The government based its right to make the assessment on the Federal Water Pollution Control Act Amendments of 1972. Should the government be able to assess Arco for the cleanup in this set of circumstances? (*United States* v. *Atlantic Richfield Co.,* 429 F. Supp. 830 [E.D. Pa. 1977].)

9. The GSA entered into a contract with a private developer for the construction of an office building to be built to GSA specifications and then leased to the GSA for five-year periods, with the leases renewable at the option of the GSA. Since the building was to be built and owned by a private developer, the GSA did not prepare an environmental impact statement. Residents of the area in which the building was to be constructed objected that this was a federal project and that an environmental impact statement was necessary. Should the developer be allowed to construct the building without an impact statement, or should the construction be halted until an impact statement is prepared, submitted, and approved? (*S. W. Neighborhood Assembly* v. *Eckard,* 445 F. Supp. 1195 [D.C. D.C. 1978].)

10. A trade association of lawn mower manufacturers sought a court order voiding the designation of lawn-mowers as a "major source of noise" and, therefore, subject to the Noise Control Act. What should result? Why? (*Outdoor Power Equipment Institute, Inc.* v. *Environmental Protection Agency,* 438 F. Supp. 1092 [D.C. 1977].)

CHAPTER 48

Labor and Fair Employment Practices

LABOR
   Federal Statutes
      The Wagner Act (1935)
      The Taft-Hartley Act (1947)
      The Landrum-Griffin Act (1959)
      Scope
   State Law
EMPLOYMENT

Fair Employment Practices Laws
The Occupational Safety and Health Act
Social Security
Unemployment Insurance
Workers' Compensation
SUMMARY
DISCUSSION QUESTIONS
CASE PROBLEMS

LABOR

Federal Statutes

Picketing Union activity in which persons stand near a place of work affected by an organizational drive or a strike in order to influence workers on union causes

Boycotts Concerted refusals to deal with firms in order to disrupt the business of those firms

Unions are a commonplace fact of life in the United States today. But it was not always so. Violence and bloody battles between employers and prounion workers marked the rise of unionism in this country. The courts were as hostile as most employers to unions. In fact, in the 1800s and early 1900s, both state and federal courts viewed workers' concerted activities (strikes, **picketing,** and the like) as common law criminal conspiracies, tortious interference with contract, or antitrust violations. Although Congress had passed the Clayton Act in 1914 in part to shield unions from liability under the antitrust laws, subsequent Supreme Court decisions had narrowed this newly won statutory protection. Congress responded to these developments by passing the Norris-LaGuardia Act in 1932. This act immunized certain activities—peaceful refusals to work, **boycotts,** and picketing, for example—from federal court action. The act barred the issuance of injunctions in the context of labor disputes and thus allowed employees to organize and to engage in collective bargaining free from employer or court intervention as long as the concerted activity did not involve **wildcat strikes,** violence, sabotage, trespass, and the like. The Norris-LaGuardia Act signaled a policy aimed at keeping the courts out of the labor field. Free from regulation, then, employees and employers fought for their respective goals by using the economic weapons appropriate to each side: from the unions, strikes, picketing, and boycotts; from the employer, discharges of employees.

The Wagner Act (1935)

Congress passed the Wagner Act, also called the National Labor Relations Act, in 1935. This legislation heralded the beginning of an affirmative — as opposed to a neutral — approach to labor organizations. In Section 7 of the Wagner Act, Congress approved the right of employees to organize themselves and "to form, join, or assist labor organizations, to bargain collectively through representatives of their own choosing, and to engage in concerted activities for the purpose of collective bargaining or other mutual aid or protection."

The right to refrain from engaging in concerted activities is protected as well. Buttressing Section 7 is Section 8, which enumerates employer **unfair labor practices,** such as coercion of or retaliation against employees who exercise their Section 7 rights, domination of unions by employers, discrimination in employment (hiring and firing, for instance) designed to discourage union activities, and refusals by employers to bargain collectively and in good faith with employee representatives (that is, with unions). Section 9 sets out the process by which the employees in the appropriate bargaining unit can conduct secret elections for choosing their representative in the collective bargaining process. The Wagner Act also established a new administrative agency, the National Labor Relations Board (NLRB or Board) to oversee such elections and also to investigate and remedy unfair labor practices. Section 10 permits judicial review of any NLRB order in the appropriate federal circuit court of appeals. A 1937 case, *NLRB* v. *Jones & Laughlin Steel Corp.,* upheld the constitutionality of the Wagner Act.[1]

The Taft-Hartley Act (1947)

Unions grew appreciably in size and power after the passage of the Wagner Act. As a result, the power balance between employees and employers became so "prounion" that in 1947 Congress passed legislation meant to counter the perceived excesses of the NLRB and pervasive court deference to its orders. The Taft-Hartley Act, also called the Labor – Management Relations Act (LMRA), attempted to curb union excesses by amending Section 8 of the Wagner Act to prohibit certain unfair labor practices by unions, including engaging in **secondary boycotts** (causing one person to stop doing business with another), forcing an employer to discriminate against employees on the basis of their union affiliation or lack of union affiliation, refusing to bargain in good faith,

Wildcat strikes
Unauthorized withholdings of services of labor during the term of a contract

Unfair labor practices
Employer *or* union activities that are prohibited by law as injurious to labor policies

Secondary boycotts
Union activities meant to pressure parties not involved in the labor dispute and to influence the affected employer

---

[1] 301 U.S. 1 (1937).

Recognitional picketing
Prohibited picketing in which a union attempts to force recognition of a union different from the currently certified bargaining representative

requiring an employer to pay for services not actually performed by an employee ("featherbedding"), and **recognitional picketing.** Congress also amended Section 7 to allow employees to refrain from joining a union and participating in its collective activities.

In addition, the Taft-Hartley Act cut back the authority of the NLRB by separating its functions: the Office of General Counsel took on prosecution of the board's unfair labor practices cases, leaving to the five-person board the decision-making (or adjudicatory) function. This significantly changed the nature of the NLRB, which, under the Wagner Act, had served simultaneously as both prosecutor and decisionmaker. The Taft-Hartley Act also empowered courts of appeals to set aside NLRB findings in unfair labor practices cases, authorized district courts to issue labor injunctions requested by the NLRB for the purpose of stopping unfair labor practices, set out the possibility of fines and imprisonment for anyone resisting NLRB orders, and provided for civil remedies for private parties damaged by secondary boycotts or various union activities.

Informational picketing   Picketing for the purpose of truthfully advising the public that an employer does not employ members of, or have a contract with, a labor organization

Other sections protect the employer's right of free speech (by refusing to characterize as unfair labor practices an employer's expressions of its opinions about unionism when they contain no threats of reprisal), preserve the employees' rights to engage in peaceful **informational picketing,** and prohibit "closed shop" agreements (contracts that obligate the employer to hire and retain only union members). "Union shop" clauses (provisions that require an employee, after being hired, to join a union in order to retain his or her job) are legal. The Taft-Hartley Act also created a Federal Mediation and Conciliation Service for settling disputes between labor and management. To foster conciliation efforts further, the act established a "cooling-off" period before strikes could occur in certain circumstances. It moreover preserved the power of states, under their "right-to-work" laws, to invalidate other union devices designed to consolidate the unions' hold on workers.

The Landrum-Griffin Act (1959)

By the 1950s, Congress had unearthed substantial corruption among union leadership. Union members had been prejudiced by officers' plundering of union treasuries and by these officers' often tyrannical treatment of the rank-and-file members. In 1959, to end these abuses, Congress responded with the Landrum-Griffin Act, also called the Labor–Management Reporting and Disclosure Act. As this latter title suggests, the act requires extensive reporting of financial affairs, allows civil and criminal sanctions for financial wrongdoings by union officers, and mandates democratic procedures in the conduct of union affairs by providing a "bill of rights" for union members regarding elections and meetings. In addition, the Landrum-Griffin Act amended portions of the Taft-Hartley Act to outlaw "hot cargo" clauses (that is, provisions in contracts requiring the employer to cease doing business with nonunion companies).

Scope

Taken together, these acts cover almost all employers and employees, excluding federal, state, and local government employers and employees; employers covered under the Railway Labor Act; agricultural workers; domestic workers; independent contractors; and most supervisors. Even though government workers are not covered, they can organize themselves under the authority of Executive Order 11491, entitled Labor-Management Relations in the Federal Service, promulgated in 1969. In addition, about two-thirds of the states have enacted laws permitting collective bargaining in the public sector for state and municipal employees. Such executive orders and statutes ordinarily forbid strikes by public employees (such as police officers and firefighters), but such strikes have nevertheless occurred in recent years. The arrival of collective bargaining in the public sector is fairly new, but it promises to have significant implications for the future as our economy becomes more service-oriented and the number of government employees accordingly proliferates.

Although it is impossible to describe fully the pervasive regulation of labor embodied in the Wagner Act, the Taft-Hartley Act, and the Landrum-Griffin Act, we shall highlight a few of the more important issues.

Questions invariably arise when the employees select their bargaining representative. The Wagner Act sets forth the procedures that must be followed during this process. Briefly, these procedures include, on a required showing of employee interest, the union's petitioning for an election that will lead to its recognition as the exclusive bargaining representative of the employees. The NLRB decides whether the election has been conducted validly and, if so, certifies the union as the exclusive bargaining agent. The employer, who ordinarily resists the election-representation process, may attempt to "decertify" the union by arguing that the employees do not constitute an appropriate bargaining unit (that is, the employees have different duties, skills, or responsibilities) or that the union has engaged in unfair labor practices. The NLRB initially adjudicates such complaints, but the circuit courts of appeals can review final NLRB orders. So, the employer may prevail. Not to be outdone, the union usually has alleged unfair labor practices by the employer during the certification process. In other words, these affairs often become real donnybrooks of contradictory allegations because each side is fighting for the economic power signified by union representation or the lack of such representation.

The certification process may raise property issues as well, since organizers ordinarily wish to distribute union literature to employees in firms where they hope ultimately to hold a certification election. The right to engage in protected activity mandated by the Wagner Act thus clashes with the employer's property rights and the efficient conduct of its business. Board decisions generally invalidate the soliciting of employees and the distributing of literature during working hours and in working areas so long as such restrictions do not unduly interfere with the free exercise of employee rights guaranteed by the Wagner Act. As mentioned earlier, during this process, it is likewise permissible for the employer to state its views about unionism unless these statements convey a threat against prounion employees or promise a benefit to antiunion employees.

Once the bargaining representative has been empowered, the Wagner Act requires *good-faith bargaining* by both the employer and the union. This is, of course, a nebulous term; but, in essence, it mandates both sides' meeting and discussing certain issues with as much objectivity as possible. The duty to bargain in good faith does not absolutely presume agreement between the parties. Under this duty, an employer cannot bypass the union to deal directly with the employees.

The Wagner Act requires good-faith bargaining over "wages, hours, and other terms and conditions of employment." Basically, then, the duty to bargain covers only those topics that have a direct impact on the employees' job security. Decisions that are not essentially related to conditions of employment but rather are managerial decisions "which lie at the core of entrepreneurial control"[2] would not be mandatory bargaining subjects. Pay differentials for different shifts, piecework and incentive plans, transfers, fringe benefits, and severance pay would be mandatory subjects. It has been more difficult for courts to classify bonuses and meals provided by the employer. Managerial decisions to terminate the company's business or to shut down a plant are ordinarily *permissive,* or nonmandatory, subjects. However, an employer might be forced to bargain about the effects of such decisions, such as **severance pay,** which impinge on the "conditions of employment."

Severance pay Wages paid on termination of one's job

Although the labor laws view collective bargaining as the parties' meeting, asserting their positions, stating their objections to the other party's position, and disclosing the information necessary for each side to arrive at an informed decision, both sides can permissibly use economic weapons outside the bargaining room. Hence, employee strikes or work stoppages and employer **lockouts** do not in themselves violate the duty to bargain in good faith. An employer's unilateral granting of a wage increase without notice to the union during the process of negotiations does constitute bad-faith bargaining, however. On the other hand, such unilateral changes made after bargaining has reached an impasse are legal.

Lockouts Plant closings or other refusals by employers to furnish work to employees during labor disputes.

The NLRB can require either side who has refused — directly or indirectly — to bargain in good faith to begin bargaining and to cease and desist from any unfair labor practice that has accompanied the "bad-faith" bargaining. The board can also use such powers for ending violations of any of the employer or union unfair labor practices enumerated earlier that have occurred outside the bargaining context. But NLRB orders are not self-enforcing and become law only when imposed by a federal circuit court of appeals. Because litigation is time-consuming, these limitations on the NLRB's enforce-

---

[2] Fibreboard Paper Products Corp. v. NLRB, 379 U.S. 203, 223 (1964).

ment powers sometimes make it difficult to police the actions of maverick employers or unions. Board hearings and resultant orders, if resisted, bring on court scrutiny. If the court affirms the NLRB order, the court issues an injunction. In the meantime, however, the allegedly unfair labor practices may have continued and may have successfully stifled the employer or employee interests at issue.

The following case illustrates some of the foregoing principles.

Pattern Makers' League of North America, AFL-CIO v. *National Labor Relations Board* 473 U.S. 95 (1985)

The Pattern Makers' League of North America, AFL-CIO (the League), a labor union, provided in its constitution that resignations were not permitted during a strike or when a strike was imminent. The League had fined ten of its members who, in violation of this provision, had resigned during a strike and had returned to work. The National Labor Relations Board (Board) held that these fines had been imposed in violation of Section 8 of the National Labor Relations Act, which states that a union commits an unfair labor practice if it restrains or coerces employees in the exercise of their Section 7 rights, including the right to "refrain from any or all [concerted] activities."

FACTS

Could the Board construe Section 8 as prohibiting the fining of employees who had tendered resignations under a union constitutional provision that made such resignations invalid?

ISSUE

Yes. The Board's construction of Section 8 was reasonable in these circumstances and the Board thus had the power to prohibit the union's imposition of fines on the individuals who had resigned in violation of the union's constitution.

HOLDING

When employee members of a union refuse to support a strike (whether or not a rule prohibits returning to work during a strike), they are refraining from "concerted activity." Therefore, the League's imposing fines on these employees for returning to work restrained the exercise of their Section 7 rights. Indeed, if the terms *refrain* and *restrain or coerce* are interpreted literally, fining employees to enforce compliance with any union rule or policy would violate the Act. Furthermore, the inconsistency between union restrictions of the right to resign and the well-established policy of voluntary unionism supported the Board's conclusion that the union's constitutional provision was invalid. The three arguments the union had advanced to support its actions — (1) union rules restricting the right to resign were protected by the proviso to Section 8(b)(1)(A); (2) the legislative history of the Act showed that Congress had not intended to protect the right of union members to resign; and (3) labor unions should be allowed to restrict the right to resign because other voluntary associations are permitted to do so — were rejected. The statutory proviso clearly states that nothing in Section 8(b)(1)(A) shall "impair the right of a labor organiza-

REASONING

tion to prescribe its own rules with respect to the acquisition or retention of membership therein." However, the union's contention that because the constitutional provision in dispute had placed restrictions on the right to withdraw from the union, it had amounted to a "rul[e] with respect to the . . . retention of membership" within the meaning of the proviso was erroneous: neither the Board nor the Court had ever interpreted the proviso as allowing unions to make rules restricting the right to resign. Rather, the operative assumption had always been that "rules with respect to the . . . retention of membership" were those that provide for the expulsion of employees from the union. In addition, the legislative history of the Taft-Hartley Act was consistent with this interpretation, and this same rationale supported the striking down of the union's second argument. Decisional law formed the basis for the rejection of the union's third contention, since the Board's interpretation of the Act takes precedence over common law statements about association members' rights. Hence, the prior judicial decisions relating to the fining of union members and the Board's consistent interpretation of Section 8(b)(1)(A) as prohibiting the imposition of fines on employees who had tendered resignations invalid under a union constitution supported deference to the Board's decision in this case.

State Law

The supremacy clause of the Constitution empowers Congress to pass laws, such as the federal labor laws, that will preempt the states' regulation of labor. Supreme Court decisions construing the labor laws (which are silent on the issue of preemption) have held that federal preemption powers are broad. Federal laws will ordinarily oust the states' jurisdiction in activities that are arguably protected or arguably prohibited by the federal labor statutes because of the NLRB's expertise and a desire for uniformity of case results. Matters that only peripherally affect the federal statutory scheme or matters that are of deep local concern may constitute legitimate state interests that state law (and courts) may therefore regulate. The law in this area is unsettled and the cases controversial; generally, however, state courts may adjudicate lawsuits involving damages from violence or other criminal or tortious activity; retaliatory discharges; and those causes of action covering all employers and employees exempted under federal statutes.

EMPLOYMENT

Fair Employment Practices Laws

In addition to the extensive federal and state regulation of labor, several federal and state statutes designed to ensure equal employment opportunity for persons historically foreclosed from the workplace have come into existence since 1964. Foremost among these laws is the Civil Rights Act of 1964. Title VII of that statute prohibits discrimination in employment on the basis of race, color, religion, sex, or national origin. Under Title VII, it is an unlawful employment practice for any employer to make decisions to hire, discharge, compensate, or establish the terms, conditions, or privileges of employment for any employee based on the categories just enumerated. In addition, an employer cannot segregate, limit, or classify employees or applicants for employment in discriminatory ways. A union cannot discriminate against or refuse to refer for employment or apprenticeship programs any individual because of race, color, religion, sex, or national origin. And employment agencies cannot discriminate with respect to referrals for jobs or use advertisements indicating a discriminatory preference or limitation. None of the three groups — employers, unions, or employment agencies — can discriminate against any individual because the individual has opposed unlawful employment practices either. An employer who relegates blacks to manual labor jobs or an employment agency or labor organization that refers only white males for executive jobs or only women for nursing or secretarial jobs will be in violation of Title VII. Title VII's coverage extends in general to employers in interstate commerce who have at least fifteen employees for at least twenty weeks per year, to any national or international labor organizations that consist of at least fifteen members or that operate a hiring hall, and to employment agencies that regularly procure employees for employers or work opportunities for potential employees. Because of amendments added in 1972, Title VII currently covers most federal, state, and local governmental and educational employees, as well.

Title VII authorized the creation of the Equal Employment Opportunity Commission (EEOC), a bipartisan, five-member group appointed by the president. Since 1979, the EEOC has become the enforcement agency for Title VII, the Equal Pay Act, the Age Discrimination in Employment Act, the Rehabilitation Act of 1973, and the like. Complaints by individual grievants or charges filed by the EEOC or state fair employment or human rights commissions may trigger the EEOC's jurisdiction.

The jurisdictional requirements for successful suits under Title VII are complex. In brief, a charge must be filed within 180 days or 300 days after the alleged discrimination has occurred, the latter time period being applicable in so-called deferral states (those that have their own fair employment practices commissions). In deferral states, the local commission has exclusive jurisdiction for sixty days, at which point the EEOC has concurrent jurisdiction over the charge. If the EEOC has retained jurisdiction for at least 180 days and has decided there is no reasonable cause to file an action on behalf of the grievant, the EEOC may issue a "right-to-sue" letter to the grievant. Within ninety days of receiving the right-to-sue letter, the grievant must file suit in the appropriate district court or lose, generally speaking, the right to sue. Practically, however, the process almost never works this quickly (the EEOC's case backlog is almost legendary). Indeed, five to six years may elapse before resolution of the allegations occurs. Moreover, because the process is oriented to grievants and because judges do not expect laypersons to write complaints that resemble legal briefs, courts give grievants considerable leeway in describing and recognizing when discrimination has arguably happened. In addition, the conciliation orientation of the process makes it possible for the grievance to be cleared up before litigation becomes necessary. Still, it is important to remember the procedural pitfalls that dot this entire area of the law.

Significant, too, is the fact that employment practices that seem neutral may in fact lead to discrimination. For instance, in the early 1970s, several cases involving testing procedures and required high school diplomas arose. These cases show that selection criteria that seem outwardly neutral may foreclose blacks and other protected persons from jobs merely because statistically fewer blacks than whites are graduated from high school. Such selection criteria as requiring a certain score on an aptitude test or a high school diploma may "operate as 'built-in' headwinds for minority groups and [may be] unrelated to measuring job capability. . . . [Title VII] proscribes not only overt discrimination but also practices that are fair in form, but discriminatory in operation. The touchstone is business necessity. If an employment practice which operates to exclude [minorities] cannot be shown to be related to job performance, the practice is prohibited."[3]

Any job requirement that prevents a disproportionate number of blacks or other minorities from securing employment or promotions has a *disparate impact* (that is, an unequal effect) on minorities and may be illegal. The employer then has the burden of proving that the requirement is job-related. The EEOC has issued guidelines for selecting employees, but these guidelines do not have the force of law. Nonetheless, courts may give these EEOC guidelines considerable deference if they so wish.

Besides liability imposed for disparate impact, employers may, in addition, be liable for *disparate treatment* of their employees. Such cases ordinarily arise when an employer allows whites or males to break rules without punishment but institutes penalties if blacks or women break the same rules. A 1976 case, *McDonald* v. *Santa Fe Trail Transportation Co.,* also held that whites can sue for racial discrimination when they receive disparate treatment.[4] In this case, the employer had accused two whites and one black of misappropriating a shipment of antifreeze. Both white employees had been fired, but the black worker had been retained. The Supreme Court concluded that Title VII prohibits all forms of racial discrimination, including **"reverse discrimination"** of this type.

Reverse discrimination
Claims by whites that they have been subjected to adverse employment decisions because of their race and the application of employment discrimination statutes designed to protect minorities

The allegations of "reverse discrimination" that spring from another source — affirmative action plans — pose some of the most controversial issues in the area of fair employment practices involving race. Title VII places on the employer the duty to maintain a racially balanced workforce. Yet if the employer takes affirmative steps to bring about such racial balance, say by slotting certain apprentice openings for blacks, such actions may adversely affect white incumbents who wish to take part in these training programs. Two diametrically opposed policies clash here: the interests of the minority candidate who has in the past been disadvantaged because of race and the white incumbent worker who has taken no part in this discrimination but who now must lose employment opportunities in order to bring about equality of opportunity for black workers. In these situations, whites have occasionally brought suits alleging "reverse discrimination." A famous 1978 case, *Regents of*

---

[3] Griggs v. Duke Power Co., 401 U.S. 424, 431–432 (1971).
[4] 427 U.S. 273 (1976).

the University of California v. *Bakke,* involved a white student who alleged that the University of California at Davis had discriminated against him on the basis of his race in violation of the Fourteenth Amendment by rejecting his application for medical school and admitting sixteen minority students with credentials inferior to his.[5] The Supreme Court, in a very complex opinion, held that university quota systems that absolutely prefer minority candidates (the university had reserved sixteen spots out of one hundred for minorities) are illegal but that a university may take race into account in the admissions process.

This issue of "reverse discrimination," as mentioned earlier, becomes even thornier in the private sector, where employers may face charges by the EEOC if they do not aggressively engage in affirmative action and may face suits by white workers alleging "reverse discrimination" if they do. In the case that follows, the Supreme Court dealt with this particular issue.

United Steelworkers of America v. *Weber*
443 U.S. 193 (1979), Rehearing Denied 444 U.S. 889 (1979)

FACTS The United Steelworkers of America and Kaiser Aluminum & Chemical Corporation had entered into a master collective bargaining agreement covering fifteen Kaiser plants. The agreement had included an affirmative action plan aimed at eliminating racial imbalances in Kaiser's workforce. This plan had reserved for black employees 50 percent of the openings in the Kaiser training programs until Kaiser's percentage of skilled black craftworkers equaled the percentage of blacks in the local labor force. Brian Weber, a white worker who had had more seniority than some of the black workers selected for the training program, was rejected as a trainee. Weber sued, alleging that Kaiser's affirmative action plan constituted "reverse discrimination" against white workers and violated Title VII's ban on discrimination because of race in the selection of apprentices for training programs.

ISSUE Did Kaiser's voluntary, race-conscious affirmative action plan violate Title VII?

HOLDING No. Title VII's prohibition against racial discrimination does not condemn all private, voluntary, race-conscious affirmative action plans.

REASONING Title VII's prohibition against racial discrimination must be read against the historical context of the Civil Rights Act of 1964. An examination of that source makes it clear that an interpretation of Title VII that forbids all race-conscious affirmative action plans must be rejected. Since one of the purposes of Title VII involves opening up job opportunities traditionally closed to blacks, Kaiser's self-evaluation efforts to eliminate its racially imbalanced workforce were appropriate. Because the Kaiser plan opened up opportunities for blacks without unnecessarily trammeling the interests of white workers, its affirmative action plan was legal.

[5] 438 U.S. 265 (1978).

Bona fide occupational qualification A defense to charges of discrimination based on religion, sex, or national origin but not to charges of racial discrimination; a situation in which one of these categories is essential to the performance of the job

Besides racial discrimination, Title VII also prohibits religious discrimination. Sincere religious beliefs (or the lack thereof) are protected under Title VII. Typically, cases involving this protected category occur when a job shift necessitates work on the day the employee considers his or her Sabbath. If a person's religion forbids work on Fridays after sundown, for instance, Title VII mandates that the employer make a "reasonable accommodation" to the employee's beliefs unless to do so would pose an "undue hardship" on the conduct of the business. A 1977 case, *Trans World Airlines, Inc.* v. *Hardison,* has severely undercut the guarantees represented by Title VII, however, by holding that an employer does not have to undertake an accommodation that requires more than a minimal expense or that violates a collective bargaining agreement.[6] Furthermore, educational institutions may make religion a **bona fide occupational qualification** (BFOQ) under other provisions of Title VII. The University of Notre Dame, for example, can hire only Catholic professors if it so wishes.

Bona fide occupational qualifications may also constitute a *limited* defense to charges of sex discrimination. It is not a violation of Title VII for a movie director to cast only women in women's roles, for instance. Issues implicating the ban on sex discrimination include stereotypes about ability to perform (such as an employer who thinks only men can be telephone "linemen" and only women can be telephone operators), height/weight requirements that are not job-related (women are usually smaller than men), and so-called sex-plus cases. In the last, the employer adds a selection criterion for women that is not added for men (as when women with preschool-aged children are not hired, but men who have such children are). One unanswered question under Title VII involves whether the theory of comparable worth, which allows employees to compare their wages to those of other workers who perform dissimilar jobs of equal value (or intrinsic worth) to the employer in order to prove sex-based wage discrimination, will ultimately enjoy widespread judicial and legislative approval. The ensuing legal developments in this area bear watching. There is little uncertainty, however, with regard to pregnancy: the Pregnancy Discrimination Act of 1978 dictates that an employer treat pregnancy in the same fashion as any other disability. To do otherwise will constitute actionable sex discrimination. Recent Title VII cases have also protected women from sexual harassment in the workplace by imposing on employers liability for sexual advances or requests for sexual favors made by their agents and supervisory employees and for sexual misconduct that creates an intimidating, hostile, or offensive working environment for women.

Title VII's ban on national origin discrimination similarly prevents harassment in the form of ethnic slurs based on the country in which one was born or the country from which one's ancestors came. Repeated Polish jokes and other derogatory statements directed at one's ethnic origins in a given case may constitute national origin discrimination. National origin discrimination

[6] 432 U.S. 63 (1977).

often takes the form of "covert discrimination." To illustrate, height/weight requirements may foreclose Spanish-surnamed Americans from employment opportunities, as may language difficulties or accents. If an employer bases an adverse employment decision on such criteria, the employer must prove that the criteria are job-related. Narrow BFOQs may exist in national origin cases. It is legal to hire a French person to be a French chef, for example. It is also legal to refuse to hire non-American citizens because the prohibition against national origin discrimination does not include citizenship.[7] Likewise, it is not a violation of Title VII for an employer to refuse to hire persons who are unable to obtain security clearances because they have relatives in Cuba, Russia, and the like.

In addition to Title VII, several other federal statutes protect various classes of persons. The Equal Pay Act of 1963 prohibits discrimination in wages on the basis of sex. Therefore, men and women performing work in the same establishment under similar working conditions must receive the same rate of pay if the work requires equal skill, equal effort, and equal responsibility. Different wages may be paid if based on seniority, merit, piecework, or any factor other than sex (for example, participation in training programs). The Age Discrimination in Employment Act of 1967 in general protects workers from age forty to age seventy from adverse employment decisions based on age. BFOQs based on safety or human and economic risks — age fifty-five retirement for police officers, for instance — may be upheld, as may differentiation in age based on a bona fide seniority system and discharges or disciplinary actions undertaken with good cause.

The Rehabilitation Act of 1973 directs federal contractors to take affirmative action with respect to "otherwise qualified" handicapped individuals. A handicapped individual includes any person who "has a physical or mental impairment which substantially limits one or more of such person's major life functions, has a record of such impairment, or is regarded as having such an impairment." The Vietnam Era Veterans' Readjustment Assistance Act, various executive orders, and the Civil Rights Acts of 1866 and 1871 form alternative bases for guaranteeing equal access to the workplace. State law often augments this extensive federal scheme, as well.

A significant case in the area of fair employment practices follows.

American Federation of State, County, and Municipal Employees (AFSCME) v. State of Washington
770 F.2d 1401 (9th Cir. 1985)

AFSCME brought a class action on behalf of 15,500 employees against the state of Washington under Title VII's sex discrimination provisions. AFSCME claimed that   **FACTS**

---

[7] Espinoza v. Farah Manufacturing Company, Inc., 414 U.S. 86 (1973).

Title VII had been violated by the state's compensating employees in jobs where females predominated at lower rates than employees in jobs where males predominated when these jobs, though dissimilar, had been identified by certain studies to be of comparable worth. In essence, AFSCME argued that sex-based wage discrimination existed if employees in job classifications occupied primarily by women were paid less than employees in job classifications filled primarily by men if the jobs were of equal value to the employer, though otherwise dissimilar. The state justified its salary scales as reflective of prevailing market rates. The trial court found the state's policies illegal under Title VII on both the disparate impact and disparate treatment theories of discrimination.

ISSUE

Did the state's decision to base its compensation on a competitive market system rather than on a theory of comparable worth establish a discriminatory motive so as to demonstrate sex discrimination on a disparate treatment theory under Title VII?

HOLDING

No. Since the state had not created the market disparity and had not been shown to have been motivated by impermissible sex-based considerations in setting salaries, the state's compensation scheme did not violate Title VII.

REASONING

The trial court's reliance on disparate impact analysis for imposing liability was inappropriate. This analysis should be confined to cases that challenge a clearly delineated employment practice applied at a single point in the job selection process. Thus, there was no authority in prior case law to support AFSCME's disparate impact theory, which had been based on the contention that the State of Washington's practice of taking prevailing market rates into account in setting wages had had an adverse impact on women, who, historically, had received lower wages than men in the labor market. A decision to base compensation on the competitive market, rather than on a theory of comparable worth, involved the assessment of a number of complex factors not easily ascertainable, an assessment too multifaceted to be appropriate for disparate impact analysis. Moreover, the compensation system in question had resulted from surveys, agency hearings, administrative recommendations, budget proposals, executive actions, and legislative enactments. Hence, a compensation system responsive to supply and demand and other complex market forces would not constitute a single practice that sufficed to support a claim under disparate impact theory. Furthermore, AFSCME's claim that the state's discriminatory motive could be inferred from studies that had concluded that the state's practice of setting salaries in reliance on market rates had created a sex-based wage disparity for jobs deemed of comparable worth was invalid. The inference of discriminatory motive which AFSCME had sought to draw from the state's participation in the market system must fail, as the state had not created the market disparity and had not been shown to have premised its salary scales on an impermissible discriminatory motive. Since AFSCME had not been able to establish the requisite element of intent by either circumstantial or direct evidence, it had not proved the disparate treatment theory either. AFSCME's proof of isolated incidents of sex segregation was insufficient both to corroborate the results of the earlier studies and to justify an inference of discriminatory motive by the state in the setting of salaries for its system as a whole. Finally, AFSCME's contention that Washington's commissioning of the compensation studies had committed the state to implement a new system of compensation based on comparable worth as defined by the studies was similarly incorrect. The state's initial reliance on a free market system in which employees in male-dominated jobs had been compensated at a higher rate than employees in dissimilar female-dominated jobs was not in and of itself a violation of Title VII, notwithstanding the studies that had deemed the positions of comparable worth. In the absence of a showing of discriminatory motive, the federal judiciary should not interfere in the market-based compensation system set for the state's employees.

Congress passed the Occupational Safety and Health Act, better known as OSHA, in 1970. This act attempts to assure safe and healthful workplace conditions for working men and women by authorizing enforcement of the standards developed under the act (through the Occupational Safety and Health Administration); by assisting and encouraging the states in their efforts to assure safe and healthful working conditions; and by providing for research, information, education, and training in the field of occupational safety and health (through NIOSH, the National Institute for Occupational Safety and Health). The act covers most employers and employees, including agricultural employees, nonprofit organizations, and professionals (such as doctors, lawyers, accountants, and brokers). In fact, the act reaches almost any employer who employs at least one employee and whose business in any way affects interstate commerce. Atomic energy workers are exempted, however.

The Occupational Safety and Health Act

Because personal illnesses and injuries arising from the workplace produce significant burdens in terms of lost production, lost wages, medical expenses, and disability payments, Congress designed an act meant to highlight the existence of such factors and to provide standards for preventing future illnesses, injuries, and losses. To this end, OSHA sets out methods by which employers can reduce workplace hazards and foster attention to safety. The act further authorizes the Secretary of Labor to set mandatory occupational safety and health standards for businesses covered under the act and to create an Occupational Safety and Health Review Commission for hearing appeals from OSHA citations and penalties.

In trying to ensure that no employee suffers diminished health, functional capacity, or life expectancy as a result of work experiences, OSHA requires each employer to furnish a safe and healthful workplace for its employees, one that is free from "recognized hazards" that may cause or are likely to cause death or serious physical harm to employees. Excessive toxic substances in the air would be an example of a "recognized hazard."

OSHA allows inspectors to enter the workplace to inspect for compliance with regulations. As the following case indicates, on an employer's refusal to admit the inspector, OSHA regulations now require a warrant. But the standards for demonstrating the need for the warrant are relatively easy to meet and do not ordinarily impede OSHA's functions very much. Employers normally do not know in advance of an inspector's arrival. By writing to the Secretary of Labor, employees may request an inspection if they believe a violation that threatens physical harm exists.

Marshall v. Barlow's, Inc.
436 U.S. 307 (1978)

FACTS   Barlow, the owner of an electrical and plumbing business in Pocatello, Idaho, refused to allow an OSHA inspector to view the working areas of his business without a search warrant. An OSHA regulation permitted such inspections without a warrant. Barlow sued the Department of Labor, asserting that such inspections violated his Fourth Amendment guarantees against unreasonable searches and seizures.

ISSUE   Did the OSHA regulation authorizing warrantless inspections violate the Fourth Amendment?

HOLDING   Yes. Such warrantless searches violate the Fourth Amendment, so OSHA will have to amend its regulations to require warrants when entry to business premises is refused.

REASONING   Warrantless searches of commercial premises are just as illegal as warrantless searches of private homes would be. The Secretary of Labor's argument that the element of surprise, so essential to the proper enforcement of OSHA, will be lost if warrants are required is therefore unsupportable. Moreover, most businesspersons will allow the search even in the absence of a warrant. Should a businessperson's refusal necessitate a warrant, OSHA can obtain one without demonstrating probable cause in the criminal sense; indeed, OSHA need not always show specific evidence of an existing violation but can show instead that the business has been chosen for inspection in accordance with an OSHA general administrative plan. Finally, OSHA is empowered to secure *ex parte warrants* (that is, warrants issued to OSHA without the businessperson's having prior notice or opportunity to object to the warrant's issuance) once entry has been refused.

Inspections typically involve a tour through the business and an examination of each work area for compliance with OSHA. After the inspector has informed the employer of the reason for the inspection, the inspector will give the employer a copy of the complaint (if one is involved) or the reason for the inspection if it results from an agency general administrative plan. When an employee has initiated the complaint, OSHA will withhold the employee's name by request. An employer representative and an employee-selected representative generally accompany the inspector on this walk-around tour. The inspector may order some violations, such as blocked aisles, locked fire exits, or unsanitary conditions, to be corrected immediately. The inspector additionally reviews the records OSHA requires the employer to maintain, including records of deaths, injuries, illnesses, and employee exposure to toxic substances. After the inspection, the inspector and employer engage in a closing conference, during which they discuss probable violations and methods for eliminating these violations. The inspector then files his or her report with the

Commission. Citations and proposed penalties may be issued to the employer, and a copy of these will be sent to the complaining party if there is one. No citation normally is issued if a violation of a standard or rule has no immediate or direct relationship to safety or health, although a notice of a minimal violation (without a proposed penalty) may be sent to the employer even in these situations. OSHA requires the prominent posting of citations in the workplace.

Penalties, when imposed, are severe: fines of up to $10,000 for each violation may be levied for willful or repeated violations. An employer will also be fined up to $1000 for each serious violation — one in which there is a "substantial probability" that the consequences of an accident resulting from the violation will be death or serious harm. Employers can defend by showing they did not, and could not with the exercise of "reasonable diligence," know about the condition or hazard. For even nonserious violations (such as a failure to paint steps and banisters or to post citations), fines of up to $1000 are possible. Prison terms are possible in the event of willful violations that cause an employee's death. The OSHA Commission assesses these penalties in light of the size of the employer's business, the seriousness of the violation, the presence or absence of employer good faith, and the past history of violations. An employer may contest any penalties by resorting to the procedures established by the Commission. In general, these require an investigation and a decision by an administrative law judge. The Commission, in turn, can review this decision. Should the employer still disagree with the decision, he or she can appeal to the appropriate federal circuit court of appeals for review.

Employers may request temporary exemptions from OSHA standards on proof of inability to comply because of unavailability of materials, equipment, or personnel to effect the changes within the required time. Permanent exemptions may be granted when the employer's method of protecting employees is as effective as that required by the standard. Needless to say, such exemptions are not granted retroactively. Other provisions of OSHA protect employees from discrimination or discharge based on filing a complaint, testifying about violations, or exercising any rights guaranteed by the act. The act prohibits employees from stopping work or walking off the job because of "potential unsafe conditions at the workplace" unless the employee, through performance of the assigned work, would subject "himself to serious injury or death from a hazardous condition at the workplace." The *Whirlpool Corp.* v. *Marshall* case, which follows, involved an interpretation of this aspect of the act and its attendant regulations.

Whirlpool Corp. v. *Marshall*
445 U.S. 1 (1980)

Two maintenance workers at the Whirlpool plant in Marion, Ohio, were told to   **FACTS**
remove objects from an overhead mesh screen designed to catch appliance compo-

nents that move along an overhead conveyor belt. Several employees had been injured in falls from the screen because it was necessary to step onto the mesh screen in order to retrieve the objects. Indeed, one employee had recently died from falling through the mesh screen. Because they feared serious injuries, the two main-tenance men refused to step onto the screen. They were given reprimands and were ordered to punch out six hours early. The Secretary of Labor sued Whirlpool for discrimination against the employees who, the Secretary believed, had merely uti-lized the rights guaranteed them under the Occupational Safety and Health Act. The Secretary had also issued a regulation that protected the right of employees to choose not to perform work because of a reasonable apprehension of injury or death when less drastic alternatives were not available. This regulation, the Secretary maintained, protected the employees from adverse employment consequences. Whirlpool argued that the Secretary had no right to promulgate this regulation.

ISSUE   Did the Secretary of Labor have the authority to promulgate a regulation that per-mitted workers' refusals to perform in hazardous situations?

HOLDING   Yes. The regulation providing for refusals to perform in dangerous situations is a right afforded by the Occupational Safety and Health Act.

REASONING   The promulgation of the regulation was a valid exercise of the authority granted the Secretary of Labor under the Occupational Safety and Health Act. Moreover, the regulation itself represented a permissible interpretation of the act in light of its fundamental purpose of preventing occupational deaths and serious injuries.

Social Security

The Social Security Act, first enacted in 1935 as part of Roosevelt's "New Deal" policies, has spawned numerous controversies. Current debate about social security centers on fears that the system will become bankrupt and on pro-posed plans to allay this possibility. By "social security," most people mean the federal old-age, survivors', and disability insurance benefits plan. Broad in scope, social security benefits today are payable to workers, their dependents, and their survivors. Through the Supplemental Security Income Program (SSI) administered by the Department of Health and Human Services, the federal social security system also makes payments to the blind, the disabled, and the aged who are in need of these benefits. The states can also supplement this pervasive federal scheme if they so choose.

In general, federal social security benefits are computed on the worker's earning records. A "fully insured" worker is one who has worked at least forty quarters (ten years). To use 1988 as an example, a worker will earn one quarter of coverage for each $470 in earnings, whether wages, farm wages, or income from self-employment, up to a maximum of four quarters. "Fully insured" workers who receive retirement benefits include retired workers, sixty-two years or older; their spouses, or divorced spouses, sixty-two or older; spouses of any age if caring for a child entitled to benefits; and children or grandchildren under eighteen (or nineteen if a student) or of any age if disabled. Additionally, survivors' benefits go to certain classes of fully insured workers, as do disability benefits for qualified workers. One should be aware, however, that computing social security benefits involves complicated arithmetical formulas noting the worker's age; date of retirement, disability, or death; and yearly earnings history. Cost-of-living escalators tied to the **consumer price index** in certain circumstances may raise benefits, as well.

Consumer price index
Measurement of how the price of a group of consumer goods changes between two time periods

Disability benefits — those granted to a worker who has been disabled at least five months — are computed in a similar manner, subject to some limitations for younger disabled workers. Additionally, for eligibility, the worker must prove that he or she can no longer engage in substantial gainful employment. The disability must be expected to last at least twelve months or to result in death. Finally, the worker must have sufficient quarters of coverage to be considered "fully insured" if near retirement age and must have worked at least twenty quarters of the last forty quarters before the disability began. Blind persons and some younger workers who become disabled face less stringent eligibility requirements. Receipt of benefits paid under workers' compensation or other federal, state, or local disability plans may lessen the amount of benefits received from social security.

Monthly payments made to a retired or disabled worker's family or to the survivors of an insured worker are equal to a certain percentage (usually 50 or 75 percent) of the worker's benefits. For example, if a worker were entitled to $379 per month in benefits, the worker's wife or divorced wife who was married to the worker for at least ten years and is not now married would receive $189.50 or $284.25 in monthly benefits. The act limits the amount one family can receive in total benefits. Similarly, benefits for a nondisabled child who is no longer attending high school normally end at age eighteen. Lump-sum death benefits to eligible persons cannot exceed $255. Earnings realized by retired persons between sixty-five and sixty-nine cannot exceed $8,400 in 1988 without loss of benefits. The Social Security Administration (SSA) will reduce from the benefits of any worker who makes more than this amount one dollar for every two dollars over the limit. Social security coverage extends to most types of employment and self-employment; among those excluded are employees of the federal government and railroad workers.

Those who have been denied benefits may utilize certain administrative steps to appeal an SSA decision. Usually, such persons file a request for reconsideration within sixty days of the date of the initial determination. The agency then conducts a thorough and independent review of the evidence. After this reconsideration, a person who remains adversely affected can file for a hearing or review by an administrative law judge. After the hearing, the administrative law judge issues a written decision that sets out his or her findings of fact in understandable language. All parties receive copies of this decision. The decision is binding unless appealed to the Appeals Council of the SSA or to a federal district court.

The taxes paid by employees and employers on wages earned by workers not only fund social security retirement benefits but also help provide qualified persons with hospital insurance. Called Medicare, this protection is normally available to persons sixty-five years or older and to some disabled persons under sixty-five. Medicare covers doctors' services, hospital care, some nursing home care, certain home health services, and hospice care. In 1988, the tax rate paid was 7.51 percent on a maximum of $45,000 in employee wages.

In addition to receiving Medicare, qualified persons can pay for a government-subsidized plan called supplementary medical insurance to cover medical services beyond hospitalization, such as doctors' services and related medical expenses involving outpatient and rehabilitation costs. Another program, Medicaid, provides broad medical assistance to "categorically needy" individuals.

Unemployment Insurance

In addition to retirement, disability, and Medicare benefits, the Social Security Program covers unemployment insurance through the Federal Unemployment Tax Act. Unemployment insurance represents a coordinated federal and state effort to provide economic security for temporarily unemployed workers. The funds used in the unemployment insurance system come from taxes, or "contributions," paid predominantly by employers. In a few states, employees also pay these taxes. Those contributing pay federal taxes, which the government uses to administer the federal/state program, as well as state taxes, which the state uses to finance the payment of weekly benefits to unemployed workers.

Various credits allowed under federal law significantly reduce the amount of taxes paid in federal contributions. Essentially, computation of the taxes is based on a specified percentage of wages paid by the employer/employees. "Wages" include anything paid as compensation for employment and thus may include salaries, fees, bonuses, and commissions. Since 1983, the amount of wages subject to federal taxes for unemployment compensation is at most $7000 for each employee per calendar year. Many states' taxable wage bases are higher than this federal figure. State contribution rates may vary, but most have set a standard rate (such as 5.4 percent).

State rates, almost without exception, utilize "experience rating" or "merit rating" systems whereby the rate employers pay reflects each individual employer's experience with unemployment. Under such systems, employers whose workers suffer the most involuntary unemployment pay higher rates than employers whose workers suffer less unemployment. Since the aim of unemployment compensation involves the achievement of regular employment and the prevention of unemployment, such systems provide incentives to employers to keep their workforces intact and thereby to perpetuate the goals of these laws.

State provisions regarding the criteria for eligibility and the amount of benefits vary greatly. For instance, in different jurisdictions, unemployment compensation may not be available to employees discharged for cause, to those who quit their jobs without cause, or to those who refuse to seek or accept a job for which they are qualified.

Workers' Compensation

Workers' compensation statutes are not the same as unemployment statutes, although both concern the welfare of workers. Workers' compensation laws in the various states attempt to reimburse workers for injuries or death arising in the employment context. "Compensation" in this area does not therefore refer to wages or salaries but rather to the money paid by the employer to indemnify the worker for employment-related injury or death. The employer usually self-insures, buys insurance, or pays money into a state insurance fund at a "merit" or "experience" rate, as discussed earlier, reflective of the employer's actual incidence of employee injuries. Injured workers then receive compensation for their injuries in the form of medical care and disability benefits, the latter often based on a specific statutory scale (such as 60 percent of average weekly wages up to $100 in average weekly wages for twenty-six weeks), through administrative proceedings in front of a workers' compensation board.

Workers' compensation acts thus impose strict liability on the employer for injuries to employees during the scope of their employment. These laws first arose out of lawmakers' concern for employees injured as a result of increased industrial mechanization, but these acts serve other functions, as well. For instance, through such statutes, employees can receive compensation without engaging in costly litigation, and the employer can recoup the costs of workers' compensation by passing these costs on to consumers. Both sides benefit, since the employee receives reimbursement for the injuries suffered and the employer's liability to the employee usually ends there; that is, the statutes ordinarily prohibit the employee from suing the employer in a court of law. Such acts, then, are grounded in public policy concerns.

The classes of employees covered by such acts depend on the particular statute involved. Agricultural, domestic, or casual laborers are often not covered because the right to compensation ordinarily depends on the nature of the work performed, the regularity of such work, and/or whether the worker was working as an independent contractor for someone else when injured. To be covered, an employee ordinarily must be a "worker" — that is, a person who performs manual labor or similar duties. For this reason, workers' compensation statutes would seemingly not cover directors, officers, or stockholders. Yet under the "dual capacity" doctrine, such persons can receive compensation if they are performing the ordinary duties of the business when injured. For example, a general manager of a tree-pruning service who is injured while pruning trees will be able to recover. If the general manager were instead working as an independent contractor (not for the corporation), he or she normally would not receive workers' compensation.

In general, however, just about any employment-related injury or disease makes the covered employee eligible for workers' compensation. For this reason, even a negligent employee usually can recover for injuries suffered while in the employment relationship. Contrast this statutory result with what would have occurred at common law: there the employer could have used the employee's contributory negligence as a complete bar to recovery. Recent decisions have allowed recoveries for occupational diseases such as asbestosis, for work-related stress, and even for injuries suffered before or after working hours. Although workers' compensation takes the place of an employee's suing the employer for the injuries suffered, employees can still maintain product liability suits against manufacturers or suppliers and can also sue any fellow employees who cause their injuries.

SUMMARY

The Wagner Act, the Taft-Hartley Act, and the Landrum-Griffin Act set out a pervasive federal scheme for the regulation of labor. This blueprint of federal labor law broadly regulates employees' rights to organize and to engage in concerted activities in furtherance of their objectives. Both employees and employers are protected from unfair labor practices. The National Labor Relations Board (NLRB or Board) retains jurisdiction over labor disputes, oversees elections, arbitrates disputes about the duty to bargain, and almost wholly preempts the states' jurisdiction over labor matters, except for criminal violations or torts, retaliatory discharges, and the like.

A host of federal statutes extensively regulates fair employment practices. Title VII of the Civil Rights Act of 1964 prohibits employment discrimination based on race, color, religion, sex, or national origin by employers, labor organizations, or employment agencies. The Equal Employment Opportunity Commission (EEOC) enforces many of these federal laws and sets out the complex procedures with which a grievant must comply. Employment criteria that have a disparate impact on minorities are illegal unless the employer can show that the criteria are job-related. Employers may also be liable for the disparate treatment of their employees. The issue of "reverse discrimination" remains controversial in the Title VII context. Limited defenses based on bona fide occupational qualifications (BFOQs) are available for the protected categories of religion, sex, and national origin; a BFOQ can never be based on race, however. The Equal Pay Act, the Age Discrimination in Employment Act, the Rehabilitation Act of 1973, and other federal statutes protect qualified individuals against employment discrimination. State law often supplements this comprehensive federal scheme.

The Occupational Safety and Health Act (OSHA) attempts to ensure safe and healthful working conditions for American workers. Inspections of the workplace provide a mechanism for realizing this statutory goal. Warrantless inspections conducted after the owner refuses entry to the inspector are illegal. Workers, in contrast, can legally walk off the job if performance of the work assignment can lead to serious injury or death.

Federal and state social security benefits aid workers, the disabled, the blind, and the aged. Computations of benefits are complex. Those who have been denied benefits may utilize certain administrative steps to appeal such agency decisions. Because both employers and employees must pay social security and hospital care taxes on wages earned by the workers, the record-keeping burdens posed by such provisions have nettled employers.

Unemployment insurance represents another aspect of federal and state labor law, one designed to provide economic security for temporarily unemployed workers. The contributions paid into the insurance fund stem from a specified percentage of wages paid by the employer or employee. State taxable wage bases may differ from the federal figure, and state provisions regarding the criteria for eligibility and the amount of benefits vary greatly.

State workers' compensation statutes attempt to reimburse workers for injuries or death resulting from the employment relationship. In return, such statutes generally prohibit the employee from suing the employer in a court of law. The classes of employees covered in such acts depend on the particular statute involved; but eligible employees may recover for occupational diseases, injuries resulting from the employee's own negligence, and injuries sustained before or after working hours. Workers' compensation statutes ordinarily do not preclude an employee's maintaining either a product liability suit against a manufacturer or a suit against a fellow employee who caused the injuries at issue.

1. List some of the rights guaranteed and the practices prohibited by the Wagner, Taft-Hartley, and Landrum-Griffin Acts.

2. Describe some of the issues and enforcement problems involved in the collective bargaining process.

3. Explain the boundaries of state regulation of labor.

4. What are the protected classes of employees under Title VII?

5. Define and describe the two methods by which an employee can show liability for discrimination on the basis of the protected categories set out in Title VII.

6. Why is the issue of "reverse discrimination" such a difficult problem?

7. Define the term *bona fide occupational qualification*.

8. Name some other statutes that guarantee fair employment.

9. Describe a typical OSHA inspection.

10. Name the classes of persons eligible for social security, unemployment insurance, and workers' compensation.

DISCUSSION QUESTIONS

1. The International Brotherhood of Electrical Workers, Local 340 (the Union) fined two of its members, Schoux and Choate, who were supervisors, for violating its constitution by working for employers that had no collective-bargaining agreements with the Union. The employers filed unfair labor practice charges with the National Labor Relations Board (NLRB), alleging that the Union had violated Section 8(b)(1)(B) of the National Labor Relations Act (Act), which makes it an unfair labor practice for a union "to restrain or coerce . . . an employer in the selection of his representatives for the purposes of collective bargaining or the adjustment of grievances." There had been no collective bargaining relationship in existence between the employers and the Union when the

CASE PROBLEMS

Union had tried to enforce its "no-contract-no-work" rule against these supervisors. Furthermore, neither Schoux nor Choate had represented their employers in collective bargaining discussions or grievance adjustments. Did the Union's discipline of its supervisor members violate Section 8(b)(1)(B)? (*NLRB* v. *International Brotherhood of Electrical Workers, Local 340*, 107 S.Ct. 2002 [1987].)

2. Section 405 of the Surface Transportation Assistance Act of 1982 forbids the discharge of employees in the commercial motor transportation industry in retaliation for refusing to operate motor vehicles that do not comply with applicable safety standards or for filing complaints alleging such noncompliance. The statute provides for the Secretary of Labor's initial investigation of an employee's discharge and, upon a finding of reasonable cause to believe that the employee was discharged in violation of the Act, requires the Secretary to order the employee's temporary reinstatement by the employer, who may then request an evidentiary hearing and a final decision from the Secretary. The statute mandates that the employer be notified of the employee's complaint but does not specify procedures for employer participation in the Secretary's initial investigation. After Roadway Express, Inc. (Roadway), a trucking company subject to Section 405's requirement, discharged one of its drivers for allegedly intentionally damaging his assigned truck, the employee filed a complaint with the Department of Labor claiming that his discharge had violated Section 405. Roadway was afforded an opportunity to meet with the Labor Department investigator and to submit a written statement detailing the basis for the employee's discharge, but it was not given the substance of the evidence collected by the investigator. Ultimately, the Secretary ordered the employee's reinstatement with backpay. Roadway then filed suit on the grounds that Section 405, to the extent that it empowers the Secretary to order temporary reinstatement without first conducting an evidentiary hearing, had deprived Roadway of procedural due process under the Fifth Amendment. How should a court rule on this claim? (*Brock* v. *Roadway Express, Inc.*, 107 S.Ct. 1740 [1987].)

3. Gene Arline (Arline) had taught elementary school in Nassau County, Florida, from 1966 until 1979, when she was discharged after having suffered a third relapse of tuberculosis within two years. Arline argued that the school board had dismissed her solely on the basis of her illness, which she contended was a handicap under the Rehabilitation Act of 1973. The school board asserted that a contagious disease was not protectable under the Act and that, in any event, Arline was not a "handicapped" individual because she was not "qualified" to teach owing to her disease. Was Arline a handicapped person under the Rehabilitation Act of 1973? (*School Board of Nassau County, Florida* v. *Arline*, 107 S.Ct. 1123 [1987], reh'g denied 107 S.Ct. 1913 [1987].)

4. After two and one-half years of working for Lawton and Company (Law-

ton), Paula Hobbie informed Lawton that she was joining the Seventh-Day Adventist Church and that, for religious reasons, she would no longer be able to work at Lawton's jewelry store on her Sabbath. When she subsequently refused to work scheduled shifts on Friday evenings and Saturdays, she was discharged. She thereupon filed a claim for unemployment compensation, which was denied by a claims examiner for "misconduct connected with [her] work" under the applicable Florida statute. The Florida Unemployment Appeals Commission (Appeals Commission) affirmed that decision. Hobbie then challenged this decision in federal court by claiming that the Appeals Commission's disqualifying her for benefits violated the Free Exercise Clause of the First Amendment that was applicable to the states through the Fourteenth Amendment. Was Hobbie correct? (*Hobbie* v. *Unemployment Appeals Commission of Florida,* 480 U.S. 136 [1987].)

5. When Mechelle Vinson met Sidney Taylor, the vice-president of Capital City Federal Saving and Loan Association (Capital City), he asked her to apply for employment with the firm. She was hired as a teller-trainee, and Taylor became her supervisor at the Northeast Branch. She was thereafter promoted successively to teller, head teller, and assistant branch manager. After Vinson had worked at the Northeast Branch for four years, she took an indefinite sick leave and was discharged two months later for excessive use of that leave. Vinson subsequently brought an action under Title VII against Taylor and Capital City, alleging that Taylor had sexually harassed her. Vinson contended that Taylor had asked her to have sexual relations with him, claiming that she "owed him" because he had obtained the job for her, and that after initially declining his invitation she had ultimately yielded, but only because she had been afraid that continued refusals would jeopardize her employment. She further asserted that thereafter she had been forced to submit to sexual advances by Taylor at the Northeast Branch both during and after business hours and that often Taylor had assaulted or raped her. In addition, she said that Taylor had caressed her on the job, had followed her into the ladies' room when she had been there alone, and at times had exposed himself to her. Capital City argued that it should not be held liable for its supervisor's sexual harassment owing to its lack of actual knowledge of the conduct. Would you agree? Also, should a successful sexual harassment case be dependent on the alleged victim's suffering a loss of employment or promotions? (*Meritor Savings Bank* v. *Vinson,* 477 U.S. 57 [1986].)

6. As part of the 1980 settlement of a Title VII lawsuit filed by Carl Stotts, a black firefighter, against the Memphis, Tennessee, Fire Department, the city agreed to a court-imposed consent decree whereby the city promised to promote thirteen individuals, to provide backpay for eighty-two others, and to increase minority representation in each job classification of the fire department to approximate the proportion of blacks in the labor force

in Shelby County, Tennessee. The 1980 decree also established hiring and promotion goals with respect to blacks. In May, 1981, owing to projected budget deficits, the city announced layoffs in city government. Layoffs were to be based on the "last-hired, first-fired" rule under which city-wide seniority, determined by each employee's length of continuous service, would be the factor in deciding who would be laid off. Following this announcement, the district court subsequently entered an order prohibiting the layoffs of black employees, which order led to the layoffs or demotions of nonminority employees who had more seniority than minority employees who had been retained. Was it legal under Title VII to deny nonminority employees the benefits of their seniority in order to provide a remedy in a case alleging a pattern or practice of discrimination where the black employees protected from layoffs were not identifiable victims of discrimination? (*Firefighters Local Union No. 1784* v. *Stotts,* 467 U.S. 561 [1984].)

7. Transportation Agency of Santa Clara County, California (the Agency) adopted an affirmative action plan that allowed it to consider sex as one factor whenever it made promotions to positions within traditionally segregated job classifications in which women had been significantly underrepresented. In selecting applicants for the position of road dispatcher, the Agency passed over Paul Johnson to promote a female applicant, Diane Joyce. Before Joyce, women had held none of the 238 skilled craftworker positions in the Agency. Although both individuals were qualified for the job, Johnson had scored slightly higher on the interview than Joyce. When the Agency nonetheless promoted Joyce, Johnson sued arguing that the Agency's affirmative action plan violated Title VII of the Civil Rights Act by taking sex into account for promotions. Was he correct? (*Johnson* v. *Transportation Agency, Santa Clara County, California,* 107 S.Ct. 1442 [1987].)

8. Reynolds Metals objected to an inspection warrant issued on a "worst-first" basis; that is, that facilities in the metal-can industry had one of the highest incidences of occupational and health accidents and injuries and thus should be inspected before other facilities. Reynolds argued that before the warrant could be issued, the Secretary of Labor must first have had probable cause to believe that specific OSHA violations existed at its facility. The Secretary asserted that probable cause could be established by demonstrating that the inspection was part of a plan designed to effectuate the purposes of the Act. Who was right? (*Reynolds Metals Company* v. *Secretary of Labor,* 442 F. Supp. 195 [W.D. Va. 1977].)

9. Fox's widow received a workers' compensation death benefits award from the Delaware Industrial Accident Board because of her husband's suicide. The board believed Fox's suicide had resulted from the severe pain and despair proximately caused by a compensable accident that had occurred at Delaware Tire Center, Fox's employer. Should suicide be

covered under workers' compensation? (*Delaware Tire Center* v. *Fox*, 411 A.2d 606 [Del. 1980].)

10. When Congress in 1978 amended the Age Discrimination in Employment Act (ADEA) to prohibit most mandatory retirements of individuals between forty and seventy, a Federal Aviation Administration regulation prohibited anyone from serving after age sixty as a captain or first officer on a commercial carrier. This regulation did not affect flight engineers. In response to the ADEA 1978 amendment, Trans World Airlines (TWA) modified its retirement procedures. Under TWA's modified plan, flight engineers were permitted to continue work after age sixty. Captains and first officers had to bid to obtain flight engineer status prior to reaching age sixty, and vacancies were filled only as they occurred. A captain who had been displaced for any reason other than age would not have to resort to the bidding procedure; these captains automatically displaced less senior flight engineers. Thurston and other captains who had been involuntarily retired upon reaching age sixty and who had thereby been denied opportunities to "bump" less senior flight engineers sued the airline, contending that its policies had violated the ADEA. Were they correct? Was TWA's retirement policy justified as either a BFOQ or as being part of a bona fide seniority system? (*Trans World Airlines, Inc.* v. *Thurston*, 469 U.S. 111 [1985].)

PART 9

Property Protection

When a society forms, it must go through certain stages. When primitive people first began to form tribes, they had a reason for seeking companionship—survival. A tribe allowed for more hunters, and therefore for more food. The larger numbers of people making up the tribe also provided for better defense, more children, and a better chance of perpetuating the species. However, tribal existence also led to internal conflicts, which led to a need for the formation of law. The earliest laws were undoubtedly designed to keep peace within the tribal unit.

Once peace was attained, and human beings began to feel personally secure, their attention shifted. Being assured of peace, they began to seek ways to acquire wealth, and to protect their wealth once they did acquire it. Thus developed the laws of property protection. And once their property was protected, human beings began to seek means for assuring that their families would be protected should some disaster befall them. From this desire came the laws of trusts, wills, estates, and insurance.

When people have no personal security, property is relatively unimportant. Once personal security is provided for, property protection becomes relatively important. This part of the text deals with the bases of property protection in our society.

CHAPTER 49

Real Property and Joint Ownership

PROPERTY RIGHTS

Property really has two meanings. One meaning is the thing that is subject to ownership, the valuable asset. The second meaning is the group of rights and interests that are protected by the law. A multitude of rights are associated with property ownership. Ownership entitles a person to use the property personally, to give someone else the use of the property, to rent the use of the property to someone else, or to use the property to secure a loan. The owner may sell the property, make improvements to the property, or abandon the property. Ownership of real estate often entitles the owner to continued use and enjoyment of the property in its present condition. For example, suppose you owned a house with a beautiful view of the mountains. If someone purchased an adjacent lot and started constructing a three-story house that would block your view, you could sue for an injunction to prohibit that person from interfering with the view. You could possibly win the case depending on state law.

REAL PROPERTY DEFINED

This chapter deals with *real property* or, as it is commonly called, real estate. There are significant differences between real and personal property. Real property is *land and things that are permanently attached to land,* including buildings, roadways, and storage structures. Personal property, on the other hand, consists of movable goods. Property that is permanently attached to buildings is also considered real property and is called a *fixture.* In determining whether an item is a fixture or a household good, courts will look at the reasonable expectations and understanding of most people. For instance, most people would be shocked if they bought a house and, when they moved in, discovered that the sellers had removed the handles on the kitchen cabinets and the plates over the light switches. The same buyers would expect the sellers to remove the tables, chairs, and other furniture. Ceiling lights are fixtures; table lamps are household goods. Plants in a flower bed are real property; plants in pots are personal property. Wall-to-wall carpeting is real property; area rugs are personal property. Refrigerators, mirrors, and paintings are generally personal property but may be real property if they are an integral part of the building.

A fixture is property that at one time was movable and independent of real estate but became attached to it. Examples would be water heaters, central air-conditioning units, furnaces, built-in ovens, installed dishwashers, bathroom sinks, and copper pipes for plumbing. A builder who is constructing a house will buy a water heater, take it to the construction site, and permanently attach it to the plumbing lines and the gas or electric lines. After it is attached, it is a fixture.

In determining whether property is personal property or a fixture, courts also consider another factor: how much damage would occur if the property in question were removed. For example, would the building be damaged by the removal of a brick fireplace? What would the wall look like after the fireplace was removed?

Real estate also includes plants that are growing on the land, such as fruit and shade trees, tomatoes, strawberries or artichokes, as well as trees that are being grown for timber. If a farmer sells land with crops still growing on it, the farmer is clearly selling real estate. Sometimes a farmer or another landowner may sell the plants but keep the land. In this case, did the landowner sell real or personal property? The common law rule was that if the plants were still growing when the **title** passed to the buyer, the sale was of real estate. If the title passed after the plants were severed from the land, the sale was of personal property. This rule was difficult to apply because in many instances the buyer and seller never discussed when title should pass.

Title The legal recognition of property ownership

For this reason, the Uniform Commercial Code uses a different test, one that is easier to apply. Under the UCC test, the determining factor is *who* is going to remove the plants or trees. If the *buyer* is going to remove them, the buyer has purchased real property. If the *seller* is going to remove them, the buyer has purchased personal property. After defining the difference between real and personal property, the UCC generally is not concerned with real estate, although some sections of the UCC do discuss fixtures and crops. A few states still follow the common law.

The laws of a state govern the real property within its boundaries regardless of the residence of the owner. For example, if you live in Utah but own land in Ohio, Ohio laws control your transactions with respect to that land.

ACQUISITION OF REAL PROPERTY

Original Occupancy

Original occupancy (original entry) occurs when the government allows *the private ownership of land that was previously owned by the government*. In the United States, title may have been acquired by grant from either the United States government or the other countries that colonized here. Original occupancy may be accomplished under an outright grant to specific people or families, or it may have occurred under **homestead entry laws.**

Voluntary Transfer by the Owner

The owner of real property may sell, trade, or give title to another by executing (signing) a deed. The recipient can be another private individual, a business entity, or a government body. In any of these cases, the transfer of title is made by the execution and delivery of a written deed of conveyance. A *deed* is the type of title evidence that is used for real estate. It indicates who owns the land. A written document is required by the Statute of Frauds. This document must adequately describe the property that is being transferred. Documents that transfer important interests in real estate must also be in writing. An example would be a loan of money secured by real estate, which is called a *mortgage*.

Homestead entry laws Laws that allowed settlers to claim public lands by entering, filing an application, and paying any fees

A deed describes the land being transferred and generally includes the following items:

1. the names of the grantor (transferor) and the grantee (transferee)
2. the amount of consideration, if any, that was paid by the grantee
3. a statement that the grantor intended to make the transfer (commonly called words of conveyance)

4. an adequate description of the property (the street address by itself will not be sufficient; usually this description contains information provided by a private or government survey)

5. a list and description of any ownership rights that are not included in the conveyance (such as mineral rights, oil rights, or **easements**)

6. the quantity of the estate conveyed

7. any covenants or warranties from the grantor or grantee (some may be implied under the state law; others may be expressed in the deed, such as the grantee shall never allow alcohol to be sold on the premises; usually the deed specifies that these convenants are binding on the grantee and his or her heirs and assigns)

8. the signature of the grantor or grantors

Easements Rights to the access and use of someone else's real estate

Warranty Deed

A warranty deed contains a number of implied covenants (or promises) made by the grantor to the effect that a good and marketable title is being conveyed. All the following covenants are included:

1. covenant of title (the grantor owns the estate or interest that he or she is purporting to convey)

2. covenant of right to convey (the grantor has the power, authority, and right to transfer this interest in the property)

3. covenant against encumbrances (there are no encumbrances on the property except for those listed on the deed; encumbrances would include easements, mortgages, and similar restrictions on ownership)

4. covenant of quiet enjoyment (the grantor promises that the grantee's possession or enjoyment of the property will not be disturbed by another person with a lawful claim of title)

5. covenant to defend (the grantor promises to defend the grantee against any lawful or reasonable claims of a third party against the title of the grantee)

Grant Deed

A grant deed contains fewer promises than a warranty deed. Basically, it includes a covenant that the grantor has not conveyed this property interest to anyone else. The grantor also promises that all the encumbrances are listed on the deed.

Quitclaim Deed

With a quitclaim deed, the grantor makes no promises about his or her interest in the property. The grantor simply releases any interest that he or she has.

Delivery of the Deed

To complete a transfer of real property, the grantor *must* deliver the deed to the grantee or have it delivered to the grantee by a third party. The delivery evidences the grantor's intention to transfer the property. This requirement was examined in the case that follows.

Rosengrant v. *Rosengrant*
629 P.2d 800 (Okla. App. 1981)

FACTS

Jay and his wife were very close to Jay's Uncle Harold and Aunt Mildred. Harold and Mildred had no children of their own, but they did have a number of nieces and nephews. They had a deed prepared naming Jay as the grantee of their farm. They executed the deed in Jay's presence, handed the deed to him, and told him that when something happened to them, he should record the deed. The deed was then handed to their banker. The banker put it in an envelope with Jay's and Harold's names on it and then stored it in the bank vault.

ISSUE

Was the delivery of the deed sufficient to transfer the ownership of the parcel?

HOLDING

No. The grantors did not intend to make a transfer at that time.

REASONING

The grantor's intention at the time of delivery is controlling. There was no evidence that Harold and Mildred wanted to transfer ownership immediately. After the delivery of the deed, the grantors continued to farm the parcel, pay taxes on it, and use it as their homestead. The evidence indicates that Mildred and Harold did not want the transfer to take effect until they both had died. Under bank policy, the bank would have returned the deed to Harold whenever he asked for it prior to his death. The ritualistic delivery of the deed did not constitute delivery at all. (Also, this deed would not be effective as a testamentary transfer because it did not comply with the state statute of wills.)

Instead of handing the deed directly to the grantee, the grantor may use a third person to make the transfer. Sometimes, in a sales transaction, it is important to use an impartial third party to assist in the transfer and to protect both the buyer and seller. This third party is charged with the obligation of supervising the transfer, including such activities as collecting the deed, collecting the funds, checking that utility bills and liens have been paid, checking that back taxes have been paid, prorating real estate taxes, prorating interest payments if a mortgage is being assumed, and checking that the parties have fulfilled any conditions such as repairs and inspections of the premises. This

Escrow Period when buyer and seller prepare for the exchange of real estate

procedure is called an **escrow** and is a common method of transferring property in some states. The person who supervises this type of delivery may be an attorney, an *escrow officer* (an employee of a bank or escrow company who oversees the escrow transaction), or another agent.

Recording of the Deed

Recording is accomplished by giving the deed to the proper authority, usually the county clerk or county recorder. The recorder files the deed or a copy of it in a deed book. Deed books are usually arranged in chronological order. The recorder also enters information about the transfer in an index, which is organized by the names of the grantors and grantees or by the location of the property. The index makes it easier to locate information about a particular parcel. The recording gives the whole world notice of the transfer to this grantee. Recording is not a legal prerequisite to the transfer, but it does establish the grantee's interest in the property, and in many states recorded deeds have priority over unrecorded deeds.

Transfer by Will of Intestate Succession

A person can arrange to leave real property by provisions in a valid will. If a person does not have a valid will, then the property will pass by the **intestate succession statute** of the state where the property is located. (Wills are discussed in Chapter 52.)

PROTECTION OF REAL PROPERTY

An owner of real property can lose the property or part of the property by operation of law or by action of the government, another person, or nature. This loss is generally involuntary on the part of the owner. To prevent it, the owner should be alert to these potential causes of loss.

Involuntary Transfers by Operation of Law

Intestate succession statute State law that determines who inherits property if there is no valid will

If the owner is in default on a mortgage or trust deed, the owner may lose the property. The lender may institute foreclosure proceedings and take possession of the real estate. The lender must follow the appropriate state laws. Usually, the property will be sold at a foreclosure sale.

If the owner has not paid a legal judgment, the judgment creditor may ask the court for a writ of execution. Following state procedures, the sheriff will attach the property and sell it at a judgment sale. (Under state law, some property, both real and personal, may be exempt from attachment under a judgment sale.)

If the owner has not paid people who supplied labor or materials for the premises, these suppliers may also be able to force a sale under state law. These workers may have mechanics' liens for the value of the supplies or services rendered to improve the property. Even if they do not force a sale of the real property, generally they can prevent a voluntary sale of the property unless they are paid from the proceeds.

Government bodies may take all or part of the owner's property by eminent domain. The government can also "take" the owner's land by restricting the manner in which it is used.

Eminent Domain

Government bodies have *the right to take private lands if they are necessary for public use.* This is called the right of *eminent domain.* Under this doctrine the government must have a legitimate public use for the land and must pay the owner a reasonable value for it.

Zoning and Planning Laws

Zoning and planning laws restrict how property may be used. They may prevent certain types of structures from being built on the property; for example, some areas may be limited to single-family residences. Or they may not allow certain industries to operate plants in particular areas because of the air pollution that these plants would cause. Sometimes they restrict the number and placement of establishments that sell alcohol. Commonly, bars are not allowed within one-quarter mile of public schools. In order to be valid, zoning and planning laws must be based on a compelling state interest, and the restrictions must be reasonable.

Adverse possession occurs when *someone tries to take title and possession of real estate from the owner.* A person who has physical possession of real property has better legal rights to that property than anyone else, except for the true owner and people who claim possession through the true owner. If the possession is of an adverse nature and if the possession is for a sufficient length of time, the adverse possessor may actually take ownership away from the true owner.

For possession to be adverse, it must be actual, open, and notorious. *Actual* possession means that the adverse possessor is actually on the land and is using the real estate in a reasonable manner for that type of land — as a residence, a farm, a ranch, or a business office. It is not sufficient that the adverse possessor states that he or she is using the land; actual use is required.

The possession must be *open* — that is, it must be obvious that the adverse possessor is on the property. It will not be sufficient if the person stays out of sight during the day and walks around the property only at night. Openness is required to reasonably put the owner and the rest of the world on notice that the adverse possessor is using the property.

The possession must also be *notorious,* which means that it is adverse or hostile to the true owner. Generally, people who occupy or use the property with the owner's permission, such as co-owners and renters, cannot be adverse possessors.

The required holding period varies from state to state and is specified by state statute. The period may range from five to thirty years. Entry under *color of title* may affect the holding period. Entering under color of title means that the holder thought that he or she had a legal right to take possession of the real property and had title to it. For example, a person with a defective deed would enter under color of title. Some states specify a shorter holding period if the holder entered under color of title and/or if the holder paid real estate taxes. In some states, the payment of real estate taxes is a necessary requirement for adverse possession; in others, color of title is required.

The possession must be continuous for the specified time period. The adverse possessor may leave the property for short periods to go to work, to classes, or on a brief vacation, for example, but he or she may not leave the property for an extended period of time.

The policy behind the doctrine of adverse possession is to encourage the use of land, a very valuable resource. The doctrine tends to encourage the use of land by someone else if the owner is not using it. As the old adage says, possession may be nine-tenths of the law. At least this applies to real property. Government land, however, may not be taken by adverse possession.

Easements

Sometimes a person may be *entitled to use the land of another in a particular manner*. This right is called an *easement*. An easement is not a right to *own* the property. It is the right to *use* the property in a particular manner. An easement may belong to a particular person, or it may run with the land. The latter means that the easement belongs to the owner of a particular parcel of land, called the *dominant parcel*. The parcel that is subject to the easement is the *servient parcel*.

An easement may be an *express* easement; that is, it was stated by the person who created the easement. Or an easement can be created by *prescription*, much like adverse possession: a person starts to use the servient parcel openly and, after the state's statutory period, will be entitled to continue the use. An easement can also be created by *necessity*, the most common example of which occurs when an owner divides a parcel and deeds a landlocked portion to someone else: the only method of access is across the servient estate. A requirement for an easement by necessity is that both parcels were originally one large parcel.

Easements can also be created by *implication*. Again, this occurs when a parcel is divided, and the owner of the dominant parcel needs to use the servient parcel. However, the need is not as great as it is for an easement by necessity. As an example of an easement by implication, suppose an owner of a parcel of land decides to sell the northeast corner of it. The owner had run a sewer system from the northeast corner to the main sewer line through the rest of the parcel. The buyer can reasonably expect to use the same sewer line when he or she owns the northeast corner. It would be *possible* to run a new sewer line to the northeast corner, but it was implied that the new owner could use the existing one. Easements are also created by *contract*, when an owner of property sells someone a right to use it. For example, an owner may sell an easement to an oil company to come onto the property to drill exploratory oil wells.

The issue in the following case was whether an easement existed.

Helms v. Tullis
398 So.2d 253 (Ala. 1981)

The Helmses owned a forty-acre tract of land. They moved a house trailer onto the land so that they could reside there. They wanted to have electrical service on the land, but it was necessary to run a power line to their property. The most efficient way to do this was to run the line over property owned by the Tullises. The Helmses told the power company that they owned all the land to the main road. The power company began installing the line and cutting down trees on the Tullises' property. The Tullises stopped them.

FACTS

Do the Helmses have the right to have a power line run across the Tullises' property?

ISSUE

No. They are not entitled to run a power line across the Tullises' property.

HOLDING

Easements are the only basis on which the Helmses would have been entitled to have a power line run across the Tullises' property. Easements may be acquired in a variety of ways, but the only two methods that would have been possible in this case are easements by necessity or by implication. Easements by necessity are recognized by the courts only when there is a real necessity. Mere convenience is not enough. Here the land could have been used even without electricity. In addition, such an easement requires that the parcel subject to the easement and the parcel entitled to the easement were originally parts of the same parcel. Easements by implication also require this original unity of ownership. In addition, there must have been open, visible, and continuous use of the one parcel for the benefit of the other. This use must be reasonably necessary to the estate needing the easement. The Helmses did not meet either set of requirements.

REASONING

The manner and type of use is restricted by the easement. A person who exceeds the amount of use that is allowed under the easement will lose the easement, and his or her rights will be extinguished. For example, suppose Mary has an easement that authorizes the use of a neighbor's road to get to her house. Mary opens a restaurant on her premises, thereby greatly increasing the traffic on her neighbor's road. This excessive use of the road will extinguish Mary's easement.

A person who owns land next to a stream or other body of water may find that soil is being lost into the water or that the water is depositing soil next to the land. If the water slowly washes the soil away, the original owner has lost the land. The person who owns the property where this soil is deposited is now the owner. The gradual building up of soil at the new site is called *accretion*. If the build-up occurs at an imperceptibly slow rate, it is called *alluvion*. *Avulsion* occurs when a severe flood or storm swiftly causes a change in the course of the

Transfers by Action of Nature

body of water. In this case, there is no change in the title. If the original owner can locate the property, he or she can reclaim it. *Reliction* occurs when the water level recedes or drops. The owner of the river bed now owns this exposed land. These rights vary from state to state. States that are subject to severe water shortages have unusual rules.

RENTAL OF REAL PROPERTY

The owner of real property may decide to allow another person or persons to use the property. The owner is willing to exchange possession of the property for money or other consideration. There are several basic types of tenancies, which are based on the length of the rental period. These include tenancies for years, periodic tenancies, tenancies at will, and tenancies at sufferance.

Tenancies for Years

A tenancy for years is for a set period of time: the beginning and the end of the tenancy are established. Generally, the Statute of Frauds requires a written lease if the tenancy is for one or more years. Such tenancies automatically end at the set time. Some states have set a maximum allowable term for a tenancy for years. If the tenant has not vacated by the end of the lease period, the landlord can execute a new lease with the tenant, or the landlord can elect to treat the tenant's action as a renewal of the lease for another term of the same length. This second term cannot exceed one year because of the Statute of Frauds.

Periodic Tenancies

A periodic tenancy starts at a specific time and continues for successive periods until terminated. It may be established to run from year to year, month to month, week to week, or for some similar period. It may be terminated by either party after proper notice. The lease normally specifies how much notice is necessary and to whom the notice should be addressed. The beginning date is specified, but the ending date is not.

Tenancies at Will

A tenancy at will can be terminated any time at the desire of either the landlord or the tenant.

Tenancies at Sufferance

A tenancy at sufferance is one in which the tenant entered into possession properly and with the landlord's permission, but wrongfully remained in possession after the period of the tenancy.

RIGHTS AND DUTIES OF TENANTS

The tenant rents the right to exclusive possession and control of the premises. This means that the tenant is the only one entitled to be in possession. At common law, the landlord is not entitled to enter the premises. However, the landlord often obtains permission from the tenant to enter the premises either on an ad hoc basis or because such a right is reserved in the lease. Even at common law, the landlord does have the right to enter the premises in case of an emergency.

If the tenant is a business, it may need to install trade fixtures, such as neon signs, commercial refrigeration units, and industrial ovens. If a tenant attaches trade fixtures to the property, the tenant is allowed to remove them before the end of the lease. But if the removal causes any damage, the tenant must repair the damage.

Under a normal lease, the landlord must put the property into good condition for the purposes specified in the lease and must maintain it in good condition. Tenants do not have an obligation to make major improvements or repairs. However, a tenant may contractually agree to make certain modifications or improvements. For example, in exchange for an exceptionally low rent, a tenant might agree to remodel a property at his or her own expense. In such a case, it is wise to specify who will pay for these improvements and who will get the benefit of them at the end of the lease.

Some states have held that in residential housing leases there is an implied warranty of habitability. This means that the landlord impliedly promises that the premises will be fit for living — for example, that the heating system will work; that there will be running water; and that there will be indoor plumbing. When the courts recognize this warranty, the tenant can use it as a basis for terminating a lease, as a means of reducing the rent, or as a defense for nonpayment of the rent.

Warranty of Habitability

Most states recognize an implied covenant that the owner will protect the tenant's right to quiet enjoyment (use) of the premises. Constructive eviction occurs when the owner does not protect this interest of the tenant, and there is a material interference with the tenant's enjoyment of the premises. Suppose, for example, that you rent an apartment and that living next door to you is a person whose habit of playing drums in the middle of the night is interfering with your sleep. Although your neighbor's behavior is in violation of the lease, the landlord will not enforce the lease provisions. The landlord's behavior constitutes constructive eviction, and you may move out without any further liability to pay rent. However, if you do not take some action promptly, the court may decide that you waived your right to complain about the noise.

Constructive Eviction

The transfer of the tenant's entire interest in the lease is an *assignment.* If the tenant transfers only part and retains some interest, the transfer is a *sublease.* (Note that this terminology is slightly different from that in Chapter 15.) Ordinarily assignments and subleases are allowed unless the lease specifically provides that they are not. Most leases do prohibit assignments and subleases without the prior written approval of the landlord.

Assignments and Subleases

The landlord has the right to retake possession of the property at the end of the lease's term. In most rental situations, the landlord expressly reserves the right to terminate the lease if the tenant breaches any promises contained in it, including the promise to adequately care for the property.

RIGHTS AND DUTIES OF THE LANDLORD

Rent

Rent is the compensation that the landlord receives from granting the right to use his or her property. Most leases require the tenant to pay the rent in advance. Many landlords require that tenants pay the first and last month's rent in advance, which provides added protection for the landlord. If the tenant is behind in paying the rent, it usually takes a number of weeks to force the tenant to leave the premises. If the tenant has not paid the rent, the landlord has a number of available options. The landlord can sue for the rent that has not been paid or can start procedures to have the tenant evicted (removed) from the premises. In some states, the landlord even has a lien on the tenant's personal belongings that are on the premises. This allows a form of self-help called a lockout: the landlord locks the tenant out of the premises while all the tenant's personal property is inside. In the following case, the court examined the legality of a lockout.

Spinks v. Taylor
278 S.E.2d 501 (N.C. 1981)

FACTS Because Spinks had not paid her rent, the landlord had her apartment padlocked when she was not there. Spinks claimed that she asked the manager to allow her to enter the apartment to get some clothes, but the manager would not allow this. The trial judge issued a decision for the landlord and did not allow the jury to decide this issue.

ISSUE Was there evidence to support the idea that the padlocking was illegal?

HOLDING Yes. The judge should have let the jury decide based on the evidence.

REASONING States use the following rules to determine the amount of self-help allowed to a landlord who is entitled to possession of the premises:

1. A landlord may use necessary and reasonable self-help.
2. A landlord must rely only on the remedies provided by the courts.
3. Or a landlord may gain possession by *peaceable* means.

North Carolina applies the last approach. Under North Carolina law, a landlord cannot retake possession against the will of the tenant. Since there was evidence that the padlocking was against Spinks's will, the court ruled that this case should be referred to a jury to determine if the landlord used peaceable means.

Damage
by the Tenant

The landlord has the right to collect from the tenant for any damage caused by the tenant. For example, if Rudy, a tenant, negligently fills his waterbed, and it leaks and causes substantial damage to the premises, then Rudy is liable for the damage. Tenants are also responsible for any damage caused to the premises by their guests. This right to collect exists at common law, and it is usually stated in the lease. The tenant is responsible for damage caused negligently or intentionally but not for ordinary wear and tear—the deterioration that occurs through ordinary usage.

Security Deposits

For protection, the landlord will usually collect a security deposit. This money is to be used to make repairs after the tenant has vacated the premises. It is for damage negligently or intentionally caused by the tenant. It is not to be used to clean the premises or to repair normal wear and tear. It generally cannot be used to repaint walls that have become dirty through normal use. It can be used to replace doors in which holes have been punched. The money that remains should be returned to the tenant within a reasonable period after the tenancy terminates. Some states have statutes that establish how long the landlord may legally keep the security deposit.

Duty to Protect Tenants and Their Guests

Landlords generally have the same responsibility to their tenants' guests as they do to the tenants themselves. The landlord does not warrant that the premises are safe, but the landlord does have the duty to warn the tenant of *latent defects*—defects that are not immediately obvious and of which the tenant may not be aware. This duty of the landlord extends only to latent defects that the landlord knew or should have known existed.

Rights After Abandonment by a Tenant

If the tenant wrongfully abandons the premises during the term of the lease, the landlord will have two options. The landlord can make a good-faith effort to find a suitable tenant, but if one cannot be found, the landlord can leave the premises vacant and collect the rent from the tenant who abandoned the premises. The tenant is legally obligated to pay the rent, and the landlord can obtain a court judgment for the payment. If the tenant can be located and is solvent, the landlord will be able to collect. If the landlord is able to rerent the premises, he or she is technically renting the premises in the tenant's behalf. If a lower rent is obtained, the tenant is liable for the difference.

Under the second option, the landlord can repossess the premises and rerent them in his or her own behalf. The original tenant who abandoned the premises is relieved of any liability for additional rent. If the landlord is able to rerent the premises for more money, that is to the landlord's benefit. As the next case indicates, there may be a factual issue whether the rerenting is for the landlord or the tenant.

Dahl v. *Comber*
444 A.2d 392 (Me. 1982)

FACTS

Dahl constructed a building for Comber's business. This building was leased to Comber for a five-year term. The business had difficult times and defaulted on the lease. Dahl tried to rent the building but was able to find only temporary tenants.

ISSUE   Did Dahl rerent the premises for his own benefit?

HOLDING   No. It was rerented for Comber.

REASONING   The lower court found that Dahl was rerenting for the benefit of his tenant. The evidence was sufficient to support this conclusion. The lease stated that any surrender had to be in writing and had to be signed by the landlord. When a tenant tries to surrender the premises to the landlord, the landlord can decide whether or not to accept the surrender. The landlord can accept the surrender and then rerent the premises in the landlord's behalf. Or the landlord can refuse the surrender and hold the tenant liable for any shortages in rent. In this case, the landlord was mitigating damages by rerenting the property in the tenant's behalf. Such an action does not disturb the tenant's underlying responsibility to pay the rent.

Legislative Trends

State landlord and tenant laws are undergoing change. Some states are very protective of the tenant's rights. Recent examples of protenant legislation include laws that require the payment of interest on security deposits and rent control statutes that prohibit landlords from raising the rent. Although rent control was intended to protect tenants, many economists argue that it does not have this protective effect. They argue that it instead creates a shortage of rental housing, because investors would prefer to make other investments that would provide a higher rate of return. The laws in some states are more protective of the landlord.

JOINT OWNERSHIP OF PROPERTY

Joint ownership exists when two or more people have title to property concurrently; that is, they own the property at the same point in time. There are four basic forms of joint ownership: tenants in common, joint tenants with rights of survivorship, tenants by the entireties, and tenants by community property. Generally, these forms of joint ownership can exist with personal property as well as with real property.

A legal characteristic of most forms of joint ownership is that each of the co-owners (the tenants) has an undivided right to use the whole property. Thus, the parcel described on the deed is not divided equally among the tenants; instead, each of them has the right to use all the property.

If there is a dispute about the use of the property that the tenants are unable to resolve among themselves, they can file their complaint with the court. The primary remedies available to resolve such a dispute are (1) to sell the property and divide the proceeds or (2) to divide the property equitably and give each tenant a separate parcel. Either of these would be considered an action for partition. Note that because the usable value of adjoining portions may differ, the separate segments may differ in size and shape.

Most of these forms of joint ownership can be created voluntarily by the tenants, or they can be created by someone else for the tenants.

A tenancy in common occurs when two or more people own the same property. Each tenant has an undivided right to use the whole property. Usually, a tenancy in common is indicated by words like "Bennett and McCormick, as tenants in common" in the deed or other evidence of title. If the deed simply says "Bennett and McCormick," most courts will presume that they are tenants in common.

There is no legal limit on the number of tenants in a tenancy in common. Practically speaking, however, if there are too many tenants, conflicts will probably arise among them regarding the use of the property. Each tenant may sell, assign, or give away his or her interest. A tenant may also will away the interest in a valid will. If the tenant has no valid will, the interest in the tenancy will pass to his or her heirs under the state intestate succession statute. A creditor of an individual tenant can attach his or her interest in the tenancy in common.

Tenants in common do not have to have equal interests in the property. For example, if there are four tenants in common, one may have a one-half interest, one may have a one-quarter interest and the other two may have a one-eighth interest each.

A joint tenancy with rights of survivorship occurs when two or more people own property together. Again, there is no legal maximum number of tenants, but, of course, the practical question of how many co-tenants can get along with each other remains. As in a tenancy in common, each tenant has an undivided right to use the whole property. Generally, each tenant has an equal interest in the property. Joint tenancies differ from tenancies in common in that when one tenant dies, his or her interest passes to the remaining co-tenants. The survivors continue to hold an undivided interest in the whole property. Generally, a will does not have any effect on a joint tenancy with right of survivorship. The interest in the property will pass from one tenant to another immediately on death by operation of law. Eventually the tenant who outlives the others will own the complete interest. In most states, corporations are not allowed to be joint tenants because corporations do not die.

Because of the survivorship feature, joint tenancies are often used as substitutes for wills. Given the potential for disputes during life, however, this practice may be unwise. In most states, if a joint tenant wrongfully causes the death of another joint tenant, he or she will not be allowed to benefit and will be prevented from taking the **decedent**'s interest.

Joint tenancies may be divided during a court action for partition. In most states, a joint tenant can sell, make a gift of, or assign his or her interest during life. A creditor of the joint tenant can attach the interest. A transferee of the joint tenant will take the interest as a tenant in common. A transferee would include a purchaser, a donee, an assignee, or a creditor who obtained rights through the attachment procedure. The transferee would not receive the survivorship rights of a joint tenant because the other joint tenants never agreed to share the risk of survivorship with the transferee.

Tenants in Common

Joint Tenants with Rights of Survivorship

Decedent A person who has died

Tenants by the Entireties

In a tenancy by the entireties, two tenants, who must be husband and wife, share the property. Each tenant is a joint owner in the whole property. This type of ownership has a survivorship feature. If one spouse dies, the survivor receives the whole property. Unlike joint tenants with rights of survivorship, many states allow a tenant who wrongfully caused the death of his or her spouse, and co-tenant, to benefit and to take title to the whole. Generally, only creditors of the family unit can attach entireties property. One spouse normally cannot unilaterally dispose of his or her interest unless the parties obtain a legal separation or a divorce. The tenants can, however, agree to sever the tenancy. A valid will does not affect distribution of entireties property. Tenancies by the entireties are not recognized in all states, especially **community property states.**

Community property states States that recognize community property for married couples

Community Property

Community property is recognized in Arizona, California, Idaho, Louisiana, Nevada, New Mexico, Texas, and Washington. This discussion will emphasize the general features of community property law. Community property laws vary from state to state. Louisiana community property law is most dissimilar, because it is based on Louisiana's French heritage. The community property laws in the other states are based predominantly on Spanish heritage.

Community property is *a form of co-ownership that can occur only between husband and wife.* It is based on the concept that financially the marriage is a partnership. One-half of most of the property that is acquired or accumulated during marriage belongs to each spouse. Technically, this assumes that one-half of each asset belongs to the husband and one-half belongs to the wife. Thus, most states require that both the husband and the wife sign any deeds to transfer real property. In most states, this requirement does not extend to personal property. In fact, the names of both spouses do not have to appear on the community property or on any title evidence to the property. For example, although a paycheck may bear the name of only one spouse, it is nonetheless community property, and as such belongs to both spouses. The primary source of community property for most couples is wages and earnings.

This is not meant to imply that a married couple will have only community property. Each may own property separately. Separate property would include the following:

1. property owned by either spouse before their marriage
2. property given to one spouse alone by gift, by will, or by intestate succession
3. property that is acquired with separate property funds

In addition, in some states—California, for example—income, rents, or profits earned from separate property is also separate property; in other states—Idaho, Texas, Louisiana—this income would be community property if received during the marriage. In Louisiana, a husband or wife can file a declaration that this income should be separate property instead of community property. All property other than that mentioned above is usually community property.

For most purposes, a husband and wife can contractually agree to split their community property into two shares of separate property. However, if they are careless and mix their respective separate properties and/or community property, it may all become community property. If the property becomes so mixed that it cannot be separated into community and separate property, the courts say that it is hopelessly commingled and treat all of it like community property. Distinguishing separate and community property was an issue in the next case.

Potthoff v. *Potthoff*
627 P.2d 708 (C.A. Ariz. 1981)

FACTS

Gertrude and Herbert Potthoff were unable to agree on a property settlement in their divorce. They maintained one basic bank account, but Herbert was the only one who could withdraw from the account. Into the account they deposited funds from Herbert's medical practice, loan proceeds, proceeds from the sale of stock, stock dividends, interest income, and proceeds from the sale of Gertrude's separate property. From this account, they paid expenses of the medical practice, living expenses, costs of investments, and costs of real estate. Before the Potthoff's marriage, Herbert had purchased property on which he built the Palm Grove Shopping Center with his separate funds. He also spent considerable time and effort there making it a successful investment.

ISSUES

Was the bank account community property? Was the Palm Grove Shopping Center separate property?

HOLDINGS

Yes, to both. The bank account was hopelessly commingled; the real property was purchased and improved with separate property funds.

REASONING

Due to the various transactions involving separate and community funds and loss of banking records, the bank account was commingled. The entire amount becomes community property if the funds become so commingled that the identity of the separate funds would be lost, which occurred in this case. The Palm Grove property, however, was purchased before the marriage and was built with separate funds. Thus, it was separate property. Under Arizona law, to the extent that separate property is improved by community funds, the community has a lien on the property for the amount of those funds. To the extent that Herbert's efforts improved the property, this increase in value was community property.

A couple begins to form community property once they are married. In most situations, they stop forming community property once they establish separate residences. In a divorce proceeding, the community property is usually divided.

Community property does not have a survivorship feature. A spouse can will his or her share of the community property to someone else. If the decedent does not have a valid will, most intestate succession statues provide that the property will pass to the surviving spouse. The National Conference of Commissioners on Uniform State Laws has drafted a proposal that, when adopted, will modify the property rights of married couples. It will make **separate property states** more like community property states.

Separate property states States that do not recognize community property rights

Distinguishing Between the Forms of Joint Ownership

The words used on the deed or other title evidence are controlling as to whether the tenants are tenants in common, joint tenants with rights of survivorship, or tenants by the entireties. If the language on the deed is not clear, under state law there will be a presumption as to the form of joint ownership. If the tenants are husband and wife, most states will presume that the property is community property or entireties property. If the state recognizes neither form of ownership, it would presume a joint tenancy with the right of survivorship. If the tenants are not related to each other by marriage, most states would presume that they are tenants in common.

SUMMARY

Property ownership includes title to the property and the right to control possession of the property. Real property consists of land, things that are built on the land, things that are growing on the land, and things that are permanently attached to the land. A fixture is property that was personal in nature before it was permanently attached to a building.

Real property can be acquired by a grant from the government or by transfer from the owner. An owner may trade, sell, give, or will the property or leave it to another person by intestate succession. Lifetime transfers will be described in a deed; the deed will be delivered to the grantee; and, in most cases, the deed will be recorded. Although not legally required, recording is for the protection of the grantee and the public.

An owner who is not careful may lose title to or use of the property. This loss can be caused by unpaid debts, by government restrictions on the use of the land, or by eminent domain. An owner may also lose his or her interest by the adverse possession of another person. Or nature may erode the owner's property.

An owner can enter into a rental agreement called a lease. Under a lease, a tenant is entitled to the exclusive possession of the owner's real estate. The lease is the contract that will govern many terms of the landlord-tenant relationship. Generally, the landlord must repair the premises. A tenant who negligently or intentionally damages the property will be liable for the cost of repairs. The landlord may require a security deposit in order to have funds for making such repairs. The tenant is justified in leaving the premises when there is constructive eviction. A landlord can evict a tenant if the tenant fails to pay the rent.

Two or more people can own an interest in the same piece of property at the same time. These people are called co-tenants. They may be tenants in common, in which case each tenant owns an undivided right in the whole parcel and there are no survivorship rights. Or they may be joint tenants with rights of survivorship. Such tenants can dispose of their interests during life; at death, their interest will pass to the remaining co-tenants by operation of law. Tenants in a tenancy by the entireties must be husband and wife. In community property states, a husband and wife can create community property. Most of the assets that they acquire during marriage will be community property.

DISCUSSION QUESTIONS

1. After Al's mother and father died, Al, who was responsible for their estate, decided to sell their home. After locating buyers for the property and entering into a sales contract with them, Al went to the premises and started to remove the petunias, his father's prize-winning roses, and a load of topsoil that was on the flower beds. The buyers were unhappy about this. Who has the right to these things? Why?

2. Are crops real or personal property? Why is this distinction important?

3. Describe the typical provisions that would be included in a deed.

4. Kim moved onto a piece of real estate in California. He began to use the property in an open, actual, and notorious manner and continued to do so for five years. He also paid the real estate taxes on this parcel. The applicable holding period is five years. Who owns this parcel? Why? Is it material that Nancy, the original owner, also paid real estate taxes? What are the legal rights of the parties? Why?

5. Jack and Rosie are neighbors. In 1970, Rosie built a fence around her property. She did not have the boundary surveyed. The fence was built four feet into Jack's property. Who owns this four-foot strip of land now? Why?

6. Why is it difficult for a lessee (tenant) to be successful as an adverse possessor?

7. How does avulsion differ from accretion?

8. Why might a person want to establish a joint tenancy with another person who is not related to him or her?

9. How is community property made or acquired in a community property state?

10. Why would a person prefer to establish a tenancy in common instead of a joint tenancy with rights of survivorship?

CASE
PROBLEMS

1. Private citizens wanted to enter upon the common areas of a multibusiness office complex to make antiabortion statements. The protesters carried signs and placards and shouted at prospective patients of Cherry Hill Women's Center, one of the ten tenants on the property. These protesters did not have the permission of the owner of the property. Does the land owner have the right to keep the protesters off the property? (*Brown* v. *Davis*, 495 A.2d 900 [N.J. Super. 1984].)

2. Jon and Marion Kubichan owned and occupied a parcel of residential property. During their ownership, they designed and built a fountain pond in their backyard. The Kubichans did not enclose the pond with a fence, but at the time of the accident it had been enclosed. The builders had not obtained the permit that was required by a city rule. Later, the Kubichans sold the property to Goldman, who then entered into a lease-option with the Reids. While the Reids occupied the property they made changes in the exterior of the pond but not in its interior. A toddler, twenty-two months old, was visiting the property with his parents and his siblings. He fell into the pond and suffered severe brain damage and quadriplegia. The pond allegedly was deceptive in nature because it appeared much shallower than it was and it lacked safety features. Is the seller liable for creating an unreasonably dangerous condition on the real estate? (*Preston* v. *Goldman*, 210 Cal. Rptr. 913 [Cal. App. 1985].)

3. Dorothy Karell purchased 18.917 acres in 1958 and received a warranty deed. Rena West and her partner purchased the adjoining 3.783-acre tract. The 18.917 acres owned by Karell was enclosed by a fence that also enclosed a portion of the 3.783 acres. Karell rented the property to various tenants from 1958 until 1972. The tenants lived in the house on the 18.917 acres. One or two of the tenants kept livestock or grew crops. In 1970 Karell contracted to sell Howl the sand and topsoil from the land enclosed in the fence. Who owns that portion of the 3.783 acres that is enclosed in the fence? Is Karell liable for the sand and topsoil that was removed by Howl? (*Karell* v. *West*, 616 S.W.2d 692 [Tex. App. 1981].)

4. Bernard Guynan owned a parcel of real estate. In September 1955, he gave his son Edward permission to build a concrete block house on a portion of the property. Edward constructed the house at his own expense and lived in it from 1957 to 1960. Then he began leasing the house and collecting the rent. When Bernard died in 1970, his wife Anne obtained title to the property. She allowed Edward to continue to rent the property to others. During this time, either Anne or Bernard had paid the real estate taxes. When a disagreement arose between Anne and Edward, Anne filed a lawsuit to have Edward and his tenants removed from the premises. Is Edward entitled to the building and real estate based on adverse possession? Why or why not? (*Guynan* v. *Guynan*, 305 N.W.2d 882 [Neb. 1981].)

5. The landlord ordered a notice to quit to be served on the tenant on 24 October 1983. A summary process action was begun on 5 December 1983.

The tenant initiated this lawsuit to require the landlord to make certain repairs. Does the tenant have the potential right to have the premises repaired? (*Rivera* v. *Santiago,* 495 A.2d 1122 [Conn. App. 1985].)

6. Mary Stoiber, a tenant of a residential parcel of real estate, sued for damages from her former landlord and the rental agents who managed the property. Stoiber was sued under an unlawful detainer action by Earley, the owner of the premises. The unlawful detainer action was filed after the Kern County Health Department ordered that the premises be vacated and destroyed within thirty days because of numerous housing code violations. Stoiber alleged that she had complained about the condition of the property to Earley's agents. She further alleged that the faulty plumbing caused discomfort and annoyance and the flooding damaged her furnishings. Did Stoiber have a cause of action for breach of the warranty of habitability? What should be her measure of damages? (*Stoiber* v. *Honeychuck,* 162 Cal. Rptr. 194 [Cal. App. 1980].)

7. The landlord owned a thirty-six-unit apartment complex. Becker, one of his tenants, slipped and fell against his glass shower door and broke his arm. The shower doors were made of untempered glass. The glass doors were installed before the landlord purchased the premises, and he didn't know that they were made of untempered glass. One of the witnesses testified that tempered glass and untempered glass look the same except for the small identification mark in one corner. It was agreed that, had the shower door been of tempered glass, the injury would have been reduced. Should the landlord be liable for latent defects in rental units when the defects existed when the tenant leased the premises? (*Becker* v. *IRM Corp.,* 698 P.2d 116 [Cal. 1985].)

8. Jackson and Chapman purchased a property on or about 5 June 1984. The property was purchased subject to the lease of the Postal Service and other tenants. The Postal Service was notified of the change of ownership of the premises. It then failed to pay rent to anyone for about six months while it waited for an official notice of the change of ownership on its own forms. The landlords filed a forcible entry and detainer action against the Postal Service. Should they win the suit? (*Jackson* v. *United States Postal Service,* 611 F. Supp. 456 [D.C. Tex. 1985].)

9. A Connecticut state statute provided that the lessee was to be given a five-day notice to quit for nonpayment of rent. The lease provided that whenever the lease terminated by the lapse of time or by breach of any of the promises in the lease, then the tenant waived all rights to notice. Did the lease provisions effectively waive the protections granted by state law? (*Sandrew* v. *Pequot Drug, Inc.,* 495 A.2d 1127 [Conn. App. 1985].)

10. Mrs. York and Mr. York were parties to an action for divorce and the division of property. Mrs. York's father testified that he meant to give the residence to her as her sole and separate property. The property was

deeded to both the husband and the wife by the wife's parents. Is the residence community property or separate property?

Originally, Mr. York and his brother purchased York Tire Company and operated it as a partnership. The partnership was owned half by the brother and half by Mr. and Mrs. York, as community property. Mrs. York traded her interest in York Tire Company for Mr. York's interest in Air Speed Oil Company. Mr. York later bought his brother's interest with a $15,000 note. He paid off the note with cash and earnings from the tire company. Later, Mr. York incorporated the business by taking the assets of the old York Tire Company and adding two service stations that were owned as community property. Is the business community property or separate property? (*Marriage of York,* 613 S.W.2d 764 [Tex. App. 1981].)

Personal Property and Bailments

OWNERSHIP OF PROPERTY

Classifications of Property

The concept of property rights discussed in the context of real property in Chapter 49 applies to personal property, as well. As we noted in that chapter, real estate is land and everything built on the land or permanently attached to it or to the buildings. All property that is not classified as real property is *personal property*.

Personal property is divided into two categories: tangible and intangible. *Tangible* personal property is property that is movable and can be felt, tasted, or seen. It has texture, color, temperature, and similar characteristics. Examples of tangible personal property include textbooks, pens, briefcases, calculators, lamps, and chairs.

Intangible personal property cannot be reduced to physical possession. It cannot be held in a person's hand. It may, however, be reduced to legal possession and is often very valuable. Intangible personal possessions include such things as patent rights, copyrights, accounts receivable, and corporate goodwill. The distinction between tangible and intangible personal property is usually not significant and does not govern the parties' legal relationships.

The traditional label for personal property is "chattels." Chattels are divided into chattels real, chattels personal, and chattels personal in action. A chattel *real* involves an interest in land, but the chattel itself is personal — for example, a leasehold or other legal right to use land. The owner of the chattel real does not own the land but does have valuable legal rights. Chattels *personal* are tangible, movable personal property, such as desks, chairs, chalk, and erasers. A chattel *personal in action,* also called a *chose in action,* is the right to file a lawsuit or to bring legal action.

Components of Ownership

The three components of ownership that are important with respect to real property are also important with respect to personal property. These components are ownership, possession, and title. *Ownership* includes all the rights related to the ownership of property. *Possession* includes the right to control the property by having it in one's custody or by directing who shall have custody of it. The concept of *title* includes both the current legal ownership of the property and the method of its acquisition. Title evidence or title also refers to the written evidence of ownership that appears on a certificate of title for such property as an automobile.

ACQUISITION OF PERSONAL PROPERTY BY INDIVIDUALS

Original Possession

Original possession occurs when the owner is the first person to possess the property. In other words, the owner created the ownership rather than receiving it by transfer from another person. One way to obtain ownership by original possession is to create the property through physical or mental labor; an artist, for example, acquires ownership through original possession by creating a painting or a sculpture.

Ownership by original possession can also be acquired by taking something that has never been owned before and reducing it to possession, as when someone pans for gold in a wilderness area and takes possession of any nuggets found.

When a person creates property, there is usually no dispute about who actually owns it. Disputes do arise, however, when people are hunting or trapping wild animals. For example, suppose that a group of hunters are about to trap a fox when a farmer spots the fox near some chicken coops and shoots it. A dispute then ensues about who owns the fox. The court would decide that the farmer owned the fox and its pelt because the hunters had not reduced the fox to their possession. The farmer had taken control over it first.

Individuals can also acquire property by having it transferred to them voluntarily by the previous owner. The transfer can occur by purchase, gift, gift causa mortis, inheritance, or intestate succession.

Purchases

The most common way to acquire property owned by another is to purchase it. When property is sold by the previous owner, there is an exchange of consideration: the buyer gives up one form of property, often money, and the seller gives up another form of property. (Sometimes the parties exchange services for the property. This form of bartering transaction is becoming increasingly popular in bartering for goods.)

Gifts

A person can also obtain ownership of property through a gift. The person who transfers the property is called the *donor* and the person who receives the property is called the *donee.*

Three requirements must be satisfied for a valid transfer by gift. First, the donor (the previous owner) must *intend* to make a gift — that is, to transfer the property without full and fair consideration. In most gift situations, the donor is freely giving up the property without receiving any consideration at all. Sometimes it is difficult to determine whether the intent of the donor was to make a gift or to sell or to lend the property. This is particularly true if the donor is now dead or if the donor and the donee had a disagreement. However, if the transfer is to be treated as a valid gift, it must be shown that the donor's intent was to make a gift.

The second requirement for a valid transfer by gift is that the donor *deliver* the gift property to the donee. When the donor hands the gift to the recipient, *actual delivery* occurs. Sometimes actual delivery is not possible owing to the situation of the parties or to the type of property given. In such situations, *constructive delivery* will be sufficient. For example, if a hospitalized man had some stocks and bonds in his safe deposit box and wanted to give them to his son, he could give his son the keys and a note that would allow him access to the box, thereby effecting constructive delivery of the gift property.

The third requirement for a valid gift is *acceptance* by the donee. The donee must be willing to take the property from the donor. In most cases, this is not a problem. However, a donee may refuse to accept a gift if the donee feels that it would "obligate" him or her to the donor, as when a sales agent making a bid for a contract offers the purchasing agent a two-week vacation in Hawaii. Sometimes a donee may refuse a gift because the gift property has no use or value to the donee or would create legal liabilities for the donee. For instance, a donee might refuse a gift of tenements that were substandard housing and had many building code violations.

A transfer by gift may be subject to a **transfer tax,** that is, a gift tax. If so, usually the donor must pay the tax. Most state and federal gift taxes also apply when the donor receives some consideration but the transfer is for less than

Transfer tax Tax on the ability to transfer assets

full and adequate consideration. For example, if a donor transfers a 5-carat diamond ring to a donee for $5, the value of the gift will be treated as the fair market value of the ring less the $5 that was paid for it. Any gift tax would be figured on this amount, and the donor would pay the tax. The gift is not subject to income tax when it is received by the donee.

If the donor intends to make a gift and delivers the property, and the donee accepts the property, the transfer is a valid gift. Once a gift has been completed, it generally cannot be revoked. The donor cannot legally take the property back from the donee, no matter how much the donor wants or needs to have it returned. For example, if Silvia gave her sister $100 as a birthday present and later Silvia lost her job and desperately needed the money, she would not be entitled to it. If her sister decided to give the money back, she would be making a separate gift, this one to Silvia. A completed gift, also called an *executed gift,* is final.

If a person promises to make a gift at some time in the future, that promise is not binding on the promisor. The promisor can change his or her mind with impunity. This situation is called an *executory promise to make a gift.* An executory promise to make a gift will be enforceable if there is promissory estoppel. (This concept was discussed in Chapter 10.)

Certain types of property require special formalities before the owner can make gifts of them. To transfer a chose in action (a right to bring legal action), the transferor must make an assignment of the right. An *assignment* is a formal transfer of a contract right. To transfer **negotiable instruments,** the transferor must make either an assignment or a negotiation. A *negotiation* is an endorsement or notation on the document that it should be paid to a specific person or that it should be paid to the bearer or holder. (The bearer or holder is the person who is in possession of the document.)

Negotiable instruments
Documents governed by the UCC, including checks, drafts, promissory notes, and certificates of deposit

Gifts fall into three categories: inter vivos gifts, testamentary gifts, or gifts causa mortis. *Inter vivos* gifts are made while the transferor is still alive; they are lifetime gifts. *Testamentary* gifts are completed when the owner dies; they are the types of gifts that a person puts in a will and are commonly called testamentary transfers. These transfers do not actually take place until death. Gifts *causa mortis* must meet special requirements about the donor's intention.

Gifts Causa Mortis

Gifts causa mortis occur while the property owner is still alive. The donor is making the gift because he or she expects to die soon. Generally the donor is contemplating death from a specific cause. The requirements for a gift causa mortis are that the donor must intend to make the gift; the gift must be made in contemplation of death; the gift property must be actually or constructively delivered; and the donor must die from the contemplated cause. If the donor does not die from the contemplated cause, the gift may be revoked. In this case, the donor or the donor's estate can reclaim the gift property. Since the donor was motivated, at least in part, by the expectation of death, it is logical that if the donor does not die, he or she should be able to get the property back.

The following hypothetical case shows the conditional nature of a gift causa mortis.

Betty, aged eighty-eight, was in the hospital and doing very poorly. The doctor told her she would probably not survive another stroke. She felt that she would very likely have another stroke before the end of the week. When her son Charles came to visit her, she told him that she wanted him to have her new color television since she would no longer need it. Charles was reluctant to take the television, but Betty insisted that she was not going to recover, and she gave him the key to go get the television.

However, Betty did recover, and when she returned home, she decided she wanted her television back. Since it was a gift causa mortis, Betty would be entitled to have it returned. She did not die as she anticipated.

Suppose Charles had gone to the hospital to take Betty home when she was discharged. While walking across the street to the car, Betty was hit and killed by a reckless driver. The gift to Charles would still be revoked because Betty did not die from the contemplated cause. If her other relatives sued to have Charles return the television, legally Charles would lose, and the television would be included with the rest of Betty's estate.

A gift causa mortis is a *legal* concept. It is not the same concept as a gift *in contemplation of death*. A gift in contemplation of death is a *tax* concept that is no longer applicable in most instances because of recent changes in the tax laws.

Inheritances

A person can also receive property from the estate of someone who dies. If the person who died had a valid will, the recipient specified in the will receives the property by inheritance. Like gifts, inheritances may be subject to state and/or federal transfer taxes.

Property Received by Intestate Succession

The property of a person who dies without a valid will is transferred to recipients by intestate succession. The people who receive this property are specified in the state intestate succession statute. As with other death-time transfers, this transfer may be subject to state or federal taxes. Transfers by wills and intestate succession statutes are discussed in greater detail in Chapter 52.

These types of voluntary transfers can occur with real property as well as personal property. These transfer taxes may be very complex and may take different forms, for example, estate tax, inheritance tax.

Sometimes the transfer of property or the custody of property to a recipient is not completely voluntary on the part of the true owner. Such a situation occurs when there is accession or confusion or when property is abandoned, lost, or mislaid.

Involuntary Transfers of Possession

Accession

Accession occurs when a person takes property that he or she does not own and adds to it. For example, a person takes some lumber and makes it into a dining room table. The legal question that arises is: who owns the dining room table? Should it be the one who owned the lumber or the one who worked on the lumber and changed its nature? The courts examine a number of factors in making their decision on this question; the most important is whether the worker knew that he or she had no right to the lumber. As with many legal problems, the courts weigh the conflicting equities.

The next hypothetical case shows one way in which accession can occur.

Ed ordered some plywood from Pay Less Hardware that was to be delivered while he was at work. When he got home from work, some plywood was piled in his driveway, and he began using it to build his children a toy chest. However, the plywood was Ed's neighbor's—it had been delivered to the wrong address.

Ed was not guilty of willful misconduct. He did not mean to misappropriate someone else's plywood. He reasonably believed that the plywood was his. Title *may* pass from the owner of the plywood to Ed because of Ed's work effort.

Title will normally remain with the rightful owner of the lumber and will not be transferred to the laborer. Depending on the circumstances, the courts may determine that the laborer is an innocent trespasser. An innocent trespasser does not acquire title simply by adding labor and additional materials. The innocent trespasser *will* acquire title under any of the following conditions:

1. Because of the work effort, the original property has lost its identity. (The innocent trespasser took iron ore and made it into steel.)

2. There is a great difference in the relative values between the original property and the new property. (The innocent trespasser took a rough diamond and cut and polished it into a beautiful pear shape.)

3. A completely new type of property has been created and the innocent trespasser added the major portion of it. (The innocent trespasser placed her notebook on a table in the library. After selecting a couple of references, the trespasser sat down and started to write her research paper. Much later the trespasser discovered that she had sat at the wrong table and used someone else's notebook.)

If the innocent trespasser does acquire title by accession, the trespasser will be obligated to pay the rightful owner for the value of the property taken. This value will be computed on the worth of the property at the time the trespasser took it. These cases are really exceptions to the general rule; the trespasser usually does not acquire title.

If title to the property stays with the original owner, the innocent trespasser can recover for the value of the services rendered in improving the property. If the owner were allowed to keep these improvements without payment, then the owner would have an unjust enrichment and the innocent trespasser would suffer an unjust loss. The owner is obligated to pay for the reasonable value of the improvements. This is similar to the theory underlying quasi contracts.

A *willful* trespasser — that is, one who knows he or she has no right to the property — cannot acquire title to the new property. The transfer of title under such conditions would permit willful trespassers to benefit from their wrongdoings and might moreover encourage them to try such an action again.

A willful trespasser is liable for any damages that he or she caused and will *not* be entitled to any compensation for improvements made to the property. Suppose, for example, Marti took some bricks that she found in a neighbor's yard. She knew she was not entitled to the bricks, but since she did not think her neighbor wanted them, she decided to go ahead and use them to build a barbecue. Although heavy, the barbecue is movable, and the neighbor is entitled to have it. Marti is not entitled to any money for her labor in building the barbecue. If the neighbor incurs any financial damages because he was planning to use the bricks in another manner, he can recover the damages from Marti.

In rare instances, title may pass to the willful trespasser because the owner decides not to contest the trespasser's title. In other words, the owner does not want the improved property. However, the original owner may collect the value of the improved property from the willful trespasser. In our example, if the neighbor decides that he does not want the barbecue, he may let the title pass to Marti by default and can collect from Marti the value of the brick barbecue instead of the value of the bricks alone. Such action will occur at the option of the original owner.

Some legal disputes involve cases in which a third party has purchased the property created by the trespasser. Generally, the dispute is between the original owner and the third-party purchaser. To be protected, the third party must be a bona fide purchaser for value. (A bona fide purchaser for value is a person who buys property in good faith, for a reasonable value, and without actual or constructive knowledge that there is anything wrong with the transfer.) The bona fide purchaser will have the same rights and liabilities as the trespasser. If the original owner could have gotten the property back from the trespasser, then he or she can get it back from the bona fide purchaser. Good-faith purchasers do have the right to remove any additions or improvements that they have made themselves if this can be done without harming the original property.

Confusion

Confusion occurs when the personal, fungible property of two or more people is mixed together and cannot be separated. *Fungible property* includes such things as sand, gravel, wheat, corn, rye, oil, and gasoline. It generally consists of very small particles or grains. When wheat of the same type and quality belonging to two different farmers is mixed together, there is confusion: the particles of wheat cannot be separated and returned to their respective owners.

Confusion may be caused by the wrongdoing of one of the owners or it may occur without any misconduct. For example, farmers often store their fungible crops, such as corn, in the same storage bin or silo. If confusion occurs *without misconduct,* the farmers will receive an undivided interest in the new confused mass. If the corn in the bin is sold, the farmers will divide the proceeds in proportion to the amount that they put into the bin. If there are any losses, the farmers will divide the losses proportionately.

If the confusion is caused by *intentional wrongdoing,* then different rules apply. If the new mixture is not divisible, title to the whole mass will pass to the innocent party. Obviously, then, it is to the wrongdoer's benefit to show that the new mass is divisible. If the wrongdoer can prove that the new mass is divisible and that the mixture has at least the same *unit value* (value per ton, pound, gallon, and the like) as the property belonging to the innocent party, then the wrongdoer will be entitled to a share of the new mass. If the wrongdoer can clearly prove how much was added, the court can award the wrongdoer that share. If the wrongdoer can only identify the relative proportion of his or her share, the wrongdoer will be allowed to recover a proportional share. In either case, the proof must be clear and convincing. The following case involved an analysis of the proof.

Exxon Corporation v. *West*
543 S.W.2d 667 (C.A. Tex. 1976)
Cert. Denied, 434 U.S. 875 (1977)

FACTS   Exxon had an agreement to take gas from the Wests' property and to pay them a royalty on it. During the contract term, the Texas Railroad Commission authorized the use of this same reservoir under the Wests' property for gas storage purposes. Exxon began injecting gas into the reservoir for storage, which created a mixture of native gas and injected gas.

ISSUE   Are the Wests entitled to royalties on all the gas drawn from the reservoir?

HOLDING   No. The gas in the reservoir had been confused, but the resulting mass could be divided.

The court held that Exxon intentionally caused confusion of the injected gas and the native gas. The Wests were entitled to royalties on the native gas. Exxon had the burden of proving how much gas was subject to the royalties. Exxon provided expert testimony by their geologist and their petroleum engineer, who studied and testified about the maximum amount of native gas and the probable amount of native gas in the reserve. Since the Wests did not offer any contradictory testimony, the court held that Exxon's witnesses had to be believed. The amount of native gas did not need to be proved with exact certainty. In such a case, reasonable certainty is sufficient.

REASONING

Abandoned Property

An owner, no longer interested in owning a piece of personal property, may *abandon* it by throwing it away without intending to reclaim it or by relinquishing it to someone else without intending to retake possession. If the property is relinquished to someone else, that person will become the new owner of the property. Generally, this type of transfer will be considered a gift. If the property is thrown away, the person who finds the property and reduces it to possession will acquire title. The property will once again be subject to original possession.

The following case involved an alleged abandonment of a property right.

Dodd, Mead & Company, Inc. v. Lilienthal
514 F. Supp. 105 (S.D. N.Y. 1981)

Lilienthal, the author of *The Zionist Connection*, contracted with Dodd, Mead & Company (Dodd, Mead) for the publication of his book. Under the contract, Dodd, Mead had the exclusive right to print, publish, and sell the book in the United States and Canada. Dodd, Mead obtained the copyright on the book. They printed and distributed 14,500 copies of it and spent more than $66,000 in manufacturing and promoting it. When the book was no longer available in bookstores or from Dodd, Mead, Lilienthal began printing it himself.

FACTS

Had Dodd, Mead abandoned their copyrighted interest in the book?

ISSUE

No. There was no evidence of a relinquishing of rights by the publisher.

HOLDING

For the holder of a copyright to abandon this property right, he or she must perform some overt act. This act must manifest an intent to surrender rights in the copyrighted material. Mere inaction is not sufficient. The court held that Dodd, Mead never abandoned the copyright and that there was no evidence

REASONING

to suggest that Dodd, Mead intended to give up its exclusive right to publish the book. Dodd, Mead was entitled to an injunction and money damages.

■■

Lost or Mislaid Property

Lost property is property that has been unintentionally lost by the true owner. The owner does not know where the property was lost or where it may be retrieved. A person who finds lost property has good title to the property. The true owner is the only one with better title than the finder. The finder of lost property is also entitled to keep possession of it.

Mislaid property is property that was intentionally set somewhere by the owner. The manner of placement and the location of the property will indicate whether the owner merely forgot to pick up the property or lost it. The owner of mislaid property usually will be able to remember where the property was left and will reclaim it. The finder of mislaid property has good title against everyone except the true owner.

There is a distinction, however, between *title* to the property and *possession* of the property. The owner of the premises where the property is found or the person in charge of the premises is entitled to hold the mislaid property. The reason is that when the true owner remembers where the mislaid property was left, he or she will return to that location to retrieve it. It is logical to leave the personal property on the premises to make it easier for the true owner to reclaim it. Note that the owner of the premises is entitled to hold mislaid property, but not lost property. If the finder of lost or mislaid property was a trespasser on the premises, the person in charge of the premises has title to the personal property that was found.

To increase the likelihood that the true owner will be able to reclaim the property, some state statutes and local ordinances require the finder of lost and/or mislaid property to complete certain steps before becoming the final owner. These statutes generally have two requirements:

1. that a specified type of notice be placed in the newspaper
2. that the property be given to the police to be claimed by the true owner

If the property is not claimed within the stated period, the police will allow the finder to claim it.

PROTECTION OF PERSONAL PROPERTY

If an owner of personal property fails to protect the property adequately, it may be taken by someone else. Sometimes this taking is legal, but often it is not. In either case, the owner will suffer a temporary or permanent loss. To protect against such a loss, the owner should be aware of the means — legal or illegal — by which property may be taken. These include conversion, escheat, judicial sale, and mortgage foreclosure or repossession of property.

Conversion occurs when one person takes the personal property of the owner. It is unauthorized and unjustified interference, permanent or temporary, with the owner's use and control of property. A very transitory interference would constitute trespass to personal property and would not be conversion. A more lengthy interference — but not necessarily a permanent one — would be conversion. Under the theory of conversion, the owner can sue the taker for the return of the property or for money to replace the property. Conversion is the tort equivalent of a number of crimes, including theft, armed robbery, embezzlement, and obtaining property by false pretenses. In a criminal proceeding, the state would protect its interest in having citizens abide by the law. In a civil proceeding, the individual would protect his or her property rights.

Conversion *can* occur when the owner of personal property voluntarily releases the property to another person, who then uses the property in a manner different from that originally authorized. For example, if the owner of an automobile left the automobile with a car dealer for repairs and the dealer used it as a demonstrator, the dealer would be liable if the automobile was damaged while a prospective customer was taking it for a test drive.

In the following case, a lessee was found to have converted the leased property.

Conversion

Swish Manufacturing Southeast
v. Manhattan Fire & Marine Insurance Company
675 F.2d 1218 (11th Cir. 1982)

Swish Manufacturing owned a corporate aircraft. Swish entered into a contract with Wings whereby Wings could lease the aircraft whenever Wings wanted it. Under the lease, Wings could not use the aircraft to transport cargo or for unlawful purposes. Swish received an insurance endorsement on the aircraft that excluded loss due to conversion. Wings took the aircraft to the Bahamas in order to smuggle marijuana. The plane was seized by Bahamian police and was damaged while in their custody.

FACTS

Was the aircraft converted by Wings?

ISSUE

Yes. The unauthorized use was a conversion.

HOLDING

Conversion is the unauthorized assumption and exercise of the right of ownership of someone else's personal property. This exercise is contrary to the owner's right. Misuse or excessive use may be conversion. Unauthorized use that causes damage to a chattel constitutes a conversion. The degree of deviation between actual use and permitted use will be important. Here the court found that the deviation was great; conversion had occurred.

REASONING

In a suit for conversion, the owner usually would like to have the personal property returned and repaired, if necessary. Another option available to the owner under the laws of most states is to force the wrongdoer to keep the personal property and to pay for it. The price will be the value at the time the property was taken. This action is performed only at the election of the owner.

Escheat

When the rightful owner of property cannot be located, the property will *escheat* to the state government. The effect of escheat is that the property is given to the government. Usually it is in someone else's custody, but possession will be transferred to the state. The policy behind the doctrine is that the state is more deserving of the property than anyone else, provided that the correct owner cannot be found. Escheat tends to occur when a person dies and the heirs or relatives cannot be located. It also tends to occur when a person does not keep careful financial records and so forgets about small bank accounts, stocks and bonds, or other assets. (Large assets are obviously rarely forgotten.) Escheat also occurs when a person dies and neither the people mentioned in the will nor the decedent's other relatives can be located. The following example shows another way in which escheat might occur.

Best Deal Bank offered charge cards to its customers. The bank had a number of credits for these charge accounts but was unable to locate the customers. The total amount of the credits was in excess of $100,000. The state wanted this money to escheat to it. As might be expected, the bank contested the escheat in court, claiming that it was still trying to locate the true owners. The bank was not successful in the lawsuit.

Escheat is governed by the appropriate state statute. Often, escheated property becomes part of the state's general fund. For a specified period after the escheat, the rightful owner can claim the property from the state. The rightful owner will need adequate proof of identity and of a right to the property.

Judicial Sale

When a person loses a civil lawsuit, the court may order that person to make payment to the other party. This is called a judgment. If the person does not make the required payment, additional action may be necessary. This action commonly consists of an execution of judgment. The person who is entitled to payment procures a writ of execution from the clerk of court's office. With this writ, the sheriff can seize the debtor's property and sell it. The money is then given to the judgment creditor to satisfy the judgment. This is called a *judicial sale* or a *sheriff's sale*. If the sale price exceeds the total owed to the judgment creditor, the costs of the sheriff's office, and the costs of the execution, the excess will usually be given to the owner. The treatment of this excess is governed by state law and by the type of judgment. Notices of judicial sales are usually included with other legal notices in the newspaper. A purchaser at a judicial sale buys the rights that the seller (the sheriff) had to sell. The sheriff's office generally does not warrant (promise) that it is entitled to sell the property. Also under state law, the true owner may have a limited period within which he or she may redeem the property, even if it is in the hands of a third-party purchaser. The amount of repayment to the third party is governed by state law.

A lender who wants to protect an interest in a loan may create a security interest in some collateral. If the lender follows the requirements for creating and perfecting a security interest, the lender will have a security interest in the property. If the borrower does not repay the loan under the terms of the contract, the lender can repossess (retake) the property. Usually the lender prefers to have cash and thus will sell the collateral. If the collateral is real estate, the loan will be called a *mortgage,* and taking possession of the property will be called a *mortgage foreclosure.* A person who buys repossessed property or foreclosed property buys only the seller's legal interest. The purchaser may lose the property if the foreclosure or repossession was wrongful.

Mortgage Foreclosure or Repossession of Property

A *bailment* arises when a person loans personal property to someone else. The *bailor* is the owner of the property, and the *bailee* is the one who has possession of the property. Whenever an owner allows another person to have custody of the owner's personal property, a bailment exists. The bailee has possession of the personal property but does not have title to or ownership of the property. It is understood that the bailee is to use the property in a specific way. For example, if the attendants of a parking garage drive a customer's car for any purpose other than parking or safeguarding it, they breach their duty as bailees. It is further understood that the bailee is to return the property at the end of the bailment.

BAILMENTS OF PERSONAL PROPERTY

If the borrower is giving up consideration, then a contract exists. However, a contract is not a requirement for a bailment. A bailment can occur gratuitously. If Elizabeth rents a car from Zeta Car Rental Company, a bailment relationship exists. Elizabeth is the bailee and Zeta Car Rental Company is the bailor. Their relationship will be governed by both the rules of bailments and the rules of contracts.

All the following elements are necessary for a bailment:

1. The bailor must retain title.
2. The possession of the property must be delivered to the bailee.
3. The bailee must accept possession.
4. The bailee must have possession of the property for a specific purpose and must have temporary control of the property.
5. The parties must intend that the property will be returned to the bailor unless the bailor directs that the property be given to another person.

A bailment is not a sale of personal property. A sale is a permanent change of possession and includes a transfer of title. Also, a sale requires an exchange of consideration, whereas a bailment does not.

A controversial question is whether parking in a garage constitutes a bailment or the rental of a space to park a car. The following is one court's opinion.

Parking Management, Inc. v. Gilder
343 A.2d 51 (D.C. App. 1975)

FACTS   Gilder parked his car in a garage managed by Parking Management, Inc. (PMI). The garage was enclosed in the Washington Hilton Hotel. When Gilder arrived at the garage, one of the attendants directed him to a space, where Gilder parked the car. Gilder took the key with him. At that time, a manager, a cashier, and three attendants were on duty. The trunk of Gilder's car was pried open while it was parked in the garage.

ISSUE   Did Gilder have a bailment relationship with PMI?

HOLDING   Yes. PMI was creating a bailment relationship under these circumstances.

REASONING   The theory that parking in a garage is a lease or a license situation is outmoded. When the owner parks the car and takes the key, the relationship is not always a lease. Unlike the usual tenant of real estate, the owner does not have an adequate opportunity to protect the car. By definition, the owner will always be away from the car once it has been parked. In addition, there is usually no fixed term for the parking of the car. The car owner cannot remove the car until the parking fee is paid. Here Gilder was under the impression that PMI was providing security. In fact, the job descriptions indicated that part of the employees' jobs included providing security. Each case must be decided on its particular facts.

Bailee's Duty of Care

Disputes often arise when the property is damaged while in the hands of the bailee. In a lawsuit, the issue would be whether or not the bailee took proper care of the property. The answer would depend on the local statutes, any bailment contract, and the type of bailment.

Classifications of Bailments

Bailments are divided into types based on who is going to benefit from the bailment relationship. The classification affects the bailee's liability if there is damage to the property.

Bailor Benefit Bailments

When the bailment is established solely to benefit the bailor, the bailee will be responsible only for gross negligence in caring for the property. For example, Daniel asks Sue to take his typewriter to the parking lot and put it in his car. Daniel is the only one benefiting from this bailment. Sue will be responsible for damage to the typewriter only if she is grossly negligent in completing the task. Suppose she carefully places the typewriter next to the trunk and opens the trunk with the key. While she is doing this, a third person steals the typewriter. Sue will not be liable because she was not grossly negligent. If she had placed the typewriter in the middle of the road before she opened the trunk, and another car had run over the typewriter, a court would probably find Sue guilty of gross negligence and therefore hold her liable. Remember that this decision will ultimately be one for the trier of fact in any court case. What is considered to be negligence will depend on the circumstances and the evidence presented.

Mutual Benefit Bailments

When a bailment is established for the benefit of both the bailor and the bailee, it is called a mutual benefit bailment. Both parties expect to gain from the bailment relationship. In such bailments, the bailee is responsible for ordinary negligence. A mutual benefit bailment occurs, for example, when the owner of a suit takes it to a dry cleaning establishment. The owner will benefit by having the suit cleaned and pressed. The dry cleaners will benefit because they are going to be paid. The dry cleaners will be responsible if they carelessly clean the suit in cleaning fluid that is too hot and the suit shrinks.

Bailee Benefit Bailments

When a bailment is established solely for the benefit of the bailee, it is called a bailee benefit bailment. The bailee will be responsible for slight negligence in caring for the property. Suppose Jeanette needed a car to drive downtown for a job interview, but her car was in the garage waiting to be repaired. Paula, her roommate, agreed to lend Jeanette her car. This bailment was created for Jeanette's benefit only. It is thus a bailee benefit bailment. If Jeanette causes an accident by driving faster than the speed limit and hitting another car, she will have to pay for the damage to Paula's car.

Restrictions on a Bailee's Liability

Some states and localities have statutes that provide maximum limits on the liability of the bailee in certain types of bailments.

If the bailment is based on a contract, the terms of the contract may increase or decrease the liability of the bailee. A bailee who is a quasi-public bailee will generally not be allowed to limit his or her liability contractually unless specifically permitted to do so by statute. A quasi-public bailee is a bailee offering services to the public, such as a common carrier, a garage, a hotel, or a public parking lot. Even when a statute permits a bailee to restrict liability, any limitation on liability must be reasonable.

A private bailee can restrict his or her liability under the terms of the agreement if this restriction does not conflict with the real purpose of the contract between the bailee and the bailor. The bailee must inform the bailor of any limitation on the bailee's liability. Most courts hold that a printed ticket stub or a posted notice on the premises does not adequately inform the bailor of the limitations *unless* the bailor's attention is directed to the sign or the ticket stub.

Termination of a Bailment

A bailment will terminate at the end of the period that the parties specify or when a specified condition occurs. If the bailment was for an indefinite time, it may be terminated at the will of either the bailor or the bailee. A bailment will also terminate when the purpose or performance of the bailment has been completed. If either party causes a material breach of the bailment relationship, the victim may terminate the bailment and the wrongdoer will be liable for any damages he or she caused. The bailment will terminate if the bailed property is destroyed or becomes unfit or unsuitable for the purpose of the bailment. Generally, a bailment will also terminate by operation of law if death, insanity, or bankruptcy of either party makes it impossible for the bailee to perform.

Bailee's Duty to Return the Property

A bailee has a general duty to return the bailor's property to the bailor. There are exceptions to this rule. The bailee is not liable to the bailor if the property is lost, destroyed, or stolen through no fault of the bailee. The bailee is not liable if the property is taken away by legal process, such as an attachment for a sheriff's sale. The bailee is not liable if the property is claimed by someone who has a better legal right to possession than the bailor has.

Sometimes a bailee has a duty to return the property to someone other than the bailor. There may be a duty to "return" the property to a transferee who has bought the property from the bailor. A common business example is when a warehouse or common carrier has an obligation to hold personal property and then transfer it to a purchaser who presents a receipt or bill of lading. These situations are discussed in detail in Chapter 20.

The following case dealt with the liability of a bailee for failure to return the property.

Vilner v. *Crocker National Bank*
152 Cal. Rptr. 850 (Cal. App. 1979)

FACTS   Vilner, the operator of a restaurant, used the Crocker National Bank's night depository on a regular basis. On the occasion in question, he unlocked the night depository at Crocker's Novato branch and placed in it a locked bag containing $7,976.36. After closing the depository, he heard what sounded like a bag dropping into the box. He reopened the depository and did not see his bag. The bag was not recovered.

Before that night, the bank had received at least four complaints by customers at other branches that deposits into the night depository were lost. On two occasions, customers had informed Crocker that bags had lodged in the depository at the Novato branch. Crocker did not take any action to correct these problems.

Is Crocker liable for not returning the bailed property? **ISSUE**

Yes. The bailee did not adequately explain its failure to return the property. **HOLDING**

If a bailor can establish that property was delivered to the bailee and that the bailor demanded its return, the bailee must explain its failure to return the property. It must explain why the bailed property disappeared and offer evidence to show that its failure to return the property was due to some specific casualty like theft or fire. When the bailee cannot redeliver on demand, it must show that it is without fault. It cannot show that it is without fault unless it can explain why it is impossible for it to redeliver the property. **REASONING**

The bailee does not have to return the property if the bailee has a lien on it. Many states have statutes that allow the bailee to keep the property in his or her possession until the bailor pays for the bailment. This is called a *possessory lien.* If the bailor fails to make payment, most statutes will permit the bailee to sell the property. A common type of bailee's lien is a mechanic's lien, which arises when services have been performed on the property. For example, if a garage repairs an automobile and the owner does not have the money to pay for the repairs, the garage can keep the automobile until the owner does pay. In most cases, the bailee will lose the lien if the bailee willingly releases the goods to the bailor — that is, if the bailor comes to reclaim the property and the bailee releases it without receiving payment. Generally, there is no bailee's lien if the bailor and bailee originally agreed that the bailor was going to pay on credit.

Personal property is classified into tangible and intangible property based on its physical characteristics. Discussions of legal interests in property revolve around ownership rights, title, and possession. Often, one person has title to property, but someone else has possession. Title to personal property can be acquired by original possession, by voluntary transfer directly from the owner to the transferee, or by involuntary transfer from the owner. A transferee of personal property will generally not have any better title than the transferor had. This will be true even though the transferee thought that the transferor **SUMMARY** had good title. This limitation on title is especially important in judicial sales, sales of repossessed property, conversion, confusion, and accession.

A bailment is a special legal relationship that occurs when the owner transfers the possession of personal property to someone else. The owner keeps title. After the purpose of the bailment has been completed, possession generally will be returned to the owner. The duty of the bailee to protect the property will be affected by whether it is a bailor benefit bailment, a mutual benefit bailment, or a bailee benefit bailment.

DISCUSSION QUESTIONS

1. What are the differences between title and possession?

2. What happens if the donor of a gift causa mortis dies but not from the expected cause? Who is likely to complain in such a situation?

3. What are the policies underlying the rules about accession?

4. James took a piece of rough turquoise stone, polished it, and set it in a silver setting in a necklace. James reasonably believed that he had found the stone on public land. In reality, he had found it on private land, where the owner, who had mined it, had placed it in a pile for polishing. Who owns the jewelry and why? What are the legal rights of the parties?

5. What rights do the owners have when confusion occurs and no one is guilty of misconduct?

6. Is an umbrella on a desk likely to be lost or mislaid property? Why? If the umbrella is on the floor, is it likely to be lost or mislaid property? Why?

7. Ric went to José's Mexican Restaurant for lunch. He hung his coat on the coat rack provided for that purpose. When he got ready to leave, Ric walked out and left his coat. Dennis found the coat. Who is entitled to title of the coat? Why? Who is entitled to possession of the coat? Why?

8. Define escheat. When would it occur?

9. What are the requirements for a bailment relationship?

10. What legal rights does a bailor have when a bailee has damaged the property or allowed someone else to damage it?

CASE PROBLEMS

1. In 1971, Treasure Salvors located an anchor from the *Nuestra Señora de Atocha*. Since that time, Treasure Salvors has continued to conduct salvage operations in the wreck area and has retrieved numerous artifacts. Frick and a number of other defendants began salvage operations 1500 yards from the location where the second anchor was discovered. Are the Treasure Salvors entitled to conduct their salvage operation free from interference from Frick? Do they have ownership rights in the wreck? (*Treasure Salvors, Inc.* v. *Unidentified Wrecked and Abandoned Sailing Vessel*, 640 F.2d 560 [5th Cir. 1981].)

2. Martha Honea was the administratrix of the estate of her father, W. E. Smith. Honea filed suit against Roger Scarbrough to recover an amount she claimed was owed by Scarbrough. Smith paid $3840 by check for a used car. Title to the car was issued in the name of Scarbrough's daughter. Scarbrough and his daughter executed a note that provided for thirty-six monthly installments of $125 each, a total of $4500. Smith gave the original copy of the note to Scarbrough's daughter and kept the carbon copy for himself. Scarbrough's daughter made one payment on the note before Smith died. This payment was made by a check, which was cashed by Smith. Did Smith intend to make a gift when he delivered the note? (*Scarbrough* v. *Honea,* 331 S.E.2d 80 [Ga. App. 1985].)

3. Herbert Kaiser wrote a check to the land title company for $14,692.16, as payment for the home his nephew was buying. He also wrote a check for $2,308 to his nephew for furnishings. The alleged oral loan agreement provided for 300 monthly payments. The nephew issued 44 monthly checks to his uncle after the transaction. A number of these checks carried the notation "for house." After Kaiser's death, the nephew quit making the monthly payments. The nephew claimed that the money advanced by Kaiser was a gift not a loan. Is the nephew correct in his assertion? (*Estate of Kaiser* v. *Gifford,* 692 S.W.2d 525 [Tex. App. 1 Dist. 1985].)

4. The personal representative of Marjorie Shepard brought a suit for amounts loaned by Shepard to Jacobson. Shepard made the loans by writing checks to Jacobson or his creditors. Some of the checks had the notation "loan" on them. The loans were not evidenced by a note. Shepard made statements during her life that the debt was forgiven. This evidence was not contradicted. Did Shepard make a valid gift to the debtor of the amount that he owed her? (*Guardian State Bank & Trust* v. *Jacobson,* 369 N.W.2d 80 [Neb. 1985].)

5. Kenneth Simkin initiated a lawsuit against his former wife, Barbara Norcross. Simkin wanted the return of his sailing vessel, a Morgan sloop. He had left the vessel tied to a jetty. He had the owner's permission to dock his vessel in this manner. It was in good condition at the time. When Simkin returned to his vessel, it was gone. It was later found in the custody of his wife. Did Simkin abandon his vessel? Did Simkin intend to give the vessel to his former wife? (*Simkin* v. *Norcross,* 610 F. Supp. 691 [D.C. Fla. 1985].)

6. Chemical Sales Company, a Missouri corporation, was engaged in the business of distributing cleaning products in the St. Louis area. Diamond Chemical Company is a New Jersey corporation engaged in the business of producing cleaning products. Diamond was the primary supplier for Chemical Sales. Chemical Sales was having financial difficulties. To ensure that they would have a continuous supply of products, Chemical Sales entered into an agreement that Diamond would manage Chemical Sales' business and receive a security interest in Chemical Sales' inventory and accounts receivable. The relationship did not work out. The key

officers of Chemical Sales quit their jobs. Diamond Chemical then terminated Chemical Sales' business and sold its assets. A demand was made on Diamond Chemical for an accounting. An accounting was not given. Did Diamond Chemical wrongfully convert Chemical Sales' property? Did Chemical Sales abandon its property? (*Chemical Sales Co., Inc.* v. *Diamond Chemical Co.,* 766 F.2d 364 [8th Cir. 1985].)

7. The Controller of the state of California, Kenneth Cory, started a lawsuit to recover funds held by the bank. The funds consisted of $157,765.47 set aside because of money orders sold by the bank that were still uncashed after seven years. The bank wanted to deduct $143,133.22 in service charges before remitting (transferring) the funds to the state. Should the funds escheat to the state of California? If so, how much should be given to the state? (*Cory* v. *Golden State Bank,* 157 Cal. Rptr. 538 [Cal. App. 1979].)

8. Goldbaum rented two safe deposit boxes in the bank. He stored rare medals and coins in these boxes. The leases for the boxes stated that "Lessors shall have no liability for loss from fire, water, radiation, the forces of nature . . . ." The bank's sprinkler system failed and the water flooded these boxes. Should the bank be liable for the damage? Was the bank a bailee? (*Goldbaum* v. *Bank Leumi Trust Company of New York,* 543 F. Supp. 434 [S.D. N.Y. 1982].)

9. Monroe rented a Roto-tiller from East Bay Rental Service. They did not give him any instructions on the proper use of the tiller and they did not warn him about the dangers involved in its use. Monroe was injured while using the tiller. Did a bailment relationship exist? If so, what type of bailment relationship existed? Should East Bay Rental Service be held liable? (*Monroe* v. *East Bay Rental Service,* 245 P.2d 9 [1st Dist., Div. 2 1952].)

10. Delta received an order from Shiba Electronic S.A. Delta obtained a cargo container from Imparca. The container was loaded and sealed by Delta and delivered to Imparca by Delta's agent. The container was placed on a vessel chartered by Imparca, and Imparca issued a clean bill of lading. The bill of lading indicated that the carrier, Imparca, discharged its responsibilities when it delivered the goods into the custody of government authorities as required by the laws of a foreign port. The twenty-foot cargo container was placed on the dock in Puerto Cabello in the custody of the Instituto Nacional De Puertos (the National Institute of Ports.) The National Institute of Ports (INP) was responsible for the operation of this port in Venezuela. INP was responsible for all the operations of this seaport including stevedoring, warehousing, and receiving and delivering cargo. Should the carrier be responsible for the disappearance of the goods? (*Allstate Insurance Co.* v. *Imparca Lines,* 646 F.2d 166 [5th Cir. 1981].)

CHAPTER 51

Insurance

THE CONCEPT OF INSURANCE

The existence of *risk* creates the need, or at least the desire, for insurance. Automobile accidents occur with alarming regularity, normally causing substantial property damage to at least one automobile and frequently to more. Fires burn down homes or businesses, presenting the owner with the potential for economic ruin. People die, leaving behind unpaid bills, and very often a family with one less wage earner. Or the death leaves a gaping hole in the management of the business that employed — and relied on — the deceased.

Risks cannot be totally avoided. When a loss occurs as a result of risk, the victim must somehow finance the loss. There are two basic ways to do so: either through self-financing or through risk sharing. Self-financing is expensive and potentially disastrous. The feared event may occur before the self-financing person has been able to **amortize** fully for the potential loss. Risk sharing therefore is a more satisfying alternative to many people. The most common form of risk sharing is through insurance.

Insurance is a type of *contract*. Basically, people who share a common risk

Amortize To provide for the gradual extinguishing of a debt by contributing funds to a sinking fund or similar account

935

contribute to a fund set up to cover the losses that will be felt if the common risk occurs. Any member of the group who suffers a loss due to the occurrence of the common risk can withdraw money from the fund to cover the loss. The amount each person contributes is based on the likelihood of the event's occurrence and also on the value of the property or other interest being protected.

Although people can form their own insurance groups, most would rather deal with a company established for the express purpose of providing insurance protection. Since insurance companies normally can provide coverage over a wider geographic area than a group of individuals could reach, the risk-sharing proportions are usually smaller for the individual insured party. And since the insurance company is an expert in the field, it can establish standards that help minimize the risk faced by members of the covered group. In addition, the insurance company's expertise allows for a more scientific rate-setting mechanism: thus, the risk funds contributed by the insured parties are likely to be as low as possible while still providing adequate coverage.

FORMATION OF THE INSURANCE CONTRACT

Because of public policy considerations, the insurance contract is heavily regulated by state law. An insurance company must comply with the applicable state law in creating the contract with the **insured.** However, because of the potential for fraud and for the huge losses being assumed by the insurance company, state statutes also give the **insurer** some special protections in the formation of the contract.

Offer and Acceptance

Insured The person protected by the insurance policy

Insurer The person or corporation who provides the protection called for by an insurance contract

Premiums The monies that the insured pays to retain an insurance contract with the insurer

The concepts of offer and acceptance are applied in a special way to insurance contracts. The insurance company has an obvious desire to control the nature and extent of its potential liability. This control is important because the company is liable for the risk insured against as soon as the contract is formed, even though most of the **premiums** the company expects to receive have not yet been paid. If the covered risk occurred at this time, the liability of the company would greatly exceed the premiums paid by the insured.

The problem is compounded when the company itself cannot analyze the insured person before the insurance goes into effect. Insurance is generally sold by an agent who represents the insurance company in its dealings with the insured. The agent is the person who speaks to the customer, but the company is the one facing the potential for liability if a claim arises. To what extent can the agent bind the company? The answer depends on the type of insurance sought by the customer.

The agent generally has the power to bind the company to an insurance contract immediately if the insurance is for *property* or *liability* coverage. When the customer completes an application, the customer has made an *offer.* When the agent accepts a premium, or even when the agent agrees to accept a premium later, the insurance company is deemed to have accepted the offer. At that point, a contract exists and the customer is immediately covered for the named risk. The reason for this immediate coverage is that under state law the insurer can cancel a property protection or liability contract fairly easily if the risk is unacceptable to the insurer.

On the other hand, the law places many restrictions on the power of the insurer to cancel a *life insurance* policy. As a result, life insurance companies prefer investigating a life insurance application before being bound to insurance coverage. When the customer completes and tenders an application for life insurance, the law treats the application as an *inquiry*. The insurance company — not the agent — then studies the application. If the company feels that the applicant presents a reasonable risk, the company makes an offer in the form of a policy. The customer can then accept the offer and create a contract by accepting delivery of the contract. Another approach is to treat the customer as an offeror and the application as an offer, but to restrict the authority of the agent. In this case, only the company is empowered to accept the offer; acceptance is shown by the issuance of a policy. In either case, the customer is *not* protected immediately, in contrast to the provisions of property insurance policies. To alleviate this problem, many life insurance companies allow the agent to issue a **binder,** a short-term life insurance policy that provides some coverage for the applicant during the insurance company's investigation of the application.

> **Binder** A short-term commitment to provide insurance coverage in some limited form pending the final entry into a permanent insurance contract

Avoiding Liability

Since insurance policies are contracts, many of the rules of contract law apply to insurance. Situations that would create voidable contracts often create voidable insurance coverage, as well. Fraud on the part of the applicant allows the insurer to avoid the contract. However, the company that provides life insurance must discover the fraud within a reasonable time (normally three years) in order to avoid the policy. After that, the **incontestability clause** makes the policy "incontestable." Fraud in the filing of a claim is also grounds for avoidance of the coverage. And intentional destruction of the insured property by the insured is not covered by most policies.

> **Incontestability clause** A clause in an insurance policy that limits the time during which the insurer may challenge coverage

Sometimes the court must decide what to do when one of the insured parties has committed a wrongful act but another insured on the same policy has not. The following case shows how one court resolved such a problem.

Ryan v. *MFA Mutual Insurance Company*
610 S.W.2d 428 (Tenn. App. 1980)

Ryan had an argument with his wife and left his home. After he left, his wife started a fire that damaged the house and some of its contents. Mr. Ryan filed a claim on the insurance policy that covered the house. The policy was in the name of Mr. and Mrs. Ryan.

FACTS

Can Mr. Ryan, an innocent coinsured, collect on a policy when the jointly insured party started the fire?

ISSUE

HOLDING   Yes. Mr. Ryan was not guilty of any wrongdoing.

REASONING   This was a case of first impression in Tennessee. A split of authority among the states had resolved the question. The former majority rule was that the innocent coinsured was barred from recovery because of the wrongdoing of the other coinsured. A new rule that allowed recovery by the innocent party had emerged over the preceding two years. Allowing the innocent party to recover would not benefit the wrongdoer in this case. When an insurance policy is ambiguous or unclear, it must be construed against the insurer. The intentional destruction of property by one of the coinsured should not be interpreted to deny recovery by the other coinsured unless the policy specifically so states. The policy here did not so state. The court held that Mr. Ryan was entitled to recovery for the damages to his property interest as covered by the policy.

One party to a normal contract is excused from performance if the other party has failed to perform. The same rule is applied in insurance. If the insured fails to pay premiums when they are due, the insurance company is justified in thereafter refusing to pay claims filed under the policy.

An insured is also normally required to provide prompt notification of any claims to be filed under the policy. The purpose is to allow the insurer an opportunity to investigate the claim and to collect any evidence it may need. Failure of the insured to provide the required notice in a timely manner may discharge the liability of the insurance company even though the occurrence is one the policy was designed to protect against.

Insurable Interest

In most states, gambling contracts are illegal and void on public policy grounds. What separates an insurance contract from a gambling contract is the requirement that a person must have an insurable interest in the object being insured for the policy to be valid and enforceable. If this requirement did not exist, it would be potentially profitable for someone to sit at the nearest airport and purchase flight insurance on the life of every passenger on a particular flight in the hope that the plane would crash. To improve the possibility of such a crash, the person might be encouraged to "arrange" a crisis on the plane. Obviously, such conduct is against public policy.

An insurable interest exists if the person purchasing the insurance has a financial or an equitable interest in the person or property being insured. That is, the purchaser must have an actual, lawful, and substantial economic interest in the safety and the preservation of the person or property being insured. An insurable interest pinpoints the exact nature of the purchaser's interest in the insured object, as well as the exact nature of the possible loss that is being protected against by the policy.

Under property and liability insurance policies, the purchaser must have an insurable interest at two distinct times: when the policy is purchased and when the loss occurs. The absence of an insurable interest at either time will void the policy, and no claims will be honored. Obviously, the owner of property has an insurable interest in that property. Less obviously, the renter of property has an insurable interest in the property rented; a lien holder has an insurable interest in the property covered by the lien; a secured creditor has an insurable interest in the collateral; and a bailee has an insurable interest in the bailed item. Furthermore, since property and liability insurance policies are designed to *indemnify* the insured party for losses actually suffered, the insurable interest is limited to the amount of loss actually suffered or to some percentage of that amount.

The requirements for an insurable interest in life insurance are slightly different from those for property and liability insurance. As will be discussed later, several types of life insurance policies are treated as investments, in contrast to the indemnity purpose of property insurance. As a result, the purchaser of a life insurance policy need have an insurable interest in the life of the insured only at the time the policy is issued. If such an interest exists at the time of issue but is later extinguished, the policy will still remain in effect and will be fully enforceable, provided that the premiums have been paid as due. Thus, the purchaser can still collect the amount of the policy on the death of the insured even though no insurable interest exists at the time of the death — unless the purchaser intentionally caused the death of the insured.

Again, it is obvious that a person has an insurable interest in his or her own life. And it is fairly obvious that a spouse has an insurable interest in the life of his or her spouse. Likewise, parents have an insurable interest in the lives of their children. And, generally, children have an insurable interest in the lives of their parents. A corporation has an insurable interest in the lives of its key executives, usually high-ranking officers on whom the corporation relies for its continued success. And a partnership, or the partners of the partnership, has an insurable interest in the life of each of the partners. Finally, a creditor has an insurable interest in the life of a debtor, but only to the extent of the debt.

Unlike property insurance, which is designed to indemnify the insured for a readily measured loss, life insurance is difficult if not impossible to value. Because there is no way to measure the value of a human life, life insurance policies are "valued" by the purchaser when the policy is purchased. Basically, the value placed on the insured life is decided by the amount the purchaser is willing to pay in premiums. The amount of the premiums is determined by the age, health, occupation, and other factors affecting the life of the insured. Life insurance policies normally are valued in increments of $1000, and a minimum amount is usually required by the company. For example, the policy may be for as little as $5000 or for as much as the national debt — provided that the purchaser is willing and able to pay the requisite premiums.

Life insurance is the one type of insurance that the insurer *knows* will have to pay off, provided that the policy remains in effect. When an insured person dies, the insurer must pay the face amount of the policy (or more) to the named

LIFE INSURANCE

Mortality tables Bases for determining the expected life span of a person of ordinary health

beneficiary. Of course, insurance companies use such things as **mortality tables** to determine the likelihood of death for any particular insured and to establish the insurance rate, or premium.

However, there is more to life insurance than the calculation of premiums. The primary purpose of most insurance policies covering the life of the purchaser is *investment*. In other words, the insured plans to pay premiums for some time period and then to receive an income or other return for the investment. There are four basic types of life insurance, three of which have investment overtones. The investments rights are spelled out in the standard provisions of the policies.

Ordinary Life Insurance

Perhaps the most common type of life insurance purchased by an individual is ordinary life insurance, also called whole life or straight life insurance. The basic concept is that the insured will pay premiums for his or her entire life, and on the insured's death the face amount of the policy will be paid to the **beneficiary.** Most insurance companies consider the age of either ninety-nine or one hundred an "entire life." Thus, if the insured pays premiums until the age of ninety-nine (or one hundred), the insurer will then pay the face amount of the policy to the insured and cancel the coverage. An ordinary life policy is also an investment policy.

Beneficiary The person named or designated by the insured as the intended recipient of any insurance proceeds or benefits if the insured risk occurs

Limited-Payment Life Insurance

A limited-payment life insurance policy is similar to a whole life policy in all respects save one. The insured pays all the premiums called for in an ordinary life policy, but pays them in a limited time. Whereas a whole life policy calls for payments until age ninety-nine, a limited-payment life policy might call for all premiums to be paid in twenty years or by age fifty-five. At that point, the insured has a fully paid policy that will be honored on the death of the insured. Or the insured can take advantage of the investment aspects of the policy.

Endowment Life Insurance

In an endowment policy, the insured pays premiums for a fixed time period; at the end of that period, the insured will receive the face amount of the policy from the insurer, and all coverage will terminate. If the insured dies during the period, the insurance company will pay the beneficiary the face amount of the policy. During the endowment period, this type of policy has an investment aspect.

Term Life Insurance

The least expensive form of life insurance is term life insurance. Most group insurance policies are term insurance. This type of insurance has no investment value; hence, the insurance company does not have to set aside funds to provide for the investment aspect required by the other types of life insurance. The term life insurance policy covers the life of the insured for a preset time period, normally for one or five years. If the insured dies during the term of the policy, the insurer must pay the face amount of the policy to the beneficiary. If the insured does not die, the policy expires at the end of the time period. No accumulated values or any coverage will remain. This type of insurance is especially appealing to young adults living on tight budgets. The coverage is inexpensive, but if something does happen to the insured, the beneficiaries will receive the full amount of the insurance.

Life insurance policies normally provide a **grace period** (usually thirty days) after the premium due date, during which the insured can pay the premium and keep the policy in effect. The policy may exclude certain risks, such as death resulting from military service and suicide by the insured. However, suicide may be excluded only for the period of time before the incontestability clause goes into effect—commonly either two or three years—because suicide is a part of the data in the mortality table. This means that if the insured commits suicide within those two or three years of the policy issue date, the company does not have to pay, but if the suicide occurs after that, the company must honor the policy as written.

Another aspect of the incontestability clause is that the insurance company must challenge any misstatements of fact or concealments by the insured within the stated period or it cannot argue them. The only things the incontestability clause does not cover are lack of an insurable interest and misstatements of age. If the insured misstates his or her age, the only thing that can be done is to modify the policy to reflect the true age of the insured.

The standard life insurance policy—except for term insurance—also contains a **nonforfeiture clause.** This clause guarantees the insured that the investment rights cannot be lost, or forfeited, after the policy has been in effect for three years. These investment rights are reflected in the **cash value** of the policy. If the insured stops paying premiums after the policy has been in effect for three full years, the insured can take the cash value built up in the policy in one of three ways:

1. *cash surrender*—giving up the coverage for the built-up cash value of the policy
2. *extended term insurance*—buying the coverage called for in the policy in term insurance for as long as the cash value will purchase it
3. *paid-up insurance*—purchasing a policy that is in effect until the death of the insured for whatever amount the cash value will cover

In addition, the insured may have options on how to treat dividends paid on the policy by the company. The dividends may be used to reduce future premiums; they may be left with the company to accrue interest; or they may be paid to the insured in cash.

Property insurance is designed as an indemnification protection against certain predetermined risks faced by the insured. The risk of loss faced by the insured is spread over a group of persons who face the same or a similar risk.

Standard Provisions

Grace period A preset time period beyond the premium due date during which the insurance remains in effect, permitting the insured to pay the premium with some delay without losing coverage

Nonforfeiture clause A contract clause assuring that the insured will not forfeit any built-up values if the policy expires or lapses

Cash value The built-up value of the policy based on its investment portion of the premiums paid

PROPERTY INSURANCE

The coverage does not normally apply if the insured intentionally destroys the insured property, but it does protect in the event the insured is negligent. The concept of insurable interest is important at two times in property insurance coverage: when the policy is issued and when the loss occurs.

Although an almost infinite number of property insurance areas exist, only three will be examined here. Property and/or liability policies have been issued against damage to the legs of dancers, against injury to the hands of pianists, and even against impairment of the fertility of thoroughbred horses "retired" to stud. Virtually anything the human mind can envision can be insured against — provided that the insured is willing to pay the premium the insurer will charge for assuming the liability if the event occurs. However, most of us are more likely to insure our house, our car, and other equally common items.

Fire Insurance

Most homes in this country are covered by fire insurance policies. The coverage provides protection in the form of indemnification for losses caused by a *hostile* fire, but not for damages caused by a *friendly* fire. In addition, extended coverage endorsements normally provide protection for damage due to smoke, heat, water, and chemicals resulting from a hostile fire. Contrary to popular belief, fires may not be hostile in every circumstance. A fire is friendly, not hostile, if it is burning where it is intended to burn. Thus, damage to a flue caused by fire in a fireplace is not covered by one's fire insurance policy. But if the fire escapes the hearth and spreads to the carpet, it has become hostile. Once it escapes the area where it is meant to be contained, it is deemed hostile, and the damage is therefore covered by a standard fire insurance policy.

Most fire insurance policies are either blanket policies or specific policies. In addition, they are either valued policies or open policies. Thus, you may have a blanket, valued policy; a blanket, open policy; a specific, valued policy; or a specific, open policy.

A *blanket* policy is applied to a class of property, normally at a specified location, rather than to specific articles of property. Coverage of furnishings or clothing would normally be blanket coverage. Coverage of a rare stamp collection would more likely be a *specific* policy, covering specified articles or things.

A *valued* policy is one with a predetermined total value for the insured property. This value is the amount to be used in case of a total loss.

An *open* policy does not predetermine the value of the insured property. Rather, it commonly establishes a maximum value the insurer will pay on total loss of the property, but the insured must establish the fair market value of the destroyed property at the date of loss. If the fair market value exceeds the maximum, the maximum will control. If the fair market value is below the maximum, the fair market value will control.

In either a valued or an open policy, if the loss is less than total, the insured can recover only the amount of the loss actually sustained up to the policy maximum.

Many fire insurance policies have a **coinsurance clause.** This clause requires the insured to maintain a minimum amount of coverage as set out in the clause, such as 80 percent of the total value of the property. If the insured maintains the minimum coverage, the company will honor the policy up to its limits. But if the insured has less than the required insurance, the insured must bear a portion of the loss personally. The following standard formula is used to determine how much of the loss must be borne by the insured:

Coinsurance clause
A clause dividing the potential risk between the insured and the insurer in the event of partial loss or destruction of the insured property

$$\text{Actual loss suffered} \times \frac{\text{amount of insurance carried}}{\text{coinsurance \% } \times \text{ value of property}} = \text{recovery}.$$

For example, George had an 80 percent coinsurance clause, property worth $50,000, insurance of $35,000, and a loss of $20,000:

$$\$20,000 \times \frac{\$35,000}{80\% \times \$50,000} = \$20,000 \times \frac{\$35,000}{\$40,000} = \$17,500.$$

George would recover $17,500 from the insurance company and would have to pay the remaining $2,500 personally. If he had maintained the 80 percent coverage required by the policy, he would have recovered the full $20,000 loss from the insurer.

Fire insurance is normally nonassignable without the prior permission of the insurance company. The coverage is deemed personal between the insured and the insurer. One of the reasons the insurance company assumed the risk is the character of the insured. To allow free substitution of the covered person with another would unduly expose the insurer to risks it might not have been willing to assume. Of course, once a loss has occurred, the proceeds are freely assignable by the insured. At that point, the duty of the insurer is fixed, and the assignment does no harm to its duty.

The insurer can cancel a fire insurance policy on delivery of notice to the insured and a refund of any unearned premium will be paid to the insured. There is usually a short time period, such as ten days, before the coverage is canceled to allow the insured time to shop for another insurer.

Marine Insurance

Marine insurance protects ships at sea and the cargo or freight on such ships from standard "perils of the sea." The coverage includes such risks as shipwreck, fire, and piracy. It excludes damage due to normal action of wind and waves and to ordinary wear and tear, as well as losses due to delays caused by ordinary weather problems. When most international business was conducted by transportation via the sea lanes, marine insurance was extremely important. Its current importance is primarily in the area of oil shipments, although many other types of cargo still move by sea.

Most marine insurance policies are valued policies; the insurer and the insured agree in advance to the value of the property insured. In addition, the policy will be either a time policy or a voyage policy. In a *time* policy, the insurance coverage is for a preset time period, at the expiration of which the insurance will lapse, even if the ship covered is in the middle of the ocean. In contrast, a *voyage* policy covers a ship until a specified voyage ends, regardless of the time it takes to complete the trip.

To obtain a marine insurance policy, the insured must warrant that the ship is seaworthy. This warranty includes at a minimum that the ship is competent to resist ordinary wind and waves, that it is properly equipped and has an adequate crew, and that the captain is both competent and of "good moral character." Breach of the warranty voids the policy coverage.

Finally, the typical marine insurance policy does not cover all contingencies; it does, however, provide for the allocation of loss when that loss is not covered by the insurance policy. If the ship or cargo is damaged, the loss will be borne proportionately in some instances and individually in others. If the loss or damage is intentionally incurred by the captain to ensure the general safety of the ship and cargo, such as when the captain must jettison some cargo in order to save the ship during a storm, the parties will share the loss. This situation is covered in a "general average" clause, which provides that the owners of the ship and the owners of the cargo will share the losses incurred in proportion to the value of property saved by the act of the captain. On the other hand, if the loss is not intentionally caused and the policy does not cover it, a "particular average" clause states that the loss is borne exclusively by the owner of the lost or damaged property.

Automobile Insurance

Automobile insurance may be the most widely owned type of insurance in the United States. Nearly every driver has insurance coverage for times when the driver is operating an automobile, either in his or her own name or on the policy of another person, such as a parent or an employer. State statutes require that a driver either have liability insurance or provide self-insurance adequate to cover potential liability that the driver may incur.

The minimum coverage any driver should have is for liability and property damage. This basic coverage protects the driver in the event that he or she causes harm to the person or property of another. That is, if the driver is at fault in an accident, the insurance coverage — at least up to the policy limits — will indemnify the driver if he or she is sued by the injured party. Most states require a minimum amount of liability and property damage coverage. For example, California requires a minimum coverage of $15,000 per person and $30,000 per accident in personal liability, and $5,000 per accident in property damage coverage; a person who is involved in an accident and does not have this minimum coverage must post a $35,000 bond or deposit in order to continue operating an automobile on California highways.

Liability and property coverage provides for protection from the "other guy" in the accident, but it does nothing for the driver or the damaged auto. For this reason, many people add at least a collision clause and often elect a comprehensive clause, as well. Collision coverage provides for insurance coverage on the driver's car in the event of an accident, even if the driver is "at fault." These clauses normally have a **deductible amount,** such as $100. Such a deductible would require the insured to pay the first $100 in collision damages before the insurance policy protection could be exercised. The deductible is designed to discourage petty claims and to help reduce the cost of the insurance.

Deductible amount
Amount of damages to be paid by the insured before any liability of the insurer can be enforced

A comprehensive coverage clause protects the automobile owner from any loss or damage except collision or accident. Thus, fire damages, theft, explosion, and vandalism are covered by this clause, and there is normally no deductible amount. Great care should be exercised in selecting this particular type of coverage. Many items are excluded by the policy, and often the insured purchases comprehensive coverage to protect only those excluded items. For example, many companies do not cover theft of tape decks, CB radios, or other electronic add-ons. Similarly, some policies do not cover "mag wheels" or other custom touches the owner has added to personalize the auto. The buyer needs to shop carefully before deciding to purchase comprehensive insurance coverage. The following case illustrates one situation in which a comprehensive policy may be worthwhile.

Edwards v. State Farm Mutual Automobile Insurance Company
296 N.W.2d 804 (Iowa 1980)

Edwards negotiated the sale of his car to Davis. Davis gave Edwards a check for $3400, the purchase price, and Edwards signed the title and gave Davis possession of the car. Davis's check was returned for lack of funds in the account. The trial court concluded, based on the testimony, that Davis had committed fraud. Neither Davis nor the car could be located. Edwards filed a claim under the comprehensive coverage of his policy.

FACTS

Is Edwards entitled to collect under the theft provisions of the policy?

ISSUE

Yes. The insured automobile was "stolen" under the terms of the policy.

HOLDING

Because the term *theft* was not defined in the policy, the court defined it broadly and in a manner most favorable to the insured. The court reasoned that the insurer could have avoided this problem by defining theft in the policy. Although lawyers would not interpret theft as including fraud or obtaining property by false pretenses, most nonlawyers would. The court believed that it should define theft according to its popular meaning. It also noted that the courts and the legislature have recently been broadening the definition of theft. The court concluded that the insurer was incorrect in arguing that this situation fell under the conditional-sale exclusion of the policy: Edwards did not intend to create a security interest in the car; he intended to sell it outright.

REASONING

Several states have moved into a contemporary area of automobile insurance known as "no-fault." The concept here is that each insured party will collect from his or her own insurance company in the event of an accident without regard to which party was the cause of the accident (that is, was "at fault"). In the event of an accident, each party submits a claim to his or her insurer, and the matter is ideally settled quickly, equitably, and inexpensively.

Finally, it is a good idea for the driver at least to consider coverage against **uninsured motorists.** This coverage protects an insured party who is unlucky enough to be involved in an accident in which the other person is both at fault and without insurance. In such an event, the insured submits a claim to the insurer, and the insurer then covers the damages incurred by the insured in the accident. The insurer then assumes the rights of the insured against the uninsured motorist who was at fault in the accident.

Uninsured motorists
Persons operating automobiles without any insurance coverage for any accidents they may cause or become party to

WARRANTIES, WAIVERS, AND ESTOPPEL

Warranties are extremely important in insurance contracts. The warranties in a policy set up the conditions that must exist, or that may not exist, before a claim made on the insurer will be valid. These warranties must be expressed in, or attached to, the policy itself. No implied warranties will be found by the courts. If the insured breaches a warranty, the insurance company has the option of avoiding the policy at its election without any challenge by the insured unless the insurer is liable because of a waiver of the warranty or an estoppel. Warranties are classified as either affirmative or continuing. An *affirmative* warranty is one that must exist at the time the policy is entered into by the parties. A *continuing* warranty is one that must be satisfied during the entire period of the insurance coverage.

Waiver comes into play when the insurer could have avoided liability but the conduct of the insurer waived this ability. Estoppel applies when the insurer is not allowed to avoid the liability (that is, is estopped from avoiding the liability). Technically, *waiver* involves voluntary conduct by the insurer in not asserting a defense. *Estoppel* means that the conduct of the insurer prevents the assertion of any power of avoidance on the policy.

Normally, a waiver will be found when the insurance company agent neglects to enforce a warranty included in the policy. For example, the agent delivers a policy to the insured even though the agent knows that the insured does not have the fire alarm system required before delivery of the policy. The lack of a fire alarm is a breach of warranty by the insured, but the conduct of the agent has waived this requirement, and the breach cannot be asserted by the insurer in the event of a claim filed by the insured.

An estoppel will normally be found in situations in which the insurer acts in a manner that the insured relies on, and subsequently the insurer attempts to deny liability because the insured failed to perform some act. Suppose, for example, that the insured is involved in an automobile accident. The insurer tells the insured that the company will gather all the evidence necessary to defend the case and that the insured needs to do nothing. Later the insurer attempts to deny liability, asserting that the insured failed to cooperate fully in the investigation. The conduct of the company would estop it from denying liability under these facts.

THE NEW EMPHASIS ON GOOD FAITH

Several cases over the past few years have imposed a new type of liability on insurance companies. These cases have held that an insurance company has a duty to act in good faith in its dealings with the insured and that a failure to do so amounts to a "civil tort" for which the insurer can be held liable for amounts beyond the maximum limits of the policy. Included have been a fire insurance coverage case in which the company refused to pay the policy amount because a replacement asset could be obtained for less than the amount of the policy; a fire insurance policy case in which the insurer refused to pay because the insured had been arrested (wrongfully) for arson, but later was acquitted; and an automobile insurance policy case in which the insurer refused to pay the claim of the insured, asserting that the uninsured motorist involved in the accident might have been insured, even though no one was aware of who that insurer was, and placing the onus on the insured to determine if that was in fact the case.

The following case was one of the first in which the issue of the good faith of the insurer was an issue. Notice how the court treated the bad faith of the insurer.

Gruenberg v. *Aetna Insurance Company*
510 P.2d 1032 (Cal. 1973)

FACTS

Gruenberg was the owner/operator of a restaurant and cocktail lounge in Los Angeles. Gruenberg purchased fire insurance on his business from several insurers, including Aetna. Seven months later the business burned. Gruenberg was informed of the fire and went to the scene. While there he argued with a member of the arson squad of the fire department and was arrested.

Investigators for Aetna informed the fire department that Gruenberg had excessive fire insurance, and on the basis of this information Gruenberg was arrested and charged with arson and with defrauding an insurance company, both felonies under California law.

The insurer demanded that Gruenberg appear to answer questions in its office before the arraignment for the felony charges. Under the advice of his attorney, Gruenberg refused to do so. The criminal charges were dismissed for lack of probable cause, but the insurance company denied liability due to Gruenberg's failure to submit to their examination as demanded.

ISSUE

Is the insurance company liable for damages for its bad-faith refusal to honor the terms of the insurance contract?

HOLDING   Yes. A failure to act in good faith by an insurance company is a breach of contract and a tort against the insured.

REASONING   An insurance policy contract carries an implied covenant of good faith and fair dealing. An unreasonable withholding of the payments due under the policy is a breach of the implied covenants and as such gives rise to a cause of action *in tort* for the breach. Further, the duty is nonconsensual in origin, being present whether the party agrees to it or not. Gruenberg had done nothing improper, and the insurer had acted in bad faith. Gruenberg was entitled to damages.

SUMMARY   Insurance is a legal and contractual arrangement for risk sharing, the spreading of risk among people who share a common potential for financial loss. The insurance contract is heavily regulated by state laws because of public policy considerations. Of special concern are the requirements of offer and acceptance and the requirement of an insurable interest in the insured before an insurance policy can be purchased.

This chapter covered two broad types of insurance: life insurance and property insurance. (Numerous other types of insurance, such as health, disability, unemployment, workers' compensation, and social security, were not covered since they are beyond the scope of this text.) Life insurance is primarily thought of as an investment by the insured. The only exception is term insurance, which has no cash or investment value.

Property insurance is primarily used to indemnify the insured if the insured event occurs. The most important types of property insurance are designed to cover fires, marine shipments, and automobiles.

Insurance companies require certain warranties as a condition to providing coverage. Breach of these warranties operates as an avoidance of liability unless the insurer is liable because of a waiver of the warranty or an estoppel.

DISCUSSION
QUESTIONS

1. Why do insurance companies use coinsurance clauses?

2. What are the differences between a coinsurance and a deductible clause?

3. How will a court interpret an ambiguous clause in an insurance contract?

4. Should a wife be allowed to recover from her insurance company for theft of her personal property if her husband was the thief and the policy was issued to the two of them as jointly insured parties?

5. In question 4, would it matter if the wife had either participated in the theft or was totally innocent of any wrongdoing?

6. Eileen has invested heavily in the stock market, partly because she believes that the president's economic policies will lead to a booming economy. She now desires a life insurance policy on the president's life to protect her investment. Does Eileen have an insurable interest in the life of the president?

7. Richard, who lives in Boston, wants to buy property insurance from Larry's of Lisbon. The policy would pay Richard $100,000 if any radioactive debris falls on Moscow, Idaho, at any time during the 1980s. Richard owns no property in Idaho, nor does he have any relatives there. What public policy arguments against the policy could be asserted?

8. Donna left her automobile in a parking lot at the local shopping center. When she returned, the automobile was gone. What types of insurance coverage should Donna have on her automobile policy in order to recover for the theft of her car?

9. Carl would like to assure his newborn son of a college education by being able to pay the tuition when his son is old enough to enter college. Carl knows that he could save enough money over the next twenty years, but he is afraid that if he dies the money will not be available. What type of life insurance policy should Carl consider to ensure that the amount will be available in twenty years or sooner if Carl should die prematurely?

10. Rhonda, a recent college graduate, has a new job. As part of her financial planning she would like to purchase as much life insurance as she can obtain for the lowest possible price. What type of policy should she purchase?

CASE PROBLEMS

1. While driving a car owned and insured by his father, Elmer was involved in an accident in which he was at fault. Elmer was covered by his father's policy. When the father reported the accident to his insurer, the insurer informed him that the policy was being canceled owing to a material misrepresentation made on the application. There was, in fact, a material misrepresentation on the application. Can the company cancel the policy after the accident has been reported? (*Hawkeye-Security Ins. Co.* v. *Government Emp. Ins. Co.,* 207 Va. 944, 154 S.E.2d 173 [1967].)

2. Scarola purchased a car in good faith and for value. However, the car was stolen before the seller received it, and Scarola therefore received void title. Scarola purchased insurance on the car, which was subsequently severely damaged in an accident. The insurance company asserted that it was not liable because Scarola had no insurable interest. Is this assertion correct? (*Scarola* v. *Insurance Company of North America,* 31 N.Y.2d 411, 340 N.Y.S.2d 630, 292 N.E.2d 776 [1972].)

3. Norman purchased a car for his cousin. The car was insured, and the policy was in the cousin's name. Some time later, the cousin returned the car to Norman and then moved away, never driving or seeing the car again. Norman allowed a prospective purchaser to test drive the car, and the prospective purchaser wrecked it. The insurer denied that the car was covered by the policy, since the cousin had moved and only he had an insurable interest. Is this assertion correct? (*Universal C.I.T. Credit Corp.* v. *Foundation Reserve Insurance Co.,* 79 N.M. 785, 450 P.2d 194 [1969].)

4. Youse had a very valuable ring insured against any damages, including

damage from fire. He accidently dropped the ring into a trash incinerator, and it was destroyed. When Youse filed a claim, the insurer denied liability since the fire was not hostile. Who should prevail? (*Youse* v. *Employers Fire Insurance Co.,* 172 Kan. 111, 238 P.2d 472 [1951].)

5. Rivers was killed in a fire. The fire started when Rivers, who was intoxicated at the time, dropped a lit cigarette in his bed. The insurer denied liability because its policy excluded death while under the influence of alcohol. The family of the deceased argued that the death was accidental and not due to intoxication. Was the death accidental and covered by the policy, or was it due to intoxication and therefore not covered? (*Rivers* v. *Conger Life Insurance Co.,* 229 So.2d 625 [Fla. App. 1969].)

6. Dixon borrowed money from Citizens Discount Company, using a truck and feed mill as collateral. Dixon then obtained a fire insurance policy on the truck and mill, naming Citizens Discount as the loss payee. A short time later, the truck and mill were destroyed in a fire and Dixon notified the insurance company, requesting the $11,000 the valued policy called for in the event of a total loss. The insurance company refused to pay the $11,000, offering instead to pay $2,000 (the value asserted by the insurance company) or to replace the lost property. Dixon refused this counteroffer and sued the insurer. How should the court resolve this case? (*Citizens Discount and Investment Corp.* v. *Dixon,* 499 S.W.2d 231 [Mo. 1973].)

7. Peterson entered into a contract with the U.S. Forest Service to build a highway beside a pipe and trestle owned by the Nevada Power Company. As part of the contract, Peterson agreed to a liquidated damages clause covering any damages done to the pipe and trestle during the construction. Peterson then obtained a liability policy from USF&G to cover the liquidated damages. During the construction some damage occurred, and Peterson notified USF&G. However, USF&G refused to pay the claim, and as a result Peterson lost the contract and then went bankrupt. Peterson has sued USF&G for consequential damages based on the bad faith of the insurer in refusing to honor the insurance policy. What should be the result? (*United States Fidelity & Guarantee Company* v. *Peterson,* 540 P.2d 1070 [Nev. 1975].)

8. Freeburg Pie Company had a fire insurance policy covering its plant and operations. A thermostat on one of the ovens malfunctioned, causing the flames within the oven to burn out of control, and as a result the oven was severely damaged. Freeburg submitted a claim to the insurer, and the insurer denied liability since the fire in question was not hostile. How should the case be decided?(*L. L. Freeburg Pie Co.* v. *St. Paul Mutual Insurance Company,* 100 N.W.2d 753 [Minn. 1960].)

9. Keddie owned a commercial fishing boat anchored in Alaska. He contacted an insurance agent about obtaining insurance for the vessel and commenced a three-sided negotiation concerning the terms and the cost of the insurance. Eventually, Keddie and the insurer reached a tentative

agreement as to the insurance coverage that was to be provided, but no policy was ever issued to Keddie. Keddie never revealed that the boat was used for commercial purposes, representing it instead as a pleasure yacht. The boat caught fire and burned after the tentative agreement was reached, but before Keddie completed the paperwork necessary to have a policy issued. Keddie claims that a contract was entered, based on the negotiations that had taken place. The insurance company denies that a contract was entered or that it is liable even if a contract was entered due to misrepresentations by Keddie. Analyze the case completely. (*Keddie* v. *Beneficial Insurance Company*, 580 P.2d 955 [Nev. 1978].)

10. Roy obtained an accidental death and dismemberment insurance policy that provided for full coverage in the event Roy lost the entire sight in either eye. Roy was in an accident that caused a traumatic cataract in one of his eyes. He had the cataract removed and thereafter had vision in the eye with a contact lens, but he could not stand the discomfort that wearing the lens caused. Without the contact lens, Roy had no effective vision. He filed a claim for full compensation for the total loss of sight due to the accident. The insurance company refused to pay since, with the contact lens, Roy had vision. Should Roy receive the payment called for in the insurance policy? (*Roy* v. *Allstate Insurance Co.*, 383 A.2d 637 [Conn. 1978].)

CHAPTER 52 ▮▮▮▮▮▮▮▮▮▮▮

Wills and Estates

THE TRANSFER OF AN ESTATE

Almost everyone has an estate, no matter how modest it might be. It may consist only of some favorite record albums, a stereo, and a ten-speed bike. At the opposite extreme, it may consist of some office buildings, rental houses, and sizable money market accounts. This chapter deals with what happens to an estate when someone dies and with techniques for transferring an estate to family members and friends. The discussion will be general because the rules vary significantly from state to state.

WILLS

Domicile One's permanent residence

In a will, a person indicates who should inherit his or her property at death. The law that controls the validity of a person's will is the law of his or her **domicile.** A will provides an excellent opportunity to name a guardian for any minor children the person may have. In fact, a will is the only way parents can specify who will raise their minor children if they both die. If parents do not use this opportunity to name a guardian, the court will appoint one, and the choice may not always be ideal. For example, grandparents may no longer be physically or emotionally capable of raising young children, but the court may still appoint them. The parents (and the courts) have the option of dividing the guardian's duties and appointing someone to care for the children's physical needs and someone else to care for their financial needs and inheritance. This option is valuable if one person is not competent in both areas.

A will is also the place to name a **personal representative** for the estate. It should also contain a **residuary clause** for all the property that is not specifically mentioned elsewhere in the will. It is not advisable to include burial instructions in a will because often the will is not located and read until after the funeral. Such instructions are better contained in a separate document, with copies distributed to the personal representative, close family members, and the attorney.

Some actions or changes in family relationships affect the validity of a will. Children who are born after a will is executed will take a share of the estate as after-born children. After-born children are generally entitled to their **intestate share.** If a marriage occurs after a will has been executed (signed), the new spouse will also take a share of the estate. A divorce will change an existing will, too. In most states, a divorce with a property settlement will revoke gifts willed to the ex-spouse; however, a few states, including California, still require a revocation by the **testator** or **testatrix.** In this chapter, we will use the term *testator* in its generic sense to include a man or a woman. In the following case, a will was revoked by a divorce.

Personal representative A person who manages the financial affairs of the estate

Residuary clause A clause that disposes of the remainder of an estate

Intestate share Portion of the estate that a person is entitled to inherit if there is no valid will

Testator A man who makes a will

Testatrix A woman who makes a will

Estate of Liles
435 A.2d 379 (D.C. App. 1981)

Roscoe and Mary Liles were married in 1945. They had no children. In 1972 Roscoe executed a will leaving his estate to his wife if she survived him. In 1975 Mary left Roscoe because he threatened her, and in 1977 she received a divorce. The divorce court divided their property. Roscoe died in 1978.

FACTS

Should the decedent's 1972 will be accepted as valid?

ISSUE

No. Roscoe's and Mary's divorce revoked this will.

HOLDING

Under common law, certain changes in the marital or family status of a decedent revoke a will. In most states, a divorce and a property division revoke a prior will leaving assets to an ex-spouse. The property agreement settles their financial obligations to each other. If they still wish assets to go to an ex-spouse, they can execute a new will. Since the will is invalid, Roscoe died intestate.

REASONING

To make changes in a will, it is not necessary to write a completely new document. The testator can simply make the desired changes in a **codicil.** The

Codicil A separate written document that changes an existing will

codicil acts as a confirmation of the will provisions that are not changed. To be valid, a codicil must satisfy the same requirements as a will. The following case shows how a court will interpret a will and a codicil together.

Matter of Estate of Eickholt
365 N.W.2d 44 (Iowa App. 1985)

FACTS

Mary Eickholt signed a will in 1980. It provided that one-half of her farm should go to her brother and one-half should go to her sister, and that the residue of her estate should be divided between them. In 1981, she signed a codicil which provided that the residue of her estate should go to four of her nephews. The same codicil directed the **executor** to sell her farm and to divide the proceeds with the rest of the residue. The attorney who drafted both documents testified at trial that Mary understood that her brother and sister would still receive the farm. The attorney could not remember if he explained to her the effect that a sale of the farm would have on this bequest.

Executor A personal representative named in a will

ISSUE

Was Mary's brother entitled to one-half of the proceeds from the farm or was there an **ademption** of that gift?

HOLDING

No. The sale proceeds were part of the residuary estate. Ademption had occurred.

REASONING

Ademption Gift in a will that is not possible because the asset is no longer in the estate

The will and the codicil do not create two residues. Testator's intention is controlling in the interpretation of a will. Outside evidence, such as the attorney's testimony, may not be presented to prove the testator's intent or to contradict the will. Courts will not use oral testimony to create a will that the testator might have desired but did not make. Courts lack the power to remake a will even if they think a different disposition of property should have been made.

When construing a will and codicil, the court interprets them as one instrument, executed on the date of the codicil. Each part should be interpreted in relation to the other. Provisions in a codicil substitute for provisions in a will only to the extent that they are incompatible with the will. The residuary clause in the codicil is clearly inconsistent with the residuary clause in the will. There can only be one residuary clause, so the one in the codicil controls since it is more recent.

[Mary's sister did not object to the interpretation of the will since most of the nephews named in the will were her sons.]

The testator may destroy the effect of a will by making a new will and stating in it that the old will is revoked. If the new will does not specifically revoke the old will, the courts in some states will try to interpret the two wills together. In such a case, the newer will revokes the older one only to the extent that they contain inconsistent provisions. A testator can also cancel an old will by physically destroying the signed original, with the intention of revoking it.

Wills can be categorized by the manner in which they were formed. Generally, wills will be formal, holographic, or nuncupative. Wills can also be categorized by the type of dispositions they contain.

The most common type of will is called a *formal,* or an attested, will. It is generally drafted by an attorney and typed by the attorney's staff. A will prepared by a competent attorney who understands the technical requirements of the applicable state statutes and the terminology of wills is more likely to achieve the desired results than one prepared by a layperson. Familiarity with the terminology of wills is important in that the words used in the will often have a special significance that differs from their ordinary meaning.

A will *can* be a very lengthy document, and it must be executed in strict compliance with the procedures specified in the state statute of wills. Generally, the testator must sign the will at the end of the document in the presence of at least two witnesses. The testator *must* ask these two individuals to act as witnesses to the will. The witnesses must be disinterested persons; that is, they must have no interest in any of the property passing under the will or by intestate succession. In most states, the will must also be dated.

California, Maine, and Wisconsin have a special type of formal will called a *statutory will.* This will is named a statutory will because it was approved by the state legislature, and the language in the will is included in the state probate statute. Printing companies in the state then print form wills using the approved language. The will is sold to an individual testator who fills in the appropriate names and executes the will. Since this is a formal will, it must be witnessed by two disinterested witnesses.

Holographic wills (called olographic wills, in some states) are required to be written, signed, and usually dated in the testator's own handwriting. Although not universally accepted, they are allowed in a number of states, including Alaska, Arizona, Arkansas, California, Idaho, Kentucky, Louisiana, Mississippi, Montana, Nevada, New Jersey, North Carolina, North Dakota, Oklahoma, Pennsylvania, South Dakota, Tennessee, Texas, Utah, Virginia, West Virginia, and Wyoming. Holographic wills are also allowed under the Uniform Probate Code, Section 2 – 503. The Uniform Probate Code is a statute drafted by the National Conference of Commissioners on Uniform State Laws for adoption by the states as their probate code at their option. (A probate code is a state statute that deals with the affairs of **decedents** and incompetents.) Eleven states have adopted the Uniform Probate Code in some form. These states are Alaska, Arizona, Colorado, Hawaii, Idaho, Minnesota, Montana, Nebraska, New Mexico, North Dakota, and Utah.

A testator who writes a holographic will runs the risk of not expressing his or her intentions properly and not complying with the technical requirements. The testator may not be able to take advantage of techniques to reduce costs and taxes because of lack of familiarity with them. An attorney or an accoun-

Formal Wills

Holographic Wills

Decedent A person who has died

tant with tax expertise may be able to make recommendations that will greatly reduce the taxes.

Most of the states that allow holographic wills require that they be dated. They do not, however, have to be witnessed. Technically, holographic wills have to be written completely in the testator's hand with no printed or typed matter included at all. Recently, some courts have become more lenient about accepting printed matter on a holographic will. A court may accept the will if the printed matter is surplusage (that is, not an integral part of the will). Many of the states that allow holographic wills require that the will be kept with the important papers of the decedent. The purpose of this requirement is to help establish the testator's intent to make a will and to ascertain that the document was important to him or her.

Nuncupative Wills

Nuncupative, or oral, wills are permitted in a number of states under limited circumstances. Usually, nuncupative wills can be used only to dispose of personal property; this is true in Kansas, Nebraska, Virginia, and Washington. However, Georgia allows real property to pass in this manner. Some states place a limit on the value of the property transferred by a nuncupative will; for example, under California Probate Code, Section 55, only $1000 of personal property can be transferred. The Uniform Probate Code makes no provision for nuncupative wills.

Nuncupative wills are limited to certain situations. Generally, an oral will is valid if made by a civilian who anticipates death from an injury received the same day or if it is made by a soldier in the field or a sailor on a ship who is in peril or in fear of death. Because of the risks of military service and duty at sea, some states recognize a separate category of wills called "soldiers' and sailors' wills." These states may exempt soldiers and sailors from the usual requirements for oral or written wills.[1]

A nuncupative will must be heard by two or three disinterested witnesses, one of whom must have been asked by the decedent to act as a witness. This requirement is helpful in distinguishing between nuncupative wills and oral instructions to change a written will or a plan to change a will. Many statutes require that the nuncupative will be written down within thirty days and/or *probated* (that is, established in probate court as genuine and valid) within six months from the time it was spoken.

Matching Wills

Wills can also be categorized by the type of dispositions they contain. Often a husband and wife have matching provisions in their wills. These wills may be mutual, joint, or contractual.

Mutual wills are separate wills in which the testators, usually a husband and wife, have matching provisions. Business partners may also decide to have matchiing provisions. Mutual wills are appropriate when both people have identical objectives. For this reason, they are also called *reciprocal* wills. For

---

[1] 79 American Jurisprudence 2d, Wills, Sections 733, 740.

example, in mutual wills, the separate will of each spouse might provide for "the transfer of my assets to my spouse. If my spouse does not survive me, then my assets shall be divided equally among my children."

In *joint* wills, two people sign the same document as their last will and testament. Usually, the dispositive provisions are the same. Joint wills are not recommended. Many state courts have difficulty analyzing the legal relationship between the two signers. The difficulty normally arises after the first person dies and the second person wants to change the will. The issue is whether the second person can change the will or is contractually obligated to leave it as it is. This conflict may cause court trials and appeals. As is the case with any lengthy trial and appeal, a large amount of the estate may be expended in trying to resolve the legal rights of the parties.

In *contractual* wills, people enter into a valid contract in which one or more of them promise to make certain dispositions in their wills. This agreement must meet the usual requirements for a valid contract, including consideration and the absence of fraud and undue influence. This arrangement lacks flexibility, but it may still be desirable in some situations. If it is desirable, it is preferable to make a separate agreement to avoid the interpretive problems of joint wills.

REQUIREMENTS FOR A VALID WILL

The requirements for a valid will vary from state to state and apply to formal, holographic, and nuncupative wills. A person must be an adult at the time the will is executed for it to be valid. The modern rule is that anyone eighteen or older can execute a valid will, but some states still require that the testator be twenty-one or older. The modern rule is included in the Uniform Probate Code and the Model Execution of Wills Act. The Model Act was also written by the National Conference of Commissioners on Uniform State Laws. It is intended as an example for states to follow in drafting their own laws.

A testator must also have **testamentary capacity.** The statement often recited in wills that the testator is of sound mind and body is not necessary. A person need not be healthy to write or sign a valid will, and a statement declaring testamentary capacity is not required. However, *actual* testamentary capacity is. When such capacity is called into question, it is narrowly defined by the courts. The common requirements are that the person understood the nature and extent of his or her assets, knew who his or her close relatives were, and understood the purpose of a will.[2] In many states, even a prior adjudication of incompetency will not invalidate a will on the grounds of insanity. If a decedent is suspected of having been incompetent, some relatives will probably contest the will. One of the purposes of the disinterested witnesses is to be able to testify about the testator's competency. In the following case, the capacity of the testator was at issue.

Testamentary capacity
Sufficient mental capability or sanity to execute a valid will

[2] Ibid., Sections 70, 71.

Koonce v. Mims
402 So.2d 942 (Ala. 1981)

FACTS   Koonce was admitted to the hospital for emphysema and heart trouble. While in the hospital, he had an attorney write a will, which he signed. His physician, who had treated him for twenty years, saw him the day after the signing of the will. This physician was permitted to testify at trial.

ISSUE   Was the trial court correct in concluding that Koonce was competent to execute a valid will?

HOLDING   Yes. Competency is presumed unless there is evidence to the contrary.

REASONING   Witnesses are allowed to testify as to competency as long as the jury makes the ultimate decision on testamentary capacity. A person contesting a will on the grounds of incompetency must present some evidence to that effect. Otherwise, it will be presumed that a person of legal age is competent. Sufficient evidence must be presented before the issue of testamentary capacity is sent to the jury.

As noted earlier, formal and holographic wills must be signed by the testator. Many states require that the signature appear at the end of the document. The following case indicates the importance of a proper signature and strict compliance with the technical requirements of the state statute of wills.

In re Pavlinko's Estate
148 A.2d 528 (Pa. 1959)

FACTS   Vasil and Hellen Pavlinko spoke very little English. They went to an attorney to have wills drawn. He discussed their wishes with them in their native language and drafted two wills. The provisions were similar. They wanted to leave their assets to each other. When both were dead, they wished to make token gifts to Vasil's brother and sister; the rest was to go to Hellen's brother. At the signing of the wills, each accidently signed the other's will.

ISSUE   Can the court accept the will Vasil signed?

HOLDING   No. The will was not signed by the testator of that will.

To be valid, a will must be signed at the end. Vasil did not sign *his* will at the end. The will that he signed was void of legal effect, and it did not make sense because of the references to "my husband." Despite Vasil's clear intentions, the statute of wills had to be given effect. Its purpose is to prevent fraud.

A person has quite a bit of freedom in the dispositions that he or she may make in a will. These provisions are very important to the testator, and the court will generally give effect to them. But a person's ability to make testamentary dispositions is not limitless. There are some restrictions. The restrictions vary from state to state, but two types of dispositions are widely prohibited. One concerns willing too much to charity to the detriment of the family. (The prohibitions on such dispositions are called *mortmain,* or fear of death, statutes, and they operate to restrict the types and amounts of charitable gifts.) The other widely prohibited disposition is a **trust** that was established for too long a period of time. (The allowable length of time is specified in the rule against perpetuities. This rule is quite complex, and a discussion of it is outside the scope of this book.) Most states do not allow the testator to will money to pets. Animals are not legal beneficiaries under wills or trusts. However, some states do allow the testator to establish an **honorary trust** for the benefit of the animal. These trusts, if allowed, are limited to an amount of assets that is not excessive with respect to the animal's reasonable needs. Obviously, a person cannot will away someone else's property (for example, the spouse's half of the **community property**) or property that passes by operation of law, as in a joint tenancy with rights of survivorship.[3] Will provisions can also be set aside if they are against public policy. Examples would be provisions that encourage beneficiaries to get divorced or that separate children from their parents.

Trust An arrangement in which one person or business holds property and invests it for another

Honorary trust An arrangement that does not meet trust requirements and thus is not enforceable, although it may be carried out voluntarily

Community property A special form of joint ownership between husband and wife

If a testator suspects that the will will be contested, a no-contest clause may be inserted in the will. Basically, such a clause indicates that if a person contests the validity of the will in court, that person will not inherit any assets from the estate. The no-contest clause is used as a threat by the testator, and in that sense it may be effective; however, many states do not enforce no-contest clauses, or they make exceptions to them. Regardless of a state's approach to no-contest clauses, if the person is successful in contesting the will, that person will inherit. Depending on the circumstances, he or she may inherit under a prior will or under the state intestate succession statute.

Contrary to popular belief, a person does not have to leave assets to family members and other relatives. In **common law states,** there is an exception to this rule for a spouse: a widow or widower who is not willed a statutory minimum amount can generally *elect against the will* (that is, choose to take a

Common law states States that do not recognize community property law

---

[3] There is a movement in the American legal community that advocates changing state laws regarding the ability to will joint tenancies and insurance policies.

preset minimum percentage of the estate rather than the amount provided by the will). Other family members may be excluded, but a testator should mention them and the fact that they are being excluded (this is often done by leaving them a nominal amount, such as $5 or $10). If the testator fails to do this, the omitted family members can claim that they were pretermitted (forgotten) **heirs.** Courts will generally award intestate shares to pretermitted heirs on the grounds that the omission was a mistake. In addition, the omission of a close family member can indicate that the testator was incompetent.

Heirs Persons who inherit property from the decedent

Actual heirs may receive their shares under different theories or philosophies. In writing a will, a testator may select between per capita or per stirpes distribution of assets. In per capita distribution, each beneficiary in the group described receives an equal share no matter how many generations he or she is below the decedent. For example, in a gift to the decedent's children and grandchildren, each one would receive an equal share. This is true whether or not the beneficiary's parent is alive. In contrast, in a per stirpes distribution to the decedent's children and grandchildren, each child of the decedent receives an equal share. If any child has already died, his or her children would equally divide that child's share. If a child is still alive, his or her offspring would not receive any assets. The latter situation is also called taking by **right of representation.** This distinction between a per stirpes and a per capita gift to children and grandchildren is shown in Figure 52.1.

Right of representation Right of children to inherit what their parent would have inherited if the parent had not died

Wills can also be set aside (ignored) by the court if they were signed because of fraud in the inducement, fraud in the execution, duress, or undue influence. The following case involved the setting aside of a will on the grounds of undue influence.

Figure 52.1 Types of Testamentary Distribution

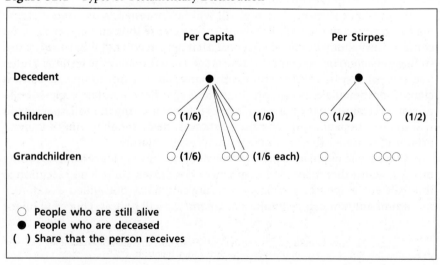

Erb v. *Lee*
430 N.E.2d 869 (Mass. App. 1982)

FACTS

The decedent, approximately eighty-five years of age, hired Bates as her housekeeper in 1969 or 1970. Erb, the decedent's attorney, was appointed her conservator in 1973. Bates began to harass the decedent for money and property, so Erb fired Bates at the decedent's request. Bates called the decedent and harassed her and demanded back wages. About five months later, Bates returned, fired her successor, and again began keeping house for the decedent. In 1974 the decedent met with her attorney because she wanted to draft a new will making Bates the primary beneficiary instead of the decedent's grandson. Bates was not present at the meeting or at the execution of the will.

ISSUE

Was the trial judge correct in deciding that Bates exerted undue influence?

HOLDING

Yes. The testatrix would not have acted in this manner of her own free will.

REASONING

The person contesting a will has the burden of proof. Undue influence will not be presumed just because of a decedent's advanced age or because someone had the opportunity to exercise undue influence. The overriding factors in this case were the decedent's weakened mental condition and Bates's threats and harassment, her meddling in the decedent's affairs, her frightening phone calls, and her domineering personality. Bates's failure to testify about her relationship with the decedent may have been construed against her. Furthermore, a person does not have to be physically present when the will is executed to exert undue influence.

INTESTATE SUCCESSION

For various reasons, many people fail to sign or to execute a valid will. States provide for the transfer of the assets of these people by the intestate succession statute. People who die without a valid will are said to have died intestate. Sometimes, especially with holographic wills, people fail to provide for the disposition of *all* their assets. In a properly drafted will, such disposition is assured by the use of a residuary clause that states: "I leave all the rest and residue of my estate to. . . ." Any assets *not* covered by the will provisions will pass by intestate succession.

The intestacy statutes vary from state to state. Passage of personal property is governed by the intestate law of the decedent's domicile. Real property is governed by the intestate law where the property is located.

Community property states provide for different chains of distribution for community property and separate property. Community property is a form of joint ownership between husband and wife. In states that allow this form of joint ownership, most property that is acquired during marriage is owned one-half by the husband and one-half by the wife. (Community property is discussed in greater detail in Chapter 49.) Some states also have separate provisions for the passage of personal property and of real property.

Generally, legislators enact a statute to dispose of property in the way they think most people would desire. For example, under the Uniform Probate Code, if the decedent leaves a surviving spouse but no surviving **issue** or parent(s), the surviving spouse takes all the intestate property.[4] If there are surviving issue who are issue of both the decedent and the surviving spouse, the spouse takes the first $50,000 plus one-half the balance of the estate. The issue would share the rest by the right of representation.[5] These provisions are applicable to separate property states and to separate property in community property states under the Uniform Probate Code.

Issue Lineal descendants, such as children, grandchildren, and great-grandchildren

ESTATE ADMINISTRATION

The concept of administering an estate is relatively simple. The representative of the estate must collect the assets of the decedent, collect money owed to the decedent, pay the debts owed by the decedent, pay the necessary expenses of administration, and pay any state or federal taxes. It is often necessary to sell assets to make these disbursements. The remaining assets are then distributed to the proper beneficiaries. A court will generally oversee this procedure through probate hearings.

A decedent's estate is usually administered by a personal representative. The representative has fiduciary duties to the lawful beneficiaries of the estate. If the decedent had a valid will that named a representative, that person will be called an *executor*. If the decedent did not have a valid will at death, the representative will be called an *administrator*. (Some localities still use the more traditional terminology of calling male representatives executors or administrators, and female representatives executrixes or administratrixes.) The administrator will be appointed by the court following any guidelines provided in the state probate code. Some states require that an executor or an administrator reside in the same state as the decedent. There is usually a minimum age of eighteen.

These personal representatives are responsible for the proper administration and probate of the estate. They must make sure that the duties previously mentioned in this section are properly completed. Personal representatives have a large responsibility for which they receive a fee. They can be *surcharged* (held personally liable) if they do not perform their duties properly. Some common areas of **malfeasance** include failure to pay taxes; failure to probate the will; failure to sell assets that are declining in value; failure to minimize taxes; failure to sell assets at a fair price; self-dealing, such as selling estate or trust assets to oneself or to a friend; and fraud. (The duties of an executor or administrator are discussed in greater detail in Chapter 53.)

Malfeasance The incorrect performance of a duty

---

[4] Uniform Probate Code, Section 2–102(1).
[5] Ibid., Section 2–103(1), (3).

Probate hearings are a series of hearings in probate court whereby the judge makes sure that the estate is being properly administered. The judge ascertains that the representative has advertised to locate the creditors of the deceased, that only lawful creditors are paid, and that the proper beneficiaries are paid. (It should be noted that if a creditor does not file a claim in a timely fashion, the claim will thereafter be barred.) The judge will conduct a hearing if any interested party contests the validity of the will. The judge confirms if the will is valid and was properly executed under state law. Even after the judge has accepted the validity of a will, the judicial order can be revoked if the will was fraudulently offered for probate. In many jurisdictions, the judge can reduce the commissions paid to the personal representative and the fees paid to the attorney and accountant if they are excessive. Executors, administrators, and, in many states, the attorneys are usually paid according to a percentage of the value of the assets in the estate. In some states, the maximum fees are established in the probate code.

Many people believe that it is wise to avoid probate. Property that is held as entireties property or as a joint tenancy with rights of survivorship, and life insurance paid to a named beneficiary are not subject to probate. If a person places assets into a trust while alive, these assets will not be probated either. Another option of the property owner is to enter into a valid contract that provides, in part, for the passage of property at the owner's death. All these arrangements may act as substitutes for a valid will and, depending on state law, may escape the technical requirements of the state statute of wills. However, even assets that are not subject to probate may still be subject to an **estate tax** and/or an **inheritance tax.**

Avoiding probate may reduce the amount of time necessary to administer an estate. In the case of joint tenancies with rights of survivorship, one owner will have immediate access to the assets at the other owner's death. Also, one can maintain more privacy by avoiding probate, which is an important consideration for many people. Probate, like most court proceedings, is part of the public record; anyone who is so inclined can read the will and the inventory of assets. Nominal costs are usually involved in the probate of an estate, such as fees for filing court documents. The amount of some fees may be based on the amount of probate assets; avoiding probate or reducing the amount of probate assets would eliminate or reduce these costs. Probate costs increase markedly when there are lawsuits concerning the validity of the will or its interpretation. These lawsuits, called *will contests,* reduce the amount of assets to be distributed to the beneficiaries. Sometimes these contests are caused by poorly drafted wills or holographic wills. Probate costs and taxes may also increase significantly if a person dies intestate or without prudent estate planning.

There are also some disadvantages to avoiding probate. The extent to which these items are disadvantageous will depend on the people involved and the method used to avoid probate. Some of the techniques — for example, establishing and operating out of a trust — require additional paperwork and attention to detail. Avoiding probate may also create a higher inheritance or

Estate tax A tax assessed on the total net value of the estate

Inheritance tax A tax assessed on individual transfers of estate assets to particular people

estate tax liability in the decedent's estate or in the estates of other family members. In probate, the creditors of the decedent are located and paid, and the estate is discharged of all further liability to them. Without probate, there is no discharge from potential creditors' claims. In addition, the purpose of probate is to protect lawful beneficiaries and creditors. This may be particularly important when beneficiaries are not knowledgeable or are confused. The court can intervene to protect them from unscrupulous people. Unfortunately, this purpose is not always served effectively under some state probate codes and procedures.

Thus, it is not always advantageous to avoid probate. As with any estate planning decision, consideration must be given to the individuals and the assets involved. One factor that is often overlooked is that an asset's status as a probate or nonprobate asset does *not* avoid the estate or inheritance taxation on it.

SUMMARY

A will states how a person would like to have property pass at his or her death. For a will to be valid, a person must intend it to be his or her will. The person must have testamentary capacity. The will must conform to the state's statutory requirements. Some legal documents, such as trusts and deeds for property, can act as substitutes for wills. In the absence of a valid will, the property will pass by intestate succession, which is controlled by state law.

A formal will, which is drafted by an attorney, or the state legislature, signed by the testator or testatrix, and witnessed by two disinterested witnesses, is the most common type of will. Some states also permit nuncupative (oral) wills and holographic (handwritten) wills.

Most estates are subject to probate proceedings. During the hearings, the probate court oversees the proper administration of the estate by the personal representative. The representative must pay debts, collect assets, pay taxes, and distribute assets to the beneficiaries.

DISCUSSION QUESTIONS

1. What is necessary for a formal will to be valid?

2. What types of wills were involved in *In re Pavlinko's Estate,* 148 A.2d 528 (Pa. 1959)?

3. What advantages do formal wills have over other types of wills?

4. List all the types of provisions that should be included in a will. Explain each one.

5. Where should a testator or testatrix keep a holographic will? Why?

6. Why does the omission of a close family member in a will create the appearance of incompetency?

7. Rachael bequeaths the remainder of her estate "to Bank of America in trust to pay all the income to Bill for life, and on Bill's death to transfer the

remainder to Bill's issue who are still alive." Bill dies without having any issue. The will has no provision controlling this situation. What will happen? Why?

8. What would be the intestate distribution under the Uniform Probate Code if a husband dies survived by his wife and their children?

9. Brian had inherited a million dollars from his parents' estate. Brian, who has an extremely low IQ, wants to have his attorney write a will leaving his estate to his gardener and excluding his nieces and nephews. Could such a will be valid? If so, under what circumstances?

10. What are the advantages and disadvantages of probating a will?

1. In the common law state of Mississippi, a husband and wife separated and established different homes. Neither one filed for a divorce or remarried. Fifteen years after the separation, the wife died testate. Her will provided gifts to three friends. Is her husband entitled to share in her estate because he received insufficient gifts in her will? Should he be so entitled? (*Tillman* v. *Williams*, 403 So.2d 880 [Miss. 1981].)

2. Clara Hicks resided in a nursing home at the time she executed a will in 1977. She was eighty-seven at that time. The will was read to her at the time of execution, and she indicated her approval of the will provisions leaving a larger share to one particular nephew. That nephew visited her at least once a week and responded to her needs and requests. Dr. Hicks, who visited her monthly in the nursing home, testified at trial that he thought that she was competent and that she understood her affairs. Did Clara Hicks have testamentary capacity? Was Clara Hicks subjected to undue influence? (*Estate of Hicks*, 327 S.E.2d 345 [S.C. 1985].)

3. George Tourville had executed a will in which one of his nephews received 25 percent of the estate; Mary, Tourville's sister and that nephew's mother, received 55 percent; and Eileen, Tourville's other living sister, received 20 percent. The nephew had managed the testator's affairs prior to death. He also helped write the paragraph of the will that left assets to himself and was present when the will was prepared. Was the nephew guilty of exerting undue influence? (*In re Estate of Tourville*, 366 N.W.2d 380 [Minn. App. 1985].)

4. Francis and Anna McGrath agreed to sell their restaurant and store. The buyers were to pay $15,000 at the time of the sale and $45 a week until the rest of the sales price was paid off. The sales contract stated that these payments would cease when both Francis and Anna had died. Must this provision comply with the statute of wills? (*McGrath* v. *McGrath*, 220 A.2d 760 [N.H. 1966].)

5. The decedent's will provided that one of his children should receive $2000 on condition that she remarry one of "true Greek blood and descent and

**CASE
PROBLEMS**

of Orthodox religion'' after her first marriage was terminated by death or divorce. On the date of the decedent's death, she was married to a man who was not Greek. Should the probate court enforce such a provision? Why or why not? (*In re Estate of Keffalas,* 233 A.2d 248 [Pa. 1967].)

6. McAboy's will was not probated when she died in 1972. This situation was discovered in 1974 by Upchurch, an attorney who was conducting a title search for a parcel of real estate. Upchurch obtained the original of McAboy's 1961 will from McAboy's attorney and a *copy* of her 1964 will from the executrix. The copy of the 1964 will was probated under the state procedures for a lost will. Three and one-half years after the probate court's order, the *original* of the 1964 will was located. On the original, the testatrix had signed a statement that this will was void and withdrawn and that her old will was republished (that is, acknowledged as valid again). Should the court order accepting the 1964 will be set aside on the grounds of fraud? (*Larkin* v. *Ruffin,* 398 So.2d 676 [Ala. 1981].)

7. Mr. and Mrs. Diller had signed *mutual* wills designating that the bulk of their estate go to their children. Mr. Diller died with an estate of approximately $6 million. He was survived by his wife, his son, and his daughter. After his death, Mrs. Diller married Mr. Friedman, who was an insurance salesman and a purported estate planner. Mr. Friedman arranged for the new Mrs. Friedman to meet with attorneys whom he had selected. These attorneys drafted wills and trusts that provided substantial benefits for Mr. Friedman to the disadvantage of Mrs. Friedman's children and other heirs. The new will included a no-contest clause. Mr. Friedman threatened to leave Mrs. Friedman if she did not sign the new will, and so she signed it. Should the daughter contest the will? Should the court enforce the no-contest clause? (*Estate of Friedman,* 161 Cal. Rptr. 311 [Cal. App. 1979].)

8. At the age of ninety, the testator had signed a will leaving his estate to his step-great-grandchildren. Ten days later the testator executed a will naming his next-door neighbor as his sole beneficiary. In this will he specifically revoked his prior wills. The neighbor did not procure the will but she did drive the testator to the attorney's office. The neighbor lived next door to the testator for ten years. During the last year or so, the neighbor was hired to provide meals and general care for the testator. The testator said that his step-great-grandchildren did not care anything about him and that he did not want them to have his money. He had also said that he wanted his money to go to someone who helped him. Was the testator competent to execute a will? Did the neighbor exert undue influence? (*Edwards* v. *Vaught,* 681 S.W.2d 322 [Ark. 1984].)

9. Mr. Nassano signed two copies of his will. The original was kept by the attorney. The copy was kept by Nassano. Nassano wrote on the duplicate copy of his will, "This *Will,* and *all* other *Wills* Made by me are *Null* and *Void*

Signed by me this Seventh Day of June 1979 Bernard Nassano June-7-
1979 BN BN." Nassano signed this statement. Did Nassano effectively
cancel his will? (*Will of Nassano,* 489 A.2d 1189 [N.J. Super. A.D. 1985].)

10. Mr. Wetzel's parents signed a single testamentary instrument in 1955. It
    was properly executed under the laws of Texas, where they lived at the
    time. This joint and mutual will provided for gifts in Wetzel's favor after
    both parents died. When Wetzel's mother died, the 1955 will was not
    probated, but Wetzel's father did accept the benefits provided for him
    under this will. Was the joint and mutual will binding on Wetzel's father,
    or could he replace it with his 1972 will? (*Wetzel* v. *Watson,* 328 S.E.2d 526
    [W.Va. 1985].)

CHAPTER 53 ▮▮▮▮▮▮▮▮▮▮▮▮▮▮▮▮▮▮▮▮

Trusts and Trust Administration

TRUST CHAR-ACTERISTICS

Trusts may be voluntary arrangements created by the property owner, or they may be legal arrangements imposed by the courts or implied by the law in order to reach a fair result. The former arrangements are known as express trusts; the latter are called implied trusts. In a trust, legal title and equitable ownership rights are split between two or more people. One person has the legal right to the asset; another person has the beneficial right to the use and enjoyment of the asset.

EXPRESS TRUSTS

Trusts that are *created voluntarily by the owner of the property* are called *express trusts*. The owner places real or personal property with a trustee for the benefit of a named person. During the period of the trust, the trustee will manage the

968

property and pay the income over to the people specified in the **trust deed.** If the trust is to take effect during the owner's life, it is called an *inter vivos* trust. If it is to take effect at death, it is called a *testamentary* trust. Testamentary trusts usually do not have a separate trust deed, but they are included as part of the will.

Generally, at least three people are needed for an express trust: a creator, a trustee, and one or more beneficiaries. A creator may also be called a settlor or a trustor. A *creator* is one who establishes the trust. The *trustee,* who may be a person or a business entity, is in charge of managing the assets. *Corpus* or *res* are the names used for the assets. The *beneficiaries* are the recipients. Depending on the trust instrument, the beneficiaries may receive the income from the assets, the assets themselves, or both. Consideration is not required to establish a trust.

To be valid, a trust must meet a few requirements. The intention or purpose of the creator must be expressed — for example, by stating that "this trust is established for my children's college educations." In many cases, though, the courts have concluded that the intention of the creator may be inferred from his or her actions if it was not expressed.

Most trust deeds must be in writing because they cannot possibly be performed within one year. Even if a writing were not required by the Statute of Frauds, it would be foolish not to write down the trust provisions. Many legal problems do not arise until after the creator has died. Trusts generally contain lengthy and complex provisions about what the trustee can and cannot do; these certainly should be reduced to writing.

A trust may terminate when its purpose is completed or when its term is over. Under some circumstances, the trust may terminate by mutual agreement of all the beneficiaries. Depending on the trust deed, the trustee, the creator, or someone else may have the power to terminate the trust.

There are various special types of express trusts. We shall discuss some of these next. A specific trust may be in more than one of these categories.

Trust deed A legal document that specifies the recipients of a trust, their interests, and how the trust should be managed; also called a deed of trust.

Charitable Trusts

A *charitable trust* is one in which *money is given to a charity for a public purpose.* A charity is a corporation organized for religious, charitable, scientific, literary, or educational purposes, including the encouragement of art and the prevention of cruelty to children or animals. Charities also include the United States or any state or political subdivision or any veterans' organization or its departments or posts.[1] Transfers to charities, either outright or in trust, may pass tax free. However, the strict requirements of the Internal Revenue Service must be met. In addition, the charitable organization must qualify under state and federal rules. An organization that qualifies for federal tax purposes may not qualify for state tax purposes. The opposite is also true. California, for example, requires that the organization be a California charity or a national charity that is going to use the assets in California. To qualify for favorable tax treatment

[1] Internal Revenue Code, Section 2055.

under federal law, a trust with charitable and noncharitable beneficiaries must meet the stringent requirements imposed by the 1969 Tax Reform Act.

If the original charitable purpose cannot be fulfilled, a court of equity may apply the *cy pres* **doctrine.** The application of the doctrine means that the court will try to follow the transferor's intention as closely as possible. This is usually accomplished by substituting another charitable beneficiary with a similar purpose for the charity initially specified. Before a substitution can occur, it must be shown that the original charity no longer exists or that the original terms no longer apply. In the following case, the *cy pres* doctrine was used to implement the creator's charitable intent.

Cy pres **doctrine**
Doctrine holding that the court will modify the trust in order to follow the creator's intention as closely as possible

---

Wesley United Methodist Church v. *Harvard College*
316 N.E.2d 620 (Mass. 1974)

FACTS Colson died in 1968. In his will, which had been written in 1957, he provided for a scholarship fund to be established and administered by the Wesley United Methodist Church Board of Trustees. The fund was to provide one $500 scholarship per year from trust income to a male member of the congregation who was attending Harvard College. The trust corpus was generating $3200 of income per year, the tuition at Harvard had risen to $2600 per year, Harvard was admitting women as well as men, and no member of the congregation had applied for the scholarship by 1973, the date the trial began. The trustees requested a modification of the trust under the *cy pres* doctrine. The family of the creator petitioned for a cancellation of the old trust and the "establishment" of an implied trust in their favor.

ISSUE Should the *cy pres* doctrine be applied to alter the terms of the original charitable trust?

HOLDING Yes. The original trust terms are now impractical, but the original charitable purpose is still valid.

REASONING The court found that the original trust terms that restricted the recipients of the scholarship to male members of the congregation and the amount of the scholarship to $500 per year were no longer realistic. The original charitable intent of the creator was obvious and the original purpose was still valid, but the original terms were too narrow. Therefore, under the *cy pres* doctrine, the court ruled that the trustees could now apply the earnings from the trust fund at their discretion, and in unlimited amount, to any deserving applicant for the scholarship. Applicants could also now be either male or female and need not be a member of the congregation of the particular church.

A *private trust* is one that is *not for the general public good*. The beneficiaries of this type of trust are individual citizens and not society as a whole. Unlike a charitable trust, on which there are no time limits, a private trust is limited in time. These limits are specified by the rule against perpetuities.

Private Trusts

A trust that will *accumulate income* is called an *accumulation trust*. The trustee will not pay out all the income to or for the use of the beneficiary or beneficiaries. The earnings will be reinvested in the trust for the period specified.

Accumulation Trusts

A *sprinkling trust* is a trust that *gives the trustee the power to determine which income beneficiaries should receive income each year and how much they should receive*. A prudent creator should provide the trustee with some standards to use in making this decision. Income that is not distributed in any particular year will be added to the corpus, as in an accumulation trust.

Sprinkling Trusts

As the name implies, a *spendthrift trust* is established when *one or more of the beneficiaries are spendthrifts* and need to be protected from their own imprudent spending habits. This type of trust may also be used if the beneficiary is unduly subject to overreaching by family members and friends. Generally, the beneficiary cannot anticipate the receipt of income or corpus from a spendthrift trust, cannot assign it to creditors or borrow against it, and will not necessarily receive all the income earned in any one year. Income will be paid to the beneficiary only when actually necessary. The trustee will often pay it directly to the creditor for services ordered by the trustee. Under some circumstances, creditors may be able to attach the trust assets.

Spendthrift Trusts

A *revocable trust* is one that *can be revoked or canceled by the creator*. In rare instances, the creator may give this power to another individual. This trust usually becomes permanent and irrevocable at the death of the creator.

Revocable Trusts

An *irrevocable trust* is one that *may not be terminated during the specified term of the trust*. Once the assets are placed in trust, they must stay there for the term of the trust under the conditions specified in the trust deed.

Irrevocable Trusts

Whether a trust is revocable or irrevocable depends on the trust document. It is always wise to specify this aspect of the trust; otherwise, the trust will be governed by state law. In most states, the trust will be irrevocable unless the creator has stated a contrary intention in the trust deed. In a minority of states, including California, it will be presumed to be revocable unless a contrary intention is expressed.

One of the advantages of trusts over other methods of transferring assets is the flexibility that trusts permit. With an outright gift, the gift property belongs to the beneficiary. If that transfer turns out to be inappropriate, the transferor cannot change it. With gifts in trust, the trustee maintains control over the

ADVANTAGES OF TRUSTS

assets under the instructions in the trust deed, and the trustee does not relinquish control for a certain period of time. For example, a trust can be established for one's children so that each will receive a third of their share of the corpus when they are twenty-five, thirty, and thirty-five.

Another aspect of the flexibility of trusts is that payment to a trust does not have to occur all at one time. A trust deed can be written to permit the creator to add assets to the trust later. In fact, the trust deed can be written so that other people can add assets to the creator's trust. Moreover, trust income can be paid out to the income beneficiaries equally, based on percentages, or based on need. They can receive the income in a lump sum at the end of the trust, annually, quarterly, monthly, or as needed.

DISADVAN-TAGES OF TRUSTS

The flexibility of trusts has been stressed as an advantage to this method of transferring assets. By the same token, lack of flexibility may be a disadvantage. If a trust is irrevocable and an emergency arises or circumstances change, the trustee will generally be bound to act as specified in the trust deed. If the trust deed did not anticipate this occurrence, then the trustee may not be able to modify his or her actions to fit the situation.

Another disadvantage of trusts is that of fees. Rarely is a trustee willing to undertake the responsibility of being a trustee without receiving a fee. The next case involved a suit for fees by the trustee.

Estate of Gump
180 Cal. Rptr. 219 (Cal. App. 1982)

FACTS Wells Fargo Bank was the trustee of a testamentary trust under Gump's will. The trustee filed its eighth annual accounting, which included a request for $32,689 compensation for the trustee. The trustee was awarded $10,000 in fees by the probate court. In accordance with the trust deed, the trustee was managing some real estate occupied by a retail store. The retail store underpaid its rent under the formula provided by the lease. The bank negligently accepted the underpayment as full payment of the rent.

ISSUE Did the probate court unduly penalize the negligent trustee?

HOLDING Yes. The probate court did not adequately compensate the trustee, and the penalty imposed was disproportionate under the circumstances.

REASONING Unless the will provides otherwise, a testamentary trustee is entitled to reasonable compensation for services. The probate court has broad discretion in this matter.

Its decision should not be disturbed unless it abuses its discretion. It may properly consider customary charges in the private sector based on the value of trust assets and the success or failure of the trustee's administration. The probate court can charge the trustee for shortages. This may be accomplished by denying part or all of the compensation rendered in conjunction with the mismanaged trust asset. In this case, the trustee was **surcharged $7300**, but the record did not disclose why. Generally, a trustee's liability is limited to the loss actually suffered by the beneficiaries, unless the trustee acted fraudulently or personally benefited. The appellate court held that that was not the situation in this case, and so the additional loss to the trustee of $7300 could not be justified.

Surcharge Required payment for failure to follow fiduciary duties.

Another disadvantage of trusts is that when a trust is established, it may increase the amount of taxes that must be paid. This depends on the nature and the terms of the trust. Under the tax codes, trusts are taxed in complex ways. Before establishing a trust, one should determine who will pay income tax on its income, who will have the advantage of any tax deductions, whether it will be subject to gift taxes, and whether it will be subject to estate or inheritance taxes when the creator or a beneficiary dies.

SELECTION OF TRUSTEES AND EXECUTORS

Since trustees and executors have broad powers and broad discretion, it is important to select them wisely. Successor trustees and executors may also be named in a trust or a will in case the first person named is unable or unwilling to serve as the personal representative. If a decedent does not have a valid will naming an executor, the probate court will appoint an administrator for the estate. In such a case, the owner of the assets will have no say in the selection. Administrators, executors, and trustees may be referred to as *fiduciaries,* since each one has a fiduciary duty to protect the rights of the creator and the beneficiaries.

The legal requirements for such fiduciaries are very simple. In most states, the fiduciary must be over eighteen years of age. Some states also require that the fiduciary be a resident of the state. It generally simplifies transactions if the fiduciary does reside in the state.

A common consideration in selecting a fiduciary is whether to select a corporate fiduciary, such as the trust department of a bank, or an individual fiduciary, such as a family member or a friend. A corporate fiduciary usually does not die or dissolve; it often has the expertise needed to do a good job; and it does not need to be bonded for the faithful performance of its duties. Although corporate trustees may last forever, individual trust officers do not. Often a creator or testator will select a bank because of past dealings with a particular trust officer. It is wise to remember that the trust officer may leave or die. Moreover, some corporate trust departments do not earn a very good rate of return on the assets that they invest. The same may be true, though, for any individual trustee. Corporate trustees also will require a fee, but they may be willing to negotiate and handle the trust for a smaller fee. If a fee is prescribed by statute, it is considered a maximum.

Individual trustees may be willing to serve without fees. They may also have more knowledge about the business and family members than corporate trustees have. In addition, they may be personally concerned for the well-being of the beneficiaries. They may, however, be biased toward certain beneficiaries. In fact, they may be so closely involved with the family that they will be subject to overreaching by family members.

A decision to choose a corporate trustee may be affected by the selection of individuals available to serve in that capacity. A trustee should be honest, mature, competent, impartial, and knowledgeable and should have the ability and time to make sound business decisions. Obviously the final selection of any personal representative should depend on the facts and circumstances of each case.

DUTIES OF TRUSTEES

A trust is a fiduciary relationship concerning specific property which is transferred to the trustee. The trustee has two primary duties in relation to this property. First, the trustee is supposed to preserve and protect the trust corpus. This includes identifying the assets, protecting them, and safeguarding them. The other primary function of the trustee is to make the assets productive. In other words, the trustee is supposed to invest and manage the assets to produce income for the beneficiaries. This must be accomplished without violating the trustee's other duties.

The trustee has some other, more specific duties. They include an obligation to follow the terms of the trust and a duty of care that must be exercised in administering someone else's property. The rule, as stated in a majority of the courts, is that a trustee must exercise the degree of *care, skill, and prudence* that a reasonably prudent businessperson would exercise in dealing with his or her own property. This standard is applied whether or not the person actually possesses the necessary skill.

Income beneficiaries
Persons with an income interest in the trust

Remainder beneficiaries Persons with an interest in what remains in the trust corpus after use by the income beneficiaries

The trustee also has a duty of loyalty. There are, in reality, two aspects of this duty. One is an obligation not to take advantage of situations involving conflicts of interest. In many instances, the trustee has an obligation to avoid even potential conflicts of interest. Obviously, then, a trustee should not personally enter into a transaction with the trust. Such a transaction is usually a breach of fiduciary duty and is voidable. The other aspect of the duty of loyalty is to be as impartial as possible among the beneficiaries. This is not always possible since there is a natural conflict between the **income beneficiaries** and the **remainder beneficiaries.**

In the following case, the trustee breached its duty of loyalty.

Northwestern Mutual Life Insurance Company v. Wiemer
421 N.E.2d 1002 (Ill. App. 1981)

Mr. and Mrs. Wiemer entered into a trust agreement with Havana Bank, as trustee, to enable them to purchase and work a farm. Later, as part of the financial arrangement, Northwestern Mutual executed a $70,000 first mortgage on the farm; Havana had the second mortgage. Mr. Weimer died. On 4 February 1976, Havana took $8000 from the trust account and paid itself part of its own second mortgage. Consequently, the trust was unable to make the April 1 payment to Northwestern. Northwestern foreclosed on the first mortgage.

FACTS

Did the trustee breach its trust duties?

ISSUE

Yes. The trustee was guilty of self-dealing in violation of its duty of loyalty.

HOLDING

Havana had drafted the trust document and was trustee under it. Havana knew the April 1 payment would be due soon. Havana had three possible options: to apply all the funds to the first mortgage; to pay the regular payment on the first mortgage and pay the rest to itself; or to pay the entire amount to Mrs. Wiemer. Instead, it applied the funds for its own personal gain. This was a classic case of self-dealing and breach of trust. It was also a violation of the trust document, which stated that the first mortgage should be paid first. The court ruled that Mrs. Wiemer was entitled to damages.

REASONING

It is commonly said that a trustee has a duty not to delegate, but this statement is really just a note of caution. Not every act of trust administration must be completed by the trustee personally. A trustee may delegate to others the performance of any act or the exercise of any power when it is consistent with the trustee's general duty of care owed to the beneficiaries. In other words, the trustee may employ agents when a reasonably prudent owner of the same type of property acting with similar objectives would employ agents. In addition, the trustee must exercise due care in selecting and supervising agents.

The trustee must be careful in selecting trust investments. This generally includes a duty to diversify the type of investments. The statutes in many states list or define what investments a trustee may make. These are often called legal investments. A creator may grant a trustee the specific power to invest in nonlegal investments. Such a provision gives the trustee broader investment power, but it does not remove the general obligation to invest wisely. Obviously, the duty to invest wisely does not imply that the trustee can guarantee that the trust will not lose money or that all investments will increase in value.

The standard test of a trustee's fulfillment of this obligation is whether other prudent investors, *at that time,* would have chosen other, better investments; the judgment should not be made by hindsight.

As pointed out in *Estate of Gump,* the trustee may be surcharged for unwise investment decisions. In these cases, the trustee must personally pay for any losses caused by negligent decisions. The trustee may not offset profits on other investments against these losses.

The trustee has a duty to maintain clear and accurate records regarding the administration of the trust. This obligation, called the *duty to account,* includes recording the location and type of assets and the receipt and expenditure of income. In some jurisdictions, the trustee must file periodic accountings with the court. In others, it is sufficient for the trustee to account to the trust beneficiaries.

The trustee must not mix his or her personal funds with trust funds, a situation known as *commingling of assets.* The trustee may not borrow money or mortgage trust property unless that power was expressly provided in the trust document. The trustee *will* have the incidental authority to carry out ordinary duties.

The trustee in the following case failed to act prudently and to protect the interests of the beneficiary.

Hatcher v. United States National Bank of Oregon
643 P.2d 359 (Or. App. 1982)

FACTS   Hatcher was a remainder beneficiary of the irrevocable inter vivos trust that her stepfather had created. The sole asset in the trust was stock in a closely held corporation. The trust owned approximately 78 percent of the outstanding shares in the corporation. The corporation offered to buy the trust's stock for $800,000, no money down, with $8\frac{1}{2}$ percent interest to be amortized by twenty equal annual payments. The corporate trustee, United States National Bank of Oregon, asked one of its financial analysts to determine whether the offer was satisfactory. The analyst was not asked for an independent evaluation of net worth, and he did not do one. He used the book value with the tax assessor's values for the real estate and reported that the offer was fair and reasonable. The trustee then made a counteroffer based on the same terms except for an $8\frac{3}{4}$ percent interest rate, which the corporation accepted. The only security for the payment was a pledge of stock. The agreement contained no controls on corporate salaries, dividends, or borrowing. Later, when the corporation had difficulty repaying loans, the trustee agreed to **subordinate** trust claims to claims of the trustee's commercial department. The commercial department would have to approve any payments to the trustee in excess of $10,000 per year. The trustee did not receive any payment in exchange for this subordination.

Subordinate Give priority to the claims of another; agree to collect only after another collects

ISSUE   Did the trustee breach its fiduciary duty to the plaintiff?

Yes. The trustee failed to act in a prudent manner.

Oregon statute ORS 128.057 requires trustees to act as reasonable and prudent persons would, "not in regard to speculation but in regard to the permanent disposition of their funds, considering the probable income as well as the probable safety of the capital." The *Restatement (Second) of Trusts*, Section 227, Comment d, suggests an additional requirement for corporate trustees: "If the trustee is a bank or trust company, it must use in selecting investments the facilities which it has or should have, and it may properly be required to show that it has made a more thorough and complete investigation than would ordinarily be expected from an individual trustee." Accordingly, the court held that Hatcher should recover for her losses due to the corporate trustee's negligence in not determining whether the price offered represented the stock's fair market value; not testing the market for other potential buyers; not following appropriate procedures to determine fair market value; not utilizing a real estate appraisal by an independent appraiser or the trustee's real estate staff; not considering the fact that this was a controlling interest; not considering the corporation's reputation (goodwill); not bargaining for better terms; not bargaining for a higher interest rate considering the terms; not anticipating the necessity to subordinate; and accepting the terms of the subordination without consideration.

POWERS OF TRUSTEES

Trustees' powers are based on two primary sources: the trust instrument and the applicable law. An additional source consists of those powers implied by law because they are necessary or appropriate to carry out the purposes of the trust. (Compare these powers with the incidental and implied powers discussed in Chapter 34.) A trustee who is uncertain about his or her powers may receive clarification from the court.

Courts have developed general concepts about the powers that may be implied under state law. These powers may vary from state to state. The most common implied powers are the power to sell assets, the power to lease assets, and the power to incur reasonable expenses. Generally, there is no power to borrow money or to mortgage property. A trustee will not have implied powers if they conflict with the trust deed or the purpose of the trust.

Unless there is an express trust provision to the contrary, the trustee will not have the power to invade the corpus. However, trust deeds commonly specify that the trustee *can* invade the corpus for the benefit of one or more of the income beneficiaries. This power generally means that assets will be converted into cash and that the cash will be taken out of the trust. The money may be given directly to the beneficiary or spent on the beneficiary's behalf. It is advisable for the trust deed to provide a standard so that the trustee and the courts can determine whether the invasion is appropriate. The common standards are called *ascertainable standards*. A body of case law enables both the trustee and the courts to know what these standards are. "The trustee can invade for the health, education, support, or maintenance of my children'' is an example of an ascertainable standard.

The trust document often includes a list of additional powers given to the trustee. The trustee may utilize these additional powers unless they are against public policy.

RIGHTS AND DUTIES OF BENEFICIARIES

Unless the beneficiary is also serving in some other capacity, he or she has no obligation to the trust. The beneficiary's rights to income and corpus are determined by the trust document and applicable state law.

IMPLIED TRUSTS

Express trusts are voluntarily and intentionally created by the owner of the assets. Implied trusts are created by operation of law. They are either implied by the law or imposed by the courts. Implied trusts may arise in the context of an express trust, but that is not a requirement.

Resulting Trusts

A *resulting trust* occurs when the owner of property disposes of the property, but the *disposition is not complete.* A portion of the owner's interest *reverts* to the owner or the owner's heirs. This situation most commonly occurs under any one of the following conditions:

1. The owner did not state who should acquire a beneficial interest, such as a remainder interest.
2. The owner did not state what should happen under certain unanticipated situations.
3. The express trust is not enforceable because it is not in the proper form — for example, the owner failed to name the beneficiaries.
4. The express trust fails completely or in part because it is illegal, impractical, or impossible or because a beneficiary refuses an interest in the trust.

Resulting trusts may also occur when a person purchases real property with his or her own money and puts the title in the name of another person. The law presumes that the purchaser intended that the recipient hold the property as "trustee" for the purchaser. This is often called a purchase money resulting trust. Such a presumption may be rebutted by evidence that the purchaser had a different intention. In many states, the courts will presume that the purchaser intended a gift if the purchaser and transferee are closely related.

Resulting trusts occur only if the proper owner has been acting in good faith and the court feels that other rules of judicial interpretation are inappropriate to resolve the confusion.

Constructive Trusts

A *constructive trust* is often more remote than a resulting trust from express trusts and other forms of property disposition. It *arises by operation of law and serves to redress a wrong or to prevent an unjust enrichment.* It is actually an equitable remedy. It is imposed by a court of equity when a person gains legal title to property but has an equitable duty to transfer the property to someone else. This can occur in any of the following situations:

1. When a person takes title as a trustee, but the trust is not enforceable. To allow the trustee to keep the property would create unjust enrichment.

2. When a person obtains property by breaching a fiduciary duty — for example, when an employee embezzles company funds.

3. When a person either is guilty of a wrong or would receive unjust enrichment. Depending on state law, the person may be guilty of fraud, conversion, theft, duress, or murder of the transferor. Some situations may involve mistake. For example, the transferor may have owned two lots and sold one lot to the transferee, but the deed mistakenly mentioned two lots. The court would impose a constructive trust on the second lot for the benefit of the transferor.

The following case illustrates one way in which the need for a constructive trust might arise.

In re Estate of Mahoney
220 A.2d 475 (Vt. 1966)

The decedent died intestate of a gunshot wound. His wife was convicted of manslaughter and sentenced to jail. The decedent was survived by his wife, his mother, and his father. His estate was worth about $3885.   **FACTS**

Can the decedent's wife inherit from his estate despite the manslaughter conviction?   **ISSUE**

Yes. The widow will inherit. The trial court may impose a constructive trust.   **HOLDING**

Under the Vermont intestacy statute, the widow would inherit the estate. Vermont does not have a "slayer's statute," which would prevent the inheritance. A slayer should not be allowed to benefit from the wrong. Legally, the title would pass to the widow. The decedent's parents could petition the court of equity to have a constructive trust imposed on the estate for their benefit. The court of equity would determine whether the widow intended to kill the decedent. If so, a trust could be imposed.   **REASONING**

As with other equitable remedies, implied trusts are created to correct unfair results.

SUMMARY

An express trust is an arrangement whereby the owner of assets voluntarily places the legal ownership in a trustee and the equitable ownership in one or more beneficiaries. The trustee is obligated to manage the trust assets prudently. Trusts can be flexible and made to accommodate numerous situations. However, they may be expensive because of trustee's fees and added tax burdens. Care must be utilized in selecting an appropriate trustee, since a trustee has a lot of discretion in how to manage the trust. The trustee must exercise due care in selecting investments for the trust. He or she may be surcharged for making the wrong selection.

The two types of implied trusts are not created voluntarily. A resulting trust occurs when a person makes an incomplete transfer of assets. Constructive trusts arise by operation of law to correct a wrong or to prevent unjust enrichment.

DISCUSSION QUESTIONS

1. What parties are involved in the formation of an express trust? What role does each party serve?

2. What is an inter vivos trust? What are some of its advantages and disadvantages?

3. How does the *cy pres* doctrine work in charitable trusts?

4. Why is a duty of loyalty imposed on a trustee? What effect does this duty have?

5. Compare and contrast spendthrift trusts and sprinkling trusts.

6. Executors and trustees may be asked to serve without fees. Why would they be reluctant to do so? Under what circumstances might they be willing to do so?

7. Are you qualified to act as executor or trustee of your parents' estate? Why or why not?

8. A constructive trust may arise when the court cannot enforce an express trust because the trust lacks a writing required by the Statute of Frauds. Explain why this would be a good application of the constructive trust doctrine.

9. Is it just to impose a high duty of care on a trustee who does not possess the necessary background? Why or why not?

10. A trustee has a duty to exercise care, skill, and prudence. What are these duties? How do they differ?

CASE PROBLEMS

1. Kemske established an irrevocable inter vivos trust for the benefit of his daughter and grandchildren. The corporate trustee was State Bank. State Bank was owned by State Bond. State Bond had three mutual funds, including Common Stock Fund. Kemske knew about the interrelationships among the three companies. The trust deed stated that the trustee

was authorized to invest in State Bond and the mutual funds of State Bond. Should this authorization be valid? Why or why not? Under what circumstances, if any, could it be valid? (*Matter of Irrevocable Inter Vivos Trust, Etc.,* 305 N.W.2d 755 [Minn. 1981].)

2. The decedent died intestate, and his wife was appointed administratrix of his estate. She continued to operate his motorcycle business for twenty months after his death. During this time, she paid herself a salary in excess of $30,000 plus fringe benefits and had the use of a company car. When the business continued to lose money, she abandoned it. She did not liquidate the remaining assets or pay corporate debts. Did the administratrix breach her fiduciary duties? Why or why not? Should a personal representative continue the operation of a business under any circumstances? If so, when and why? (*In re Estate of Kurkowski,* 409 A.2d 357 [Pa. 1979].)

3. Decedent's trustees, Lamb and Millikan (decedent's attorney), loaned two-thirds of the decedent's trust funds to a borrower and took as security a second mortgage on a parcel of real estate. The trustees based the loan on casual conversations with the borrower and did not require a credit check of the borrower or an appraisal of the property. The borrower, who was another client of Millikan, was having financial difficulty because another lender reneged on a loan commitment. There were six notices of default and three lawsuits pending against the borrower at the time of the loan. Did the trustees violate their duty to act as prudent investors? (*Matter of Estate of Collins,* 139 Cal. Rptr. 644 [Cal. App. 1977].)

4. Parker was trustee of Hamon's testamentary trust. As such, she loaned trust funds secured by real estate. The trustee did not speak to the borrower until after the loan had been made. The trustee did receive a written application from the borrower, which was approved by the trustee's attorney. She did not inspect the land herself. Her main source of information was Muncy, whom she had known for thirty years. She also received a written report about the land from three men she did not know. Based on this information, she loaned a substantial amount of money on practically valueless land. Did Parker violate her duty to the trust beneficiary? (*Estate of Hamon,* 60 Cal. App. 154 [1922].)

5. Fidelity National Bank was named as the original trustee of Dunham's testamentary trusts. When it refused to serve, the court appointed Louisiana National Bank as trustee, but the trust funds were never transferred to this trustee. A number of suits were filed and are still pending before the Supreme Court. They concern the partition of the trusts and the court-ordered removal of two individual co-trustees. Provisional trustees were named for the purpose of the lawsuits. Was Louisiana National Bank in breach of its duty because it did not demand that funds be transferred to it? Why or why not? (*Matter of Succession of Dunham,* 399 So.2d 221 [La. App. 1981].)

6. Devon National Bank was the trustee of the Zarkins' land trust. The trust property was the Zarkin's residence. Home Federal Savings and Loan held the first mortgage, and Devon held the second mortgage. Devon purchased the trust property after there had been a decree of foreclosure caused by the first mortgagee. Did the trustee breach its duties to the Zarkinses? If so, what remedies should the Zarkinses have and why? (*Home Federal Savings and Loan Association of Chicago* v. *Zarkins,* 432 N.E.2d 841 [Ill. 1982].)

7. Security Pacific National Bank was named as the trustee of the decedent's testamentary trust. It decided to sell the lemon groves. Another branch of the bank loaned $115,000 of the bank's funds to the ultimate purchaser of this land and took back a deed of trust covering the trust property. This loan enabled the purchaser to acquire the trust property. The bank earned between $2,004.50 and $2,274.00 interest on this loan. The trust did not earn income or interest while the property was in escrow because the trustee surrendered the right to collect income. Did Security Pacific violate its duty to the trust by dealing with the trust property for its own benefit? Did it breach its duty of loyalty? Should the fact that the bank did not know its action was wrong be relevant to a lawsuit based on a trustee's duty to avoid self-dealing in connection with trust property? (*Estate of Pitzer,* 202 Cal. Rptr. 855 [Cal. App. 1984].)

8. The trust of Roberta Switzer provided for her children and contained a spendthrift provision. It stated that the interests of the beneficiaries shall not be subject to claims of the beneficiaries' creditors or to legal process, nor shall the interests be voluntarily or involuntarily assigned, alienated, or encumbered. It also stated that the trustees should use their discretion in paying as much as necessary for the maintenance, support, and education of each living child. Her son, George, filed a petition in bankruptcy. He was twenty-seven at the time, and under the trust he was not entitled to receive a share of the trust assets yet. Should the court allow the attachment of George's interest to pay for the necessities provided to George? Should public policy favor the trust provisions or the bankruptcy trustee? (*Erickson* v. *Bank of California, N.A.,* 643 P.2d 670 [Wash. 1982].)

9. Bernard Guynan owned a parcel of real estate. In September, 1955, he gave his son Edward permission to construct a concrete block house on a portion of the property. Edward constructed the house at his own expense and lived in it from 1957 to 1960, after which time he rented the house and collected the rentals. When Bernard died in 1970, his wife, Anne, obtained title to the property. Anne allowed Edward to continue to rent the property to others. Because of a disagreement between Anne and her son, Anne filed a lawsuit to have Edward and his tenants removed from the premises. Should the court impose a resulting trust or a constructive trust in Edward's favor? Why or why not? (*Guynan* v. *Guynan,* 305 N.W.2d 882 [Neb. 1981].)

10. Tenna Manufacturing Company was considering selling small motors to a buyer on credit. An agent for Tenna contacted Columbia Union National Bank by phone about the buyer's credit-worthiness. Tenna was going to be an unsecured creditor. A bank employee assured Tenna that the buyer had good credit, was current on loans, had good customers, and had a good balance on its account. At least some of this information was misleading in a material way. About two months after Tenna sold the small motors to the buyer, the bank called its secured loan to the buyer and seized all the buyer's assets, including the motors. When the motors were sold, the bank received the proceeds. Does Tenna have any legal recourse against the bank? What legal theory or theories should apply? (*Tenna Manufacturing Co.* v. *Columbia Union National Bank,* 484 F. Supp. 1214 [W.D. Mo. 1980].)

PART 10

The Emerging Business Environment

The world has become smaller in the twentieth century. Advances in communications and in travel have made the entire planet readily accessible to many people and to many businesses. In addition, the reconstruction following World War II has led to a great deal of international trade. Investors today are willing and able to invest in business opportunities in foreign nations as well as in domestic businesses.

No longer of necessity exclusively tied to one nation, businesses today commonly own plants in several nations. Because of the increasingly multinational character of business, no text on business law can be truly complete or comprehensive without at least touching on international business. This final part of the text introduces the topic and some of the problems that the area presents to the legal system. While the coverage is brief, at least the seed is planted. Serious students can easily expand their knowledge through independent study.

In addition, the computer age has spawned an entirely new era, with new legal problems, as well. Many of these "new" problems merely require a redefined application of "old" principles. In the last chapter, the era of computers and the law is introduced.

International Business

Marshall McLuhan once said that modern media, especially television, allow us to live in a "global village." As a result, the ordinary rules of commerce that you have learned may some day be applicable to international business transactions. In 1986, the United States alone exported $217 billion in goods and imported $387 billion in goods. The United States' major trading partners are West Germany, Japan, and the United Kingdom, which had exports of $242 billion, $209 billion, and $107 billion, respectively, and imports of $189

BUSINESS IN A GLOBAL VILLAGE

billion, $126 billion, and $126 billion, respectively.[1] Investment in the United States has quadrupled in the three year period 1983–1986.[2] The United States currently imports thirteen of the thirty-six minerals considered to be essential for our military weaponry. Although the United States is the "bread basket" of the world, our import of foods grew from $20 billion in 1985 to $22 billion in 1986. So Marshall McLuhan was right. We are so economically interdependent on one another that we do live in a global village.

UNITED STATES ANTITRUST LAWS

Does the law of the United States, or of any other sovereign nation, end at its borders? You have seen movie scenes of automobile chases in which the sheriff of one county has to stop his hot pursuit at the border of his county and depend on the cooperation of the sheriff of the adjoining county to take up the chase in order to apprehend the person he was chasing. Do nations work that way too, or is there some other way that "domestic" law can be applied internationally? The following case attempted to answer that question.

France v. Turkey (The S. S. Lotus)
P.C.I.J. Ser. A, No. 10 (1927)

FACTS A collision occurred on the high seas between the French steamer *Lotus* and the Turkish steamer *BozKourt.* On the arrival of the *Lotus* at Istanbul, a criminal proceeding was instituted against Lieutenant Demons, the officer on watch on board the *Lotus* at the time of the collision.

ISSUE Does the Turkish court have jurisdiction over a French citizen involved in an event that happened on the high seas?

HOLDING Yes, provided that the French citizen is subject to a Turkish court's jurisdiction.

REASONING International law governs relations between states. In general, one nation's law cannot be exercised in the territory of another nation without the second nation's permission. On the other hand, international law does not prohibit one nation from exercising jurisdiction in its own territory concerning acts that took place outside its territory. Independent nations have wide discretion to act, provided that their actions are not limited by international treaties or are not in conflict with an established rule of international law.

---

[1] United Nations, *Monthly Bulletin of Statistics,* June, 1987.
[2] U.S. Department of Commerce, *Survey of Current Business,* May, 1987.

Accordingly, the United States does have laws that have extraterritorial application. These laws fall into two broad categories: crimes and torts. Since the United States antitrust laws fall into both categories, they do have extraterritorial implications.

The Sherman Act states in its first section that "every contract, combination . . . or conspiracy in restraint of trade or commerce among the several States, or with foreign nations, is declared to be illegal." United States courts have not been in full agreement, however, on the meaning of that statute with respect to international commerce. Among American courts, there is no consensus on how far the jurisdiction should extend. Some courts use the "direct and substantial effect" test. That test examines the effect on United States foreign commerce as a prerequisite for proper jurisdiction. Other courts have used a different test that looks at whether there is a conspiracy that adversely affects American commerce. In general, however, most courts prefer to evaluate and balance the relevant considerations in each case. The courts determine whether the contacts and interests of the United States are sufficient to support the exercise of extraterritorial jurisdiction. However, in the following case, the Supreme Court allowed an alleged violation of the Sherman Act to be decided by a Japanese arbitration.

Mitsubishi Motors Corp. v. *Soler Chrysler-Plymouth, Inc.*
473 U.S. 614 (1985)

A Puerto Rican corporation entered into a contract with a Swiss corporation and a Japanese corporation. The Japanese corporation was a joint venture between the Swiss corporation and another Japanese corporation. The contract provided that in the event of a dispute it would be referred to the Japanese Arbitration Association for resolution. A dispute arose and the Japanese corporation sought a U.S. District Court order compelling arbitration in Japan. The Puerto Rican corporation stated that antitrust claims could not be settled by arbitration. The district court ordered arbitration. The court of appeals reversed the district court. The case was then heard by the Supreme Court.

FACTS

Are antitrust claims subject to arbitration clauses?

ISSUE

Yes. Claims arising under the Sherman Act are arbitrable.

HOLDING

The court was asked "whether an American court should enforce an agreement to resolve antitrust claims by arbitration when that agreement arises from an international transaction." There is a federal policy that favors arbitration, and "(t)here is no reason to depart from these guidelines when a party bound by an arbitration agreement raises claims founded on statutory rights."

REASONING

THE "RULES OF THE GAME"

At one time, it was necessary to know the laws of all the countries involved in an international transaction. Because of the complexity of that matter as well as the increased number of countries in the world since the end of World War II, countries in common geographical areas have banded together to form economic unions in order to facilitate and expedite world trade. French-speaking African countries formed the Union Douanière et Economique de l'Afrique Centrale (UDEAC); Eastern European countries, the Council for Mutual Economic Assistance (COMECON); Caribbean countries, the Caribbean Community (CARICOM); and European countries, the European Common Market (EEC). We will examine the EEC since it is the most developed of the groups just mentioned. Recent court opinions reflect the same extraterritorial effect of EEC antitrust laws as is the case with American antitrust laws.

European Economic Community

The EEC was created by the Treaty of Rome in 1957. The member states are Belgium, Denmark, France, Greece, West Germany, Ireland, Italy, Luxembourg, The Netherlands, The United Kingdom, Spain, and Portugal. The EEC has its own legislative, executive, and judicial branches. The purpose of the community is to establish a common customs tariff for outside nations and to eliminate tariffs among EEC members. The treaty also covers the free movement of workers, goods, and capital. It is aimed at accomplishing international cooperation. The EEC is governed by the Council of Ministers, the Commission, the Assembly, and the Court of Justice.

The Council of Ministers

Each member nation sends a representative to the Council of Ministers. The council coordinates the economic policies of the member nations so that they will be in accord with the Treaty of Rome.

The Commission

The Commission is composed of persons from each member nation, but they do not represent that nation as do the members of the Council of Ministers. Rather, they represent the EEC as a whole. The Commission is charged with the responsibility of implementing the Treaty of Rome by issuing regulations and directives. The Commission can either make decisions by itself or it can make formal proposals to the Council of Ministers.

The Assembly

The Assembly is sometimes referred to as the European Parliament, since its members are chosen directly by popular election in each member nation. The Assembly oversees the activities of both the Council of Ministers and the Commission by offering its opinion on various matters.

The Court of Justice

The Court of Justice functions in much the same way as the United States Supreme Court does; it is the final arbiter of all disputes. *Once the Court of Justice makes a ruling, it becomes the domestic law of all the member nations.* In order to accomplish this tremendous feat, all the member nations had to give up some of their sovereignty. The law is now applied in all ten countries and to their approximately 300 million citizens; as such, its market is larger than that of the United States. The following case illustrates the type of subject matter brought before the court.

Van Duyn v. *The "Home Office"*
4 December 1974, Case No. 41/74

A woman of Dutch nationality arrived in Great Britain to take up employment as a secretary with the Church of Scientology, of which she was a practicing member. She was refused entry into Great Britain on the grounds that the government considered the church to be a social danger and therefore a harmful body.

FACTS

Is the provision of the Treaty of Rome relating to freedom of movement for workers, entailing the abolition of any discrimination based on the nationality of workers, applicable if one nation chooses to exclude a worker on the basis of public policy?

ISSUE

No. Domestic public policy considerations allow the exclusion of some people.

HOLDING

The right to freedom of movement contained in the Treaty of Rome has been limited by a council directive that allows member nations to exclude certain persons on the basis of public policy, public safety, and public health. Although past association cannot be considered with respect to a person's present or future behavior, active and avowed association may constitute such a criterion. International law allows a nation to exclude certain persons from its borders.

REASONING

Figure 54.1 depicts the European Economic Community.

Workers

Article 48 of the Treaty of Rome prohibits "any discrimination based on nationality, between workers of the member states, as regards employment, remuneration, and other conditions of work and employment." The EEC has interpreted that article to mean, among other things, that all workers must be given the same tax advantages, access to public schools, and housing as citizens of the nation enjoy.

Goods

The EEC has a customs union that is designed to eliminate customs duties among all member nations. In addition, the union has a common tariff with

Figure 54.1   The European Economic Community

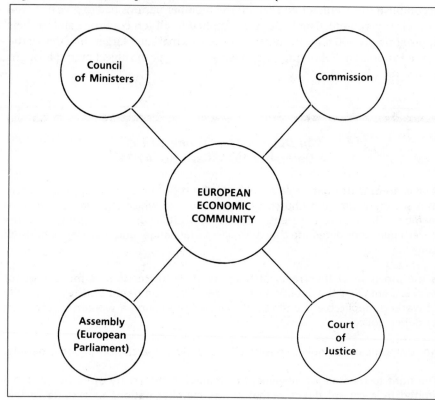

respect to trade between member nations and nonmember nations. As a result, no burdens are placed on trade between member nations, but a burden is placed on trade with countries outside the EEC.

Capital

The European Monetary System (EMS) was created in 1979. Its purpose is to allow only limited fluctuations in the currencies of various member nations from preset parity prices. This is accomplished through a joint credit facility that lends support to an EMS currency when it needs an infusion of capital.

EEC Rules of Business Competition

Article 85

Article 85 of the Treaty of Rome declares null and void any agreement or practice that has as its goal the prevention, restriction, or distortion of competition within the EEC. The thrust of the article is to prohibit price fixing, allocating markets, and the creation of unequal terms that result in competitive advantages.

Article 86

Article 86 prohibits one or more entities that have a "dominant" market position within a substantial segment of the EEC from taking "improper" advantage of such a position. The term *dominant* has been the source of much litigation. In the *United Brands* case of 14 February 1978, it was determined that a market share of 40 percent created a dominant position.

CBEM, S.A. v. Compagnie Luxembourgeoise De Telediffusion, S.A., Case No. 311/84
European Court of Justice (1985–8) (ECR 3261)

FACTS

CBEM advertised on Belgium RTL television station beginning in 1982. The defendant operated the station. In 1983, IPB (also a defendant and a subsidiary of the other defendant) granted CBEM the exclusive right to advertise its product on RTL. The agreement expired in 1984. CBEM alleged that it created the market for television advertising on RTL and that it should be allowed to continue instead of IPB.

ISSUES

(1) Did the defendants occupy a 'dominant position' within the meaning of Article 86 of the EEC Treaty? (2) If so, was the dominant position abused?

HOLDINGS

(1) Yes. (2) Yes.

REASONING

An enterprise "occupies a dominant position for the purposes of Article 86 where it enjoys a position of economic strength which enables it to hinder the maintenance of effective competition on the relevant market by allowing it to behave to an appreciable extent independently of its competitors and customers and ultimately of consumers . . . " An abuse of a dominant position is committed when an enterprise reserves to itself an activity, for example, advertising that could be carried out by another enterprise.

Negative Clearance

The Council of Ministers issued a regulation whereby a business could obtain from the Commission a "negative clearance." Its effect is that the economic activity in question does not violate either Article 85 or Article 86.

Extraterritoriality

The EEC position on extraterritoriality is approximately the same as the American position. In the *J.R. Geigy, A.G.* v. *Commission* case of 14 July 1972, it was decided that Geigy violated Article 85 on the basis of a company-owned subsidiary located inside the EEC, even though the alleged acts in violation of the Treaty of Rome took place outside EEC territory.

THE GENERAL AGREEMENT ON TARIFFS AND TRADE

The General Agreement on Tariffs and Trade (GATT) involves discussions among eighty-four countries. It is aimed at lowering tariff and trade barriers. Ultimately, it is hoped, free trade will result and there will no longer be any trade barriers. As a result of GATT's efforts, tariffs have been reduced to 70 percent of what they were twenty years ago. They have been reduced through meetings called "Rounds." The first five Rounds proceeded item by item, but beginning in 1964 the now famous "Kennedy Round" achieved an across-the-board tariff reduction.

IMPORTS

All goods imported into a country must "pass" customs. Passing customs usually means paying a certain sum of money at the port of entry based on the type and value of the goods. For example, when Subaru imported the BRAT motor vehicle into this country, it had to be decided whether the BRAT was a truck or a sports car since the duty that had to be paid would differ depending on the category to which it rightfully belonged. Once the type of import that is in question is determined, the analysis turns to its valuation. Is the proper valuation its wholesale value at point of origin or destination, its retail value at point of origin or destination, or a combination of all those factors? In general, the transaction value of the goods is used. The *transaction value* is the price the importer paid for the goods plus certain other necessary and related expenses. The U.S. Customs Court has exclusive jurisdiction over civil actions challenging administrative decisions of the U.S. Customs Service.[3]

EXPORTS

United States policy with respect to export "controls" is reflected in the Export Administration Act of 1979 (50 U.S.C. 2401 et seq.), in which it is stated that controls will be used as follows:

§2401. Congressional findings

The Congress makes the following findings:

(1)   The ability of United States citizens to engage in international commerce is a fundamental concern of United States policy.

(2)   Exports contribute significantly to the economic well-being of the United States and the stability of the world economy by increasing employment and production in the United States, and by earning foreign exchange, thereby contributing favorably to the trade balance. The restriction of exports from the United States can have serious adverse effects on the balance of payments and on domes-

---

[3] 28 U.S.C. 1582 (a).

tic employment, particularly when restrictions applied by the United States are more extensive than those imposed by other countries.

(3)   It is important for the national interest of the United States that both the private sector and the Federal Government place a high priority on exports, consistent with the economic, security, and foreign policy objectives of the United States.

(4)   The availability of certain materials at home and abroad varies so that the quantity and composition of United States exports and their distribution among importing countries may affect the welfare of the domestic economy and may have an important bearing upon fulfillment of the foreign policy of the United States.

(5)   Exports of goods or technology without regard to whether they make a significant contribution to the military potential of individual countries or combinations of countries may adversely affect the national security of the United States.

(6)   Uncertainty of export control policy can inhibit the efforts of the United States business and work to the detriment of the overall attempt to improve the trade balance of the United States.

(7)   Unreasonable restrictions on access to world supplies can cause worldwide political and economic instability, interfere with free international trade, and retard the growth and development of nations.

(8)   It is important that the administration of export controls imposed for national security purposes give special emphasis to the need to control exports of technology (and goods which contribute significantly to the transfer of such technology) which could make a significant contribution to the military potential of any country or combination of countries which would be detrimental to the national security of the United States.

(9)   Minimization of restrictions on exports of agricultural commodities and products is of critical importance to the maintenance of a sound agricultural sector, to a positive contribution to the balance of payments, to reducing the level of Federal expenditures for agricultural support programs, and to United States cooperation in efforts to eliminate malnutrition and world hunger.

(10)   It is important that the administration of export controls imposed for foreign policy purposes give special emphasis to the need to control exports of goods and substances hazardous to the public health and the environment which are banned or severely restricted for use in the United States, and which, if exported, could affect the international reputation of the United States as a responsible trading partner.

(11)   The acquisition of national security, sensitive goods, and technology by the Soviet Union and other countries, the actions and policies of which run counter to the national security interests of the United States, has led to the significant enhancement of Soviet bloc military-industrial capabilities. This enhancement poses a threat to the security of the United States, its allies, and other friendly nations, and places additional demands on the defense budget of the United States.

(12)   Availability to controlled countries of goods and technology from foreign sources is a fundamental concern of the United States and should be eliminated through negotiations and other appropriate means whenever possible.

(13)   Excessive dependence of the United States, its allies, or countries sharing

common strategic objectives with the United States, on energy and other crucial resources from potential adversaries can be harmful to the mutual and individual security of all those countries.

To implement this legislation, the Department of Commerce maintains a "commodity control list" of all goods and technology that have been defined by the federal government as subject to the act.

LABOR

Do United States labor laws have extraterritorial application? Early cases suggested that the answer was no, but more recent cases suggest that we may be moving toward an extraterritorial application of our labor laws. The following case demonstrates that view.

Vermilya-Brown Co. v. Connell
335 U.S. 377 (1948)

FACTS The plaintiffs were hired in New York City and employed by the defendant in Bermuda. Suit was brought with respect to overtime pay based on the Fair Labor Standards Act.

ISSUE Do United States labor laws have extraterritorial jurisdiction?

HOLDING Yes, if the workers are working in United States–controlled areas.

REASONING A controversy as to the geographical application of the statute had to be considered together with an executive agreement that authorized the United States to enact legislation with respect to United States–leased areas in Bermuda. Since the United States can regulate the actions of United States citizens outside the United States, the leased areas within Bermuda were subject to the legislation.

MONEY

Money is the oil that lubricates the machinery of international commercial transactions. Money that moves from one country to another must move within the framework of the international monetary system. That system recognizes the regulations and restrictions that various countries impose on the movement of their money.

Most international transactions with the United States are denominated in dollars since the American dollar is considered to be a "hard" currency. For example, if an importer in country X wanted to buy some widgets from an American company, he would have to pay for the widgets in dollars. Country X does not use dollars in its local economy. Therefore, the importer would have to go to his bank and request that the money he has on deposit in the national currency of country X be converted into dollars in sufficient amount to pay for the widgets. Depending on the strength or weakness of country X's currency, the dollars will be either easy or difficult to obtain. Furthermore, before any funds leave the country, the government will, in one form or another, have to approve the transfer of dollars out of the country. For example, because of the fall in the price of oil and excessive borrowing by the Mexican government, all conversions of pesos into dollars were stopped in 1982. Trade between Mexico and all other countries ceased until the government could stabilize the peso with help from the International Monetary Fund.

Federal law provides criminal liability for failure to report the export or import of money without reporting it in accordance with the Currency and Foreign Transactions Reporting Act (32 USC 5316). The reporting requirements formerly applied to all transactions in excess of $5,000. The amount was raised to $10,000 in 1982 when the statute was amended. In the following case, one of the issues was whether a cashier's check was money.

United States v. Dichne
612 F.2d 632 (2d Cir. 1979)

The defendant was in the import–export business. He boarded a plane in Los Angeles bound for London. During the time that he was in the boarding area of the airport announcements were made over the public address system on four separate occasions concerning monetary reporting requirements. Also, there were a number of large posters in the area carrying the same information. At no time did he request or complete a report on the $375,000 in the form of a cashier's check he had on his person. The check was eventually presented for payment in Europe.

FACTS

Is a cashier's check money?

ISSUE

Yes.

HOLDING

The announcements stated that currency or monetary instruments in excess of $5,000 were required to be reported. A cashier's check is a monetary instrument and is recognized as such by Article 3 of the Uniform Commercial Code. "It is implausible that he was unaware that such a check constituted a 'monetary instrument' within the meaning of the warning announcements and posters."

REASONING

At one time, there was no worldwide protection with respect to patents, trademarks, copyrights, and trade names. Although various attempts had been made, true protection was at best limited to a few countries working

INFORMATION

together. Authors from Mark Twain's time to the recent present complained bitterly about how their intellectual property had been used in other countries without any compensation paid to them. The only solution to the problem was for the owners of intellectual property to seek protection separately in each country. Because of the highly impractical nature of this solution, the problem persisted. For example, the Coca-Cola Co. could not register the Coca-Cola bottle as a trademark in Great Britain. Much of Japanese technology has been built on American technology. During President Reagan's second term, he called for international patent and copyright protection. Today, we have the Patent Cooperation Treaty, which was enacted into U.S. law on 6 November 1986. As of 1988, thirty-nine countries had signed the treaty, which provides for simultaneous filings of patents in all countries that have signed the treaty. The following case illustrates the practical problem that businesses used to face with respect to this issue.

Deepsouth Packing Co. v. Laitram Corp.
406 U.S. 518 (1972)

FACTS Both the plaintiff and the defendant held patents on machines that devein shrimp more efficiently than other machines or hand labor. Laitram's patent claim was superior to Deepsouth's in this country but not outside the United States.

ISSUE Is Deepsouth Packing's absence from the United States market because of Laitram's superior patent rights also preventing it from exporting its machines overseas?

HOLDING No. United States patent laws apply only within the United States.

REASONING The patent statute (35 U.S.C. 154) entitles a patentee to a grant throughout the United States only. United States patents do not apply to United States competition in international commerce. Since there is no common law right, only a statutory one, it is clear that the power of the statute pertains to United States territory only.

NATIONALIZA-TION

Nationalization of privately owned business entities is a risk that exists primarily in developing countries. *Nationalization* is the act of converting privately owned businesses into governmentally owned businesses. In general, international trade can be carried on without fear of nationalization; the exporter merely ensures that payment is guaranteed before shipment of goods. However, international investment is not so simple a matter. To build and operate an aluminum plant or an oil refinery requires a large investment of capital. If, during the time the investment is paying for itself, it is nationalized, the result is usually a loss to the investor. It is for that reason, as well as for others, that international investment decisions usually require a shorter payback period than national investment decisions.

Is nationalization legal? It depends on your perspective. For the most part, from the viewpoint of the country that nationalizes a private property, some act of the legislature or head of state makes it "legal" within that country. From the viewpoint of international law, however, it may not be legal. If it does not comply with international law, it is termed a **confiscation,** not a nationalization. If it does comply with international law, it is called an **expropriation.** The key element is whether the state had a proper public purpose and, in addition, whether "just compensation" was paid for the property. No matter what it is called, there is precious little that can be done about it, should it occur.

One means of insuring an investment against the risk of loss is by utilizing the facilities of the Overseas Private Investment Corporation (OPIC). OPIC furnishes low-cost insurance against nationalization; confiscation; lack of convertibility of foreign earnings; and general loss due to insurrection, revolution, or war. OPIC currently insures over 400 projects in fifty countries.

Confiscation A taking of private property by the government in violation of international law

Expropriation A taking of private property by the government not in violation of international law

One reason for the importance of seeking insurance protection for overseas investments is the Act of State doctrine. The doctrine states that every sovereign state is bound to respect the independence of every other sovereign state, and the courts of one country will not sit in judgment on the acts of the government of another performed within its own borders. The concept of the Act of State doctrine is imbedded in the notion of sovereign immunity. Certainly each sovereign state recognizes all other states' sovereignty. But the Act of State doctrine is not a specific rule of international law. International law does not require that nations follow this rule, and in the United States, the Constitution does not require it. Judicial decisions of the United States, however, have recognized the doctrine. The doctrine is based on the theory that each nation is not qualified to question the actions of other nations taken on their own soil. In fact, denouncing the public decisions of other nations can have a decidedly adverse effect on the conduct of a nation's foreign policy. The following case illustrates a modern application of the doctrine.

ACT OF STATE DOCTRINE

Banco Nacional de Cuba v. *Sabbatino*
376 U.S. 398 (1964)

Cuba expropriated the property of a Cuban corporation, the capital stock of which was principally owned by United States residents. The American residents filed suit to recover proceeds in a United States district court against the corporation, which was an instrumentality of the Cuban government.

FACTS

ISSUE   Will the judiciary of one country examine the validity of a taking of property within the territory of another country?

HOLDING   No. There is a lack of jurisdiction in such a case.

REASONING   The judiciary will not examine the validity of a taking of property by a foreign government if that taking was within its own territory. This is applicable if the United States diplomatically recognizes the foreign government at the time of the taking. The only grounds on which the United States could examine the taking is if a treaty or other unambiguous agreement gave it the power to do so. Furthermore, this is true if the taking is alleged to be in violation of international law.

But what about a situation in which an American bank held promissory notes issued by a group of Costa Rican banks payable in the United States in United States dollars? Would there be a lack of jurisdiction if the Costa Rican government, after the notes were signed, refused to make the payments in United States dollars? Does the "Act of State" doctrine apply? The Second Circuit said an emphatic "no" when it held that the situs (location) of the debt was in the United States and not Costa Rica, therefore, the doctrine did not apply. See *Allied Bank* v. *Banco Credito,* 757 F.2d 516 (2d Cir. 1985).

SOVEREIGN IMMUNITY

Whereas the Act of State doctrine is not a rule of international law, sovereign immunity is. Simply put, a state cannot be "sued" by another state unless it allows itself to be sued. This is true with respect to individuals suing as well. The traditional view is that a state cannot be sued in any of its own courts without permission. But when one state recognizes the "immunity" of another state from suit in that state's own courts, does that immunity apply to the courts of other nations? In the latter situation, it is said that the matter goes beyond a question of immunity to that of "comity." **Comity** is merely the informal and voluntary recognition of the sovereignty of another nation. In this sense, it is a manifestation of judicial restraint — voluntarily choosing not to exercise jurisdiction. That voluntariness was ended in 1976 when Congress enacted the Foreign Sovereign Immunities Act. The act became effective in 1977 and provides a rule that states are not immune from suit in courts other than their own if the subject of the litigation is over "commercial" activities. Accordingly, states are not immune from suit if it involves commercial property.

Comity The informal and voluntary recognition of the sovereignty of another nation

DISPUTES

The best method of resolving an international dispute is by providing for that contingency at the time of creating the international transaction. Three principal options for settling a dispute are available: the International Court of Justice, national courts, and arbitration.

A private person has no standing before the International Court of Justice (ICJ). Only nations may appear before the court. A private person who has a grievance against a state not his own must first secure the agreement of his own state to espouse his claim. If his state asserts his claim, the issue then becomes whether the other state wants to allow the matter to appear before the ICJ for resolution. If it does not, that is the end of the matter. This procedure is established in the United Nations Charter, since the ICJ is an agency of the United Nations. Each state must agree to be bound by the court's decision; if they do not so agree, there is no jurisdiction to hear the claim. Figure 54.2 lists the authorities the Court uses in reaching its decisions.

The International Court of Justice

A private person usually can resort to settlement of a dispute with a foreign nation by seeking redress through the courts of that state. Private persons can

National Courts

Figure 54.2 The International Court of Justice

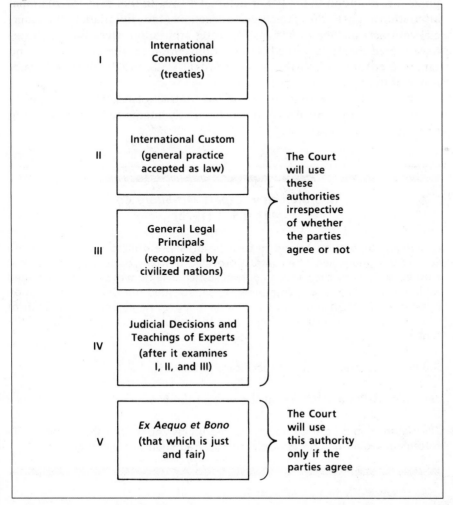

I — International Conventions (treaties)

II — International Custom (general practice accepted as law)

III — General Legal Principals (recognized by civilized nations)

IV — Judicial Decisions and Teachings of Experts (after it examines I, II, and III)

The Court will use these authorities irrespective of whether the parties agree or not

V — Ex Aequo et Bono (that which is just and fair)

The Court will use this authority only if the parties agree

sometimes seek adequate relief in their native state's judicial system. For example, a favorable judgment from a United States court may be filed in another country and, under certain conditions, can execute on assets in the foreign country on the basis of the other country's judicial decision. In the landmark case of *Hilton* v. *Guyot,* 159 U.S. 113 (1895) the Court said that the court of one country may be respected in the courts of another country if four conditions are met.

1. The court was one of competent jurisdiction.
2. The record reflects adequate proof.
3. The defendant must have had the opportunity to defend himself.
4. The record must be clear and unequivocal.

Arbitration

For a variety of reasons, a particular international dispute may not be appropriate for resolution in the ICJ or national courts. In that case, international arbitration might be the correct course of action. Many international commercial contracts include provisions for using arbitration. Over fifty countries have signed the 1958 United Nations Convention on the Recognition and Enforcement of Foreign Arbitration Awards (T.I.A.S. 6997). The United States is one of the signatories.

The specification in an international contract of referral of disputes to arbitration or to a particular court may be strictly interpreted, as the following case illustrates.

M/S Bremen v. Zapata Off-Shore Co.
407 U.S. 1 (1972)

FACTS   A German corporation agreed to tow the off-shore drilling rig of the Zapata Co. to the Adriatic Sea. The contract provided that any dispute arising from it must be decided by the London Court of Justice. The rig was seriously damaged while being towed, and a dispute arose. Zapata sued the German corporation in a United States district court in Florida, alleging negligence and breach of contract. The German corporation moved to dismiss the suit on the basis of the contract clause.

ISSUE   Should the contract clause be specifically enforced?

HOLDING   Yes. Both parties agreed to it at the time of the contract.

REASONING   The clause should be specifically enforced unless Zapata can show that its enforcement would be unreasonable, unjust, fraudulent, or overreaching.

We live in an interdependent world. Consequently, businesspersons should be aware of the international implications of their business dealings and of the fact that United States antitrust and labor laws have the *potential* to be applied extraterritorially.

SUMMARY

International transactions are expedited through the use of regional cooperative unions, such as the European Economic Community (EEC). The EEC was created by the Treaty of Rome. The General Agreement on Tariffs and Trade (GATT) has done more in the past twenty years to stimulate world trade than was accomplished in all the years of international commerce preceding it.

Nationalization is the taking of private property. If the nationalization complies with international law, it is called an expropriation. If it does not, it is called a confiscation. The Act of State doctrine is used to justify the position that one country will not stand in judgment on the actions of other countries carried on within their own territories.

Sovereign immunity is a rule of international law that states that a country cannot be sued unless it allows itself to be sued.

International law provides three mechanisms for the resolution of international disputes. The International Court of Justice (ICJ) is the appropriate forum when one nation sues another, provided that each nation agrees to the suit. Domestic courts are used for the resolution of disputes between citizens of different nations. Lastly, arbitration is used in international as well as domestic disputes.

DISCUSSION QUESTIONS

1. How would you apply the term *global village* to international business?

2. What arguments can you make for restricting a nation's laws to its territorial limits?

3. What is the modern significance of the Treaty of Rome?

4. Did the Court of Justice properly render its verdict in the *Van Duyn* case, or should it have interpreted the treaty more broadly?

5. What is "negative clearance"?

6. Two corporations, one organized in Belgium and the other in Great Britain, seek to merge. They are both in the computer software business. The Belgium corporation has 15 percent of the EEC market, and the British corporation has 30 percent. What problems do these facts raise with respect to the Treaty of Rome?

7. An American corporation wishes to export a new computer microchip outside the United States. Do you envision any problems in complying with United States law?

8. You are an executive with an international publishing house. What steps would you take to ensure that your publishing and royalty rights were protected in the world markets?

9. You are a financial adviser to a multinational manufacturing corporation.

What considerations would enter into your thinking with respect to a decision to invest $500 million in the nation of Chad?

10. The president has the power under current federal law to enter into foreign trade agreements with foreign governments. In so doing, the president can modify existing duties and import restrictions. Should the president use that power if country X is flooding the United States market with goods that are cheaper than similar United States-made goods? Discuss. (19 U.S.C. § 1351.)

11. The Foreign Corrupt Practices Act (see Chapter 44) provides criminal penalties for United States corporations that pay anything of value (bribe) to any foreign official for the purpose of obtaining or retaining business in a foreign country. Why is there an exception for "grease" payments? Discuss.

CASE PROBLEMS

1. Is a nationalization a sovereign act, or is it commercial in nature? (*Carey* v. *National Oil Corp.,* 453 F. Supp. 1097 [S.D. N.Y. 1978].)

2. During the Spanish-American War, United States naval vessels captured two Spanish fishing vessels and their cargoes as prizes of war. If a rule of international law is that fishing vessels are exempt from capture as prizes of war, how should a United States court decide the fate of the fishing vessels? (*The Paquette Habana* v. *The Lola,* 175 U.S. 677 [1900].)

3. During Prohibition, the United States Coast Guard seized two vessels nineteen miles off the coast of the United States. The vessels were seized because they were carrying cargoes of whiskey bound for the United States. If the cargo had arrived in the United States, it would have violated federal law, which prohibited alcohol as a subject of commerce. At the time of the seizure, boundaries of the United States extended to twelve miles off the coast. Was the seizure valid? (*The Over the Top Schroeder* v. *Bissell* (5 F.2d 838 [D. Conn. 1925].)

4. Should nations use their status as nation-states in the international community to protect the private business interests of their citizens in international legal tribunals, or should they leave private interests alone? (*Barcelona Traction, Light, & Power Co., Ltd., Belgium* v. *Spain* [1970 I.C.J. Rep. 3].)

5. The American Civil Liberties Union sued on behalf of itself and other bank depositors to restrain the enforcement of the foreign transaction reporting requirements of the Currency and Foreign Transactions Reporting Act as a violation of the Fourth Amendment. Is the reporting requirement a general search warrant? Why or why not? (*California Bankers Association* v. *Shultz,* 416 U.S. 21 [1974].)

CHAPTER 55

Computers and the Law

INTRODUCTION

The pervasity of the influence of computers on our lives probably defies description. The strange words that pepper our everyday speech — *software, hardware, bytes, input, output, electronic bulletin boards, mainframes, minis* — graphically illustrate the primacy of computers in our world. We use computers in the classroom, in our public libraries, for our own personal uses, and for numerous other daily activities, including medical diagnoses. Without computers, the telecommunications, financial, insurance, airline, and newspaper industries and a myriad of other businesses and multinational corporations would undoubtedly grind to a near halt. The government itself holds so much information about us on computer tapes that Congress and state legislatures have passed statutes designed to protect our privacy. And no one believes the amount of computer-generated data will decrease in the foreseeable future. Although authorities had estimated that the information industry would grow by 15 percent annually (from the 3.9 percent of the U.S. gross national product attributable to this industry in 1984) to reach $300 billion in worldwide total revenues in 1985 and a whopping $1 trillion in the early 1990s,[1] the slump of 1984–1986 may preclude the attainment of these optimistic levels.[2] Still, experts continue to believe that the information processing industry will dominate all other industries in the world by the end of the century; and if it does not already affect the daily life of every person now, the information industry will certainly affect all our lives by the end of the century.

Given these facts, computers represent, to use the vernacular, "big bucks." Estimated computer shipments in 1987 totalled $72.2 billion and will probably amount to $122 billion in 1989.[3] As the products in the industry continue to show improvements in price and performance levels and as new technologies overtake the old, producers like IBM, Burroughs, Honeywell, Hewlett-Packard, NCR, and Sperry will face fierce competition in their struggle for market shares. The same is, moreover, true of producers of **peripherals** and **software,** since these firms encounter equally brutal competition not only domestically but internationally as well, most notably from the Japanese. In short, the "boom" days of the early 1980s are over for U.S.-based computer vendors.

Peripherals Mechanical devices connected to computers, e.g., printers, terminals, and disk drives

Software Computer programs (or instructions)

Besides competition, the computer industry also raises noneconomic issues involving regulation/deregulation, privacy, equity, and sovereignty. In fact, these issues have led in many instances to the erection of nontariff trade barriers to transborder data flows. It is easy to forget that we as Americans view privacy much differently from others in our "global village." For example, even though we would probably reject governmental restrictions meant to impede the free flow of information across our country and across national borders, many other countries do not share our misgivings about this type of regulation of information. These countries would also generally favor the creation of governmental commissions to administer privacy laws and to protect citizens' interests, while we would very likely balk at the institution of such governmental controls. In a related vein, the lesser-developed, so-called third-world countries fear the United States's telecommunications dominance, especially our power in the "information era." Their "have not" status alarms them because they believe their lack of access to computer technologies carries with it significant cultural and economic repercussions. Similarly, other countries view U.S.-generated data processing as a threat to their sovereignty owing to the challenges these **data banks** pose to these countries' comparatively fledgling information industries. Canadian banking legislation, for instance, requires that all data processing leading to the preparation of banking statements be carried out in Canada. Not only does such legislation protect Canadian jobs, it also avoids the effects of what Canada has dubbed "cultural imperialism," or "Americanized" interpretations of data. As Ameri-

Data banks Central depositories for information

---

[1] *Standard & Poor's Industry Surveys,* June 6, 1985, p. C73.

[2] Ibid., October 1, 1987, p. C75.

[3] Ibid., *Industry Surveys,* June 6, 1985, p. C73.

can technology increasingly permits the beaming of the latest merchandise lines and items across international borders through "electronic catalogues," or teletext and videotext technologies, we can expect such criticisms to proliferate. Since many countries do not welcome this type of information, the erection of further barriers to impede such transborder data flows may follow as a consequence. Indeed, for some American firms these barriers are already a reality. For example, Japan in the late 1970s made it difficult for American firms to connect to its international record carrier unless each leased circuit terminated at a single facility in the U.S. Similarly, France has recently proposed to levy taxes on information flows across its borders. A host of international organizations and numerous committees within the executive and legislative branches of our government therefore are directing their concerted efforts to a consideration of the problems spawned by the computer age. You will presumably be able to witness the resolution of these profound issues as they unfold on the world stage.

Interesting though it is to ponder the multifaceted questions arising from the computer age, we shall confine our examination of this important topic to the legal issues inherent in this subject. We can divide these issues into five main areas: the intellectual property aspects of computers (copyrights, patents, trade secrets, and unfair competition); contract law, particularly the Uniform Commercial Code; tort law; statutory protection (invasion of privacy, antitrust, and criminal law); and constitutional law. The national movement toward total computer literacy for all Americans presupposes an understanding of the legal ramifications spawned by the information era. Hence, this chapter's focus upon some of the more significant elements of computers and the law should facilitate your comprehension of this noteworthy topic.

INTELLECTUAL PROPERTY ASPECTS OF COMPUTERS

Copyrights

As we learned in Chapter 46, federal law protects the holders of copyrights and patents. Congress as early as 1790 exercised the power granted to it by the Constitution in conferring statutory protection on artistic works created by writers, artists, and composers. The copyright laws protect "any original works of authorship fixed in any tangible medium of expression [including literary works]. . . . "[4] Hence, copyright laws traditionally have protected only *expressions* of ideas, not the ideas themselves. Plans, methods, systems, or devices are not copyrightable, either.

The most important of the early copyright laws, the Copyright Act of 1909, remained virtually unchanged until 1 January 1978, when the present copyright statute, the Copyright Act of 1976, became effective. (Vestiges of the 1909 Act in reality remain with us, since it still covers works created prior to 1 January 1978.) Although it was unclear whether computer programs were copyrightable under the 1909 Act, the Copyright Office began accepting computer programs for registration as books as early as 1964, despite the misgiv-

---

[4] 17 U.S.C. §102 (West 1985).

ings of Register officials.[5] At the time of the passage of the 1976 Act, the "jury" (in the form of the National Commission on New Technological Uses [CONTU]) was still out on the copyrightability of computer software. However, the Computer Software Copyright Act of 1980 amended the 1976 Act by adding the phrase "computer program" and certain other provisions exempting the copying of computer programs from the Act's infringement provisions. As a result of these amendments, few doubts remain today as to the copyrightability of computer programs, despite the omission of this phrase from the listed categories of proper subject matters for copyright protection. Under the 1980 amendments, "[a]'computer program' is a set of statements or instructions to be used directly or indirectly in a computer in order to bring about a certain result."[6] According to the 1980 amendments, computer data bases are also copyrightable under Section 103(b) as "compilations" or "derivative works." Infringements of copyrights (for example, unauthorized copying, distribution, or derivation) do not occur if the owner (i.e., a copyright holder) of a copy of a computer program only makes or authorizes the making of a new copy (or adaption) when the copy is an essential step in the utilization of the program in conjunction with a machine (i.e., for use with the owner's computer) or for archival purposes (i.e., for making backup copies in case the original copy is accidentally destroyed).[7] The "fair use" doctrine (whereby, for instance, your professor uses computer software for an in-class performance or display) and the right of libraries to reproduce and distribute copyrighted works, including computer software in some circumstances, apparently do not constitute infringements either.[8] The Act presently does not differentiate between human-readable or machine-readable copies for infringement purposes; copies in either form may constitute infringements unless the copying falls into one of these exemptions.

Yet controversies still abound owing to the fact that the 1976 Act continues the longstanding expression/idea dichotomy of copyright law. This duality (i.e., that the program as written is protectable but the unique ideas contained in the program are not) of course looms as a significant impediment to software developers who wish to copyright their manuals, since it is easy to produce competing products once the ideas underlying the original package become known. Thus, even though the manuals will be copyrightable upon the developers' meeting the required statutory criteria, the formats may not be. Similarly, the audiovisual display aspects of a video game may be copyrightable whereas the idea (a crazy character that "munches" everything, for instance) behind the game (or the game per se) will ordinarily be ineligible for copyright protection.[9] The same may be true in general of flowcharts, compo-

---

[5] Scott, *Computer Law*, at 3–6. Copyright © 1984 John Wiley & Sons, Inc.
[6] 17 U.S.C. Section 101 (West 1985).
[7] Ibid. at Section 117.
[8] Ibid. at Sections 107 and 108.
[9] Scott, *Computer Law*, at 3–89–90. Copyright © 1984 John Wiley & Sons, Inc.

nents of machines, and printed circuit boards that do not have computer programs embedded in them: these are normally uncopyrightable.[10] The unsettled state of the law in this area merely complicates developers' problems.

But the case that follows represents one of the most significant recent decisions regarding the application of the copyright laws to computer software, particularly computer operating systems. Note that the opinion addresses the important issue of whether *object code,* which is not readable by people, is a "writing" within the Copyright Act's coverage and hence copyrightable or instead, given its normal use, a "method of operation" or a "system," which would be uncopyrightable.

Apple Computer, Inc. v. *Franklin Computer Corp.*
714 F.2d 1240 (3d Cir. 1983), Cert. Dismissed, 464 U.S. 1033 (1984)

Apple Computer, Inc. (Apple), filed suit against Franklin Computer Corp. (Franklin) for copyright infringement owing to Franklin's copying of fourteen of Apple's **operating system computer programs** for use with Franklin's ACE 100 personal computer. Franklin admitted it had copied Apple's programs and **ROM chips** but argued it had done so because it had not been feasible for Franklin to write its own operating system programs. Franklin also asserted that the Apple programs did not constitute copyrightable subject matter because the **object code** on which the programs relied was not a "writing" and that the programs were "processes," "systems," or "methods of operation" unprotected by law.

Were the Apple programs protected under the copyright laws?

Yes. Computer programs, whether in **source code** or in object code embedded in ROM chips, are "literary works" protected under the Copyright Act of 1976 from unauthorized copying from either their object code or source code version.

The lower court had been wrong in stating, in effect, that programs expressed in object code, as distinguished from source code, were uncopyrightable. Rather, the legislative history of the Copyright Act and recent amendments supported the conclusion that a computer program, whether in object code or source code, is a "literary work" protected from unauthorized copying from either its object or source code version. Thus, earlier holdings that a computer program in object code embedded in a ROM chip is an appropriate subject of copyright protection were reaffirmed. Franklin's contention that computer operating systems, as opposed to application programs, are nonproper subjects of the copyright laws regardless of the language or medium in which they are fixed because they are either "processes," "systems," or "methods of operation" that are per se excluded from protection under Section 102(b) of the Copyright Act was incorrect. Moreover, Franklin's concession that application programs (which generally perform a certain task for the

FACTS

Operating system computer programs
Collections of systems software programs designed to help someone else program or use a computer and which allow the computer to execute programs and manage programming tasks

ISSUE

HOLDING

REASONING

ROM chips (Read Only Memory chips)
Computer chips on which the data and information used to run computer operating systems are affixed; chips that can be "read" by a computer program but generally cannot be changed or altered

Object code Translation of source code into lower-level language, consisting of numbers and symbols that the computer interprets into electronic impulses (machine language)

---

[10] Ibid. at 3–32.

Source code Human-readable version of the program that gives instructions to the computer

computer user, such as word processing or checkbook balancing) are appropriate subjects for copyright protection was inconsistent with its position that operating system programs are not. Since both types of programs instruct the computer to do something, it therefore makes no difference whether the instructions involve directions to do a certain task or the translation of high-level language from source code to object code. The fact that the instructions are etched in a ROM chip and are used to activate the computer did not make the operating system program either a "process," "system," or "method of operation," or part of a "machine," all of which are statutorily uncopyrightable. Franklin's argument that the ROM chip is a utilitarian device whose practical usage precludes copyrightability was equally unconvincing. But Franklin's contention that a systems operating program amounts to an idea rather than the means of the expression of an idea was more persuasive. If other programs can be written or created that perform the same functions as the copyright holder's operating system program, the program is an expression of an idea and hence copyrightable. Because the lower court had made no findings as to whether some or all of Apple's operating programs represented the only means of expression of the ideas underlying them, this issue was not fit for appellate review but could be decided on remand. Since Franklin had been unable to prove its contentions that operating system programs are per se uncopyrightable, the lower court's denial of Apple's request for a preliminary injunction to stop Franklin's copying of Apple's programs was reversed.

Patents

The same provision of the Constitution that provides the basis for copyright protection furnishes the grounds for patents. Congress has the power to promote the progress of science and the useful arts by securing to inventors (rather than authors) the exclusive right to their respective discoveries (rather than writings). Today, most experts lump the terms *useful arts, inventors,* and *discoveries* with patent rights and leave the promotion of science through writings to copyright law.

Since the first patent statute in 1790, the statutory categories of patentable subject matter have consisted of (1) any process (the earlier term was *art,* but the term *process* now includes a process, art, or method); (2) machine; (3) manufacture; (4) composition of matter; and (5) any new and useful improvement thereon.[11] Neither the old law nor the significant amendments to the patent laws contemplated the inclusion of computer or program-related inventions within these classifications. As a result, by the 1960s, the Patent Office (PO) and the Court of Customs and Patent Appeals (CCPA) had drawn strict battle lines regarding the patentability of computer programs and other software. The CCPA was for it; the PO against it.[12] Although it was clear that computer programs could fill the first requirement of patentability, that is, that they could potentially arise under one of the four categories of patentable subject matter ("process" or "machine," presumably), doubts existed as to

[11] Ibid. at 4–5.
[12] Ibid. at 4–3.

whether software could fulfill the remaining four conditions of patentability: (1) utility, (2) novelty, (3) nonobviousness, and (4) adequate disclosure. Those arguing for patentability viewed computer systems consisting of both hardware and software as either a process (i.e., a method for operating a machine) or as a physical component of the hardware itself and thus protected by the "machine" requirement, with the program being one element in the overall apparatus. Other authorities, however, relegated computer software to areas lying outside patent protection by characterizing software as ideas standing alone, laws of nature, scientific truths or principles, algorithms (mathematical formulas), mental steps, printed matter, functions of a machine, and/or methods of doing business.[13] Indeed, for many years that was the fate that befell program-related invention cases, since questions arose as to whether an invention containing as one of its elements a computer program implementing such an algorithm was patentable.

Many precedents relied upon the so-called preemption test in which the PO was obliged to examine whether the patent claim on the software would wholly **preempt** the other uses of the algorithm (i.e., calculations, formulas, or equations). If so, the invention fell into one of the categories of nonstatutory subject matter and was unpatentable because the claim merely recited a mathematical algorithm. If, instead, the algorithm was but one of several steps or procedures leading to the transformation of the data into a wholly different state or thing, the invention complied with the statutory subject matter and was patentable. After several cases in the 1970s holding computer-related inventions unpatentable, the Supreme Court in the following case accepted the preemption test in holding the claim patentable.

Preempt Seize upon to the exclusion of others

Diamond v. *Diehr*
450 U.S. 175 (1981)

Diehr filed a patent application for a process for molding raw, uncured synthetic rubber into cured precision products. Diehr claimed its invention ensured the production of molded articles that were properly cured by a process that fed temperatures inside mold presses into a computer. Repeated calculations of the cure time through use of a mathematical equation enabled the computer to signal a device to open the press at the proper time. Diehr contended that this process of measuring temperatures inside the mold cavity, feeding the information to a digital computer for constant recalculation of the cure time, and the signaling by the computer to open the press were all new in the art. The patent examiner characterized Diehr's claim as being based on a computer program for operating a rubber-molding process and thus rejected it as one predicated on nonstatutory subject matter. However, the Court of Customs and Patent Appeals reversed, owing to its view that Diehr's claim

FACTS

[13] Ibid. at 4–10.

did not constitute a mathematical algorithm or an improved method of calculation but rather an improved process for molding rubber articles by solving a practical problem that had arisen in the molding of rubber products.

ISSUE

Was a process for curing synthetic rubber that included in several of its steps the use of a mathematical formula and a programmed digital computer patentable subject matter?

HOLDING

Yes. Because Diehr was not attempting to patent a mathematical formula but instead an industrial process that implemented or applied that mathematical formula as a means of transforming or reducing an article to a different state or thing, Diehr's claim constituted patentable subject matter under the Patent Act.

REASONING

Answering this issue involved construing Section 101 of the patent laws, which provides that: "Whoever invents or discovers any new and useful process, machine, manufacture, or composition of matter, or any new and useful improvement thereof, may obtain a patent therefor, subject to the conditions and requirements of this title." Earlier cases had defined a "process" as an act or series of acts performed upon the subject matter to be transformed and reduced to a different state or thing. If new and useful, these cases had declared, a process was just as patentable as a piece of machinery; and it mattered not whether the machinery suitable for performing the process was new or patentable. Therefore, industrial processes such as Diehr's were among the types that had historically been eligible to receive the protection of the patent laws. The fact that several steps of the process had used a mathematical equation and a programmed digital computer would not alter this conclusion. Even though mathematical formulas, like laws of nature, natural phenomena, and abstract ideas, are nonpatentable subject matter, Diehr had not sought to patent a mathematical formula; rather, Diehr had requested patent protection for a process of curing synthetic rubber. And, although Diehr's process had employed a well-known mathematical equation, Diehr had not endeavored to preempt (or foreclose from others) the use of that equation except in conjunction with all of the other steps in the claimed process. In addition, a claim encompassing subject matter otherwise statutory would not become nonstatutory simply because it had used a mathematical formula, computer program, or digital computer. The engrafting of Section 102's requirement of novelty and Section 103's requirement of nonobviousness onto Section 101's last phrase was unnecessary; hence, a rejection of patent protection on either of these grounds would not affect the determination of whether the invention fell into a category of protectable subject matter under Section 101. Whenever a claim containing a mathematical formula implements or applies that formula in a structure or process that, when considered as a whole, is performing a function which the patent laws were designed to protect (i.e., transforming or reducing an article to a different state or thing), then the claim satisfies Section 101. Because Diehr's claim was not an attempt to patent a mathematical formula but rather a claim involving an industrial process for the molding of rubber products, the judgment of the Court of Customs and Patent Appeals was affirmed.

Note that *Diamond* v. *Diehr* involved the question of the patentability of a computer program used as an integral part of a machine. A subsequent CCPA decision, *In re Pardo*,[14] answered the question of whether a **compiler program,** one designed to translate source code to object code, could alone constitute patentable subject matter by holding that it could.

Compiler program One that converts a high-level programming language into binary or machine code

We have already seen some of the limitations on protection of software under copyright law (only the written expression of the software and not the ideas embodied in it are protectable) and patent law (strict compliance with statutory requirements is necessary for patentability). However, various state and common law doctrines, such as trade secrets, unfair competition, and misappropriation, may apply to certain aspects of software, including know-how, information, and ideas, and thus encompass concepts too nebulous for copyright or patent protection. These doctrines may also cover computer hardware, as well.

Trade Secrets

According to the *Restatement (First) of Torts,* Section 757, Comment (b), a trade secret may include:

> any formula, pattern, device or compilation of information which is used in one's business, and which gives [one] an opportunity to obtain an advantage over competitors who do not know or use it. The subject matter of a trade secret must be secret . . . so that, except by the use of improper means, there would be difficulty in acquiring the information. In determining whether given information is a trade secret courts generally consider:

1. The extent to which the information is known outside the owner's business
2. The extent to which it is known by employees and others involved in the business
3. The extent of measures taken by the owner to guard the secrecy of the information
4. The value of the information to the owner and to its competitors
5. The amount of effort or money expended by the owner in developing the information
6. The ease or difficulty with which the information could be properly acquired or duplicated by others.

The owner of software who decides to resort to trade secret protection may find it advantageous, since it avoids the public registration required to devise and enforce rights under the patent and copyright laws.[15] However, because maintaining the secrecy of the proprietary information in question may be difficult and because lack of secrecy constitutes one of the primary defenses to

[14] 684 F.2d 912 (CCPA 1982).
[15] The Kewanee Oil Co. v. Bicron Corp. case, 416 U.S. 470 (1974), held that federal patent laws do not preempt state trade secret laws.

a charge of trade secret misappropriation, the owner of the trade secret should implement various mechanisms to ensure secrecy. Actions that employers can take to protect trade secrets about software (or hardware) include the creation of nondisclosure, noncompete, and confidentiality agreements with employees. Employers should also limit physical access to areas where the development of **proprietary** software is taking place as well as to storage areas. All software and documents containing trade secrets should bear proprietary labels, and the software should use **encrypted code** so that only those who have the key for unscrambling it can make the program intelligible. Constant reminders to employees about secrecy obligations and exit interviews with departing employees as to the information the company considers proprietary constitute recommended policies for employers intent on ensuring secrecy as well.

Proprietary Characterized by private, exclusive ownership

Encrypted code Code typed in one set of symbols and interpreted by the machine as another; used for security

The licensing of software mandates special steps by the owner of the software in order to preserve secrecy. Besides restricting disclosures by the licensee, the licensor/owner should limit the rights the licensee retains in the software by virtue of the license, prohibit copying except for use or archival purposes, formulate special coding techniques to identify misappropriated software, distribute the software in object code as opposed to source code, and stipulate that the breach of any confidentiality provision will result in the immediate termination of the licensing agreement.

Courts in fact base trade secret protection on several theories — property, contract, and tort — although courts prefer to utilize the latter two in deciding disputes about computer software. (Indeed, courts often apply the two theories interchangeably.) It is easier for a court to discern a relationship between the owner of the trade secret and the person or entity using or disclosing the trade secret than it is for a court to ascribe property concepts to the trade secret owing to the difficulty of determining where general information (which is unprotectable) leaves off and proprietary information in the form of the trade secret (which is protectable) begins. Courts often derive these relationships impliedly from the parties' status as employer/employee, vendor/buyer, and the like. However, the parties cannot enjoy a confidential relationship unless a protectable trade secret first exists. Once it does, though, the trade secret may last perpetually until the owner loses the differential advantage it affords. This loss may occur through another party's independent discovery of the secret or any other legitimate means, such as reverse engineering or the public dissemination of the knowledge underlying the trade secret through either a failure to keep the information secret or flaws in the methods the owner has employed to ensure secrecy. Mass distribution of software copies to those with whom the software owner has a confidential relationship generally does not eliminate trade secret protection as long as the owner has otherwise taken precautions to preserve secrecy.

Unfair Competition

Although our system of law allows rather free-wheeling activities under the rubric of "competition," some conduct goes so far beyond the pale that courts will give remedies to those injured by such activities as soliciting a former employer's customers or employees, an employee's competing with his or her employer while still in the employ of the latter, wrongful terminations by the employer, and "palming off" one's goods as those of another.[16] The common law and statutory restrictions on "unfair competition" oftentimes form the legal bases upon which aggrieved persons sue in these circumstances. Misappropriation, another basis for relief, derives from the common law principles of unfair competition and often becomes a "catch-all" theory used in situations in which patent, copyright, and trade secret law do not cover the aspect of the business in dispute. In the context of computer software, then, courts may find actionable misappropriation if the plaintiff has invested substantial amounts of time and money in developing the software (that is, a property interest is present) and the defendant has appropriated the software with a minimum of effort and expense to the injury of the plaintiff. Courts are sensitive to the time and effort necessary to develop software systems and, thus, during litigation (under the so-called head start doctrine) sometimes issue injunctions against a competitor's use of the software for at least the time it would have taken the competitor to develop the software independently.

However, this area of the law remains unsettled because of the ambiguities arising from fairly recent Supreme Court holdings and the 1976 Copyright Act. Under the so-called *Sears-Compco* doctrine,[17] even though the states retain an interest in preventing their citizens from being misled as to the source of the goods, state unfair competition laws cannot impose liability for, or prohibit the copying of, unpatented or uncopyrighted items. Thus, in certain cases federal law preempts state law claims based on unfair competition doctrines. But these decisions leave us with scant guidance as to when this preemption occurs. Similarly, the 1976 Copyright Act provides for the preemption of state law whenever state law creates legal or equitable rights that are equivalent to any of the exclusive rights enumerated under certain provisions of the Act.[18] Yet courts are split on the issue of when to apply the preemption doctrine in cases of alleged unfair competition and misappropriation. Caution is therefore warranted in these areas.

Congress's enactment of the Semiconductor Chip Protection Act of 1984, which took effect on 8 January 1985,[19] as an amendment to the copyright laws, affords developers of integrated circuits a ten-year monopoly over their resultant semiconductor chips. Although it contains ideas common to copyright, patent, and trade secret law, this Act creates a new class of intellectual property law. Congress directed the legislation at chip pirates (both domestic and international), who in the past had merely taken chips apart, had reconstructed the circuit design on the chip (known as the mask), and then made

The Semiconductor Chip Protection Act of 1984

---

[16] Scott, *Computer Law,* at 5–26–27. Copyright © 1984 John Wiley & Sons, Inc.

[17] Sears, Roebuck & Co. v. Stiffel Co., 376 U.S. 225 (1964); Compco Corporation v. Day-Brite Lighting, Inc., 376 U.S. 234 (1964).

[18] 17 U.S.C. Section 301 (West 1985).

[19] Ibid. at Section 913(a).

copies of the original chip. Obviously, as long as copyright law did not protect semiconductor chips (they were deemed utilitarian articles and hence uncopyrightable even though the circuit diagrams might be), the incentive for pirates to reap profits by copying while at the same time avoiding the mammoth costs associated with developing the chips clearly existed. The Act eliminates this result by prohibiting reverse engineering that has as its end purpose the copying of the chip but preserves current law by allowing reverse engineering leading to the creation of a new chip.[20] The Act itself protects only mask works, or the layouts of the integrated circuits that appear on the chips; it does not protect the semiconductor chips themselves; any other product that performs the function of chips (such as circuit boards); or works embodied in mask works (such as computer programs).[21] Indeed, not all mask works are protected, either. For instance, if the mask work is not "fixed" in a semiconductor chip (as would be the case in information merely stored on diskettes) or if, analogous to the patent law's requirements of novelty and nonobviousness, the mask work embodies designs that are commonplace and not original, no protection exists.[22] The duration of the protection is ten years from the time of registration or the first commercial exploitation of the mask work, whichever occurs first.[23] The process of registration contains special procedures for protecting proprietary information. The same remedies generally available under the copyright laws relating to infringement (injunctions, damages, attorneys' fees, and import exclusion and seizure) apply in this context, except criminal sanctions are unavailable.[24] Some provisions of the Act protect the mask works of nonpirating foreign companies under certain circumstances, as well. Although interpretive questions will undoubtedly arise as the first cases begin to appear under this Act, you should particularly note this statute because it represents the first federal intellectual property law in over one hundred years.

CONTRACT LAW

General Considerations

Boilerplate Standard contract language found in all instruments of a like nature

Since the law of contracts concerning computers should theoretically vary little from contracting for any other kind of equipment or goods, you should be fairly familiar with this dimension of computer law from our discussions in Parts II and III of this text. In practice, however, computer-related contract law encompasses some pitfalls not common to the rest of contract law owing to the technology, the structure of the computer industry, and the relationship between the vendor and the purchaser. For instance, vendors of computers especially benefit from the **boilerplate** phrases you have encountered in our earlier examination of contract principles because the wide array of main-

---

[20] Ibid. at Section 906.

[21] Scott, *Computer Law*, at 12–9. Copyright © 1984 John Wiley & Sons, Inc.

[22] Ibid. at 12–10.

[23] 17 U.S.C. Section 904(a), (b) (West 1985).

[24] Ibid. at Sections 910 and 911. The Act also contains a statutory damages provision (the amount awarded cannot exceed more than $250,000) as an alternative to a lawsuit for actual damages.

frames, minis, and micros — not to mention the numerous peripherals — may overwhelm even the bravest soul among us. Choosing a computer, as you well know, can be a very intimidating experience. Hence, when the sales representative presents you with a preprinted standard form contract containing confusing and ambiguous jargon, you may lack the knowledge and familiarity with computers to enable you to question or interpret its provisions. Moreover, since the relationship between the vendor and buyer presupposes continuity (in that the vendor typically assumes the responsibility for the ongoing maintenance of the hardware and software), adding to the buyer's worries is the fact that the vendor may go out of business in the future and thus fail to provide the maintenance responsibilities contemplated in their initial agreement. To use the jargon of the industry, the "shakeouts" that have caused major companies (including Xerox, General Electric, and RCA), as well as numerous other producers of mainframes, micros, minis, and personal computers to leave the industry, reinforce the validity of these types of apprehensions. And, in some cases, the buyer's virtual dependence on the computer for the firm's survival as a business places even more of a burden on the purchaser, since a series of computer malfunctions (or "system crashes") may lead eventually to the firm's bankruptcy and dissolution. Thus, we cannot reemphasize enough the importance of understanding in advance your firm's (or your personal) current and future data processing needs.

If the purchase of a system is afoot, senior executive and technical people (or a hired consultant), in addition to an attorney who has experience in computer contracts, should spearhead this effort by ascertaining such information as the computer's slowest acceptable response time, the highest number of customers for the next ten years, or the largest number of pages of information needed within any twenty-four hour period of time. Once the buyer has defined the minimum and maximum requirements of the system, ordinarily the buyer sends requests for proposals to potential vendors. Negotiations — sometimes long and drawn-out — usually follow. If the parties can reach agreement on these and other issues, the vendor and buyer then enter into a contract reflecting those terms and the schedule for implementing the contract. In addition to price and the items and services the vendor must provide, including hardware, software, and maintenance, the contract should list the payment schedule (with the final payment's being contingent upon the system's being properly installed, thoroughly tested, and fully operational); the functional specifications of the system's elements; a timetable for each aspect of the system mentioned in the contract (including remedies for failure to live up to the timetable); acceptable testing procedures for each element of the system; and general remedies covering each party's failure to perform completely all of the steps enumerated in the contract. Once the contract embodies the phases contemplated by the parties, the contract itself becomes the document to which the parties (especially the buyer) can resort for guidance during the implementation phase. Lastly, the contract should set out the terms of the parties' relationship during the post-acceptance portion of the contract. This is reached when the system is up and functioning in accordance with the contractual provisions but during which the buyer's use may necessitate maintenance or other support services by the vendor. One who plans to lease rather than purchase the system should take into account the foregoing general considerations and in addition bear in mind the contract's assignment provisions; the existence of "hell or high water" clauses (those stating that the vendor or lessor's default will not release the buyer or lessee from its unconditional obligation to pay according to the terms of the contract); and terms relating to maintenance and return condition; taxes, loss, and insurance responsibilities; purchase options; and so forth.[25]

The Uniform Commercial Code

As we saw in Part 3 of this text, the Uniform Commercial Code (UCC) in Article Two applies to transactions in goods. Generally, this means sales of goods, or "all things (including specially manufactured goods) which are movable at the time of identification to the contract for sale."[26] Computer hardware is clearly a type of goods. This remains true even though the transactions relating to hardware may also involve the provision of services, such as installation, training, and maintenance. As long as the "goods" component of the transaction predominates over the "services" aspect, most courts allow the Code to cover the transaction. The law is not as clear, however, with regard to software, since software ordinarily involves both tangible property (the medium upon which the software is stored) and the previously mentioned services. In this case, courts make distinctions based on the types of software: bundled (whether prewritten or custom) and unbundled. Bundled software refers to the practice of selling computer hardware, software, and support services for one price. (Bundling, because it may violate the antitrust laws in that buyers or lessees who do not want certain components of the bundling must nonetheless pay the full price, is not as common as it once was). Courts also split on whether Article Two of the Code covers leases of equipment and software licenses, but in general courts will more readily apply Article Two in the former context than in the latter. The warranty provisions of the Code involving express warranties and the implied warranty of merchantability ordinarily apply to computer hardware and software. The implied warranty of fitness for a particular purpose, which usually involves the buyer's reliance on the seller to furnish or select suitable goods and the seller's knowledge of the buyer's particular purpose, may in a given case be especially relevant to transactions involving hardware and software. Although the UCC permits the exclusion of warranties in certain circumstances, courts are sometimes hostile to these attempted exclusions. Thus, both vendor and buyer should check carefully any purported warranty disclaimers. "Shrink-wrap" or "box-top" licenses, through which vendors attempt to limit the further distribution of their software sold in retail stores by placing a copy of the licensing agreement

---

25 Scott, *Computer Law,* at 6–17. Copyright © 1984 John Wiley & Sons, Inc.
26 Uniform Commercial Code, Section 2–105.

inside the package, pose similar problems of enforceability for vendors, since courts may deem these agreements adhesion contracts because of the lack of any meaningful bargaining power on the purchaser's part.

Buyers may also utilize the remedies sections of the UCC, namely rejection and revocation of acceptance, for example; and upon breach of the contract (by the vendor's negligent performance or complete nonperformance of the contract) may sue the vendor for damages, including incidental and consequential damages if warranted by the circumstances. Vendors may in general limit these remedies by contract unless a court subsequently construes the limitation as unconscionable or the remedy fails of its essential purpose. Nonetheless, reasonable liquidated damages clauses, whereby the parties agree in advance that upon breach a certain sum of money will be paid to the injured party, seem particularly inappropriate in computer contracts because losses accruing from late delivery, nondelivery, or malfunctions involve damages that are by definition difficult to determine with certainty beforehand. Courts may also order specific performance, injunctive relief, restitution, rescission, and replevin in a given case.

TORT LAW

Although there are comparatively few cases involving tort law in the computer field, as we learned in Chapter 3, tort law can form the basis for civil (as opposed to criminal) liability. Vendors of computers, then, may become the objects of lawsuits alleging negligence, intentional torts (such as conversion, defamation, fraud, and invasion of privacy), and strict liability. Defective hardware or improperly designed software, one's negligent use of a computer in circumstances in which a third party relies on computer-generated data and as a result suffers losses, and negligent nonuse of a computer in such areas as air or railroad traffic control, stock trading, and hospital care may lead to liability as well if losses ensue. Thus, failure to acquire sufficient insurance coverage based on an appraisal that used computer-generated, incorrect data may lead to the imposition of liability for damages incurred as a result of the failure to act. But whether computer programmers are professionals and thus potentially liable under malpractice theories remains an open question.

However, the law is clearer in other contexts. For example, computer salespersons must be careful not to become overly zealous in their representations about the system's capabilities because such statements, coupled with the seller's knowledge that the statements are false and the buyer's justifiable reliance on the representations to his or her detriment, may leave the vendor open to liability under fraud. The damages courts have awarded in fraud cases have even included punitive damages. The intentional tort of conversion occurs whenever former employees appropriate computer programs owned by their former employers. Similarly, court actions involving defamation can possibly derive from computer messages displayed on terminals and perhaps even from mathematical configurations as long as their defamatory content is discernible and no privilege covers the generation of the information. Credit reporting agencies should accordingly take special care in this context.

In addition to such intentional torts, defectively manufactured computer equipment may give rise to strict liability as well. The health care profession's increasing reliance on sophisticated computerized equipment exposes both the profession and the manufacturer to liability if, for instance, a CAT scanner or intensive-care monitoring equipment should malfunction. The imposition of strict liability in situations involving only economic harm as opposed to personal injury may be more questionable, however.

STATUTORY PROTECTION

The common law theories that we have just examined are fully applicable to computers and have enriched the legal environment of this important industry. But legislative enactments relating to privacy, antitrust, and criminal law represent an increasingly significant source of law for this area, as well.

Invasion of Privacy

Invasion of privacy, although it may give rise to liability under intentional tort common law theories, is more appropriately discussed in the statutory context. But even though numerous statutes concern themselves with this subject nowadays, the concept of privacy, jealously guarded by each of us individually, has evolved slowly in the law. Indeed, the Constitution does not even mention the term. The Supreme Court did not recognize the concept until the mid-sixties, but since that time Congress has enacted several significant privacy laws that affect not only us as citizens but also the computer industry. These statutes include: the Freedom of Information Act (which, with some exceptions, opens up federal governmental records to public inspection); the Fair Credit Reporting Act of 1970 (which regulates the information practices of consumer reporting agencies like credit bureaus and the practices of those who use these reports); the Family Educational Rights and Privacy Act of 1974 (which affords parents of dependent students and students over eighteen the right to inspect, correct, and control somewhat the disclosure of information in educational records); the Privacy Act of 1974 (which assures informational privacy in computerized record-keeping systems by agencies of the executive branch, independent regulatory agencies, and the Federal Reserve Bank and provides remedies for violations including injunctive relief, damages, and attorneys' fees as well as criminal sanctions); the Right to Financial Privacy Act of 1978 (which specifies the circumstances in which the government, including the Internal Revenue Service, can gain access to individuals and partnerships' financial records and sets out the civil remedies available against violators); and the Electronic Fund Transfer Act of 1978 (which regulates the rights, liabilities, and responsibilities of participants in electronic fund transfer systems in order to promote individual consumers' rights and makes available civil and criminal remedies for violations).[27] These laws attempt to balance

----

[27] Scott, *Computer Law*, at 7–39–43; 48–50. Copyright © 1984 John Wiley & Sons, Inc.

individuals' rights to privacy with government's and other institutions' legitimate needs to collect and maintain information about people by guaranteeing to these individuals the right to know how other entities are using information about them and by protecting the individual from unwarranted or excessive collection or dissemination of personal information. And although it has always been difficult to safeguard privacy, the pervasity of high-speed, low-cost computers in business and homes has elevated computer-related privacy violations to a national concern.

Intrusion, whether by unauthorized access to a data base contained on one's computer, unwanted collection of data on one's personal habits or lifestyle, or unauthorized removal of data from a computer, either electronically or manually (through the removal of the software containing the data from the system itself), is one type of violation. The emergence of "hackers" or "electronic vandals" who engage in such activities for amusement has occupied the public press's attention for the last few years. Besides intrusion, interception of information consisting of unauthorized access by an employee or other person at the computer site, unauthorized access from a different location through a remote terminal, or monitoring and interception of information flowing between computers raises additional privacy issues. Finally, the existence of large aggregations of information in the form of tax, credit, military, medical, employment, and governmental records (such as census tracts and vital statistics) leaves open the possible misuse of information. In this context, you may have already experienced the annoyances that result when a group to which you belong sells your name and address to another entity. As we have already seen in the coverage of specific statutes, a corollary of this potential problem of misuse is the individual's right to be informed of the content of the information being maintained about him or her, who has access to it, and the right to correct erroneous information contained in the data files. This aspect of privacy also covers the right of the individual to demand that certain information (say credit ratings) be included in these records to facilitate the individual's daily affairs. Because the technology itself makes such storage and retrieval of information speedy and relatively cheap and because existing technology allows the storage of a twenty-page dossier on every American on a magnetic tape less than a mile long, the safeguards mentioned earlier of limiting access to these data and assuring mechanisms to correct erroneous information and to eliminate "stale" information become all the more significant.

Antitrust Law

Besides privacy statutes, the federal and state antitrust statutes we examined in Chapter 46 may also cover the activities of firms in the computer field. For instance, the Sherman Act prohibits price-fixing, group boycotts, monopolization, tying arrangements, and certain wrongful terminations of distributors. The Clayton Act augments this extensive federal regulatory scheme by also prohibiting tie-ins and certain exclusive dealing arrangements as well as mergers that would substantially lessen competition or tend to create a monopoly. Bundling, or the practice of selling a number of products or services for a single price, may raise antitrust concerns if courts construe the practice as an illegal tying arrangement. To constitute such an arrangement there must be two separate and distinct products, and the seller must condition the sale of the desired product (the tying product) on the purchase of the less desirable product (the tied product). Generally, before courts will find violations of the antitrust laws, the seller must wield sufficient economic power in the market for the tying product to restrain competition appreciably in the market for the tied product and the seller's activities must affect a not insubstantial amount of commerce in that market. The Robinson-Patman Act prohibits price discrimination unless the price differential is cost-justified or made in good faith to meet (but not beat) the price offered by a competitor. Similarly, the Federal Trade Commission Act makes illegal unfair methods of competition and unfair or deceptive trade practices in or affecting interstate commerce. The Supreme Court's recent sanctioning of the application of the Racketeer Influenced and Corrupt Organizations (RICO) Act in the civil law context holds wide-ranging implications for the possible imposition of liability in computer-related fields if, for example, a sales representative uses the mail or a telephone to engage in fraudulent representations about computer products.

The following case illustrates some of these points.

Digidyne Corporation v. Data General Corporation
734 F.2d 1336 (9th Cir. 1984)
Rehearing Denied 473 U.S. 926 (1985)

FACTS

Central processing units
The main units of the computer hardware that control the interpretation and execution of program instructions, including memory

Data General Corporation (Data General) manufactured a computer system known as NOVA, consisting of NOVA **central processing units** (CPUs) designed to perform a particular "instruction set" or group of tasks and a copyrighted NOVA operating system called RDOS containing the basic commands for operating the system. Digidyne Corporation (Digidyne) produced NOVA CPUs designed to perform the NOVA instruction set and thus to make use of Data General's RDOS.

ISSUE

Did Data General's refusal to license its NOVA operating system software except to purchasers of its NOVA CPUs constitute an unlawful tying arrangement under Section One of the Sherman Act and Section Three of the Clayton Act?

HOLDING

Yes. Data General's copyright, its reliance on trade secrecy, and its policies gave it sufficient economic power over NOVA purchasers to constitute an illegal tie-in.

REASONING

The settled rule is that a tying arrangement is illegal if it unreasonably restrains competition or is illegal per se without the showing of an unreasonable restraint on competition if: (1) the arrangement involves separate products and the purchase of the other (the tied product); (2) sufficient economic power with respect to the tying product to restrain competition appreciably in the tied product exists; and (3) the arrangement affects a substantial amount of commerce in the tied product. The evidence was persuasive, therefore, that Digidyne had proved a per se violation in this case. Moreover, proof of the seller's power to fix prices was not required to show per se illegality. Rather, what was required was the seller's special ability — usually called *market power* or *leverage* — to force a purchaser to do something it would not do in a competitive market. This need not consist of a restraint on competition that is substantial in terms of the entire market for the tied product but instead only that a substantial amount of volume (a dollar-volume that is not merely *de minimis*) is foreclosed. Here, there was abundant evidence showing that Data General's RDOS was distinctive, particularly desirable to a number of buyers, and not readily reproducible by other sellers. The fact that the RDOS could not be produced without infringing Data General's copyright and utilizing Data General's trade secrets had satisfied the rule that the requisite economic power would be presumed when the tying product is patented or copyrighted. The fact that many of Data General's customers were also "locked into" the use of RDOS, since, as **original equipment manufacturers (OEMs)** they had combined RDOS and NOVA CPUs with their application software and thus could abandon their application software that was compatible with Data General's RDOS only at a substantial cost, had magnified Data General's leverage power. Data General's potential power to coerce had also been evident from its requiring all licensees either to purchase its CPUs and a set antity of other peripheral hardware as a condition of receiving RDOS or to pay a program license charge, which was in the nature of a penalty. Hence, despite the availability of comparable or functionally equivalent operating systems, Data General's RDOS, which was available only from the defendant, had been sufficiently attractive to some customers to enable the defendant to require those who had wished to buy it also to buy from Data General NOVA instruction set CPUs they might otherwise have bought from others. Accordingly, this power had constituted evidence of an illegal tying arrangement under the Sherman and Clayton Acts.

Original equipment manufacturers (OEMs)
A misnomer referring to vendors who assemble computer systems from components originally manufactured by other suppliers

Criminal Law

The criminal law also addresses computer-related crimes. For the imposition of criminal liability, the state or federal government must prove criminal intent and an act that violates a statute. In the late 1970s, as the first cases involving computer-related crimes arose, the coverage of many state laws failed to encompass such things as theft of computer time or services because the statutes in question applied only to the theft of tangible, not intangible, property. Another limitation on the imposition of liability flowed from many statutes' requirement that the theft involve something worth a particular dollar value. Consequently, it was difficult to say whether a given computer theft involved only the value of the paper (which would in most states amount only to a misdemeanor) or instead the value of the intellectual property represented in the paper (which would sometimes amount to a felony whenever certain computer programs worth millions of dollars were involved). Nowadays, federal statutes and statutes in about three-fifths of the states address these issues in making theft of computer time and services actionable under the criminal law.

Unauthorized access by use of false pretenses or wiretapping for the purpose of committing criminal acts such as embezzlement constitute illegal

Fictitious payee A recipient of payments who has no right to the payments

acts in most jurisdictions. Similarly, instances of so-called data diddling, or the introduction of fraudulent data into a computer system for criminal purposes such as payments to a **fictitious payee** or through vandalism, as demonstrated by recent cases in which teenage "hackers" have invaded corporate and military files, violate criminal statutes. Crimes involving programming have spawned a variety of colorful names to describe the scams — "the Trojan Horse" (alteration of instructions in the program prior to the program's execution so that instructions self-destruct upon the program's execution); "the logic bomb" (an addition to a computer system timed to be executed at a scheduled moment to effect transfer of funds or to sabotage systems by erasing tapes or crashing the system); "the trapdoor" (compromises of a system effected by unauthorized access to passwords or the like); and "the salami technique" (hard-to-detect theft accomplished by "small slices," for example, by rounding down interest in accounts by minuscule amounts and depositing these amounts in the account of the perpetrator).[28] Many of these so-called computer "viruses" that can erase, alter, or destroy data and software have "infected" national research and business computer networks in recent years. Computer experts are currently working hard to develop failsafe "antidotes" for these "outbreaks." Estimates of the cost of computer crime range from $100 million to $3 billion per year.[29] The physical destruction of data by disgruntled employees, political protestors, or terrorists, though usually covered by existing vandalism statutes, has resulted in the enactment of special statutes in many jurisdictions. The Counterfeit Access Device and Computer Fraud and Abuse Act of 12 October 1984 in addition establishes criminal liability for unauthorized access to or use of a computer to obtain national security information or financial information protected by the Right to Financial Privacy Act or the Fair Credit Reporting Act. This law also criminalizes conduct used to modify or destroy information in or otherwise affect government computers or their operations. Although this enactment represents the first federal crime law dealing solely with computers per se, you should recall that numerous federal statutes, in addition to specific state laws covering computer-related crimes, apply directly or indirectly to these sorts of activities.

CONSTITU-TIONAL LAW

You may remember that we discussed some of the constitutional aspects of the regulation of business in Chapter 45. As of this time, however, the constitutional law dimensions of computers has received only slight attention. Nonetheless, you should be aware that the electronic publishing aspects of computer-related technologies (teletext and videotext systems, for example) raise not only privacy concerns of the type we examined earlier but also First Amendment issues. Should we regulate these systems as we would any other

---

[28] Ibid. at 8–10–11.

[29] Bureau of Justice, U.S. Department of Justice, *Computer Crime: Electronic Fund Transfer Systems and Crime* (Washington, D.C.: U.S. Government Printing Office, 1982), p. 83.

communications medium like television, or should we instead analogize these systems to newspapers, which we have traditionally exempted from governmental regulation?

Besides the First Amendment, the Fourth Amendment may apply to the computer industry as well. Although some precedents already exist, courts in the future will undoubtedly continue to grapple with such issues as whether the Fourth Amendment protects computer records from unreasonable searches and seizures and whether it is possible to base warrants on the strength of computer-generated (as opposed to personal) information. In addition, they will also need to decide the specificity of detail required for the lawful search of a computer or facilities containing computerized records and the evidentiary issues that underlie these types of records (e.g., does the Fourth Amendment permit law enforcement officers to use civilian computer experts to facilitate such searches?).

The Due Process Clause may protect those who have been deprived of property, for example, as a result of computer-generated shut-off notices and the subsequent shut-offs of utilities. The same may be true of persons deprived of governmental benefits by computer-generated erroneous information without the persons' having an opportunity to correct the records that formed the basis for the adverse decisions.

SUMMARY

The pervasity of the influence of computers in our lives conjures up a whole host of economic and noneconomic issues as well as legal questions. Despite early doubts about the copyrightability of computer programs, these programs merit copyright protection today. No infringement of the copyright laws occurs when the copy is made for use with a machine or for archival purposes. Moreover, computer-related programs can be patentable as long as the claim does more than merely recite a mathematical algorithm; it must instead use an algorithm (or a mathematical formula) as one of the steps leading to the transformation of the data into a wholly different state or thing. Various state and common law doctrines, such as trade secrets, unfair competition, and misappropriation may apply to certain aspects of software and form the basis for protecting the owner's interest in the software in circumstances in which copyright or patent protection would be unavailable. The Semiconductor Chip Protection Act of 1984 protects most mask works, or the layouts of the integrated circuits embedded on the chips, for a period of ten years. The only new intellectual property law in over one hundred years, this Act should reduce the incidence of domestic and international chip piracy. Computer-related contract law encompasses some pitfalls not common to contract law in general owing to the technology, the structure of the industry, and the special relationship between the vendor and the purchaser. The Uniform Commercial Code applies to the sale of computer hardware and may cover the sale of software, as well. Vendors' attempts to exclude warranties and to force "shrink-wrap" licenses on buyers may be legally unenforceable. Tort law may also apply to computer-related transactions. Various statutes exist to protect the individual from invasions of privacy that may occur from the collection and maintenance of computer data. Furthermore, federal and state antitrust laws may cover the activities of firms in the computer field as well. Illegal tying arrangements represent one common type of antitrust violation in this area. Various state and federal laws address the problem of computer-related crimes. The constitutional law dimensions of computers will merit increased attention in the future as computer technology becomes even more pervasive in our daily lives.

DISCUSSION QUESTIONS

1. Discuss some of the economic and noneconomic issues computers pose.
2. In what two circumstances will the copying of computer programs be statutorily exempt from claims of copyright infringement?
3. What were the bases for the early doubts about the patentability of computer programs?
4. List five steps the owners of trade secrets can take to ensure secrecy.
5. Discuss some of the special concerns that underlie the contracting process for computers.
6. What are software "shrink-wrap" or "box-top" licenses? Are they enforceable against the buyers of such software?
7. Name at least three methods by which computers can be used to invade one's privacy.
8. Explain how an illegal tying arrangement may crop up in the sale of computers and related software.
9. What were the early limitations on the law's ability to impose liability for computer-related crimes?
10. Briefly discuss the constitutional dimensions of computer law.

CASE PROBLEMS

1. Michael McGraw worked for the City of Indianapolis as a computer operator. Because the City leased computer services on a fixed charge or flat rate basis, the expense to it was not dependent on use. The City provided McGraw with a terminal at his desk and assigned a portion of the computer's information storage capacity, called a "private library," for his utilization in performing his duties. McGraw, when hired, had received a handbook that spelled out the general prohibition against the unauthorized use of City property. Although other City employees sometimes used the computer for personal convenience, unbeknownst to the City, McGraw began a business venture and used the City's computer to store his personal business records. After his supervisor became aware of his unauthorized activities and reprimanded him several times, McGraw was

discharged for unsatisfactory job performance. However, McGraw's use of the computer had not been cited as a basis for this discharge. Following his discharge, McGraw asked a former co-worker to secure for him a "print-out" of his business data and to erase them from McGraw's library. The coworker instead turned the "print-out" over to McGraw's former supervisor. As a result, McGraw was subsequently charged with theft under the criminal law. In Indiana, the statutory elements of theft include the unauthorized control over another's property with the intent to deprive the other of any part of its value or use. Had McGraw, by his unauthorized use of the City's computer, intended to deprive the City of any part of its value or use? (*State* v. *McGraw*, 480 N.E.2d 552 [Ind. 1985].)

2. Kevin Martin was a passenger in a car that had been driven through a red light. When the driver was arrested, Martin was asked for identification and thereupon gave his driver's license to the arresting officer. A computer check on the license revealed an outstanding Alabama warrant for Martin's arrest. Based on this warrant, the officer arrested Martin and searched him. This search subsequently revealed a brown pouch containing heroin. There was actually no outstanding warrant on Martin, as he had served time in Alabama and had been released some months earlier. However, the computer records had not been corrected until the day after Martin's arrest. Was Martin's arrest invalid because it was based on erroneous computer information? (*Martin* v. *State*, 424 So.2d 994 [Fla. App. 1983].)

3. Abele had made improvements to existing computerized axial tomography, or CAT scans, by reducing the exposure to x-rays while enhancing the reliability of the images produced. Abele admitted that his application had used algorithms, or mathematical calculations, but only after an x-ray beam produced by a CAT scan had passed through an object and had been detected upon its exit. After these data-gathering steps had occurred, the mathematical algorithm portion of the invention (a computer) was used to obtain data that were then displayed on a television screen for diagnostic purposes. Did Abele's application constitute patentable subject matter? (*In re Abele*, 684 F.2d 902 [C.C.P.A. 1982].)

4. During 1973–1974, Bernard Tureen had a health insurance policy with the All-American Insurance Company (All-American). In those years, Tureen had two heart attacks and made disability claims against All-American for benefits. All-American hired Equifax, Inc. (Equifax), a consumer reports firm that investigates and provides information to employers, insurers, and merchants for their use in decision making, to investigate Tureen's claims. Equifax searched its own files and reported to All-American that Tureen had applied for insurance twenty-three times since 1949. All-American retained this report in its claims department and did not disseminate its contents to anyone else. Tureen sued Equifax for invasion of privacy on the basis of the investigative report and the

statements about his past insurance history. Had Equifax, by collecting and retaining Tureen's past insurance history, commited this tort? (*Tureen* v. *Equifax, Inc.*, 571 F.2d 411 [8th Cir. 1978].)

5. Atari, Inc. (Atari), sued JS&A Group, Inc. (JS&A), for copyright infringement. JS&A, a retailer of electronic products, had marketed "PROM BLASTER," a device used for duplication of those video games that were compatible with the Atari 2600 home computer, such as PAC-MAN and CENTIPEDE. JS&A had also marketed nine games of its own. Because JS&A had urged consumers to protect their investments in video game cartridges by making copies in case the cartridges were ruined, JS&A argued that the copying was permissible archival copying. Atari, however, characterized JS&A's actions as actively inducing the making of infringing copies of Atari's copyrighted home video games without any other substantial noninfringing use. Was Atari correct? (*Atari, Inc.* v. *JS&A Group, Inc.*, 597 F. Supp. 5 [E.D. Ill. 1983].)

6. AccuSystems, Inc. (AccuSystems), and its sole shareholder William Selden sued Honeywell Information Systems, Inc. (Honeywell), for fraud arising out of the sale of computer hardware and software to AccuSystems. Beard, a Honeywell salesperson, had made a visit to Selden's former employer's payroll processing operations and had told Selden that Honeywell's TL-6 system would be better-suited to the firm's business, as it could handle thirty-two terminals on line. Beard had also stated that the TL-6 system had been extensively tested and furnished to other locations where it was working well. When Selden shortly thereafter formed AccuSystems, he bought a TL-6 system. Unfortunately, following installation, AccuSystems experienced serious difficulties with the TL-6 system: it failed when more than three terminals were in operation, and it could only process simple programs. The evidence revealed that AccuSystems had been the first installation site for the TL-6 system, and no testing of the system had been undertaken until a year after AccuSystems's purchases. Could AccuSystems prove fraud in these circumstances? (*AccuSystems, Inc.* v. *Honeywell Information Systems, Inc.*, 580 F. Supp. 474 [S.D. N.Y. 1984].)

7. Convoy Company (Convoy) entered into a contract with a firm named WOFAC whereby WOFAC agreed to design a computerized load makeup and rerouting system for use in Convoy's motor vehicle transport business. Convoy then entered into a second contract with Univac (Sperry Rand Corporation) for the computer hardware to be used with WOFAC's software. Because the system never functioned properly, Convoy sued WOFAC for $516,129.09 in actual damages and more than $1,000,000 in lost profits and punitive damages. After Convoy settled with WOFAC for $354,500, Convoy then sued Univac for $216,398.61 in actual damages. The trial judge reentered judgment for Convoy against Univac for that amount, which included the electronic data processing staff and salaried supervisory staff costs associated with the unsatisfactory computer sys-

tem. Were these costs recoverable as damages? (*Convoy Company* v. *Sperry Rand Corporation,* 601 F.2d 385 [9th Cir. 1979], modified in part 672 F.2d 781 [9th Cir. 1982].)

8. Apple Computer, Inc. (Apple), manufactures small computers that it markets through a network of independent local outlets. Apple banned mail order sales of computers to ensure the proper support for the buyer after the sale. Apple contended that only through face-to-face transactions would its retail dealers be able to assess the needs of prospective purchasers, assemble the particular packages to meet those needs, supply hands-on instruction and training, and follow up on any servicing needs. Apple also meant its policy as protection of its dealers against the profit erosion caused by "free-riding" mail order dealers. O.S.C. Corporation (O.S.C.), one of the authorized dealers Apple had terminated owing to O.S.C.'s violation of the ban, sued Apple for alleged antitrust violations. Should a court find in O.S.C.'s favor? (*O.S.C. Corporation* v. *Apple Computer, Inc.,* 792 F.2d 1464 [9th Cir. 1986].)

9. Triangle Underwriters, Inc. (Triangle), sued Honeywell, Inc. (Honeywell), under contract and tort theories (specifically fraud) after the turn-key system (one which is prepared and can be plugged in and made ready to function immediately) that Triangle had purchased from Honeywell failed to perform. Triangle had planned to use the Honeywell system in its insurance business; however, errors appeared on the system's very first run in January, 1971, and cropped up repeatedly in the various runs of invoices and other insurance-related documents. Triangle argued that these errors and the resulting billing complaints caused the collapse of its business. The trial court dismissed the contract claims because Triangle had filed suit after the UCC's four-year statute of limitations had run. Triangle argued the contract had been for services rather than for the sale of goods and that it therefore had had six years in which to sue under New York law. Was Triangle correct? (*Triangle Underwriters, Inc.* v. *Honeywell, Inc.,* 604 F.2d 737 [2nd Cir. 1979], aff'd on other grounds 651 F.2d 132 [2nd Cir. 1981].)

10. A. I. Root Company (Root) sued Computer/Dynamics, Inc. (CDI), for antitrust violations allegedly resulting from CDI's proposed sale of software to Root. Root had been using a set of computer programs known as the Basic Operating Software System (BOSS) to operate machines that it had purchased from MAI dealers (including CDI). These programs constituted the operating software necessary to operate the computer generally and to support applications software (or programs that performed specific data-processing tasks). Root had approached CDI for the reconfigured BOSS software necessary to operate properly its newly-purchased Basic Four Model 730B. Root alleged that CDI had offered to sell the reconfigured BOSS software only if Root would sign licensing agreements concerning the applications software that would require Root to: (1) use only

computer hardware manufactured by MAI with Root's applications software; and (2) purchase for a "transfer fee" CDI's programming services each time Root acquired an updated or different Basic Four computer. Root contended that these terms constituted an unlawful tying arrangement by conditioning the sale of the reconfigured BOSS software (the tying product) upon Root's signing the application software license (the tied product). Should a court agree with Root's claim? (*A. I. Root Company v. Computer/Dynamics, Inc.,* 806 F.2d 673 [6th Cir. 1986].)

The Uniform Commercial Code

ARTICLE 1

GENERAL PROVISIONS

PART 1

Short Title, Construction, Application and Subject Matter of the Act

Section 1–101. Short Title

This Act shall be known and may be cited as Uniform Commercial Code.

Section 1–102. Purposes; Rules of Construction; Variation by Agreement

(1) This Act shall be liberally construed and applied to promote its underlying purposes and policies.

(2) Underlying purposes and policies of this Act are

(a) to simplify, clarify and modernize the law governing commercial transactions;

(b) to permit the continued expansion of commercial practices through custom, usage and agreement of the parties;

(c) to make uniform the law among the various jurisdictions.

(3) The effect of provisions of this Act may be varied by agreement, except as otherwise provided in this Act and except that the obligations of good faith, diligence, reasonableness and care prescribed by this Act may not be disclaimed by agreement but the parties may by agreement determine the standards by which the performance of such obligations is to be measured if such standards are not manifestly unreasonable.

(4) The presence in certain provisions of this Act of the words "unless otherwise agreed" or words of similar import does not imply that the effect of other provisions may not be varied by agreement under subsection (3).

(5) In this Act unless the context otherwise requires

(a) words in the singular number include the plural, and in the plural include the singular;

(b) words of the masculine gender include the feminine and the neuter, and when the sense so indicates words of the neuter gender may refer to any gender.

Section 1–103. Supplementary General Principles of Law Applicable

Unless displaced by the particular provisions of this Act, the principles of law and equity, including the law merchant and the law relative to capacity to contract, principal and agent, estoppel, fraud, misrepresentation, duress, coercion, mistake, bankruptcy, or other validating or invalidating cause shall supplement its provisions.

Section 1–104. Construction Against Implicit Repeal

This Act being a general act intended as a unified coverage of its subject matter, no part of it shall be deemed to be impliedly repealed by subsequent legislation if such construction can reasonably be avoided.

Section 1–105. Territorial Application of the Act; Parties' Power to Choose Applicable Law

(1) Except as provided hereafter in this section, when a transaction bears a reasonable relation to this state and also to another state or nation the parties may agree that the law either of this state or of such other state or nation shall govern their rights and duties. Failing such agreement this Act applies to transactions bearing an appropriate relation to this state.

(2) Where one of the following provisions of this Act specifies the applicable law, that provision governs and a contrary agreement is effective only to the extent permitted by the law (including the conflict of laws rules) so specified:

> Rights of creditors against sold goods. Section 2–402.
>
> Applicability of the Article on Bank Deposits and Collections. Section 4–102.
>
> Bulk transfers subject to the Article on Bulk Transfers. Section 6–102.
>
> Applicability of the Article on Investment Securities. Section 8–106.
>
> Policy and scope of the Article on Secured Transactions. Section 9–103. ′

Section 1–106. Remedies to Be Liberally Administered

(1) The remedies provided by this Act shall be liberally administered to the end that the aggrieved party may be put in as good a position as if the other party had fully performed but neither consequential or special nor penal damages may be had except as specifically provided in this Act or by other rule of law.

(2) Any right or obligation declared by this Act is enforceable by action unless the provision declaring it specifies a different and limited effect.

Section 1–107. Waiver or Renunciation of Claim or Right After Breach

Any claim or right arising out of an alleged breach can be discharged in whole or in part without consideration by a written waiver or renunciation signed and delivered by the aggrieved party.

Section 1–108. Severability

If any provision or clause of this Act or application thereof to any person or circumstances is held invalid, such invalidity shall not affect other provisions or applications of the Act which can be given effect without the invalid provision or application, and to this end the provisions of this Act are declared to be severable.

Section 1–109. Section Captions

Section captions are parts of this Act.

PART 2

General Definitions and Principles of Interpretation

Section 1–201. General Definitions

Subject to additional definitions contained in the subsequent Articles of this Act which are applicable to specific Articles or Parts thereof, and unless the context otherwise requires, in this Act:

(1) "Action" in the sense of a judicial proceeding includes recoupment, counterclaim, setoff, suit in equity and any other proceedings in which rights are determined.

(2) "Aggrieved party" means a party entitled to resort to a remedy.

(3) "Agreement" means the bargain of the parties in fact as found in their language or by implication from other circumstances including course of dealing or usage of trade or course of performance as provided in this Act (Sections 1–205 and 2–208). Whether an agreement has legal consequences is determined by the provisions of this Act, if applicable; otherwise by the law of contracts (Section 1–103). (Compare "Contract".)

(4) "Bank" means any person engaged in the business of banking.

(5) "Bearer" means the person in possession of an instrument, document of title, or security payable to bearer or indorsed in blank.

(6) "Bill of lading" means a document evidencing the receipt of goods for shipment issued by a person engaged in the business of transporting or forwarding goods, and includes an airbill. "Airbill" means a document serving for air transportation as a bill of lading does for marine or rail transportation, and includes an air consignment note or air waybill.

(7) "Branch" includes a separately incorporated foreign branch of a bank.

(8) "Burden of establishing" a fact means the burden of persuading the triers of fact that the existence of the fact is more probable than its non-existence.

(9) "Buyer in ordinary course of business" means a person who in good faith and without knowledge that the sale to him is in violation of the ownership rights or security interest of a third party in the goods buys in ordinary course from a person in the business of selling goods of that kind but does not include a pawnbroker. All persons who sell minerals or the like (including oil and gas) at wellhead or minehead shall be deemed to be persons in the business of selling goods of that kind. "Buying" may be for cash or by exchange of other property or on secured or unsecured credit and includes receiving goods or documents of title under a pre-existing contract for sale but does not include a transfer in bulk or as security for or in total or partial satisfaction of a money debt.

(10) "Conspicuous": A term or clause is conspicuous when it is so written that a reasonable person against whom it is to operate ought to have noticed it. A printed heading in capitals (as: Non-Negotiable Bill of Lading) is conspicuous. Language in the body of a form is "conspicuous" if it is in larger or other contrasting type or color. But in a telegram any stated term is "conspicuous." Whether a term or clause is "conspicuous" or not is for decision by the court.

(11) "Contract" means the total legal obligation which results from the parties' agreement as affected by this Act and any other applicable rules of law. (Compare "Agreement.")

(12) "Creditor" includes a general creditor, a secured creditor, a lien creditor and any representative of creditors, including an assignee for the benefit of creditors, a trustee in bankruptcy, a receiver in equity and an executor or administrator of an insolvent debtor's or assignor's estate.

(13) "Defendant" includes a person in the position of defendant in a cross-action or counterclaim.

(14) "Delivery" with respect to instruments, documents of title, chattel paper or securities means voluntary transfer of possession.

(15) "Document of title" includes bill of lading, dock warrant, dock receipt, warehouse receipt or order for the delivery of goods, and also any other document which in the regular course of business or financing is treated as adequately evidencing that the person in possession of it is entitled to receive, hold and dispose of the document and the goods it covers. To be a document of title a document must purport to be issued by or addressed to a bailee and purport to cover goods in the bailee's possession which are either identified or are fungible portions of an identified mass.

(16) "Fault" means wrongful act, omission or breach.

(17) "Fungible" with respect to goods or securities means goods or securities of which any unit is, by nature or usage of trade, the equivalent of any other like unit. Goods which are not fungible shall be deemed fungible for the purposes of this Act to the extent that under a particular agreement or document unlike units are treated as equivalents.

(18) "Genuine" means free of forgery or counterfeiting.

(19) "Good faith" means honesty in fact in the conduct or transaction concerned.

(20) "Holder" means a person who is in possession of a document of title or an instrument or an investment security drawn, issued or indorsed to him or to his order or to bearer or in blank.

(21) To "honor" is to pay or to accept and pay, or where a credit so engages to purchase or discount a draft complying with the terms of the credit.

(22) "Insolvency proceedings" includes any assignment for the benefit of creditors or other proceedings intended to liquidate or rehabilitate the estate of the person involved.

(23) A person is "insolvent" who either has ceased to pay his debts in the ordinary course of business or cannot pay his debts as they become due or is insolvent within the meaning of the federal bankruptcy law.

(24) "Money" means a medium of exchange authorized or adopted by a domestic or foreign government as a part of its currency.

(25) A person has "notice" of a fact when

(a) he has actual knowledge of it; or

(b) he has received a notice or notification of it; or

(c) from all the facts and circumstances known to him at the time in question he has reason to know that it exists.

A person "knows" or has "knowledge" of a fact when he has actual knowledge of it. "Discover" or "learn" or a word or phrase of similar import refers to knowledge rather than to reason to know. The time and circumstances under which a notice or notification may cease to be effective are not determined by this Act.

(26) A person "notifies" or "gives" a notice or notification to another by taking such steps as may be reasonably required to inform the other in ordinary course whether or not such other actually comes to know of it. A person "receives" a notice or notification

when

(a) it comes to his attention; or

(b) it is duly delivered at the place of business through which the contract was made or at any other place held out by him as the place for receipt of such communications.

(27) Notice, knowledge or a notice or notification received by an organization is effective for a particular transaction from the time when it is brought to the attention of the individual conducting that transaction, and in any event from the time when it would have been brought to his attention if the organization had exercised due diligence. An organization exercises due diligence if it maintains reasonable routines for communicating significant information to the person conducting the transaction and there is reasonable compliance with the routines. Due diligence does not require an individual acting for the organization to communicate information unless such communication is part of his regular duties or unless he has reason to know of the transaction and that the transaction would be materially affected by the information.

(28) "Organization" includes a corporation, government or governmental subdivision or agency, business trust, estate, trust, partnership or association, two or more persons having a joint or common interest, or any other legal or commercial entity.

(29) "Party", as distinct from "third party", means a person who has engaged in a transaction or made an agreement within this Act.

(30) "Person" includes an individual or an organization (See Section 1–102).

(31) "Presumption" or "presumed" means that the trier of fact must find the existence of the fact presumed unless and until evidence is introduced which would support a finding of its nonexistence.

(32) "Purchase" includes taking by sale, discount, negotiations, mortgage, pledge, lien, issue or re-issue, gift or any other voluntary transaction creating an interest in property.

(33) "Purchaser" means a person who takes by purchase.

(34) "Remedy" means any remedial right to which an aggrieved party is entitled with or without resort to a tribunal.

(35) "Representative" includes an agent, an officer of a corporation or association, and a trustee, executor or administrator of an estate, or any other person empowered to act for another.

(36) "Rights" includes remedies.

(37) "Security interest" means an interest in personal property or fixtures which secures payment or performance of an obligation. The retention or reservation of title by a seller of goods notwithstanding shipment or delivery to the buyer (Section 2–401) is limited in effect to a reservation of a "security interest". The term also includes any interest of a buyer of accounts or chattel paper which is subject to Article 9. The special property interest of a buyer of goods on identification of such goods to a contract for sale under Section 2–401 is not a "security interest", but a buyer may also acquire a "security interest" by complying with Article 9. Unless a lease or consignment is intended as security, reservation of title thereunder is not a "security interest" but a consignment is in any event subject to the provisions on consignment sales (Section 2–326). Whether a lease is intended as security is to be determined by the facts of each case; however, (a) the inclusion of an option to purchase does not of itself make the lease one intended for security, and (b) an agreement that upon compliance with the terms of the lease the lessee shall become or has the option to become the owner of the property for no additional consideration or for a nominal consideration does make the lease one intended for security.

(38) "Send" in connection with any writing or notice means to deposit in the mail or deliver for transmission by any other usual means of communication with postage or cost of transmission provided for and properly addressed and in the case of an instrument to an address specified thereon or otherwise agreed, or if there be none to any address reasonable under the circumstances. The receipt of any writing or notice within the time at which it would have arrived if properly sent has the effect of a proper sending.

(39) "Signed" includes any symbol executed or adopted by a party with present intention to authenticate a writing.

(40) "Surety" includes guarantor.

(41) "Telegram" includes a message transmitted by radio, teletype, cable, any mechanical method of transmission, or the like.

(42) "Term" means that portion of an agreement which relates to a particular matter.

(43) "Unauthorized" signature or indorsement means one made without actual, implied or apparent authority and includes a forgery.

(44) "Value". Except as otherwise provided with respect to negotiable instruments and bank collections (Sections

3–303, 4–208 and 4–209) a person gives "value" for rights if he acquires them

(a)   in return for a binding commitment to extend credit or for the extension of immediately available credit whether or not drawn upon and whether or not a charge-back is provided for in the event of difficulties in collection; or

(b)   as security for or in total or partial satisfaction of a pre-existing claim; or

(c)   by accepting delivery pursuant to a pre-existing contract for purchase; or

(d)   generally, in return for any consideration sufficient to support a simple contract.

(45) "Warehouse receipt" means a receipt issued by a person engaged in the business of storing goods for hire.

(46) "Written" or "writing" includes printing, typewriting or any other intentional reduction to tangible form.

Section 1–202.   Prima Facie Evidence by Third Party Documents

A document in due form purporting to be a bill of lading, policy or certificate of insurance, official weigher's or inspector's certificate, consular invoice, or any other document authorized or required by the contract to be issued by a third party shall be prima facie evidence of its own authenticity and genuineness and of the facts stated in the document by the third party.

Section 1–203.   Obligation of Good Faith

Every contract or duty within this Act imposes an obligation of good faith in its performance or enforcement.

Section 1–204.   Time; Reasonable Time; "Seasonably"

(1)   Whenever this Act requires any action to be taken within a reasonable time, any time which is not manifestly unreasonable may be fixed by agreement.

(2)   What is a reasonable time for taking any action depends on the nature, purpose and circumstances of such action.

(3)   An action is taken "seasonably" when it is taken at or within the time agreed or if no time is agreed at or within a reasonable time.

Section 1–205.   Course of Dealing and Usage of Trade

(1)   A course of dealing is a sequence of previous conduct between the parties to a particular transaction which is fairly to be regarded as establishing a common basis of understanding for interpreting their expressions and other conduct.

(2)   A usage of trade is any practice or method of dealing having such regularity of observance in a place, vocation or trade as to justify an expectation that it will be observed with respect to the transaction in question. The existence and scope of such a usage are to be proved as facts. If it is established that such a usage is embodied in a written trade code or similar writing the interpretation of the writing is for the court.

(3)   A course of dealing between parties and any usage of trade in the vocation or trade in which they are engaged or of which they are or should be aware give particular meaning to and supplement or qualify terms of an agreement.

(4)   The express terms of an agreement and an applicable course of dealing or usage of trade shall be construed wherever reasonable as consistent with each other; but when such construction is unreasonable express terms control both course of dealing and usage of trade and course of dealing controls usage of trade.

(5)   An applicable usage of trade in the place where any part of performance is to occur shall be used in interpreting the agreement as to that part of the performance.

(6)   Evidence of a relevant usage of trade offered by one party is not admissible unless and until he has given the other party such notice as the court finds sufficient to prevent unfair surprise to the latter.

Section 1–206.   Statute of Frauds for Kinds of Personal Property Not Otherwise Covered

(1)   Except in the cases described in subsection (2) of this section a contract for the sale of personal property is not enforceable by way of action or defense beyond five thousand dollars in amount or value of remedy unless there is some writing which indicates that a contract for sale has been made between the parties at a defined or stated price, reasonably identifies the subject matter, and is signed by the party against whom enforcement is sought or by his authorized agent.

(2)   Subsection (1) of this section does not apply to contracts for the sale of goods (Section 2–201) nor

of securities (Section 8–319) nor to security agreements (Section 9–203).

Section 1–207. Performance or Acceptance Under Reservation of Rights

A party who with explicit reservation of rights performs or promises performance or assents to performance in a manner demanded or offered by the other party does not thereby prejudice the rights reserved. Such words as "without prejudice", "under protest" or the like are sufficient.

Section 1–208. Option to Accelerate at Will

A term providing that one party or his successor in interest may accelerate payment or performance or require collateral or additional collateral "at will" or "when he deems himself insecure" or in words of similar import shall be construed to mean that he shall have power to do so only if he in good faith believes that the prospect of payment or performance is impaired. The burden of establishing lack of good faith is on the party against whom the power has been exercised.

Section 1–209. Subordinated Obligations

An obligation may be issued as subordinated to payment of another obligation of the person obligated, or a creditor may subordinate his right to payment of an obligation by agreement with either the person obligated or another creditor of the person obligated. Such a subordination does not create a security interest as against either the common debtor or a subordinated creditor. This section shall be construed as declaring the law as it existed prior to the enactment of this section and not as modifying it. Added 1966.

Note: *This new section is proposed as an optional provision to make it clear that a subordination agreement does not create a security interest unless so intended.*

ARTICLE **2**

SALES

PART **1**

Short Title, Construction and Subject Matter

Section 2–101. Short Title

This Article shall be known and may be cited as Uniform Commercial Code — Sales.

Section 2–102. Scope; Certain Security and Other Transactions Excluded from This Article

Unless the context otherwise requires, this Article applies to transactions in goods; it does not apply to any transaction which although in the form of an unconditional contract to sell or present sale is intended to operate only as a security transaction nor does this Article impair or repeal any statute regulating sales to consumers, farmers or other specified classes of buyers.

Section 2–103. Definitions and Index of Definitions

(1) In this Article unless the context otherwise requires

(a) "Buyer" means a person who buys or contracts to buy goods.

(b) "Good faith" in the case of a merchant means honesty in fact and the observance of reasonable commercial standards of fair dealing in the trade.

(c) "Receipt" of goods means taking physical possession of them.

(d) "Seller" means a person who sells or contracts to sell goods.

(2) Other definitions applying to this Article or to specified Parts thereof, and the sections in which they appear are:

"Acceptance." Section 2–606.
"Banker's credit." Section 2–325.
"Between merchants." Section 2–104.
"Cancellation." Section 2–106(4).
"Commercial unit." Section 2–105.
"Confirmed credit." Section 2–325.
"Conforming to contract." Section 2–106.
"Contract for sale." Section 2–106.
"Cover." Section 2–712.
"Entrusting." Section 2–403.
"Financing agency." Section 2–104.
"Future goods." Section 2–105.
"Goods." Section 2–105.
"Identification." Section 2–501.
"Installment contract." Section 2–612.
"Letter of credit." Section 2–325.
"Lot." Section 2–105.
"Merchant." Section 2–104.
"Overseas." Section 2–323.
"Person in position of seller." Section 2–707.
"Present sale." Section 2–106.
"Sale." Section 2–106.
"Sale on approval." Section 2–326.

"Sale or return." Section 2–326.
"Termination." Section 2–106.

(3) The following definitions in other articles apply to this Article:

"Check." Section 3–104.
"Consignee." Section 7–102.
"Consignor." Section 7–102.
"Consumer goods." Section 9–109.
"Dishonor." Section 3–507.
"Draft." Section 3–104.

(4) In addition Article 1 contains general definitions and principles of construction and interpretation applicable throughout this Article.

Section 2–104. Definitions: "Merchant"; "Between Merchants"; "Financing Agency"

(1) "Merchant" means a person who deals in goods of the kind or otherwise by his occupation holds himself out as having knowledge or skill peculiar to the practices or goods involved in the transaction or to whom such knowledge or skill may be attributed by his employment of an agent or broker or other intermediary who by his occupation holds himself out as having such knowledge or skill.

(2) "Financing agency" means a bank, finance company or other person who in the ordinary course of business makes advances against goods or documents of title or who by arrangement with either the seller or the buyer intervenes in ordinary course to make or collect payment due or claimed under the contract for sale, as by purchasing or paying the seller's draft or making advances against it or by merely taking it for collection whether or not documents of title accompany the draft. "Financing agency" includes also a bank or other person who similarly intervenes between persons who are in the position of seller and buyer in respect to the goods (Section 2–707).

(3) "Between merchants" means in any transaction with respect to which both parties are chargeable with the knowledge or skill of merchants.

Section 2–105. Definitions: Transferability; "Goods"; "Future" Goods; "Lot"; "Commercial Unit"

(1) "Goods" means all things (including specially manufactured goods) which are movable at the time of identification to the contract for sale other than the money in which the price is to be paid, investment securities (Article 8) and things in action. "Goods" also includes the unborn young of animals and growing crops and other identified things attached to realty as described in the section on goods to be severed from realty (Section 2–107).

(2) Goods must be both existing and identified before any interest in them can pass. Goods which are not both existing and identified are "future" goods. A purported present sale of future goods or of any interest therein operates as a contract to sell.

(3) There may be a sale of a part interest in existing identified goods.

(4) An undivided share in an identified bulk of fungible goods is sufficiently identified to be sold although the quantity of the bulk is not determined. Any agreed proportion of such a bulk or any quantity thereof agreed upon by number, weight or other measure may to the extent of the seller's interest in the bulk be sold to the buyer who then becomes an owner in common.

(5) "Lot" means a parcel or a single article which is the subject matter of a separate sale or delivery, whether or not it is sufficient to perform the contract.

(6) "Commercial unit" means such a unit of goods as by commercial usage is a single whole for purposes of sale and division of which materially impairs its character or value on the market or in use. A commercial unit may be a single article (as a machine) or a set of articles (as a suite of furniture or an assortment of sizes) or a quantity (as a bale, gross, or carload) or any other unit treated in use or in the relevant market as a single whole.

Section 2–106. Definitions: "Contract"; "Agreement"; "Contract for Sale"; "Sale"; "Present Sale"; "Conforming" to Contract; "Termination"; "Cancellation"

(1) In this Article unless the context otherwise requires "contract" and "agreement" are limited to those relating to the present or future sale of goods. "Contract for sale" includes both a present sale of goods and a contract to sell goods at a future time. A "sale" consists in the passing of title from the seller to the buyer for a price (Section 2–401). A "present sale" means a sale which is accomplished by the making of the contract.

(2) Goods or conduct including any part of a performance are "conforming" or conform to the contract when they are in accordance with the obligations under the contract.

(3) "Termination" occurs when either party pursuant to a power created by agreement or law puts an end

to the contract otherwise than for its breach. On "termination" all obligations which are still executory on both sides are discharged but any right based on prior breach or performance survives.

(4) "Cancellation" occurs when either party puts an end to the contract for breach by the other and its effect is the same as that of "termination" except that the cancelling party also retains any remedy for breach of the whole contract or any unperformed balance.

Section 2–107. Goods to Be Severed from Realty; Recording

(1) A contract for the sale of minerals or the like (including oil and gas) or a structure or its materials to be removed from realty is a contract for the sale of goods within this Article if they are to be severed by the seller but until severance a purported present sale thereof which is not effective as a transfer of an interest in land is effective only as a contract to sell.

(2) A contract for the sale apart from the land of growing crops or other things attached to realty and capable of severance without material harm thereto but not described in subsection (1) or of timber to be cut is a contract for the sale of goods within this Article whether the subject matter is to be severed by the buyer or by the seller even though it forms part of the realty at the time of contracting, and the parties can by identification effect a present sale before severance.

(3) The provisions of this section are subject to any third party rights provided by the law relating to realty records, and the contract for sale may be executed and recorded as a document transferring an interest in land and shall then constitute notice to third parties of the buyer's rights under the contract for sale.

PART **2**

Form, Formation and Readjustment of Contract

Section 2–201. Formal Requirements; Statute of Frauds

(1) Except as otherwise provided in this section a contract for the sale of goods for the price of $500 or more is not enforceable by way of action or defense unless there is some writing sufficient to indicate that a contract for sale has been made between the parties and signed by the party against whom enforcement is sought or by his authorized agent or broker. A writing is not insufficient because it omits or incorrectly states a term agreed upon but the contract is not enforceable under this paragraph beyond the quantity of goods shown in such writing.

(2) Between merchants if within a reasonable time a writing in confirmation of the contract and sufficient against the sender is received and the party receiving it has reason to know its contents, it satisfies the requirements of subsection (1) against such party unless written notice of objection to its contents is given within ten days after it is received.

(3) A contract which does not satisfy the requirements of subsection (1) but which is valid in other respects is enforceable

(a) if the goods are to be specially manufactured for the buyer and are not suitable for sale to others in the ordinary course of the seller's business and the seller, before notice of repudiation is received and under circumstances which reasonably indicate that the goods are for the buyer, has made either a substantial beginning of their manufacture or commitments for their procurement; or

(b) if the party against whom enforcement is sought admits in his pleading, testimony or otherwise in court that a contract for sale was made, but the contract is not enforceable under this provision beyond the quantity of goods admitted; or

(c) with respect to goods for which payment has been made and accepted or which have been received and accepted (Section 2–606).

Section 2–202. Final Written Expression: Parol or Extrinsic Evidence

Terms with respect to which the confirmatory memoranda of the parties agree or which are otherwise set forth in a writing intended by the parties as a final expression of their agreement with respect to such terms as are included therein may not be contradicted by evidence of any prior agreement or of a contemporaneous oral agreement but may be explained or supplemented

(a) by course of dealing or usage of trade (Section 1–205) or by course of performance (Section 2–208); and

(b) by evidence of consistent additional terms unless the court finds the writing to have been intended also as a complete and exclusive statement of the terms of the agreement.

Section 2–203. Seals Inoperative

The affixing of a seal to a writing evidencing a contract for sale or an offer to buy or sell goods does not constitute the writing of a sealed instrument and the law with respect to sealed instruments does not apply to such a contract or offer.

Section 2–204. Formation in General

(1) A contract for sale of goods may be made in any manner sufficient to show agreement, including conduct by both parties which recognizes the existence of such a contract.

(2) An agreement sufficient to constitute a contract for sale may be found even though the moment of its making is undetermined.

(3) Even though one or more terms are left open a contract for sale does not fail for indefiniteness if the parties have intended to make a contract and there is a reasonably certain basis for giving an appropriate remedy.

Section 2–205. Firm Offers

An offer by a merchant to buy or sell goods in a signed writing which by its terms gives assurance that it will be held open is not revocable, for lack of consideration, during the time stated or if no time is stated for a reasonable time, but in no event may such period of irrevocability exceed three months; but any such term of assurance on a form supplied by the offeree must be separately signed by the offeror.

Section 2–206. Offer and Acceptance in Formation of Contract

(1) Unless otherwise unambiguously indicated by the language or circumstances

  (a) an offer to make a contract shall be construed as inviting acceptance in any manner and by any medium reasonable in the circumstances;

  (b) an order or other offer to buy goods for prompt or current shipment shall be construed as inviting acceptance either by a prompt promise to ship or by the prompt or current shipment of conforming or non-conforming goods, but such a shipment of non-conforming goods does not constitute an acceptance if the seller seasonably notifies the buyer that the shipment is offered only as an accommodation to the buyer.

(2) Where the beginning of a requested performance is a reasonable mode of acceptance an offeror who is not notified of acceptance within a reasonable time may treat the offer as having lapsed before acceptance.

Section 2–207. Additional Terms in Acceptance or Confirmation

(1) A definite and seasonable expression of acceptance or a written confirmation which is sent within a reasonable time operates as an acceptance even though it states terms additional to or different from those offered or agreed upon, unless acceptance is expressly made conditional on assent to the additional or different terms.

(2) The additional terms are to be construed as proposals for addition to the contract. Between merchants such terms become part of the contract unless:

  (a) the offer expressly limits acceptance to the terms of the offer;

  (b) they materially alter it; or

  (c) notification of objection to them has already been given or is given within a reasonable time after notice of them is received.

(3) Conduct by both parties which recognizes the existence of a contract is sufficient to establish a contract for sale although the writings of the parties do not otherwise establish a contract. In such case the terms of the particular contract consist of those terms on which the writings of the parties agree, together with any supplementary terms incorporated under any other provisions of this Act.

Section 2–208. Course of Performance or Practical Construction

(1) Where the contract for sale involves repeated occasions for performance by either party with knowledge of the nature of the performance and opportunity for objection to it by the other, any course of performance accepted or acquiesced in without objection shall be relevant to determine the meaning of the agreement.

(2) The express terms of the agreement and any such course of performance, as well as any course of dealing and usage of trade, shall be construed whenever reasonable as consistent with each other; but when such construction is unreasonable, express terms shall control course of performance and course of performance shall control both course of dealing and usage of trade (Section 1–205).

(3) Subject to the provisions of the next section on modification and waiver, such course of performance shall be relevant to show a waiver or modification of any term inconsistent with such course of performance.

Section 2–209. Modification, Rescission and Waiver

(1) An agreement modifying a contract within this Article needs no consideration to be binding.

(2) A signed agreement which excludes modification or rescission except by a signed writing cannot be otherwise modified or rescinded, but except as between

merchants such a requirement on a form supplied by the merchant must be separately signed by the other party.

(3) The requirements of the statute of frauds section of this Article (Section 2–201) must be satisfied if the contract as modified is within its provisions.

(4) Although an attempt at modification or rescission does not satisfy the requirements of subsection (2) or (3) it can operate as a waiver.

(5) A party who has made a waiver affecting an executory portion of the contract may retract the waiver by reasonable notification received by the other party that strict performance will be required of any term waived, unless the retraction would be unjust in view of a material change of position in reliance on the waiver.

Section 2–210. Delegation of Performance; Assignment of Rights

(1) A party may perform his duty through a delegate unless otherwise agreed or unless the other party has a substantial interest in having his original promisor perform or control the acts required by the contract. No delegation of performance relieves the party delegating of any duty to perform or any liability for breach.

(2) Unless otherwise agreed all rights of either seller or buyer can be assigned except where the assignment would materially change the duty of the other party, or increase materially the burden or risk imposed on him by his contract, or impair materially his chance of obtaining return performance. A right to damages for breach of the whole contract or a right arising out of the assignor's due performance of his entire obligation can be assigned despite agreement otherwise.

(3) Unless the circumstances indicate the contrary a prohibition of assignment of "the contract" is to be construed as barring only the delegation to the assignee of the assignor's performance.

(4) An assignment of "the contract" or of "all my rights under the contract" or an assignment in similar general terms is an assignment of rights and unless the language or the circumstances (as in an assignment for security) indicate the contrary, it is a delegation of performance of the duties of the assignor and its acceptance by the assignee constitutes a promise by him to perform those duties. This promise is enforceable by either the assignor or the other party to the original contract.

(5) The other party may treat any assignment which delegates performance as creating reasonable grounds

for insecurity and may without prejudice to his rights against the assignor demand assurances from the assignee (Section 2–609).

PART 3

General Obligation and Construction of Contract

Section 2–301. General Obligations of Parties

The obligation of the seller is to transfer and deliver and that of the buyer is to accept and pay in accordance with the contract.

Section 2–302. Unconscionable Contract or Clause

(1) If the court as a matter of law finds the contract or any clause of the contract to have been unconscionable at the time it was made the court may refuse to enforce the contract, or it may enforce the remainder of the contract without the unconscionable clause, or it may so limit the application of any unconscionable clause as to avoid any unconscionable result.

(2) When it is claimed or appears to the court that the contract or any clause thereof may be unconscionable the parties shall be afforded a reasonable opportunity to present evidence as to its commercial setting, purpose and effect to aid the court in making the determination.

Section 2–303. Allocation or Division of Risks

Where this Article allocates a risk or a burden as between the parties "unless otherwise agreed", the agreement may not only shift the allocation but may also divide the risk or burden.

Section 2–304. Price Payable in Money, Goods, Realty, or Otherwise

(1) The price can be made payable in money or otherwise. If it is payable in whole or in part in goods each party is a seller of the goods which he is to transfer.

(2) Even though all or part of the price is payable in an interest in realty the transfer of the goods and the seller's obligations with reference to them are subject to this Article but not the transfer of the interest in realty or the transferor's obligations in connection therewith.

Section 2–305. Open Price Term

(1) The parties if they so intend can conclude a contract for sale even though the price is not settled. In such a case the price is a reasonable price at the time for delivery if

  (a) nothing is said as to price; or

  (b) the price is left to be agreed by the parties and they fail to agree; or

  (c) the price is to be fixed in terms of some agreed market or other standard as set or recorded by a third person or agency and it is not so set or recorded.

(2) A price to be fixed by the seller or by the buyer means a price for him to fix in good faith.

(3) When a price left to be fixed otherwise than by agreement of the parties fails to be fixed through fault of one party the other may at his option treat the contract as cancelled or himself fix a reasonable price.

(4) Where, however, the parties intend not to be bound unless the price be fixed or agreed and it is not fixed or agreed there is no contract. In such a case the buyer must return any goods already received or if unable so to do must pay their reasonable value at the time of delivery and the seller must return any portion of the price paid on account.

Section 2–306. Output, Requirements and Exclusive Dealings

(1) A term which measures the quantity by the output of the seller or the requirements of the buyer means such actual output or requirements as may occur in good faith, except that no quantity unreasonably disproportionate to any stated estimate or in the absence of a stated estimate to any normal or otherwise comparable prior output or requirements may be tendered or demanded.

(2) A lawful agreement by either the seller or the buyer for exclusive dealing in the kind of goods concerned imposes unless otherwise agreed an obligation by the seller to use best efforts to supply the goods and by the buyer to use best efforts to promote their sale.

Section 2–307. Delivery in Single Lot or Several Lots

Unless otherwise agreed all goods called for by a contract for sale must be tendered in a single delivery and payment is due only on such tender but where the circumstances give either party the right to make or demand delivery in lots the price if it can be apportioned may be demanded for each lot.

Section 2–308. Absence of Specified Place for Delivery

Unless otherwise agreed

  (a) the place for delivery of goods is the seller's place of business or if he has none his residence; but

  (b) in a contract for sale of identified goods which to the knowledge of the parties at the time of contracting are in some other place, that place is the place for their delivery; and

  (c) documents of title may be delivered through customary banking channels.

Section 2–309. Absence of Specific Time Provisions; Notice of Termination

(1) The time for shipment or delivery or any other action under a contract if not provided in this Article or agreed upon shall be a reasonable time.

(2) Where the contract provides for successive performances but is indefinite in duration it is valid for a reasonable time but unless otherwise agreed may be terminated at any time by either party.

(3) Termination of a contract by one party except on the happening of an agreed event requires that reasonable notification be received by the other party and an agreement dispensing with notification is invalid if its operation would be unconscionable.

Section 2–310. Open Time for Payment or Running of Credit; Authority to Ship Under Reservation

Unless otherwise agreed

  (a) payment is due at the time and place at which the buyer is to receive the goods even though the place of shipment is the place of delivery; and

  (b) if the seller is authorized to send the goods he may ship them under reservation, and may tender the documents of title, but the buyer may inspect the goods after their arrival before payment is due unless such inspection is inconsistent with the terms of the contract (Section 2–513); and

  (c) if delivery is authorized and made by way of documents of title otherwise than by subsection (b) then payment is due at the time and place at which the buyer is to receive the documents regardless of where the goods are to be received; and

(d) where the seller is required or authorized to ship the goods on credit the credit period runs from the time of shipment but post-dating the invoice or delaying its dispatch will correspondingly delay this starting of the credit period.

Section 2–311. Options and Cooperation Respecting Performance

(1) An agreement for sale which is otherwise sufficiently definite (subsection (3) of Section 2–204) to be a contract is not made invalid by the fact that it leaves particulars of performance to be specified by one of the parties. Any such specification must be made in good faith and within limits set by commercial reasonableness.

(2) Unless otherwise agreed specifications relating to assortment of the goods are at the buyer's option and except as otherwise provided in subsections (1)(c) and (3) of Section 2–319 specifications or arrangements relating to shipment are at the seller's option.

(3) Where such specification would materially affect the other party's performance but is not seasonably made or where one party's cooperation is necessary to the agreed performance of the other but is not seasonably forthcoming, the other party in addition to all other remedies

(a) is excused for any resulting delay in his own performance; and

(b) may also either proceed to perform in any reasonable manner or after the time for a material part of his own performance treat the failure to specify or to cooperate as a breach by failure to deliver or accept the goods.

Section 2–312. Warranty of Title and Against Infringement; Buyer's Obligation Against Infringement

(1) Subject to subsection (2) there is in a contract for sale a warranty by the seller that

(a) the title conveyed shall be good, and its transfer rightful; and

(b) the goods shall be delivered free from any security interest or other lien or encumbrance of which the buyer at the time of contracting has no knowledge.

(2) A warranty under subsection (1) will be excluded or modified only by specific language or by circumstances which give the buyer reason to know that the person selling does not claim title in himself or that he is purporting to sell only such right or title as he or a third person may have.

(3) Unless otherwise agreed a seller who is a merchant regularly dealing in goods of the kind warrants that the goods shall be delivered free of the rightful claim of any third person by way of infringement or the like but a buyer who furnishes specifications to the seller must hold the seller harmless against any such claim which arises out of compliance with the specifications.

Section 2–313. Express Warranties by Affirmation, Promise, Description, Sample

(1) Express warranties by the seller are created as follows:

(a) Any affirmation of fact or promise made by the seller to the buyer which relates to the goods and becomes part of the basis of the bargain creates an express warranty that the goods shall conform to the affirmation or promise.

(b) Any description of the goods which is made part of the basis of the bargain creates an express warranty that the goods shall conform to the description.

(c) Any sample or model which is made part of the basis of the bargain creates an express warranty that the whole of the goods shall conform to the sample or model.

(2) It is not necessary to the creation of an express warranty that the seller use formal words such as "warrant" or "guarantee" or that he have a specific intention to make a warranty, but an affirmation merely of the value of the goods or a statement purporting to be merely the seller's opinion or commendation of the goods does not create a warranty.

Section 2–314. Implied Warranty: Merchantability; Usage of Trade

(1) Unless excluded or modified (Section 2–316), a warranty that the goods shall be merchantable is implied in a contract for their sale if the seller is a merchant with respect to goods of that kind. Under this section the serving for value of food or drink to be consumed either on the premises or elsewhere is a sale.

(2) Goods to be merchantable must be at least such as

(a)   pass without objection in the trade under the contract description; and

(b)   in the case of fungible goods, are of fair average quality within the description; and

(c)   are fit for the ordinary purposes for which such goods are used; and

(d)   run, within the variations permitted by the agreement, of even kind, quality and quantity within each unit and among all units involved; and

(e)   are adequately contained, packaged, and labeled as the agreement may require; and

(f)   conform to the promises or affirmations of fact made on the container or label if any.

(3)   Unless excluded or modified (Section 2–316) other implied warranties may arise from course of dealing or usage of trade.

Section 2–315.   Implied Warranty: Fitness for Particular Purpose

Where the seller at the time of contracting has reason to know any particular purpose for which the goods are required and that the buyer is relying on the seller's skill or judgment to select or furnish suitable goods, there is unless excluded or modified under the next section an implied warranty that the goods shall be fit for such purpose.

Section 2–316.   Exclusion or Modification of Warranties

(1)   Words or conduct relevant to the creation of an express warranty and words or conduct tending to negate or limit warranty shall be construed wherever reasonable as consistent with each other; but subject to the provisions of this Article on parol or extrinsic evidence (Section 2–202) negation or limitation is inoperative to the extent that such construction is unreasonable.

(2)   Subject to subsection (3), to exclude or modify the implied warranty of merchantability or any part of it the language must mention merchantability and in case of a writing must be conspicuous, and to exclude or modify any implied warranty of fitness the exclusion must be by a writing and conspicuous. Language to exclude all implied warranties of fitness is sufficient if it states, for example, that "There are no warranties which extend beyond the description on the face hereof."

(3)   Notwithstanding subsection (2)

(a)   unless the circumstances indicate otherwise, all implied warranties are excluded by expressions like "as is", "with all faults" or other language which in common understanding calls the buyer's attention to the exclusion of warranties and makes plain that there is no implied warranty; and

(b)   when the buyer before entering into the contract has examined the goods or the sample or model as fully as he desired or has refused to examine the goods there is no implied warranty with regard to defects which an examination ought in the circumstances to have revealed to him; and

(c)   an implied warranty can also be excluded or modified by course of dealing or course of performance or usage of trade.

(4)   Remedies for breach of warranty can be limited in accordance with the provisions of this Article on liquidation or limitation of damages and on contractual modification of remedy (Sections 2–718 and 2–719).

Section 2–317.   Cumulation and Conflict of Warranties Express or Implied

Warranties whether express or implied shall be construed as consistent with each other and as cumulative, but if such construction is unreasonable the intention of the parties shall determine which warranty is dominant. In ascertaining that intention the following rules apply:

(a)   Exact or technical specifications displace an inconsistent sample or model or general language of description.

(b)   A sample from an existing bulk displaces inconsistent general language of description.

(c)   Express warranties displace inconsistent implied warranties other than an implied warranty of fitness for a particular purpose.

Section 2–318.   Third Party Beneficiaries of Warranties Express or Implied

Note: *If this Act is introduced in the Congress of the United States, this section should be omitted. (States to select one alternative.)*

Alternative A

A seller's warranty whether express or implied extends to any natural person who is in the family or household of his buyer or who is a guest in his home if it is reasonable to expect that such person may use, consume or be affected by the goods and who is injured in person by breach of the warranty. A seller may not exclude or limit the operation of this section.

Alternative B

A seller's warranty whether express or implied extends to any natural person who may reasonably be expected to use, consume or be affected by the goods and who is injured in person by breach of the warranty. A seller may not exclude or limit the operation of this section.

Alternative C

A seller's warranty whether express or implied extends to any person who may reasonably be expected to use, consume or be affected by the goods and who is injured by breach of the warranty. A seller may not exclude or limit the operation of this section with respect to injury to the person of an individual to whom the warranty extends. As amended 1966.

Section 2–319.   F.O.B. and F.A.S. Terms

(1) Unless otherwise agreed the term F.O.B. (which means "free on board") at a named place, even though used only in connection with the stated price, is a delivery term under which

   (a)   when the term is F.O.B. the place of shipment, the seller must at that place ship the goods in the manner provided in this Article (Section 2–504) and bear the expense and risk of putting them into the possession of the carrier; or

   (b)   when the term is F.O.B. the place of destination, the seller must at his own expense and risk transport the goods to that place and there tender delivery of them in the manner provided in this Article (Section 2–503);

   (c)   when under either (a) or (b) the term is also F.O.B. vessel, car or other vehicle, the seller must in addition at his own expense and risk load the goods on board. If the term is F.O.B. vessel the buyer must name the vessel and in an appropriate case the seller must comply with the provisions of this Article on the form of bill of lading (Section 2–323).

(2) Unless otherwise agreed the term F.A.S. vessel (which means "free alongside") at a named port, even though used only in connection with the stated price, is a delivery term under which the seller must

   (a)   at his own expense and risk deliver the goods alongside the vessel in the manner usual in that port or on a dock designated and provided by the buyer; and

   (b)   obtain and tender a receipt for the goods in exchange for which the carrier is under a duty to issue a bill of lading.

(3) Unless otherwise agreed in any case falling within subsection (1)(a) or (c) or subsection (2) the buyer must seasonably give any needed instructions for making delivery, including when the term is F.A.S. or F.O.B. the loading berth of the vessel and in an appropriate case its name and sailing date. The seller may treat the failure of needed instructions as a failure of cooperation under this Article (Section 2–311). He may also at his option move the goods in any reasonable manner preparatory to delivery or shipment.

(4) Under the term F.O.B. vessel or F.A.S. unless otherwise agreed the buyer must make payment against tender of the required documents and the seller may not tender nor the buyer demand delivery of the goods in substitution for the documents.

Section 2–320.   C.I.F. and C. & F. Terms

(1) The term C.I.F. means that the price includes in a lump sum the cost of the goods and the insurance and freight to the named destination. The term C. & F. or C.F. means that the price so includes cost and freight to the named destination.

(2) Unless otherwise agreed and even though used only in connection with the stated price and destination, the term C.I.F. destination or its equivalent requires the seller at his own expense and risk to

   (a)   put the goods into the possession of a carrier at the port for shipment and obtain a negotiable bill or bills of lading covering the entire transportation to the named destination; and

   (b)   load the goods and obtain a receipt from the carrier (which may be contained in the bill of lading) showing that the freight has been paid or provided for; and

   (c)   obtain a policy or certificate of insurance, including any war risk insurance, of a kind and on terms then current at the port of shipment in the usual amount, in the currency of the contract, shown to cover the same goods covered by the bill of lading and providing for payment of loss to the order of the buyer or for the account of whom it may concern; but the seller may add to the price the amount of the premium for any such war risk insurance; and

(d)   prepare an invoice of the goods and procure any other documents required to effect shipment or to comply with the contract; and

(e)   forward and tender with commercial promptness all the documents in due form and with any indorsement necessary to perfect the buyer's rights.

(3)   Unless otherwise agreed the term C. & F. or its equivalent has the same effect and imposes upon the seller the same obligations and risks as a C.I.F. term except the obligation as to insurance.

(4)   Under the term C.I.F. or C. & F. unless otherwise agreed the buyer must make payment against tender of the required documents and the seller may not tender nor the buyer demand delivery of the goods in substitution for the documents.

Section 2–321.   C.I.F. or C. & F.: "Net Landed Weights"; "Payment on Arrival"; Warranty of Condition on Arrival

Under a contract containing a term C.I.F. or C. & F.

(1)   Where the price is based on or is to be adjusted according to "net landed weights", "delivered weights", "out turn" quantity or quality or the like, unless otherwise agreed the seller must reasonably estimate the price. The payment due on tender of the documents called for by the contract is the amount so estimated, but after final adjustment of the price a settlement must be made with commercial promptness.

(2)   An agreement described in subsection (1) or any warranty of quality or condition of the goods on arrival places upon the seller the risk of ordinary deterioration, shrinkage and the like in transportation but has no effect on the place or time or identification to the contract for sale or delivery or on the passing of the risk of loss.

(3)   Unless otherwise agreed where the contract provides for payment on or after arrival of the goods the seller must before payment allow such preliminary inspection as is feasible; but if the goods are lost delivery of the documents and payment are due when the goods should have arrived.

Section 2–322.   Delivery "Ex-Ship"

(1)   Unless otherwise agreed a term for delivery of goods "ex-ship" (which means from the carrying vessel) or in equivalent language is not restricted to a particular ship and requires delivery from a ship which has reached a place at the named port of destination where goods of the kind are usually discharged.

(2)   Under such a term unless otherwise agreed

(a)   the seller must discharge all liens arising out of the carriage and furnish the buyer with a direction which puts the carrier under a duty to deliver the goods; and

(b)   the risk of loss does not pass to the buyer until the goods leave the ship's tackle or are otherwise properly unloaded.

Section 2–323.   Form of Bill of Lading Required in Overseas Shipment; "Overseas"

(1)   Where the contract contemplates overseas shipment and contains a term C.I.F. or C. & F. or F.O.B. vessel, the seller unless otherwise agreed must obtain a negotiable bill of lading stating that the goods have been loaded on board or, in the case of a term C.I.F. or C. & F., received for shipment.

(2)   Where in a case within subsection (1) a bill of lading has been issued in a set of parts, unless otherwise agreed if the documents are not to be sent from abroad the buyer may demand tender of the full set; otherwise only one part of the bill of lading need be tendered. Even if the agreement expressly requires a full set

(a)   due tender of a single part is acceptable within the provisions of the Article on cure of improper delivery (subsection (1) of Section 2–508); and

(b)   even though the full set is demanded, if the documents are sent from abroad the person tendering an incomplete set may nevertheless require payment upon furnishing an indemnity which the buyer in good faith deems adequate.

(3)   A shipment by water or by air or a contract contemplating such shipment is "overseas" insofar as by usage of trade or agreement it is subject to the commercial, financing or shipping practices characteristic of international deep water commerce.

Section 2–324.   "No Arrival, No Sale" Term

Under a term "no arrival, no sale" or terms of like meaning, unless otherwise agreed,

(a) the seller must properly ship conforming goods and if they arrive by any means he must tender them on arrival but he assumes an obligation that the goods will arrive unless he had caused the non-arrival; and

(b) where without fault of the seller the goods are in part lost or have so deteriorated as no longer to conform to the contract or arrive after the contract time, the buyer may proceed as if there had been casualty to identified goods (Section 2–613).

Section 2–325. "Letter of Credit" Term; "Confirmed Credit"

(1) Failure of the buyer seasonably to furnish an agreed letter of credit is a breach of the contract for sale.

(2) The delivery to seller of a proper letter of credit suspends the buyer's obligation to pay. If the letter of credit is dishonored, the seller may on seasonable notification to the buyer require payment directly from him.

(3) Unless otherwise agreed the term "letter of credit" or "banker's credit" in a contract for sale means an irrevocable credit issued by a financing agency of good repute and, where the shipment is overseas, of good international repute. The term "confirmed credit" means that the credit must also carry the direct obligation of such an agency which does business in the seller's financial market.

Section 2–326. Sale on Approval and Sale or Return; Consignment Sales and Rights of Creditors

(1) Unless otherwise agreed, if delivered goods may be returned by the buyer even though they conform to the contract, the transaction is

(a) a "sale on approval" if the goods are delivered primarily for use, and

(b) a "sale or return" if the goods are delivered primarily for resale.

(2) Except as provided in subsection (3), goods held on approval are not subject to the claims of the buyer's creditors until acceptance; goods held on sale or return are subject to such claims while in the buyer's possession.

(3) Where goods are delivered to a person for sale and such person maintains a place of business at which he deals in goods of the kind involved, under a name other than the name of the person making delivery, then with respect to claims of creditors of the person conducting the business the goods are deemed to be on sale or return. The provisions of this subsection are applicable even though an agreement purports to reserve title to the person making delivery until payment or resale or uses such words as "on consignment" or "on memorandum". However, this subsection is not applicable if the person making delivery

(a) complies with an applicable law providing for a consignor's interest or the like to be evidenced by a sign, or

(b) establishes that the person conducting the business is generally known by his creditors to be substantially engaged in selling the goods of others, or

(c) complies with the filing provisions of the Article on Secured Transactions (Article 9).

(4) Any "or return" term of a contract for sale is to be treated as a separate contract for sale within the statute of frauds section of this Article (Section 2–201) and as contradicting the sale aspect of the contract within the provisions of this Article on parol or extrinsic evidence (Section 2–202).

Section 2–327. Special Incidents of Sale on Approval and Sale or Return

(1) Under a sale on approval unless otherwise agreed

(a) although the goods are identified to the contract the risk of loss and the title do not pass to the buyer until acceptance; and

(b) use of the goods consistent with the purpose of trial is not acceptance but failure seasonably to notify the seller of election to return the goods is acceptance, and if the goods conform to the contract acceptance of any part is acceptance of the whole; and

(c) after due notification of election to return, the return is at the seller's risk and expense but a merchant buyer must follow any reasonable instructions.

(2) Under a sale or return unless otherwise agreed

(a) the option to return extends to the whole or any commercial unit of the goods while in substantially their original condition, but must be exercised seasonably; and

(b) the return is at the buyer's risk and expense.

Section 2–328. Sale by Auction

(1) In a sale by auction if goods are put up in lots each lot is the subject of a separate sale.

(2) A sale by auction is complete when the auctioneer so announces by the fall of the hammer or in other customary manner. Where a bid is made while the hammer is falling in acceptance of a prior bid the auctioneer may in his discretion reopen the bidding or declare the goods sold under the bid on which the hammer was falling.

(3) Such a sale is with reserve unless the goods are in explicit terms put up without reserve. In an auction with reserve the auctioneer may withdraw the goods at any time until he announces completion of the sale. In an auction without reserve, after the auctioneer calls for bids on an article or lot, that article or lot cannot be withdrawn unless no bid is made within a reasonable time. In either case a bidder may retract his bid until the auctioneer's announcement of completion of the sale, but a bidder's retraction does not revive any previous bid.

(4) If the auctioneer knowingly receives a bid on the seller's behalf or the seller makes or procures such a bid, and notice has not been given that liberty for such bidding is reserved, the buyer may at his option avoid the sale or take the goods at the price of the last good faith bid prior to the completion of the sale. This subsection shall not apply to any bid at a forced sale.

PART **4**

Title, Creditors and Good Faith Purchasers

Section 2–401. Passing of Title; Reservation for Security; Limited Application of This Section

Each provision of this Article with regard to the rights, obligations and remedies of the seller, the buyer, purchasers or other third parties applies irrespective of title to the goods except where the provision refers to such title. Insofar as situations are not covered by the other provisions of this Article and matters concerning title became material the following rules apply:

(1) Title to goods cannot pass under a contract for sale prior to their identification to the contract (Section 2–501), and unless otherwise explicitly agreed the buyer acquires by their identification a special property as limited by this Act. Any retention or reservation by the seller of the title (property) in goods shipped or delivered to the buyer is limited in effect to a reservation of a security interest. Subject to these provisions and to the provisions of the Article on Secured Transactions (Article 9), title to goods passes from the seller to the buyer in any manner and on any conditions explicitly agreed on by the parties.

(2) Unless otherwise explicitly agreed title passes to the buyer at the time and place at which the seller completes his performance with reference to the physical delivery of the goods, despite any reservation of a security interest and even though a document of title is to be delivered at a different time or place, and in particular and despite any reservation of a security interest by the bill of lading

> (a) if the contract requires or authorizes the seller to send the goods to the buyer but does not require him to deliver them at destination, title passes to the buyer at the time and place of shipment; but

> (b) if the contract requires delivery at destination, title passes on tender there.

(3) Unless otherwise explicitly agreed where delivery is to be made without moving the goods,

> (a) if the seller is to deliver a document of title, title passes at the time when and the place where he delivers such document; or

> (b) if the goods are at the time of contracting already identified and no documents are to be delivered, title passes at the time and place of contracting.

(4) A rejection or other refusal by the buyer to receive or retain the goods, whether or not justified, or a justified revocation of acceptance revests title to the goods in the seller. Such revesting occurs by operation of law and is not a "sale".

Section 2–402. Rights of Seller's Creditors Against Sold Goods

(1) Except as provided in subsections (2) and (3), rights of unsecured creditors of the seller with respect to goods which have been identified to a contract for sale are subject to the buyer's rights to recover the goods under this Article (Sections 2–502 and 2–716).

(2) A creditor of the seller may treat a sale or an identification of goods to a contract for sale as void if as against him a retention of possession by the seller is fraudulent under any rule of law of the state where the goods are situated, except that retention of possession in good faith and current course of trade by

a merchant-seller for a commercially reasonable time after a sale or identification is not fraudulent.

(3) Nothing in this Article shall be deemed to impair the rights of creditors of the seller

(a) under the provisions of the Article on Secured Transactions (Article 9); or

(b) where identification to the contract or delivery is made not in current course of trade but in satisfaction of or as security for a pre-existing claim for money, security or the like and is made under circumstances which under any rule of law of the state where the goods are situated would apart from this Article constitute the transaction a fraudulent transfer or voidable preference.

Section 2–403. Power to Transfer; Good Faith Purchase of Goods; "Entrusting"

(1) A purchaser of goods acquires all title which his transferor had or had power to transfer except that a purchaser of a limited interest acquires rights only to the extent of the interest purchased. A person with voidable title has power to transfer a good title to a good faith purchaser for value. When goods have been delivered under a transaction of purchase the purchaser has such power even though

(a) the transferor was deceived as to the identity of the purchaser, or

(b) the delivery was in exchange for a check which is later dishonored, or

(c) it was agreed that the transaction was to be a "cash sale", or

(d) the delivery was procured through fraud punishable as larcenous under the criminal law.

(2) Any entrusting of possession of goods to a merchant who deals in goods of that kind gives him power to transfer all rights of the entruster to a buyer in ordinary course of business.

(3) "Entrusting" includes any delivery and any acquiescence in retention of possession regardless of any condition expressed between the parties to the delivery or acquiescence and regardless of whether the procurement of the entrusting or the possessor's disposition of the goods have been such as to be larcenous under the criminal law.

(4) The rights of other purchasers of goods and of lien creditors are governed by the Articles on Secured

Transactions (Article 9), Bulk Transfers (Article 6) and Documents of Title (Article 7).

PART 5

Performance

Section 2–501. Insurable Interest in Goods; Manner of Identification of Goods

(1) The buyer obtains a special property and an insurable interest in goods by identification of existing goods as goods to which the contract refers even though the goods so identified are non-conforming and he has an option to return or reject them. Such identification can be made at any time and in any manner explicitly agreed to by the parties. In the absence of explicit agreement identification occurs

(a) when the contract is made if it is for the sale of goods already existing and identified;

(b) if the contract is for the sale of future goods other than those described in paragraph (c), when goods are shipped, marked or otherwise designated by the seller as goods to which the contract refers;

(c) when the crops are planted or otherwise become growing crops or the young are conceived if the contract is for the sale of unborn young to be born within twelve months after contracting or for the sale of crops to be harvested within twelve months or the next normal harvest season after contracting whichever is longer.

(2) The seller retains an insurable interest in goods so long as title to or any security interest in the goods remains in him and where the identification is by the seller alone he may until default or insolvency or notification to the buyer that the identification is final substitute other goods for those identified.

(3) Nothing in this section impairs any insurable interest recognized under any other statute or rule of law.

Section 2–502. Buyer's Right to Goods on Seller's Insolvency

(1) Subject to subsection (2) and even though the goods have not been shipped a buyer who has paid a part or all of the price of goods in which he has a special property under the provisions of the immediately preceding section may on making and keeping good a tender of any unpaid portion of their prices recover

them from the seller if the seller becomes insolvent within ten days after receipt of the first installment on their price.

(2) If the identification creating his special property has been made by the buyer he acquires the right to recover the goods only if they conform to the contract for sale.

Section 2–503. Manner of Seller's Tender of Delivery

(1) Tender of delivery requires that the seller put and hold conforming goods at the buyer's disposition and give the buyer any notification reasonably necessary to enable him to take delivery. The manner, time and place for tender are determined by the agreement and this Article, and in particular

(a) tender must be at a reasonable hour, and if it is of goods they must be kept available for the period reasonably necessary to enable the buyer to take possession; but

(b) unless otherwise agreed the buyer must furnish facilities reasonably suited to the receipt of the goods.

(2) Where the case is within the next section respecting shipment tender requires that the seller comply with its provisions.

(3) Where the seller is required to deliver at a particular destination tender requires that he comply with subsection (1) and also in any appropriate case tender documents as described in subsections (4) and (5) of this section.

(4) Where goods are in the possession of a bailee and are to be delivered without being moved

(a) tender requires that the seller either tender a negotiable document of title covering such goods or procure acknowledgment by the bailee of the buyer's right to possession of the goods; but

(b) tender to the buyer of a non-negotiable document of title or of a written direction to the bailee to deliver is sufficient tender unless the buyer seasonably objects, and receipt by the bailee of notification of the buyer's rights fixes those rights as against the bailee and all third persons; but risk of loss of the goods and of any failure by the bailee to honor the non-negotiable document of title or to obey the direction remains on the seller until the buyer has had a reasonable time to present the document or direction, and a

refusal by the bailee to honor the document or to obey the direction defeats the tender.

(5) Where the contract requires the seller to deliver documents

(a) he must tender all such documents in correct form, except as provided in this Article with respect to bills of lading in a set (subsection (2) of Section 2–323); and

(b) tender through customary banking channels is sufficient and dishonor of a draft accompanying the documents constitutes non-acceptance or rejection.

Section 2–504. Shipment by Seller

Where the seller is required or authorized to send the goods to the buyer and the contract does not require him to deliver them at a particular destination, then unless otherwise agreed he must

(a) put the goods in the possession of such a carrier and make such a contract for their transportation as may be reasonable having regard to the nature of the goods and other circumstances of the case; and

(b) obtain and promptly deliver or tender in due form any document necessary to enable the buyer to obtain possession of the goods or otherwise required by the agreement or by usage of trade; and

(c) promptly notify the buyer of the shipment.

Failure to notify the buyer under paragraph (c) or to make a proper contract under paragraph (a) is a ground for rejection only if material delay or loss ensues.

Section 2–505. Seller's Shipment Under Reservation

(1) Where the seller has identified goods to the contract by or before shipment:

(a) his procurement of a negotiable bill of lading to his own order or otherwise reserves in him a security interest in the goods. His procurement of the bill to the order of a financing agency or of the buyer indicates in addition only the seller's expectation of transferring that interest to the person named.

(b) a non-negotiable bill of lading to himself or his nominee reserves possession of the goods as security but except in a case of conditional delivery (subsection (2) of Section 2–507) a non-negotiable bill of lading naming the buyer as consignee reserves no security interest even though the seller retains possession of the bill of lading.

(2) When shipment by the seller with reservation of a security interest is in violation of the contract for sale it constitutes an improper contract for transportation within the preceding section but impairs neither the rights given to the buyer by shipment and identification of the goods to the contract nor the seller's powers as a holder of a negotiable document.

Section 2–506. Rights of Financing Agency

(1) A financing agency by paying or purchasing for value a draft which relates to a shipment of goods acquires to the extent of the payment or purchase and in addition to its own rights under the draft and any document of title securing it any rights of the shipper in the goods including the right to stop delivery and the shipper's right to have the draft honored by the buyer.

(2) The right to reimbursement of a financing agency which has in good faith honored or purchased the draft under commitment to or authority from the buyer is not impaired by subsequent discovery of defects with reference to any relevant document which was apparently regular on its face.

Section 2–507. Effect of Seller's Tender; Delivery on Condition

(1) Tender of delivery is a condition to the buyer's duty to accept the goods and, unless otherwise agreed, to his duty to pay for them. Tender entitles the seller to acceptance of the goods and to payment according to the contract.

(2) Where payment is due and demanded on the delivery to the buyer of goods or documents of title, his right as against the seller to retain or dispose of them is conditional upon his making the payment due.

Section 2–508. Cure by Seller of Improper Tender or Delivery; Replacement

(1) Where any tender or delivery by the seller is rejected because non-conforming and the time for performance has not yet expired, the seller may seasonably notify the buyer of his intention to cure and may then within the contract time make a conforming delivery.

(2) Where the buyer rejects a non-conforming tender which the seller had reasonable grounds to believe would be acceptable with or without money allowance the seller may if he seasonably notifies the buyer have a further reasonable time to substitute a conforming tender.

Section 2–509. Risk of Loss in the Absence of Breach

(1) Where the contract requires or authorizes the seller to ship the goods by carrier

(a) if it does not require him to deliver them at a particular destination, the risk of loss passes to the buyer when the goods are duly delivered to the carrier even though the shipment is under reservation (Section 2–505); but

(b) if it does require him to deliver them at a particular destination and the goods are there duly tendered while in the possession of the carrier, the risk of loss passes to the buyer when the goods are there duly so tendered as to enable the buyer to take delivery.

(2) Where the goods are held by a bailee to be delivered without being moved, the risk of loss passes to the buyer

(a) on his receipt of a negotiable document of title covering the goods; or

(b) on acknowledgment by the bailee of the buyer's right to possession of the goods; or

(c) after his receipt of a non-negotiable document of title or other written direction to deliver, as provided in subsection (4)(b) of Section 2–503.

(3) In any case not within subsection (1) or (2), the risk of loss passes to the buyer on his receipt of the goods if the seller is a merchant; otherwise the risk passes to the buyer on tender of delivery.

(4) The provisions of this section are subject to contrary agreement of the parties and to the provisions of this Article on sale on approval (Section 2–327) and on effect of breach on risk of loss (Section 2–510).

Section 2–510. Effect of Breach on Risk of Loss

(1) Where a tender or delivery of goods so fails to conform to the contract as to give a right of rejection the risk of their loss remains on the seller until cure or acceptance.

(2) Where the buyer rightfully revokes acceptance he may to the extent of any deficiency in his effective

insurance coverage treat the risk of loss as having rested on the seller from the beginning.

(3) Where the buyer as to conforming goods already identified to the contract for sale repudiates or is otherwise in breach before risk of their loss has passed to him, the seller may to the extent of any deficiency in his effective insurance coverage treat the risk of loss as resting on the buyer for a commercially reasonable time.

Section 2–511. Tender of Payment by Buyer; Payment by Check

(1) Unless otherwise agreed tender of payment is a condition to the seller's duty to tender and complete any delivery.

(2) Tender of payment is sufficient when made by any means or in any manner current in the ordinary course of business unless the seller demands payment in legal tender and gives any extension of time reasonably necessary to procure it.

(3) Subject to the provisions of this Act on the effect of an instrument on an obligation (Section 3–802), payment by check is conditional and is defeated as between the parties by dishonor of the check on due presentment.

Section 2–512. Payment by Buyer Before Inspection

(1) Where the contract requires payment before inspection non-conformity of the goods does not excuse the buyer from so making payment unless

(a) the non-conformity appears without inspection; or

(b) despite tender of the required documents the circumstances would justify injunction against honor under the provisions of this Act (Section 5–114).

(2) Payment pursuant to subsection (1) does not constitute an acceptance of goods or impair the buyer's right to inspect or any of his remedies.

Section 2–513. Buyer's Right to Inspection of Goods

(1) Unless otherwise agreed and subject to subsection (3), where goods are tendered or delivered or identified to the contract for sale, the buyer has a right before payment or acceptance to inspect them at any reasonable place and time and in any reasonable manner.

When the seller is required or authorized to send the goods to the buyer, the inspection may be after their arrival.

(2) Expenses of inspection must be borne by the buyer but may be recovered from the seller if the goods do not conform and are rejected.

(3) Unless otherwise agreed and subject to the provisions of this Article on C.I.F. contracts (subsection (3) of Section 2–321), the buyer is not entitled to inspect the goods before payment of the price when the contract provides

(a) for delivery "C.O.D." or on other like terms; or

(b) for payment against documents of title, except where such payment is due only after the goods are to become available for inspection.

(4) A place or method of inspection fixed by the parties is presumed to be exclusive but unless otherwise expressly agreed it does not postpone identification or shift the place for delivery or for passing the risk of loss. If compliance becomes impossible, inspection shall be as provided in this section unless the place or method fixed was clearly intended as an indispensable condition failure of which avoids the contract.

Section 2–514. When Documents Deliverable on Acceptance; When on Payment

Unless otherwise agreed documents against which a draft is drawn are to be delivered to the drawee on acceptance of the draft if it is payable more than three days after presentment; otherwise, only on payment.

Section 2–515. Preserving Evidence of Goods in Dispute

In furtherance of the adjustment of any claim or dispute

(a) either party on reasonable notification to the other and for the purpose of ascertaining the facts and preserving evidence has the right to inspect, test and sample the goods including such of them as may be in the possession or control of the other; and

(b) the parties may agree to a third party inspection or survey to determine the conformity or condition of the goods and may agree that the findings shall be binding upon them in any subsequent litigation or adjustment.

PART **6**

Breach, Repudiation and Excuse

Section 2–601. Buyer's Rights on Improper Delivery

Subject to the provisions of this Article on breach in installment contracts (Section 2–612) and unless otherwise agreed under the sections on contractual limitations of remedy (Sections 2–718 and 2–719), if the goods or the tender of delivery fail in any respect to conform to the contract, the buyer may

(a) reject the whole; or

(b) accept the whole; or

(c) accept any commercial unit or units and reject the rest.

Section 2–602. Manner and Effect of Rightful Rejection

(1) Rejection of goods must be within a reasonable time after their delivery or tender. It is ineffective unless the buyer seasonably notifies the seller.

(2) Subject to the provisions of the two following sections on rejected goods (Sections 2–603 and 2–604),

(a) after rejection any exercise of ownership by the buyer with respect to any commercial unit is wrongful as against the seller; and

(b) if the buyer has before rejection taken physical possession of goods in which he does not have a security interest under the provisions of this Article (subsection (3) of Section 2–711), he is under a duty after rejection to hold them with reasonable care at the seller's disposition for a time sufficient to permit the seller to remove them; but

(c) the buyer has no further obligations with regard to goods rightfully rejected.

(3) The seller's rights with respect to goods wrongfully rejected are governed by the provisions of this Article on seller's remedies in general (Section 2–703).

Section 2–603. Merchant Buyer's Duties as to Rightfully Rejected Goods

(1) Subject to any security interest in the buyer (subsection (3) of Section 2–711), when the seller has no agent or place of business at the market of rejection a merchant buyer is under a duty after rejection of goods in his possession or control to follow any reasonable instructions received from the seller with respect

to the goods and in the absence of such instructions to make reasonable efforts to sell them for the seller's account if they are perishable or threaten to decline in value speedily. Instructions are not reasonable if on demand indemnity for expenses is not forthcoming.

(2) When the buyer sells goods under subsection (1), he is entitled to reimbursement from the seller or out of the proceeds for reasonable expenses of caring for and selling them, and if the expenses include no selling commission then to such commission as is usual in the trade or if there is none to a reasonable sum not exceeding ten per cent on the gross proceeds.

(3) In complying with this section the buyer is held only to good faith and good faith conduct hereunder is neither acceptance nor conversion nor the basis of an action for damages.

Section 2–604. Buyer's Options as to Salvage of Rightfully Rejected Goods

Subject to the provisions of the immediately preceding section on perishables if the seller gives no instructions within a reasonable time after notification of rejection the buyer may store the rejected goods for the seller's account or reship them to him or resell them for the seller's account with reimbursement as provided in the preceding section. Such action is not acceptance or conversion.

Section 2–605. Waiver of Buyer's Objections by Failure to Particularize

(1) The buyer's failure to state in connection with rejection a particular defect which is ascertainable by reasonable inspection precludes him from relying on the unstated defect to justify rejection or to establish breach

(a) where the seller could have cured it if stated seasonably; or

(b) between merchants when the seller has after rejection made a request in writing for a full and final written statement of all defects on which the buyer proposes to rely.

(2) Payment against documents made without reservation of rights precludes recovery of the payment for defects apparent on the face of the documents.

Section 2–606. What Constitutes Acceptance of Goods

(1) Acceptance of goods occurs when the buyer

(a) after a reasonable opportunity to inspect the goods signifies to the seller that the goods are conforming or that he will take or retain them in spite of their nonconformity; or

(b)   fails to make an effective rejection (subsection (1) of Section 2–602), but such acceptance does not occur until the buyer has had a reasonable opportunity to inspect them; or

(c)   does any act inconsistent with the seller's ownership; but if such act is wrongful as against the seller it is an acceptance only if ratified by him.

(2)   Acceptance of a part of any commercial unit is acceptance of that entire unit.

Section 2–607.   Effect of Acceptance; Notice of Breach; Burden of Establishing Breach After Acceptance; Notice of Claim or Litigation to Person Answerable Over

(1)   The buyer must pay at the contract rate for any goods accepted.

(2)   Acceptance of goods by the buyer precludes rejection of the goods accepted and if made with knowledge of a non-conformity cannot be revoked because of it unless the acceptance was on the reasonable assumption that the non-conformity would be seasonably cured but acceptance does not of itself impair any other remedy provided by this Article for non-conformity.

(3)   Where a tender has been accepted

(a)   the buyer must within a reasonable time after he discovers or should have discovered any breach notify the seller of breach or be barred from any remedy; and

(b)   if the claim is one for infringement or the like (subsection (3) of Section 2–312) and the buyer is sued as a result of such a breach he must so notify the seller within a reasonable time after he receives notice of the litigation or be barred from any remedy over for liability established by the litigation.

(4)   The burden is on the buyer to establish any breach with respect to the goods accepted.

(5)   Where the buyer is sued for breach of a warranty or other obligation for which his seller is answerable over

(a)   he may give his seller written notice of the litigation. If the notice states that the seller may come in and defend and that if the seller does not do so he will be bound in any action against him by his buyer by any determination of fact common to the two litigations, then unless the seller after seasonable receipt of the notice does come in and defend he is so bound.

(b)   if the claim is one for infringement or the like (subsection (3) of Section 2–312) the original seller may demand in writing that his buyer turn over to him control of the litigation including settlement or else be barred from any remedy over and if he also agrees to bear all expense and to satisfy any adverse judgment, then unless the buyer after seasonable receipt of the demand does turn over control the buyer is so barred.

(6)   The provisions of subsections (3), (4) and (5) apply to any obligation of a buyer to hold the seller harmless against infringement or the like (subsection (3) of Section 2–312).

Section 2–608.   Revocation of Acceptance in Whole or in Part

(1)   The buyer may revoke his acceptance of a lot or commercial unit whose non-conformity substantially impairs its value to him if he has accepted it

(a)   on the reasonable assumption that its non-conformity would be cured and it has not been seasonably cured; or

(b)   without discovery of such non-conformity if his acceptance was reasonably induced either by the difficulty of discovery before acceptance or by the seller's assurances.

(2)   Revocation of acceptance must occur within a reasonable time after the buyer discovers or should have discovered the ground for it and before any substantial change in condition of the goods which is not caused by their own defects. It is not effective until the buyer notifies the seller of it.

(3)   A buyer who so revokes has the same rights and duties with regard to the goods involved as if he had rejected them.

Section 2–609.   Right to Adequate Assurance of Performance

(1)   A contract for sale imposes an obligation on each party that the other's expectation of receiving due performance will not be impaired. When reasonable grounds for insecurity arise with respect to the performance of either party the other may in writing demand adequate assurance of due performance and until he receives such assurance may if commercially

reasonable suspend any performance for which he has not already received the agreed return.

(2) Between merchants the reasonableness of grounds for insecurity and the adequacy of any assurance offered shall be determined according to commercial standards.

(3) Acceptance of any improper delivery or payment does not prejudice the aggrieved party's right to demand adequate assurance of future performance.

(4) After receipt of a justified demand failure to provide within a reasonable time not exceeding thirty days such assurance of due performance as is adequate under the circumstances of the particular case is a repudiation of the contract.

Section 2–610.   Anticipatory Repudiation

When either party repudiates the contract with respect to a performance not yet due the loss of which will substantially impair the value of the contract to the other, the aggrieved party may

> (a)   for a commercially reasonable time await performance by the repudiating party; or

> (b)   resort to any remedy for breach (Section 2–703 or Section 2–711), even though he has notified the repudiating party that he would await the latter's performance and has urged retraction; and

> (c)   in either case suspend his own performance or proceed in accordance with the provisions of this Article on the seller's right to identify goods to the contract notwithstanding breach or to salvage unfinished goods (Section 2–704).

Section 2–611.   Retraction of Anticipatory Repudiation

(1) Until the repudiating party's next performance is due he can retract his repudiation unless the aggrieved party has since the repudiation cancelled or materially changed his position or otherwise indicated that he considers the repudiation final.

(2) Retraction may be by any method which clearly indicates to the aggrieved party that the repudiating party intends to perform, but must include any assurance justifiably demanded under the provisions of this Article (Section 2–609).

(3) Retraction reinstates the repudiating party's rights under the contract with due excuse and allowance to the aggrieved party for any delay occasioned by the repudiation.

Section 2–612.   "Installment Contract"; Breach

(1) An "installment contract" is one which requires or authorizes the delivery of goods in separate lots to be separately accepted, even though the contract contains a clause "each delivery is a separate contract" or its equivalent.

(2) The buyer may reject any installment which is non-conforming if the non-conformity substantially impairs the value of that installment and cannot be cured or if the non-conformity is a defect in the required documents; but if the non-conformity does not fall within subsection (3) and the seller gives adequate assurance of its cure the buyer must accept that installment.

(3) Whenever non-conformity or default with respect to one or more installments substantially impairs the value of the whole contract there is a breach of the whole. But the aggrieved party reinstates the contract if he accepts a non-conforming installment without seasonably notifying of cancellation or if he brings an action with respect only to past installments or demands performance as to future installments.

Section 2–613.   Casualty to Identified Goods

Where the contract requires for its performance goods identified when the contract is made, and the goods suffer casualty without fault of either party before the risk of loss passes to the buyer, or in a proper case under a "no arrival, no sale" term (Section 2–324) then

> (a)   if the loss is total the contract is avoided; and

> (b)   if the loss is partial or the goods have so deteriorated as no longer to conform to the contract the buyer may nevertheless demand inspection and at his option either treat the contract as avoided or accept the goods with due allowance from the contract price for the deterioration or the deficiency in quantity but without further right against the seller.

Section 2–614.   Substituted Performance

(1) Where without fault of either party the agreed berthing, loading, or unloading facilities fail or an agreed type of carrier becomes unavailable or the agreed manner of delivery otherwise becomes commercially impracticable but a commercially reasonable substitute is available, such substitute performance must be tendered and accepted.

(2) If the agreed means or manner of payment fails because of domestic or foreign governmental regulation, the seller may withhold or stop delivery unless the buyer provides a means or manner of payment which is commercially a substantial equivalent. If delivery has already been taken, payment by the means or in the manner provided by the regulation discharges the buyer's obligation unless the regulation is discriminatory, oppressive or predatory.

Section 2–615. Excuse by Failure of Presupposed Conditions

Except so far as a seller may have assumed a greater obligation and subject to the preceding section on substituted performance:

(a) Delay in delivery or non-delivery in whole or in part by a seller who complies with paragraphs (b) and (c) is not a breach of his duty under a contract for sale if performance as agreed has been made impracticable by the occurrence of a contingency the non-occurrence of which was a basic assumption on which the contract was made or by compliance in good faith with any applicable foreign or domestic governmental regulation or order whether or not it later proves to be invalid.

(b) Where the causes mentioned in paragraph (a) affect only a part of the seller's capacity to perform, he must allocate production and deliveries among his customers but may at his option include regular customers not then under contract as well as his own requirements for further manufacture. He may so allocate in any manner which is fair and reasonable.

(c) The seller must notify the buyer seasonably that there will be delay or non-delivery and, when allocation is required under paragraph (b), of the estimated quota thus made available for the buyer.

Section 2–616. Procedure on Notice Claiming Excuse

(1) Where the buyer receives notification of a material or indefinite delay or an allocation justified under the preceding section he may by written notification to the seller as to any delivery concerned, and where the prospective deficiency substantially impairs the value of the whole contract under the provisions of this Article relating to breach of installment contracts (Section 2–612), then also as to the whole,

(a) terminate and thereby discharge any unexecuted portion of the contract; or

(b) modify the contract by agreeing to take his available quota in substitution.

(2) If after receipt of such notification from the seller the buyer fails so to modify the contract within a reasonable time not exceeding thirty days the contract lapses with respect to any deliveries affected.

(3) The provisions of this section may not be negated by agreement except in so far as the seller has assumed a greater obligation under the preceding section.

PART 7

Remedies

Section 2–701. Remedies for Breach of Collateral Contracts Not Impaired

Remedies for breach of any obligation or promise collateral or ancillary to a contract for sale are not impaired by the provisions of this Article.

Section 2–702. Seller's Remedies on Discovery of Buyer's Insolvency

(1) Where the seller discovers the buyer to be insolvent he may refuse delivery except for cash including payment for all goods theretofore delivered under the contract, and stop delivery under this Article (Section 2–705).

(2) Where the seller discovers that the buyer has received goods on credit while insolvent he may reclaim the goods upon demand made within ten days after the receipt, but if misrepresentation of solvency has been made to the particular seller in writing within three months before delivery the ten day limitation does not apply. Except as provided in this subsection the seller may not base a right to reclaim goods on the buyer's fraudulent or innocent misrepresentation of solvency or of intent to pay.

(3) The seller's right to reclaim under subsection (2) is subject to the rights of a buyer in ordinary course or other good faith purchaser under this Article (Section 2–403). Successful reclamation of goods excludes all other remedies with respect to them.

Section 2–703. Seller's Remedies in General

Where the buyer wrongfully rejects or revokes acceptance of goods or fails to make a payment due on or before delivery or repudiates with respect to a part or the whole, then with respect to any goods directly affected and, if the breach is of the whole contract

(Section 2–612), then also with respect to the whole undelivered balance, the aggrieved seller may

(a) withhold delivery of such goods;

(b) stop delivery by any bailee as hereafter provided (Section 2–705);

(c) proceed under the next section respecting goods still unidentified to the contract;

(d) resell and recover damages as hereafter provided (Section 2–706);

(e) recover damages for non-acceptance (Section 2–708) or in a proper case the price (Section 2–709);

(f) cancel.

Section 2–704. Seller's Right to Identify Goods to the Contract Notwithstanding Breach or to Salvage Unfinished Goods

(1) An aggrieved seller under the preceding section may

(a) identify to the contract conforming goods not already identified if at the time he learned of the breach they are in his possession or control;

(b) treat as the subject of resale goods which have demonstrably been intended for the particular contract even though those goods are unfinished.

(2) Where the goods are unfinished an aggrieved seller may in the exercise of reasonable commercial judgment for the purposes of avoiding loss and of effective realization either complete the manufacture and wholly identify the goods to the contract or cease manufacture and resell for scrap or salvage value or proceed in any other reasonable manner.

Section 2–705. Seller's Stoppage of Delivery in Transit or Otherwise

(1) The seller may stop delivery of goods in the possession of a carrier or other bailee when he discovers the buyer to be insolvent (Section 2–702) and may stop delivery of carload, truckload, planeload or larger shipments of express or freight when the buyer repudiates or fails to make a payment due before delivery or if for any other reason the seller has a right to withhold or reclaim the goods.

(2) As against such buyer the seller may stop delivery until

(a) receipt of the goods by the buyer; or

(b) acknowledgment to the buyer by any bailee of the goods except a carrier that the bailee holds the goods for the buyer; or

(c) such acknowledgment to the buyer by a carrier by reshipment or as warehouseman; or

(d) negotiation to the buyer of any negotiable document of title covering the goods.

(3) (a) To stop delivery the seller must so notify as to enable the bailee by reasonable diligence to prevent delivery of the goods.

(b) After such notification the bailee must hold and deliver the goods according to the directions of the seller but the seller is liable to the bailee for any ensuing charges or damages.

(c) If a negotiable document of title has been issued for goods the bailee is not obliged to obey a notification to stop until surrender of the document.

(d) A carrier who has issued a non-negotiable bill of lading is not obliged to obey a notification to stop received from a person other than the consignor.

Section 2–706. Seller's Resale Including Contract for Resale

(1) Under the conditions stated in Section 2–703 on seller's remedies, the seller may resell the goods concerned or the undelivered balance thereof. Where the resale is made in good faith and in a commercially reasonable manner the seller may recover the difference between the resale price and the contract price together with any incidental damages allowed under the provisions of this Article (Section 2–710), but less expenses saved in consequence of the buyer's breach.

(2) Except as otherwise provided in subsection (3) or unless otherwise agreed resale may be at public or private sale including sale by way of one or more contracts to sell or of identification to an existing contract of the seller. Sale may be as a unit or in parcels and at any time and place and on any terms but every aspect of the sale including the method, manner, time, place and terms must be commercially reasonable. The resale must be reasonably identified as referring to the broken contract, but it is not necessary that the goods be in existence or that any or all of them have been identified to the contract before the breach.

(3)   Where the resale is at private sale the seller must give the buyer reasonable notification of his intention to resell.

(4)   Where the resale is at public sale

(a)   only identified goods can be sold except where there is a recognized market for a public sale of futures in goods of the kind; and

(b)   it must be made at a usual place or market for public sale if one is reasonably available and except in the case of goods which are perishable or threaten to decline in value speedily the seller must give the buyer reasonable notice of the time and place of the resale; and

(c)   if the goods are not to be within the view of those attending the sale the notification of sale must state the place where the goods are located and provide for their reasonable inspection by prospective bidders; and

(d)   the seller may buy.

(5)   A purchaser who buys in good faith at a resale takes the goods free of any rights of the original buyer even though the seller fails to comply with one or more of the requirements of this section.

(6)   The seller is not accountable to the buyer for any profit made on any resale. A person in the position of a seller (Section 2–707) or a buyer who has rightfully rejected or justifiably revoked acceptance must account for any excess over the amount of his security interest, as hereinafter defined (subsection (3) of Section 2–711).

Section 2–707.   "Person in the Position of a Seller"

(1)   A "person in the position of a seller" includes as against a principal an agent who has paid or become responsible for the price of goods on behalf of his principal or anyone who otherwise holds a security interest or other right in goods similar to that of a seller.

(2)   A person in the position of a seller may as provided in this Article withhold or stop delivery (Section 2–705) and resell (Section 2–706) and recover incidental damages (Section 2–710).

Section 2–708.   Seller's Damages for Non-Acceptance or Repudiation

(1)   Subject to subsection (2) and to the provisions of this Article with respect to proof of market price (Section

2–723), the measure of damages for non-acceptance or repudiation by the buyer is the difference between the market price at the time and place for tender and the unpaid contract price together with any incidental damages provided in this Article (Section 2–710), but less expenses saved in consequence of the buyer's breach.

(2)   If the measure of damages provided in subsection (1) is inadequate to put the seller in as good a position as performance would have done then the measure of damages is the profit (including reasonable overhead) which the seller would have made from full performance by the buyer, together with any incidental damages provided in this Article (Section 2–710), due allowance for costs reasonably incurred and due credit for payments or proceeds of resale.

Section 2–709.   Action for the Price

(1)   When the buyer fails to pay the price as it becomes due the seller may recover, together with any incidental damages under the next section, the price

(a)   of goods accepted or of conforming goods lost or damaged within a commercially reasonable time after risk of their loss has passed to the buyer; and

(b)   of goods identified to the contract if the seller is unable after reasonable effort to resell them at a reasonable price or the circumstances reasonably indicate that such effort will be unavailing.

(2)   Where the seller sues for the price he must hold for the buyer any goods which have been identified to the contract and are still in his control except that if resale becomes possible he may resell them at any time prior to the collection of the judgment. The net proceeds of any such resale must be credited to the buyer and payment of the judgment entitles him to any goods not resold.

(3)   After the buyer has wrongfully rejected or revoked acceptance of the goods or has failed to make a payment due or has repudiated (Section 2–610), a seller who is held not entitled to the price under this section shall nevertheless be awarded damages for non-acceptance under the preceding section.

Section 2–710.   Seller's Incidental Damages

Incidental damages to an aggrieved seller include any commercially reasonable charges, expenses or commissions incurred in stopping delivery, in the transportation, care and custody of goods after the buyer's breach, in connection with return or resale of the goods or otherwise resulting from the breach.

Section 2–711. Buyer's Remedies in General; Buyer's Security Interest in Rejected Goods

(1) Where the seller fails to make delivery or repudiates or the buyer rightfully rejects or justifiably revokes acceptance then with respect to any goods involved, and with respect to the whole if the breach goes to the whole contract (Section 2–612), the buyer may cancel and whether or not he has done so may in addition to recovering so much of the price as has been paid

(a) "cover" and have damages under the next section as to all the goods affected whether or not they have been identified to the contract; or

(b) recover damages for non-delivery as provided in this Article (Section 2–713).

(2) Where the seller fails to deliver or repudiates the buyer may also

(a) if the goods have been identified recover them as provided in this Article (Section 2–502); or

(b) in a proper case obtain specific performance or replevy the goods as provided in this Article (Section 2–716).

(3) On rightful rejection or justifiable revocation of acceptance a buyer has a security interest in goods in his possession or control for any payments made on their price and any expenses reasonably incurred in their inspection, receipt, transportation, care and custody and may hold such goods and resell them in like manner as an aggrieved seller (Section 2–706).

Section 2–712. "Cover"; Buyer's Procurement of Substitute Goods

(1) After a breach within the preceding section the buyer may "cover" by making in good faith and without unreasonable delay any reasonable purchase of or contract to purchase goods in substitution for those due from the seller.

(2) The buyer may recover from the seller as damages the difference between the cost of cover and the contract price together with any incidental or consequential damages as hereinafter defined (Section 2–715), but less expenses saved in consequence of the seller's breach.

(3) Failure of the buyer to effect cover within this section does not bar him from any other remedy.

Section 2–713. Buyer's Damages for Non-Delivery or Repudiation

(1) Subject to the provisions of this Article with respect to proof of market price (Section 2–723), the measure of damages for non-delivery or repudiation by the seller is the difference between the market price at the time when the buyer learned of the breach and the contract price together with any incidental and consequential damages provided in this Article (Section 2–715), but less expense saved in consequence of the seller's breach.

(2) Market price is to be determined as of the place for tender or, in cases of rejection after arrival or revocation of acceptance, as of the place of arrival.

Section 2–714. Buyer's Damages for Breach in Regard to Accepted Goods

(1) Where the buyer has accepted goods and given notification (subsection (3) of Section 2–607) he may recover as damages for any non-conformity of tender the loss resulting in the ordinary course of events from the seller's breach as determined in any manner which is reasonable.

(2) The measure of damages for breach of warranty is the difference at the time and place of acceptance between the value of the goods accepted and the value they would have had if they had been as warranted, unless special circumstances show proximate damages of a different amount.

(3) In a proper case any incidental and consequential damages under the next section may also be recovered.

Section 2–715. Buyer's Incidental and Consequential Damages

(1) Incidental damages resulting from the seller's breach include expenses reasonably incurred in inspection, receipt, transportation and care and custody of goods rightfully rejected, any commercially reasonable charges, expenses or commissions in connection with effecting cover and any other reasonable expense incident to the delay or other breach.

(2) Consequential damages resulting from the seller's breach include

(a) any loss resulting from general or particular requirements and needs of which the seller at the time of contracting had reason to know and which could not reasonably be prevented by cover or otherwise; and

(b) injury to person or property proximately resulting from any breach of warranty.

Section 2–716. Buyer's Right to Specific Performance or Replevin

(1) Specific performance may be decreed where the goods are unique or in other proper circumstances.

(2) The decree for specific performance may include such terms and conditions as to payment of the price, damages, or other relief as the court may deem just.

(3) The buyer has a right of replevin for goods identified to the contract if after reasonable effort he is unable to effect cover for such goods or the circumstances reasonably indicate that such effort will be unavailing or if the goods have been shipped under reservation and satisfaction of the security interest in them has been made or tendered.

Section 2–717. Deduction of Damages from the Price

The buyer on notifying the seller of his intention to do so may deduct all or any part of the damages resulting from any breach of the contract from any part of the price still due under the same contract.

Section 2–718. Liquidation or Limitation of Damages; Deposits

(1) Damages for breach by either party may be liquidated in the agreement but only at an amount which is reasonable in the light of the anticipated or actual harm caused by the breach, the difficulties of proof of loss, and the inconvenience or nonfeasibility of otherwise obtaining an adequate remedy. A term fixing unreasonably large liquidated damages is void as a penalty.

(2) Where the seller justifiably withholds delivery of goods because of the buyer's breach, the buyer is entitled to restitution of any amount by which the sum of his payments exceeds

(a) the amount to which the seller is entitled by virtue of terms liquidating the seller's damages in accordance with subsection (1), or

(b) in the absence of such terms, twenty per cent of the value of the total performance for which the buyer is obligated under the contract or $500, whichever is smaller.

(3) The buyer's right to restitution under subsection (2) is subject to offset to the extent that the seller establishes

(a) a right to recover damages under the provisions of this Article other than subsection (1), and

(b) the amount or value of any benefits received by the buyer directly or indirectly by reason of the contract.

(4) Where a seller has received payment in goods their reasonable value or the proceeds of their resale shall be treated as payments for the purposes of subsection (2); but if the seller has notice of the buyer's breach before reselling goods received in part performance, his resale is subject to the conditions laid down in this Article on resale by an aggrieved seller (Section 2–706).

Section 2–719. Contractual Modification or Limitation of Remedy

(1) Subject to the provisions of subsections (2) and (3) of this section and of the preceding section on liquidation and limitation of damages,

(a) the agreement may provide for remedies in addition to or in substitution for those provided in this Article and may limit or alter the measure of damages recoverable under this Article, as by limiting the buyer's remedies to return of the goods and repayment of the price or to repair and replacement of non-conforming goods or parts; and

(b) resort to a remedy as provided is optional unless the remedy is expressly agreed to be exclusive, in which case it is the sole remedy.

(2) Where circumstances cause an exclusive or limited remedy to fail of its essential purpose, remedy may be had as provided in this Act.

(3) Consequential damages may be limited or excluded unless the limitations or exclusion is unconscionable. Limitation of consequential damages for injury to the person in the case of consumer goods is prima facie unconscionable but limitation of damages where the loss is commercial is not.

Section 2–720. Effect of "Cancellation" or "Rescission" on Claims for Antecedent Breach

Unless the contrary intention clearly appears, expressions of "cancellation" or "rescission" of the contract or the like shall not be construed as a renunciation or discharge of any claim in damages for an antecedent breach.

Section 2–721. Remedies for Fraud

Remedies for material misrepresentation or fraud include all remedies available under this Article for nonfraudulent breach. Neither rescission or a claim for rescission of the contract for sale nor rejection or return of the goods shall bar or be deemed inconsistent with a claim for damages or other remedy.

Section 2–722. Who Can Sue Third Parties for Injury to Goods

Where a third party so deals with goods which have been identified to a contract for sale as to cause actionable injury to a party to that contract

(a)   a right of action against the third party is in either party to the contract for sale who has title to or a security interest or a special property or an insurable interest in the goods; and if the goods have been destroyed or converted a right of action is also in the party who either bore the risk of loss under the contract for sale or has since the injury assumed the risk as against the other;

(b)   if at the time of the injury the party plaintiff did not bear the risk of loss as against the other party to the contract for sale and there is no arrangement between them for disposition of the recovery, his suit or settlement is, subject to his own interest, as a fiduciary for the other party to the contract;

(c)   either party may with the consent of the other sue for the benefit of whom it may concern.

Section 2–723. Proof of Market Price: Time and Place

(1) If an action based on anticipatory repudiation comes to trial before the time for performance with respect to some or all of the goods, any damages based on market price (Section 2–708 or Section 2–713) shall be determined according to the price of such goods prevailing at the time when the aggrieved party learned of the repudiation.

(2) If evidence of a price prevailing at the times or places described in this Article is not readily available the price prevailing within any reasonable time before or after the time described or at any other place which in commercial judgment or under usage of trade would serve as a reasonable substitute for the one described may be used, making any proper allowance for the cost of transporting the goods to or from such other place.

(3) Evidence of a relevant price prevailing at a time or place other than the one described in this Article offered by one party is not admissible unless and until he has given the other party such notice as the court finds sufficient to prevent unfair surprise.

Section 2–724. Admissibility of Market Quotations

Whenever the prevailing price or value of any goods regularly bought and sold in any established commodity market is in issue, reports in official publications or trade journals or in newspapers or periodicals of general circulation published as the reports of such market shall be admissible in evidence. The circumstances of the preparation of such a report may be shown to affect its weight but not its admissibility.

Section 2–725. Statute of Limitations in Contracts for Sale

(1) An action for breach of any contract for sale must be commenced within four years after the cause of action has accrued. By the original agreement the parties may reduce the period of limitation to not less than one year but may not extend it.

(2) A cause of action accrues when the breach occurs, regardless of the aggrieved party's lack of knowledge of the breach. A breach of warranty occurs when tender of delivery is made, except that where a warranty explicitly extends to future performance of the goods and discovery of the breach must await the time of such performance the cause of action accrues when the breach is or should have been discovered.

(3) Where an action commenced within the time limited by subsection (1) is so terminated as to leave available a remedy by another action for the same breach such other action may be commenced after the expiration of the time limited and within six months after the termination of the first action unless the termination resulted from voluntary discontinuance or from dismissal for failure or neglect to prosecute.

(4) This section does not alter the law on tolling of the statute of limitations nor does it apply to causes of action which have accrued before this Act becomes effective.

ARTICLE **3**

COMMERCIAL PAPER

PART **1**

Short Title, Form and Interpretation

Section 3–101.   Short Title

This Article shall be known and may be cited as Uniform Commercial Code — Commercial Paper.

Section 3–102.   Definitions and Index of Definitions

(1) In this Article unless the context otherwise requires

(a)   "Issue" means the first delivery of an instrument to a holder or a remitter.

(b)   An "order" is a direction to pay and must be more than an authorization or request. It must identify the person to pay with reasonable certainty. It may be addressed to one or more such persons jointly or in the alternative but not in succession.

(c)   A "promise" is an undertaking to pay and must be more than an acknowledgment of an obligation.

(d)   "Secondary party" means a drawer or endorser.

(e)   "Instrument" means a negotiable instrument.

(2) Other definitions applying to this Article and the sections in which they appear are:

"Acceptance." Section 3–410.
"Accommodation party." Section 3–415.
"Alteration." Section 3–407.
"Certificate of deposit." Section 3–104.
"Certification." Section 3–411.
"Check." Section 3–104.
"Definite time." Section 3–109.
"Dishonor." Section 3–507.
"Draft." Section 3–104.
"Holder in due course." Section 3–302.
"Negotiation." Section 3–202.
"Note." Section 3–104.
"Notice of dishonor." Section 3–508.

"On demand." Section 3–108.
"Presentment." Section 3–504.
"Protest." Section 3–509.
"Restrictive indorsement." Section 3–205.
"Signature." Section 3–401.

(3) The following definitions in other Articles apply to this Article:

"Account." Section 4–104.
"Banking day." Section 4–104.
"Clearing house." Section 4–104.
"Collecting bank." Section 4–105.
"Customer." Section 4–104.
"Depositary bank." Section 4–105.
"Documentary draft." Section 4–104.
"Intermediary bank." Section 4–105.
"Item." Section 4–104.
"Midnight deadline." Section 4–104.
"Payor bank." Section 4–105.

(4)   In addition, Article 1 contains general definitions and principles of construction and interpretation applicable throughout this Article.

Section 3–103.   Limitations on Scope of Article

(1)   This Article does not apply to money, documents of title or investment securities.

(2)   The provisions of this Article are subject to the provisions of the Article on Bank Deposits and Collections (Article 4) and Secured Transactions (Article 9).

Section 3–104.   Form of Negotiable Instruments; "Draft"; "Check"; "Certificate of Deposit"; "Note"

(1)   Any writing to be a negotiable instrument within this Article must

(a)   be signed by the maker or drawer; and

(b)   contain an unconditional promise or order to pay a sum certain in money and no other promise, order, obligation or power given by the maker or drawer except as authorized by this Article; and

(c)   be payable on demand or at a definite time; and

(d)   be payable to order or to bearer.

(2) A writing which complies with the requirements of this section is

    (a) a "draft" ("bill of exchange") if it is an order;

    (b) a "check" if it is a draft drawn on a bank and payable on demand;

    (c) a "certificate of deposit" if it is an acknowledgment by a bank of receipt of money with an engagement to repay it;

    (d) a "note" if it is a promise other than a certificate of deposit.

(3) As used in other Articles of this Act, and as the context may require, the terms "draft", "check", "certificate of deposit" and "note" may refer to instruments which are not negotiable within this Article as well as to instruments which are so negotiable.

Section 3–105. When Promise or Order Unconditional

(1) A promise or order otherwise unconditional is not made conditional by the fact that the instrument

    (a) is subject to implied or constructive conditions; or

    (b) states its consideration, whether performed or promised, or the transaction which gave rise to the instrument, or that the promise or order is made or the instrument matures in accordance with or "as per" such transaction; or

    (c) Refers to or states that it arises out of a separate agreement or refers to a separate agreement for rights as to prepayment or acceleration; or

    (d) states that it is drawn under a letter of credit; or

    (e) states that it is secured, whether by mortgage, reservation of title or otherwise; or

    (f) indicates a particular account to be debited or any other fund or source from which reimbursement is expected; or

    (g) is limited to payment out of a particular fund or the proceeds of a particular source, if the instrument is issued by a government or governmental agency or unit; or

    (h) is limited to payment out of the entire assets of a partnership, unincorporated association, trust or estate by or on behalf of which the instrument is issued.

(2) A promise or order is not unconditional if the instrument

    (a) states that it is subject to or governed by any other agreement; or

    (b) states that it is to be paid only out of a particular fund or source except as provided in this section.

Section 3–106. Sum Certain

(1) The sum payable is a sum certain even though it is to be paid

    (a) with stated interest or by stated installments; or

    (b) with stated different rates of interest before and after default or a specified date; or

    (c) with a stated discount or addition if paid before or after the date fixed for payment; or

    (d) with exchange or less exchange, whether at a fixed rate or at the current rate; or

    (e) with costs of collection or an attorney's fee or both upon default.

(2) Nothing in this section shall validate any term which is otherwise illegal.

Section 3–107. Money

(1) An instrument is payable in money if the medium of exchange in which it is payable is money at the time the instrument is made. An instrument payable in "currency" or "current funds" is payable in money.

(2) A promise or order to pay a sum stated in a foreign currency is for a sum certain in money and, unless a different medium of payment is specified in the instrument, may be satisfied by payment of that number of dollars which the stated foreign currency will purchase at the buying sight rate for that currency on the day on which the instrument is payable or, if payable on demand, on the day of demand. If such an instrument specifies a foreign currency as the medium of payment the instrument is payable in that currency.

Section 3–108. Payable on Demand

Instruments payable on demand include those payable at sight or on presentation and those in which no time for payment is stated.

Section 3–109. Definite Time

(1) An instrument is payable at a definite time if by its terms it is payable

(a) on or before a stated date or at a fixed period after a stated date; or

(b) at a fixed period after sight; or

(c) at a definite time subject to any acceleration; or

(d) at a definite time subject to extension at the option of the holder, or to extension to a further definite time at the option of the maker or acceptor or automatically upon or after a specified act or event.

(2) An instrument which by its terms is otherwise payable only upon an act or event uncertain as to time of occurrence is not payable at a definite time even though the act or event has occurred.

Section 3–110. Payable to Order

(1) An instrument is payable to order when by its terms it is payable to the order or assigns of any person therein specified within reasonable certainty, or to him or his order, or when it is conspicuously designated on its face as "exchange" or the like and names a payee. It may be payable to the order of

(a) the maker or drawer; or

(b) the drawee; or

(c) a payee who is not maker, drawer or drawee; or

(d) two or more payees together or in the alternative; or

(e) an estate, trust or fund, in which case it is payable to the order of the representative of such estate, trust or fund or his successors; or

(f) an office, or an officer by his title as such in which case it is payable to the principal but the incumbent of the office or his successors may act as if he or they were the holder; or

(g) a partnership or unincorporated association, in which case it is payable to the partnership or association and may be indorsed or transferred by any person thereto authorized.

(2) An instrument not payable to order is not made so payable by such words as "payable upon return of this instrument properly indorsed."

(3) An instrument made payable both to order and to bearer is payable to order unless the bearer words are handwritten or typewritten.

Section 3–111. Payable to Bearer

An instrument is payable to bearer when by its terms it is payable to

(a) bearer or the order of bearer; or

(b) a specified person or bearer; or

(c) "cash" or the order of "cash", or any other indication which does not purport to designate a specific payee.

Section 3–112. Terms and Omissions Not Affecting Negotiability

(1) The negotiability of an instrument is not affected by

(a) the omission of a statement of any consideration or of the place where the instrument is drawn or payable; or

(b) a statement that collateral has been given to secure obligations either on the instrument or otherwise of an obligor on the instrument or that in case of default on those obligations the holder may realize on or dispose of the collateral; or

(c) a promise or power to maintain or protect collateral or to give additional collateral; or

(d) a term authorizing a confession of judgment on the instrument if it is not paid when due; or

(e) a term purporting to waive the benefit or any law intended for the advantage or protection of any obligor; or

(f) a term in a draft providing that the payee by indorsing or cashing it acknowledges full satisfaction of an obligation of the drawer; or

(g) a statement in a draft drawn in a set of parts (Section 3–801) to the effect that the order is effective only if no other part has been honored.

(2) Nothing in this section shall validate any term which is otherwise illegal.

Section 3–113. Seal

An instrument otherwise negotiable is within this Article even though it is under a seal.

Section 3–114.   Date, Antedating, Postdating

(1) The negotiability of an instrument is not affected by the fact that it is undated, antedated or postdated.

(2) Where an instrument is antedated or postdated the time when it is payable is determined by the stated date if the instrument is payable on demand or at a fixed period after date.

(3) Where the instrument or any signature thereon is dated, the date is presumed to be correct.

Section 3–115.   Incomplete Instruments

(1) When a paper whose contents at the time of signing show that it is intended to become an instrument is signed while still incomplete in any necessary respect it cannot be enforced until completed, but when it is completed in accordance with authority given it is effective as completed.

(2) If the completion is unauthorized the rules as to material alteration apply (Section 3–407), even though the paper was not delivered by the maker or drawer; but the burden of establishing that any completion is unauthorized is on the party so asserting.

Section 3–116.   Instruments Payable to Two or More Persons

An instrument payable to the order of two or more persons

    (a) if in the alternative is payable to any one of them and may be negotiated, discharged or enforced by any of them who has possession of it;

    (b) if not in the alternative is payable to all of them and may be negotiated, discharged or enforced only by all of them.

Section 3–117.   Instruments Payable with Words of Description

An instrument made payable to a named person with the addition of words describing him

    (a) as agent or officer of a specified person is payable to his principal but the agent or officer may act as if he were the holder;

    (b) as any other fiduciary for a specified person or purpose is payable to the payee and may be negotiated, discharged or enforced by him;

    (c) in any other manner is payable to the payee unconditionally and the additional words are without effect on subsequent parties.

Section 3–118.   Ambiguous Terms and Rules of Construction

The following rules apply to every instrument:

    (a) Where there is doubt whether the instrument is a draft or a note the holder may treat it as either. A draft drawn on the drawer is effective as a note.

    (b) Handwritten terms control typewritten and printed terms, and typewritten control printed.

    (c) Words control figures except that if the words are ambiguous figures control.

    (d) Unless otherwise specified a provision for interest means interest at the judgment rate at the place of payment from the date of the instrument, or if it is undated from the date of issue.

    (e) Unless the instrument otherwise specifies two or more persons who sign as maker, acceptor or drawer or indorser and as a part of the same transaction are jointly and severally liable even though the instrument contains such words as "I promise to pay."

    (f) Unless otherwise specified consent to extension authorizes a single extension for not longer than the original period. A consent to extension, expressed in the instrument, is binding on secondary parties and accommodation makers. A holder may not exercise his option to extend an instrument over the objection of a maker or acceptor or other party who in accordance with Section 3–604 tenders full payment when the instrument is due.

Section 3–119.   Other Writings Affecting Instrument

(1) As between the obligor and his immediate obligee or any transferee the terms of an instrument may be modified or affected by any other written agreement executed as a part of the same transaction, except that a holder in due course is not affected by any limitation of his rights arising out of the separate written agreement if he had no notice of the limitation when he took the instrument.

(2) A separate agreement does not affect the negotiability of an instrument.

Section 3–120. Instruments "Payable Through" Bank

An instrument which states that it is "payable through" a bank or the like designates that bank as a collecting bank to make presentment but does not of itself authorize the bank to pay the instrument.

Section 3–121. Instruments Payable at Bank

Note: *If this Act is introduced in the Congress of the United States, this section should be omitted. (States to select either alternative.)*

Alternative A

A note or acceptance which states that it is payable at a bank is the equivalent of a draft drawn on the bank payable when it falls due out of any funds of the maker or acceptor in current account or otherwise available for such payment.

Alternative B

A note or acceptance which states that it is payable at a bank is not of itself an order or authorization to the bank to pay it.

Section 3–122. Accrual of Cause of Action

(1) A cause of action against a maker or an acceptor accrues

   (a) in the case of a time instrument on the day after maturity;

   (b) in the case of a demand instrument upon its date or, if no date is stated, on the date of issue.

(2) A cause of action against the obligor of a demand or time certificate of deposit accrues upon demand, but demand on a time certificate may not be made until on or after the date of maturity.

(3) A cause of action against a drawer of a draft or an indorser of any instrument accrues upon demand following dishonor of the instrument. Notice of dishonor is a demand.

(4) Unless an instrument provides otherwise, interest runs at a rate provided by law for a judgment

   (a) in the case of a maker, acceptor or other primary obligor of a demand instrument, from the date of demand;

   (b) in all other cases from the date of accrual or the cause of action.

PART 2

Transfer and Negotiation

Section 3–201. Transfer: Right to Indorsement

(1) Transfer of an instrument vests in the transferee such rights as the transferor has therein, except that a transferee who has himself been a party to any fraud or illegality affecting the instrument or who as a prior holder had notice of a defense or claim against it cannot improve his position by taking from a later holder in due course.

(2) A transfer of a security interest in an instrument vests the foregoing rights in the transferee to the extent of the interest transferred.

(3) Unless otherwise agreed any transfer for value of an instrument not then payable to bearer gives the transferee the specifically enforceable right to have the unqualified indorsement of the transferor. Negotiation takes effect only when the indorsement is made and until that time there is no presumption that the transferee is the owner.

Section 3–202. Negotiation

(1) Negotiation is the transfer of an instrument in such form that the transferee becomes a holder. If the instrument is payable to order it is negotiated by delivery with any necessary indorsement; if payable to bearer it is negotiated by delivery.

(2) An indorsement must be written by or on behalf of the holder and on the instrument or on a paper so firmly affixed thereto as to become a part thereof.

(3) An indorsement is effective for negotiation only when it conveys the entire instrument or any unpaid residue. If it purports to be of less it operates only as a partial assignment.

(4) Words of assignment, condition, waiver, guaranty, limitation or disclaimer of liability and the like accompanying an indorsement do not affect its character as an indorsement.

Section 3–203. Wrong or Misspelled Name

Where an instrument is made payable to a person under a misspelled name or one other than his own he may indorse in that name or his own or both; but signature in both names may be required by a person paying or giving value for the instrument.

Section 3-204. Special Indorsement; Blank Indorsement

(1) A special indorsement specifies the person to whom or to whose order it makes the instrument payable. Any instrument specially indorsed becomes payable to the order of the special indorsee and may be further negotiated only by his indorsement.

(2) An indorsement in blank specifies no particular indorsee and may consist of a mere signature. An instrument payable to order and indorsed in blank becomes payable to bearer and may be negotiated by delivery alone until specially indorsed.

(3) The holder may convert a blank indorsement into a special indorsement by writing over the signature of the indorser in blank any contract consistent with the character of the indorsement.

Section 3-205. Restrictive Indorsements

An indorsement is restrictive which either

   (a)   is conditional; or

   (b)   purports to prohibit further transfer of the instrument; or

   (c)   includes the words "for collection", "for deposit", "pay any bank", or like terms signifying a purpose of deposit or collection; or

   (d)   otherwise states that it is for the benefit or use of the indorser or of another person.

Section 3-206. Effect of Restrictive Indorsement

(1) No restrictive indorsement prevents further transfer or negotiation of the instrument.

(2) An intermediary bank, or a payor bank which is not the depository bank, is neither given notice nor otherwise affected by a restrictive indorsement of any person except the bank's immediate transferor or the person presenting for payment.

(3) Except for an intermediary bank, any transferee under an indorsement which is conditional or includes the words "for collection", "for deposit", "Pay any bank", or like terms (subparagraphs (a) and (c) of Section 3-205) must pay or apply any value given by him for or on the security of the instrument consistently with the indorsement and to the extent that he does so he becomes a holder for value. In addition such transferee is a holder in due course if he otherwise complies with the requirements of Section 3-302 on what constitutes a holder in due course.

(4) The first taker under an indorsement for the benefit of the indorser or another person (subparagraph (d) of Section 3-205) must pay or apply any value given by him for or on the security of the instrument consistently with the indorsement and to the extent that he does so he becomes a holder for value. In addition such taker is a holder in due course if he otherwise complies with the requirements of Section 3-302 on what constitutes a holder in due course. A later holder for value is neither given notice nor otherwise affected by such restrictive indorsement unless he has knowledge that a fiduciary or other person has negotiated the instrument in any transaction for his own benefit or otherwise in breach of duty (subsection (2) of Section 3-304).

Section 3-207. Negotiation Effective Although It May Be Rescinded

(1) Negotiation is effective to transfer the instrument although the negotiation is

   (a)   made by an infant, a corporation exceeding its powers, or any other person without capacity; or

   (b)   obtained by fraud, duress or mistake of any kind; or

   (c)   part of an illegal transaction; or

   (d)   made in breach of duty.

(2) Except as against a subsequent holder in due course such negotiation is in an appropriate case subject to rescission, the declaration of a constructive trust or any other remedy permitted by law.

Section 3-208. Reacquisition

Where an instrument is returned to or reacquired by a prior party he may cancel any indorsement which is not necessary to his title and reissue or further negotiate the instrument, but any intervening party is discharged as against the reacquiring party and subsequent holders not in due course and if his indorsement has been cancelled is discharged as against subsequent holders in due course as well.

PART **3**

Rights of a Holder

Section 3-301. Rights of a Holder

The holder of an instrument whether or not he is the owner may transfer or negotiate it and, except as otherwise provided in Section 3–603 on payment or satisfaction, discharge it or enforce payment in his own name.

Section 3–302.   Holder in Due Course

(1) A holder in due course is a holder who takes the instrument

(a)   for value; and

(b)   in good faith; and

(c)   without notice that it is overdue or has been dishonored or of any defense against or claim to it on the part of any person.

(2) A payee may be a holder in due course.

(3) A holder does not become a holder in due course of an instrument:

(a)   by purchase of it at judicial sale or by taking it under legal process; or

(b)   by acquiring it in taking over an estate; or

(c)   by purchasing it as part of a bulk transaction not in regular course of business of the transferor.

(4) A purchaser of a limited interest can be a holder in due course only to the extent of the interest purchased.

Section 3–303.   Taking for Value

A holder takes the instrument for value

(a)   to the extent that the agreed consideration has been performed or that he acquires a security interest in or a lien on the instrument otherwise than by legal process; or

(b)   when he takes the instrument in payment of or as security for an antecedent claim against any person whether or not the claim is due; or

(c)   when he gives a negotiable instrument for it or makes an irrevocable commitment to a third person.

Section 3–304.   Notice to Purchaser

(1) The purchaser has notice of a claim or defense if

(a)   the instrument is so incomplete, bears such visible evidence of forgery or alteration, or is otherwise so irregular as to call into question its validity, terms or ownership or to create an ambiguity as to the party to pay; or

(b)   the purchaser has notice that the obligation of any party is voidable in whole or in part, or that all parties have been discharged.

(2) The purchaser has notice of a claim against the instrument when he has knowledge that a fiduciary has negotiated the instrument in payment of or as security for his own debt or in any transaction for his own benefit or otherwise in breach of duty.

(3) The purchaser has notice that an instrument is overdue if he has reason to know

(a)   that any part of the principal amount is overdue or that there is an uncured default in payment of another instrument of the same series; or

(b)   that acceleration of the instrument has been made; or

(c)   that he is taking a demand instrument after demand has been made or more than a reasonable length of time after its issue. A reasonable time for a check drawn and payable within the states and territories of the United States and the District of Columbia is presumed to be thirty days.

(4) Knowledge of the following facts does not of itself give the purchaser notice of a defense or claim

(a)   that the instrument is antedated or postdated;

(b)   that it was issued or negotiated in return for an executory promise or accompanied by a separate agreement, unless the purchaser has notice that a defense or claim has arisen from the terms thereof;

(c)   that any party has signed for accommodation;

(d)   that an incomplete instrument has been completed, unless the purchaser has notice of any improper completion;

(e)   that any person negotiating the instrument is or was a fiduciary;

(f)   that there has been default in payment of interest on the instrument or in payment of any other instrument, except one of the same series.

(5) The filing or recording of a document does not of itself constitute notice within the provisions of this Article to a person who would otherwise be a holder in due course.

(6) To be effective notice must be received at such time and in such manner as to give a reasonable opportunity to act on it.

Section 3–305. Rights of a Holder in Due Course

To the extent that a holder is a holder in due course he takes the instrument free from

(1) all claims to it on the part of any person; and

(2) all defenses of any party to the instrument with whom the holder has not dealt except

(a) infancy, to the extent that it is a defense to a simple contract; and

(b) such other incapacity, or duress, or illegality of the transaction, as renders the obligation of the party a nullity; and

(c) such misrepresentation as has induced the party to sign the instrument with neither knowledge nor reasonable opportunity to obtain knowledge of its character or its essential terms; and

(d) discharge in insolvency proceedings; and

(e) any other discharge of which the holder has notice when he takes the instrument.

Section 3–306. Rights of One Not Holder in Due Course

Unless he has the rights of a holder in due course any person takes the instrument subject to

(a) all valid claims to it on the part of any person; and

(b) all defenses of any party which would be available in an action on a simple contract; and

(c) the defenses of want or failure of consideration, non-performance of any condition precedent, non-delivery, or delivery for a special purpose (Section 3–408); and

(d) the defense that he or a person through whom he holds the instrument acquired it by theft, or that payment or satisfaction to such holder would be inconsistent with the terms of a restrictive indorsement. The claim of any third person to the instrument is not otherwise available as a defense to any party liable thereon unless the third person himself defends the action for such party.

Section 3–307. Burden of Establishing Signatures, Defenses and Due Course

(1) Unless specifically denied in the pleadings each signature on an instrument is admitted. When the effectiveness of a signature is put in issue

(a) the burden of establishing it is on the party claiming under the signature; but

(b) the signature is presumed to be genuine or authorized except where the action is to enforce the obligation of a purported signer who has died or become incompetent before proof is required.

(2) When signatures are admitted or established, production of the instrument entitles a holder to recover on it unless the defendant establishes a defense.

(3) After it is shown that a defense exists a person claiming the rights of a holder in due course has the burden of establishing that he or some person under whom he claims is in all respects a holder in due course.

PART **4**

Liability of Parties

Section 3–401. Signature

(1) No person is liable on an instrument unless his signature appears thereon.

(2) A signature is made by use of any name, including any trade or assumed name, upon an instrument, or by any word or mark used in lieu of a written signature.

Section 3–402. Signature in Ambiguous Capacity

Unless the instrument clearly indicates that a signature is made in some other capacity it is an indorsement.

Section 3–403. Signature by Authorized Representative

(1) A signature may be made by any agent or other representative, and his authority to make it may be established as in other cases of representation. No particular form of appointment is necessary to establish such authority.

(2) An authorized representative who signs his own name to an instrument

(a) is personally obligated if the instrument neither names the person represented nor shows that the representative signed in a representative capacity;

(b) except as otherwise established between the immediate parties, is personally obligated if the instrument names the person represented but does not show that the representative signed in a representative capacity, or if the instrument does not name the person represented but does show that the representative signed in a representative capacity.

(3) Except as otherwise established the name of an organization preceded or followed by the name and office of an authorized individual is a signature made in a representative capacity.

Section 3–404. Unauthorized Signatures

(1) Any unauthorized signature is wholly inoperative as that of the person whose name is signed unless he ratifies it or is precluded from denying it; but it operates as the signature of the unauthorized signer in favor of any person who in good faith pays the instrument or takes it for value.

(2) Any unauthorized signature may be ratified for all purposes of this Article. Such ratification does not of itself affect any rights of the person ratifying against the actual signer.

Section 3–405. Impostors; Signature in Name of Payee

(1) An indorsement by any person in the name of a named payee is effective if

    (a) an impostor by use of the mails or otherwise has induced the maker or drawer to issue the instrument to him or his confederate in the name of the payee; or

    (b) a person signing as or on behalf of a maker or drawer intends the payee to have no interest in the instrument; or

    (c) an agent or employee of the maker or drawer has supplied him with the name of the payee intending the latter to have no such interest.

(2) Nothing in this section shall affect the criminal or civil liability of the person so indorsing.

Section 3–406. Negligence Contributing to Alteration or Unauthorized Signature

Any person who by his negligence substantially contributes to a material alteration of the instrument or to the making of an unauthorized signature is precluded from asserting the alteration or lack of authority against a holder in due course or against a drawee or other payor who pays the instrument in good faith and in accordance with the reasonable commercial standards of the drawee's or payor's business.

Section 3–407. Alteration

(1) Any alteration of an instrument is material which changes the contract of any party thereto in any respect, including any such change in

    (a) the number or relations of the parties; or

    (b) an incomplete instrument, by completing it otherwise than as authorized; or

    (c) the writing as signed, by adding to it or by removing any part of it.

(2) As against any person other than a subsequent holder in due course

    (a) alteration by the holder which is both fraudulent and material discharges any party whose contract is thereby changed unless that party assents or is precluded from asserting the defense;

    (b) no other alteration discharges any party and the instrument may be enforced according to its original tenor, or as to incomplete instruments according to the authority given.

(3) A subsequent holder in due course may in all cases enforce the instrument according to its original tenor, and when an incomplete instrument has been completed, he may enforce it as completed.

Section 3–408. Consideration

Want or failure of consideration is a defense as against any person not having the rights of a holder in due course (Section 3–305), except that no consideration is necessary for an instrument or obligation thereon given in payment of or as security for an antecedent obligation of any kind. Nothing in this section shall be taken to displace any statute outside this Act under which a promise is enforceable notwithstanding lack or failure of consideration. Partial failure of consideration is a defense pro tanto whether or not the failure is in an ascertained or liquidated amount.

Section 3–409. Draft Not an Assignment

(1) A check or other draft does not of itself operate as an assignment of any funds in the hands of the drawee available for its payment, and the drawee is not liable on the instrument until he accepts it.

(2) Nothing in this section shall affect any liability in contract, tort or otherwise arising from any letter of

credit or other obligation or representation which is not an acceptance.

Section 3–410.   Definition and Operation of Acceptance

(1) Acceptance is the drawee's signed engagement to honor the draft as presented. It must be written on the draft, and may consist of his signature alone. It becomes operative when completed by delivery or notification.

(2) A draft may be accepted although it has not been signed by the drawer or is otherwise incomplete or is overdue or has been dishonored.

(3) Where the draft is payable at a fixed period after sight and the acceptor fails to date his acceptance the holder may complete it by supplying a date in good faith.

Section 3–411.   Certification of a Check

(1) Certification of a check is acceptance. Where a holder procures certification the drawer and all prior indorsers are discharged.

(2) Unless otherwise agreed a bank has no obligation to certify a check.

(3) A bank may certify a check before returning it for lack of proper indorsement. If it does so the drawer is discharged.

Section 3–412.   Acceptance Varying Draft

(1) Where the drawee's preferred acceptance in any manner varies the draft as presented the holder may refuse the acceptance and treat the draft as dishonored in which case the drawee is entitled to have his acceptance cancelled.

(2) The terms of the draft are not varied by an acceptance to pay at any particular bank or place in the United States, unless the acceptance states that the draft is to be paid only at such bank or place.

(3) Where the holder assents to an acceptance varying the terms of the draft each drawer and indorser who does not affirmatively assent is discharged.

Section 3–413.   Contract of Maker, Drawer and Acceptor

(1) The maker or acceptor engages that he will pay the instrument according to its tenor at the time of his engagement or as completed pursuant to Section 3–115 on incomplete instruments.

(2) The drawer engages that upon dishonor of the draft and any necessary notice of dishonor or protest he will pay the amount of the draft to the holder or to any indorser who takes it up. The drawer may disclaim this liability by drawing without recourse.

(3) By making, drawing or accepting the party admits as against all subsequent parties including the drawee the existence of the payee and his then capacity to indorse.

Section 3–414.   Contract of Indorser; Order of Liability

(1) Unless the indorsement otherwise specifies (as by such words as "without recourse") every indorser engages that upon dishonor and any necessary notice of dishonor and protest he will pay the instrument according to its tenor at the time of his indorsement to the holder or to any subsequent indorser who takes it up, even though the indorser who takes it up was not obligated to do so.

(2) Unless they otherwise agree indorsers are liable to one another in the order in which they indorse, which is presumed to be the order in which their signatures appear on the instrument.

Section 3–415.   Contract of Accommodation Party

(1) An accommodation party is one who signs the instrument in any capacity for the purpose of lending his name to another party to it.

(2) When the instrument has been taken for value before it is due the accommodation party is liable in the capacity in which he has signed even though the taker knows of the accommodation.

(3) As against a holder in due course and without notice of the accommodation oral proof of the accommodation is not admissible to give the accommodation party the benefit of discharges dependent on his character as such. In other cases the accommodation character may be shown by oral proof.

(4) An indorsement which shows that it is not in the chain of title is notice of its accommodation character.

(5) An accommodation party is not liable to the party accommodated, and if he pays the instrument has a right of recourse on the instrument against such party.

Section 3–416.   Contract of Guarantor

(1) "Payment guaranteed" or equivalent words added to a signature mean that the signer engages that if the

instrument is not paid when due he will pay it according to its tenor without resort by the holder to any other party.

(2) "Collection guaranteed" or equivalent words added to a signature mean that the signer engages that if the instrument is not paid when due he will pay it according to its tenor, but only after the holder has reduced his claim against the maker or acceptor to judgment and execution has been returned unsatisfied, or after the maker or acceptor has become insolvent or it is otherwise apparent that it is useless to proceed against him.

(3) Words of guaranty which do not otherwise specify guarantee payment.

(4) No words of guaranty added to the signature of a sole maker or acceptor affect his liability on the instrument. Such words added to the signature of one of two or more makers or acceptors create a presumption that the signature is for the accommodation of the others.

(5) When words of guaranty are used presentment, notice of dishonor and protest are not necessary to charge the user.

(6) Any guaranty written on the instrument is enforcible notwithstanding any statute of frauds.

Section 3–417. Warranties on Presentment and Transfer

(1) Any person who obtains payment or acceptance and any prior transferor warrants to a person who in good faith pays or accepts that

   (a)   he has a good title to the instrument or is authorized to obtain payment or acceptance on behalf of one who has a good title; and

   (b)   he has no knowledge that the signature of the maker or drawer is unauthorized, except that this warranty is not given by a holder in due course acting in good faith

       (i)   to a maker with respect to the maker's own signature; or

       (ii)   to a drawer with respect to the drawer's own signature, whether or not the drawer is also the drawee; or

       (iii)   to an acceptor of a draft if the holder in due course took the draft after the acceptance or obtained the acceptance without knowledge that the drawer's signature was unauthorized; and

   (c)   the instrument has not been materially altered, except that this warranty is not given by a holder in due course acting in good faith

       (i)   to the maker of a note; or

       (ii)   to the drawer of a draft whether or not the drawer is also the drawee; or

       (iii)   to the acceptor of a draft with respect to an alteration made prior to the acceptance if the holder in due course took the draft after the acceptance, even though the acceptance provided "payable as originally drawn" or equivalent terms; or

       (iv)   to the acceptor of a draft with respect to an alteration made after the acceptance.

(2) Any person who transfers an instrument and receives consideration warrants to his transferee and if the transfer is by indorsement to any subsequent holder who takes the instrument in good faith that

   (a)   he has a good title to the instrument or is authorized to obtain payment or acceptance on behalf of one who has good title and the transfer is otherwise rightful; and

   (b)   all signatures are genuine or authorized; and

   (c)   the instrument has not been materially altered; and

   (d)   no defense of any party is good against him; and

   (e)   he has no knowledge of any insolvency proceeding instituted with respect to the maker or acceptor or the drawer of an unaccepted instrument.

(3) By transferring "without recourse" the transferor limits the obligation stated in subsection (2)(d) to a warranty that he has no knowledge of such a defense.

(4) A selling agent or broker who does not disclose the fact that he is acting only as such gives the warranties provided in this section, but if he makes such disclosure warrants only his good faith and authority.

Section 3–418. Finality of Payment or Acceptance

Except for recovery of bank payments as provided in the Article on Bank Deposits and Collections (Article 4) and except for liability for breach of warranty on presentment under the preceding section, payment or acceptance of any instrument is final in favor of a holder in due course, or a person who has in good faith changed his position in reliance on the payment.

Section 3–419. Conversion of Instrument; Innocent Representative

(1) An instrument is converted when

(a) a drawee to whom it is delivered for acceptance refuses to return it on demand; or

(b) any person to whom it is delivered for payment refuses on demand either to pay or to return it; or

(c) it is paid on a forged indorsement.

(2) In an action against a drawee under subsection (1) the measure of the drawee's liability is the face amount of the instrument. In any other action under subsection (1) the measure of liability is presumed to be the face amount of the instrument.

(3) Subject to provisions of this Act concerning restrictive indorsements a representative, including a depositary or collecting bank, who has in good faith and in accordance with the reasonable commercial standards applicable to the business of such representative dealt with an instrument or its proceeds on behalf of one who was not the true owner is not liable in conversion or otherwise to the true owner beyond the amount of any proceeds remaining in his hands.

(4) An intermediary bank or payor bank which is not a depositary bank is not liable in conversion solely by reason of the fact that proceeds of an item indorsed restrictively (Sections 3–205 and 3–206) are not paid or applied consistently with the restrictive indorsement of an indorser other than its immediate transferor.

PART 5

Presentment, Notice of Dishonor and Protest

Section 3–501. When Presentment, Notice of Dishonor, and Protest Necessary or Permissible

(1) Unless excused (Section 3–511) presentment is necessary to charge secondary parties as follows:

(a) presentment for acceptance is necessary to charge the drawer and indorsers of a draft where the draft so provides, or is payable elsewhere than at the residence or place of business of the drawee, or its date of payment depends upon such presentment. The holder may at his option present for acceptance any other draft payable at a stated date;

(b) presentment for payment is necessary to charge any indorser;

(c) in the case of any drawer, the acceptor of a draft payable at a bank or the maker of a note payable at a bank, presentment for payment is necessary, but failure to make presentment discharges such drawer, acceptor or maker only as stated in Section 3–502 (1)(b).

(2) Unless excused (Section 3–511)

(a) notice of any dishonor is necessary to charge any indorser;

(b) in the case of any drawer, the acceptor of a draft payable at a bank or the maker of a note payable at a bank, notice of any dishonor is necessary, but failure to give such notice discharges such drawer, acceptor or maker only as stated in Section 3–502 (1)(b).

(3) Unless excused (Section 3–511) protest of any dishonor is necessary to charge the drawer and indorsers of any draft which on its face appears to be drawn or payable outside of the states, territories, dependencies, and possessions of the United States, the District of Columbia and the Commonwealth of Puerto Rico. The holder may at his option make protest of any dishonor of any other instrument and in the case of a foreign draft may on insolvency of the acceptor before maturity make protest for better security.

(4) Notwithstanding any provision of this section, neither presentment nor notice of dishonor nor protest is necessary to charge an indorser who has indorsed an instrument after maturity.

Section 3–502. Unexcused Delay; Discharge

(1) Where without excuse any necessary presentment or notice of dishonor is delayed beyond the time when it is due

(a) any indorser is discharged; and

(b) any drawer or the acceptor of a draft payable at a bank or the maker of a note payable at a bank who because the drawee or payor bank becomes insolvent during the delay is deprived of funds maintained with the drawee or payor bank to cover the instrument may discharge his liability by written assignment to the holder of his rights against the drawee or payor bank in respect of such funds, but such drawer, acceptor or maker is not otherwise discharged.

(2) Where without excuse a necessary protest is delayed beyond the time when it is due any drawer or indorser is discharged.

Section 3–503. Time of Presentment

(1) Unless a different time is expressed in the instrument the time for any presentment is determined as follows:

(a) where an instrument is payable at or a fixed period after a stated date any presentment for acceptance must be made on or before the date it is payable;

(b) where an instrument is payable after sight it must either be presented for acceptance or negotiated within a reasonable time after date or issue whichever is later;

(c) where an instrument shows the date on which it is payable presentment for payment is due on that date;

(d) where an instrument is accelerated presentment for payment is due within a reasonable time after the acceleration;

(e) with respect to the liability of any secondary party presentment for acceptance or payment of any other instrument is due within a reasonable time after such party becomes liable thereon.

(2) A reasonable time for presentment is determined by the nature of the instrument, any usage of banking or trade and the facts of the particular case. In the case of an uncertified check which is drawn and payable within the United States and which is not a draft drawn by a bank the following are presumed to be reasonable periods within which to present for payment or to initiate bank collection:

(a) with respect to the liability of the drawer, thirty days after date or issue whichever is later; and

(b) with respect to the liability of an indorser, seven days after his indorsement.

(3) Where any presentment is due on a day which is not a full business day for either the person making presentment or the party to pay or accept, presentment is due on the next following day which is a full business day for both parties.

(4) Presentment to be sufficient must be made at a reasonable hour, and if at a bank during its banking day.

Section 3–504. How Presentment Made

(1) Presentment is a demand for acceptance or payment made upon the maker, acceptor, drawee or other payor by or on behalf of the holder.

(2) Presentment may be made

(a) by mail, in which event the time of presentment is determined by the time of receipt of the mail; or

(b) through a clearing house; or

(c) at the place of acceptance of payment specified in the instrument or if there be none at the place of business or residence of the party to accept or pay. If neither the party to accept r pay nor anyone authorized to act for him is present or accessible at such place presentment is excused.

(3) It may be made

(a) to any one of two or more makers, acceptors, drawees or other payors; or

(b) to any person who has authority to make or refuse the acceptance of payment.

(4) A draft accepted or a note made payable at a bank in the United States must be presented at such bank.

(5) In the cases described in Section 4–210 presentment may be made in the manner and with the result stated in that section.

Section 3–505. Rights of Party to Whom Presentment Is Made

(1) The party to whom presentment is made may without dishonor require

(a) exhibition of the instrument; and

(b) reasonable identification of the person making presentment and evidence of his authority to make it if made for another; and

(c) that the instrument be produced for acceptance or payment at a place specified in it, or if there be none at any place reasonable in the circumstances; and

(d) a signed receipt on the instrument for any partial or full payment and its surrender upon full payment.

(2) Failure to comply with any such requirement invalidates the presentment but the person presenting

has a reasonable time in which to comply and the time for acceptance or payment runs from the time of compliance.

Section 3–506.   Time Allowed for Acceptance or Payment

(1) Acceptance may be deferred without dishonor until the close of the next business day following presentment. The holder may also in a good faith effort to obtain acceptance and without either dishonor of the instrument or discharge of secondary parties allow postponement of acceptance for an additional business day.

(2) Except as a longer time is allowed in the case of documentary drafts drawn under a letter of credit, and unless an earlier time is agreed to by the party to pay, payment of an instrument may be deferred without dishonor pending reasonable examination to determine whether it is properly payable, but payment must be made in any event before the close of business on the day of presentment.

Section 3–507.   Dishonor; Holder's Right of Recourse; Term Allowing Re-Presentment

(1) An instrument is dishonored when

(a)   a necessary or optional presentment is duly made and due acceptance or payment is refused or cannot be obtained within the prescribed time or in case of bank collections the instrument is seasonably returned by the midnight deadline (Section 4–301); or

(b)   presentment is excused and the instrument is not duly accepted or paid.

(2) Subject to any necessary notice of dishonor and protest, the holder has upon dishonor an immediate right of recourse against the drawers and indorsers.

(3) Return of an instrument for lack of proper indorsement is not dishonor.

(4) A term in a draft or an indorsement thereof allowing a stated time for re-presentment in the event of any dishonor of the draft by nonacceptance if a time draft or by nonpayment if a sight draft gives the holder as against any secondary party bound by the term an option to waive the dishonor without affecting the liability of the secondary party and he may present again up to the end of the stated time.

Section 3–508.   Notice of Dishonor

(1) Notice of dishonor may be given to any person who may be liable on the instrument by or on behalf of the holder or any party who has himself received notice, or any other party who can be compelled to pay the instrument. In addition an agent or bank in whose hands the instrument is dishonored may give notice to his principal or customer or to another agent or bank from which the instrument was received.

(2) Any necessary notice must be given by a bank before its midnight deadline and by any other person before midnight of the third business day after dishonor or receipt of notice of dishonor.

(3) Notice may be given in any reasonable manner. It may be oral or written and in any terms which identify the instrument and state that it has been dishonored. A misdescription which does not mislead the party notified does not vitiate the notice. Sending the instrument bearing a stamp, ticket or writing stating that acceptance or payment has been refused or sending a notice of debit with respect to the instrument is sufficient.

(4) Written notice is given when sent although it is not received.

(5) Notice to one partner is notice to each although the firm has been dissolved.

(6) When any party is in insolvency proceedings instituted after the issue of the instrument notice may be given either to the party or to the representative of his estate.

(7) When any party is dead or incompetent notice may be sent to his last known address or given to his personal representative.

(8) Notice operates for the benefit of all parties who have rights on the instrument against the party notified.

Section 3–509.   Protest; Noting for Protest

(1) A protest is a certificate of dishonor made under the hand and seal of a United States consul or vice consul or a notary public or other person authorized to certify dishonor by the law of the place where dishonor occurs. It may be made upon information satisfactory to such person.

(2) The protest must identify the instrument and certify either that due presentment has been made or the reason why it is excused and that the instrument has been dishonored by nonacceptance or nonpayment.

(3) The protest may also certify that notice of dishonor has been given to all parties or to specified parties.

(4) Subject to subsection (5) any necessary protest is due by the time that notice of dishonor is due.

(5) If, before protest is due, an instrument has been noted for protest by the officer to make protest, the protest may be made at any time thereafter as of the date of the noting.

Section 3–510. Evidence of Dishonor and Notice of Dishonor

The following are admissible as evidence and create a presumption of dishonor and of any notice of dishonor therein shown:

(a) a document regular in form as provided in the preceding section which purports to be a protest;

(b) the purported stamp or writing of the drawee, payor bank or presenting bank on the instrument or accompanying it stating that acceptance or payment has been refused for reasons consistent with dishonor;

(c) any book or record of the drawee, payor bank, or any collecting bank kept in the usual course of business which shows dishonor, even though there is no evidence of who made the entry.

Section 3–511. Waived or Excused Presentment, Protest or Notice of Dishonor or Delay Therein

(1) Delay in presentment, protest or notice of dishonor is excused when the party is without notice that it is due or when the delay is caused by circumstances beyond his control and he exercises reasonable diligence after the cause of the delay ceases to operate.

(2) Presentment or notice or protest as the case may be is entirely excused when

(a) the party to be charged has waived it expressly or by implication either before or after it is due; or

(b) such party has himself dishonored the instrument or has countermanded payment or otherwise has no reason to expect or right to require that the instrument be accepted or paid; or

(c) by reasonable diligence the presentment or protest cannot be made or the notice given.

(3) Presentment is also entirely excused when

(a) the maker, acceptor or drawee of any instrument except a documentary draft is dead or in insolvency proceedings instituted after the issue of the instrument; or

(b) acceptance or payment is refused but not for want of proper presentment.

(4) Where a draft has been dishonored by nonacceptance a later presentment for payment and any notice of dishonor and protest for nonpayment are excused unless in the meantime the instrument has been accepted.

(5) A waiver of protest is also a waiver of presentment and of notice of dishonor even though protest is not required.

(6) Where a waiver of presentment or notice or protest is embodied in the instrument itself it is binding upon all parties; but where it is written above the signature of an indorser it binds him only.

PART 6

Discharge

Section 3–601. Discharge of Parties

(1) The extent of the discharge of any party from liability on an instrument is governed by the sections on

(a) payment or satisfaction (Section 3–603); or

(b) tender of payment (Section 3–604); or

(c) cancellation or renunciation (Section 3–605); or

(d) impairment of right of recourse or of collateral (Section 3–606); or

(e) reacquisition of the instrument by a prior party (Section 3–208); or

(f) fraudulent and material alteration (Section 3–407); or

(g) certification of a check (Section 3–411); or

(h) acceptance varying a draft (Section 3–412); or

(i) unexcused delay in presentment or notice of dishonor or protest (Section 3–502).

(2) Any party is also discharged from his liability on an instrument to another party by any other act or agreement with such party which would discharge his simple contract for the payment of money.

(3) The liability of all parties is discharged when any party who has himself no right of action or recourse on the instrument

(a) reacquires the instrument in his own right; or

(b) is discharged under any provision of this Article, except as otherwise provided with respect to discharge for impairment of recourse or of collateral (Section 3–606).

Section 3–602. Effect of Discharge Against Holder in Due Course

No discharge of any party provided by this Article is effective against a subsequent holder in due course unless he has notice thereof when he takes the instrument.

Section 3–603. Payment or Satisfaction

(1) The liability of any party is discharged to the extent of his payment or satisfaction to the holder even though it is made with knowledge of a claim of another person to the instrument unless prior to such payment or satisfaction the person making the claim either supplies indemnity deemed adequate by the party seeking the discharge or enjoins payment or satisfaction by order of a court of competent jurisdiction in an action in which the adverse claimant and the holder are parties. This subsection does not, however, result in the discharge of the liability

(a) of a party who in bad faith pays or satisfies a holder who acquired the instrument by theft or who (unless having the rights of a holder in due course) holds through one who so acquired it; or

(b) of a party (other than an intermediary bank or a payor bank which is not a depositary bank) who pays or satisfies the holder of an instrument which has been restrictively indorsed in a manner not consistent with the terms of such restrictive indorsement.

(2) Payment or satisfaction may be made with the consent of the holder by any person including a stranger to the instrument. Surrender of the instrument to such a person gives him the rights of a transferee (Section 3–201).

Section 3–604. Tender of Payment

(1) Any party making tender of full payment to a holder when or after it is due is discharged to the extent of all subsequent liability for interest, costs and attorney's fees.

(2) The holder's refusal of such tender wholly discharges any party who has a right of recourse against the party making the tender.

(3) Where the maker or acceptor of an instrument payable otherwise than on demand is able and ready to pay at every place of payment specified in the instrument when it is due, it is equivalent to tender.

Section 3–605. Cancellation and Renunciation

(1) The holder of an instrument may even without consideration discharge any party

(a) in any manner apparent on the face of the instrument or the indorsement, as by intentionally cancelling the instrument or the party's signature by destruction or mutilation, or by striking out the party's signature; or

(b) by renouncing his rights by a writing signed and delivered or by surrender of the instrument to the party to be discharged.

(2) Neither cancellation nor renunciation without surrender of the instrument affects the title thereto.

Section 3–606. Impairment of Recourse or of Collateral

(1) The holder discharges any party to the instrument to the extent that without such party's consent the holder

(a) without express reservation of rights releases or agrees not to sue any person against whom the party has to the knowledge of the holder a right of recourse or agrees to suspend the right to enforce against such person the instrument or collateral or otherwise discharges such person, except that failure or delay in effecting any required presentment, protest or notice of dishonor with respect to any such person does not discharge any party as to whom presentment, protest or notice of dishonor is effective or unnecessary; or

(b) unjustifiably impairs any collateral for the instrument given by or on behalf of the party or any person against whom he has a right of recourse.

(2) By express reservation of rights against a party with a right of recourse the holder preserves

(a) all his rights against such party as of the time when the instrument was originally due; and

(b) the right of the party to pay the instrument as of that time; and

(c) all rights of such party to recourse against others.

PART 7

Advice of International Sight Draft

Section 3–701. Letter of Advice of International Sight Draft

(1) A "letter of advice" is a drawer's communication to the drawee that a described draft has been drawn.

(2) Unless otherwise agreed when a bank receives from another bank a letter of advice of an international sight draft the drawee bank may immediately debit the drawer's account and stop the running of interest pro tanto. Such a debit and any resulting credit to any account covering outstanding drafts leaves in the drawer full power to stop payment or otherwise dispose of the amount and creates no trust or interest in favor of the holder.

(3) Unless otherwise agreed and except where a draft is drawn under a credit issued by the drawee, the drawee of an international sight draft owes the drawer no duty to pay an unadvised draft but if it does so and the draft is genuine, may appropriately debit the drawer's account.

PART 8

Miscellaneous

Section 3–801. Drafts in a Set

(1) Where a draft is drawn in a set of parts, each of which is numbered and expressed to be an order only if no other part has been honored, the whole of the parts constitutes one draft but a taker of any part may become a holder in due course of the draft.

(2) Any person who negotiates, indorses or accepts a single part of a draft drawn in a set thereby becomes liable to any holder in due course of that part as if it were the whole set, but as between different holders in due course to whom different parts have been ne-

gotiated the holder whose title first accrues has all rights to the draft and its proceeds.

(3) As against the drawee the first presented part of a draft drawn in a set is the part entitled to payment, or if a time draft to acceptance and payment. Acceptance of any subsequently presented part renders the drawee liable thereon under subsection (2). With respect both to a holder and to the drawer payment of a subsequently presented part of a draft payable at sight has the same effect as payment of a check notwithstanding an effective stop order (Section 4–407).

(4) Except as otherwise provided in this section, where any part of a draft in a set is discharged by payment or otherwise the whole draft is discharged.

Section 3–802. Effect of Instrument on Obligation for Which It Is Given

(1) Unless otherwise agreed where an instrument is taken for an underlying obligation

(a) the obligation is pro tanto discharged if a bank is a drawer, maker or acceptor of the instrument and there is no recourse on the instrument against the underlying obligor; and

(b) in any other case the obligation is suspended pro tanto until the instrument is due or if it is payable on demand until its presentment. If the instrument is dishonored action may be maintained on either the instrument or the obligation; discharge of the underlying obligor on the instrument also discharges him on the obligation.

(2) The taking in good faith of a check which is not postdated does not of itself so extend the time on the original obligation as to discharge a surety.

Section 3–803. Notice to Third Party

Where a defendant is sued for breach of an obligation for which a third person is answerable over under this Article he may give the third person written notice of the litigation, and the person notified may then give similar notice to any other person who is answerable over to him under this Article. If the notice states that the person notified may come in and defend and that if the person notified does not do so he will in any action against him by the person giving the notice be bound by any determination of fact common to the two litigations, then unless after seasonable receipt of the notice the person notified does come in and defend he is so bound.

Section 3–804. Lost, Destroyed or Stolen Instruments

The owner of an instrument which is lost, whether by destruction, theft or otherwise, may maintain an action in his own name and recover from any party liable thereon upon due proof of his ownership, the facts which prevent his production of the instrument and its terms. The court may require security indemnifying the defendant against loss by reason of further claims on the instrument.

Section 3–805. Instruments Not Payable to Order or to Bearer

This Article applies to any instrument whose terms do not preclude transfer and which is otherwise negotiable within this Article but which is not payable to order or to bearer, except that there can be no holder in due course of such an instrument.

ARTICLE 4
BANK DEPOSITS AND COLLECTIONS

PART 1
General Provisions and Definitions

Section 4–101. Short Title

This Article shall be known and may be cited as Uniform Commercial Code — Bank Deposits and Collections.

Section 4–102. Applicability

(1) To the extent that items within this Article are also within the scope of Articles 3 and 8, they are subject to the provisions of those Articles. In the event of conflict the provisions of this Article govern those of Article 3 but the provisions of Article 8 govern those of this Article.

(2) The liability of a bank for action or nonaction with respect to any item handled by it for purposes of presentment, payment or collection is governed by the law of the place where the bank is located. In the case of action or non-action by or at a branch or separate office of a bank, its liability is governed by the law of the place where the branch or separate office is located.

Section 4–103. Variation by Agreement; Measure of Damages; Certain Action Constituting Ordinary Care

(1) The effect of the provisions of this Article may be varied by agreement except that no agreement can disclaim a bank's responsibility for its own lack of good faith or failure to exercise ordinary care or can limit the measure of damages for such lack or failure; but the parties may by agreement determine the standards by which such responsibility is to be measured if such standards are not manifestly unreasonable.

(2) Federal Reserve regulations and operating letters, clearing house rules, and the like, have the effect of agreements under subsection (1), whether or not specifically assented to by all parties interested in items handled.

(3) Action or non-action approved by this Article or pursuant to Federal Reserve regulations or operating letters constitutes the exercise of ordinary care and, in the absence of special instructions, action or non-action consistent with clearing house rules and the like or with a general banking usage not disapproved by this Article, prima facie constitutes the exercise of ordinary care.

(4) The specification or approval of certain procedures by this Article does not constitute disapproval of other procedures which may be reasonable under the circumstances.

(5) The measure of damages for failure to exercise ordinary care in handling an item is the amount of the item reduced by an amount which could not have been realized by the use of ordinary care, and where there is bad faith it includes other damages, if any, suffered by the party as a proximate consequence.

Section 4–104. Definitions and Index of Definitions

(1) In this Article unless the context otherwise requires

(a) "Account" means any account with a bank and includes a checking, time, interest or savings account;

(b) "Afternoon" means the period of a day between noon and midnight;

(c) "Banking day" means that part of any day on which a bank is open to the public for carrying on substantially all of its banking functions;

(d) "Clearing house" means any association of banks or other payors regularly clearing items;

(e) "Customer" means any person having an account with a bank or for whom a bank has agreed to collect items and includes a bank carrying an account with another bank;

(f) "Documentary draft" means any negotiable or nonnegotiable draft with accompanying documents, securities or other papers to be delivered against honor of the draft;

(g) "Item" means any instrument for the payment of money even though it is not negotiable but does not include money;

(h) "Midnight deadline" with respect to a bank is midnight on its next banking day following the banking day on which it receives the relevant item or notice or from which the time for taking action commences to run, whichever is later;

(i) "Properly payable" includes the availability of funds for payment at the time of decision to pay or dishonor;

(j) "Settle" means to pay in cash, by clearing house settlement, in a charge or credit or by remittance, or otherwise as instructed. A settlement may be either provisional or final;

(k) "Suspends payments" with respect to a bank means that it has been closed by order of the supervisory authorities, that a public officer has been appointed to take it over or that it ceases or refuses to make payments in the ordinary course of business.

(2) Other definitions applying to this Article and the sections in which they appear are:

"Collecting bank." Section 4–105.
"Depositary bank." Section 4–105.
"Intermediary bank." Section 4–105.
"Payor bank." Section 4–105.
"Presenting bank." Section 4–105.
"Remitting bank." Section 4–105.

(3) The following definitions in other Articles apply to this Article:

"Acceptance." Section 3–410.
"Certificate of deposit." Section 3–104.
"Certification." Section 3–411.
"Check." Section 3–104.
"Draft." Section 3–104.
"Holder in due course." Section 3–302.
"Notice of dishonor." Section 3–508.
"Presentment." Section 3–504.
"Protest." Section 3–509.
"Secondary party." Section 3–102.

(4) In addition Article 1 contains general definitions and principles of construction and interpretation applicable throughout this Article.

Section 4–105. **"Depositary Bank";**
"Intermediary Bank";
"Collecting Bank"; "Payor
Bank"; "Presenting Bank";
"Remitting Bank"

In this Article unless the context otherwise requires:

(a) "Depositary bank" means the first bank to which an item is transferred for collection even though it is also the payor bank;

(b) "Payor bank" means a bank by which an item is payable as drawn or accepted;

(c) "Intermediary bank" means any bank to which an item is transferred in course of collection except the depositary or payor bank;

(d) "Collecting bank" means any bank handling the item for collection except the payor bank;

(e) "Presenting bank" means any bank presenting an item except a payor bank;

(f) "Remitting bank" means any payor or intermediary bank remitting for an item.

Section 4–106. **Separate Office of a Bank**

A branch or separate office of a bank [maintaining its own deposit ledgers] is a separate bank for the purpose of computing the time within which and determining the place at or to which action may be taken or notices or orders shall be given under this Article and under Article 3.

Note: *The brackets are to make it optional with the several states whether to require a branch to maintain its own deposit ledgers in order to be considered to be a separate bank for certain purposes under Article 4. In some states, "maintaining its own deposit ledgers" is a satisfactory test. In others, branch banking practices are such that this test would not be suitable.*

Section 4–107. **Time of Receipt of Items**

(1) For the purpose of allowing time to process items, prove balances and make the necessary entries on its books to determine its position for the day, a bank may fix an afternoon hour of two P.M. or later as a cut-off hour for the handling of money and items and the making of entries on its books.

(2) Any item or deposit of money received on any

day after a cut-off hour so fixed or after the close of the banking day may be treated as being received at the opening of the next banking day.

Section 4–108. Delays

(1) Unless otherwise instructed, a collecting bank in a good faith effort to secure payment may, in the case of specific items and with or without the approval of any person involved, waive, modify or extend time limits imposed or permitted by this Act for a period not in excess of an additional banking day without discharge of secondary parties and without liability to its transferor or any prior party.

(2) Delay by a collecting bank or payor bank beyond time limits prescribed or permitted by this Act or by instructions is excused if caused by interruption of communication facilities, suspension of payments by another bank, war, emergency conditions or other circumstances beyond the control of the bank provided it exercises such diligence as the circumstances require.

Section 4–109. Process of Posting

The "process of posting" means the usual procedure followed by a payor bank in determining to pay an item and in recording the payment including one or more of the following or other steps as determined by the bank:

(a)   verification of any signature;

(b)   ascertaining that sufficient funds are available;

(c)   affixing a "paid" or other stamp;

(d)   entering a charge or entry to a customer's account;

(e)   correcting or reversing an entry or erroneous action with respect to the item.

PART **2**

Collection of Items: Depositary and Collecting Banks

Section 4–201. Presumption and Duration of Agency Status of Collecting Banks and Provisional Status of Credits; Applicability of Article; Item Indorsed "Pay Any Bank"

(1) Unless a contrary intent clearly appears and prior to the time that a settlement given by a collecting bank for an item is or becomes final (subsection (3)

of Section 4–211 and Sections 4–212 and 4–213) the bank is an agent or sub-agent of the owner of the item and any settlement given for the item is provisional. This provision applies regardless of the form of indorsement or lack of indorsement and even though credit given for the item is subject to immediate withdrawal as of right or is in fact withdrawn; but the continuance of ownership of an item by its owner and any rights of the owner to proceeds of the item are subject to rights of a collecting bank such as those resulting from outstanding advances on the item and valid rights of setoff. When an item is handled by banks for purposes of presentment, payment and collection, the relevant provisions of this Article apply even though action of parties clearly establishes that a particular bank has purchased the item and is the owner of it.

(2) After an item has been indorsed with the words "pay any bank" or the like, only a bank may acquire the rights of a holder

(a)   until the item has been returned to the customer initiating collection; or

(b)   until the item has been specially indorsed by a bank to a person who is not a bank.

Section 4–202. Responsibility for Collection; When Action Seasonable

(1) A collecting bank must use ordinary care in

(a)   presenting an item or sending it for presentment; and

(b)   sending notice of dishonor or non-payment or returning an item other than a documentary draft to the bank's transferors (or directly to the depositary bank under subsection (2) of Section 4–212; see note to Section 4–212) after learning that the item has not been paid or accepted as the case may be; and

(c)   settling for an item when the bank receives final settlement; and

(d)   making or providing for any necessary protest; and

(e)   notifying its transferor of any loss or delay in transit within a reasonable time after discovery thereof.

(2) A collecting bank taking proper action before its midnight deadline following receipt of an item or payment acts seasonably; taking proper action within a reasonably longer time may be seasonable but the bank has the burden of so establishing.

(3) Subject to subsection (1)(a), a bank is not liable for the insolvency, neglect, misconduct, mistake or default of another bank or person or for loss or destruction of an item in transit or in the possession of others.

Section 4–203.   Effect of Instructions

Subject to the provisions of Article 3 concerning conversion of instruments (Section 3–419) and the provisions of both Article 3 and this Article concerning restrictive indorsements only a collecting bank's transferor can give instructions which affect the bank or constitute notice to it and a collecting bank is not liable to prior parties for any action taken pursuant to such instructions or in accordance with any agreement with its transferor.

Section 4–204.   Methods of Sending and Presenting; Sending Direct to Payor Bank

(1)   A collecting bank must send items by reasonably prompt method taking into consideration any relevant instructions, the nature of the item, the number of such items on hand, and the cost of collection involved and the method generally used by it or others to present such items.

(2)   A collecting bank may send

(a)   any item direct to the payor bank;

(b)   any item to any non-bank payor if authorized by its transferor; and

(c)   any item other than documentary drafts to any non-bank payor, if authorized by Federal Reserve regulation or operating letter, clearing house rule or the like.

(3)   Presentment may be made by a presenting bank at a place where the payor bank has requested that presentment be made.

Section 4–205.   Supplying Missing Indorsement; No Notice from Prior Indorsement

(1)   A depositary bank which has taken an item for collection may supply any indorsement of the customer which is necessary to title unless the item contains the words "payee's indorsement required" or the like. In the absence of such a requirement a statement placed on the item by the depositary bank to the effect that the item was deposited by a customer or credited to his account is effective as the customer's indorsement.

(2)   An intermediary bank, or payor bank which is not a depositary bank, is neither given notice nor otherwise affected by a restrictive indorsement of any person except the bank's immediate transferor.

Section 4–206.   Transfer Between Banks

Any agreed method which identifies the transferor bank is sufficient for the item's further transfer to another bank.

Section 4–207.   Warranties of Customer and Collecting Bank on Transfer or Presentment of Items; Time for Claims

(1)   Each customer or collecting bank who obtains payment or acceptance of an item and each prior customer and collecting bank warrants to the payor bank or other payor who in good faith pays or accepts the item that

(a)   he has a good title to the item or is authorized to obtain payment or acceptance on behalf of one who has a good title; and

(b)   he has no knowledge that the signature of the maker or drawer is unauthorized, except that this warranty is not given by any customer or collecting bank that is a holder in due course and acts in good faith

(i)   to a maker with respect to the maker's own signature; or

(ii)   to a drawer with respect to the drawer's own signature, whether or not the drawer is also the drawee; or

(iii)   to an acceptor of an item if the holder in due course took the item after the acceptance or obtained the acceptance without knowledge that the drawer's signature was unauthorized; and

(c)   the item has not been materially altered, except that this warranty is not given by any customer or collecting bank that is a holder in due course and acts in good faith

(i)   to the maker of a note; or

(ii)   to the drawer of a draft whether or not the drawer is also the drawee; or

(iii)   to the acceptor of an item with respect to an alteration made prior to the acceptance if the holder in due course took the item after the acceptance, even though the acceptance provided "payable as originally drawn" or equivalent terms; or

(iv) to the acceptor of an item with respect to an alteration made after the acceptance.

(2) Each customer and collecting bank who transfers an item and receives a settlement or other consideration for it warrants to his transferee and to any subsequent collecting bank who takes the item in good faith that

(a) he has a good title to the item or is authorized to obtain payment or acceptance on behalf of one who has a good title and the transfer is otherwise rightful; and

(b) all signatures are genuine or authorized; and

(c) the item has not been materially altered; and

(d) no defense of any party is good against him; and

(e) he has no knowledge of an insolvency proceeding instituted with respect to the maker or acceptor or the drawer of an unaccepted item.

In addition each customer and collecting bank so transferring an item and receiving a settlement or other consideration engages that upon dishonor and any necessary notice of dishonor and protest he will take up the item.

(3) The warranties and the engagement to honor set forth in the two preceding subsections arise notwithstanding the absence of indorsement or words of guaranty or warranty in the transfer or presentment and a collecting bank remains liable for their breach despite remittance to its transferor. Damages for breach of such warranties or engagement to honor shall not exceed the consideration received by the customer or collecting bank responsible plus finance charges and expenses related to the item, if any.

(4) Unless a claim for breach of warranty under this section is made within a reasonable time after the person claiming learns of the breach, the person liable is discharged to the extent of any loss caused by the delay in making claim.

Section 4–208. Security Interest of Collecting Bank in Items, Accompanying Documents and Proceeds

(1) A bank has a security interest in an item and any accompanying documents or the proceeds of either

(a) in case of an item deposited in an account to the extent to which credit given for the item has been withdrawn or applied;

(b) in case of an item for which it has given credit available for withdrawal as of right, to the extent of the credit given whether or not the credit is drawn upon and whether or not there is a right of charge-back; or

(c) if it makes an advance on or against the item.

(2) When credit which has been given for several items received at one time or pursuant to a single agreement is withdrawn or applied in part the security interest remains upon all the items, any accompanying documents or the proceeds of either. For the purpose of this section, credits first given are first withdrawn.

(3) Receipt by a collecting bank of a final settlement for an item is a realization on its security interest in the item, accompanying documents and proceeds. To the extent and so long as the bank does not receive final settlement for the item or give up possession of the item or accompanying documents for purposes other than collection, the security interest continues and is subject to the provisions of Article 9 except that

(a) no security agreement is necessary to make the security interest enforceable (subsection (1)(b) of Section 9–203); and

(b) no filing is required to perfect the security interest; and

(c) the security interest has priority over conflicting perfected security interests in the item, accompanying documents or proceeds.

Section 4–209. When Bank Gives Value for Purposes of Holder in Due Course

For purposes of determining its status as a holder in due course, the bank has given value to the extent that it has a security interest in an item provided that the bank otherwise complies with the requirements of Section 3–302 on what constitutes a holder in due course.

Section 4–210. Presentment by Notice of Item Not Payable by, Through or at a Bank; Liability of Secondary Parties

(1) Unless otherwise instructed, a collecting bank may present an item not payable by, through or at a bank by sending to the party to accept or pay a written notice that the bank holds the item for acceptance or payment. The notice must be sent in time to be received on or before the day when presentment is due and the bank must meet any requirement of the party to

accept or pay under Section 3–505 by the close of the bank's next banking day after it knows of the requirement.

(2) Where presentment is made by notice and neither honor nor request for compliance with a requirement under Section 3–505 is received by the close of business on the day after maturity or in the case of demand items by the close of business on the third banking day after notice was sent, the presenting bank may treat the time as dishonored and charge any secondary party by sending him notice of the facts.

Section 4–211. Media of Remittance; Provisional and Final Settlement in Remittance Cases

(1) A collecting bank may take in settlement of an item

(a)   a check of the remitting bank or of another bank on any bank except the remitting bank; or

(b)   a cashier's check or similar primary obligation of a remitting bank which is a member of or clears through a member of the same clearing house or group as the collecting bank; or

(c)   appropriate authority to charge an account of the remitting bank or of another bank with the collecting bank; or

(d)   if the item is drawn upon or payable by a person other than a bank, a cashier's check, certified check or other bank check or obligation.

(2) If before its midnight deadline the collecting bank properly dishonors a remittance check or authorization to charge on itself or presents or forwards for collection a remittance instrument of or on another bank which is of a kind approved by subsection (1) or has not been authorized by it, the collecting bank is not liable to prior parties in the event of the dishonor of such check, instrument or authorization.

(3) A settlement for an item by means of a remittance instrument or authorization to charge is or becomes a final settlement as to both the person making and the person receiving the settlement

(a)   if the remittance instrument or authorization to charge is of a kind approved by subsection (1) or has not been authorized by the person receiving the settlement and in either case the person receiving the settlement acts seasonably before its midnight deadline in presenting, forwarding for collection or paying the instrument or authorization, — at the time the remittance instrument

or authorization is finally paid by the payor by which it is payable;

(b)   if the person receiving the settlement has authorized remittance by a nonbank check or obligation or by a cashier's check or similar primary obligation of or a check upon the payor or other remitting bank which is not of a kind approved by subsection (1)(b), — at the time of the receipt of such remittance check or obligation; or

(c)   if in a case not covered by sub-paragraphs (a) or (b) the person receiving the settlement fails to seasonably present, forward for collection, pay or return a remittance instrument or authorization to it to charge before its midnight deadline — at such midnight deadline.

Section 4–212. Right of Charge-Back or Refund

(1) If a collecting bank has made provisional settlement with its customer for an item and itself fails by reason of dishonor, suspension of payments by a bank or otherwise to receive a settlement for the item which is or becomes final, the bank may revoke the settlement given by it, charge back the amount of any credit given for the item to its customer's account or obtain refund from its customer whether or not it is able to return the items if by its midnight deadline or within a longer reasonable time after it learns the facts it returns the item or sends notification of the facts. These rights to revoke, charge-back and obtain refund terminate if and when a settlement for the item received by the bank is or becomes final (subsection (3) of Section 4–211 and subsections (2) and (3) of Section 4–213).

[(2) Within the time and manner prescribed by this section and Section 4–301, an intermediary or payor bank, as the case may be, may return an unpaid item directly to the depositary bank and may send for collection a draft on the depositary bank and obtain reimbursement. In such case, if the depositary bank has received provisional settlement for the item, it must reimburse the bank drawing the draft and any provisional credits for the item between banks shall become and remain final.]

Note: *Direct returns is recognized as an innovation that is not yet established bank practice, and therefore Paragraph 2 has been bracketed. Some lawyers have doubts whether it should be included in legislation or left to development by agreement.*

(3) A depositary bank which is also the payor may charge-back the amount of an item to its customer's account or obtain refund in accordance with the section

governing return of an item received by a payor bank for credit on its books (Section 4–301).

(4)   The right to charge-back is not affected by

(a)   prior use of the credit given for the item; or

(b)   failure by any bank to exercise ordinary care with respect to the item but any bank so failing remains liable.

(5)   A failure to charge-back or claim refund does not affect other rights of the bank against the customer or any other party.

(6)   If credit is given in dollars as the equivalent of the value of an item payable in a foreign currency the dollar amount of any charge-back or refund shall be calculated on the basis of the buying sight rate for the foreign currency prevailing on the day when the person entitled to the charge-back or refund learns that it will not receive payment in ordinary course.

Section 4–213.   Final Payment of Item by Payor Bank; When Provisional Debits and Credits Become Final; When Certain Credits Become Available for Withdrawal

(1)   An item is finally paid by a payor bank when the bank has done any of the following, whichever happens first:

(a)   paid the item in cash; or

(b)   settled for the item without reserving a right to revoke the settlement and without having such right under statute, clearing house rule or agreement; or

(c)   completed the process of posting the item to the indicated account of the drawer, maker or other person to be charged therewith; or

(d)   made a provisional settlement for the item and failed to revoke the settlement in the time and manner permitted by statute, clearing house rule or agreement.

Upon a final payment under subparagraphs (b), (c) or (d) the payor bank shall be accountable for the amount of the item.

(2)   If provisional settlement for an item between the presenting and payor banks is made through a clearing house or by debits or credits in an account between them, then to the extent that provisional debits or credits for the item are entered in accounts between the presenting and payor banks or between the pre-

senting and successive prior collecting banks seriatim, they become final upon final payment of the item by the payor bank.

(3)   If a collecting bank receives a settlement for an item which is or becomes final (subsection (3) of Section 4–211, subsection (2) of Section 4–213) the bank is accountable to its customer for the amount of the item and any provisional credit given for the item in an account with its customer becomes final.

(4)   Subject to any right of the bank to apply the credit to an obligation of the customer, credit given by a bank for an item in an account with its customer becomes available for withdrawal as of right

(a)   in any case where the bank has received a provisional settlement for the item, — when such settlement becomes final and the bank has had a reasonable time to learn that the settlement is final;

(b)   in any case where the bank is both a depositary bank and a payor bank and the item is finally paid, — at the opening of the bank's second banking day following receipt of the item.

(5)   A deposit of money in a bank is final when made but, subject to any right of the bank to apply the deposit to an obligation of the customer, the deposit becomes available for withdrawal as of right at the opening of the bank's next banking day following receipt of the deposit.

Section 4–214.   Insolvency and Preference

(1)   Any item in or coming into the possession of a payor or collecting bank which suspends payment and which item is not finally paid shall be returned by the receiver, trustee or agent in charge of the closed bank to the presenting bank or the closed bank's customer.

(2)   If a payor bank finally pays an item and suspends payments without making a settlement for the item with its customer or the presenting bank which settlement is or becomes final, the owner of the item has a preferred claim against the payor bank.

(3)   If a payor bank gives or a collecting bank gives or receives a provisional settlement for an item and thereafter suspends payments, the suspension does not prevent or interfere with the settlement becoming final if such finality occurs automatically upon the lapse of certain time or the happening of certain events (subsection (3) of Section 4–211, subsections (1)(d), (2) and (3) of Section 4–213).

(4)   If a collecting bank receives from subsequent parties

settlement for an item which settlement is or becomes final and suspends payments without making a settlement for the item with its customer which is or becomes final, the owner of the item has a preferred claim against such collecting bank.

PART **3**

Collection of Items: Payor Banks

Section 4–301. Deferred Posting; Recovery of Payment by Return of Items; Time of Dishonor

(1) Where an authorized settlement for a demand item (other than a documentary draft) received by a payor bank otherwise than for immediate payment over the counter has been made before midnight of the banking day of receipt the payor bank may revoke the settlement and recover any payment if before it has made final payment (subsection (1) of Section 4–213) and before its midnight deadline it

(a) returns the item; or

(b) sends written notice of dishonor or nonpayment if the item is held for protest or is otherwise unavailable for return.

(2) If a demand item is received by a payor bank for credit on its books it may return such item or send notice of dishonor and may revoke any credit given or recover the amount thereof withdrawn by its customer, if it acts within the time limit and in the manner specified in the preceding subsection.

(3) Unless previous notice of dishonor has been sent an item is dishonored at the time when for purposes of dishonor it is returned or notice sent in accordance with this section.

(4) An item is returned:

(a) as to an item received through a clearing house, when it is delivered to the presenting or last collecting bank or to the clearing house or is sent or delivered in accordance with its rules; or

(b) in all other cases, when it is sent or delivered to the bank's customer or transferor or pursuant to his instructions.

Section 4–302. Payor Bank's Responsibility for Late Return of Item

In the absence of a valid defense such as breach of a presentment warranty (subsection (1) of Section 4–207), settlement effected or the like, if an item is presented on and received by a payor bank the bank is accountable for the amount of

(a) a demand item other than a documentary draft whether properly payable or not if the bank, in any case where it is not also the depositary bank, retains the item beyond midnight of the banking day of receipt without settling for it or, regardless of whether it is also the depositary bank, does not pay or return the item or send notice of dishonor until after its midnight deadline; or

(b) any other properly payable item unless within the time allowed for acceptance or payment of that item the bank either accepts or pays the item or returns it and accompanying documents.

Section 4–303. When Items Subject to Notice, Stop-Order, Legal Process or Setoff; Order in Which Items May Be Charged or Certified

(1) Any knowledge, notice of stop-order received by, legal process served upon or setoff exercised by a payor bank, whether or not effective under other rules of law to terminate, suspend or modify the bank's right or duty to pay an item or to charge its customer's account for the item, comes too late to so terminate, suspend or modify such right or duty if the knowledge, notice, stop-order or legal process is received or served and a reasonable time for the bank to act thereon expires or the setoff is exercised after the bank has done any of the following:

(a) accepted or certified the item;

(b) paid the item in cash;

(c) settled for the item without reserving a right to revoke the settlement and without having such right under statute, clearing house rule or agreement;

(d) completed the process of posting the item to the indicated account of the drawer, maker or other person to be charged therewith or otherwise has evidenced by examination of such indicated account and by action its decision to pay the item; or

(e) become accountable for the amount of the item under subsection (1)(d) of Section 4–213 and Section 4–302 dealing with the payor bank's responsibility for late return of items.

(2) Subject to the provisions of subsection (1) items may be accepted, paid, certified or charged to the

indicated account of its customer in any order convenient to the bank.

PART 4

Relationship Between Payor Bank and Its Customer

Section 4–401. When Bank May Charge Customer's Account

(1) As against its customer, a bank may charge against his account any item which is otherwise properly payable from that account even though the charge creates an overdraft.

(2) A bank which in good faith makes payment to a holder may charge the indicated account of its customer according to

(a) the original tenor of his altered item; or

(b) the tenor of his completed item, even though the bank knows the item has been completed unless the bank has notice that the completion was improper.

Section 4–402. Bank's Liability to Customer for Wrongful Dishonor

A payor bank is liable to its customer for damages proximately caused by the wrongful dishonor of an item. When the dishonor occurs through mistake liability is limited to actual damages proved. If so proximately caused and proved damages may include damages for an arrest or prosecution of the customer or other consequential damages. Whether any consequential damages are proximately caused by the wrongful dishonor is a question of fact to be determined in each case.

Section 4–403. Customer's Right to Stop Payment; Burden of Proof of Loss

(1) A customer may by order to his bank stop payment of any item payable for his account but the order must be received at such time and in such manner as to afford the bank a reasonable opportunity to act on it prior to any action by the bank with respect to the item described in Section 4–303.

(2) An oral order is binding upon the bank only for fourteen calendar days unless confirmed in writing within that period. A written order is effective for only six months unless renewed in writing.

(3) The burden of establishing the fact and amount of loss resulting from the payment of an item contrary to a binding stop payment order is on the customer.

Section 4–404. Bank Not Obligated to Pay Check More than Six Months Old

A bank is under no obligation to a customer having a checking account to pay a check, other than a certified check, which is presented more than six months after its date, but it may charge its customer's account for a payment made thereafter in good faith.

Section 4–405. Death or Incompetence of Customer

(1) A payor or collecting bank's authority to accept, pay or collect an item or to account for proceeds of its collection if otherwise effective is not rendered ineffective by incompetence of a customer of either bank existing at the time the item is issued or its collection is undertaken if the bank does not know of an adjudication of incompetence. Neither death nor incompetence of a customer revokes such authority to accept, pay, collect or account until the bank knows of the fact of death or of an adjudication of incompetence and has reasonable opportunity to act on it.

(2) Even with knowledge a bank may for ten days after the date of death pay or certify checks drawn on or prior to that date unless ordered to stop payment by a person claiming an interest in the account.

Section 4–406. Customer's Duty to Discover and Report Unauthorized Signature or Alteration

(1) When a bank sends to its customer a statement of account accompanied by items paid in good faith in support of the debit entries or holds the statement and items pursuant to a request or instructions of its customer or otherwise in a reasonable manner makes the statement and items available to the customer, the customer must exercise reasonable care and promptness to examine the statement and items to discover his unauthorized signature or any alteration on an item and must notify the bank promptly after discovery thereof.

(2) If the bank establishes that the customer failed with respect to an item to comply with the duties imposed on the customer by subsection (1) the customer is precluded from asserting against the bank

(a) his unauthorized signature or any alteration

on the item if the bank also establishes that it suffered a loss by reason of such failure; and

(b) an unauthorized signature or alteration by the same wrongdoer on any other item paid in good faith by the bank after the first item and statement was available to the customer for a reasonable period not exceeding fourteen calendar days and before the bank receives notification from the customer of any such unauthorized signature or alteration.

(3) The preclusion under subsection (2) does not apply if the customer establishes lack of ordinary care on the part of the bank in paying the item(s).

(4) Without regard to care or lack of care of either the customer or the bank a customer who does not within one year from the time the statement and items are made available to the customer (subsection (1)) discover and report his unauthorized signature or any alteration on the face or back of the item or does not within three years from that time discover and report any unauthorized indorsement is precluded from asserting against the bank such unauthorized signature or indorsement or such alteration.

(5) If under this section a payor bank has a valid defense against a claim of a customer upon or resulting from payment of an item and waives or fails upon request to assert the defense the bank may not assert against any collecting bank or other prior party presenting or transferring the item a claim based upon the unauthorized signature of alteration giving rise to the customer's claim.

Section 4–407. Payor Bank's Right to Subrogation on Improper Payment

If a payor bank has paid an item over the stop payment order of the drawer or maker or otherwise under circumstances giving a basis for objection by the drawer or maker, to prevent unjust enrichment and only to the extent necessary to prevent loss to the bank by reason of its payment of the item, the payor bank shall be subrogated to the rights

(a) of any holder in due course on the item against the drawer or maker; and

(b) of the payee or any other holder of the item against the drawer or maker either on the item or under the transaction out of which the item arose; and

(c) of the drawer or maker against the payee or

any other holder of the item with respect to the transaction out of which the item arose.

PART 5

Collection of Documentary Drafts

Section 4–501. Handling of Documentary Drafts; Duty to Send for Presentment and to Notify Customer of Dishonor

A bank which takes a documentary draft for collection must present or send the draft and accompanying documents for presentment and upon learning that the draft has not been paid or accepted in due course must seasonably notify its customer of such fact even though it may have discounted or bought the draft or extended credit available for withdrawal as of right.

Section 4–502. Presentment of "On Arrival" Drafts

When a draft or the relevant instructions require presentment "on arrival", "when goods arrive" or the like, the collecting bank need not present until in its judgment a reasonable time for arrival of the goods has expired. Refusal to pay or accept because the goods have not arrived is not dishonor; the bank must notify its transferor of such refusal but need not present the draft again until it is instructed to do so or learns of the arrival of the goods.

Section 4–503. Responsibility of Presenting Bank for Documents and Goods; Report of Reasons for Dishonor; Referee in Case of Need

Unless otherwise instructed and except as provided in Article 5 a bank presenting a documentary draft

(a) must deliver the documents to the drawee on acceptance of the draft if it is payable more than three days after presentment; otherwise, only on payment; and

(b) upon dishonor, either in the case of presentment for acceptance or presentment for payment, may seek and follow instructions from any referee in case of need designated in the draft or if the presenting bank does not choose to utilize his services it must use diligence and good faith to ascertain the reason for dishonor, must notify its transferor of the dishonor and of the results of its effort to ascertain the reasons therefor and must request instructions.

But the presenting bank is under no obligation with respect to goods represented by the documents except to follow any reasonable instructions seasonably received; it has a right to reimbursement for any expense incurred in following instructions and to prepayment of or indemnity for such expenses.

Section 4–504. Privilege of Presenting Bank to Deal with Goods; Security Interest for Expenses

(1) A presenting bank which, following the dishonor of a documentary draft, has seasonably requested instructions but does not receive them within a reasonable time may store, sell, or otherwise deal with the goods in any reasonable manner.

(2) For its reasonable expenses incurred by action under subsection (1) the presenting bank has a lien upon the goods or their proceeds, which may be foreclosed in the same manner as an unpaid seller's lien.

ARTICLE 5

LETTERS OF CREDIT

Section 5–101. Short Title

This Article shall be known and may be cited as Uniform Commercial Code — Letters of Credit.

Section 5–102. Scope

(1) This Article applies

(a) to a credit issued by a bank if the credit requires a documentary draft or a documentary demand for payment; and

(b) to a credit issued by a person other than a bank if the credit requires that the draft or demand for payment be accompanied by a document of title; and

(c) to a credit issued by a bank or other person if the credit is not within subparagraphs (a) or (b) but conspicuously states that it is a letter of credit or is conspicuously so entitled.

(2) Unless the engagement meets the requirements of subsection (1), this Article does not apply to engagements to make advances or to honor drafts or demands for payment, to authorities to pay or purchase, to guarantees or to general agreements.

(3) This Article deals with some but not all of the rules and concepts of letters of credit as such rules or concepts have developed prior to this act or may hereafter develop. The fact that this Article states a rule does not by itself require, imply or negate application of the same or a converse rule to a situation not provided for or to a person not specified by this Article.

Section 5–103. Definitions

(1) In this Article unless the context otherwise requires

(a) "Credit" or "letter of credit" means an engagement by a bank or other person made at the request of a customer and of a kind within the scope of this Article (Section 5–102) that the issuer will honor drafts or other demands for payment upon compliance with the conditions specified in the credit. A credit may be either revocable or irrevocable. The engagement may be either an agreement to honor or a statement that the bank or other person is authorized to honor.

(b) A "documentary draft" or a "documentary demand for payment" is one honor of which is conditioned upon the presentation of a document or documents. "Document" means any paper including document of title, security, invoice, certificate, notice of default and the like.

(c) An "issuer" is a bank or other person issuing a credit.

(d) A "beneficiary" of a credit is a person who is entitled under its terms to draw or demand payment.

(e) An "advising bank" is a bank which gives notification of the issuance of a credit by another bank.

(f) A "confirming bank" is a bank which engages either that it will itself honor a credit already issued by another bank or that such a credit will be honored by the issuer or a third bank.

(g) A "customer" is a buyer or other person who causes an issuer to issue a credit. The term also includes a bank which procures issuance or confirmation on behalf of that bank's customer.

(2) Other definitions applying to this Article and the sections in which they appear are:

"Notation of credit." Section 5–108.
"Presenter." Section 5–112(3).

(3) Definitions in other Articles applying to this Article and the sections in which they appear are:

"Accept" or "acceptance." Section 3–410.
"Contract for sale." Section 2–106.
"Draft." Section 3–104.

"Holder in due course." Section 3–302.
"Midnight deadline." Section 4–104.
"Security." Section 8–102.

(4) In addition, Article 1 contains general definitions and principles of construction and interpretation applicable throughout this Article.

Section 5–104. Formal Requirements; Signing

(1) Except as otherwise required in subsection (1)(c) of Section 5–102 on scope, no particular form of phrasing is required for a credit. A credit must be in writing and signed by the issuer and a confirmation must be in writing and signed by the confirming bank. A modification of the terms of a credit or confirmation must be signed by the issuer or confirming bank.

(2) A telegram may be a sufficient signed writing if it identifies its sender by an authorized authentication. The authentication may be in code and the authorized naming of the issuer in an advice of credit is a sufficient signing.

Section 5–105. Consideration

No consideration is necessary to establish a credit or to enlarge or otherwise modify its terms.

Section 5–106. Time and Effect of Establishment of Credit

(1) Unless otherwise agreed a credit is established

    (a) as regards the customer as soon as a letter of credit is sent to him or the letter of credit or an authorized written advice of its issuance is sent to the beneficiary; and

    (b) as regards the beneficiary when he receives a letter of credit or an authorized written advice of its issuance.

(2) Unless otherwise agreed once an irrevocable credit is established as regards the customer it can be modified or revoked only with the consent of the customer and once it is established as regards the beneficiary it can be modified or revoked only with his consent.

(3) Unless otherwise agreed after a revocable credit is established it may be modified or revoked by the issuer without notice to or consent from the customer or beneficiary.

(4) Notwithstanding any modification or revocation of a revocable credit any person authorized to honor or negotiate under the terms of the original credit is entitled to reimbursement for or honor of any draft

or demand for payment duly honored or negotiated before receipt of notice of the modification or revocation and the issuer in turn is entitled to reimbursement from its customer.

Section 5–107. Advice of Credit; Confirmation; Error in Statement of Terms

(1) Unless otherwise specified an advising bank by advising a credit issued by another bank does not assume any obligation to honor drafts drawn or demands for payment made under the credit but it does assume obligation for the accuracy of its own statement.

(2) A confirming bank by confirming a credit becomes directly obligated on the credit to the extent of its confirmation as though it were its issuer and acquires the rights of an issuer.

(3) Even though an advising bank incorrectly advises the terms of a credit it has been authorized to advise the credit is established as against the issuer to the extent of its original terms.

(4) Unless otherwise specified the customer bears as against the issuer all risks of transmission and reasonable translation or interpretation of any message relating to a credit.

Section 5–108. "Notation Credit"; Exhaustion of Credit

(1) A credit which specifies that any person purchasing or paying drafts drawn or demands for payment made under it must note the amount of the draft or demand on the letter or advice of credit is a "notation credit".

(2) Under a notation credit

    (a) a person paying the beneficiary or purchasing a draft or demand for payment from him acquires a right to honor only if the appropriate notation is made and by transferring or forwarding for honor the documents under the credit such a person warrants to the issuer that the notation has been made; and

    (b) unless the credit or a signed statement that an appropriate notation has been made accompanies the draft or demand for payment the issuer may delay honor until evidence of notation has been procured which is satisfactory to it but its obligation and that of its customer continue for a reasonable time not exceeding thirty days to obtain such evidence.

(3) If the credit is not a notation credit

(a) the issuer may honor complying drafts or demands for payment presented to it in the order in which they are presented and is discharged pro tanto by honor of any such draft or demand;

(b) as between competing good faith purchasers of complying drafts or demands the person first purchasing has priority over a subsequent purchaser even though the later purchased draft or demand has been first honored.

Section 5–109.   Issuer's Obligation to Its Customer

(1) An issuer's obligation to its customer includes good faith and observance of any general banking usage but unless otherwise agreed does not include liability or responsibility

(a) for performance of the underlying contract for sale or other transaction between the customer and the beneficiary; or

(b) for any act or omission of any person other than itself or its own branch or for loss or destruction of a draft, demand or document in transit or in the possession of others; or

(c) based on knowledge or lack of knowledge of any usage or any particular trade.

(2) An issuer must examine documents with care so as to ascertain that on their face they appear to comply with the terms of the credit but unless otherwise agreed assumes no liability or responsibility for the genuineness, falsification or effect of any document which appears on such examination to be regular on its face.

(3) A non-bank issuer is not bound by any banking usage of which it has no knowledge.

Section 5–110.   Availability of Credit in Portions; Presenter's Reservation of Lien or Claim

(1) Unless otherwise specified a credit may be used in portions in the discretion of the beneficiary.

(2) Unless otherwise specified a person by presenting a documentary draft or demand for payment under a credit relinquishes upon its honor all claims to the documents and a person by transferring such draft or demand or causing such presentment authorizes such relinquishment. An explicit reservation of claim makes the draft or demand non-complying.

Section 5–111.   Warranties on Transfer and Presentment

(1) Unless otherwise agreed the beneficiary by transferring or presenting a documentary draft or demand for payment warrants to all interested parties that the necessary conditions of the credit have been complied with. This is in addition to any warranties arising under Articles 3, 4, 7 and 8.

(2) Unless otherwise agreed a negotiating, advising, confirming, collecting or issuing bank presenting or transferring a draft or demand for payment under a credit warrants only the matters warranted by a collecting bank under Article 4 and any such bank transferring a document warrants only the matters warranted by an intermediary under Articles 7 and 8.

Section 5–112.   Time Allowed for Honor or Rejection; Withholding Honor or Rejection by Consent; "Presenter"

(1) A bank to which a documentary draft or demand for payment is presented under a credit may without dishonor of the draft, demand or credit

(a) defer honor until the close of the third banking day following receipt of the documents; and

(b) further defer honor if the presenter has expressly or impliedly consented thereto.

Failure to honor within the time here specified constitutes dishonor of the draft or demand and of the credit [except as otherwise provided in subsection (4) of Section 5–114 on conditional payment].

Note: *The bracketed language in the last sentence of subsection (1) should be included only if the optional provisions of Section 5–114 (4) and (5) are included.*

(2) Upon dishonor the bank may unless otherwise instructed fulfill its duty to return the draft or demand and the documents by holding them at the disposal of the presenter and sending him an advice to that effect.

(3) "Presenter" means any person presenting a draft or demand for payment for honor under a credit even though that person is a confirming bank or other correspondent which is acting under an issuer's authorization.

Section 5–113.   Indemnities

(1) A bank seeking to obtain (whether for itself or another) honor, negotiation or reimbursement under

a credit may give an indemnity to induce such honor, negotiation or reimbursement.

(2) An indemnity agreement inducing honor, negotiation or reimbursement

(a) unless otherwise explicitly agreed applies to defects in the documents but not in the goods; and

(b) unless a longer time is explicitly agreed expires at the end of ten business days following receipt of the documents by the ultimate customer unless notice of objection is sent before such expiration date. The ultimate customer may send notice of objection to the person from whom he received the documents and any bank receiving such notice is under a duty to send notice to its transferor before its midnight deadline.

Section 5–114. Issuer's Duty and Privilege to Honor; Right to Reimbursement

(1) An issuer must honor a draft or demand for payment which complies with the terms of the relevant credit regardless of whether the goods or documents conform to the underlying contract for sale or other contract between the customer and the beneficiary. The issuer is not excused from honor of such a draft or demand by reason of an additional general term that all documents must be satisfactory to the issuer, but an issuer may require that specified documents must be satisfactory to it.

(2) Unless otherwise agreed when documents appear on their face to comply with the terms of a credit but a required document does not in fact conform to the warranties made on negotiation or transfer of a document of title (Section 7–507) or of a security (Section 8–306) or is forged or fraudulent or there is fraud in the transaction

(a) the issuer must honor the draft or demand for payment if honor is demanded by a negotiating bank or other holder of the draft or demand which has taken the draft or demand under the credit and under circumstances which would make it a holder in due course (Section 3–302) and in an appropriate case would make it a person to whom a document of title has been duly negotiated (Section 7–502) or a bona fide purchaser of a security (Section 8–302); and

(b) in all other cases as against its customer, an issuer acting in good faith may honor the draft

or demand for payment despite notification from the customer of fraud, forgery or other defect not apparent on the face of the documents but a court of appropriate jurisdiction may enjoin such honor.

(3) Unless otherwise agreed an issuer which has duly honored a draft or demand for payment is entitled to immediate reimbursement of any payment made under the credit and to be put in effectively available funds not later than the day before maturity of any acceptance made under the credit.

[(4) When a credit provides for payment by the issuer on receipt of notice that the required documents are in the possession of a correspondent or other agent of the issuer

(a) any payment made on receipt of such notice is conditional; and

(b) the issuer may reject documents which do not comply with the credit if it does so within three banking days following its receipt of the documents; and

(c) in the event of such rejection, the issuer is entitled by charge back or otherwise to return of the payment made.]

[(5) In the case covered by subsection (4) failure to reject documents within the time specified in subparagraph (b) constitutes acceptance of the documents and makes the payment final in favor of the beneficiary.]

Note: *Subsections (4) and (5) are bracketed as optional. If they are included, the bracketed language in the last sentence of Section 5–112(1) should also be included.*

Section 5–115. Remedy for Improper Dishonor or Anticipatory Repudiation

(1) When an issuer wrongfully dishonors a draft or demand for payment presented under a credit the person entitled to honor has with respect to any documents the rights of a person in the position of a seller (Section 2–707) and may recover from the issuer the face amount of the draft or demand together with incidental damages under Section 2–710 on seller's incidental damages and interest but less any amount realized by resale or other use or disposition of the subject matter of the transaction. In the event no resale or other utilization is made the documents, goods or other subject matter involved in the transaction must be turned over to the issuer on payment of judgment.

(2) When an issuer wrongfully cancels or otherwise

repudiates a credit before presentment of a draft or demand for payment drawn under it the beneficiary has the rights of a seller after anticipatory repudiation by the buyer under Section 2–610 if he learns of the repudiation in time reasonably to avoid procurement of the required documents. Otherwise the beneficiary has an immediate right of action for wrongful dishonor.

Section 5–116. Transfer and Assignment

(1) The right to draw under a credit can be transferred or assigned only when the credit is expressly designated as transferable or assignable.

(2) Even though the credit specifically states that it is nontransferable or nonassignable the beneficiary may before performance of the conditions of the credit assign his right to proceeds. Such an assignment is an assignment of an account right under Article 9 on Secured Transactions and is governed by that Article except that

    (a)   the assignment is ineffective until the letter of credit or advice of credit is delivered to the assignee which delivery constitutes perfection of the security interest under Article 9; and

    (b)   the issuer may honor drafts or demands for payment drawn under the credit until it receives a notification of the assignment signed by the beneficiary which reasonably identifies the credit involved in the assignment and contains a request to pay the assignee; and

    (c)   after what reasonably appears to be such a notification has been received the issuer may without dishonor refuse to accept or pay even to a person otherwise entitled to honor until the letter of credit or advice of credit is exhibited to the issuer.

(3) Except where the beneficiary has effectively assigned his right to draw or his right to proceeds, nothing in this section limits his right to transfer or negotiate drafts of demands drawn under the credit.

Section 5–117. Insolvency of Bank Holding Funds for Documentary Credit

(1) Where an issuer or an advising or confirming bank or a bank which has for a customer procured issuance of a credit by another bank becomes insolvent before final payment under the credit and the credit is one to which this Article is made applicable by paragraphs (a) or (b) of Section 5–102(1) on scope, the receipt or allocation of funds or collateral to secure or meet obligations under the credit shall have the following results:

    (a)   to the extent of any funds or collateral turned over after or before the insolvency as indemnity against or specifically for the purpose of payment of drafts or demands for payment drawn under the designated credit, the drafts or demands are entitled to payment in preference over depositors or other general creditors of the issuer or bank; and

    (b)   on expiration of the credit or surrender of the beneficiary's rights under it unused any person who has given such funds or collateral is similarly entitled to return thereof; and

    (c)   a charge to a general or current account with a bank if specifically consented to for the purpose of indemnity against or payment of drafts or demands for payment drawn under the designated credit falls under the same rules as if the funds had been drawn out in cash and then turned over with specific instructions.

(2) After honor or reimbursement under this section the customer or other person for whose account the insolvent bank has acted is entitled to receive the documents involved.

ARTICLE 6

BULK TRANSFERS

Section 6–101. Short Title

This Article shall be known and may be cited as Uniform Commercial Code — Bulk Transfers.

Section 6–102. "Bulk Transfer"; Transfers of Equipment; Enterprises Subject to This Article; Bulk Transfers Subject to This Article

(1) A "bulk transfer" is any transfer in bulk and not in the ordinary course of the transferor's business of a major part of the materials, supplies, merchandise or other inventory (Section 9–109) of an enterprise subject to this Article.

(2) A transfer of a substantial part of the equipment (Section 9–109) of such an enterprise is a bulk transfer if it is made in connection with a bulk transfer of inventory, but not otherwise.

(3) The enterprises subject to this Article are all those whose principal business is the sale of merchandise from stock, including those who manufacture what they sell.

(4) Except as limited by the following section all bulk transfers of goods located within this state are subject to this Article.

Section 6–103. Transfers Excepted from This Article

The following transfers are not subject to this Article:

(1) Those made to give security for the performance of an obligation;

(2) General assignments for the benefit of all the creditors of the transferor, and subsequent transfers by the assignee thereunder;

(3) Transfers in settlement or realization of a lien or other security interest;

(4) Sales by executors, administrators, receivers, trustees in bankruptcy, or any public officer under judicial process;

(5) Sales made in the course of judicial or administrative proceedings for the dissolution or reorganization of a corporation and of which notice is sent to the creditors of the corporation pursuant to order of the court or administrative agency;

(6) Transfers to a person maintaining a known place of business in this State who becomes bound to pay the debts of the transferor in full and gives public notice of that fact, and who is solvent after becoming so bound;

(7) A transfer to a new business enterprise organized to take over and continue the business, if public notice of the transaction is given and the new enterprise assumes the debts of the transferor and he receives nothing from the transaction except an interest in the new enterprise junior to the claims of creditors;

(8) Transfers of property which is exempt from execution.

Public notice under subsection (6) or subsection (7) may be given by publishing once a week for two consecutive weeks in a newspaper of general circulation where the transferor had its principal place of business in this state an advertisement including the names and addresses of the transferor and transferee and the effective date of the transfer.

Section 6–104. Schedule of Property, List of Creditors

(1) Except as provided with respect to auction sales (Section 6–108), a bulk transfer subject to this Article is ineffective against any creditor of the transferor unless:

(a) The transferee requires the transferor to furnish a list of his existing creditors prepared as stated in this section; and

(b) The parties prepare a schedule of the property transferred sufficient to identify it; and

(c) The transferee preserves the list and schedule for six months next following the transfer and permits inspection of either or both and copying therefrom at all reasonable hours by any creditor of the transferor, or files the list and schedule in (*a public office to be here identified*).

(2) The list of creditors must be signed and sworn to or affirmed by the transferor or his agent. It must contain the names and business addresses of all creditors of the transferor, with the amounts when known, and also the names of all persons who are known to the transferor to assert claims against him even though such claims are disputed. If the transferor is the obligor of an outstanding issue of bonds, debentures or the like as to which there is an indenture trustee, the list of creditors need include only the name and address of the indenture trustee and the aggregate outstanding principal amount of the issue.

(3) Responsibility for the completeness and accuracy of the list of creditors rests on the transferor, and the transfer is not rendered ineffective by errors or omissions therein unless the transferee is shown to have had knowledge.

Section 6–105. Notice to Creditors

In addition to the requirements of the preceding section, any bulk transfer subject to this Article except one made by auction sale (Section 6–108) is ineffective against any creditor of the transferor unless at least ten days before he takes possession of the goods or pays for them, whichever happens first, the transferee gives notice of the transfer in the manner and to the persons hereafter provided (Section 6–107).

[Section 6–106. Application of the Proceeds

In addition to the requirements of the two preceding sections:

(1) Upon every bulk transfer subject to this Article

for which new consideration becomes payable except those made by sale at auction it is the duty of the transferee to assure that such consideration is applied so far as necessary to pay those debts of the transferor which are either shown on the list furnished by the transferor (Section 6–104) or filed in writing in the place stated in the notice (Section 6–107) within thirty days after the mailing of such notice. This duty of the transferee runs to all the holders of such debts, and may be enforced by any of them for the benefit of all.

(2) If any of said debts are in dispute the necessary sum may be withheld from distribution until the dispute is settled or adjudicated.

(3) If the consideration payable is not enough to pay all of the said debts in full distribution shall be made pro rata.]

Note: *This section is bracketed to indicate division of opinion as to whether or not it is a wise provision, and to suggest that this is a point on which State enactments may differ without serious damage to the principle of uniformity.*

In any State where this section is omitted, the following parts of sections, also bracketed in the text, should also be omitted, namely: Sections 6–107(2)(e), 6–108(3)(c), and 6–109(2). In any State where this section is enacted, these other provisions should be also.

Optional Subsection (4)

[(4) The transferee may within ten days after he takes possession of the goods pay the consideration into the (specify court) in the county where the transferor had its principal place of business in this state and thereafter may discharge his duty under this section by giving notice by registered or certified mail to all the persons to whom the duty runs that the consideration has been paid into that court and that they should file their claims there. On motion of any interested party, the court may order the distribution of the consideration to the persons entitled to it.]

Note: *Optional subsection (4) is recommended for those states which do not have a general statute providing for payment of money into court.*

Section 6–107.   The Notice

(1) The notice to creditors (Section 6–105) shall state:

(a)   that a bulk transfer is about to be made; and

(b)   the names and business addresses of the transferor and transferee, and all other business names and addresses used by the transferor within three years last past so far as known to the transferee; and

(c)   whether or not all the debts of the transferor are to be paid in full as they fall due as a result of the transaction, and if so, the address to which creditors should send their bills.

(2) If the debts of the transferor are not to be paid in full as they fall due or if the transferee is in doubt on that point then the notice shall state further:

(a)   the location and general description of the property to be transferred and the estimated total of the transferor's debts;

(b)   the address where the schedule of property and list of creditors (Section 6–104) may be inspected;

(c)   whether the transfer is to pay existing debts and if so the amount of such debts and to whom owing;

(d)   whether the transfer is for new consideration and if so the amount of such consideration and the time and place of payment; [and]

[(e) if for new consideration the time and place where creditors of the transferor are to file their claims.]

(3) The notice in any case shall be delivered personally or sent by registered or certified mail to all the persons shown on the list of creditors furnished by the transferor (Section 6–104) and to all other persons who are known to the transferee to hold or assert claims against the transferor.

Section 6–108.   Auction Sales; "Auctioneer"

(1) A bulk transfer is subject to this Article even though it is by sale at auction, but only in the manner and with the results stated in this section.

(2) The transferor shall furnish a list of his creditors and assist in the preparation of a schedule of the property to be sold, both prepared as before stated (Section 6–104).

(3) The person or persons other than the transferor who direct, control or are responsible for the auction are collectively called the "auctioneer". The auctioneer shall:

(a)   receive and retain the list of creditors and prepare and retain the schedule of property for the period stated in this Article (Section 6–104);

(b)   give notice of the auction personally or by registered or certified mail at least ten days before it occurs to all persons shown on the list of creditors and to all other persons who are known to him to hold or assert claims against the transferor; [and]

[(c) assure that the net proceeds of the auction are applied as provided in this Article (Section 6–106).]

(4) Failure of the auctioneer to perform any of these duties does not affect the validity of the sale or the title of the purchasers, but if the auctioneer knows that the auction constitutes a bulk transfer such failure renders the auctioneer liable to the creditors of the transferor as a class for the sums owing to them from the transferor up to but not exceeding the net proceeds of the auction. If the auctioneer consists of several persons their liability is joint and several.

Section 6–109. What Creditors Protected [Credit for Payment to Particular Creditors]

(1) The creditors of the transferor mentioned in this Article are those holding claims based on transactions or events occurring before the bulk transfer, but creditors who become such after notice to creditors is given (Sections 6–105 and 6–107) are not entitled to notice.

[(2) Against the aggregate obligation imposed by the provisions of this Article concerning the application of the proceeds (Section 6–106 and subsection (3)(c) of 6–108) the transferee or auctioneer is entitled to credit for sums paid to particular creditors of the transferor, not exceeding the sums believed in good faith at the time of the payment to be properly payable to such creditors.]

Section 6–110. Subsequent Transfers

When the title of a transferee to property is subject to a defect by reason of his non-compliance with the requirements of this Article, then:

(1) a purchaser of any of such property from such transferee who pays no value or who takes with notice of such non-compliance takes subject to such defect, but

(2) a purchaser for value in good faith and without such notice takes free of such defect.

Section 6–111. Limitation of Actions and Levies

No action under this Article shall be brought nor levy made more than six months after the date on which the transferee took possession of the goods unless the transfer has been concealed. If the transfer has been concealed, actions may be brought on levies made within six months after its discovery.

Note to Article 6: *Section 6–106 is bracketed to indicate division of opinion as to whether or not it is a wise provision, and to suggest that this is a point on which State enactments may differ without serious damage to the principle of uniformity.*

In any State where Section 6–106 is not enacted, the following parts of sections, also bracketed in the text, should also be omitted, namely: Sections 6–107(2)(e), 6–108(3)(c), and 6–109(2). In any State where Section 6–106 is enacted, these other provisions should be also.

ARTICLE **7**

WAREHOUSE RECEIPTS, BILLS OF LADING AND OTHER DOCUMENTS OF TITLE

PART **1**

General

Section 7–101. Short Title

This Article shall be known and may be cited as Uniform Commercial Code — Documents of Title.

Section 7–102. Definitions and Index of Definitions

(1) In this Article, unless the context otherwise requires:

(a) "Bailee" means the person who by a warehouse receipt, bill of lading or other document of title acknowledges possession of goods and contracts to deliver them.

(b) "Consignee" means the person named in a bill to whom or to whose order the bill promises delivery.

(c) "Consignor" means the person named in a bill as the person from whom the goods have been received for shipment.

(d) "Delivery order" means a written order to deliver goods directed to a warehouseman, carrier or other person who in the ordinary course of business issues warehouse receipts or bills of lading.

(e) "Document" means document of title as defined in the general definitions in Article 1 (Section 1–201).

(f) "Goods" means all things which are treated

as movable for the purposes of a contract of storage or transportation.

(g) "Issuer" means a bailee who issues a document except that in relation to an unaccepted delivery order it means the person who orders the possessor of goods to deliver. Issuer includes any person for whom an agent or employee purports to act in issuing a document if the agent or employee has real or apparent authority to issue documents, notwithstanding that the issuer received no goods or that the goods were misdescribed or that in any other respect the agent or employee violated his instructions.

(h) "Warehouseman" is a person engaged in the business of storing goods for hire.

(2) Other definitions applying to this Article or to specified Parts thereof, and the sections in which they appear are:

"Duly negotiate." Section 7–501.
"Person entitled under the document." Section 7–403(4).

(3) Definitions in other Articles applying to this Article and the sections in which they appear are:

"Contract for sale." Section 2–106.
"Overseas." Section 2–323.
"Receipt" of goods. Section 2–103.

(4) In addition Article 1 contains general definitions and principles of construction and interpretation applicable throughout this Article.

Section 7–103. Relation of Article to Treaty, Statute, Tariff, Classification or Regulation

To the extent that any treaty or statute of the United States, regulatory statute of this State or tariff, classification or regulation filed or issued pursuant thereto is applicable, the provisions of this Article are subject thereto.

Section 7–104. Negotiable and Non-Negotiable Warehouse Receipt, Bill of Lading or Other Document of Title

(1) A warehouse receipt, bill of lading or other document of title is negotiable

(a) if by its terms the goods are to be delivered to bearer or to the order of a named person; or

(b) where recognized in overseas trade, if it runs to a named person or assigns.

(2) Any other document is non-negotiable. A bill of lading in which it is stated that the goods are consigned to a named person is not made negotiable by a provision that the goods are to be delivered only against a written order signed by the same or another named person.

Section 7–105. Construction Against Negative Implication

The omission from either Part 2 or Part 3 of this Article of a provision corresponding to a provision made in the other Part does not imply that a corresponding rule of law is not applicable.

PART 2
Warehouse Receipts: Special Provisions

Section 7–201. Who May Issue a Warehouse Receipt; Storage Under Government Bond

(1) A warehouse receipt may be issued by any warehouseman.

(2) Where goods including distilled spirits and agricultural commodities are stored under a statute requiring a bond against withdrawal or a license for the issuance of receipts in the nature of warehouse receipts, a receipt issued for the goods has like effect as a warehouse receipt even though issued by a person who is the owner of the goods and is not a warehouseman.

Section 7–202. Form of Warehouse Receipt; Essential Terms; Optional Terms

(1) A warehouse receipt need not be in any particular form.

(2) Unless a warehouse receipt embodies within its written or printed terms each of the following, the warehouseman is liable for damages caused by the omission to a person injured thereby:

(a) the location of the warehouse where the goods are stored;

(b) the date of issue of the receipt;

(c) the consecutive number of the receipt;

(d) a statement whether the goods received will be delivered to the bearer, to a specified person, or to a specified person or his order;

(e) the rate of storage and handling charges, except that where goods are stored under a field warehousing arrangement a statement of that fact is sufficient on a non-negotiable receipt;

(f) a description of the goods or of the packages containing them;

(g) the signature of the warehouseman, which may be made by his authorized agent;

(h) if the receipt is issued for goods of which the warehouseman is owner, either solely or jointly or in common with others, the fact of such ownership; and

(i) a statement of the amount of advances made and of liabilities incurred for which the warehouseman claims a lien or security interest (Section 7–209). If the precise amount of such advances made or of such liabilities incurred is, at the time of the issue of the receipt, unknown to the warehouseman or to his agent who issues it, a statement of the fact that advances have been made or liabilities incurred and the purpose thereof is sufficient.

(3) A warehouseman may insert in his receipt any other terms which are not contrary to the provisions of this Act and do not impair his obligation of delivery (Section 7–403) or his duty of care (Section 7–204). Any contrary provisions shall be ineffective.

Section 7–203. Liability for Non-Receipt or Misdescription

A party to or purchaser for value in good faith of a document of title other than a bill of lading relying in either case upon the description therein of the goods may recover from the issuer damages caused by the non-receipt or misdescription of the goods, except to the extent that the document conspicuously indicates that the issuer does not know whether any part or all of the goods in fact were received or conform to the description, as where the description is in terms of marks or labels or kind, quantity or condition, or the receipt or description is qualified by "contents, condition and quality unknown", "said to contain" or the like, if such indication be true, or the party or purchaser otherwise has notice.

Section 7–204. Duty of Care; Contractual Limitation of Warehouseman's Liability

(1) A warehouseman is liable for damages for loss of or injury to the goods caused by his failure to exercise such care in regard to them as a reasonably careful man would exercise under like circumstances but unless otherwise agreed he is not liable for damages which could not have been avoided by the exercise of such care.

(2) Damages may be limited by a term in the warehouse receipt or storage agreement limiting the amount of liability in case of loss or damage, and setting forth a specific liability per article or item, or value per unit of weight, beyond which the warehouseman shall not be liable; provided, however, that such liability may on written request of the bailor at the time of signing such storage agreement or within a reasonable time after receipt of the warehouse receipt be increased on part or all of the goods thereunder, in which event increased rates may be charged based on such increased valuation, but that no such increase shall be permitted contrary to a lawful limitation of liability contained in the warehouseman's tariff, if any. No such limitation is effective with respect to the warehouseman's liability for conversion to his own use.

(3) Reasonable provisions as to the time and manner of presenting claims and instituting actions based on the bailment may be included in the warehouse receipt or tariff.

(4) This section does not impair or repeal . . .

Note: *Insert in subsection (4) a reference to any statute which imposes a higher responsibility upon the warehouseman or invalidates contractual limitations which would be permissible under this Article.*

Section 7–205. Title Under Warehouse Receipt Defeated in Certain Cases

A buyer in the ordinary course of business of fungible goods sold and delivered by a warehouseman who is also in the business of buying and selling such goods takes free of any claim under a warehouse receipt even though it has been duly negotiated.

Section 7–206. Termination of Storage at Warehouseman's Option

(1) A warehouseman may on notifying the person on whose account the goods are held and any other person known to claim an interest in the goods require payment of any charges and removal of the goods from the warehouse at the termination of the period of storage fixed by the document, or, if no period is fixed, within a stated period not less than thirty days after the notification. If the goods are not removed before the date specified in the notification, the warehouseman may sell them in accordance with the provisions of the section on enforcement of a warehouseman's lien (Section 7–210).

(2) If a warehouseman in good faith believes that the goods are about to deteriorate or decline in value to less than the amount of his lien within the time prescribed in subsection (1) for notification, advertisement and sale, the warehouseman may specify in the notification any reasonable shorter time for removal of the goods and in case the goods are not removed, may sell them at public sale held not less than one week after a single advertisement or posting.

(3) If as a result of a quality or condition of the goods of which the warehouseman had no notice at the time of deposit the goods are a hazard to other property or to the warehouse or to persons, the warehouseman may sell the goods at public or private sale without advertisement on reasonable notification to all persons known to claim an interest in the goods. If the warehouseman after a reasonable effort is unable to sell the goods he may dispose of them in any lawful manner and shall incur no liability by reason of such disposition.

(4) The warehouseman must deliver the goods to any person entitled to them under this Article upon due demand made at any time prior to sale or other disposition under this section.

(5) The warehouseman may satisfy his lien from the proceeds of any sale or disposition under this section but must hold the balance for delivery on the demand of any person to whom he would have been bound to deliver the goods.

Section 7–207. Goods Must Be Kept Separate; Fungible Goods

(1) Unless the warehouse receipt otherwise provides, a warehouseman must keep separate the goods covered by each receipt so as to permit at all times identification and delivery of those goods except that different lots of fungible goods may be commingled.

(2) Fungible goods so commingled are owned in common by the persons entitled thereto and the warehouseman is severally liable to each owner for that owner's share. Where because of overissue a mass of fungible goods is insufficient to meet all the receipts which the warehouseman has issued against it, the persons entitled include all holders to whom overissued receipts have been duly negotiated.

Section 7–208. Altered Warehouse Receipts

Where a blank in a negotiable warehouse receipt has been filled in without authority, a purchaser for value and without notice of the want of authority may treat the insertion as authorized. Any other unauthorized alteration leaves any receipt enforceable against the issuer according to its original tenor.

Section 7–209. Lien of Warehouseman

(1) A warehouseman has a lien against the bailor on the goods covered by a warehouse receipt or on proceeds thereof in his possession for charges for storage or transportation (including demurrage and terminal charges), insurance, labor, or charges present or future in relation to the goods, and for expenses necessary for preservation of the goods or reasonably incurred in their sale pursuant to law. If the person on whose account the goods are held is liable for like charges or expenses in relation to other goods whenever deposited and it is stated in the receipt that a lien is claimed for charges and expenses in relation to other goods, the warehouseman also has a lien against him for such charges and expenses whether or not the other goods have been delivered by the warehouseman. But against a person to whom a negotiable warehouse receipt is duly negotiated a warehouseman's lien is limited to charges in an amount or at a rate specified on the receipt or if no charges are so specified then to a reasonable charge for storage of the goods covered by the receipt subsequent to the date of the receipt.

(2) The warehouseman may also reserve a security interest against the bailor for a maximum amount specified on the receipt for charges other than those specified in subsection (1), such as for money advanced and interest. Such a security interest is governed by the Article on Secured Transactions (Article (9).

(3) (a) A warehouseman's lien for charges and expenses under subsection (1) or a security interest under subsection (2) is also effective against any person who so entrusted the bailor with possession of the goods that a pledge of them by him to a good faith purchaser for value would have been valid but is not effective against a person as to whom the document confers no right in the goods covered by it under Section 7–503.

(b) A warehouseman's lien on household goods for charges and expenses in relation to the goods under subsection (1) is also effective against all persons if the depositor was the legal possessor of the goods at the time of deposit. ''Household goods'' means furniture, furnishings and personal effects used by the depositor in a dwelling.

(4) A warehouseman loses his lien on any goods which he voluntarily delivers or which he unjustifiably refuses to deliver.

Section 7–210. Enforcement of Warehouseman's Lien

(1) Except as provided in subsection (2), a warehouseman's lien may be enforced by public or private

sale of the goods in block or in parcels, at any time or place and on any terms which are commercially reasonable, after notifying all persons know to claim an interest in the goods. Such notification must include a statement of the amount due, the nature of the proposed sale and the time and place of any public sale. The fact that a better price could have been obtained by a sale at a different time or in a different method from that selected by the warehouseman is not of itself sufficient to establish that the sale was not made in a commercially reasonable manner. If the warehouseman either sells the goods in the usual manner in any recognized market therefor, or if he sells at the price current in such market at the time of his sale, or if he has otherwise sold in conformity with commercially reasonable practices among dealers in the type of goods sold, he has sold in a commercially reasonable manner. A sale of more goods than apparently necessary to be offered to insure satisfaction of the obligation is not commercially reasonable except in cases covered by the preceding sentence.

(2) A warehouseman's lien on goods other than goods stored by a merchant in the course of his business may be enforced only as follows:

(a) All persons known to claim an interest in the goods must be notified.

(b) The notification must be delivered in person or sent by registered or certified letter to the last known address of any person to be notified.

(c) The notification must include an itemized statement of the claim, a description of the goods subject to the lien, a demand for payment within a specified time not less than ten days after receipt of the notification, and a conspicuous statement that unless the claim is paid within the time the goods will be advertised for sale and sold by auction at a specified time and place.

(d) The sale must conform to the terms of the notification.

(e) The sale must be held at the nearest suitable place to that where the goods are held or stored.

(f) After the expiration of the time given in the notification, an advertisement of the sale must be published once a week for two weeks consecutively in a newspaper of general circulation where the sale is to be held. The advertisement must include a description of the goods, the name of the person on whose account they are being held, and the time and place of the sale. The sale must take place at least fifteen days after the first publication. If there is no newspaper of general circulation

where the sale is to be held, the advertisement must be posted at least ten days before the sale in not less than six conspicuous places in the neighborhood of the proposed sale.

(3) Before any sale pursuant to this section any person claiming a right in the goods may pay the amount necessary to satisfy the lien and the reasonable expenses incurred under this section. In that event the goods must not be sold, but must be retained by the warehouseman subject to the terms of the receipt and this Article.

(4) The warehouseman may buy at any public sale pursuant to this section.

(5) A purchaser in good faith of goods sold to enforce a warehouseman's lien takes the goods free of any rights of persons against whom the lien was valid, despite noncompliance by the warehouseman with the requirements of this section.

(6) The warehouseman may satisfy his lien from the proceeds of any sale pursuant to this section but must hold the balance, if any, for delivery on demand to any person to whom he would have been bound to deliver the goods.

(7) The rights provided by this section shall be in addition to all other rights allowed by law to a creditor against his debtor.

(8) Where a lien is on goods stored by a merchant in the course of his business the lien may be enforced in accordance with either subsection (1) or (2).

(9) The warehouseman is liable for damages caused by failure to comply with the requirements for sale under this section and in case of willful violation is liable for conversion.

PART **3**

Bills of Lading: Special Provisions

Section 7–301. Liability for Non-Receipt or Misdescription; "Said to Contain"; "Shipper's Load and Count"; Improper Handling

(1) A consignee of a non-negotiable bill who has given value in good faith or a holder to whom a negotiable bill has been duly negotiated relying in either case upon the description therein of the goods, or upon the date therein shown, may recover from the issuer damages caused by the misdating of the bill or the nonreceipt or misdescription of the goods, except to the extent that the document indicates that the

issuer does not know whether any part or all of the goods in fact were received or conform to the description, as where the description is in terms of marks or labels or kind, quantity, or condition or the receipt or description is qualified by "contents or condition of contents of packages unknown", "said to contain", "shipper's weight, load and count" or the like, if such indication be true.

(2) When goods are loaded by an issuer who is a common carrier, the issuer must count the packages of goods if package freight and ascertain the kind and quantity if bulk freight. In such cases "shipper's weight, load and count" or other words indicating that the description was made by the shipper are ineffective except as to freight concealed by packages.

(3) When bulk freight is loaded by a shipper who makes available to the issuer adequate facilities for weighing such freight, an issuer who is a common carrier must ascertain the kind and quantity within a reasonable time after receiving the written request of the shipper to do so. In such cases "shipper's weight" or other words of like purport are ineffective.

(4) The issuer may by inserting in the bill the words "shipper's weight, load and count" or other words of like purport indicate that the goods were loaded by the shipper; and if such statement be true the issuer shall not be liable for damages caused by the improper loading. But their omission does not imply liability for such damages.

(5) The shipper shall be deemed to have guaranteed to the issuer the accuracy at the time of shipment of the description, marks, labels, number, kind, quantity, condition and weight as furnished by him; and the shipper shall indemnify the issuer against damage caused by inaccuracies in such particulars. The right of the issuer to such indemnity shall in no way limit his responsibility and liability under the contract of carriage to any person other than the shipper.

Section 7–302. Through Bills of Lading and Similar Documents

(1) The issuer of a through bill of lading or other document embodying an undertaking to be performed in part by persons acting as its agents or by connecting carriers is liable to anyone entitled to recover on the document for any breach by such other persons or by a connecting carrier of its obligation under the document but to the extent that the bill covers an undertaking to be performed overseas or in territory not contiguous to the continental United States or an undertaking including matters other than transportation this liability may be varied by agreement of the parties.

(2) Where goods covered by a through bill of lading or other document embodying an undertaking to be performed in part by persons other than the issuer are received by any such person, he is subject with respect to his own performance while the goods are in his possession to the obligation of their issuer. His obligation is discharged by delivery of the goods to another such person pursuant to the document, and does not include liability for breach by any other such persons or by the issuer.

(3) The issuer of such through bill of lading or other document shall be entitled to recover from the connecting carrier or such other person in possession of the goods when the breach of the obligation under the document occurred, the amount it may be required to pay to anyone entitled to recover on the document therefor, as may be evidenced by any receipt, judgment, or transcript thereof, and the amount of any expense reasonably incurred by it in defending any action brought by anyone entitled to recover on the document therefor.

Section 7–303. Diversion; Reconsignment; Change of Instructions

(1) Unless the bill of lading otherwise provides, the carrier may deliver the goods to a person or destination other than that stated in the bill or may otherwise dispose of the goods on instructions from

(a) the holder of a negotiable bill; or

(b) the consignor on a non-negotiable bill notwithstanding contrary instructions from the consignee; or

(c) the consignee on a non-negotiable bill in the absence of contrary instructions from the consignor, if the goods have arrived at the billed destination or if the consignee is in possession of the bill; or

(d) the consignee on a non-negotiable bill if he is entitled as against the consignor to dispose of them.

(2) Unless such instructions are noted on a negotiable bill of lading, a person to whom the bill is duly negotiated can hold the bailee according to the original terms.

Section 7–304. Bills of Lading in a Set

(1) Except where customary in overseas transportation, a bill of lading must not be issued in a set of parts. The issuer is liable for damages caused by violation of this subsection.

(2) Where a bill of lading is lawfully drawn in a set

of parts, each of which is numbered and expressed to be valid only if the goods have not been delivered against any other part, the whole of the parts constitute one bill.

(3) Where a bill of lading is lawfully issued in a set of parts and different parts are negotiated to different persons, the title of the holder to whom the first due negotiation is made prevails as to both the document and the goods even though any later holder may have received the goods from the carrier in good faith and discharged the carrier's obligation by surrender of his part.

(4) Any person who negotiates or transfers a single part of a bill of lading drawn in a set is liable to holders of that part as if it were the whole set.

(5) The bailee is obliged to deliver in accordance with Part 4 of this Article against the first presented part of a bill of lading lawfully drawn in a set. Such delivery discharges the bailee's obligation on the whole bill.

Section 7–305. Destination Bills

(1) Instead of issuing a bill of lading to the consignor at the place of shipment a carrier may at the request of the consignor procure the bill to be issued at destination or at any other place designated in the request.

(2) Upon request of anyone entitled as against the carrier to control the goods while in transit and on surrender of any outstanding bill of lading or other receipt covering such goods, the issuer may procure a substitute bill to be issued at any place designated in the request.

Section 7–306. Altered Bills of Lading

An unauthorized alteration or filling in of a blank in a bill of lading leaves the bill enforceable according to its original tenor.

Section 7–307. Lien of Carrier

(1) A carrier has a lien on the goods covered by a bill of lading for charges subsequent to the date of its receipt of the goods for storage or transportation (including demurrage and terminal charges) and for expenses necessary for preservation of the goods incident to their transportation or reasonably incurred in their sale pursuant to law. But against a purchaser for value of a negotiable bill of lading a carrier's lien is limited to charges stated in the bill or the applicable tariffs, or if no charges are stated then to a reasonable charge.

(2) A lien for charges and expenses under subsection (1) on goods which the carrier was required by law to receive for transportation is effective against the consignor or any person entitled to the goods unless the carrier had notice that the consignor lacked authority to subject the goods to such charges and expenses. Any other lien under subsection (1) is effective against the consignor and any person who permitted the bailor to have control or possession of the goods unless the carrier had notice that the bailor lacked such authority.

(3) A carrier loses his lien on any goods which he voluntarily delivers or which he unjustifiably refuses to deliver.

Section 7–308.   Enforcement of Carrier's Lien

(1) A carrier's lien may be enforced by public or private sale of the goods, in bloc or in parcels, at any time or place and on any terms which are commercially reasonable, after notifying all persons known to claim an interest in the goods. Such notification must include a statement of the amount due, the nature of the proposed sale and the time and place of any public sale. The fact that a better price could have been obtained by a sale at a different time or in a different method from that selected by the carrier is not of itself sufficient to establish that the sale was not made in a commercially reasonable manner. If the carrier either sells the goods in the usual manner in any recognized market therefor or if he sells at the price current in such market at the time of his sale or if he has otherwise sold in conformity with commercially reasonable practices among dealers in the type of goods sold he has sold in a commercially reasonable manner. A sale of more goods than apparently necessary to be offered to ensure satisfaction of the obligation is not commercially reasonable except in cases covered by the preceding sentence.

(2) Before any sale pursuant to this section any person claiming a right in the goods may pay the amount necessary to satisfy the lien and the reasonable expenses incurred under this section. In that event the goods must not be sold, but must be retained by the carrier subject to the terms of the bill and this Article.

(3) The carrier may buy at any public sale pursuant to this section.

(4) A purchaser in good faith of goods sold to enforce a carrier's lien takes the goods free of any rights of persons against whom the lien was valid, despite noncompliance by the carrier with the requirements of this section.

(5) The carrier may satisfy his lien from the proceeds of any sale pursuant to this section but must hold the balance, if any, for delivery on demand to any person

to whom he would have been bound to deliver the goods.

(6) The rights provided by this section shall be in addition to all other rights allowed by law to a creditor against his debtor.

(7) A carrier's lien may be enforced in accordance with either subsection (1) or the procedure set forth in subsection (2) of Section 7–210.

(8) The carrier is liable for damages caused by failure to comply with the requirements for sale under this section and in case of willful violation is liable for conversion.

Section 7–309. Duty of Care; Contractual Limitation of Carrier's Liability

(1) A carrier who issues a bill of lading whether negotiable or non-negotiable must exercise the degree of care in relation to the goods which a reasonably careful man would exercise under like circumstances. This subsection does not repeal or change any law or rule of law which imposes liability upon a common carrier for damages not caused by its negligence.

(2) Damages may be limited by a provision that the carrier's liability shall not exceed a value stated in the document if the carrier's rates are dependent upon value and the consignor by the carrier's tariff is afforded an opportunity to declare a higher value or a value as lawfully provided in the tariff, or where no tariff is filed he is otherwise advised of such opportunity; but no such limitation is effective with respect to the carrier's liability for conversion to its own use.

(3) Reasonable provisions as to the time and manner of presenting claims and instituting actions based on the shipment may be included in a bill of lading or tariff.

PART 4

Warehouse Receipts and Bills of Lading: General Obligations

Section 7–401. Irregularities in Issue of Receipt or Bill or Conduct of Issuer

The obligations imposed by this Article on an issuer apply to a document of title regardless of the fact that

(a) the document may not comply with the requirements of this Article or of any other law or

regulation regarding its issue, form or content; or

(b) the issuer may have violated laws regulating the conduct of his business; or

(c) the goods covered by the document were owned by the bailee at the time the document was issued; or

(d) the person issuing the document does not come within the definition of warehouseman if it purports to be a warehouse receipt.

Section 7–402. Duplicate Receipt or Bill; Overissue

Neither a duplicate nor any other document of title purporting to cover goods already represented by an outstanding document of the same issuer confers any right in the goods, except as provided in the case of bills in a set, overissue of documents for fungible goods and substitutes for lost, stolen or destroyed documents. But the issuer is liable for damages caused by his overissue or failure to identify a duplicate document as such by conspicuous notation on its face.

Section 7–403. Obligation of Warehouseman or Carrier to Deliver; Excuse

(1) The bailee must deliver the goods to a person entitled under the document who complies with subsections (2) and (3), unless and to the extent that the bailee establishes any of the following:

(a) delivery of the goods to a person whose receipt was rightful as against the claimant;

(b) damage to or delay, loss or destruction of the goods for which the bailee is not liable [, but the burden of establishing negligence in such cases is on the person entitled under the document];

Note: *The brackets in (1)(b) indicate that State enactments may differ on this point without serious damage to the principle of uniformity.*

(c) previous sale or other disposition of the goods in lawful enforcement of a lien or on warehouseman's lawful termination of storage;

(d) the exercise by a seller of his right to stop delivery pursuant to the provisions of the Article on Sales (Section 2–705);

(e) a diversion, reconsignment or other disposition pursuant to the provisions of this Article (Section 7–303) or tariff regulating such right;

(f) release, satisfaction or any other fact affording a personal defense against the claimant;

(g)   any other lawful excuse.

(2)   A person claiming goods covered by a document of title must satisfy the bailee's lien where the bailee so requests or where the bailee is prohibited by law from delivering the goods until the charges are paid.

(3)   Unless the person claiming is one against whom the document confers no right under Section 7–503(1), he must surrender for cancellation or notation of partial deliveries any outstanding negotiable document covering the goods, and the bailee must cancel the document or conspicuously note the partial delivery thereon or be liable to any person to whom the document is duly negotiated.

(4)   "Person entitled under the document" means holder in the case of a negotiable document or the person to whom delivery is to be made by the terms of or pursuant to written instructions under a non-negotiable document.

Section 7–404.   No Liability for Good Faith Delivery Pursuant to Receipt or Bill

A bailee who in good faith including observance of reasonable commercial standards has received goods and delivered or otherwise disposed of them according to the terms of the document of title or pursuant to this Article is not liable therefor. This rule applies even though the person from whom he received the goods had no authority to procure the document or to dispose of the goods and even though the person to whom he delivered the goods had no authority to receive them.

PART 5

Warehouse Receipts and Bills of Lading: Negotiation and Transfer

Section 7–501.   Form of Negotiation and Requirements of "Due Negotiation"

(1)   A negotiable document of title running to the order of a named person is negotiated by his indorsement and delivery. After his indorsement in blank or to bearer any person can negotiate it by delivery alone.

(2)   (a)   A negotiable document of title is also negotiated by delivery alone when by its original terms it runs to bearer.

(b)   When a document running to the order of a named person is delivered to him the effect is the same as if the document had been negotiated.

(3)   Negotiation of a negotiable document of title after it has been indorsed to a specified person requires indorsement by the special indorsee as well as delivery.

(4)   A negotiable document of title is "duly negotiated" when it is negotiated in the manner stated in this section to a holder who purchases it in good faith without notice of any defense against or claim to it on the part of any person and for value, unless it is established that the negotiation is not in the regular course of business or financing or involves receiving the document in settlement or payment of a money obligation.

(5)   Indorsement of a non-negotiable document neither makes it negotiable nor adds to the transferee's rights.

(6)   The naming in a negotiable bill of a person to be notified of the arrival of the goods does not limit the negotiability of the bill nor constitute notice to a purchaser thereof of any interest of such person in the goods.

Section 7–502.   Rights Acquired by Due Negotiation

(1)   Subject to the following section and to the provisions of Section 7–205 on fungible goods, a holder to whom a negotiable document of title has been duly negotiated acquires thereby:

(a)   title to the document;

(b)   title to the goods;

(c)   all rights accruing under the law of agency or estoppel, including rights to goods delivered to the bailee after the document was issued; and

(d)   the direct obligation of the issuer to hold or deliver the goods according to the terms of the document free of any defense or claim by him except those arising under the terms of the document or under this Article. In the case of a delivery order the bailee's obligation accrues only upon acceptance and the obligation acquired by the holder is that the issuer and any indorser will procure the acceptance of the bailee.

(2)   Subject to the following section, title and rights so acquired are not defeated by any stoppage of the goods represented by the document or by surrender of such goods by the bailee, and are not impaired even though the negotiation or any prior negotiation constituted a breach of duty or even though any person has been deprived of possession of the document by misrepresentation, fraud, accident, mistake, duress, loss, theft or conversion, or even though a previous sale

or other transfer of the goods or document has been made to a third person.

Section 7–503. Document of Title to Goods Defeated in Certain Cases

(1) A document of title confers no right in goods against a person who before issuance of the document had a legal interest or a perfected security interest in them and who neither

> (a) delivered or entrusted them or any document of title covering them to the bailor or his nominee with actual or apparent authority to ship, store or sell or with power to obtain delivery under this Article (Section 7–403) or with power of disposition under this Act (Sections 2–403 and 9–307) or other statute or rule of law; nor

> (b) acquiesced in the procurement by the bailor or his nominee of any document of title.

(2) Title to goods based upon an unaccepted delivery order is subject to the rights of anyone to whom a negotiable warehouse receipt or bill of lading covering the goods has been duly negotiated. Such a title may be defeated under the next section to the same extent as the rights of the issuer or a transferee from the issuer.

(3) Title to goods based upon a bill of lading issued to a freight forwarder is subject to the rights of anyone to whom a bill issued by the freight forwarder is duly negotiated; but delivery by the carrier in accordance with Part 4 of this Article pursuant to its own bill of lading discharges the carrier's obligation to deliver.

Section 7–504. Rights Acquired in the Absence of Due Negotiation; Effect of Diversion; Seller's Stoppage of Delivery

(1) A transferee of a document, whether negotiable or non-negotiable, to whom the document has been delivered but not duly negotiated, acquires the title and rights which his transferor had or had actual authority to convey.

(2) In the case of a non-negotiable document, until but not after the bailee receives notification of the transfer, the rights of the transferee may be defeated

> (a) by those creditors of the transferor who could treat the sale as void under Section 2–402; or

> (b) by a buyer from the transferor in ordinary course of business if the bailee has delivered the goods to the buyer or received notification of his rights; or

> (c) as against the bailee by good faith dealings of the bailee with the transferor.

(3) A diversion or other change of shipping instructions by the consignor in a non-negotiable bill of lading which causes the bailee not to deliver to the consignee defeats the consignee's title to the goods if they have been delivered to a buyer in ordinary course of business and in any event defeats the consignee's rights against the bailee.

(4) Delivery pursuant to a non-negotiable document may be stopped by a seller under Section 2–705, and subject to the requirement of due notification there provided. A bailee honoring the seller's instructions is entitled to be indemnified by the seller against any resulting loss or expense.

Section 7–505. Indorser Not a Guarantor for Other Parties

The indorsement of a document of title issued by a bailee does not make the indorser liable for any default by the bailee or by previous indorsers.

Section 7–506. Delivery Without Indorsement: Right to Compel Indorsement

The transferee of a negotiable document of title has a specifically enforceable right to have his transferor supply any necessary indorsement but the transfer becomes a negotiation only as of the time the indorsement is supplied.

Section 7–507. Warranties on Negotiation or Transfer of Receipt or Bill

Where a person negotiates or transfers a document of title for value otherwise than as a mere intermediary under the next following section, then unless otherwise agreed he warrants to his immediate purchaser only in addition to any warranty made in selling the goods

> (a) that the document is genuine; and

> (b) that he had no knowledge of any fact which would impair its validity or worth; and

> (c) that his negotiation or transfer is rightful and fully effective with respect to the title to the document and the goods it represents.

Section 7–508. Warranties of Collecting Bank as to Documents

A collecting bank or other intermediary known to be entrusted with documents on behalf of another or with collection of a draft or other claim against delivery of documents warrants by such delivery of the documents only its own good faith and authority. This rule applies even though the intermediary has purchased or made advances against the claim or draft to be collected.

Section 7–509. Receipt or Bill: When Adequate Compliance with Commercial Contract

The question whether a document is adequate to fulfill the obligations of a contract for sale or the conditions of a credit is governed by the Articles on Sales (Article 2) and on Letters of Credit (Article 5).

PART **6**

Warehouse Receipts and Bills of Lading: Miscellaneous Provisions

Section 7–601. Lost and Missing Documents

(1) If a document has been lost, stolen or destroyed, a court may order delivery of the goods or issuance of a substitute document and the bailee may without liability to any person comply with such order. If the document was negotiable the claimant must post security approved by the court to indemnify any person who may suffer loss as a result of non-surrender of the document. If the document was not negotiable, such security may be required at the discretion of the court. The court may also in its discretion order payment of the bailee's reasonable costs and counsel fees.

(2) A bailee who without court order delivers goods to a person claiming under a missing negotiable document is liable to any person injured thereby, and if the delivery is not in good faith becomes liable for conversion. Delivery in good faith is not conversion if made in accordance with a filed classification or tariff or, where no classification or tariff is filed, if the claimant posts security with the bailee in an amount at least double the value of the goods at the time of posting to indemnify any person injured by the delivery who files a notice of claim within one year after the delivery.

Section 7–602. Attachment of Goods Covered by a Negotiable Document

Except where the document was originally issued upon delivery of the goods by a person who had no power to dispose of them, no lien attaches by virtue of any judicial process to goods in the possession of a bailee for which a negotiable document of title is outstanding unless the document be first surrendered to the bailee

or its negotiation enjoined, and the bailee shall not be compelled to deliver the goods pursuant to process until the document is surrendered to him or impounded by the court. One who purchases the document for value without notice of the process or injunction takes free of the lien imposed by judicial process.

Section 7–603. Conflicting Claims; Interpleader

If more than one person claims title or possession of the goods, the bailee is excused from delivery until he has had a reasonable time to ascertain the validity of the adverse claims or to bring an action to compel all claimants to interplead and may compel such interpleader, either in defending an action for nondelivery of the goods, or by original action, whichever is appropriate.

ARTICLE **8**

INVESTMENT SECURITIES

PART **1**

Short Title and General Matters

Section 8–101. Short Title

This Article shall be known and may be cited as Uniform Commercial Code — Investment Securities.

Section 8–102. Definitions and Index of Definitions

(1) In this Article unless the context otherwise requires

   (a) A "security" is an instrument which

      (i) is issued in bearer or registered form; and

      (ii) is of a type commonly dealt in upon securities exchanges or markets or commonly recognized in any area in which it is issued or dealt in as a medium for investment; and

      (iii) is either one of a class or series or by its terms is divisible into a class or series of instruments; and

      (iv) evidences a share, participation or other interest in property or in an enterprise or evidences an obligation of the issuer.

   (b) A writing which is a security is governed by this Article and not by Uniform Commercial Code — Commercial Paper even though it also meets the requirements of that Article. This Article does not apply to money.

(c)   A security is in "registered form" when it specifies a person entitled to the security or to the rights it evidences and when its transfer may be registered upon books maintained for that purpose by or on behalf of an issuer or the security so states.

(d)   A security is in "bearer form" when it runs to bearer according to its terms and not by reason of any indorsement.

(2) A "subsequent purchaser" is a person who takes other than by original issue.

(3) A "clearing corporation" is a corporation all of the capital stock of which is held by or for a national securities exchange or association registered under a statute of the United States such as the Securities Exchange Act of 1934.

(4) A "custodian bank" is any bank or trust company which is supervised and examined by state or federal authority having supervision over banks and which is acting as custodian for a clearing corporation.

(5) Other definitions applying to this Article or to specified Parts thereof and the sections in which they appear are:

> "Adverse claim." Section 8–301.
> "Bona fide purchaser." Section 8–302.
> "Broker." Section 8–303.
> "Guarantee of the signature." Section 8–402.
> "Intermediary bank." Section 4–105.
> "Issuer." Section 8–201.
> "Overissue." Section 8–104.

(6) In addition Article 1 contains general definitions and principles of construction and interpretation applicable throughout this Article.

Section 8–103.   Issuer's Lien

A lien upon a security in favor of an issuer thereof is valid against a purchaser only if the right of the issuer to such lien is noted conspicuously on the security.

Section 8–104.   Effect of Overissue; "Overissue"

(1) The provisions of this Article which validate a security or compel its issue or reissue do not apply to the extent that validation, issue or reissue would result in overissue; but

> (a)   if an identical security which does not constitute an overissue is reasonably available for

purchase, the person entitled to issue or validation may compel the issuer to purchase and deliver such a security to him against surrender of the security, if any, which he holds; or

> (b)   if a security is not so available for purchase, the person entitled to issue or validation may recover from the issuer the price he or the last purchaser for value paid for it with interest from the date of his demand.

(2) "Overissue" means the issue of securities in excess of the amount which the issuer has corporate power to issue.

Section 8–105.   Securities Negotiable; Presumptions

(1) Securities governed by this Article are negotiable instruments.

(2) In any action on a security

> (a)   unless specifically denied in the pleadings, each signature on the security or in a necessary indorsement is admitted;

> (b)   when the effectiveness of a signature is put in issue the burden of establishing it is on the party claiming under the signature but the signature is presumed to be genuine or authorized;

> (c)   when signatures are admitted or established production of the instrument entitles a holder to recover on it unless the defendant establishes a defense or a defect going to the validity of the security; and

> (d)   after it is shown that a defense or defect exists the plaintiff has the burden of establishing that he or some person under whom he claims is a person against whom the defense or defect is ineffective (Section 8–202).

Section 8–106.   Applicability

The validity of a security and the rights and duties of the issuer with respect to registration of transfer are governed by the law (including the conflict of laws rules) of the jurisdiction of organization of the issuer.

Section 8–107.   Securities Deliverable; Action for Price

(1) Unless otherwise agreed and subject to any applicable law or regulation respecting short sales, a person obligated to deliver securities may deliver any security of the specified issue in bearer form or registered in the name of the transferee or indorsed to him or in blank.

(2) When the buyer fails to pay the price as it comes due under a contract of sale the seller may recover the price

(a)   of securities accepted by the buyer; and

(b)   of other securities if efforts at their resale would be unduly burdensome or if there is no readily available market for their resale.

PART 2
Issue — Issuer

Section 8–201.   "Issuer"

(1)   With respect to obligations on or defenses to a security "issuer" includes a person who

(a)   places or authorizes the placing of his name on a security (otherwise than an authenticating trustee, registrar, transfer agent or the like) to evidence that it represents a share, participation or other interest in his property or in an enterprise or to evidence his duty to perform an obligation evidenced by the security; or

(b)   directly or indirectly creates fractional interests in his rights or property which fractional interests are evidenced by securities; or

(c)   becomes responsible for or in place of any other person described as an issuer in this section.

(2)   With respect to obligations on or defenses to a security a guarantor is an issuer to the extent of his guaranty whether or not his obligation is noted on the security.

(3)   With respect to registration of transfer (Part 4 of this Article) "issuer" means a person on whose behalf transfer books are maintained.

Section 8–202.   Issuer's Responsibility and Defenses; Notice of Defect or Defense

(1)   Even against a purchaser for value and without notice, the terms of a security include those stated on the security and those made part of the security by reference to another instrument, indenture or document or to a constitution, statute, ordinance, rule, regulation, order or the like to the extent that the terms so referred to do not conflict with the stated terms. Such a reference does not of itself charge a purchaser for value with notice of a defect going to the validity of the security even though the security expressly states that a person accepting it admits such notice.

(2)   (a). A security other than one issued by a government or governmental agency or unit even though issued with a defect going to its validity is valid in the hands of a purchaser for value and without notice of the particular defect unless the defect involves a violation of constitutional provisions in which case the security is valid in the hands of a subsequent purchaser for value and without notice of the defect.

(b)   The rule of subparagraph (a) applies to an issuer which is a government or governmental agency or unit only if either there has been substantial compliance with the legal requirements governing the issue or the issuer has received a substantial consideration for the issue as a whole or for the particular security and a stated purpose of the issue is one for which the issuer has power to borrow money or issue the security.

(3)   Except as otherwise provided in the case of certain unauthorized signatures on issue (Section 8–205), lack of genuineness of a security is a complete defense even against a purchaser for value and without notice.

(4)   All other defenses of the issuer including nondelivery and conditional delivery of the security are ineffective against a purchaser for value who has taken without notice of the particular defense.

(5)   Nothing in this section shall be construed to affect the right of a party to a "when, as and if issued" or a "when distributed" contract to cancel the contract in the event of a material change in the character of the security which is the subject of the contract or in the plan or arrangement pursuant to which such security is to be issued or distributed.

Section 8–203.   Staleness as Notice of Defects or Defenses

(1)   After an act or event which creates a right to immediate performance of the principal obligation evidenced by the security or which sets a date on or after which the security is to be presented or surrendered for redemption or exchange, a purchaser is charged with notice of any defect in its issue or defense of the issuer

(a)   if the act or event is one requiring the payment of money or the delivery of securities or both on presentation or surrender of the security and such funds or securities are available on the date set for payment or exchange and he takes the security more than one year after that date; and

(b)   if the act or event is not covered by paragraph (a) and he takes the security more than two years after the date set for surrender or presentation or the date on which such performance became due.

(2) A call which has been revoked is not within subsection (1).

Section 8–204. Effect of Issuer's Restrictions on Transfer

Unless noted conspicuously on the security a restriction on transfer imposed by the issuer even though otherwise lawful is ineffective except against a person with actual knowledge of it.

Section 8–205. Effect of Unauthorized Signature on Issue

An unauthorized signature placed on a security prior to or in the course of issue is ineffective except that the signature is effective in favor of a purchaser for value and without notice of the lack of authority if the signing has been done by

(a) an authenticating trustee, registrar, transfer agent or other person entrusted by the issuer with the signing of the security or of similar securities or their immediate preparation for signing; or

(b) an employee of the issuer or of any of the foregoing entrusted with responsible handling of the security.

Section 8–206. Completion or Alteration of Instrument

(1) Where a security contains the signatures necessary to its issue or transfer but is incomplete in any other respect

(a) any person may complete it by filling in the blanks as authorized; and

(b) even though the blanks are incorrectly filled in, the security as completed is enforceable by a purchaser who took it for value and without notice of such incorrectness.

(2) A complete security which has been improperly altered even though fraudulently remains enforceable but only according to its original terms.

Section 8–207. Rights of Issuer with Respect to Registered Owners

(1) Prior to due presentment for registration of transfer of a security in registered form the issuer or indenture trustee may treat the registered owner as the person exclusively entitled to vote, to receive notifications and otherwise to exercise all rights and powers of an owner.

(2) Nothing in this Article shall be construed to affect the liability of the registered owner of a security for calls, assessments or the like.

Section 8–208. Effect of Signature of Authenticating Trustee, Registrar or Transfer Agent

(1) A person placing his signature upon a security as authenticating trustee, registrar, transfer agent or the like warrants to a purchaser for value without notice of the particular defect that

(a) the security is genuine; and

(b) his own participation in the issue of the security is within his capacity and within the scope of the authorization received by him from the issuer; and

(c) he has reasonable grounds to believe that the security is in the form and within the amount the issuer is authorized to issue.

(2) Unless otherwise agreed, a person by so placing his signature does not assume responsibility for the validity of the security in other respects.

PART **3**

Purchase

Section 8–301. Rights Acquired by Purchaser; "Adverse Claim"; Title Acquired by Bona Fide Purchaser

(1) Upon delivery of a security the purchaser acquires the rights in the security which his transferor had or had actual authority to convey except that a purchaser who has himself been a party to any fraud or illegality affecting the security or who as a prior holder had notice of an adverse claim cannot improve his position by taking from a later bona fide purchaser. "Adverse claim" includes a claim that a transfer was or would be wrongful or that a particular adverse person is the owner of or has an interest in the security.

(2) A bona fide purchaser in addition to acquiring the rights of a purchaser also acquires the security free of any adverse claim.

(3) A purchaser of a limited interest acquires rights only to the extent of the interest purchased.

Section 8–302. "Bona Fide Purchaser"

A "bona fide purchaser" is a purchaser for value in good faith and without notice of any adverse claim who takes delivery of a security in bearer form or of one in registered form issued to him or indorsed to him or in blank.

Section 8–303. "Broker"

"Broker" means a person engaged for all or part of his time in the business of buying and selling securities, who in the transaction concerned acts for, or buys a security from or sells a security to a customer. Nothing in this Article determines the capacity in which a person acts for purposes of any other statute or rule to which such person is subject.

Section 8–304. Notice to Purchaser of Adverse Claims

(1) A purchaser (including a broker for the seller or buyer but excluding an intermediary bank) of a security is charged with notice of adverse claims if

    (a) the security whether in bearer or registered form has been indorsed "for collection" or "for surrender" or for some other purpose not involving transfer; or

    (b) the security is in bearer form and has on it an unambiguous statement that it is the property of a person other than the transferor. The mere writing of a name on a security is not such a statement.

(2) The fact that the purchaser (including a broker for the seller or buyer) has notice that the security is held for a third person or is registered in the name of or indorsed by a fiduciary does not create a duty of inquiry into the rightfulness of the transfer or constitute notice of adverse claims. If, however, the purchaser (excluding an intermediary bank) has knowledge that the proceeds are being used or that the transaction is for the individual benefit of the fiduciary or otherwise in breach of duty, the purchaser is charged with notice of adverse claims.

Section 8–305. Staleness as Notice of Adverse Claims

An act or event which creates a right to immediate performance of the principal obligation evidenced by the security or which sets a date on or after which the security is to be presented or surrendered for redemption or exchange does not of itself constitute any notice of adverse claims except in the case of a purchase

    (a) after one year from any date set for such presentment or surrender for redemption or exchange; or

    (b) after six months from any date set for payment of money against presentation or surrender of the security if funds are available for payment on that date.

Section 8–306. Warranties on Presentment and Transfer

(1) A person who presents a security for registration of transfer or for payment or exchange warrants to the issuer that he is entitled to the registration, payment or exchange. But a purchaser for value without notice of adverse claims who receives a new, reissued or re-registered security on registration of transfer warrants only that he has no knowledge of any unauthorized signature (Section 8–311) in a necessary indorsement.

(2) A person by transferring a security to a purchaser for value warrants only that

    (a) his transfer is effective and rightful; and

    (b) the security is genuine and has not been materially altered; and

    (c) he knows no fact which might impair the validity of the security.

(3) Where a security is delivered by an intermediary known to be entrusted with delivery of the security on behalf of another or with collection of a draft or other claim against such delivery, the intermediary by such delivery warrants only his own good faith and authority even though he has purchased or made advances against the claim to be collected against the delivery.

(4) A pledgee or other holder for security who re-delivers the security received, or after payment and on order of the debtor delivers that security to a third person makes only the warranties of an intermediary under subsection (3).

(5) A broker gives to his customer and to the issuer and a purchaser the warranties provided in this section and has the rights and privileges of a purchaser under this section. The warranties of and in favor of the broker acting as an agent are in addition to applicable warranties given by and in favor of his customer.

Section 8–307. Effect of Delivery Without Indorsement; Right to Compel Indorsement

Where a security in registered form has been delivered to a purchaser without a necessary indorsement he may become a bona fide purchaser only as of the time the indorsement is supplied, but against the transferor the transfer is complete upon delivery and the purchaser has a specifically enforceable right to have any necessary indorsement supplied.

Section 8–308.   Indorsement, How Made; Special Indorsement; Indorser Not a Guarantor; Partial Assignment

(1) An indorsement of a security in registered form is made when an appropriate person signs on it or on a separate document an assignment or transfer of the security or a power to assign or transfer it or when the signature of such person is written without more upon the back of the security.

(2) An indorsement may be in blank or special. An indorsement in blank includes an indorsement to bearer. A special indorsement specifies the person to whom the security is to be transferred, or who has power to transfer it. A holder may convert a blank indorsement into a special indorsement.

(3) "An appropriate person" in subsection (1) means

   (a)   the person specified by the security or by special indorsement to be entitled to the security; or

   (b)   where the person so specified is described as a fiduciary but is no longer serving in the described capacity — either that person or his successor; or

   (c)   where the security or indorsement so specifies more than one person as fiduciaries and one or more are no longer serving in the described capacity, — the remaining fiduciary or fiduciaries, whether or not a successor has been appointed or qualified; or

   (d)   when the person so specified is an individual and is without capacity to act by virtue of death, incompetence, infancy or otherwise, — his executor, administrator, guardian or like fiduciary; or

   (e)   where the security or indorsement so specifies more than one person as tenants by the entirety or with right of survivorship and by reason of death all cannot sign, — the survivor or survivors; or

   (f)   a person having power to sign under applicable law or controlling instrument; or

   (g)   to the extent that any of the foregoing persons may act through an agent, — his authorized agent.

(4) Unless otherwise agreed the indorser by his indorsement assumes no obligation that the security will be honored by the issuer.

(5) An indorsement purporting to be only of part of a security representing units intended by the issuer to be separately transferable is effective to the extent of the indorsement.

(6) Whether the person signing is appropriate is determined as of the date of signing and an indorsement by such a person does not become unauthorized for the purposes of this Article by virtue of any subsequent change of circumstances.

(7) Failure of a fiduciary to comply with a controlling instrument or with the law of the state having jurisdiction of the fiduciary relationship, including any law requiring the fiduciary to obtain court approval of the transfer, does not render his indorsement unauthorized for the purposes of this Article.

Section 8–309.   Effect of Indorsement Without Delivery

An indorsement of a security whether special or in blank does not constitute a transfer until delivery of the security on which it appears or if the indorsement is on a separate document until delivery of both the document and the security.

Section 8–310.   Indorsement of Security in Bearer Form

An indorsement of a security in bearer form may give notice of adverse claims (Section 8–304) but does not otherwise affect any right to registration the holder may possess.

Section 8–311.   Effect of Unauthorized Indorsement

Unless the owner has ratified an unauthorized indorsement or is otherwise precluded from asserting its ineffectiveness

   (a)   he may assert its ineffectiveness against the issuer or any purchaser other than a purchaser for value and without notice of adverse claims who has in good faith received a new, reissued or re-registered security on registration of transfer; and

   (b)   an issuer who registers the transfer of a security upon the unauthorized indorsement is subject to liability for improper registration (Section 8–404).

Section 8–312.　Effect of Guaranteeing Signature or Indorsement

(1)　Any person guaranteeing a signature of an indorser of a security warrants that at the time of signing

(a)　the signature was genuine; and

(b)　the signer was an appropriate person to indorse (Section 8–308); and

(c)　the signer had legal capacity to sign.

But the guarantor does not otherwise warrant the rightfulness of the particular transfer.

(2)　Any person may guarantee an indorsement of a security and by so doing warrants not only the signature (subsection 1) but also the rightfulness of the particular transfer in all respects. But no issuer may require a guarantee of indorsement as a condition to registration of transfer.

(3)　The foregoing warranties are made to any person taking or dealing with the security in reliance on the guarantee and the guarantor is liable to such person for any loss resulting from breach of the warranties.

Section 8–313.　When Delivery to the Purchaser Occurs; Purchaser's Broker as Holder

(1)　Delivery to a purchaser occurs when

(a)　he or a person designated by him acquires possession of a security; or

(b)　his broker acquires possession of a security specially indorsed to or issued in the name of the purchaser; or

(c)　his broker sends him confirmation of the purchase and also by book entry or otherwise identifies a specific security in the broker's possession as belonging to the purchaser; or

(d)　with respect to an identified security to be delivered while still in the possession of a third person when that person acknowledges that he holds for the purchaser.

(e)　appropriate entries on the books of a clearing corporation are made under Section 8–320.

(2)　The purchaser is the owner of a security held for him by his broker, but is not the holder except as specified in subparagraphs (b), (c) and (e) of subsection (1). Where a security is part of a fungible bulk the purchaser is the owner of a proportionate property interest in the fungible bulk.

(3)　Notice of an adverse claim received by the broker or by the purchaser after the broker takes delivery as a holder for value is not effective either as to the broker or as to the purchaser. However, as between the broker and the purchaser the purchaser may demand delivery of an equivalent security as to which no notice of an adverse claim has been received.

Section 8–314.　Duty to Deliver, When Completed

(1)　Unless otherwise agreed where a sale of a security is made on an exchange or otherwise through brokers

(a)　the selling customer fulfills his duty to deliver when he places such a security in the possession of the selling broker or of a person designated by the broker or if requested causes an acknowledgment to be made to the selling broker that it is held for him; and

(b)　the selling broker including a correspondent broker acting for a selling customer fulfills his duty to deliver by placing the security or a like security in the possession of the buying broker or a person designated by him or by effecting clearance of the sale in accordance with the rules of the exchange on which the transaction took place.

(2)　Except as otherwise provided in this section and unless otherwise agreed, a transferor's duty to deliver a security under a contract of purchase is not fulfilled until he places the security in form to be negotiated by the purchaser in the possession of the purchaser or of a person designated by him or at the purchaser's request causes an acknowledgment to be made to the purchaser that it is held for him. Unless made on an exchange a sale to a broker purchasing for his own account is within this subsection and not within subsection (1).

Section 8–315.　Action Against Purchaser Based upon Wrongful Transfer

(1)　Any person against whom the transfer of a security is wrongful for any reason, including his incapacity, may against any one except a bona fide purchaser reclaim possession of the security or obtain possession of any new security evidencing all or part of the same rights or have damages.

(2)　If the transfer is wrongful because of an unauthorized indorsement, the owner may also reclaim or obtain possession of the security or new security even from a bona fide purchaser if the ineffectiveness of the purported indorsement can be asserted against him under the provisions of this Article on unauthorized indorsements (Section 8–311).

(3) The right to obtain or reclaim possession of a security may be specifically enforced and its transfer enjoined and the security impounded pending the litigation.

Section 8–316. Purchaser's Right to Requisites for Registration of Transfer on Books

Unless otherwise agreed the transferor must on due demand supply his purchaser with any proof of his authority to transfer or with any other requisite which may be necessary to obtain registration of the transfer of the security but if the transfer is not for value a transferor need not do so unless the purchaser furnishes the necessary expenses. Failure to comply with a demand made within a reasonable time gives the purchaser the right to reject or rescind the transfer.

Section 8–317. Attachment or Levy upon Security

(1) No attachment or levy upon a security or any share or other interest evidenced thereby which is outstanding shall be valid until the security is actually seized by the officer making the attachment or levy but a security which has been surrendered to the issuer may be attached or levied upon at the source.

(2) A creditor whose debtor is the owner of a security shall be entitled to such aid from courts of appropriate jurisdiction, by injunction or otherwise, in reaching such security or in satisfying the claim by means thereof as is allowed at law or in equity in regard to property which cannot readily be attached or levied upon by ordinary legal process.

Section 8–318. No Conversion by Good Faith Delivery

An agent or bailee who in good faith (including observance of reasonable commercial standards if he is in the business of buying, selling or otherwise dealing with securities) has received securities and sold, pledged or delivered them according to the instructions of his principal is not liable for conversion or for participation in breach of fiduciary duty although the principal had no right to dispose of them.

Section 8–319. Statute of Frauds

A contract for the sale of securities is not enforceable by way of action or defense unless

(a) there is some writing signed by the party against whom enforcement is sought or by his authorized agent or broker sufficient to indicate that a contract has been made for sale of a stated quantity of described securities at a defined or stated price; or

(b) delivery of the security has been accepted or payment has been made but the contract is enforceable under this provision only to the extent of such delivery or payment; or

(c) within a reasonable time a writing in confirmation of the sale or purchase and sufficient against the sender under paragraph (a) has been received by the party against whom enforcement is sought and he has failed to send written objection to its contents within ten days after its receipt; or

(d) the party against whom enforcement is sought admits in his pleading, testimony or otherwise in court that a contract was made for sale of a stated quantity of described securities at a defined or stated price.

Section 8–320. Transfer or Pledge Within a Central Depository System

(1) If a security

(a) is in the custody of a clearing corporation or of a custodian bank or a nominee of either subject to the instructions of the clearing corporation; and

(b) is in bearer form or indorsed in blank by an appropriate person or registered in the name of the clearing corporation or custodian bank or a nominee of either; and

(c) is shown on the account of a transferor or pledgor on the books of the clearing corporation;

then, in addition to other methods, a transfer or pledge of the security or any interest therein may be effected by the making of appropriate entries on the books of the clearing corporation reducing the account of the transferor or pledgor and increasing the account of the transferee or pledgee by the amount of the obligation or the number of shares or rights transferred or pledged.

(2) Under this section entries may be with respect to like securities or interests therein as a part of a fungible bulk and may refer merely to a quantity of a particular security without reference to the name of the registered owner, certificate or bond number or the like and, in appropriate cases, may be on a net basis taking into account other transfers or pledges of the same security.

(3) A transfer of pledge under this section has the effect of a delivery of a security in bearer form or duly indorsed in blank (Section 8–301) representing the amount of the obligation or the number of shares or rights transferred or pledged. If a pledge or the creation of a security interest is intended, the making of entries has the effect of a taking of delivery by the pledgee or a secured party (Sections 9–304 and 9–305). A transferee or pledgee under this section is a holder.

(4) A transfer or pledge under this section does not constitute a registration of transfer under Part 4 of this Article.

(5) That entries made on the books of the clearing corporation as provided in subsection (1) are not appropriate does not affect the validity or effect of the entries nor the liabilities or obligations of the clearing corporation to any person adversely affected thereby.

PART 4
Registration

Section 8–401. Duty of Issuer to Register Transfer

(1) Where a security in registered form is presented to the issuer with a request to register transfer, the issuer is under a duty to register the transfer as requested if

(a) the security is indorsed by the appropriate person or persons (Section 8–308); and

(b) reasonable assurance is given that those indorsements are genuine and effective (Section 8–402); and

(c) the issuer has no duty to inquire into adverse claims or has discharged any such duty (Section 8–403); and

(d) any applicable law relating to the collection of taxes has been complied with; and

(e) the transfer is in fact rightful or is to a bona fide purchaser.

(2) Where an issuer is under a duty to register a transfer of a security the issuer is also liable to the person presenting it for registration or his principal for loss resulting from any unreasonable delay in registration or from failure or refusal to register the transfer.

Section 8–402. Assurance that Indorsements Are Effective

(1) The issuer may require the following assurance that each necessary indorsement (Section 8–308) is genuine and effective:

(a) in all cases, a guarantee of the signature (subsection (1) of Section 8–312) of the person indorsing; and

(b) where the indorsement is by an agent, appropriate assurance of authority to sign;

(c) where the indorsement is by a fiduciary, appropriate evidence of appointment or incumbency;

(d) where there is more than one fiduciary, reasonable assurance that all who are required to sign have done so;

(e) where the indorsement is by a person not covered by any of the foregoing, assurance appropriate to the case corresponding as nearly as may be to the foregoing.

(2) A "guarantee of the signature" in subsection (1) means a guarantee signed by or on behalf of a person reasonably believed by the issuer to be responsible. The issuer may adopt standards with respect to responsibility provided such standards are not manifestly unreasonable.

(3) "Appropriate evidence of appointment or incumbency" in subsection (1) means

(a) in the case of a fiduciary appointed or qualified by a court, a certificate issued by or under the direction or supervision of that court or an officer thereof and dated within sixty days before the date of presentation for transfer; or

(b) in any other case, a copy of a document showing the appointment or a certificate issued by or on behalf of a person reasonably believed by the issuer to be responsible or, in the absence of such a document or certificate, other evidence reasonably deemed by the issuer to be appropriate. The issuer may adopt standards with respect to such evidence provided such standards are not manifestly unreasonable. The issuer is not charged with notice of the contents of any document obtained pursuant to this paragraph (b) except to the extent that the contents relate directly to the appointment or incumbency.

(4) The issuer may elect to require reasonable assurance beyond that specified in this section but if it does so and for a purpose other than that specified in subsection 3(b) both requires and obtains a copy of a will, trust, indenture, articles of co-partnership, by-laws or other controlling instrument it is charged with notice of all matters contained therein affecting the transfer.

Section 8–403.   Limited Duty of Inquiry

(1) An issuer to whom a security is presented for registration is under a duty to inquire into adverse claims if

(a)   a written notification of an adverse claim is received at a time and in a manner which affords the issuer a reasonable opportunity to act on it prior to the issuance of a new, reissued or re-registered security and the notification identifies the claimant, the registered owner and the issue of which the security is a part and provides an address for communications directed to the claimant; or

(b)   the issuer is charged with notice of an adverse claim from a controlling instrument which it has elected to require under subsection (4) of Section 8–402.

(2) The issuer may discharge any duty of inquiry by any reasonable means, including notifying an adverse claimant by registered or certified mail at the address furnished by him or if there be no such address at his residence or regular place of business that the security has been presented for registration of transfer by a named person, and that the transfer will be registered unless within thirty days from the date of mailing the notification, either

(a)   an appropriate restraining order, injunction or other process issues from a court of competent jurisdiction; or

(b)   an indemnity bond sufficient in the issuer's judgment to protect the issuer and any transfer agent, registrar or other agent of the issuer involved, from any loss which it or they may suffer by complying with the adverse claim is filed with the issuer.

(3) Unless an issuer is charged with notice of an adverse claim from a controlling instrument which it has elected to require under subsection (4) of Section 8–402 or receives notification of an adverse claim under subsection (1) of this section, where a security presented for registration is indorsed by the appropriate person or persons the issuer is under no duty to inquire into adverse claims. In particular

(a)   an issuer registering a security in the name of a person who is a fiduciary or who is described as a fiduciary is not bound to inquire into the existence, extent, or correct description of the fiduciary relationship and thereafter the issuer may assume without inquiry that the newly registered owner continues to be the fiduciary until the issuer receives written notice that the fiduciary is no longer acting as such with respect to the particular security;

(b)   an issuer registering transfer on an indorsement by a fiduciary is not bound to inquire whether the transfer is made in compliance with a controlling instrument or with the law of the state having jurisdiction of the fiduciary relationship, including any law requiring the fiduciary to obtain court approval of the transfer; and

(c)   the issuer is not charged with notice of the contents of any court record or file or other recorded or unrecorded document even though the document is in its possession and even though the transfer is made on the indorsement of a fiduciary to the fiduciary himself or to his nominee.

Section 8–404.   Liability and Non-Liability for Registration

(1) Except as otherwise provided in any law relating to the collection of taxes, the issuer is not liable to the owner or any other person suffering loss as a result of the registration of a transfer of a security if

(a)   there were on or with the security the necessary indorsements (Section 8–308); and

(b)   the issuer had no duty to inquire into adverse claims or has discharged any such duty (Section 8–403).

(2) Where an issuer has registered a transfer of a security to a person not entitled to it the issuer on demand must deliver a like security to the true owner unless

(a)   the registration was pursuant to subsection (1); or

(b)   the owner is precluded from asserting any claim for registering the transfer under subsection (1) of the following section; or

(c)   such delivery would result in overissue, in which case the issuer's liability is governed by Section 8–104.

Section 8–405.   Lost, Destroyed and Stolen Securities

(1) Where a security has been lost, apparently destroyed or wrongfully taken and the owner fails to

notify the issuer of that fact within a reasonable time after he has notice of it and the issuer registers a transfer of the security before receiving such a notification, the owner is precluded from asserting against the issuer any claim for registering the transfer under the preceding section or any claim to a new security under this section.

(2) Where the owner of a security claims that the security has been lost, destroyed or wrongfully taken, the issuer must issue a new security in place of the original security if the owner

(a) so requests before the issuer has notice that the security has been acquired by a bona fide purchaser; and

(b) files with the issuer a sufficient indemnity bond; and

(c) satisfies any other reasonable requirements imposed by the issuer.

(3) If, after the issue of the new security, a bona fide purchaser of the original security presents it for registration of transfer, the insurer must register the transfer unless registration would result in overissue, in which event the issuer's liability is governed by Section 8–104. In addition to any rights on the indemnity bond, the issuer may recover the new security from the person to whom it was issued or any person taking under him except a bona fide purchaser.

Section 8–406. Duty of Authenticating Trustee, Transfer Agent or Registrar

(1) Where a person acts as authenticating trustee, transfer agent, registrar, or other agent for an issuer in the registration of transfers of its securities or in the issue of new securities or in the cancellation of surrendered securities

(a) he is under a duty to the issuer to exercise good faith and due diligence in performing his functions; and

(b) he has with regard to the particular functions he performs the same obligation to the holder or owner of the security and has the same rights and privileges as the issuer has in regard to those functions.

(2) Notice to an authenticating trustee, transfer agent, registrar or other such agent is notice to the issuer with respect to the functions performed by the agent.

ARTICLE 9
SECURED TRANSACTIONS; SALES OF ACCOUNTS AND CHATTEL PAPER

PART 1
Short Title, Applicability and Definitions

Section 9–101. Short Title

This Article shall be known and may be cited as Uniform Commercial Code — Secured Transactions.

Section 9–102. Policy and Subject Matter of Article

(1) Except as otherwise provided in Section 9–104 on excluded transactions this Article applies

(a) to any transaction (regardless of its form) which is intended to create a security interest in personal property or fixtures including goods, documents, instruments, general intangibles, chattel paper or accounts; and also

(b) to any sale of accounts or chattel paper.

(2) This Article applies to security interests created by contract including pledge, assignment, chattel mortgage, chattel trust, trust deed, factor's lien, equipment trust, conditional sale, trust receipt, other lien or title retention contract and lease or consignment intended as security. This Article does not apply to statutory liens except as provided in Section 9–310.

(3) The application of this Article to a security interest in a secured obligation is not affected by the fact that the obligation is itself secured by a transaction or interest to which this Article does not apply.

Section 9–103. Perfection of Security Interest in Multiple State Transactions

(1) Documents, instruments and ordinary goods.

(a) This subsection applies to documents and instruments and to goods other than those covered by a certificate of title described in subsection (2), mobile goods described in subsection (3), and minerals described in subsection (5).

(b) Except as otherwise provided in this subsection, perfection and the effect of perfection or non-perfection of a security interest in collateral are governed by the law of the jurisdiction where the collateral is when the last event occurs on which is based the assertion that the security interest is perfected or unperfected.

(c)   If the parties to a transaction creating a purchase money security interest in goods in one jurisdiction understand at the time that the security interest attaches that the goods will be kept in another jurisdiction, then the law of the other jurisdiction governs the perfection and the effect of perfection or non-perfection of the security interest from the time it attaches until thirty days after the debtor receives possession of the goods and thereafter if the goods are taken to the other jurisdiction before the end of the thirty-day period.

(d)   When collateral is brought into and kept in this state while subject to a security interest perfected under the law of the jurisdiction from which the collateral was removed, the security interest remains perfected, but if action is required by Part 2 of this Article to perfect the security interest,

(i)   if the action is not taken before the expiration of the period of perfection in the other jurisdiction or the end of four months after the collateral is brought into this state, whichever period first expires, the security interest becomes unperfected at the end of that period and is thereafter deemed to have been unperfected as against a person who became a purchaser after removal;

(ii)   if the action is taken before the expiration of the period specified in subparagraph (i), the security interest continues perfected thereafter;

(iii)   for the purpose of priority over a buyer of consumer goods (subsection (2) of Section 9–307), the period of the effectiveness of a filing in the jurisdiction from which the collateral is removed is governed by the rules with respect to perfection in subparagraphs (i) and (ii).

(2)   Certificate of title.

(a)   This subsection applies to goods covered by a certificate of title issued under a statute of this state or of another jurisdiction under the law of which indication of a security interest on the certificate is required as a condition of perfection.

(b)   Except as otherwise provided in this subsection, perfection and the effect of perfection or non-perfection of the security interest are governed by the law (including the conflict of laws rules) of the jurisdiction issuing the certificate until four

months after the goods are removed from that jurisdiction and thereafter until the goods are registered in another jurisdiction, but in any event not beyond surrender of the certificate. After the expiration of that period, the goods are not covered by the certificate of title within the meaning of this section.

(c)   Except with respect to the rights of a buyer described in the next paragraph, a security interest, perfected in another jurisdiction otherwise than by notation on a certificate of title, in goods brought into this state and thereafter covered by a certificate of title issued by this state is subject to the rules stated in paragraph (d) of subsection (1).

(d)   If goods are brought into this state while a security interest therein is perfected in any manner under the law of the jurisdiction from which the goods are removed and a certificate of title is issued by this state and the certificate does not show that the goods are subject to the security interest or that they may be subject to security interests not shown on the certificate, the security interest is subordinate to the rights of a buyer of the goods who is not in the business of selling goods of that kind to the extent that he gives value and receives delivery of the goods after issuance of the certificate and without knowledge of the security interest.

(3)   Accounts, general intangibles and mobile goods.

(a)   This subsection applies to accounts (other than an account described in subsection (5) on minerals) and general intangibles (other than uncertificated securities) and to goods which are mobile and which are of a type normally used in more than one jurisdiction, such as motor vehicles, trailers, rolling stock, airplanes, shipping containers, road building and construction machinery and commercial harvesting machinery and the like, if the goods are equipment or are inventory leased or held for lease by the debtor to others, and are not covered by a certificate of title described in subsection (2).

(b)   The law (including the conflict of laws rules) of the jurisdiction in which the debtor is located governs the perfection and the effect of perfection or non-perfection of the security interest.

(c)   If, however, the debtor is located in a jurisdiction which is not a part of the United States, and which does not provide for perfection of the security interest by filing or recording in that jurisdiction, the law of the jurisdiction in the United

States in which the debtor has its major executive office in the United States governs the perfection and the effect of perfection or non-perfection of the security interest through filing. In the alternative, if the debtor is located in a jurisdiction which is not a part of the United States or Canada and the collateral is accounts or general intangibles for money due or to become due, the security interest may be perfected by notification to the account debtor. As used in this paragraph, "United States" includes its territories and possessions and the Commonwealth of Puerto Rico.

(d) A debtor shall be deemed located at his place of business if he has one, at his chief executive office if he has more than one place of business, otherwise at his residence. If, however, the debtor is a foreign air carrier under the Federal Aviation Act of 1958, as amended, it shall be deemed located at the designated office of the agent upon whom service of process may be made on behalf of the foreign air carrier.

(e) A security interest perfected under the law of the jurisdiction of the location of the debtor is perfected until the expiration of four months after a change of the debtor's location to another jurisdiction, or until perfection would have ceased by the law of the first jurisdiction, whichever period first expires. Unless perfected in the new jurisdiction before the end of that period, it becomes unperfected thereafter and is deemed to have been unperfected as against a person who became a purchaser after the change.

(4) Chattel paper.

The rules stated for goods in subsection (1) apply to a possessory security interest in chattel paper. The rules stated for accounts in subsection (3) apply to a non-possessory security interest in chattel paper, but the security interest may not be perfected by notification to the account debtor.

(5) Minerals.

Perfection and the effect of perfection or non-perfection of a security interest which is created by a debtor who has an interest in minerals or the like (including oil and gas) before extraction and which attaches thereto as extracted, or which attaches to an account resulting from the sale thereof at the wellhead or minehead are governed by the law (including the conflict of laws rules) of the jurisdiction wherein the wellhead or minehead is located.

(6) Uncertificated securities.

The law (including the conflict of laws rules) of the jurisdiction of organization of the issuer governs the perfection and the effect of perfection or nonperfection of a security interest in uncertificated securities. Amended in 1972 and 1977.

Section 9–104. Transactions Excluded from Article

This Article does not apply

(a) to a security interest subject to any statute of the United States to the extent that such statute governs the rights of parties to and third parties affected by transactions in particular types of property; or

(b) to a landlord's lien; or

(c) to a lien given by statute or other rule of law for services or materials except as provided in Section 9–310 on priority of such liens; or

(d) to a transfer of a claim for wages, salary or other compensation of an employee; or

(e) to a transfer by a government or governmental subdivision or agency; or

(f) to a sale of accounts or chattel paper as part of a sale of the business out of which they arose, or an assignment of accounts or chattel paper which is for the purpose of collection only, or a transfer of a right to payment under a contract to an assignee who is also to do the performance under the contract or a transfer of a single account to an assignee in whole or partial satisfaction of a pre-existing indebtedness; or

(g) to a transfer of an interest in or claim in or under any policy of insurance, except as provided with respect to proceeds (Section 9–306) and priorities in proceeds (Section 9–312); or

(h) to a right represented by a judgment (other than a judgment taken on a right to payment which was collateral); or

(i) to any right of set-off; or

(j) except to the extent that provision is made for fixtures in Section 9–313, to the creation or transfer of an interest in or lien on real estate, including a lease or rents thereunder; or

(k) to a transfer in whole or in part of any claim arising out of tort; or

(l) to a transfer of an interest in any deposit account (subsection (1) of Section 9–105), except as provided with respect to proceeds (Section 9–306) and priorities in proceeds (Section 9–312).

Section 9–105. Definitions and Index of Definitions

(1) In this Article unless the context otherwise requires:

(a) "Account debtor" means the person who is obligated on an account, chattel paper or general intangible;

(b) "Chattel paper" means a writing or writings which evidence both a monetary obligation and a security interest in or a lease of specific goods, but a charter or other contract involving the use or hire of a vessel is not chattel paper. When a transaction is evidenced both by such a security agreement or a lease and by an instrument or a series of instruments, the group of writings taken together constitutes chattel paper;

(c) "Collateral" means the property subject to a security interest, and includes accounts and chattel paper which have been sold;

(d) "Debtor" means the person who owes payment or other performance of the obligation secured, whether or not he owns or has rights in the collateral, and includes the seller of accounts or chattel paper. Where the debtor and the owner of the collateral are not the same person, the term "debtor" means the owner of the collateral in any provision of the Article dealing with the collateral, the obligor in any provision dealing with the obligation, and may include both where the context so requires;

(e) "Deposit account" means a demand, time, savings, passbook or like account maintained with a bank, savings and loan association, credit union or like organization, other than an account evidenced by a certificate of deposit;

(f) "Document" means document of title as defined in the general definitions of Article 1 (Section 1–201), and a receipt of the kind described in subsection (2) of Section 7–201;

(g) "Encumbrance" includes real estate mortgages and other liens on real estate and all other rights in real estate that are not ownership interests;

(h) "Goods" includes all things which are movable at the time the security interest attaches or which are fixtures (Section 9–313), but does not include money, documents, instruments, accounts, chattel paper, general intangibles, or minerals or the like (including oil and gas) before extraction.

"Goods" also includes standing timber which is to be cut and removed under a conveyance or contract for sale, the unborn young of animals, and growing crops;

(i) "Instrument" means a negotiable instrument (defined in Section 3–104), or a certificated security (defined in Section 8–102) or any other writing which evidences a right to the payment of money and is not itself a security agreement or lease and is of a type which is in ordinary course of business transferred by delivery with any necessary indorsement or assignment;

(j) "Mortgage" means a consensual interest created by a real estate mortgage, a trust deed on real estate, or the like;

(k) An advance is made "pursuant to commitment" if the secured party has bound himself to make it, whether or not a subsequent event of default or other event not within his control has relieved or may relieve him from his obligation;

(l) "Security agreement" means an agreement which creates or provides for a security interest;

(m) "Secured party" means a lender, seller or other person in whose favor there is a security interest, including a person to whom accounts or chattel paper have been sold. When the holders of obligations issued under an indenture of trust, equipment trust agreement or the like are represented by a trustee or other person, the representative is the secured party;

(n) "Transmitting utility" means any person primarily engaged in the railroad, street railway or trolley bus business, the electric or electronics communications transmission business, the transmission of goods by pipeline, or the transmission or the production and transmission of electricity, steam, gas or water, or the provision of sewer service.

(2) Other definitions applying to this Article and the sections in which they appear are:

"Account." Section 9–106.
"Attach." Section 9–203.
"Construction mortgage." Section 9–313(1).
"Consumer goods." Section 9–109(1).
"Equipment." Section 9–109(2).
"Farm products." Section 9–109(3).
"Fixture." Section 9–313(1).
"Fixture filing." Section 9–313(1).
"General intangibles." Section 9–106.
"Inventory." Section 9–109(4).
"Lien creditor." Section 9–301(3).

"Proceeds." Section 9–306(1).
"Purchase money security interest." Section 9–107.
"United States." Section 9–103.

(3) The following definitions in other Articles apply to this Article:

"Check." Section 3–104.
"Contract for sale." Section 2–106.
"Holder in due course." Section 3–302.
"Note." Section 3–104.
"Sale." Section 2–106.

(4) In addition Article 1 contains general definitions and principles of construction and interpretation applicable throughout this Article. Amended in 1972 and 1977.

Section 9–106. Definitions: "Account"; "General Intangibles"

"Account" means any right to payment for goods sold or leased or for services rendered which is not evidenced by an instrument or chattel paper, whether or not it has been earned by performance. "General intangibles" means any personal property (including things in action) other than goods, accounts, chattel paper, documents, instruments, and money. All rights to payment earned or unearned under a charter or other contract involving the use or hire of a vessel and all rights incident to the charter or contract are accounts.

Section 9–107. Definitions: "Purchase Money Security Interest"

A security interest is a "purchase money security interest" to the extent that it is

(a) taken or retained by the seller of the collateral to secure all or part of its price; or

(b) taken by a person who by making advances or incurring an obligation gives value to enable the debtor to acquire rights in or the use of collateral if such value is in fact so used.

Section 9–108. When After-Acquired Collateral Not Security for Antecedent Debt

Where a secured party makes an advance, incurs an obligation, releases a perfected security interest, or otherwise gives new value which is to be secured in whole or in part by after-acquired property his security interest in the after-acquired collateral shall be deemed to be taken for new value and not as security for an antecedent debt if the debtor acquires his rights in such collateral either in the ordinary course of his business or under a contract of purchase made pursuant to the security agreement within a reasonable time after new value is given.

Section 9–109. Classification of Goods; "Consumer Goods"; "Equipment"; "Farm Products"; "Inventory"

Goods are

(1) "consumer goods" if they are used or bought for use primarily for personal, family or household purposes;

(2) "equipment" if they are used or bought for use primarily in business (including farming or a profession) or by a debtor who is a non-profit organization or a governmental subdivision or agency or if the goods are not included in the definitions of inventory, farm products or consumer goods;

(3) "farm products" if they are crops or livestock or supplies used or produced in farming operations or if they are products of crops or livestock in their unmanufactured states (such as ginned cotton, woolclip, maple syrup, milk and eggs), and if they are in the possession of a debtor engaged in raising, fattening, grazing or other farming operations. If goods are farm products they are neither equipment nor inventory;

(4) "inventory" if they are held by a person who holds them for sale or lease or to be furnished under contracts of service or if he has so furnished them, or if they are raw materials, work in process or materials used or consumed in a business. Inventory of a person is not to be classified as his equipment.

Section 9–110. Sufficiency of Description

For the purposes of this Article any description of personal property or real estate is sufficient whether or not it is specific if it reasonably identifies what is described.

Section 9–111. Applicability of Bulk Transfer Laws

The creation of a security interest is not a bulk transfer under Article 6 (see Section 6–103).

Section 9–112. Where Collateral Is Not Owned by Debtor

Unless otherwise agreed, when a secured party knows that collateral is owned by a person who is not the debtor, the owner of the collateral is entitled to receive from the secured party any surplus under Section 9–502(2) or under Section 9–504(1), and is not liable for the debt or for any deficiency after resale, and he has the same right as the debtor

(a)   to receive statements under Section 9–208;

(b)   to receive notice of and to object to a secured party's proposal to retain the collateral in satisfaction of the indebtedness under Section 9–505;

(c)   to redeem the collateral under Section 9–506;

(d)   to obtain injunctive or other relief under Section 9–507(1); and

(e)   to recover losses caused to him under Section 9–208(2).

Section 9–113.   Security Interest Arising Under Article on Sales

A security interest arising solely under the Article on Sales (Article 2) is subject to the provisions of this Article except that to the extent that and so long as the debtor does not have or does not lawfully obtain possession of the goods

(a)   no security agreement is necessary to make the security interest enforceable; and

(b)   no filing is required to perfect the security interest; and

(c)   the rights of the secured party on default by the debtor are governed by the Article on Sales (Article 2).

Section 9–114.   Consignment

(1) A person who delivers goods under a consignment which is not a security interest and who would be required to file under this Article by paragraph (3)(c) of Section 2–326 has priority over a secured party who is or becomes a creditor of the consignee and who would have a perfected security interest in the goods if they were the property of the consignee, and also has priority with respect to identifiable cash proceeds received on or before delivery of the goods to a buyer, if

(a)   the consignor complies with the filing provision of the Article on Sales with respect to consignments (paragraph (3)(c) of Section 2–326) before the consignee receives possession of the goods; and

(b)   the consignor gives notification in writing to the holder of the security interest if the holder has filed a financing statement covering the same

types of goods before the date of the filing made by the consignor; and

(c)   the holder of the security interest receives the notification within five years before the consignee receives possession of the goods; and

(d)   the notification states that the consignor expects to deliver goods on consignment to the consignee, describing the goods by item or type.

(2) In the case of a consignment which is not a security interest and in which the requirements of the preceding subsection have not been met, a person who delivers goods to another is subordinate to a person who would have a perfected security interest in the goods if they were the property of the debtor.

PART 2
Validity of Security Agreement and Rights of Parties Thereto

Section 9–201.   General Validity of Security Agreement

Except as otherwise provided by this Act a security agreement is effective according to its terms between the parties, against purchasers of the collateral and against creditors. Nothing in this Article validates any charge or practice illegal under any statute or regulation thereunder governing usury, small loans, retail installment sales, or the like, or extends the application of any such statute or regulation to any transaction not otherwise subject thereto.

Section 9–202.   Title to Collateral Immaterial

Each provision of this Article with regard to rights, obligations and remedies applies whether title to collateral is in the secured party or in the debtor.

Section 9–203.   Attachment and Enforceability of Security Interest; Proceeds; Formal Requisites

(1) Subject to the provisions of Section 4–208 on the security interest of a collecting bank, Section 8–321 on security interests in securities and Section 9–113 on a security interest arising under the Article on Sales, a security interest is not enforceable against the debtor or third parties with respect to the collateral and does not attach unless:

(a)   the collateral is in the possession of the secured party pursuant to agreement, or the debtor has signed a security agreement which contains a description of the collateral and in addition, when the security interest covers crops growing or to be grown or timber to be cut, a description of the land concerned;

(b)   value has been given; and

(c)   the debtor has rights in the collateral.

(2) A security interest attaches when it becomes enforceable against the debtor with respect to the collateral. Attachment occurs as soon as all of the events specified in subsection (1) have taken place unless explicit agreement postpones the time of attaching.

(3) Unless otherwise agreed a security agreement gives the secured party the rights to proceeds provided by Section 9–306.

(4) A transaction, although subject to this Article, is also subject to . . . . ,* and in the case of conflict between the provisions of this Article and any such statute, the provisions of such statute control. Failure to comply with any applicable statute has only the effect which is specified therein.

Note: *At* * *in subsection (4), insert reference to any local statute regulating small loans, retail installment sales and the like.*

Section 9–204.   After-Acquired Property; Future Advances

(1) Except as provided in subsection (2), a security agreement may provide that any or all obligations covered by the security agreement are to be secured by after-acquired collateral.

(2) No security interest attaches under an after-acquired property clause to consumer goods other than accessions (Section 9–314) when given as additional security unless the debtor acquires rights in them within ten days after the secured party gives value.

(3) Obligations covered by a security agreement may include future advances or other value whether or not the advances or value are given pursuant to commitment (subsection (1) of Section 9–105).

Section 9–205.   Use or Disposition of Collateral Without Accounting Permissible

A security interest is not invalid or fraudulent against creditors by reason of liberty in the debtor to use, commingle or dispose of all or part of the collateral (including returned or repossessed goods) or to collect or compromise accounts or chattel paper, or to accept the return of goods or make repossessions, or to use,

commingle or dispose of proceeds, or by reason of the failure of the secured party to require the debtor to account for proceeds or replace collateral. This section does not relax the requirements of possession where perfection of a security interest depends upon possession of the collateral by the secured party or by a bailee.

Section 9–206.   Agreement Not to Assert Defenses Against Assignee; Modification of Sales Warranties Where Security Agreement Exists

(1) Subject to any statute or decision which establishes a different rule for buyers or lessees of consumer goods, an agreement by a buyer or lessee that he will not assert against an assignee any claim or defense which he may have against the seller or lessor is enforceable by an assignee who takes his assignment for value, in good faith and without notice of a claim or defense, except as to defenses of a type which may be asserted against a holder in due course of a negotiable instrument under the Article on Commercial Paper (Article 3). A buyer who as part of one transaction signs both a negotiable instrument and a security agreement makes such an agreement.

(2) When a seller retains a purchase money security interest in goods the Article on Sales (Article 2) governs the sale and any disclaimer, limitation or modification of the seller's warranties.

Section 9–207.   Rights and Duties When Collateral Is in Secured Party's Possession

(1) A secured party must use reasonable care in the custody and preservation of collateral in his possession. In the case of an instrument or chattel paper reasonable care includes taking necessary steps to preserve rights against prior parties unless otherwise agreed.

(2) Unless otherwise agreed, when collateral is in the secured party's possession

(a)   reasonable expenses (including the cost of any insurance and payment of taxes or other charges) incurred in the custody, preservation, use or operation of the collateral are chargeable to the debtor and are secured by the collateral;

(b)   the risk of accidental loss or damage is on the debtor to the extent of any deficiency in any effective insurance coverage;

(c)   the secured party may hold as additional security any increase or profits (except money) received from the collateral, but money so received, unless remitted to the debtor, shall be applied in reduction of the secured obligation;

(d)   the secured party must keep the collateral identifiable but fungible collateral may be commingled;

(e)   the secured party may repledge the collateral upon terms which do not impair the debtor's right to redeem it.

(3)   A secured party is liable for any loss caused by his failure to meet any obligation imposed by the preceding subsections but does not lose his security interest.

(4)   A secured party may use or operate the collateral for the purpose of preserving the collateral or its value or pursuant to the order of a court of appropriate jurisdiction or, except in the case of consumer goods, in the manner and to the extent provided in the security agreement.

Section 9–208.   Request for Statement of Account or List of Collateral

(1)   A debtor may sign a statement indicating what he believes to be the aggregate amount of unpaid indebtedness as of a specified date and may send it to the secured party with a request that the statement be approved or corrected and returned to the debtor. When the security agreement or any other record kept by the secured party identifies the collateral a debtor may similarly request the secured party to approve or correct a list of the collateral.

(2)   The secured party must comply with such a request within two weeks after receipt by sending a written correction or approval. If the secured party claims a security interest in all of a particular type of collateral owned by the debtor he may indicate that fact in his reply and need not approve or correct an itemized list of such collateral. If the secured party without reasonable excuse fails to comply he is liable for any loss caused by the debtor thereby; and if the debtor has properly included in his request a good faith statement of the obligation or a list of the collateral or both the secured party may claim a security interest only as shown in the statement against persons misled by his failure to comply. If he no longer has an interest in the obligation or collateral at the time the request is received he must disclose the name and address of any successor in interest known to him and he is liable for any loss caused to the debtor as a result of failure to disclose. A successor in interest is not subject to this section until a request is received by him.

(3)   A debtor is entitled to such a statement once every six months without charge. The secured party may require payment of a charge not exceeding $10 for each additional statement furnished.

PART 3

Rights of Third Parties: Perfected and Unperfected Security Interests; Rules of Priority

Section 9–301.   Persons Who Take Priority over Unperfected Security Interests; Rights of "Lien Creditor"

(1)   Except as otherwise provided in subsection (2), an unperfected security interest is subordinate to the rights of

(a)   persons entitled to priority under Section 9–312;

(b)   a person who becomes a lien creditor before the security interest is perfected;

(c)   in the case of goods, instruments, documents, and chattel paper, a person who is not a secured party and who is a transferee in bulk or other buyer not in ordinary course of business or is a buyer of farm products in ordinary course of business, to the extent that he gives value and receives delivery of the collateral without knowledge of the security interest and before it is perfected;

(d)   in the case of accounts and general intangibles, a person who is not a secured party and who is a transferee to the extent that he gives value without knowledge of the security interest and before it is perfected.

(2)   If the secured party files with respect to a purchase money security interest before or within ten days after the debtor receives possession of the collateral, he takes priority over the rights of a transferee in bulk or of a lien creditor which arise between the time the security interest attaches and the time of filing.

(3)   A "lien creditor" means a creditor who has acquired a lien on the property involved by attachment, levy or the like and includes an assignee for benefit of creditors from the time of assignment, and a trustee in bankruptcy from the date of the filing of the petition or a receiver in equity from the time of appointment.

(4)   A person who becomes a lien creditor while a security interest is perfected takes subject to the security

interest only to the extent that it secures advances made before he becomes a lien creditor or within 45 days thereafter or made without knowledge of the lien or pursuant to a commitment entered into without knowledge of the lien.

Section 9–302. When Filing Is Required to Perfect Security Interest; Security Interests to Which Filing Provisions of This Article Do Not Apply

(1) A financing statement must be filed to perfect all security interests except the following:

(a) a security interest in collateral in possession of the secured party under Section 9–305;

(b) a security interest temporarily perfected in instruments or documents without delivery under Section 9–304 or in proceeds for a 10 day period under Section 9–306;

(c) a security interest created by an assignment of a beneficial interest in a trust or a decedent's estate;

(d) a purchase money security interest in consumer goods; but filing is required for a motor vehicle required to be registered; and fixture filing is required for priority over conflicting interests in fixtures to the extent provided in Section 9–313;

(e) an assignment of accounts which does not alone or in conjunction with other assignments to the same assignee transfer a significant part of the outstanding accounts of the assignor;

(f) a security interest of a collecting bank (Section 4–208) or in securities (Section 8–321) or arising under the Article on Sales (see Section 9–113) or covered in subsection (3) of this section;

(g) an assignment for the benefit of all the creditors of the transferor, and subsequent transfers by the assignee thereunder.

(2) If a secured party assigns a perfected security interest, no filing under this Article is required to order to continue the perfected status of the security interest against creditors of and transferees from the original debtor.

(3) The filing of a financing statement otherwise required by this Article is not necessary or effective to perfect a security interest in property subject to

(a) a statute or treaty of the United States which provides for a national or international registration or a national or international certificate or title or which specifies a place of filing different from that specified in this Article for filing of the security interest; or

(b) the following statutes of this state; [list any certificate of title statute covering automobiles, trailers, mobile homes, boats, farm tractors, or the like, and any central filing statute*.]; but during any period in which collateral is inventory held for sale by a person who is in the business of selling goods of that kind, the filing provisions of this Article (Part 4) apply to a security interest in that collateral created by him as debtor; or

Note: *It is recommended that the provisions of certificate of title acts for perfection of security interests by notation on the certificates should be amended to exclude coverage of inventory held for sale.*

(c) a certificate of title statute of another jurisdiction under the law of which indication of a security interest on the certificate is required as a condition of perfection (subsection (2) of Section 9–103).

(4) Compliance with a statute or treaty described in subsection (3) is equivalent to the filing of a financing statement under this Article, and a security interest in property subject to the statute or treaty can be perfected only by compliance therewith except as provided in Section 9–103 on multiple state transactions. Duration and renewal or perfection of a security interest perfected by compliance with the statute or treaty are governed by the provisions of the statute or treaty; in other respects the security interest is subject to this Article.

Section 9–303. When Security Interest Is Perfected; Continuity of Perfection

(1) A security interest is perfected when it has attached and when all of the applicable steps required for perfection have been taken. Such steps are specified in Sections 9–302, 9–304, 9–305 and 9–306. If such steps are taken before the security interest attaches, it is perfected at the time when it attaches.

(2) If a security interest is originally perfected in any way permitted under this Article and is subsequently perfected in some other way under this Article, without an intermediate period when it is unperfected, the security interest shall be deemed to be perfected continuously for the purposes of this Article.

Section 9–304. Perfection of Security Interest in Instruments, Documents, and Goods Covered by Documents; Perfection by Permissive Filing; Temporary Perfection Without Filing or Transfer of Possession

(1) A security interest in chattel paper or negotiable documents may be perfected by filing. A security interest in money or instruments (other than certificated securities or instruments which constitute part of chattel papers can be perfected only by the secured party's taking possession, except as provided in subsections (4) and (5) of this section and subsections (2) and (3) of Section 9–306 on proceeds.

(2) During the period that goods are in the possession of the issuer of a negotiable document therefor, a security interest in the goods is perfected by perfecting a security interest in the document, and any security interest in the goods otherwise perfected during such period is subject thereto.

(3) A security interest in goods in the possession of a bailee other than one who has issued a negotiable document therefor is perfected by issuance of a document in the name of the secured party or by the bailee's receipt of notification of the secured party's interest or by filing as to the goods.

(4) A security interest in instruments (other than certificated securities) or negotiable documents is perfected without filing or the taking of possession for a period of 21 days from the time it attaches to the extent that it arises for new value given under a written security agreement.

(5) A security interest remains perfected for a period of 21 days without filing where a secured party having a perfected security interest in an instrument (other than a certificated security), a negotiable document or goods in possession of a bailee other than one who has issued a negotiable document therefor

　　(a) makes available to the debtor the goods or documents representing the goods for the purpose of ultimate sale or exchange or for the purpose of loading, unloading, storing, shipping, transshipping, manufacturing, processing or otherwise dealing with them in a manner preliminary to their sale or exchange, but priority between conflicting security interests in the goods is subject to subsection (3) of Section 9–312; or

　　(b) delivers the instrument to the debtor for the purpose of ultimate sale or exchange or of presentation, renewal, or registration of transfer.

(6) After the 21 day period in subsections (4) and (5) perfection depends upon compliance with applicable provisions of this Article. Amended in 1972 and 1977.

Section 9–305. When Possession by Secured Party Perfects Security Interest Without Filing

A security interest in letters of credit and advices of credit (subsection (2)(a) of Section 5–116), goods, instruments (other than certificated securities), money, negotiable documents or chattel paper may be perfected by the secured party's taking possession of the collateral. If such collateral other than goods covered by a negotiable document is held by a bailee, the secured party is deemed to have possession from the time the bailee receives notification of the secured party's interest. A security interest is perfected by possession from the time possession is taken without relation back and continues only so long as possession is retained, unless otherwise specified in this Article. The security interest may be otherwise perfected as provided in this Article before or after the period of possession by the secured party. Amended in 1972 and 1977.

Section 9–306. "Proceeds"; Secured Party's Rights on Disposition of Collateral

(1) "Proceeds" includes whatever is received upon the sale, exchange, collection or other disposition of collateral or proceeds. Insurance payable by reason of loss or damage to the collateral is proceeds, except to the extent that it is payable to a person other than a party to the security agreement. Money, checks, deposit accounts, and the like are "cash proceeds". All other proceeds are "non-cash proceeds".

(2) Except where this Article otherwise provides, a security interest continues in collateral notwithstanding sale, exchange or other disposition thereof unless the disposition was authorized by the secured party in the security agreement or otherwise, and also continues in any identifiable proceeds including collections received by the debtor.

(3) The security interest in proceeds is a continuously perfected security interest if the interest in the original collateral was perfected but it ceases to be a perfected security interest and becomes unperfected ten days after receipt of the proceeds by the debtor unless

(a) a filed financing statement covers the original collateral and the proceeds are collateral in which a security interest may be perfected by filing in the office or offices where the financing statement has been filed and, if the proceeds are acquired with cash proceeds, the description of collateral in the financing statement indicates the types of property constituting the proceeds; or

(b) a filed financing statement covers the original collateral and the proceeds are identifiable cash proceeds; or

(c) the security interest in the proceeds is perfected before the expiration of the ten day period.

Except as provided in this section, a security interest in proceeds can be perfected only by the methods or under the circumstances permitted in this Article for original collateral of the same type.

(4) In the event of insolvency proceedings instituted by or against a debtor, a secured party with a perfected security interest in proceeds has a perfected security interest only in the following proceeds:

(a) in identifiable non-cash proceeds and in separate deposit accounts containing only proceeds;

(b) in identifiable cash proceeds in the form of money which is neither commingled with other money nor deposited in a deposit account prior to the insolvency proceedings;

(c) in identifiable cash proceeds in the form of checks and the like which are not deposited in a deposit account prior to the insolvency proceedings; and

(d) in all cash and deposit accounts of the debtor in which proceeds have been commingled with other funds, but the perfected security interest under this paragraph (d) is

(i) subject to any right to set-off; and

(ii) limited to an amount not greater than the amount of any cash proceeds received by the debtor within ten days before the institution of the insolvency proceedings less the sum of (I) the payments to the secured party on account of cash proceeds received by the debtor during such period and (II) the cash proceeds received by the debtor during such period to which the secured party is entitled under paragraphs (a) through (c) of this subsection (4).

(5) If a sale of goods results in an account or chattel paper which is transferred by the seller to a secured party, and if the goods are returned to or are repossessed by the seller or the secured party, the following rules determine priorities:

(a) If the goods were collateral at the time of sale, for an indebtedness of the seller which is still unpaid, the original security interest attaches again to the goods and continues as a perfected security interest if it was perfected at the time when the goods were sold. If the security interest was originally perfected by a filing which is still effective, nothing further is required to continue the perfected status; in any other case, the secured party must take possession of the returned or repossessed goods or must file.

(b) An unpaid transferee of the chattel paper has a security interest in the goods against the transferor. Such security interest is prior to a security interest inserted under paragraph (a) to the extent that the transferee of the chattel paper was entitled to priority under Section 9–308.

(c) An unpaid transferee of the account has a security interest in the goods against the transferor. Such security interest is subordinate to a security interest asserted under paragraph (a).

(d) A security interest of an unpaid transferee asserted under paragraph (b) or (c) must be perfected for protection against creditors of the transferor and purchasers of the returned or repossessed goods.

Section 9–307. Protection of Buyers of Goods

(1) A buyer in ordinary course of business (subsection (9) of Section 1–201) other than a person buying farm products from a person engaged in farming operations takes free of a security interest created by his seller even though the security interest is perfected and even though the buyer knows of its existence.

(2) In the case of consumer goods, a buyer takes free of a security interest even though perfected if he buys without knowledge of the security interest, for value and for his own personal, family or household purposes unless prior to the purchase the secured party has filed a financing statement covering goods.

(3) A buyer other than a buyer in ordinary course of business (subsection (1) of this section) takes free of a security interest to the extent that it secures future advances made after the secured party acquires knowl-

edge of the purchase, or more than 45 days after the purchase, whichever first occurs, unless made pursuant to a commitment entered into without knowledge of the purchase and before the expiration of the 45 day period.

Section 9–308.   Purchase of Chattel Paper and Instruments

A purchaser of chattel paper or an instrument who gives new value and takes possession of it in the ordinary course of his business has priority over a security interest in the chattel paper or instrument

> (a)   which is perfected under Section 9–304 (permissive filing and temporary perfection) or under Section 9–306 (perfection as to proceeds) if he acts without knowledge that the specific paper or instrument is subject to a security interest; or
>
> (b)   which is claimed merely as proceeds of inventory subject to a security interest (Section 9–306) even though he knows that the specific paper or instrument is subject to the security interest.

Section 9–309.   Protection of Purchasers of Instruments, Documents and Securities

Nothing in this Article limits the rights of a holder in due course of a negotiable instrument (Section 3–302) or a holder to whom a negotiable document of title has been duly negotiated (Section 7–501) or a bona fide purchaser of a security (Section 8–302) and such holders or purchasers take priority over an earlier security interest even though perfected. Filing under this Article does not constitute notice of the security interest to such holders or purchasers. Amended in 1977.

Section 9–310.   Priority of Certain Liens Arising by Operation of Law

When a person in the ordinary course of his business furnishes services or materials with respect to goods subject to a security interest, a lien upon goods in the possession of such person given by statute or rule of law for such materials or services takes priority over a perfected security interest unless the lien is statutory and the statute expressly provides otherwise.

Section 9–311.   Alienability of Debtor's Rights: Judicial Process

The debtor's rights in collateral may be voluntarily or involuntarily transferred (by way of sale, creation of a security interest, attachment, levy, garnishment or other judicial process) notwithstanding a provision in the security agreement prohibiting any transfer or making the transfer constitute a default.

Section 9–312.   Priorities Among Conflicting Security Interests in the Same Collateral

(1)   The rules of priority stated in other sections of this Part and in the following sections shall govern when applicable: Section 4–208 with respect to the security interests of collecting banks in items being collected, accompanying documents and proceeds; Section 9–103 on security interests related to other jurisdictions; Section 9–114 on consignments.

(2)   A perfected security interest in crops for new value given to enable the debtor to produce the crops during the production season and given not more than three months before the crops become growing crops by planting or otherwise takes priority over an earlier perfected security interest to the extent that such earlier interest secures obligations due more than six months before the crops become growing crops by planting or otherwise, even though the person giving new value had knowledge of the earlier security interest.

(3)   A perfected purchase money security interest in inventory has priority over a conflicting security interest in the same inventory and also has priority in identifiable cash proceeds received on or before the delivery of the inventory to a buyer if

> (a)   the purchase money security interest is perfected at the time the debtor receives possession of the inventory; and
>
> (b)   the purchase money secured party gives notification in writing to the holder of the conflicting security interest if the holder had filed a financing statement covering the same types of inventory (i) before the date of the filing made by the purchase money secured party, or (ii) before the beginning of the 21 day period where the purchase money security interest is temporarily perfected without filing or possession (subsection (5) of Section 9–304); and
>
> (c)   the holder of the conflicting security interest receives the notification within five years before the debtor receives possession of the inventory; and
>
> (d)   the notification states that the person giving the notice has or expects to acquire a purchase money security interest in inventory of the debtor, describing such inventory by item or type.

(4) A purchase money security interest in collateral other than inventory has priority over a conflicting security interest in the same collateral or its proceeds if the purchase money security interest is perfected at the time the debtor receives possession of the collateral or within ten days thereafter.

(5) In all cases not governed by other rules stated in this section (including cases of purchase money security interests which do not qualify for the special priorities set forth in subsections (3) and (4) of this section), priority between conflicting security interests in the same collateral shall be determined according to the following rules:

(a) Conflicting security interests rank according to priority in time of filing or perfection. Priority dates from the time a filing is first made covering the collateral or the time the security interest is first perfected, whichever is earlier, provided that there is no period thereafter when there is neither filing nor perfection.

(b) So long as conflicting security interests are unperfected, the first to attach has priority.

(6) For purposes of subsection (5) a date of filing or perfection as to collateral is also a date of filing or perfection as to proceeds.

(7) If future advances are made while a security interest is perfected by filing, the taking of possession, or under Section 8–321 on securities, the security interest has the same priority for the purposes of subsection (5) with respect to the future advances as it does with respect to the first advance. If a commitment is made before or while the secured interest is so perfected, the security interest has the same priority with respect to advances made pursuant thereto. In other cases a perfected security interest has priority from the date the advance is made. Amended in 1972 and 1977.

Section 9–313. Priority of Security Interests in Fixtures

(1) In this section and in the provisions of Part 4 of this Article referring to fixture filing, unless the context otherwise requires

(a) goods are "fixtures" when they become so related to particular real estate that an interest in them arises under real estate law;

(b) a "fixture filing" is the filing in the office where a mortgage on the real estate would be filed or recorded of a financing statement covering goods which are or are to become fixtures and conforming to the requirements of subsection (5) of Section 9–102;

(c) a mortgage is a "construction mortgage" to the extent that it secures an obligation incurred for the construction of an improvement on land including the acquisition cost of the land, if the recorded writing so indicates.

(2) A security interest under this Article may be created in goods which are fixtures or may continue in goods which become fixtures, but no security interest exists under this Article in ordinary building materials incorporated into an improvement on land.

(3) This Article does not prevent creation of an encumbrance upon fixtures pursuant to real estate law.

(4) A perfected security interest in fixtures has priority over the conflicting interest of an encumbrancer or owner of the real estate where

(a) the security interest is a purchase money security interest, the interest of the encumbrancer or owner arises before the goods become fixtures, the security interest is perfected by a fixture filing before the goods become fixtures or within ten days thereafter, and the debtor has an interest of record in the real estate or is in possession of the real estate; or

(b) the security interest is perfected by a fixture filing before the interest of the encumbrancer or owner is of record, the security interest has priority over any conflicting interest of a predecessor in title of the encumbrancer or owner, and the debtor has an interest of record in the real estate or is in possession of the real estate; or

(c) the fixtures are readily removable factory or office machines or readily removable replacements of domestic appliances which are consumer goods, and before the goods become fixtures the security interest is perfected by any method permitted by this Article; or

(d) the conflicting interest is a lien on the real estate obtained by legal or equitable proceedings after the security interest was perfected by any method permitted by this Article.

(5) A security interest in fixtures, whether or not perfected, has priority over the conflicting interest of an encumbrancer or owner of the real estate where

(a) the encumbrancer or owner has consented in writing to the security interest or has disclaimed an interest in the goods as fixtures; or

(b) the debtor has a right to remove the goods as against the encumbrancer or owner. If the debtor's right terminates, the priority of the security interest continues for a reasonable time.

(6) Notwithstanding paragraph (a) of subsection (4) but otherwise subject to subsections (4) and (5), a security interest in fixtures is subordinate to a construction mortgage recorded before the goods become fixtures if the goods become fixtures before the completion of the construction. To the extent that it is given to refinance a construction mortgage, a mortgage has this priority to the same extent as the construction mortgage.

(7) In cases not within the preceding subsections, a security interest in fixtures is subordinate to the conflicting interest of an encumbrancer or owner of the related real estate who is not the debtor.

(8) When the secured party has priority over all owners and encumbrancers of the real estate, he may, on default, subject to the provisions of Part 5, remove his collateral from the real estate but he must reimburse any encumbrancer or owner of the real estate who is not the debtor and who has not otherwise agreed for the cost of repair of any physical injury, but not for any diminution in value of the real estate caused by the absence of the goods removed or by any necessity of replacing them. A person entitled to reimbursement may refuse permission to remove until the secured party gives adequate security for the performance of this obligation.

Section 9–314.   Accessions

(1) A security interest in goods which attaches before they are installed in or affixed to other goods takes priority as to the goods installed or affixed (called in this section "accessions") over the claims of all persons to the whole except as stated in subsection (3) and subject to Section 9–315(1).

(2) A security interest which attaches to goods after they become part of a whole is valid against all persons subsequently acquiring interests in the whole except as stated in subsection (3) but is invalid against any person with an interest in the whole at the time the security interest attaches to the goods who has not in writing consented to the security interest or disclaimed an interest in the goods as part of the whole.

(3) The security interests described in subsections (1) and (2) do not take priority over

(a) a subsequent purchaser for value of any interest in the whole; or

(b) a creditor with a lien on the whole subsequently obtained by judicial proceedings; or

(c) a creditor with a prior perfected security interest in the whole to the extent that he makes subsequent advances

if the subsequent purchase is made, the lien by judicial proceedings obtained or the subsequent advance under the prior perfected security interest is made or contracted for without knowledge of the security interest and before it is perfected. A purchaser of the whole at a foreclosure sale other than the holder of a perfected security interest purchasing at his own foreclosure sale is a subsequent purchaser within this section.

(4) When under subsections (1) or (2) and (3) a secured party has an interest in accessions which has priority over the claims of all persons who have interests in the whole, he may on default subject to the provisions of Part 5 remove his collateral from the whole but he must reimburse any encumbrancer or owner of the whole who is not the debtor and who has not otherwise agreed for the cost of repair of any physical injury but not for any diminution in value of the whole caused by the absence of the goods removed or by any necessity for replacing them. A person entitled to reimbursement may refuse permission to remove until the secured party gives adequate security for the performance of this obligation.

Section 9–315.   Priority When Goods Are Commingled or Processed

(1) If a security interest in goods was perfected and subsequently the goods or a part thereof have become part of a product or mass, the security interest continues in the product or mass if

(a) the goods are so manufactured, processed, assembled or commingled that their identity is lost in the product or mass; or

(b) a financing statement covering the original goods also covers the product into which the goods have been manufactured, processed or assembled.

In a case to which paragraph (b) applies, no separate security interest in that part of the original goods which has been manufactured, processed or assembled into the product may be claimed under Section 9–314.

(2) When under subsection (1) more than one security interest attaches to the product or mass, they rank equally according to the ratio that the cost of the goods to which each interest originally attached bears to the cost of the total product or mass.

Section 9–316. Priority Subject to Subordination

Nothing in this Article prevents subordination by agreement by any person entitled to priority.

Section 9–317. Secured Party Not Obligated on Contract of Debtor

The mere existence of a security interest or authority given to the debtor to dispose of or use collateral does not impose contract or tort liability upon the secured party for the debtor's acts or omissions.

Section 9–318. Defenses Against Assignee; Modification of Contract After Notification of Assignment; Term Prohibiting Assignment Ineffective; Identification and Proof of Assignment

(1) Unless an account debtor has made an enforceable agreement not to assert defenses or claims arising out of a sale as provided in Section 9–206 the rights of an assignee are subject to

(a) all the terms of the contract between the account debtor and assignor and any defense or claim arising therefrom; and

(b) any other defense or claim of the account debtor against the assignor which accrues before the account debtor receives notification of the assignment.

(2) So far as the right to payment or a part thereof under an assigned contract has not been fully earned by performance, and notwithstanding notification of the assignment, any modification of or substitution for the contract made in good faith and in accordance with reasonable commercial standards is effective against an assignee unless the account debtor has otherwise agreed but the assignee acquires corresponding rights under the modified or substituted contract. The assignment may provide that such modification or substitution is a breach by the assignor.

(3) The account debtor is authorized to pay the assignor until the account debtor receives notification that the amount due or to become due has been assigned and that payment is to be made to the assignee. A notification which does not reasonably identify the rights assigned is ineffective. If requested by the account debtor, the assignee must seasonably furnish reasonable proof that the assignment has been made and unless he does so the account debtor may pay the assignor.

(4) A term in any contract between an account debtor and an assignor is ineffective if it prohibits assignment of an account or prohibits creation of a security interest in a general intangible for money due or to become due or requires the account debtor's consent to such assignment or security interest.

PART 4

Filing

Section 9–401. Place of Filing; Erroneous Filing; Removal of Collateral

First Alternative Subsection (1)

(1) The proper place to file in order to perfect a security interest is as follows:

(a) when the collateral is timber to be cut or is minerals of the like (including oil and gas) or accounts subject to subsection (5) of Section 9–103, or when the financing statement is filed as a fixture filing (Section 9–313) and the collateral is goods which are or are to become fixtures, then in the office where a mortgage on the real estate would be filed or recorded;

(b) in all other cases, in the office of the [Secretary of State].

Second Alternative Subsection (1)

(1) The proper place to file in order to perfect a security interest is as follows:

(a) when the collateral is equipment used in farming operations, or farm products, or accounts or general intangibles arising from or relating to the sale of farm products by a farmer, or consumer goods, then in the office of the . . . . in the county of the debtor's residence or if the debtor is not a resident of this state then in the office of the . . . . in the county where the goods are kept, and in addition when the collateral is crops growing or to be grown in the office of the . . . . in the county where the land is located;

(b) when the collateral is timber to be cut or is minerals or the like (including oil and gas) or accounts subject to subsection (5) of Section 9–103, or when the financing statement is filed as a fixture filing (Section 9–313) and the collateral is goods which are or are to become fixtures, then in the office where a mortgage on the real estate would be filed or recorded;

(c)   in all other cases, in the office of the [Secretary of State].

Third Alternative Subsection (1)

(1) The proper place to file in order to perfect a security interest is as follows:

(a) when the collateral is equipment used in farming operations, or farm products, or accounts or general intangibles arising from or relating to the sale of farm products by a farmer, or consumer goods, then in the office of the . . . . in the county of the debtor's residence or if the debtor is not a resident of this state then in the office of the . . . . in the county where the goods are kept, and in addition when the collateral is crops growing or to be grown in the office of the . . . . in the county where the land is located;

(b) when the collateral is timber to be cut or is minerals or the like (including oil and gas) or accounts subject to subsection (5) of Section 9–103, or when the financing statement is filed as a fixture filing (Section 9–313) and the collateral is goods which are or are to become fixtures, then in the office where a mortgage on the real estate would be filed or recorded;

(c)   in all other cases, in the office of the [Secretary of State] and in addition, if the debtor has a place of business in only one county of this state, also in the office of . . . . of such county, or, if the debtor has no place of business in this state, but resides in the state, also in the office of . . . . of the county in which he resides.

Note: *One of the three alternatives should be selected as subsection (1).*

(2) A filing which is made in good faith in an improper place or not in all of the places required by this section is nevertheless effective with regard to any collateral as to which the filing complied with the requirements of this Article and is also effective with regard to collateral covered by the financing statement against any person who has knowledge of the contents of such financing statement.

(3) A filing which is made in the proper place in this state continues effective even though the debtor's residence or place of business or the location of the collateral or its use, whichever controlled the original filing, is thereafter changed.

Alternative Subsection (3)

[(3) A filing which is made in the proper county continues effective for four months after a change to another county of the debtor's residence or place of business or the location of the collateral, whichever controlled the original filing. It becomes ineffective thereafter unless a copy of the financing statement signed by the secured party is filed in the new county within said period. The security interest may also be perfected in the new county after the expiration of the four-month period; in such case perfection dates from the time of perfection in the new county. A change in the use of the collateral does not impair the effectiveness of the original filing.]

(4) The rules in Section 9–103 determine whether filing is necessary in this state.

(5) Notwithstanding the preceding subsections, and subject to subsection (3) of Section 9–302, the proper place to file in order to perfect a security interest in collateral, including fixtures, of a transmitting utility is the office of the [Secretary of State]. This filing constitutes a fixture filing (Section 9–313) as to the collateral described therein which is or is to become fixtures.

(6) For the purposes of this section, the residence of an organization is its place of business if it has one or its chief executive office if it has more than one place of business.

Note: *Subsection (6) should be used only if the state chooses the Second or Third Alternative Subsection (1).*

Section 9–402.   Formal Requisites of Financing Statement; Amendments; Mortgage as Financing Statement

(1) A financing statement is sufficient if it gives the name of the debtor and the secured party, is signed by the debtor, gives an address of the secured party from which information concerning the security interest may be obtained, gives a mailing address of the debtor and contains a statement indicating the types, or describing the items, of collateral. A financing statement may be filed before a security agreement is made or a security interest otherwise attaches. When the financing statement covers crops growing or to be grown, the statement must also contain a description of the real estate concerned. When the financing statement covers timber to be cut or covers minerals or the like (including oil and gas) or accounts subject to subsection (5) of Section 9–103, or when the financing statement is filed as a fixture filing (Section 9–313) and the collateral is goods which are or are to become fixtures, the statement must also comply with subsection (5). A copy of the security agreement is sufficient as a financing statement if it contains the above information and is signed by the debtor. A carbon, photographic

or other reproduction of a security agreement or a financing statement is sufficient as a financing statement if the security agreement so provides or if the original has been filed in this state.

(2) A financing statement which otherwise complies with subsection (1) is sufficient when it is signed by the secured party instead of the debtor if it is filed to perfect a security interest in

(a) collateral already subject to a security interest in another jurisdiction when it is brought into this state, or when the debtor's location is changed to this state. Such a financing statement must state that the collateral was brought into this state or that the debtor's location was changed to this state under such circumstances; or

(b) proceeds under Section 9–306 if the security interest in the original collateral was perfected. Such a financing statement must describe the original collateral; or

(c) collateral as to which the filing has lapsed; or

(d) collateral acquired after a change of name, identity or corporate structure of the debtor (subsection (7)).

(3) A form substantially as follows is sufficient to comply with subsection (1):

Name of debtor (or assignor) ....
Address ....
Name of secured party (or assignee) ....
Address ....

1. This financing statement covers the following types (or items) of property:

(Describe)........................

2. (If collateral is crops) The above crops are growing or are to be grown on:

(Describe Real Estate) ....

3. (If applicable) The above goods are to become fixtures on (Where appropriate substitute either "The above timber is standing on . . ." or "The above minerals or the like (including oil and gas) or accounts will be financed at the wellhead or minehead of the well or mine located on . . .")

(Describe Real Estate) ....

and this financing statement is to be filed [for record] in the real estate records. (If the debtor does not have an interest of record) The name of a record owner is...................

4. (If products of collateral are claimed) Products of the collateral are also covered.

(use whichever is applicable)

....
Signature of Debtor (or Assignor)

....
Signature of Secured Party (or Assignee)

(4) A financing statement may be amended by filing a writing signed by both the debtor and the secured party. An amendment does not extend the period of effectiveness of a financing statement. If any amendment adds collateral, it is effective as to the added collateral only from the filing date of the amendment. In this Article, unless the context otherwise requires, the term "financing statement" means the original financing statement and any amendments.

(5) A financing statement covering timber to be cut or covering minerals or the like (including oil and gas) or accounts subject to subsection (5) of Section 9–103, or a financing statement filed as a fixture filing (Section 9–313) where the debtor is not a transmitting utility, must show that it covers this type of collateral, must recite that it is to be filed [for record] in the real estate records, and the financing statement must contain a description of the real estate [sufficient if it were contained in a mortgage of the real estate to give constructive notice of the mortgage under the law of this state]. If the debtor does not have an interest of record in the real estate, the financing statement must show the name of a record owner.

(6) A mortgage is effective as a financing statement filed as a fixture filing from the date of its recording if

(a) the goods are described in the mortgage by item or type; and

(b) the goods are or are to become fixtures related to the real estate described in the mortgage; and

(c) the mortgage complies with the requirements for a financing statement in this section other than a recital that it is to be filed in the real estate records; and

(d) the mortgage is duly recorded.

No fee with reference to the financing statement is required other than the regular recording and satisfaction fees with respect to the mortgage.

(7) A financing statement sufficiently shows the name of the debtor if it gives the individual, partnership or corporate name of the debtor, whether or not it adds other trade names or names of partners. Where the debtor so changes his name or in the case of an or-

ganization its name, identity or corporate structure that a filed financing statement becomes seriously misleading, the filing is not effective to perfect a security interest in collateral acquired by the debtor more than four months after the change, unless a new appropriate financing statement is filed before the expiration of that time. A filed financing statement remains effective with respect to collateral transferred by the debtor even though the secured party knows of or consents to the transfer.

(8) A financing statement substantially complying with the requirements of this section is effective even though it contains minor errors which are not seriously misleading.

Section 9–403. What Constitutes Filing; Duration of Filing; Effect of Lapsed Filing; Duties of Filing Officer

(1) Presentation for filing of a financing statement and tender of the filing fee or acceptance of the statement by the filing officer constitutes filing under this Article.

(2) Except as provided in subsection (6) a filed financing statement is effective for a period of five years from the date of filing. The effectiveness of a filed financing statement lapses on the expiration of the five year period unless a continuation statement is filed prior to the lapse. If a security interest perfected by filing exists at the time insolvency proceedings are commenced by or against the debtor, the security interest remains perfected until termination of the insolvency proceedings and thereafter for a period of sixty days or until expiration of the five year period, whichever occurs later. Upon lapse the security interest becomes unperfected, unless it is perfected without filing. If the security interest becomes unperfected upon lapse, it is deemed to have been unperfected as against a person who became a purchaser or lien creditor before lapse.

(3) A continuation statement may be filed by the secured party within six months prior to the expiration of the five year period specified in subsection (2). Any such continuation statement must be signed by the secured party, identify the original statement by file number and state that the original statement is still effective. A continuation statement signed by a person other than the secured party of record must be accompanied by a separate written statement of assignment signed by the secured party of record and complying with subsection (2) of Section 9–405, including payment of the required fee. Upon timely filing of the continuation statement, the effectiveness of the original

statement is continued for five years after the last date to which the filing was effective whereupon it lapses in the same manner as provided in subsection (2) unless another continuation statement is filed prior to such lapse. Succeeding continuation statements may be filed in the same manner to continue the effectiveness of the original statement. Unless a statute on disposition of public records provides otherwise, the filing officer may remove a lapsed statement from the files and destroy it immediately if he has retained a microfilm or other photographic record, or in other cases after one year after the lapse. The filing officer shall so arrange matters by physical annexation of financing statements to continuation statements or other related filings, or by other means, that if he physically destroys the financing statements of a period more than five years past, those which have been continued by a continuation statement or which are still effective under subsection (6) shall be retained.

(4) Except as provided in subsection (7) a filing officer shall mark each statement with a file number and with the date and hour of filing and shall hold the statement or a microfilm or other photographic copy thereof for public inspection. In addition the filing officer shall index the statement according to the name of the debtor and shall note in the index the file number and the address of the debtor given in the statement.

(5) The uniform fee for filing and indexing and for stamping a copy furnished by the secured party to show the date and place of filing for an original financing statement or for a continuation statement shall be $ . . . . if the statement is in the standard form prescribed by the [Secretary of State] and otherwise shall be $ . . . . , plus in each case, if the financing statement is subject to subsection (5) of Section 9–402, $ . . . . The uniform fee for each name more than one required to be indexed shall be $ . . . . The secured party may at his option show a trade name for any person and an extra uniform indexing fee of $ . . . . shall be paid with respect thereto.

(6) If the debtor is a transmitting utility (subsection (5) of Section 9–401) and a filed financing statement so states, it is effective until a termination statement is filed. A real estate mortgage which is effective as a fixture filing under subsection (6) of Section 9–402 remains effective as a fixture filing until the mortgage is released or satisfied of record or its effectiveness otherwise terminates as to the real estate.

(7) When a financing statement covers timber to be cut or covers minerals or the like (including oil and gas) or accounts subject to subsection (5) of Section

9–103, or is filed as a fixture filing, [it shall be filed for record and] the filing officer shall index it under the names of the debtor and any owner of record shown on the financing statement in the same fashion as if they were the mortgagors in a mortgage of the real estate described, and, to the extent that the law of this state provides for indexing of mortgages under the name of the mortgagee, under the name of the secured party as if he were the mortgagee thereunder, or where indexing is by description in the same fashion as if the financing statement were a mortgage of the real estate described.

Note: *In states in which writings will not appear in the real estate records and indices unless actually recorded, the bracketed language in subsection (7) should be used.*

Section 9–404. Termination Statement

(1) If a financing statement covering consumer goods is filed on or after . . . . , then within one month or within ten days following written demand by the debtor after there is no outstanding secured obligation and no commitment to make advances, incur obligations or otherwise give value, the secured party must file with each filing officer with whom the financing statement was filed, a termination statement to the effect that he no longer claims a security interest under the financing statement, which shall be identified by file number. In other cases whenever there is no outstanding secured obligation and no commitment to make advances, incur obligations or otherwise give value, the secured party must on written demand by the debtor send the debtor, for each filing officer with whom the financing statement was filed, a termination statement to the effect that he no longer claims a security interest under the financing statement, which shall be identified by file number. A termination statement signed by a person other than the secured party of record must be accompanied by a separate written statement of assignment signed by the secured party of record and complying with subsection (2) of Section 9–405, including payment of the required fee. If the affected secured party fails to file such a termination statement as required by this subsection, or to send such a termination statement within ten days after proper demand therefor, he shall be liable to the debtor for one hundred dollars, and in addition for any loss caused to the debtor by such failure.

(2) On presentation to the filing officer of such a termination statement he must note it in the index. If he has received the termination statement in duplicate, he shall return one copy of the termination statement to the secured party stamped to show the time of receipt thereof. If the filing officer has a microfilm or other photographic record of the financing statement, and of any related continuation statement, statement of assignment and statement of release, he may remove the originals from the files at any time after receipt of the termination statement, or if he has no such record, he may remove them from the files at any time after one year after receipt of the termination statement.

(3) If the termination statement is in the standard form prescribed by the [Secretary of State], the uniform fee for filing and indexing the termination statement shall be $ . . . . and otherwise shall be $ . . . . , plus in each case an additional fee of $ . . . . for each name more than one against which the termination statement is required to be indexed.

Note: *The date to be inserted should be the effective date of the revised Article 9.*

Section 9–405. Assignment of Security Interest; Duties of Filing Officer; Fees

(1) A financing statement may disclose an assignment of a security interest in the collateral described in the financing statement by indication in the financing statement of the name and address of the assignee or by an assignment itself of a copy thereof on the face or back of the statement. On presentation to the filing officer of such a financing statement the filing officer shall mark the same as provided in Section 9–403(4). The uniform fee for filing, indexing and furnishing filing data for a financing statement so indicating an assignment shall be $ . . . . if the statement is in the standard form prescribed by the [Secretary of State] and otherwise shall be $ . . . . , plus in each case an additional fee of $ . . . . for each name more than one against which the financing statement is required to be indexed.

(2) A secured party may assign of record all or part of his rights under a financing statement by the filing in the place where the original financing statement was filed of a separate written statement of assignment signed by the secured party of record and setting forth the name of the secured party of record and the debtor, the file number and the date of filing of the financing statement and the name and address of the assignee and containing a description of the collateral assigned. A copy of the assignment is sufficient as a separate statement if it complies with the preceding sentence. On presentation to the filing officer of such a separate statement, the filing officer shall mark such separate statement with the date and hour of the filing. He

shall note the assignment on the index of the financing statement, or in the case of a fixture filing, or a filing covering timber to be cut, or covering minerals or the like (including oil and gas) or accounts subject to subsection (5) of Section 9–103, he shall index the assignment under the name of the assignor as grantor and, to the extent that the law of this state provides for indexing the assignment of a mortgage under the name of the assignee, he shall index the assignment of the financing statement under the name of the assignee. The uniform fee for filing, indexing and furnishing filing data about such a separate statement of assignment shall be $ . . . . if the statement is in the standard form prescribed by the [Secretary of State] and otherwise shall be $ . . . . , plus in each case an additional fee of $ . . . . for each name more than one against which the statement of assignment is required to be indexed. Notwithstanding the provisions of this subsection, an assignment of record of a security interest in a fixture contained in a mortgage effective as a fixture filing (subsection (6) of Section 9–402) may be made only by an assignment of the mortgage in the manner provided by the law of the state other than this Act.

(3) After the disclosure or filing of an assignment under this section, the assignee is the secured party of record.

Section 9–406.   Release of Collateral; Duties of Filing Officer; Fees

A secured party of record may by his signed statement release all or a part of any collateral described in a filed financing statement. The statement of release is sufficient if it contains a description of the collateral being released, the name and address of the debtor, the name and address of the secured party, and the file number of the financing statement. A statement of release signed by a person other than the secured party of record must be accompanied by a separate written statement of assignment signed by the secured party of record and complying with subsection (2) of Section 9–405, including payment of the required fee. Upon presentation of such a statement of release to the filing officer he shall mark the statement with the hour and date of filing and shall note the same upon the margin of the index of the filing of the financing statement. The uniform fee for filing and noting such a statement of release shall be $ . . . . if the statement is in the standard form prescribed by the [Secretary of State] and otherwise shall be $ . . . . , plus in each case an additional fee of $ . . . . for each name more than one against which the statement of release is required to be indexed.

[Section 9–407.   Information from Filing Officer]

[(1) If the person filing any financing statement, termination statement, statement of assignment, or statement of release, furnishes the filing officer a copy thereof, the filing officer shall upon request note upon the copy the file number and date and hour of the filing of the original and deliver or send the copy to such person.]

[(2) Upon request of any person, the filing officer shall issue his certificate showing whether there is on file on the date and hour stated therein, any presently effective financing statement naming a particular debtor and any statement of assignment thereof and if there is, giving the date and hour of filing of each such statement and the names and addresses of each secured party therein. The uniform fee for such a certificate shall be $ . . . . if the request for the certificate is in the standard form prescribed by the [Secretary of State] and otherwise shall be $ . . . . Upon request the filing officer shall furnish a copy of any filed financing statement or statement of assignment for a uniform fee of $ . . . . per page.]

Note: *This section is proposed as an optional provision to require filing officers to furnish certificates. Local law and practices should be consulted with regard to the advisability of adoption.*

Section 9–408.   Financing Statements Covering Consigned or Leased Goods

A consignor or lessor of goods may file a financing statement using the terms "consignor," "consignee," "lessor," "lessee" or the like instead of the terms specified in Section 9–402. The provisions of this Part shall apply as appropriate to such a financing statement but its filing shall not of itself be a factor in determining whether or not the consignment or lease is intended as security (Section 1–201(37)). However, if it is determined for other reasons that the consignment or lease is so intended, a security interest of the consignor or lessor which attaches to the consigned or leased goods is perfected by such filing. Added in 1972.

PART 5

Default

Section 9–501.   Default; Procedure When Security Agreement Covers Both Real and Personal Property

(1) When a debtor is in default under a security agreement, a secured party has the rights and remedies

provided in this Part and except as limited by subsection (3) those provided in the security agreement. He may reduce his claim to judgment, foreclose or otherwise enforce the security interest by any available judicial procedure. If the collateral is documents the secured party may proceed either as to the documents or as to the goods covered thereby. A secured party in possession has the rights, remedies and duties provided in Section 9–207. The rights and remedies referred to in this subsection are cumulative.

(2) After default, the debtor has the rights and remedies provided in this Part, those provided in the security agreement and those provided in Section 9–207.

(3) To the extent that they give rights to the debtor and impose duties on the secured party, the rules stated in the subsections referred to below may not be waived or varied except as provided with respect to compulsory disposition of collateral (subsection (3) of Section 9–504 and Section 9–505) and with respect to redemption of collateral (Section 9–506) but the parties may by agreement determine the standards by which the fulfillment of these rights and duties is to be measured if such standards are not manifestly unreasonable:

    (a) subsection (2) of Section 9–502 and subsection (2) of Section 9–504 insofar as they require accounting for surplus proceeds of collateral;

    (b) subsection (3) of Section 9–504 and subsection (1) of Section 9–505 which deal with disposition of collateral;

    (c) subsection (2) of Section 9–505 which deals with acceptance of collateral as discharge of obligation;

    (d) Section 9–506 which deals with redemption of collateral; and

    (e) subsection (1) of Section 9–507 which deals with the secured party's liability for failure to comply with this Part.

(4). If the security agreement covers both real and personal property, the secured party may proceed under this Part as to the personal property or he may proceed as to both the real and the personal property in accordance with his rights and remedies in respect of the real property in which case the provisions of this Part do not apply.

(5) When a secured party has reduced his claim to judgment the lien of any levy which may be made upon his collateral by virtue of any execution based upon the judgment shall relate back to the date of the perfection of the security interest in such collateral. A judicial sale, pursuant to such execution, is a foreclosure

of the security interest by judicial procedure within the meaning of this section, and the secured party may purchase at the sale and thereafter hold the collateral free of any other requirements of this Article.

Section 9–502. Collection Rights of Secured Party

(1) When so agreed and in any event on default the secured party is entitled to notify an account debtor or the obligor on an instrument to make payment to him whether or not the assignor was therefore making collections on the collateral, and also to take control of any proceeds to which he is entitled under Section 9–306.

(2) A secured party who by agreement is entitled to charge back uncollected collateral or otherwise to full or limited recourse against the debtor and who undertakes to collect from the account debtors or obligors must proceed in a commercially reasonable manner and may deduct his reasonable expenses of realization from the collections. If the security agreement secures an indebtedness, the secured party must account to the debtor for any surplus, and unless otherwise agreed, the debtor is liable for any deficiency. But, if the underlying transaction was a sale of accounts or chattel paper, the debtor is entitled to any surplus or is liable for any deficiency only if the security agreement so provides.

Section 9–503. Secured Party's Right to Take Possession After Default

Unless otherwise agreed a secured party has on default the right to take possession of the collateral. In taking possession a secured party may proceed without judicial process if this can be done without breach of the peace or may proceed by action. If the security agreement so provides the secured party may require the debtor to assemble the collateral and make it available to the secured party at a place to be designated by the secured party which is reasonably convenient to both parties. Without removal a secured party may render equipment unusable, and may dispose of collateral on the debtor's premises under Section 9–504.

Section 9–504. Secured Party's Right to Dispose of Collateral After Default; Effect of Disposition

(1) A secured party after default may sell, lease or otherwise dispose of any or all of the collateral in its then condition or following any commercially reasonable preparation or processing. Any sale of goods is subject to the Article on Sales (Article 2). The proceeds of disposition shall be applied in the order following to

(a)   the reasonable expenses of retaking, holding, preparing for sale or lease, selling, leasing and the like and, to the extent provided for in the agreement and not prohibited by law, the reasonable attorneys' fees and legal expenses incurred by the secured party;

(b)   the satisfaction indebtedness secured by the security interest under which the disposition is made;

(c)   the satisfaction of indebtedness secured by any subordinate security interest in the collateral if written notification of demand therefor is received before distribution of the proceeds is completed. If requested by the secured party, the holder of a subordinate security interest must seasonably furnish reasonable proof of his interest, and unless he does so, the secured party need not comply with his demand.

(2)   If the security interest secures an indebtedness, the secured party must account to the debtor for any surplus, and, unless otherwise agreed, the debtor is liable for any deficiency. But if the underlying transaction was a sale of accounts or chattel paper, the debtor is entitled to any surplus or is liable for any deficiency only if the security agreement so provides.

(3)   Disposition of the collateral may be by public or private proceedings and may be made by way of one or more contracts. Sale or other disposition may be as a unit or in parcels and at any time and place and on any terms but every aspect of the disposition including the method, manner, time, place and terms must be commercially reasonable. Unless collateral is perishable or threatens to decline speedily in value or is of a type customarily sold on a recognized market, reasonable notification of the time and place of any public sale or reasonable notification of the time after which any private sale or other intended disposition is to be made shall be sent by the secured party to the debtor, if he has not signed after default a statement renouncing or modifying his right to notification of sale. In the case of consumer goods no other notification need be sent. In other cases notification shall be sent to any other secured party from whom the secured party has received (before sending his notification to the debtor or before the debtor's renunciation of his rights) written notice of a claim of an interest in the collateral. The secured party may buy at any public sale and if the collateral is of a type customarily sold in a recognized market or is of a type which is the subject of widely distributed standard price quotations he may buy at private sale.

(4)   When collateral is disposed of by a secured party after default, the disposition transfers to a purchaser for value all of the debtor's rights therein, discharges the security interest under which it is made and any security interest or lien subordinate thereto. The purchaser takes free of all such rights and interests even though the secured party fails to comply with the requirements of this Part or of any judicial proceedings

(a)   in the case of a public sale, if the purchaser has no knowledge of any defects in the sale and if he does not buy in collusion with the secured party, other bidders or the person conducting the sale; or

(b)   in any other case, if the purchaser acts in good faith.

(5)   A person who is liable to a secured party under a guaranty, indorsement, repurchase agreement or the like and who receives a transfer of collateral from the secured party or is subrogated to his rights has thereafter the rights and duties of the secured party. Such a transfer of collateral is not a sale or disposition of the collateral under this Article.

Section 9–505.   Compulsory Disposition of Collateral; Acceptance of the Collateral as Discharge of Obligation

(1)   If the debtor has paid sixty per cent of the cash price in the case of a purchase money security interest in consumer goods or sixty per cent of the loan in the case of another security interest in consumer goods, and has not signed after default a statement renouncing or modifying his rights under this Part a secured party who has taken possession of collateral must dispose of it under Section 9–504 and if he fails to do so within ninety days after he takes possession the debtor at his option may recover in conversion or under Section 9–507(1) on secured party's liability.

(2)   In any other case involving consumer goods or any other collateral a secured party in possession may, after default, propose to retain the collateral in satisfaction of the obligation. Written notice of such proposal shall be sent to the debtor if he has not signed after default a statement renouncing or modifying his rights under this subsection. In the case of consumer goods no other notice need be given. In other cases notice shall be sent to any other secured party from whom the secured party has received (before sending his notice to the debtor or before the debtor's renunciation of his rights) written notice of a claim of an interest in the collateral. If the secured party receives

objection in writing from a person entitled to receive notification within twenty-one days after the notice was sent, the secured party must dispose of the collateral under Section 9–504. In the absence of such written objection the secured party may retain the collateral in satisfaction of the debtor's obligation.

Section 9–506. Debtor's Right to Redeem Collateral

At any time before the secured party has disposed of collateral or entered into a contract for its disposition under Section 9–504 or before the obligation has been discharged under Section 9–505(2) the debtor or any other secured party may unless otherwise agreed in writing after default redeem the collateral by tendering fulfillment of all obligations secured by the collateral as well as the expenses reasonably incurred by the secured party in retaking, holding and preparing the collateral for disposition, in arranging for the sale, and to the extent provided in the agreement and not prohibited by law, his reasonable attorneys' fees and legal expenses.

Section 9–507. Secured Party's Liability for Failure to Comply with This Part

(1) If it is established that the secured party is not proceeding in accordance with the provisions of this Part disposition may be ordered or restrained on appropriate terms and conditions. If the disposition has occurred the debtor or any person entitled to notification or whose security interest has been made known to the secured party prior to the disposition has a right to recover from the secured party any loss caused by a failure to comply with the provisions of this Part. If the collateral is consumer goods, the debtor has a right to recover in any event an amount not less than the credit service charge plus ten per cent of the principal amount of the debt or the time price differential plus ten per cent of the cash price.

(2) The fact that a better price could have been obtained by a sale at a different time or in a different method from that selected by the secured party is not of itself sufficient to establish that the sale was not made in a commercially reasonable manner. If the secured party either sells the collateral in the usual manner in any recognized market therefor or if he sells at the price current in such market at the time of his sale or if he has otherwise sold in conformity with reasonable commercial practices among dealers the type of property sold he has sold in a commercially reasonable manner. The principles stated in the two preceding sentences with respect to sales also apply as may be appropriate to other types of disposition. A disposition which has been approved in any judicial proceeding or by any bona fide creditors' committee or representative of creditors shall conclusively be deemed to be commercially reasonable, but this sentence does not indicate that any such approval must be obtained in any case nor does it indicate that any disposition not so approved is not commercially reasonable.

[Articles 10 and 11 are not included.]

APPENDIX B

The Constitution of the United States of America

We the people of the United States, in Order to form a more perfect Union, establish Justice, insure domestic Tranquility, provide for the common defense, promote the general Welfare, and secure the Blessings of Liberty to ourselves and our posterity, do ordain and establish this Constitution for the United States of America.

ARTICLE I

Section 1. All legislative Powers herein granted shall be vested in a Congress of the United States, which shall consist of a Senate and House of Representatives.

Section 2. The House of Representatives shall be composed of Members chosen every second Year by the People of the several States, and the Electors in each State shall have the Qualifications requisite for Electors of the most numerous Branch of the State Legislature.

No person shall be a Representative who shall not have attained to the Age of twenty five Years, and been seven Years a Citizen of the United States, and who shall not, when elected, be an Inhabitant of that State in which he shall be chosen.

Representatives and direct Taxes shall be apportioned among the several States which may be included within this Union, according to their respective Numbers, *which shall be determined by adding to the whole Number of free Persons, including those bound to Service for a Term of Years,* and excluding Indians not taxed, *three fifths of all other Persons.*[1] The actual Enumeration shall be made within three Years after the first Meeting of the Congress of the United States, and within every subsequent Term of ten Years, in such Manner as they shall by Law direct. The Number of Representatives shall not exceed one for every thirty Thousand, but each State shall have at Least one Representative; and until such enumeration shall be made, the State of New Hampshire shall be entitled to chuse three, Massachusetts eight, Rhode-Island and Providence Plantations one, Connecticut five, New-York six, New Jersey four, Pennsylvania eight, Delaware one, Maryland six, Virginia ten, North Carolina five, South Carolina five, and Georgia three.

When vacancies happen in the Representation from any State, the Executive Authority thereof shall issue Writs of Election to fill such Vacancies.

The House of Representatives shall chuse their Speaker and other Officers; and shall have the sole Power of Impeachment.

Section 3. The Senate of the United States shall be composed of two Senators from each State *chosen by the Legislature thereof,*[2] for six Years; and each Senator shall have one Vote.

Immediately after they shall be assembled in Consequence of the first Election, they shall be divided as

---

[1] See Amendment XIV. Throughout, italics indicate passages altered by amendments.

[2] See Amendment XVII.

equally as may be into three Classes. The Seats of the Senators of the first Class shall be vacated at the Expiration of the second Year, of the second Class at the Expiration of the fourth Year, and of the third Class at the Expiration of the sixth Year, so that one third may be chosen every second Year *and if Vacancies happen by Resignation, or otherwise, during the Recess of the Legislature of any State, the Executive thereof may make temporary Appointments until the next Meeting of the Legislature, which shall then fill such Vacancies.*[3]

No Person shall be a Senator who shall not have attained to the Age of thirty Years, and been nine Years a Citizen of the United States, and who shall not, when elected, be an Inhabitant of that State for which he shall be chosen.

The Vice President of the United States shall be President of the Senate, but shall have no Vote, unless they be equally divided.

The Senate shall chuse their other Officers, and also a President pro tempore, in the Absence of the Vice President, or when he shall exercise the Office of President of the United States.

The Senate shall have the sole Power to try all Impeachments. When sitting for that Purpose, they shall be on Oath or Affirmation. When the President of the United States is tried, the Chief Justice shall preside: And no Person shall be convicted without the Concurrence of two thirds of the Members present.

Judgment in Cases of Impeachment shall not extend further than to removal from Office, and disqualification to hold and enjoy any Office of honor, Trust or Profit under the United States; but the Party convicted shall nevertheless be liable and subject to Indictment, Trial, Judgment and Punishment, according to Law.

Section 4.   The Times, Places and Manner of holding Elections for Senators and Represenatives, shall be prescribed in each State by the Legislature thereof; but the Congress may at any time by Law make or alter such Regulations, except as to the Places of chusing Senators.

The Congress shall assemble at least once in every Year, and such Meeting shall be on the first Monday in December, unless they shall by Law appoint a different Day.[4]

Section 5.   Each House shall be the Judge of the Elections, Returns and Qualifications of its own Members, and a Majority of each shall constitute a Quorum to do Business; but a smaller Number may adjourn from day to day, and may be authorized to compel the Attendance of absent Members, in such Manner, and under such Penalties as each House may provide.

[3] Ibid.
[4] See Amendment XX.

Each House may determine the Rules of its Proceedings, punish its Members for disorderly Behaviour, and, with the Concurrence of two thirds, expel a Member.

Each House shall keep a Journal of its Proceedings, and from time to time publish the same, excepting such Parts as may in their Judgment require Secrecy; and the Yeas and Nays of the Membership of either House on any question shall, at the desire of one fifth of those present, be entered on the Journal.

Neither House, during the Session of Congress, shall, without the Consent of the other, *adjourn* for more than three days, nor to any other Place than that in which the two Houses shall be sitting.

Section 6.   The Senators and Representatives shall receive a Compensation for their Services, to be ascertained by Law, and paid out of the Treasury of the United States. They shall in all Cases, except Treason, Felony and Breach of the Peace, be privileged from Arrest during their Attendance at the Session of their respective Houses, and in going to and returning from the same; and for any Speech or Debate in either House, they shall not be questioned in any other Place.

No Senator or Representative shall, during the Time for which he was elected, be appointed to any civil Office under the Authority of the United States, which shall have been created, on the Emoluments whereof shall have been encreased during such time; and no Person holding any Office under the United States, shall be a Member of either House during his Continuance in Office.

Section 7.   All Bills for raising Revenue shall originate in the House of Representatives; but the Senate may propose or concur with Amendments as on other Bills.

Every Bill which shall have passed the House of Representatives and the Senate, shall, before it become a Law, be presented to the President of the United States; if he approve he shall sign it, but if not he shall return it, with his Objections to that House in which it shall have originated, who shall enter the Objections at large on their Journal, and proceed to reconsider it. If after such Reconsideration two thirds of that House shall agree to pass the Bill, it shall be sent, together with the Objections, to the other House, by which it shall likewise be reconsidered, and if approved by two thirds of that House, it shall become a Law. But in all such Cases the Votes of both Houses shall be determined by Yeas and Nays, and the Names of the Persons voting for and against the Bill shall be entered on the Journal of each House respectively. If any Bill shall not be returned by the President within ten Days (Sundays excepted) after it shall have been presented to him, the Same shall be a Law, in like Manner as if he had signed it, unless the Congress by their Adjournment prevent its Return, in which Case it shall not be a Law.

Every Order, Resolution, or Vote to which the Concurrence of the Senate and House of Representatives may be necessary (except on a question of Adjournment) shall be presented to the President of the United States; and before the Same shall take Effect, shall be approved by him, or being disapproved by him, shall be repassed by two thirds of the Senate and House of Representatives, according to the Rules and Limitations prescribed in the Case of a Bill.

Section 8. The Congress shall have Power To lay and collect Taxes, Duties, Imposts and Excises, to pay the Debts and provide for the common Defence and general Welfare of the United States; but all Duties, Imposts and Excises shall be uniform throughout the United States;

To borrow Money on the credit of the United States;

To regulate Commerce with foreign Nations, and among the several States, and with the Indian Tribes;

To establish a uniform Rule of Naturalization, and uniform Laws on the subject of Bankruptcies throughout the United States;

To coin Money, regulate the Value thereof, and of foreign Coin, and fix the Standard of Weights and Measures;

To provide for the Punishment of counterfeiting the Securities and current Coin of the United States;

To establish Post Offices and post Roads;

To promote the Progress of Science and useful Arts, by securing for limited Times to Authors and Inventors the exclusive Right to their respective Writings and Discoveries;

To constitute Tribunals inferior to the supreme Court;

To define and punish Piracies and Felonies committed on the high Seas, and Offences against the Law of Nations;

To declare War, grant Letters of Marque and Reprisal, and make Rules concerning Captures on Land and Water;

To raise and support Armies, but no Appropriation of Money to that Use shall be for a longer Term than two Years;

To provide and maintain a Navy;

To make Rules for the Government and Regulation of the land and naval Forces;

To provide for calling forth the Militia to execute the Laws of the Union, suppress Insurrections and repel Invasions;

To provide for organizing, arming, and disciplining,

the Militia, and for governing such Part of them as may be employed in the Service of the United States, reserving to the States respectively, the Appointment of the Officers, and the Authority of training the Militia according to the discipline prescribed by Congress;

To exercise exclusive Legislation in all Cases whatsoever, over such District (not exceeding ten Miles square) as may, by Cession of particular States, and the Acceptance of Congress, become the Seat of the Government of the United States, and to exercise like Authority over all Places purchased by the Consent of the Legislature of the State in which the Same shall be, for the Erection of Forts, Magazines, Arsenals, dock-Yards, and other needful buildings; — And

To make all Laws which shall be necessary and proper for carrying into Execution the foregoing Powers, and all other Powers vested by this Constitution in the Government of the United States, or in any Department or Officer thereof.

Section 9. The Migration or Importation of such Persons as any of the States now existing shall think proper to admit, shall not be prohibited by the Congress prior to the Year one thousand eight hundred and eight, but a Tax or duty may be imposed on such Importation, not exceeding ten dollars for each Person.

The Privilege of the Writ of Habeas Corpus shall not be suspended, unless when in Cases of Rebellion or Invasion the public Safety may require it.

No Bill of Attainder or ex post facto Law shall be passed.

No Capitation, or other direct, Tax shall be laid, unless in Proportion to the Census or Enumeration herein before directed to be taken.[5]

No Tax or Duty shall be laid on Articles exported from any State.

No Preference shall be given by any Regulation of Commerce or Revenue to the Ports of one State over those of another; nor shall Vessels bound to, or from, one State, be obliged to enter, clear, or pay Duties in another.

No Money shall be drawn from the Treasury, but in Consequence of Appropriations made by Law; and a regular Statement and Account of the Receipts and Expenditures of all public Money shall be published from time to time.

No Title of Nobility shall be granted by the United States; And no Person holding any Office of Profit or Trust under them, shall, without the Consent of the Congress, accept of any present, Emolument, Office, or Title, of any kind whatever, from any King, Prince, or foreign State.

[5]See Amendment XVI.

Section 10. No State shall enter into any Treaty, Alliance, or Confederation; grant Letters of Marque and Reprisal; coin Money; emit Bills of Credit; make any Thing but gold and silver Coin a Tender in Payment of Debts; pass any Bill of Attainder, ex post facto Law, or Law impairing the Obligation of Contracts, or grant any Title of Nobility.

No State shall, without the Consent of the Congress, lay any Imposts or Duties on Imports or Exports, except what may be absolutely necessary for executing its inspection Laws; and the net Produce of all Duties and Imposts, laid by any State on Imports or Exports, shall be for the Use of the Treasury of the United States; and all such Laws shall be subject to the Revision and Controul of the Congress.

No State shall, without the Consent of Congress, lay any Duty of Tonnage, keep Troops, or Ships of War in time of Peace, enter into any Agreement or Compact with another State, or with a foreign Power, or engage in War, unless actually invaded, or in such imminent Danger as will not admit of delay.

ARTICLE II

Section 1. The executive Power shall be vested in a President of the United States of America. He shall hold his Office during the Term of four Years, and, together with the Vice President, chosen for the Same Term, be elected, as follows.

Each State shall appoint, in such Manner as the Legislature thereof may direct, a Number of Electors, equal to the whole Number of Senators and Representatives to which the State may be entitled in the Congress; but no Senator or Representative, or Person holding an Office of Trust or Profit under the United States, shall be appointed an Elector.

The Electors shall meet in their respective States, and vote by Ballot for two Persons of whom one at least shall not be an Inhabitant of the same State with themselves. And they shall make a List of all the Persons voted for, and of the Number of Votes for each; which List they shall sign and certify, and transmit sealed to the Seat of the Government of the United States, directed to the President of the Senate. The President of the Senate shall, in the Presence of the Senate and House of Representatives, open all the Certificates, and the Votes shall then be counted. The Person having the greatest Number of Votes shall be the President, if such Number be a Majority of the whole Number of Electors appointed; and if there be more than one who have such Majority, and have an equal Number of Votes, then the House of Representatives shall immediately chuse by Ballot one of them for President; and if no Person have a Majority, then from the five highest on the List the said House shall in like Manner chuse the President. But in chusing the President, the Votes shall be taken by States, the Representation from each State having one Vote; a quorum for this Purpose shall consist of a Member or Members from two thirds of the States, and a Majority of all the States shall be necessary to a Choice. In every Case, after the Choice of the President, the Person having the greatest Number of Votes of the Electors shall be the Vice President. But if there should remain two or more who have equal Votes, the Senate shall chuse from them by Ballot the Vice President.[6]

The Congress may determine the Time of chusing the Electors, and the Day on which they shall give their Votes; which Day shall be the same throughout the United States.

No Person except a natural born Citizen, or a Citizen of the United States, at the time of the Adoption of this Constitution, shall be eligible to the Office of President; neither shall any Person be eligible to that Office who shall not have attained the Age of thirty five Years, and been fourteen Years a Resident within the United States.

In Case of the Removal of the President from Office, or of his Death, Resignation, or Inability to discharge the Powers and Duties of the said Office, the same shall devolve on the Vice President, and the Congress may by Law provide for the Case of Removal, Death, Resignation or Inability, both of the President and Vice President, declaring what Officer shall then act as President, and such Officer shall act accordingly, until the Disability be removed, or a President shall be elected.[7]

The President shall, at stated Times, receive for his Services, a Compensation, which shall neither be encreased nor diminished during the Period for which he shall have been elected, and he shall not receive within that Period any other Emolument from the United States, or any of them.

Before he enter on the Execution of his Office, he shall take the following Oath or Affirmation: — "I do solemnly swear (or affirm) that I will faithfully execute the Office of President of the United States, and will to the best of my Ability, preserve, protect and defend the Constitution of the United States."

Section 2. The President shall be Commander in Chief of the Army and Navy of the United States, and of the Militia of the several States, when called into the actual Service of the United States; he may require the Opinion, in writing, of the principal Officer in each of the executive Departments, upon any Subject relating to the Duties of their respective Offices, and

---

6See Amendment XII.

7See Amendment XXV.

he shall have Power to grant Reprieves and Pardons for Offences against the United States, except in Cases of Impeachment.

He shall have Power, by and with the Advice and Consent of the Senate, to make Treaties, provided two thirds of the Senators present concur; and he shall nominate, and by and with the Advice and Consent of the Senate, shall appoint Ambassadors, other public Ministers and Consuls, Judges of the supreme Court, and all other Officers of the United States, whose Appointments are not herein otherwise provided for, and which shall be established by Law; but the Congress may by Law vest the Appointment of such inferior Officers, as they think proper, in the President alone, in the Courts of Law, or in the Heads of Departments.

The President shall have Power to fill up all Vacancies that may happen during the Recess of the Senate, by granting Commissions which shall expire at the End of their next Session.

Section 3. He shall from time to time give to the Congress Information of the State of the Union, and recommend to their Consideration such Measures as he shall judge necessary and expedient; he may, on extraordinary Occasions, convene both Houses, or either of them, and in Case of Disagreement between them, with Respect to the Time of Adjournment, he may adjourn them to such Time as he shall think proper; he shall receive Ambassadors and other public Ministers; he shall take Care that the Laws be faithfully executed, and shall Commission all the Officers of the United States.

Section 4. The President, Vice President and all civil Officers of the United States, shall be removed from Office on Impeachment for, and Conviction of, Treason, Bribery, or other high Crimes and Misdemeanors.

ARTICLE III

Section 1. The judicial Power of the United States, shall be vested in one supreme Court, and in such inferior Courts as the Congress may from time to time ordain and establish. The Judges, both of the supreme and inferior Courts, shall hold their Offices during good Behaviour, and shall, at stated Times, receive for their Services, a Compensation, which shall not be diminished during their Continuance in Office.

Section 2. The judicial Power shall extend to all Cases, in Law and Equity, arising under this Constitution, the Laws of the United States, and Treaties

made, or which shall be made, under their Authority; — to all Cases affecting Ambassadors, other public Ministers and Consuls; — to all Cases of admiralty and maritime Jurisdiction; — to Controversies to which the United States shall be a Party; — to Controversies between two or more States, — *between a State and Citizens of another State,*[8] — between Citizens of different States, — between Citizens of the same State claiming Lands under Grants of different States, *and between a state, or the Citizens thereof, and foreign States, Citizens or Subjects.*[9]

In all Cases affecting Ambassadors, other public Ministers and Consuls, and those in which a State shall be Party, the supreme Court shall have original Jurisdiction. In all other Cases before mentioned, the supreme Court shall have appellate Jurisdiction, both as to Law and Fact, with such Exceptions, and under such Regulations as the Congress shall make.

The Trial of all Crimes, except in Cases of Impeachment, shall be by Jury; and such Trial shall be held in the State where the said Crimes shall have been committed; but when not committed within any State, the Trial shall be at such Place or Places as the Congress may by Law have directed.

Section 3. Treason against the United States, shall consist only in levying War against them, or in adhering to their Enemies, giving them Aid and Comfort. No Person shall be convicted of Treason unless on the Testimony of two Witnesses to the same overt Act, or on Confession in open Court.

The Congress shall have Power to declare the Punishment of Treason, but no Attainder of Treason shall work Corruption of Blood, or Forfeiture except during the Life of the Person attainted.

ARTICLE IV

Section 1. Full Faith and Credit shall be given in each State to the public Acts, Records, and judicial Proceedings of every other State. And the Congress may by general Laws prescribe the Manner in which such Acts, Records and Proceedings shall be proved, and the Effect thereof.

Section 2. The Citizens of each State shall be entitled to all Privileges and Immunities of Citizens in the several States.

A Person charged in any State with Treason, Felony, or other Crime, who shall flee from Justice, and be found in another State, shall on Demand of the ex-

---

[8] See Amendment XI.
[9] Ibid.

ecutive Authority of the State from which he fled, be delivered up, to be removed to the State having Jurisdiction of the Crime.

No Person held to Service or Labour in one State under the Laws thereof, escaping into another, shall, in Consequence of any Law or Regulation therein, be discharged from such Service or Labour, but shall be delivered up on Claim of the Party to whom such Service or Labour may be due.[10]

Section 3. New States may be admitted by the Congress into this Union; but no new State shall be formed or erected within the Jurisdiction of any other State; nor any State be formed by the Junction of two or more States, or Parts of States, without the Consent of the Legislatures of the States concerned as well as of the Congress.

The Congress shall have Power to dispose of and make all needful Rules and Regulations respecting the Territory or other Property belonging to the United States; and nothing in this Constitution shall be so construed as to Prejudice any Claims of the United States, or of any particular State.

Section 4. The United States shall guarantee to every State in this Union a Republican Form of Government, and shall protect each of them against Invasion, and on Application of the Legislature, or of the Executive (when the Legislature cannot be convened) against domestic Violence.

ARTICLE V

The Congress, whenever two thirds of both Houses shall deem it necessary, shall propose Amendments to this Constitution, or on the Application of the Legislatures of two thirds of the several States, shall call a Convention for proposing Amendments, which, in either Case, shall be valid to all Intents and Purposes, as Part of this Constitution, when ratified by the Legislatures of three fourths of the several States, or by Conventions in three fourths thereof, as the one or the other Mode of Ratification may be proposed by the Congress; Provided that no Amendment which may be made prior to the Year One thousand eight hundred and eight shall in any Manner affect the first and fourth Clauses in the Ninth Section of the first Article; and that no State, without its Consent, shall be deprived of its equal Suffrage in the Senate.

ARTICLE VI

All Debts contracted and Engagements entered into, before the Adoption of this Constitution, shall be as

[10]See Amendment XIII.

valid against the United States under this Constitution, as under the Confederation.

This Constitution, and the laws of the United States which shall be made in Pursuance thereof; and all Treaties made, or which shall be made, under the Authority of the United States, shall be the supreme Law of the Land; and the Judges in every State shall be bound thereby, any Thing in the Constitution or Laws of any State on the Contrary notwithstanding.

The Senators and Representatives before mentioned, and the Members of the several State Legislatures, and all executive and judicial Officers, both of the United States and of the several States, shall be bound by Oath or Affirmation, to support this Constitution; but no religious Test shall ever be required as a Qualification to any Office or public Trust under the United States.

ARTICLE VII

The Ratification of the Conventions of nine States, shall be sufficient for the Establishment of this Constitution between the States so ratifying the Same.

Done in Convention by the Unanimous Consent of the States present the Seventeenth Day of September in the Year of our Lord one thousand seven hundred and Eighty seven and of the Independence of the United States of America the Twelfth. IN WITNESS whereof we have hereunto subscribed our Names. [Signatures omitted.]

Articles in Addition to, and Amendment of, the Constitution of the United States of America, Proposed by Congress and Ratified by the Legislatures of the Several States, Pursuant to the Fifth Article of the Original Constitution

AMENDMENT I

Congress shall make no law respecting an establishment of religion, or prohibiting the free exercise thereof; or abridging the freedom of speech, or of the press; or the right of the people peaceably to assemble, and to petition the Government for a redress of grievances. [The first ten amendments were ratified on 15 December 1791.]

AMENDMENT II

A well regulated militia, being necessary to the security of a free State, the right of the people to keep and bear arms, shall not be infringed.

AMENDMENT III

No Soldier shall, in time of peace be quartered in any house, without the consent of the owner, nor in time of war, but in a manner to be prescribed by law.

AMENDMENT IV

The right of the people to be secure in their persons, houses, papers, and effects, against unreasonable searches and seizures, shall not be violated, and no warrants shall issue, but upon probable cause, supported by oath or affirmation, and particularly describing the place to be searched, and the persons or things to be seized.

AMENDMENT V

No person shall be held to answer for a capital, or otherwise infamous crime, unless on a presentment or indictment of a Grand Jury, except in cases arising in the land or naval forces, or in the militia, when in actual service in time of war or public danger; nor shall any person be subject for the same offense to be twice put in jeopardy of life or limb; nor shall be compelled in any criminal case to be a witness against himself, nor be deprived of life, liberty, or property, without due process of law; nor shall private property be taken for public use, without just compensation.

AMENDMENT VI

In all criminal prosecutions, the accused shall enjoy the right to a speedy and public trial, by an impartial jury of the State and district wherein the crime shall have been committed, which district shall have been previously ascertained by law, and to be informed of the nature and cause of the accusation; to be confronted with the witnesses against him; to have compulsory process for obtaining witnesses in his favor, and to have the assistance of counsel for his defence.

AMENDMENT VII

In Suits at common law, where the value in controversy shall exceed twenty dollars, the right of trial by jury shall be preserved, and no fact tried by a jury, shall be otherwise reexamined in any Court of the United States, than according to the rules of the common law.

AMENDMENT VIII

Excessive bail should not be required, nor excessive fines imposed, nor cruel and unusual punishment inflicted.

AMENDMENT IX

The enumeration in the Constitution, of certain rights, shall not be construed to deny or disparage others retained by the people.

AMENDMENT X

The powers not delegated to the United States by the Constitution, nor prohibited by it to the States, are reserved to the States respectively, or to the people.

AMENDMENT XI (1798)

The Judicial power of the United States shall not be construed to extend to any suit in law or equity, commenced or prosecuted against one of the United States by Citizens of another State, or by Citizens or Subjects of any Foreign State.

AMENDMENT XII (1804)

The Electors shall meet in their respective states, and vote by ballot for President and Vice-President, one of whom, at least, shall not be an inhabitant of the same state with themselves; they shall name in their ballots the person voted for as President, and in distinct ballots the person voted for as Vice-President, and they shall make distinct lists of all persons voted for as President, and of all persons voted for as Vice-President, and of the number of votes for each, which lists they shall sign and certify, and transmit sealed to the seat of the government of the United States, directed to the President of the Senate; — The President of the

Senate shall, in the presence of the Senate and House of Representatives, open all the certificates and the votes shall then be counted; — The person having the greatest number of votes for President, shall be the President, if such number be a majority of the whole number of Electors appointed; and if no person have such majority, then from the persons having the highest numbers not exceeding three on the list of those voted for as President, the House of Representatives shall choose immediately, by ballot, the President. But in choosing the President, the votes shall be taken by states, the representation from each state having one vote; a quorum for this purpose shall consist of a member or members from two-thirds of the states, and a majority of all the states shall be necessary to a choice. *And if the House of Representatives shall not choose a President whenever the right of choice shall devolve upon them, before the fourth day of March next following, then the Vice-President shall act as President, as in the case of the death or other constitutional disability of the President.*[11] — The person having the greatest number of votes as Vice-President, shall be the Vice-President, if such number be a majority of the whole number of Electors appointed, and if no person have a majority, then from the two highest numbers on the list, the Senate shall choose the Vice-President; a quorum for the purpose shall consist of two-thirds of the whole number of Senators, and a majority of the whole number shall be necessary to a choice. But no person constitutionally ineligible to the office of President shall be eligible to that of Vice-President of the United States.

AMENDMENT XIII (1865)

Section 1. Neither slavery nor involuntary servitude, except as a punishment for crime whereof the party shall have been duly convicted, shall exist within the United States, or any place subject to their jurisdiction.

Section 2. Congress shall have power to enforce this article by appropriate legislation.

AMENDMENT XIV (1868)

Section 1. All persons born or naturalized in the United States, and subject to the jurisdiction thereof, are citizens of the United States and of the State wherein they reside. No State shall make or enforce any law which shall abridge the privileges or immunities of citizens of the United States; nor shall any State deprive

[11]See Amendment XX.

any person of life, liberty, or property, without due process of law; nor deny to any person within its jurisdiction the equal protection of the laws.

Section 2. Representatives shall be apportioned among the several States according to their respective numbers, counting the whole number of persons in each State, excluding Indians not taxed. But when the right to vote at any election for the choice of electors for President and Vice President of the United States, Representatives in Congress, the Executive and Judicial officers of a State, or the members of the Legislature thereof, is denied to any of the male inhabitants of such state, being twenty-one years of age, and citizens of the United States, or in any way abridged, except for participation in rebellion, or other crime, the basis of representation therein shall be reduced in the proportion which the number of such male citizens shall bear to the whole number of male citizens twenty-one years of age in such State.

Section 3. No person shall be a Senator or Representative in Congress, or elector of President and Vice President, or hold any office, civil or military, under the United States, or under any State, who, having previously taken an oath, as a member of Congress, or as an officer of the United States, or as a member of any State legislature, or as an executive or judicial officer of any State, to support the Constitution of the United States, shall be engaged in insurrection or rebellion against the same, or given aid or comfort to the enemies thereof. But Congress may by a vote of two-thirds of each House, remove such disability.

Section 4. The validity of the public debt of the United States, authorized by law, including debts incurred for payment of pensions and bounties for services in suppressing insurrection or rebellion, shall not be questioned. But neither the United States nor any State shall assume or pay any debt or obligation incurred in aid of insurrection or rebellion against the United States, or any claim for the loss or emancipation of any slave, but all such debts, obligations and claims shall be held illegal and void.

Section 5. The Congress shall have power to enforce, by appropriate legislation, the provisions of this article.

AMENDMENT XV (1870)

Section 1. The right of citizens of the United States to vote shall not be denied or abridged by the United States or by any State on account of race, color, or previous condition of servitude.

Section 2. The Congress shall have the power to enforce this article by appropriate legislation.

AMENDMENT XVI (1913)

The Congress shall have power to lay and collect taxes on incomes, from whatever source derived, without apportionment among the several States, and without regard to any census or enumeration.

AMENDMENT XVII (1913)

The Senate of the United States shall be composed of two Senators from each State, elected by the people thereof, for six years; and each Senator shall have one vote. The electors in each State shall have the qualifications requisite for electors of the most numerous branch of the State legislatures.

When vacancies happen in the representation of any State in the Senate, the executive authority of such State shall issue writs of election to fill such vacancies: *Provided,* That the legislature of any State may empower the executive thereof to make temporary appointments until the people fill the vacancies by election as the legislature may direct.

This amendment shall not be so construed as to affect the election or term of any Senator chosen before it becomes valid as a part of the Constitution.

AMENDMENT XVIII (1919)

Section 1. *After one year from the ratification of this article the manufacture, sale, or transportation of intoxicating liquors within, the importation thereof into, or the exportation thereof from the United States and all territory subject to the jurisdiction thereof for beverage purposes is hereby prohibited.*

Section 2. *The Congress and the several States shall have concurrent power to enforce this article by appropriate legislation.*

Section 3. *This article shall be inoperative unless it shall have been ratified as an amendment to the Constitution by the legislatures of the several States, as provided in the Constitution, within seven years from the date of the submission hereof to the States by the Congress.*[12]

[12]See Amendment XXI.

AMENDMENT XIX (1920)

The right of citizens of the United States to vote shall not be denied or abridged by the United States or by any State on account of sex.

Congress shall have the power to enforce this article by appropriate legislation.

AMENDMENT XX (1933)

Section 1. The terms of the President and Vice President shall end at noon on the 20th day of January, and the terms of Senators and Representatives at noon on the 3rd day of January, of the years in which such terms would have ended if this article had not been ratified, and the terms of their successors shall then begin.

Section 2. The Congress shall assemble at least once in every year, and such meeting shall begin at noon on the 3rd day of January, unless they shall by law appoint a different day.

Section 3. If, at the time fixed for the beginning of the term of the President, the President elect shall have died, the Vice President elect shall become President. If a President shall not have been chosen before the time fixed for the beginning of his term, or if the President elect shall have failed to qualify, then the Vice President elect shall act as President until a President shall have qualified; and the Congress may by law provide for the case wherein neither a President elect nor a Vice President elect shall have qualified, declaring who shall then act as President, or the manner in which one who is to act shall be selected, and such person shall act accordingly until a President or Vice President shall have qualified.

Section 4. The Congress may by law provide for the case of the death of any of the persons from whom the House of Representatives may choose a President whenever the rights of choice shall have devolved upon them, and for the case of the death of any of the persons from whom the Senate may choose a Vice President whenever the right of choice shall have devolved upon them.

Section 5. Sections 1 and 2 shall take effect on the 15th day of October following the ratification of this article.

Section 6. This article shall be inoperative unless it shall have been ratified as an amendment to the Constitution by the legislatures of three-fourths of the several States within seven years from the date of its submission.

AMENDMENT XXI (1933)

Section 1. The eighteenth article of amendment to the Constitution of the United States is hereby repealed.

Section 2. The transportation or importation into any State, Territory, or possession of the United States for delivery or use therein of intoxicating liquors, in violation of the laws thereof, is hereby prohibited.

Section 3. This article shall be inoperative unless it shall be ratified as an amendment to the Constitution by conventions in the several States, as provided in the Constitution, within seven years from the date of the submission hereof to the States by the Congress.

AMENDMENT XXII (1951)

Section 1. No person shall be elected to the office of the President more than twice, and no person who has held the office of President, or acted as President, for more than two years of a term to which some other person was elected President shall be elected to the office of the President more than once. But this Article shall not apply to any person holding the office of President when this Article was proposed by the Congress, and shall not prevent any person who may be holding the office of President, or acting as President, during the term within which this Article becomes operative from holding the office of President or acting as President during the remainder of such term.

Section 2. This article shall be inoperative unless it shall have been ratified as an amendment to the Constitution by the legislatures of three-fourths of the several States within seven years from the date of its submission to the States by the Congress.

AMENDMENT XXIII (1961)

Section 1. The District constituting the seat of Government of the United States shall appoint in such manner as the Congress may direct:

A number of electors of President and Vice President equal to the whole number of Senators and Representatives in Congress to which the District would be entitled if it were a State, but in no event more than the least populous State; they shall be in addition to those appointed by the States, but they shall be considered, for the purposes of the election of President and Vice President, to be electors appointed by a State; and they shall meet in the District and perform such duties as provided by the twelfth article of amendment.

Section 2. The Congress shall have power to enforce this article by appropriate legislation.

AMENDMENT XXIV (1964)

Section 1. The right of citizens of the United States to vote in any primary or other election for President or Vice President, for electors for President or Vice President, or for Senator or Representative in Congress, shall not be denied or abridged by the United States or by any State by reason of failure to pay any poll tax or other tax.

Section 2. The Congress shall have power to enforce this article by appropriate legislation.

AMENDMENT XXV (1967)

Section 1. In case of the removal of the President from office or of his death or resignation, the Vice President shall become President.

Section 2. Whenever there is a vacancy in the office of the Vice President, the President shall nominate a Vice President who shall take office upon confirmation by a majority vote of both Houses of Congress.

Section 3. Whenever the President transmits to the President pro tempore of the Senate and the Speaker of the House of Representatives his written declaration that he is unable to discharge the powers and duties of his office, and until he transmits to them a written declaration to the contrary, such powers and duties shall be discharged by the Vice President as Acting President.

Section 4. Whenever the Vice President and a majority of either the principal officers of the executive departments or of such other body as Congress may by law provide, transmit to the President pro tempore of the Senate and the Speaker of the House of Representatives their written declaration that the President is unable to discharge the powers and duties of his office, the Vice President shall immediately assume the powers and duties of the office as Acting President.

Thereafter, when the President transmits to the President pro tempore of the Senate and the Speaker of the House of Representatives his written declaration that no inability exists, he shall resume the powers and duties of his office unless the Vice President and a majority of either the principal officers of the executive department or of such other body as Congress may by law provide, transmit within four days to the President pro tempore of the Senate and the Speaker of the House of Representatives their written declaration that the President is unable to discharge the powers and duties of his office. Thereupon Congress shall decide the issue, assembling within forty-eight hours for that purpose if not in session. If the Congress, within twenty-one days after receipt of the latter written declaration, or, if Congress is not in session, within twenty-one days after Congress is required to assemble, determines by two-thirds vote of both Houses that the President is unable to discharge the powers and duties of his office, the Vice President shall continue to discharge the same as Acting President; otherwise, the President shall resume the powers and duties of his office.

AMENDMENT XXVI (1971)

Section 1. The right of citizens of the United States, who are eighteen years of age or older, to vote shall not be denied or abridged by the United States or by any State on account of age.

Section 2. The Congress shall have the power to enforce this article by appropriate legislation.

Proposed Amendment (1972)

Resolved by the Senate and House of Representatives of the United States of America in Congress assembled (two-thirds of each House concurring therein), That the following article is proposed as an amendment to the Constitution of the United States, which shall be valid to all intents and purposes as part of the Constitution when ratified by the legislatures of three-fourths of the several States within seven years from the date of its submission by the Congress.[13]

Section 1. Equality of rights under the law shall not be denied or abridged by the United States or by any State on account of sex.

Section 2. The Congress shall have the power to enforce, by appropriate legislation, the provisions of this article.

Section 3. This amendment shall take effect two years after the date of ratification.

Proposed Amendment (1978)

Section 1. For purposes of representation in the Congress, election of the President and Vice President, and article V of this Constitution, the District constituting the seat of government of the United States shall be treated as though it were a State.

Section 2. The exercise of the rights and powers conferred under this article shall be by the people of the District constituting the seat of government, and as shall be provided by the Congress.

Section 3. The twenty-third article of amendment to the Constitution of the United States is hereby repealed.

Section 4. This article shall be inoperative, unless it shall have been ratified as an amendment to the Constitution by the legislatures of three-fourths of the several States within seven years from the date of its submission.

---

[13]In 1978 Congress extended the deadline for ratification of the Equal Rights Amendment to 30 June 1982; although defeated at that time, it is still active as a proposed amendment.

APPENDIX C

The Uniform Partnership Act[1]

[1] Source: National Conference of Commissioners of Uniform State Laws.

PART 1

Preliminary Provisions

Section 1. Name of Act

This act may be cited as Uniform Partnership Act.

Section 2. Definition of Terms

In this act, "Court" includes every court and judge having jurisdiction in the case.

"Business" includes every trade, occupation, or profession.

"Person" includes individuals, partnerships, corporations, and other associations.

"Bankrupt" includes bankrupt under the Federal Bankruptcy Act or insolvent under any state insolvent act.

"Conveyance" includes every assignment, lease, mortgage, or encumbrance.

"Real property" includes land and any interest or estate in land.

Section 3. Interpretation of Knowledge and Notice

(1) A person has "knowledge" of a fact within the meaning of this act not only when he has actual knowledge thereof, but also when he has knowledge of such other facts as in the circumstances shows bad faith.

(2) A person has "notice" of a fact within the meaning of this act when the person who claims the benefit of the notice:

(a) states the fact to such person; or

(b) delivers through the mail, or by other means of communication, a written statement of the fact to such person or to a proper person at his place of business or residence.

Section 4. Rules of Construction

(1) The rule that statutes in derogation of the common law are to be strictly construed shall have no application to this act.

(2) The law of estoppel shall apply under this act.

(3) The law of agency shall apply under this act.

(4) This act shall be so interpreted and construed as to effect its general purpose to make uniform the law of those states which enact it.

(5) This act shall not be construed so as to impair the obligations of any contract existing when the act goes into effect, nor to affect any action or proceedings begun or right accrued before this act takes effect.

Section 5. Rules for Cases Not Provided for in This Act

In any case not provided for in this act the rules of law and equity, including the law merchant, shall govern.

1151

PART 2

Nature of Partnership

Section 6. Partnership Defined

(1) A partnership is an association of two or more persons to carry on as co-owners a business for profit.

(2) But any association formed under any other statute of this state, or any statute adopted by authority, other than the authority of this state, is not a partnership under this act, unless such association would have been a partnership in this state prior to the adoption of this act; but this act shall apply to limited partnerships except in so far as the statutes relating to such partnerships are inconsistent herewith.

Section 7. Rules for Determining the Existence of a Partnership

In determining whether a partnership exists, these rules shall apply:

(1) Except as provided by section 16, persons who are not partners as to each other are not partners as to third persons.

(2) Joint tenancy, tenancy in common, tenancy by the entireties, joint property, common property, or part ownership does not of itself establish a partnership, whether such co-owners do or do not share any profits made by the use of the property.

(3) The sharing of gross returns does not of itself establish a partnership, whether or not the persons sharing them have a joint or common right or interest in any property from which the returns are derived.

(4) The receipt by a person of a share of the profits of a business is prima facie evidence that he is a partner in the business, but no such inference shall be drawn if such profits were received in payment:

   (a)   as a debt by installments or otherwise,

   (b)   as wages of an employee or rent to a landlord,

   (c)   as an annuity to a widow or representative of a deceased partner,

   (d)   as interest on a loan, though the amount of payment vary with the profits of the business,

   (e)   as the consideration for the sale of a goodwill of a business or other property by installments or otherwise.

Section 8. Partnership Property

(1) All property originally brought into the partnership stock or subsequently acquired by purchase or otherwise, on account of the partnership, is partnership property.

(2) Unless the contrary intention appears, property acquired with partnership funds is partnership property.

(3) Any estate in real property may be acquired in the partnership name. Title so acquired can be conveyed only in the partnership name.

(4) A conveyance to a partnership in the partnership name, though without words of inheritance, passes the entire estate of the grantor unless a contrary intent appears.

PART 3

Relations of Partners to Persons Dealing with the Partnership

Section 9. Partner Agent of Partnership as to Partnership Business

(1) Every partner is an agent of the partnership for the purpose of its business, and the act of every partner, including the execution in the partnership name of any instrument, for apparently carrying on in the usual way the business of the partnership of which he is a member binds the partnership, unless the partner so acting has in fact no authority to act for the partnership in the particular matter, and the person with whom he is dealing has knowledge of the fact that he has no such authority.

(2) An act of a partner which is not apparently for the carrying on of the business of the partnership in the usual way does not bind the partnership unless authorized by the other partners.

(3) Unless authorized by the other partners or unless they have abandoned the business, one or more but less than all the partners have no authority to:

   (a)   assign the partnership property in trust for creditors or on the assignee's promise to pay the debts of the partnership,

   (b)   dispose of the good-will of the business,

   (c)   do any other act which would make it impossible to carry on the ordinary business of a partnership,

   (d)   confess a judgment,

   (e)   submit a partnership claim or liability to arbitration or reference.

(4) No act of a partner in contravention of a restriction

on authority shall bind the partnership to persons having knowledge of the restriction.

Section 10. Conveyance of Real Property of the Partnership

(1) Where title to real property is in the partnership name, any partner may convey title to such property by a conveyance executed in the partnership name; but the partnership may recover such property unless the partner's act binds the partnership under the provisions of paragraph (1) of section 9, or unless such property has been conveyed by the grantee or a person claiming through such grantee to a holder for value without knowledge that the partner, in making the conveyance, has exceeded his authority.

(2) Where title to real property is in the name of the partnership, a conveyance executed by a partner, in his own name, passes the equitable interest of the partnership, provided the act is one within the authority of the partner under the provisions of paragraph (1) of section 9.

(3) Where title to real property is in the name of one or more but not all the partners, and the record does not disclose the right of partnership, the partners in whose name the title stands may convey title to such property, but the partnership may recover such property if the partners' act does not bind the partnership under the provisions of paragraph (1) of section 9, unless the purchaser or his assignee, is a holder for value, without knowledge.

(4) Where the title to real property is in the name of one or more or all the partners, or in a third person in trust for the partnership, a conveyance executed by a partner in the partnership name, or in his own name, passes the equitable interest of the partnership, provided the act is one within the authority of the partner under the provisions of paragraph (1) of section 9.

(5) Where the title to real property is in the names of all the partners a conveyance executed by all the partners passes all their rights in such property.

Section 11. Partnership Bound by Admission of Partner

An admission or representation made by any partner concerning partnership affairs within the scope of his authority as conferred by this act is evidence against the partnership.

Section 12. Partnership Charged with Knowledge of or Notice to Partner

Notice to any partner of any matter relating to partnership affairs, and the knowledge of the partner acting in the particular matter, acquired while a partner or then present to his mind, and the knowledge of any other partner who reasonably could and should have communicated it to the acting partner, operate as notice to or knowledge of the partnership, except in the case of a fraud on the partnership committed by or with the consent of that partner.

Section 13. Partnership Bound by Partner's Wrongful Act

Where, by any wrongful act or omission of any partner acting in the ordinary course of the business of the partnership or with the authority of his co-partners, loss or injury is caused to any person, not being a partner in the partnership, or any penalty is incurred, the partnership is liable therefor to the same extent as the partner so acting or omitting to act.

Section 14. Partnership Bound by Partner's Breach of Trust

The partnership is bound to make good the loss:

(a) where one partner acting within the scope of his apparent authority receives money or property of a third person and misapplies it; and

(b) where the partnership in the course of its business receives money or property of a third person and the money or property so received is misapplied by any partner while it is in the custody of the partnership.

Section 15. Nature of Partner's Liability

All partners are liable

(a) jointly and severally for everything chargeable to the partnership under sections 13 and 14.

(b) jointly for all other debts and obligations of the partnership; but any partner may enter into a separate obligation to perform a partnership contract.

Section 16. Partner by Estoppel

(1) When a person, by words spoken or written or by conduct, represents himself, or consents to another representing him to any one, as a partner in an existing partnership or with one or more persons not actual partners, he is liable to any such person to whom such representation has been made, who has, on the faith of such representation, given credit to the actual or apparent partnership, and if he has made such representation or consented to its being made in a public manner he is liable to such person, whether the representation has or has not been made or communicated to such

person so giving credit by or with the knowledge of the apparent partner making the representation or consenting to its being made.

(a) When a partnership liability results, he is liable as though he were an actual member of the partnership.

(b) When no partnership liability results, he is liable jointly with the other persons, if any, so consenting to the contract or representation as to incur liability, otherwise separately.

(2) When a person has been thus represented to be a partner in an existing partnership, or with one or more persons not actual partners, he is an agent of the persons consenting to such representation to bind them to the same extent and in the same manner as though he were a partner in fact, with respect to persons who rely upon the representation. Where all the members of the existing partnership consent to the representation, a partnership act or obligation results; but in all other cases it is the joint act or obligation of the person acting and the persons consenting to the representation.

Section 17. Liability of Incoming Partner

A person admitted as a partner into an existing partnership is liable for all the obligations of the partnership arising before his admission as though he had been a partner when such obligations were incurred, except that this liability shall be satisfied only out of partnership property.

PART 4

Relations of Partners to One Another

Section 18. Rules Determining Rights and Duties of Partners

The rights and duties of the partners in relation to the partnership shall be determined, subject to any agreement between them, by the following rules:

(a) Each partner shall be repaid his contributions, whether by way of capital or advances to the partnership property and share equally in the profits and surplus remaining after all liabilities, including those to partners, are satisfied; and must contribute towards the losses, whether of capital or otherwise, sustained by the partnership according to this share in the profits.

(b) The partnership must indemnify every partner in respect of payments made and personal liabilities reasonably incurred by him in the ordinary and proper conduct of its business, or for the preservation of its business or property.

(c) A partner, who in aid of the partnership makes any payment or advance beyond the amount of capital which he agreed to contribute, shall be paid interest from the date of the payment or advance.

(d) A partner shall receive interest on the capital contributed by him only from the date when repayment should be made.

(e) All partners have equal rights in the management and conduct of the partnership business.

(f) No partner is entitled to remuneration for acting in the partnership business, except that a surviving partner is entitled to reasonable compensation for his services in winding up the partnership affairs.

(g) No person can become a member of a partnership without the consent of all the partners.

(h) Any difference arising as to ordinary matters connected with the partnership business may be decided by a majority of the partners; but no act in contravention of any agreement between the partners may be done rightfully without the consent of all the partners.

Section 19. Partnership Books

The partnership books shall be kept, subject to any agreement between the partners, at the principal place of business of the partnership, and every partner shall at all times have access to and may inspect and copy any of them.

Section 20. Duty of Partners to Render Information

Partners shall render on demand true and full information of all things affecting the partnership to any partner or the legal representative of any deceased partner or partner under legal disability.

Section 21. Partner Accountable as a Fiduciary

(1) Every partner must account to the partnership for any benefit, and hold as trustee for it any profits derived by him without the consent of the other partners from any transaction connected with the formation, conduct, or liquidation of the partnership or from any use by him of its property.

(2) This section applies also to the representatives of a deceased partner engaged in the liquidation of the af-

fairs of the partnership as the personal representatives of the last surviving partner.

Section 22. Right to an Account

Any partner shall have the right to a formal account as to partnership affairs:

(a) if he is wrongfully excluded from the partnership business or possession of its property by his co-partners,

(b) if the right exists under the terms of any agreement,

(c) as provided by section 21,

(d) whenever other circumstances render it just and reasonable.

Section 23. Continuation of Partnership Beyond Fixed Term

(1) When a partnership for a fixed term or particular undertaking is continued after the termination of such term or particular undertaking without any express agreement, the rights and duties of the partners remain the same as they were at such termination, so far as is consistent with a partnership at will.

(2) A continuation of the business by the partners or such of them as habitually acted therein during the term, without any settlement or liquidation of the partnership affairs, is prima facie evidence of a continuation of the partnership.

PART 5

Property Rights of a Partner

Section 24. Extent of Property Rights of a Partner

The property rights of a partner are (1) his rights in specific partnership property, (2) his interest in the partnership, and (3) his right to participate in the management.

Section 25. Nature of a Partner's Right in Specific Partnership Property

(1) A partner is co-owner with his partners of specific partnership property holding as a tenant in partnership.

(2) The incidents of this tenancy are such that:

(a) A partner, subject to the provisions of this act and to any agreement between the partners, has an equal right with his partners to possess specific partnership property for partnership purposes; but he has no right to possess such property for any other purpose without the consent of his partners.

(b) A partner's right in specific partnership property is not assignable except in connection with the assignment of rights of all the partners in the same property.

(c) A partner's right in specific partnership property is not subject to attachment or execution, except on a claim against the partnership. When partnership property is attached for a partnership debt the partners, or any of them, or the representatives of a deceased partner, cannot claim any right under the homestead or exemption laws.

(d) On the death of a partner his right in specific partnership property vests in the surviving partner or partners, except where the deceased was the last surviving partner, when his right in such property vests in his legal representative. Such surviving partner or partners, or the legal representative of the last surviving partner, has no right to possess the partnership property for any but a partnership purpose.

(e) A partner's right in specific partnership property is not subject to dower, curtesy, or allowances to widows, heirs, or next of kin.

Section 26. Nature of Partner's Interest in the Partnership

A partner's interest in the partnership is his share of the profits and surplus, and the same is personal property.

Section 27. Assignment of Partner's Interest

(1) A conveyance by a partner of his interest in the partnership does not of itself dissolve the partnership, nor, as against the other partners in the absence of agreement, entitle the assignee, during the continuance of the partnership, to interfere in the management or administration of the partnership business or affairs, or to require any information or account of partnership transactions, or to inspect the partnership books; but it merely entitles the assignee to receive in accordance with his contract the profits to which the assigning partner would otherwise be entitled.

(2) In case of a dissolution of the partnership, the assignee is entitled to receive his assignor's interest and may require an account from the date only of the last account agreed to by all the partners.

Section 28.   Partner's Interest Subject to Charging Order

(1) On due application to a competent court by any judgment creditor of a partner, the court which entered the judgment, order, or decree, or any other court, may charge the interest of the debtor partner with payment of the unsatisfied amount of such judgment debt with interest thereon; and may then or later appoint a receiver of his share of the profits, and of any other money due or to fall due to him in respect of the partnership, and make all other orders, directions, accounts and inquiries which the debtor partner might have made, or which the circumstances of the case may require.

(2) The interest charged may be redeemed at any time before foreclosure, or in case of a sale being directed by the court may be purchased without thereby causing a dissolution:

> (a) with separate property, by any one or more of the partners, or
>
> (b) with partnership property, by any one or more of the partners with the consent of all the partners whose interests are not so charged or sold.

(3) Nothing in this act shall be held to deprive a partner of his right, if any, under the exemption laws, as regards his interest in the partnership.

PART 6

Dissolution and Winding Up

Section 29.   Dissolution Defined

The dissolution of a partnership is the change in the relation of the partners caused by any partner ceasing to be associated in the carrying on as distinguished from the winding up of the business.

Section 30.   Partnership Not Terminated by Dissolution

On dissolution the partnership is not terminated, but continues until the winding up of partnership affairs is completed.

Section 31.   Causes of Dissolution

Dissolution is caused:

(1) without violation of the agreement between the partners,

> (a) by the termination of the definite term or particular undertaking specified in the agreement,
>
> (b) by the express will of any partner when no definite term or particular undertaking is specified,
>
> (c) by the express will of all the partners who have not assigned their interests or suffered them to be charged for their separate debts, either before or after the termination of any specified term or particular undertaking,
>
> (d) by the expulsion of any partner from the business bona fide in accordance with such a power conferred by the agreement between the partners.

(2) in contravention of the agreement between the partners, where the circumstances do not permit a dissolution under any other provision of this section, by the express will of any partner at any time;

(3) by any event which makes it unlawful for the business of the partnership to be carried on or for the members to carry it on in partnership;

(4) by the death of any partner;

(5) by the bankruptcy of any partner or the partnership;

(6) by decree of court under section 32.

Section 32.   Dissolution by Decree of Court

(1) On application by or for a partner the court shall decree a dissolution whenever;

> (a) a partner has been declared a lunatic in any judicial proceeding or is shown to be of unsound mind,
>
> (b) a partner becomes in any other way incapable of performing his part of the partnership contract,
>
> (c) a partner has been guilty of such conduct as tends to affect prejudicially the carrying on of the business,
>
> (d) a partner wilfully or persistently commits a breach of the partnership agreement, or otherwise so conducts himself in matters relating to the partnership business that it is not reasonably practicable to carry on the business in partnership with him,
>
> (e) the business of the partnership can only be carried on at a loss,

(f) other circumstances render a dissolution equitable.

(2) On the application of the purchaser of a partner's interest under sections 27 and 28:

(a) after the termination of the specified term or particular undertaking,

(b) at any time if the partnership was a partnership at will when the interest was assigned or when the charging order was issued.

Section 33. General Effect of Dissolution on Authority of Partner

Except so far as may be necessary to wind up partnership affairs or to complete transactions begun but not then finished, dissolution terminates all authority of any partner to act for the partnership,

(1) with respect to the partners,

(a) when the dissolution is not by the act, bankruptcy or death of a partner; or

(b) when the dissolution is by such act, bankruptcy or death of a partner, in cases where section 34 so requires.

(2) with respect to persons not partners, as declared in section 35.

Section 34. Right of Partner to Contribution from Co-Partners after Dissolution

Where the dissolution is caused by the act, death or bankruptcy of a partner, each partner is liable to his co-partners for his share of any liability created by any partner acting for the partnership as if the partnership had not been dissolved unless

(a) the dissolution being by act of any partner, the partner acting for the partnership had knowledge of the dissolution, or

(b) the dissolution being by the death or bankruptcy of a partner, the partner acting for the partnership had knowledge or notice of the death or bankruptcy.

Section 35. Power of Partner to Bind Partnership to Third Persons after Dissolution

(1) After dissolution a partner can bind the partnership except as provided in Paragraph (3)

(a) by any act appropriate for winding up partnership affairs or completing transactions unfinished at dissolution;

(b) by any transaction which would bind the partnership if dissolution had not taken place, provided the other party to the transaction

(i) had extended credit to the partnership prior to dissolution and had no knowledge or notice of the dissolution; or

(ii) though he had not so extended credit, had nevertheless known of the partnership prior to dissolution, and, having no knowledge or notice of dissolution, the fact of dissolution had not been advertised in a newspaper of general circulation in the place (or in each place if more than one) at which the partnership business was regularly carried on.

(2) The liability of a partner under Paragraph (1b) shall be satisfied out of partnership assets alone when such partner had been prior to dissolution

(a) unknown as a partner to the person with whom the contract is made; and

(b) so far unknown and inactive in partnership affairs that the business reputation of the partnership could not be said to have been in any degree due to his connection with it.

(3) The partnership is in no case bound by any act of a partner after dissolution

(a) where the partnership is dissolved because it is unlawful to carry on the business, unless the act is appropriate for winding up partnership affairs; or

(b) where the partner has become bankrupt; or

(c) where the partner has no authority to wind up partnership affairs; except by a transaction with one who

(i) had extended credit to the partnership prior to dissolution and had no knowledge or notice of his want of authority; or

(ii) had not extended credit to the partnership prior to dissolution, and, having no knowledge or notice of his want of authority, the fact of his want of authority has not been advertised in the manner provided for advertising the fact of dissolution in Paragraph (1b ii).

(4) Nothing in this section shall affect the liability under Section 16 of any person who after dissolution represents himself or consents to another representing him as a partner in a partnership engaged in carrying on business.

Section 36. Effect of Dissolution on Partner's Existing Liability

(1) The dissolution of the partnership does not of itself discharge the existing liability of any partner.

(2) A partner is discharged from any existing liability upon dissolution of the partnership by an agreement to that effect between himself, the partnership creditor and the person or partnership continuing the business; and such agreement may be inferred from the course of dealing between the creditor having knowledge of the dissolution and the person or partnership continuing the business.

(3) Where a person agrees to assume the existing obligations of a dissolved partnership, the partners whose obligations have been assumed shall be discharged from any liability to any creditor of the partnership who, knowing of the agreement, consents to a material alteration in the nature or time of payment of such obligations.

(4) The individual property of a deceased partner shall be liable for all obligations of the partnership incurred while he was a partner but subject to the prior payment of his separate debts.

Section 37. Right to Wind Up

Unless otherwise agreed the partners who have not wrongfully dissolved the partnership or the legal representative of the last surviving partner, not bankrupt, has the right to wind up the partnership affairs; provided, however, that any partner, his legal representative or his assignee, upon cause shown, may obtain winding up by the court.

Section 38. Rights of Partners to Application of Partnership Property

(1) When dissolution is caused in any way, except in contravention of the partnership agreement, each partner, as against his co-partners and all persons claiming through them in respect of their interests in the partnership, unless otherwise agreed, may have the partnership property applied to discharge its liabilities, and the surplus applied to pay in cash the net amount owing to the respective partners. But if dissolution is caused by expulsion of a partner, bona fide under the partnership agreement and if the expelled partner is discharged from all partnership liabilities, either by payment or agreement under section 36(2), he shall receive in cash only the net amount due him from the partnership.

(2) When dissolution is caused in contravention of the partnership agreement the rights of the partners shall be as follows:

(a) Each partner who has not caused dissolution wrongfully shall have,

(i) all the rights specified in paragraph (1) of this section, and

(ii) the right, as against each partner who has caused the dissolution wrongfully, to damages for breach of the areement.

(b) The partners who have not caused the dissolution wrongfully, if they all desire to continue the business in the same name, either by themselves or jointly with others, may do so, during the agreed term for the partnership and for that purpose may possess the partnership property, provided they secure the payment by bond approved by the court, or pay to any partner who has caused the dissolution wrongfully, the value of his interest in the partnership at the dissolution, less any damages recoverable under clause (2a ii) of this section, and in like manner indemnify him against all present or future partnership liabilities.

(c) A partner who has caused the dissolution wrongfully shall have:

(i) if the business is not continued under the provisions of paragraph (2b) all the rights of a partner under paragraph (1), subject to clause (2a ii), of this section,

(ii) if the business is continued under paragraph (2b) of this section the right as against his co-partners and all claiming through them in respect of their interests in the partnership, to have the value of his interest in the partnership, less any damages caused to his co-partners by the dissolution, ascertained and paid to him in cash, or the payment secured by bond approved by the court, and to be released from all existing liabilities of the partnership; but in ascertaining the value of the partner's interest the value of the good-will of the business shall not be considered.

Section 39. Rights Where Partnership Is Dissolved for Fraud or Misrepresentation

Where a partnership contract is rescinded on the ground of the fraud or misrepresentation of one of the parties thereto, the party entitled to rescind is, without prejudice to any other right, entitled,

(a) to a lien on, or a right of retention of, the surplus of the partnership property after satisfying the partnership liabilities to third persons for any sum of money paid by him for the purchase of an interest in the partnership and for any capital or advances contributed by him; and

(b) to stand, after all liabilities to third persons have been satisfied, in the place of the creditors of the partnership for any payments made by him in respect of the partnership liabilities; and

(c) to be indemnified by the person guilty of the fraud or making the representation against all debts and liabilities of the partnership.

Section 40. Rules for Distribution

In settling accounts between the partners after dissolution, the following rules shall be observed, subject to any agreement to the contrary:

(a) The assets of the partnership are:

(i) the partnership property,

(ii) the contributions of the partners necessary for the repayment of all the liabilities specified in clause (b) of this paragraph.

(b) The liabilities of the partnership shall rank in order of payment, as follows:

(i) those owing to creditors other than partners,

(ii) those owing to partners other than for capital and profits,

(iii) those owing to partners in respect of capital,

(iv) those owing to partners in respect of profits.

(c) The assets shall be applied in the order of their declaration in clause (a) of this paragraph to the satisfaction of the liabilities.

(d) The partners shall contribute, as provided by section 18(a) the amount necessary to satisfy the liabilities; but if any, but not all, of the partners are insolvent, or, not being subject to process, refuse to contribute, the other partners shall contribute their share of the liabilities, and, in the relative proportions in which they share the profits, the additional amount necessary to pay the liabilities.

(e) An assignee for the benefit of creditors or any person appointed by the court shall have the right to enforce the contributions specified in clause (d) of this paragraph.

(f) Any partner or his legal representtive shall have the right to enforce the contributions specified in clause (d) of this paragraph, to the extent of the amount which he has paid in excess of his share of the liability.

(g) The individual property of a deceased partner shall be liable for the contributions specified in clause (d) of this paragraph.

(h) When partnership property and the individual properties of the partners are in possession of a court for distribution, partnership creditors shall have priority on partnership property and separate creditors on individual property, saving the rights of lien or secured creditors as heretofore.

(i) Where a partner has become bankrupt or his estate is insolvent the claims against his separate property shall rank in the following order:

(i) those owing to separate creditors,

(ii) those owing to partnership creditors,

(iii) those owing to partners by way of contribution.

Section 41. Liability of Persons Continuing the Business in Certain Cases

(1) When any new partner is admitted into an existing partnership, or when any partner retires and assigns (or the representative of the deceased partner assigns) his rights in partnership property to two or more of the partners, or to one or more of the partners and one or more third persons, if the business is continued without liquidation of the partnership affairs, creditors of the first or dissolved partnership are also creditors of the partnership so continuing the business.

(2) When all but one partner retire and assign (or the representative of a deceased partner assigns) their rights in partnership property to the remaining partner, who continues the business without liquidation of partnership affairs, either alone or with others,

creditors of the dissolved partnership are also creditors of the person or partnership so continuing the business.

(3)   When any partner retires or dies and the business of the dissolved partnership is continued as set forth in paragraphs (1) and (2) of this section, with the consent of the retired partners or the representative of the deceased partner, but without any assignment of his right in partnership property, rights of creditors of the dissolved partnersip and of the creditors of the person or partnership continuing the business shall be as if such assignment has been made.

(4)   When all the partners or their representatives assign their rights in partnership property to one or more third persons who promise to pay the debts and who continue the business of the dissolved partnership, creditors of the dissolved partnership are also creditors of the person or partnership continuing the business.

(5)   When any partner wrongfully causes a dissolution and the remaining partners continue the business under the provisions of section 38(2b), either alone or with others, and without liquidation of the partnership affairs, creditors of the dissolved partnership are also creditors of the person or partnership continuing the business.

(6)   When a partner is expelled and the remaining partners continue the business either alone or with others, without liquidation of the partnership affairs, creditors of the dissolved partnership are also creditors of the person or partnership continuing the business.

(7)   The liability of a third person becoming a partner in the partnership continuing the business, under this section, to the creditors of the dissolved partnership, shall be satisfied out of partnership property only.

(8)   When the business of a partnership after dissolution is continued under any conditions set forth in this section the creditors of the dissolved partnership, as against the separate creditors of the retiring or deceased partner or the representative of the deceased partner, have a prior right to any claim of the retired partner or the representative of the deceased partner against the person or partnership continuing the business, on account of the retired or deceased partner's interest in the dissolved partnership or on account of any consideration promised for such interest or for his right in partnership property.

(9)   Nothing in this section shall be held to modify any right of creditors to set aside any assignment on the ground of fraud.

(10) The use by the person or partnership continuing the business of the partnership name, or the name of a deceased partner as part thereof, shall not of itself make the individual property of the deceased partner liable for any debts contracted by such person or partnership.

Section 42.   Rights of Retiring or Estate of Deceased Partner When the Business Is Continued

When any partner retires or dies, and the business is continued under any of the conditions set forth in section 41(1, 2, 3, 5, 6), or section 38(2b) without any settlement of accounts as between him or his estate and the person or partnership continuing the business, unless otherwise agreed, he or his legal representative as against such persons or partnership may have the value of his interest at the date of dissolution ascertained, and shall receive as an ordinary creditor an amount equal to the value of his interest in the dissolved partnership with interest, or, at his option or at the option of his legal representative, in lieu of interest, the profits attributable to the use of his right in the property of the dissolved partnership; provided that the creditors of the dissolved partnership as against the separate creditors, or the representative of the retired or deceased partner, shall have priority on any claim arising under this section, as provided by section 41(8) of this act.

Section 43.   Accrual of Actions

The right to an account of his interest shall accrue to any partner, or his legal representative, as against the winding up partners or the surviving partners or the person or partnership continuing the business, at the date of dissolution, in the absence of any agreement to the contrary.

PART 7
Miscellaneous Provisions

Section 44.   When Act Takes Effect

This act shall take effect on the . . . . day of . . . . one thousand nine hundred and . . . .

Section 45.   Legislation Repealed

All acts or parts of acts inconsistent with this act are hereby repealed.

The Revised Uniform Limited Partnership Act with the 1985 Amendments[1]

ARTICLE 1

GENERAL PROVISIONS

Section 101. Definitions

As used in this [Act], unless the context otherwise requires:

(1) "Certificate of limited partnership" means the certificate referred to in Section 201, and the certificate as amended or restated.

(2) "Contribution" means any cash, property, services rendered, or a promissory note or other binding obligation to contribute cash or property or to perform services, which a partner contributes to a limited partnership in his capacity as a partner.

(3) "Event of withdrawal of a general partner" means an event that causes a person to cease to be a general partner as provided in Section 402.

(4) "Foreign limited partnership" means a partnership formed under the laws of any state other than this State and having as partners one or more general partners and one or more limited partners.

(5) "General partner" means a person who has been admitted to a limited partnership as a general partner in accordance with the partnership agreement and named in the certificate of limited partnership as a general partner.

(6) "Limited partner" means a person who has been admitted to a limited partnership as a limited partner in accordance with the partnership agreement.

(7) "Limited partnership" and "domestic limited partnership" mean a partnership formed by two or more persons under the laws of this State and having one or more general partners and one or more limited partners.

(8) "Partner" means a limited or general partner.

(9) "Partnership agreement" means any valid agreement, written or oral, of the partners as to the affairs of a limited partnership and the conduct of its business.

(10) "Partnership interest" means a partner's share of the profits and losses of a limited partnership and the right to receive distribution of partnership assets.

(11) "Person" means a natural person, partnership, limited partnership (domestic or foreign), trust, estate, association, or corporation.

(12) "State" means a state, territory, or possession of the United States, the District of Columbia, or the Commonwealth of Puerto Rico.

Section 102. Name

The name of each limited partnership as set forth in its certificate of limited partnership:

(1) shall contain without abbreviation the words "limited partnership";

(2) may not contain the name of a limited partner

---

[1] Source: National Conference of Commissioners on Uniform State Laws.

unless (i) it is also the name of a general partner or the corporate name of a corporate general partner, or (ii) the business of the limited partnership had been carried on under that name before the admission of that limited partner;

(3) may not be the same as, or deceptively similar to, the name of any corporation or limited partnership organized under the laws of this State or licensed or registered as a foreign corporation or limited partnership in this State; and

(4) may not contain the followng words [here insert prohibited words].

Section 103. Reservation of Name

(a) The exclusive right to the use of a name may be reserved by:

(1) any person intending to organize a limited partnership under this [Act] and to adopt that name;

(2) any domestic limited partnership or any foreign limited partnership registered in this State which, in either case, intends to adopt that name;

(3) any foreign limited partnership intending to register in this State and adopt that name; and

(4) any person intending to organize a foreign limited partnership and intending to have it register in this State and adopt that name.

(b) The reservation shall be made by filing with the Secretary of State an application, executed by the applicant, to reserve a specified name. If the Secretary of State finds that the name is available for use by a domestic or foreign limited partnership, he [or she] shall reserve the name for the exclusive use of the applicant for a period of 120 days. Once having so reserved a name, the same applicant may not again reserve the same name until more than 60 days after the expiration of the last 120-day period for which that applicant reserved that name. The right to the exclusive use of a reserved name may be transferred to any other person by filing in the office of the Secretary of State a notice of the transfer, executed by the applicant for whom the name was reserved and specifying the name and address of the transferee.

Section 104. Specified Office and Agent

Each limited partnership shall continuously maintain in this State:

(1) an office, which may but need not be a place of its business in this State, at which shall be kept the records required by Section 105 to be maintained; and

(2) an agent for service of process on the limited partnership, which agent must be an individual resident of this State, a domestic corporation, or a foreign corporation authorized to do business in this State.

Section 105. Records to Be Kept

(a) Each limited partnership shall keep at the office referred to in Section 104(1) the following:

(1) a current list of the full name and last known business address of each partner, separately identifying the general partners (in alphabetical order) and the limited partners (in alphabetical order);

(2) a copy of the certificate of limited partnership and all certificates of amendment thereto, together with executed copies of any powers of attorney pursuant to which any certificate has been executed;

(3) copies of the limited partnership's federal, state and local income tax returns and reports, if any, for the three most recent years;

(4) copies of any then effective written partnership agreements and of any financial statements of the limited partnership for the three most recent years; and

(5) unless contained in a written partnership agreement, a writing setting out:

(i) the amount of cash and a description and statement of the agreed value of the other property or services contributed by each partner and which each partner has agreed to contribute;

(ii) the times at which or events on the happening of which any additional contributions agreed to be made by each partner are to be made;

(iii) any right of a partner to receive, or of a general partner to make, distributions to a partner which include a return of all or any part of the partner's contribution; and

(iv) any events upon the happening of which the limited partnership is to be dissolved and its affairs wound up.

(b) Records kept under this section are subject to inspection and copying at the reasonable request and at the expense of any partner during ordinary business hours.

Section 106.   Nature of Business

A limited partnership may carry on any business that a partnership without limited partners may carry on except [here designate prohibited activities].

Section 107.   Business Transactions of Partner with Partnership

Except as provided in the partnership agreement, a partner may lend money to and transact other business with the limited partnership and, subject to other applicable law, has the same rights and obligations with respect thereto as a person who is not a partner.

ARTICLE 2

FORMATION; CERTIFICATE OF LIMITED PARTNERSHIP

Section 201.   Certificate of Limited Partnership

(a)   In order to form a limited partnership, a certificate of limited partnership must be executed and filed in the office of the Secretary of State. The certificate shall set forth:

(1)   the name of the limited partnership;

(2)   the address of the office and the name and address of the agent for service of process required to be maintained by Section 104;

(3)   the name and the business address of each general partner;

(4)   the latest date upon which the limited partnership is to dissolve; and

(5)   any other matters the general partners determine to include therein.

(b)   A limited partnership is formed at the time of the filing of the certificate of limited partnership in the office of the Secretary of State or at any later time specified in the certificate of limited partnership if, in either case, there has been substantial compliance with the requirements of this section.

Section 202.   Amendment to Certificate

(a)   A certificate of limited partnership is amended by filing a certificate of amendment thereto in the office

of the Secretary of State. The certificate shall set forth:

(1)   the name of the limited partnership;

(2)   the date of filing the certificate; and

(3)   the amendment to the certificate.

(b)   Within 30 days after the happening of any of the following events, an amendment to a certificate of limited partnership reflecting the occurrence of the event or events shall be filed:

(1)   the admission of a new general partner;

(2)   the withdrawal of a general partner; or

(3)   the continuation of the business under Section 801 after an event of withdrawal of a general partner.

(c)   A general partner who becomes aware that any statement in a certificate of limited partnership was false when made or that any arrangements or other facts described have changed, making the certificate inaccurate in any respect, shall promptly amend the certificate.

(d)   A certificate of limited partnership may be amended at any time for any other proper purpose the general partners determine.

(e)   No person has any liability because an amendment to a certificate of limited partnership has not been filed to reflect the occurrence of any event referred to in subsection (b) of this section if the amendment is filed within the 30-day period specified in subsection (b).

(f)   A restated certificate of limited partnership may be executed and filed in the same manner as a certificate of amendment.

Section 203.   Cancellation of Certificate

A certificate of limited partnership shall be cancelled upon the dissolution and the commencement of winding up of the partnership or at any other time there are no limited partners. A certificate of cancellation shall be filed in the office of the Secretary of State and set forth:

(1)   the name of the limited partnership;

(2)   the date of filing of its certificate of limited partnership;

(3)   the reason for filing the certificate of cancellation;

(4)   the effective date (which shall be a date certain) of

cancellation if it is not to be effective upon the filing of the certificate; and

(5)   any other information the general partners filing the certificate determine.

Section 204.   Execution of Certificates

(a)   Each certificate required by this Article to be filed in the office of the Secretary of State shall be executed in the following manner:

(1)   an original certificate of limited partnership must be signed by all general partners;

(2)   a certificate of amendment must be signed by at least one general partner and by each other general partner designated in the certificate as a new general partner; and

(3)   a certificate of cancellation must be signed by all general partners.

(b)   Any person may sign a certificate by an attorney-in-fact, but a power of attorney to sign a certificate relating to the admission of a general partner must specifically describe the admission.

(c)   The execution of a certificate by a general partner constitutes an affirmation under the penalties of perjury that the facts stated therein are true.

Section 205.   Execution by Judicial Act

If a person required by Section 204 to execute any certificate fails or refuses to do so, any other person who is adversely affected by the failure or refusal may petition the [designate the appropriate court] to direct the execution of the certificate. If the court finds that it is proper for the certificate to be executed and that any person so designated has failed or refused to execute the certificate, it shall order the Secretary of State to record an appropriate certificate.

Section 206.   Filing in Office of Secretary of State

(a)   Two signed copies of the certificate of limited partnership and of any certificates of amendment or cancellation (or of any judicial decree of amendment or cancellation) shall be delivered to the Secretary of State. A person who executes a certificate as an agent of fiduciary need not exhibit evidence of his [or her] authority as a prerequisite to filing. Unless the Secretary of State finds that any certificate does not conform to law, upon receipt of all filing fees required by law he [or she] shall:

(1)   endorse on each duplicate original the word

"Filed" and the day, month and year of the filing thereof;

(2)   file one duplicate original in his [or her] office; and

(3)   return the other duplicate original to the person who filed it or his [or her] representative.

(b)   Upon the filing of a certificate of amendment (or judicial decree of amendment) in the office of the Secretary of State, the certificate of limited partnership shall be amended as set forth therein, and upon the effective date of a certificate of cancellation (or a judicial decree thereof), the certificate of limited partnership is cancelled.

Section 207.   Liability for False Statement in Certificate

If any certificate of limited partnership or certificate of amendment or cancellation contains a false statement, one who suffers loss by reliance on the statement may recover damages for the loss from:

(1)   any person who executes the certificate, or causes another to execute it on his behalf, and knew, and any general partner who knew or should have known, the statement to be false at the time the certificate was executed; and

(2)   any general partner who thereafter knows or should have known that any arrangement or other fact described in the certificate has changed, making the statement inaccurate in any respect within a sufficient time before the statement was relied upon reasonably to have enabled that general partner to cancel or amend the certificate, or to file a petition for its cancellation or amendment under Section 205.

Section 208.   Scope of Notice

The fact that a certificate of limited partnership is on file in the office of the Secretary of State is notice that the partnership is a limited partnership and the persons designated therein as general partners are general partners, but it is not notice of any other fact.

Section 209.   Delivery of Certificates to Limited Partners

Upon the return by the Secretary of State pursuant to Section 206 of a certificate marked "Filed," the general partners shall promptly deliver or mail a copy of the certificate of limited partnership and each certificate of amendment or cancellation to each limited partner unless the partnership agreement provides otherwise.

ARTICLE 3

LIMITED PARTNERS

Section 301.   Admission of Limited Partners

(a)   A person becomes a limited partner:

   (1)   at the time the limited partnership is formed; or

   (2)   at any later time specified in the records of the limited partnership for becoming a limited partner.

(b)   After the filing of a limited partnership's original certificate of limited partnership, a person may be admitted as an additional limited partner:

   (1)   in the case of a person acquiring a partnership interest directly from the limited partnership, upon compliance with the partnership agreement or, if the partnership agreement does not so provide, upon the written consent of all partners; and

   (2)   in the case of an assignee of a partnership interest of a partner who has the power, as provided in Section 704, to grant the assignee the right to become a limited partner, upon the exercise of that power and compliance with any conditions limiting the grant or exercise of the power.

Section 302.   Voting

Subject to Section 303, the partnership agreement may grant to all or a specified group of the limited partners the right to vote (on a per capita or other basis) upon any matter.

Section 303.   Liability to Third Parties

(a)   Except as provided in subsection (d), a limited partner is not liable for the obligations of a limited partnership unless he [or she] is also a general partner or, in addition to the exercise of his [or her] rights and powers as a limited partner, he [or she] participates in the control of the business. However, if the limited partner participates in the control of the business, he [or she] is liable only to persons who transact business with the limited partnership reasonably believing, based upon the limited partner's conduct, that the limited partner is a general partner.

(b)   A limited partner does not participate in the control of the business within the meaning of subsection (a) solely by doing one or more of the following:

   (1)   being a contractor for or an agent or employee of the limited partnership or of a general partner or being an officer, director, or shareholder of a general partner that is a corporation;

   (2)   consulting with and advising a general partner with respect to the business of the limited partnership;

   (3)   acting as surety for the limited partnership or guaranteeing or assuming one or more specific obligations of the limited partnership;

   (4)   taking any action required or permitted by law to bring or pursue a derivative action in the right of the limited partnership;

   (5)   requesting or attending a meeting of partners;

   (6)   proposing, approving, or disapproving, by voting or otherwise, one or more of the following matters:

      (i)   the dissolution and winding up of the limited partnership;

      (ii)   the sale, exchange, lease, mortgage, pledge, or other transfer of all or substantially all of the assets of the limited partnership;

      (iii) the incurrence of indebtedness by the limited partnership other than in the ordinary course of its business;

      (iv)   a change in the nature of the business;

      (v)   the admission or removal of a general partner;

      (vi)   the admission or removal of a limited partner;

      (vii) a transaction involving an actual or potential conflict of interest between a general partner and the limited partnership or the limited partners;

      (viii) an amendment to the partnership agreement or certificate of limited partnership; or

      (ix)   matters related to the business of the limited partnership not otherwise enumerated in this subsection (b), which the partnership agreement states in writing may be subject to the approval or disapproval of limited partners;

   (7)   winding up the limited partnership pursuant to Section 804; or

(8) exercising any right or power permitted to limited partners under this [Act] and not specifically enumerated in this subsection (b).

(c) The enumeration in subsection (b) does not mean that the possession or exercise of any other powers by a limited partner constitutes participation by him [or her] in the business of the limited partnership.

(d) A limited partner who knowingly permits his [or her] name to be used in the name of the limited partnership, except under circumstances permitted by Section 102(2), is liable to creditors who extend credit to the limited partnership without actual knowledge that the limited partner is not a general partner.

Section 304.   Person Erroneously Believing Himself [or Herself] Limited Partner

(a) Except as provided in subsection (b), a person who makes a contribution to a business enterprise and erroneously but in good faith believes that he [or she] has become a limited partner in the enterprise is not a general partner in the enterprise and is not bound by its obligations by reason of making the contribution, receiving distributions from the enterprise, or exercising any rights of a limited partner, if, on ascertaining the mistake, he [or she];

(1) causes an appropriate certificate of limited partnership or a certificate of amendment to be executed and filed; or

(2) withdraws from future equity participation in the enterprise by executing and filing in the office of the Secretary of State a certificate declaring withdrawal under this section.

(b) A person who makes a contribution of the kind described in subsection (a) is liable as a general partner to any third party who transacts business with the enterprise (i) before the person withdraws and an appropriate certificate is filed to show withdrawal, or (ii) before an appropriate certificate is filed to show that he [or she] is not a general partner, but in either case only if the third party actually believed in good faith that the person was a general partner at the time of the transaction.

Section 305.   Information

Each limited partner has the right to:

(1) inspect and copy any of the partnership records required to be maintained by Section 105; and

(2) obtain from the general partners from time to time

upon reasonable demand (i) true and full information regarding the state of the business and financial condition of the limited partnership, (ii) promptly after becoming available, a copy of the limited partnership's federal, state and local income tax returns for each year, and (iii) other information regarding the affairs of the limited partnership as is just and reasonable.

ARTICLE 4

GENERAL PARTNERS

Section 401.   Admission of Additional General Partners

After the filing of a limited partnership's original certificate of limited partnership, additional general partners may be admitted as provided in writing in the partnership agreement or, if the partnership agreement does not provide in writing for the admission of additional general partners, with the written consent of all partners.

Section 402.   Events of Withdrawal

Except as approved by the specific written consent of all partners at the time, a person ceases to be a general partner of a limited partnership upon the happening of any of the following events:

(1) the general partner withdraws from the limited partnership as provided in Section 602;

(2) the general partner ceases to be a member of the limited partnership as provided in Section 702;

(3) the general partner is removed as a general partner in accordance with the partnership agreement;

(4) unless otherwise provided in writing in the partnership agreement, the general partner: (i) makes an assignment for the benefit of creditors; (ii) files a voluntary petition in bankruptcy; (iii) is adjudicated a bankrupt or insolvent; (iv) files a petition or answer seeking for himself [or herself] any reorganization, arrangement, composition, readjustment, liquidation, dissolution or similar relief under any statute, law, or regulation; (v) files an answer or other pleading admitting or failing to contest the material allegations of a petition filed against him [or her] in any proceeding of this nature; or (vi) seeks, consents to, or acquiesces in the appointment of a trustee, receiver, or liquidator of the general partner or of all or any substantial part of his [or her] properties;

(5) unless otherwise provided in writing in the partnership agreement, [120] days after the commencement of any proceeding against the general partner seeking reorganization, arrangement, composition, readjustment, liquidation, dissolution or similar relief under any statute, law, or regulation, the proceeding has not been dismissed, or if within [90] days after the appointment without his [or her] consent or acquiescence of a trustee, receiver, or liquidator of the general partner or of all or any substantial part of his [or her] properties, the appointment is not vacated or stayed or within [90] days after the expiration of any such stay, the appointment is not vacated;

(6) in the case of a general partner who is a natural person,

(i) his [or her] death; or

(ii) the entry of an order by a court of competent jurisdiction adjudicating him [or her] incompetent to manage his [or her] person or his [or her] estate;

(7) in the case of a general partner who is acting as a general partner by virtue of being a trustee of a trust, the termination of the trust (but not merely the substitution of a new trustee);

(8) in the case of a general partner that is a separate partnership, the dissolution and commencement of winding up of the separate partnership;

(9) in the case of a general partner that is a corporation, the filing of a certificate of dissolution, or its equivalent, for the corporation or the revocation of its charter; or

(10) in the case of an estate, the distribution by the fiduciary of the estate's entire interest in the partnership.

Section 403. General Powers and Liabilities

(a) Except as provided in this [Act] or in the partnership agreement, a general partner of a limited partnership has the rights and powers and is subject to the restrictions of a partner in a partnership without limited partners.

(b) Except as provided in this [Act], a general partner of a limited partnership has the liabilities of a partner in a partnership without limited partners to persons other than the partnership and the other partners. Except as provided in this [Act] or in the partnership agreement, a general partner of a limited partnership has the liabilities of a partner in a partnership without limited partners to the partnership and to the other partners.

Section 404. Contributions by General Partner

A general partner of a limited partnership may make contributions to the partnership and share in the profits and losses of, and in distributions from, the limited partnership as a general partner. A general partner also may make contributions to and share in profits, losses, and distributions as a limited partner. A person who is both a general partner and a limited partner has the rights and powers, and is subject to the restrictions and liabilities, of a general partner and, except as provided in the partnership agreement, also has the powers, and is subject to the restrictions, of a limited partner to the extent of his [or her] participation in the partnership as a limited partner.

Section 405. Voting

The partnership agreement may grant to all or certain identified general partners the right to vote (on a per capita or any other basis), separately or with all or any class of the limited partners, on any matter.

ARTICLE 5

FINANCE

Section 501. Form of Contribution

The contribution of a partner may be in cash, property, or services rendered, or a promissory note or other obligation to contribute cash or property or to perform services.

Section 502. Liability for Contribution

(a) A promise by a limited partner to contribute to the limited partnership is not enforceable unless set out in a writing signed by the limited partner.

(b) Except as provided in the partnership agreement, a partner is obligated to the limited partnership to perform any enforceable promise to contribute cash or property or to perform services, even if he [or she] is unable to perform because of death, disability, or any other reason. If a partner does not make the required contribution of property or services, he [or she] is obligated at the option of the limited partnership to contribute cash equal to that portion of the value, as stated in the partnership records required to be kept pursuant to Section 105, of the stated contribution which has not been made.

(c) Unless otherwise provided in the partnership agreement, the obligation of a partner to make a contribution or return money or other property paid or distributed in violation of this [Act] may be compromised only by consent of all partners. Notwithstanding the compromise, a creditor of a limited partnership who extends credit or otherwise acts in reliance on that obligation after the partner signs a writing which reflects the obligation and before the amendment or cancellation thereof to reflect the compromise may enforce the original obligation.

Section 503.   Sharing of Profits and Losses

The profits and losses of a limited partnership shall be allocated among the partners, and among classes of partners, in the manner provided in writing in the partnership agreement. If the partnership agreement does not so provide in writing, profits and losses shall be allocated on the basis of the value, as stated in the partnership records required to be kept pursuant to Section 105, of the contributions made by each partner to the extent they have been received by the partnership and have not been returned.

Section 504.   Sharing of Distributions

Distributions of cash or other assets of a limited partnership shall be allocated among the partners and among classes of partners in the manner provided in writing in the partnership agreement. If the partnership agreement does not so provide in writing, distributions shall be made on the basis of the value, as stated in the partnership records required to be kept pursuant to Section 105, of the contributions made by each partner to the extent they have been received by the partnership and have not been returned.

ARTICLE 6

DISTRIBUTIONS AND WITHDRAWAL

Section 601.   Interim Distributions

Except as provided in this Article, a partner is entitled to receive distributions from a limited partnership before his [or her] withdrawal from the limited partnership and before the dissolution and winding up thereof to the extent and at the times or upon the happening of the events specified in the partnership agreement.

Section 602.   Withdrawal of General Partner

A general partner may withdraw from a limited partnership at any time by giving written notice to the other partners, but if the withdrawal violates the part-

nership agreement, the limited partnership may recover from the withdrawing general partner damages for breach of the partnership agreement and offset the damages against the amount otherwise distributable to him [or her].

Section 603.   Withdrawal of Limited Partner

A limited partner may withdraw from a limited partnership at the time or upon the happening of events specified in writing in the partnership agreement. If the agreement does not specify in writing the time or the events upon the happening of which a limited partner may withdraw or a definite time for the dissolution and winding up of the limited partnership, a limited partner may withdraw upon not less than six months' prior written notice to each general partner at his [or her] address on the books of the limited partnership at its office in this State.

Section 604.   Distribution upon Withdrawal

Except as provided in this Article, upon withdrawal any withdrawing partner is entitled to receive any distribution to which he [or she] is entitled under the partnership agreement and, if not otherwise provided in the agreement, he [or she] is entitled to receive, within a reasonable time after withdrawal, the fair value of his [or her] interest in the limited partnership as of the date of withdrawal based upon his [or her] right to share in distributions from the limited partnership.

Section 605.   Distribution in Kind

Except as provided in writing in the partnership agreement, a partner, regardless of the nature of his [or her] contribution, has no right to demand and receive any distribution from a limited partnership in any form other than cash. Except as provided in writing in the partnership agreement, a partner may not be compelled to accept a distribution of any asset in kind from a limited partnership to the extent that the percentage of the asset distributed to him [or her] exceeds a percentage of that asset which is equal to the percentage in which he [or she] shares in distributions from the limited partnership.

Section 606.   Right to Distribution

At the time a partner becomes entitled to receive a distribution, he [or she] has the status of, and is entitled to all remedies available to, a creditor of the limited partnership with respect to the distribution.

Section 607.   Limitations on Distribution

A partner may not receive a distribution from a limited partnership to the extent that, after giving effect to the distribution, all liabilities of the limited partnershp, other than liabilities to partners on account of their partnership interests, exceed the fair value of the partnership assets.

Section 608.   Liability upon Return of Contribution

(a) If a partner has received the return of any part of his [or her] contribution without violation of the partnership agreement or this [Act], he [or she] is liable to the limited partnership for a period of one year thereafter for the amount of the returned contribution, but only to the extent necessary to discharge the limited partnership's liabilities to creditors who extended credit to the limited partnership during the period the contribution was held by the partnership.

(b) If a partner has received the return of any part of his [or her] contribution in violation of the partnership agreement or this [Act], he [or she] is liable to the limited partnership for a period of six years thereafter for the amount of the contribution wrongfully returned.

(c) A partner receives a return of his [or her] contribution to the extent that a distribution to him [or her] reduces his [or her] share of the fair value of the net assets of the limited partnership below the value, as set forth in the partnership records required to be kept pursuant to Section 105, of his contribution which has not been distributed to him [or her].

ARTICLE 7

ASSIGNMENT OF PARTNERSHIP INTERESTS

Section 701.   Nature of Partnership Interest

A partnership interest is personal property.

Section 702.   Assignment of Partnership Interest

Except as provided in the partnership agreement, a partnership interest is assignable in whole or in part. An assignment of a partnership interest does not dissolve a limited partnership or entitle the assignee to become or to exercise any rights of a partner. An assignment entitles the assignee to receive, to the extent assigned, only the distribution to which the assignor would be entitled. Except as provided in the partnership agreement, a partner ceases to be a partner upon assignment of all his [or her] partnership interest.

Section 703.   Rights of Creditor

On application to a court of competent jurisdiction by any judgment creditor of a partner, the court may charge the partnership interest of the partner with payment of the unsatisfied amount of the judgment with interest. To the extent so charged, the judgment creditor has only the rights of an assignee of the partnership interest. This [Act] does not deprive any partner of the benefit of any exemption laws applicable to his [or her] partnership interest.

Section 704.   Right of Assignee to Become Limited Partner

(a) An assignee of a partnership interest, including an assignee of a general partner, may become a limited partner if and to the extent that (i) the assignor gives the assignee that right in accordance with authority described in the partnership agreement, or (ii) all other partners consent.

(b) An assignee who has become a limited partner has, to the extent assigned, the rights and powers, and is subject to the restrictions and liabilities, of a limited partner under the partnership agreement and this [Act]. An assignee who becomes a limited partner also is liable for the obligations of his [or her] assignor to make and return contributions as provided in Articles 5 and 6. However, the assignee is not obligated for liabilities unknown to the assignee at the time he [or she] became a limited partner.

(c) If an assignee of a partnership interest becomes a limited partner, the assignor is not released from his [or her] liability to the limited partnership under Sections 207 and 502.

Section 705.   Power of Estate of Deceased or Incompetent Partner

If a partner who is an individual dies or a court of competent jurisdiction adjudges him [or her] to be incompetent to manage his [or her] person or his [or her] property, the partner's executor, administrator, guardian, conservator, or other legal representative may exercise all the partner's rights for the purpose of settling his [or her] estate or administering his [or her] property, including any power the partner had to give an assignee the right to become a limited partner. If a partner is a corporation, trust, or other entity and is dissolved or terminated, the powers of that partner may be exercised by its legal representative or successor.

ARTICLE 8

DISSOLUTION

Section 801.   Nonjudicial Dissolution

A limited partnership is dissolved and its affairs shall be wound up upon the happening of the first to occur of the following:

(1)   at the time specified in the certificate of limited partnership;

(2)   upon the happening of events specified in writing in the partnership agreement;

(3)   written consent of all partners;

(4)   an event of withdrawal of a general partner unless at the time there is at least one other general partner and the written provisions of the partnership agreement permit the business of the limited partnership to be carried on by the remaining general partner and that partner does so, but the limited partnership is not dissolved and is not required to be wound up by reason of any event of withdrawal if, within 90 days after the withdrawal, all partners agree in writing to continue the business of the limited partnership and to the appointment of one or more additional general partners if necessary or desired; or

(5)   entry of a decree of judicial dissolution under Section 802.

Section 802.   Judicial Dissolution

On application by or for a partner the [designate the appropriate court] court may decree dissolution of a limited partnership whenever it is not reasonably practicable to carry on the business in conformity with the partnership agreement.

Section 803.   Winding Up

Except as provided in the partnership agreement, the general partners who have not wrongfully dissolved a limited partnership or, if none, the limited partners, may wind up the limited partnership's affairs; but the [designate the appropriate court] court may wind up the limited partnership's affairs upon application of any partner, his [or her] legal representative, or assignee.

Section 804.   Distribution of Assets

Upon the winding up of a limited partnership, the assets shall be distributed as follows:

(1)   to creditors, including partners who are creditors, to the extent permitted by law, in satisfaction of liabilities of the limited partnership other than liabilities for distributions to partners under Section 601 or 604;

(2)   except as provided in the partnership agreement, to partners and former partners in satisfaction of liabilities for distributions under Section 601 or 604; and

(3)   except as provided in the partnership agreement, to partners first for the return of their contributions and secondly respecting their partnership interests, in the proportions in which the partners share in distributions.

ARTICLE 9

FOREIGN LIMITED PARTNERSHIPS

Section 901.   Law Governing

Subject to the Constitution of this State, (i) the laws of the state under which a foreign limited partnership is organized govern its organization and internal affairs and the liability of its limited partners, and (ii) a foreign limited partnership may not be denied registration by reason of any difference between those laws and the laws of this State.

Section 902.   Registration

Before transacting business in this State, a foreign limited partnership shall register with the Secretary of State. In order to register, a foreign limited partnership shall submit to the Secretary of State, in duplicate, an application for registration as a foreign limited partnership, signed and sworn to be a general partner and setting forth:

(1)   the name of the foreign limited partnership and, if different, the name under which it proposes to register and transact business in this State;

(2)   the State and date of its formation;

(3)   the name and address of any agent for service of process on the foreign limited partnership whom the foreign limited partnership elects to appoint; the agent must be an individual resident of this State, a domestic corporation, or a foreign corporation having a place of business in, and authorized to do business in, this State;

(4) a statement that the Secretary of State is appointed the agent of the foreign limited partnership for service of process if no agent has been appointed under paragraph (3) or, if appointed, the agent's authority has been revoked or if the agent cannot be found or served with the exercise of reasonable diligence;

(5) the address of the office required to be maintained in the state of its organization by the laws of that state or, if not so required, of the principal office of the foreign limited partnership;

(6) the name and business address of each general partner; and

(7) the address of the office at which is kept a list of the names and addresses of the limited partners and their capital contributions, together with an undertaking by the foreign limited partnership to keep those records until the foreign limited partnership's registration in this State is cancelled or withdrawn.

Section 903. Issuance of Registration

(a) If the Secretary of State finds that an application for registration conforms to law and all requisite fees have been paid, he [or she] shall:

(1) endorse on the application the word "Filed," and the month, day and year of the filing thereof;

(2) file in his [or her] office a duplicate original of the application; and

(3) issue a certificate of registration to transact business in this State.

(b) The certificate of registration, together with a duplicate original of the application, shall be returned to the person who filed the application or his [or her] representative.

Section 904. Name

A foreign limited partnership may register with the Secretary of State under any name, whether or not it is the name under which it is registered in its state of organization, that includes without abbreviation the words "limited partnership" and that could be registered by a domestic limited partnership.

Section 905. Changes and Amendments

If any statement in the application for registration of a foreign limited partnership was false when made or any arrangements or other facts described have changed, making the application inaccurate in any respect, the foreign limited partnership shall promptly file in the office of the Secretary of State a certificate, signed and sworn to by a general partner, correcting such statement.

Section 906. Cancellation of Registration

A foreign limited partnership may cancel its registration by filing with the Secretary of State a certificate of cancellation signed and sworn by a general partner. A cancellation does not terminate the authority of the Secretary of State to accept service of process on the foreign limited partnership with respect to [claims for relief] [causes of action] arising out of the transactions of business in this State.

Section 907. Transaction of Business Without Registration

(a) A foreign limited partnership transacting business in this State may not maintain any action, suit, or proceeding in any court of this State until it has registered in this State.

(b) The failure of a foreign limited partnership to register in this State does not impair the validity of any contract or act of the foreign limited partnership or prevent the foreign limited partnership from defending any action, suit, or proceeding in any court of this State.

(c) A limited partner of a foreign limited partnership is not liable as a general partner of the foreign limited partnership solely by reason of having transacted business in this State without registration.

(d) A foreign limited partnership, by transacting business in this State without registration, appoints the Secretary of State as its agent for service of process with respect to [claims for relief] [causes of action] arising out of the transaction of business in this State.

Section 908. Action by [Appropriate Official]

The [designate the appropriate official] may bring an action to restrain a foreign limited partnership from transacting business in this State in violation of this Article.

ARTICLE 10

DERIVATIVE ACTIONS

Section 1001. Right of Action

A limited partner may bring an action in the right of a limited partnership to recover a judgment in its favor if general partners with authority to do so have refused to bring the action or if an effort to cause those general partners to bring the action is not likely to succeed.

Section 1002.   Proper Plaintiff

In a derivative action, the plaintiff must be a partner at the time of bringing the action and (i) must have been a partner at the time of the transaction of which he [or she] complains or (ii) his [or her] status as a partner must have devolved upon him [or her] by operation of law or pursuant to the terms of the partnership agreement from a person who was a partner at the time of the transaction.

Section 1003.   Pleading

In a derivative action, the complaint shall set forth with particularity the effort of the plaintiff to secure initiation of the action by a general partner or the reasons for not making the effort.

Section 1004.   Expenses

If a derivative action is successful, in whole or in part, or if anything is received by the plaintiff as a result of a judgment, compromise or settlement of an action or claim, the court may award the plaintiff reasonable expenses, including reasonable attorney's fees, and shall direct him [or her] to remit to the limited partnership the remainder of those proceeds received by him [or her].

ARTICLE 11

MISCELLANEOUS

Section 1101.   Construction and Application

This [Act] shall be so applied and construed to effectuate its general purpose to make uniform the law with respect to the subject of this [Act] among states enacting it.

Section 1102.   Short Title

This [Act] may be cited as the Uniform Limited Partnership Act.

Section 1103.   Severability

If any provision of this [Act] or its application to any person or circumstance is held invalid, the invalidity does not affect other provisions or applications of the [Act] which can be given effect without the invalid provision or application, and to this end the provisions of this Act are severable.

Section 1104.   Effective Date, Extended Effective Date, and Repeal

Except as set forth below, the effective date of this [Act] is _____ and the following acts [list existing limited partnership acts] are hereby repealed:

(1) The existing provisions for execution and filing of certificates of limited partnerships and amendments thereunder and cancellations thereof continue in effect until [specify time required to create central filing system], the extended effective date, and Sections 102, 103, 104, 105, 201, 202, 203, 204 and 206 are not effective until the extended effective date.

(2) Section 402, specifying the conditions under which a general partner ceases to be a member of a limited partnership, is not effective until the extended effective date, and the applicable provisions of existing law continue to govern until the extended effective date.

(3) Sections 501, 502 and 608 apply only to contributions and distributions made after the effective date of this [Act].

(4) Section 704 applies only to assignments made after the effective date of this [Act].

(5) Article 9, dealing with registration of foreign limited partnerships, is not effective until the extended effective date.

(6) Unless otherwise agreed by the partners, the applicable provisions of existing law governing allocation of profits and losses (rather than the provisions of Section 503), distributions to a withdrawing partner (rather than the provisions of Section 604), and distribution of assets upon the winding up of a limited partnership (rather than the provisions of Section 804) govern limited partnerships formed before the effective date of this [Act].

Section 1105.   Rules for Cases Not Provided for in This [Act]

In any case not provided for in this [Act] the provisions of the Uniform Partnership Act govern.

Section 1106.   Savings Clause

The repeal of any statutory provision by this Act does not impair, or otherwise affect, the organization or the continued existence of a limited partnership existing at the effective date of this Act, nor does the repeal of any existing statutory provision by this Act impair any contract or affect any right accrued before the effective date of this Act.

Glossary

A

Abandoned property Property that the owner has discarded with no intention of ever again reclaiming any rights or interests in it.

Abet To assist or support in the performance of an act or the attainment of a purpose.

Acceleration clause A clause in a contract that advances the date for payment on the occurrence of a condition or the breach of a duty.

Acceleration of payment The speeding up of the due date for payment for a contract or for a commercial instrument.

Accept To agree to, as in an offer.

Acceptance Compliance with the terms of an offer; the action of a buyer in taking the goods tendered by a seller; the act whereby a drawee agrees to honor a negotiable instrument upon due presentment.

Acceptor A person who accepts a negotiable instrument or otherwise agrees to be primarily liable for the instrument.

Accession The acquisition of additional property due to the growth or increase of property already possessed.

Accommodation party A party who signs a commercial paper for the purpose of lending his or her name to another party to the instrument.

Accord An agreement between two or more parties on the degree of performance that will operate as a full discharge of an obligation.

Accord and satisfaction The making of a new agreement between two or more parties and the performance of that agreement by the parties (normally used in the area of disputed claims).

Account To furnish a justifying explanation or analysis for monies spent or actions taken.

Accretion An addition by growing, especially in the area of real property, where land increases by natural actions and causes.

Actionable Affording grounds for an action, such as a suit at law.

Actual cause The act that brings about some end result.

Actual fraud See **Fraud.**

Adhesion A firm attachment; a sticking together. When used in reference to a contract, it means a contract whose terms are not open to negotiation — the offeree must "take it or leave it."

Adjudicate To determine through a judicial proceeding.

Adjunct Added or joined to another.

Administrative law The branch of public law that deals with administrative agencies and their actions.

The definitions given here are accurate as far as they go, but space limitations prevent complete technical definitions. A student who wants a more detailed definition is advised to consult a legal dictionary such as *Black's Law Dictionary* or *Ballantine's Law Dictionary.*

Administrator (administratrix) A man (woman) who has been empowered by an appropriate court to handle the estate of a deceased person; a manager of the affairs of another person, in the name of the person so managed.

Admission Agreement or concession concerning evidence or pleadings without the need to introduce proof.

Adverse possession A method for gaining title to property by possession/occupancy for a predetermined statutory period. Adverse possession requires that the possessor occupy the property openly, notoriously, hostilely, and continuously for a period specified by state statute.

Advisory opinion A formal opinion issued by a court at the request of a legislative body or of a government officer concerning a hypothetical fact situation.

Affidavit A written, sworn statement declaring the facts contained in the statement to be true.

Affirmative defense A defense to a cause of action that must be raised by the defendant.

After-acquired property Property gained or possessed following a certain date or event; that which is attained later.

Agency A legal relationship in which one person is empowered and authorized to represent another, normally in the formation of contracts.

Agent A person authorized to act for or on behalf of another in the formation of contracts.

Aid To assist; to provide a person with things necessary to the attainment of a desired end.

Alien Foreign; owing allegiance to another government.

Alleged Asserted to be true or factual without any showing of proof.

Allonge A piece of paper permanently attached to a negotiable instrument to accommodate additional endorsements when the original instrument has no more room for endorsements.

Alluvion An increase in land by the gradual deposit of substances from the flow of water against the shore. The land so added becomes the property of the owner of the land where the new substances are deposited.

Ambiguity Doubtful meaning or uncertainty due to obscurity or lack of distinctness.

Amortize To provide for the gradual extinction of a debt or obligation by periodic contributions to a sinking fund or similar device.

Annuitant The beneficiary of an annuity.

Annuity A sum of money payable periodically, commonly annually, to a named person; the contract that creates the obligation to pay the annuitant the periodic payments.

Answer Any sort of pleading filed by the defendant in a cause of action, but especially the written statement that sets forth the defenses asserted.

Antedated Predated; given an earlier date than the date on which the event occurred (normally used with reference to a negotiable instrument).

Anticipatory breach A refusal or rejection by one party to a contract before the time for performance that permits the other party to treat the repudiation as an immediate breach of the contract. Also known as *anticipatory repudiation*.

Antitrust laws Legislation opposed to the formation or use of trusts or combinations; statutes designed to protect commerce from unfair trade practices or monopolies.

Apparent authority Authority that the agent appears to possess because of the conduct of the principal and on which the third person relies as being authorized; authority that the agent does not in fact possess but that the third person has been caused to believe does exist.

Appellant A party who takes an appeal from one court to another.

Appellate court A court that has the authority to review the action of inferior courts upon proper appeal or writ; a reviewing court.

Appellee The party in a case against whom an appeal has been taken.

Appraisal right The right in certain extraordinary corporate activities to have a security evaluated and the appraised value paid to the owner.

Appurtenant Belonging to; annexed to; adjoining and necessary to the enjoyment of.

Arbitration A nonjudicial settlement of a case or controversy whereby the parties submit the issues to an independent person chosen by the parties or appointed by statutory authority.

Arraignment The calling of a defendant before the court to answer to a charge of having committed a crime.

Arson At common law, the intentional burning of the house or outbuilding of another person. Today, a number of state statutes also include as arson the malicious burning of one's own house or outbuildings.

Articles of incorporation The legal document that must be filed with a designated state official in order to do business as a corporation. The articles must comply with state statutes and must be approved by the state before the corporation legally exists.

Assault An intentional threat to harm another by use of force, together with the apparent means to accomplish the threat, which causes fear that the harm will occur.

Assignee The grantee, or recipient, of an assignment.

Assignment The legal transfer to another of one's rights under a contract.

Assignment for the benefit of creditors An assignment by a debtor of the debtor's assets to a trustee to be used in the satisfaction of the claims of creditors.

Assignor A person who makes an assignment.

Association A voluntary joining together of two or more persons to achieve a common goal.

Assumption of the risk A legal defense to a tort action in which the plaintiff is said to have voluntarily chosen to face the risk or danger that occurred and therefore has no right to complain of its occurrence.

Assurance A guaranty; a promise; a statement that inspires confidence that the assured thing will occur.

Attach To seize property in order to bring it within the jurisdiction of the court.

Attachment The act of attaching; a writ or judicial order directing the taking of persons or property in order to assure jurisdiction by the court.

At will Without a set time period; for as long as is mutually agreeable.

Auction A public sale in which the property being sold goes to the highest bidder.

Avoid To cancel an obligation or duty.

Avulsion The removal of land from the property of one person and the addition of that land to the property of another person by the action of water.

Award The decision entered by an arbitrator or other nonjudicial person in the matter submitted for resolution.

B

Bail Security given for the appearance of a defendant/prisoner in order to secure a release from imprisonment pending the trial.

Bailee The person to whom property is delivered in a bailment, with the understanding that that person will return the property at a later time or will dispose of it according to the directions of the bailor.

Bailment A delivery of goods from one party to another in trust, with no transfer of title occurring.

Bailor The person who delivers the property involved in a bailment to the bailee. A bailor does not need to be the owner of the bailed goods in order to create a valid bailment.

Bankruptcy An area of law designed to give an "honest debtor" a fresh start; the proceedings undertaken against a person or a firm under the bankruptcy laws.

Bar The complete and permanent destruction of an action at law; also, the entire body of attorneys permitted to practice law in a particular jurisdiction.

Bargain (Noun) an agreement between parties that specifies what each is to receive and what each is to perform or deliver. (Verb) to come to terms.

Battery The unauthorized touching of the person of another without legal excuse or the consent of the person so touched.

Beneficiary A person for whom a trust is created; a person designated to receive the proceeds of an insurance policy; a person who receives advantages or profits from another.

Benefit An advantage, profit, or gain; a legal right received from another.

Beyond a reasonable doubt A standard of proof required in criminal proceedings, meaning proof to a moral certainty, proof that is entirely convincing, proof not subject to any other *reasonable* interpretation.

Bilateral Two-sided; reciprocal.

Bilateral contract A contract formed by the exchange of promises by the two parties to the contract; a promise in exchange for a promise.

Binder A temporary contract to provide insurance coverage pending the processing of an application and the issuance of a formal policy.

Blank endorsement A type of endorsement in which the endorser merely writes his or her name without designating the next holder and leaving the instrument payable to bearer.

Board of directors The managers of a corporation; the official governing body of a private corporation elected by the stockholders at the annual meeting of the stockholders.

Bona fide In good faith; honestly; without deceit; innocently.

Bona fide occupational qualification (BFOQ) A legally justifiable limitation concerning the ability to perform a particular job.

Bona fide purchaser A person who purchases in good faith, for value, and without notice of any defects or defenses affecting the sale or transaction.

Bond A written evidence of indebtedness, usually bearing interest, issued by a public or private corporation, and payable at a fixed future date.

Book value The value of a business, arrived at by deducting liabilities from assets.

Boycott A concerted refusal to have any dealings with a person or a firm; a conspiracy to disrupt the business of a person or firm.

Breach The breaking of a duty or right, whether by act or omission; the failure to honor a promise, or any part of a promise, that forms the basis of a contract.

Bribe Anything of value given or accepted with the corrupt intention of influencing a person in the performance of a public duty or the carrying out of any official actions.

Bulk sale The sale of all or a substantial part of a merchant's stock in trade not made in the ordinary course of business. Also known as *bulk transfer*.

Burden of proof The legal duty to prove the truth of facts in dispute in a cause of action in order to prevail in the cause; the amount of proof necessary to carry one's case, such as "beyond a reasonable doubt," or "clear and convincing evidence."

Burglary The crime of breaking into a building with an intent to steal; at common law, the act of breaking into a dwelling at night with an intent to commit a felony.

Buyer in the ordinary course of business A purchaser who buys goods or services from a merchant seller in a standard (as opposed to an extraordinary) transaction.

Bylaws The rules and regulations adopted by a corporation or other association for the purpose of self-regulation, especially of day-to-day matters not covered by other documents.

C

Cancel To delete or annul; to strike out or obliterate; to revoke.

Cancellation Any action shown on the face of a contract that indicates an intent to destroy the obligation of the contract.

Capacity Legal ability to perform an act or to assume an obligation; legal measurement of power, competence, or ability.

Capital contribution The money invested in a business venture by the owners in return for their shares of ownership; the value of any assets invested in a business venture in lieu of money.

Carrier See **Common carrier**.

Cases and controversies Judicial proceedings between parties involving an actual fact situation on justiciable issues, and excluding advisory opinions or hypothetical situations.

Cash Money; legal tender; official currency.

Cashier's check A check that is issued by a bank and drawn against the bank's own funds and that is accepted upon issue.

Cash value The actual market value a thing is worth in a private sale for cash, with no portion of the payment deferred.

Causa mortis In contemplation of death (normally used in reference to a gift made by the donor because of the donor's expectation of death).

Caveat emptor Literally, let the buyer beware, meaning that the buyer needs to exercise caution since he or she assumes any and all risks in the transaction.

Caveat venditor Literally, let the seller beware, meaning that the seller is responsible for any and all defects or deficiencies in the goods being sold.

Certification The act of certifying something, such as a check, in order to guarantee the signature and the amount appearing on its face.

Certiorari Literally, to be made informed of; the name of a writ issued by a court in order to review the action of an inferior court in a proceeding.

Charging order A court order that allows a judgment creditor to receive the profits otherwise owed to the debtor from the operation of a business in which the debtor has an interest, especially the profits of a partnership in which the debtor is a partner.

Charitable subscription A written and signed commitment to contribute money to a charity.

Charter A grant by the government that authorizes the creation and operation of a corporation.

Chattel Articles of personal (as opposed to real) property; any interest in property that is less than a freehold or a fee interest in land.

Chattel mortgage A mortgage used to create a lien on some right or personal property as security for the payment of a debt or the performance of an obligation.

Chose in action See **Things in action.**

Circumscribe To restrict the range or activity of something clearly and definitely.

Civil rights The personal rights and freedoms guaranteed to the citizens of the United States by the Constitution.

Class action A lawsuit filed by some members of a group on behalf of all the members of the same group.

Clear and convincing proof A measure of the burden of proof that must be satisfied in a civil case, which is more than a mere preponderance of the evidence but less than the degree of proof required in a criminal case; proof that is very convincing but not necessarily conclusive.

Clearinghouse An association of banks and financial institutions that "clears" items, adjusting and paying items among the banks in the city or region.

Closed shop A business in which the employees must be members of a labor union in order to hold their employment.

Codicil An addition to a preexisting will used to explain, modify, or supplement the will.

Coinsurance clause A clause on fire insurance policies that requires that the insured maintain a predetermined percentage of the risk, based on the value of the property, or suffer a reduced coverage from the insurer in the event of a loss.

Collateral Supplementary; additional; added to; secondary. A collateral *promise* is made secondarily and is added to the primary, or original, promise made by another. Collateral also refers to *security*, things that are given as further assurance that a promise or performance will be forthcoming.

Collective bargaining Contract negotiations between the management of a company and representatives of labor, or the employees, which determines such things as working conditions, wages, hours, and so on.

Comity The informal and voluntary recognition of the sovereignty of another nation.

Commercial frustration Excuse of performance in a contract when the contract depends on the existence of a person or thing and the person or thing ceases to exist; excuse of performance when a contract becomes impossible to perform because of an act of God or a change in the law.

Commercial paper Negotiable instruments; checks, drafts, notes, and certificates of deposit; instruments that are used as credit instruments and/or as substitutes for money and that are governed by Article 3 of the UCC.

Commercial unit The size or quantity of packaged goods called for in a contract, such as a *dozen* eggs, a *ton* of coal, and so on.

Commission A fee paid to an agent or employee for the performance of some task or service; especially, a fee paid as a percentage of the total monies to be received.

Common carrier A person or firm offering to the general public, for compensation, the service of transporting people or goods.

Common law Unwritten law; the law as developed by the use of precedent and stare decisis, whereby the court uses the opinions in earlier, similar cases to reach a verdict in a current case.

Common stock The basic and only necessary ownership class of stock.

Communication The exchange of knowledge or information between parties; a statement made by one party to another.

Community property Property held jointly by a husband and wife; normally, property acquired during the marriage and excluding gifts or inheritances received by one spouse only.

Comparative negligence A means of measuring negligence whereby the negligence of the plaintiff is compared with that of the defendant, and the award to the plaintiff is reduced by the amount of negligence attributed to the plaintiff.

Compensation Indemnification; payment for services rendered; payment for damages suffered.

Compensatory damages Those damages necessary to compensate the injured party or to make the injured party whole; actual damages.

Competitors Persons who offer to perform the same, or a very similar, service and who normally attempt to distinguish their own services on the basis of price, quality, or other differences.

Complaint The first formal filing of a plaintiff in a civil case, setting out the alleged cause of action and a prayer for relief.

Composition An agreement between a debtor and his or her creditors whereby each creditor agrees to accept less than is owed in exchange for an earlier payment, and a discharge is granted to the debtor upon the performance of the agreed consideration.

Conclusive presumption   A presumption whose establishment precludes any further evidence or argument to the contrary.

Concurrent jurisdiction   Jurisdiction among several different courts, with the appropriate court being decided by the party who files suit.

Condemnation   The process by which privately held land is taken for a public use despite the owner's objection and lack of consent. See also **Eminent domain.**

Condition   An event whose occurrence will create the obligation to perform a contractual promise or will excuse the performance of a contractual promise.

Conditional sales contract   A sales contract in which the transfer of title to the buyer is subject to a condition, most commonly the payment of the full purchase price by the buyer.

Condition precedent   A condition that must occur before the obligation to perform will exist.

Conditions concurrent   Conditions that are mutually dependent and that must occur at or very near the same time.

Condition subsequent   A condition whose occurrence will excuse the performance of a contractual obligation.

Confession of judgment   A judgment in which the defendant has given the plaintiff written permission to enter a judgment in favor of the plaintiff against the defendant in the event of a lawsuit.

Confirmation   The supporting of a statement with proof; the ratification of a contract that was avoidable; a firming up or finalizing of an agreement that was in doubt.

Confiscation   A taking of private property by the government in violation of international law.

Conforming   In agreement; matching the description; acceptable.

Confusion   A blending, intermixing, or commingling that causes the individual parts to become obscured.

Consent   Voluntary approval of or agreement with the conduct done by, or proposed to be done by, another.

Consent decree   A decree entered by agreement of the parties and in the form of a solemn contract.

Consequential damages   Indirect damages; damages that arise as a consequence of an act or omission and not as a direct result.

Consideration   The legal benefit conferred or the legal detriment assumed as the result of the creation of a contract; the legal measure of value given in a contract.

Consignee   A person to whom goods are shipped.

Consignment   A bailment for the sale of goods. The consignor ships goods to the consignee so that the consignee can sell those goods to purchasers.

Consignor   A person who ships goods to another person.

Consolidate   To combine; to join together; to merge.

Conspicuous   Reasonably calculated to be seen and noticed; expected to convey the information to be imparted; obvious to the eye.

Conspiracy   A combining of two or more persons for the purpose of performing an unlawful act or of violating public policy.

Constitution   A written document that is the supreme law of the jurisdiction it purports to govern.

Constructive condition   A condition imposed by law.

Construction eviction   An inability of the purchasee or lessee to obtain possession or occupancy because of an outstanding claim.

Constructive fraud   An act or omission that operates as would a virtual fraud to the detriment of another or to the detriment of public policy even though the actor did not intend it to be a fraud.

Constructive notice   Information of which a person should have been aware from a review of all the facts and circumstances; information that a person is treated as knowing, whether actually known or not.

Constructive trust   A trust imposed by law to prevent the unjust enrichment of the purported owner of the "trust" property.

Consumer   A user; a person who utilizes economic goods, especially for personal or household use.

Consumer goods   Goods purchased for personal or household use, in contrast to goods purchased for inventory or equipment use.

Consumer price index   Measurement of how the price of a group of consumer goods changes between two time periods.

Contingent   Possible but not assured or definite; subject to the occurrence of a condition.

Contract   A legally enforceable agreement between two or more persons, supported by adequate consideration and having the requisite legal form.

Contract of adhesion   See **Adhesion.**

Contributory negligence   Negligent conduct by the

plaintiff that, taken together with the negligence of the defendant, makes up the proximate cause of the accident; a defense to a lawsuit for negligence in which the defendant shows that the plaintiff was at fault in the occurrence.

Conversion   The unauthorized and wrongful exercise of dominion and control over the personal property of another to the harm of that other person.

Convert   To change the nature of, as from real property to personal property.

Conveyance   A transfer of legal or equitable title.

Copyright   A legally protected, exclusive right to sell, to publish, or to reproduce artistic, musical or literary works for the life of the author plus fifty years.

Corporate charter   The right to conduct business granted to the corporation by the state in which the firm was incorporated, as evidenced by the formal legal papers and documents shown as the charter.

Corporation   An artificial person created under the statutes of a state or federal government, organized for the purpose set out in the application for corporate existence.

Corpus   Literally, body; the principal sum contributed, as to a trust, as distinguished from the income generated by that principal sum.

Counteroffer   A reply to an offer in which the offeree rejects the original offer and substitutes a *new* offer, whereby the former offeree becomes the offeror.

Court of equity   A separate court system developed at common law to administer justice and fairness in cases that were not actionable "at law."

Covenant   A promise, often in writing and under seal, pledging that something has been done or will be done.

Covenant not to compete   A clause in a contract whereby one party agrees not to compete with the other party after the termination of the contract.

Cover   In the law of sales, to purchase similar goods from another source upon the breach of a sales contract by the seller; in insurance, to agree to insure a named asset or thing of value.

Creator   A person who establishes a trust by transferring assets (the corpus) to a trustee for the welfare of the beneficiary.

Credit   The ability to purchase goods or services on time; the opposite of a debt, or a debt looked at from the perspective of the creditor.

Creditor   A person to whom a debt is owed.

Creditor beneficiary   A third party who is designated to receive the benefits of a promise or a performance in satisfaction of a legal obligation owed by one of the parties to the contract.

Crime   An act or conduct against society or the state that is subject to penal sanctions.

Criminal law   The body of law that is designed to protect society at large rather than the individual members of society. Criminal law provides for penal treatment of convicted offenders of the law.

Cruel and unusual punishment   Any punishment or penalty that is disproportionate to the offense, that amounts to barbaric treatment, or that shocks the community standards.

Cumulative voting   A voting method that allows voters to take the total number of votes they are authorized to cast and allocate them in any manner they see fit. They may cast all their votes for one candidate or allocate them in any proportion among the various candidates.

Cure   In the law of sales, the right of the seller to correct any nonconformity of the goods tendered to the buyer in order to avoid a breach of contract.

Current rate   The interest rate that financial institutions are currently charging on loans.

***Cy pres* doctrine**   Literally, as near as possible; a doctrine utilized in equity to carry out the wishes of a testator or of a trustee when the original wish is impossible or when it violates public policy (used especially in the area of charitable trusts when the original beneficiary has been improperly described or has ceased to exist).

D

Damages   Compensation and/or indemnification recovered in a court proceeding for injuries suffered by one person at the hands or by the conduct of another.

D/b/a   Abbreviation for "doing business as"; the name under which a business is conducted.

Deadlock   A tie; a standstill.

Debt   An amount of money owed to another; an obligation.

Debtor   A person who owes an obligation to a creditor.

Debtor in possession   A term used in bankruptcy proceedings to signify that the debtor in a reorganization proceeding is still in control of the business and its assets during the course of the bankruptcy process.

Deceased   A person who has died.

Decedent   Deceased.

Deductible   That which is to be subtracted; a clause in an insurance contract that relieves the insurer of any liability for a specified initial amount of loss.

Deed   The legal instrument by which an owner of land transfers the land to a grantee.

De facto   In fact; in deed; in reality. Contrasted with *de jure*, which means in law, *de facto* normally implies that something is being treated as a fact when it is not technically complete.

Defalcation   A misappropriation or misapplication of monies held by a fiduciary in a fiduciary capacity.

Defamation   A communication, oral or written, that holds a person up to ridicule, humilation, or scorn; a false and malicious attack upon the reputation of another.

Default   A failure to do what should be done, especially in the performance of a contractual obligation, without legal excuse or justification for the nonperformance.

Default judgment   A judgment rendered against a party because of that party's nonappearance in court.

Defendant   The person being sued in a civil action or being charged with a crime in a criminal action; the person from whom remedies or damages are being sought.

Defense   The reason, justification, or excuse for the conduct of the defendant, acceptance of which would shelter the defendant from the damages or remedies being sought in the action.

Defraud   To cheat; to trick; to take property or things of value from another by intentional deception.

De jure   Rightfully; legally; lawfully. Contrasted with *de facto*, *de jure* means in full compliance with all the requisite technicalities.

Delegate   To assign responsibility or authority to another; to have another act on one's behalf; to transfer the duty to perform to a third party.

Delivery   The intentional transfer of possession to another; the transfer of some thing or some right to another person.

Demand   The assertion of a legal right.

Demand instrument   An instrument that is due and payable at any time; an instrument that can be enforced immediately.

Deposition   Testimony of a witness taken outside of a trial and reduced to a writing and authenticated. A deposition may be used to preserve the testimony of a witness who is not available at trial or to impeach the testimony offered by a witness during the trial.

Depositor   A person who makes a deposit; a bank customer who places funds into an account with the bank for later personal use.

Derivative action   A suit filed by a shareholder on behalf of the corporation to enforce a corporate cause of action.

Destination contract   A contract for the transportation of goods by a common or independent carrier in which the seller remains liable for any losses or damages to the goods until the goods have reached a named destination.

Deterrent   Something that discourages or prevents the occurrence of an act.

Detriment   Loss or harm suffered to a person or a person's property; the forbearance of a legal right.

Diligence   Prudence; care; attention to details and surroundings.

Directors   Persons elected by the shareholders of a corporation to act as a board in managing the affairs of that corporation; managers; supervisors.

Disaffirm   To revoke a prior commitment or promise; to decline to perform what one had previously agreed to perform (most often used in the area of contract law when the disaffirming party asserts a lack of capacity to have entered the contract that is being repudiated).

Discharge   To release from obligation or liability; to excuse from any further duty to perform.

Disclaim   To deny; to renounce; to disavow.

Disclaimer   A statement by a seller, often in writing, that attempts to deny the existence of certain warranty protections that are normally afforded to the buyer.

Disclosed principal   A principal whose existence and identity are made known to the third person with whom the agent is dealing.

Disclosure   A revealing of what would otherwise be unknown.

Discovery   A pretrial procedure for allowing the parties to the litigation to narrow the issues by making one another aware of certain requested information, documents, and so on, and that includes the use of depositions, interrogatories, requests for admissions, and a number of other devices.

Discretion Wise conduct; caution; exercise of care and concern.

Dishonor A refusal to accept and/or to pay a negotiable instrument upon due and proper presentment to the drawee or maker.

Dissent The minority opinion in a court case; the reasoning of the judges who disagreed with the majority position.

Dissolution The termination of existence of a corporation or partnership, at least in the form previously known and followed. Dissolution does not necessarily mean that the business will cease to operate, only that the prior form no longer exists.

Diversification The addition of variety, as by the inclusion of a new product line or entry into a new business area; an expansion into new fields and areas of interest.

Diversity of citizenship A jurisdictional aspect of trials in federal courts wherein the parties on the different sides of a lawsuit are residents of different states.

Divest To take away from; to deprive; the opposite of invest.

Dividends A portion of a corporation's profits paid out to its shareholders on a pro rata basis, as voted by the board of directors; in insurance, the refund of excess premiums paid into the company by the policyholders, who are also the owners of the insurance company.

Document An instrument that may be used as evidence.

Document of title Written evidence of the legal ownership of a particular asset.

Domestic Relating to a home, a domicile, or the place of birth or origin.

Domicile The legal home or residence of a person; the state of incorporation of a corporation.

Donee The recipient of a gift or a bequest.

Donee beneficiary A third party who receives the benefits of a contract between two other parties for no reason except the donative intent of the donor.

Donor A person who gives a gift or makes a bequest.

Double jeopardy A second prosecution for the same offense or conduct, which is prohibited by the Constitution.

Drawee The person against whom an order instrument is drawn and who is expected to accept the instrument and to pay it upon maturity and proper presentment.

Drawer The person who issues an order instrument and who gives the order to pay the instrument to the drawee.

Due diligence The degree of prudence and care that can reasonably be expected from an ordinary, prudent person under the same circumstances.

Due process A measure of the appropriateness of a legal proceeding from the perspective of both the court and the individual; the proper exercise of power and authority by the court and the legislature within the rules and principles established by the courts.

Duress An unlawful imposition whereby a person loses the free exercise of his or her will because of an improper threat made upon the person or upon any other person or thing that is of sufficient importance to the person to constrain the exercise of free will.

Duty That which a person is expected and required to perform; a legal obligation to perform in a certain manner or to refrain from performing in a certain manner.

E

Easement The right to use the land of another person, as for ingress and egress; a limited right to use and enjoy the land of another.

Emancipate To free from the control or power of another; to release from parental care and to make legally independent.

Embezzlement The fraudulent appropriation of money by a person entrusted with the money.

Eminent domain The power of a government body to take private property for a public use or benefit, subject to compliance with due process requirements and payment of a fair value.

Employee A person who occupies some permanent position; a person who accepts a job for wages and operates under the control of the employer.

Employer One who uses the services of another, usually by hiring the other person to perform for wages.

Employment The act of hiring employees; the work environment.

Encumbrance A claim or a right against property owned by another, such as a mortgage or a lien.

Endorsee A person to whom a document or instrument is endorsed.

Endorsement The signing of one's name on the

back of a negotiable instrument in order to properly negotiate it to the next holder; a provision added to an insurance contract that alters the nature or the risk of the basic policy.

Endorser   A person who endorses, as by signing his or her name on the back of a negotiable instrument in order to further negotiate it.

Endowment   A life insurance policy that calls for the payment of the face amount of the policy to the insured at a certain age or date or for the payment of the face amount to the beneficiary if the insured dies before that time; the establishment of a fund for the use and benefit of a charitable institution.

Enjoin   To order by means of an injunction.

Entity   A separate being; a thing with a separate and independent legal existence.

Entrustment   The transfer of possession to another person of something that one owns or to which one is entitled, without any transfer of title, as in a consignment.

Equal protection   The requirement that the courts and laws of a state shall apply to all persons within the jurisdiction of the state in like manner, without regard to any extraneous factors such as race, age, or sex; the equality of treatment of all persons who come before the court.

Equipment   The fixed assets of a business, excluding lands and buildings; those assets that a business needs to carry out its commercial function.

Equitable   Fair; just; being a matter for a court of equity and not for a court of law.

Equity   A branch of the legal system designed to provide remedies where no remedy existed at common law; a system designed to provide "fairness" when there was no suitable remedy "at law."

Escheat   The reversion of lands to the state which occurs when a decedent has no legal heirs.

Escrow   A conditional delivery of a deed or of property to a trustee or escrow holder, who in turn delivers it to the grantee upon final performance.

Estate   The assets of a bankrupt; the assets owned by a decedent at the time of death; the interests a person holds in land.

Estoppel   A legal bar that prevents a person from alleging or denying a fact because that person's previous conduct or statements preclude the denial of facts contrary to the conduct or statements.

Eviction   The deprivation of one's right to possess land by court action or order.

Evidence   Any type of proof presented at trial to support a position advocated by the presenting party.

Examiner   A person appointed by the court to look into the affairs and the financial condition of a debtor in a bankruptcy proceeding.

Exchange   To trade; to give something to another, receiving something of equivalent value from the other; to trade foreign currency for domestic currency and domestic currency for foreign currency.

Exclusive-dealing contract   A contract that, by its terms, obligates the promisee to deal with only the promisor in a designated area of trade or commerce.

Exclusive jurisdiction   The right of one court to hear a particular case or controversy, to the exclusion of any and all other courts.

Exculpatory clause   A part of an agreement in which a prospective plaintiff agrees in advance not to seek to hold the prospective defendant liable for certain things for which that person would otherwise be liable.

Excuse   The reason given for not having done something that was to have been done; the rationalization of a nonperformance.

Executed contract   A contract that has been fully performed by all parties to it.

Execution   The full and complete carrying out of some act; a legal remedy for the enforcement of a court's verdict or judgment.

Executor (executrix)   The man (woman) named and appointed in a will by a testator to carry out the administration of the estate as established by the will.

Executory contract   A contract that has been less than fully performed, with performance still to occur.

Exemplary damages   See **Punitive damages.**

Exempt   Excused from a duty or obligation generally imposed on other persons in similar circumstances.

Ex parte   For one party only; without notice to the other side.

Expelled   Ejected; put out; removed.

Expert   A person qualified to testify or to speak as an authority on a given subject because of special skill, training, or knowledge in the subject area.

Export   To send out of the country, especially goods or articles of commerce.

Ex post facto   Literally, after the fact. An ex post facto law is enacted after the action has occurred and often is designed to be retroactive.

Express   Actually stated; clear and definite.

Express authority   Authority actually and truly given to the agent by the principal in the creation of an agency.

Express condition   A condition specifically mentioned in a contract.

Express warranty   A statement about the quality or condition of goods that the seller gives to the buyer at the time of the sale and that is intended as a part of the contract.

Expropriation   A taking of private property by government that is not in violation of international law.

Extension   An addition to something that already exists, as in the granting of additional time to complete a performance or to make a payment.

Extraterritoriality   The state of being exempt from the jurisdiction of local laws or local jurisdiction.

F

Face value   The value dictated by the face of an instrument or document without reference to any external documents.

Fact   Something actual; an actual occurrence.

Factor's lien   A claim or encumbrance on property held by a consignee for compensation owed by the principal.

False imprisonment   The unlawful arrest or detention of a person without permission, a warrant, or legal justification for doing so.

Farm goods   Goods produced by or used in the operation of a farm.

Fellow servant doctrine   A common law defense to a claim for damages by an employee injured on the job; a rule that protects the employer from liability to an employee for job-related injuries caused by a fellow employee.

Felony   A crime punishable by death or incarceration in a penitentiary.

Fiduciary   One who holds a special position of trust or confidence and who is thereby expected to act with the utmost good faith and loyalty.

Filing   The act of placing upon file; the act of depositing something in the custody of a public official to be held as a matter of record.

Finance charge   The consideration paid for the privilege of paying over time rather than paying cash at the time of contract performance; interest on a loan.

Financing statement   A legal document signed by the parties to a secured transaction that describes the collateral involved and that is filed with the appropriate state officials.

Firm offer   An offer made by a merchant to a merchant calling for an irrevocable period in which the offer may be accepted and during which the offer may not be revoked even though there is no consideration for holding it open.

Fixture   An item that was personal property but that has become so permanently attached to real property as to be a part of the real property.

Forbearance   A refraining from acting; the condition of not doing what one would otherwise legally be entitled to do.

Foreclosure   A legal proceeding designed to bar or to extinguish the rights of a mortgagor to the property mortgaged.

Foreign bill   A negotiable bill of exchange drawn in one state or country upon a drawee in another state or country.

Foreign corporation   A corporation incorporated in one state or country and doing business in another state or country.

Foreseeable   Capable of being anticipated as the reasonable result of a particular course of action or of a lack of action.

Forfeiture   The loss of a right or privilege as a penalty for certain conduct.

Forgery   The fraudulent making or altering of a written document or instrument with the intent of affecting the rights and duties of another; the signing of another person's name without permission or authority.

Formal   Of a particular form, as required by law, in order to be valid and enforceable.

Formal will   A testamentary document prepared in strict conformity with the state statute for the preparation of such a document and published and witnessed in its execution.

Franchise   A special privilege granted by a corporation to conduct business under the corporate name.

Fraud   The intentional misstatement of a material fact made for the purpose of inducing the other party to enter an agreement in reliance on the misstated fact; the intentional concealment of a defect whose existence should have been made known to the other party.

Fraudulent conveyance   A transfer of property

made with the intent of defrauding a creditor, of hindering a creditor's efforts to obtain the property transferred, or of placing such property beyond the reach of the creditor.

Fungible　Virtually identical; interchangeable; descriptive of things that belong to a class and that are not identifiable individually.

Future advances clause　A clause commonly used in secured transactions that provides for currently pledged collateral to cover any future credit extended by the covered creditor without need to resort to a subsequent security agreement.

G

Garnishment　A legal proceeding in which assets of a debtor that are in the hands of a third person are ordered held by the third person or turned over to the creditor in full or partial satisfaction of the debt.

General partnership　See **Partnership.**

Gift　An intentional, gratuitous transfer of property from a donor to a donee.

Good faith　Honesty in fact in the transaction; a lack of evil intent or motive.

Goods　Tangible, personal property; things that have a physical being and are movable.

Goodwill　The reputation of a business; the name value of a business; an intangible asset based on community perceptions.

Grace period　An insurance term designating the time period permitted after a premium payment is due during which the insured may tender the premium and retain the insurance coverage.

Grand jury　A jury convened for the purpose of hearing evidence to decide if there is probable cause to believe that a crime has been committed and to issue indictments if it finds the requisite probable cause.

Grant　To bestow on, confer on, or deliver to someone other than the party making the grant.

Grant deed　A deed that transfers an estate in land but with no warranties made by the grantor in the transfer.

Grantee　The recipient of a grant.

Grantor　The person who makes the transfer in a grant.

Gratuitous　Without consideration; not governed by contract law.

Guarantor　One who offers a guaranty by agreeing

to pay the debts of another if that person does not pay; a collateral obligor.

Guaranty　A promise to pay the debts or defaults of another on condition that the creditor first attempt to collect the debt from the debtor and be unable to do so.

Guardian　A person legally responsible for taking care of the affairs of another who lacks the legal capacity to do.

H

Habeus corpus　Literally, you should have the body; the technical name for a number of common law writs used to bring a person before a court and subject to its jurisdiction; the right to obtain such a writ as a protection against unlawful imprisonment.

Habitability　Suitability of premises for human occupancy.

Handwritten　Manually subscribed; written by hand, as opposed to being typed, preprinted, or otherwise inscribed by machine.

Harm　Physical or mental damage or injury.

Heir　A person who is designated by statute to receive the assets that are not disposed of by a decedent's will.

Holder　A person who has legally acquired possession of a negotiable instrument by endorsement and/or delivery.

Holder in due course　A holder of a negotiable instrument who acquired possession for value, in good faith, and without notice of any defects or defenses that affect liability on the instrument.

Holographic　Entirely handwritten.

Holographic will　A type of will that is entirely handwritten by the testator, personally and manually, and is dated and signed.

Horizontal merger　A merger between two or more firms at the same level of the distributive chain; a merger between competing firms.

I

Illusory　Falacious; nominal as opposed to substantial; of false appearance.

Impair　To lessen or diminish; to make worse; to interfere with a legal right or remedy.

Impeach　As an aspect of evidence, to challenge the veracity of a witness by using evidence that refutes the witness or his or her testimony.

Implied   Assumed or gathered by a consideration of all the circumstances; not expressed; deduced.

Implied authority   That authority actually given by a principal to an agent but not expressed; the authority reasonably expected to be used and to be necessary in carrying out the purpose of the agency.

Implied consent   Agreement presumed to exist because of the actions or inactions of a party to the agreement.

Implied contract   A contract imposed by law because of the conduct of the parties.

Implied warranty   A warranty protection that unless properly disclaimed by the warrantor is imposed by operation of law because of the nature of the transaction.

Import   Goods or property brought into one country from another country.

Impossibility   Something that cannot possibly be performed because of natural or legal restrictions.

Imposter   A person who assumes a name or an identity not his or her own for the purpose of deceiving another.

Impracticable   Not capable of being performed by the means currently available; commercially unreasonable.

Incidental authority   Actual authority possessed by an agent in minor areas for which no specific directions were given.

Incidental beneficiary   A person who happens to benefit from a contract between two other parties but who was not intended to benefit and who has no legal recourse if the contract is not performed.

Incontestability clause   A clause in an insurance policy that removes the right of the insurer to challenge the application information after some predetermined time period.

Incorporation   The act of forming a corporation by compliance with the applicable state statutes.

Incorporators   Persons who originate a corporation.

Indemnification   Reimbursement to a person for losses sustained; protection from losses or harm.

Independent contractor   A person hired to perform a task for another and who totally controls the means to be used in attaining the desired results, being subject to control of the employer only in regard to the ends to be attained.

Indictment   A formal accusation of criminal conduct issued by a grand jury and then tried before a petit jury.

Informal   Not according to any specific legal form.

Infringement   A violation of a property right of another, especially in the areas of copyrights and patents; an unauthorized use of property belonging to another.

In gross   Personal; not annexed to another person or thing.

Inheritance   Property that a person receives from the estate of a decedent.

Injunction   A writ issued by a court of equity ordering a person to do or to refrain from doing some specified act.

Injury   Wrong or damages done to a person or a person's property or reputation.

In pari delicto   Equally at fault; equally guilty.

In personam   Against a particular person.

Inquiry   A request for information; a question concerning terms or conditions.

In rem   Against a thing; done without regard to any particular person and thus done "against the entire world."

Insane   Of unsound mind; deranged; mad. The term *insane* has many meanings in law, depending upon the circumstances in which it is used. In contract law, it may mean committed to an institution or unable to look out for one's best interests.

Insanity   The state of being insane.

Insider   A person in a position of power; one who has access to information not generally available to the public.

Insolvent   A person unable to pay debts as they come due; one who has liabilities in excess of assets.

Installment note   A negotiable instrument that calls for periodic payments of a debt at predetermined times.

Insurable interest   A legal or equitable interest in the insured property or life; a sufficient connection to the insured property or life to ensure that the contract is to provide for reimbursement of loss and is not a wagering proposition.

Insurance   A method of providing for risk sharing among persons facing the same sort of risk by paying premiums into a fund to be used to reimburse those members of the group harmed by the occurrence of the risk.

Insured   A person protected by an insurance policy.

Insurer   A person who issues an insurance policy.

Intangible property   An asset that does not have physical form or existence.

Intangible right   A right that may be represented

by something such as a writing but that is of value in and of itself without regard to the writing.

Integration   The act of making whole or entire; the entire writing or writings entered into by the parties as their final and complete contract agreement.

Intended beneficiary   A third party who was clearly meant to benefit from the contract by one of the original parties to the contract.

Intent   The purpose for which a person acts; meaning.

Intentional tort   A private or civil wrong done willfully or with reckless disregard for the results that ensue.

Interest   The cost imposed by a creditor for the use of money over time.

Interpretation   The defining, discovering, and explaining of unclear language.

Interrogatory   A series of written questions issued to a party and answered under oath as a portion of the pretrial discovery stage of a lawsuit.

Interstate   Between two or more states or between one state and a foreign country.

Inter vivos   Between living persons; during life.

Intestate   Without a will; a person who dies without leaving a will.

Intestate share   The amount a person inherits from the estate of a decedent who left no valid will; the inheritance provided for in the state statute of descent and distribution.

Intestate succession statute   The state law governing the distribution of the estate of a decedent who left no valid will.

Intoxication   Drunkenness; lack of sobriety; the condition of being under the influence of alcoholic beverages. A number of states also consider being under the influence of a narcotic or illegal controlled substance (drug) as intoxication.

In transit   On the way; being delivered.

Intrastate   Wholly within the borders of one state.

Invasion of privacy   Infringement of the right to be left alone, free from disturbance by others.

Inventory   Stock in trade; goods held for the purpose of resale to customers in the ordinary course of business.

Investigation   A detailed search; a legal inquiry or examination.

Investment security   Bonds, notes, certificates, and other instruments or contracts from which one expects to receive a return primarily from the efforts of others.

Involuntary   Without will; against one's will; not done freely.

Issue   (Noun) one's offspring, progeny. (Verb) to send forth; to originate; to put into circulation. In commercial paper, the issue is the original transfer of a negotiable instrument to the payee or to a remitter.

Issuer   One who officially distributes an item.

J

Jargon   The technical terminology of a particular profession.

Joint and several liability   The liability faced when a creditor may elect to sue each of the debtors individually or to sue all of them together.

Joint liability   The liability faced when a creditor must sue a collection of debtors together and not individually.

Joint tenants   Tenants who acquired title to property at the same time, from the same person, in the same interest, and with the same rights to possession and usage.

Joint venture   A commercial undertaking by two or more persons with a limited time or purpose, which is similar to a partnership but without the continuous nature of a partnership.

Judge   (Noun) the officer who presides over a court of law or equity. (Verb) to decide judicially (properly, to adjudge).

Judgment   The final finding, or opinion, of a court at the conclusion of an action.

Judgment creditor   A creditor who has obtained a court verdict that allows the enforcement of an execution.

Judgment NOV   A judgment *non obstante verdicto*, meaning notwithstanding the verdict; a judgment entered by the court in direct contravention of the jury verdict, normally so entered because the jury verdict is unreasonable under all the facts and circumstances of the case.

Judgment rate   The interest rate imposed and to be paid on a judgment ordered by a court.

Judicial restraint   A doctrine under which the court refuses to enter certain areas in official opinions; the exercise of discretion by a court in determining which cases to hear or which cases to decide.

Judicial review   The examination and hearing of a case, especially by an appellate court.

Junior secured party   Any secured party whose

security interest is subordinate to that of the priority secured party.

Jurisdiction The power of the court to hear a certain cause of action; the power the court may exercise over a person or thing.

Jurisprudence The general philosophy of law and the legal system.

Jury In general, a panel of persons sworn to inquire into certain matters of fact and to render a verdict thereon. Included among the various types of juries are petit juries and grand juries.

Justice A judge appointed or elected to sit on an appellate court; the conformity of a person's actions to the requirements of law.

Justification Legal excuse for a course of conduct.

K

Knocking down The acceptance of a bid made at an auction, signified by a blow of the auctioneer's hammer.

Knowledge Those things of which a person is aware through perception, experience, education, or exposure.

L

Laissez-faire A government philosophy of minimizing regulation as much as possible; a government attitude of keeping "hands off" business.

Landlord A person who owns and leases or rents land to another.

Lapse The expiration or the loss of an opportunity because of the passage of a time limit within which the opportunity had to be exercised.

Larceny A felonious taking of the personal property of another person with the intent to deprive the owner of possession and to convert it to one's own use.

Law merchant A system of laws developed by merchants to regulate commercial transactions at early common law, before such transactions were covered by the courts of either law or equity; the predecessor of modern commercial law.

Lease Any agreement that establishes a landlord-tenant relationship; contracts that grant the right to use and occupy realty.

Legality Lawfulness.

Lessee The person to whom a lease is granted; the tenant.

Lessor The person who grants a lease; the landlord.

Levy execution To seize and sell property to satisfy a judgment.

Liability insurance An insurance policy that protects the insured from a designated potential liability.

Liable Responsible; subject to an adverse contingency or action.

Libel A defamation based on the written publication of something that injures the reputation of the plaintiff.

License Permission; the written document that evidences permission to perform certain acts; the right to use land belonging to another in some manner despite a lack of any estate or title to so use the land.

Lien A legal charge or encumbrance against property.

Life insurance An insurance policy that provides for the payment of an amount of money in the event the insured dies during the term of the policy. A number of investment aspects of many life insurance policies distinguish this type of insurance from property and liability insurance.

Limited partner A partner in a limited partnership who has contributed capital and filed the necessary forms to be classified as limited but who has no voice in management and who faces no personal liability for the debts or other liabilities of the firm.

Limited partnership A partnership consisting of at least one limited partner, whose risk is restricted to the amount of capital contributed to the firm and who may not take part in the management of the business, and at least one general partner, who is responsible for the management of the firm.

Liquidated Agreed upon; settled; not in dispute.

Liquidated damages Damages agreed upon in advance by the parties to a contract and included in the contract as the appropriate measure of damages in the event of a breach; damages preset by the parties because of the anticipated difficulty of establishing damages in the event of a breach.

Liquidated debts Debts whose amounts are agreed upon by the parties.

Liquidation The winding up of the affairs of a business in order to go out of business; the marshaling of assets and the subsequent reduction of those assets to cash in order to pay the claims of creditors.

Logotype An identifying symbol.

Loss   The harm or injury that results from a separation; a decrease in size or amount; the amount of a financial liability or setback.

Lost property   Property that is accidentally or unintentionally lost by the owner and whose location is unknown and whose recovery is difficult.

Loyalty   Faithfulness; adherence to the concept of supporting another over any competing interests; single-minded support and purpose.

M

Maker   In negotiable instruments, the person who promises to pay the note or certificate of deposit; the person who developes, creates, or causes to exist.

Mala in se   Morally wrong; wrong in and of itself.

Mala prohibita   Made wrong by law; pertaining to statutory offenses.

Malfeasance   The performance of an illegal act or a morally wrongful act; wrongful conduct.

Mandamus   The name of a writ issued by a court of competent jurisdiction ordering the performance of some act, in which the order is directed to an inferior court or to a person or a corporation.

Marshaling of assets   The arrangement of a debtor's assets in such a manner as to maximize the protection of the creditors; the gathering and grouping of the assets of the debtor.

Master   A principal who has the right to control an agent.

Material   Important, essential, or necessary.

Material fact   A fact that is a part of the basis of the bargain; a fact without which the contract as entered would not have been made.

Mechanics' lien   A statutory protection given to certain builders, artisans, and providers of materials providing for a lien on the building and the land that they have improved.

Mens rea   "Guilty mind"; criminal intent; the mental intent that must be shown in order to convict a person of a crime.

Mental distress   Suffering in the mind, as opposed to the body; such threats as remove free will.

Merchant   A person involved in the trade or commerce of a particular type of goods; one who claims to be an expert in certain types of goods; one who employs an expert in certain types of goods.

Merchantability   An implied warranty of quality that warrants to the buyer that the goods are of fair average quality, are fit for their normal use and purpose, and are adequately contained, packaged, and labeled.

Merge   To blend; to come together; to combine into one thing.

Merger   The absorbing of one thing into another so that only one remains after the merging; in contract law, the extinction of one contract by absorption into another; in corporate and antitrust law, the combining of two or more firms into one resulting firm.

Midnight deadline   With respect to a bank, midnight of the next banking day after the day on which it receives the item in question or the notice on which it is acting.

Mining partnership   A special form of co-venture that is neither a joint venture nor a partnership in the literal sense and that involves a joint effort to develop a mine or to develop oil or gas leases, with a sharing of profits and a sharing of expenses.

Minor   One not yet of legal age; an infant in the law; one lacking the statutory age to be considered an adult.

Minority   The period before a person reaches the legal age of majority; the period of legal infancy; the justices who disagree with the majority opinion; the dissent.

Misdemeanor   A criminal offense of less severity than a felony and normally punishable by fine or imprisonment in other than a penitentiary.

Misdescription   A false description of the subject matter of a contract that causes harm to one of the parties.

Misfeasance   Improper performance of some act that could be lawfully performed.

Mislaid property   Property placed somewhere and then forgotten by the owner; property intentionally placed but not recovered.

Misrepresentation   The misstatement of a material fact in the formation of a contract, made without an intent to deceive.

Mistake   An error regarding the truth of facts or of law that causes a person to act or to refrain from acting in a manner other than he or she would have acted had the truth been known.

Mitigation   A reduction or a minimizing of loss, liability, or penalty imposed by law.

Money   Legal currency issued by a recognized government entity; legal media of exchange.

Monopolize   To assume complete control over; to attempt to gain or to retain a monopoly.

Monopoly   The power of a firm exclusively to carry on a business or a trade to the exclusion of all competitors.

Moot   Subject to argument; not settled or decided.

Mortgage   A conditional transfer of property as security for a debt; an estate in land created by the granting of the estate but intended as security and becoming void if the debt is repaid.

Mortgagee   The person who receives a mortgage; the creditor.

Mortgage insurance   An insurance policy taken out by a mortgagor to pay off the debt in the event that the insured risk occurs during the mortgage period.

Mortgage note   A promissory note issued in conjunction with a mortgage specifying the terms for repayment of the loan by the debtor in order to cancel the mortgage.

Mortgagor   The person who gives a mortgage as security; the debtor.

N

Nationalization   The act of a government in proclaiming that a business or other property has become the property of the government and that individual owners have been removed from or deprived of the property.

Navigable waters   The commercial waterways of a nation; those streams, rivers, and lakes capable of use in commerce.

Necessary   Needed; inevitable; unavoidable.

Necessity   A controlling force or compulsion that allows for no other course of conduct.

Negligence   A failure to exercise due care under circumstances that require due care and that results in harm to another person.

Negligence per se   Negligence in and of itself without reference to any external factors.

Negligently   Without proper caution and care.

Negotiability   The quality of being transferable by endorsement or delivery.

Negotiable   Transferable by endorsement and delivery so as to give the recipient the rights of the transferor.

Negotiable instruments   Legal instruments governed by Article 3 of the UCC and consisting of notes, drafts, checks, and certificates of deposit.

Negotiation   The act of transferring a negotiable instrument by endorsement or delivery in such a manner that the transferee becomes a holder.

Nolo contendere   A plea of "no contest" entered in a criminal case whereby the defendant agrees to suffer the punishment for the crime charged but does not plead guilty and whereby the case cannot be used as evidence in any later proceedings on the same issue.

Nominal damages   Damages in name; the award given to a plaintiff when no substantial injuries are suffered, consisting of a token sum that the defendant is required to pay in acknowledgment of the wrongful conduct.

Nonassignable   Not subject to being assigned. In contract law, certain rights are nonassignable because of the personal nature of the duty.

Nonconforming   Not in compliance with the terms of the agreement or description.

Nonexempt assets   Those assets of the debtor that may not be protected and retained in a bankruptcy proceeding; those assets that will be liquidated in bankruptcy in order to satisfy the claims of creditors.

Nonforfeiture clause   A clause used in life insurance policies that specifies that certain rights and options of the insured will not be taken away should the policy lapse.

Nonjusticiable   Not properly subject to court action.

No-par value stock   Corporate stock not designated as having a par value; unvalued stock that is sold at some stated value, which is decided by the board of directors at the time of issue.

Notice   The information of which a person should be aware on the basis of knowledge or general observation.

Notorious   Of general notice or knowledge; widely known.

Novation   The substitution of a new contract in place of a preexisting one, whether between the same parties or with new parties replacing one or more of the original ones.

Nuisance   An annoyance or disturbance of a person's use, occupancy, and enjoyment of property that makes the ordinary use or enjoyment uncomfortable or bothersome.

Nuncupative   Oral; verbal; spoken.

Nuncupative will   A will made orally by the testator during his or her last illness or while facing impending death.

O

Obligation   Something a person is bound to do or to refrain from doing; a duty imposed by law or by contract.

Obligee   The person who is to receive the benefit from an obligation or from the performance of an obligation.

Obligor   The person bound by an obligation; the person who is to carry out the duty or to render the benefit.

Occupany   The taking of possession of property in order to assert a right of ownership; in real property, the exercise of control over land.

Offer   The presentation for acceptance or rejection of a power to create a contract made to the offeree.

Offeree   The person to whom an offer is made.

Offeror   The person who makes an offer to enter into a contract.

Oligopoly   An economic condition in which a small number of firms dominate the market but no one firm controls it.

Omission   A failure to perform; especially, a failure to perform an act required by law.

Operation of law   Certain automatic results that must occur following certain actions or facts because of established legal principles and not as the result of any voluntary choice by the parties involved.

Option   A privilege given to the offeree, for consideration, to accept an offer at any time during a preset period, with the understanding that the offer cannot be revoked during the stated period; a contract to keep an offer open for some agreed-upon time period.

Order   A command or direction; an administrative agency's rules and regulations; a category of negotiable paper in which the drawer commands the drawee to pay a named person.

Order for relief   A bankruptcy judge's decree that the debtor is properly before the court and that control over the procedures to be followed thereafter lies with the bankruptcy court.

Ordinance   A law enacted by a municipal authority.

Output contract   A contract that calls for the buyer to purchase all of the production of the seller during the term of the contract.

Overdraft   A check or draft, honored by the drawee, in excess of the funds to which the drawer is entitled.

Overdue   Not paid when payment was due; delayed beyond maturity; unperformed at the date performance was to have been completed.

P

Paid-in capital   The property contributed to a business venture by the owners of the business as their contributions to the formation of the firm.

Parol evidence   Oral evidence; verbal testimony of witnesses.

Parol evidence rule   A rule that prohibits the introduction of oral evidence that contradicts a complete written contract or agreement unless there is evidence that the writing was the result of fraud, mistake, or accident.

Partially disclosed principal   A principal whose existence is known to the third person at the time of negotiation with the agent but whose identity is not.

Partial performance   Performance of a contractual obligation that is less than full or complete.

Participate   To take part in; to share; to divide in equal shares or proportions.

Partnership   An association of two or more persons as co-owners to carry on a business for profit; a voluntary joining of two or more persons to own and to operate a business venture as equal members.

Party   A person who is directly involved in the performance of any contract or agreement or in the trial, prosecution, or defense of any legal action.

Par value   The face value of a share of stock, not necessarily the same as the price for which the share can be sold.

Past consideration   Purported consideration but in fact no consideration; an attempt to use past conduct as consideration for a present contract.

Patent   (Noun) a government grant of monopoly power to make, to use, or otherwise to enjoy the fruits of one's inventions, provided the invention is new, useful, and not obvious to one of ordinary skill in the field. (Adjective) obvious; manifest; apparent.

Payee   The person designated by the maker or drawer of a negotiable instrument as the person to receive payment or to continue negotiation of the instrument; the person to whose order a negotiable instrument is originally drawn or issued.

Perfection The act of completing and of moving beyond challenge or defect; in secured transactions, the act of a creditor that serves as notice to the rest of the world that the security interest exists in his or her favor, as by filing.

Performance The carrying out of what one has agreed to do; the satisfaction of an obligation or contract.

Peril The risk or hazard against which an insurance policy is issued to the insured.

Perjury The making of false statements while under oath.

Per se By itself; taken alone; unconnected to other matters.

Personal defense In negotiable instruments, a defense that exists between the drawer or maker and the payee or some other party but that does not directly affect the instrument itself; a defense that attacks the underlying obligation but not the validity of the instrument.

Personal property Anything capable of being owned except land or anything permanently attached to land.

Personal representative The executor or administrator of a decedent's estate.

Petit jury "Twelve men good and true"; the ordinary jury called for in a civil or criminal trial; the finders of fact.

Plaintiff The person who commences a civil cause of action by filing suit against the defendant.

Plea bargaining A device used in a criminal proceeding whereby the state accepts a guilty plea on a lesser offense in exchange for not bringing the defendant to trial on the greater offense with which he or she was originally charged.

Pledge A form of perfection in secured transactions whereby the debtor creates a bailment with the creditor, allowing the creditor to retain possession of the collateral until the debt is repaid.

Police power The authority conferred upon the government to enact the laws necessary to ensure domestic tranquility; the power inherent in the state to protect the lives, health, and property of its citizens by enacting and enforcing laws.

Political question A nonjusticiable issue; a matter that is purely political in nature and as such is not germane to any legal issues or actions within the jurisdiction of a court.

Pollution Contamination of the environment; impurity.

Pooling agreement An agreement between two or more parties to place funds into a common "pool" for allocation for certain uses, as for coverage of losses contemplated and faced by the members of the pooling group.

Possession The exercise of exclusive physical control over an asset regardless of ownership; physical dominion.

Possessory lien A statutory claim on property evidenced by the physical control and possession of the creditor and perfected for as long as the creditor retains possession.

Postdated Dated for a time later than the time of issuance or creation.

Power The ability or the right to do something. Power does not necessarily mean right; a person may have the power to do a certain thing but doing so will involve the violation of a private civil duty.

Preemption A seizing for oneself to the exclusion of all others; the right to purchase before others; in corporate law, the right of present stockholders to purchase a new issue of stock before the stock is offered to the general public.

Preference In bankruptcy, a transfer by the debtor to an unsecured creditor that allows that creditor to receive a greater percentage of his or her claim than is received by other creditors of the same class.

Preferred stock A class of corporate stock that has rights superior to those of common stock in the areas of dividends and the distribution of corporate assets.

Premium The cost of insurance coverage paid by the insured to the insurer.

Prepayment clause A contract clause that allows the debtor to pay the debt before it is due without penalty.

Preponderance of proof A degree of proof that seems to outweigh that offered by the other side.

Prescription In real property, the acquisition of an easement by the open, notorious, continuous, and hostile use of the property of another as a matter of right.

Presenter A person who presents; one who makes a presentment.

Presentment A demand upon the primary party by the holder of a negotiable instrument for payment and/or acceptance of the instrument.

Price discrimination The charging of different prices to different purchasers when the price differential is not justified by cost differentials.

Price fixing An agreement between two or more competing merchants to charge a certain price for goods or services without regard to market pressures or concepts of competition; a per se violation of the Sherman Act when done in interstate commerce.

Price leadership A position enjoyed by certain firms, by virtue of size, innovations, or ability, to set prices in certain channels of commerce with the understanding or expectation that competing firms will price their products accordingly; the ability to direct the pricing policies of an industry.

Prima facie At first sight; on its face; something presumed to be true because of its appearance unless disproved by evidence to the contrary.

Primary liability The liability of the person to be looked to first for payment, who, in commercial paper, is the maker of promise paper or the drawee on order paper.

Principal In agency law, the person who appoints an agent and bestows authority upon the agent for the purposes set out in the agency agreement.

Priority Precedence; higher rights; the right to come before another.

Privacy See **Invasion of privacy.**

Private trust A trust created for a private purpose and having certain named or readily identifiable beneficiaries.

Privilege A benefit or advantage enjoyed by some members of a group beyond that enjoyed by the general public; the right enjoyed by certain persons to have particular types of communications treated as confidential, not subject to disclosure.

Privity of contract The relationship of two or more persons by virtue of the existence of the contract between them.

Probate (Noun) the legal procedure for establishing that a given written document was the last will and testament of a decedent and that the document is valid. (Adjective) relating to wills and the proof thereof.

Probate court A court having jurisiction over the estates of decedents.

Procedural law The body of law that governs *how* legal proceedings are to be conducted.

Proceeds The property, especially money, received from the sale or disposal of assets.

Profits The excess in income over expenditures; the gain made in the sale of assets or services; the benefits a person receives from the use of land.

Promise A showing of an intent to act or to refrain from acting in a certain way made in such a way that the promisee is aware of the commitment.

Promisee One to whom a promise is made.

Promisor One who makes a promise.

Promissory estoppel A doctrine that prohibits a promisor from denying the making of a promise or from escaping the liability for that promise because of the justifiable reliance of the promisee that the promise would be kept.

Promissory note A written promise to pay a certain sum of money at a future time unconditionally.

Promoter A person who begins the process of forming a corporation by procuring subscribers for the stock or by taking other affirmative steps toward incorporating.

Property Anything capable of being owned; anything that has value.

Property insurance Insurance that covers personal property or buildings and fixtures against certain predetermined risks and hazards.

Proprietorship The designation for an unincorporated business that has a single owner/manager.

Pro rata Proportionately; according to percentages.

Prospectus A document presented by a corporation or its agents announcing the issue of corporate securities, stating the nature of the securities and the financial status of the issuing firm, and asking the general public to purchase the securities covered.

Protest A formal notice of dishonor of a negotiable instrument made before and attested to by a notary public or a consul of an embassy; a formal declaration of dissent or disagreement regarding some act that has occurred or that is about to occur.

Provable Capable of being proved; susceptible to being proved.

Proximate cause An act that naturally and foreseeably leads to harm or injury to another or to an event that injures another.

Proxy A person appointed and designated to act for another, especially at a public meeting, such as a meeting of the shareholders of a corporation; the document or instrument used to appoint someone to act in a representative capacity as a proxy.

Proxy solicitation A request contained in the notice of a shareholders' meeting that the shareholder allow some person to act as a proxy for that shareholder at the meeting.

Public corporation A corporation formed by a federal or state government to carry out a government purpose.

Public domain   All the land owned by the federal government and all land occupied by federal building, arsenals, and docks or for other federal purposes.

Public policy   The general attitude of the public toward certain conduct; the public sense of morality, good conduct, and acceptable behavior to which citizens must conform.

Published   Made public; made generally known.

Punitive damages   Damages awarded to a plaintiff over and above those to which he or she would normally be entitled because of the excessive wrongfulness of the defendant's conduct; damages designed to punish and to make an example of the defendant as a means of discouraging similar conduct by others. Also known as *exemplary damages*.

Purchase money security interest   A security interest in which the credit extended is used to purchase the collateral that is being used as security.

Purchaser   One who acquires property by buying it from a seller for money; one who acquires real property by any method except inheritance.

Q

Qualification   A skill or trait necessary to perform a certain task or to hold a certain office; a modification or limitation of terms used to restrict the scope or meaning of language.

Qualified endorsement   A type of endorsement used on negotiable instruments to remove the contractual liability of the endorsement should the instrument be dishonored.

Quantifiable   Capable of exact statement; measurable; verifiable.

Quasi contract   An equitable remedy to prevent unjust enrichment when no contract was formed but one of the parties has received value knowingly and has not prevented performance by the other party.

Quasi-judicial   "As if" done by a judicial body; pertaining to the hearings, investigations, and ascertaining of facts by administrative bodies in controversies involving administrative agencies in the performance of the duties delegated to them by Congress.

Quasi-legislative   "As if" done by a legislative body; pertaining to the exercise of administrative agencies in enacting regulations within the delegation of authority the agency received from Congress.

Question of fact   A question to be determined by a jury.

Question of law   A question to be decided by the court, in contrast to a question of fact, which is to be determined by the jury.

Quid pro quo   Literally, something for something; the consideration given by each party to a contract in exchange for the consideration given by the other; the bargain element of the contract.

Quiet enjoyment   The right and expectation of a tenant or a purchaser of land to use and enjoy the premises without disturbances or interferences from others; a covenant that is included in leases and deeds.

Quitclaim deed   A deed conveying from the grantor to the grantee such rights as the grantor possesses, if any; a deed of conveyance that carries no warranties or assurances of its validity or genuineness.

Quorum   The number of members or the number of shares that must be present and/or represented at a meeting in order for the meeting to be properly convened and for any business to be properly and legally conducted.

R

Ratification   The acceptance of and the binding to an act that was unauthorized when committed and that was voidable before the ratification. Ratification must be of the *entire* act, not just those parts of benefit to the person who is accepting.

Ratify   To approve and formally sanction.

Real defense   In commercial paper, a defense that attacks the validity of the instrument itself, allowing the maker or drawer to escape liability on the instrument regardless of the status of the holder.

Real property   Land or anything permanently attached to land.

Reasonable and prudent person   A person who before acting gives thought to the consequences of acting; a careful and thoughtful person.

Rebuttable presumption   An assumption of the truth of a matter, based on evidence, that will be accepted as true unless shown to be untrue by other convincing evidence.

Receiver   An unbiased person appointed by a court to receive, preserve, and manage the funds and property of a party involved in litigation.

Receivership   An equitable remedy whereby the court appoints a receiver to manage the property involved pending the outcome of the case.

Reckless   Lacking proper caution; negligent; careless.

Reclaim   To obtain the return of something; to get back.

Reconcile   To make consistent; to settle or resolve; to put into balance or harmony.

Recoupment   A withholding of something that is due; a reduction in the amount allegedly owed because of a counterclaim or a setoff.

Redeem   To buy back; to remove a security interest or a mortgage by paying the total debt due.

Redemption   The act of redeeming or repurchasing; the revocation of a conditional sale by performance of the condition that provided for the revocation.

Reformation   An equitable remedy whereby the court "reforms" a contract in order to remove a mistake and to make the agreement conform to the terms to which the parties originally agreed.

Registered agent   A person designated by a foreign corporation as the proper person upon whom to serve process.

Registration statement   A formal statement complying with statutory information standards that is filed by a corporation in order to offer an issue of securities for sale.

Regulation   An authoritative rule that deals with procedures; an executive rule or order that has the effect of law.

Reimbursement   Repayment for expenditures incurred; indemnification.

Rejection   A refusal to accept what is offered.

Relative   (Noun) kin; family member; a relation by blood or marriage. (Adjective) not capable of exact statement; comparative.

Release   The surrender of a right or claim by the person possessing it to the person who would be obligated to perform; the surrender of a legal claim.

Relevant market   The total market in which a firm operates, including its geographic scope and all competing or substitute products.

Reliance   Dependence; expectation of truth or occurrence.

Reliction   Land that is uncovered by the gradual receding of water.

Remainder beneficiary   The person who is to receive the benefit after the expiration of a prior interest granted in the property, with both interests created at the same time and in the same instrument.

Remand   To send a case back to an inferior court for further action; to return a prisoner to custody pending trial.

Remedy   A method for enforcing a right or preventing a violation of a right; the result of a successful action.

Remitter   The person to whom a bank draft or cashier's check is issued before it is delivered to the payee; the purchaser of such a bank draft or cashier's check.

Remuneration   Salary; wages; compensation.

Renunciation   The abandonment of a right by the possessor of the right.

Reorganization   The restructuring of an insolvent corporation so that the interests of its creditors can be protected and the corporation can continue to exist.

Repentance   A feeling of regret or contrition for past wrongdoing.

Replevin   An action taken to acquire possession of goods that are not necessarily unique but that are currently unavailable in the open market; in the law of sales, a remedy of the buyer when cover is not available and specific performance is not appropriate.

Replevy   To take goods under a writ for replevin.

Repossession   The act of regaining possession; the act of taking possession of collateral upon the default of the debtor in a secured transaction.

Representation   A statement made by an applicant for insurance coverage that allows the insurer to assess the risk and that, if false and material, may allow the insurer to cancel the policy; a statement made to influence the other party to act or to refrain from acting.

Repudiate   To reject, refuse, deny, or disclaim; to refuse to acknowledge or pay.

Repudiation   A rejection; a refusal; a denial of a right or a refusal to perform a duty.

Requirement contract   A contract in which the seller agrees to provide as much of a product or service as the buyer needs during the contract term.

Rescission   An annulment or cancellation; a termination of a contract through restoration of the parties to the status quo.

Reservation of title   A contract clause that leaves title to the sold object with the seller until the buyer has paid the entire purchase price. In secured transaction law, such an effort is treated as a mere security interest, with title transferred to the buyer.

Residuary Pertaining to the surplus of a decedent's estate after all the debts have been paid and all the legacies distributed and discharged.

Residuary clause A clause in a will that provides for the disposal of any property left after all bequests and divisions of the estate have been made.

Res judicata A thing already decided by a judicial action or opinion and that having been decided is final.

Respondeat superior Literally, let the master answer; a legal doctrine that holds the master liable for the wrongs of the servant, and the principal liable for the wrongs of the agent, provided the wrong was committed in the course and scope of employment.

Restatement Part of the title of compilations dealing with various areas of law, such as torts and contracts, which detail how the different states have treated topics covered in the volumes and which are used to provide guidance to the courts in resolving cases and controversies in these different areas of law.

Restitution The return of something; in contract law, the return of any consideration given upon a breach, upon rescission, or upon avoidance of the contract.

Restraint of trade Any conduct that serves to limit the development of commerce or to interfere with the free flow of commerce.

Restrictive covenant A promise in a deed whereby the grantee agrees not to do certain things or to use the land in certain ways.

Restrictive endorsement A type of endorsement that purports to limit or terminate any further negotiation of the instrument; an endorsement that restricts future negotiations to a particular field of commerce, such as banking.

Resulting trust A trust created by implication of law based on the *presumed* intention of the parties involved, which is inferred from the surrounding facts and circumstances.

Retract To take back or withdraw, as an offer before its acceptance.

Revenue Profit; return on investments; income; yield.

Revert To return to; to go back.

Revest To vest again; to acquire a right or interest a second time; to regain.

Revocation The cancellation, rescission, or annulment of something previously done or offered.

Right A legal power or privilege to do something; justice; that to which a person is entitled.

Risk of loss Legal responsibility for any damages, loss, or destruction of the subject matter of a contract.

Robbery A criminal and felonious taking of personal property from a person by force or the threat of force.

Royalty fee Payment made in exchange for the grant of a right or a license.

Rule against perpetuities A requirement that an interest in property must vest within a specified time — a life in existence plus twenty-one years — or the interest becomes invalid on the basis of its being contrary to public policy. The rule refers to present possessory interests and not to future interests.

Rule of reason A defense to an antitrust action used to show that the conduct complained of was reasonable under the circumstances and was the least objectionable of the alternative courses of conduct available to the actor.

S

Sale The passing of title from the seller to the buyer for a price.

Sale on approval A sale in which the buyer is allowed some preset time period to test the product before the sale is final.

Sale or return A sale in which the buyer is allowed to return any goods not resold by the buyer for credit to the buyer's account.

Sanction (Noun) the penalty imposed for a violation of law as a means of helping in the enforcement of the law. (Verb) to make valid by a formal procedure.

Scienter Knowledge; especially, one party's prior knowledge of the cause of a subsequent injury to another person.

Seasonably As quickly as practical; within the appropriate time.

Secondary liability A liability that does not arise or attach until the occurrence of a condition; the liability faced by each endorser on a negotiable instrument upon proper presentment and dishonor of the instrument.

Secured creditor A creditor who has access to collateral as a resource to cover the debt upon the default of the debtor.

Secured transactions Credit arrangements, covered by Article 9 of the UCC, in which the creditor has a security interest in certain assets of the debtor.

Security Something of value given or pledged to assure the performance of an obligation or the repayment of a debt.

Security agreement The document executed by the debtor and the creditor in establishing a secured transaction.

Security interest An interest in personal property or fixtures that secures payment or performance of an obligation.

Seller A person who transfers property in a contract for the sale of property.

Servant A person employed to perform services for a master under the control of the master.

Service charge A fee charged for the performance of a particular service, often added to a basic fee; the charge imposed by a bank on its customer for particular services, such as certifying a check or stopping payment on a check.

Service mark A distinctive symbol designating the service offered by a particular business or individual.

Service of process The delivery of a writ or summons to the party or to the address of the party to which it is directed.

Setoff A demand that the defendant has against the plaintiff and that is deducted from the amount the defendant is to pay to the plaintiff in settlement of the claim.

Settlement An agreement that settles a dispute as to what each party owes the other.

Settlor One who creates a trust.

Several liability The liability faced by each of the parties when the plaintiff may sue any of them and recover the entire judgment from those sued, without having to sue all of the potential defendants.

Share A proportional ownership of a corporate venture with proportionate rights to management, to profits of the corporation, and to corporate assets upon dissolution.

Shareholder The owner of a share of a corporation's stock; an investor in a corporation whose investment is made up of ownership shares.

Shipment contract A contract whereby the seller agrees to put conforming goods into the hands of a shipper and the buyer assumes risk of loss during transit of the goods.

Short-swing profits Profits made by officers, 10 percent shareholders, insiders, and tippees by the purchase and sale of corporate securities within six months, by matching the high sale and the low purchase prices, and by disregarding any losses.

Signature Any mark, symbol, or device used with the present intent to authenticate a writing.

Silence A forbearance from speaking.

Slander An oral defamation of character; an oral communication that causes a person's reputation to be held up to scorn or ridicule and that is made to any person except the person so scorned or ridiculed.

Sovereign One possessing supreme power within a given sphere; the government.

Sovereign immunity The doctrine that protects the state from liability for the performance of its sovereign role; an absolute defense available to the state in lawsuits, provided the government was involved in a government function.

Special endorsement A type of endorsement used in negotiable instruments whereby the holder designates the next holder of the instrument and another endorsement is needed to further negotiate the instrument.

Specific performance An equitable remedy provided by the courts when monetary damages would be insufficient and the object of the contract is unique and in which the court orders performance of the contract exactly as agreed.

Standing The legal right to commence an action based on a showing that the plaintiff has a substantial legal interest that needs to be protected.

Stare decisis "Let the decision stand"; the policy followed by the courts in deciding current cases on the basis of precedent, thereby not disturbing established policy.

Statement A declaration of matters of fact; an allegation.

Statute A law enacted by the legislative branch of the government.

Statute of Frauds A statute requiring that certain specified types of contracts be in writing in order to be enforceable in court.

Statute of limitations A statute that provides for a definite time period during which certain legal actions must be commenced and after which they will be barred.

Statutory Related to or created by statute.

Statutory standard The general conduct expected of an individual as established by law; the legal measurement of conduct for a given set of circumstances.

Statutory warranties The warranty protections imposed by law upon the parties to a contract; the quality standards to which a product must adhere in order to comply with the statutory provisions.

Stipend   A fixed sum of money paid periodically.

Stock   The capital fund of a corporation acquired by the sale and distribution of corporate shares; the different classes of shares that a corporation issues to its owners.

Stop payment order   An order given by a drawer of a check to the drawee that a designated check be dishonored upon presentment to the drawee. An oral stop payment order is valid for fourteen days; a written one for six months.

Strict foreclosure   A means of foreclosure that precludes the right of the debtor to redeem the property and that vests title in the creditor.

Strict liability   Liability without fault; liability for which there is no defense assertable by the defendant.

Subject matter jurisdiction   The power of a court to hear only the classes of cases and controversies that are within its jurisdiction, especially important in courts of limited jurisdiction.

Sublease   The lease of all or part of the premises by the lessee for some portion of the unexpired lease period of the lessee's occupancy.

Subpoena duces tecum   An order issued by a court to some designated party to produce specified documents at a trial.

Subrogate   To substitute one person in place of another with reference to rights or claims.

Subscription   The act of writing one's name on a legal document; a written contract in which the subscriber agrees to pay money in exchange for some designated benefit or purpose.

Subsidiary   A corporation controlled by another corporation that owns a majority of the subsidiary corporation's stock.

Substantial performance   Performance of a contract that is less than perfect but that is in compliance with the essential portions of the contract; a good-faith effort to perform a contract, with performance satisfactory and the deviations minor or technical.

Substantive law   The portion of the law that deals with and regulates rights.

Suit   Any legal action in which a plaintiff seeks the enforcement of rights or the granting of remedies.

Sum certain   An amount of money to be paid on a negotiable instrument, with the total amount calculable from the information contained on the face of the instrument.

Summary judgment   A judgment entered by the court when there is no substantial issue of fact present; a judgment by the court on the basis of depositions, discovery, and other nonevidential matters.

Summons   A writ requiring a sheriff to inform the person named that an action has been filed against that person and ordering the person to appear in court to answer the action.

Supremacy clause   The clause in the Constitution that specifies that the federal government is supreme to the state governments and that federal law controls over state law if the federal law is valid.

Surcharge   Required payment for failure to follow fiduciary duties.

Surety   A person who promises to pay or to perform in the event that the principal fails to do so.

Suretyship contract   A contract in which a surety agrees to answer for the debt of another upon the default of the other and in which the surety is entitled to indemnification upon the performance of the obligation.

Suspend   To delay a performance temporarily, with the expectation that performance will occur later.

T

Tenancy   An interest in or possession of land in any manner.

Tenancy in partnership   A form of ownership of partnership property by the partners, with a right of survivorship.

Tenant   One who possesses land belonging to another; the holder of a leasehold estate.

Tenants by the entireties   An estate held by a husband and wife jointly by conveyance and that carries a right of survivorship.

Tenants in common   Co-ownership of real property by two or more persons, with the owners having undivided interests in the land but with title passing to them from different grantors, at different times, or in differing amounts.

Tender   An offer of performance.

Term insurance   A form of life insurance with no investment properties or characteristics that provides coverage for a fixed time period and that is paid only if the loss occurs during that time period.

Testament   The disposition of a testator's personal property according to his or her wishes upon the death of the testator.

Testamentary   Pertaining to a will.

Testamentary capacity   The mental capability required by law in order to make a valid will; the state of being of sufficient age to execute a will and of being aware of the nature of the act.

Testator (testatrix)   A man (woman) who makes a will.

Things in action   A right to receive or to recover money or personal property as the result of a judicial proceeding.

Third-party beneficiary   A person who is not a party to a contract but who will benefit from the performance of the contract; one who derives some gain or benefit from the contractual performance of the parties to the contract.

Time instrument   A negotiable instrument payable at some future, determinable time and not payable upon demand.

Time-price differential sales contract   A contract with a difference in price based on the date of payment, with one price for an immediate payment and another price if the payment is at a later date.

Tippee   One who is not an insider but who receives from an insider information not yet available to the general public; one who receives a tip.

Title   The legal right of ownership and possession of property.

Tort   The breaching of a civil duty that is the proximate cause of harm to some person or the property of some person; failure to exercise due care.

Tort feasor   A person who commits a tort.

Tortious   Wrongful; pertaining to torts.

Trademark   A distinctive mark or symbol used to identify a particular company or its products.

Transferable   Capable of being assigned, transferred, negotiated, or passed from party to party with all the rights of the original holder or party being retained.

Treason   An attempt to overthrow the government by overt acts; betrayal of the government to a foreign government.

Treasury stock   Stock that has been issued by a corporation and then reacquired by the corporation as a part of its treasury.

Treaty   A written contract or agreement entered into by two or more nations for the general welfare of the nations involved.

Treble damages   A statutory remedy in antitrust actions that allows the successful plaintiff to recover three times the damages suffered as a result of the antitrust violation.

Trespass   An unlawful act committed on the person, property, or rights of another; unlawful entry on another's land.

Trial court   The court of first impression; the court in which a cause of action is initiated and that hears evidence and testimony in reaching its verdict.

Trust   A legal relationship in which one party — the trustee — holds legal title to the property, while another party — the beneficiary — holds equitable title to the same property; a combination formed by several corporations by mutual agreement.

Trust deed   A security agreement similar to a mortgage in which a deed is conveyed to a trustee as security for the payment of a debt, with the trustee having the power of sale upon default in the repayment of the debt.

Trustee   The person responsible for performing the purpose of a trust and who administers the trust property for the beneficiary.

Trustee in bankruptcy   The person appointed by the bankruptcy court to act as trustee of the debtor's property for the benefit and protection of the creditors.

Tying arrangement   A contract that requires the buyer to purchase one product from the seller in order to be allowed to purchase a second, difficult-to-obtain product from the same seller.

U

Ultra vires   Beyond the scope or legal power of a corporation as established by the corporation's charter or by state statute.

Unconditional   Not subject to any conditions; under every set of facts or circumstances; in every instance.

Unconscionable   Blatantly unfair and one-sided; so unfair as to shock the conscience.

Unconstitutional   Contrary to a constitution; in violation of a constitution.

Underwriter   The insurer; one who insures another against some risk.

Undisclosed principal   A principal whose existence and identity are unknown to the third person at the time the third person is dealing with the principal's agent.

Undue influence   The control of the free will of another person by unfair or improper persuasion.

Unenforceable   Not subject to performance by judicial intervention; not capable of being implemented under judicial direction.

Unfair trade practice   Any commercial practice that does not allow for the free exercise of trade by competitors; a false, deceptive, or unfair method of gaining trade at the expense of others.

Unilateral   One-sided.

Unilateral contract   A contract in which only one party makes a promise, with the other party's being expected to perform an act in order to accept and thereby create a contract.

Uninsured motorist   An operator of a motor vehicle who is not covered by a valid automobile or vehicular liability insurance policy.

Union shop   A place of employment where only members of a labor union are employed.

Unjust enrichment   The receiving of something of value to which the recipient is not entitled by law or equity; the possession of something to which one is not entitled.

Unliquidated   Not agreed upon; in dispute; subject to controversy or disagreement.

Unqualified endorsement   A type of endorsement that does not qualify the liability of the endorser to the endorsee in the event that the instrument is dishonored.

Unsecured creditor   A general creditor; a creditor who has not entered into a security agreement with the debtor and who does not have specific collateral to rely on in the event of a default by the debtor.

Usage of trade   A practice common to the trade or industry involved or having a generally recognized meaning within the trade or industry.

Usurious contract   A contract that calls for the payment of interest at a rate higher than that permitted under state law.

Usury   The charging of an interest rate in excess of the statutory maximum; the charging of excessive interest.

V

Valid   Legally enforceable; properly executed and formed; legally sufficient.

Value   The worth of an object in terms of money; the consideration necessary to support a simple contract.

Venue   The geographic area in which an action is held and from which the jurors are selected; the court in which an action may be commenced, based upon the convenience of the parties.

Vertical merger   A merger between firms at different levels of the distributive chain.

Vest   To grant a fixed right concerning present or future use; to place in the possession of some authority or person.

Vicarious   Serving in place of someone or something else; acting as a substitute for.

Void   Of no legal effect; invalid; null.

Voidable   Capable of being avoided; cancelable at the option of the disadvantaged party.

Voidable preference   The act of an insolvent debtor of paying one creditor of a class, allowing that creditor to obtain a larger percentage of the debt than other creditors of the same class, within four months of the bankruptcy petition.

Voir dire   The examination of a prospective witness or juror to determine that person's acceptability.

Voluntary   Of one's own free will; spontaneous; intentional.

Voting trust   A commitment by stockholders of a corporation to place their shares in trust so that the shares can be voted as a bloc; a device used to increase the voting power of a group.

W

Waiver   The voluntary surrender of a legal right; the intentional surrender of a right.

Waiver of defenses clause   A clause in a contract whereby one party agrees in advance not to assert certain defenses should a breach occur.

Warehouseman   A person engaged in the business of receiving and storing the goods of others for a fee.

Warranty   A representation that becomes a part of the contract and that is made by a seller of goods at the time of the sale as to the character, quality, or nature of the goods.

Warranty deed   A deed that contains warranties of title from the grantor to the grantee.

Watered stock   Shares of a corporation that are issued as fully paid when in fact the full par or stated value has not been paid by the purchaser.

Will   A written document prepared by a testator to provide for the disposition of the testator's estate upon his or her death.

Winding up   The termination of a business enterprise by marshaling and liquidating the assets and distributing the proceeds according to state law.

Workers' compensation   A type of insurance required by statute to protect workers in the event of injury or illness arising on the job and used in lieu of workers' lawsuits against the employer for such injury or illness.

Working papers   The papers prepared by an accountant in the course of employment that are used to prepare the final reports and that serve as evidence of the care and skill exercised by the accountant in the performance of the job.

Writ   A legal instrument, prepared in the form of a letter and addressed to a sheriff, to some other officer of the court, or to the person directly affected, that requires the performance of a specified act under order of the court.

Writ of execution   A writ used to enforce the judgment of a court.

Writing   A reduction to tangible form.

Wrong   A violation of the legal rights of some other person.

Z

Zoning   A division of the land governed by a city, with certain designated uses being permitted for each area and other uses being declared improper and impermissible; government regulation of permissible land use for the general welfare of the community.

Case Index

---

a = case citation, annotation
b = briefed case
c = case problem

Topical Index